Andrea Danese
617-944-3700
ext 2791

LINEAR ALGEBRA and Its Applications

INSTRUCTOR'S EDITION

David C. Lay
University of Maryland

Addison-Wesley Publishing Company
Reading, Massachusetts • Menlo Park, California • New York
Don Mills, Ontario • Wokingham, England • Amsterdam • Bonn
Sydney • Singapore • Tokyo • Madrid • San Juan • Milan • Paris

Sponsoring Editor: Jerome Grant
Production Supervisor: Karen Wernholm/Mona Zeftel
Marketing Manager: Andrew Fisher
Development Editor: Lenore Parens
Copy Editor: Joyce Grandy
Cover Designer: Leslie Haimes
Manufacturing Manager: Roy Logan

Photo/illustration credits

Pages 95, 96 Courtesy of Ford Motor Company. Page 122 Copyright © Chips and Technologies, Inc., 1993. Reprinted with permission of the copyright owners. All rights reserved. Page 152 Photo by Bo Strain. Reprinted by permission of The University of North Carolina at Chapel Hill. Page 190 Courtesy of Rockwell International Corporation, Space Systems Division. Page 331 The Bettmann Archive. Page 332 From *North American Datum of 1983,* editor Charles Schwartz, National Geodetic Information Center. Page 379 Adapted from Goldstein/Lay/Schneider, *Calculus and Its Applications* 5/E, © 1990, p. 23. Reprinted by permission of Prentice-Hall, Inc., Englewood Cliffs, N.J. Page 403 Adapted with permission from Earth Observation Satellite Company, Lanham, MD USA. Page 404 GEOPIC® images courtesy of Earth Satellite Corporation, Rockville, MD.

Library of Congress Cataloging-in-Publication Data

Lay, David C.
Linear algebra and its applications / David C. Lay.
p. cm.
Includes index.
ISBN 0-201-52031-1 ISBN 0-201-52032-X (Instructor's Edition)
1. Algebras, Linear. I. Title.
QA184.L397 1993
512'.5—dc20 93-31730
CIP

1 2 3 4 5 6 7 8 9 10-CRW-96959493

*To my wife, **Lillian,** and our children,*
Christina, Deborah, and Melissa,
whose support, encouragement, and faithful
prayers made this book possible

About the Author

David C. Lay holds a B.A. from Aurora University (Illinois), and an M.A. and Ph.D. from the University of California at Los Angeles. Lay has been an educator and research mathematician since 1966, mostly at the University of Maryland, College Park. He has also served as a visiting professor at the University of Amsterdam, the Free University, Amsterdam, and the University of Kaiserslautern, Germany. He has over 30 research articles published in functional analysis and linear algebra.

As a founding member of the NSF-sponsored Linear Algebra Curriculum Study Group, Lay has been a leader in the current movement to modernize the linear algebra curriculum. Lay is also a co-author of several mathematics texts, including *Introduction to Functional Analysis,* with Angus E. Taylor, *Calculus and Its Applications,* with L. J. Goldstein and D. I. Schneider, and *Mathematics for the Management, Life, and Social Sciences,* with L. J. Goldstein and D. I. Schneider.

A top-notch educator, Professor Lay has received three university awards for teaching excellence. He has been elected by university students to membership in Alpha Lambda Delta National Scholastic Honor Society and Golden Key National Honor Society. In 1989, Aurora University conferred on him the Outstanding Alumnus award. Lay is a member of the American Mathematical Society, the International Linear Algebra Society, the Mathematical Association of America, Sigma Xi, and the Society for Industrial and Applied Mathematics. Since 1992, he has been on the national board of the Association of Christians in the Mathematical Sciences.

Contents

Note to the Instructor

This note, which is not included in the standard student edition, offers some information that may help you organize your course.

DESIGNING THE COURSE

The text is written for a one-semester course meeting three or four times per week. However, a one-quarter survey is described later, in the list of sample syllabi. The topical organization table on the next two pages shows how the text can accommodate a variety of courses. In most cases, all of the core topics should be covered. Some of the supplementary topics will be considered as core topics by many instructors, but they are optional in the technical sense that subsequent sections make no essential use of them. All application sections are optional. Some supplementary topics, such as Sections 4.2 and 6.4, do depend on earlier supplementary topics. A section-by-section commentary identifies such interdependencies. The balance between supplementary topics and applications will vary according to your own course objectives.

Extensive class testing over several years has verified that each core section and supplementary section can be covered easily in one 50-minute period, with time for some discussion of homework. Longer application sections have subsections that can be covered in one period or less. When a substantial number of the theoretical problems are assigned, allowance must be made for extra discussion the next day, and the pace of one section per day may have to slow down a bit.

SAMPLE SYLLABI

The first three syllabi are for semester-length courses, with at least 39 lecture periods of 50 minutes, including time for homework discussions and occasional

Topical Organization of Linear Algebra and Its Applications

	Core Topics	Supplementary Topics	Applications
1.	1.1 Systems of Linear Equations		
2.	1.2 Row Reduction and Echelon Forms		1.3 Applications of Linear Systems
3.	2.1 Vectors in $\mathbb{R}^n$		
4.	2.2 The Equation $A\mathbf{x} = \mathbf{b}$		
5.	2.3 Solution Sets of Linear Systems		
6.	2.4 Linear Independence		
7.	2.5 Linear Transformations		
8.	2.6 The Matrix of a Linear Transformation		2.7 Nutrition and Population Movement
9.	3.1 Matrix Operations		
10.	3.2 Inverse of a Matrix		
11.	3.3 Characterizations of Invertible Matrices	3.4 Partitioned Matrices	
		3.5 Matrix Factorizations	
		3.6 Iterative Solutions of Linear Systems	3.7 The Leontief Input–Output Model
			3.8 Computer Graphics
		4.1 Introduction to Determinants	
		4.2 Properties of Determinants	4.3 Cramer's Rule, Volume, Linear Transformations
12.	5.1 Vector Spaces and Subspaces		
13.	5.2 Null Spaces, Column Spaces, and Linear Transformations		
14.	5.3 Linearly Independent Sets; Bases		
15.	5.4 Coordinate Systems		
16.	5.5 Dimension of a Vector Space		
17.	5.6 Rank	5.7 Change of Basis	5.8 Applications to Difference Equations
			5.9 Applications to Markov Chains
18.	6.1 Eigenvectors and Eigenvalues		
19.	6.2 The Characteristic Equation		
20.	6.3 Diagonalization	6.4 Eigenvectors and Linear Transformations	
		6.5 Complex Eigenvalues	6.6 Applications to Dynamical Systems
		6.7 Iterative Estimates for Eigenvalues	

	Core Topics	Supplementary Topics	Applications
21.	7.1 Inner Product, Length, and Orthogonality		
22.	7.2 Orthogonal Sets		
23.	7.3 Orthogonal Projections	7.4 Gram–Schmidt Process	
24.	7.5 Least-Squares Problems		7.6 Applications to Linear Models
		7.7 Inner Product Spaces	7.8 Applications of Inner Product Spaces
25.	8.1 Diagonalization of Symmetric Matrices		
26.	8.2 Quadratic Forms	8.3 Constrained Optimization	
		8.4 The Singular Value Decomposition	8.5 Applications to Image Processing and Statistics

quizzes, but not counting days for hour exams or the final examination. I have class tested the text three to five times in each of these courses. The 39-day schedule is based on a 15-week semester, with three or four exams and two or three days' slack time, to allow for unplanned delays or digressions that often occur when a textbook is used for the first time. Extra review days, if any, should be planned within the 39-day schedule.

The fourth syllabus is for a short course and it describes how to omit up to five of the core topics. The final syllabus shows how to incorporate the topics recommended by the Linear Algebra Curriculum Study Group into a semester course.

Course 1. A 39-lecture class for freshmen and sophomores, with a wide variety of majors.

Such a course could include all 26 core topics and perhaps six of the following supplementary topics:

3.4 Partitioned Matrices
3.5 Matrix Factorizations
4.1 Introduction to Determinants
4.2 Properties of Determinants
5.7 Change of Basis
6.4 Eigenvectors and Linear Transformations
6.5 Complex Eigenvalues
7.4 Gram–Schmidt Process and QR Factorization

In addition to these 32 class days, you can probably fit in four or more applications and still have three review days. I recommend one application from each of Chapters 1, 2, 3, and 5. They are spread out to provide welcome relief from the theory. Early introduction of applications seems especially beneficial in a course for younger students.

Some courses, such as our course at the University of Maryland, are four credits instead of three. In this case, another 10 or so supplementary and application sections can be covered.

Course 2. A 39-lecture course for juniors who have already seen determinants and brief glimpses of matrix algebra in other courses and have had multivariable calculus.

This course can go a little faster through Sections 1.1, 1.2, and 2.1, covering all three sections in two days, with students reading a lot on their own. (Later, the class will also speed through Section 7.1.) Applications are not as important for students who are already aware that linear algebra is useful. Also, Chapter 4 can be skipped entirely, and the brief treatment in Section 6.2 used instead. As a result, the 26 core sections can be covered easily in 25 days, and perhaps nine of the supplementary sections can be covered, still leaving time for four or five days on the applications in Chapters 5 through 8. In a 15-week course, I usually get as far as the singular value decomposition (Section 8.4).

Course 3. A 39-lecture course for juniors and seniors in the social and management sciences who are aiming at graduate school and will likely take a course later in multivariate statistics.

Cover all core sections except for Section 2.6. In Chapter 5 focus on $\mathbb{R}^n$, with some work on $\mathbb{P}_n$. (The commentary on Section 2.6 identifies the effect of omitting that section.) For supplementary topics, you might select partitioned matrices (Section 3.4), inner product Examples 1–6 of Section 7.7, constrained optimization (Section 8.3), and perhaps one or two other sections. That should leave room for applications from Sections 1.3 (Examples 1 and 5), 2.7, 3.7, 5.9, 7.6, 7.8 (Examples 1 and 2), and 8.5, plus two days for review.

Course 4. A 27-lecture short course.

Any course this brief will of necessity short-change the students, but some departments have been forced into this unpleasant situation. Nevertheless, a good survey can be taught from this text.

Cover 21 of the 26 core sections, omitting Sections 2.6, 5.4, 7.3, 7.5, and 8.2, and treating Section 5.5 somewhat lightly. (You might discuss Theorem 8 in Section 2.6 but assign no homework, and prove Theorem 8 in Section 5.4, because that proof helps students understand the essential properties of a basis.) See the section commentaries for the effects of these omissions.

There is now room for you to choose a few supplementary topics (perhaps

Sections 4.1 and 4.2) and one or two applications. For applications, I would suggest quickly covering population movement in Section 2.8, to get something applied into the first half of the course. Later, a day could be spent either on Markov chains in Section 5.9 or on part of Section 6.6, in order to give some more time to eigenvalues. The total time would be about 25 days. I would not attempt more the first time through the text.

Course 5. A course that covers the basic syllabus recommended by the Linear Algebra Curriculum Study Group.

The LACSG "core" topics are all included in any course that covers all 26 topics listed in this text as core topics, plus the following sections:

3.4 Partitioned Matrices

3.5 Matrix Factorizations

4.1 Introduction to Determinants

4.2 Properties of Determinants
plus Theorem 7 and Example 1 from Section 4.3

7.4 The Gram–Schmidt Process

7.6 Applications to Linear Models (Example 1 only)

This 32-lecture schedule is about four days longer than the LACSG time estimates, but the 32 days include more time on linear transformations and time for general vector spaces and positive definite matrices. Another five or six sections can be selected to fill out some of the supplementary topics and applications suggested by the LACSG. If you are using MATLAB, one or both of Sections 3.6 and 6.7 would be natural choices.

SECTION COMMENTARIES

The commentaries below point out connections between a given section and those that follow it. Obvious connections are usually not mentioned. Some subsections of core material are identified as optional when their omission will cause no serious problem later. The commentaries also list exercises that are particularly valuable pedagogically, anticipate future discussions, or treat an optional supplementary topic.

SECTION 1.1 Introduction to Linear Systems

This section and the next form the foundation for the row reduction algorithm used throughout the text. The existence and uniqueness questions introduced here are of fundamental importance and appear at several points later in the text. The exercises focus only on the existence question. Systems with many solutions are treated in Section 1.2.

Key Exercises: 27–30.

SECTION 1.2 Row Reduction and Echelon Forms

The pivot positions in a matrix will play an essential role in several theorems—on spanning, linear independence, invertibility, the determinant, and rank. Theorem 1 is fundamental. Example 3 is helpful but need not be presented in class. The parametric descriptions of solution sets are written in vector form in Section 2.3. The solution method is reviewed in Section 5.2.

Key Exercises: 22–34.

SECTION 1.3 Applications of Linear Systems

The three separate applications—network flow, electrical networks, and Leontief Economic Models—are not used elsewhere. If only one is covered, you should have plenty of time to get a good start on Section 2.1.

SECTION 2.1 Vectors in $\mathbb{R}^n$

The traditional "arrow" interpretation of a vector is a handicap to understanding and visualizing Span $\{\mathbf{u},\mathbf{v}\}$ as well as the set $\{\mathbf{p} + t\mathbf{v} : t \text{ in } \mathbb{R}\}$, discussed in Section 2.3. The set of free arrows in $\mathbb{R}^3$ is discussed in Section 5.1. Until then, a vector is a list of numbers, represented geometrically by a point. Sometimes an arrow is added to draw attention to the point.

Part or all of Section 7.1 could be inserted here, of course, along with more vector geometry, but the danger in doing so is that students will start to perceive the course as largely computational. I think that students' opinions of the course are set somewhere in the first two weeks, and they need to feel the conceptual emphasis early in the course. Forcing students to deal with Span $\{\mathbf{v}_1,\ldots,\mathbf{v}_p\}$ has that effect. Example 6 is optional, but it is used in Example 6 of Section 2.5. There are no other applications in between.

Key Exercises: 15–26. A discussion of Exercise 25 will help students understand $[\mathbf{a}_1 \;\; \mathbf{a}_2 \;\; \mathbf{a}_3]$, $\{\mathbf{a}_1, \mathbf{a}_2, \mathbf{a}_3\}$, and Span $\{\mathbf{a}_1, \mathbf{a}_2, \mathbf{a}_3\}$.

SECTION 2.2 The Equation $A\mathbf{x} = \mathbf{b}$

First impressions are often lasting. That is why the connection between $A\mathbf{x}$ and a linear combination of vectors must be made immediately. The value of this definition is far greater than one might expect. Nothing in the section is optional. The connection between Theorem 2(a) and an *existence* question could be made here, but I think it is better made when reviewing for an exam.

Key Exercises: 17–28, 35, 36. Students should be writing explanations as part of their answers.

SECTION 2.3 Solution Sets of Linear Systems

The material on translation is placed at the beginning, to avoid a digression during the discussion of solution sets. The geometry helps students understand Span $\{\mathbf{u}, \mathbf{v}\}$. Nonhomogeneous *difference* equations are discussed in Section 5.8, using a figure like Fig. 7 here.

SECTION 2.4 Linear Independence

The second half of Theorem 5 will be used several times later in the text. Exercise 36 could be stated as a theorem, in parallel with Theorem 2, but students *must* know the proof, to avoid confusing the two results.

SECTION 2.5 Introduction to Linear Transformations

The connection with existence and uniqueness problems is made here and in Section 2.6. Introducing linear transformations here raises the level of the first part of the course and simplifies the work later in the course. Linear transformations appear in the following sections in the next three chapters:

3.1 The definition of AB is motivated by linear transformations.

3.3 Invertible transformations are discussed.

3.5 Matrix factorization is explained via linear transformations.

3.8 Linear transformations are at the heart of computer graphics.

4.3 The volume-change effect of a linear transformation is measured by a determinant.

5.2 General linear transformations are introduced without fanfare, because students are already familiar with concrete matrix transformations.

5.4 The coordinate mapping is a one-to-one linear mapping of V onto $\mathbb{R}^n$.

5.5 The coordinate mapping provides a transparent proof of the key theorem needed to discuss the dimension of a vector space.

5.8 This section is a showcase of the power of linear algebra, mainly because linear transformations can be used in the explanations.

Linear transformations appear frequently, too, in Chapters 6 and 8. Exercise 24 is used in Section 3.8, Computer Graphics. Exercise 21 leads nicely into Section 2.6.

SECTION 2.6 The Matrix of a Linear Transformation

The proof of Theorem 9 applies to any linear transformation, in case you want to discuss this later in Chapter 5. Theorem 10 is used in parts of the Invertible Matrix Theorem in Section 3.3, and in the subsection of Section 3.3 regarding invertible linear transformations. The notions of one-to-one and onto prepare students for the discussion of the coordinate mapping in Section 5.4. Also, Section 2.6 provides a background for Section 6.4.

Exercises 25–36 offer fairly easy writing practice.

SECTION 2.7 Applications to Nutrition and Population Movement

One purpose of this section is to give the students a break from the concentrated material in the previous sections. The nutrition problem is not mentioned later in the text. However, if you plan to treat Markov chains later in Section 5.9, then you should present the population movement examples. By considering population sizes here and population distributions in Section 5.9, you can sidestep a discussion of probabilities.

It is desirable to discuss some examples of difference equations before Chapter 6. However, the chapter introductory example will suffice, if you choose to omit Sections 2.7, 5.8, and 5.9. Section 6.6 and a few other places earlier in the chapter also treat difference equations, so you have quite a variety from which to choose.

SECTION 3.1 Matrix Operations

The definition here of a matrix product AB is not only well motivated, but it also gives the proper view of AB for nearly all matrix calculations. The dual fact about the rows of A and the rows of AB is seldom used, mainly because vectors here are usually written as columns.

Although the section is long, it is easy and quite a bit can be assigned as outside reading. Exercises 31 and 32 are optional, but they are mentioned in Example 4 of Section 3.4. Outer products also appear in Exercises 31–34 of Section 5.6 and in the spectral decomposition of a symmetric matrix, in Section 8.1.

SECTION 3.2 The Inverse of a Matrix

The proof of Theorem 5 is important; students need to see that both uniqueness and existence must be proved. Elementary matrices are used in Sections 3.5, Matrix Factorizations, and in Section 4.2. The algorithm for finding A^{-1} is popular because it is so familiar and leads to easy exam questions. However, in most courses, time is better spent on the LU factorization in Section 3.5, for instance. (The LU factorization takes longer to present.)

Exercise 9 is useful and indicates how matrix products involving inverses are actually computed in practice. This exercise can be used in Section 5.7, to compute a change-of-coordinates matrix, and the exercise is mentioned in a numerical note in Section 6.4. Exercise 10 is referenced in Section 3.3, after the proof of Theorem 8.

SECTION 3.3 Characterizations of Invertible Matrices

The Invertible Matrix Theorem ties together most of the concepts studied thus far. Additional statements are added to the theorem in Sections 5.6 and 6.1. The subsection on invertible linear transformations is optional.

Key Exercises: 14–20.

SECTION 3.4 Partitioned Matrices

This section should be part of any modern course in linear algebra because partitioned matrix notation is widely used today in disciplines that employ linear algebra. I made it optional only because it is not yet a standard topic in many linear algebra courses. Block matrix multiplication is used to obtain the spectral decomposition of a symmetric matrix in Section 8.1 and the reduced singular value decomposition in Section 8.4.

Key Exercises: 13 and 14. Formula (7) leads to an inverse of the matrix A when A_{11} and its Schur complement are both invertible. Exercises 1–10 provide excellent practice with matrix algebra and the Invertible Matrix Theorem. Exercises 17 and 18 are mentioned at the end of Section 3.5.

SECTION 3.5 Matrix Factorizations

Modern algorithms in numerical linear algebra are often described using matrix factorizations. For practical work, this section is more important than Sections 5.7 and 6.4, even though matrix factorizations can be explained nicely in terms of change of bases. See Exercises 22–26.

SECTION 3.6 Iterative Solutions of Linear Systems

This section is well suited for a course that includes a computer or supercalculator component. The section could also be used in an out-of-class project. In any case, the *existence* of iterative methods should be at least mentioned in every course.

SECTION 3.7 The Leontief Input–Output Model

This section is independent of Section 1.3. The material here makes a good backdrop for the series expansion of $(I - C)^{-1}$, because this formula is actually used in some practical economic work. Exercise 8 gives an interpretation to entries of an inverse matrix that could be stated without the economic context.

SECTION 3.8 Applications to Computer Graphics

This section seems to have had universal appeal in the classes I have taught. A five- or ten-minute video demonstration of computer graphics will heighten student interest. The section is fun to teach and it provides practice with composition of linear transformations. A common student mistake is to reverse the order of the matrices.

SECTION 4.1 Introduction to Determinants

Because Chapter 4 is mainly computational, it gives students time to absorb the theory from earlier chapters before they plunge into Chapter 5. Theorem 1 in Section 4.1 enables you to get into the subject quickly. This is important, because a typical first course cannot afford to spend more than a week on determinants. Exercises 33–36 provide the first step in the inductive proof of Theorem 3, in the next section.

SECTION 4.2 Properties of Determinants

The development here is more efficient than some presentations, because the hard work is all packed into the proof of Theorem 3. The characterization of $\det A$ via pivots gives a concrete interpretation to the standard bizarre calculations with cofactors. Theorems 4 and 6 are important for later work.

SECTION 4.3 Cramer's Rule, Volume, and Linear Transformations

There are several independent topics here from which to choose. I tend to prefer the geometric interpretation of the determinant, because of its connection with calculus. But who can resist presenting the wonderful proof of Cramer's Rule? I learned it from Roger Horn and Charles Johnson. See their book, *Matrix Analysis*, Cambridge University Press, Cambridge, 1985, page 21.

SECTION 5.1 Vector Spaces and Subspaces

The space $\mathbb{S}$ of signals is used in Section 5.8. The spaces of polynomials, $\mathbb{P}_n$, are used in many sections of Chapters 5 and 7. I designed this section to avoid the standard exercises in which a student is asked to check ten axioms on an array of sets (some of which may be artificially weird). In fact, Theorem 2 provides the main homework tool in this section for showing that a set is a subspace. Students could be taught how to check the closure axioms, of course, but I think the time for that is spent better elsewhere in a first course.

The exercises in the next few sections emphasize $\mathbb{R}^n$, to give students time to absorb the abstract concepts.

SECTION 5.2 Null Spaces, Column Spaces, and Linear Transformations

This section provides a review of Chapter 2 using the new terminology. Linear transformations are introduced without fuss, because the students are already comfortable with the idea for $\mathbb{R}^n$. The comments for Section 2.5 list the sections in Chapter 5 where linear transformations are used.

Key Exercises: 21–28. They are simple but helpful. The idea in Exercises 7–18 is to use Theorems 2 and 3, not the Subspace Test, to show that a given set is a subspace.

SECTION 5.3 Linearly Independent Sets; Bases

The definition of basis is given initially for subspaces because this emphasizes that the basis elements must be in the subspace. Students often overlook this point when the definition is given only for a vector space. The subsection on bases for $\text{Nul}\,A$ and $\text{Col}\,A$ is essential for Sections 5.5 and 5.6.

Key Exercises: 23–25.

SECTION 5.4 Coordinate Systems

Section 5.7 depends heavily on this section, as does Section 6.4. It is possible to cover the $\mathbb{R}^n$ parts of the two later sections, however, if the first half of Section 5.4 (and perhaps Example 7) is covered. The linearity of the coordinate mapping is used in Section 5.5, to prove Theorem 10, and in Section 6.4 to find the matrix of a transformation relative to two bases. The change-of-coordinates matrix appears in Section 6.4, Theorem 8 and Exercise 27. The concept of an isomorphism is needed in the proof of Theorem 18 in Section 5.8.

Exercise 25 is used in Section 5.7 to show that the change-of-coordinates matrix is invertible.

SECTION 5.5 The Dimension of a Vector Space

Theorem 10 is true because a vector space isomorphic to $\mathbb{R}^n$ has the same algebraic properties as $\mathbb{R}^n$. A proof may not be needed to convince the class. If you skipped Theorem 9 in Section 5.4, you could give a proof such as the one on page 111 of *Introduction to Linear Algebra,* 2d ed., by Serge Lang, Springer-Verlag, New York, 1986. Theorem 13 is used in Section 5.8, to verify when enough vectors for a basis have been found, and in the Gram–Schmidt process, in Section 7.4.

Exercise 34 is mentioned in the proof of Theorem 18 in Section 5.8.

SECTION 5.6 Rank

Figure 1, connected with Example 4, prepares the way for Theorem 3 in Section 7.1. Exercises 27–29 are optional, but they tie in neatly with Example 6 of Section 8.4.

SECTION 5.7 Change of Basis

The row reduction algorithm that produces $\underset{\mathscr{C}\leftarrow\mathscr{B}}{P}$ can also be deduced from Exercise 9 in Section 3.2. The change-of-coordinates matrix here is interpreted in Section 6.4 as the matrix of the identity transformation relative to two bases.

SECTION 5.8 Applications to Difference Equations

This is an important section for engineering students and worth two days of class time, if you can arrange that. To spend only one day, you could cover up through Example 5, but assign Example 3 for reading (because it takes some time to present in class). Example 3 is needed for Exercise 24 in Section 7.5.

SECTION 5.9 Markov Chains

The migration matrix is examined again in Section 6.2, where an eigenvector decomposition shows explicitly why the sequence of state vectors $\mathbf{x}_k$ tends to a steady-state vector. The discussion in Section 6.2 does not depend on prior knowledge of Section 5.9.

SECTION 6.1 Eigenvectors and Eigenvalues

The subsection on eigenvectors and difference equations anticipates the discussion that follows in Section 6.2. Also, see Exercises 31 and 32.

SECTION 6.2 The Characteristic Equation

The idea of similarity, introduced here, is discussed again in Section 6.4, along with eight more exercises. The subsection on dynamical systems provides a short introduction to the subject. The calculations here eliminate the need to supply details for the eigenvector decomposition (2) in Section 6.6.

If you covered partitioned matrices in Chapter 3, you might connect Exercise 13 in Section 3.4 with Supplementary Exercises 10–12 in Chapter 6.

SECTION 6.3 Diagonalization

This section is essential for the diagonalization of symmetric matrices, in Section 8.1. Theorem 7 is needed for Practice Problem 3 and Exercises 21–24, but is not used elsewhere. A number of exercises in later sections are stated for diagonalizable matrices, because the proofs are simpler for this class of matrices. (See Exercise 25 in Section 6.4, for example.)

SECTION 6.4 Eigenvectors and Linear Transformations

Students should be encouraged to review Section 5.4 before the lecture here. To simplify Section 6.4, the focus is on the matrix for a linear transformation relative to a single basis, and no special notation is given to the matrix for a transformation that acts between two different spaces. If you wish to further simplify the discussion, you could derive the matrix formula (4) only for the case when $T: \mathbb{R}^n \to \mathbb{R}^n$, and then skip to Theorem 8.

SECTION 6.5 Complex Eigenvalues

Although some applications, such as in electrical engineering, naturally involve complex vector spaces, the majority of applications accessible to undergraduates requires only real vector spaces. For that reason, I have chosen to discuss complex eigenvalues only for real matrices. A discussion of eigenvalues for complex matrices would take more time than most first courses have available. Moreover, in such discussions, the important case of a real matrix acting on $\mathbb{R}^n$ seldom receives the attention it deserves.

Even if there is no time for this section, students can be encouraged to look at the pictures! Figure 5 in Section 6.6 could be examined, too.

Exercises 23 and 24 provide the proof that a real symmetric matrix has only real eigenvalues. These exercises, together with the (real) Schur factorization described in Supplementary Exercise 14 in Chapter 7, and Exercise 32 in Section 8.1, give you the pieces from which you can construct a proof of the spectral theorem for symmetric matrices, if you wish.

SECTION 6.6 Applications to Dynamical Systems

The results here are easier to describe than those for differential equations, and the discrete case deserves more attention in the undergraduate curriculum than it commonly now receives.

A brief treatment of this material could cover Example 1, the discussion following it, and some of Exercises 1–6. The last subsection on the spotted owls could be added to this, requiring only a little hand-waving if you have not discussed complex eigenvalues.

For my classes that follow the Course Syllabus 2, I leave the ecology for outside reading and spend one day on the graphical description of trajectories, change of variable, and complex eigenvalues. Usually, two or three engineers in my class have already seen state-space methods, and their comments help to spark considerable enthusiasm for this material, particularly the change of variable that decouples a system.

SECTION 6.7 Iterative Estimates for Eigenvalues

Example 5 of Section 6.2 and the eigenvector decomposition in Section 6.6 both flow naturally into the power method. When discussing the power method, be careful to *avoid* the following incorrect statements: (1) for sufficiently large k, the vector $A^k\mathbf{x}$ is a good approximation to an eigenvector of A corresponding to the strictly dominant eigenvalue, λ_1; and (2) for large k, the vector $A(A^k\mathbf{x})$ is a good approximation to $\lambda_1(A^k\mathbf{x})$.

In Example 1, the points $A^k\mathbf{x}$ lie on a line parallel to the eigenspace for $\lambda = 2$. So statement (1) is false. In fact, $\mathbf{x} = (.1)\mathbf{v}_1 + \mathbf{v}_2$, where $\mathbf{v}_2$ is an eigenvector for $\lambda = 1$. Thus $A^k\mathbf{x} = 2^k(.1)\mathbf{v}_1 + \mathbf{v}_2$ and $A^{k+1}\mathbf{x} - 2A^k\mathbf{x} = -\mathbf{v}_2$ for all k. Hence statement (2) is false. Also, see Exercise 21.

One or both statements essentially appear in a majority of the leading linear algebra texts that cover the power method. (However, their final algorithms for the power method itself are correct.) The statements are true when the second largest eigenvalue is less than 1 in magnitude. But in general, the sequence $\{A^k\mathbf{x}\}$ *must* be scaled to a sequence of unit vectors (in some convenient norm). The scaling is not simply a matter of keeping numbers from getting too large or too small.

SECTION 7.1 Inner Product, Length, and Orthogonality

The general material on orthogonal complements is essential for later work. Theorem 3 is an important general fact, but it is needed only for Supplementary Exercise 11 at the end of the chapter and in Section 8.4. The optional material on angles is not used later. Exercises 27–31 concern facts used later.

SECTION 7.2 Orthogonal Sets

The nonsquare matrices in Theorems 6 and 7 are needed for the QR factorization, in Section 7.4. It is important to emphasize that the term *orthogonal* matrix applies only to certain *square* matrices. The subsection on orthogonal projections not only sets the stage for the general case in Section 7.3, it also provides what is needed for the orthogonal diagonalization exercises in Section 8.1, because none of the eigenspaces there have dimension greater than 2. For this reason, the Gram–Schmidt process (Section 7.4) is not really needed in Chapter 8. Exercises 19 and 20 set the stage for Section 7.3.

SECTION 7.3 Orthogonal Projections

Example 1 seems to help students understand Theorem 8. Of course, Theorem 8 is needed for the Gram–Schmidt process. Theorems 8 and 9 are needed for the discussions of least-squares in Sections 7.5 and 7.6. Theorem 10 is used with the QR factorization to provide a good numerical method for solving least-squares problems, in Section 7.5.

Key Exercises: 19, 20. They lead naturally into the Gram–Schmidt process.

SECTION 7.4 The Gram–Schmidt Process

The QR factorization encapsulates the essential outcome of the Gram–Schmidt process, just as the LU factorization describes the result of a row reduction process. For practical use of linear algebra, the factorizations are more important than the algorithms that produce them. In fact, the Gram–Schmidt process is *not* the appropriate way to compute the QR factorization. (See the Numerical Notes.) For that reason, one should consider deemphasizing the hand calculation of the Gram–Schmidt process, even though it provides easy exam questions.

The Gram–Schmidt process is used in Sections 7.7 and 7.8, in connection with various sets of orthogonal polynomials. The process is mentioned in Sections 8.1 and 8.4, but the one-dimensional projection constructed in Section 7.2 will suffice. The QR factorization is used in an optional subsection of Section 7.5, and it is needed in Supplementary Exercise 7 of Chapter 8 to produce the Cholesky factorization of a positive definite matrix.

SECTION 7.5 Least-Squares Problems

This is a core section, but it need not take a full day. Each example provides a stopping place. Theorem 13 and Example 1 are all that is needed for Section 7.6. Theorem 15, however, gives an illustration of why the QR factorization is important. Example 4 is related to Exercise 17 in Section 7.6.

SECTION 7.6 Applications to Linear Models

All science students will benefit from Example 1. The general linear model and the subsequent examples are aimed at students who may take a multivariate statistics course. In a general sophomore class, that may include more students than one might expect.

SECTION 7.7 Inner Product Spaces

The three types of inner products described here are matched by applications in Section 7.8. It is possible to spend just one day on selected portions of both sections. Example 1 matches the weighted least-squares in Section 7.8. Examples 2–6 are applied to trend analysis in Section 7.8. This material is aimed at students who have not had much calculus or who intend to take more than one course in statistics.

For students who have seen some calculus, Example 7 is needed for the Fourier series in Section 7.8. Example 2 is used to motivate the inner product on $C[a,b]$. The Cauchy–Schwarz and triangle inequalities are not used later, but they should be part of the training of every mathematics student.

SECTION 7.8 Applications of Inner Product Spaces

The connections with Section 7.7 have already been identified. For my junior-level course (see Syllabus 2), I spend three days on the following topics: Theorems 13 and 15 in Section 7.5, plus Examples 1, 3, and 5; Example 1 in Section 7.6; Examples 2 and 7 in Section 7.7, with the motivation for the definite integral; and Fourier series in Section 7.8.

SECTION 8.1 Diagonalization of Symmetric Matrices

Theorems 1 and 2 and the calculations in Examples 2 and 3 are important for the sections that follow. Note that "symmetric matrix" means "real symmetric matrix," because all matrices in the text have real entries, as mentioned at the beginning of this chapter.

Theorem 2 is easily proved for the 2×2 case:

$$\text{If } A = \begin{bmatrix} a & b \\ b & d \end{bmatrix}, \text{ then } \lambda = \frac{1}{2}\left(a + d \pm \sqrt{(a-d)^2 + 4b^2}\right)$$

If $b = 0$, then A *is* diagonal. Otherwise, there are two distinct eigenvalues, so A must be diagonalizable. In this case an eigenvector for λ is $(d - \lambda, -b)$.

SECTION 8.2 Quadratic Forms

This section can provide a good conclusion to the course, because the mathematics here is widely used in applications. For instance, Exercises 17 and 18 can be used to develop the second derivative test for functions of two variables. However, if time permits, some interesting applications still lie ahead. Theorem 4 is used to prove Theorem 6 in Section 8.3, which in turn is used to develop the singular value decomposition.

SECTION 8.3 Constrained Optimization

Theorem 6 is the main result needed in the next two sections. Theorem 7 is mentioned in Example 2 of Section 8.4. Theorem 8 is needed for Exercise 22 in Section 8.4 and at the very end of Section 8.5. The economic principles in Example 6 should be familiar to students who have had a course in economics.

SECTION 8.4 The Singular Value Decomposition

This section presents a modern topic of great importance in applications, particularly in computer calculations. Moreover, the singular value decomposition explains much about the structure of matrix transformations. The SVD does for an arbitrary matrix almost what an orthogonal diagonalization does for a symmetric matrix.

SECTION 8.5 Applications to Image Processing and Statistics

The application here has turned out to be of interest to a wide variety of students, including engineers. I cover this in Course 3, described above, but I only have time to mention the idea briefly to my other classes.

I hope you enjoy using the text.

D.C.L.

Preface

This text provides a modern elementary introduction to linear algebra and some of its interesting applications, accessible to students with the maturity that should come from successfully completing two semesters of college-level mathematics, usually calculus.

The main goal of the text is to help students master the basic concepts and skills they will use later in their careers. The topics here follow the recommendations of the Linear Algebra Curriculum Study Group, which were based on a careful investigation of the real needs of the students and a consensus among professionals in many disciplines that use linear algebra. Hopefully, this course will be one of the most useful and interesting mathematics classes taken as an undergraduate.

DISTINCTIVE FEATURES

Early Introduction of Key Concepts

The text features a gradual but steady development of the subject—from simple ideas about systems of equations and their matrix representation to more challenging concepts in linear algebra. Each topic moves from elementary examples to general principles. Certain key ideas are introduced early in $\mathbb{R}^n$ and gradually examined from different points of view. Later generalizations of these concepts appear as natural extensions of familiar ideas, visualized through the geometric intuition developed in Chapter 2. A major achievement of the text, I believe, is that the level of difficulty for the students is fairly even throughout the course.

A Modern View of Matrix Multiplication

Good notation is crucial, and the text reflects the way scientists and engineers actually use linear algebra in practice. The definitions and proofs focus on the columns of a matrix rather than on the matrix entries. This approach simplifies many arguments, and it permits vector space ideas to be tied into the study of linear systems. For instance, students can find spanning and linear independence difficult to understand, even in the context of $\mathbb{R}^n$. However, after years of experimentation, I have found that the initial contact with these ideas is easier when students have a proper understanding of matrix-vector multiplication, viewing $A\mathbf{x}$ as a linear combination of the columns of A.

Linear Transformations

Linear transformations form a "thread" that is woven into the fabric of the text. Their use enhances the geometric flavor of the text. In Chapter 2, for instance, linear transformations provide a dynamic and graphical view of matrix-vector multiplication. Then, linear transformations appear repeatedly as new concepts are discussed. This gradual and concrete approach eventually leads to a solid understanding of a fairly difficult yet essential topic.

Eigenvalues and Dynamical Systems

Too often, eigenvalues are treated hurriedly at the end of a linear algebra course. In this text, students study eigenvalues in both Chapters 6 and 8. Because this material is spread over several weeks, students have more time than usual to absorb and review these critical concepts. The discussion in Chapter 6 is motivated by and applied to discrete dynamical systems. I believe that the graphical descriptions of such systems, including those with complex eigenvalues, appear here for the first time in an elementary linear algebra text.

Orthogonality and Least-Squares Problems

These topics receive a more comprehensive treatment than is commonly found in beginning texts. The Linear Algebra Curriculum Study Group has emphasized the need for a substantial unit on orthogonality and least-squares problems, because orthogonality plays such an important role in computer calculations and numerical linear algebra and because inconsistent linear systems arise so often in practical work. The foundation for this material is laid in Sections 7.1 to 7.3. After that a variety of topics, such as the QR factorization, can be covered as time permits. General inner product spaces are treated in the last two sections of Chapter 7.

PEDAGOGICAL FEATURES

Applications

A broad selection of applications illustrates the power of linear algebra to explain fundamental principles and simplify calculations in engineering, computer science, mathematics, physics, biology, economics, and statistics. Each chapter opens with an introductory vignette that sets the stage for some application of linear algebra and provides a motivation for developing the mathematics that follows. Later, the text returns to that application in a section near the end of the chapter. Shorter applications are scattered throughout the text, and some chapters have more than one application section at the end.

A Strong Geometric Emphasis

Every major concept in the course is given a geometric interpretation, because many students learn better when they can visualize an idea. There are substantially more drawings here than usual, and some of the figures have never appeared before in a linear algebra text.

Examples

This text devotes a larger proportion of its expository material to examples than most linear algebra texts. There are more examples than one would ordinarily present in class. But because the examples are written carefully, with lots of detail, students can read them on their own.

Theorems and Proofs

Important results are stated as theorems. Other useful facts are displayed in blue-tinted boxes, for easy reference. These boxed facts are usually justified in an informal discussion, as are several of the theorems. In a few cases, the essential calculations of a proof are exhibited in a carefully chosen example. Most of the theorems, however, have formal proofs, written with the beginning student in mind. The proofs illustrate how various concepts and definitions are used in arguments, and they provide model arguments for students who are learning to construct proofs. A few routine verifications are saved for exercises, when they will benefit students. The only two central facts stated without proof concern cofactor expansions of a determinant and the orthogonal diagonalization of a symmetric matrix.

Practice Problems

One to four carefully selected problems appear just before each exercise set. Complete solutions follow the exercise set. These problems either focus on potential trouble spots in the exercise set or provide a "warm-up" to the exercises, and the solutions often contain helpful hints or warnings about the homework.

Exercises

The abundant supply of exercises ranges from routine computations to conceptual questions that require more thought. A good number of innovative questions pinpoint conceptual difficulties that I have found on student papers over the years. Each exercise set is carefully arranged, leading from one idea to the next, in the same general order as the text; homework assignments are readily available when only part of a section is discussed. A notable feature of the exercises is their numerical simplicity. Problems "unfold" quickly, so students spend little time on numerical calculations. The exercises concentrate on teaching understanding rather than mechanical calculations.

Writing Exercises

An ability to write coherent mathematical statements in English is essential for all students of linear algebra, not just those who may go to graduate school in mathematics. Engineers and scientists need to be able to communicate *why* something is true, to say precisely what they mean. For example, an engineer may need to justify to a superior why a new design will work, or a scientist may want to prepare a research grant proposal.

To develop this ability to write, I have included many exercises for which a written justification is part of the answer. Some questions are open-ended; some are true/false/justify. Conceptual exercises that require a short proof usually contain hints that help a student get started. Or, an exercise is broken down into simple steps. For all odd-numbered writing exercises, either a solution is included at the back of the text, or a hint is given and the solution is in the Study Guide, described below.

Computational Topics

The text stresses the impact of the computer on both the development and practice of linear algebra in science and engineering. Frequent "Numerical Notes" draw attention to issues in computing and distinguish between theoretical concepts, such as matrix inversion, and computer implementations such as LU factorizations. Forty-five exercises, in application sections and in two sections on iterative methods, require a computer or supercalculator for their solutions.

SUPPLEMENTS

Study Guide

I wrote this paperback student supplement to be an integral part of the course. It complements the text in several ways. Detailed solutions are given to every third odd problem: 1, 7, 13, . . . , and most key exercises are covered in this way. Instructors can refer students to these explanations whenever the class discussion time is limited. Also, solutions are given to *every* odd-numbered writing exercise whenever the text's answer is only a "Hint."

The Study Guide, however, is much more than a solutions manual. It contains numerous warnings about common student errors, along with other hints and suggestions for studying, written the way I talk to my own students; it provides a separate glossary for each chapter, to help students prepare for exams; and it includes explanations of how various proofs are designed and logically arranged, to assist those students who are learning to construct proofs. Also, since more and more students are using MATLAB each year, the Study Guide describes the appropriate MATLAB commands when they are first needed.

MATLAB Data Bank

Data for over 700 numerical exercises is available in MATLAB readable M-files, to encourage the use of MATLAB. Since these files eliminate the need to enter and check data, their use can save time on homework, even though most of the exercises involve minimal calculations. The M-files are on a disk supplied with the Instructor's Edition; also included are special M-files that make MATLAB more useful in a teaching environment. Students can obtain a free copy of all the M-files directly from The MathWorks, which produces MATLAB, by mailing a card attached to the Study Guide.

Instructor's Edition

For the convenience of instructors, this special edition includes brief answers to all exercises. A *Note to the Instructor* at the beginning of the text provides a commentary on the design and organization of the text, to help instructors plan their course. Suggestions for course syllabi are given, based on a topical division of the text into 26 core sections, 13 supplementary sections, and 11 applications sections.

ACKNOWLEDGMENTS

I am indeed grateful to many groups of people who have helped me over the years with various aspects of this book.

First, I sincerely thank Israel Gohberg and Robert Ellis for the nearly fifteen years of research collaboration in linear algebra, which has so greatly shaped my view of linear algebra. Because our research has had connections with problems in signal processing and engineering control, I have had opportunities to see firsthand the importance of linear algebra in science and engineering.

Next, I express my appreciation to my other good friends and colleagues at College Park, with whom I have had many fruitful conversations about linear algebra during the past ten to fifteen years: Ellen Correl, Jerome Dancis, Seymour Goldberg, Richard Good, Denny Gulick, Garry Helzer, and also Paul Smith, who has helped me greatly with the various applications to statistics that are now in the text. I appreciate, too, the valuable suggestions received from Der-Chen Chang, Robert Ellis, and John Horváth, while teaching from my text several times in recent years.

I am indebted to the mathematics department at the University of Maryland for giving me opportunities to teach many small classes of linear algebra and then to try out my material several times in the large lecture format. Also, I am thankful for the comments of the hundreds of students who have used photocopied versions of the text over the past six years. Two such "students" were Professors Joann and Harvey Keselman, on sabbatical leave from the University of Manitoba, who audited my course and made numerous helpful suggestions, particularly about statistical applications.

It has been my privilege to work with David Carlson, Charles Johnson, and Duane Porter, on the Linear Algebra Curriculum Study Group. Their ideas about teaching linear algebra, along with contributions of the other members of the William and Mary Workshop, have influenced this text in several important ways.

For assistance with the chapter opening examples and subsequent discussions, I thank Professor Wassily Leontief, Institute for Economic Analysis,

New York University; Clopper Almon, University of Maryland; Edward F. Moylan, Ford Motor Company; Roland Lamberson, Humboldt State University; and Russell Hardie and Chris Peterson, both of Earth Satellite Corporation. Each person named was very generous with time, advice, and materials such as photographs and data. Also, I thank Michael Butler, of the College of the Redwoods, for suggesting the spotted owl research in California.

The text has been reviewed at several stages, and I sincerely thank the following faculty for their careful analyses and constructive suggestions:

Susan Jane Colley, Oberlin College
Murray Eisenberg, University of Massachusetts at Amherst
Laxmi N. Gupta, Rochester Institute of Technology
James F. Hurley, University of Connecticut
Mohammed Kazemi, University of North Carolina
Andrzej Kedzierawski, Delaware State College
Robert A. Maynard, Tidewater Community College
Chris Nieman, Belleville Area College
Michael A. Penna, Indiana University—Purdue University at Indianapolis
Stephen Pennell, University of Massachusetts at Lowell
Carlos A. Pereira, The King's College
John Rhodes, Bates College
James Rowell, University of Minnesota—Duluth
Joseph B. Stephen, Northern Illinois University
Mo Tavakoli, Chaffey College
W. Vance Underhill, East Texas State University
Monte J. Zerger, Adams State College

Over the past three years, I have been fortunate to have many faculty class-test the manuscript. Their comments have been most useful, and I am happy to express my appreciation to:

Wayne Barrett, Brigham Young University
Jane Day, San Jose State University
Diane Doyle, Adirondack Community College
Luz DeAlba, Drake University
Evarist Giné, University of Connecticut
William Hager, University of Florida
Gaston Hernandez, University of Connecticut
James F. Hurley, University of Connecticut
Jonathan King, University of Florida
Israel Koltracht, University of Connecticut
Walter B. Lowrie, University of Connecticut

Wolodymyr Madych, University of Connecticut
Michael Menaker, University of Maryland University College
Michael Neumann, University of Connecticut
Richard Orr, Rochester Institute of Technology
Richard Pfeifer, San Jose State University
Leiba Rodman, The College of William and Mary
James Rowell, University of Minnesota—Duluth
Jon Scott, Montgomery College (Takoma Park)
Rick Smith, University of Florida
Margaret Suchow, Adirondack Community College
Gilbert Sward, Montgomery College (Rockville)
Linda Valdes, San Jose State University

A number of persons checked the accuracy of the text, and I really appreciate their work. William Gragg, of the Naval Postgraduate School, read the numerical notes and related topics and offered many good suggestions. Jon Scott, of Montgomery College, and Richard Good, of the University of Maryland, read the galleys and checked the numerical calculations in the text and examples. Professor Good was also very helpful in his careful review of the glossary and the solutions to the writing exercises. Some of my best students in recent years checked and double checked all the answers in the final manuscript: Yougandh Chitre, Leigh Ann Stuart, and Jennifer Yuin, together with graduate students Jawad Al-Khal and Ashvina Kulkarni.

Finally, I sincerely thank the staff at Addison-Wesley for their superb work on the book, especially Jerome Grant, senior mathematics editor, who orchestrated the entire publishing effort, and Lenore Parens, developmental editor, who took the students' point of view when reading and rereading the entire manuscript. My thanks also go to the rest of the team at Addison-Wesley responsible for my book: Karen Wernholm and Mona Zeftel, senior production supervisors, Meredith Nightingale, art coordinator, Andy Fisher, marketing manager, and Jim Behnke, President of Addison-Wesley Higher Education Group.

David C. Lay

A Note to Students

This course is potentially the most interesting and valuable undergraduate mathematics course you will study. The following remarks offer some advice and information to help you master the material and enjoy the course.

In linear algebra, the *concepts* are as important as the *computations*. The simple numerical exercises that begin each exercise set only help you check your understanding of basic procedures. Later in your career, computers will do the calculations, but you will have to choose the calculations, know how to interpret the results, and then explain the results to other people. For this reason, many exercises in the text ask you to explain or justify your calculations. A written explanation is often required as part of the answer. For odd-numbered exercises, you will find either the desired explanation or at least a good hint. You must avoid the temptation to look at such answers until you have tried to write out the solution yourself. Otherwise, you are likely to think you understand something when in fact you do not.

To master the concepts of linear algebra, you will have to read and reread the text carefully. New terms are in boldface type, sometimes enclosed in a definition box. A glossary of terms is included at the end of the text. Important facts are stated as theorems or are enclosed in tinted boxes, for easy reference.

In a practical sense, linear algebra is a language. You must learn this language the same way you would study a foreign language—with daily work. Material presented in one section is not easily understood unless you have thoroughly studied the text and worked the exercises for the preceding sections. Keeping up with the course will save you lots of time and distress!

Study Guide

To help you succeed in this course, I have written a Study Guide to accompany the text. It contains detailed solutions to every third odd-numbered exercise, plus solutions to all odd-numbered exercises that only give a hint in the answer section. The Study Guide also provides warnings of common errors, helpful hints that call attention to key exercises and potential exam questions, and a separate glossary of terms for each chapter (invaluable when reviewing for an exam). Further, the Study Guide shows you how to use MATLAB (a computer program) to save hours of homework time. A postcard in the Study Guide entitles you to a free disk with data for over 700 exercises in the text. One simple command in MATLAB will retrieve all the data you need for a problem. If you have access to MATLAB (not included with the data disk), you will want to use this powerful aid.

1

Systems of Linear Equations

Introductory Example: Linear Models in Economics and Engineering

It was late summer in 1949. Harvard Professor Wassily Leontief was carefully feeding the last of his punched cards into the university's Mark II computer. The cards contained economic information about the U.S. economy and represented a summary of more than 250,000 pieces of information produced by the U.S. Bureau of Labor Statistics after two years of intensive work. Leontief had divided the U.S. economy into 500 "sectors," such as the coal industry, the automotive industry, communications, and so on. For each sector, he had written a linear equation that described how the sector distributed its output to the other sectors of the economy. Because the Mark II, one of the largest computers of its day, could not handle the resulting system of 500 equations in 500 unknowns, Leontief had distilled the problem into a system of 42 equations in 42 unknowns.

Programming the Mark II computer for Leontief's 42 equations had required several months of effort, and he was anxious to see how long the computer would take to solve the problem. The Mark II hummed and blinked for 56 hours before finally producing a solution. We will discuss the nature of this solution in Sections 1.3 and 3.7.

Leontief, who was awarded the 1973 Nobel Prize in Economic Science, opened the door to a new era in mathematical modeling in economics. His efforts at Harvard in 1949 marked one of the first significant uses of computers to analyze what was then a large-scale mathematical model. Since that time, researchers in many other fields have employed computers to analyze mathematical models. Because of the massive amounts of data involved, the models are usually *linear*; that is, they are described by *systems of linear equations.*

The importance of linear algebra for applications has risen in direct proportion to the increase in computing power, with each new generation of hardware and software triggering a demand for even greater capabilities. Computer science is thus intricately linked with linear algebra through the explosive growth of parallel processing and large-scale computations.

Scientists and engineers now work on problems far more complex than even dreamed possible a few decades ago. Today, linear algebra has more potential value for students in many scientific and business fields than any other undergraduate mathematics subject! The material in this text provides the foundation for further work in many interesting areas. Here are a few possibilities; others will be described later.

- *Oil exploration.* When a ship searches for offshore oil deposits, its computers solve thousands of separate systems of linear equations *every day.* The seismic data for the equations are obtained from underwater shock waves created by explosions from air guns. The waves bounce off subsurface rocks and are measured by geophones attached to mile-long cables behind the ship.
- *Linear programming.* Many important management decisions today are made on the basis of linear programming models that utilize hundreds of variables. The airline industry, for instance, employs linear programs that schedule flight crews, monitor the locations of aircraft, or plan the varied schedules of support services such as maintenance and terminal operations.
- *Electrical networks.* Engineers use simulation software to design electrical circuits and microchips involving millions of transistors. The software relies on linear algebra techniques and systems of linear equations.

A central concern of linear algebra is the study of systems of linear equations. Sections 1.1 and 1.2 present a systematic method for solving such systems. With only minor technical modifications, this method is the one used in most computer programs that solve systems of linear equations. Many of the examples and exercises here are so simple numerically that they could be solved by a variety of algebraic techniques. However, the method presented here must be mastered; it will be needed throughout the text.

1.1 INTRODUCTION TO SYSTEMS OF LINEAR EQUATIONS

A **linear equation** in the variables $x_1, \ldots, x_n$ is an equation that can be written in the form

$$a_1x_1 + a_2x_2 + \cdots + a_nx_n = b \tag{1}$$

where b and the **coefficients** $a_1, \ldots, a_n$ are real numbers, usually known in advance. The subscript n may be any positive integer. In textbook examples and exercises, n is normally between 2 and 5. In real-life problems, n might be 50 or 5000, or even larger.

The equations

$$4x_1 - 5x_2 + 2 = x_1 \quad \text{and} \quad x_2 = 2\left(\sqrt{6} - x_1\right) + x_3$$

are both linear because they may be rearranged algebraically as in Eq. (1):

$$3x_1 - 5x_2 = -2 \quad \text{and} \quad 2x_1 + x_2 - x_3 = 2\sqrt{6}$$

The equations

$$4x_1 - 5x_2 = x_1x_2 \quad \text{and} \quad x_2 = 2\sqrt{x_1} - 6$$

are not linear because of the presence of x_1x_2 in the first equation and $\sqrt{x_1}$ in the second.

A **system of linear equations** (or a **linear system**) is a collection of one or more linear equations involving the same set of variables, say, $x_1, \ldots, x_n$. An example is

$$\begin{aligned} 2x_1 - x_2 + 1.5x_3 &= 8 \\ x_1 \qquad - 4x_3 &= -7 \end{aligned} \tag{2}$$

A **solution** of the system is a list $(s_1, s_2, \ldots, s_n)$ of numbers that makes each equation a true statement when the values $s_1, \ldots, s_n$ are substituted for $x_1, \ldots, x_n$, respectively. For instance, (5, 6.5, 3) is a solution of system (2) because, when these values are substituted in (2) for x_1, x_2, x_3, respectively, the equations simplify to $8 = 8$ and $-7 = -7$.

The set of all possible solutions is called the **solution set** of the linear system. Two linear systems are called **equivalent** if they have the same solution set. That is, each solution of the first system is a solution of the second system, and each solution of the second system is a solution of the first.

Finding the solution set of a system of two linear equations in two variables is easy because it amounts to finding the intersection of two lines. A typical problem is

$$\begin{aligned} x_1 - 2x_2 &= -1 \\ -x_1 + 3x_2 &= 3 \end{aligned}$$

The graphs of these equations are lines, which we denote by l_1 and l_2. A pair of numbers (x_1, x_2) satisfies *both* equations in the system if and only if the point (x_1, x_2) lies on both l_1 and l_2. In the system above, the solution is the single point (3, 2), as you can easily verify. See Fig. 1.

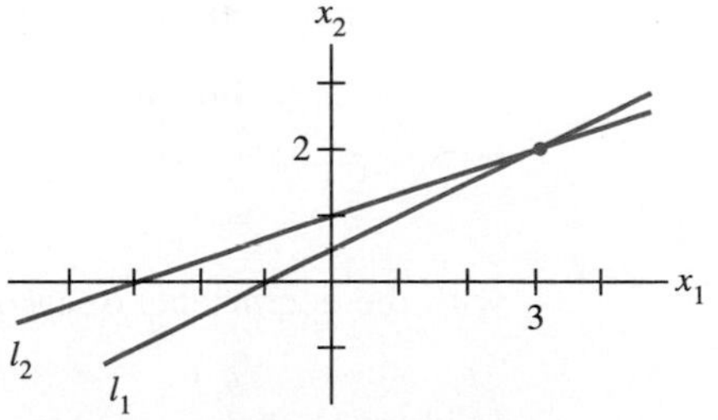

FIGURE 1 Exactly one solution.

Of course, two lines need not intersect in a single point—they could be parallel, or they could coincide and hence "intersect" at every point on the line. Figure 2 shows the graphs that correspond to the following systems:

$$\text{(a)}\quad \begin{aligned} x_1 - 2x_2 &= -1 \\ -x_1 + 2x_2 &= 3 \end{aligned} \qquad \text{(b)}\quad \begin{aligned} x_1 - 2x_2 &= -1 \\ -x_1 + 2x_2 &= 1 \end{aligned}$$

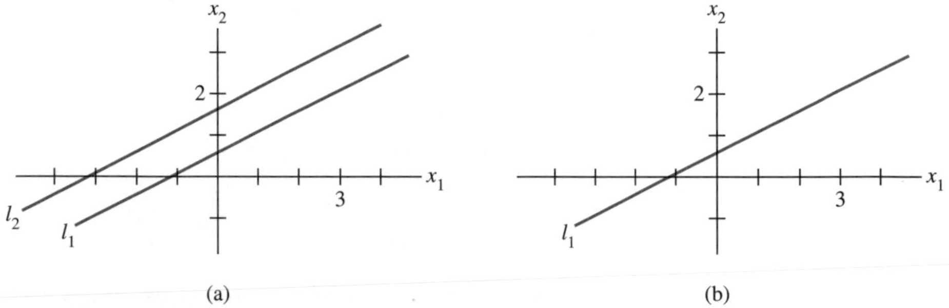

FIGURE 2 (a) No solution. (b) Infinitely many solutions.

Figures 1 and 2 illustrate the following general fact about linear systems, to be verified in Section 1.2.

A system of linear equations has either

1. no solution, or

2. exactly one solution, or

3. infinitely many solutions.

We say that a linear system is **consistent** if it has either one solution or infinitely many solutions; a system is **inconsistent** if it has no solution.

Matrix Notation

The essential information of a linear system can be recorded compactly in a rectangular array called a **matrix**. Given the system

$$\begin{aligned} x_1 - 2x_2 + x_3 &= 0 \\ 2x_2 - 8x_3 &= 8 \\ -4x_1 + 5x_2 + 9x_3 &= -9 \end{aligned} \tag{3}$$

with the coefficients of each variable aligned in columns, the matrix

$$\begin{bmatrix} 1 & -2 & 1 \\ 0 & 2 & -8 \\ -4 & 5 & 9 \end{bmatrix}$$

is called the **coefficient matrix** (or **matrix of coefficients**) of the system (3), and

$$\begin{bmatrix} 1 & -2 & 1 & 0 \\ 0 & 2 & -8 & 8 \\ -4 & 5 & 9 & -9 \end{bmatrix} \tag{4}$$

is called the **augmented matrix** of the system. (The second row here contains a zero because the second equation could be written as $0 \cdot x_1 + 2x_2 - 8x_3 = 8$.)

An augmented matrix of a system consists of the coefficient matrix with an added column containing the constants from the right sides of the equations.

The **size** of a matrix tells how many rows and columns it has. The augmented matrix (4) above has 3 rows and 4 columns and is called a 3×4 (read "3 by 4") matrix. If m and n are positive integers, an $\boldsymbol{m \times n}$ **matrix** is a rectangular array of numbers with m rows and n columns. (The number of rows always comes first.) Matrix notation will simplify the calculations in the examples that follow.

Solving a Linear System

This section and the next describe an algorithm or a systematic procedure for solving linear systems. The basic strategy is *to replace one system with an equivalent system (i.e., one with the same solution set) that is easier to solve.*

Roughly speaking, we use the x_1 term in the first equation of a system to eliminate the x_1 terms in the other equations. Then we use the x_2 term in the second equation to eliminate the x_2 terms in the other equations, and so on, until we finally obtain a very simple equivalent system of equations.

Three basic operations are used to simplify a linear system: Replace one equation by the sum of itself and a multiple of another equation, interchange two equations, and multiply all the terms in an equation by a nonzero constant. After the first example, we will see why these three operations do not change the solution set of the system.

EXAMPLE 1 Solve system (3).

Solution We perform the elimination procedure with and without matrix notation, and place the results side by side for comparison:

$$\begin{aligned} x_1 - 2x_2 + x_3 &= 0 \\ 2x_2 - 8x_3 &= 8 \\ -4x_1 + 5x_2 + 9x_3 &= -9 \end{aligned} \qquad \begin{bmatrix} 1 & -2 & 1 & 0 \\ 0 & 2 & -8 & 8 \\ -4 & 5 & 9 & -9 \end{bmatrix}$$

We want to keep x_1 *in the first equation and eliminate it from the other equations.* To do so, add 4 times equation 1 to equation 3. After some practice, the following calculation is usually performed mentally:

$$\begin{array}{rr} 4\cdot\text{[equation 1]:} & 4x_1 - 8x_2 + 4x_3 = 0 \\ +\text{[equation 3]:} & -4x_1 + 5x_2 + 9x_3 = -9 \\ \hline \text{[new equation 3]:} & -3x_2 + 13x_3 = -9 \end{array}$$

The result of this calculation is written in place of the original third equation:

$$\begin{aligned} x_1 - 2x_2 + x_3 &= 0 \\ 2x_2 - 8x_3 &= 8 \\ -3x_2 + 13x_3 &= -9 \end{aligned} \qquad \begin{bmatrix} 1 & -2 & 1 & 0 \\ 0 & 2 & -8 & 8 \\ 0 & -3 & 13 & -9 \end{bmatrix}$$

Next, multiply equation 2 by $1/2$ in order to obtain 1 as the coefficient for x_2. (This will simplify the arithmetic in the next step.)

$$\begin{aligned} x_1 - 2x_2 + x_3 &= 0 \\ x_2 - 4x_3 &= 4 \\ -3x_2 + 13x_3 &= -9 \end{aligned} \qquad \begin{bmatrix} 1 & -2 & 1 & 0 \\ 0 & 1 & -4 & 4 \\ 0 & -3 & 13 & -9 \end{bmatrix}$$

Use the x_2 in equation 2 to eliminate the $-3x_2$ in equation 3. The "mental" computation is

$$\begin{array}{rr} 3\cdot[\text{equation 2}]: & 3x_2 - 12x_3 = 12 \\ +\,[\text{equation 3}]: & -3x_2 + 13x_3 = -9 \\ \hline [\text{new equation 3}]: & x_3 = 3 \end{array}$$

The new system has a *triangular* form:[1]

$$\begin{aligned} x_1 - 2x_2 + x_3 &= 0 \\ x_2 - 4x_3 &= 4 \\ x_3 &= 3 \end{aligned} \qquad \begin{bmatrix} 1 & -2 & 1 & 0 \\ 0 & 1 & -4 & 4 \\ 0 & 0 & 1 & 3 \end{bmatrix}$$

Eventually, we want to eliminate the $-2x_2$ term from equation 1, but it is more efficient to use the x_3 in equation 3 first, to eliminate the $-4x_3$ and $+x_3$ terms in equations 2 and 1. The two "mental" calculations are

$$\begin{array}{rr} 4\cdot[\text{eq. 3}]: & 4x_3 = 12 \\ +\,[\text{eq. 2}]: & x_2 - 4x_3 = 4 \\ \hline [\text{new eq. 2}]: & x_2 \qquad = 16 \end{array} \qquad \begin{array}{rr} -1\cdot[\text{eq. 3}]: & -x_3 = -3 \\ +\,[\text{eq. 1}]: & x_1 - 2x_2 + x_3 = 0 \\ \hline [\text{new eq. 1}]: & x_1 - 2x_2 \qquad = -3 \end{array}$$

We combine the results of these two operations:

$$\begin{aligned} x_1 - 2x_2 \qquad &= -3 \\ x_2 \qquad &= 16 \\ x_3 &= 3 \end{aligned} \qquad \begin{bmatrix} 1 & -2 & 0 & -3 \\ 0 & 1 & 0 & 16 \\ 0 & 0 & 1 & 3 \end{bmatrix}$$

Now, having cleaned out the column above the x_3 in equation 3, we move back to the x_2 in equation 2 and use it to eliminate the $-2x_2$ above it. Because of our previous work with x_3, there is now no arithmetic involving x_3 terms. Adding 2 times equation 2 to equation 1, we obtain the system:

$$\begin{aligned} x_1 \qquad &= 29 \\ x_2 \qquad &= 16 \\ x_3 &= 3 \end{aligned} \qquad \begin{bmatrix} 1 & 0 & 0 & 29 \\ 0 & 1 & 0 & 16 \\ 0 & 0 & 1 & 3 \end{bmatrix}$$

[1]The intuitive term *triangular* will be replaced by a precise term in the next section.

We're essentially done! Our work indicates that the only solution of the original system is (29, 16, 3). Since we made so many calculations, however, it is a good practice to check our work. To verify that (29, 16, 3) *is* a solution, substitute these values into the left side of the original system, and compute:

$$\begin{aligned} (29) - 2(16) + (3) &= 29 - 32 + 3 = 0 \\ 2(16) - 8(3) &= 32 - 24 = 8 \\ -4(29) + 5(16) + 9(3) &= -116 + 80 + 27 = -9 \end{aligned}$$

The results agree with the right side of the original system, so (29, 16, 3) is a solution of the system. ▮

Example 1 illustrates how operations on equations in a linear system correspond to operations on the appropriate rows of the augmented matrix. The three basic operations listed earlier correspond to the following operations on the augmented matrix.

Elementary Row Operations:

1. (Replacement) Replace one row by the sum of itself and a multiple of another row.[2]
2. (Interchange) Interchange two rows.
3. (Scaling) Multiply all entries in a row by a nonzero constant.

Row operations may be applied to any matrix, not merely to one that arises as the augmented matrix of a linear system. We say two matrices are **row equivalent** if there is a sequence of row operations that transforms one matrix into the other.

It is important to note that row operations are *reversible*. If two rows are interchanged, they may be returned to their original positions by another interchange. If a row is scaled by a nonzero constant c, then multiplying the new row by $1/c$ produces the original row. Finally, consider a replacement operation involving two rows, say, rows 1 and 2, and suppose that c times row 1 is added to row 2 to produce a new row 2. To "reverse" this operation, add $-c$ times row 1 to (new) row 2 and obtain the original row 2. See Exercises 31–34 at the end of this section.

At the moment, we are interested in row operations on the augmented matrix of a system of linear equations. Suppose that a system is changed to a new one via row operations. By considering each type of row operation, it is easy to see that any solution of the original system remains a solution of the new system. Conversely, since the original system can be produced via row operations on the new system, each solution of the new system is also a solution of the original system. This discussion justifies the following fact.

[2] A common paraphrase of row replacement is, "Add to one row a multiple of another row."

If the augmented matrices of two linear systems are row equivalent, then the two systems have the same solution set.

Though Example 1 is lengthy, you will find that after some practice, the calculations go quickly. Fortunately, in many cases later in the text, you will not need to find the solution of a linear system. Instead, you will only want to know something about the size of the solution set.

Existence and Uniqueness Questions

In Section 1.2, we'll see why a solution set for a linear system contains either no solution, one solution, or infinitely many solutions. To determine which possibility is true for a particular system, we ask two questions.

Two Fundamental Questions About a Linear System:

1. Is the system consistent; that is, does at least one solution *exist?*
2. If a solution exists, is it the *only* one; that is, is the solution *unique?*

These two questions will appear throughout the text, in many different guises. In this section and the next, we show how to answer these questions via row operations on the augmented matrix.

EXAMPLE 2 Determine if the following system is consistent.

$$\begin{aligned} x_1 - 2x_2 + x_3 &= 0 \\ 2x_2 - 8x_3 &= 8 \\ -4x_1 + 5x_2 + 9x_3 &= -9 \end{aligned}$$

Solution This is the system from Example 1. Suppose that we have performed the row operations necessary to obtain the triangular form

$$\begin{aligned} x_1 - 2x_2 + x_3 &= 0 \\ x_2 - 4x_3 &= 4 \\ x_3 &= 3 \end{aligned} \qquad \begin{bmatrix} 1 & -2 & 1 & 0 \\ 0 & 1 & -4 & 4 \\ 0 & 0 & 1 & 3 \end{bmatrix}$$

At this point we know x_3. Were we to substitute the value of x_3 into equation 2, we would know x_2 and hence could determine x_1 from equation 1. So a solution exists; the system is consistent. (In fact, x_2 is uniquely determined by equation 2 since x_3 has only one possible value, and x_1 is therefore uniquely determined by equation 1. So the solution is unique.)

EXAMPLE 3 Determine if the following system is consistent.

$$\begin{aligned} x_2 - 4x_3 &= 8 \\ 2x_1 - 3x_2 + 2x_3 &= 1 \\ 5x_1 - 8x_2 + 7x_3 &= 1 \end{aligned} \tag{5}$$

Solution The augmented matrix is

$$\begin{bmatrix} 0 & 1 & -4 & 8 \\ 2 & -3 & 2 & 1 \\ 5 & -8 & 7 & 1 \end{bmatrix}$$

To obtain an x_1 in the first equation, interchange rows 1 and 2:

$$\begin{bmatrix} 2 & -3 & 2 & 1 \\ 0 & 1 & -4 & 8 \\ 5 & -8 & 7 & 1 \end{bmatrix}$$

To eliminate the $5x_1$ term in the third equation, add $-5/2$ times row 1 to row 3:

$$\begin{bmatrix} 2 & -3 & 2 & 1 \\ 0 & 1 & -4 & 8 \\ 0 & -1/2 & 2 & -3/2 \end{bmatrix} \tag{6}$$

Next, use the x_2 term in the second equation to eliminate the $-(1/2)x_2$ term from the third equation. Add 1/2 times row 2 to row 3:

$$\begin{bmatrix} 2 & -3 & 2 & 1 \\ 0 & 1 & -4 & 8 \\ 0 & 0 & 0 & 5/2 \end{bmatrix} \tag{7}$$

The augmented matrix is now in triangular form. To interpret it correctly, go back to equation notation:

$$\begin{aligned} 2x_1 - 3x_2 + 2x_3 &= 1 \\ x_2 - 4x_3 &= 8 \\ 0 &= 5/2 \end{aligned} \tag{8}$$

The equation $0 = 5/2$ is a short form of $0x_1 + 0x_2 + 0x_3 = 5/2$. This system in triangular form obviously has a built-in contradiction. There are no values of x_1, x_2, x_3 that satisfy (8) because the equation $0 = 5/2$ is never true. Since (8) and (5) have the same solution set, the original system is inconsistent (i.e., has no solution).

Pay close attention to the augmented matrix in (7). Its last row is typical of an inconsistent system in triangular form.

Numerical Notes

1. Row operations in the text and exercises will usually be extremely easy to perform, allowing you to focus on the underlying concepts. Still, you must learn to perform row operations accurately because they will be used throughout the text.
2. The data for most numerical exercises are already entered into MATLAB M-files. You can obtain a free copy of all the M-files directly from The MathWorks, which produces MATLAB, by mailing a card attached to the Study Guide. The use of MATLAB or another matrix utility will often reduce the time you spend on exercises.
3. In realistic problems, systems of linear equations are solved by a computer. Most computer programs use the elimination algorithm given here and in Section 1.2, modified slightly for improved accuracy.

PRACTICE PROBLEMS

Throughout the text, practice problems should be attempted before working the exercises. Solutions appear after each exercise set.

In Problems 1 and 2, state in words the next elementary "row" operation that should be performed on the system in order to solve it. (More than one answer is possible in Problem 1.)

1. $$\begin{aligned} x_1 + 4x_2 - 2x_3 + 8x_4 &= 12 \\ x_2 - 7x_3 + 2x_4 &= -4 \\ 5x_3 - x_4 &= 7 \\ x_3 + 3x_4 &= -5 \end{aligned}$$

2. $$\begin{aligned} x_1 - 3x_2 + 5x_3 - 2x_4 &= 0 \\ x_2 + 8x_3 \quad &= -4 \\ 2x_3 \quad &= 3 \\ x_4 &= 1 \end{aligned}$$

3. The augmented matrix of a linear system has been transformed by row operations into the form below. Determine if the system is consistent.

$$\begin{bmatrix} 1 & 5 & 2 & -6 \\ 0 & 4 & -7 & 2 \\ 0 & 0 & 5 & 0 \end{bmatrix}$$

4. Is $(3, 4, -2)$ a solution of the system below?

$$\begin{aligned} 5x_1 - x_2 + 2x_3 &= 7 \\ -2x_1 + 6x_2 + 9x_3 &= 0 \\ -7x_1 + 5x_2 - 3x_3 &= -7 \end{aligned}$$

1.1 EXERCISES

Solve each system in Exercises 1–4 by using elementary row operations on the equations or on the augmented matrix.

1. $$\begin{aligned} x_1 + 7x_2 &= 4 \\ -2x_1 - 9x_2 &= 2 \end{aligned}$$

2. $$\begin{aligned} 2x_1 + 6x_2 &= -6 \\ 5x_1 + 7x_2 &= 1 \end{aligned}$$

3. $$\begin{aligned} x_1 - 3x_2 &= 4 \\ -3x_1 + 9x_2 &= 8 \end{aligned}$$

4. $$\begin{aligned} 4x_2 &= 6 \\ x_1 - 6x_2 &= 3 \end{aligned}$$

Consider each matrix in Exercises 5–8 as the augmented matrix of a linear system. State in words the next elementary row operation that should be performed in the process of solving the system.

5. $$\begin{bmatrix} 1 & -4 & 2 & 7 \\ 0 & 0 & 3 & 6 \\ 0 & 1 & -3 & -4 \end{bmatrix}$$

6. $$\begin{bmatrix} 1 & 8 & 2 & -7 \\ 0 & 1 & -1 & 9 \\ 0 & 4 & 5 & 0 \end{bmatrix}$$

7. $$\begin{bmatrix} 1 & 3 & 0 & 5 & -5 \\ 0 & 1 & -6 & 9 & 0 \\ 0 & 0 & 2 & 7 & 1 \\ 0 & 0 & 1 & 4 & -2 \end{bmatrix}$$

8. $$\begin{bmatrix} 1 & 4 & 3 & 0 & 5 \\ 0 & 1 & -2 & 0 & 7 \\ 0 & 0 & 1 & 0 & -6 \\ 0 & 0 & 0 & 1 & 4 \end{bmatrix}$$

In Exercises 9–14, the augmented matrix of a linear system has been reduced by row operations to the form shown. In each case, continue the appropriate row operations and describe the solution set of the original system.

9. $$\begin{bmatrix} 1 & 0 & 4 & 7 \\ 0 & 1 & -2 & -1 \\ 0 & 0 & 1 & 3 \end{bmatrix}$$

10. $$\begin{bmatrix} 1 & 2 & 0 & 1 \\ 0 & 1 & 4 & 5 \\ 0 & 0 & 1 & 2 \end{bmatrix}$$

11. $$\begin{bmatrix} 1 & -3 & 0 & 0 \\ 0 & 1 & 5 & 0 \\ 0 & 0 & 0 & 1 \\ 0 & 0 & 1 & -2 \end{bmatrix}$$

12. $$\begin{bmatrix} 1 & -5 & 7 & 0 \\ 0 & 1 & 3 & 0 \\ 0 & 0 & 1 & 0 \end{bmatrix}$$

13. $$\begin{bmatrix} 1 & -1 & 0 & 0 & -5 \\ 0 & 1 & -2 & 0 & -7 \\ 0 & 0 & 1 & -3 & -2 \\ 0 & 0 & 0 & 1 & 4 \end{bmatrix}$$

14. $$\begin{bmatrix} 1 & 2 & 0 & -3 & -9 \\ 0 & 1 & 0 & 4 & 2 \\ 0 & 0 & 1 & 0 & 5 \\ 0 & 0 & 0 & 1 & -1 \end{bmatrix}$$

The augmented matrices for the systems in Exercises 15–26 are already entered in the MATLAB M-file x1s1. See the Study Guide for details. Solve the systems in Exercises 15–20.

15. $$\begin{aligned} x_1 + 5x_2 + 2x_3 &= 1 \\ -x_1 - 4x_2 + x_3 &= 6 \\ x_1 + 3x_2 - 3x_3 &= -9 \end{aligned}$$

16. $$\begin{aligned} x_2 + x_3 &= 3 \\ 3x_1 + 5x_2 + 9x_3 &= -2 \\ x_1 + 2x_2 + 3x_3 &= 3 \end{aligned}$$

17. $$\begin{aligned} x_1 + 2x_2 \quad\quad &= 4 \\ -x_1 + 3x_2 + 3x_3 &= -2 \\ x_2 + x_3 &= 0 \end{aligned}$$

18. $$\begin{aligned} x_1 - 5x_2 + 4x_3 &= -3 \\ 2x_1 - 7x_2 + 3x_3 &= -2 \\ -2x_1 + x_2 + 7x_3 &= -1 \end{aligned}$$

19. $$\begin{aligned} x_2 + 5x_3 &= -4 \\ x_1 + 4x_2 + 3x_3 &= -2 \\ 2x_1 + 7x_2 + x_3 &= -1 \end{aligned}$$

20. $$\begin{aligned} 2x_1 \quad\quad - 4x_3 &= -10 \\ x_2 + 3x_3 &= 2 \\ 3x_1 + 5x_2 + 8x_3 &= -6 \end{aligned}$$

Determine if the systems in Exercises 21–26 are consistent. Do not completely solve the systems.

21. $$\begin{aligned} x_1 - 5x_2 - 4x_3 &= 0 \\ -x_1 + 6x_2 + 6x_3 &= -3 \\ -2x_1 + 6x_2 + 3x_3 &= 7 \end{aligned}$$

22. $$\begin{aligned} x_1 + 2x_2 - 4x_3 &= -3 \\ -3x_1 - 5x_2 + 8x_3 &= 7 \\ -x_1 + x_2 - 3x_3 &= 0 \end{aligned}$$

23. $$\begin{aligned} -2x_1 - 3x_2 + 4x_3 &= 5 \\ x_2 - 2x_3 &= 4 \\ x_1 + 3x_2 - x_3 &= 2 \end{aligned}$$

24. $$\begin{aligned} x_1 - 6x_2 \quad\quad\quad\quad &= 5 \\ x_2 - 4x_3 + x_4 &= 0 \\ -x_1 + 6x_2 + x_3 + 5x_4 &= 3 \\ -x_2 + 5x_3 + 4x_4 &= 0 \end{aligned}$$

25. $$\begin{aligned} 2x_2 + 2x_3 \quad\quad &= 0 \\ x_1 \quad\quad\quad\quad - 2x_4 &= -3 \\ x_3 + 3x_4 &= -4 \\ -2x_1 + 3x_2 + 2x_3 + x_4 &= 5 \end{aligned}$$

26. $$\begin{aligned} x_1 \quad - 2x_3 \quad\quad &= -1 \\ x_2 \quad\quad - x_4 &= 2 \\ -3x_2 + 2x_3 \quad\quad &= 0 \\ -4x_1 \quad\quad\quad + 7x_4 &= -5 \end{aligned}$$

In Exercises 27–30, determine the value(s) of h such that the matrix is the augmented matrix of a consistent linear system.

27. $\begin{bmatrix} 1 & -3 & h \\ -2 & 6 & -5 \end{bmatrix}$

28. $\begin{bmatrix} 1 & 4 & -2 \\ 3 & h & -6 \end{bmatrix}$

29. $\begin{bmatrix} 1 & h & -2 \\ -4 & 2 & 10 \end{bmatrix}$

30. $\begin{bmatrix} 2 & -6 & -3 \\ -4 & 12 & h \end{bmatrix}$

In Exercises 31–34, find the elementary row operation that transforms the first matrix into the second, and then find the reverse row operation that transforms the second matrix into the first.

31. $\begin{bmatrix} 1 & 3 & -1 \\ 0 & 2 & -4 \\ 0 & -3 & 4 \end{bmatrix}, \begin{bmatrix} 1 & 3 & -1 \\ 0 & 1 & -2 \\ 0 & -3 & 4 \end{bmatrix}$

32. $\begin{bmatrix} 0 & 5 & -3 \\ 1 & 5 & -2 \\ 2 & 1 & 8 \end{bmatrix}, \begin{bmatrix} 1 & 5 & -2 \\ 0 & 5 & -3 \\ 2 & 1 & 8 \end{bmatrix}$

33. $\begin{bmatrix} 1 & 3 & -1 & 5 \\ 0 & 1 & -4 & 2 \\ 0 & 2 & -5 & -1 \end{bmatrix}, \begin{bmatrix} 1 & 3 & -1 & 5 \\ 0 & 1 & -4 & 2 \\ 0 & 0 & 3 & -5 \end{bmatrix}$

34. $\begin{bmatrix} 1 & -2 & 0 & 3 \\ 0 & 3 & 5 & 1 \\ 3 & -4 & 7 & 2 \end{bmatrix}, \begin{bmatrix} 1 & -2 & 0 & 3 \\ 0 & 3 & 5 & 1 \\ 0 & 2 & 7 & -7 \end{bmatrix}$

SOLUTIONS TO PRACTICE PROBLEMS

1. For "hand computation," the best choice is to interchange equations 3 and 4. Another possibility is to multiply equation 3 by 1/5. Or, replace equation 4 by its sum with $-1/5$ times row 3. (In any case, do not use the x_2 in equation 2 to eliminate the $4x_2$ in equation 1. Wait until a triangular form is reached and the x_3 terms and x_4 terms are eliminated from the first two equations.)

2. The system is in triangular form. Further simplification begins with the x_4 in the fourth equation. Use the x_4 to eliminate all x_4 terms above it. The appropriate step now is to add 2 times equation 4 to equation 1. (After that, move up to equation 3, multiply it by 1/2, and then use the equation to eliminate the x_3 terms above it.)

3. The system corresponding to the augmented matrix is

$$\begin{aligned} x_1 + 5x_2 + 2x_3 &= -6 \\ 4x_2 - 7x_3 &= 2 \\ 5x_3 &= 0 \end{aligned}$$

The third equation makes $x_3 = 0$, which is certainly an allowable value for x_3. After eliminating the x_3 terms in equations 1 and 2, we could go on to solve for unique values for x_2 and x_1. Hence a solution exists and it is unique. Contrast this situation with that in Example 3.

4. It is easy to check if a specific list of numbers is a solution. Setting $x_1 = 3$, $x_2 = 4$, and $x_3 = -2$, we find that

$$\begin{aligned} 5(3) - (4) + 2(-2) &= 15 - 4 - 4 = 7 \\ -2(3) + 6(4) + 9(-2) &= -6 + 24 - 18 = 0 \\ -7(3) + 5(4) - 3(-2) &= -21 + 20 + 6 = 5 \end{aligned}$$

Although the first two equations are satisfied, the third is not, so $(3, 4, -2)$ is not a solution to the system. Notice the use of parentheses when making the substitutions. They are strongly recommended as a guard against arithmetic errors.

1.2 ROW REDUCTION AND ECHELON FORMS

In this section, we refine the method of Section 1.1 into a row reduction algorithm that will enable us to solve any system of linear equations.[1] By using only the first part of the algorithm, we will be able to answer the fundamental existence and uniqueness questions posed in Section 1.1.

The algorithm applies to any matrix, whether or not the matrix is viewed as an augmented matrix for a linear system. So the first part of the section concerns an arbitrary rectangular matrix. We begin by introducing two important classes of matrices that include the "triangular" matrices of Section 1.1. In the definitions that follow, a *nonzero* row or column in a matrix means a row or column that contains at least one nonzero entry; a *leading entry* of a row refers to the leftmost nonzero entry (in a nonzero row).

DEFINITION

A rectangular matrix is in **echelon form** (or **row echelon form**) if it has the following three properties:

1. All nonzero rows are above any rows of all zeros.
2. Each leading entry of a row is in a column to the right of the leading entry of the row above it.
3. All entries in a column below a leading entry are zero.

If a matrix in echelon form satisfies the following additional conditions, then it is in **reduced echelon form**:

4. The leading entry in each nonzero row is 1.
5. Each leading 1 is the only nonzero entry in its column.

An **echelon matrix** (respectively, **reduced echelon matrix**) is one that is in echelon form (respectively, reduced echelon form). Property 2 says that the leading entries form an *echelon* ("steplike") pattern that moves down and to the right through the matrix. Property 3 is a simple consequence of property 2, but we include it for emphasis.

The "triangular" matrices of Section 1.1, such as

$$\begin{bmatrix} 2 & -3 & 2 & 1 \\ 0 & 1 & -4 & 8 \\ 0 & 0 & 0 & 5/2 \end{bmatrix} \quad \text{and} \quad \begin{bmatrix} 1 & 0 & 0 & 29 \\ 0 & 1 & 0 & 16 \\ 0 & 0 & 1 & 3 \end{bmatrix}$$

are in echelon form. In fact, the second matrix is in reduced echelon form. Here are additional examples.

---

[1] Our algorithm is a variant of what is commonly called *Gaussian elimination.* A similar elimination method for linear systems was used by Chinese mathematicians in about 250 B.C. The process was unknown in Western culture until the nineteenth century, when a famous German mathematician, Carl Friedrich Gauss, discovered it. A German engineer, Wilhelm Jordan, popularized the algorithm in an 1888 text on geodesy.

EXAMPLE 1 The following matrices are in echelon form. The leading entries, ■, may have any nonzero value; the starred entries may have any values (including zero).

$$\begin{bmatrix} \blacksquare & * & * & * \\ 0 & \blacksquare & * & * \\ 0 & 0 & 0 & 0 \\ 0 & 0 & 0 & 0 \end{bmatrix}, \quad \begin{bmatrix} 0 & \blacksquare & * & * & * & * & * & * & * & * \\ 0 & 0 & 0 & \blacksquare & * & * & * & * & * & * \\ 0 & 0 & 0 & 0 & \blacksquare & * & * & * & * & * \\ 0 & 0 & 0 & 0 & 0 & \blacksquare & * & * & * & * \\ 0 & 0 & 0 & 0 & 0 & 0 & 0 & 0 & \blacksquare & * \end{bmatrix}$$

The following matrices are in reduced echelon form because the leading entries are 1's, and there are 0's below *and above* each leading 1.

$$\begin{bmatrix} 1 & 0 & * & * \\ 0 & 1 & * & * \\ 0 & 0 & 0 & 0 \\ 0 & 0 & 0 & 0 \end{bmatrix}, \quad \begin{bmatrix} 0 & 1 & * & 0 & 0 & 0 & * & * & 0 & * \\ 0 & 0 & 0 & 1 & 0 & 0 & * & * & 0 & * \\ 0 & 0 & 0 & 0 & 1 & 0 & * & * & 0 & * \\ 0 & 0 & 0 & 0 & 0 & 1 & * & * & 0 & * \\ 0 & 0 & 0 & 0 & 0 & 0 & 0 & 0 & 1 & * \end{bmatrix}$$

A matrix may be **row reduced** (that is, transformed by elementary row operations) into more than one matrix in echelon form, using different sequences of row operations. However, the reduced echelon form one obtains from a matrix is unique. The following theorem is proved in Appendix A at the end of the text.

THEOREM 1

Uniqueness of the Reduced Echelon Form

Each matrix is row equivalent to one and only one reduced echelon matrix.

If a matrix A is row equivalent to an echelon matrix U, we call U **an echelon form of A**; if U is in reduced echelon form, we call U **the reduced echelon form of A**.

Pivot Positions

When row operations on a matrix produce an echelon form, further row operations to obtain the reduced echelon form do not change the positions of the leading entries. Since the reduced echelon form is unique, *the leading entries are always in the same positions in any echelon form obtained from a given matrix.* These locations are called **pivot positions**, and the columns that contain them are **pivot columns**. [The squares (■) in Example 1 identify the pivot positions.] Many fundamental concepts in the next four chapters will be connected in one way or another with pivot positions in a matrix.

EXAMPLE 2 Row reduce the following matrix to echelon form, and locate the pivot columns.

$$\begin{bmatrix} 0 & -3 & -6 & 4 & 9 \\ -1 & -2 & -1 & 3 & 1 \\ -2 & -3 & 0 & 3 & -1 \\ 1 & 4 & 5 & -9 & -7 \end{bmatrix}$$

Solution Use the same basic strategy as in Section 1.1. The top of the leftmost nonzero column is the first pivot position. A nonzero entry, or *pivot*, must be placed in this position. A good choice is to interchange rows 1 and 4 (because the mental computations in the next step will not involve fractions).

Pivot

$$\begin{bmatrix} 1 & 4 & 5 & -9 & -7 \\ -1 & -2 & -1 & 3 & 1 \\ -2 & -3 & 0 & 3 & -1 \\ 0 & -3 & -6 & 4 & 9 \end{bmatrix}$$

Pivot column

Create zeros below the pivot "1" by adding multiples of the first row to the rows below, and obtain matrix (1) below. The pivot position in the second row must be as far left as possible, namely, in the second column. We'll choose the 2 in this position as the next pivot.

Pivot

$$\begin{bmatrix} 1 & 4 & 5 & -9 & -7 \\ 0 & 2 & 4 & -6 & -6 \\ 0 & 5 & 10 & -15 & -15 \\ 0 & -3 & -6 & 4 & 9 \end{bmatrix} \tag{1}$$

Next pivot column

Add $-5/2$ times row 2 to row 3, and add $3/2$ times row 2 to row 4:

$$\begin{bmatrix} 1 & 4 & 5 & -9 & -7 \\ 0 & 2 & 4 & -6 & -6 \\ 0 & 0 & 0 & 0 & 0 \\ 0 & 0 & 0 & -5 & 0 \end{bmatrix} \tag{2}$$

The matrix in (2) is different from any encountered in Section 1.1. There is no way to create a leading entry in column 3! (We can't use rows 1 or 2 because doing so would destroy the echelon arrangement of the leading entries already produced.) However, if we interchange rows 3 and 4, we can produce a leading entry in column 4.

Pivot

$$\begin{bmatrix} 1 & 4 & 5 & -9 & -7 \\ 0 & 2 & 4 & -6 & -6 \\ 0 & 0 & 0 & -5 & 0 \\ 0 & 0 & 0 & 0 & 0 \end{bmatrix} \qquad \text{General form: } \begin{bmatrix} \blacksquare & * & * & * & * \\ 0 & \blacksquare & * & * & * \\ 0 & 0 & 0 & \blacksquare & * \\ 0 & 0 & 0 & 0 & 0 \end{bmatrix}$$

Pivot columns

The matrix is in echelon form, with the pivot columns indicated. Any other echelon matrix that is row equivalent to the original matrix has the same pivot positions and the same general form. ∎

A **pivot**, as illustrated in Example 2, is a nonzero number in a pivot position that is used as needed to create zeros via row operations. In some hand computations, it may be convenient to change a pivot to a leading 1 in order to simplify later arithmetic. For instance, we could have divided the second row in (1) by the pivot before creating the zeros below the pivot position. Or it may be possible to interchange two rows in order to select a 1 as a pivot. (See the first step in Example 2.)

With Example 2 as a guide, we are ready to describe an efficient procedure for transforming a matrix into an echelon or reduced echelon matrix. A careful study and mastery of the procedure now will pay rich dividends later in the course.

The Row Reduction Algorithm

The algorithm that follows consists of four steps, and it produces a matrix in echelon form. A fifth step produces a matrix in reduced echelon form. We illustrate the algorithm by an example.

EXAMPLE 3 Apply elementary row operations to transform the following matrix first into echelon form and then into reduced echelon form.

$$\begin{bmatrix} 0 & 3 & -6 & 6 & 4 & -5 \\ 3 & -7 & 8 & -5 & 8 & 9 \\ 3 & -9 & 12 & -9 & 6 & 15 \end{bmatrix}$$

Solution

> **Step 1.** Begin with the leftmost nonzero column. This is a pivot column. The pivot position is at the top.

$$\begin{bmatrix} 0 & 3 & -6 & 6 & 4 & -5 \\ 3 & -7 & 8 & -5 & 8 & 9 \\ 3 & -9 & 12 & -9 & 6 & 15 \end{bmatrix}$$

↑ Pivot column

> **Step 2.** Select a nonzero entry in the pivot column as a pivot. If necessary, interchange rows to move this entry into the pivot position.

Interchange rows 1 and 3. (We could have interchanged rows 1 and 2 instead.)

Pivot (→ the entry 3 in row 1, column 1)

$$\begin{bmatrix} 3 & -9 & 12 & -9 & 6 & 15 \\ 3 & -7 & 8 & -5 & 8 & 9 \\ 0 & 3 & -6 & 6 & 4 & -5 \end{bmatrix}$$

> **Step 3.** Use row replacement operations to create zeros in all positions below the pivot.

As a preliminary step, we could divide the top row by the pivot, 3. But with two 3's in column 1, it is just as easy to add -1 times row 1 to row 2.

Pivot

$$\begin{bmatrix} 3 & -9 & 12 & -9 & 6 & 15 \\ 0 & 2 & -4 & 4 & 2 & -6 \\ 0 & 3 & -6 & 6 & 4 & -5 \end{bmatrix}$$

> **Step 4.** Cover the row containing the pivot position and cover all rows, if any, above it. Apply steps 1–3 to the submatrix that remains. Repeat the process until there are no more nonzero rows to modify.

With row 1 covered, step 1 shows that column 2 is the next pivot column; for step 2, we'll select as a pivot the "top" entry in that column.

Pivot

$$\begin{bmatrix} 3 & -9 & 12 & -9 & 6 & 15 \\ 0 & 2 & -4 & 4 & 2 & -6 \\ 0 & 3 & -6 & 6 & 4 & -5 \end{bmatrix}$$

New pivot column

For step 3, we could insert an optional step of dividing the "top" row of the submatrix by the pivot, 2. Instead, we add $-3/2$ times the "top" row to the row below. This produces

$$\begin{bmatrix} 3 & -9 & 12 & -9 & 6 & 15 \\ 0 & 2 & -4 & 4 & 2 & -6 \\ 0 & 0 & 0 & 0 & 1 & 4 \end{bmatrix}$$

When we cover the row containing the second pivot position for step 4, we are left with a new submatrix having only one row:

$$\begin{bmatrix} 3 & -9 & 12 & -9 & 6 & 15 \\ 0 & 2 & -4 & 4 & 2 & -6 \\ 0 & 0 & 0 & 0 & 1 & 4 \end{bmatrix}$$

Pivot

Steps 1 to 3 require no work for this submatrix, and we have reached an echelon form of the full matrix. If we want the reduced echelon form, we perform one more step.

> **Step 5.** Beginning with the rightmost pivot, and working upward and to the left, create zeros above each pivot. If a pivot is not 1, make it 1 by a scaling operation.

The rightmost pivot is in row 3. Create 0's above it, adding suitable multiples of row 3 to rows 2 and 1.

$$\begin{bmatrix} 3 & -9 & 12 & -9 & 0 & -9 \\ 0 & 2 & -4 & 4 & 0 & -14 \\ 0 & 0 & 0 & 0 & 1 & 4 \end{bmatrix} \begin{matrix} \leftarrow \text{Row } 1 + (-6)\cdot\text{row } 3 \\ \leftarrow \text{Row } 2 + (-2)\cdot\text{row } 3 \\ \end{matrix}$$

The next pivot is in row 2. Scale this row, dividing by the pivot.

$$\begin{bmatrix} 3 & -9 & 12 & -9 & 0 & -9 \\ 0 & 1 & -2 & 2 & 0 & -7 \\ 0 & 0 & 0 & 0 & 1 & 4 \end{bmatrix} \leftarrow \text{Row scaled by } \tfrac{1}{2}$$

Create a 0 in column 2 by adding 9 times row 2 to row 1.

$$\begin{bmatrix} 3 & 0 & -6 & 9 & 0 & -72 \\ 0 & 1 & -2 & 2 & 0 & -7 \\ 0 & 0 & 0 & 0 & 1 & 4 \end{bmatrix} \begin{matrix} \leftarrow \text{Row } 1 + 9\cdot\text{row } 2 \\ \\ \end{matrix}$$

Finally, scale row 1, dividing by the pivot, 3.

$$\begin{bmatrix} 1 & 0 & -2 & 3 & 0 & -24 \\ 0 & 1 & -2 & 2 & 0 & -7 \\ 0 & 0 & 0 & 0 & 1 & 4 \end{bmatrix} \begin{matrix} \leftarrow \text{Row scaled by } \tfrac{1}{3} \\ \\ \end{matrix}$$

This is the reduced echelon form of the original matrix. ∎

The combination of steps 1–4 is called the **forward phase** of the row reduction algorithm. Step 5, which produces the unique reduced echelon form, is called the **backward phase**.

Numerical Note

In step 2, a computer program usually selects as a pivot the entry in a column having the largest absolute value. This strategy, called **partial pivoting**, tends to reduce roundoff errors in the calculations.

Solutions of Linear Systems

The row reduction algorithm leads directly to an explicit description of the solution set of a linear system when the algorithm is applied to the augmented matrix of the system.

Suppose, for example, that the augmented matrix of a linear system has been changed into the equivalent *reduced* echelon form

$$\begin{bmatrix} 1 & 0 & -5 & 1 \\ 0 & 1 & 1 & 4 \\ 0 & 0 & 0 & 0 \end{bmatrix} \tag{3}$$

There are three variables because the augmented matrix has four columns. The associated system of equations is

$$\begin{aligned} x_1 \quad\quad -5x_3 &= 1 \\ x_2 + \ x_3 &= 4 \\ 0 \ &= 0 \end{aligned} \tag{4}$$

The variables x_1 and x_2 corresponding to pivot columns in the matrix are called **basic variables**.[2] The other variable, x_3, is called a **free variable**.

We shall describe the solution set of the system by solving these equations for the basic variables in terms of the free variables. This operation is possible because the reduced echelon form (3) places each basic variable in one and only one equation. We can solve the first equation for x_1 and the second for x_2. (The third equation is ignored; it offers no restriction on the variables.)

$$\begin{cases} x_1 = 1 + 5x_3 \\ x_2 = 4 - \ x_3 \\ x_3 \text{ is free} \end{cases} \tag{5}$$

By saying that x_3 is "free," we mean that we are free to choose any value for x_3. Once that is done, the formulas in (5) determine the values for x_1 and x_2. For instance, if we take $x_3 = 0$, we get the solution $(1, 4, 0)$; if we take $x_3 = 1$, we get $(6, 3, 1)$. *Each different choice of* x_3 *determines a (different) solution of the system, and every solution of the system is determined by a choice of* x_3.

The solution in (5) is called a **general solution** of the system because it gives an explicit description of *all* solutions.

EXAMPLE 4 Find the general solution of the linear system whose augmented matrix has been reduced to

$$\begin{bmatrix} 1 & 6 & 2 & -5 & -2 & -4 \\ 0 & 0 & 2 & -8 & -1 & 3 \\ 0 & 0 & 0 & 0 & 1 & 7 \end{bmatrix}$$

Solution The matrix is in echelon form, but we want the reduced echelon form before solving for the basic variables. The row reduction is completed next. The symbol "$\sim$" before a matrix indicates that the matrix is row equivalent to the preceding matrix.

$$\begin{bmatrix} 1 & 6 & 2 & -5 & -2 & -4 \\ 0 & 0 & 2 & -8 & -1 & 3 \\ 0 & 0 & 0 & 0 & 1 & 7 \end{bmatrix} \sim \begin{bmatrix} 1 & 6 & 2 & -5 & 0 & 10 \\ 0 & 0 & 2 & -8 & 0 & 10 \\ 0 & 0 & 0 & 0 & 1 & 7 \end{bmatrix}$$

$$\sim \begin{bmatrix} 1 & 6 & 2 & -5 & 0 & 10 \\ 0 & 0 & 1 & -4 & 0 & 5 \\ 0 & 0 & 0 & 0 & 1 & 7 \end{bmatrix} \sim \begin{bmatrix} 1 & 6 & 0 & 3 & 0 & 0 \\ 0 & 0 & 1 & -4 & 0 & 5 \\ 0 & 0 & 0 & 0 & 1 & 7 \end{bmatrix}$$

[2] Some texts use the term *leading variables* because they correspond to the columns containing leading entries.

There are five variables since the augmented matrix has six columns. The associated system now is

$$\begin{aligned} x_1 + 6x_2 \quad + 3x_4 \quad &= 0 \\ x_3 - 4x_4 \quad &= 5 \\ x_5 &= 7 \end{aligned} \tag{6}$$

The pivot columns of the matrix are 1, 3, and 5, so the basic variables are x_1, x_3, and x_5. The remaining variables, x_2 and x_4, must be free. Solving for the basic variables, we obtain the general solution:

$$\begin{cases} x_1 = -6x_2 - 3x_4 \\ x_2 \text{ is free} \\ x_3 = 5 + 4x_4 \\ x_4 \text{ is free} \\ x_5 = 7 \end{cases} \tag{7}$$

Observe that the value of x_5 is already fixed by the third equation in system (6). ∎

Parametric Descriptions of Solution Sets

The descriptions in (5) and (7) are *parametric descriptions* of solution sets in which the free variables act as parameters. *Solving a system* amounts to finding a parametric description of the solution set.

Whenever there are free variables in a consistent system, a solution set has many parametric descriptions. For instance, in system (4), we may add 5 times equation 2 to equation 1 and obtain the equivalent system

$$\begin{aligned} x_1 + 5x_2 \qquad &= 21 \\ x_2 + x_3 &= \ \ 4 \end{aligned}$$

We could treat x_2 as a parameter and solve for x_1 and x_3 in terms of x_2, and we would have an accurate description of the solution set. However, to be consistent, we make the (arbitrary) convention of always using the free variables as the parameters for describing a solution set. (The answer section at the end of the text also reflects this convention.)

Back-Substitution

Consider the following system whose augmented matrix is in echelon form but is *not* in reduced echelon form.

$$\begin{aligned} x_1 - 7x_2 + 2x_3 - 5x_4 + 8x_5 &= \ \ 10 \\ x_2 - 3x_3 + 3x_4 + \ \ x_5 &= -5 \\ x_4 - \ \ x_5 &= \ \ 4 \end{aligned}$$

Many texts would solve this system by back-substitution, *without matrix notation.* That is, solve equation 3 for x_4 in terms of x_5 and substitute the expression for x_4 into equation 2; solve equation 2 for x_2; and then substitute the expressions for x_2 and x_4 into equation 1 and solve for x_1.

The backward phase of the row reduction algorithm, which produces the reduced echelon form, is equivalent to back-substitution. But the discipline of the matrix format substantially reduces the likelihood of errors during "hand" computations. I *strongly* recommend that you use only the *reduced* echelon form to solve a system!

The Study Guide that accompanies this text discusses the problems of back-substitution in greater detail. Several other helpful suggestions for performing row operations accurately and rapidly are also given.

Existence and Uniqueness Questions

Although a nonreduced echelon form is a poor tool for solving a system, this form is just the right device for answering two fundamental questions about systems posed in Section 1.1.

EXAMPLE 5 Determine the existence and uniqueness of the solutions to the system

$$\begin{aligned} 3x_2 - 6x_3 + 6x_4 + 4x_5 &= -5 \\ 3x_1 - 7x_2 + 8x_3 - 5x_4 + 8x_5 &= 9 \\ 3x_1 - 9x_2 + 12x_3 - 9x_4 + 6x_5 &= 15 \end{aligned}$$

Solution The augmented matrix of this system was row reduced in Example 3 to

$$\begin{bmatrix} 3 & -9 & 12 & -9 & 6 & 15 \\ 0 & 2 & -4 & 4 & 2 & -6 \\ 0 & 0 & 0 & 0 & 1 & 4 \end{bmatrix} \tag{8}$$

The basic variables are x_1, x_2, and x_5; the free variables are x_3 and x_4. There is no equation such as $0 = 1$ that would create an inconsistent system, so we could use back-substitution to find a solution. But the *existence* of a solution is already clear in (8). Also, the solution is *not unique* because there are free variables. Each different choice of x_3 and x_4 determines a different solution. Thus the system has infinitely many solutions. ∎

When a system is in echelon form and contains no equation of the form $0 = b$, with b nonzero, every nonzero equation contains a basic variable with a nonzero coefficient. Either the basic variables are completely determined (with no free variables), or at least one of the basic variables may be expressed in terms of one or more free variables. In the former case, there is a unique solution; in the latter case, there are infinitely many solutions (one for each choice of values for the free variables).

These remarks justify the following theorem.

THEOREM 2 **Existence and Uniqueness Theorem**

A linear system is consistent if and only if the rightmost column of the augmented matrix is *not* a pivot column, that is, if and only if an echelon form of the augmented matrix has *no* row of the form

$$[0 \quad \cdots \quad 0 \quad b] \qquad \text{with } b \text{ nonzero}$$

If a linear system is consistent, then the solution set contains either (i) a unique solution, when there are no free variables, or (ii) infinitely many solutions, when there is at least one free variable.

The following procedure outlines how to find and describe all solutions of a linear system.

Using Row Reduction to Solve a Linear System

1. Write the augmented matrix of the system.
2. Use the row reduction algorithm to obtain an equivalent augmented matrix in echelon form. Decide whether the system is consistent. If there is no solution, stop; otherwise, go to the next step.
3. Continue row reduction to obtain the reduced echelon form.
4. Write the system of equations corresponding to the matrix obtained in step 3.
5. Rewrite each nonzero equation from step 4 so that its one basic variable is expressed in terms of any free variables appearing in the equation.

PRACTICE PROBLEMS

1. Find the general solution of the linear system whose augmented matrix is

$$\begin{bmatrix} 1 & -3 & -5 & 0 \\ 0 & 1 & 1 & 3 \end{bmatrix}$$

2. Find the general solution of the system

$$\begin{aligned} x_1 - 2x_2 - x_3 + 3x_4 &= 0 \\ -2x_1 + 4x_2 + 5x_3 - 5x_4 &= 3 \\ 3x_1 - 6x_2 - 6x_3 + 8x_4 &= 2 \end{aligned}$$

1.2 EXERCISES

In Exercises 1–4, determine which matrices are in reduced echelon form and which others are in echelon form (but not in reduced echelon form).

1. a. $\begin{bmatrix} 1 & 0 & 0 & 0 \\ 0 & 1 & 0 & 0 \\ 0 & 0 & 1 & 0 \end{bmatrix}$ b. $\begin{bmatrix} 1 & 0 & 0 & 0 \\ 0 & 1 & 1 & 0 \\ 0 & 0 & 0 & 1 \end{bmatrix}$

c. $\begin{bmatrix} 0 & 1 & 1 \\ 0 & 0 & 1 \\ 0 & 0 & 0 \end{bmatrix}$ d. $\begin{bmatrix} 0 & 0 & 0 \\ 1 & 0 & 0 \\ 0 & 1 & 0 \end{bmatrix}$

2. a. $\begin{bmatrix} 1 & 1 & 1 & 0 \\ 0 & 0 & 0 & 1 \\ 0 & 0 & 0 & 0 \end{bmatrix}$ b. $\begin{bmatrix} 1 & 0 & 1 & 0 \\ 0 & 0 & 1 & 1 \\ 0 & 0 & 0 & 1 \end{bmatrix}$

c. $\begin{bmatrix} 1 & 0 & 1 \\ 0 & 0 & 0 \\ 0 & 1 & 0 \end{bmatrix}$ d. $\begin{bmatrix} 1 & 1 & 1 \\ 0 & 0 & 0 \\ 0 & 0 & 0 \end{bmatrix}$

3. a. $\begin{bmatrix} 1 & 1 & 0 & 0 & 0 \\ 0 & 1 & 1 & 0 & 0 \\ 0 & 0 & 1 & 1 & 0 \\ 0 & 0 & 0 & 1 & 1 \end{bmatrix}$

b. $\begin{bmatrix} 1 & 2 & 3 & 4 & 5 \\ 0 & 2 & 3 & 4 & 5 \\ 0 & 0 & 3 & 4 & 5 \\ 0 & 0 & 0 & 4 & 5 \end{bmatrix}$

c. $\begin{bmatrix} 0 & 1 & 0 & 0 & 0 \\ 0 & 0 & 1 & 2 & 0 \\ 0 & 0 & 0 & 0 & 1 \\ 0 & 0 & 0 & 0 & 0 \end{bmatrix}$

4. a. $\begin{bmatrix} 1 & 0 & 0 & 0 & 0 \\ 1 & 1 & 0 & 0 & 0 \\ 0 & 1 & 1 & 0 & 0 \\ 0 & 0 & 1 & 1 & 0 \end{bmatrix}$

b. $\begin{bmatrix} 0 & 2 & 3 & 4 & 5 \\ 0 & 0 & 3 & 4 & 5 \\ 0 & 0 & 0 & 0 & 5 \\ 0 & 0 & 0 & 0 & 0 \end{bmatrix}$

c. $\begin{bmatrix} 1 & 2 & 3 & 4 & 5 \\ 0 & 1 & 2 & 3 & 4 \\ 0 & 0 & 1 & 2 & 3 \\ 0 & 0 & 0 & 1 & 2 \end{bmatrix}$

Row reduce the matrices in Exercises 5 and 6 to reduced echelon form, and list the pivot columns.

5. a. $\begin{bmatrix} 1 & 2 & 3 \\ 0 & 1 & 2 \\ 0 & 0 & 1 \end{bmatrix}$

b. $\begin{bmatrix} 1 & 2 & 3 & 4 \\ 5 & 6 & 7 & 8 \\ 9 & 10 & 11 & 12 \end{bmatrix}$

c. $\begin{bmatrix} 1 & 3 & 0 & 0 & 3 \\ 0 & 0 & 1 & 0 & 0 \\ 0 & 0 & 0 & 0 & 0 \\ 0 & 0 & 0 & 3 & 1 \end{bmatrix}$

6. a. $\begin{bmatrix} 1 & 1 & 1 \\ 0 & 2 & 2 \\ 0 & 0 & 3 \end{bmatrix}$

b. $\begin{bmatrix} 1 & 4 & 7 & 10 \\ 2 & 5 & 8 & 11 \\ 3 & 6 & 9 & 12 \end{bmatrix}$

c. $\begin{bmatrix} 1 & 0 & 1 & 0 & 0 \\ 0 & 0 & 1 & 0 & 1 \\ 0 & 1 & 0 & 1 & 0 \\ 0 & 0 & 0 & 1 & 1 \end{bmatrix}$

Find the general solutions of the systems whose augmented matrices are given in Exercises 7–21.

7. $\begin{bmatrix} 1 & 0 & 2 & 5 \\ 2 & 0 & 3 & 6 \end{bmatrix}$ **8.** $\begin{bmatrix} 1 & -3 & 0 & -5 \\ -3 & 7 & 0 & 9 \end{bmatrix}$

9. $\begin{bmatrix} 0 & 3 & 6 & 9 \\ -1 & 1 & -2 & -1 \end{bmatrix}$ **10.** $\begin{bmatrix} 1 & 3 & -3 & 7 \\ 3 & 9 & -4 & 1 \end{bmatrix}$

11. $\begin{bmatrix} 1 & 4 & 2 & 3 \\ -2 & -8 & -1 & 9 \end{bmatrix}$ **12.** $\begin{bmatrix} 1 & 3 & 6 & 9 \\ -1 & 1 & -2 & -1 \end{bmatrix}$

13. $\begin{bmatrix} 2 & -4 & 3 \\ -6 & 12 & -9 \\ 4 & -8 & 6 \end{bmatrix}$ **14.** $\begin{bmatrix} 1 & 2 & 4 \\ -2 & -3 & -5 \\ 2 & 1 & -1 \end{bmatrix}$

15. $\begin{bmatrix} 1 & 2 & -7 \\ -1 & -1 & 1 \\ 2 & 1 & 5 \end{bmatrix}$ **16.** $\begin{bmatrix} 1 & 0 & 0 & 8 & -3 \\ 0 & 1 & 0 & 4 & -6 \\ 0 & 0 & 1 & -7 & 5 \\ 0 & 0 & 0 & 0 & 0 \end{bmatrix}$

17. $\begin{bmatrix} 1 & 0 & -9 & 0 & 4 \\ 0 & 1 & 3 & 0 & -1 \\ 0 & 0 & 0 & 1 & -7 \\ 0 & 0 & 0 & 0 & 1 \end{bmatrix}$

18. $\begin{bmatrix} 1 & 5 & 0 & 0 & 3 \\ 0 & 0 & 1 & 0 & -2 \\ 0 & 0 & 0 & 1 & 6 \\ 0 & 0 & 0 & 0 & 1 \end{bmatrix}$

19. $\begin{bmatrix} 1 & -2 & 0 & 0 & 7 & -3 \\ 0 & 1 & 0 & 0 & -3 & 1 \\ 0 & 0 & 0 & 1 & 5 & -4 \\ 0 & 0 & 0 & 0 & 0 & 0 \end{bmatrix}$

20. $\begin{bmatrix} 1 & 0 & -5 & 0 & -8 & 3 \\ 0 & 1 & 4 & -1 & 0 & 6 \\ 0 & 0 & 0 & 0 & 1 & 0 \\ 0 & 0 & 0 & 0 & 0 & 0 \end{bmatrix}$

21. $\begin{bmatrix} 1 & 0 & -2 & 0 & 0 & 0 \\ 0 & 1 & 6 & -3 & -2 & 7 \\ 0 & 0 & 0 & 1 & 0 & -5 \\ 0 & 0 & 0 & 0 & 1 & 0 \end{bmatrix}$

In Exercises 22–25, determine the value(s) of h such that the matrix is the augmented matrix of a consistent linear system.

22. $\begin{bmatrix} 1 & 4 & 2 \\ -3 & h & -1 \end{bmatrix}$

23. $\begin{bmatrix} 1 & -1 & 4 \\ -2 & 3 & h \end{bmatrix}$

24. $\begin{bmatrix} 1 & -3 & 1 \\ h & 6 & -2 \end{bmatrix}$

25. $\begin{bmatrix} 1 & h & 3 \\ 2 & 8 & 1 \end{bmatrix}$

In Exercises 26–27, choose h and k such that the system has (a) no solution, (b) a unique solution, and (c) many solutions. Give separate answers for each part.

26. $\begin{aligned} x_1 + hx_2 &= 1 \\ 2x_1 + 3x_2 &= k \end{aligned}$

27. $\begin{aligned} x_1 - 3x_2 &= 1 \\ 2x_1 + hx_2 &= k \end{aligned}$

28. Suppose that a 3×5 *coefficient* matrix for a system has three pivot columns. Is the system consistent? Why?

29. Suppose that a system of linear equations has a 3×5 *augmented* matrix whose fifth column is a pivot column. Is the system consistent? Why?

30. A system of linear equations with more equations than unknowns is sometimes called an *overdetermined* system. Can such a system be consistent? Illustrate your answer with a specific system of three equations in two unknowns.

31. A system of linear equations with fewer equations than unknowns is sometimes called an *underdetermined system.* Suppose that such a system happens to be consistent. Explain why there must be an infinite number of solutions.

32. Give an example of an inconsistent underdetermined system of two equations in three unknowns.

33. Restate the last sentence in Theorem 2 using the concept of pivot columns: "If a linear system is consistent, then the solution is unique if and only if ______ ."

34. What would you have to know about the pivot columns in an augmented matrix in order to know that the linear system is consistent and has a unique solution?

SOLUTIONS TO PRACTICE PROBLEMS

1. The reduced echelon form of the augmented matrix and the corresponding system are

$$\begin{bmatrix} 1 & 0 & -2 & 9 \\ 0 & 1 & 1 & 3 \end{bmatrix} \quad \text{and} \quad \begin{aligned} x_1 \qquad - 2x_3 &= 9 \\ x_2 + \ x_3 &= 3 \end{aligned}$$

The basic variables are x_1 and x_2, and the general solution is

$$\begin{cases} x_1 = 9 + 2x_3 \\ x_2 = 3 - x_3 \\ x_3 \text{ is free} \end{cases}$$

Note: It is essential that the general solution describe each variable, with any parameters clearly identified. The following statement does *not* describe the solution:

$$\begin{cases} x_1 = 9 + 2x_3 \\ x_2 = 3 - x_3 \\ x_3 = 3 - x_2 \quad \text{(incorrect solution)} \end{cases}$$

This description implies that x_2 and x_3 are *both* free, which certainly is not the case.

2. When we row reduce the system's augmented matrix, we obtain

$$\begin{bmatrix} 1 & -2 & -1 & 3 & 0 \\ -2 & 4 & 5 & -5 & 3 \\ 3 & -6 & -6 & 8 & 2 \end{bmatrix} \sim \begin{bmatrix} 1 & -2 & -1 & 3 & 0 \\ 0 & 0 & 3 & 1 & 3 \\ 0 & 0 & -3 & -1 & 2 \end{bmatrix}$$

$$\sim \begin{bmatrix} 1 & -2 & -1 & 3 & 0 \\ 0 & 0 & 3 & 1 & 3 \\ 0 & 0 & 0 & 0 & 5 \end{bmatrix}$$

This echelon matrix shows that the system is *inconsistent*, because its rightmost column is a pivot column; the third row corresponds to the equation $0 = 5$. There is no need to perform any more row operations. Note that the presence of the free variables in this problem is irrelevant because the system is inconsistent.

1.3 APPLICATIONS OF LINEAR SYSTEMS

It's time to see some linear equations in action! The problems discussed here provide a glimpse into two of the areas mentioned in the chapter introduction—networks and economic models. Later, with more linear algebra concepts at our disposal, we'll examine many other applications of linear systems.

Network Flow

Systems of linear equations arise naturally when scientists, engineers, or economists study the flow of some quantity through a network. For instance, urban planners and traffic engineers monitor the pattern of traffic flow in a grid of city streets. Electrical engineers calculate current flow through electrical circuits. And economists analyze the distribution of products from manufacturers to consumers through a network of wholesalers and retailers. For many networks, the systems of equations involve hundreds or even thousands of variables and equations.

A *network* consists of a set of points called *junctions* or *nodes*, with lines or arcs called *branches* connecting some or all of the junctions. The direction of flow in each branch is indicated, and the flow amount (or rate) is either shown or is denoted by a variable.

The basic assumption of network flow is that the total flow into the network equals the total flow out of the network and that the total flow into a junction equals the total flow out of the junction. For example, Fig. 1 shows 30 units flowing into a junction through one branch, with x_1 and x_2 the flows out of the junction through other branches. Since the flow is "conserved" at each junction, we must have $x_1 + x_2 = 30$. In a similar fashion, the flow at each junction is described by a linear equation. The problem of network analysis is to determine the flow in each branch when partial information (such as the input to the network) is known.

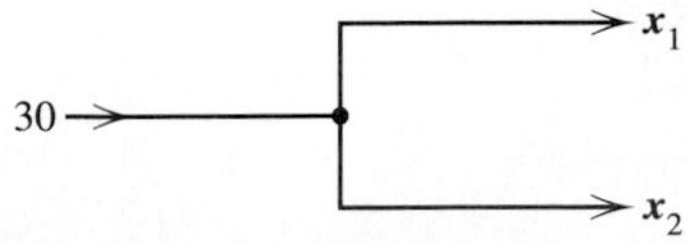

FIGURE 1 A junction or node.

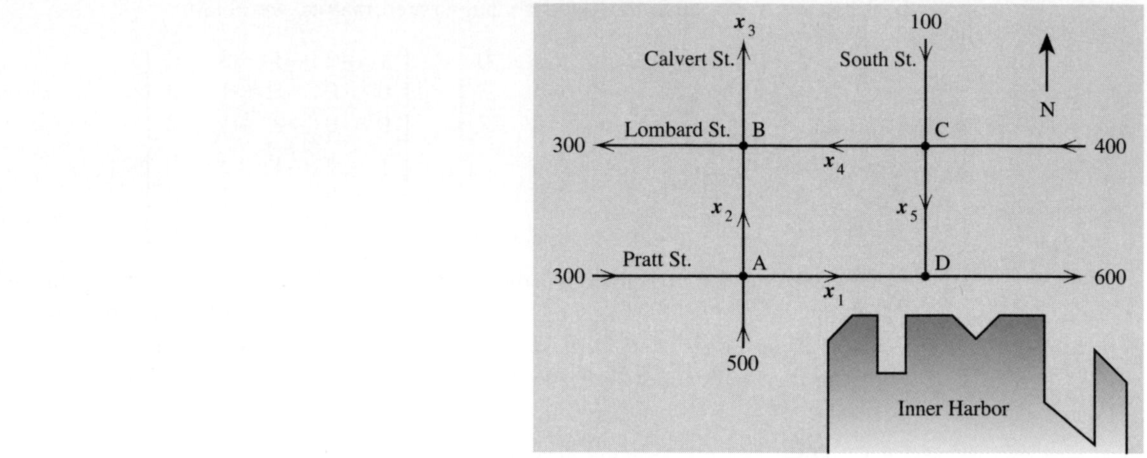

FIGURE 2 Baltimore streets.

EXAMPLE 1 The network in Fig. 2 shows the traffic flow (in vehicles per hour) over several one-way streets in downtown Baltimore during a typical early afternoon. Determine the general flow pattern for the network.

Solution We'll write equations that describe the flow and then find the general solution of the system. Label the street intersections ("junctions") and the unknown flows in the branches, as shown in Fig. 2. At each intersection, set the flow in equal to the flow out.

Intersection	Flow in		Flow out
A	$300 + 500$	$=$	$x_1 + x_2$
B	$x_2 + x_4$	$=$	$300 + x_3$
C	$100 + 400$	$=$	$x_4 + x_5$
D	$x_1 + x_5$	$=$	600

Also, the total flow into the network $(500 + 300 + 100 + 400)$ equals the total flow out of the network $(300 + x_3 + 600)$ which simplifies to $x_3 = 400$. Combining this equation with a rearrangement of the first four equations, we obtain the following system of equations.

$$\begin{aligned}
x_1 + x_2 \qquad\qquad\qquad &= 800 \\
x_2 - x_3 + x_4 \qquad &= 300 \\
x_4 + x_5 &= 500 \\
x_1 \qquad\qquad\qquad + x_5 &= 600 \\
x_3 \qquad\qquad &= 400
\end{aligned}$$

Row reduction of the associated augmented matrix leads to

$$\begin{aligned} x_1 \qquad\qquad &+ x_5 = 600 \\ x_2 \qquad\quad &- x_5 = 200 \\ x_3 \qquad &\quad\;\; = 400 \\ x_4 &+ x_5 = 500 \end{aligned}$$

The general flow pattern for the network is described by

$$\begin{cases} x_1 = 600 - x_5 \\ x_2 = 200 + x_5 \\ x_3 = 400 \\ x_4 = 500 - x_5 \\ x_5 \text{ is free} \end{cases}$$

A negative flow in a network branch corresponds to flow in the direction opposite to that shown on the model. Since the streets in this problem are one-way, none of the variables here can be negative. This fact leads easily to certain limitations on the possible values of the variables. For instance, $x_5 \leq 500$ because x_4 can't be negative. Other constraints on the variables are considered in Practice Problem 1. ∎

Once a model for traffic flow is available, city planners can see which streets are critical to a smooth flow of traffic. For instance, in the example above, the section of South Street corresponding to x_5 could be closed without disrupting the overall flow; however, since the solution requires x_3 to be 400, any restriction to the flow on Calvert north of Lombard would force a change in the overall flow into the downtown area.

Electrical Networks

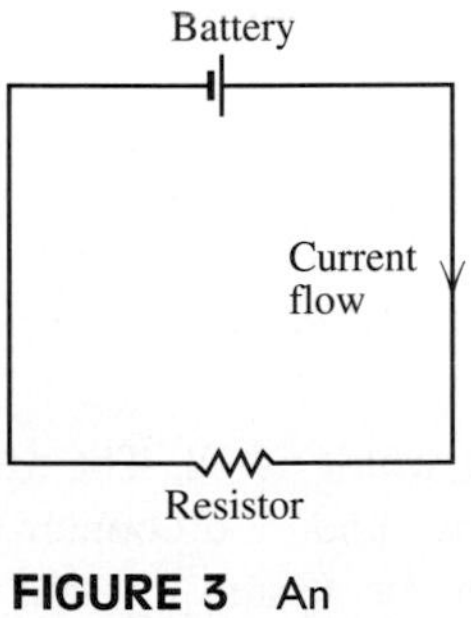

FIGURE 3 An electrical network.

The simplest sort of electrical network involves only batteries and resistors. Examples of resistors include light bulbs, motors, and heaters. See Fig. 3.

A voltage source such as a battery forces a current of electrons to flow through the network or circuit. Each resistor in the circuit retards the current flow and "uses up" some of the voltage in the circuit. According to *Ohm's law*, this "voltage drop" across a resistor equals the product of the resistance R and the current flow I:

$$\{\text{Voltage drop}\} = V = RI$$

The voltage is measured in *volts*, the resistance in *ohms*, and the current flow in amperes (*amps*, for short).

Current flow in the electrical networks considered here is governed by two laws. The second law refers to a **loop**, which is a closed path over a sequence of branches that begins and ends at the same node.

> **Kirchhoff's Laws**
>
> **1.** (Current Law) The current flow into a node equals the current flow out of the node.
>
> **2.** (Voltage Law) The algebraic sum of the RI voltage drops in one direction around a loop equals the algebraic sum of the voltage sources in the same direction around the loop.

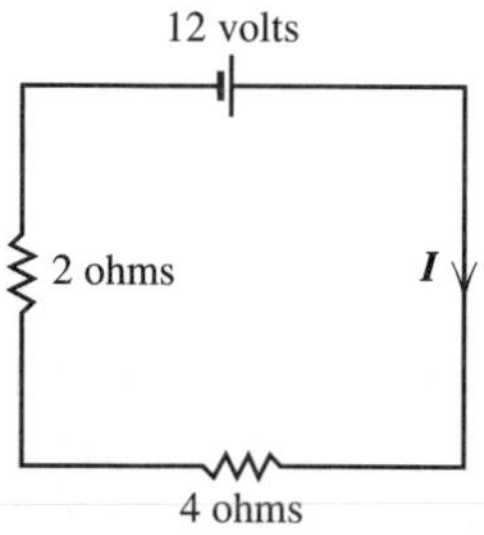

FIGURE 4

EXAMPLE 2 Determine the current I in the circuit in Fig. 4.

Solution Tracing the circuit in the direction of the flow, we compute the voltage drop across the bottom resistor as $RI = 4I$ volts. The second voltage drop is $2I$ volts. Since the voltage supplied by the battery is 12 volts, Kirchhoff's voltage law gives $4I + 2I = 12$, and $I = 2$ amps.

The direction of current flow shown in a network branch is arbitrary, but, by convention, whenever possible we show the direction of current away from the longer (positive) side of a battery around to the shorter (negative) side.

The flow directions shown in a network influence how the RI products and voltages are recorded when using Kirchhoff's voltage law. In Example 2, we could have traversed the circuit in a counterclockwise direction. In that case, we pass through the resistors in a direction opposite to that shown on the network. So we record the voltage "drops" as negative, as $-2I$ and $-4I$. Likewise, we pass through the battery in a direction opposite to the indicated current flow, so we record the voltage as a negative 12 volts. Then, by Kirchhoff, $-2I - 4I = -12$, and $I = 2$, as before.

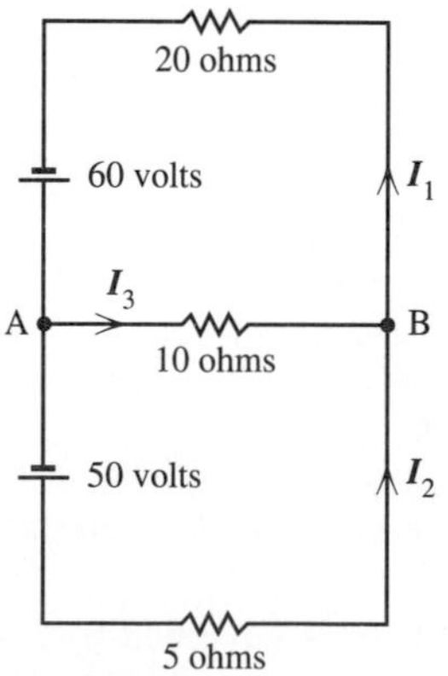

FIGURE 5

EXAMPLE 3 Determine the branch currents I_1, I_2, and I_3 in the network shown in Fig. 5.

Solution Kirchhoff's current law provides one equation for each node:

Node	Current In		Current Out	
A	I_1	$=$	$I_2 + I_3$	(1)
B	$I_2 + I_3$	$=$	I_1	

Observe that the second equation is redundant, so we won't use it. The voltage law provides one equation for each loop. In the top loop, we choose a counter-clockwise direction, which coincides with the directions shown for I_1 and I_3, and gives the conventional current flow from the battery. So we have

RI Voltage Drops		Voltage Sources	
$20I_1 + 10I_3$	$=$	60	(2)

In the bottom loop, a counterclockwise direction coincides with the direction of I_2 but is opposite to the direction for I_3. So we give the RI product for I_3 a negative sign:

RI Voltage Drops		Voltage Sources	
$5I_2 - 10I_3$	$=$	50	(3)

There is a third large outside loop for which we choose a counterclockwise direction. The RI products are both positive, and so are the voltages for the batteries. By Kirchhoff's voltage law,

$$20I_1 + 5I_2 = 60 + 50$$

Notice that this equation may be obtained by adding corresponding terms in (2) and (3), so this equation offers no new information about the currents.

Rearranging the essential restrictions (1), (2), and (3) on the currents, we have

$$\begin{aligned} I_1 - I_2 - I_3 &= 0 \\ 20I_1 \qquad + 10I_3 &= 60 \\ 5I_2 - 10I_3 &= 50 \end{aligned}$$

The solution of this system of equations is $I_1 = 4$ amps, $I_2 = 6$ amps, $I_3 = -2$ amps. The negative sign for I_3 means that the current I_3 flows in the direction opposite to that shown on the network. ■

Example 3 shows that the equations derived from the shortest possible loops in a network can be combined to produce the equations for the longer loops. This holds true for all networks in this text. So we need consider only the "minimal" loops.

Leontief Economic Models

The system of 500 equations in 500 variables, mentioned in this chapter's introduction, is now known as a Leontief "input–output" (or "production") model.[1] Section 3.7 will examine this model in more detail, when we have more theory and better notation available. For now, we look at a simpler "exchange model," also due to Leontief.

Suppose a nation's economy is divided into many sectors, such as various manufacturing, communication, entertainment, and service industries. Suppose that for each sector we know its total output for one year and we know exactly how this output is divided or "exchanged" among the other sectors of the economy. Let the total dollar value of a sector's output be called the **price** of that output. Leontief proved the following result.

> There exist *equilibrium prices* that can be assigned to the total outputs of the various sectors in such a way that the income of each sector exactly balances its expenses.

The following example shows how to find the equilibrium prices.

[1] See Wassily W. Leontief, *Scientific American*, "Input–Output Economics," October 1951, pp. 15–21.

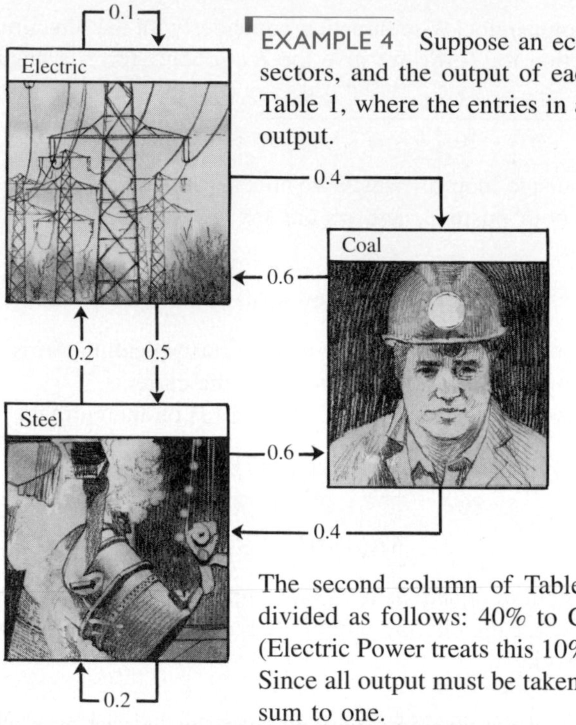

EXAMPLE 4 Suppose an economy consists of the Coal, Electric (Power), and Steel sectors, and the output of each sector is distributed among the various sectors as in Table 1, where the entries in a column represent the fractional parts of a sector's total output.

TABLE 1 A Simple Economy

Distribution of output from:			
Coal	Electric	Steel	Purchased by:
.0	.4	.6	Coal
.6	.1	.2	Electric
.4	.5	.2	Steel

The second column of Table 1, for instance, says that the total Electric output is divided as follows: 40% to Coal, 50% to Steel, and the remaining 10% to Electric. (Electric Power treats this 10% as an expense it incurs in order to operate its business.) Since all output must be taken into account, the decimal fractions in each column must sum to one.

Denote the prices (i.e., dollar values) of the total annual outputs of the Coal, Electric Power, and Steel sectors by p_c, p_e, and p_s, respectively. If possible, find equilibrium prices that make each sector's income match its expenditures.

Solution A sector looks down a column to see where its output goes, and it looks across a row to see what it needs as inputs. For instance, the first row of Table 1 says that Coal receives (and pays for) 40% of the Electric output and 60% of the Steel output. Since the respective values of the total outputs are p_e and p_s, Coal must spend $.4p_e$ dollars for its share of Electric's output and $.6p_s$ for its share of Steel's output. That is,

$$\left\{\begin{matrix}\text{expenses}\\ \text{of}\\ \text{Coal}\end{matrix}\right\} = \left\{\begin{matrix}\text{purchases}\\ \text{from}\\ \text{Electric}\end{matrix}\right\} + \left\{\begin{matrix}\text{purchases}\\ \text{from}\\ \text{Steel}\end{matrix}\right\} = .4p_e + .6p_s$$

To make Coal's income, p_c, equal to its expenses, we want

$$p_c = .4p_e + .6p_s \tag{4}$$

From the second row of the exchange table, we find that

$$\begin{aligned}\left\{\begin{matrix}\text{expenses}\\ \text{of}\\ \text{Electric}\end{matrix}\right\} &= \left\{\begin{matrix}\text{purchases}\\ \text{from}\\ \text{Coal}\end{matrix}\right\} + \left\{\begin{matrix}\text{purchases}\\ \text{from}\\ \text{Electric}\end{matrix}\right\} + \left\{\begin{matrix}\text{purchases}\\ \text{from}\\ \text{Steel}\end{matrix}\right\}\\ &= \quad .6p_c \quad + \quad .1p_e \quad + \quad .2p_s\end{aligned}$$

Hence the income/expense requirement for Electric Power is

$$p_e = .6p_c + .1p_e + .2p_s \tag{5}$$

Finally, the third row of the exchange table leads to the final requirement:

$$p_s = .4p_c + .5p_e + .2p_s \tag{6}$$

To solve the system of equations (4), (5), and (6), we move all the unknowns to the left sides of the equations and combine like terms. [For instance, on the left of (5) we write $p_e - .1p_e$ as $.9p_e$.]

$$\begin{aligned} p_c - .4p_e - .6p_s &= 0 \\ -.6p_c + .9p_e - .2p_s &= 0 \\ -.4p_c - .5p_e + .8p_s &= 0 \end{aligned}$$

Row reduction is next. For simplicity here, we arbitrarily round all decimals to two decimal places.

$$\begin{bmatrix} 1 & -.4 & -.6 & 0 \\ -.6 & .9 & -.2 & 0 \\ -.4 & -.5 & .8 & 0 \end{bmatrix} \sim \begin{bmatrix} 1 & -.4 & -.6 & 0 \\ 0 & .66 & -.56 & 0 \\ 0 & -.66 & .56 & 0 \end{bmatrix} \sim \begin{bmatrix} 1 & -.4 & -.6 & 0 \\ 0 & .66 & -.56 & 0 \\ 0 & 0 & 0 & 0 \end{bmatrix}$$

$$\sim \begin{bmatrix} 1 & -.4 & -.6 & 0 \\ 0 & 1 & -.85 & 0 \\ 0 & 0 & 0 & 0 \end{bmatrix} \sim \begin{bmatrix} 1 & 0 & -.94 & 0 \\ 0 & 1 & -.85 & 0 \\ 0 & 0 & 0 & 0 \end{bmatrix}$$

The general solution is $p_c = .94p_s$, $p_e = .85p_s$, and p_s is free. If, for instance, we take p_s to be 100 (or 100 million), then $p_c = 94$ and $p_e = 85$. The incomes and expenditures of each sector will be equal if the output of coal is priced at \$94 million, the electric output at \$85 million, and the steel at \$100 million. ∎

PRACTICE PROBLEMS

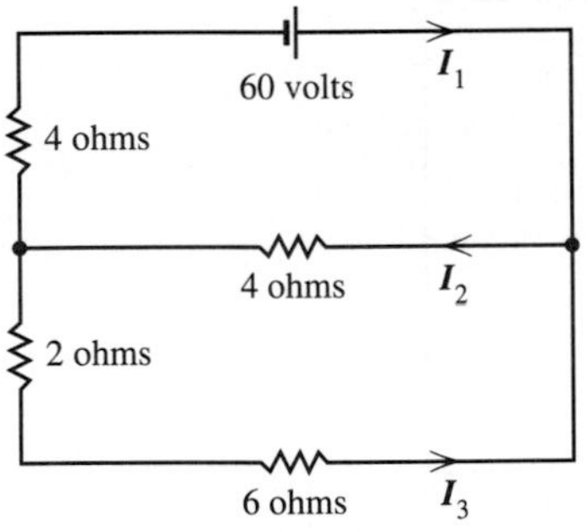

1. Consider the network flow studied in Example 1. Determine the possible range of values of x_1 and x_2. [*Hint:* The example showed that $x_5 \le 500$. What does this imply about x_1 and x_2? Also, use the fact that $x_5 \ge 0$.]
2. Determine the branch currents in the network shown here.
3. Suppose an economy has three sectors, Agriculture, Mining, and Manufacturing. Agriculture sells 5% of its output to Mining, 30% to Manufacturing, and retains the rest. Mining sells 20% of its output to Agriculture, 70% to Manufacturing, and retains the rest. Manufacturing sells 20% of its output to Agriculture, 30% to Mining, and retains the rest.

   Determine the exchange table for this economy, where the columns describe how the output of each sector is exchanged among the three sectors.

1.3 EXERCISES

1. Find the general flow pattern of the network at the right. Assuming that the flows are all nonnegative, what is the largest possible value for x_3?

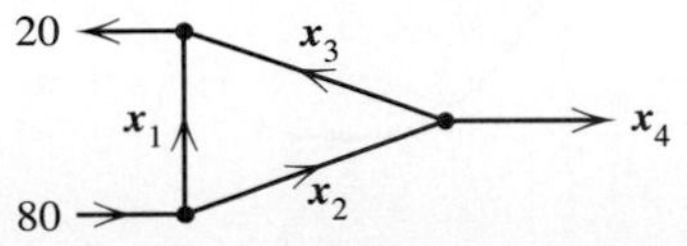

2. a. Find the general traffic pattern in the freeway network below. (Flow rates: cars/minute.)

b. Describe the general traffic pattern when the road whose flow is x_4 is closed.

c. When $x_4 = 0$, what is the minimum value of x_1?

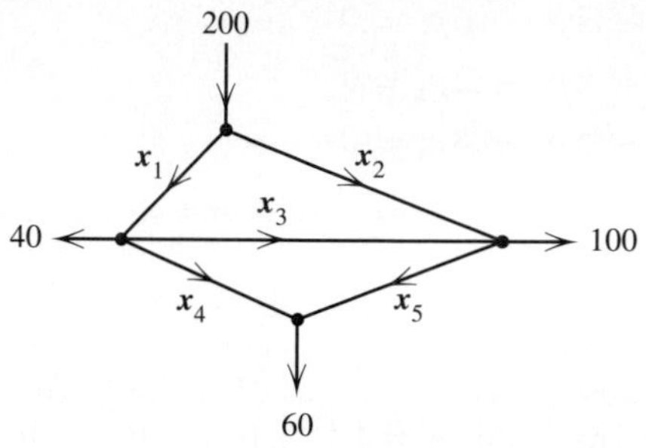

3. a. Find the general flow pattern in the network below.

b. Assuming that the flow must be in the directions indicated, find the minimum flows in the branches denoted by x_2, x_3, x_4, and x_5.

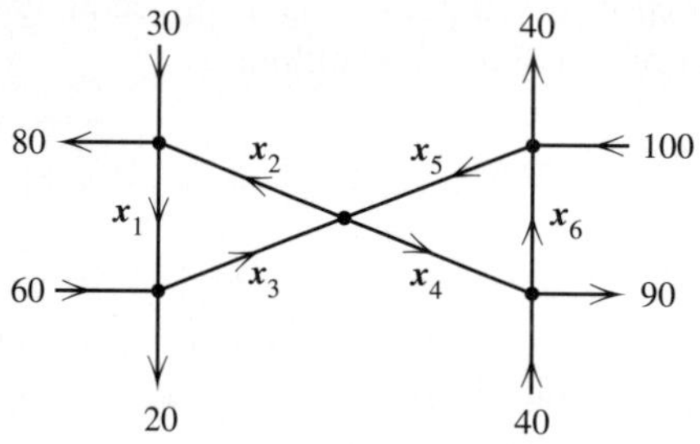

4. Intersections in England are often constructed as a one-way "roundabout," such as shown in the figure below. Assume that traffic must travel in the directions shown. Find the general solution of the network flow. Find the smallest possible value for x_6.

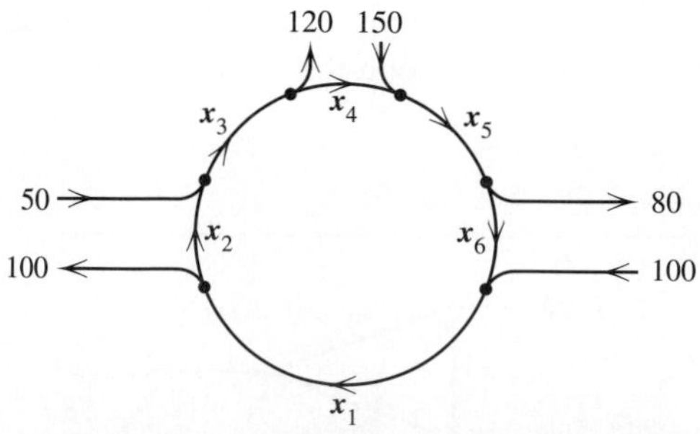

In Exercises 5–10, use Kirchhoff's laws to set up a system of equations that determines the branch currents in the network. Then solve the system.

5.

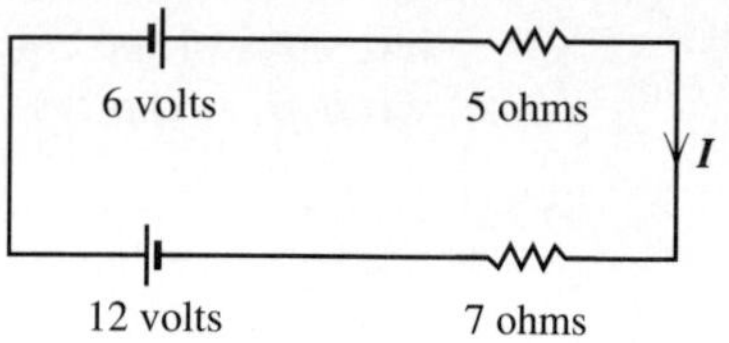

6.

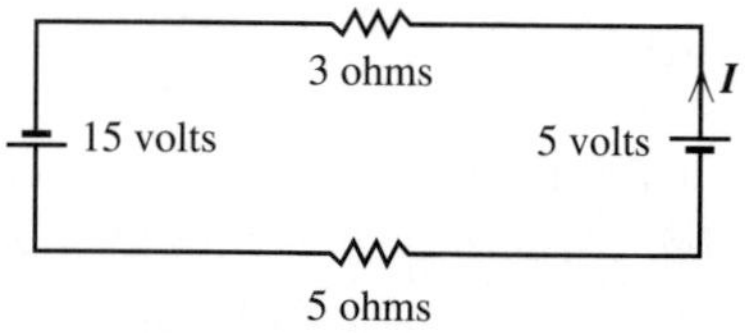

7.

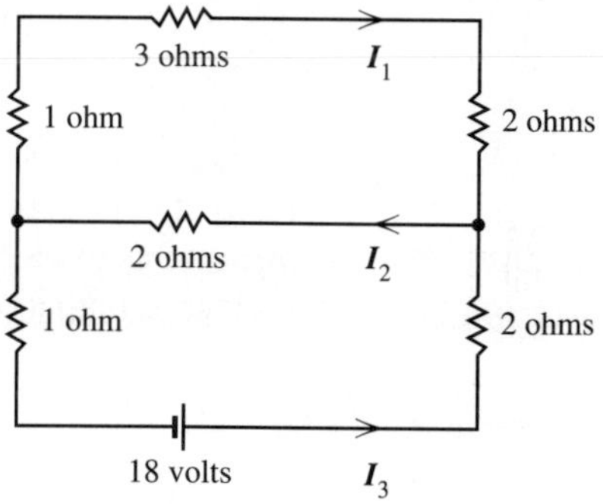

8.

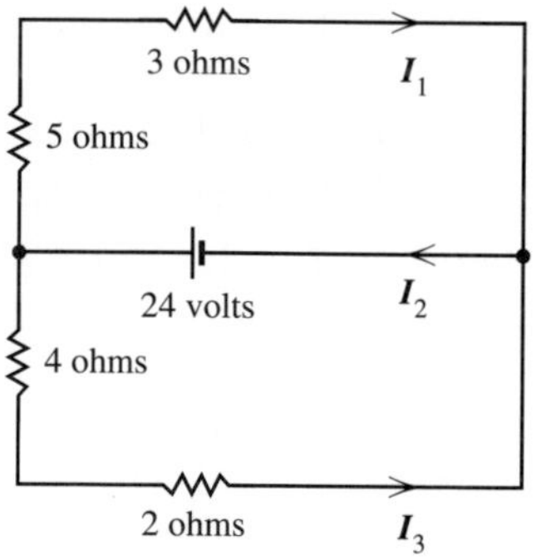

9.

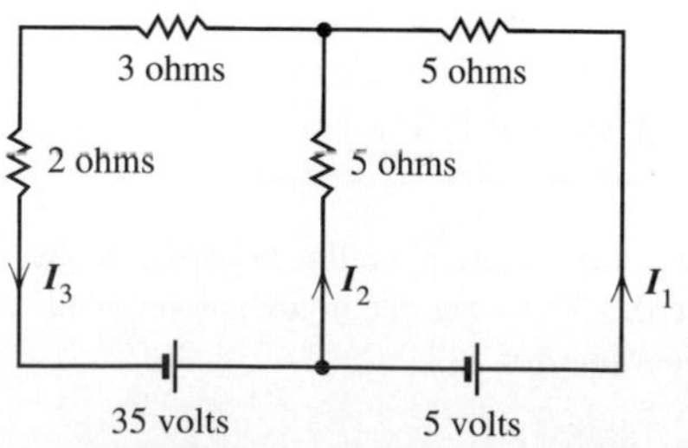

10.

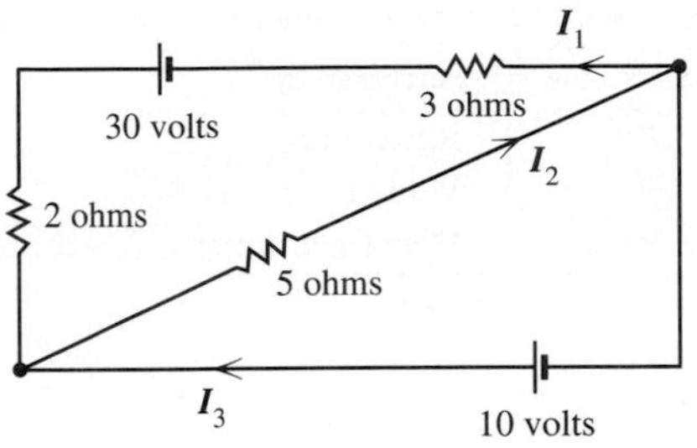

11. Suppose an economy has only two sectors, Goods and Services. Each year, Goods sells 80% of its output to Services and keeps the rest, while Services sells 70% of its output to Goods and retains the rest. Find equilibrium prices for the annual output of the Goods and Services sectors that make each sector's income match its expenditures.

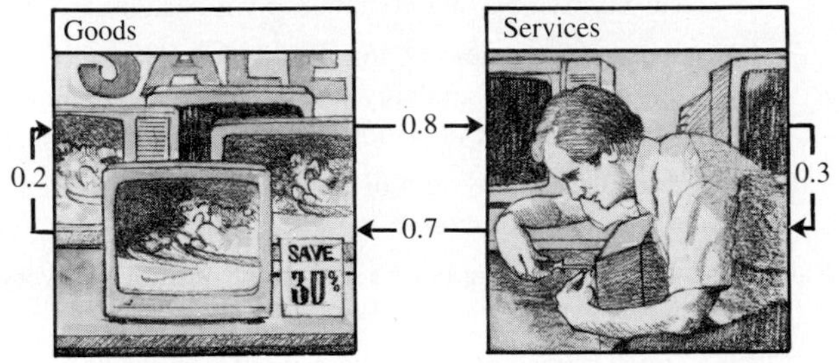

12. Find another set of equilibrium prices for the economy in Example 4. Suppose the same economy used German marks instead of dollars to measure the value of the various sectors' outputs. Would this change the problem in any way? Discuss.

13. Consider an economy with three sectors, Chemicals & Metals, Fuels & Power, and Machinery. Chemicals sells 30% of its output to Fuels, 50% to Machinery, and retains the rest. Fuels sells 80% of its output to Chemicals, 10% to Machinery, and retains the rest. Machinery sells 40% to Chemicals, 40% to Fuels, and retains the rest.

a. Construct the exchange table for this economy.

b. Develop a system of equations that leads to prices at which each sector's income matches its expenses. Then write the augmented matrix that can be row reduced to find these prices.

c. *Optional:* Use MATLAB to find a set of equilibrium prices when the price for the Machinery output is 100 units.

14. Use MATLAB to find a set of equilibrium prices for the economy in Practice Problem 3.

SOLUTIONS TO PRACTICE PROBLEMS

1. Since $x_5 \le 500$, the equations for x_1 and x_2 imply that $x_1 \ge 100$ and $x_2 \le 700$. The fact that $x_5 \ge 0$ implies that $x_1 \le 600$ and $x_2 \ge 200$. So $100 \le x_1 \le 600$, and $200 \le x_2 \le 700$.

2. At the right node, the current law produces the equation $I_1 + I_3 = I_2$. The left node produces an equivalent equation, so we omit it. Tracing the upper loop clockwise and the lower loop counterclockwise, we use the voltage law to obtain

$$\begin{aligned} 4I_1 + 4I_2 &= 60 \\ 4I_2 + 8I_3 &= 0 \quad \text{(No voltage source in lower loop)} \end{aligned}$$

Rearranging the three equations, we have

$$\begin{aligned} I_1 - I_2 + I_3 &= 0 \\ 4I_1 + 4I_2 &= 60 \\ 4I_2 + 8I_3 &= 0 \end{aligned}$$

Row operations lead to $I_1 = 9$ amps, $I_2 = 6$ amps, and $I_3 = -3$ amps.

3. Write the percentages as decimals. Since all output must be taken into account, each column sum must be 1. This fact helps us fill in any missing entries.

Distribution of Output			
Agriculture	Mining	Manufacturing	Purchased by
.65	.20	.20	Agriculture
.05	.10	.30	Mining
.30	.70	.50	Manufacturing

CHAPTER 1 SUPPLEMENTARY EXERCISES

1. Mark each statement True or False. Justify each answer. (If true, cite appropriate facts or theorems. If false, explain why or give a "counterexample" that shows why the statement is false. Complete answers are given in the Study Guide.)

___ a. If a matrix B is obtained from A by elementary row operations, then A can be obtained from B by elementary row operations.

___ b. Every matrix is row equivalent to a unique matrix in echelon form.

___ c. One elementary row operation is multiplication of all entries in a row by a constant.

___ d. If two augmented matrices are row equivalent, then the associated systems of linear equations have the same solution set.

___ e. Any system of n linear equations in n variables has at most n solutions.

___ f. If a system of linear equations has two different solutions, it must have infinitely many solutions.

___ g. If a system of linear equations has no free variables, then it has a unique solution.

___ h. An underconstrained linear system (with fewer equations than variables) cannot have a unique solution.

___ i. An overconstrained linear system (with more equations than variables) cannot have a unique solution.

___ j. If the coefficient matrix of a consistent system of linear equations has a pivot position in every column, then the solution must be unique.

___ k. A system of linear equations has infinitely many solutions if and only if at least one column in the coefficient matrix does not contain a pivot position.

___ l. A consistent system of linear equations has infinitely many solutions if and only if at least one column in the coefficient matrix does not contain a pivot position.

___ m. An inconsistent system of linear equations sometimes has a unique solution.

___ n. A 5×7 matrix cannot have a pivot position in every row.

___ o. A 6×5 matrix cannot have a pivot position in every row.

2. Let a and b represent real numbers. Describe the possible solution sets of the (linear) equation $ax = b$. (Hint: The number of solutions depends on a and b.)

3. The set of solutions of a single linear equation

$$a_1x + a_2y + a_3z = b$$

is represented in a rectangular xyz-coordinate system by a plane (when a_1, a_2, a_3 are not all zero). What types of linear systems and what types of solution sets are illustrated by the sets of planes shown in the accompanying figures?

Three planes intersecting in a line

(a)

Three planes intersecting in a point

(b)

Three planes with no intersection

(c)

4. What types of solution sets do you expect to find in a system of two linear equations in three variables? Draw figures (involving planes) to illustrate the possibilities.

5. What is the difference between a matrix in echelon form and one in reduced echelon form?

6. What kinds of questions can be answered from information displayed by an echelon form of an augmented matrix? For what kind of problem is a reduced echelon form more appropriate?

7. Suppose the coefficient matrix of a system of linear equations has a pivot position in every row. Explain why the system is consistent.

8. Suppose the coefficient matrix of a linear system of three equations in three variables has a pivot in each column. Explain why the system has a unique solution.

9. Determine h and k so that the solution set of the system (i) is empty, (ii) contains a unique solution, and (iii) contains infinitely many solutions.

a. $$\begin{aligned} x_1 + 2x_2 &= k \\ 4x_1 + hx_2 &= 5 \end{aligned}$$

b. $$\begin{aligned} -3x_1 + hx_2 &= 1 \\ 6x_1 + kx_2 &= -3 \end{aligned}$$

10. Determine if each system is consistent for *all* possible h and k. Justify your answers.

a. $$\begin{aligned} 2x_1 - x_2 &= h \\ -6x_1 + 2x_2 &= k \end{aligned}$$

b. $$\begin{aligned} 2x_1 - x_2 &= h \\ -6x_1 + 3x_2 &= k \end{aligned}$$

11. Find a condition on g, h, k that makes the system consistent.

a. $$\begin{aligned} x_1 - 4x_2 + 7x_3 &= g \\ 3x_2 - 5x_3 &= h \\ -2x_1 + 5x_2 - 9x_3 &= k \end{aligned}$$

b. $$\begin{aligned} 2x_1 + 5x_2 - 3x_3 &= g \\ 4x_1 + 7x_2 - 4x_3 &= h \\ -6x_1 - 3x_2 + x_3 &= k \end{aligned}$$

12. Solve the systems below. The decimal coefficients are typical of some exercises that will arise later in applications.

a. $$\begin{aligned} x_1 + x_2 &= 1 \\ .2x_1 - .5x_2 &= 0 \\ -.2x_1 + .5x_2 &= 0 \end{aligned}$$

b. $$\begin{aligned} .1x_1 - .3x_2 - .4x_3 &= 0 \\ -.1x_1 + .6x_2 - .2x_3 &= 0 \\ -.3x_2 + .6x_3 &= 0 \end{aligned}$$

Suppose experimental data are represented by a set of points in the plane. An **interpolating polynomial** for the data is a polynomial whose graph passes through every point. In scientific work, such a polynomial can be used, for example, to estimate values between the known data points. Another use is to create curves for graphical images on a computer screen. One method for finding an interpolating polynomial is to solve a system of linear equations.

13. Find the interpolating polynomial $p(t) = a_0 + a_1t + a_2t^2$ for the data (1, 12), (2, 15), (3, 16). That is, find a_0, a_1, a_2 such that

$$\begin{aligned} a_0 + a_1(1) + a_2(1)^2 &= 12 \\ a_0 + a_1(2) + a_2(2)^2 &= 15 \\ a_0 + a_1(3) + a_2(3)^2 &= 16 \end{aligned}$$

14. Use MATLAB to find the interpolating polynomial $a_0 + a_1t + a_2t^2 + a_3t^3$ for the data (1, 4.5), (2, 2.2), (3, 4.1), (4, 6.0).

2

Vector and Matrix Equations

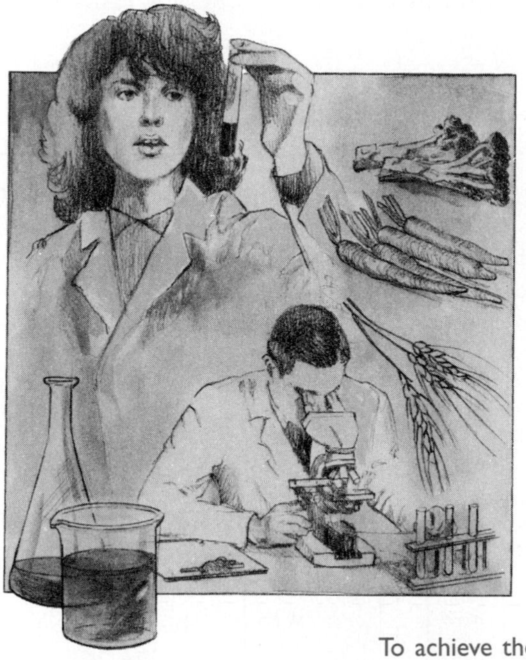

Introductory Example: Nutrition Problems

The formula for the Cambridge Diet, a popular diet in the 1980s, was based on years of research. A team of scientists headed by Dr. Alan H. Howard developed this diet at Cambridge University after more than eight years of clinical work with obese patients.[1] The very low-calorie powdered formula diet combines a precise balance of carbohydrate, high-quality protein, and fat, together with vitamins, minerals, trace elements, and electrolytes. Millions of persons have used the diet in recent years to achieve rapid and substantial weight loss.

To achieve the desired amounts and proportions of nutrients, Dr. Howard had to incorporate a large variety of foodstuffs in the diet. Each foodstuff supplied several of the required ingredients, but not in the correct proportions. For instance, nonfat milk was a major source of protein but contained too much calcium. So soy flour was used for part of the protein because soy flour contains little calcium. However, soy flour contains proportionally too much fat, so whey was added since it supplies less fat in relation to calcium. Unfortunately, whey contains too much carbohydrate .... Obviously, the delicate problem of balancing nutrients is complex.

Problems of formulating specialized diets for humans and livestock arise frequently. Typically the data for such problems consist of many lists or "vectors," one for each foodstuff, that describe the various nutrients supplied by the foodstuffs. As we shall see in Section 2.7, these vectors are easily combined into an equation that gives a useful description of the nutrition problem and leads to its solution.

---

[1]The first announcement of this rapid weight-loss regimen was given in the *International Journal of Obesity* (1978) 2, 321–332.

Systems of linear equations may appear in a problem in at least three different forms: as an ordinary system of the type studied in Chapter 1, as a single *vector equation* involving several vectors, or as a *matrix equation* containing at least one matrix and several vectors.

In this chapter, we show how these three types of equations are related and how to convert from one type to another. This skill will permit us to transfer knowledge about systems of equations to problems involving vectors and matrices. In so doing, we will be able to examine many of the central concepts of linear algebra in a simple and concrete setting. The theoretical results in Chapter 5 will flow easily from our work here and in Chapter 3.

2.1 VECTORS IN $\mathbb{R}^n$

Important properties of linear systems can be described with the concept and notation of vectors. This section introduces vectors and the two basic operations on them. The term *vector* appears in a variety of mathematical and physical contexts, which we will discuss in Chapter 5, "Vector Spaces." Until then, we will use *vector* to mean *a list of numbers*. This simple idea enables us to get to interesting and important applications as quickly as possible.

Vectors in $\mathbb{R}^2$

A matrix with only one column is called a **column vector**, or simply a **vector**. Examples of vectors with two entries are

$$\mathbf{u} = \begin{bmatrix} 3 \\ -1 \end{bmatrix}, \qquad \mathbf{v} = \begin{bmatrix} .2 \\ .3 \end{bmatrix}, \qquad \mathbf{w} = \begin{bmatrix} w_1 \\ w_2 \end{bmatrix}$$

where w_1 and w_2 are any real numbers. The set of all vectors with two entries is denoted by $\mathbb{R}^2$ (read "r-two"). The $\mathbb{R}$ stands for the real numbers that appear as entries in the vectors, and the exponent 2 indicates that the vectors each contain two entries.[1]

Two vectors in $\mathbb{R}^2$ are **equal** if and only if their corresponding entries are equal. Thus $\begin{bmatrix} 4 \\ 7 \end{bmatrix}$ and $\begin{bmatrix} 7 \\ 4 \end{bmatrix}$ are *not* equal. We say that vectors in $\mathbb{R}^2$ are *ordered pairs* of real numbers.

Given two vectors $\mathbf{u}$ and $\mathbf{v}$ in $\mathbb{R}^2$, their **sum** is the vector $\mathbf{u}+\mathbf{v}$ obtained by adding corresponding entries of $\mathbf{u}$ and $\mathbf{v}$. For example,

$$\begin{bmatrix} 1 \\ -2 \end{bmatrix} + \begin{bmatrix} 2 \\ 5 \end{bmatrix} = \begin{bmatrix} 1+2 \\ -2+5 \end{bmatrix} = \begin{bmatrix} 3 \\ 3 \end{bmatrix}$$

Given a vector $\mathbf{u}$ and a real number c, the **scalar multiple** of $\mathbf{u}$ by c is the vector $c\mathbf{u}$

[1] Most of the text concerns vectors and matrices that have only real entries. In part of Chapter 6 we will allow entries from the complex number field, $\mathbb{C}$, and change notation accordingly.

obtained by multiplying each entry in **u** by c. For instance,

$$\text{if}\quad \mathbf{u}=\begin{bmatrix}3\\-1\end{bmatrix}\quad\text{and}\quad c=5,\quad\text{then}\quad c\mathbf{u}=5\begin{bmatrix}3\\-1\end{bmatrix}=\begin{bmatrix}15\\-5\end{bmatrix}$$

The number c in $c\mathbf{u}$ is called a **scalar**; it is written in lightface type to distinguish it from the boldface vector **u**.

The operations of scalar multiplication and vector addition can be combined, as in the following example.

EXAMPLE 1 Given $\mathbf{u}=\begin{bmatrix}1\\-2\end{bmatrix}$ and $\mathbf{v}=\begin{bmatrix}2\\-5\end{bmatrix}$, find $4\mathbf{u}$, $(-3)\mathbf{v}$, and $4\mathbf{u}+(-3)\mathbf{v}$.

Solution

$$4\mathbf{u}=\begin{bmatrix}4\\-8\end{bmatrix},\qquad (-3)\mathbf{v}=\begin{bmatrix}-6\\15\end{bmatrix}$$

and

$$4\mathbf{u}+(-3)\mathbf{v}=\begin{bmatrix}4\\-8\end{bmatrix}+\begin{bmatrix}-6\\15\end{bmatrix}=\begin{bmatrix}-2\\7\end{bmatrix}$$

Sometimes for convenience (and also to save space), we write a column vector such as $\begin{bmatrix}3\\-1\end{bmatrix}$ in the form $(3, -1)$. In this case, we use parentheses and a comma to distinguish the vector $(3, -1)$ from the 1×2 row matrix $[\,3\quad -1\,]$, written with brackets and no comma. Thus

$$\begin{bmatrix}3\\-1\end{bmatrix}\neq[\,3\quad -1\,]$$

because the matrices have different shapes, even though they have the same entries.

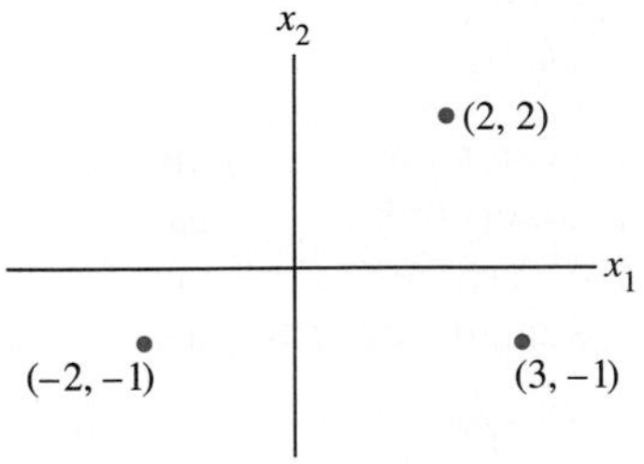

FIGURE 1 Vectors as points.

Geometric Descriptions of $\mathbb{R}^2$

Consider a rectangular coordinate system in the plane. Because each point in the plane is determined by an ordered pair of numbers, *we can identify a geometric point* (a,b) *with the column vector* $\begin{bmatrix}a\\b\end{bmatrix}$. So we may regard $\mathbb{R}^2$ as the set of all points in the plane. See Fig. 1.

The geometric visualization of a vector such as $\begin{bmatrix}3\\-1\end{bmatrix}$ is often aided by including an arrow (directed line segment) from the origin (0, 0) to the point $(3, -1)$, as in Fig. 2. In this case, the individual points along the arrow itself have no special significance.[2]

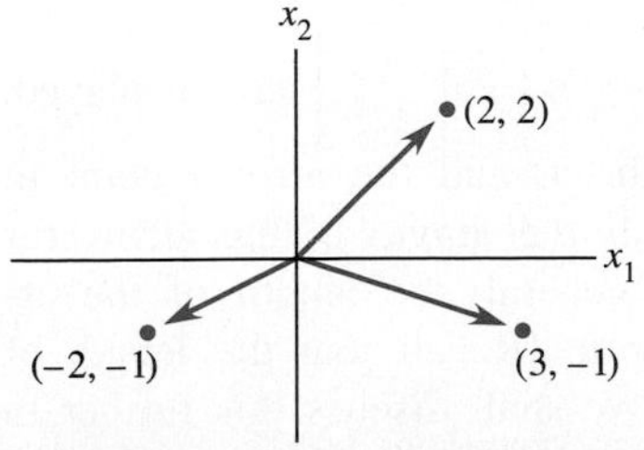

FIGURE 2 Vectors with arrows.

[2] In physics, "arrows" can represent forces and usually are free to move about in space. This interpretation of vectors will be discussed in Section 5.1.

The sum of two vectors has a useful geometric representation. The following rule can be verified by analytic geometry.

Parallelogram Rule for Addition. If $\mathbf{u}$ and $\mathbf{v}$ in $\mathbb{R}^2$ are represented as points in the plane, then $\mathbf{u} + \mathbf{v}$ corresponds to the fourth vertex of the parallelogram whose other vertices are $\mathbf{u}$, $\mathbf{0}$, and $\mathbf{v}$. See Fig. 3.

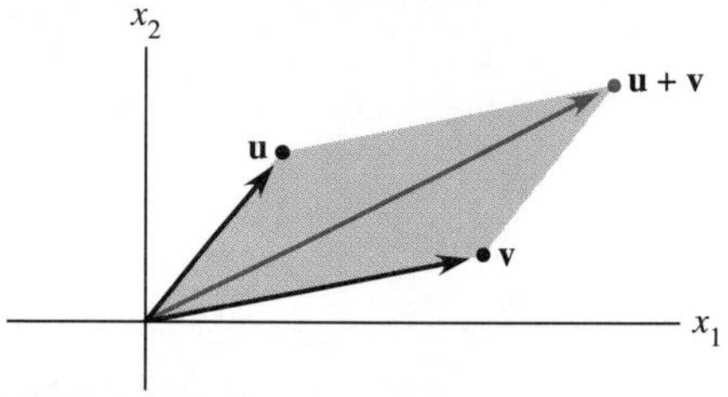

FIGURE 3 The parallelogram rule.

EXAMPLE 2 The vectors $\mathbf{u} = \begin{bmatrix} 2 \\ 2 \end{bmatrix}$, $\mathbf{v} = \begin{bmatrix} -6 \\ 1 \end{bmatrix}$, and $\mathbf{u}+\mathbf{v} = \begin{bmatrix} -4 \\ 3 \end{bmatrix}$ are displayed in Fig. 4. ∎

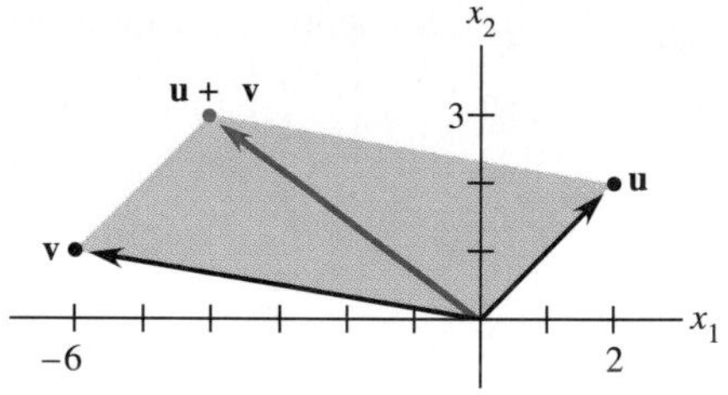

FIGURE 4

The next example illustrates the fact that the set of all scalar multiples of one fixed vector is a line through the origin.

EXAMPLE 3 Let $\mathbf{u} = \begin{bmatrix} 3 \\ -1 \end{bmatrix}$. Display the vectors $\mathbf{u}$, $2\mathbf{u}$, and $-\frac{2}{3}\mathbf{u}$ on a graph.

Solution See Fig. 5, where $\mathbf{u}$, $2\mathbf{u} = \begin{bmatrix} 6 \\ -2 \end{bmatrix}$, and $-\frac{2}{3}\mathbf{u} = \begin{bmatrix} -2 \\ 2/3 \end{bmatrix}$ are displayed. The arrow for $2\mathbf{u}$ is twice as long as the arrow for $\mathbf{u}$, and the arrows point in the same direction. The arrow for $-\frac{2}{3}\mathbf{u}$ is two-thirds the length of the arrow for $\mathbf{u}$, and the arrows point in opposite directions. In general, the length of the arrow for $c\mathbf{u}$ is $|c|$ times the length of the arrow for $\mathbf{u}$. [Recall that the length of the line segment from $(0, 0)$ to (a, b) is $\sqrt{a^2 + b^2}$. We shall discuss this further in Chapter 7.] ∎

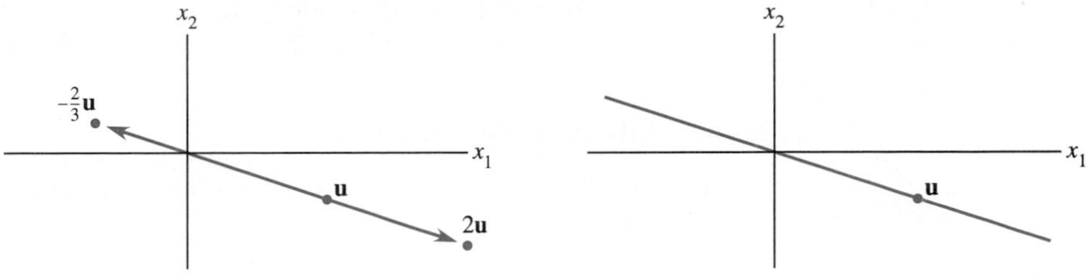

Typical multiples of **u**   The set of all multiples of **u**

FIGURE 5

Vectors in $\mathbb{R}^3$

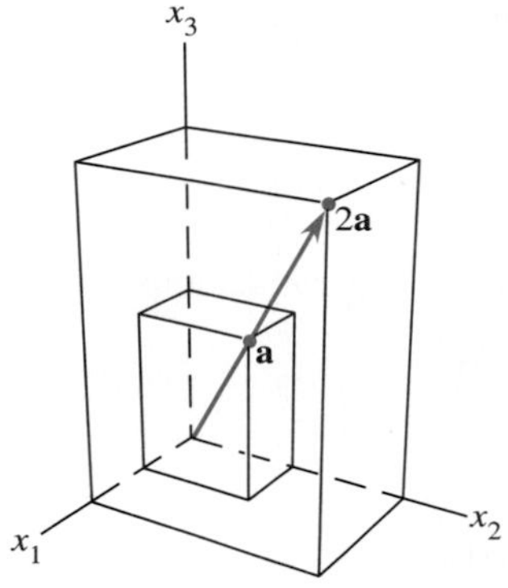

FIGURE 6 Scalar multiples in $\mathbb{R}^3$.

Vectors in $\mathbb{R}^3$ are 3×1 column matrices with three entries. They are represented geometrically by points in a three-dimensional coordinate space, with arrows from the origin sometimes included for visual clarity. The vectors $\mathbf{a} = \begin{bmatrix} 2 \\ 3 \\ 4 \end{bmatrix}$ and $2\mathbf{a}$ are displayed in Fig. 6.

Vectors in $\mathbb{R}^n$

If n is a positive integer, $\mathbb{R}^n$ (read "r-n") denotes the collection of all lists (or *ordered n-tuples*) of n real numbers, usually written as $n\times1$ column matrices, such as

$$\mathbf{u} = \begin{bmatrix} u_1 \\ u_2 \\ \vdots \\ u_n \end{bmatrix}$$

The vector whose entries are all zero is called the **zero vector** and is denoted by **0**. (The number of entries in **0** will be clear from the context.)

Equality of vectors in $\mathbb{R}^n$ and the operations of scalar multiplication and vector addition in $\mathbb{R}^n$ are defined entry by entry just as in $\mathbb{R}^2$. These operations on vectors have the following properties, which can be verified directly from the corresponding properties for real numbers. See Practice Problem 1 and Exercise 30 at the end of this section.

Algebraic Properties of $\mathbb{R}^n$. For all $\mathbf{u}, \mathbf{v}, \mathbf{w}$ in $\mathbb{R}^n$ and all scalars c and d:

(i) $\mathbf{u}+\mathbf{v}=\mathbf{v}+\mathbf{u}$
(ii) $(\mathbf{u}+\mathbf{v})+\mathbf{w}=\mathbf{u}+(\mathbf{v}+\mathbf{w})$
(iii) $\mathbf{u}+\mathbf{0}=\mathbf{0}+\mathbf{u}=\mathbf{u}$
(iv) $\mathbf{u}+(-\mathbf{u})=-\mathbf{u}+\mathbf{u}=\mathbf{0}$, where $-\mathbf{u}$ denotes $(-1)\mathbf{u}$
(v) $c(\mathbf{u}+\mathbf{v})=c\mathbf{u}+c\mathbf{v}$
(vi) $(c+d)\mathbf{u}=c\mathbf{u}+d\mathbf{u}$
(vii) $c(d\mathbf{u})=(cd)(\mathbf{u})$
(viii) $1\mathbf{u}=\mathbf{u}$.

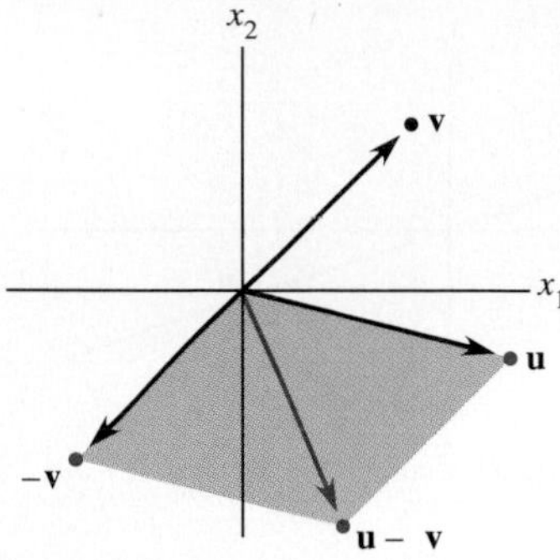

FIGURE 7 Vector subtraction.

For simplicity of notation, we also use "vector subtraction" and write $\mathbf{u} - \mathbf{v}$ in place of $\mathbf{u} + (-1)\mathbf{v}$. Figure 7 shows $\mathbf{u} - \mathbf{v}$ as the sum of $\mathbf{u}$ and $-\mathbf{v}$.

Linear Combinations

Given vectors $\mathbf{v}_1, \mathbf{v}_2, \ldots, \mathbf{v}_p$ in $\mathbb{R}^n$ and given scalars $c_1, c_2, \ldots, c_p$, the vector $\mathbf{y}$ defined by

$$\mathbf{y} = c_1\mathbf{v}_1 + \cdots + c_p\mathbf{v}_p$$

is called a **linear combination** of $\mathbf{v}_1, \ldots, \mathbf{v}_p$ using **weights** $c_1, \ldots, c_p$. Property (ii) above permits us to omit parentheses when forming such a linear combination. Some (or even all) of the weights may be zero.

EXAMPLE 4 Let $\mathbf{u}, \mathbf{v}, \mathbf{w}, \mathbf{z}$ be vectors in $\mathbb{R}^4$ such that

$$2\mathbf{u} - 3\mathbf{v} = \mathbf{w} + 4\mathbf{z}$$

Express $\mathbf{u}$ as a linear combination of $\mathbf{v}$, $\mathbf{w}$, and $\mathbf{z}$.

Solution The algebraic properties above justify the following calculations.

$$2\mathbf{u} - 3\mathbf{v} + 3\mathbf{v} = \mathbf{w} + 4\mathbf{z} + 3\mathbf{v}$$

$$2\mathbf{u} = 3\mathbf{v} + \mathbf{w} + 4\mathbf{z}$$

$$\left(\frac{1}{2}\right)2\mathbf{u} = \frac{1}{2}(3\mathbf{v} + \mathbf{w} + 4\mathbf{z})$$

$$\mathbf{u} = \frac{3}{2}\mathbf{v} + \frac{1}{2}\mathbf{w} + 2\mathbf{z}$$

Thus $\mathbf{u}$ is a linear combination of $\mathbf{v}$, $\mathbf{w}$, and $\mathbf{z}$, using weights 3/2, 1/2, and 2.

DEFINITION

If $\mathbf{v}_1, \ldots, \mathbf{v}_p$ are vectors in $\mathbb{R}^n$, then the set of all possible linear combinations of $\mathbf{v}_1, \ldots, \mathbf{v}_p$ is called the **subset of $\mathbb{R}^n$ spanned** (or **generated**) **by** $\{\mathbf{v}_1, \ldots, \mathbf{v}_p\}$ and is denoted by Span $\{\mathbf{v}_1, \ldots, \mathbf{v}_p\}$.

Span $\{\mathbf{v}_1, \ldots, \mathbf{v}_p\}$ is the collection of all vectors that can be written in the form $x_1\mathbf{v}_1 + x_2\mathbf{v}_2 + \cdots + x_p\mathbf{v}_p$, with $x_1, \ldots, x_p$ scalars. For instance, the following vectors are all in Span $\{\mathbf{v}_1, \mathbf{v}_2\}$:

$$\mathbf{v}_1 + \mathbf{v}_2, \qquad \mathbf{v}_1 - \mathbf{v}_2, \qquad 3\mathbf{v}_1 + 5\mathbf{v}_2, \qquad \frac{1}{4}\mathbf{v}_1 + \frac{3}{4}\mathbf{v}_2$$

Notice that the scalar 0 times any vector is the zero vector. Hence $\mathbf{v}_1 = 1 \cdot \mathbf{v}_1 + 0 \cdot \mathbf{v}_2$, which shows that $\mathbf{v}_1$ is a linear combination of $\mathbf{v}_1$ and $\mathbf{v}_2$ (in a trivial sort of way). Thus $\mathbf{v}_1$ itself is in Span $\{\mathbf{v}_1, \mathbf{v}_2\}$. In fact, any scalar multiple of $\mathbf{v}_1$ is in Span $\{\mathbf{v}_1, \mathbf{v}_2\}$ because for any scalar c we have $c\mathbf{v}_1 = c\mathbf{v}_1 + 0 \cdot \mathbf{v}_2$.

A Geometric Description of Span $\{\mathbf{v}\}$ and Span $\{\mathbf{u}, \mathbf{v}\}$

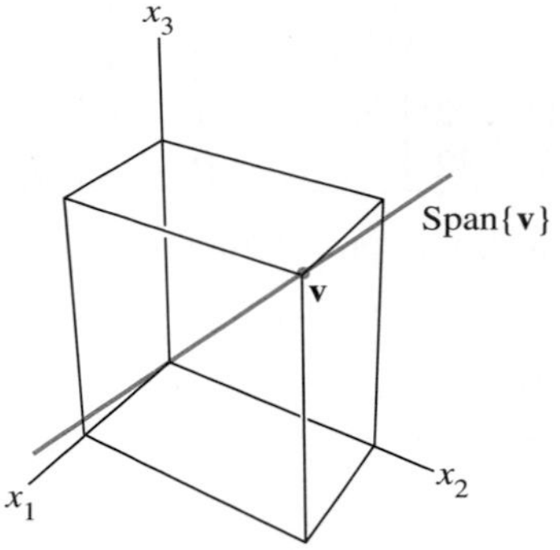

FIGURE 8 Span $\{\mathbf{v}\}$ as a line through the origin.

Let $\mathbf{v}$ be a nonzero vector in $\mathbb{R}^3$. Then Span $\{\mathbf{v}\}$ is the set of all scalar multiples of $\mathbf{v}$, and we visualize it as the set of points on the line in $\mathbb{R}^3$ through $\mathbf{v}$ and $\mathbf{0}$. See Fig. 8.

If $\mathbf{u}$ and $\mathbf{v}$ are nonzero vectors in $\mathbb{R}^3$, with $\mathbf{v}$ not a multiple of $\mathbf{u}$, then Span $\{\mathbf{u}, \mathbf{v}\}$ is the plane in $\mathbb{R}^3$ that contains $\mathbf{u}$, $\mathbf{v}$, and $\mathbf{0}$. In particular, Span $\{\mathbf{u}, \mathbf{v}\}$ contains the line in $\mathbb{R}^3$ through $\mathbf{u}$ and $\mathbf{0}$ and the line through $\mathbf{v}$ and $\mathbf{0}$. See Fig. 9.

EXAMPLE 5 Let $\mathbf{a}_1 = \begin{bmatrix} 1 \\ -2 \\ -5 \end{bmatrix}$, $\mathbf{a}_2 = \begin{bmatrix} 2 \\ 5 \\ 6 \end{bmatrix}$, and $\mathbf{b} = \begin{bmatrix} 7 \\ 4 \\ -3 \end{bmatrix}$. Show that $\mathbf{b}$ is in the plane spanned by $\mathbf{a}_1$ and $\mathbf{a}_2$; that is, find weights x_1, x_2 such that

$$x_1\mathbf{a}_1 + x_2\mathbf{a}_2 = \mathbf{b} \tag{1}$$

Solution Use the definitions of scalar multiplication and vector addition to rewrite the vector equation

$$\underset{\uparrow \atop \mathbf{a}_1}{x_1\begin{bmatrix} 1 \\ -2 \\ -5 \end{bmatrix}} + \underset{\uparrow \atop \mathbf{a}_2}{x_2\begin{bmatrix} 2 \\ 5 \\ 6 \end{bmatrix}} = \underset{\uparrow \atop \mathbf{b}}{\begin{bmatrix} 7 \\ 4 \\ -3 \end{bmatrix}}$$

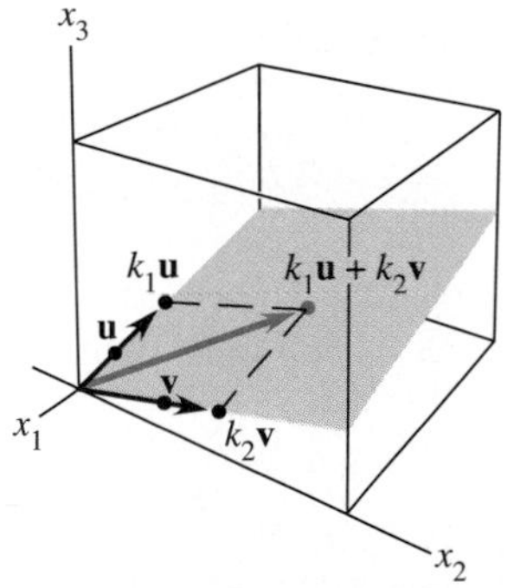

FIGURE 9 Span $\{\mathbf{u}, \mathbf{v}\}$ as a plane through the origin.

which is the same as

$$\begin{bmatrix} x_1 \\ -2x_1 \\ -5x_1 \end{bmatrix} + \begin{bmatrix} 2x_2 \\ 5x_2 \\ 6x_2 \end{bmatrix} = \begin{bmatrix} 7 \\ 4 \\ -3 \end{bmatrix}$$

and

$$\begin{bmatrix} x_1 + 2x_2 \\ -2x_1 + 5x_2 \\ -5x_1 + 6x_2 \end{bmatrix} = \begin{bmatrix} 7 \\ 4 \\ -3 \end{bmatrix} \tag{2}$$

The vectors on the left and right sides of (2) are equal if and only if their corresponding entries are both equal. That is, x_1 and x_2 make the vector equation (1) true if and only if x_1 and x_2 satisfy the system

$$\begin{aligned} x_1 + 2x_2 &= 7 \\ -2x_1 + 5x_2 &= 4 \\ -5x_1 + 6x_2 &= -3 \end{aligned} \tag{3}$$

We solve this system by row reducing the augmented matrix of the system as follows:[3]

$$\begin{bmatrix} 1 & 2 & 7 \\ -2 & 5 & 4 \\ -5 & 6 & -3 \end{bmatrix} \sim \begin{bmatrix} 1 & 2 & 7 \\ 0 & 9 & 18 \\ 0 & 16 & 32 \end{bmatrix} \sim \begin{bmatrix} 1 & 2 & 7 \\ 0 & 1 & 2 \\ 0 & 16 & 32 \end{bmatrix} \sim \begin{bmatrix} 1 & 0 & 3 \\ 0 & 1 & 2 \\ 0 & 0 & 0 \end{bmatrix}$$

The solution of (3) is $x_1 = 3$ and $x_2 = 2$. Hence $\mathbf{b}$ is a linear combination of $\mathbf{a}_1$ and $\mathbf{a}_2$, with weights $x_1 = 3$ and $x_2 = 2$. That is,

$$3\begin{bmatrix} 1 \\ -2 \\ -5 \end{bmatrix} + 2\begin{bmatrix} 2 \\ 5 \\ 6 \end{bmatrix} = \begin{bmatrix} 7 \\ 4 \\ -3 \end{bmatrix}$$

Observe in Example 5 that the original vectors $\mathbf{a}_1, \mathbf{a}_2$, and $\mathbf{b}$ are the columns of the augmented matrix we row reduced:

$$\begin{bmatrix} 1 & 2 & 7 \\ -2 & 5 & 4 \\ -5 & 6 & -3 \end{bmatrix}$$
$$\begin{matrix} \uparrow & \uparrow & \uparrow \\ \mathbf{a}_1 & \mathbf{a}_2 & \mathbf{b} \end{matrix}$$

Let us write this matrix in a way that calls attention to its columns, namely,

$$[\,\mathbf{a}_1 \quad \mathbf{a}_2 \quad \mathbf{b}\,] \tag{4}$$

It is clear how to write the augmented matrix immediately from the vector equation (1), without going through the intermediate steps of Example 5. Simply take the vectors in the order in which they appear in (1) and place them into the columns of a matrix as in (4).

The discussion above is easily modified to establish the following fundamental fact.

A vector equation

$$x_1\mathbf{a}_1 + x_2\mathbf{a}_2 + \cdots + x_n\mathbf{a}_n = \mathbf{b}$$

has the same solution set as the linear system whose augmented matrix is

$$[\,\mathbf{a}_1 \quad \mathbf{a}_2 \quad \cdots \quad \mathbf{a}_n \quad \mathbf{b}\,] \tag{5}$$

In particular, $\mathbf{b}$ is in Span $\{\mathbf{a}_1, \ldots, \mathbf{a}_n\}$ if and only if the linear system corresponding to (5) is consistent.

[3] The symbol "$\sim$" between matrices denotes row equivalence (Section 1.2).

Linear Combinations in Applications

The final example shows how scalar multiples and linear combinations can arise when a quantity such as "cost" is broken down into several categories. The basic principle for the example concerns the cost of producing several units of an item when the cost per unit is known:

$$\begin{Bmatrix} \text{number} \\ \text{of units} \end{Bmatrix} \cdot \begin{Bmatrix} \text{cost} \\ \text{per unit} \end{Bmatrix} = \begin{Bmatrix} \text{total} \\ \text{cost} \end{Bmatrix}$$

EXAMPLE 6 A company manufactures two products. For one dollar's worth of product B, the company spends \$.45 on materials, \$.25 on labor, and \$.15 on overhead. For one dollar's worth of product C, the company spends \$.40 on materials, \$.30 on labor, and \$.15 on overhead. Let

$$\mathbf{b} = \begin{bmatrix} .45 \\ .25 \\ .15 \end{bmatrix} \quad \text{and} \quad \mathbf{c} = \begin{bmatrix} .40 \\ .30 \\ .15 \end{bmatrix}$$

Then **b** and **c** represent the "costs per dollar of income" for the two products.

a. What economic interpretation may be given to the vector 100**b**?

b. Suppose the company wishes to manufacture x_1 dollars worth of product B and x_2 dollars worth of product C. Give a vector that describes the various costs the company will have (for materials, labor, and overhead).

Solution

a. We have

$$100\mathbf{b} = 100 \begin{bmatrix} .45 \\ .25 \\ .15 \end{bmatrix} = \begin{bmatrix} 45 \\ 25 \\ 15 \end{bmatrix}$$

The vector 100**b** lists the various costs for producing \$100 worth of product B, namely, \$45 for materials, \$25 for labor, and \$15 for overhead.

b. The costs of manufacturing x_1 dollars worth of B are given by the vector $x_1\mathbf{b}$, and the costs of manufacturing x_2 dollars worth of C are given by $x_2\mathbf{c}$. Hence the total costs for both products are given by the vector $x_1\mathbf{b} + x_2\mathbf{c}$.

PRACTICE PROBLEMS

1. Prove that $\mathbf{u} + \mathbf{v} = \mathbf{v} + \mathbf{u}$ for any $\mathbf{u}$ and $\mathbf{v}$ in $\mathbb{R}^n$.
2. For what value(s) of h will $\mathbf{y}$ be in Span $\{\mathbf{v}_1, \mathbf{v}_2, \mathbf{v}_3\}$, if

$$\mathbf{v}_1 = \begin{bmatrix} 1 \\ -1 \\ -2 \end{bmatrix}, \quad \mathbf{v}_2 = \begin{bmatrix} 5 \\ -4 \\ -7 \end{bmatrix}, \quad \mathbf{v}_3 = \begin{bmatrix} -3 \\ 1 \\ 0 \end{bmatrix}, \quad \text{and} \quad \mathbf{y} = \begin{bmatrix} -4 \\ 3 \\ h \end{bmatrix}$$

2.1 EXERCISES

In Exercises 1 and 2, compute $\mathbf{u}+\mathbf{v}$ and $\mathbf{u}-2\mathbf{v}$.

1. $\mathbf{u}=\begin{bmatrix}3\\2\end{bmatrix}, \mathbf{v}=\begin{bmatrix}2\\-1\end{bmatrix}$ **2.** $\mathbf{u}=\begin{bmatrix}-1\\2\end{bmatrix}, \mathbf{v}=\begin{bmatrix}-3\\-1\end{bmatrix}$

In Exercises 3 and 4, display the following vectors with arrows on an xy-graph: $\mathbf{u}, \mathbf{v}, -\mathbf{v}, -2\mathbf{v}, \mathbf{u}+\mathbf{v}, \mathbf{u}-\mathbf{v}$, and $\mathbf{u}-2\mathbf{v}$.

3. $\mathbf{u}$ and $\mathbf{v}$ as in Exercise 1

4. $\mathbf{u}$ and $\mathbf{v}$ as in Exercise 2

5. Let $\mathbf{a}, \mathbf{b}, \mathbf{c}$ be vectors in $\mathbb{R}^8$ such that $4\mathbf{a}+5\mathbf{b}+6\mathbf{c}=\mathbf{0}$. Express $\mathbf{a}$ as a linear combination of $\mathbf{b}$ and $\mathbf{c}$.

6. Let $\mathbf{u}, \mathbf{v}, \mathbf{w}, \mathbf{x}$ be in $\mathbb{R}^6$ such that $3(\mathbf{x}-\mathbf{u})=2(\mathbf{v}-3\mathbf{w})$. Express $\mathbf{x}$ as a linear combination of $\mathbf{u}$, $\mathbf{v}$, and $\mathbf{w}$.

7. Find s and t if $\begin{bmatrix}s\\2\end{bmatrix}=\begin{bmatrix}5\\s-t\end{bmatrix}$.

8. Find s and t if $s\begin{bmatrix}3\\-4\end{bmatrix}=3\begin{bmatrix}2\\t\end{bmatrix}$.

Solve the equations in Exercises 9 and 10 for the vector $\mathbf{x}$.

9. $x+\begin{bmatrix}1\\-3\\5\end{bmatrix}=\begin{bmatrix}7\\3\\-1\end{bmatrix}$ **10.** $4\mathbf{x}+\begin{bmatrix}6\\-3\\-9\end{bmatrix}=\mathbf{x}$

In Exercises 11 and 12, write a system of equations that is equivalent to the given vector equation.

11. $x_1\begin{bmatrix}3\\1\\-5\end{bmatrix}+x_2\begin{bmatrix}-2\\0\\4\end{bmatrix}=\begin{bmatrix}8\\-6\\3\end{bmatrix}$

12. $x_1\begin{bmatrix}2\\3\end{bmatrix}+x_2\begin{bmatrix}-1\\4\end{bmatrix}+x_3\begin{bmatrix}-7\\1\end{bmatrix}=\begin{bmatrix}0\\0\end{bmatrix}$

In Exercises 13 and 14, write a vector equation that is equivalent to the given system of equations.

13. $\begin{aligned}2x_1 - x_2 + 5x_3 &= 3\\ x_1 - 8x_2 + 2x_3 &= 5\\ 4x_2 - 4x_3 &= 5\end{aligned}$ **14.** $\begin{aligned}x_1 + 6x_2 + 2x_3 &= 5\\ 5x_1 \qquad - 6x_3 &= 7\\ 3x_1 - x_2 + 4x_3 &= -1\end{aligned}$

In Exercises 15 and 16, determine if $\mathbf{b}$ is in Span $\{\mathbf{a}_1, \mathbf{a}_2, \mathbf{a}_3\}$.

15. $\mathbf{a}_1=\begin{bmatrix}1\\0\\1\end{bmatrix}, \mathbf{a}_2=\begin{bmatrix}-2\\1\\-2\end{bmatrix}, \mathbf{a}_3=\begin{bmatrix}-6\\3\\-5\end{bmatrix}, \mathbf{b}=\begin{bmatrix}11\\-5\\9\end{bmatrix}$

16. $\mathbf{a}_1=\begin{bmatrix}1\\0\\-2\end{bmatrix}, \mathbf{a}_2=\begin{bmatrix}-4\\3\\8\end{bmatrix}, \mathbf{a}_3=\begin{bmatrix}2\\5\\-4\end{bmatrix}, \mathbf{b}=\begin{bmatrix}3\\-7\\-3\end{bmatrix}$

In Exercises 17–20, determine if $\mathbf{b}$ is a linear combination of the columns of the matrix A.

17. $A=\begin{bmatrix}1 & 2\\2 & 7\\-3 & -9\end{bmatrix}, \mathbf{b}=\begin{bmatrix}-1\\-3\\8\end{bmatrix}$

18. $A=\begin{bmatrix}1 & 0\\-1 & -2\\5 & 4\end{bmatrix}, \mathbf{b}=\begin{bmatrix}1\\2\\-1\end{bmatrix}$

19. $A=\begin{bmatrix}1 & 0 & 2\\-2 & 1 & 0\\2 & 1 & 8\end{bmatrix}, \mathbf{b}=\begin{bmatrix}-5\\11\\-7\end{bmatrix}$

20. $A=\begin{bmatrix}1 & 0 & 5\\-2 & 1 & -6\\0 & 2 & 8\end{bmatrix}, \mathbf{b}=\begin{bmatrix}2\\-1\\6\end{bmatrix}$

21. Let $\mathbf{a}_1=\begin{bmatrix}1\\3\\-1\end{bmatrix}, \mathbf{a}_2=\begin{bmatrix}-5\\-8\\2\end{bmatrix}$ and $\mathbf{b}=\begin{bmatrix}3\\-5\\h\end{bmatrix}$. For what value(s) of h will $\mathbf{b}$ be in the plane spanned by $\mathbf{a}_1$ and $\mathbf{a}_2$?

22. Let $\mathbf{v}_1=\begin{bmatrix}1\\0\\-2\end{bmatrix}, \mathbf{v}_2=\begin{bmatrix}-2\\1\\7\end{bmatrix}$, and $\mathbf{y}=\begin{bmatrix}h\\-3\\-5\end{bmatrix}$. For what value(s) of h will $\mathbf{y}$ be in the plane spanned by $\mathbf{v}_1$ and $\mathbf{v}_2$?

23. Let $\mathbf{u}=\begin{bmatrix}2\\-1\end{bmatrix}$ and $\mathbf{v}=\begin{bmatrix}2\\1\end{bmatrix}$. Show that $\begin{bmatrix}h\\k\end{bmatrix}$ is in Span $\{\mathbf{u}, \mathbf{v}\}$ for all h and k.

24. Repeat Exercise 23 for $\mathbf{u}=\begin{bmatrix}2\\-6\end{bmatrix}$ and $\mathbf{v}=\begin{bmatrix}1\\5\end{bmatrix}$.

25. Let $A=\begin{bmatrix}1 & 0 & -4\\0 & 1 & -2\\-2 & 3 & 3\end{bmatrix}$ and $\mathbf{b}=\begin{bmatrix}4\\1\\-4\end{bmatrix}$. Denote the columns of A by $\mathbf{a}_1, \mathbf{a}_2, \mathbf{a}_3$, and let $W=\text{Span}\,\{\mathbf{a}_1, \mathbf{a}_2, \mathbf{a}_3\}$.

a. Is $\mathbf{b}$ in $\{\mathbf{a}_1, \mathbf{a}_2, \mathbf{a}_3\}$? How many vectors are in $\{\mathbf{a}_1, \mathbf{a}_2, \mathbf{a}_3\}$?

b. Is $\mathbf{b}$ in W? How many vectors are in W?

c. Show that $\mathbf{a}_1$ is in W. [*Hint*: Row operations are unnecessary.]

26. Let $A=\begin{bmatrix}2 & 0 & 6\\-1 & 8 & 5\\1 & -2 & 1\end{bmatrix}$, let $\mathbf{b}=\begin{bmatrix}10\\3\\3\end{bmatrix}$, and let W be the set of all linear combinations of the columns of A.

a. Is $\mathbf{b}$ in W?

b. Show that the third column of A is in W.

27. A mining company has two mines. One day's operation at mine #1 produces ore that contains 20 metric tons of copper and 550 kilograms of silver, while one day's operation at mine #2 produces ore that contains 30 metric tons of copper and 500 kilograms of silver. Let $\mathbf{v}_1 = \begin{bmatrix} 20 \\ 550 \end{bmatrix}$ and $\mathbf{v}_2 = \begin{bmatrix} 30 \\ 500 \end{bmatrix}$. Then $\mathbf{v}_1$ and $\mathbf{v}_2$ represent the "output per day" of mines #1 and #2, respectively.

a. What physical interpretation may be given to the vector $5\mathbf{v}_1$?

b. Suppose the company operates mine #1 for x_1 days and mine #2 for x_2 days. Write a vector equation whose solution gives the number of days each mine should operate in order to produce 150 tons of copper and 2825 kilograms of silver. Do not solve the equation.

28. A steam plant burns two types of coal: anthracite (A) and bituminous (B). For each ton of A burned, the plant produces 27.6 million Btu of heat, 3100 grams (g) of sulfur dioxide, and 250 g of particulate matter (solid particle pollutants). For each ton of B burned, the plant produces 30.2 million Btu, 6400 g of sulfur dioxide, and 360 g of particulate matter.

a. How much heat does the steam plant produce when it burns x_1 tons of A and x_2 tons of B?

b. Suppose that the output of the steam plant is described by a vector that lists the amounts of heat, sulfur dioxide, and particulate matter. Express this output as a linear combination of two vectors, assuming that the plant burns x_1 tons of A and x_2 tons of B.

29. Let $\mathbf{v}_1, \ldots, \mathbf{v}_k$ be points in $\mathbb{R}^3$ and suppose that for $j = 1, \ldots, k$ an object with mass m_j is located at point $\mathbf{v}_j$. Physicists call such objects *point masses*. The total mass of the system of point masses is

$m = m_1 + \cdots + m_k$

The *center of gravity* (or *center of mass*) of the system is

$\bar{\mathbf{v}} = \frac{1}{m}[m_1\mathbf{v}_1 + \cdots + m_k\mathbf{v}_k]$

Compute the center of gravity of the system consisting of the following point masses:

Point	Mass
$\mathbf{v}_1 = (5, -4, 3)$	2 g
$\mathbf{v}_2 = (4, 3, -2)$	5 g
$\mathbf{v}_3 = (-4, -3, -1)$	2 g
$\mathbf{v}_4 = (-9, 8, 6)$	1 g

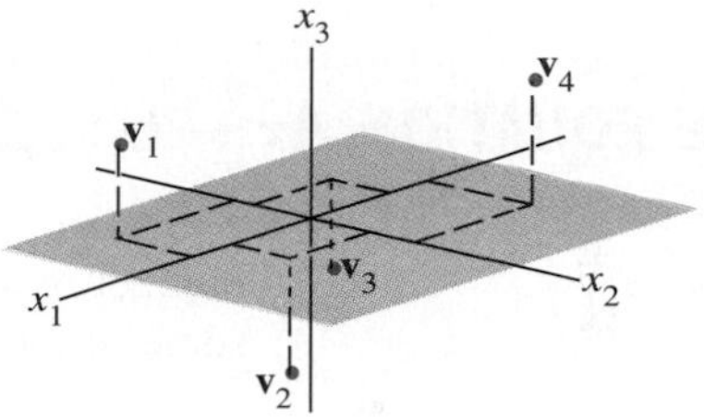

30. Use the vectors $\mathbf{u} = (u_1, \ldots, u_n)$, $\mathbf{v} = (v_1, \ldots, v_n)$, and $\mathbf{w} = (w_1, \ldots, w_n)$ to verify the following algebraic properties of $\mathbb{R}^n$.

a. $(\mathbf{u} + \mathbf{v}) + \mathbf{w} = \mathbf{u} + (\mathbf{v} + \mathbf{w})$

b. $\mathbf{u} + (-\mathbf{u}) = (-\mathbf{u}) + \mathbf{u} = \mathbf{0}$

c. $c(\mathbf{u} + \mathbf{v}) = c\mathbf{u} + c\mathbf{v}$

d. $c(d\mathbf{u}) = (cd)\mathbf{u}$

SOLUTIONS TO PRACTICE PROBLEMS

1. Take arbitrary vectors $\mathbf{u} = (u_1, \ldots, u_n)$ and $\mathbf{v} = (v_1, \ldots, v_n)$ in $\mathbb{R}^n$, and compute

$$\begin{aligned} \mathbf{u} + \mathbf{v} &= (u_1 + v_1, \ldots, u_n + v_n) && \text{Definition of vector addition} \\ &= (v_1 + u_1, \ldots, v_n + u_n) && \text{Commutativity of addition in } \mathbb{R} \\ &= \mathbf{v} + \mathbf{u} && \text{Definition of vector addition} \end{aligned}$$

2. The vector $\mathbf{y}$ belongs to Span $\{\mathbf{v}_1, \mathbf{v}_2, \mathbf{v}_3\}$ if and only if there exist scalars x_1, x_2, x_3 such that

$$x_1 \begin{bmatrix} 1 \\ -1 \\ -2 \end{bmatrix} + x_2 \begin{bmatrix} 5 \\ -4 \\ -7 \end{bmatrix} + x_3 \begin{bmatrix} -3 \\ 1 \\ 0 \end{bmatrix} = \begin{bmatrix} -4 \\ 3 \\ h \end{bmatrix}$$

This vector equation is equivalent to a system of three equations in three unknowns. If we row reduce the augmented matrix for this system, we find that

$$\begin{bmatrix} 1 & 5 & -3 & -4 \\ -1 & -4 & 1 & 3 \\ -2 & -7 & 0 & h \end{bmatrix} \sim \begin{bmatrix} 1 & 5 & -3 & -4 \\ 0 & 1 & -2 & -1 \\ 0 & 3 & -6 & h-8 \end{bmatrix} \sim \begin{bmatrix} 1 & 5 & -3 & -4 \\ 0 & 1 & -2 & -1 \\ 0 & 0 & 0 & h-5 \end{bmatrix}$$

The system is consistent if and only if there is no pivot in the fourth column. That is, $h - 5$ must be 0. So $\mathbf{y}$ is in Span $\{\mathbf{v}_1, \mathbf{v}_2, \mathbf{v}_3\}$ if and only if $h = 5$.

Remember: The presence of a free variable in a system does not guarantee that the system is consistent.

2.2 THE EQUATION $A\mathbf{x} = \mathbf{b}$

A fundamental idea in linear algebra is to view a linear combination of vectors as the product of a matrix and a vector. The following definition will permit us to rephrase some of the concepts of Section 2.1 in new ways.

DEFINITION

If A is an $m \times n$ matrix, with columns $\mathbf{a}_1, \ldots, \mathbf{a}_n$, and if x is in $\mathbb{R}^n$, then the vector $A\mathbf{x}$ is **the linear combination of the columns of A using the corresponding entries in x as weights**, that is,

$$A\mathbf{x} = [\,\mathbf{a}_1 \quad \mathbf{a}_2 \quad \cdots \quad \mathbf{a}_n\,] \begin{bmatrix} x_1 \\ \vdots \\ x_n \end{bmatrix} = x_1\mathbf{a}_1 + x_2\mathbf{a}_2 + \cdots + x_n\mathbf{a}_n$$

Note that $A\mathbf{x}$ is defined only if the number of columns of A equals the number of entries in $\mathbf{x}$.

EXAMPLE 1

a.

$$\begin{bmatrix} 1 & 2 & -1 \\ 0 & -5 & 3 \end{bmatrix} \begin{bmatrix} 4 \\ 3 \\ 7 \end{bmatrix} = 4\begin{bmatrix} 1 \\ 0 \end{bmatrix} + 3\begin{bmatrix} 2 \\ -5 \end{bmatrix} + 7\begin{bmatrix} -1 \\ 3 \end{bmatrix}$$

$$= \begin{bmatrix} 4 \\ 0 \end{bmatrix} + \begin{bmatrix} 6 \\ -15 \end{bmatrix} + \begin{bmatrix} -7 \\ 21 \end{bmatrix} = \begin{bmatrix} 3 \\ 6 \end{bmatrix}$$

b.

$$\begin{bmatrix} 2 & -3 \\ 8 & 0 \\ -5 & 2 \end{bmatrix} \begin{bmatrix} 4 \\ 7 \end{bmatrix} = 4\begin{bmatrix} 2 \\ 8 \\ -5 \end{bmatrix} + 7\begin{bmatrix} -3 \\ 0 \\ 2 \end{bmatrix} = \begin{bmatrix} 8 \\ 32 \\ -20 \end{bmatrix} + \begin{bmatrix} -21 \\ 0 \\ 14 \end{bmatrix} = \begin{bmatrix} -13 \\ 32 \\ -6 \end{bmatrix}$$

In Section 2.1, we learned how to write a system of linear equations as a vector equation involving a linear combination of vectors. For example, we know that the system

$$\begin{aligned} x_1 + 2x_2 - x_3 &= 4 \\ -5x_2 + 3x_3 &= 1 \end{aligned} \tag{1}$$

is equivalent to

$$x_1\begin{bmatrix}1\\0\end{bmatrix} + x_2\begin{bmatrix}2\\-5\end{bmatrix} + x_3\begin{bmatrix}-1\\3\end{bmatrix} = \begin{bmatrix}4\\1\end{bmatrix} \tag{2}$$

Let us think of the three vectors on the left side of (2) as the columns of a matrix, namely,

$$A = \begin{bmatrix}1 & 2 & -1\\0 & -5 & 3\end{bmatrix}$$

Using the definition of a matrix times a vector, we may rewrite (2) in the form $A\mathbf{x} = \mathbf{b}$, namely,

$$\begin{bmatrix}1 & 2 & -1\\0 & -5 & 3\end{bmatrix}\begin{bmatrix}x_1\\x_2\\x_3\end{bmatrix} = \begin{bmatrix}4\\1\end{bmatrix} \tag{3}$$

Even though the equation $A\mathbf{x} = \mathbf{b}$ involves two vectors as well as a matrix, we shall refer to it as a **matrix equation**, to distinguish it from a vector equation such as is shown in (2).

Notice how the matrix in (3) is just the matrix of coefficients of the system (1). Similar calculations show that any system of linear equations, or any vector equation such as (2), can be written as an equivalent matrix equation in the form $A\mathbf{x} = \mathbf{b}$. This simple observation will be used repeatedly throughout the text.

Here is the formal result.

THEOREM 1

Given an $m \times n$ matrix A, with columns $\mathbf{a}_1, \ldots, \mathbf{a}_n$, and given $\mathbf{b}$ in $\mathbb{R}^m$, the matrix equation

$$A\mathbf{x} = \mathbf{b} \tag{4}$$

has the same solution set as the vector equation

$$x_1\mathbf{a}_1 + x_2\mathbf{a}_2 + \cdots + x_n\mathbf{a}_n = \mathbf{b} \tag{5}$$

which, in turn, has the same solution set as the system of linear equations whose augmented matrix is

$$[\mathbf{a}_1 \quad \mathbf{a}_2 \quad \cdots \quad \mathbf{a}_n \quad \mathbf{b}] \tag{6}$$

Theorem 1 provides a powerful tool for gaining insight into problems in linear algebra because we may now view a system of linear equations in three different but equivalent ways: as a matrix equation, as a vector equation, or as a system of linear equations. When we construct a mathematical model of a problem in real life, we are free to choose whichever viewpoint is most natural. Then we may switch from one formulation of a problem to another whenever it is convenient. In any case, the matrix equation, the vector equation, and the system of equations are all solved in the same way—by row reducing the augmented matrix (6). Other methods of solution will be discussed later.

Existence of Solutions

The equivalence of (4) and (5) leads immediately to the following important fact.

> The equation $A\mathbf{x} = \mathbf{b}$ has a solution if and only if $\mathbf{b}$ is a linear combination of the columns of A.

In Section 2.1, we considered the existence question, "Is $\mathbf{b}$ in Span $\{\mathbf{a}_1, \ldots, \mathbf{a}_n\}$?" Equivalently, "Is $A\mathbf{x} = \mathbf{b}$ consistent?" A harder existence problem is to determine whether the equation $A\mathbf{x} = \mathbf{b}$ is consistent *for all* possible $\mathbf{b}$.

EXAMPLE 2 Let $A = \begin{bmatrix} 1 & -2 & -1 \\ -3 & 1 & 9 \\ -1 & 7 & -5 \end{bmatrix}$ and $\mathbf{b} = \begin{bmatrix} b_1 \\ b_2 \\ b_3 \end{bmatrix}$. Is the equation $A\mathbf{x} = \mathbf{b}$ consistent for all possible b_1, b_2, b_3?

Solution Row reduce the augmented matrix for $A\mathbf{x} = \mathbf{b}$:

$$\begin{bmatrix} 1 & -2 & -1 & b_1 \\ -3 & 1 & 9 & b_2 \\ -1 & 7 & -5 & b_3 \end{bmatrix} \sim \begin{bmatrix} 1 & -2 & -1 & b_1 \\ 0 & -5 & 6 & b_2 + 3b_1 \\ 0 & 5 & -6 & b_3 + b_1 \end{bmatrix}$$

$$\sim \begin{bmatrix} 1 & -2 & -1 & b_1 \\ 0 & -5 & 6 & b_2 + 3b_1 \\ 0 & 0 & 0 & b_3 + 4b_1 + b_2 \end{bmatrix}$$

The equation $A\mathbf{x} = \mathbf{b}$ is *not* consistent for every $\mathbf{b}$ because some choices of $\mathbf{b}$ can make $4b_1 + b_2 + b_3$ nonzero.

The reduced matrix in Example 2 provides a description of all $\mathbf{b}$ for which the equation $A\mathbf{x} = \mathbf{b}$ *is* consistent: The entries in $\mathbf{b}$ must satisfy

$$4b_1 + b_2 + b_3 = 0$$

This is the equation of a plane through the origin in $\mathbb{R}^3$. The plane is the set of all linear combinations of the columns of A.

The equation $A\mathbf{x} = \mathbf{b}$ in Example 2 fails to be consistent for all $\mathbf{b}$ because the echelon form of A has a row of zeros. If A had a pivot in all three rows, we would not care about the calculations in the augmented column because in this case an echelon form of the augmented matrix could not have a row such as $[0 \quad 0 \quad 0 \quad 1]$.

In the next theorem, when we say that **the columns of A span $\mathbb{R}^m$**, we mean that every $\mathbf{b}$ in $\mathbb{R}^m$ is a linear combination of the columns of A. In general, a set of vectors $\{\mathbf{v}_1, \dots, \mathbf{v}_p\}$ in $\mathbb{R}^m$ **spans** $\mathbb{R}^m$ if $\text{Span}\{\mathbf{v}_1, \dots, \mathbf{v}_p\} = \mathbb{R}^m$.

THEOREM 2

Let A be an $m\times n$ matrix. Then the following statements are logically equivalent. That is, for a particular A, either they are all true statements or they are all false.

a. For each $\mathbf{b}$ in $\mathbb{R}^m$, the equation $A\mathbf{x} = \mathbf{b}$ is consistent.

b. The columns of A span $\mathbb{R}^m$.

c. A has a pivot position in every row.

The fact that statements (a) and (b) are equivalent follows easily from Theorem 1. The fact that (a) and (c) are equivalent is suggested by the discussion above. The details are given at the end of the section. The exercises will provide examples of how Theorem 2 is used.

Warning: Theorem 2 is about a *coefficient matrix*, not an augmented matrix. If an augmented matrix $[\,A \quad \mathbf{b}\,]$ has a pivot position in every row, then the equation $A\mathbf{x} = \mathbf{b}$ may or may not be consistent.

Computation of $A\mathbf{x}$

The calculations in Example 1 were based on the definition of the product of a matrix A and a vector $\mathbf{x}$. The following simple example will lead to a more efficient method for calculating the entries in $A\mathbf{x}$ when working problems by hand.

EXAMPLE 3 Compute $A\mathbf{x}$, where $A = \begin{bmatrix} 2 & 3 & 4 \\ -1 & 5 & -3 \\ 6 & -2 & 8 \end{bmatrix}$ and $\mathbf{x} = \begin{bmatrix} x_1 \\ x_2 \\ x_3 \end{bmatrix}$.

Solution From the definition,

$$\begin{aligned}
\begin{bmatrix} 2 & 3 & 4 \\ -1 & 5 & -3 \\ 6 & -2 & 8 \end{bmatrix}\begin{bmatrix} x_1 \\ x_2 \\ x_3 \end{bmatrix} &= x_1\begin{bmatrix} 2 \\ -1 \\ 6 \end{bmatrix} + x_2\begin{bmatrix} 3 \\ 5 \\ -2 \end{bmatrix} + x_3\begin{bmatrix} 4 \\ -3 \\ 8 \end{bmatrix} \\
&= \begin{bmatrix} 2x_1 \\ -x_1 \\ 6x_1 \end{bmatrix} + \begin{bmatrix} 3x_2 \\ 5x_2 \\ -2x_2 \end{bmatrix} + \begin{bmatrix} 4x_3 \\ -3x_3 \\ 8x_3 \end{bmatrix} \qquad (7) \\
&= \begin{bmatrix} 2x_1 + 3x_2 + 4x_3 \\ -x_1 + 5x_2 - 3x_3 \\ 6x_1 - 2x_2 + 8x_3 \end{bmatrix}
\end{aligned}$$

The first entry in the product $A\mathbf{x}$ is a sum of products, using the first row of A and the entries in $\mathbf{x}$. That is,

$$\begin{bmatrix} 2 & 3 & 4 \\ & & \\ & & \end{bmatrix} \begin{bmatrix} x_1 \\ x_2 \\ x_3 \end{bmatrix} = \begin{bmatrix} 2x_1 + 3x_2 + 4x_3 \\ \\ \end{bmatrix}$$

This matrix shows how to compute the first entry in $A\mathbf{x}$ directly, without writing down all the calculations shown in (7). Similarly, the second entry in $A\mathbf{x}$ may be calculated at once by multiplying the entries in the second row of A by the corresponding entries in $\mathbf{x}$ and then summing the resulting products:

$$\begin{bmatrix} & & \\ -1 & 5 & -3 \\ & & \end{bmatrix} \begin{bmatrix} x_1 \\ x_2 \\ x_3 \end{bmatrix} = \begin{bmatrix} \\ -x_1 + 5x_2 - 3x_3 \\ \\ \end{bmatrix}$$

Likewise, the third entry in $A\mathbf{x}$ may be calculated from the third row of A and the entries in $\mathbf{x}$.

Rule for Computing $A\mathbf{x}$. If the product $A\mathbf{x}$ is defined, then the ith entry in $A\mathbf{x}$ is the sum of the products of corresponding entries from row i of A and from the vector $\mathbf{x}$.

EXAMPLE 4

a. $$\begin{bmatrix} 1 & 2 & -1 \\ 0 & -5 & 3 \end{bmatrix} \begin{bmatrix} 4 \\ 3 \\ 7 \end{bmatrix} = \begin{bmatrix} 1\cdot 4 + 2\cdot 3 + (-1)\cdot 7 \\ 0\cdot 4 + (-5)\cdot 3 + 3\cdot 7 \end{bmatrix} = \begin{bmatrix} 3 \\ 6 \end{bmatrix}$$

b. $$\begin{bmatrix} 2 & -3 \\ 8 & 0 \\ -5 & 2 \end{bmatrix} \begin{bmatrix} 4 \\ 7 \end{bmatrix} = \begin{bmatrix} 2\cdot 4 + (-3)\cdot 7 \\ 8\cdot 4 + 0\cdot 7 \\ (-5)\cdot 4 + 2\cdot 7 \end{bmatrix} = \begin{bmatrix} -13 \\ 32 \\ -6 \end{bmatrix}$$

c. $$\begin{bmatrix} 1 & 0 & 0 \\ 0 & 1 & 0 \\ 0 & 0 & 1 \end{bmatrix} \begin{bmatrix} r \\ s \\ t \end{bmatrix} = \begin{bmatrix} 1\cdot r + 0\cdot s + 0\cdot t \\ 0\cdot r + 1\cdot s + 0\cdot t \\ 0\cdot r + 0\cdot s + 1\cdot t \end{bmatrix} = \begin{bmatrix} r \\ s \\ t \end{bmatrix}$$

By definition, the matrix in Example 4(c) with 1's on the diagonal and 0's elsewhere is called an **identity matrix** and is denoted by I. The calculation in part 4(c) shows that $I\mathbf{x} = \mathbf{x}$ for every $\mathbf{x}$ in $\mathbb{R}^3$. There is an analogous $n \times n$ identity matrix, sometimes written as I_n. As in part (c), $I_n\mathbf{x} = \mathbf{x}$ for every $\mathbf{x}$ in $\mathbb{R}^n$.

Properties of the Matrix-Vector Product $A\mathbf{x}$

The facts in the next theorem are important and will be used throughout the text.

THEOREM 3

If A is an $m \times n$ matrix, $\mathbf{u}$ and $\mathbf{v}$ are vectors in $\mathbb{R}^n$, and c is a scalar, then

a. $A(\mathbf{u} + \mathbf{v}) = A\mathbf{u} + A\mathbf{v}$
b. $A(c\mathbf{u}) = c(A\mathbf{u})$.

Proof For simplicity, take $n = 3$, $A = [\mathbf{a}_1 \ \ \mathbf{a}_2 \ \ \mathbf{a}_3]$, and $\mathbf{u}$, $\mathbf{v}$ in $\mathbb{R}^3$. (The proof of the general case is similar.) For $i = 1, 2, 3$, let u_i and v_i be the ith entries in $\mathbf{u}$ and $\mathbf{v}$, respectively. To prove statement (a), compute $A(\mathbf{u} + \mathbf{v})$ as a linear combination of the columns of A using the entries in $\mathbf{u} + \mathbf{v}$ as weights.

$$A(\mathbf{u}+\mathbf{v}) = [\mathbf{a}_1 \ \ \mathbf{a}_2 \ \ \mathbf{a}_3]\begin{bmatrix} u_1 + v_1 \\ u_2 + v_2 \\ u_3 + v_3 \end{bmatrix}$$

Entries in $\mathbf{u} + \mathbf{v}$

$$= (u_1 + v_1)\mathbf{a}_1 + (u_2 + v_2)\mathbf{a}_2 + (u_3 + v_3)\mathbf{a}_3$$

Columns of A

$$= (u_1\mathbf{a}_1 + u_2\mathbf{a}_2 + u_3\mathbf{a}_3) + (v_1\mathbf{a}_1 + v_2\mathbf{a}_2 + v_3\mathbf{a}_3)$$

$$= A\mathbf{u} + A\mathbf{v}$$

To prove statement (b), compute $A(c\mathbf{u})$ as a linear combination of the columns of A using the entries in $c\mathbf{u}$ as weights.

$$A(c\mathbf{u}) = [\mathbf{a}_1 \ \ \mathbf{a}_2 \ \ \mathbf{a}_3]\begin{bmatrix} cu_1 \\ cu_2 \\ cu_3 \end{bmatrix} = (cu_1)\mathbf{a}_1 + (cu_2)\mathbf{a}_2 + (cu_3)\mathbf{a}_3$$

$$= c(u_1\mathbf{a}_1) + c(u_2\mathbf{a}_2) + c(u_3\mathbf{a}_3)$$

$$= c(u_1\mathbf{a}_1 + u_2\mathbf{a}_2 + u_3\mathbf{a}_3)$$

$$= c(A\mathbf{u})$$ ∎

Numerical Note

To optimize a computer algorithm to compute $A\mathbf{x}$, the sequence of calculations should involve data stored in contiguous memory locations. The most widely used professional algorithms for matrix computations are written in Fortran, a language that stores a matrix as a set of columns. Such algorithms compute $A\mathbf{x}$ as a linear combination of the columns of A. In contrast, if a program is written in the popular language "C," which stores matrices by rows, $A\mathbf{x}$ should be computed via the alternative rule that uses the rows of A.

Proof of Theorem 2 By Theorem 1, statement (a) is the same as saying that for each $\mathbf{b}$ in $\mathbb{R}^m$, the vector equation $x_1\mathbf{a}_1 + \cdots + x_n\mathbf{a}_n = \mathbf{b}$ is consistent, which is another way of phrasing statement (b). Thus (a) and (b) are either both true or both false. To complete the proof, it suffices to show (for an arbitrary matrix A) that (a) and (c) are either both true or both false. For in this case, (a), (b), and (c) will be either all true or all false at the same time.

Let U be an echelon form of A. Given $\mathbf{b}$ in $\mathbb{R}^m$, we may row reduce the augmented matrix $[A \ \ \mathbf{b}]$ to an augmented matrix $[U \ \ \mathbf{d}]$ for some $\mathbf{d}$ in $\mathbb{R}^m$:

$$[A \ \ \mathbf{b}] \sim \cdots \sim [U \ \ \mathbf{d}]$$

If statement (c) is true, then each row of U contains a pivot position and there can be no pivot in the augmented column. So $A\mathbf{x} = \mathbf{b}$ is consistent for any $\mathbf{b}$ and statement (a) is true. If statement (c) is false, U has a row of zeros. Let $\mathbf{d}$ be any vector with a 1 in that row. Then $[U \quad \mathbf{d}]$ represents an *inconsistent* system. Since row operations are reversible, $[U \quad \mathbf{d}]$ may be transformed into the form $[A \quad \mathbf{b}]$. The new system $A\mathbf{x} = \mathbf{b}$ is also inconsistent, and statement (a) is false. ∎

PRACTICE PROBLEMS

1. Let $A = \begin{bmatrix} 1 & 5 & -2 & 0 \\ -3 & 1 & 9 & -5 \\ 4 & -8 & -1 & 7 \end{bmatrix}$, $\mathbf{x} = \begin{bmatrix} 3 \\ -2 \\ 0 \\ -4 \end{bmatrix}$, and $\mathbf{b} = \begin{bmatrix} -7 \\ 9 \\ 0 \end{bmatrix}$. It can be shown that $A\mathbf{x} = \mathbf{b}$. Use this fact to exhibit $\mathbf{b}$ as a specific linear combination of the columns of A.

2. Let $A = \begin{bmatrix} 2 & 5 \\ 3 & 1 \end{bmatrix}$, $\mathbf{u} = \begin{bmatrix} 4 \\ -1 \end{bmatrix}$, and $\mathbf{v} = \begin{bmatrix} -3 \\ 5 \end{bmatrix}$. Verify Theorem 3(a) in this case by computing $A(\mathbf{u} + \mathbf{v})$ and $A\mathbf{u} + A\mathbf{v}$.

2.2 EXERCISES

Compute the products in Exercises 1–6 by using (i) the definition, as in Example 1, and (ii) the rule for computing $A\mathbf{x}$. If a product is undefined, say so.

1. $\begin{bmatrix} 2 & 4 \\ 3 & 5 \end{bmatrix}\begin{bmatrix} 5 \\ -3 \end{bmatrix}$

2. $\begin{bmatrix} 4 & 1 \\ 2 & -5 \\ 0 & 6 \end{bmatrix}\begin{bmatrix} 5 \\ 2 \end{bmatrix}$

3. $\begin{bmatrix} 5 & 2 & 1 \\ -4 & 4 & 7 \end{bmatrix}\begin{bmatrix} 1 \\ 1 \\ 1 \end{bmatrix}$

4. $\begin{bmatrix} 3 & -8 \\ -1 & 5 \\ 2 & -3 \end{bmatrix}\begin{bmatrix} -4 \\ 1 \\ 0 \end{bmatrix}$

5. $\begin{bmatrix} -2 \\ 9 \\ 0 \end{bmatrix}\begin{bmatrix} r \\ s \end{bmatrix}$

6. $\begin{bmatrix} 0 & 0 & 1 \\ 0 & 1 & 0 \\ 1 & 0 & 0 \end{bmatrix}\begin{bmatrix} r \\ s \\ t \end{bmatrix}$

Write the systems in Exercises 7 and 8 in the form $A\mathbf{x} = \mathbf{b}$.

7. $$\begin{aligned} 3x_1 - x_2 + 4x_3 &= 1 \\ -4x_1 + x_2 - 5x_3 &= 0 \\ x_2 - 3x_3 &= 6 \end{aligned}$$

8. $$\begin{aligned} 3x_2 - 2x_3 + x_4 &= 0 \\ x_1 - 2x_2 + 6x_3 &= 0 \\ 7x_1 + x_2 - 5x_3 - 8x_4 &= 0 \end{aligned}$$

Given A and $\mathbf{b}$ in Exercises 9 and 10, write $A\mathbf{x} = \mathbf{b}$ as a vector equation.

9. $A = \begin{bmatrix} 2 & 4 & -6 \\ 0 & 1 & 3 \\ -3 & -5 & 7 \end{bmatrix}$, $\mathbf{b} = \begin{bmatrix} 2 \\ 5 \\ -3 \end{bmatrix}$

10. $A = \begin{bmatrix} 0 & 5 & 3 \\ 1 & 2 & 1 \\ -3 & -1 & 2 \end{bmatrix}$, $\mathbf{b} = \begin{bmatrix} -1 \\ 0 \\ 1 \end{bmatrix}$

11. Solve the equation $A\mathbf{x} = \mathbf{b}$, with A and $\mathbf{b}$ as in Exercise 9. Write the solution as a vector.

12. Solve the equation $A\mathbf{x} = \mathbf{b}$, with A and $\mathbf{b}$ as in Exercise 10. Write the solution as a vector.

In Exercises 13–16, write the matrix equation as a vector equation, or vice-versa.

13. $\begin{bmatrix} 4 & -2 & -5 & 9 \\ -7 & 1 & -8 & -3 \end{bmatrix}\begin{bmatrix} 2 \\ 6 \\ -1 \\ 0 \end{bmatrix} = \begin{bmatrix} 1 \\ 0 \end{bmatrix}$

14. $\begin{bmatrix} 6 & -2 \\ 1 & 3 \\ -5 & 4 \\ 9 & -3 \end{bmatrix}\begin{bmatrix} -3 \\ -7 \end{bmatrix} = \begin{bmatrix} 4 \\ -24 \\ 13 \\ -6 \end{bmatrix}$

15. $x_1\begin{bmatrix}-4\\1\\4\end{bmatrix}+x_2\begin{bmatrix}3\\-5\\2\end{bmatrix}=\begin{bmatrix}-2\\0\\3\end{bmatrix}$

16. $y_1\begin{bmatrix}3\\1\end{bmatrix}+y_2\begin{bmatrix}-5\\2\end{bmatrix}+y_3\begin{bmatrix}0\\-1\end{bmatrix}=\begin{bmatrix}-4\\7\end{bmatrix}$

17. Let $\mathbf{u}=\begin{bmatrix}-5\\-3\\-6\end{bmatrix}$ and $A=\begin{bmatrix}3&5\\1&1\\-2&-8\end{bmatrix}$. Is $\mathbf{u}$ in the plane in $\mathbb{R}^3$ spanned by the columns of A? (See the accompanying figure.) Why or why not?

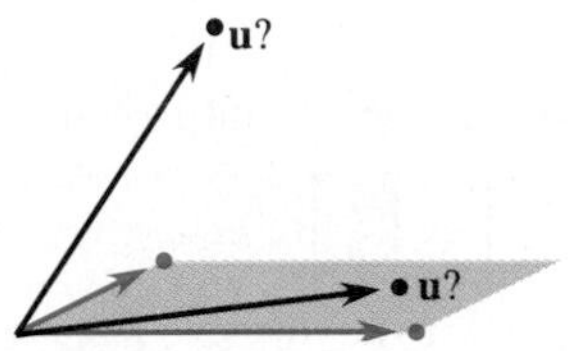

Where is **u**?

18. Let $\mathbf{u}=\begin{bmatrix}8\\2\\3\end{bmatrix}$ and $A=\begin{bmatrix}4&3&5\\0&1&-1\\1&2&0\end{bmatrix}$. Is $\mathbf{u}$ in the subset of $\mathbb{R}^3$ spanned by the columns of A? Why or why not?

19. Let $A=\begin{bmatrix}-3&1\\6&-2\end{bmatrix}$ and $\mathbf{b}=\begin{bmatrix}b_1\\b_2\end{bmatrix}$. Show that the equation $A\mathbf{x}=\mathbf{b}$ is not consistent for all possible $\mathbf{b}$, and describe the set of all $\mathbf{b}$ for which $A\mathbf{x}=\mathbf{b}$ *is* consistent.

20. Repeat Exercise 19: $A=\begin{bmatrix}1&3&-4\\3&2&-6\\-5&-1&8\end{bmatrix}$, $\mathbf{b}=\begin{bmatrix}b_1\\b_2\\b_3\end{bmatrix}$.

21. How many rows of $A=\begin{bmatrix}1&3&-2&-2\\0&1&-1&5\\-1&-2&1&7\\1&1&0&-6\end{bmatrix}$ contain pivot positions?

22. If a 5×6 matrix A has four pivot columns, how many rows of A contain a pivot position? Why?

In Exercises 23–28, explain *why* your calculations justify your answer, and mention an appropriate theorem.

23. Do the columns of the matrix in Exercise 20 span $\mathbb{R}^3$?

24. Do the columns of the matrix in Exercise 21 span $\mathbb{R}^4$?

25. Do the columns of $\begin{bmatrix}0&0&2\\0&-5&1\\4&6&-3\end{bmatrix}$ span $\mathbb{R}^3$?

26. Do the columns of the matrix in Exercise 17 span $\mathbb{R}^3$?

27. Let $\mathbf{v}_1=\begin{bmatrix}1\\0\\-1\\0\end{bmatrix}$, $\mathbf{v}_2=\begin{bmatrix}0\\1\\0\\-1\end{bmatrix}$, $\mathbf{v}_3=\begin{bmatrix}1\\0\\0\\-1\end{bmatrix}$. Does $\{\mathbf{v}_1,\mathbf{v}_2,\mathbf{v}_3\}$ span $\mathbb{R}^4$?

28. Let $\mathbf{v}_1=\begin{bmatrix}1\\0\\-1\end{bmatrix}$, $\mathbf{v}_2=\begin{bmatrix}-1\\3\\7\end{bmatrix}$, $\mathbf{v}_3=\begin{bmatrix}3\\-2\\-2\end{bmatrix}$. Does $\{\mathbf{v}_1,\mathbf{v}_2,\mathbf{v}_3\}$ span $\mathbb{R}^3$?

29. It can be shown that $\begin{bmatrix}4&1&2\\-2&0&8\\3&5&-6\end{bmatrix}\begin{bmatrix}-1\\4\\2\end{bmatrix}=\begin{bmatrix}4\\18\\5\end{bmatrix}$. Use this fact (and no row operations) to find scalars c_1, c_2, c_3 such that

$$\begin{bmatrix}4\\18\\5\end{bmatrix}=c_1\begin{bmatrix}4\\-2\\3\end{bmatrix}+c_2\begin{bmatrix}1\\0\\5\end{bmatrix}+c_3\begin{bmatrix}2\\8\\-6\end{bmatrix}$$

30. Let $\mathbf{u}=\begin{bmatrix}3\\8\\4\end{bmatrix}$, $\mathbf{v}=\begin{bmatrix}1\\3\\1\end{bmatrix}$, and $\mathbf{w}=\begin{bmatrix}1\\1\\3\end{bmatrix}$. It can be shown that $2\mathbf{u}-5\mathbf{v}-\mathbf{w}=\mathbf{0}$. Use this fact (and no row operations) to solve the equation $\begin{bmatrix}3&1\\8&3\\4&1\end{bmatrix}\begin{bmatrix}x_1\\x_2\end{bmatrix}=\begin{bmatrix}1\\1\\3\end{bmatrix}$.

31. Let $\mathbf{u}=\begin{bmatrix}1\\3\\3\end{bmatrix}$, $\mathbf{v}=\begin{bmatrix}-2\\1\\0\end{bmatrix}$, and $A=\begin{bmatrix}5&1&-3\\7&-2&1\end{bmatrix}$. Compute $A(\mathbf{u}+\mathbf{v})$, and $A\mathbf{u}+A\mathbf{v}$ without using Theorem 3.

32. Compute $5\mathbf{u}$, $A(5\mathbf{u})$, and $5(A\mathbf{u})$, where $\mathbf{u}$ and A are given in Exercise 31. Do not use Theorem 3 for the calculations.

33. Let A be a 3×4 matrix, let $\mathbf{y}_1$ and $\mathbf{y}_2$ be vectors in $\mathbb{R}^3$, and let $\mathbf{w}=\mathbf{y}_1+\mathbf{y}_2$. Suppose that $\mathbf{y}_1=A\mathbf{x}_1$ and $\mathbf{y}_2=A\mathbf{x}_2$ for some vectors $\mathbf{x}_1$ and $\mathbf{x}_2$ in $\mathbb{R}^4$. What fact allows you to conclude that the system $A\mathbf{x}=\mathbf{w}$ is consistent? (*Note*: $\mathbf{x}_1$ and $\mathbf{x}_2$ denote vectors, not scalar entries in vectors.)

34. Let A be a 5×3 matrix, let $\mathbf{y}$ be a vector in $\mathbb{R}^3$ and $\mathbf{z}$ a vector in $\mathbb{R}^5$. Suppose that $A\mathbf{y}=\mathbf{z}$. What fact allows you to conclude that the system $A\mathbf{x}=4\mathbf{z}$ is consistent?

35. Let A be a 3×2 matrix. Explain why the equation $A\mathbf{x}=\mathbf{b}$ cannot be consistent for all $\mathbf{b}$ in $\mathbb{R}^3$. Generalize your argument to the case of an arbitrary A with more rows than columns.

36. Could a set of three vectors in $\mathbb{R}^4$ span all of $\mathbb{R}^4$? Explain. What about n vectors in $\mathbb{R}^m$ when m is greater than n?

SOLUTIONS TO PRACTICE PROBLEMS

1. The matrix equation

$$\begin{bmatrix} 1 & 5 & -2 & 0 \\ -3 & 1 & 9 & -5 \\ 4 & -8 & -1 & 7 \end{bmatrix} \begin{bmatrix} 3 \\ -2 \\ 0 \\ -4 \end{bmatrix} = \begin{bmatrix} -7 \\ 9 \\ 0 \end{bmatrix}$$

is equivalent to the vector equation

$$3\begin{bmatrix} 1 \\ -3 \\ 4 \end{bmatrix} - 2\begin{bmatrix} 5 \\ 1 \\ -8 \end{bmatrix} + 0\begin{bmatrix} -2 \\ 9 \\ -1 \end{bmatrix} - 4\begin{bmatrix} 0 \\ -5 \\ 7 \end{bmatrix} = \begin{bmatrix} -7 \\ 9 \\ 0 \end{bmatrix}$$

which expresses $\mathbf{b}$ as a linear combination of the columns of A.

2.

$$\mathbf{u}+\mathbf{v} = \begin{bmatrix} 4 \\ -1 \end{bmatrix} + \begin{bmatrix} -3 \\ 5 \end{bmatrix} = \begin{bmatrix} 1 \\ 4 \end{bmatrix}$$

$$A(\mathbf{u}+\mathbf{v}) = \begin{bmatrix} 2 & 5 \\ 3 & 1 \end{bmatrix}\begin{bmatrix} 1 \\ 4 \end{bmatrix} = \begin{bmatrix} 2+20 \\ 3+4 \end{bmatrix} = \begin{bmatrix} 22 \\ 7 \end{bmatrix}$$

$$A\mathbf{u}+A\mathbf{v} = \begin{bmatrix} 2 & 5 \\ 3 & 1 \end{bmatrix}\begin{bmatrix} 4 \\ -1 \end{bmatrix} + \begin{bmatrix} 2 & 5 \\ 3 & 1 \end{bmatrix}\begin{bmatrix} -3 \\ 5 \end{bmatrix}$$

$$= \begin{bmatrix} 3 \\ 11 \end{bmatrix} + \begin{bmatrix} 19 \\ -4 \end{bmatrix} = \begin{bmatrix} 22 \\ 7 \end{bmatrix}$$

2.3 SOLUTION SETS OF LINEAR SYSTEMS

Vectors can be used to give an explicit and geometric description of the solution set of a system of linear equations. In $\mathbb{R}^2$ or $\mathbb{R}^3$, a solution set is a plane, a line, a single point, the empty set, or (rarely) all of $\mathbb{R}^2$ or $\mathbb{R}^3$. These same geometric objects will also serve well as mental images of solution sets in $\mathbb{R}^n$ when $n > 3$. As a preliminary, we examine translations of lines.

Vector Addition as Translation

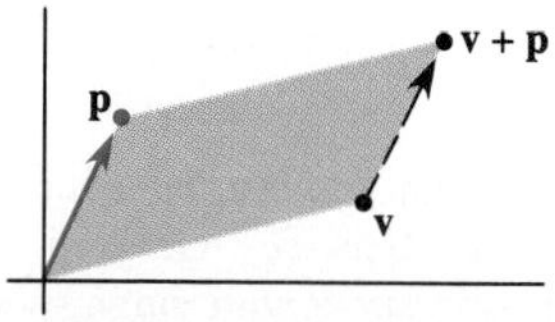

FIGURE 1 Adding $\mathbf{p}$ to $\mathbf{v}$ translates $\mathbf{v}$ to $\mathbf{v}+\mathbf{p}$.

In dynamic terms, the operation of vector addition is a translation. Given $\mathbf{v}$ and $\mathbf{p}$ in $\mathbb{R}^2$ or $\mathbb{R}^3$, the effect of adding $\mathbf{p}$ to $\mathbf{v}$ is to *move* $\mathbf{v}$ in a direction parallel to $\mathbf{p}$. We say that $\mathbf{v}$ is **translated by p** to $\mathbf{v}+\mathbf{p}$. We may think of "$+\mathbf{p}$" as a "translation operator" that acts on $\mathbf{v}$ to produce $\mathbf{v}+\mathbf{p}$. See Fig. 1, where the arrow from $\mathbf{v}$ to $\mathbf{v}+\mathbf{p}$ shows the action of the operator $+\mathbf{p}$.[1]

If each point on a line L in $\mathbb{R}^2$ or $\mathbb{R}^3$ is translated by a vector $\mathbf{p}$, the result is a line parallel to L, which we write as $L+\mathbf{p}$. See Fig. 2. In general, two lines L and M are said to be parallel if there is a $\mathbf{p}$ such that $M = L+\mathbf{p}$.

[1]Physicists often call the arrow in Fig. 1 from $\mathbf{v}$ to $\mathbf{v}+\mathbf{p}$ a *free vector* and the arrow from $\mathbf{0}$ to $\mathbf{p}$ a *bound vector* or a *position vector*.

Suppose L goes through the origin $\mathbf{0}$, and take any nonzero point $\mathbf{v}$ on L. The line $L+\mathbf{p}$ passes through $\mathbf{p}$ and $\mathbf{v}+\mathbf{p}$. See Fig. 3. We say that $L+\mathbf{p}$ is **the line through p parallel to v**.

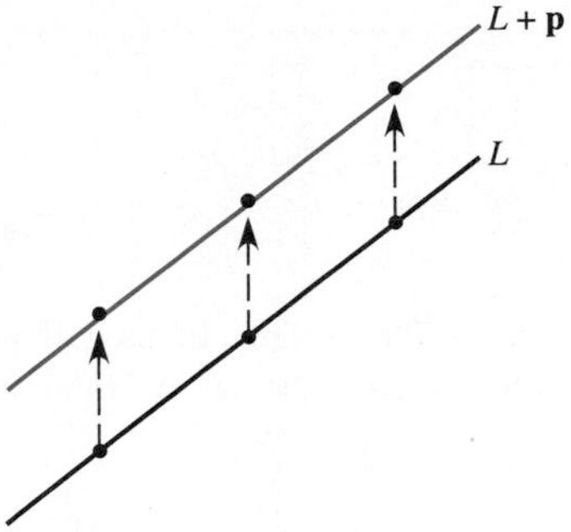

FIGURE 2 Translated line.

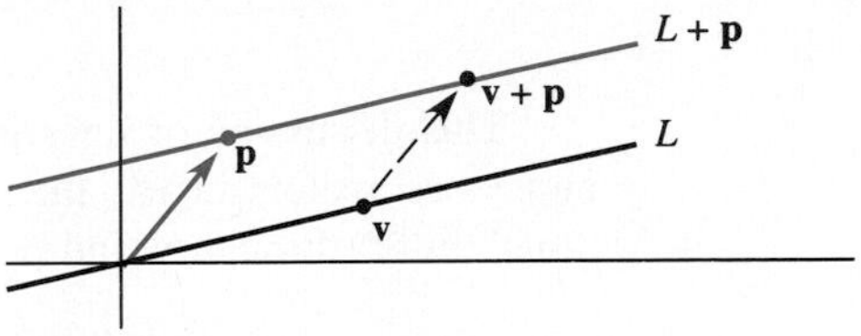

FIGURE 3 Adding $\mathbf{p}$ to L translates L to $L+\mathbf{p}$.

The L in Fig. 3 is the set of all multiples of $\mathbf{v}$—namely, points of the form $t\mathbf{v}$, where t is in $\mathbb{R}$. The translated line contains the points of the form $t\mathbf{v}+\mathbf{p}$, which can also be written as $\mathbf{p}+t\mathbf{v}$. If $\mathbf{x}$ represents an arbitrary vector in $L+\mathbf{p}$, then there must be a t in $\mathbb{R}$ such that

$$\mathbf{x} = \mathbf{p} + t\mathbf{v}$$

This equation is called a **parametric equation** of the line because each point in $L+\mathbf{p}$ is determined uniquely by the parameter t.

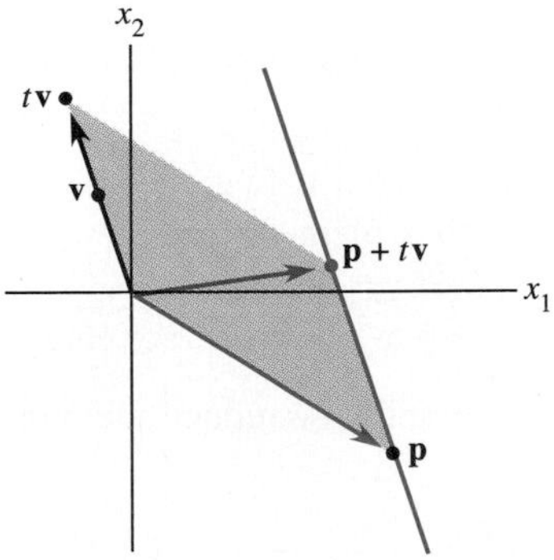

FIGURE 4

EXAMPLE 1 Let $\mathbf{p} = \begin{bmatrix} 8 \\ -5 \end{bmatrix}$ and $\mathbf{v} = \begin{bmatrix} -1 \\ 3 \end{bmatrix}$. Find a parametric equation

Solution See Fig. 4. One parametric equation is

$$\underset{\mathbf{x}}{\underset{\uparrow}{\begin{bmatrix} x_1 \\ x_2 \end{bmatrix}}} = \underset{\mathbf{p}}{\underset{\uparrow}{\begin{bmatrix} 8 \\ -5 \end{bmatrix}}} + t\underset{\mathbf{v}}{\underset{\uparrow}{\begin{bmatrix} -1 \\ 3 \end{bmatrix}}}$$

The line may also be described by a system of parametric equations,

$$\begin{cases} x_1 &= 8 - t \\ x_2 &= -5 + 3t \end{cases}$$

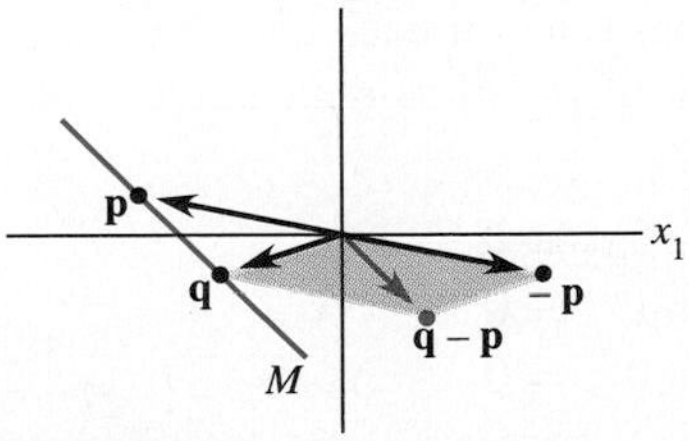

FIGURE 5 The line through $\mathbf{p}$ and $\mathbf{q}$.

EXAMPLE 2 Let $\mathbf{p} = \begin{bmatrix} -5 \\ 1 \end{bmatrix}$ and $\mathbf{q} = \begin{bmatrix} -3 \\ -1 \end{bmatrix}$. Find a parametric equation of the line M in $\mathbb{R}^2$ through $\mathbf{p}$ and $\mathbf{q}$. See Fig. 5.

Solution Translation by $-\mathbf{p}$ moves the line M to a line through the origin and $\mathbf{q}-\mathbf{p}$. So M is parallel to the vector

$$\mathbf{q} - \mathbf{p} = \begin{bmatrix} -3 \\ -1 \end{bmatrix} - \begin{bmatrix} -5 \\ 1 \end{bmatrix} = \begin{bmatrix} 2 \\ -2 \end{bmatrix}$$

Hence a parametric equation of M is

$$\mathbf{x} = \mathbf{p} + t(\mathbf{q} - \mathbf{p}) \quad \text{or} \quad \begin{bmatrix} x_1 \\ x_2 \end{bmatrix} = \begin{bmatrix} -5 \\ 1 \end{bmatrix} + t\begin{bmatrix} 2 \\ -2 \end{bmatrix}$$

This discussion of lines in $\mathbb{R}^2$ obviously carries over to lines in $\mathbb{R}^3$. In fact, if $\mathbf{p}$ and $\mathbf{v}$ are vectors in $\mathbb{R}^n$, then it is natural to think of the set $\{\mathbf{p} + t\mathbf{v} : t \text{ in } \mathbb{R}\}$ as a "line" in $\mathbb{R}^n$ through $\mathbf{p}$ and parallel to $\mathbf{v}$.

Homogeneous Linear Systems

A system of linear equations is said to be **homogeneous** if it can be written in the form $A\mathbf{x} = \mathbf{0}$, where A is an $m \times n$ matrix and $\mathbf{0}$ is the zero vector in $\mathbb{R}^m$. Such a system $A\mathbf{x} = \mathbf{0}$ *always* has at least one solution, namely, $\mathbf{x} = \mathbf{0}$ (the zero vector in $\mathbb{R}^n$). This zero solution is usually called the **trivial solution**. For a given equation $A\mathbf{x} = \mathbf{0}$, the important question is whether there exists a **nontrivial solution**, that is, a nonzero vector $\mathbf{x}$ that satisfies $A\mathbf{x} = \mathbf{0}$. The existence and uniqueness theorem in Section 1.2 (Theorem 2) leads immediately to the following fact.

The homogeneous system $A\mathbf{x} = \mathbf{0}$ has a nontrivial solution if and only if the system has at least one free variable.

EXAMPLE 3 Determine if the following homogeneous system has a nontrivial solution. Then describe the solution set.

$$\begin{aligned} 3x_1 + 5x_2 - 4x_3 &= 0 \\ -3x_1 - 2x_2 + 4x_3 &= 0 \\ 6x_1 + x_2 - 8x_3 &= 0 \end{aligned}$$

Solution Let A be the matrix of coefficients of the system and row reduce the augmented matrix $[A \quad \mathbf{0}]$ to echelon form.

$$\begin{bmatrix} 3 & 5 & -4 & 0 \\ -3 & -2 & 4 & 0 \\ 6 & 1 & -8 & 0 \end{bmatrix} \sim \begin{bmatrix} 3 & 5 & -4 & 0 \\ 0 & 3 & 0 & 0 \\ 0 & -9 & 0 & 0 \end{bmatrix} \sim \begin{bmatrix} 3 & 5 & -4 & 0 \\ 0 & 3 & 0 & 0 \\ 0 & 0 & 0 & 0 \end{bmatrix}$$

Since x_3 is a free variable, $A\mathbf{x} = \mathbf{0}$ has nontrivial solutions (one for each choice of x_3). To describe the solution set, continue the row reduction of $[A \quad \mathbf{0}]$ to *reduced* echelon form:

$$\begin{bmatrix} 1 & 0 & -\frac{4}{3} & 0 \\ 0 & 1 & 0 & 0 \\ 0 & 0 & 0 & 0 \end{bmatrix} \qquad \begin{aligned} x_1 \qquad - \tfrac{4}{3}x_3 &= 0 \\ x_2 \qquad\quad &= 0 \\ 0 &= 0 \end{aligned}$$

Solve for the basic variables x_1 and x_2 and obtain $x_1 = \frac{4}{3}x_3$, $x_2 = 0$, with x_3 free. As a vector, the general solution of $A\mathbf{x} = \mathbf{0}$ has the form

$$\mathbf{x} = \begin{bmatrix} x_1 \\ x_2 \\ x_3 \end{bmatrix} = \begin{bmatrix} \frac{4}{3}x_3 \\ 0 \\ x_3 \end{bmatrix} = x_3 \begin{bmatrix} \frac{4}{3} \\ 0 \\ 1 \end{bmatrix} = x_3\mathbf{v}, \quad \text{where } \mathbf{v} = \begin{bmatrix} \frac{4}{3} \\ 0 \\ 1 \end{bmatrix}$$

Here the parameter x_3 is factored out of the expression for the general solution vector. This shows that every solution of $A\mathbf{x} = \mathbf{0}$ in this case is a multiple of $\mathbf{v}$. The trivial solution is obtained by choosing $x_3 = 0$. Geometrically, the solution set is a line through $\mathbf{0}$ in $\mathbb{R}^3$. ∎

Notice that a nontrivial solution $\mathbf{x}$ can have some zero entries as long as not all of its entries are zero.

EXAMPLE 4 The single equation for a plane in $\mathbb{R}^3$ can be treated as a very simple system of equations. Describe all solutions of the homogeneous "system"

$$2x_1 - 3x_2 + x_3 = 0 \tag{1}$$

Solution There is no need for matrix notation. Solve for the basic variable x_1 in terms of the free variables. The general solution is $x_1 = \frac{3}{2}x_2 - \frac{1}{2}x_3$, with x_2 and x_3 free. As a vector, the general solution is

$$\mathbf{x} = \begin{bmatrix} x_1 \\ x_2 \\ x_3 \end{bmatrix} = \begin{bmatrix} \frac{3}{2}x_2 - \frac{1}{2}x_3 \\ x_2 \\ x_3 \end{bmatrix} = \begin{bmatrix} \frac{3}{2}x_2 \\ x_2 \\ 0 \end{bmatrix} + \begin{bmatrix} -\frac{1}{2}x_3 \\ 0 \\ x_3 \end{bmatrix} = x_2 \underset{\substack{\uparrow \\ \mathbf{u}}}{\begin{bmatrix} \frac{3}{2} \\ 1 \\ 0 \end{bmatrix}} + x_3 \underset{\substack{\uparrow \\ \mathbf{v}}}{\begin{bmatrix} -\frac{1}{2} \\ 0 \\ 1 \end{bmatrix}} \tag{2}$$

This calculation shows that every solution of $A\mathbf{x} = \mathbf{0}$ is a linear combination of the vectors $\mathbf{u}$, $\mathbf{v}$, shown in (2). That is, the solution set is Span $\{\mathbf{u}, \mathbf{v}\}$. ∎

The original equation (1) for the plane in Example 4 is an *implicit* description of the plane. Solving this equation amounts to finding an *explicit* description of the plane as the set spanned by $\mathbf{u}$ and $\mathbf{v}$. Equation (2), $\mathbf{x} = x_2\mathbf{u} + x_3\mathbf{v}$, is called a **parametric equation** of the plane. Whenever a solution set is described explicitly with vectors as in Examples 3 and 4, we say that the solution is in *parametric vector form.*

Examples 3 and 4, along with the exercises, illustrate the fact that the solution set of a homogeneous equation $A\mathbf{x} = \mathbf{0}$ can always be expressed explicitly as Span $\{\mathbf{v}_1, \ldots, \mathbf{v}_p\}$ for suitable vectors $\mathbf{v}_1, \ldots, \mathbf{v}_p$. If the only solution is the zero vector, then the solution set is Span $\{\mathbf{0}\}$. Even when $n > 3$, or when there are more than two vectors in the spanning set, our mental image of the solution set of $A\mathbf{x} = \mathbf{0}$ is either a line or plane *through the origin* or just the origin by itself.

Solutions of Nonhomogeneous Systems

When a nonhomogeneous system has many solutions, the general solution can be written in parametric vector form as one vector plus an arbitrary linear combination of vectors that satisfy the corresponding homogeneous system.

EXAMPLE 5 Describe all solutions of $A\mathbf{x} = \mathbf{b}$, where

$$A = \begin{bmatrix} 3 & 5 & -4 \\ -3 & -2 & 4 \\ 6 & 1 & -8 \end{bmatrix} \quad \text{and} \quad \mathbf{b} = \begin{bmatrix} 7 \\ -1 \\ -4 \end{bmatrix}$$

Solution Here A is the matrix of coefficients from Example 3. Row operations on $[A \quad \mathbf{b}]$ produce

$$\begin{bmatrix} 3 & 5 & -4 & 7 \\ -3 & -2 & 4 & -1 \\ 6 & 1 & -8 & -4 \end{bmatrix} \sim \begin{bmatrix} 1 & 0 & -\frac{4}{3} & -1 \\ 0 & 1 & 0 & 2 \\ 0 & 0 & 0 & 0 \end{bmatrix}, \qquad \begin{aligned} x_1 \quad - \tfrac{4}{3}x_3 &= -1 \\ x_2 \qquad &= 2 \\ 0 &= 0 \end{aligned}$$

Thus $x_1 = -1 + \frac{4}{3}x_3$, $x_2 = 2$, and x_3 is free. As a vector, the general solution of $A\mathbf{x} = \mathbf{b}$ has the form

$$\mathbf{x} = \begin{bmatrix} x_1 \\ x_2 \\ x_3 \end{bmatrix} = \begin{bmatrix} -1 + \frac{4}{3}x_3 \\ 2 \\ x_3 \end{bmatrix} = \begin{bmatrix} -1 \\ 2 \\ 0 \end{bmatrix} + \begin{bmatrix} \frac{4}{3}x_3 \\ 0 \\ x_3 \end{bmatrix} = \underset{\substack{\uparrow \\ \mathbf{p}}}{\begin{bmatrix} -1 \\ 2 \\ 0 \end{bmatrix}} + x_3 \underset{\substack{\uparrow \\ \mathbf{v}}}{\begin{bmatrix} \frac{4}{3} \\ 0 \\ 1 \end{bmatrix}} \tag{3}$$

The solutions of $A\mathbf{x} = \mathbf{b}$ have the form $\mathbf{x} = \mathbf{p} + t\mathbf{v}$, where t is the same as x_3. The solution set is *the line in* $\mathbb{R}^3$ *through* $\mathbf{p}$ *parallel to* $\mathbf{v}$.

The vector $\mathbf{p}$ itself is the solution of $A\mathbf{x} = \mathbf{b}$ corresponding to $x_3 = 0$. Also, from Example 3, $\mathbf{v}$ spans the solution set of the homogeneous equation $A\mathbf{x} = \mathbf{0}$. *The solution sets of* $A\mathbf{x} = \mathbf{b}$ *and* $A\mathbf{x} = \mathbf{0}$ *are parallel lines.* (Fig. 6 shows a typical case.)

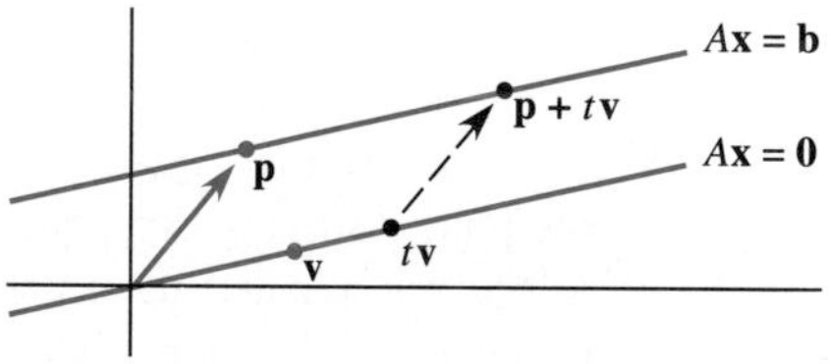

FIGURE 6 Parallel solution sets of $A\mathbf{x} = \mathbf{b}$ and $A\mathbf{x} = \mathbf{0}$.

The phenomenon described in Example 5 generalizes to any *consistent* equation $A\mathbf{x} = \mathbf{b}$, with $\mathbf{b} \neq \mathbf{0}$, although the solution set will be larger than a line when there are several free variables. The following theorem gives the precise statement. See Exercise 25 for a proof.

THEOREM 4

Suppose the equation $A\mathbf{x} = \mathbf{b}$ is consistent for some given $\mathbf{b}$, and let $\mathbf{p}$ be a solution. Then the solution set of $A\mathbf{x} = \mathbf{b}$ is the set of all vectors of the form $\mathbf{w} = \mathbf{p} + \mathbf{v}_h$, where $\mathbf{v}_h$ is any solution of the homogeneous equation $A\mathbf{x} = \mathbf{0}$.

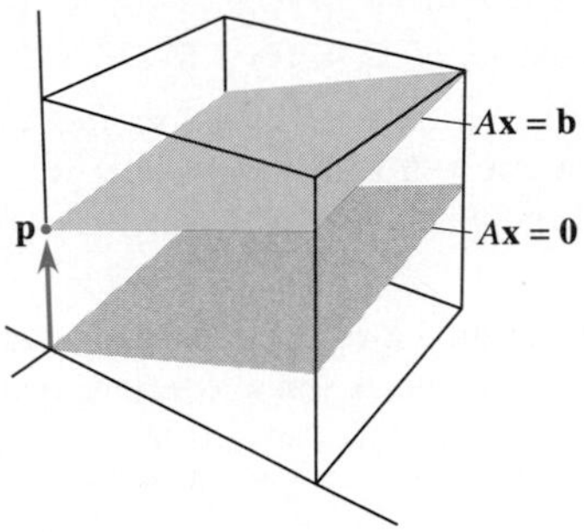

FIGURE 7 Parallel solution sets of $A\mathbf{x} = \mathbf{b}$ and $A\mathbf{x} = \mathbf{0}$.

Theorem 4 says that the solution set of $A\mathbf{x} = \mathbf{b}$ is obtained by translating the solution set of $A\mathbf{x} = \mathbf{0}$, using any particular solution $\mathbf{p}$ of $A\mathbf{x} = \mathbf{b}$ for the translation. Figure 7 illustrates the case when there are two free variables. Even when $n > 3$, our mental image of the solution set of a consistent system $A\mathbf{x} = \mathbf{b}$ (with $\mathbf{b} \neq \mathbf{0}$) is either a single nonzero point or a line or plane not passing through the origin.

The following algorithm outlines the calculations shown in Examples 3, 4 and 5.

> **Writing a Solution Set (of a consistent system) in Parametric Vector Form.**
>
> 1. Row reduce the augmented matrix to reduced echelon form.
> 2. Express each basic variable in terms of any free variables appearing in an equation.
> 3. Write a typical solution $\mathbf{x}$ as a vector whose entries depend on the free variables, if any.
> 4. Decompose $\mathbf{x}$ into a linear combination of vectors (with numeric entries) using the free variables as parameters.

PRACTICE PROBLEMS

1. Each of the following equations determines a plane in $\mathbb{R}^3$. Do the two planes intersect? If so, describe their intersection.

$$\begin{aligned} x_1 + 4x_2 - 5x_3 &= 0 \\ 2x_1 - x_2 + 8x_3 &= 9 \end{aligned}$$

2. Write the general solution of $2x_1 - 3x_2 + x_3 = 7$ in parametric vector form, and relate the solution set to the one found in Example 4.

2.3 EXERCISES

In Exercises 1 and 2, find the parametric equation of the line through $\mathbf{a}$ parallel to $\mathbf{b}$.

1. $\mathbf{a} = \begin{bmatrix} 3 \\ -8 \end{bmatrix}$, $\mathbf{b} = \begin{bmatrix} -1 \\ 5 \end{bmatrix}$ **2.** $\mathbf{a} = \begin{bmatrix} -4 \\ 0 \end{bmatrix}$, $\mathbf{b} = \begin{bmatrix} 2 \\ -3 \end{bmatrix}$

In Exercises 3 and 4, find a parametric equation of the line through $\mathbf{a}$ and $\mathbf{b}$.

3. $\mathbf{a} = \begin{bmatrix} -1 \\ 4 \end{bmatrix}$, $\mathbf{b} = \begin{bmatrix} 0 \\ 7 \end{bmatrix}$ **4.** $\mathbf{a} = \begin{bmatrix} 9 \\ -5 \end{bmatrix}$, $\mathbf{b} = \begin{bmatrix} 2 \\ -1 \end{bmatrix}$

In Exercises 5–8, determine if the system has a nontrivial solution. Try to use as few row operations as possible.

5. $$\begin{aligned} x_1 - 5x_2 + 9x_3 &= 0 \\ -x_1 + 4x_2 - 3x_3 &= 0 \\ 2x_1 - 8x_2 + 9x_3 &= 0 \end{aligned}$$

6. $$\begin{aligned} 3x_1 + 6x_2 - 4x_3 - x_4 &= 0 \\ -5x_1 \qquad + 8x_3 + 3x_4 &= 0 \\ 8x_1 - x_2 \qquad + 7x_4 &= 0 \end{aligned}$$

7. $$\begin{aligned} 5x_1 - x_2 + 3x_3 &= 0 \\ 4x_1 - 3x_2 + 7x_3 &= 0 \end{aligned}$$

8. $$\begin{aligned} 4x_1 - 2x_2 &= 0 \\ 6x_1 + 3x_2 &= 0 \end{aligned}$$

In Exercises 9 and 10, follow the method of Examples 3 and 4 to write the solution set of the given homogeneous system in parametric vector form.

9.
$$\begin{aligned} x_1 - 3x_2 - 2x_3 &= 0 \\ x_2 - x_3 &= 0 \\ -2x_1 + 3x_2 + 7x_3 &= 0 \end{aligned}$$

10.
$$\begin{aligned} x_1 + 2x_2 - 7x_3 &= 0 \\ -2x_1 - 3x_2 + 9x_3 &= 0 \\ -2x_2 + 10x_3 &= 0 \end{aligned}$$

In Exercises 11–16, describe all solutions of $A\mathbf{x} = \mathbf{0}$ in parametric vector form where A is row equivalent to the matrix shown.

11. $\begin{bmatrix} 1 & -2 & -5 & 5 \\ 0 & 0 & -3 & 2 \end{bmatrix}$ **12.** $\begin{bmatrix} 1 & 5 & 16 & 7 \\ 0 & 2 & 6 & 3 \end{bmatrix}$

13. $\begin{bmatrix} 1 & -5 & 0 & 2 & 0 & -4 \\ 0 & 0 & 0 & 1 & 0 & -3 \\ 0 & 0 & 0 & 0 & 1 & 5 \\ 0 & 0 & 0 & 0 & 0 & 0 \end{bmatrix}$

14. $\begin{bmatrix} 1 & 6 & 0 & 8 & -1 & -2 \\ 0 & 0 & 1 & -3 & 4 & 6 \\ 0 & 0 & 0 & 0 & 0 & 1 \\ 0 & 0 & 0 & 0 & 0 & 0 \end{bmatrix}$

15. $[2 \ -8 \ \ 6]$ **16.** $[1 \ -5 \ \ 0 \ \ 4]$

17. Suppose that the solution set of a certain system of equations can be described as $x_1 = 4 - 3x_3$, $x_2 = -1 + 6x_3$, with x_3 free. Use vectors to describe this set as a line in $\mathbb{R}^3$.

18. Suppose that the solution set of a certain system of equations can be described as $x_1 = 7 + x_4$, $x_2 = -5 - 2x_4$, $x_3 = 1 - 3x_4$, with x_4 free. Use vectors to describe this set as a "line" in $\mathbb{R}^4$.

19. Follow the method of Example 5 to describe the solutions of the following system. Also, give a geometric description of the solution set and compare it with that in Exercise 9.
$$\begin{aligned} x_1 - 3x_2 - 2x_3 &= -5 \\ x_2 - x_3 &= 4 \\ -2x_1 + 3x_2 + 7x_3 &= -2 \end{aligned}$$

20. As in Exercise 19, describe the solutions of the following system, and provide a geometric comparison with the solution set in Exercise 10.
$$\begin{aligned} x_1 + 2x_2 - 7x_3 &= 0 \\ -2x_1 - 3x_2 + 9x_3 &= 4 \\ -2x_2 + 10x_3 &= -8 \end{aligned}$$

21. Describe the solution set in $\mathbb{R}^3$ of $x_1 - 4x_2 + 3x_3 = 0$, and compare it with the solution set of $x_1 - 4x_2 + 3x_3 = 7$.

22. Describe the solution set in $\mathbb{R}^3$ of $x_1 + 3x_2 - 8x_3 = 0$; compare it with the solution set of $x_1 + 3x_2 - 8x_3 = -1$.

23. Let A be an $m \times n$ matrix and let $\mathbf{u}$ and $\mathbf{v}$ be vectors in $\mathbb{R}^n$ with the property that $A\mathbf{u} = \mathbf{0}$ and $A\mathbf{v} = \mathbf{0}$. Let $\mathbf{w} = \mathbf{u} + \mathbf{v}$. Compute $A\mathbf{w}$ and show that $A\mathbf{w} = \mathbf{0}$. What fact do you need to do this?

24. Let A be an $m \times n$ matrix, let $\mathbf{u}$ be a vector in $\mathbb{R}^n$ such that $A\mathbf{u} = \mathbf{0}$. Let $\mathbf{w} = 5\mathbf{u}$. What fact allows you to conclude that $A\mathbf{w} = \mathbf{0}$?

25. Prove Theorem 4:

a. Suppose that $\mathbf{p}$ is a solution of $A\mathbf{x} = \mathbf{b}$, so that $A\mathbf{p} = \mathbf{b}$. Let $\mathbf{v}_h$ be any solution of the homogeneous equation $A\mathbf{x} = \mathbf{0}$ and let $\mathbf{w} = \mathbf{p} + \mathbf{v}_h$. Show that $\mathbf{w}$ is a solution of $A\mathbf{x} = \mathbf{b}$.

b. Let $\mathbf{w}$ be any solution of $A\mathbf{x} = \mathbf{b}$ and define $\mathbf{v}_h = \mathbf{w} - \mathbf{p}$. Show that $\mathbf{v}_h$ is a solution of $A\mathbf{x} = \mathbf{0}$. This shows that every solution of $A\mathbf{x} = \mathbf{b}$ has the form $\mathbf{w} = \mathbf{p} + \mathbf{v}_h$, with $\mathbf{p}$ a particular solution of $A\mathbf{x} = \mathbf{b}$ and $\mathbf{v}_h$ a solution of $A\mathbf{x} = \mathbf{0}$.

26. Suppose $A\mathbf{x} = \mathbf{b}$ has a solution. Use Theorem 4 to explain why the solution is unique precisely when $A\mathbf{x} = \mathbf{0}$ has only the trivial solution.

27. Suppose A is the 3×3 *zero* matrix (with all zero entries). Describe the solution set of the equation $A\mathbf{x} = \mathbf{0}$.

28. If $\mathbf{b} \neq \mathbf{0}$, can the solution set of $A\mathbf{x} = \mathbf{b}$ be a plane through the origin? Explain.

In Exercises 29–32, (a) does the equation $A\mathbf{x} = \mathbf{0}$ have a nontrivial solution and (b) does the equation $A\mathbf{x} = \mathbf{b}$ have at least one solution for every possible $\mathbf{b}$?

29. A is a 3×3 matrix with three pivot positions.

30. A is a 3×3 matrix with two pivot positions.

31. A is a 3×2 matrix with two pivot positions.

32. A is a 2×4 matrix with two pivot positions.

33. Given $A = \begin{bmatrix} 5 & 10 \\ -8 & -16 \\ 7 & 14 \end{bmatrix}$, find one nontrivial solution of $A\mathbf{x} = \mathbf{0}$ by inspection. [*Hint*: Think of the equation as $x_1\mathbf{a}_1 + x_2\mathbf{a}_2 = \mathbf{0}$.]

34. Given $A = \begin{bmatrix} 1 & 3 \\ 2 & 6 \\ 3 & 9 \end{bmatrix}$, find a nontrivial solution of $A\mathbf{x} = \mathbf{0}$ by inspection.

SOLUTIONS TO PRACTICE PROBLEMS

1. Row reduce the augmented matrix:

$$\begin{bmatrix} 1 & 4 & -5 & 0 \\ 2 & -1 & 8 & 9 \end{bmatrix} \sim \begin{bmatrix} 1 & 4 & -5 & 0 \\ 0 & -9 & 18 & 9 \end{bmatrix} \sim \begin{bmatrix} 1 & 0 & 3 & 4 \\ 0 & 1 & -2 & -1 \end{bmatrix}$$

$$\begin{aligned} x_1 \qquad + 3x_3 &= 4 \\ x_2 - 2x_3 &= -1 \end{aligned}$$

Thus $x_1 = 4 - 3x_3$, $x_2 = -1 + 2x_3$, with x_3 free. The general solution in parametric vector form is

$$\begin{bmatrix} x_1 \\ x_2 \\ x_3 \end{bmatrix} = \begin{bmatrix} 4 - 3x_3 \\ -1 + 2x_3 \\ x_3 \end{bmatrix} = \underset{\mathbf{p}}{\underset{\uparrow}{\begin{bmatrix} 4 \\ -1 \\ 0 \end{bmatrix}}} + x_3 \underset{\mathbf{v}}{\underset{\uparrow}{\begin{bmatrix} -3 \\ 2 \\ 1 \end{bmatrix}}}$$

The intersection of the two planes is the line through $\mathbf{p}$ in the direction of $\mathbf{v}$.

2. The augmented matrix $[\,2 \quad -3 \quad 1 \quad 7\,]$ is row equivalent to $[\,1 \quad -\frac{3}{2} \quad \frac{1}{2} \quad \frac{7}{2}\,]$, and the general solution is $x_1 = \frac{7}{2} + \frac{3}{2}x_2 - \frac{1}{2}x_3$, with x_2 and x_3 free. That is

$$\mathbf{x} = \begin{bmatrix} x_1 \\ x_2 \\ x_3 \end{bmatrix} = \begin{bmatrix} \frac{7}{2} + \frac{3}{2}x_2 - \frac{1}{2}x_3 \\ x_2 \\ x_3 \end{bmatrix} = \begin{bmatrix} \frac{7}{2} \\ 0 \\ 0 \end{bmatrix} + x_2 \begin{bmatrix} \frac{3}{2} \\ 1 \\ 0 \end{bmatrix} + x_3 \begin{bmatrix} -\frac{1}{2} \\ 0 \\ 1 \end{bmatrix}$$

$$= \mathbf{p} \quad + \quad x_2\mathbf{u} \quad + \quad x_3\mathbf{v}$$

The solution set of the nonhomogeneous equation $A\mathbf{x} = \mathbf{b}$ is the translated plane $\mathbf{p}$ + Span $\{\mathbf{u}, \mathbf{v}\}$, which passes through $\mathbf{p}$ and is parallel to the solution set of the homogeneous equation in Example 4.

2.4 LINEAR INDEPENDENCE

The homogeneous equations of Section 2.3 can be studied from a different perspective by writing them as vector equations. In this way the focus shifts from the unknown solutions of $A\mathbf{x} = \mathbf{0}$ to the vectors that appear in the vector equations.

For instance, consider the equation

$$x_1 \begin{bmatrix} 1 \\ 2 \\ 3 \end{bmatrix} + x_2 \begin{bmatrix} 4 \\ 5 \\ 6 \end{bmatrix} + x_3 \begin{bmatrix} 2 \\ 1 \\ 0 \end{bmatrix} = \begin{bmatrix} 0 \\ 0 \\ 0 \end{bmatrix} \tag{1}$$

This equation has a trivial solution, of course, where $x_1 = x_2 = x_3 = 0$. As in Section 2.3, the main issue is whether the trivial solution is the *only one*.

DEFINITION

A set of vectors $\{\mathbf{v}_1, \ldots, \mathbf{v}_k\}$ in $\mathbb{R}^n$ is said to be **linearly independent** if the vector equation

$$x_1\mathbf{v}_1 + x_2\mathbf{v}_2 + \cdots + x_k\mathbf{v}_k = \mathbf{0}$$

has only the trivial solution. The set $\{\mathbf{v}_1, \ldots, \mathbf{v}_k\}$ is said to be **linearly dependent** if there exist weights $c_1, \ldots, c_k$, not all zero, such that

$$c_1\mathbf{v}_1 + c_2\mathbf{v}_2 + \cdots + c_k\mathbf{v}_k = \mathbf{0} \tag{2}$$

Equation (2) is called a **linear dependence relation** among $\mathbf{v}_1, \ldots, \mathbf{v}_k$ when the weights are not all zero. A set is linearly dependent if and only if it is not linearly independent. For brevity, we may say that $\mathbf{v}_1, \ldots, \mathbf{v}_k$ are linearly dependent when we mean that $\{\mathbf{v}_1, \ldots, \mathbf{v}_k\}$ is a linearly dependent set. We use analogous terminology for linearly independent sets.

EXAMPLE 1 Let $\mathbf{v}_1 = \begin{bmatrix} 1 \\ 2 \\ 3 \end{bmatrix}$, $\mathbf{v}_2 = \begin{bmatrix} 4 \\ 5 \\ 6 \end{bmatrix}$, $\mathbf{v}_3 = \begin{bmatrix} 2 \\ 1 \\ 0 \end{bmatrix}$.

a. Determine if the set $\{\mathbf{v}_1, \mathbf{v}_2, \mathbf{v}_3\}$ is linearly independent.

b. If possible, find a linear dependence relation among $\mathbf{v}_1, \mathbf{v}_2, \mathbf{v}_3$.

Solution

a. We must determine if there is a nontrivial solution of Eq. (1) above. Row operations on the associated augmented matrix show that

$$\begin{bmatrix} 1 & 4 & 2 & 0 \\ 2 & 5 & 1 & 0 \\ 3 & 6 & 0 & 0 \end{bmatrix} \sim \begin{bmatrix} 1 & 4 & 2 & 0 \\ 0 & -3 & -3 & 0 \\ 0 & 0 & 0 & 0 \end{bmatrix}$$

Clearly, x_1 and x_2 are basic variables and x_3 is free. Each nonzero value of x_3 determines a nontrivial solution of (1). Hence $\mathbf{v}_1, \mathbf{v}_2, \mathbf{v}_3$ are linearly dependent (and not linearly independent).

b. To find a linear dependence relation among $\mathbf{v}_1, \mathbf{v}_2, \mathbf{v}_3$, completely row reduce the augmented matrix and write the new system:

$$\begin{bmatrix} 1 & 0 & -2 & 0 \\ 0 & 1 & 1 & 0 \\ 0 & 0 & 0 & 0 \end{bmatrix} \qquad \begin{aligned} x_1 \qquad - 2x_3 &= 0 \\ x_2 + \ x_3 &= 0 \\ 0 &= 0 \end{aligned}$$

Thus $x_1 = 2x_3$, $x_2 = -x_3$, and x_3 is free. Choose any nonzero value for x_3, say, $x_3 = 5$. Then $x_1 = 10$, and $x_2 = -5$. Substitute these values into (1) and obtain

$$10\mathbf{v}_1 - 5\mathbf{v}_2 + 5\mathbf{v}_3 = \mathbf{0}$$

This is one (out of infinitely many) possible linear dependence relations among $\mathbf{v}_1, \mathbf{v}_2, \mathbf{v}_3$. ∎

Linear Independence of Matrix Columns

Suppose that we begin with a matrix $A = [\mathbf{a}_1 \quad \cdots \quad \mathbf{a}_n]$ instead of a set of vectors. The matrix equation $A\mathbf{x} = \mathbf{0}$ may be written as

$$x_1\mathbf{a}_1 + x_2\mathbf{a}_2 + \cdots + x_n\mathbf{a}_n = \mathbf{0}$$

Each linear dependence relation among the columns of A *corresponds to a nontrivial solution of* $A\mathbf{x} = \mathbf{0}$. Thus we have the following important fact.

> The columns of a matrix A are linearly independent if and only if the equation $A\mathbf{x} = \mathbf{0}$ has *only* the trivial solution. (3)

EXAMPLE 2 Determine if the columns of $A = \begin{bmatrix} 0 & 1 & 4 \\ 1 & 2 & -1 \\ 5 & 8 & 0 \end{bmatrix}$ are linearly independent.

Solution To study $A\mathbf{x} = \mathbf{0}$, row reduce the augmented matrix:

$$\begin{bmatrix} 0 & 1 & 4 & 0 \\ 1 & 2 & -1 & 0 \\ 5 & 8 & 0 & 0 \end{bmatrix} \sim \begin{bmatrix} 1 & 2 & -1 & 0 \\ 0 & 1 & 4 & 0 \\ 5 & 8 & 0 & 0 \end{bmatrix} \sim \begin{bmatrix} 1 & 2 & -1 & 0 \\ 0 & 1 & 4 & 0 \\ 0 & -2 & 5 & 0 \end{bmatrix}$$

$$\sim \begin{bmatrix} 1 & 2 & -1 & 0 \\ 0 & 1 & 4 & 0 \\ 0 & 0 & 13 & 0 \end{bmatrix}$$

At this point, it is clear that there are three basic variables and no free variables. So the equation $A\mathbf{x} = \mathbf{0}$ has only the trivial solution, and the columns of A are linearly independent. ∎

Sets of One or Two Vectors

A set containing only one vector—say, $\mathbf{v}$—is linearly independent if and only if $\mathbf{v}$ is not the zero vector. This is because the vector equation $x_1\mathbf{v} = \mathbf{0}$ has only the trivial solution when $\mathbf{v} \neq \mathbf{0}$. The zero vector is linearly dependent because $x_1\mathbf{0} = \mathbf{0}$ has many nontrivial solutions.

The next example will explain the nature of a linearly dependent set of two vectors.

EXAMPLE 3 Determine if the following sets of vectors are linearly independent.

a. $\mathbf{v}_1 = \begin{bmatrix} 3 \\ 1 \end{bmatrix}, \quad \mathbf{v}_2 = \begin{bmatrix} 6 \\ 2 \end{bmatrix}$ b. $\mathbf{v}_1 = \begin{bmatrix} 3 \\ 2 \end{bmatrix}, \quad \mathbf{v}_2 = \begin{bmatrix} 6 \\ 2 \end{bmatrix}$

Solution

a. Notice that $\mathbf{v}_2$ is a multiple of $\mathbf{v}_1$, namely, $\mathbf{v}_2 = 2\mathbf{v}_1$. Hence $-2\mathbf{v}_1 + \mathbf{v}_2 = \mathbf{0}$, which shows that $\{\mathbf{v}_1, \mathbf{v}_2\}$ is linearly dependent.

b. $\mathbf{v}_1$ and $\mathbf{v}_2$ are certainly *not* multiples of one another. Could they be linearly dependent? Suppose c and d satisfy

$$c\mathbf{v}_1 + d\mathbf{v}_2 = \mathbf{0}$$

If $c \neq 0$, then we can solve for $\mathbf{v}_1$ in terms of $\mathbf{v}_2$, namely, $\mathbf{v}_1 = (-d/c)\mathbf{v}_2$. This result is impossible because $\mathbf{v}_1$ is *not* a multiple of $\mathbf{v}_2$. So c must be zero. Similarly, d must also be zero. Thus $\{\mathbf{v}_1, \mathbf{v}_2\}$ is a linearly independent set. ∎

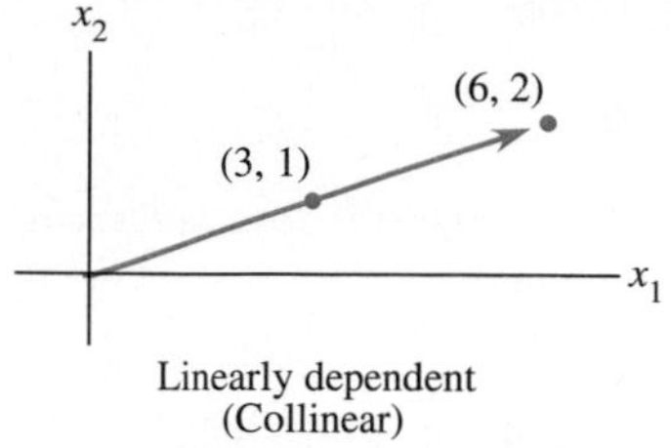

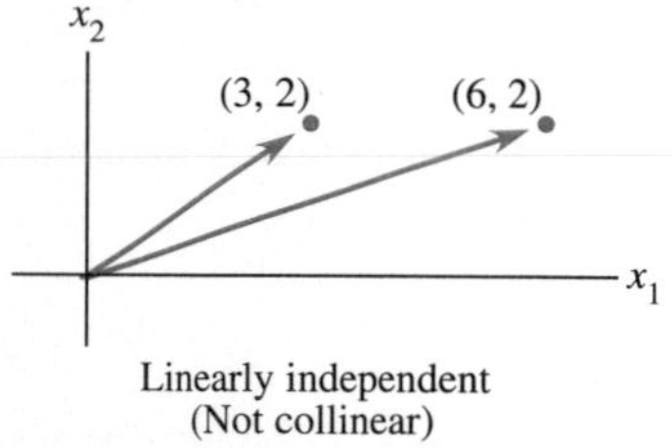

FIGURE 1

The arguments in Example 3 show that we can always decide *by inspection* when a set of two vectors is linearly dependent. Row operations are unnecessary. Simply check whether one vector is a multiple of the other.

A set of two vectors $\{\mathbf{v}_1, \mathbf{v}_2\}$ is linearly dependent if and only if one of the vectors is a multiple of the other.

In geometric terms, two vectors are linearly dependent if and only if they lie on the same line through the origin. Such vectors are sometimes said to be **collinear.** Figure 1 shows the vectors from Example 3.

Sets of Two or More Vectors

The proof of the next theorem is similar to the solution of Example 3. Details are given at the end of this section.

THEOREM 5

Characterization of Linearly Dependent Sets

A set $S = \{\mathbf{v}_1, \dots, \mathbf{v}_p\}$ of two or more vectors is linearly dependent if and only if at least one of the vectors in S is a linear combination of the others. In fact, if S is linearly dependent, and $\mathbf{v}_1 \neq \mathbf{0}$, then some $\mathbf{v}_j$ (with $j > 1$) is a linear combination of the preceding vectors, $\mathbf{v}_1, \dots, \mathbf{v}_{j-1}$.

Warning: Theorem 5 does *not* say that *every* vector in a linearly dependent set is a linear combination of the preceding vectors. A vector in a linearly dependent set may fail to be a linear combination of the other vectors. See Practice Problem 3.

EXAMPLE 4 Let $\mathbf{u} = \begin{bmatrix} 3 \\ 1 \\ 0 \end{bmatrix}$ and $\mathbf{v} = \begin{bmatrix} 1 \\ 6 \\ 0 \end{bmatrix}$. Describe the set spanned by $\mathbf{u}$ and $\mathbf{v}$, and explain why a vector $\mathbf{w}$ is in Span $\{\mathbf{u}, \mathbf{v}\}$ if and only if $\{\mathbf{u}, \mathbf{v}, \mathbf{w}\}$ is linearly dependent.

Solution The vectors **u** and **v** are linearly independent because neither vector is a multiple of the other, and so they span a plane in $\mathbb{R}^3$. (See Section 2.1.) In fact, Span {**u**, **v**} is the x_1x_2-plane (with $x_3 = 0$). If **w** is a linear combination of **u** and **v**, then {**u**, **v**, **w**} is linearly dependent, by Theorem 5. Conversely, suppose that {**u**, **v**, **w**} is linearly dependent. By Theorem 5, some vector in {**u**, **v**, **w**} is a linear combination of the preceding vectors (since $\mathbf{u} \neq \mathbf{0}$). That vector must be **w**, since **v** is not a multiple of **u**. So **w** is in Span {**u**, **v**}. See Fig. 2. ▮

Linearly dependent, **w** in Span {**u**, **v**}

Linearly independent, **w** *not* in Span {**u**, **v**}

FIGURE 2 Linear dependence in $\mathbb{R}^3$.

Example 4 obviously generalizes to any set {**u**, **v**, **w**} in $\mathbb{R}^3$ with **u** and **v** linearly independent. The set {**u**, **v**, **w**} will be linearly dependent if and only if **w** is in the plane spanned by **u** and **v**.

The next two theorems often provide a quick way to see that a set of vectors is linearly dependent. Moreover, Theorem 6 will be a key result for work in later chapters.

THEOREM 6

If a set contains more vectors than there are entries in each vector, then the set is linearly dependent. That is, any set $\{\mathbf{v}_1, \ldots, \mathbf{v}_p\}$ in $\mathbb{R}^n$ is linearly dependent if $p > n$.

Proof Let $A = [\,\mathbf{v}_1 \;\; \cdots \;\; \mathbf{v}_p\,]$. Then A is $n \times p$, and the equation $A\mathbf{x} = \mathbf{0}$ corresponds to a system of n equations in p unknowns. If $p > n$, there are more variables than equations, so there must be a free variable. Hence $A\mathbf{x} = \mathbf{0}$ has a nontrivial solution and the columns of A are linearly dependent. See Fig. 3 for a matrix version of this theorem. ▮

$$\overset{p}{n\begin{bmatrix} * & * & * & * & * \\ * & * & * & * & * \\ * & * & * & * & * \end{bmatrix}}$$

FIGURE 3 If $p > n$, the columns are linearly dependent.

Warning: Theorem 6 says nothing about the case when the number of vectors in the set does *not* exceed the number of entries in each vector.

EXAMPLE 5 The vectors $\begin{bmatrix} 3 \\ 1 \end{bmatrix}, \begin{bmatrix} 6 \\ -1 \end{bmatrix}, \begin{bmatrix} -2 \\ 2 \end{bmatrix}$ are linearly dependent by Theorem 6, because there are three vectors in the set and there are only two entries in each vector. Notice, however, that none of the vectors is a multiple of one of the other vectors. No two of the vectors are collinear. See Fig. 4. ▮

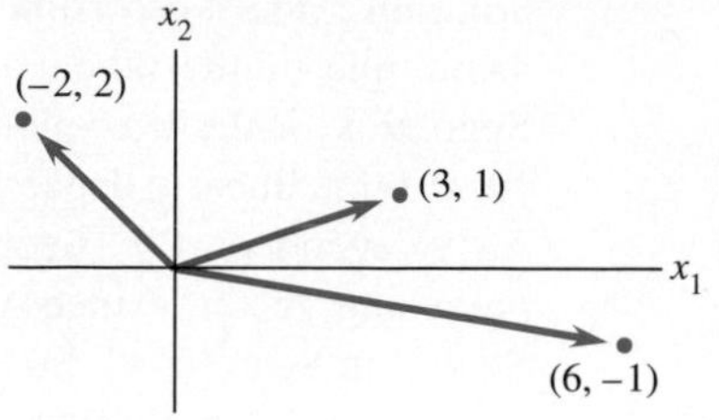

FIGURE 4 A linearly dependent set in $\mathbb{R}^2$.

THEOREM 7

> If a set $S = \{\mathbf{v}_1, \ldots, \mathbf{v}_p\}$ in $\mathbb{R}^n$ contains the zero vector, then the set is linearly dependent.

Proof By renumbering the vectors, we may suppose that $\mathbf{v}_1 = \mathbf{0}$. Then the equation $1 \cdot \mathbf{v}_1 + 0\mathbf{v}_2 + \cdots + 0\mathbf{v}_p = \mathbf{0}$ shows that S is linearly dependent. ∎

EXAMPLE 6 Determine by inspection if the given set is linearly dependent.

a. $\begin{bmatrix} 1 \\ 7 \\ 6 \end{bmatrix}, \begin{bmatrix} 2 \\ 0 \\ 9 \end{bmatrix}, \begin{bmatrix} 3 \\ 1 \\ 5 \end{bmatrix}, \begin{bmatrix} 4 \\ 1 \\ 8 \end{bmatrix}$ b. $\begin{bmatrix} 2 \\ 3 \\ 5 \end{bmatrix}, \begin{bmatrix} 0 \\ 0 \\ 0 \end{bmatrix}, \begin{bmatrix} 1 \\ 1 \\ 8 \end{bmatrix}$ c. $\begin{bmatrix} -2 \\ 4 \\ 6 \\ 10 \end{bmatrix}, \begin{bmatrix} 3 \\ -6 \\ -9 \\ 15 \end{bmatrix}$

Solution

a. The set contains four vectors that each have only three entries. So the set is linearly dependent by Theorem 6.

b. Theorem 6 does not apply here because the number of vectors does not exceed the number of entries in each vector. Since the zero vector is in the set, the set is linearly dependent by Theorem 7.

c. As we compare corresponding entries of the two vectors, the second vector seems to be $-3/2$ times the first vector. This relation holds for the first three pairs of entries, but fails for the fourth pair. Thus neither of the vectors is a multiple of the other, and hence they are linearly independent. ∎

The concept of linear independence is not usually assimilated in one reading. Understanding should come as you work through problems and proofs. The following proof is worth reading carefully because it shows how the definition of linear independence can be used in a proof.

Proof of Theorem 5 If some $\mathbf{v}_j$ in S equals a linear combination of the other vectors, then $\mathbf{v}_j$ can be subtracted from both sides of the equation, producing a linear dependence relation with a nonzero weight (-1) on $\mathbf{v}_j$. [For instance, if $\mathbf{v}_1 = c_2\mathbf{v}_2 + c_3\mathbf{v}_3$, then $\mathbf{0} = (-1)\mathbf{v}_1 + c_2\mathbf{v}_2 + c_3\mathbf{v}_3 + 0\mathbf{v}_4 + \cdots + 0\mathbf{v}_p$.] Thus S is linearly dependent.

Conversely, if S is linearly dependent, then there exist weights $c_1, \ldots, c_p$, not all zero, such that

$$c_1\mathbf{v}_1 + c_2\mathbf{v}_2 + \cdots + c_p\mathbf{v}_p = \mathbf{0}$$

Let j be the largest subscript for which $c_j \neq 0$. If $j = 1$, then $c_1\mathbf{v}_1 = \mathbf{0}$, which is impossible because $\mathbf{v}_1 \neq \mathbf{0}$. So $j > 1$, and

$$c_1\mathbf{v}_1 + \cdots + c_j\mathbf{v}_j + 0\mathbf{v}_{j+1} + \cdots + 0\mathbf{v}_p = \mathbf{0}$$

$$c_j\mathbf{v}_j = -c_1\mathbf{v}_1 - \cdots - c_{j-1}\mathbf{v}_{j-1}$$

$$\mathbf{v}_j = (-\frac{c_1}{c_j})\mathbf{v}_1 + \cdots + \left(-\frac{c_{j-1}}{c_j}\right)\mathbf{v}_{j-1}$$

∎

PRACTICE PROBLEMS

Let $\mathbf{u} = \begin{bmatrix} 3 \\ 2 \\ -4 \end{bmatrix}$, $\mathbf{v} = \begin{bmatrix} -6 \\ 1 \\ 7 \end{bmatrix}$, $\mathbf{w} = \begin{bmatrix} 0 \\ -5 \\ 2 \end{bmatrix}$, and $\mathbf{z} = \begin{bmatrix} 3 \\ 7 \\ -5 \end{bmatrix}$.

1. Are the sets $\{\mathbf{u}, \mathbf{v}\}$, $\{\mathbf{u}, \mathbf{w}\}$, $\{\mathbf{u}, \mathbf{z}\}$, $\{\mathbf{v}, \mathbf{w}\}$, $\{\mathbf{v}, \mathbf{z}\}$, and $\{\mathbf{w}, \mathbf{z}\}$ each linearly independent? Why?
2. Does the answer to Problem (1) imply that $\{\mathbf{u}, \mathbf{v}, \mathbf{w}, \mathbf{z}\}$ is linearly independent?
3. To determine if $\{\mathbf{u}, \mathbf{v}, \mathbf{w}, \mathbf{z}\}$ is linearly dependent, is it wise to check if, say, $\mathbf{w}$ is a linear combination of $\mathbf{u}$, $\mathbf{v}$, and $\mathbf{z}$?
4. Is $\{\mathbf{u}, \mathbf{v}, \mathbf{w}, \mathbf{z}\}$ linearly dependent?

2.4 EXERCISES

Decide if the sets in Exercises 1–6 are linearly independent.

1. $\begin{bmatrix} 3 \\ 0 \\ 0 \end{bmatrix}, \begin{bmatrix} -3 \\ 2 \\ 3 \end{bmatrix}, \begin{bmatrix} 6 \\ 4 \\ 0 \end{bmatrix}$

2. $\begin{bmatrix} -2 \\ 0 \\ 0 \end{bmatrix}, \begin{bmatrix} 8 \\ 0 \\ -5 \end{bmatrix}, \begin{bmatrix} -1 \\ 0 \\ 3 \end{bmatrix}$

3. $\begin{bmatrix} 1 \\ -5 \end{bmatrix}, \begin{bmatrix} -2 \\ 10 \end{bmatrix}$

4. $\begin{bmatrix} -4 \\ 1 \end{bmatrix}, \begin{bmatrix} 12 \\ -3 \end{bmatrix}$

5. $\begin{bmatrix} 0 \\ -6 \\ 1 \end{bmatrix}, \begin{bmatrix} 0 \\ 4 \\ -2 \end{bmatrix}, \begin{bmatrix} -8 \\ -4 \\ 3 \end{bmatrix}$

6. $\begin{bmatrix} 1 \\ 3 \\ -2 \end{bmatrix}, \begin{bmatrix} -3 \\ -5 \\ 6 \end{bmatrix}, \begin{bmatrix} 0 \\ 5 \\ -6 \end{bmatrix}$

For Exercises 7–12, determine if the columns of the given matrix form a linearly dependent set.

7. $\begin{bmatrix} 1 & 3 & -2 & 0 \\ 3 & 10 & -7 & 1 \\ -5 & -5 & 3 & 7 \end{bmatrix}$

8. $\begin{bmatrix} 0 & 2 & 6 & 8 \\ 1 & -3 & -4 & 1 \\ -1 & 4 & 7 & 3 \end{bmatrix}$

9. $\begin{bmatrix} 3 & 4 & 3 \\ -1 & -7 & 7 \\ 1 & 3 & -2 \\ 0 & 2 & -6 \end{bmatrix}$

10. $\begin{bmatrix} 3 & 4 & 9 \\ -2 & -7 & 7 \\ 1 & 2 & -2 \\ 0 & 2 & -6 \end{bmatrix}$

11. $\begin{bmatrix} 1 & 1 & 0 & 4 \\ -1 & 0 & 3 & -1 \\ 0 & -2 & 1 & 1 \\ 1 & 0 & -1 & 3 \end{bmatrix}$

12. $\begin{bmatrix} 1 & -1 & -3 & 0 \\ 0 & 1 & 5 & 4 \\ -1 & 2 & 8 & 5 \\ 3 & -1 & 1 & 3 \end{bmatrix}$

In Exercises 13 and 14, (a) for what values of h is $\mathbf{v}_3$ in Span $\{\mathbf{v}_1, \mathbf{v}_2\}$ and (b) for what values of h is $\{\mathbf{v}_1, \mathbf{v}_2, \mathbf{v}_3\}$ linearly dependent?

13. $\mathbf{v}_1 = \begin{bmatrix} 1 \\ 3 \\ -2 \end{bmatrix}$, $\mathbf{v}_2 = \begin{bmatrix} -2 \\ -6 \\ 4 \end{bmatrix}$, $\mathbf{v}_3 = \begin{bmatrix} 1 \\ 2 \\ h \end{bmatrix}$

14. $\mathbf{v}_1 = \begin{bmatrix} 1 \\ 3 \\ 3 \end{bmatrix}, \mathbf{v}_2 = \begin{bmatrix} 3 \\ 9 \\ -1 \end{bmatrix}, \mathbf{v}_3 = \begin{bmatrix} -2 \\ -6 \\ h \end{bmatrix}$

In Exercises 15–18, find the value(s) of h for which the set of vectors is linearly dependent.

15. $\begin{bmatrix} 1 \\ 3 \\ -3 \end{bmatrix}, \begin{bmatrix} -2 \\ -4 \\ 1 \end{bmatrix}, \begin{bmatrix} -1 \\ 1 \\ h \end{bmatrix}$

16. $\begin{bmatrix} 0 \\ 1 \\ -2 \end{bmatrix}, \begin{bmatrix} 2 \\ -5 \\ 7 \end{bmatrix}, \begin{bmatrix} 2 \\ 0 \\ h \end{bmatrix}$

17. $\begin{bmatrix} 1 \\ -5 \\ -2 \end{bmatrix}, \begin{bmatrix} -3 \\ 8 \\ 6 \end{bmatrix}, \begin{bmatrix} 4 \\ h \\ -8 \end{bmatrix}$

18. $\begin{bmatrix} 1 \\ -5 \end{bmatrix}, \begin{bmatrix} 4 \\ 7 \end{bmatrix}, \begin{bmatrix} -2 \\ h \end{bmatrix}$

Determine by inspection which sets in Exercises 19–24 are linearly independent. Give reasons for your answers.

19. $\begin{bmatrix} 5 \\ 5 \end{bmatrix}, \begin{bmatrix} 6 \\ 1 \end{bmatrix}, \begin{bmatrix} 2 \\ 4 \end{bmatrix}, \begin{bmatrix} 3 \\ 6 \end{bmatrix}$

20. $\begin{bmatrix} 16 \\ -8 \\ 12 \end{bmatrix}, \begin{bmatrix} -4 \\ 2 \\ -4 \end{bmatrix}$

21. $\begin{bmatrix} 2 \\ -5 \\ 1 \end{bmatrix}, \begin{bmatrix} -6 \\ 5 \\ 3 \end{bmatrix}, \begin{bmatrix} 0 \\ 0 \\ 0 \end{bmatrix}$

22. $\begin{bmatrix} 1 \\ -6 \\ 3 \end{bmatrix}, \begin{bmatrix} 0 \\ 0 \\ 0 \end{bmatrix}, \begin{bmatrix} -5 \\ 4 \\ -8 \end{bmatrix}$

23. $\begin{bmatrix} 6 \\ 2 \\ -8 \end{bmatrix}, \begin{bmatrix} 3 \\ 1 \\ -2 \end{bmatrix}$

24. $\begin{bmatrix} 3 \\ 1 \end{bmatrix}, \begin{bmatrix} 9 \\ 1 \end{bmatrix}, \begin{bmatrix} 6 \\ 7 \end{bmatrix}, \begin{bmatrix} 3 \\ 4 \end{bmatrix}$

25. Construct 3×2 matrices A and B such that $A\mathbf{x} = \mathbf{0}$ has only the trivial solution and $B\mathbf{x} = \mathbf{0}$ has a nontrivial solution.

26. Repeat Exercise 25 with 2×2 matrices.

Exercises 27 and 28 should be solved *without performing row operations*. [*Hint*: Write $A\mathbf{x} = \mathbf{0}$ as a vector equation.]

27. Given $A = \begin{bmatrix} 2 & 3 & 5 \\ -5 & 1 & -4 \\ -3 & -1 & -4 \\ 1 & 0 & 1 \end{bmatrix}$, observe that the third column is the sum of the first two columns. Find a nontrivial solution of $A\mathbf{x} = \mathbf{0}$.

28. Given $A = \begin{bmatrix} 4 & 1 & 6 \\ -7 & 5 & 3 \\ 9 & -3 & 3 \end{bmatrix}$, observe that the first column plus twice the second column equals the third column. Find a nontrivial solution of $A\mathbf{x} = \mathbf{0}$.

Each statement in Exercises 29–34 is either true (in all cases) or false (for at least one example). If false, construct a specific example to show that the statement is not always true. Such an example is called a *counterexample* to the statement. If true, give a justification. (One specific example cannot explain why a statement is always true.)

29. If $\mathbf{v}_1, \ldots, \mathbf{v}_4$ are in $\mathbb{R}^4$ and $\mathbf{v}_3 = 2\mathbf{v}_1 + \mathbf{v}_2$, then $\{\mathbf{v}_1, \mathbf{v}_2, \mathbf{v}_3, \mathbf{v}_4\}$ is linearly dependent.

30. If $\mathbf{v}_1, \ldots, \mathbf{v}_4$ are in $\mathbb{R}^4$ and $\mathbf{v}_3 = \mathbf{0}$, then $\{\mathbf{v}_1, \mathbf{v}_2, \mathbf{v}_3, \mathbf{v}_4\}$ is linearly dependent.

31. If the vectors $\mathbf{v}_1, \mathbf{v}_2, \mathbf{v}_3$ lie on a line in $\mathbb{R}^2$, then they are linearly dependent.

32. If $\mathbf{v}_1, \ldots, \mathbf{v}_4$ are in $\mathbb{R}^4$ and $\mathbf{v}_3$ is *not* a linear combination of $\mathbf{v}_1, \mathbf{v}_2, \mathbf{v}_4$, then $\{\mathbf{v}_1, \mathbf{v}_2, \mathbf{v}_3, \mathbf{v}_4\}$ is linearly independent.

33. If $\mathbf{v}_1, \ldots, \mathbf{v}_4$ are in $\mathbb{R}^4$ and $\{\mathbf{v}_1, \mathbf{v}_2, \mathbf{v}_3\}$ is linearly dependent, then $\{\mathbf{v}_1, \mathbf{v}_2, \mathbf{v}_3, \mathbf{v}_4\}$ is also linearly dependent.

34. If $\mathbf{v}_1, \ldots, \mathbf{v}_4$ are linearly independent vectors in $\mathbb{R}^4$, then $\{\mathbf{v}_1, \mathbf{v}_2, \mathbf{v}_3\}$ is also linearly independent. [*Hint*: Think about $x_1\mathbf{v}_1 + x_2\mathbf{v}_2 + x_3\mathbf{v}_3 + 0\cdot\mathbf{v}_4 = \mathbf{0}$.]

35. Let A be a 7×5 matrix. How many pivot columns must A have so that its columns will be linearly independent?

36. a. Fill in the blank in the following statement: "If A is an $m\times n$ matrix, then the columns of A are linearly independent if and only if A has ______ pivot columns."

    b. Explain why the statement in (a) is true.

37. Suppose that A is an $m\times n$ matrix with the property that for all $\mathbf{b}$ in $\mathbb{R}^m$ the equation $A\mathbf{x} = \mathbf{b}$ has at most one solution. Use the definition of linear independence to explain why the columns of A must be linearly independent.

38. Suppose that an $m\times n$ matrix A has n pivot columns. Explain why for each $\mathbf{b}$ in $\mathbb{R}^m$ the equation $A\mathbf{x} = \mathbf{b}$ has at most one solution. [*Hint*: Explain why $A\mathbf{x} = \mathbf{b}$ cannot have infinitely many solutions.]

SOLUTIONS TO PRACTICE PROBLEMS

1. Yes. In each case, the two vectors are not collinear. Thus each set is linearly independent.

2. No. The observation in Problem 1, by itself, says nothing about the linear independence of {**u**, **v**, **w**, **z**}.

3. No. When testing for linear independence, it is usually a poor idea to check if one selected vector is a linear combination of the others. It may happen that the selected vector is not a linear combination of the others and yet the whole set of vectors is linearly dependent. In this practice problem, **w** is not a linear combination of **u**, **v**, and **z**.

4. Yes, by Theorem 6. There are more vectors (four) than entries (three) in them.

2.5 INTRODUCTION TO LINEAR TRANSFORMATIONS

The difference between a matrix equation $A\mathbf{x} = \mathbf{b}$ and the associated vector equation $x_1\mathbf{a}_1 + \cdots + x_n\mathbf{a}_n = \mathbf{b}$ is merely a matter of notation. However, a matrix equation $A\mathbf{x} = \mathbf{b}$ can arise in linear algebra (and in applications) in a way that is not directly connected with linear combinations of vectors. This happens when we think of the matrix A as an object that "acts" on a vector $\mathbf{x}$ by multiplication to produce a new vector called $A\mathbf{x}$.

For instance, the equations

$$\underset{\uparrow \atop A}{\begin{bmatrix} 4 & -3 & 1 & 3 \\ 2 & 0 & 5 & 1 \end{bmatrix}} \underset{\uparrow \atop \mathbf{x}}{\begin{bmatrix} 1 \\ 1 \\ 1 \\ 1 \end{bmatrix}} = \underset{\uparrow \atop \mathbf{b}}{\begin{bmatrix} 5 \\ 8 \end{bmatrix}} \quad \text{and} \quad \underset{\uparrow \atop A}{\begin{bmatrix} 4 & -3 & 1 & 3 \\ 2 & 0 & 5 & 1 \end{bmatrix}} \underset{\uparrow \atop \mathbf{u}}{\begin{bmatrix} 1 \\ 4 \\ -1 \\ 3 \end{bmatrix}} = \underset{\uparrow \atop \mathbf{0}}{\begin{bmatrix} 0 \\ 0 \end{bmatrix}}$$

say that multiplication by A transforms $\mathbf{x}$ into $\mathbf{b}$, and transforms $\mathbf{u}$ into the zero vector. See Fig. 1.

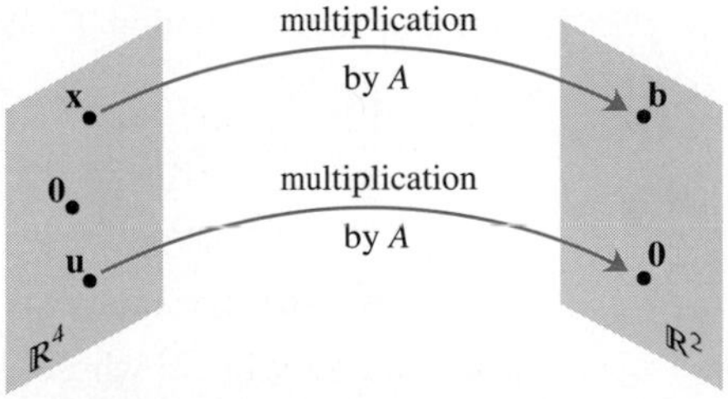

FIGURE 1 Transforming vectors via matrix multiplication.

From this new point of view, solving the equation $A\mathbf{x} = \mathbf{b}$ amounts to finding all vectors $\mathbf{x}$ in $\mathbb{R}^4$ that are transformed into the vector $\mathbf{b}$ in $\mathbb{R}^2$ under the "action" of multiplication by A.

The correspondence from $\mathbf{x}$ to $A\mathbf{x}$ is a *function* from one set of vectors to another. This concept generalizes the common notion of a function as a rule that transforms one real number into another.

A **transformation** (or **function** or **mapping**) T from $\mathbb{R}^n$ to $\mathbb{R}^m$ is a rule that assigns to each vector $\mathbf{x}$ in $\mathbb{R}^n$ a unique vector $T(\mathbf{x})$ in $\mathbb{R}^m$. The vector $T(\mathbf{x})$ is called the **image** of $\mathbf{x}$ (under the action of T). The set $\mathbb{R}^n$ is called the **domain** of T, and the set of all images $T(\mathbf{x})$ in $\mathbb{R}^m$ is called the **range** of T. We write $T : \mathbb{R}^n \to \mathbb{R}^m$ to indicate that the domain of T is $\mathbb{R}^n$ and that the range of T is contained in $\mathbb{R}^m$. See Fig. 2. (Sometimes the range is *all* of $\mathbb{R}^m$.)

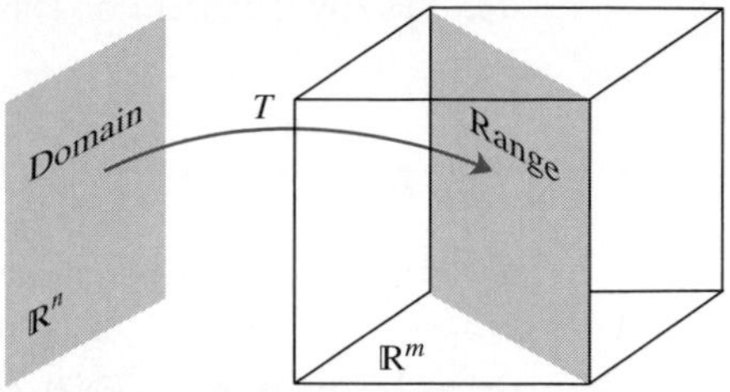

FIGURE 2 Domain and range of T: $\mathbb{R}^n \to \mathbb{R}^m$.

Matrix Transformations

The rest of this section focuses on mappings associated with matrix multiplication. For each $\mathbf{x}$ in $\mathbb{R}^n$, $T(\mathbf{x})$ is computed as $A\mathbf{x}$, where A is an $m \times n$ matrix. For simplicity, we sometimes denote such a *matrix transformation* by $\mathbf{x} \mapsto A\mathbf{x}$. Observe that the domain of T is $\mathbb{R}^n$ when A has n columns and that the range of T lies in $\mathbb{R}^m$ when each column of A has m entries.

EXAMPLE 1 Let $A = \begin{bmatrix} 1 & -3 \\ 3 & 5 \\ -1 & 7 \end{bmatrix}$, $\mathbf{u} = \begin{bmatrix} 2 \\ -1 \end{bmatrix}$, $\mathbf{b} = \begin{bmatrix} 3 \\ 2 \\ -5 \end{bmatrix}$, $\mathbf{c} = \begin{bmatrix} 3 \\ 2 \\ 5 \end{bmatrix}$, and define a transformation $T : \mathbb{R}^2 \to \mathbb{R}^3$ by $T(\mathbf{x}) = A\mathbf{x}$, so that

$$T(\mathbf{x}) = A\mathbf{x} = \begin{bmatrix} 1 & -3 \\ 3 & 5 \\ -1 & 7 \end{bmatrix} \begin{bmatrix} x_1 \\ x_2 \end{bmatrix} = \begin{bmatrix} x_1 - 3x_2 \\ 3x_1 + 5x_2 \\ -x_1 + 7x_2 \end{bmatrix}$$

a. Find $T(\mathbf{u})$, the image of $\mathbf{u}$ under the transformation T.

b. Find an $\mathbf{x}$ in $\mathbb{R}^2$ whose image under T is $\mathbf{b}$.

c. Is there more than one $\mathbf{x}$ whose image under T is $\mathbf{b}$?

d. Determine if $\mathbf{c}$ is in the range of the transformation T.

Solution

a. Compute

$$T(\mathbf{u}) = A\mathbf{u} = \begin{bmatrix} 1 & -3 \\ 3 & 5 \\ -1 & 7 \end{bmatrix} \begin{bmatrix} 2 \\ -1 \end{bmatrix} = \begin{bmatrix} 5 \\ 1 \\ -9 \end{bmatrix}$$

b. Solve $T(\mathbf{x}) = \mathbf{b}$ for $\mathbf{x}$. That is, solve $A\mathbf{x} = \mathbf{b}$, or

$$\begin{bmatrix} 1 & -3 \\ 3 & 5 \\ -1 & 7 \end{bmatrix} \begin{bmatrix} x_1 \\ x_2 \end{bmatrix} = \begin{bmatrix} 3 \\ 2 \\ -5 \end{bmatrix} \tag{1}$$

Using the method of Section 2.2, row reduce the augmented matrix:

$$\begin{bmatrix} 1 & -3 & 3 \\ 3 & 5 & 2 \\ -1 & 7 & -5 \end{bmatrix} \sim \begin{bmatrix} 1 & -3 & 3 \\ 0 & 14 & -7 \\ 0 & 4 & -2 \end{bmatrix} \sim \begin{bmatrix} 1 & -3 & 3 \\ 0 & 1 & -.5 \\ 0 & 0 & 0 \end{bmatrix} \sim \begin{bmatrix} 1 & 0 & 1.5 \\ 0 & 1 & -.5 \\ 0 & 0 & 0 \end{bmatrix} \tag{2}$$

Hence $x_1 = 1.5$, $x_2 = -.5$, and $\mathbf{x} = \begin{bmatrix} 1.5 \\ -.5 \end{bmatrix}$. The image of this $\mathbf{x}$ under T is the given vector $\mathbf{b}$.

c. Any $\mathbf{x}$ whose image under T is $\mathbf{b}$ must satisfy (1). From (2) it is clear that Eq. (1) has a unique solution. So there is exactly one $\mathbf{x}$ whose image is $\mathbf{b}$.

d. The vector $\mathbf{c}$ is in the range of T if $\mathbf{c}$ is the image of some $\mathbf{x}$ in $\mathbb{R}^2$, that is, if $\mathbf{c} = T(\mathbf{x})$ for some $\mathbf{x}$. This is just another way of asking if the system $A\mathbf{x} = \mathbf{c}$ is consistent. To find the answer, row reduce the augmented matrix:

$$\begin{bmatrix} 1 & -3 & 3 \\ 3 & 5 & 2 \\ -1 & 7 & 5 \end{bmatrix} \sim \begin{bmatrix} 1 & -3 & 3 \\ 0 & 14 & -7 \\ 0 & 4 & 8 \end{bmatrix} \sim \begin{bmatrix} 1 & -3 & 3 \\ 0 & 1 & 2 \\ 0 & 14 & -7 \end{bmatrix} \sim \begin{bmatrix} 1 & -3 & 3 \\ 0 & 1 & 2 \\ 0 & 0 & -35 \end{bmatrix}$$

The third equation, $0 = -35$, shows that the system is inconsistent. So $\mathbf{c}$ is *not* in the range of T. ▮

The question in Example 1(c) is a *uniqueness* problem for a system of linear equations, translated now into the language of matrix transformations: Is $\mathbf{b}$ the image of a *unique* $\mathbf{x}$ in $\mathbb{R}^n$? Similarly, Example 1(d) is an *existence* problem: Does there *exist* an $\mathbf{x}$ whose image is $\mathbf{c}$?

The next two matrix transformations can be viewed geometrically. They reinforce the dynamic view of a matrix as something that transforms vectors into other vectors. Section 3.8 contains other interesting examples connected with computer graphics.

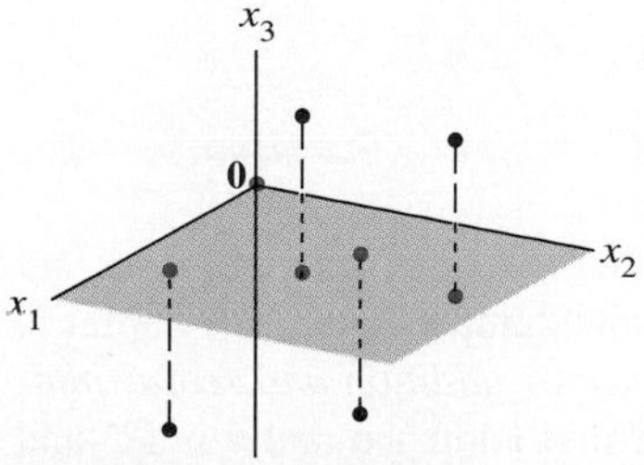

FIGURE 3 A projection transformation.

EXAMPLE 2 If $A = \begin{bmatrix} 1 & 0 & 0 \\ 0 & 1 & 0 \\ 0 & 0 & 0 \end{bmatrix}$, then the transformation $\mathbf{x} \mapsto A\mathbf{x}$ *projects* points in $\mathbb{R}^3$ onto the x_1x_2-coordinate plane because

$$\begin{bmatrix} x_1 \\ x_2 \\ x_3 \end{bmatrix} \mapsto \begin{bmatrix} 1 & 0 & 0 \\ 0 & 1 & 0 \\ 0 & 0 & 0 \end{bmatrix} \begin{bmatrix} x_1 \\ x_2 \\ x_3 \end{bmatrix} = \begin{bmatrix} x_1 \\ x_2 \\ 0 \end{bmatrix}$$

See Fig. 3. ▮

EXAMPLE 3 Let $A = \begin{bmatrix} 1 & 3 \\ 0 & 1 \end{bmatrix}$. The transformation $T : \mathbb{R}^2 \rightarrow \mathbb{R}^2$ defined by $T(\mathbf{x}) = A\mathbf{x}$ is called a **shear transformation**. It can be shown that if T acts on each point in the 2×2 square shown in Fig. 4, then the set of images forms the shaded parallelogram. The key idea is to show that T maps line segments onto line segments (as shown in Exercise 24) and then to check that the corners of the square map onto the vertices of the parallelogram. For instance, the image of the point $\mathbf{u} = \begin{bmatrix} 0 \\ 2 \end{bmatrix}$ is $T(\mathbf{u}) = \begin{bmatrix} 1 & 3 \\ 0 & 1 \end{bmatrix}\begin{bmatrix} 0 \\ 2 \end{bmatrix} = \begin{bmatrix} 6 \\ 2 \end{bmatrix}$, and the image of $\begin{bmatrix} 2 \\ 2 \end{bmatrix}$ is $\begin{bmatrix} 1 & 3 \\ 0 & 1 \end{bmatrix}\begin{bmatrix} 2 \\ 2 \end{bmatrix} = \begin{bmatrix} 8 \\ 2 \end{bmatrix}$. T deforms the square as if the top of the square were pushed to the right while the base is held fixed. Shear transformations arise in physics, geology, and crystallography.

sheep

sheared sheep

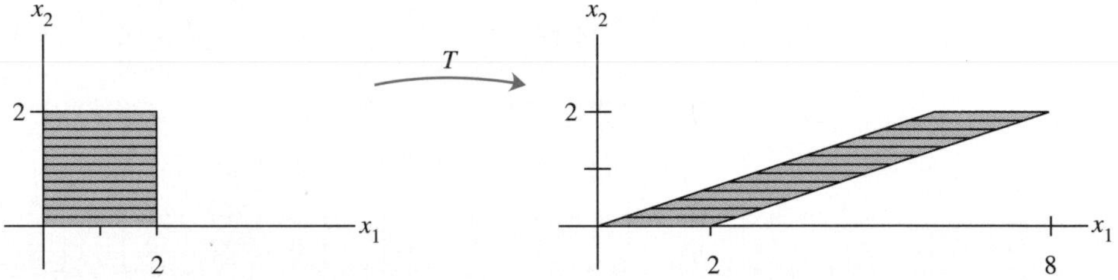

FIGURE 4 A shear transformation.

Linear Transformations

Theorem 3 in Section 2.2 shows that if A is $m \times n$, then the transformation $\mathbf{x} \mapsto A\mathbf{x}$ has the properties

$$A(\mathbf{u} + \mathbf{v}) = A\mathbf{u} + A\mathbf{v} \quad \text{and} \quad A(c\mathbf{u}) = cA\mathbf{u}$$

for all $\mathbf{u}, \mathbf{v}$ in $\mathbb{R}^n$ and all scalars c. These properties, written in function notation, identify the most important class of transformations in linear algebra.

DEFINITION

A transformation (or mapping) T is **linear** if

i. $T(\mathbf{u} + \mathbf{v}) = T(\mathbf{u}) + T(\mathbf{v})$ for all $\mathbf{u}, \mathbf{v}$ in the domain of T,

ii. $T(c\mathbf{u}) = cT(\mathbf{u})$ for all $\mathbf{u}$ and all scalars c.

For the time being, the only examples of linear mappings of interest to us are matrix transformations, but we will study other important examples later, in Chapter 5.

Linear transformations *preserve the operations of vector addition and scalar multiplication.* Property (i) says that the result $T(\mathbf{u}+\mathbf{v})$ of first adding $\mathbf{u}$ and $\mathbf{v}$ in $\mathbb{R}^n$ and then applying T is the same as applying T first to $\mathbf{u}$ and $\mathbf{v}$ and then adding $T(\mathbf{u})$ and $T(\mathbf{v})$ in $\mathbb{R}^m$. These two properties lead easily to the following useful facts.

If T is a linear transformation, then

$$T(\mathbf{0}) = \mathbf{0} \tag{3}$$

and

$$T(c\mathbf{u} + d\mathbf{v}) = cT(\mathbf{u}) + dT(\mathbf{v}) \tag{4}$$

for all vectors $\mathbf{u}, \mathbf{v}$ in the domain of T and all scalars c, d.

Property (3) follows from (ii), because $T(\mathbf{0}) = T(0\mathbf{u}) = 0T(\mathbf{u}) = \mathbf{0}$. Property (4) requires both (i) and (ii):

$$T(c\mathbf{u} + d\mathbf{v}) = T(c\mathbf{u}) + T(d\mathbf{v}) = cT(\mathbf{u}) + dT(\mathbf{v})$$

Observe that *if a transformation satisfies* (4) *for all* $\mathbf{u}, \mathbf{v}$ *and* c, d, *it must be linear.* (Take $c = d = 1$ for preservation of addition, and take $d = 0$ for preservation of scalar multiplication.) Repeated application of (4) produces a useful generalization:

$$T(c_1\mathbf{v}_1 + \cdots + c_p\mathbf{v}_p) = c_1T(\mathbf{v}_1) + \cdots + c_pT(\mathbf{v}_p) \tag{5}$$

In engineering and physics, (5) is referred to as a *superposition principle.* Think of $\mathbf{v}_1, \ldots, \mathbf{v}_p$ as signals that go into a system or process and $T(\mathbf{v}_1), \ldots, T(\mathbf{v}_p)$ as the responses of that system to the signals. The system satisfies the superposition principle if whenever an input is expressed as a linear combination of such signals, the system's response is *the same* linear combination of the responses to the individual signals. We will return to this idea in Chapter 5.

EXAMPLE 4 Given a scalar r, define $T : \mathbb{R}^2 \to \mathbb{R}^2$ by $T(\mathbf{x}) = r\mathbf{x}$. T is called a **contraction** when $0 \le r \le 1$ and a **dilation** when $r > 1$. Let $r = 3$ and show that T is a linear transformation.

Solution Let $\mathbf{u}, \mathbf{v}$ be in $\mathbb{R}^2$ and let c, d be scalars. Then

$$\begin{aligned} T(c\mathbf{u} + d\mathbf{v}) &= 3(c\mathbf{u} + d\mathbf{v}) && \text{Definition of } T \\ &= 3c\mathbf{u} + 3d\mathbf{v} && \text{Vector arithmetic} \\ &= c(3\mathbf{u}) + d(3\mathbf{v}) && \\ &= cT(\mathbf{u}) + dT(\mathbf{v}) \end{aligned}$$

Thus T is a linear transformation because it satisfies (4). See Fig. 5.

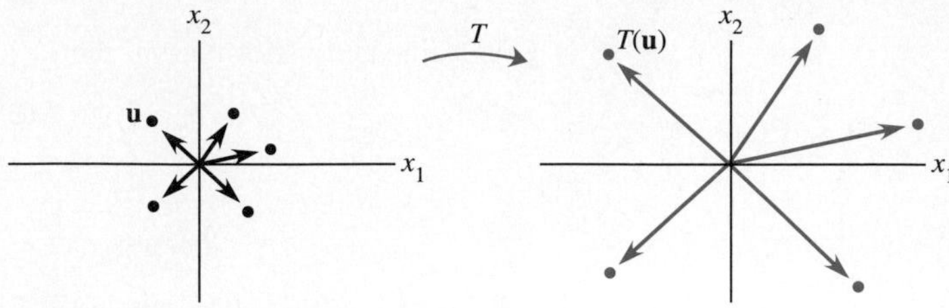

FIGURE 5 A dilation transformation.

EXAMPLE 5 Define a linear transformation $T : \mathbb{R}^2 \to \mathbb{R}^2$ by

$$T(\mathbf{x}) = \begin{bmatrix} 0 & -1 \\ 1 & 0 \end{bmatrix} \begin{bmatrix} x_1 \\ x_2 \end{bmatrix} = \begin{bmatrix} -x_2 \\ x_1 \end{bmatrix}$$

Find the images under T of $\mathbf{u} = \begin{bmatrix} 4 \\ 1 \end{bmatrix}$, $\mathbf{v} = \begin{bmatrix} 2 \\ 3 \end{bmatrix}$, and $\mathbf{u} + \mathbf{v} = \begin{bmatrix} 6 \\ 4 \end{bmatrix}$.

Solution

$$T(\mathbf{u}) = \begin{bmatrix} 0 & -1 \\ 1 & 0 \end{bmatrix} \begin{bmatrix} 4 \\ 1 \end{bmatrix} = \begin{bmatrix} -1 \\ 4 \end{bmatrix}, \qquad T(\mathbf{v}) = \begin{bmatrix} 0 & -1 \\ 1 & 0 \end{bmatrix} \begin{bmatrix} 2 \\ 3 \end{bmatrix} = \begin{bmatrix} -3 \\ 2 \end{bmatrix}$$

$$T(\mathbf{u} + \mathbf{v}) = \begin{bmatrix} 0 & -1 \\ 1 & 0 \end{bmatrix} \begin{bmatrix} 6 \\ 4 \end{bmatrix} = \begin{bmatrix} -4 \\ 6 \end{bmatrix}$$

Notice that $T(\mathbf{u}+\mathbf{v})$ is obviously equal to $T(\mathbf{u}) + T(\mathbf{v})$. It appears from Fig. 6 that T rotates $\mathbf{u}$, $\mathbf{v}$, and $\mathbf{u} + \mathbf{v}$ counterclockwise through 90°. In fact, T transforms the entire parallelogram determined by $\mathbf{u}$ and $\mathbf{v}$ into the one determined by $T(\mathbf{u})$ and $T(\mathbf{v})$. (See Exercise 26.)

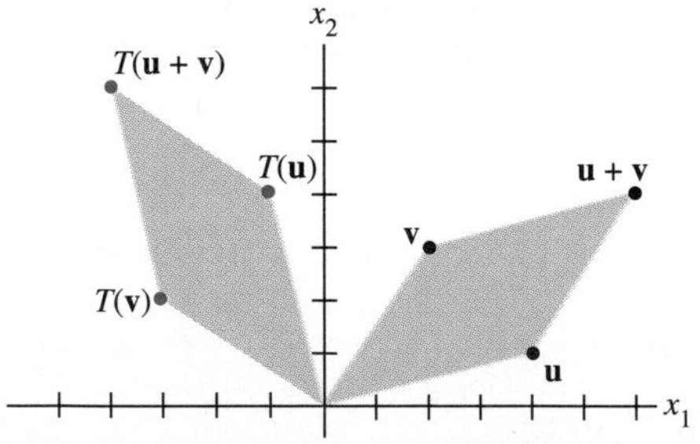

FIGURE 6 A rotation transformation.

The final example is not geometrical; instead it shows how a linear mapping can transform one type of data into another.

EXAMPLE 6 A company manufactures two products, B and C. Using data from Example 6 in Section 2.1, we construct a "unit cost" matrix, $U = [\mathbf{b} \quad \mathbf{c}]$, whose columns describe the "costs per dollar of output" for the products:

$$\begin{array}{c} \text{Product} \\ \begin{array}{cc} \text{B} & \text{C} \end{array} \end{array}$$
$$U = \begin{bmatrix} .45 & .40 \\ .25 & .35 \\ .15 & .15 \end{bmatrix} \begin{array}{l} \text{Materials} \\ \text{Labor} \\ \text{Overhead} \end{array}$$

Let $\mathbf{x} = (x_1, x_2)$ be a "production" vector, corresponding to x_1 dollars of product B and x_2 dollars of product C, and define $T : \mathbb{R}^2 \to \mathbb{R}^3$ by

$$T(\mathbf{x}) = U\mathbf{x} = x_1 \begin{bmatrix} .45 \\ .25 \\ .15 \end{bmatrix} + x_2 \begin{bmatrix} .40 \\ .35 \\ .15 \end{bmatrix} = \begin{bmatrix} \text{Total cost of materials} \\ \text{Total cost of labor} \\ \text{Total cost of overhead} \end{bmatrix}$$

The mapping T transforms a list of production quantities (measured in dollars) into a list of total costs. The linearity of this mapping is reflected in two ways:

1. If production is increased by a factor of, say, 4 from $\mathbf{x}$ to $4\mathbf{x}$, then the costs will increase by the same factor, from $T(\mathbf{x})$ to $4T(\mathbf{x})$.
2. If $\mathbf{x}$ and $\mathbf{y}$ are production vectors, then the total cost vector associated with the combined production $\mathbf{x} + \mathbf{y}$ is precisely the sum of the cost vectors $T(\mathbf{x})$ and $T(\mathbf{y})$.

PRACTICE PROBLEMS

1. Suppose that $T : \mathbb{R}^5 \to \mathbb{R}^2$ and $T(\mathbf{x}) = A\mathbf{x}$ for some matrix A and each $\mathbf{x}$ in $\mathbb{R}^5$. How many rows and columns does A have?
2. Let $A = \begin{bmatrix} 1 & 0 \\ 0 & -1 \end{bmatrix}$. Give a geometric description of the transformation $\mathbf{x} \mapsto A\mathbf{x}$.
3. The line segment from $\mathbf{0}$ to a vector $\mathbf{u}$ is the set of points of the form $t\mathbf{u}$ where $0 \le t \le 1$. Show that a linear transformation T maps this segment into the segment between $\mathbf{0}$ and $T(\mathbf{u})$.

2.5 EXERCISES

1. For $A = \begin{bmatrix} 3 & 0 \\ 0 & 3 \end{bmatrix}$, define $T : \mathbb{R}^2 \to \mathbb{R}^2$ by $T(\mathbf{x}) = A\mathbf{x}$. Find the images under T of $\mathbf{u} = \begin{bmatrix} 1 \\ 5 \end{bmatrix}$ and $\mathbf{v} = \begin{bmatrix} -4 \\ -1 \end{bmatrix}$.

2. Let $A = \begin{bmatrix} 2 & 0 & 0 \\ 0 & 2 & 0 \\ 0 & 0 & 2 \end{bmatrix}$, $\mathbf{u} = \begin{bmatrix} 1 \\ 0 \\ -3 \end{bmatrix}$, $\mathbf{v} = \begin{bmatrix} 5 \\ -1 \\ 4 \end{bmatrix}$. Define $T : \mathbb{R}^3 \to \mathbb{R}^3$ by $T(\mathbf{x}) = A\mathbf{x}$. Find $T(\mathbf{u})$ and $T(\mathbf{v})$.

In Exercises 3–6, with T defined by $T(\mathbf{x}) = A\mathbf{x}$, find an $\mathbf{x}$ whose image under T is $\mathbf{b}$, and determine if $\mathbf{x}$ is unique.

3. $A = \begin{bmatrix} 1 & 0 & -1 \\ 3 & 1 & -5 \\ -4 & 2 & 1 \end{bmatrix}$, $\mathbf{b} = \begin{bmatrix} 0 \\ -5 \\ -6 \end{bmatrix}$

4. $A = \begin{bmatrix} 1 & 2 & -1 \\ 2 & 3 & 1 \\ 0 & 3 & -8 \end{bmatrix}$, $\mathbf{b} = \begin{bmatrix} 5 \\ 9 \\ 4 \end{bmatrix}$

5. $A = \begin{bmatrix} 1 & 0 & 3 \\ -2 & 1 & -3 \end{bmatrix}$, $\mathbf{b} = \begin{bmatrix} -4 \\ 9 \end{bmatrix}$

6. $A = \begin{bmatrix} 1 & 0 & 3 \\ 0 & 1 & -4 \\ 3 & 2 & 1 \\ -2 & -1 & -2 \end{bmatrix}$, $\mathbf{b} = \begin{bmatrix} 1 \\ -5 \\ -7 \\ 3 \end{bmatrix}$

7. Let A be a 7×5 matrix. What must a and b be in order to define $T : \mathbb{R}^a \to \mathbb{R}^b$ by $T(\mathbf{x}) = A\mathbf{x}$?

8. How many rows and columns must a matrix A have in order to define a mapping from $\mathbb{R}^3$ into $\mathbb{R}^4$ by the rule $T(\mathbf{x}) = A\mathbf{x}$?

For Exercises 9 and 10, find all $\mathbf{x}$ in $\mathbb{R}^4$ that are mapped into the zero vector by the transformation $\mathbf{x} \mapsto A\mathbf{x}$.

9. $A = \begin{bmatrix} 1 & 3 & 4 & -3 \\ 0 & 1 & 3 & -2 \\ 3 & 7 & 6 & -5 \end{bmatrix}$

10. $A = \begin{bmatrix} 1 & 2 & -7 & 5 \\ 0 & 1 & -4 & 0 \\ 1 & 0 & 1 & 6 \\ 2 & -1 & 6 & 8 \end{bmatrix}$

11. Let $\mathbf{b} = \begin{bmatrix} 1 \\ -1 \\ 7 \end{bmatrix}$ and let A be the matrix in Exercise 9. Is $\mathbf{b}$ in the range of the linear transformation $\mathbf{x} \mapsto A\mathbf{x}$?

12. Let $\mathbf{b} = \begin{bmatrix} 9 \\ 5 \\ 0 \\ -9 \end{bmatrix}$ and let A be the matrix in Exercise 10. Is $\mathbf{b}$ in the range of the linear transformation $\mathbf{x} \mapsto A\mathbf{x}$?

13. Let $A = \begin{bmatrix} -1 & 0 \\ 0 & -1 \end{bmatrix}$, $\mathbf{u} = \begin{bmatrix} 5 \\ 2 \end{bmatrix}$, $\mathbf{v} = \begin{bmatrix} -3 \\ -1 \end{bmatrix}$. Let $T(\mathbf{x}) = A\mathbf{x}$ for $\mathbf{x}$ in $\mathbb{R}^2$.
   a. On a rectangular coordinate system, plot the vectors $\mathbf{u}, \mathbf{v}, T(\mathbf{u})$, and $T(\mathbf{v})$.
   b. Give a geometric description of what T does to a vector $\mathbf{x}$ in $\mathbb{R}^2$.

14. Let $A = \begin{bmatrix} 0 & 0 \\ 0 & 1 \end{bmatrix}$, $\mathbf{u} = \begin{bmatrix} 2 \\ 4 \end{bmatrix}$, $\mathbf{v} = \begin{bmatrix} 5 \\ -1 \end{bmatrix}$. Let $T(\mathbf{x}) = A\mathbf{x}$ for $\mathbf{x}$ in $\mathbb{R}^2$.
   a. On a rectangular coordinate system, plot the vectors $\mathbf{u}, \mathbf{v}, T(\mathbf{u})$, and $T(\mathbf{v})$.
   b. Give a geometric description of what T does to a vector $\mathbf{x}$ in $\mathbb{R}^2$.

In Exercises 15–18, use a rectangular coordinate system to plot $\begin{bmatrix} 4 \\ 2 \end{bmatrix}$, $\begin{bmatrix} -5 \\ -2 \end{bmatrix}$, and their images under the transformation T. (Make a separate sketch for each exercise.) Give a geometric description of what T does to a vector $\mathbf{x}$ in $\mathbb{R}^2$.

15. $T(\mathbf{x}) = \begin{bmatrix} .5 & 0 \\ 0 & .5 \end{bmatrix} \begin{bmatrix} x_1 \\ x_2 \end{bmatrix}$

16. $T(\mathbf{x}) = \begin{bmatrix} -1 & 0 \\ 0 & 1 \end{bmatrix} \begin{bmatrix} x_1 \\ x_2 \end{bmatrix}$

17. $T(\mathbf{x}) = \begin{bmatrix} 0 & 1 \\ 1 & 0 \end{bmatrix} \begin{bmatrix} x_1 \\ x_2 \end{bmatrix}$

18. $T(\mathbf{x}) = \begin{bmatrix} 2 & 0 \\ 0 & 1 \end{bmatrix} \begin{bmatrix} x_1 \\ x_2 \end{bmatrix}$

19. Let $T : \mathbb{R}^2 \to \mathbb{R}^2$ be a linear transformation that maps $\mathbf{u} = \begin{bmatrix} 1 \\ 5 \end{bmatrix}$ into $\begin{bmatrix} 2 \\ 0 \end{bmatrix}$ and maps $\mathbf{v} = \begin{bmatrix} 3 \\ 1 \end{bmatrix}$ into $\begin{bmatrix} 1 \\ -4 \end{bmatrix}$. Use the fact that T is linear to find the images under T of $2\mathbf{u}$, $3\mathbf{v}$, and $2\mathbf{u} + 3\mathbf{v}$.

20. Let $T : \mathbb{R}^2 \to \mathbb{R}^3$ be a linear transformation that maps $\mathbf{u} = \begin{bmatrix} 1 \\ 0 \end{bmatrix}$ into $\begin{bmatrix} 7 \\ -3 \\ 1 \end{bmatrix}$ and maps $\mathbf{v} = \begin{bmatrix} 1 \\ 1 \end{bmatrix}$ into $\begin{bmatrix} 2 \\ 0 \\ 4 \end{bmatrix}$. Use the fact that T is linear to find the images under T of $3\mathbf{u}$, $-2\mathbf{v}$, and $3\mathbf{u} - 2\mathbf{v}$.

21. Let $\mathbf{e}_1 = \begin{bmatrix} 1 \\ 0 \end{bmatrix}$, $\mathbf{e}_2 = \begin{bmatrix} 0 \\ 1 \end{bmatrix}$, $\mathbf{y}_1 = \begin{bmatrix} 3 \\ -5 \end{bmatrix}$, and $\mathbf{y}_2 = \begin{bmatrix} -2 \\ 7 \end{bmatrix}$, and let $T : \mathbb{R}^2 \to \mathbb{R}^2$ be a linear transformation that maps $\mathbf{e}_1$ into $\mathbf{y}_1$ and maps $\mathbf{e}_2$ into $\mathbf{y}_2$. Find the images of $\begin{bmatrix} 7 \\ 6 \end{bmatrix}$ and $\begin{bmatrix} x_1 \\ x_2 \end{bmatrix}$.

22. Let $T : \mathbb{R} \to \mathbb{R}$ be a linear transformation, and let $m = T(1)$. Use a property of a linear transformation to show that $T(x) = mx$ for all x in $\mathbb{R}$.

23. Given $\mathbf{v} \neq \mathbf{0}$ and $\mathbf{p}$ in $\mathbb{R}^n$, show that a linear transformation $T : \mathbb{R}^n \to \mathbb{R}^n$ maps the line through $\mathbf{p}$ in the direction of $\mathbf{v}$ onto a line, or onto a single point (a *degenerate line*).

24. a. Show that the line through vectors $\mathbf{p}$ and $\mathbf{q}$ in $\mathbb{R}^n$ may be written in the parametric form $\mathbf{x} = (1 - t)\mathbf{p} + t\mathbf{q}$.
   b. The line segment from $\mathbf{p}$ to $\mathbf{q}$ is the set of points of the form $(1 - t)\mathbf{p} + t\mathbf{q}$ for $0 \leq t \leq 1$ (as shown in the figure). Show that a linear transformation T maps this line segment onto a line segment or onto a single point.

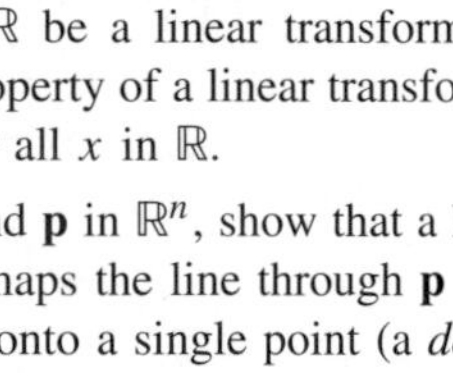

25. Let $T : \mathbb{R}^n \to \mathbb{R}^m$ be a linear transformation and let $\{\mathbf{v}_1, \mathbf{v}_2, \mathbf{v}_3\}$ be a linearly dependent set in $\mathbb{R}^n$. Explain why the set $\{T(\mathbf{v}_1), T(\mathbf{v}_2), T(\mathbf{v}_3)\}$ is linearly dependent.

26. Let $\mathbf{u}$ and $\mathbf{v}$ be vectors in $\mathbb{R}^n$. It can be shown that the set P of all points in the parallelogram determined by $\mathbf{u}$ and $\mathbf{v}$ has the form $a\mathbf{u} + b\mathbf{v}$, for $0 \le a \le 1, 0 \le b \le 1$. Let $T : \mathbb{R}^n \to \mathbb{R}^m$ be a linear transformation. Explain why the image of a point in P under the transformation T lies in the parallelogram determined by $T(\mathbf{u})$ and $T(\mathbf{v})$.

27. Define $f : \mathbb{R} \to \mathbb{R}$ by $f(x) = mx + b$.

a. Show that f is a linear transformation when $b = 0$.

b. Find a property of a linear transformation that is violated when $b \neq 0$.

c. Why is f called a linear function?

28. Show that the mapping T defined by $T(x_1, x_2) = (4x_1 - 2x_2,\ 3|x_2|)$ is not linear.

29. Show that the mapping T defined by $T(x_1, x_2) = (2x_1 - 3x_2,\ x_1 + 4,\ 5x_2)$ is not linear.

30. An *affine transformation* $T : \mathbb{R}^n \to \mathbb{R}^m$ has the form $T(x) = A\mathbf{x} + \mathbf{b}$, with A an $m \times n$ matrix and $\mathbf{b}$ in $\mathbb{R}^m$. Show that T is *not* a linear transformation when $\mathbf{b} \neq \mathbf{0}$. (Affine transformations are important in computer graphics.)

SOLUTIONS TO PRACTICE PROBLEMS

1. A must have five columns for $A\mathbf{x}$ to be defined. A must have two rows for the range of T to be in $\mathbb{R}^2$.
2. Plot some random points (vectors) on graph paper to see what happens. A point such as (4,1) maps into (4, −1). The transformation $\mathbf{x} \mapsto A\mathbf{x}$ reflects points through the x-axis (or x_1-axis).
3. Let $\mathbf{x} = t\mathbf{u}$ for some t such that $0 \le t \le 1$. Since T is linear, $T(t\mathbf{u}) = tT(\mathbf{u})$, which is a point on the line segment between $\mathbf{0}$ and $T(\mathbf{u})$.

2.6 THE MATRIX OF A LINEAR TRANSFORMATION

In this section we show that every linear transformation $T : \mathbb{R}^n \to \mathbb{R}^m$ is a matrix transformation $\mathbf{x} \mapsto A\mathbf{x}$, and we examine how important properties of T are related to familiar properties of A. The key to finding A is to observe that T is completely determined by what it does to the columns of the identity matrix in $\mathbb{R}^n$.

EXAMPLE 1 The columns of $I_2 = \begin{bmatrix} 1 & 0 \\ 0 & 1 \end{bmatrix}$ are $\mathbf{e}_1 = \begin{bmatrix} 1 \\ 0 \end{bmatrix}$ and $\mathbf{e}_2 = \begin{bmatrix} 0 \\ 1 \end{bmatrix}$. Suppose T is a linear transformation from $\mathbb{R}^2$ into $\mathbb{R}^3$ such that

$$T(\mathbf{e}_1) = \begin{bmatrix} 5 \\ -7 \\ 2 \end{bmatrix}, \qquad T(\mathbf{e}_2) = \begin{bmatrix} -3 \\ 8 \\ 0 \end{bmatrix}$$

With no additional information, find a formula for the image of an arbitrary $\mathbf{x}$ in $\mathbb{R}^2$.

Solution Write

$$\mathbf{x} = \begin{bmatrix} x_2 \\ x_2 \end{bmatrix} = x_1 \begin{bmatrix} 1 \\ 0 \end{bmatrix} + x_2 \begin{bmatrix} 0 \\ 1 \end{bmatrix} = x_1\mathbf{e}_1 + x_2\mathbf{e}_2 \tag{1}$$

Since T is a *linear* transformation,

$$T(\mathbf{x}) = x_1 T(\mathbf{e}_1) + x_2 T(\mathbf{e}_2) \tag{2}$$
$$= x_1 \begin{bmatrix} 5 \\ -7 \\ 2 \end{bmatrix} + x_2 \begin{bmatrix} -3 \\ 8 \\ 0 \end{bmatrix} = \begin{bmatrix} 5x_1 - 3x_2 \\ -7x_1 + 8x_2 \\ 2x_1 + 0 \end{bmatrix}$$

The step from (1) to (2) explains why knowledge of $T(\mathbf{e}_1)$ and $T(\mathbf{e}_2)$ is sufficient to determine $T(\mathbf{x})$ for any $\mathbf{x}$. Moreover, since (2) expresses $T(\mathbf{x})$ as a linear combination of vectors, we may put these vectors into the columns of a matrix A and write (2) as

$$T(\mathbf{x}) = \begin{bmatrix} T(\mathbf{e}_1) & T(\mathbf{e}_2) \end{bmatrix} \begin{bmatrix} x_1 \\ x_2 \end{bmatrix} = A\mathbf{x}$$

THEOREM 8

Let $T : \mathbb{R}^n \to \mathbb{R}^m$ be a linear transformation. Then there exists a unique matrix A such that

$$T(\mathbf{x}) = A\mathbf{x} \quad \text{for all } \mathbf{x} \text{ in } \mathbb{R}^n$$

In fact, A is the $m \times n$ matrix whose jth column is the vector $T(\mathbf{e}_j)$, where $\mathbf{e}_j$ is the jth column of the identity matrix in $\mathbb{R}^n$.

$$A = [T(\mathbf{e}_1) \quad \cdots \quad T(\mathbf{e}_n)] \tag{3}$$

Proof Write $\mathbf{x} = I_n\mathbf{x} = [\mathbf{e}_1 \quad \cdots \quad \mathbf{e}_n]\mathbf{x} = x_1\mathbf{e}_1 + \cdots + x_n\mathbf{e}_n$, and use the linearity of T to compute

$$T(\mathbf{x}) = T(x_1\mathbf{e}_1 + \cdots + x_n\mathbf{e}_n) = x_1 T(\mathbf{e}_1) + \cdots + x_n T(\mathbf{e}_n)$$
$$= [T(\mathbf{e}_1) \quad \cdots \quad T(\mathbf{e}_n)] \begin{bmatrix} x_1 \\ \vdots \\ x_n \end{bmatrix} = A\mathbf{x}$$

The uniqueness of A is treated in Exercise 33.

The matrix A in (3) is called the **standard matrix for the linear transformation T**.

We know now that every linear transformation from $\mathbb{R}^n$ to $\mathbb{R}^m$ is a matrix transformation and vice versa. The term *linear transformation* focuses on a property of a mapping, while *matrix transformation* describes how such a mapping is implemented, as the next examples illustrate.

EXAMPLE 2 Find the standard matrix A for the dilation transformation $T(\mathbf{x}) = 3\mathbf{x}$, for $\mathbf{x}$ in $\mathbb{R}^2$.

Solution Write

$$T(\mathbf{e}_1) = 3\mathbf{e}_1 = \begin{bmatrix} 3 \\ 0 \end{bmatrix} \text{ and } T(\mathbf{e}_2) = 3\mathbf{e}_2 = \begin{bmatrix} 0 \\ 3 \end{bmatrix}$$

$$A = \begin{bmatrix} 3 & 0 \\ 0 & 3 \end{bmatrix}$$

EXAMPLE 3 Let $T : \mathbb{R}^2 \to \mathbb{R}^2$ be the transformation that rotates each point in $\mathbb{R}^2$ through an angle φ, with counterclockwise rotation for a positive angle. We could show geometrically that such a transformation is linear. (See Fig. 6 in Section 2.5.) Find the standard matrix A of this transformation.

Solution $\begin{bmatrix} 1 \\ 0 \end{bmatrix}$ rotates into $\begin{bmatrix} \cos\varphi \\ \sin\varphi \end{bmatrix}$, and $\begin{bmatrix} 0 \\ 1 \end{bmatrix}$ rotates into $\begin{bmatrix} -\sin\varphi \\ \cos\varphi \end{bmatrix}$. See Fig. 1. By Theorem 8,

$$A = \begin{bmatrix} \cos\varphi & -\sin\varphi \\ \sin\varphi & \cos\varphi \end{bmatrix}$$

Example 5 in Section 2.5 is a special case of this transformation, with $\varphi = \pi/2$.

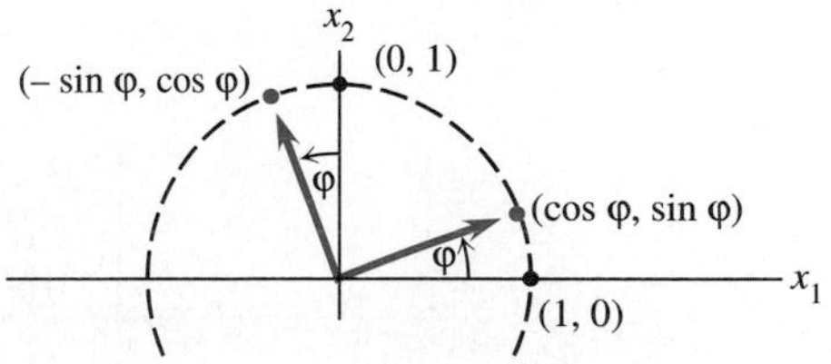

FIGURE 1 A rotation transformation.

Existence and Uniqueness Questions

Two general existence and uniqueness questions are appropriate for any linear transformation. Both questions require new vocabulary.

DEFINITION

A mapping $T : \mathbb{R}^n \to \mathbb{R}^m$ is said to be **onto** $\mathbb{R}^m$ if each $\mathbf{b}$ in $\mathbb{R}^m$ is the image of *at least one* $\mathbf{x}$ in $\mathbb{R}^n$.

Equivalently, T is onto $\mathbb{R}^m$ if for each $\mathbf{b}$ in $\mathbb{R}^m$ there exists at least one solution of $T(\mathbf{x}) = \mathbf{b}$. "Does T map $\mathbb{R}^n$ onto $\mathbb{R}^m$?" is an existence question.

The mapping T is *not* onto when there is some $\mathbf{b}$ in $\mathbb{R}^m$ such that the equation $T(\mathbf{x}) = \mathbf{b}$ has no solution. See Fig. 2.

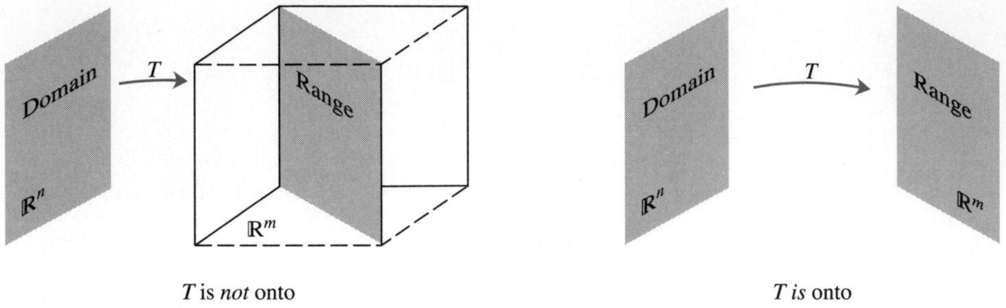

FIGURE 2 Is the range of T all of $\mathbb{R}^m$?

DEFINITION

A mapping $T : \mathbb{R}^n \to \mathbb{R}^m$ is said to be **one-to-one** (or **1:1**) if each $\mathbf{b}$ in $\mathbb{R}^m$ is the image of *at most one* $\mathbf{x}$ in $\mathbb{R}^n$.

Equivalently, T is one-to-one if for each $\mathbf{b}$ in $\mathbb{R}^m$ the equation $T(\mathbf{x}) = \mathbf{b}$ has either a unique solution or none at all. "Is T one-to-one?" is a uniqueness question.

The mapping T is *not* one-to-one when some $\mathbf{b}$ in $\mathbb{R}^m$ is the image of more than one vector in $\mathbb{R}^n$. If there is no such $\mathbf{b}$, then T is one-to-one. See Fig. 3.

These two function properties relate easily to concepts developed earlier in the chapter.

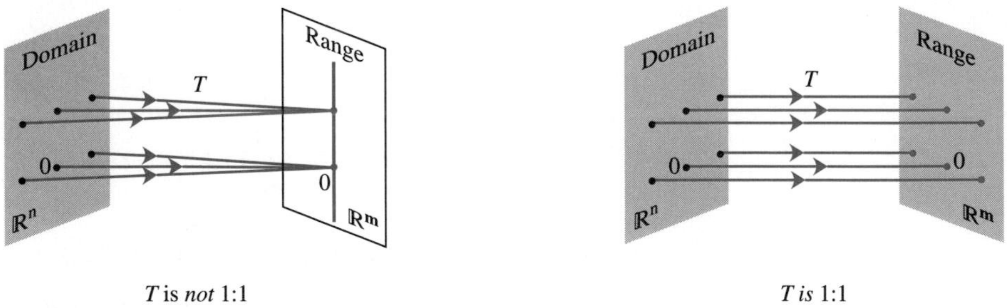

FIGURE 3 Is every $\mathbf{b}$ the image of at most one vector?

EXAMPLE 4 Let T be the linear transformation whose standard matrix is

$$A = \begin{bmatrix} 1 & -4 & 8 & 1 \\ 0 & 2 & -1 & 3 \\ 0 & 0 & 0 & 5 \end{bmatrix}$$

Does T map $\mathbb{R}^4$ onto $\mathbb{R}^3$? Is T a one-to-one mapping?

Solution Since A happens to be in echelon form, we can see at once that A has a pivot position in each row. By Theorem 2, for each $\mathbf{b}$ in $\mathbb{R}^3$ the equation $A\mathbf{x} = \mathbf{b}$ is consistent. In other words, the linear transformation T maps $\mathbb{R}^4$ (its domain) onto $\mathbb{R}^3$. However, since the equation $A\mathbf{x} = \mathbf{b}$ has a free variable (because there are four variables and only three basic variables), each $\mathbf{b}$ is the image of more than one $\mathbf{x}$. That is, T is *not* one-to-one. ∎

THEOREM 9

Let $T : \mathbb{R}^n \to \mathbb{R}^m$ be a linear transformation. Then T is one-to-one if and only if the equation $T(\mathbf{x}) = \mathbf{0}$ has only the trivial solution.

Proof Since T is linear, $T(\mathbf{0}) = \mathbf{0}$. If T is one-to-one, then the equation $T(\mathbf{x}) = \mathbf{0}$ has at most one solution and hence only the trivial solution. If T is not one-to-one, then there is a $\mathbf{b}$ that is the image of at least two different vectors in $\mathbb{R}^n$, say $\mathbf{u}$ and $\mathbf{v}$. That is, $T(\mathbf{u}) = \mathbf{b}$ and $T(\mathbf{v}) = \mathbf{b}$. But then, since T is linear,

$$T(\mathbf{u} - \mathbf{v}) = T(\mathbf{u}) - T(\mathbf{v}) = \mathbf{b} - \mathbf{b} = \mathbf{0}$$

The vector $\mathbf{u} - \mathbf{v}$ is not zero, since $\mathbf{u} \neq \mathbf{v}$. Hence the equation $T(\mathbf{x}) = \mathbf{0}$ has more than one solution. So either the two conditions mentioned in the theorem are both true or they are both false. ∎

THEOREM 10

Let $T : \mathbb{R}^n \to \mathbb{R}^m$ be a linear transformation and let A be the standard matrix for T. Then

a. T maps $\mathbb{R}^n$ onto $\mathbb{R}^m$ if and only if the columns of A span $\mathbb{R}^m$,

b. T is one-to-one if and only if the columns of A are linearly independent.

Proof

a. By Theorem 2, the columns of A span $\mathbb{R}^m$ if and only if for each $\mathbf{b}$ the equation $A\mathbf{x} = \mathbf{b}$ is consistent—in other words, if and only if for every $\mathbf{b}$, the equation $T(\mathbf{x}) = \mathbf{b}$ has at least one solution. This is true if and only if T maps $\mathbb{R}^n$ onto $\mathbb{R}^m$.

b. The equations $T(\mathbf{x}) = \mathbf{0}$ and $A\mathbf{x} = \mathbf{0}$ are the same except for notation. So, by Theorem 9, T is one-to-one if and only if $A\mathbf{x} = \mathbf{0}$ has only the trivial solution. This happens if and only if the columns of A are linearly independent, as was already noted in the boxed statement (3) in Section 2.4. ∎

In the next example and in some exercises that follow, we write column vectors in rows, using parentheses and commas. Also, when we apply a linear transformation T to a vector—say, $\mathbf{x} = \begin{bmatrix} x_1 \\ x_2 \end{bmatrix} = (x_1, x_2)$—we write $T(x_1, x_2)$ instead of the more formal $T((x_1, x_2))$.

EXAMPLE 5 Let $T(x_1, x_2) = (3x_1 + x_2,\ 0,\ x_1 + 3x_2)$. Show that T is a one-to-one linear transformation. Does T map $\mathbb{R}^2$ onto $\mathbb{R}^3$?

Solution When $\mathbf{x}$ and $T(\mathbf{x})$ are written as column vectors, it is easy to see that T is described by the equation

$$\begin{bmatrix} 3 & 1 \\ 0 & 0 \\ 1 & 3 \end{bmatrix} \begin{bmatrix} x_1 \\ x_2 \end{bmatrix} = \begin{bmatrix} 3x_1 + x_2 \\ 0 \\ x_1 + 3x_2 \end{bmatrix} \tag{4}$$

so T is indeed a linear transformation, with its standard matrix A shown in (4). The columns of A are linearly independent because they are not multiples. By Theorem 10(b), T is one-to-one. To decide if T is onto $\mathbb{R}^3$, we examine the span of the columns of A. Since A is 3×2, the columns of A span $\mathbb{R}^3$ if and only if A has 3 pivot positions, by Theorem 2. This is impossible, since A has only 2 columns. So the columns of A do not span $\mathbb{R}^3$ and the associated linear transformation is not onto $\mathbb{R}^3$.

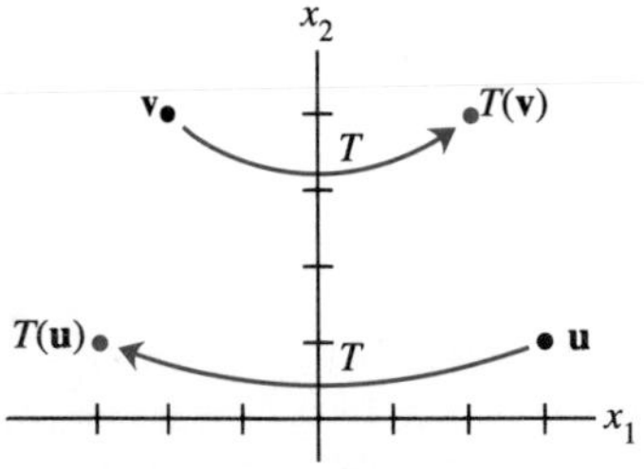

A reflection transformation.

PRACTICE PROBLEM

Let $T : \mathbb{R}^2 \to \mathbb{R}^2$ be the transformation that reflects each point in the vertical axis. For instance, if $\mathbf{u} = \begin{bmatrix} 3 \\ 1 \end{bmatrix}$, then $T(\mathbf{u}) = \begin{bmatrix} -3 \\ 1 \end{bmatrix}$; if $\mathbf{v} = \begin{bmatrix} -2 \\ 4 \end{bmatrix}$, then $T(\mathbf{v}) = \begin{bmatrix} 2 \\ 4 \end{bmatrix}$. (See the accompanying figure.) Find a matrix A that implements T, and thereby show that T is a linear transformation.

2.6 EXERCISES

In Exercises 1–14, assume that T is a linear transformation. Find the standard matrix of T.

1. $T : \mathbb{R}^2 \to \mathbb{R}^3$
$T(1, 0) = (4, -1, 2)$ and $T(0, 1) = (-5, 3, -6)$
2. $T : \mathbb{R}^2 \to \mathbb{R}^2$, $T(1, 0) = (3, 3)$, and $T(0, 1) = (-2, 5)$
3. $T : \mathbb{R}^3 \to \mathbb{R}^2$, $T(\mathbf{e}_1) = (1, 4)$, $T(\mathbf{e}_2) = (-2, 9)$, and $T(\mathbf{e}_3) = (3, -8)$, where $\mathbf{e}_1, \mathbf{e}_2, \mathbf{e}_3$ are the columns of the 3×3 identity matrix
4. $T : \mathbb{R}^2 \to \mathbb{R}^4$
$T(\mathbf{e}_1) = (1, 2, 0, 5)$ and $T(\mathbf{e}_2) = (3, -6, 1, 0)$, where $\mathbf{e}_1$ and $\mathbf{e}_2$ are the columns of the 2×2 identity matrix
5. $T : \mathbb{R}^2 \to \mathbb{R}^2$ rotates points clockwise through π radians
6. $T : \mathbb{R}^2 \to \mathbb{R}^2$ rotates points clockwise through $\pi/2$ radians
7. $T : \mathbb{R}^2 \to \mathbb{R}^2$ reflects points through the horizontal x_1-axis
8. $T : \mathbb{R}^2 \to \mathbb{R}^2$ reflects points through the line $x_1 = x_2$
9. $T : \mathbb{R}^2 \to \mathbb{R}^2$ reflects points through the line $x_1 = -x_2$
10. $T : \mathbb{R}^2 \to \mathbb{R}^2$ reflects each point through the origin
11. $T : \mathbb{R}^3 \to \mathbb{R}^3$ projects each point (x_1, x_2, x_3) vertically onto the x_1x_2-plane (where $x_3 = 0$)
12. $T : \mathbb{R}^3 \to \mathbb{R}^3$ projects each point (x_1, x_2, x_3) onto the x_2x_3-plane (where $x_1 = 0$)
13. $T : \mathbb{R}^2 \to \mathbb{R}^2$ is a "vertical shear" transformation that maps $\mathbf{e}_1$ into $\mathbf{e}_1 + 2\mathbf{e}_2$ but leaves the vector $\mathbf{e}_2$ unchanged
14. $T : \mathbb{R}^2 \to \mathbb{R}^2$ is a "horizontal shear" transformation that maps $\mathbf{e}_2$ into $\mathbf{e}_2 - 3\mathbf{e}_1$ but leaves the vector $\mathbf{e}_1$ unchanged

In Exercises 15 and 16, fill in the missing entries of the matrix, assuming that the equation holds for all values of the variables.

15. $$\begin{bmatrix} ? & ? & ? \\ ? & ? & ? \\ ? & ? & ? \end{bmatrix} \begin{bmatrix} x_1 \\ x_2 \\ x_3 \end{bmatrix} = \begin{bmatrix} 2x_2 - x_3 \\ x_1 + x_2 - x_3 \\ x_1 \end{bmatrix}$$

16. $\begin{bmatrix} ? & ? \\ ? & ? \\ ? & ? \end{bmatrix}\begin{bmatrix} x_1 \\ x_2 \end{bmatrix} = \begin{bmatrix} 5x_1 - 6x_2 \\ x_2 \\ 2x_1 - 2x_2 \end{bmatrix}$

In Exercises 17–22, show that T is a linear transformation T by finding a matrix that implements the mapping. Note that $x_1, x_2, \ldots$ are not vectors but are entries in vectors.

17. $T(x_1, x_2, x_3) = (x_3,\ x_2,\ x_1)$
18. $T(x_1, x_2) = (5x_2 - x_1,\ 0,\ 3x_1 + x_2,\ x_1)$
19. $T(x_1, x_2, x_3) = (3x_2 - x_3,\ x_1 + 4x_2 + x_3)$
20. $T(x_1, x_2, x_3) = (x_1,\ x_2 + 4x_1,\ x_3)$
21. $T(x_1, x_2, x_3, x_4) = (x_1 + x_2,\ x_2 + x_3,\ x_3 + x_4,\ 0)$
22. $T(x_1, x_2, x_3, x_4) = 3x_1 - 4x_2 + 8x_4$ $[T : \mathbb{R}^4 \to \mathbb{R}]$
23. Let $T : \mathbb{R}^2 \to \mathbb{R}^2$ be a linear transformation such that $T(x_1, x_2) = (x_1 + x_2,\ 4x_1 + 7x_2)$. Find $\mathbf{x}$ such that $T(\mathbf{x}) = (-2, -5)$.
24. Let $T : \mathbb{R}^2 \to \mathbb{R}^3$ be a linear transformation such that $T(x_1, x_2) = (x_1 + 2x_2,\ -x_1 - 3x_2,\ -3x_1 - 2x_2)$. Find $\mathbf{x}$ such that $T(\mathbf{x}) = (-4, 7, 0)$.
25. Determine if the linear transformation in Exercise 3 is one-to-one.
26. Determine if the linear transformation in Exercise 4 is one-to-one.
27. Determine if the linear transformation in Exercise 3 maps $\mathbb{R}^3$ onto $\mathbb{R}^2$.
28. Determine if the linear transformation in Exercise 4 maps $\mathbb{R}^2$ onto $\mathbb{R}^4$.
29. Determine if the linear transformation in Exercise 21 is one-to-one and if the transformation is onto.
30. Repeat Exercise 29 for the transformation in Exercise 20.
31. Let $T : \mathbb{R}^n \to \mathbb{R}^m$ be a linear transformation, with A its standard matrix. Complete the following statement to make it true: "T is one-to-one if and only if A has ___ pivot columns." Explain why the statement is true. [*Hint*: Look in the exercises for Section 2.4.]
32. Let $T : \mathbb{R}^n \to \mathbb{R}^m$ be a linear transformation, with A its standard matrix. Complete the following statement to make it true: "T maps $\mathbb{R}^n$ onto $\mathbb{R}^m$ if and only if A has ___ pivot columns." Find some theorems that explain why the statement is true.
33. Verify the uniqueness of A in Theorem 8. Let $T : \mathbb{R}^n \to \mathbb{R}^m$ be a linear transformation such that $T(\mathbf{x}) = B\mathbf{x}$ for some $m \times n$ matrix B. Show that if A is the standard matrix for T, then $A = B$. [*Hint*: Show that A and B have the same columns.]
34. Why is the question "Is the linear transformation T onto?" an existence question?
35. If a linear transformation $T : \mathbb{R}^n \to \mathbb{R}^m$ maps $\mathbb{R}^n$ *onto* $\mathbb{R}^m$, what can you say about m and n?
36. If a linear transformation $T : \mathbb{R}^n \to \mathbb{R}^m$ is one-to-one, what can you say about m and n?

SOLUTION TO PRACTICE PROBLEM

The geometric description of T implies that T changes (x_1, x_2) into $(-x_1, x_2)$. The matrix A that does this is found by inspection. Since the equation

$$\begin{bmatrix} ? & ? \\ ? & ? \end{bmatrix}\begin{bmatrix} x_1 \\ x_2 \end{bmatrix} = \begin{bmatrix} -x_1 \\ x_2 \end{bmatrix}$$

must hold for all (x_1, x_2), it is clear that $A = \begin{bmatrix} -1 & 0 \\ 0 & 1 \end{bmatrix}$, and $T(\mathbf{x}) = A\mathbf{x}$ for all $\mathbf{x}$. By properties of matrix multiplication (Theorem 3 in Section 2.2), T must be a linear transformation.

2.7 APPLICATIONS TO NUTRITION AND POPULATION MOVEMENT

The two applications in this section illustrate the usefulness of vector and matrix equations. We address the nutrition problem mentioned at the beginning of the chapter, and then we turn to a mathematical model of population movement. This second application also serves to introduce the concept of a difference equation, a powerful mathematical tool for studying dynamic processes in a wide variety of fields such as engineering, ecology, economics, telecommunications, and the management sciences.

Constructing a Nutritious Weight Loss Diet

The problem of selecting the proper combination of ingredients to provide a reasonably safe and effective diet food product was described in the chapter introduction. For the Cambridge Diet, the problem was to supply 31 nutrients in precise amounts. The manufacturer was able to do this using only 33 ingredients. Listed in Table 1 are three of the ingredients in the diet, together with the amounts of certain nutrients supplied by 100 grams of each ingredient.[1]

TABLE 1

Nutrient (grams)	Amounts (grams) supplied per 100 g of ingredient: Nonfat milk	Soy flour	Whey	Amounts supplied by the Cambridge Diet in one day
Protein	36	51	13	33
Carbohydrate	52	34	74	45
Fat	0	7	1.1	3

EXAMPLE 1 If possible, find some combination of nonfat milk, soy flour, and whey to provide the exact amounts of protein, carbohydrate, and fat supplied by the diet in one day (Table 1).

Solution Let x_1, x_2, and x_3, respectively, denote the number of units (100 grams) of these foodstuffs. One approach to the problem is to derive equations for each nutrient separately. For instance, the product

$$\left\{\begin{matrix} x_1 \text{ units of} \\ \text{nonfat milk} \end{matrix}\right\} \cdot \left\{\begin{matrix} \text{protein per unit} \\ \text{of nonfat milk} \end{matrix}\right\}$$

gives the amount of protein supplied by x_1 units of nonfat milk. To this amount, we would then add similar products for soy flour and whey and set the resulting sum equal to the amount of protein we need. Analogous calculations would have to be made for each nutrient.

A more efficient method, and one that is conceptually simpler, is to consider a "nutrient vector" for each foodstuff and build just one vector equation. The amount of nutrients supplied by x_1 units of nonfat milk is the scalar multiple

[1] Ingredients in the diet as of 1984; nutrient data for ingredients adapted from USDA Agricultural Handbooks No. 8-1 and 8-6, 1976.

$$\overset{\text{Scalar}}{\begin{Bmatrix} x_1 \text{ units of} \\ \text{nonfat milk} \end{Bmatrix}} \cdot \overset{\text{Vector}}{\begin{Bmatrix} \text{nutrients per unit} \\ \text{of nonfat milk} \end{Bmatrix}} = x_1\mathbf{a}_1$$

where $\mathbf{a}_1$ is the first column in Table 1. Let $\mathbf{a}_2$ and $\mathbf{a}_3$ be the corresponding vectors for soy flour and whey, respectively, and let $\mathbf{b}$ be the vector that lists the total nutrients required (the last column of the table). Then $x_2\mathbf{a}_2$ and $x_3\mathbf{a}_3$ give the nutrients supplied by x_2 units of soy flour and x_3 units of whey, respectively. So the equation we want is

$$x_1\mathbf{a}_1 + x_2\mathbf{a}_2 + x_3\mathbf{a}_3 = \mathbf{b} \tag{1}$$

When we row reduce the augmented matrix for the corresponding system of equations, we obtain

$$\begin{bmatrix} 36 & 51 & 13 & 33 \\ 52 & 34 & 74 & 45 \\ 0 & 7 & 1.1 & 3 \end{bmatrix} \sim \cdots \sim \begin{bmatrix} 1 & 0 & 0 & .277 \\ 0 & 1 & 0 & .392 \\ 0 & 0 & 1 & .233 \end{bmatrix}$$

To three significant digits, we need .277 units of nonfat milk, .392 units of soy flour, and .233 units of whey in order to provide the desired amounts of protein, carbohydrate, and fat. ∎

It is important that the values of x_1, x_2, and x_3 found above are nonnegative. This is necessary for the solution to be physically feasible. (How could you use $-.233$ units of whey, for instance?) With a large number of nutrient requirements, it may be necessary to use a larger number of foodstuffs in order to produce a system of equations with a "nonnegative" solution. Thus many, many different combinations of foodstuffs may need to be examined in order to find a system of equations with such a solution. In addition, other factors such as the cost of the ingredients must be considered.

Example 1 falls within a general class of problems that are usually treated by linear programming techniques. Our method of constructing vector equations often simplifies the task of formulating such problems.

Population Movement

A subject of interest to demographers is the movement of populations or groups of people from one region to another. We consider here a simple model of the changes in the population of a certain city and its surrounding suburbs over a period of years.

Fix an initial year, say 1990, and denote the populations of the city and suburbs that year by r_0 and s_0, respectively. Let $\mathbf{x}_0$ be the population vector

$$\mathbf{x}_0 = \begin{bmatrix} r_0 \\ s_0 \end{bmatrix} \begin{array}{l} \text{City population, 1990} \\ \text{Suburban population, 1990} \end{array}$$

For 1991 and subsequent years, denote the population of the city and suburbs by the vectors

$$\mathbf{x}_1 = \begin{bmatrix} r_1 \\ s_1 \end{bmatrix}, \quad \mathbf{x}_2 = \begin{bmatrix} r_2 \\ s_2 \end{bmatrix}, \quad \mathbf{x}_3 = \begin{bmatrix} r_3 \\ s_3 \end{bmatrix}, \ldots$$

Our goal is to describe mathematically how these vectors might be related.

Suppose demographic studies show that each year about 5% of the city's population moves to the suburbs (and 95% remain in the city), while 3% of the suburban population moves to the city (and 97% remain in the suburbs). See Fig. 1.

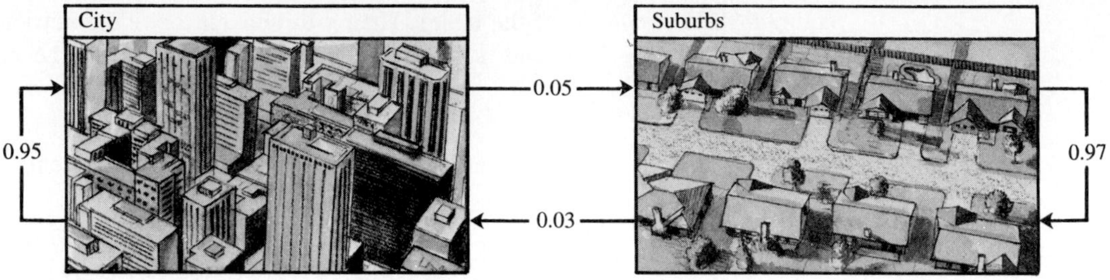

FIGURE 1 Annual percentage migration between city and suburbs.

After one year, the original r_0 persons in the city are now distributed between city and suburbs as

$$\begin{bmatrix} .95r_0 \\ .05r_0 \end{bmatrix} = r_0 \begin{bmatrix} .95 \\ .05 \end{bmatrix} \begin{matrix} \text{Remain in city} \\ \text{Move to suburbs} \end{matrix} \tag{2}$$

The s_0 persons in the suburbs in 1990 are distributed one year later as

$$s_0 \begin{bmatrix} .03 \\ .97 \end{bmatrix} \begin{matrix} \text{Move to city} \\ \text{Remain in suburbs} \end{matrix} \tag{3}$$

The vectors in (2) and (3) account for all of the population in 1991.[2] Thus

$$\begin{bmatrix} r_1 \\ s_1 \end{bmatrix} = r_0 \begin{bmatrix} .95 \\ .05 \end{bmatrix} + s_0 \begin{bmatrix} .03 \\ .97 \end{bmatrix} = \begin{bmatrix} .95 & .03 \\ .05 & .97 \end{bmatrix} \begin{bmatrix} r_0 \\ s_0 \end{bmatrix}$$

That is,

$$\mathbf{x}_1 = M\mathbf{x}_0 \tag{4}$$

where M is the **migration matrix** determined by the following table:

$$\begin{matrix} & \text{From} & \\ \text{City} & \text{Suburbs} & \text{To} \end{matrix}$$
$$\begin{bmatrix} .95 & .03 \\ .05 & .97 \end{bmatrix} \begin{matrix} \text{City} \\ \text{Suburbs} \end{matrix}$$

Equation (4) describes how the population changes from 1990 to 1991. If the migration percentages remain constant, then the change from 1991 to 1992 is given by

$$\mathbf{x}_2 = M\mathbf{x}_1$$

[2]For now we ignore other influences on the population such as migration out of the city/suburban region.

and similarly for 1992 to 1993 and subsequent years. In general,

$$\mathbf{x}_{k+1} = M\mathbf{x}_k \quad \text{for } k = 0, 1, 2, \ldots \tag{5}$$

The sequence of vectors $\{\mathbf{x}_0, \mathbf{x}_1, \mathbf{x}_2, \ldots\}$ describes the population of the city/suburban region over a period of years, and the change in the population from one year to the next is given by (5).

EXAMPLE 2 Compute the population of the region just described for the years 1991 and 1992, given that the population in 1990 was 600,000 in the city and 400,000 in the suburbs.

Solution The initial population in 1990 is $\mathbf{x}_0 = \begin{bmatrix} 600{,}000 \\ 400{,}000 \end{bmatrix}$. For 1991,

$$\mathbf{x}_1 = \begin{bmatrix} .95 & .03 \\ .05 & .97 \end{bmatrix}\begin{bmatrix} 600{,}000 \\ 400{,}000 \end{bmatrix} = \begin{bmatrix} 582{,}000 \\ 418{,}000 \end{bmatrix}$$

For 1992,

$$\mathbf{x}_2 = M\mathbf{x}_1 = \begin{bmatrix} .95 & .03 \\ .05 & .97 \end{bmatrix}\begin{bmatrix} 582{,}000 \\ 418{,}000 \end{bmatrix} = \begin{bmatrix} 565{,}440 \\ 434{,}560 \end{bmatrix}$$

Population Movement with External Migration

The population movement model is easily adapted to take into account migration into and out of the city/suburban region. Suppose that each year 14,000 persons move into the city from outside the region and 5000 persons from the city leave the region. Then there is a *net* movement of 9000 persons into the city from outside the region. Also, suppose there is a net movement of 13,000 persons annually into the suburbs from outside the region. We can adjust (5) for this annual population increase by writing

$$\mathbf{x}_{k+1} = M\mathbf{x}_k + \mathbf{v} \quad \text{for } k = 0, 1, 2, \ldots \tag{6}$$

where $\mathbf{v} = \begin{bmatrix} 9{,}000 \\ 13{,}000 \end{bmatrix}$.

EXAMPLE 3 Use the revised model in (6) to compute the 1991 and 1992 populations for the same initial data $\mathbf{x}_0$ as in Example 2.

Solution

$$\begin{aligned} \mathbf{x}_1 &= M\mathbf{x}_0 + \mathbf{v} \\ &= \begin{bmatrix} .95 & .03 \\ .05 & .97 \end{bmatrix}\begin{bmatrix} 600{,}000 \\ 400{,}000 \end{bmatrix} + \begin{bmatrix} 9{,}000 \\ 13{,}000 \end{bmatrix} \end{aligned}$$

$$= \begin{bmatrix} 582{,}000 \\ 418{,}000 \end{bmatrix} + \begin{bmatrix} 9{,}000 \\ 13{,}000 \end{bmatrix} = \begin{bmatrix} 591{,}000 \\ 431{,}000 \end{bmatrix}$$

$$\mathbf{x}_2 = M\mathbf{x}_1 + \mathbf{v}$$

$$= \begin{bmatrix} .95 & .03 \\ .05 & .97 \end{bmatrix} \begin{bmatrix} 591{,}000 \\ 431{,}000 \end{bmatrix} + \begin{bmatrix} 9{,}000 \\ 13{,}000 \end{bmatrix}$$

$$= \begin{bmatrix} 574{,}380 \\ 447{,}620 \end{bmatrix} + \begin{bmatrix} 9{,}000 \\ 13{,}000 \end{bmatrix} = \begin{bmatrix} 583{,}380 \\ 460{,}620 \end{bmatrix}$$

Difference Equations

Equations such as (5) and (6) that involve a sequence $\{\mathbf{x}_0, \mathbf{x}_1, \mathbf{x}_2, \ldots\}$ of vectors are called **linear difference equations** or **recurrence relations**. Difference equations are widely used in such diverse areas as ecology, economics, and electrical engineering. They provide mathematical models of dynamic processes that change over time, when the process is described or measured only at specified points in time. Difference equations are the discrete analogs of the (continuous) differential equations studied in calculus. The discrete case is discussed further in Sections 5.8, 5.9, and 6.6.

PRACTICE PROBLEM

Find a matrix A and vectors $\mathbf{x}$ and $\mathbf{b}$ such that the problem in Example 1 amounts to solving the equation $A\mathbf{x} = \mathbf{b}$.

2.7 EXERCISES

1. The container of a breakfast cereal usually lists the number of calories and the amounts of protein, carbohydrate, and fat contained in one serving of the cereal. The amounts for two common cereals are given.

	Nutrition Information per Serving	
Nutrient	General Mills Cheerios	Quaker 100% Natural Cereal
Calories	110	130
Protein (g)	4	3
Carbohydrate (g)	20	18
Fat (g)	2	5

Suppose a mixture of these two cereals is to be prepared that contains exactly 295 calories, 9 g protein, 48 g carbohydrate, and 8 g fat.

a. Set up a vector equation for this problem. Include a statement that says what your variables in the equation represent.

b. Write an equivalent matrix equation and then determine if the desired mixture of the two cereals can be prepared.

2. One serving (28 g) of Kellogg's Cracklin' Oat Bran supplies 110 calories, 3 g of protein, 21 g of carbohydrate, and 3 g of fat. One serving of Kellogg's Crispix supplies 110 calories, 2 g of protein, 25 g of carbohydrate, and no fat. Set up a matrix B and a vector $\mathbf{u}$ such that $B\mathbf{u}$ gives the amounts of calories, protein, carbohydrate, and fat contained in a mixture of three servings of Cracklin' Oat Bran and two servings of Crispix.

3. The Cambridge Diet supplies .8 g of calcium per day, in addition to the nutrients listed in Example 1. The amounts of calcium supplied by one unit (100 g) of the three ingredients in the Cambridge Diet are as follows: 1.26 g from nonfat milk, .19 g from soy flour, and .8 g from whey. Another ingredient in the diet mixture is isolated soy protein, which provides the following nutrients in one unit: 80 g of protein, 0 g of carbohydrate, 3.4 g of fat, and .18 g of calcium.

Set up a matrix equation whose solution determines the amounts of nonfat milk, soy flour, whey, and isolated soy protein necessary to supply the precise amounts of protein, carbohydrate, fat, and calcium in the Cambridge Diet. State what the variables in the equation represent. Then solve the equation, if you have MATLAB or another matrix utility program available. Discuss your answer.

4. A dietician is planning a meal that supplies certain quantities of vitamin C, calcium, and magnesium. Three foods will be used, their quantities measured in appropriate units. The nutrients supplied by these foods and the dietary requirements are given.

	Milligrams of Nutrients per unit of Food			Total Nutrients Required
Nutrient	Food 1	Food 2	Food 3	(in mg)
Vitamin C	10	20	20	100
Calcium	50	40	10	300
Magnesium	30	10	40	200

a. Write a vector equation for this problem. State what the variables represent.

b. Solve the equation.

5. In a certain region, about 4% of the city's population moves to the surrounding suburbs each year and about 3% of the suburban population moves into the city. In 1990 there were 600,000 residents in the city and 400,000 in the suburbs.

a. Set up a difference equation that describes this situation, where $\mathbf{x}_0$ is the initial population in 1990.

b. Estimate the population in the city and in the suburbs two years later in 1992. (Ignore other factors that might influence the population sizes.)

6. In a certain region, about 6% of the city's population moves to the surrounding suburbs each year and about 4% of the suburban population moves into the city. In addition, due to movement into and out of the region, there is a net increase in the city population each year of 10,000 persons and a net increase in the suburban population of 8000 persons. In 1990 there were 800,000 residents in the city and 500,000 in the suburbs.

a. Set up a difference equation that describes this situation, where $\mathbf{x}_0$ is the initial population in 1990.

b. Estimate the population in the city and in the suburbs two years later, in 1992.

7. In 1990, the population of California was 29,716,000 and the population living in the United States but *outside* California was 218,994,000. During the year, 509,500 persons moved from California to elsewhere in the United States, while 564,100 persons moved into California from elsewhere in the United States.[3]

a. Set up the migration matrix for this situation, using 4 significant decimal places for the migration into and out of California.

b. Use MATLAB to compute the projected populations in the year 2000 for California and elsewhere in the United States.

c. In 1990, approximately 11.95% of the total U.S. population lived in California. Convert the population data from (b) into percentages. This calculation will give a better picture of the situation because total population *growth* during the 10 years was not included in the model for part (b).

8. Budget Rent A Car in Wichita, Kansas, has a fleet of about 450 cars, at three locations. A car rented at one location may be returned to any of the three locations. The various fractions of cars returned to each location are shown in the table below. Suppose that on Monday, there are 304 cars at the airport (or rented from there), 48 cars at the east side office, and 98 cars at the west side office. What will be the approximate distribution of cars on Wednesday?

Cars Rented From: Airport	East	West	Returned To
.97	.05	.10	Airport
.00	.90	.05	East
.03	.05	.85	West

9. Let M be the migration matrix in Example 2.

a. Use MATLAB to compute the population vectors $\mathbf{x}_k$ for $k = 1, \ldots, 20$. Discuss what you find.

b. Repeat (a) with an initial population of 350,000 in the city and 650,000 in the suburbs. What do you find?

[3] Migration data supplied by the Demographic Research Unit of the California State Department of Finance.

SOLUTION TO PRACTICE PROBLEM

$$A = \begin{bmatrix} 36 & 51 & 13 \\ 52 & 34 & 74 \\ 0 & 7 & 1.1 \end{bmatrix}, \quad \mathbf{x} = \begin{bmatrix} x_1 \\ x_2 \\ x_3 \end{bmatrix}, \quad \mathbf{b} = \begin{bmatrix} 33 \\ 45 \\ 3 \end{bmatrix}$$

CHAPTER 2 SUPPLEMENTARY EXERCISES

1. Mark each statement True or False. Justify each answer.

____ a. If an augmented matrix $[A \;\; \mathbf{b}]$ is transformed into $[C \;\; \mathbf{d}]$ by elementary row operations, then the equations $A\mathbf{x} = \mathbf{b}$ and $C\mathbf{x} = \mathbf{d}$ have exactly the same solution sets.

____ b. If A is a 3×2 matrix, the equation $A\mathbf{x} = \mathbf{0}$ necessarily has a nontrivial solution.

____ c. If a system $A\mathbf{x} = \mathbf{0}$ has a solution, so does the system $A\mathbf{x} = \mathbf{b}$.

____ d. If a system $A\mathbf{x} = \mathbf{b}$ has more than one solution, then so does the system $A\mathbf{x} = \mathbf{0}$.

____ e. If A is $m \times n$ and the equation $A\mathbf{x} = \mathbf{b}$ is consistent, then the columns of A span $\mathbb{R}^m$.

____ f. If an augmented matrix $[A \;\; \mathbf{b}]$ can be transformed by elementary row operations into reduced echelon form, then the equation $A\mathbf{x} = \mathbf{b}$ is consistent.

____ g. The equation $A\mathbf{x} = \mathbf{0}$ has the trivial solution if and only if there are no free variables.

____ h. If A is $m \times n$ and the equation $A\mathbf{x} = \mathbf{b}$ is consistent for every $\mathbf{b}$ in $\mathbb{R}^m$, then A must have n pivot columns.

____ i. If an $m \times n$ matrix A has m pivot columns, then the equation $A\mathbf{x} = \mathbf{b}$ has a unique solution for every $\mathbf{b}$ in $\mathbb{R}^m$.

____ j. If none of the $\mathbb{R}^3$ vectors in the set $S = \{\mathbf{v}_1, \mathbf{v}_2, \mathbf{v}_3\}$ is a multiple of one of the other vectors, then S is linearly independent.

____ k. In some cases, it is possible for four vectors to span $\mathbb{R}^5$.

____ l. If $\{\mathbf{u}, \mathbf{v}, \mathbf{w}\}$ is a linearly independent set, then $\mathbf{u}$, $\mathbf{v}$, and $\mathbf{w}$ are not in $\mathbb{R}^2$.

____ m. Suppose $\mathbf{u}, \mathbf{v}, \mathbf{w}$ are nonzero vectors in $\mathbb{R}^5$, $\mathbf{v}$ is not a multiple of $\mathbf{u}$, and $\mathbf{w}$ is not a linear combination of $\mathbf{u}$ and $\mathbf{v}$. Then $\{\mathbf{u}, \mathbf{v}, \mathbf{w}\}$ is linearly independent.

____ n. A linear transformation is a function.

____ o. If A is a 5×4 matrix, the linear transformation $\mathbf{x} \mapsto A\mathbf{x}$ cannot map $\mathbb{R}^4$ onto $\mathbb{R}^5$.

2. Consider the problem of determining whether the following system of equations is consistent:

$$\begin{aligned} 3x_1 - x_2 + 2x_3 &= 1 \\ -6x_1 + 3x_2 - 7x_3 &= 5 \end{aligned}$$

a. Define appropriate vectors, and restate the problem in terms of linear combinations. Then solve the problem.

b. Define an appropriate matrix, and restate the problem using the phrase "columns of A."

c. Define an appropriate linear transformation T using the matrix in (b), and restate the problem in terms of T.

3. Consider the problem of determining if the following system of equations is consistent for all b_1, b_2, b_3:

$$\begin{aligned} x_1 - 2x_2 &= b_1 \\ -5x_1 + 3x_2 &= b_2 \\ 3x_1 + x_2 &= b_3 \end{aligned}$$

a. Define appropriate vectors, and restate the problem in terms of Span $\{\mathbf{v}_1, \mathbf{v}_2\}$. Then solve the problem.

b. Define an appropriate matrix A, and restate the problem using the phrase "columns of A."

c. Define an appropriate linear transformation T using the matrix in (b), and restate the problem in terms of T.

4. Let A be a 3×3 matrix with the property that the linear transformation $\mathbf{x} \mapsto A\mathbf{x}$ maps $\mathbb{R}^3$ onto $\mathbb{R}^3$. Explain why the transformation must be one-to-one. [*Hint*: Think about pivot positions.]

5. Let $T : \mathbb{R}^n \to \mathbb{R}^m$ be a linear transformation and suppose $T(\mathbf{u}) = \mathbf{v}$. Show that $T(-\mathbf{u}) = -\mathbf{v}$.

6. Use a theorem to explain why the columns of

$$\begin{bmatrix} 1 & 0 & 0 & 0 \\ 2 & 5 & 0 & 0 \\ 3 & 6 & 8 & 0 \\ 4 & 7 & 9 & 10 \end{bmatrix}$$

are linearly independent. [*Hint*: Label the columns from right to left as $\mathbf{v}_1, \ldots, \mathbf{v}_4$.]

7. Suppose $\mathbf{v}_1, \mathbf{v}_2, \mathbf{v}_3$ are distinct points on one line in $\mathbb{R}^3$. The line need not pass through the origin. Show that $\{\mathbf{v}_1, \mathbf{v}_2, \mathbf{v}_3\}$ is linearly dependent.

8. Let $T : \mathbb{R}^3 \to \mathbb{R}^3$ be the linear transformation that reflects each vector in the plane $x_2 = 0$. That is, $T(x_1, x_2, x_3) = (x_1, -x_2, x_3)$. Find the matrix A that implements this transformation.

9. A *Givens rotation* is a linear transformation from $\mathbb{R}^n$ to $\mathbb{R}^n$ used in computer programs to create a zero entry in a vector (usually a column of a matrix). The standard matrix of a Givens rotation in $\mathbb{R}^2$ has the form

$$\begin{bmatrix} a & -b \\ b & a \end{bmatrix}, \qquad a^2 + b^2 = 1$$

Find a and b such that $\begin{bmatrix} 4 \\ 3 \end{bmatrix}$ is rotated into $\begin{bmatrix} 5 \\ 0 \end{bmatrix}$.

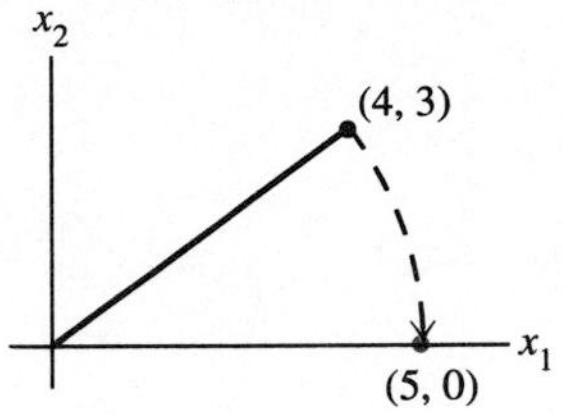

A Givens rotation in $\mathbb{R}^2$.

10. The following equation describes a Givens rotation in $\mathbb{R}^3$. Find a and b.

$$\begin{bmatrix} a & 0 & -b \\ 0 & 1 & 0 \\ b & 0 & a \end{bmatrix} \begin{bmatrix} 2 \\ 3 \\ 4 \end{bmatrix} = \begin{bmatrix} 2\sqrt{5} \\ 3 \\ 0 \end{bmatrix}, \qquad a^2 + b^2 = 1$$

3

Matrix Algebra

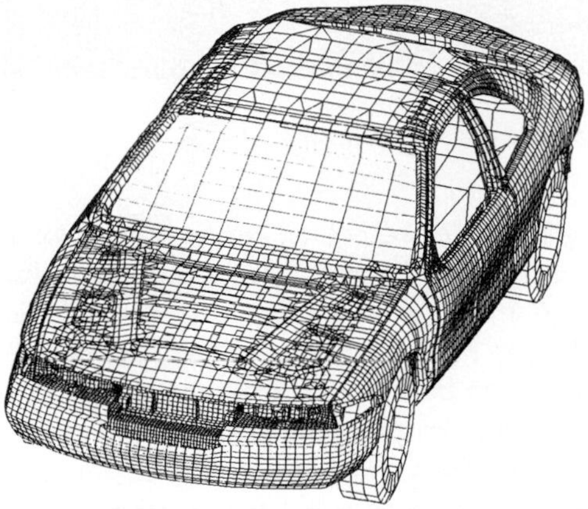

Introductory Example: Computer Graphics in Automotive Design

Computer-aided design (CAD) saves Ford Motor Company millions of dollars each year. First adopted by Ford in the early 1970s, CAD and CAM (computer-aided manufacturing) have revolutionized the automotive industry. Today, computer graphics forms the heart, and linear algebra the soul, of modern car design.

Many months before a new car model is built, engineers design and construct a mathematical car—a wire-frame model that exists only in computer memory and on graphics display terminals. (The 1993 Lincoln Mark VIII is shown above.) This mathematical model organizes and influences each step of the design and manufacture of the car. Working at more than 2600 graphics workstations, Ford engineers refine the original design, sculpt the flowing lines of the body, test the ability of metal sheets to withstand the forming and bending needed to produce the body, adjust the interior seating arrangements, plan and lay out mechanical parts, and produce the engineering drawings for thousands of components that suppliers will manufacture. The engineers even road test the suspension of the mathematical car, place the car in a mathematical wind tunnel, and repeatedly crash-test the car on the computer!

The wire-frame car model is stored as data in many matrices for each major component. Each column of a matrix lists the coordinates of one point on the component's surface. Additional columns describe which points to connect by curves. A three-dimensional scanner generates the original data points by passing sensors across a full-scale clay model of the car. Individual parts inside the car are stored as data matrices, too. The smallest components are sketched with computer graphics software at the computer screen, and large parts are formed by mathematically assembling smaller components.

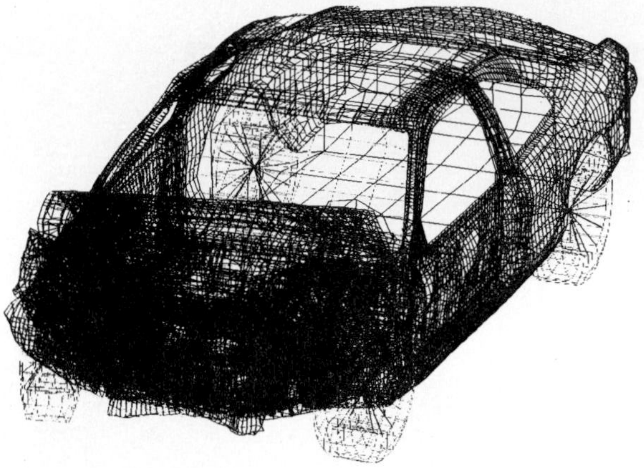

Wire-frame model in crash test.

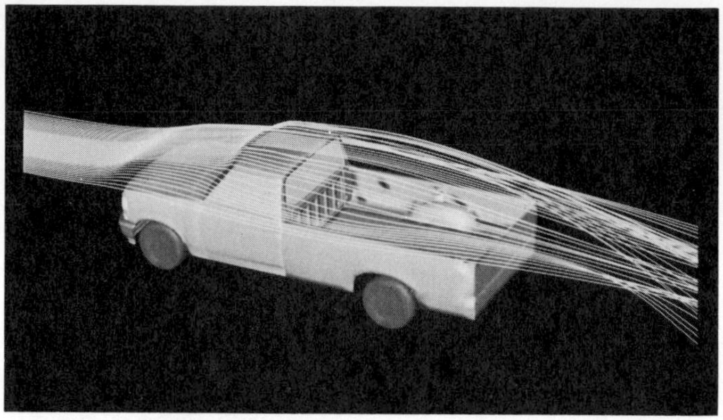

Truck in a mathematical wind tunnel.

Later, mathematical programs generate more points, curves, and color data to *render* the exterior car surfaces, making the mathematical car appear so realistic that it appears on the screen as if it were a real car in a dealer's showroom. Potential customers give their opinions as the car rotates on the "showroom floor." If the customers don't like the car, the design can be changed *before* the actual car is built.

Whether working on the overall body design, or modifying a small component part, engineers perform several basic operations on graphics images, such as changing the orientation or scale of a figure, zooming in on some small region, or switching between two- and three-dimensional views. Linear algebra is indeed the "soul" of the graphics software because all the manipulations of screen images are accomplished via linear algebra techniques. Section 3.8 (Computer Graphics) looks at the mathematics involved.

Our ability to analyze and solve equations will be greatly enhanced when we can perform algebraic operations with matrices. Furthermore, the definitions and theorems in this chapter provide some basic tools for handling the many applications of linear algebra that involve two or more matrices. For square matrices, the Invertible Matrix Theorem in Section 3.3 ties together most of the concepts treated earlier in the text. Sections 3.4 and 3.5 examine partitioned matrices and matrix factorizations, which appear in most modern uses of linear algebra. The chapter closes with two interesting applications of matrix algebra, to economics and computer graphics.

3.1 MATRIX OPERATIONS

If A is an $m \times n$ matrix—that is, a matrix with m rows and n columns—then the scalar entry in the ith row and jth column of A is denoted by a_{ij} and is called the (i, j)-entry of A. See Fig. 1. For instance, the $(3, 2)$-entry is the number a_{32} in the third row, second column. The columns of A are vectors in $\mathbb{R}^m$ and are denoted by (boldface) $\mathbf{a}_1, \ldots, \mathbf{a}_n$. We focus attention on these columns when we write

$$A = [\,\mathbf{a}_1 \quad \mathbf{a}_2 \quad \cdots \quad \mathbf{a}_n\,]$$

Observe that the number a_{ij} is the ith entry (from the top) of the jth column vector $\mathbf{a}_j$.

$$\begin{array}{ccc} & \begin{array}{c}\text{Column}\\ j\end{array} & \\ \text{Row i} & \begin{bmatrix} a_{11} & \cdots & a_{1j} & \cdots & a_{1n} \\ \vdots & & \vdots & & \vdots \\ a_{i1} & \cdots & a_{ij} & \cdots & a_{in} \\ \vdots & & \vdots & & \vdots \\ a_{m1} & \cdots & a_{mj} & \cdots & a_{mn} \end{bmatrix} & = \text{A} \\ & \begin{array}{ccccc} \uparrow & \quad & \uparrow & \quad & \uparrow \\ \mathbf{a}_1 & & \mathbf{a}_j & & \mathbf{a}_n \end{array} & \end{array}$$

FIGURE 1 Matrix notation.

Sums and Scalar Multiples

The arithmetic for vectors described earlier has a natural extension to matrices. We say that two matrices are **equal** if they have the same **size** (i.e., the same number of rows and columns) and if their corresponding entries are equal. If A and B are $m \times n$ matrices, then the **sum** $A + B$ is the $m \times n$ matrix whose columns are the sums of the corresponding columns in A and B. Since vector addition of the columns is done entrywise, each entry in $A + B$ is the sum of the corresponding entries in A and B. The sum $A + B$ is defined only when A and B are the same size.

EXAMPLE 1 Let

$$A = \begin{bmatrix} 4 & 0 & 5 \\ -1 & 3 & 2 \end{bmatrix}, \qquad B = \begin{bmatrix} 1 & 1 & 1 \\ 3 & 5 & 7 \end{bmatrix}, \qquad C = \begin{bmatrix} 2 & -3 \\ 0 & 1 \end{bmatrix}$$

Then

$$A + B = \begin{bmatrix} 5 & 1 & 6 \\ 2 & 8 & 9 \end{bmatrix}$$

but $A + C$ is not defined, since A and C are of different sizes.

If r is a scalar and A is a matrix, then the **scalar multiple** rA is the matrix whose columns are r times the corresponding columns in A. As with vectors, we define $-A$ to mean $(-1)A$, and we write $A - B$ in place of $A + (-1)B$. A matrix whose entries are all zeros is called a **zero matrix** and is written as 0. The size of 0 is usually clear from the context.

EXAMPLE 2 Let A and B be the matrices in Example 1. Compute $2B$ and $A - 2B$.

Solution

$$2B = 2\begin{bmatrix} 1 & 1 & 1 \\ 3 & 5 & 7 \end{bmatrix} = \begin{bmatrix} 2 & 2 & 2 \\ 6 & 10 & 14 \end{bmatrix}$$

$$A - 2B = \begin{bmatrix} 4 & 0 & 5 \\ -1 & 3 & 2 \end{bmatrix} - \begin{bmatrix} 2 & 2 & 2 \\ 6 & 10 & 14 \end{bmatrix} = \begin{bmatrix} 2 & -2 & 3 \\ -7 & -7 & -12 \end{bmatrix}$$

It was unnecessary in Example 2 to compute $A - 2B$ as $A + (-1)2B$ because the usual rules of algebra apply to sums and scalar multiples of matrices, as we see in the following theorem.

THEOREM 1

Let A, B, C be matrices of the same size, and let r and s be scalars.

a. $A + B = B + A$
b. $(A + B) + C = A + (B + C)$
c. $A + 0 = A$
d. $r(A + B) = rA + rB$
e. $(r + s)A = rA + sA$
f. $r(sA) = (rs)A$.

Each equality in Theorem 1 is verified by showing that the matrix on the left side has the same size as the matrix on the right and that corresponding columns are equal. Size is no problem because A, B, and C are equal in size. The equality of columns follows immediately from analogous properties of vectors. For instance, if the jth columns of A, B, and C, are $\mathbf{a}_j$, $\mathbf{b}_j$, and $\mathbf{c}_j$, respectively, then the jth columns of $(A + B) + C$ and $A + (B + C)$ are

$$(\mathbf{a}_j + \mathbf{b}_j) + \mathbf{c}_j \qquad \text{and} \qquad \mathbf{a}_j + (\mathbf{b}_j + \mathbf{c}_j)$$

respectively. Since these two vector sums are equal for each j, property (b) is verified.

Because of the associative property of addition, we may simply write $A + B + C$ for the sum, which may be computed either as $(A + B) + C$ or as $A + (B + C)$. The same applies to sums of four or more matrices.

Matrix Multiplication

When a matrix B multiplies a vector $\mathbf{x}$, it transforms $\mathbf{x}$ into the vector $B\mathbf{x}$. If this vector is then multiplied in turn by a matrix A, the resulting vector is $A(B\mathbf{x})$. See Fig. 2. Thus $A(B\mathbf{x})$ is produced from $\mathbf{x}$ by a *composition* of mappings, the linear transformations studied in Section 2.5. Our goal is to represent this composite mapping as multiplication by a single matrix, denoted by AB, so that

$$A(B\mathbf{x}) = (AB)\mathbf{x} \tag{1}$$

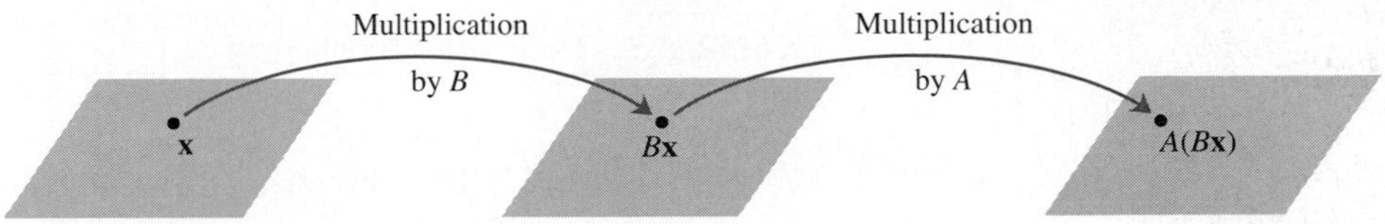

FIGURE 2 Multiplication by B and then A.

See Fig. 3.

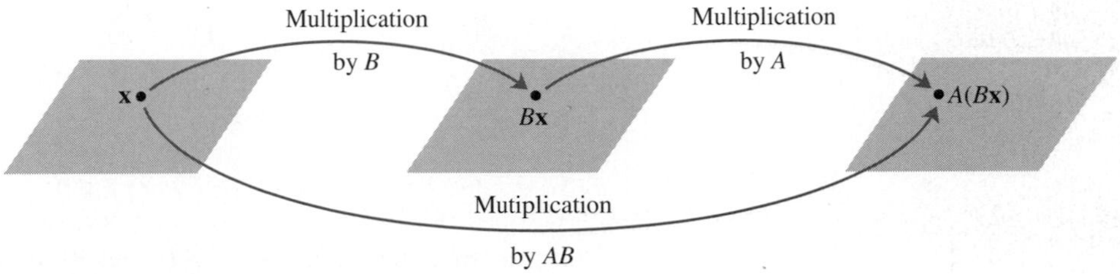

FIGURE 3 Multiplication by AB.

If A is $m \times n$, B is $n \times p$, and $\mathbf{x}$ is in $\mathbb{R}^p$, denote the columns of B by $\mathbf{b}_1, \ldots, \mathbf{b}_p$ and the entries in $\mathbf{x}$ by $x_1, \ldots, x_p$. Then

$$B\mathbf{x} = x_1\mathbf{b}_1 + \cdots + x_p\mathbf{b}_p$$

By the linearity of multiplication by A,

$$\begin{aligned} A(B\mathbf{x}) &= A(x_1\mathbf{b}_1) + \cdots + A(x_p\mathbf{b}_p) \\ &= x_1 A\mathbf{b}_1 + \cdots + x_p A\mathbf{b}_p \end{aligned}$$

The vector $A(B\mathbf{x})$ is a linear combination of the vectors $A\mathbf{b}_1, \ldots, A\mathbf{b}_p$, using the entries in $\mathbf{x}$ as weights. If we rewrite these vectors as the columns of a matrix, we have

$$A(B\mathbf{x}) = [\, A\mathbf{b}_1 \quad A\mathbf{b}_2 \quad \cdots \quad A\mathbf{b}_p \,]\mathbf{x}$$

Thus multiplication by $[\, A\mathbf{b}_1 \quad A\mathbf{b}_2 \quad \cdots \quad A\mathbf{b}_p \,]$ transforms $\mathbf{x}$ into $A(B\mathbf{x})$. We have found the matrix we sought!

DEFINITION

If A is an $m \times n$ matrix, and if B is an $n \times p$ matrix with columns $\mathbf{b}_1, \ldots, \mathbf{b}_p$, then AB is the $m \times p$ matrix whose columns are $A\mathbf{b}_1, \ldots, A\mathbf{b}_p$. That is,

$$AB = A[\, \mathbf{b}_1 \quad \mathbf{b}_2 \quad \cdots \quad \mathbf{b}_p \,] = [\, A\mathbf{b}_1 \quad A\mathbf{b}_2 \quad \cdots \quad A\mathbf{b}_p \,]$$

This definition makes (1) true for all $\mathbf{x}$ in $\mathbb{R}^p$. Equation (1) proves that the composite mapping in Fig. 3 is a linear transformation and that its standard matrix is AB. *Multiplication of matrices corresponds to composition of linear transformations.*

EXAMPLE 3 Compute AB, where $A = \begin{bmatrix} 2 & 3 \\ 1 & -5 \end{bmatrix}$ and $B = \begin{bmatrix} 4 & 3 & 6 \\ 1 & -2 & 3 \end{bmatrix}$.

Solution Write $B = [\mathbf{b}_1 \ \ \mathbf{b}_2 \ \ \mathbf{b}_3]$, and compute:

$$A\mathbf{b}_1 = \begin{bmatrix} 2 & 3 \\ 1 & -5 \end{bmatrix}\begin{bmatrix} 4 \\ 1 \end{bmatrix} = \begin{bmatrix} 11 \\ -1 \end{bmatrix}, \quad A\mathbf{b}_2 = \begin{bmatrix} 2 & 3 \\ 1 & -5 \end{bmatrix}\begin{bmatrix} 3 \\ -2 \end{bmatrix} = \begin{bmatrix} 0 \\ 13 \end{bmatrix}, \quad A\mathbf{b}_3 = \begin{bmatrix} 2 & 3 \\ 1 & -5 \end{bmatrix}\begin{bmatrix} 6 \\ 3 \end{bmatrix} = \begin{bmatrix} 21 \\ -9 \end{bmatrix}$$

Then

$$AB = A[\mathbf{b}_1 \ \ \mathbf{b}_2 \ \ \mathbf{b}_3] = \begin{bmatrix} 11 & 0 & 21 \\ -1 & 13 & -9 \end{bmatrix}$$

$$\uparrow \qquad \uparrow \qquad \uparrow$$
$$A\mathbf{b}_1 \quad A\mathbf{b}_2 \quad A\mathbf{b}_3$$

Observe from the definition of AB that its first column, $A\mathbf{b}_1$, is a linear combination of the columns of A using the entries in $\mathbf{b}_1$ as weights. The same holds true for each column of AB.

> Each column of AB is a linear combination of the columns of A using weights from the corresponding column of B.

Obviously, the number of columns of A must match the number of rows in B in order for a linear combination such as $A\mathbf{b}_1$ to be defined. Also, the definition of AB shows that *AB has the same number of rows as* A *and the same number of columns as* B.

EXAMPLE 4 If A is a 3×5 matrix and B is a 5×2 matrix, what are the sizes of AB and BA, if they are defined?

Solution Since A has 5 columns and B has 5 rows, the product AB is defined and is a 3×2 matrix:

$$\underset{3\times5}{\overset{A}{\begin{bmatrix} * & * & * & * & * \\ * & * & * & * & * \\ * & * & * & * & * \end{bmatrix}}} \underset{5\times2}{\overset{B}{\begin{bmatrix} * & * \\ * & * \\ * & * \\ * & * \\ * & * \end{bmatrix}}} = \underset{3\times2}{\overset{AB}{\begin{bmatrix} * & * \\ * & * \\ * & * \end{bmatrix}}}$$

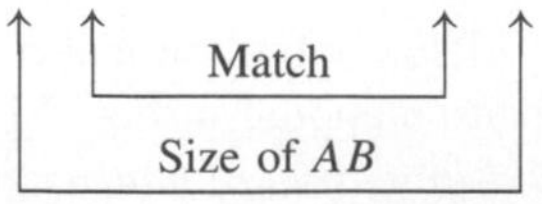

The product BA is *not* defined because the 2 columns of B do not match the 3 rows of A.

The definition of AB is important for theoretical work and applications, but the following rule provides a more efficient method for calculating the individual entries in AB when working small problems by hand.

Row–Column Rule for Computing AB. If the product AB is defined, then the entry in row i and column j of AB is the sum of the products of corresponding entries from row i of A and column j of B. If $(AB)_{ij}$ denotes the (i, j)-entry in AB, and if A is an $m \times n$ matrix, then

$$(AB)_{ij} = a_{i1}b_{1j} + a_{i2}b_{2j} + \cdots + a_{in}b_{nj}$$

To verify this rule, let $B = [\mathbf{b}_1 \ \cdots \ \mathbf{b}_p]$. Column j of AB is $A\mathbf{b}_j$, and we can compute $A\mathbf{b}_j$ by the "Rule for Computing $A\mathbf{x}$" from Section 2.2. The ith entry in $A\mathbf{b}_j$ is the sum of the products of corresponding entries from row i of A and the vector $\mathbf{b}_j$, which is precisely the computation described in the rule for computing the (i, j)-entry of AB.

EXAMPLE 5 Use the row–column rule to compute two of the entries in AB for the matrices in Example 3. An inspection of the numbers involved will make it clear how the two methods for calculating AB produce the same matrix.

Solution To find the entry in row 1 and column 3 of AB, consider row 1 of A and column 3 of B. Multiply corresponding entries and add the results, as shown below:

$$AB = \rightarrow \begin{bmatrix} 2 & 3 \\ 1 & -5 \end{bmatrix} \begin{bmatrix} 4 & 3 & \overset{\downarrow}{6} \\ 1 & -2 & 3 \end{bmatrix} = \begin{bmatrix} \square & \square & 2(6)+3(3) \\ \square & \square & \square \end{bmatrix} = \begin{bmatrix} \square & \square & 21 \\ \square & \square & \square \end{bmatrix}$$

For the entry in row 2 and column 2 of AB, use row 2 of A and column 2 of B:

$$\begin{array}{c} \\ \rightarrow \end{array} \begin{bmatrix} 2 & 3 \\ 1 & -5 \end{bmatrix} \begin{bmatrix} 4 & \overset{\downarrow}{3} & 6 \\ 1 & -2 & 3 \end{bmatrix} = \begin{bmatrix} \square & \square & 21 \\ \square & 1(3)+-5(-2) & \square \end{bmatrix} = \begin{bmatrix} \square & \square & 21 \\ \square & 13 & \square \end{bmatrix}$$

EXAMPLE 6 Find the entries in the second row of AB, where

$$A = \begin{bmatrix} 2 & -5 & 0 \\ -1 & 3 & -4 \\ 6 & -8 & -7 \\ -3 & 0 & 9 \end{bmatrix}, \quad B = \begin{bmatrix} 4 & -6 \\ 7 & 1 \\ 3 & 2 \end{bmatrix}$$

Solution By the row–column rule, the entries of the second row of AB come from row 2 of A (and the columns of B):

$$\rightarrow \begin{bmatrix} 2 & -5 & 0 \\ -1 & 3 & -4 \\ 6 & -8 & -7 \\ -3 & 0 & 9 \end{bmatrix} \begin{bmatrix} 4 & -6 \\ 7 & 1 \\ 3 & 2 \end{bmatrix}$$

$$= \begin{bmatrix} \square & \square \\ -4+21-12 & 6+3-8 \\ \square & \square \\ \square & \square \end{bmatrix} = \begin{bmatrix} \square & \square \\ 5 & 1 \\ \square & \square \\ \square & \square \end{bmatrix}$$

Notice that since Example 6 only requested the second row of AB, we could have written just the second row of A to the left of B and computed

$$\begin{bmatrix} -1 & 3 & -4 \end{bmatrix} \begin{bmatrix} 4 & -6 \\ 7 & 1 \\ 3 & 2 \end{bmatrix} = \begin{bmatrix} 5 & 1 \end{bmatrix}$$

This observation about rows of AB is true in general and follows immediately from the rule for computing AB stated above.

The ith row of AB is the ith row of A times B.

Properties of Matrix Multiplication

The following theorem lists the standard properties of matrix multiplication. Recall that I_m represents the $m \times m$ identity matrix and $I_m\mathbf{x} = \mathbf{x}$ for all $\mathbf{x}$ in $\mathbb{R}^m$.

THEOREM 2

Let A be $m \times n$ and let B and C have sizes for which the indicated sums and products are defined.

a. $A(BC) = (AB)C$ (associative law of multiplication)
b. $A(B + C) = AB + AC$ (left distributive law)
c. $(B + C)A = BA + CA$ (right distributive law)
d. $r(AB) = (rA)B = A(rB)$ for any scalar r
e. $I_mA = A = AI_n$ (identity for matrix multiplication)

Proof Properties (b)–(e) are considered in the exercises. Property (a) follows from the fact that matrix multiplication corresponds to composition of linear transformations (which are functions), and it is known (or easy to check) that the composition of functions is associative. Here is another proof of (a) that rests on the "column definition" of the product of two matrices. Let

$$C = [\mathbf{c}_1 \quad \cdots \quad \mathbf{c}_p]$$

By definition of matrix multiplication

$$\begin{aligned} BC &= [\,B\mathbf{c}_1 \quad \cdots \quad B\mathbf{c}_p\,] \\ A(BC) &= [\,A(B\mathbf{c}_1) \quad \cdots \quad A(B\mathbf{c}_p)\,] \end{aligned}$$

Recall from (1) that the definition of AB makes $A(B\mathbf{x}) = (AB)\mathbf{x}$ for all $\mathbf{x}$, so

$$A(BC) = [\,(AB)\mathbf{c}_1 \quad \cdots \quad (AB)\mathbf{c}_p\,] = (AB)C$$ ∎

The associative and distributive laws in Theorems 1 and 2 say essentially that pairs of parentheses in matrix expressions may be inserted and deleted in the same way as in the algebra of real numbers. In particular, we may write ABC for the product, that may be computed either as $A(BC)$ or as $(AB)C$.[1] Similarly, a product $ABCD$ of four matrices may be computed as $A(BCD)$ or $(ABC)D$ or $A(BC)D$, and so on. It does not matter how we group the matrices when computing the product, as long as the left-to-right order of the matrices is preserved.

The left-to-right order in products is critical because, in general, AB and BA are not the same. This is not surprising, because the columns of AB are linear combinations of the columns of A, while the columns of BA are constructed from the columns of B. If $AB = BA$, we say that A and B **commute** with one another.

EXAMPLE 7 Let $A = \begin{bmatrix} 5 & 1 \\ 3 & -2 \end{bmatrix}$ and $B = \begin{bmatrix} 2 & 0 \\ 4 & 3 \end{bmatrix}$. Show that these matrices do not commute. That is, verify that $AB \neq BA$.

Solution

$$AB = \begin{bmatrix} 5 & 1 \\ 3 & -2 \end{bmatrix}\begin{bmatrix} 2 & 0 \\ 4 & 3 \end{bmatrix} = \begin{bmatrix} 14 & 3 \\ -2 & -6 \end{bmatrix}$$

$$BA = \begin{bmatrix} 2 & 0 \\ 4 & 3 \end{bmatrix}\begin{bmatrix} 5 & 1 \\ 3 & -2 \end{bmatrix} = \begin{bmatrix} 10 & 2 \\ 29 & -2 \end{bmatrix}$$

∎

For emphasis, we include the remark about commutativity with the following list of important differences between matrix algebra and ordinary algebra of real numbers. See Exercises 16–18 for examples of these situations.

[1] When B is square and C has fewer columns than A has rows, it is more efficient to compute $A(BC)$ instead of $(AB)C$.

Warnings

1. In general, $AB \neq BA$.
2. The cancellation laws do *not* hold for matrix multiplication. That is, if $AB = AC$, then it is *not* true in general that $B = C$.
3. If a product AB is the zero matrix, you *cannot* conclude in general that either $A = 0$ or $B = 0$.

Powers of a Matrix

If A is an $n \times n$ matrix and if k is a nonnegative integer k, we write A^k for the product of k copies of A times the identity, that is

$$A^k = \underbrace{A \cdots A}_{k} \cdot I$$

This definition includes the case $A^0 = I$. We will use powers of matrices for applications in Section 3.7 and later in the text.

The Transpose of a Matrix

Given an $m \times n$ matrix A, the **transpose** of A is the $n \times m$ matrix, denoted by A^T, whose columns are formed from the corresponding rows of A.

EXAMPLE 8 Let

$$A = \begin{bmatrix} a & b \\ c & d \end{bmatrix}, \quad B = \begin{bmatrix} -5 & 2 \\ 1 & -3 \\ 0 & 4 \end{bmatrix}, \quad C = \begin{bmatrix} 1 & 1 & 1 & 1 \\ -3 & 5 & -2 & 7 \end{bmatrix}$$

Then

$$A^T = \begin{bmatrix} a & c \\ b & d \end{bmatrix}, \quad B^T = \begin{bmatrix} -5 & 1 & 0 \\ 2 & -3 & 4 \end{bmatrix}, \quad C^T = \begin{bmatrix} 1 & -3 \\ 1 & 5 \\ 1 & -2 \\ 1 & 7 \end{bmatrix}$$

THEOREM 3

Let A and B denote matrices whose sizes are appropriate for the following sums and products.

a. $(A^T)^T = A$
b. $(A + B)^T = A^T + B^T$
c. For any scalar r, $(rA)^T = rA^T$
d. $(AB)^T = B^T A^T$

Proofs of (a)–(c) are straightforward and are omitted. For (d), see Exercise 43. The generalization of (d) to products of more than two factors may be stated in words as follows.

> The transpose of a product of matrices equals the product of their transposes in the reverse order.

The exercises contain numerical examples that illustrate properties of transposes.

> **Numerical Notes**
>
> 1. The fastest way to obtain AB on a computer depends on the way the computer stores matrices in its memory. The standard high-performance algorithms, such as in LINPACK, calculate AB by columns as in our definition of the product.
> 2. The definition of AB lends itself well to parallel processing on a computer. The columns of B are assigned individually or in groups to different processors, which independently and hence simultaneously compute the corresponding columns of AB.

PRACTICE PROBLEMS

1. Since vectors in $\mathbb{R}^n$ may be regarded as $n\times 1$ matrices, the properties of transposes in Theorem 3 apply to vectors, too. Let

$$A = \begin{bmatrix} 1 & -3 \\ -2 & 4 \end{bmatrix} \quad \text{and} \quad \mathbf{x} = \begin{bmatrix} 5 \\ 3 \end{bmatrix}$$

Compute $(A\mathbf{x})^T$, $\mathbf{x}^TA^T$, $\mathbf{x}\mathbf{x}^T$, and $\mathbf{x}^T\mathbf{x}$. Is $A^T\mathbf{x}^T$ defined?

2. Let A be a 4×4 matrix and let $\mathbf{x}$ be a vector in $\mathbb{R}^4$. What is the fastest way to compute $A^2\mathbf{x}$? Count the multiplications.

3.1 EXERCISES

In Exercises 1–8, find the indicated matrix if it is defined; if it is undefined, explain why. Let

$$A = \begin{bmatrix} 7 & 0 & -1 \\ -1 & 5 & 2 \end{bmatrix}, \quad B = \begin{bmatrix} -1 & 4 & 1 \\ 5 & -3 & 0 \end{bmatrix},$$

$$C = \begin{bmatrix} 1 & 4 \\ -4 & 0 \end{bmatrix}, \quad D = \begin{bmatrix} 1 & 0 \\ -2 & 1 \end{bmatrix}, \quad E = \begin{bmatrix} 7 \\ -3 \end{bmatrix}$$

1. $-2A$
2. $A + B$
3. $B - 2A$
4. $3C - E$
5. AC
6. CB
7. CD
8. EB
9. Let $A = \begin{bmatrix} 4 & -1 \\ 3 & -2 \end{bmatrix}$. Compute $3I_2 - A$ and $(3I_2)A$.
10. Compute $A - I_3$ and $A - 2I_3$, when

$$A = \begin{bmatrix} 4 & -5 & 3 \\ 5 & 7 & -2 \\ -3 & 2 & -1 \end{bmatrix}$$

In Exercises 11 and 12, compute the product AB in two ways: (1) by the definition, where $A\mathbf{b}_1$ and $A\mathbf{b}_2$ are computed separately; and (2) by the rule for computing a product.

11. $A = \begin{bmatrix} 1 & 3 \\ 0 & 4 \\ -2 & 1 \end{bmatrix}$, $B = \begin{bmatrix} 2 & 3 \\ 1 & -1 \end{bmatrix}$

12. $A = \begin{bmatrix} 3 & 4 \\ 5 & 0 \\ 1 & 2 \end{bmatrix}$, $B = \begin{bmatrix} 3 & -1 \\ -1 & 2 \end{bmatrix}$

13. If a matrix A is 3×5 and the product AB is 3×7, what is the size of B?

14. How many rows does B have if BA is a 2×6 matrix?

15. With C, D, and E as in Exercises 1–8, compute $(CD)E$ and $C(DE)$. Which product requires fewer multiplications?

16. Let $A = \begin{bmatrix} 3 & -4 \\ -5 & 1 \end{bmatrix}$, $B = \begin{bmatrix} 7 & 4 \\ 5 & k \end{bmatrix}$. What value(s) of k, if any, will make $AB = BA$?

17. Let $A = \begin{bmatrix} 1 & 2 \\ 3 & 6 \end{bmatrix}$, $B = \begin{bmatrix} 3 & -8 \\ 2 & 3 \end{bmatrix}$, $C = \begin{bmatrix} 5 & 2 \\ 1 & -2 \end{bmatrix}$. Verify that $AB = AC$ and yet $B \neq C$.

18. Let $A = \begin{bmatrix} 2 & -6 \\ -1 & 3 \end{bmatrix}$. Find a 2×2 matrix B such that $AB = 0$. Use two different nonzero columns for B.

The **diagonal entries** in a matrix $A = [a_{ij}]$ are those with equal row and column indices, $a_{11}, a_{22}, a_{33}, \ldots$. A **diagonal matrix** is a square matrix whose nondiagonal entries are all zero.

19. Let $A = \begin{bmatrix} 1 & 1 & 1 \\ 1 & 2 & 3 \\ 1 & 4 & 5 \end{bmatrix}$ and $D = \begin{bmatrix} 2 & 0 & 0 \\ 0 & 3 & 0 \\ 0 & 0 & 4 \end{bmatrix}$. Compute AD and DA. Explain how the columns or rows of A change when A is multiplied by D on the right and on the left. Find a 3×3 diagonal matrix B (with $B \neq I$) such that $AB = BA$.

20. Choose two 3×3 diagonal matrices, and check if they commute.

In Exercises 21–26, assume that the matrix product AB is defined.

21. Suppose that the first two columns of B, $\mathbf{b}_1$ and $\mathbf{b}_2$, are equal. What does this tell you about the columns of AB? Why?

22. Suppose that the first and third rows of A are equal. What does this tell you about the rows of AB? Why?

23. Suppose that the third column of B is the sum of the first two columns. What can you say about the third column of AB? Why?

24. Suppose that the second column of B is all zeros. What can you say about the second column of AB?

25. Suppose that the last column of AB is entirely zero but B itself has no column of zeros. What can you say about the columns of A?

26. If $A = \begin{bmatrix} 1 & -2 \\ -2 & 5 \end{bmatrix}$ and $AB = \begin{bmatrix} -1 & 2 & -1 \\ 6 & -9 & 3 \end{bmatrix}$, determine the first and second columns of B.

Compute the indicated quantities in Exercises 27–30 using

$$A = \begin{bmatrix} 1 & 2 \\ -3 & 4 \end{bmatrix}, \quad B = \begin{bmatrix} -8 & 4 \\ -7 & 5 \end{bmatrix}, \quad \mathbf{u} = \begin{bmatrix} 5 \\ -2 \end{bmatrix}$$

Do not use Theorem 3 to simplify your work, but rather use these exercises to verify that Theorem 3 is correct for the vectors and matrices listed here.

27. A^T, B^T, $A^T + B^T$, $(A+B)^T$

28. $A\mathbf{u}$, $(A\mathbf{u})^T$, $\mathbf{u}^T A^T$

29. AB, $(AB)^T$, $A^T B^T$, $B^T A^T$

30. $(3A)^T$ and $3A^T$

In Exercises 31 and 32, view vectors in $\mathbb{R}^n$ as $n\times 1$ matrices. For $\mathbf{u}$, $\mathbf{v}$ in $\mathbb{R}^n$, the matrix product $\mathbf{u}^T\mathbf{v}$ is a 1×1 matrix, called the **scalar product**, or **inner product**, of $\mathbf{u}$ and $\mathbf{v}$. It is usually written as a single real number without brackets. The matrix product $\mathbf{u}\mathbf{v}^T$ is an $n\times n$ matrix, called the **outer product** of $\mathbf{u}$ and $\mathbf{v}$. The products $\mathbf{u}^T\mathbf{v}$ and $\mathbf{u}\mathbf{v}^T$ will appear later in the text.

31. Let $\mathbf{u} = \begin{bmatrix} -2 \\ 3 \\ -4 \end{bmatrix}$, $\mathbf{v} = \begin{bmatrix} a \\ b \\ c \end{bmatrix}$. Compute $\mathbf{u}^T\mathbf{v}$, $\mathbf{v}^T\mathbf{u}$, $\mathbf{u}\mathbf{v}^T$, and $\mathbf{v}\mathbf{u}^T$.

32. If $\mathbf{u}$ and $\mathbf{v}$ are in $\mathbb{R}^n$, how are $\mathbf{u}^T\mathbf{v}$ and $\mathbf{v}^T\mathbf{u}$ related? How are $\mathbf{u}\mathbf{v}^T$ and $\mathbf{v}\mathbf{u}^T$ related?

33. Let A and B be matrices with sizes 5×2 and 2×5, respectively. Give the sizes of the following matrices, if they are defined: AB, BA, $(AB)^T$, $(BA)^T$, $A^T B^T$, and $B^T A^T$. Why is it true in this case that $(AB)^T$ cannot equal $A^T B^T$?

34. Let $A = \begin{bmatrix} a & b \\ 0 & a \end{bmatrix}$ and $C = \begin{bmatrix} c & d \\ 0 & c \end{bmatrix}$. Compute $(AC)^T$ and $A^T C^T$.

35. Prove Theorem 1(d).

36. Prove Theorem 1(e).

37. Prove Theorem 2(b). Use the row–column rule. The (i, j)-entry in $A(B+C)$ may be written as

$$a_{i1}(b_{1j}+c_{1j})+\cdots+a_{in}(b_{nj}+c_{nj}) \quad \text{or} \quad \sum_{k=1}^{n} a_{ik}(b_{kj}+c_{kj})$$

38. Prove Theorem 2(c). [*Hint*: Use the row-column rule.]

39. Prove Theorem 2(d). [*Hint*: The (i, j)-entry in $(rA)B$ is $(ra_{i1})b_{1j} + \cdots + (ra_{in})b_{nj}$.]

40. Show that $I_m A = A$ when A is an $m \times n$ matrix. You may assume $I_m \mathbf{x} = \mathbf{x}$ for all $\mathbf{x}$ in $\mathbb{R}^m$.

41. Show that $AI_n = A$ when A is an $m \times n$ matrix. [*Hint*: Use the (column) definition of AI_n.]

42. Prove Theorem 3(b). [*Hint*: The (i, j)-entry of $(A + B)^T$ is the (j, i)-entry of $A + B$.]

43. Prove Theorem 3(d). [*Hint*: Consider the jth row of $(AB)^T$.]

44. Give a formula for $(AB\mathbf{x})^T$, where $\mathbf{x}$ is a vector and A and B are matrices of appropriate sizes.

SOLUTIONS TO PRACTICE PROBLEMS

1. $A\mathbf{x} = \begin{bmatrix} 1 & -3 \\ -2 & 4 \end{bmatrix}\begin{bmatrix} 5 \\ 3 \end{bmatrix} = \begin{bmatrix} -4 \\ 2 \end{bmatrix}$. So $(A\mathbf{x})^T = [\,-4 \quad 2\,]$. Also, $\mathbf{x}^T A^T = [\,5 \quad 3\,]\begin{bmatrix} 1 & -2 \\ -3 & 4 \end{bmatrix} = [\,-4 \quad 2\,]$. The quantities $(A\mathbf{x})^T$ and $\mathbf{x}^T A^T$ are equal, as we expect from Theorem 3(d). Next,

$$\mathbf{x}\mathbf{x}^T = \begin{bmatrix} 5 \\ 3 \end{bmatrix}[\,5 \quad 3\,] = \begin{bmatrix} 25 & 15 \\ 15 & 9 \end{bmatrix}$$

$$\mathbf{x}^T\mathbf{x} = [\,5 \quad 3\,]\begin{bmatrix} 5 \\ 3 \end{bmatrix} = [25 + 9] = 34$$

A 1×1 matrix such as $\mathbf{x}^T\mathbf{x}$ is usually written without the brackets. Finally, $A^T\mathbf{x}^T$ is not defined, because $\mathbf{x}^T$ does not have two rows to match the two columns of A^T.

2. The fastest way to compute $A^2\mathbf{x}$ is to compute $A(A\mathbf{x})$. The product $A\mathbf{x}$ requires 16 multiplications, 4 for each entry, and $A(A\mathbf{x})$ requires 16 more. In contrast, the product A^2 requires 64 multiplications, 4 for each of the 16 entries in A^2. After that, $A^2\mathbf{x}$ takes 16 more multiplications, for a total of 80.

3.2 THE INVERSE OF A MATRIX

In this section and the next, we consider only square matrices and we investigate the matrix analogue of the reciprocal or multiplicative inverse of a nonzero real number.

If A is an $n \times n$ matrix, it often happens that there is another $n \times n$ matrix C such that

$$AC = I \quad \text{and} \quad CA = I$$

where I is the $n \times n$ identity matrix. In this case, we say that A is **invertible** and we call C an **inverse** of A. If B were another inverse of A, then we would have $B = BI = B(AC) = (BA)C = IC = C$. Thus when A is invertible, its inverse is unique. We denote it by A^{-1}, so that

$$AA^{-1} = I \quad \text{and} \quad A^{-1}A = I$$

EXAMPLE 1 If $A = \begin{bmatrix} 2 & 5 \\ -3 & -7 \end{bmatrix}$ and $C = \begin{bmatrix} -7 & -5 \\ 3 & 2 \end{bmatrix}$, then

$$AC = \begin{bmatrix} 2 & 5 \\ -3 & -7 \end{bmatrix}\begin{bmatrix} -7 & -5 \\ 3 & 2 \end{bmatrix} = \begin{bmatrix} 1 & 0 \\ 0 & 1 \end{bmatrix} \quad \text{and}$$

$$CA = \begin{bmatrix} -7 & -5 \\ 3 & 2 \end{bmatrix}\begin{bmatrix} 2 & 5 \\ -3 & -7 \end{bmatrix} = \begin{bmatrix} 1 & 0 \\ 0 & 1 \end{bmatrix}$$

Thus $C = A^{-1}$.

Here is a simple formula for the inverse of a 2×2 matrix, along with a test to tell if the inverse exists.

THEOREM 4

Let $A = \begin{bmatrix} a & b \\ c & d \end{bmatrix}$. If $ad - bc \neq 0$, then A is invertible and

$$A^{-1} = \frac{1}{ad - bc}\begin{bmatrix} d & -b \\ -c & a \end{bmatrix}$$

If $ad - bc = 0$, then A is not invertible.

The simple proof of Theorem 4 is outlined in Exercises 21–22. The quantity $ad - bc$ is called the **determinant** of A, and we write

$$\det A = ad - bc$$

Theorem 4 says that a 2×2 matrix A is invertible if and only if $\det A \neq 0$.

EXAMPLE 2 Find the inverse of $A = \begin{bmatrix} 3 & 4 \\ 5 & 6 \end{bmatrix}$.

Solution We have $\det A = 3(6) - 4(5) = -2 \neq 0$. Hence A is invertible, and

$$A^{-1} = \frac{1}{-2}\begin{bmatrix} 6 & -4 \\ -5 & 3 \end{bmatrix} = \begin{bmatrix} 6/(-2) & -4/(-2) \\ -5/(-2) & 3/(-2) \end{bmatrix} = \begin{bmatrix} -3 & 2 \\ 5/2 & -3/2 \end{bmatrix}$$

Invertible matrices are indispensable in linear algebra—mainly for algebraic calculations and formula derivations, as in the next theorem. There are also occasions when an inverse matrix provides insight into a mathematical model of a real-life situation, as in Example 3.

THEOREM 5

If A is an invertible $n\times n$ matrix, then for each $\mathbf{b}$ in $\mathbb{R}^n$, the equation $A\mathbf{x} = \mathbf{b}$ has the unique solution $\mathbf{x} = A^{-1}\mathbf{b}$.

Proof Take any **b** in $\mathbb{R}^n$. A solution exists because, when $A^{-1}\mathbf{b}$ is substituted for **x**, we have $A\mathbf{x} = A(A^{-1}\mathbf{b}) = (AA^{-1})\mathbf{b} = I\mathbf{b} = \mathbf{b}$. So $A^{-1}\mathbf{b}$ is a solution. To prove the solution is unique, we show that if **u** is any solution, then **u** in fact must be $A^{-1}\mathbf{b}$. Indeed, if $A\mathbf{u} = \mathbf{b}$, we can multiply both sides by A^{-1} and obtain

$$A^{-1}A\mathbf{u} = A^{-1}\mathbf{b}, \qquad I\mathbf{u} = A^{-1}\mathbf{b}, \qquad \text{and} \qquad \mathbf{u} = A^{-1}\mathbf{b}$$ ∎

EXAMPLE 3 A horizontal elastic beam is supported at each end and is subjected to forces at points 1, 2, 3, as in Fig. 1. Let **f** in $\mathbb{R}^3$ list the forces at these points, and let **y** in $\mathbb{R}^3$ list the amounts of deflection (that is, movement) of the beam at the three points. Using Hooke's law in physics, it can be shown that

$$\mathbf{y} = D\mathbf{f}$$

where D is a *flexibility matrix*. Its inverse is called the *stiffness matrix*. Describe the physical significance of the columns of D and D^{-1}.

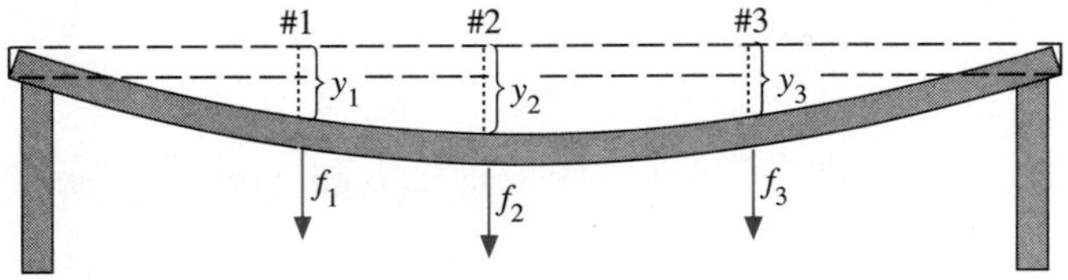

FIGURE 1 Deflection of an elastic beam.

Solution The vector $\mathbf{f} = (1, 0, 0)$ corresponds to a single force of 1 unit at point 1. The corresponding deflection vector is

$$\mathbf{y} = D\mathbf{f} = [\,\mathbf{d}_1 \quad \mathbf{d}_2 \quad \mathbf{d}_3\,]\begin{bmatrix}1\\0\\0\end{bmatrix} = 1\cdot\mathbf{d}_1 + 0\cdot\mathbf{d}_2 + 0\cdot\mathbf{d}_3 = \mathbf{d}_1$$

So the first column, $\mathbf{d}_1$, lists the deflections due to a force of 1 unit at point 1. Similar interpretations hold for $\mathbf{d}_2$ and $\mathbf{d}_3$.

To study the stiffness matrix, write $D^{-1} = [\,\mathbf{w}_1 \quad \mathbf{w}_2 \quad \mathbf{w}_3\,]$ and consider the deflection vector $\mathbf{y} = (1, 0, 0)$. By Theorem 5, the corresponding force vector is

$$\mathbf{f} = D^{-1}\mathbf{y} = [\,\mathbf{w}_1 \quad \mathbf{w}_2 \quad \mathbf{w}_3\,]\begin{bmatrix}1\\0\\0\end{bmatrix} = 1\cdot\mathbf{w}_1 + 0\cdot\mathbf{w}_2 + 0\cdot\mathbf{w}_3 = \mathbf{w}_1$$

The first column of D^{-1} gives the forces that must be applied at the three points in order to produce a deflection of 1 unit at point 1 and zero deflection at the other points. Similarly, $\mathbf{w}_2$ and $\mathbf{w}_3$ list the forces required to produce deflections of 1 unit at points 2 and 3, respectively. In each case, one or two of the forces will have to be negative (point upward) to produce the 1 unit deflections. If the flexibility is measured, for example, in inches of deflection per pound of load, then the stiffness matrix entries are given in pounds of load per inch of deflection.

The formula of Theorem 5 is seldom used to solve an equation $A\mathbf{x} = \mathbf{b}$ numerically because row reduction of $[A \quad \mathbf{b}]$ is nearly always faster. (Row reduction is usually more accurate, too, when computations involve rounding off numbers.) One possible exception is the 2×2 case. Mental computations to solve $A\mathbf{x} = \mathbf{b}$ are sometimes easier using the formula for A^{-1}, as in the next example.

EXAMPLE 4 Use the inverse of the matrix A in Example 2 to solve the system

$$\begin{aligned} 3x_1 + 4x_2 &= 3 \\ 5x_1 + 6x_2 &= 7 \end{aligned}$$

Solution This system is equivalent to $A\mathbf{x} = \mathbf{b}$, so

$$\mathbf{x} = A^{-1}\mathbf{b} = \begin{bmatrix} -3 & 2 \\ 5/2 & -3/2 \end{bmatrix} \begin{bmatrix} 3 \\ 7 \end{bmatrix} = \begin{bmatrix} 5 \\ -3 \end{bmatrix}$$

The next theorem provides three useful facts about invertible matrices.

THEOREM 6

a. If A is an invertible matrix, then A^{-1} is invertible and

$$(A^{-1})^{-1} = A$$

b. If A and B are $n \times n$ invertible matrices, then so is AB, and the inverse of AB is the product of the inverses of A and B in the reverse order. That is,

$$(AB)^{-1} = B^{-1}A^{-1}$$

c. If A is an invertible matrix, then so is A^T, and the inverse of A^T is the transpose of A^{-1}. That is,

$$(A^T)^{-1} = (A^{-1})^T$$

Proof

a. To show that A^{-1} is invertible, we must find a matrix C such that

$$A^{-1}C = I \qquad \text{and} \qquad CA^{-1} = I$$

However, we already know that these equations are satisfied with A in place of C. Hence A^{-1} is invertible and A is its inverse.

b. Using the associative law for multiplication, we find that

$$(AB)(B^{-1}A^{-1}) = A(BB^{-1})A^{-1} = AIA^{-1} = AA^{-1} = I$$

A similar calculation shows that $(B^{-1}A^{-1})(AB) = I$. Hence AB is invertible, and its inverse is $B^{-1}A^{-1}$. Part (c) is Exercise 20. ∎

The following generalization of Theorem 6(b) is needed later.

> The product of $n \times n$ invertible matrices is invertible, and the inverse is the product of their inverses in the reverse order.

There is an important connection between invertible matrices and row operations that leads to a method for computing inverses. As we shall see, an invertible matrix A is row equivalent to an identity matrix, and we can find A^{-1} by *watching the row reduction of* A *to* I.

Elementary Matrices

An **elementary matrix** is one that is obtained by performing a single elementary row operation on an identity matrix. The next example illustrates the three kinds of elementary matrices.

EXAMPLE 5 Let $E_1 = \begin{bmatrix} 1 & 0 & 0 \\ 0 & 1 & 0 \\ -4 & 0 & 1 \end{bmatrix}$, $E_2 = \begin{bmatrix} 0 & 1 & 0 \\ 1 & 0 & 0 \\ 0 & 0 & 1 \end{bmatrix}$, $E_3 = \begin{bmatrix} 1 & 0 & 0 \\ 0 & 1 & 0 \\ 0 & 0 & 5 \end{bmatrix}$. Compute E_1A, E_2A, and E_3A, where $A = \begin{bmatrix} a & b & c \\ d & e & f \\ g & h & i \end{bmatrix}$, and describe how these products may be obtained by elementary row operations on A.

Solution We have

$$E_1A = \begin{bmatrix} a & b & c \\ d & e & f \\ g-4a & h-4b & i-4c \end{bmatrix}, \quad E_2A = \begin{bmatrix} d & e & f \\ a & b & c \\ g & h & i \end{bmatrix}$$

$$E_3A = \begin{bmatrix} a & b & c \\ d & e & f \\ 5g & 5h & 5i \end{bmatrix}$$

Addition of -4 times row 1 of A to row 3 produces E_1A. (This is a row replacement operation.) An interchange of rows 1 and 2 of A produces E_2A, and multiplication of row 3 of A by 5 produces E_3A. ∎

Left-multiplication (that is, multiplication on the left) by E_1 in Example 5 has the same effect on any $3 \times n$ matrix. It adds -4 times row 1 to row 3. In particular, since $E_1 \cdot I = E_1$, we see that E_1 *itself* is produced by this same row operation on the identity. Thus Example 5 illustrates the following general fact about elementary matrices. See Exercises 23–28.

> If an elementary row operation is performed on an $m \times n$ matrix A, the resulting matrix may be written as EA, where E is created by performing the same row operation on I_m.

Since row operations are reversible, as we showed in Section 1.1, elementary matrices are invertible, for if E is produced by a row operation on I, then there is another row operation of the same type that will change E back into I. Hence there is an elementary matrix F such that $FE = I$. Since E and F correspond to reverse operations, $EF = I$, too.

> Each elementary matrix E is invertible. The inverse of E is the elementary matrix of the same type that transforms E back into I.

EXAMPLE 6 Find the inverse of $E_1 = \begin{bmatrix} 1 & 0 & 0 \\ 0 & 1 & 0 \\ -4 & 0 & 1 \end{bmatrix}$.

Solution To transform E_1 into I, add +4 times row 1 to row 3. The elementary matrix that does this is

$$E_1^{-1} = \begin{bmatrix} 1 & 0 & 0 \\ 0 & 1 & 0 \\ +4 & 0 & 1 \end{bmatrix}$$

Using elementary matrices, we can prove the following theorem, which leads immediately to a method for finding the inverse of a matrix.

THEOREM 7

> An $n \times n$ matrix A is invertible if and only if A is row equivalent to I_n, and in this case, any sequence of elementary row operations that reduces A to I_n also transforms I_n into A^{-1}.

Proof Suppose A is invertible. Then, since the equation $A\mathbf{x} = \mathbf{b}$ has a solution for each $\mathbf{b}$ (Theorem 5), A has a pivot position in every row (Theorem 2 in Section 2.2). Because A is square, the n pivot positions must be on the diagonal, which implies that the reduced echelon form of A is I_n. That is, $A \sim I_n$.

Now suppose, conversely, that $A \sim I_n$. Then, since each step of the row reduction of A corresponds to left-multiplication by an elementary matrix, there exist elementary matrices $E_1, \dots, E_p$ such that

$$A \sim E_1 A \sim E_2 E_1 A \sim \cdots \sim E_p \cdots E_1 A = I_n \tag{1}$$

Since the product $E_p \cdots E_1$ of invertible matrices is invertible, the equation at the end of (1) leads to

$$\begin{aligned}(E_p \cdots E_1)^{-1}(E_p \cdots E_1)A &= (E_p \cdots E_1)^{-1}I_n \\ A &= (E_p \cdots E_1)^{-1}\end{aligned}$$

Thus A is invertible, as it is the inverse of an invertible matrix (Theorem 6). Also,

$$A^{-1} = [(E_p \cdots E_1)^{-1}]^{-1} = E_p \cdots E_1$$

Then $A^{-1} = E_p \cdots E_1 \cdot I$, which says that A^{-1} results from applying $E_1, \ldots, E_p$ successively to I_n. This is the same sequence in (1) that reduced A to I_n. ▮

An Algorithm for Finding A^{-1}

If we place A and I side-by-side to form an augmented matrix $[\,A \quad I\,]$, then row operations on this matrix produce identical operations on A and on I. By Theorem 7, either there are row operations that transform A to I_n, and I_n to A^{-1}, or else A is not invertible.

> **Algorithm for Finding A^{-1}.** Row reduce the augmented matrix $[\,A \quad I\,]$. If A is row equivalent to I, then $[\,A \quad I\,]$ is row equivalent to $[\,I \quad A^{-1}\,]$. Otherwise, A does not have an inverse.

EXAMPLE 7 Find the inverse of the matrix $A = \begin{bmatrix} 0 & 1 & 2 \\ 1 & 0 & 3 \\ 4 & -3 & 8 \end{bmatrix}$, if it exists.

Solution

$$[\,A \quad I\,] = \begin{bmatrix} 0 & 1 & 2 & 1 & 0 & 0 \\ 1 & 0 & 3 & 0 & 1 & 0 \\ 4 & -3 & 8 & 0 & 0 & 1 \end{bmatrix} \sim \begin{bmatrix} 1 & 0 & 3 & 0 & 1 & 0 \\ 0 & 1 & 2 & 1 & 0 & 0 \\ 4 & -3 & 8 & 0 & 0 & 1 \end{bmatrix}$$

$$\sim \begin{bmatrix} 1 & 0 & 3 & 0 & 1 & 0 \\ 0 & 1 & 2 & 1 & 0 & 0 \\ 0 & -3 & -4 & 0 & -4 & 1 \end{bmatrix} \sim \begin{bmatrix} 1 & 0 & 3 & 0 & 1 & 0 \\ 0 & 1 & 2 & 1 & 0 & 0 \\ 0 & 0 & 2 & 3 & -4 & 1 \end{bmatrix}$$

$$\sim \begin{bmatrix} 1 & 0 & 3 & 0 & 1 & 0 \\ 0 & 1 & 2 & 1 & 0 & 0 \\ 0 & 0 & 1 & 3/2 & -2 & 1/2 \end{bmatrix}$$

$$\sim \begin{bmatrix} 1 & 0 & 0 & -9/2 & 7 & -3/2 \\ 0 & 1 & 0 & -2 & 4 & -1 \\ 0 & 0 & 1 & 3/2 & -2 & 1/2 \end{bmatrix}$$

Since $A \sim I$, we conclude that A is invertible by Theorem 7, and

$$A^{-1} = \begin{bmatrix} -9/2 & 7 & -3/2 \\ -2 & 4 & -1 \\ 3/2 & -2 & 1/2 \end{bmatrix}$$

It is a good idea to check the final answer:

$$AA^{-1} = \begin{bmatrix} 0 & 1 & 2 \\ 1 & 0 & 3 \\ 4 & -3 & 8 \end{bmatrix} \begin{bmatrix} -9/2 & 7 & -3/2 \\ -2 & 4 & -1 \\ 3/2 & -2 & 1/2 \end{bmatrix} = \begin{bmatrix} 1 & 0 & 0 \\ 0 & 1 & 0 \\ 0 & 0 & 1 \end{bmatrix}$$

It is not necessary to check that $A^{-1}A = I$ since A is invertible. ∎

Another View of Matrix Inversion

Denote the columns of I_n by $\mathbf{e}_1, \ldots, \mathbf{e}_n$. Then row reduction of $[\,A \quad I\,]$ to $[\,I \quad A^{-1}\,]$ may be viewed as the simultaneous solution of the n systems

$$A\mathbf{x} = \mathbf{e}_1, \quad A\mathbf{x} = \mathbf{e}_2, \quad \ldots, \quad A\mathbf{x} = \mathbf{e}_n \tag{2}$$

where the "augmented columns" of these systems have all been placed next to A to form $[\,A \quad \mathbf{e}_1 \quad \mathbf{e}_2 \quad \cdots \quad \mathbf{e}_n\,] = [\,A \quad I\,]$. The equation $AA^{-1} = I$ and the definition of matrix multiplication show that the columns of A^{-1} are precisely the solutions of the systems in (2). This observation is useful because in some applied problems one may only need to find one or two columns of A^{-1}. In this case, only the corresponding systems in (2) need be solved.

PRACTICE PROBLEMS

1. Use determinants to determine which of the following matrices are invertible.

   a. $\begin{bmatrix} 3 & -9 \\ 2 & 6 \end{bmatrix}$ b. $\begin{bmatrix} 4 & -9 \\ 0 & 5 \end{bmatrix}$ c. $\begin{bmatrix} 6 & -9 \\ -4 & 6 \end{bmatrix}$

2. Find the inverse of the matrix $A = \begin{bmatrix} 1 & -2 & -1 \\ -1 & 5 & 6 \\ 5 & -4 & 5 \end{bmatrix}$, if it exists.

3.2 EXERCISES

Find the inverses of the matrices in Exercises 1–4.

1. $\begin{bmatrix} 3 & -8 \\ -1 & 3 \end{bmatrix}$

2. $\begin{bmatrix} -4 & -5 \\ 5 & 6 \end{bmatrix}$

3. $\begin{bmatrix} 3 & -7 \\ -6 & 13 \end{bmatrix}$

4. $\begin{bmatrix} 7 & 9 \\ -6 & -8 \end{bmatrix}$

5. Use the inverse found in Exercise 1 to solve the system:

$$3x_1 - 8x_2 = 5$$
$$-x_1 + 3x_2 = 2$$

6. Use the inverse found in Exercise 3 to solve the system

$$3x_1 - 7x_2 = -4$$
$$-6x_1 + 13x_2 = 1$$

7. Let $A = \begin{bmatrix} 1 & 2 \\ 3 & 8 \end{bmatrix}$, $\mathbf{b}_1 = \begin{bmatrix} 5 \\ 7 \end{bmatrix}$, $\mathbf{b}_2 = \begin{bmatrix} -2 \\ -2 \end{bmatrix}$, $\mathbf{b}_3 = \begin{bmatrix} 3 \\ 5 \end{bmatrix}$, $\mathbf{b}_4 = \begin{bmatrix} 1 \\ 7 \end{bmatrix}$.

a. Find A^{-1}, and use it to solve the four equations

$$A\mathbf{x} = \mathbf{b}_1, \quad A\mathbf{x} = \mathbf{b}_2, \quad A\mathbf{x} = \mathbf{b}_3, \quad A\mathbf{x} = \mathbf{b}_4$$

b. The four equations in part (a) may be solved by the *same* set of row operations, since the coefficient matrix is the same in each case. Solve the four equations in part (a) by row reducing the augmented matrix $[\,A \quad \mathbf{b}_1 \quad \mathbf{b}_2 \quad \mathbf{b}_3 \quad \mathbf{b}_4\,]$.

8. Let $A = \begin{bmatrix} 5 & 13 \\ 3 & 8 \end{bmatrix}$, $\mathbf{b}_1 = \begin{bmatrix} 1 \\ -1 \end{bmatrix}$, $\mathbf{b}_2 = \begin{bmatrix} -2 \\ 1 \end{bmatrix}$, $\mathbf{b}_3 = \begin{bmatrix} 4 \\ 2 \end{bmatrix}$, $\mathbf{b}_4 = \begin{bmatrix} 1 \\ 1 \end{bmatrix}$.

a. Find A^{-1} and use it to solve the four equations

$$A\mathbf{x} = \mathbf{b}_1, \qquad A\mathbf{x} = \mathbf{b}_2, \qquad A\mathbf{x} = \mathbf{b}_3, \qquad A\mathbf{x} = \mathbf{b}_4$$

b. Solve the four equations in part (a), using the method of Exercise 7(b). Observe that the arithmetic is unpleasant by hand. What conclusions can you draw about the relative merits of the two methods?

9. Let A be an invertible $n \times n$ matrix, and let B be $n \times p$.

a. Show that the equation $AX = B$ has a unique solution, $A^{-1}B$.

b. Explain why $A^{-1}B$ can be computed by row reduction:

> If $[\,A \quad B\,] \sim \cdots \sim [\,I \quad X\,]$, then $X = A^{-1}B$.

If A is larger than 2×2, then row reduction of $[\,A \quad B\,]$ is much faster than computing both A^{-1} and $A^{-1}B$.

10. Use matrix algebra to show that if A is invertible and C satisfies $AC = I$, then $C = A^{-1}$.

11. Explain why the equation $A\mathbf{x} = \mathbf{0}$ has only the trivial solution when A is invertible.

12. Explain why the columns of A are linearly independent when A is invertible.

13. Suppose $AB = AC$, where B and C are $n \times p$ matrices and A is invertible. Show that $B = C$. Is this true, in general, if A is not invertible?

14. Suppose $(B - C)A = 0$, where B and C are $m \times n$ matrices and A is invertible. Show that $B = C$.

15. Suppose A, B, and C are invertible $n \times n$ matrices. Show that ABC is also invertible by producing a matrix D such that $(ABC)D = I$ and $D(ABC) = I$.

16. Suppose A and B are $n \times n$, B is invertible, and AB is invertible. Show that A is invertible. [*Hint*: Let $C = AB$, and solve this equation for A.]

17. Solve the equation $AB = BC$ for A, assuming that A, B, and C are square and B is invertible.

18. Suppose P is invertible and $A = PBP^{-1}$. Solve for B in terms of A.

19. Solve the equation $C^{-1}(A + X)B^{-1} = I$ for X, assuming that A, B, and C are all $n \times n$ invertible matrices.

20. Verify Theorem 6(c).

Exercises 21 and 22 prove Theorem 4 for $A = \begin{bmatrix} a & b \\ c & d \end{bmatrix}$.

21. Show that if $ad - bc = 0$, then the equation $A\mathbf{x} = \mathbf{0}$ has more than one solution. Why does this imply that A is not invertible? [*Hint*: If a and b are not both zero, consider the vector $\mathbf{x} = \begin{bmatrix} -b \\ a \end{bmatrix}$.]

22. Show that if $ad - bc \neq 0$, the formula for A^{-1} works.

The matrices described in Exercises 23–28 illustrate the three basic kinds of elementary matrices. The matrices I and A mentioned in these problems refer to the 4×4 matrix I and

$$A = \begin{bmatrix} 1 & 0 & 0 & 0 \\ 2 & 1 & 0 & 0 \\ 3 & 2 & 1 & 0 \\ 4 & 3 & 2 & 1 \end{bmatrix}$$

23. Construct E by interchanging two rows of I. (You choose the rows.) Then compute EA. What effect on A does multiplication on the left by E produce? Would the same conclusion be true for any 4×4 matrix A?

24. With E as in Exercise 23, find a matrix F such that left-multiplication by F transforms E back into I, that is, $FE = I$.

25. Construct E by multiplying the third row of I by 5. Then compute EA. What effect on A does left-multiplication by E produce? Would the same conclusion be true for any 4×4 matrix A?

26. Find the inverse of the matrix E in Exercise 25.

27. Construct E by adding -3 times row 2 of I to row 4. Then compute EA. What effect on A does left-multiplication by E produce? Would the same conclusion be true for any 4×4 matrix?

28. With E as in Exercise 27, find a matrix F such that left-multiplication by F transforms E back into I, that is, $FE = I$. Verify that $EF = I$.

Find the inverses of the matrices in Exercises 29–34, when they exist. Use the method of this section.

29. $\begin{bmatrix} 1 & 2 \\ 5 & 9 \end{bmatrix}$

30. $\begin{bmatrix} -3 & 6 \\ -1 & 3 \end{bmatrix}$

31. $\begin{bmatrix} 1 & 0 & 5 \\ 1 & 1 & 0 \\ 3 & 2 & 6 \end{bmatrix}$

32. $\begin{bmatrix} 1 & 4 & -3 \\ -2 & -7 & 6 \\ 1 & 7 & -2 \end{bmatrix}$

33. $\begin{bmatrix} 1 & 3 & -1 \\ 0 & 1 & 2 \\ -1 & 0 & 8 \end{bmatrix}$ **34.** $\begin{bmatrix} 1 & 5 & 0 \\ -2 & -7 & 6 \\ 1 & 3 & -4 \end{bmatrix}$

35. Let $A = \begin{bmatrix} -1 & -5 & -7 \\ 2 & 5 & 6 \\ 1 & 3 & 4 \end{bmatrix}$. Find the third column of A^{-1} without computing the other columns.

36. With A as in Exercise 35, find the second column of A^{-1} without computing the other columns.

Exercises 37 and 38 concern the flexibility matrix D described in Example 3, with flexibility measured in inches per pound, and

$$D = \begin{bmatrix} .005 & .002 & .001 \\ .002 & .004 & .002 \\ .001 & .002 & .005 \end{bmatrix}$$

37. Suppose forces of 20, 50, and 10 pounds are applied at points 1, 2, and 3, respectively, in Fig. 1 on page 109. Find the corresponding deflections.

38. Compute the stiffness matrix D^{-1}. List the forces needed to produce a deflection of .08 in. at point 1, with zero deflection at the other points.

39. Let $A = \begin{bmatrix} 2 & 5 \\ -1 & -3 \\ 2 & 4 \end{bmatrix}$ and let $C = \begin{bmatrix} 1 & 3 & 1 \\ 1 & 0 & -1 \end{bmatrix}$. Verify that $CA = I$. Is A invertible? Why or why not?

40. Let $A = \begin{bmatrix} 1/3 & -2/3 & 2/3 \\ 2/3 & 2/3 & 1/3 \end{bmatrix}$ and let $D = A^T$. Verify that $AD = I$. Is A invertible? Why or why not?

SOLUTIONS TO PRACTICE PROBLEMS

1. a. $\det \begin{bmatrix} 3 & -9 \\ 2 & 6 \end{bmatrix} = 3\cdot 6 - (-9)\cdot 2 = 18 + 18 = 36$. The determinant is nonzero, so the matrix is invertible.

b. $\det \begin{bmatrix} 4 & -9 \\ 0 & 5 \end{bmatrix} = 4\cdot 5 - (-9)\cdot 0 = 20 \neq 0$. The matrix is invertible.

c. $\det \begin{bmatrix} 6 & -9 \\ -4 & 6 \end{bmatrix} = 6\cdot 6 - (-9)(-4) = 36 - 36 = 0$. The matrix is not invertible.

2.

$$[\,A \quad I\,] \sim \begin{bmatrix} 1 & -2 & -1 & 1 & 0 & 0 \\ -1 & 5 & 6 & 0 & 1 & 0 \\ 5 & -4 & 5 & 0 & 0 & 1 \end{bmatrix} \sim \begin{bmatrix} 1 & -2 & -1 & 1 & 0 & 0 \\ 0 & 3 & 5 & 1 & 1 & 0 \\ 0 & 6 & 10 & -5 & 0 & 1 \end{bmatrix}$$

$$\sim \begin{bmatrix} 1 & -2 & -1 & 1 & 0 & 0 \\ 0 & 3 & 5 & 1 & 1 & 0 \\ 0 & 0 & 0 & -7 & -2 & 1 \end{bmatrix}$$

We have obtained a matrix of the form $[\,B \quad D\,]$ where B is square and has a row of zeros. Further row operations will not transform B into I, so we stop. A does not have an inverse.

3.3 CHARACTERIZATIONS OF INVERTIBLE MATRICES

This section provides a review of most of the concepts introduced in the first three chapters of the text, in relation to systems of n linear equations in n unknowns and to *square* matrices. The main result is Theorem 8.

THEOREM 8

The Invertible Matrix Theorem

Let A be a square $n \times n$ matrix. Then the following statements are equivalent. That is, for given A, the statements are either all true or all false.

a. A is an invertible matrix.

b. A is row equivalent to the $n \times n$ identity matrix.

c. A is a product of elementary matrices.

d. The equation $A\mathbf{x} = \mathbf{0}$ has only the trivial solution.

e. The equation $A\mathbf{x} = \mathbf{b}$ has at least one solution for each $\mathbf{b}$ in $\mathbb{R}^n$.

f. There is an $n \times n$ matrix C such that $AC = I$.

g. There is an $n \times n$ matrix D such that $DA = I$.

h. A^T is an invertible matrix.

Several other statements are easily added to Theorem 8. Because A is square, statement (b) is equivalent to

b′. A has n pivot positions.

We know from Section 2.4 that statement (d) is equivalent to

d′. The columns of A form a linearly independent set.

Now consider the statement:

e′. The equation $A\mathbf{x} = \mathbf{b}$ has a *unique* solution for each $\mathbf{b}$ in $\mathbb{R}^n$.

This statement certainly implies the formally "weaker" statement (e). By Theorem 8 (still to be proved), (e) implies that A is invertible, which in turn implies (e′) again, by Theorem 5 in Section 3.2. So (e) and (e′) are equivalent if Theorem 8 is true. Next, observe from Theorem 2 in Section 2.2 that (e) is equivalent to

e″. The columns of A span $\mathbb{R}^n$.

Furthermore, if we view A as implementing a linear transformation, then Theorem 10 in Section 2.6 says that (d′) and (e″) are equivalent, respectively, to

d″. The linear transformation $\mathbf{x} \mapsto A\mathbf{x}$ is one-to-one.

e‴. The linear transformation $\mathbf{x} \mapsto A\mathbf{x}$ maps $\mathbb{R}^n$ onto $\mathbb{R}^n$.

Finally, if (a) is equivalent to (h), each of the other statements about A gives rise to an analogous statement about A^T. We will refrain from writing them unless we have need for such results.

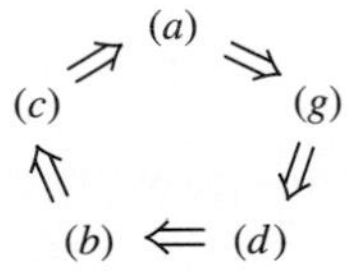

FIGURE 1

Proof of Theorem 8 First we need some notation (also used later in the text). If statement (b) is true whenever statement (a) is true, we say that (a) *implies* (b), and we write (a) ⇒ (b). We will establish a "circle" of implications, as shown in Fig. 1. If any one of these five statements is true, then so are the others. Then we will link the remaining statements to the statements in this circle.

(a) ⇒ (g) ⇒ (d)

If (a) is true, then A^{-1} works for D in (g), so (a) ⇒ (g). If (g) is true and if $\mathbf{x}$ satisfies $A\mathbf{x} = \mathbf{0}$, then left-multiplying by D and using (g), we have $DA\mathbf{x} = D\mathbf{0}$, so

$I\mathbf{x} = \mathbf{0}$. Thus $\mathbf{x} = \mathbf{0}$, which shows that (d) is true whenever (g) is true. So (g) $\Rightarrow$ (d).

(d) $\Rightarrow$ (b) If (d) is true, then the equation $A\mathbf{x} = \mathbf{0}$ has no free variables and n basic variables, which means that A is row equivalent to a reduced echelon matrix R with n leading ones. Since A and R are square, R must be the $n \times n$ identity matrix, I_n. Thus (d) implies (b).

(b) $\Rightarrow$ (c) $\Rightarrow$ (a) If (b) is true, there exist elementary matrices such that $(E_p \cdots E_1)A = I_n$. Hence $A = (E_p \cdots E_1)^{-1} I_n = E_1^{-1} \cdots E_p^{-1}$, by Theorem 6 in Section 3.2. Since $E_1^{-1}, \ldots, E_p^{-1}$ are elementary matrices, (c) is true. Also, if A is a product of elementary matrices (which are always invertible), then A itself is invertible, by Theorem 6. Thus (b) $\Rightarrow$ (c) and (c) $\Rightarrow$ (a). This completes the circle in Fig. 1.

(b) $\Rightarrow$ (e) and (e) $\Rightarrow$ (b) Since A is square, the equivalence of (b) and (e) follows from Theorem 2 in Section 2.2.

(f) $\Rightarrow$ (h) $\Rightarrow$ (a) $\Rightarrow$ (f) Finally, suppose (f) is true and $AC = I$. Then $C^TA^T = (AC)^T = I^T = I$. Applying the already known equivalence of (a) and (g) to A^T, we conclude that A^T is invertible. So (f) $\Rightarrow$ (h). Using Theorem 6 with A^T in place of A, we conclude that (h) $\Rightarrow$ (a). Since (a) obviously implies (f), we have linked (f) and (h) into the other statements, and the proof is complete. ∎

The next fact follows easily from Theorem 8 and Exercise 10 in Section 3.2.

> Let A and B be square matrices. If either $BA = I$ or $AB = I$, then A and B are invertible, with $B = A^{-1}$ and $A = B^{-1}$.

The Invertible Matrix Theorem divides the set of all $n \times n$ matrices into two disjoint classes: (I) the invertible matrices and (II) the noninvertible matrices. Each of the statements in the theorem is a description of every matrix in class I. Matrices in class II are described by the negations of the statements in the Invertible Matrix Theorem. Some of these negations are considered in the exercises.

EXAMPLE 1 Use the Invertible Matrix Theorem to decide if A is invertible, where

$$A = \begin{bmatrix} 1 & 0 & -2 \\ 3 & 1 & -2 \\ -5 & -1 & 9 \end{bmatrix}$$

Solution

$$A \sim \begin{bmatrix} 1 & 0 & -2 \\ 0 & 1 & 4 \\ 0 & -1 & -1 \end{bmatrix} \sim \begin{bmatrix} 1 & 0 & -2 \\ 0 & 1 & 4 \\ 0 & 0 & 3 \end{bmatrix}$$

Thus each column of A is a pivot column. So A is invertible, by the Invertible Matrix Theorem (statement b′). ∎

The power of the Invertible Matrix Theorem lies in the connections it provides between so many important concepts, such as linear independence of columns of a matrix A and the existence of solutions to equations of the form $A\mathbf{x} = \mathbf{b}$. It should be emphasized, however, that the Invertible Matrix Theorem *applies only to square matrices*. For example, if the columns of a 4×3 matrix are linearly independent, we cannot use the Invertible Matrix Theorem to conclude anything about the existence or nonexistence of solutions to equations of the form $A\mathbf{x} = \mathbf{b}$.

Invertible Linear Transformations

Recall from Section 3.1 that matrix multiplication corresponds to composition of linear transformations. When a matrix A is invertible, the equation $A^{-1}A\mathbf{x} = \mathbf{x}$ may be viewed as a statement about linear transformations. See Fig. 2.

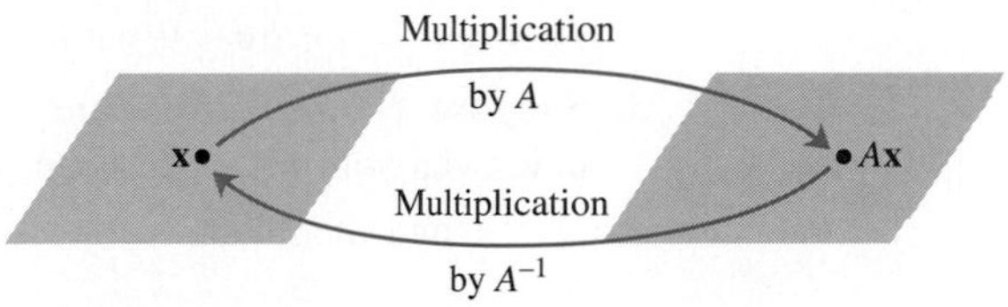

FIGURE 2 A^{-1} transforms $A\mathbf{x}$ back to $\mathbf{x}$.

A linear transformation $T : \mathbb{R}^n \to \mathbb{R}^n$ is said to be **invertible** if there exists a function $S : \mathbb{R}^n \to \mathbb{R}^n$ such that

$$S(T(\mathbf{x})) = \mathbf{x} \quad \text{for all } \mathbf{x} \text{ in } \mathbb{R}^n \tag{1}$$
$$T(S(\mathbf{x})) = \mathbf{x} \quad \text{for all } \mathbf{x} \text{ in } \mathbb{R}^n \tag{2}$$

The next theorem shows that if such an S exists, it is unique and must be a linear transformation. We call S the **inverse** of T and write it as T^{-1}.

THEOREM 9

Let $T : \mathbb{R}^n \to \mathbb{R}^n$ be a linear transformation and let A be the standard matrix for T. Then T is invertible if and only if A is an invertible matrix. In that case, the linear transformation S given by $S(\mathbf{x}) = A^{-1}\mathbf{x}$ is the unique function satisfying (1) and (2).

Proof Suppose that T is invertible. Then (2) shows that T is onto $\mathbb{R}^n$, for if $\mathbf{b}$ is in $\mathbb{R}^n$ and $\mathbf{x} = S(\mathbf{b})$, then $T(\mathbf{x}) = T(S(\mathbf{b})) = \mathbf{b}$, so each $\mathbf{b}$ is in the range of T. Thus A is invertible, by the Invertible Matrix Theorem (statement e‴).

Conversely, suppose that A is invertible, and let $S(\mathbf{x}) = A^{-1}\mathbf{x}$. Then, S is a linear transformation, and S obviously satisfies (1) and (2). For instance,

$$S(T(\mathbf{x})) = S(A\mathbf{x}) = A^{-1}(A\mathbf{x}) = \mathbf{x}$$

Thus T is invertible. The proof that S is unique is outlined in Exercise 31. ∎

EXAMPLE 2 What can you say about a one-to-one linear transformation T from $\mathbb{R}^n$ into $\mathbb{R}^n$?

Solution The columns of the standard matrix A of T are linearly independent (by Theorem 10 in Section 2.6). So A is invertible, by the Invertible Matrix Theorem, and T maps $\mathbb{R}^n$ *onto* $\mathbb{R}^n$. Also, T is invertible, by Theorem 9.

PRACTICE PROBLEMS

1. Determine if $A = \begin{bmatrix} 2 & 3 & 4 \\ 2 & 3 & 4 \\ 2 & 3 & 4 \end{bmatrix}$ is invertible.
2. Suppose that for a certain $n \times n$ matrix A, statement (e) in the Invertible Matrix Theorem is *not* true. What can you say about equations of the form $A\mathbf{x} = \mathbf{b}$?
3. Suppose that A and B are $n \times n$ matrices and the equation $AB\mathbf{x} = \mathbf{0}$ has a nontrivial solution. What can you say about the matrix AB?

3.3 EXERCISES

Unless otherwise specified, all matrices in these exercises are assumed to be $n \times n$. Determine which of the matrices in Exercises 1–12 are invertible. Use as few calculations as possible. Justify your answers.

1. $\begin{bmatrix} 6 & -12 \\ -2 & 4 \end{bmatrix}$

2. $\begin{bmatrix} -4 & 16 \\ 3 & -9 \end{bmatrix}$

3. $\begin{bmatrix} 5 & 0 & 3 \\ 7 & 0 & 2 \\ 9 & 0 & 1 \end{bmatrix}$

4. $\begin{bmatrix} 5 & 3 & 2 \\ 0 & 7 & 1 \\ 0 & 0 & 9 \end{bmatrix}$

5. $\begin{bmatrix} 1 & -7 & 5 \\ 1 & -4 & -1 \\ -2 & 8 & -3 \end{bmatrix}$

6. $\begin{bmatrix} 0 & 2 & 5 \\ -2 & 0 & 7 \\ 1 & 3 & 4 \end{bmatrix}$

7. $\begin{bmatrix} 5 & -9 & 3 \\ 0 & 3 & 4 \\ 1 & 0 & 3 \end{bmatrix}$

8. $\begin{bmatrix} 1 & 4 & 2 \\ 2 & 7 & 3 \\ 1 & 7 & 5 \end{bmatrix}$

9. $\begin{bmatrix} 1 & 3 & 0 & -1 \\ 0 & 1 & -2 & -1 \\ -2 & -6 & 3 & 2 \\ 3 & 5 & 8 & -3 \end{bmatrix}$

10. $\begin{bmatrix} 1 & 2 & 3 & 4 \\ 0 & 5 & 6 & 7 \\ 0 & 0 & 8 & 9 \\ 0 & 0 & 0 & 10 \end{bmatrix}$

11. $\begin{bmatrix} 1 & 0 & 0 & 0 \\ 2 & 5 & 0 & 0 \\ 3 & 6 & 8 & 0 \\ 4 & 7 & 9 & 10 \end{bmatrix}$

12. $\begin{bmatrix} 1 & 3 & -5 \\ 0 & 2 & -3 \\ 0 & -4 & 7 \\ -1 & 5 & -8 \end{bmatrix}$

13. Examine Exercises 10 and 11, and consider what would happen if one of the diagonal entries were zero. Make a conjecture about when a square upper triangular matrix is invertible. What about a square lower triangular matrix?

14. If the equation $A\mathbf{x} = \mathbf{0}$ has the trivial solution, do the columns of A span $\mathbb{R}^n$? Why or why not?

15. If a 4×4 matrix G cannot be row reduced to I_4, what can you say about the columns of G? Why?

16. If H is 7×7 and the equation $H\mathbf{x} = \mathbf{v}$ is consistent for every $\mathbf{v}$ in $\mathbb{R}^7$, is it possible that for some $\mathbf{v}$ the equation $H\mathbf{x} = \mathbf{v}$ has more than one solution? Why or why not?

17. If the columns of a 5×5 matrix P are linearly independent, what can you say about solutions of $P\mathbf{x} = \mathbf{b}$? Why?

18. Is it possible for a 6×6 matrix Q to be invertible when its columns do not span $\mathbb{R}^6$? Why or why not?

19. If the equation $B\mathbf{x} = \mathbf{c}$ is inconsistent for some $\mathbf{c}$ in $\mathbb{R}^n$, what can you say about the equation $B\mathbf{x} = \mathbf{0}$?

20. If the equation $C\mathbf{x} = \mathbf{y}$ has more than one solution for some $\mathbf{y}$ in $\mathbb{R}^n$, do the columns of C span $\mathbb{R}^n$? Why or why not?

21. Explain why A^2 is invertible whenever A is invertible.

22. If A is invertible, the columns of A^{-1} are linearly independent. Explain why.

23. Verify the boxed statement preceding Example 1. (It is enough to suppose that $AB = I$, because the roles of A and B may be reversed.)

24. If A has linearly independent columns, then its rows are linearly independent, too. Explain why.

25. Show that if AB is invertible, so is A. [*Hint*: Use Theorem 8 with $C = B(AB)^{-1}$. You cannot use Theorem 6(b), because you cannot *assume* that A and B are invertible.]

26. Show that if AB is invertible, so is B.

27. Let $T : \mathbb{R}^n \to \mathbb{R}^n$ be an invertible linear transformation. Explain why T is both one-to-one and onto $\mathbb{R}^n$. Use Eqs. (1) and (2). Then give a second explanation using one or more theorems.

28. Let T be a linear transformation that maps $\mathbb{R}^n$ onto $\mathbb{R}^n$. Show that T is invertible.

In Exercises 29 and 30, T is a linear transformation from $\mathbb{R}^2$ into $\mathbb{R}^2$. Show that T is invertible and find a formula for T^{-1}.

29. $T(x_1, x_2) = (-5x_1 + 9x_2, 4x_1 - 7x_2)$

30. $T(x_1, x_2) = (6x_1 - 8x_2, -5x_1 + 7x_2)$

31. Let $T : \mathbb{R}^n \to \mathbb{R}^n$ be an invertible linear transformation, and let S and U be functions from $\mathbb{R}^n$ into $\mathbb{R}^n$ such that $S(T(\mathbf{x})) = \mathbf{x}$ and $U(T(\mathbf{x})) = \mathbf{x}$ for all $\mathbf{x}$ in $\mathbb{R}^n$. Show that $U(\mathbf{v}) = S(\mathbf{v})$ for all $\mathbf{v}$ in $\mathbb{R}^n$. This will show that T has a unique inverse, as asserted in Theorem 9. [*Hint*: Given any $\mathbf{v}$ in $\mathbb{R}^n$, we may write $\mathbf{v} = T(\mathbf{x})$ for some $\mathbf{x}$. Why? Compute $S(\mathbf{v})$ and $U(\mathbf{v})$.]

32. Suppose that T and S satisfy (1) and (2), where T is a linear transformation. Show directly that S is a linear transformation. [*Hint*: Given $\mathbf{u}, \mathbf{v}$ in $\mathbb{R}^n$, let $\mathbf{x} = S(\mathbf{u}), \mathbf{y} = S(\mathbf{v})$. Then $T(\mathbf{x}) = \mathbf{u}, T(\mathbf{y}) = \mathbf{v}$. Why? Apply S to both sides of the equation $T(\mathbf{x}) + T(\mathbf{y}) = T(\mathbf{x} + \mathbf{y})$. Also, consider $T(c\mathbf{x}) = cT(\mathbf{x})$.]

SOLUTIONS TO PRACTICE PROBLEMS

1. The columns of A are obviously linearly dependent because columns 2 and 3 are multiples of column 1. Hence A cannot be invertible, by the Invertible Matrix Theorem.
2. If (e) is *not* true, then the equation $A\mathbf{x} = \mathbf{b}$ is inconsistent for at least one $\mathbf{b}$ in $\mathbb{R}^n$.
3. Apply the Invertible Matrix Theorem to the matrix AB in place of A. Then statement (c) becomes: $AB\mathbf{x} = \mathbf{0}$ has only the trivial solution. This is not true. So AB is not invertible.

3.4 PARTITIONED MATRICES

A key feature of our work with matrices has been the ability to regard a matrix A as a list of column vectors rather than just a rectangular array of numbers. This point of view has been so useful that we wish to consider other **partitions** of A, indicated by horizontal and vertical dividing rules, as in Example 1 below. Partitioned matrices appear often in modern applications of linear algebra because the notation simplifies many discussions and highlights essential structure in matrix calculations.

EXAMPLE 1 The matrix

$$A = \left[\begin{array}{ccc|cc|c} 3 & 0 & -1 & 5 & 9 & -2 \\ -5 & 2 & 4 & 0 & -3 & 1 \\ \hline -8 & -6 & 3 & 1 & 7 & -4 \end{array}\right]$$

can also be written as the 2×3 **partitioned** (or **block**) **matrix**

$$A = \begin{bmatrix} A_{11} & A_{12} & A_{13} \\ A_{21} & A_{22} & A_{23} \end{bmatrix}$$

whose entries are the *blocks* or *submatrices*

$$A_{11} = \begin{bmatrix} 3 & 0 & -1 \\ -5 & 2 & 4 \end{bmatrix}, \quad A_{12} = \begin{bmatrix} 5 & 9 \\ 0 & -3 \end{bmatrix}, \quad A_{13} = \begin{bmatrix} -2 \\ 1 \end{bmatrix}$$

$$A_{21} = \begin{bmatrix} -8 & -6 & 3 \end{bmatrix}, \quad A_{22} = \begin{bmatrix} 1 & 7 \end{bmatrix}, \quad A_{23} = \begin{bmatrix} -4 \end{bmatrix}$$

EXAMPLE 2 When a matrix A appears in a mathematical model of a physical system such as an electrical network, a transportation system, or a large corporation, it may be natural to regard A as a partitioned matrix. For instance, if a microcomputer circuit board consists mainly of three VLSI (very large-scale integrated) microchips, then the matrix for the circuit board might have the general form

$$A = \left[\begin{array}{c|c|c} A_{11} & A_{12} & A_{13} \\ \hline A_{21} & A_{22} & A_{23} \\ \hline A_{31} & A_{32} & A_{33} \end{array}\right]$$

The submatrices on the "diagonal" of A—namely, A_{11}, A_{22}, and A_{33}—concern the three VLSI chips, while the other submatrices depend on the interconnections among those microchips.

Addition and Scalar Multiplication

If matrices A and B are the same size and are partitioned in exactly the same way, then it is natural to make the same partition of the ordinary matrix sum $A + B$. In this case, each block of $A + B$ is the (matrix) sum of the corresponding blocks of A and B. Multiplication of a partitioned matrix by a scalar is also computed block-by-block.

Multiplication of Partitioned Matrices

Partitioned matrices may be multiplied by the usual row–column rule as if the block entries were scalars, provided that for a product AB, the column partition of A matches the row partition of B.

EXAMPLE 3 Let

$$A = \left[\begin{array}{ccc|cc} 2 & -3 & 1 & 0 & -4 \\ 1 & 5 & -2 & 3 & -1 \\ \hline 0 & -4 & -2 & 7 & -1 \end{array}\right] = \begin{bmatrix} A_{11} & A_{12} \\ A_{21} & A_{22} \end{bmatrix}, \quad B = \left[\begin{array}{cc} 6 & 4 \\ -2 & 1 \\ -3 & 7 \\ \hline -1 & 3 \\ 5 & 2 \end{array}\right] = \begin{bmatrix} B_1 \\ B_2 \end{bmatrix}$$

The 5 columns of A are partitioned into a set of 3 columns and then a set of 2 columns. The 5 rows of B are partitioned in the same way—into a set of 3 rows and then a set of 2 rows. We say that the partitions of A and B are **conformable** for **block**

multiplication. It can be shown that the ordinary product AB may be written as

$$AB = \begin{bmatrix} A_{11} & A_{12} \\ A_{21} & A_{22} \end{bmatrix} \begin{bmatrix} B_1 \\ B_2 \end{bmatrix} = \begin{bmatrix} A_{11}B_1 + A_{12}B_2 \\ A_{21}B_1 + A_{22}B_2 \end{bmatrix} = \left[\begin{array}{cc} -5 & 4 \\ -6 & 2 \\ \hline 2 & 1 \end{array}\right]$$

It is important that each smaller product in the expression for AB is written with the submatrix from A on the left, since matrix multiplication is not commutative. For instance,

$$A_{11}B_1 = \begin{bmatrix} 2 & -3 & 1 \\ 1 & 5 & -2 \end{bmatrix} \begin{bmatrix} 6 & 4 \\ -2 & 1 \\ -3 & 7 \end{bmatrix} = \begin{bmatrix} 15 & 12 \\ 2 & -5 \end{bmatrix}$$

$$A_{12}B_2 = \begin{bmatrix} 0 & -4 \\ 3 & -1 \end{bmatrix} \begin{bmatrix} -1 & 3 \\ 5 & 2 \end{bmatrix} = \begin{bmatrix} -20 & -8 \\ -8 & 7 \end{bmatrix}$$

Hence the top block in AB is

$$A_{11}B_1 + A_{12}B_2 = \begin{bmatrix} 15 & 12 \\ 2 & -5 \end{bmatrix} + \begin{bmatrix} -20 & -8 \\ -8 & 7 \end{bmatrix} = \begin{bmatrix} -5 & 4 \\ -6 & 2 \end{bmatrix}$$

The row–column rule for multiplication of block matrices provides the most general way to view the product of two matrices. Each of the following views of a product has already been described using simple partitions of matrices: (1) the definition of $A\mathbf{x}$ using the columns of A; (2) the column definition of AB; (3) the row–column rule for computing AB; and (4) the rows of AB as products of the rows of A and the matrix B. A fifth view of AB, again using partitions, follows in Theorem 10 below.

The calculations in the next example prepare the way for Theorem 10. Here $\text{col}_k(A)$ is the kth column of A and $\text{row}_k(B)$ is the kth row of B.

EXAMPLE 4 Let $A = \begin{bmatrix} -3 & 1 & 2 \\ 1 & -4 & 5 \end{bmatrix}$ and $B = \begin{bmatrix} a & b \\ c & d \\ e & f \end{bmatrix}$. Verify that

$$AB = \text{col}_1(A)\text{row}_1(B) + \text{col}_2(A)\text{row}_2(B) + \text{col}_3(A)\text{row}_3(B)$$

Solution Each term above is an *outer product*. (See Exercises 31 and 32 in Section 3.1.) By the ordinary row–column rule,

$$\text{col}_1(A)\text{row}_1(B) = \begin{bmatrix} -3 \\ 1 \end{bmatrix} [a \quad b] = \begin{bmatrix} -3a & -3b \\ a & b \end{bmatrix}$$

$$\text{col}_2(A)\text{row}_2(B) = \begin{bmatrix} 1 \\ -4 \end{bmatrix} [c \quad d] = \begin{bmatrix} c & d \\ -4c & -4d \end{bmatrix}$$

$$\text{col}_3(A)\text{row}_3(B) = \begin{bmatrix} 2 \\ 5 \end{bmatrix} [e \quad f] = \begin{bmatrix} 2e & 2f \\ 5e & 5f \end{bmatrix}$$

Thus

$$\sum_{k=1}^{3} \text{col}_k(A)\text{row}_k(B) = \begin{bmatrix} -3a + c + 2e & -3b + d + 2f \\ a - 4c + 5e & b - 4d + 5f \end{bmatrix}$$

This matrix is obviously AB. Notice that the $(1,1)$-entry in AB is the sum of the $(1,1)$-entries in the three outer products, the $(1,2)$-entry in AB is the sum of the $(1,2)$-entries in the three outer products, and so on.

THEOREM 10 **Column-Row Expansion of AB**

If A is $m\times n$ and B is $n\times p$, then

$$AB = [\,\mathrm{col}_1(A) \quad \mathrm{col}_2(A) \quad \cdots \quad \mathrm{col}_n(A)\,]\begin{bmatrix} \mathrm{row}_1(B) \\ \mathrm{row}_2(B) \\ \vdots \\ \mathrm{row}_n(B) \end{bmatrix} \tag{1}$$
$$= \mathrm{col}_1(A)\mathrm{row}_1(B) + \cdots + \mathrm{col}_n(A)\mathrm{row}_n(B)$$

Proof For each row index i and column index j, the (i,j)-entry in $\mathrm{col}_k(A)\mathrm{row}_k(B)$ is the product of a_{ik} from $\mathrm{col}_k(A)$ and b_{kj} from $\mathrm{row}_k(B)$. Hence the (i,j)-entry in the sum shown in (1) is

$$\underset{(k=1)}{a_{i1}b_{1j}} + \underset{(k=2)}{a_{i2}b_{2j}} + \cdots + \underset{(k=n)}{a_{in}b_{nj}}$$

This sum is also the (i,j)-entry in AB, by the row–column rule. ∎

Inverses of Partitioned Matrices

The next example illustrates calculations involving inverses and partitioned matrices.

EXAMPLE 5 A matrix of the form

$$A = \begin{bmatrix} A_{11} & A_{12} \\ 0 & A_{22} \end{bmatrix}$$

is said to be *block upper triangular*. Assume that A_{11} is $p\times p$, A_{22} is $q\times q$, and A is invertible. Find a formula for A^{-1}.

Solution Denote A^{-1} by B and partition B so that

$$\begin{bmatrix} A_{11} & A_{12} \\ 0 & A_{22} \end{bmatrix}\begin{bmatrix} B_{11} & B_{12} \\ B_{21} & B_{22} \end{bmatrix} = \begin{bmatrix} I_p & 0 \\ 0 & I_q \end{bmatrix} \tag{2}$$

This matrix equation provides four equations that will lead to the unknown submatrices $B_{11}, \ldots, B_{22}$. Compute the product on the left of (2) to obtain

$$A_{11}B_{11} + A_{12}B_{21} = I_p \tag{3}$$
$$A_{11}B_{12} + A_{12}B_{22} = 0 \tag{4}$$
$$A_{22}B_{21} = 0 \tag{5}$$
$$A_{22}B_{22} = I_q \tag{6}$$

By itself, (6) does not say that A_{22} is invertible, because we do not yet know that $B_{22}A_{22} = I_q$. But, using the Invertible Matrix Theorem and the fact that A_{22} is square, we *can* conclude that A_{22} is invertible and $B_{22} = A_{22}^{-1}$. Now we can use (5) to find

$$B_{21} = A_{22}^{-1}0 = 0$$

so that (3) simplifies to

$$A_{11}B_{11} + 0 = I_p$$

This shows that A_{11} is invertible and $B_{11} = A_{11}^{-1}$. Finally, from (4),

$$A_{11}B_{12} = -A_{12}B_{22} = -A_{12}A_{22}^{-1}, \qquad \text{and} \qquad B_{12} = -A_{11}^{-1}A_{12}A_{22}^{-1}$$

Thus

$$A^{-1} = \begin{bmatrix} A_{11} & A_{12} \\ 0 & A_{22} \end{bmatrix}^{-1} = \begin{bmatrix} A_{11}^{-1} & -A_{11}^{-1}A_{12}A_{22}^{-1} \\ 0 & A_{22}^{-1} \end{bmatrix}$$

A **block diagonal matrix** is a partitioned matrix with zero blocks off the main diagonal (of blocks). Such a matrix is invertible if and only if each block on the diagonal is invertible. See Exercises 12 and 13.

Numerical Notes

1. When matrices are too large to fit in a computer's high-speed memory, partitioning permits a computer to work only with two or three submatrices at a time. For instance, in recent work on linear programming, a research team simplified a problem by partitioning the matrix into 837 rows and 51 columns. The problem's solution took about 4 minutes on a Cray supercomputer.[1]
2. Some high-speed computers, particularly those with vector pipeline architecture, perform matrix calculations more efficiently when the algorithms use partitioned matrices.[2]
3. The latest professional software for high-performance numerical linear algebra, LAPACK, makes intensive use of partitioned matrix calculations.

The exercises that follow give practice with matrix algebra and illustrate typical calculations found in applications.

[1]The solution time doesn't sound too impressive until you learn that each of the 51 block columns contained about 250,000 individual columns. The original problem had 837 equations and over 12,750,000 variables! Nearly 100 million of the more than 10 billion entries in the matrix were nonzero. See Bixby, Robert E., et al., "Very Large-Scale Linear Programming: A Case Study in Combining Interior Point and Simplex Methods," *Operations Research*, 40, no. 5 (1992):885–897.

[2]The importance of block matrix algorithms for computer calculations is described in *Matrix Computations,* 2d ed., by Gene H. Golub and Charles F. van Loan, Johns Hopkins University Press, Baltimore, 1989, pp. 25, 36–37, 45–47.

PRACTICE PROBLEMS

1. Show that $\begin{bmatrix} I & 0 \\ A & I \end{bmatrix}$ is invertible and find its inverse.
2. Compute $X^T X$, when X is partitioned as $[\, X_1 \quad X_2 \,]$.

3.4 EXERCISES

In Exercises 1–8, assume that the matrices are partitioned conformably for the indicated multiplication. Compute the products shown in Exercises 1–4.

1. $\begin{bmatrix} I & 0 \\ E & I \end{bmatrix}\begin{bmatrix} A & B \\ C & D \end{bmatrix}$

2. $\begin{bmatrix} A & 0 \\ 0 & B \end{bmatrix}\begin{bmatrix} C & D \\ E & F \end{bmatrix}$

3. $\begin{bmatrix} 0 & I \\ I & 0 \end{bmatrix}\begin{bmatrix} A & B \\ C & D \end{bmatrix}$

4. $\begin{bmatrix} I & -X \\ 0 & I \end{bmatrix}\begin{bmatrix} A & B \\ C & D \end{bmatrix}$

5. Suppose A is invertible. Find matrices X and Y so that

$$\begin{bmatrix} I & 0 \\ X & I \end{bmatrix}\begin{bmatrix} A & B \\ C & D \end{bmatrix} = \begin{bmatrix} A & B \\ 0 & Y \end{bmatrix}$$

6. Suppose A, B, C are square. Find X, Y, and Z so that

$$\begin{bmatrix} A & B \\ C & 0 \end{bmatrix}\begin{bmatrix} I & 0 \\ X & Y \end{bmatrix} = \begin{bmatrix} 0 & I \\ Z & 0 \end{bmatrix}$$

7. Suppose that A_{11} is an invertible matrix. Find matrices X and Y such that the product below has the form indicated. Also, compute B_{22}. [*Hint*: Compute the product on the left, and set it equal to the right side.]

$$\begin{bmatrix} I & 0 & 0 \\ X & I & 0 \\ Y & 0 & I \end{bmatrix}\begin{bmatrix} A_{11} & A_{12} \\ A_{21} & A_{22} \\ A_{31} & A_{32} \end{bmatrix} = \begin{bmatrix} B_{11} & B_{12} \\ 0 & B_{22} \\ 0 & B_{32} \end{bmatrix}$$

8. Suppose that A_{11} and A_{22} are invertible. Find matrices X and Y such that the product below has the form shown.

$$\begin{bmatrix} A_{11} & A_{12} & A_{13} \\ A_{21} & A_{22} & A_{23} \\ A_{31} & A_{32} & A_{33} \end{bmatrix}\begin{bmatrix} I & X & 0 \\ 0 & I & Y \\ 0 & 0 & I \end{bmatrix} = \begin{bmatrix} B_{11} & 0 & B_{13} \\ B_{21} & B_{22} & 0 \\ B_{31} & B_{32} & B_{33} \end{bmatrix}$$

9. The inverse of $\begin{bmatrix} I & A & B \\ 0 & I & 0 \\ 0 & 0 & I \end{bmatrix}$ is $\begin{bmatrix} I & X & Y \\ 0 & I & Z \\ 0 & 0 & I \end{bmatrix}$. Find X, Y, and Z.

10. The inverse of $\begin{bmatrix} I & 0 & 0 \\ C & I & 0 \\ A & B & I \end{bmatrix}$ is $\begin{bmatrix} I & 0 & 0 \\ Z & I & 0 \\ X & Y & I \end{bmatrix}$. Find X, Y, and Z.

11. Let A be an $m \times p$ matrix, B an $m \times q$ matrix, and $\mathbf{u}, \mathbf{v}, \mathbf{y}$ vectors in $\mathbb{R}^p$, $\mathbb{R}^q$, and $\mathbb{R}^m$, respectively. Write the vector equation below as a matrix equation involving a partitioned matrix (and a partitioned vector).

$A\mathbf{u} + B\mathbf{v} = \mathbf{y}$

12. Let $A = \begin{bmatrix} B & 0 \\ 0 & C \end{bmatrix}$, where B and C are square. Show that A is invertible if and only if both B and C are invertible.

13. Show that a block upper-triangular matrix A partitioned as in Example 5 is invertible if and only if both A_{11} and A_{22} are invertible. [*Hint*: Verify that if both A_{11} and A_{22} are invertible, the formula for A^{-1} given in Example 5 actually works as the inverse of A.] This fact about A is an important part of several computer algorithms that estimate eigenvalues of matrices. Eigenvalues are discussed in Chapter 6.

14. Suppose A_{11} is invertible. Find X and Y so that

$$\begin{bmatrix} A_{11} & A_{12} \\ A_{21} & A_{22} \end{bmatrix} = \begin{bmatrix} I & 0 \\ X & I \end{bmatrix}\begin{bmatrix} A_{11} & 0 \\ 0 & S \end{bmatrix}\begin{bmatrix} I & Y \\ 0 & I \end{bmatrix} \tag{7}$$

where $S = A_{22} - A_{21}A_{11}^{-1}A_{12}$. The matrix S is called the **Schur complement** of A_{11}. Likewise, if A_{22} is invertible, the matrix $A_{11} - A_{12}A_{22}^{-1}A_{21}$ is called the Schur complement of A_{22}. Such expressions occur frequently in the theory of systems engineering, and elsewhere.

15. When a deep space probe is launched, corrections may be necessary to place the probe on a precisely calculated trajectory. Radar monitoring provides a stream of vectors, $\mathbf{x}_1, \ldots, \mathbf{x}_k$, giving information at different times about how the probe's position compares with its planned trajectory. Let X_k be the matrix $[\, \mathbf{x}_1 \ \cdots \ \mathbf{x}_k \,]$. The matrix $G_k = X_k X_k^T$ is computed as the radar data are analyzed. When $\mathbf{x}_{k+1}$ arrives, a new G_{k+1} must be computed. Since the data vectors arrive at high speed, the computational burden could be severe. But partitioned matrix multiplication helps tremendously. Compute the column–row expansions of G_k and G_{k+1}, and describe what must be computed in order to *update* G_k to form G_{k+1}.

The probe Galileo was launched October 18, 1989, and should arrive near Jupiter in December 1995.

16. Let X be an $m \times n$ data matrix such that X^TX is invertible, and let $M = I_m - X(X^TX)^{-1}X^T$. Add a column $\mathbf{x}_0$ to the data and form

$$W = [\, X \quad \mathbf{x}_0 \,]$$

Compute W^TW. The (1, 1)-entry is X^TX. Show that the Schur complement (Exercise 14) of X^TX may be written in the form $\mathbf{x}_0^T M \mathbf{x}_0$. It can be shown that the quantity $(\mathbf{x}_0^T M \mathbf{x}_0)^{-1}$ is the (2, 2)-entry in $(W^TW)^{-1}$. This entry has a useful statistical interpretation, under appropriate hypotheses.

In the study of engineering control of physical systems, a standard set of differential equations is transformed by Laplace transforms into the following system of linear equations:

$$\begin{bmatrix} A - sI_n & B \\ C & I_m \end{bmatrix} \begin{bmatrix} \mathbf{x} \\ \mathbf{u} \end{bmatrix} = \begin{bmatrix} \mathbf{0} \\ \mathbf{y} \end{bmatrix} \tag{8}$$

where A is $n \times n$, B is $n \times m$, C is $m \times n$, and s is a variable. The vector $\mathbf{u}$ in $\mathbb{R}^m$ is the "input" to the system, $\mathbf{y}$ in $\mathbb{R}^m$ is the "output," and $\mathbf{x}$ in $\mathbb{R}^n$ is the "state" vector. (Actually, the vectors $\mathbf{x}, \mathbf{u}, \mathbf{y}$ are functions of s, but we suppress this fact because it does not affect the algebraic calculations in Exercises 17 and 18.)

17. Assume that $A - sI_n$ is invertible and view (8) as a system of two vector equations. Solve the top equation for $\mathbf{x}$ and substitute into the bottom equation. The result is an equation of the form $W(s)\mathbf{u} = \mathbf{y}$, where $W(s)$ is a matrix that depends on s. $W(s)$ is called the *transfer function* of the system because it transforms the input $\mathbf{u}$ into the output $\mathbf{y}$. Find $W(s)$ and describe how it is related to the partitioned *system matrix* on the left side of (8). See Exercise 14.

18. Suppose that the transfer function $W(s)$ in Exercise 17 is invertible for some s. It can be shown that the inverse transfer function $W(s)^{-1}$, which transforms outputs into inputs, is the Schur complement of $A - BC - sI_n$ for the matrix below. Find this Schur complement. See Exercise 14.

$$\begin{bmatrix} A - BC - sI_n & B \\ -C & I_m \end{bmatrix}$$

19. Use partitioned matrices to prove by induction that the product of two lower triangular matrices is again lower triangular. [*Hint*: A $(k+1)\times(k+1)$ lower triangular matrix A may be written in the form below where a is a scalar, $\mathbf{x}$ is in $\mathbb{R}^k$, and A_1 is a $k\times k$ lower triangular matrix. See the Study Guide for help with induction.]

$$A = \begin{bmatrix} a & 0^T \\ \mathbf{x} & A_1 \end{bmatrix}$$

20. Find a formula for the inverse of an invertible 2×2 block lower triangular matrix.

SOLUTIONS TO PRACTICE PROBLEMS

1. If $\begin{bmatrix} I & 0 \\ A & I \end{bmatrix}$ is invertible, its inverse has the form $\begin{bmatrix} W & X \\ Y & Z \end{bmatrix}$. We compute $\begin{bmatrix} I & 0 \\ A & I \end{bmatrix} \begin{bmatrix} W & X \\ Y & Z \end{bmatrix} = \begin{bmatrix} W & X \\ AW + Y & AX + Z \end{bmatrix}$. So W, X, Y, Z must satisfy $W = I$, $X = 0$, $AW + Y = 0$, and $AX + Z = I$. It follows that $Y = -A$ and $Z = I$. Hence

$$\begin{bmatrix} I & 0 \\ A & I \end{bmatrix} \begin{bmatrix} I & 0 \\ -A & I \end{bmatrix} = \begin{bmatrix} I & 0 \\ 0 & I \end{bmatrix}$$

By the Invertible Matrix Theorem (don't forget to mention it),

$$\begin{bmatrix} I & 0 \\ A & I \end{bmatrix}^{-1} = \begin{bmatrix} I & 0 \\ -A & I \end{bmatrix}$$

2. $X^T X = \begin{bmatrix} X_1^T \\ X_2^T \end{bmatrix} [X_1 \quad X_2] = \begin{bmatrix} X_1^T X_1 & X_1^T X_2 \\ X_2^T X_1 & X_2^T X_2 \end{bmatrix}$. The partitions of X^T and X are automatically conformable for multiplication because the columns of X^T are the rows of X. This partition of $X^T X$ is used in several computer algorithms for matrix computations.

3.5 MATRIX FACTORIZATIONS

A *factorization* of a matrix A is an equation that expresses A as a product of two or more matrices. Whereas matrix multiplication involves a *synthesis* of data (combining the effect of two or more linear transformations into a single matrix), matrix factorization is an *analysis* of data. In the language of computer science, the expression of A as a product amounts to a *preprocessing* of the data in A, organizing that data into two or more parts whose structures are more useful in some way, perhaps more accessible for computation.

Matrix factorizations and, later, factorizations of linear transformations, will appear at a number of key points throughout the text. This section focuses on a factorization that lies at the heart of several important computer programs widely used in applications. Several other factorizations, to be studied later, are introduced in the exercises.

The LU Factorization

An $m \times n$ matrix A **admits an LU factorization** if it can be written in the form $A = LU$, where L is an $m \times m$ lower triangular matrix with 1's on the diagonal and U is upper triangular.[1] For instance, see Fig. 1. The matrix L is invertible and is called a *unit* lower triangular matrix.

$$A = \underbrace{\begin{bmatrix} 1 & 0 & 0 & 0 \\ * & 1 & 0 & 0 \\ * & * & 1 & 0 \\ * & * & * & 1 \end{bmatrix}}_{L} \underbrace{\begin{bmatrix} * & * & * & * & * \\ 0 & * & * & * & * \\ 0 & 0 & * & * & * \\ 0 & 0 & 0 & 0 & * \end{bmatrix}}_{U}$$

FIGURE 1 An LU factorization.

The reason for considering a factorization $A = LU$ is that it dramatically speeds up a solution of $A\mathbf{x} = \mathbf{b}$ that uses row reduction, provided that L and U are known. If we write $A\mathbf{x} = \mathbf{b}$ as $LU\mathbf{x} = \mathbf{b}$, and if we denote $U\mathbf{x}$ by $\mathbf{y}$, then we can find $\mathbf{x}$ by

[1] All entries in U below the diagonal entries, u_{11}, u_{22}, and so on, are zero. This definition makes sense even when U is not square.

solving the *pair* of equations

$$\boxed{\begin{aligned} L\mathbf{y} &= \mathbf{b} \\ U\mathbf{x} &= \mathbf{y} \end{aligned}} \tag{1}$$

First solve $L\mathbf{y} = \mathbf{b}$ for $\mathbf{y}$ and then solve $U\mathbf{x} = \mathbf{y}$ for $\mathbf{x}$. See Fig. 2. Each equation is easy to solve because L and U are triangular.

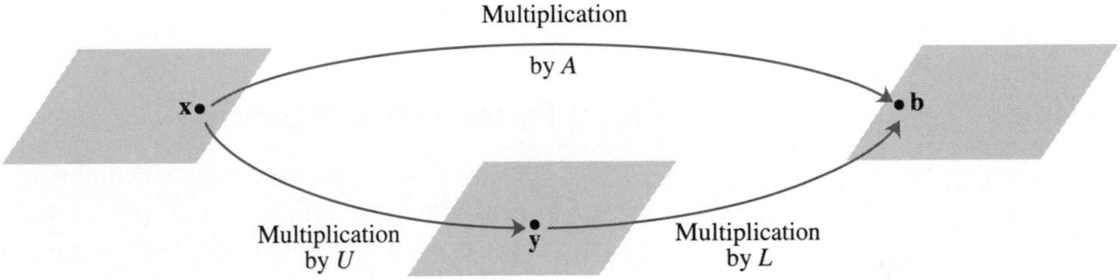

FIGURE 2 Factorization of the mapping $\mathbf{x} \mapsto A\mathbf{x}$.

EXAMPLE 1 It may be verified that

$$A = \begin{bmatrix} 3 & -7 & -2 & 2 \\ -3 & 5 & 1 & 0 \\ 6 & -4 & 0 & -5 \\ -9 & 5 & -5 & 12 \end{bmatrix} = \begin{bmatrix} 1 & 0 & 0 & 0 \\ -1 & 1 & 0 & 0 \\ 2 & -5 & 1 & 0 \\ -3 & 8 & 3 & 1 \end{bmatrix} \begin{bmatrix} 3 & -7 & -2 & 2 \\ 0 & -2 & -1 & 2 \\ 0 & 0 & -1 & 1 \\ 0 & 0 & 0 & -1 \end{bmatrix} = LU$$

Use this LU factorization of A to solve $A\mathbf{x} = \mathbf{b}$, where $\mathbf{b} = \begin{bmatrix} -9 \\ 5 \\ 7 \\ 11 \end{bmatrix}$.

Solution The solution of $L\mathbf{y} = \mathbf{b}$ needs only 6 multiplications and 6 additions, because the arithmetic takes place only in column 5:

$$[\,L \quad \mathbf{b}\,] = \begin{bmatrix} 1 & 0 & 0 & 0 & -9 \\ -1 & 1 & 0 & 0 & 5 \\ 2 & -5 & 1 & 0 & 7 \\ -3 & 8 & 3 & 1 & 11 \end{bmatrix} \sim \begin{bmatrix} 1 & 0 & 0 & 0 & -9 \\ 0 & 1 & 0 & 0 & -4 \\ 0 & 0 & 1 & 0 & 5 \\ 0 & 0 & 0 & 1 & 1 \end{bmatrix} = [\,I \quad \mathbf{y}\,]$$

Then, for $U\mathbf{x} = \mathbf{y}$, the "backwards" phase of row reduction requires 4 divisions, 6 multiplications, and 6 additions. (For instance, creating the zeros in column 4 of $[\,U \quad \mathbf{y}\,]$ requires 1 division in row 4 and 3 multiplication–addition pairs to add multiples of row 4 to the rows above.)

$$[\,U \quad \mathbf{y}\,] = \begin{bmatrix} 3 & -7 & -2 & 2 & -9 \\ 0 & -2 & -1 & 2 & -4 \\ 0 & 0 & -1 & 1 & 5 \\ 0 & 0 & 0 & -1 & 1 \end{bmatrix} \sim \begin{bmatrix} 1 & 0 & 0 & 0 & 3 \\ 0 & 1 & 0 & 0 & 4 \\ 0 & 0 & 1 & 0 & -6 \\ 0 & 0 & 0 & 1 & -1 \end{bmatrix}, \qquad \mathbf{x} = \begin{bmatrix} 3 \\ 4 \\ -6 \\ -1 \end{bmatrix}$$

The total "operation count," excluding the cost of finding L and U, is 16 multiplications and divisions. For simplicity, we ignore additions because they take less computer time. In contrast, row reduction of $[\,A \quad \mathbf{b}\,]$ to $[\,I \quad \mathbf{x}\,]$ takes 36 operations (multiplications and divisions). Even worse, computing A^{-1} and $A^{-1}\mathbf{b}$ takes 80 operations! ∎

The computational efficiency of the LU factorization depends on knowing L and U. The next algorithm shows that the row reduction of A to an echelon form U amounts to an LU factorization because it produces L with essentially no extra work. After the first row reduction, L and U are available for solving additional equations whose coefficient matrix is A.

An LU Factorization Algorithm

Suppose that A can be reduced to an echelon form U using *only row replacement operations*, in which a multiple of one row is added to another row below it. In this case there exist lower triangular elementary matrices $E_1, \ldots, E_p$ such that

$$E_p \cdots E_1 A = U \tag{2}$$

Then we can write

$$A = (E_p \cdots E_1)^{-1} U = LU$$

where

$$L = (E_p \cdots E_1)^{-1} \tag{3}$$

It can be shown that products and inverses of lower triangular matrices are also lower triangular. (For instance, see Exercise 19.) Thus L is lower triangular. Of course, U is upper triangular because it is in echelon form.

Observe that the row operations in (2), which reduce A to U, also reduce the L in (3) to I, because $E_p \cdots E_1 L = (E_p \cdots E_1)(E_p \cdots E_1)^{-1} = I$. This observation is the key to *finding L*.

Strategy for an LU Factorization

1. Reduce A to an echelon form U by a sequence of row replacement operations, if possible.
2. Place entries in L such that the *same sequence of row operations* reduces L to I.

Step 1 is not always possible, but if it is, the argument above shows that an LU factorization exists. Example 2 will show how to implement step 2. By construction, L will satisfy

$$(E_p \cdots E_1)L = I$$

using the same $E_1, \ldots, E_p$ as in (2). Thus L will be invertible, by the Invertible Matrix Theorem, with $(E_p \cdots E_1) = L^{-1}$. From (2), $L^{-1}A = U$, and $A = LU$. So step 2 will produce an acceptable L.

EXAMPLE 2 Find an LU factorization of

$$A = \begin{bmatrix} 2 & 4 & -1 & 5 & -2 \\ -4 & -5 & 3 & -8 & 1 \\ 2 & -5 & -4 & 1 & 8 \\ -6 & 0 & 7 & -3 & 1 \end{bmatrix}$$

Solution Since A has four rows, L should be 4×4. The first column of L is the first column of A divided by the top pivot entry:

$$L = \begin{bmatrix} 1 & 0 & 0 & 0 \\ -2 & 1 & 0 & 0 \\ 1 & & 1 & 0 \\ -3 & & & 1 \end{bmatrix}$$

Compare the first columns of A and L. *The row operations that create zeros in the first column of* A *will also create zeros in the first column of* L. We want this same correspondence of row operations to hold for the rest of L, so we watch a row reduction of A to an echelon form U:

$$A = \begin{bmatrix} 2 & 4 & -1 & 5 & -2 \\ -4 & -5 & 3 & -8 & 1 \\ 2 & -5 & -4 & 1 & 8 \\ -6 & 0 & 7 & -3 & 1 \end{bmatrix} \sim \begin{bmatrix} 2 & 4 & -1 & 5 & -2 \\ 0 & 3 & 1 & 2 & -3 \\ 0 & -9 & -3 & -4 & 10 \\ 0 & 12 & 4 & 12 & -5 \end{bmatrix} = A_1 \tag{4}$$

$$\sim A_2 = \begin{bmatrix} 2 & 4 & -1 & 5 & -2 \\ 0 & 3 & 1 & 2 & -3 \\ 0 & 0 & 0 & 2 & 1 \\ 0 & 0 & 0 & 4 & 7 \end{bmatrix} \sim \begin{bmatrix} 2 & 4 & -1 & 5 & -2 \\ 0 & 3 & 1 & 2 & -3 \\ 0 & 0 & 0 & 2 & 1 \\ 0 & 0 & 0 & 0 & 5 \end{bmatrix} = U$$

The highlighted entries above determine the row reduction of A to U. At each pivot column, divide the highlighted entries by the pivot and place the result into L:

$$\begin{bmatrix} 2 \\ -4 \\ 2 \\ -6 \end{bmatrix} \quad \begin{bmatrix} 3 \\ -9 \\ 12 \end{bmatrix} \quad \begin{bmatrix} 2 \\ 4 \end{bmatrix} \quad \begin{bmatrix} 5 \end{bmatrix}$$

$$\div 2 \qquad \div 3 \qquad \div 2 \qquad \div 5$$

$$\downarrow \qquad \downarrow \qquad \downarrow \qquad \downarrow$$

$$\begin{bmatrix} 1 & & & \\ -2 & 1 & & \\ 1 & -3 & 1 & \\ -3 & 4 & 2 & 1 \end{bmatrix}, \quad \text{and} \quad L = \begin{bmatrix} 1 & 0 & 0 & 0 \\ -2 & 1 & 0 & 0 \\ 1 & -3 & 1 & 0 \\ -3 & 4 & 2 & 1 \end{bmatrix}$$

An easy calculation verifies that this L and U satisfy $LU = A$.

If A cannot be row reduced without row interchanges, or if interchanges are desired for numerical reasons, then the procedure above can be modified to produce an L that is *permuted lower triangular*, in the sense that a rearrangement (called a permutation) of the rows of L will make L lower triangular. The resulting *permuted LU factorization* will solve $A\mathbf{x} = \mathbf{b}$ in the same way as before, except that the reduction of $[\,L \quad \mathbf{b}\,]$ to $[\,I \quad \mathbf{y}\,]$ follows the order of the pivots in L from left to right, starting with the pivot in the first column. For details, see the Study Guide.

Numerical Notes

Assuming that an $n \times n$ matrix has an LU factorization, $A = LU$, the relative efficiency of using L and U for calculations may be estimated by counting arithmetic operations (multiplications and divisions only).[2] Assume that n is moderately large, say $n \geq 30$.

1. Any $n \times n$ triangular system may be solved in about $n^2/2$ operations. So the solution of $L\mathbf{y} = \mathbf{b}$ and $U\mathbf{x} = \mathbf{y}$ requires about n^2 operations.
2. Row reduction of $[\,A \quad \mathbf{b}\,]$ to $[\,U \quad \mathbf{y}\,]$ requires about $n^3/3$ operations.
3. Calculation of A^{-1} requires about n^3 operations, and multiplication of $\mathbf{b}$ by A^{-1} requires another n^2 operations.

A Matrix Factorization in Electrical Engineering

Matrix factorization is intimately related to the problem of constructing an electrical network with specified properties. The following discussion gives just a glimpse of the connection between factorization and circuit design.

Suppose the box in Fig. 3 represents some sort of electric circuit, with an input and output. Record the input voltage and current by $\begin{bmatrix} v_1 \\ i_1 \end{bmatrix}$ (with voltage v in volts and current i in amps), and record the output voltage and current by $\begin{bmatrix} v_2 \\ i_2 \end{bmatrix}$. Frequently, the transformation $\begin{bmatrix} v_1 \\ i_1 \end{bmatrix} \mapsto \begin{bmatrix} v_2 \\ i_2 \end{bmatrix}$ is linear. That is, there is a matrix A, called the *transfer matrix,* such that

$$\begin{bmatrix} v_2 \\ i_2 \end{bmatrix} = A \begin{bmatrix} v_1 \\ i_1 \end{bmatrix}$$

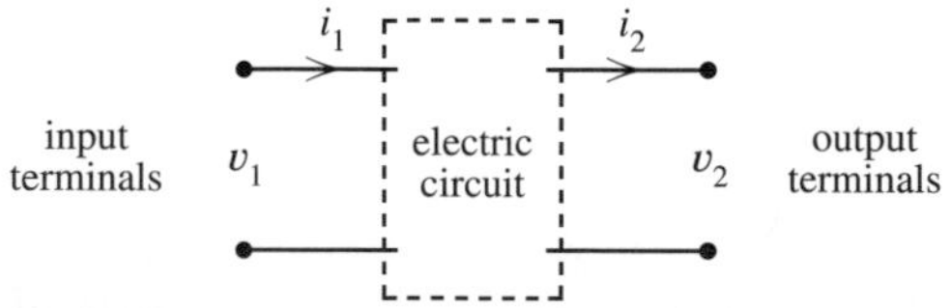

FIGURE 3 A circuit with input and output terminals.

[2]See Section 3.8 in *Applied Linear Algebra*, 3d ed., by Ben Noble and James W. Daniel, Prentice-Hall, Englewood Cliffs, 1988.

Fig. 4 shows a *ladder network*, where two circuits (there could be more) are connected in series, so that the output of one circuit becomes the input of the next circuit. The left circuit in Fig. 4 is called a *series circuit*, with resistance R_1 (in ohms); the right circuit is a *shunt circuit*, with resistance R_2. Using Ohm's law and Kirchhoff's laws, one can show that the transfer matrices of the series and shunt circuits, respectively, are

$$\begin{bmatrix} 1 & -R_1 \\ 0 & 1 \end{bmatrix} \quad \text{and} \quad \begin{bmatrix} 1 & 0 \\ -1/R_2 & 1 \end{bmatrix}$$

Transfer matrix of series circuit — Transfer matrix of shunt circuit

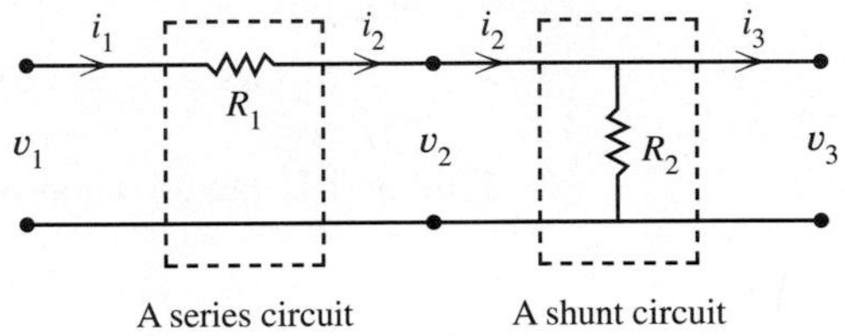

FIGURE 4 A ladder network.

EXAMPLE 3

a. Compute the transfer matrix of the ladder network in Fig. 4.

b. Design a ladder network whose transfer matrix is $\begin{bmatrix} 1 & -8 \\ -.5 & 5 \end{bmatrix}$.

Solution

a. Let A_1 and A_2 be the transfer matrices of the series and shunt circuits, respectively. Then an input vector $\mathbf{x}$ is transformed first into $A_1\mathbf{x}$ and then into $A_2(A_1\mathbf{x})$. The series connection of the circuits corresponds to composition of linear transformations; and the transfer matrix of the ladder network is (note the order)

$$A_2A_1 = \begin{bmatrix} 1 & 0 \\ -1/R_2 & 1 \end{bmatrix}\begin{bmatrix} 1 & -R_1 \\ 0 & 1 \end{bmatrix} = \begin{bmatrix} 1 & -R_1 \\ -1/R_2 & 1 + R_1/R_2 \end{bmatrix} \tag{5}$$

b. We seek to factor the matrix $\begin{bmatrix} 1 & -8 \\ -.5 & 5 \end{bmatrix}$ into the product of transfer matrices, such as in (5). So we look for R_1 and R_2 in Fig. 4 to satisfy

$$\begin{bmatrix} 1 & -R_1 \\ -1/R_2 & 1 + R_1/R_2 \end{bmatrix} = \begin{bmatrix} 1 & -8 \\ -.5 & 5 \end{bmatrix}$$

From the (1, 2)-entries, $R_1 = 8$ ohms, and from the (2, 1)-entries, $1/R_2 = .5$ ohms and $R_2 = 1/.5 = 2$ ohms. With these values, the network in Fig. 4 has the desired transfer matrix. ∎

A network transfer matrix summarizes the input–output behavior (the "design specifications") of the network without reference to the interior circuits. To physically build a network with specified properties, an engineer first determines if such a network can be constructed (or *realized*). Then the engineer tries to factor the transfer matrix into matrices corresponding to smaller circuits that perhaps are already manufactured and ready for assembly. In the common case of alternating current, the entries in the transfer matrix are usually rational complex-valued functions. (See Exercises 17 and 18 in Section 3.4 and Example 4 in Section 4.3.) A standard problem is to find a *minimal realization* that uses the smallest number of electrical components.

PRACTICE PROBLEM

Find an LU factorization of $A = \begin{bmatrix} 2 & -4 & -2 & 3 \\ 6 & -9 & -5 & 8 \\ 2 & -7 & -3 & 9 \\ 4 & -2 & -2 & -1 \\ -6 & 3 & 3 & 4 \end{bmatrix}$.

Note: It will turn out that A has only three pivot columns, so the method of Example 2 will produce only the first three columns of L. The remaining two columns of L come from I_5.

3.5 EXERCISES

In Exercises 1–6, solve the equation $A\mathbf{x} = \mathbf{b}$ by using the LU factorization given for A. In Exercises 1 and 2, also solve $A\mathbf{x} = \mathbf{b}$ by ordinary row reduction.

1. $A = \begin{bmatrix} 3 & -7 & -2 \\ -3 & 5 & 1 \\ 6 & -4 & 0 \end{bmatrix}$, $\mathbf{b} = \begin{bmatrix} -7 \\ 5 \\ 2 \end{bmatrix}$

$A = \begin{bmatrix} 1 & 0 & 0 \\ -1 & 1 & 0 \\ 2 & -5 & 1 \end{bmatrix} \begin{bmatrix} 3 & -7 & -2 \\ 0 & -2 & -1 \\ 0 & 0 & -1 \end{bmatrix}$

2. $A = \begin{bmatrix} 4 & 3 & -5 \\ -4 & -5 & 7 \\ 8 & 6 & -8 \end{bmatrix}$, $\mathbf{b} = \begin{bmatrix} 2 \\ -4 \\ 6 \end{bmatrix}$

$A = \begin{bmatrix} 1 & 0 & 0 \\ -1 & 1 & 0 \\ 2 & 0 & 1 \end{bmatrix} \begin{bmatrix} 4 & 3 & -5 \\ 0 & -2 & 2 \\ 0 & 0 & 2 \end{bmatrix}$

3. $A = \begin{bmatrix} 2 & -1 & 2 \\ -6 & 0 & -2 \\ 8 & -1 & 5 \end{bmatrix}$, $\mathbf{b} = \begin{bmatrix} 1 \\ 0 \\ 4 \end{bmatrix}$

$A = \begin{bmatrix} 1 & 0 & 0 \\ -3 & 1 & 0 \\ 4 & -1 & 1 \end{bmatrix} \begin{bmatrix} 2 & -1 & 2 \\ 0 & -3 & 4 \\ 0 & 0 & 1 \end{bmatrix}$

4. $A = \begin{bmatrix} 2 & -2 & 4 \\ 1 & -3 & 1 \\ 3 & 7 & 5 \end{bmatrix}$, $\mathbf{b} = \begin{bmatrix} 0 \\ -5 \\ 7 \end{bmatrix}$

$A = \begin{bmatrix} 1 & 0 & 0 \\ 1/2 & 1 & 0 \\ 3/2 & -5 & 1 \end{bmatrix} \begin{bmatrix} 2 & -2 & 4 \\ 0 & -2 & -1 \\ 0 & 0 & -6 \end{bmatrix}$

5. $A = \begin{bmatrix} 1 & -2 & -4 & -3 \\ 2 & -7 & -7 & -6 \\ -1 & 2 & 6 & 4 \\ -4 & -1 & 9 & 8 \end{bmatrix}$, $\mathbf{b} = \begin{bmatrix} 1 \\ 7 \\ 0 \\ 3 \end{bmatrix}$

$A = \begin{bmatrix} 1 & 0 & 0 & 0 \\ 2 & 1 & 0 & 0 \\ -1 & 0 & 1 & 0 \\ -4 & 3 & -5 & 1 \end{bmatrix} \begin{bmatrix} 1 & -2 & -4 & -3 \\ 0 & -3 & 1 & 0 \\ 0 & 0 & 2 & 1 \\ 0 & 0 & 0 & 1 \end{bmatrix}$

6. $A = \begin{bmatrix} 1 & 3 & 4 & 0 \\ -3 & -6 & -7 & 2 \\ 3 & 3 & 0 & -4 \\ -5 & -3 & 2 & 9 \end{bmatrix}$, $\mathbf{b} = \begin{bmatrix} 1 \\ -2 \\ -1 \\ 2 \end{bmatrix}$

$$A = \begin{bmatrix} 1 & 0 & 0 & 0 \\ -3 & 1 & 0 & 0 \\ 3 & -2 & 1 & 0 \\ -5 & 4 & -1 & 1 \end{bmatrix} \begin{bmatrix} 1 & 3 & 4 & 0 \\ 0 & 3 & 5 & 2 \\ 0 & 0 & -2 & 0 \\ 0 & 0 & 0 & 1 \end{bmatrix}$$

Find an LU factorization of the matrices in Exercises 7–16. Note that MATLAB will usually produce a permuted LU factorization because it uses partial pivoting for numerical accuracy, interchanging rows when necessary to select as pivots the column entries with the largest absolute values.

7. $\begin{bmatrix} 2 & 5 \\ -3 & -4 \end{bmatrix}$

8. $\begin{bmatrix} 6 & 9 \\ 4 & 5 \end{bmatrix}$

9. $\begin{bmatrix} 3 & -1 & 2 \\ -3 & -2 & 10 \\ 9 & -5 & 6 \end{bmatrix}$

10. $\begin{bmatrix} -5 & 3 & 4 \\ 10 & -8 & -9 \\ 15 & 1 & 2 \end{bmatrix}$

11. $\begin{bmatrix} 3 & -6 & 3 \\ 6 & -7 & 2 \\ -1 & 7 & 0 \end{bmatrix}$

12. $\begin{bmatrix} 2 & -4 & 2 \\ 1 & 5 & -4 \\ -6 & -2 & 4 \end{bmatrix}$

13. $\begin{bmatrix} 1 & 3 & -5 & -3 \\ -1 & -5 & 8 & 4 \\ 4 & 2 & -5 & -7 \\ -2 & -4 & 7 & 5 \end{bmatrix}$

14. $\begin{bmatrix} 1 & 4 & -1 & 5 \\ 3 & 7 & -2 & 9 \\ -2 & -3 & 1 & -4 \\ -1 & 6 & -1 & 7 \end{bmatrix}$

15. $\begin{bmatrix} 2 & -4 & 4 & -2 \\ 6 & -9 & 7 & -3 \\ -1 & -4 & 8 & 0 \end{bmatrix}$

16. $\begin{bmatrix} 2 & -6 & 6 \\ -4 & 5 & -7 \\ 3 & 5 & -1 \\ -6 & 4 & -8 \\ 8 & -3 & 9 \end{bmatrix}$

17. When A is invertible, MATLAB finds A^{-1} by factoring $A = LU$ (where L may be permuted lower triangular), inverting L and U, and then computing $U^{-1}L^{-1}$. Use this method to compute the inverse of A in Exercise 2. (Apply the algorithm of Section 3.2 to L and U.)

18. Find A^{-1} as in Exercise 17, if $A = \begin{bmatrix} 1 & 2 & 2 \\ -6 & -11 & -12 \\ 1 & -4 & 3 \end{bmatrix}$.

19. Let A be a lower triangular $n \times n$ matrix with nonzero entries on the diagonal. Show that A is invertible and A^{-1} is lower triangular:

a. Explain why A can be changed into I using only row replacements and scaling. [*Hint*: Where are the pivots?]

b. Explain why the row operations that reduce A to I change I into a lower-triangular matrix.

20. Let $A = LU$ be an LU factorization. Explain why A may be row reduced to U using only replacement operations. (This fact is the converse of what was proved in the text.)

21. Suppose $A = BC$, where B is invertible. Show that any sequence of row operations that reduces B to I also reduces A to C. The converse is not true, since the zero matrix may be factored $0 = B \cdot 0$.

Exercises 22–26 provide a glimpse of some widely used matrix factorizations, some of which are discussed later in the text.

22. (Reduced LU Factorization) With A as in the Practice Problem, find a 5×3 matrix B and a 3×4 matrix C such that $A = BC$. Generalize this idea to the case where A is $m \times n$, $A = LU$, and U has only 3 nonzero rows.

23. (Rank Factorization) Suppose that an $m \times n$ matrix admits a factorization $A = CD$ where C is $m \times 4$ and D is $4 \times n$.

a. Show that A is the sum of four outer products. (See Section 3.4.)

b. Let $m = 400$ and $n = 100$. Explain why a computer programmer might prefer to store the data from A in the form of two matrices C and D.

24. (QR Factorization) Suppose that $A = QR$, where Q and R are $n \times n$, R is invertible and upper triangular, and Q has the property that $Q^TQ = I$. Show that for each $\mathbf{b}$ in $\mathbb{R}^n$ the equation $A\mathbf{x} = \mathbf{b}$ has a unique solution. Describe an algorithm for producing the solution. [*Hint*: First explain why Q is invertible.]

25. (Singular Value Decomposition) Suppose $A = UDV^T$, where U and V are $n \times n$ matrices with the property that $U^TU = I$ and $V^TV = I$, and where D is a diagonal matrix with nonzero numbers $\sigma_1, \ldots, \sigma_n$ on the diagonal. Show that A is invertible and find a formula for A^{-1}.

26. (Spectral Factorization) Suppose a 3×3 matrix A admits a factorization as $A = PDP^{-1}$, where P is some invertible 3×3 matrix and D is the diagonal matrix

$$D = \begin{bmatrix} 1 & 0 & 0 \\ 0 & 1/2 & 0 \\ 0 & 0 & 1/3 \end{bmatrix}$$

Show that this factorization is useful when computing high powers of A. Find fairly simple formulas for A^2, A^3, and A^k (k a positive integer), using P and the entries in D.

27. Design two different ladder networks that each output 9 volts and 4 amps when the input is 12 volts and 6 amps.

28. Show that if three shunt circuits (with resistances R_1, R_2, R_3) are connected in series, the resulting network has the same transfer matrix as a single shunt circuit. Find a formula for the resistance in that circuit.

29. a. Compute the transfer matrix of the network in the figure below.

b. Let $A = \begin{bmatrix} 4/3 & -12 \\ -1/4 & 3 \end{bmatrix}$. Design a ladder network whose transfer matrix is A by finding a suitable matrix factorization of A.

30. Find a different factorization of the A in Exercise 29, and thereby design a different ladder network whose transfer matrix is A.

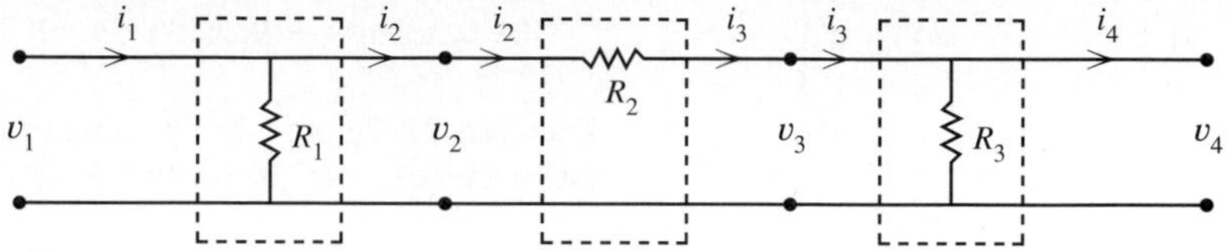

SOLUTION TO PRACTICE PROBLEM

$$A = \begin{bmatrix} 2 & -4 & -2 & 3 \\ 6 & -9 & -5 & 8 \\ 2 & -7 & -3 & 9 \\ 4 & -2 & -2 & -1 \\ -6 & 3 & 3 & 4 \end{bmatrix} \sim \begin{bmatrix} 2 & -4 & -2 & 3 \\ 0 & 3 & 1 & -1 \\ 0 & -3 & -1 & 6 \\ 0 & 6 & 2 & -7 \\ 0 & -9 & -3 & 13 \end{bmatrix}$$

$$\sim \begin{bmatrix} 2 & -4 & -2 & 3 \\ 0 & 3 & 1 & -1 \\ 0 & 0 & 0 & 5 \\ 0 & 0 & 0 & -5 \\ 0 & 0 & 0 & 10 \end{bmatrix} \sim \begin{bmatrix} 2 & -4 & -2 & 3 \\ 0 & 3 & 1 & -1 \\ 0 & 0 & 0 & 5 \\ 0 & 0 & 0 & 0 \\ 0 & 0 & 0 & 0 \end{bmatrix} = U$$

Divide the entries in each highlighted column by the pivot at the top. The resulting columns form the first three columns in the lower half of L. This suffices to make row reduction of L to I correspond to reduction of A to U. Use the last two columns of I_5 to make L unit lower triangular.

$$\begin{bmatrix} 2 \\ 6 \\ 2 \\ 4 \\ -6 \end{bmatrix} \quad \begin{bmatrix} 3 \\ -3 \\ 6 \\ -9 \end{bmatrix} \quad \begin{bmatrix} 5 \\ -5 \\ 10 \end{bmatrix}$$

$$\div 2 \qquad \div 3 \qquad \div 5$$

$$\downarrow \qquad \downarrow \qquad \downarrow$$

$$\begin{bmatrix} 1 & & & \\ 3 & 1 & & \\ 1 & -1 & 1 & \cdots \\ 2 & 2 & -1 & \\ -3 & -3 & 2 & \end{bmatrix}, \qquad L = \begin{bmatrix} 1 & 0 & 0 & 0 & 0 \\ 3 & 1 & 0 & 0 & 0 \\ 1 & -1 & 1 & 0 & 0 \\ 2 & 2 & -1 & 1 & 0 \\ -3 & -3 & 2 & 0 & 1 \end{bmatrix}$$

3.6 ITERATIVE SOLUTIONS OF LINEAR SYSTEMS

Consistent linear systems in real life are solved in one of two ways: by direct calculation (using a matrix factorization, for example) or by an iterative procedure that generates a sequence of vectors that approach the exact solution. When the coefficient matrix is large and *sparse* (with a high proportion of zero entries), iterative algorithms can be more rapid than direct methods and can require less computer memory. Also, an iterative process may be stopped as soon as an approximate solution is sufficiently accurate for practical work.

The simple iterative methods below were discovered long ago, but they provided the foundation for what today is an active area of research at the interface of mathematics and computer science.

General Framework for an Iterative Solution of $A\mathbf{x} = \mathbf{b}$

Throughout the section, A is an invertible matrix. The goal of an iterative algorithm is to produce a sequence of vectors,

$$\mathbf{x}^{(0)}, \mathbf{x}^{(1)}, \ldots, \mathbf{x}^{(k)}, \ldots$$

that converges to the unique solution of $A\mathbf{x} = \mathbf{b}$, say $\mathbf{x}^*$, in the sense that the entries in $\mathbf{x}^{(k)}$ are as close as desired to the corresponding entries in $\mathbf{x}^*$ for all k sufficiently large.

To describe a recursion algorithm that produces $\mathbf{x}^{(k+1)}$ from $\mathbf{x}^{(k)}$, we write $A = M - N$ for suitable matrices M and N, and then rewrite the equation $A\mathbf{x} = \mathbf{b}$ as $M\mathbf{x} - N\mathbf{x} = \mathbf{b}$ and

$$M\mathbf{x} = N\mathbf{x} + \mathbf{b}$$

If a sequence $\{\mathbf{x}^{(k)}\}$ satisfies

$$\boxed{M\mathbf{x}^{(k+1)} = N\mathbf{x}^{(k)} + \mathbf{b} \qquad (k = 0, 1, \ldots)} \tag{1}$$

and if the sequence converges to some vector $\mathbf{x}^*$, then it can be shown that $A\mathbf{x}^* = \mathbf{b}$. [The vector on the left in (1) approaches $M\mathbf{x}^*$, while the vector on the right in (1) approaches $N\mathbf{x}^* + \mathbf{b}$. This implies that $M\mathbf{x}^* = N\mathbf{x}^* + \mathbf{b}$ and $A\mathbf{x}^* = \mathbf{b}$.]

For $\mathbf{x}^{(k+1)}$ to be uniquely specified in (1), M must be invertible. Also, M should be chosen so that $\mathbf{x}^{(k+1)}$ is easy to calculate. The iterative methods below illustrate two simple choices for M.

Jacobi's Method

This method assumes that the diagonal entries of A are all nonzero. Let D be the diagonal matrix formed from the diagonal entries of A. Jacobi's method uses D for M and $D - A$ for N in (1), so that

$$D\mathbf{x}^{(k+1)} = (D - A)\mathbf{x}^{(k)} + \mathbf{b} \qquad (k = 0, 1, \ldots)$$

In a real-life problem, available information may suggest a value for $\mathbf{x}^{(0)}$. For simplicity, we take the zero vector as $\mathbf{x}^{(0)}$.

EXAMPLE 1 Apply Jacobi's method to the system

$$\begin{aligned} 10x_1 + x_2 - x_3 &= 18 \\ x_1 + 15x_2 + x_3 &= -12 \\ -x_1 + x_2 + 20x_3 &= 17 \end{aligned} \tag{2}$$

Take $\mathbf{x}^{(0)} = (0, 0, 0)$ as an initial approximation to the solution, and use six iterations (that is, compute $\mathbf{x}^{(1)}, \ldots, \mathbf{x}^{(6)}$).

Solution For some k, denote the entries in $\mathbf{x}^{(k)}$ by (x_1, x_2, x_3) and the entries in $\mathbf{x}^{(k+1)}$ by (y_1, y_2, y_3). The recursion

$$\underset{D}{\begin{bmatrix} 10 & 0 & 0 \\ 0 & 15 & 0 \\ 0 & 0 & 20 \end{bmatrix}} \underset{\mathbf{x}^{(k+1)}}{\begin{bmatrix} y_1 \\ y_2 \\ y_3 \end{bmatrix}} = \underset{(D-A)}{\begin{bmatrix} 0 & -1 & 1 \\ -1 & 0 & -1 \\ 1 & -1 & 0 \end{bmatrix}} \underset{\mathbf{x}^{(k)}}{\begin{bmatrix} x_1 \\ x_2 \\ x_3 \end{bmatrix}} + \underset{\mathbf{b}}{\begin{bmatrix} 18 \\ -12 \\ 17 \end{bmatrix}}$$

can be written as

$$\begin{aligned} 10y_1 &= \quad\;\; - x_2 + x_3 + 18 \\ 15y_2 &= -x_1 \quad\;\; - x_3 - 12 \\ 20y_3 &= \;\; x_1 - x_2 \quad\;\; + 17 \end{aligned}$$

and

$$\begin{aligned} y_1 &= (-x_2 + x_3 + 18)/10 \\ y_2 &= (-x_1 - x_3 - 12)/15 \\ y_3 &= (x_1 - x_2 + 17)/20 \end{aligned} \tag{3}$$

A faster way to get (3) is to solve the first equation in (2) for x_1, the second equation for x_2, the third for x_3, and then rename the variables on the left as y_1, y_2, and y_3, respectively.

For $k = 0$, take $\mathbf{x}^{(0)} = (x_1, x_2, x_3) = (0, 0, 0)$, and compute

$$\mathbf{x}^{(1)} = (y_1, y_2, y_3) = (18/10, -12/15, 17/20) = (1.8, -.8, .85)$$

For $k = 1$, use the entries in $\mathbf{x}^{(1)}$ as x_1, x_2, x_3 in (3) and compute the new y_1, y_2, y_3:

$$\begin{aligned} y_1 &= [-(-.8) + (.85) + 18]/10 = 1.965 \\ y_2 &= [-(1.8) - (.85) - 12]/15 = -.9767 \\ y_3 &= [(1.8) - (-.8) + 17]/20 = .98 \end{aligned}$$

Thus $\mathbf{x}^{(2)} = (1.965, -.9767, .98)$. The entries in $\mathbf{x}^{(2)}$ are used on the right in (3) to compute the entries in $\mathbf{x}^{(3)}$, and so on. Here are the results, with calculations using

MATLAB and results reported to four decimal places:

$$\begin{array}{ccccccc} \mathbf{x}^{(0)} & \mathbf{x}^{(1)} & \mathbf{x}^{(2)} & \mathbf{x}^{(3)} & \mathbf{x}^{(4)} & \mathbf{x}^{(5)} & \mathbf{x}^{(6)} \\ \begin{bmatrix} 0 \\ 0 \\ 0 \end{bmatrix} & \begin{bmatrix} 1.8 \\ -.8 \\ .85 \end{bmatrix} & \begin{bmatrix} 1.965 \\ -.9767 \\ .98 \end{bmatrix} & \begin{bmatrix} 1.9957 \\ -.9963 \\ .9971 \end{bmatrix} & \begin{bmatrix} 1.9993 \\ -.9995 \\ .9996 \end{bmatrix} & \begin{bmatrix} 1.9999 \\ -.9999 \\ .9999 \end{bmatrix} & \begin{bmatrix} 2.0000 \\ -1.0000 \\ 1.0000 \end{bmatrix} \end{array}$$

If we decide to stop when the entries in $\mathbf{x}^{(k)}$ and $\mathbf{x}^{(k-1)}$ differ by less than .001, then we need five iterations ($k = 5$).

The Gauss–Seidel Method

This method uses the recursion (1) with M the *lower triangular part* of A. That is, M has the same entries as A on the diagonal and below, and M has zeros above the diagonal. See Fig. 1. As in Jacobi's method, the diagonal entries of A must be nonzero for M to be invertible.

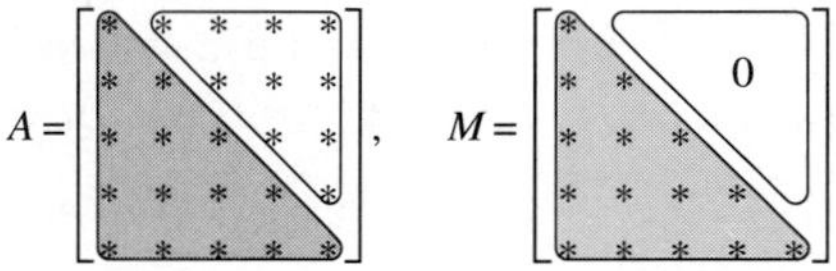

FIGURE 1 The lower triangular part of A.

EXAMPLE 2 Apply the Gauss–Seidel method to the system in Example 1 with $\mathbf{x}^{(0)} = \mathbf{0}$ and six iterations.

$$\begin{aligned} 10x_1 + x_2 - x_3 &= 18 \\ x_1 + 15x_2 + x_3 &= -12 \\ -x_1 + x_2 + 20x_3 &= 17 \end{aligned} \tag{4}$$

Solution With M the lower triangular part of A and $N = M - A$, the recursion relation is

$$\underset{\substack{\uparrow \\ M}}{\begin{bmatrix} 10 & 0 & 0 \\ 1 & 15 & 0 \\ -1 & 1 & 20 \end{bmatrix}} \underset{\substack{\uparrow \\ \mathbf{x}^{(k+1)}}}{\begin{bmatrix} y_1 \\ y_2 \\ y_3 \end{bmatrix}} = \underset{\substack{\uparrow \\ (M-A)}}{\begin{bmatrix} 0 & -1 & 1 \\ 0 & 0 & -1 \\ 0 & 0 & 0 \end{bmatrix}} \underset{\substack{\uparrow \\ \mathbf{x}^{(k)}}}{\begin{bmatrix} x_1 \\ x_2 \\ x_3 \end{bmatrix}} + \underset{\substack{\uparrow \\ \mathbf{b}}}{\begin{bmatrix} 18 \\ -12 \\ 17 \end{bmatrix}}$$

or

$$\begin{aligned} 10y_1 &= -x_2 + x_3 + 18 \\ y_1 + 15y_2 &= -x_3 - 12 \\ -y_1 + y_2 + 20y_3 &= 17 \end{aligned}$$

We will work with one equation at a time. When we reach the second equation, y_1 will be already known, so we can move it to the right side. Likewise, in the third equation y_1 and y_2 will be known, so we move them to the right. Dividing by the coefficients of the terms remaining on the left, we obtain

$$\begin{aligned} y_1 &= (-x_2 + x_3 + 18)/10 \\ y_2 &= (-y_1 - x_3 - 12)/15 \\ y_3 &= (y_1 - y_2 + 17)/20 \end{aligned} \tag{5}$$

Another way to view (5) is to solve each equation in (4) for x_1, x_2, x_3, respectively, and regard the highlighted x's as the *new* values:

$$\begin{aligned} x_1 &= (-x_2 + x_3 + 18)/10 \\ x_2 &= (-x_1 - x_3 - 12)/15 \\ x_3 &= (x_1 - x_2 + 17)/20 \end{aligned} \tag{6}$$

Use the first equation to calculate the *new* x_1 [called y_1 in (5)] from x_2 and x_3. Then use this *new* x_1 along with x_3 in the second equation to compute the *new* x_2. Finally, in the third equation, use the *new values* for x_1 and x_2 to compute x_3. In this way, the latest information about the variables is used to compute new values. [A computer program would use statements corresponding to the equations in (6).]

From $\mathbf{x}^{(0)} = (0, 0, 0)$, we obtain

$$x_1 = [-(0) + (0) + 18]/10 = 1.8$$

$$x_2 = [-(1.8) - (0) - 12]/15 = -.92$$

$$x_3 = [+(1.8) - (-.92) + 17]/20 = .986$$

Thus $\mathbf{x}^{(1)} = (1.8, -.92, .986)$. The entries in $\mathbf{x}^{(1)}$ are used in (6) to produce $\mathbf{x}^{(2)}$, and so on. Here are the MATLAB calculations reported to four decimal places:

$$\begin{array}{ccccccc} \mathbf{x}^{(0)} & \mathbf{x}^{(1)} & \mathbf{x}^{(2)} & \mathbf{x}^{(3)} & \mathbf{x}^{(4)} & \mathbf{x}^{(5)} & \mathbf{x}^{(6)} \\ \begin{bmatrix} 0 \\ 0 \\ 0 \end{bmatrix} & \begin{bmatrix} 1.8 \\ -.92 \\ .986 \end{bmatrix} & \begin{bmatrix} 1.9906 \\ -.9984 \\ .9995 \end{bmatrix} & \begin{bmatrix} 1.9998 \\ -.9999 \\ 1.0000 \end{bmatrix} & \begin{bmatrix} 2.0000 \\ -1.0000 \\ 1.0000 \end{bmatrix} & \begin{bmatrix} 2.0000 \\ -1.0000 \\ 1.0000 \end{bmatrix} & \begin{bmatrix} 2.0000 \\ -1.0000 \\ 1.0000 \end{bmatrix} \end{array}$$

Observe that when k is 4, the entries in $\mathbf{x}^{(k)}$ and $\mathbf{x}^{(k-1)}$ differ by less than .001. The values in $\mathbf{x}^{(6)}$ in this case happen to be accurate to eight decimal places.

∎

There exist examples where Jacobi's method is faster than the Gauss–Seidel method, but usually a Gauss–Seidel sequence converges faster, as in Example 2. (If parallel processing is available, Jacobi might be faster because the entries in $\mathbf{x}^{(k)}$ can be computed simultaneously.) There are also examples where one or both methods fail to produce a convergent sequence, and other examples where a sequence is convergent, but converges too slowly for practical use.

Fortunately, there is a simple condition that guarantees (but is not essential for) the convergence of both Jacobi and Gauss–Seidel sequences. This condition is often satisfied, for instance, in large-scale systems that can arise during numerical solutions of partial differential equations (such as Laplace's equation for steady-state heat flow).

An $n \times n$ matrix A is said to be **strictly diagonally dominant** if the absolute value of each diagonal entry exceeds the *sum* of the absolute values of the other entries in the same row. In this case it can be shown that A is invertible and that both the Jacobi and Gauss–Seidel sequences converge to the unique solution of $A\mathbf{x} = \mathbf{b}$, for any initial $\mathbf{x}^{(0)}$. (The speed of the convergence depends on how much the diagonal entries dominate the corresponding row sums.)

The coefficient matrix in Examples 1 and 2 is strictly diagonally dominant, but the following matrix is not. Examine each row:

$$\begin{bmatrix} -6 & 2 & -3 \\ 1 & 4 & -2 \\ 3 & -5 & 8 \end{bmatrix} \qquad \begin{aligned} |-6| &> |2| + |-3| \\ |4| &> |1| + |-2| \\ |8| &= |3| + |-5| \end{aligned}$$

The problem lies in the third row, because $|8|$ is not *larger* than the sum of the magnitudes of the other entries. The practice problem below suggests a trick that sometimes works when a system is not strictly diagonally dominant.

PRACTICE PROBLEM

Show that the Gauss–Seidel method *will* produce a sequence converging to the solution of the following system, provided the equations are arranged properly:

$$\begin{aligned} x_1 - 3x_2 + x_3 &= -2 \\ -6x_1 + 4x_2 + 11x_3 &= 1 \\ 5x_1 - 2x_2 - 2x_3 &= 9 \end{aligned}$$

3.6 EXERCISES

Solve the systems in Exercises 1–4 using Jacobi's method, with $\mathbf{x}^{(0)} = \mathbf{0}$ and three iterations. MATLAB: Repeat the iterations until two successive approximations agree within a tolerance of .001 in each entry.

1. $\begin{aligned} 4x_1 + x_2 &= 7 \\ -x_1 + 5x_2 &= -7 \end{aligned}$

2. $\begin{aligned} 10x_1 - x_2 &= 25 \\ x_1 + 8x_2 &= 43 \end{aligned}$

3. $\begin{aligned} 3x_1 + x_2 &= 11 \\ -x_1 - 5x_2 + 2x_3 &= 15 \\ 3x_1 + 7x_3 &= 17 \end{aligned}$

4. $\begin{aligned} 50x_1 - x_2 &= 149 \\ x_1 - 100x_2 + 2x_3 &= -101 \\ 2x_2 + 50x_3 &= -98 \end{aligned}$

In Exercises 5–8, use the Gauss–Seidel method, with $\mathbf{x}^{(0)} = \mathbf{0}$ and two iterations. MATLAB: Compare the number of iterations needed by Gauss-Seidel and Jacobi to make two successive approximations agree within a tolerance of .001.

5. The system in Exercise 1.

6. The system in Exercise 2.

7. The system in Exercise 3.

8. The system in Exercise 4.

Determine which of the matrices in Exercises 9 and 10 are diagonally dominant.

9. a. $\begin{bmatrix} 5 & 4 \\ 4 & 3 \end{bmatrix}$ b. $\begin{bmatrix} 9 & -5 & 2 \\ 5 & -8 & -1 \\ -2 & 1 & 4 \end{bmatrix}$

10. a. $\begin{bmatrix} 3 & -2 \\ 2 & 3 \end{bmatrix}$ b. $\begin{bmatrix} 5 & 3 & 1 \\ 3 & 6 & -4 \\ 1 & -4 & 7 \end{bmatrix}$

Neither iteration method of this section works for the systems as written in Exercises 11 and 12. Compute the first three iterates for Gauss–Seidel, with $\mathbf{x}^{(0)} = \mathbf{0}$. Then rearrange the equations to make Gauss–Seidel work, and compute two iterations. MATLAB: Find an approximation accurate to three decimal places.

11. $\begin{aligned} 2x_1 + 6x_2 &= 4 \\ 5x_1 - x_2 &= 6 \end{aligned}$

12. $\begin{aligned} -x_1 + 4x_2 - x_3 &= 3 \\ 4x_1 - x_2 \phantom{{}+4x_3} &= 10 \\ -x_2 + 4x_3 &= 6 \end{aligned}$

The systems in Exercises 13 and 14 are not strictly diagonally dominant, and no rearrangement of the equations will make them so. Nevertheless, both Jacobi and Gauss–Seidel produce convergent sequences. MATLAB: Find how many Gauss–Seidel iterations are needed to produce an approximation accurate to three decimal places. Set $\mathbf{x}^{(0)} = \mathbf{0}$.

13. $\begin{aligned} 4x_1 - 2x_2 &= 10 \\ -5x_1 + 4x_2 &= -2 \end{aligned}$

14. $\begin{aligned} 5x_1 - 3x_2 + 2x_3 &= -19 \\ -x_1 + 5x_2 + 3x_3 &= 10 \\ x_1 - 4x_2 - 4x_3 &= 18 \end{aligned}$

MATLAB: In Exercises 15 and 16, try both Jacobi's method and the Gauss–Seidel method and describe what happens. Set $\mathbf{x}^{(0)} = \mathbf{0}$. If a sequence seems to converge, try to find two successive approximations that agree within a tolerance of .001.

15. $\begin{aligned} x_1 \phantom{{}-2x_2} + x_3 &= 6 \\ x_1 - x_2 \phantom{{}+x_3} &= 3 \\ x_1 + 2x_2 - 3x_3 &= 9 \end{aligned}$

16. $\begin{aligned} 3x_1 - 2x_2 + 2x_3 &= 10 \\ -2x_1 + 3x_2 - 2x_3 &= -7 \\ 2x_1 - 2x_2 + 3x_3 &= 4 \end{aligned}$

17. The main focus of Section 3.7 will be the equation $\mathbf{x} = C\mathbf{x} + \mathbf{d}$. Under suitable hypotheses on C, this equation can be solved by an iterative scheme using the recursion relation

$$\mathbf{x}^{(k+1)} = C\mathbf{x}^{(k)} + \mathbf{d} \tag{7}$$

a. Show that (7) is a special case of (1). What are M, N, and A?

b. Take $\mathbf{x}^{(0)} = \mathbf{0}$ and use (7) to find a formula for $\mathbf{x}^{(2)}$ not involving $\mathbf{x}^{(1)}$.

c. Verify by induction that if $\mathbf{x}^{(0)} = \mathbf{0}$, then

$$\mathbf{x}^{(k)} = \mathbf{d} + C\mathbf{d} + C^2\mathbf{d} + \cdots + C^{k-1}\mathbf{d} \qquad (k = 1, 2, \ldots)$$

18. Suppose $\mathbf{x}^*$ satisfies $A\mathbf{x} = \mathbf{b}$ and $\mathbf{x}^{(k)}$ is determined by the recursion relation (1), where A is invertible, $A = M - N$, and M is invertible. The vector $\mathbf{e}^{(k)} = \mathbf{x}^{(k)} - \mathbf{x}^*$ is the error in the approximation of $\mathbf{x}^*$ by $\mathbf{x}^{(k)}$. The steps below imply that if $(M^{-1}N)^k \to 0$ as $k \to \infty$, then $\mathbf{e}^{(k)} \to \mathbf{0}$, which means that the sequence $\{\mathbf{x}^{(k)}\}$ converges to the solution $\mathbf{x}^*$.

a. Show that $\mathbf{e}^{(k+1)} = (M^{-1}N)\mathbf{e}^{(k)}$.

b. Prove by induction that $\mathbf{e}^{(k)} = (M^{-1}N)^k\mathbf{e}^{(0)}$.

SOLUTION TO PRACTICE PROBLEM

The system is not strictly diagonally dominant, so neither Jacobi nor Gauss-Seidel is guaranteed to work. In fact, both iterative methods produce sequences that fail to converge, even though the system has the unique solution $x_1 = 3, x_2 = 2, x_3 = 1$. However, the equations can be rearranged as

$$\begin{aligned} 5x_1 - 2x_2 - 2x_3 &= 9 \\ x_1 - 3x_2 + x_3 &= -2 \\ -6x_1 + 4x_2 + 11x_3 &= 1 \end{aligned}$$

Now the coefficient matrix is strictly diagonally dominant, so we know Gauss–Seidel works with any initial vector. In fact, if $\mathbf{x}^{(0)} = \mathbf{0}$, then $\mathbf{x}^{(8)} = (2.9987, 1.9992, .9996)$.

3.7 THE LEONTIEF INPUT–OUTPUT MODEL

Linear algebra played an essential role in the Nobel prize-winning work of Wassily Leontief, as mentioned at the beginning of Chapter 1. The economic model described in this section is the basis for more elaborate models used now in many parts of the world.

Suppose the nation's economy is divided into n sectors that produce goods or services, and let $\mathbf{x}$ be a **production** vector in $\mathbb{R}^n$ that lists the output of each sector for one year. Also, suppose another part of the economy (called the *open sector)* does not produce goods or services but only consumes them, and let $\mathbf{d}$ be a **final demand vector** (or **bill of final demands)** that lists the value of the goods and services demanded from the various sectors by the nonproductive part of the economy. The vector $\mathbf{d}$ can represent consumer demand, government consumption, surplus production, exports, or other external demand.

As the various sectors produce goods to meet consumer demand, the producers themselves create additional **intermediate demand** for goods they need as inputs for their own production. The interrelations between the sectors is very complex, and the connection between the final demand and the production is unclear. Leontief asked if there is a production level $\mathbf{x}$ such that the amounts produced (or "supplied") will exactly balance the total demand for that production, so that

$$\left\{\begin{matrix}\text{amount}\\ \text{produced}\\ \mathbf{x}\end{matrix}\right\} = \left\{\begin{matrix}\text{intermediate}\\ \text{demand}\end{matrix}\right\} + \left\{\begin{matrix}\text{final}\\ \text{demand}\\ \mathbf{d}\end{matrix}\right\} \tag{1}$$

The basic assumption of Leontief's input–output model is that for each sector there is a **unit consumption vector** in $\mathbb{R}^n$ that lists the inputs needed *per unit of output* of the sector. All input and output units are measured in millions of dollars, rather than in quantities such as tons or bushels. (Prices of goods and services are held constant.)

As a simple example, suppose the economy consists of three sectors—manufacturing, agriculture, and services, with unit consumption vectors $\mathbf{c}_1, \mathbf{c}_2, \mathbf{c}_3$ shown in the table below:

Purchased from:	Inputs Consumed Per Unit of Output Manufacturing	Agriculture	Services
Manufacturing	.50	.40	.20
Agriculture	.20	.30	.10
Services	.10	.10	.30
	↑ $\mathbf{c}_1$	↑ $\mathbf{c}_2$	↑ $\mathbf{c}_3$

EXAMPLE 1 What amounts will be consumed by the manufacturing sector if it decides to produce 100 units?

Solution Compute

$$100\mathbf{c}_1 = 100\begin{bmatrix}.50\\ .20\\ .10\end{bmatrix} = \begin{bmatrix}50\\ 20\\ 10\end{bmatrix}$$

To produce 100 units, manufacturing will order (i.e., "demand") and consume 50 units from other parts of the manufacturing sector, 20 units from agriculture, and 10 units from services.

If manufacturing decides to produce x_1 units of output, then $x_1\mathbf{c}_1$ represents the *intermediate demands* of manufacturing, because the amounts in $x_1\mathbf{c}_1$ will be consumed in the process of creating the x_1 units of output. Likewise, if x_2 and x_3 denote the planned outputs of the agriculture and services sectors, $x_2\mathbf{c}_2$ and $x_3\mathbf{c}_3$ list their corresponding intermediate demands. The total intermediate demand from all three sectors is given by

$$\begin{aligned}\{\text{intermediate demand}\} &= x_1\mathbf{c}_1 + x_2\mathbf{c}_2 + x_3\mathbf{c}_3 \\ &= C\mathbf{x} \end{aligned} \tag{2}$$

where C is the **consumption matrix** $[\mathbf{c}_1 \quad \mathbf{c}_2 \quad \mathbf{c}_3]$, namely,

$$C = \begin{bmatrix} .50 & .40 & .20 \\ .20 & .30 & .10 \\ .10 & .10 & .30 \end{bmatrix} \tag{3}$$

Equations (1) and (2) yield Leontief's model.

The Leontief Input–Output Model, or Production Equation

$$\underset{\substack{\text{Amount}\\ \text{produced}}}{\mathbf{x}} = \underset{\substack{\text{Intermediate}\\ \text{demand}}}{C\mathbf{x}} + \underset{\substack{\text{Final}\\ \text{demand}}}{\mathbf{d}} \tag{4}$$

Writing $\mathbf{x}$ as $I\mathbf{x}$ and using matrix algebra, we can rewrite (4):

$$\begin{aligned} I\mathbf{x} - C\mathbf{x} &= \mathbf{d} \\ (I - C)\mathbf{x} &= \mathbf{d} \end{aligned} \tag{5}$$

EXAMPLE 2 Consider the economy whose consumption matrix is given by (3). Suppose the external demand is 50 units for manufacturing, 30 units for agriculture, and 20 units for services. Find the production level $\mathbf{x}$ that will satisfy this demand.

Solution The coefficient matrix in (5) is

$$I - C = \begin{bmatrix} 1 & 0 & 0 \\ 0 & 1 & 0 \\ 0 & 0 & 1 \end{bmatrix} - \begin{bmatrix} .5 & .4 & .2 \\ .2 & .3 & .1 \\ .1 & .1 & .3 \end{bmatrix} = \begin{bmatrix} .5 & -.4 & -.2 \\ -.2 & .7 & -.1 \\ -.1 & -.1 & .7 \end{bmatrix}$$

To solve (5), row reduce the augmented matrix

$$\begin{bmatrix} .5 & -.4 & -.2 & 50 \\ -.2 & .7 & -.1 & 30 \\ -.1 & -.1 & .7 & 20 \end{bmatrix} \sim \begin{bmatrix} 5 & -4 & -2 & 500 \\ -2 & 7 & -1 & 300 \\ -1 & -1 & 7 & 200 \end{bmatrix} \sim \cdots \sim \begin{bmatrix} 1 & 0 & 0 & 226 \\ 0 & 1 & 0 & 119 \\ 0 & 0 & 1 & 78 \end{bmatrix}$$

The last column is rounded to the nearest whole unit. Manufacturing must produce approximately 226 units, agriculture 119 units, and services only 78 units.

If the matrix $I-C$ is invertible, then we can apply Theorem 5 in Section 3.2, with A replaced by $(I-C)$, and from the equation $(I-C)\mathbf{x} = \mathbf{d}$ obtain $\mathbf{x} = (I-C)^{-1}\mathbf{d}$. The theorem below shows that in most practical cases, $I-C$ *is* invertible and the production vector $\mathbf{x}$ is economically feasible, in the sense that the entries in $\mathbf{x}$ are nonnegative.

In the theorem, the term **column sum** denotes the sum of the entries in a column of a matrix. Under ordinary circumstances, the column sums of a consumption matrix are less than one because a sector should require less than one unit's worth of inputs to produce one unit of output.

THEOREM 11

Let C be the consumption matrix for an economy and let $\mathbf{d}$ be the final demand. If C and $\mathbf{d}$ have nonnegative entries and if each column sum of C is less than one, then $(I - C)^{-1}$ exists and the production vector

$$\mathbf{x} = (I - C)^{-1}\mathbf{d}$$

has nonnegative entries and is the unique solution of

$$\mathbf{x} = C\mathbf{x} + \mathbf{d}$$

The following discussion will suggest why the theorem is true and will lead to a new way to compute $(I - C)^{-1}$.

A Formula for $(I - C)^{-1}$

Imagine that the demand represented by $\mathbf{d}$ is presented to the various industries at the beginning of the year, and the industries respond by setting their production levels at $\mathbf{x} = \mathbf{d}$, which will exactly meet the external demand. As the industries prepare to produce $\mathbf{d}$, they send out orders for their raw materials and other inputs. This creates an intermediate demand of $C\mathbf{d}$ for inputs.

To meet the additional demand of $C\mathbf{d}$, the industries will need as additional inputs the amounts in $C(C\mathbf{d}) = C^2\mathbf{d}$. Of course, this creates a second round of intermediate demand, and when the industries decide to produce even more to meet this new demand, they create a third round of demand, namely, $C(C^2\mathbf{d}) = C^3\mathbf{d}$. And so it goes.

Theoretically, we can imagine this process continuing indefinitely, although in real life it would not take place in such a rigid sequence of events. We can diagram this hypothetical situation as follows:

	Demand That Must Be Met	Inputs Needed to Meet This Demand
Final demand	$\mathbf{d}$	$C\mathbf{d}$
Intermediate demand		
1st round	$C\mathbf{d}$	$C(C\mathbf{d}) = C^2\mathbf{d}$
2d round	$C^2\mathbf{d}$	$C(C^2\mathbf{d}) = C^3\mathbf{d}$
3d round	$C^3\mathbf{d}$	$C(C^3\mathbf{d}) = C^4\mathbf{d}$
	$\vdots$	$\vdots$

The production level $\mathbf{x}$ that will meet all of this demand is

$$\begin{aligned}\mathbf{x} &= \mathbf{d} + C\mathbf{d} + C^2\mathbf{d} + C^3\mathbf{d} + \cdots \\ &= (I + C + C^2 + C^3 + \cdots)\mathbf{d}\end{aligned} \tag{6}$$

To make sense of (6), we use the following algebraic identity:

$$(I - C)(I + C + C^2 + \cdots + C^{m-1}) = I - C^m \tag{7}$$

It can be shown that if the column sums in C are all strictly less than 1, then C^m approaches the zero matrix as m gets arbitrarily large, and $I - C^m \to I$. (This fact is analogous to the fact that if a positive number t is less than 1, then $t^m \to 0$ as m increases.) In such a case $(I - C)$ is invertible, and using (7), we write

$$(I - C)^{-1} = I + C + C^2 + C^3 + \cdots$$
provided that $C^m \to 0$ as $m \to \infty$. (8)

We interpret (8) as meaning that the right side may be made as close to $(I - C)^{-1}$ as desired by taking m sufficiently large.

In actual input–output models, powers of the consumption matrix approach the zero matrix rather quickly. So (8) really provides a practical way to compute $(I-C)^{-1}$. Likewise, for any $\mathbf{d}$, the vector $C^m\mathbf{d}$ approaches the zero vector quickly, and (6) is a practical way to solve $(I - C)\mathbf{x} = \mathbf{d}$. If the entries in C and $\mathbf{d}$ are nonnegative, then (6) shows that the entries in $\mathbf{x}$ are nonnegative, too.

The Economic Importance of Entries in $(I - C)^{-1}$

The entries in $(I - C)^{-1}$ are significant because they can be used to predict how the production $\mathbf{x}$ will have to change when the final demand $\mathbf{d}$ changes. In fact, the entries in column j of $(I - C)^{-1}$ are the *increased* amounts the various sectors will have to produce in order to satisfy *an increase of 1 unit* in the final demand for output from sector j. See Exercise 8.

PRACTICE PROBLEM

Suppose an economy has two sectors, goods and services. One unit of output from goods requires inputs of .2 unit from goods and .5 unit from services. A unit of output from services requires inputs of .4 unit from goods and .3 unit from services. There is a final demand of 20 units of Goods and 30 units of Services. Set up the Leontief input–output model for this situation.

3.7 EXERCISES

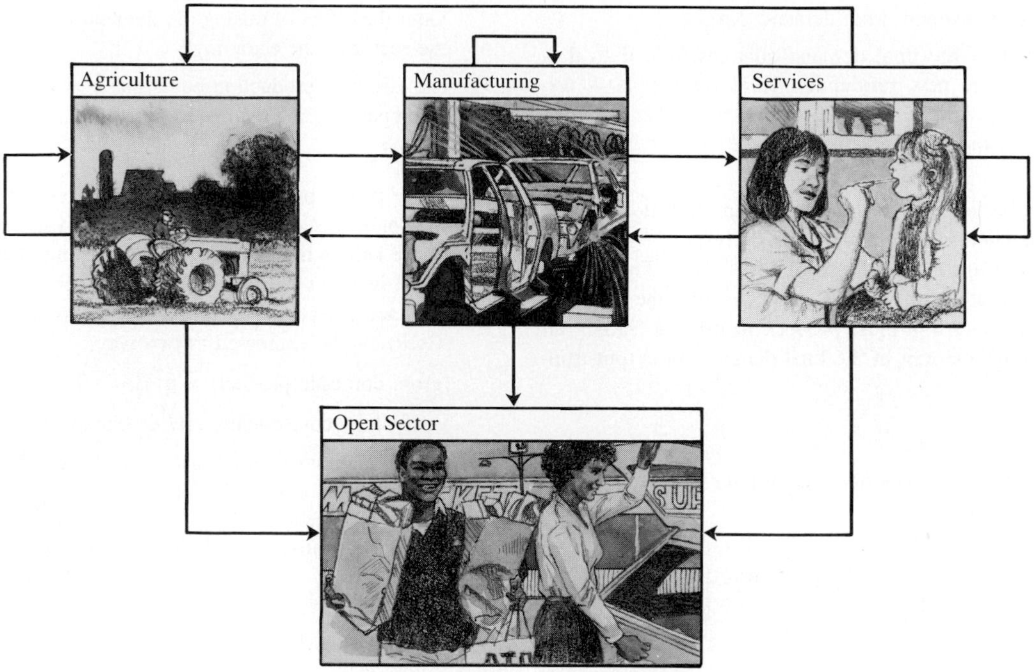

Exercises 1–4 refer to an economy that is divided into three sectors—manufacturing, agriculture, and services. For each unit of output, manufacturing requires .10 unit from other companies in the sector, .30 unit from agriculture, and .30 from services. For each unit of output, agriculture uses .20 unit of its own output, .60 unit from manufacturing, and .10 unit of services. For each unit of output, the services sector consumes .10 unit of services, .60 unit from manufacturing, but no agricultural products.

1. Construct the consumption matrix for this economy, and determine what intermediate demands are created if agriculture plans to produce 100 units.

2. Determine the production levels needed to satisfy a final demand of 18 units for agriculture, with no final demand for the other sectors. (Do not compute an inverse matrix.)

3. Determine the production levels needed to satisfy a final demand of 18 units for manufacturing, with no final demand for the other sectors. (Do not compute an inverse matrix.)

4. The total of the entries in the production vector **x** found in Exercise 2 is greater than the total of the entries in the **x** for Exercise 3. Explain why this should be expected if one examines the consumption matrix.

5. Consider the production model $\mathbf{x} = C\mathbf{x} + \mathbf{d}$ for an economy with two sectors, where

$$C = \begin{bmatrix} .0 & .5 \\ .6 & .2 \end{bmatrix}, \qquad \mathbf{d} = \begin{bmatrix} 50 \\ 30 \end{bmatrix}$$

Use an inverse matrix to determine the production level necessary to satisfy the final demand.

6. Repeat Exercise 5 with $C = \begin{bmatrix} .1 & .6 \\ .5 & .2 \end{bmatrix}$ and $\mathbf{d} = \begin{bmatrix} 18 \\ 11 \end{bmatrix}$.

7. Let C and $\mathbf{d}$ be as in Exercise 5.
   a. Determine the production level necessary to satisfy a final demand of 1 unit of output of sector 1.
   b. Use an inverse matrix to determine the production level necessary to satisfy a final demand of $\begin{bmatrix} 51 \\ 30 \end{bmatrix}$.
   c. Use the fact that $\begin{bmatrix} 51 \\ 30 \end{bmatrix} = \begin{bmatrix} 50 \\ 30 \end{bmatrix} + \begin{bmatrix} 1 \\ 0 \end{bmatrix}$ to explain how and why the answers to parts (a) and (b) and to Exercise 5 are related.

8. Let C be an $n \times n$ consumption matrix whose column sums are less than one. Let $\mathbf{x}$ be the production vector that satisfies a final demand $\mathbf{d}$, and let $\Delta\mathbf{x}$ be a production vector that satisfies a different final demand $\Delta\mathbf{d}$.

a. Show that if the final demand changes from $\mathbf{d}$ to $\mathbf{d} + \Delta\mathbf{d}$, then the new production level must be $\mathbf{x} + \Delta\mathbf{x}$. Thus $\Delta\mathbf{x}$ gives the amounts by which production must *change* in order to accommodate the *change* $\Delta\mathbf{d}$ in demand.

b. Let $\Delta\mathbf{d}$ be the vector in $\mathbb{R}^n$ with 1 in the first entry and 0's elsewhere. Explain why the corresponding production $\Delta\mathbf{x}$ is the first column of $(I - C)^{-1}$. This shows that the first column of $(I - C)^{-1}$ gives the amounts the various sectors must produce in order to satisfy an increase of one unit in the final demand for output from sector 1.

9. Solve the Leontief production equation for an economy with three sectors, given that

$$C = \begin{bmatrix} .2 & .2 & .0 \\ .3 & .1 & .3 \\ .1 & .0 & .2 \end{bmatrix} \quad \text{and} \quad \mathbf{d} = \begin{bmatrix} 40 \\ 60 \\ 80 \end{bmatrix}$$

10. The consumption matrix C for the United States economy in 1972 has the property that *every entry* in the matrix $(I - C)^{-1}$ is nonzero (and positive).[1] What does that say about the effect of raising the demand for the output of just one sector of the economy?

11. The Leontief production equation, $\mathbf{x} = C\mathbf{x} + \mathbf{d}$, is usually accompanied by a dual **price equation,**

$$\mathbf{p} = C^T\mathbf{p} + \mathbf{v}$$

where $\mathbf{p}$ is a **price vector** whose entries list the price per unit for each sector's output, and $\mathbf{v}$ is a **value added vector** whose entries list the value added per unit of output. (Value added includes wages, profit, depreciation, etc.) An important fact in economics is that the gross domestic product (GDP) can be expressed in two ways:

$$\{\text{gross domestic product}\} = \mathbf{p}^T\mathbf{d} = \mathbf{v}^T\mathbf{x}$$

Verify the second equality. [*Hint*: Compute $\mathbf{p}^T\mathbf{x}$ in two ways.]

12. Let C be a consumption matrix such that $C^m \to 0$ as $m \to \infty$, and for $m = 1, 2, \ldots$, let $D_m = I + C + \cdots + C^m$. Find a difference equation that relates D_m and D_{m+1} and thereby obtain an iterative procedure for computing formula (8) for $(I - C)^{-1}$.

[1]From Wassily W. Leontief, "The World Economy of the Year 2000," *Scientific American*, September 1980, pp. 206–231.

SOLUTION TO PRACTICE PROBLEM

The following data are given:

Purchased From	Inputs Needed per Unit of Output: Goods	Services	External Demand
Goods	.2	.4	20
Services	.5	.3	30

The Leontief input–output model is $\mathbf{x} = C\mathbf{x} + \mathbf{d}$, where

$$C = \begin{bmatrix} .2 & .4 \\ .5 & .3 \end{bmatrix}, \qquad \mathbf{d} = \begin{bmatrix} 20 \\ 30 \end{bmatrix}$$

3.8 APPLICATIONS TO COMPUTER GRAPHICS

Computer graphics are images displayed or animated on a computer screen. Applications of computer graphics are widespread and growing rapidly. For instance, computer-aided design is an integral part of many engineering processes, such as the automobile production described in the chapter introduction. The entertainment industry has made the most spectacular use of computer graphics—from the special effects in *Star Wars* to Nintendo and arcade games.

Most interactive computer software for business and industry employs computer graphics in the screen displays and for other functions, such as graphical display of data, desktop publishing, and slide production for commercial and educational presentations. Consequently, anyone studying a computer language invariably spends time learning how to use at least two-dimensional (2D) graphics.

This section examines some of the basic mathematics used to manipulate and display graphical images such as a wire-frame model of a car. Such an image (or picture) consists of a number of points, connecting lines or curves, and information about how to fill in closed regions bounded by the lines and curves. Often, curved lines are approximated by short straight-line segments, and a figure is defined mathematically by a list of points.

Among the simplest 2D graphics symbols are letters used for labels on the screen. Some letters are stored as wire-frame objects; others that have curved portions are stored with additional mathematical formulas for the curves.

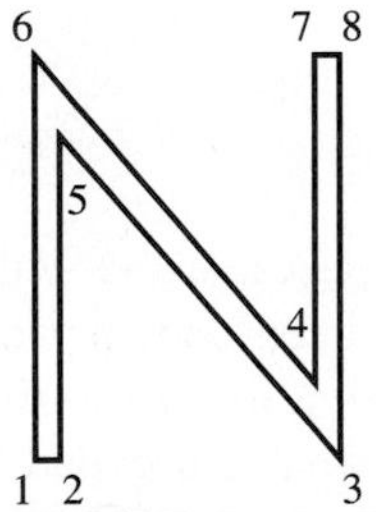

FIGURE 1
Regular N.

EXAMPLE 1 The capital letter N in Fig. 1 is determined by eight points, or *vertices*. The coordinates of the points can be stored in a data matrix, D.

$$\begin{array}{r} \\ \\ x\text{-coordinate} \\ y\text{-coordinate} \end{array} \begin{array}{c} \text{Vertex:} \\ \begin{array}{cccccccc} 1 & 2 & 3 & 4 & 5 & 6 & 7 & 8 \end{array} \\ \begin{bmatrix} 0 & .5 & 6 & 5.5 & .5 & 0 & 5.5 & 6 \\ 0 & 0 & 0 & 1.58 & 6.42 & 8 & 8 & 8 \end{bmatrix} = D \end{array}$$

In addition to D, it is necessary to specify which vertices are connected by lines, but we omit this detail.

The main reason graphical objects are described by collections of straight-line segments is that the standard transformations in computer graphics map line segments onto other line segments. (For instance, see Exercise 24 in Section 2.5.) Once the vertices that describe an object have been transformed, their images can be connected with the appropriate straight lines to produce the complete image of the original object.

EXAMPLE 2 Given $A = \begin{bmatrix} 1 & .25 \\ 0 & 1 \end{bmatrix}$, describe the effect of the shear transformation $\mathbf{x} \mapsto A\mathbf{x}$ on the letter N in Example 1.

Solution By definition of matrix multiplication, the columns of the product AD contain the images of the vertices of the letter N.

$$\begin{array}{cccccccc} 1 & 2 & 3 & 4 & 5 & 6 & 7 & 8 \end{array}$$
$$AD = \begin{bmatrix} 0 & .5 & 6 & 5.895 & 2.105 & 2 & 7.5 & 8 \\ 0 & 0 & 0 & 1.580 & 6.420 & 8 & 8 & 8 \end{bmatrix}$$

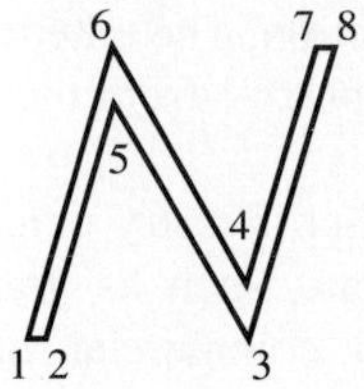

FIGURE 2
Slanted N.

The transformed vertices are plotted in Fig. 2, along with connecting line segments that correspond to those in the original figure. ∎

The italic N in Fig. 2 looks a bit too wide. To compensate, we can shrink the width by a scale transformation.

EXAMPLE 3 Compute the matrix of the transformation that performs a shear transformation as in Example 2, and then scales all x-coordinates by a factor of .75.

Solution The matrix that multiplies the x-coordinate of a point by .75 is

$$S = \begin{bmatrix} .75 & 0 \\ 0 & 1 \end{bmatrix}$$

So the matrix of the composite transformation is

$$SA = \begin{bmatrix} .75 & 0 \\ 0 & 1 \end{bmatrix} \begin{bmatrix} 1 & .25 \\ 0 & 1 \end{bmatrix} = \begin{bmatrix} .75 & .1875 \\ 0 & 1 \end{bmatrix}$$

The result of this composite transformation is shown in Fig. 3. ∎

FIGURE 3 Composite transformation of N.

The mathematics of computer graphics is intimately connected with matrix multiplication. Unfortunately, translating an object on a screen does not correspond directly to matrix multiplication, because translation is not a linear transformation. The standard way to avoid this difficulty is to introduce what are called *homogeneous coordinates*.

Homogeneous Coordinates

Each point (x, y) in $\mathbb{R}^2$ can be identified with the point $(x, y, 1)$ on the plane in $\mathbb{R}^3$ that lies one unit above the xy-plane. We say that (x, y) has *homogeneous coordinates* $(x, y, 1)$. For instance, the point $(0, 0)$ has homogeneous coordinates $(0, 0, 1)$. Homogeneous coordinates for points are not added or multiplied by scalars, but they can be transformed via multiplication by 3×3 matrices.

EXAMPLE 4 A translation of the form $(x, y) \mapsto (x + h, y + k)$ is written in homogeneous coordinates as $(x, y, 1) \mapsto (x + h, y + k, 1)$. This transformation can be computed via matrix multiplication:

$$\begin{bmatrix} 1 & 0 & h \\ 0 & 1 & k \\ 0 & 0 & 1 \end{bmatrix} \begin{bmatrix} x \\ y \\ 1 \end{bmatrix} = \begin{bmatrix} x+h \\ y+k \\ 1 \end{bmatrix}$$

∎

EXAMPLE 5 Any linear transformation on $\mathbb{R}^2$ is represented with respect to homogeneous coordinates by a partitioned matrix of the form $\begin{bmatrix} A & 0 \\ 0 & 1 \end{bmatrix}$ where A is a 2×2 matrix. Typical examples are:

$$\begin{bmatrix} \cos\vartheta & -\sin\vartheta & 0 \\ \sin\vartheta & \cos\vartheta & 0 \\ 0 & 0 & 1 \end{bmatrix}, \quad \begin{bmatrix} 0 & 1 & 0 \\ 1 & 0 & 0 \\ 0 & 0 & 1 \end{bmatrix}, \quad \begin{bmatrix} s & 0 & 0 \\ 0 & t & 0 \\ 0 & 0 & 1 \end{bmatrix}$$

Counterclockwise rotation about the origin, angle ϑ — Reflection in $y = x$ — Scale x by s and y by t

Composite Transformations

The movement of a figure on a computer screen often requires two or more basic transformations. The composition of such transformations corresponds to matrix multiplication when homogeneous coordinates are used.

EXAMPLE 6 Find the 3×3 matrix that corresponds to the composite transformation of a scaling by .3, a rotation of 90°, and finally a translation that adds $(-.5, 2)$ to each point of a figure.

Solution If $\vartheta = \pi/2$, then $\sin\vartheta = 1$ and $\cos\vartheta = 0$. From Examples 4 and 5, we have

$$\begin{bmatrix} x \\ y \\ 1 \end{bmatrix} \xrightarrow{\text{Scale}} \begin{bmatrix} .3 & 0 & 0 \\ 0 & .3 & 0 \\ 0 & 0 & 1 \end{bmatrix} \begin{bmatrix} x \\ y \\ 1 \end{bmatrix}$$

$$\xrightarrow{\text{Rotate}} \begin{bmatrix} 0 & -1 & 0 \\ 1 & 0 & 0 \\ 0 & 0 & 1 \end{bmatrix} \begin{bmatrix} .3 & 0 & 0 \\ 0 & .3 & 0 \\ 0 & 0 & 1 \end{bmatrix} \begin{bmatrix} x \\ y \\ 1 \end{bmatrix}$$

$$\xrightarrow{\text{Translate}} \begin{bmatrix} 1 & 0 & -.5 \\ 0 & 1 & 2 \\ 0 & 0 & 1 \end{bmatrix} \begin{bmatrix} 0 & -1 & 0 \\ 1 & 0 & 0 \\ 0 & 0 & 1 \end{bmatrix} \begin{bmatrix} .3 & 0 & 0 \\ 0 & .3 & 0 \\ 0 & 0 & 1 \end{bmatrix} \begin{bmatrix} x \\ y \\ 1 \end{bmatrix}$$

The matrix for the composite transformation is

$$\begin{bmatrix} 1 & 0 & -.5 \\ 0 & 1 & 2 \\ 0 & 0 & 1 \end{bmatrix} \begin{bmatrix} 0 & -1 & 0 \\ 1 & 0 & 0 \\ 0 & 0 & 1 \end{bmatrix} \begin{bmatrix} .3 & 0 & 0 \\ 0 & .3 & 0 \\ 0 & 0 & 1 \end{bmatrix}$$

$$= \begin{bmatrix} 0 & -1 & -.5 \\ 1 & 0 & 2 \\ 0 & 0 & 1 \end{bmatrix} \begin{bmatrix} .3 & 0 & 0 \\ 0 & .3 & 0 \\ 0 & 0 & 1 \end{bmatrix} = \begin{bmatrix} 0 & -.3 & -.5 \\ .3 & 0 & 2 \\ 0 & 0 & 1 \end{bmatrix}$$

3D Computer Graphics

Some of the newest and most exciting work in computer graphics is connected with molecular modeling. With 3D graphics, a biologist can examine a simulated protein molecule and search for active sites that might accept a drug molecule. The biologist can rotate and translate an experimental drug and attempt to attach it to the protein. This ability to *visualize* potential chemical reactions is vital to modern drug and cancer research. In fact, advances in drug design depend to some extent upon progress in the ability of computer graphics to construct realistic simulations of molecules and their interactions.[1]

FIGURE 4 Molecular modeling in virtual reality. (Computer Science Department, University of North Carolina at Chapel Hill. Photo by Bo Strain.)

Current research in molecular modeling is focused on *virtual reality*, an environment in which a researcher can see and *feel* the drug molecule slide into the protein. In Fig. 4, such tactile feedback is provided by a force-displaying remote manipulator. Another design for virtual reality involves a helmet and glove that detect head, hand, and finger movements. The helmet contains two tiny computer screens, one for each eye. Making this virtual environment more realistic is a challenge to engineers, scientists, and mathematicians. The mathematics we examine here barely opens the door to this interesting field of research.

Homogeneous 3D Coordinates

By analogy with the 2D case, we say that $(x, y, z, 1)$ are homogeneous coordinates for the $\mathbb{R}^3$ point (x, y, z). In general, (X, Y, Z, H) are **homogeneous coordinates** for

[1]Robert Pool, "Computing in Science," *Science* 256, 3 April 1992, p. 45.

(x, y, z) if $H \neq 0$ and

$$x = \frac{X}{H}, \qquad y = \frac{Y}{H}, \qquad \text{and} \qquad z = \frac{Z}{H} \tag{1}$$

Each nonzero scalar multiple of $(x, y, z, 1)$ gives a set of homogeneous coordinates for (x, y, z). For instance, both $(10, -6, 14, 2)$ and $(-15, 9, -21, -3)$ are homogeneous coordinates for $(5, -3, 7)$.

The next example illustrates the transformations used in molecular modeling to move a drug into a protein molecule.

EXAMPLE 7 Give 4×4 matrices for the following transformations:

a. Rotation about the y-axis through an angle of 30°. (By convention, a positive angle is the counterclockwise direction when looking toward the origin from the positive half of the axis of rotation—in this case, the y-axis.)
b. Translation by the vector $\mathbf{p} = (-6, 4, 5)$.

Solution

a. First construct the 3×3 matrix for the rotation. The vector $\mathbf{e}_1$ rotates down toward the negative z-axis, stopping at $(\cos 30°, 0, -\sin 30°) = (\sqrt{3}/2, 0, -.5)$. The vector $\mathbf{e}_2$ on the y-axis does not move, but $\mathbf{e}_3$ on the z-axis rotates down toward the positive x-axis, stopping at $(\sin 30°, 0, \cos 30°) = (.5, 0, \sqrt{3}/2)$. See Fig. 5. From Section 2.6, the standard matrix for this rotation is

$$A = \begin{bmatrix} \sqrt{3}/2 & 0 & .5 \\ 0 & 1 & 0 \\ -.5 & 0 & \sqrt{3}/2 \end{bmatrix}$$

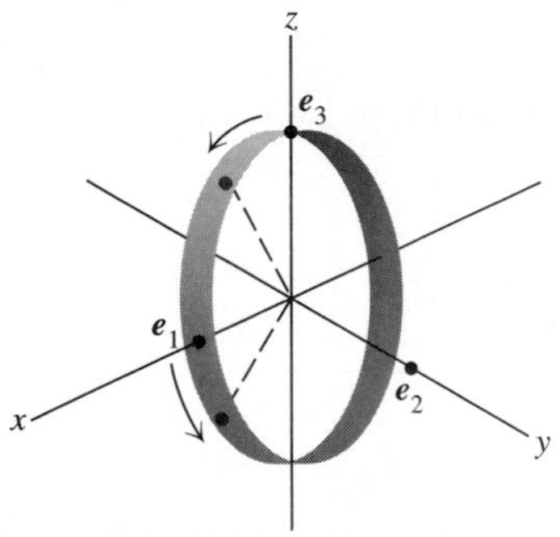

FIGURE 5

So the rotation matrix for homogeneous coordinates is

$$\begin{bmatrix} \sqrt{3}/2 & 0 & .5 & 0 \\ 0 & 1 & 0 & 0 \\ -.5 & 0 & \sqrt{3}/2 & 0 \\ 0 & 0 & 0 & 1 \end{bmatrix}$$

b. We want $(x, y, z, 1)$ to map to $(x - 6, y + 4, z + 5, 1)$. The matrix that does this is

$$\begin{bmatrix} 1 & 0 & 0 & -6 \\ 0 & 1 & 0 & 4 \\ 0 & 0 & 1 & 5 \\ 0 & 0 & 0 & 1 \end{bmatrix}$$

Perspective Projections

A three-dimensional object is represented on the two-dimensional computer screen by projecting the object onto a *viewing plane*. (We ignore other important steps, such as selecting the portion of the viewing plane to display on the screen.) For simplicity, let the xy-plane represent the computer screen, and imagine that the eye of a viewer is along the positive z-axis, at a point $(0, 0, d)$. A *perspective projection* maps each point (x, y, z) onto an image point $(x^*, y^*, 0)$ so that the two points and the eye position, called the *center of projection*, are on a line. See Fig. 6(a).

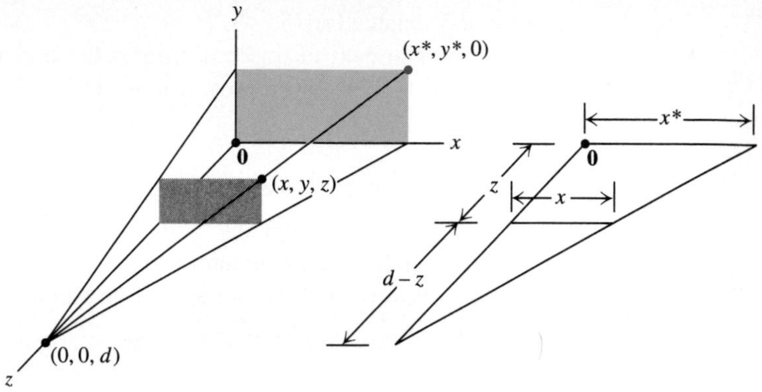

(a) (b)

FIGURE 6 Perspective projection of (x, y, z) onto $(x^*, y^*, 0)$.

The triangle in the xz-plane in Fig. 6(a) is redrawn in part (b) to show the lengths of line segments. Similar triangles show that

$$\frac{x^*}{d} = \frac{x}{d-z} \quad \text{and} \quad x^* = \frac{dx}{d-z} = \frac{x}{1-z/d}$$

Similarly,

$$y^* = \frac{y}{1-z/d}$$

Using homogeneous coordinates, we can represent the perspective projection by a matrix, say, P. We want $(x, y, z, 1)$ to map into $\left(\frac{x}{1-z/d}, \frac{y}{1-z/d}, 0, 1\right)$. Scaling these coordinates by $1 - z/d$, we can also use $(x, y, 0, 1 - z/d)$ as homogeneous coordinates for the image. Now it is easy to display P. In fact,

$$P\begin{bmatrix} x \\ y \\ z \\ 1 \end{bmatrix} = \begin{bmatrix} 1 & 0 & 0 & 0 \\ 0 & 1 & 0 & 0 \\ 0 & 0 & 0 & 0 \\ 0 & 0 & -1/d & 1 \end{bmatrix}\begin{bmatrix} x \\ y \\ z \\ 1 \end{bmatrix} = \begin{bmatrix} x \\ y \\ 0 \\ 1-z/d \end{bmatrix}$$

Other perspective projections, with the center of projection in other locations, result in 4×4 matrices having various nonzero entries in the fourth row.

EXAMPLE 8 Let S be the box with vertices $(3, 1, 5)$, $(5, 1, 5)$, $(5, 0, 5)$, $(3, 0, 5)$, $(3, 1, 4)$, $(5, 1, 4)$, $(5, 0, 4)$ and $(3, 0, 4)$. Find the image of S under the perspective projection with center of projection at $(0, 0, 10)$.

Solution Let P be the projection matrix and let D be the data matrix for S using homogeneous coordinates. The data matrix for the image of S is

$$PD = \begin{bmatrix} 1 & 0 & 0 & 0 \\ 0 & 1 & 0 & 0 \\ 0 & 0 & 0 & 0 \\ 0 & 0 & -1/10 & 1 \end{bmatrix} \overset{\text{Vertex:}}{\overset{\begin{matrix} 1 & 2 & 3 & 4 & 5 & 6 & 7 & 8 \end{matrix}}{\begin{bmatrix} 3 & 5 & 5 & 3 & 3 & 5 & 5 & 3 \\ 1 & 1 & 0 & 0 & 1 & 1 & 0 & 0 \\ 5 & 5 & 5 & 5 & 4 & 4 & 4 & 4 \\ 1 & 1 & 1 & 1 & 1 & 1 & 1 & 1 \end{bmatrix}}}$$

$$= \begin{bmatrix} 3 & 5 & 5 & 3 & 3 & 5 & 5 & 3 \\ 1 & 1 & 0 & 0 & 1 & 1 & 0 & 0 \\ 0 & 0 & 0 & 0 & 0 & 0 & 0 & 0 \\ .5 & .5 & .5 & .5 & .6 & .6 & .6 & .6 \end{bmatrix}$$

To obtain $\mathbb{R}^3$ coordinates, use (1) and divide the top three entries in each column by the corresponding entry in the fourth row:

$$\overset{\text{Vertex:}}{\overset{\begin{matrix} 1 & 2 & 3 & 4 & 5 & 6 & 7 & 8 \end{matrix}}{\begin{bmatrix} 6 & 10 & 10 & 6 & 5 & 8.3 & 8.3 & 5 \\ 2 & 2 & 0 & 0 & 1.7 & 1.7 & 0 & 0 \\ 0 & 0 & 0 & 0 & 0 & 0 & 0 & 0 \end{bmatrix}}}$$

In summary, a typical computer graphics transformation on $\mathbb{R}^3$ is represented with respect to homogeneous coordinates by a 4×4 matrix of the form

$$\begin{bmatrix} A & \mathbf{p} \\ \mathbf{q}^T & r \end{bmatrix}$$

where A is a 3×3 matrix that produces a linear transformation (usually rotation, shearing, or scaling), $\mathbf{p}$ is an $\mathbb{R}^3$ vector that translates points, $\mathbf{q}$ is an $\mathbb{R}^3$ vector associated with a perspective transformation, and r is a scalar (usually 1).

Numerical Note

Continuous movement of graphical 3D objects requires intensive computation with 4×4 matrices, particularly when the surfaces are *rendered* to appear realistic, with texture and appropriate lighting. *Graphics workstations* have 4×4 matrix operations and graphics algorithms embedded in their microchips and circuitry. Such workstations can perform the more than 50 million multiplications per second needed for color animation.[2]

[2] See "High-Performance Polygon Rendering," by Kurt Akeley and Tom Jermoluk, *Computer Graphics*, 22, no. 4, (1988), 239–246.

Further Reading

Computer Graphics: Principles and Practice, 2nd ed., by James D. Foley, Andries van Dam, Steven K. Feiner, and John F. Hughes, Reading, Mass.: Addison-Wesley, 1990, Chapters 5 and 6.

PRACTICE PROBLEM

Rotation of a figure about a point **p** in $\mathbb{R}^2$ is accomplished by first translating the figure by $-\mathbf{p}$, rotating about the origin, and then translating back by **p**. See Fig. 7. Construct the 3×3 matrix that rotates points $-30°$ about the point $(-2, 6)$, using homogeneous coordinates.

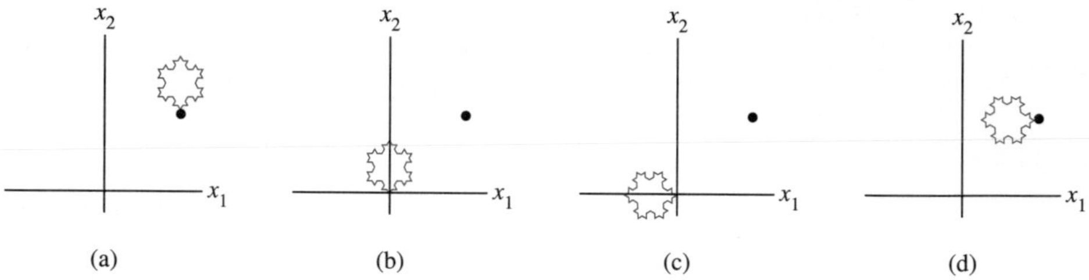

FIGURE 7 Rotation of figure about point **p**.

3.8 EXERCISES

1. What 3×3 matrix will have the same effect on homogeneous coordinates for $\mathbb{R}^2$ that the shear matrix A has in Example 2?
2. Use matrix multiplication to find the image of the triangle with data matrix $D = \begin{bmatrix} 5 & 2 & 4 \\ 0 & 2 & 3 \end{bmatrix}$ under the transformation that reflects points in the y-axis. Sketch both the original triangle and its image.

In Exercises 3–8, find the 3×3 matrices that produce the described composite 2D transformations, using homogeneous coordinates.

3. Translate by (3, 1), and then rotate 45° about the origin.
4. Translate by $(-2, 3)$, and then scale the x-coordinate by .8 and the y-coordinate by 1.2.
5. Reflect points in the x-axis, and then rotate 30° about the origin.
6. Rotate points 30°, and then reflect in the x-axis.
7. Rotate points through 60° about the point (6, 8).
8. Rotate points through 45° about the point (3, 7).
9. A 2×200 data matrix D contains the coordinates of 200 points. Compute the number of multiplications required to transform these points using two arbitrary 2×2 matrices A and B. Consider the two possibilities $A(BD)$ and $(A)D$. Discuss the implications of your results for computer graphics calculations.
10. Consider the following geometric 2D transformations: D a dilation (in which x-coordinates and y-coordinates are scaled by the same factor), R a rotation, and T a translation. Does D *commute* with R? That is, is $D(R(\mathbf{x})) = R(D(\mathbf{x}))$ for all $\mathbf{x}$ in $\mathbb{R}^2$? Does D commute with T? Does R commute with T?
11. A rotation on a computer screen is sometimes implemented as the product of two shear-and-scale transformations, which can speed up calculations that determine how a graphic image actually appears in terms of screen pixels. (The screen consists of rows and columns of small dots, called pixels.) The first transformation translates vertically and then compresses each column of pixels; the second translates horizontally and then stretches each row of pixels. Let

$$A_1 = \begin{bmatrix} 1 & 0 & 0 \\ \sin\varphi & \cos\varphi & 0 \\ 0 & 0 & 1 \end{bmatrix},$$

$$A_2 = \begin{bmatrix} \sec\varphi & -\tan\varphi & 0 \\ 0 & 1 & 0 \\ 0 & 0 & 1 \end{bmatrix}$$

Show that the composition of the two transformations is a rotation in $\mathbb{R}^2$.

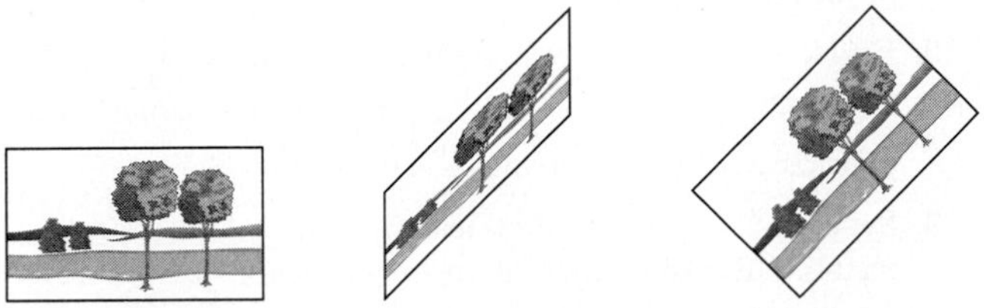

12. A rotation in $\mathbb{R}^2$ usually requires four multiplications. Compute the product below, and show that the matrix for a rotation can be factored into three shear transformations (each of which requires only one multiplication).

$$\begin{bmatrix} 1 & -\tan\varphi/2 & 0 \\ 0 & 1 & 0 \\ 0 & 0 & 1 \end{bmatrix} \begin{bmatrix} 1 & 0 & 0 \\ \sin\varphi & 1 & 0 \\ 0 & 0 & 1 \end{bmatrix} \cdot \begin{bmatrix} 1 & -\tan\varphi/2 & 0 \\ 0 & 1 & 0 \\ 0 & 0 & 1 \end{bmatrix}$$

13. The usual transformations on homogeneous coordinates for 2D computer graphics involve 3×3 matrices of the form
$$\begin{bmatrix} A & \mathbf{p} \\ 0 & 1 \end{bmatrix}$$
where A is a 2×2 matrix and $\mathbf{p}$ is in $\mathbb{R}^2$. Show that such a transformation amounts to a linear transformation on $\mathbb{R}^2$ followed by a translation. [*Hint*: Find an appropriate matrix factorization involving partitioned matrices.]

14. Show that the transformation in Exercise 7 is equivalent to a rotation about the origin followed by a translation by $\mathbf{p}$. Find $\mathbf{q}$ and $\mathbf{p}$.

15. What vector in $\mathbb{R}^3$ has homogeneous coordinates $(\frac{1}{2}, -\frac{1}{4}, \frac{1}{8}, \frac{1}{24})$?

16. Are $(1, -2, 3, 4)$ and $(10, -20, 30, 40)$ homogeneous coordinates for the same point in $\mathbb{R}^3$? Why or why not?

17. Give the 4×4 matrix that rotates points in $\mathbb{R}^3$ about the x-axis through an angle of 60°.

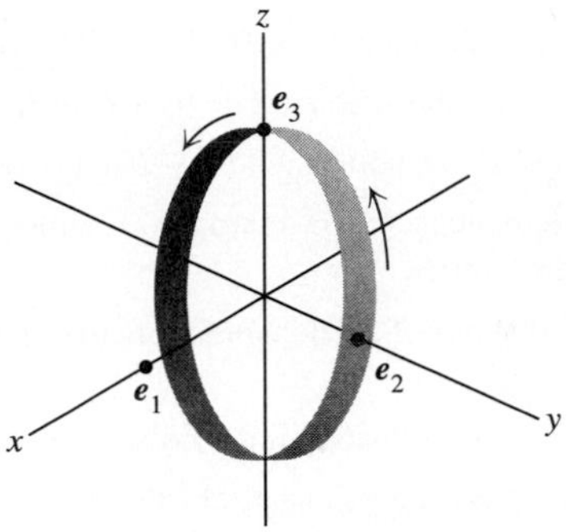

18. Give the 4×4 matrix that rotates points in $\mathbb{R}^3$ about the z-axis through an angle of $-30°$ and then translates by $\mathbf{p} = (5, -2, 1)$.

19. Let S be the triangle with vertices $(4.2, 1.2, 4)$, $(6, 4, 2)$, $(2, 2, 6)$. Find the image of S under the perspective projection with center of projection at $(0, 0, 10)$.

20. Let S be the triangle with vertices $(9, 3, -5)$, $(12, 8, 2)$, $(1.8, 2.7, 1)$. Find the image of S under the perspective projection with center of projection at $(0, 0, 10)$.

SOLUTION TO PRACTICE PROBLEM

Assemble the matrices right-to-left for the three operations. Using $\mathbf{p} = (-2, 6)$, $\cos(-30°) = \sqrt{3}/2$, and $\sin(-30°) = -.5$, we have:

$$\underset{\text{back by } p}{\overset{\text{Translate}}{\begin{bmatrix} 1 & 0 & -2 \\ 0 & 1 & 6 \\ 0 & 0 & 1 \end{bmatrix}}} \underset{\text{the origin}}{\overset{\text{Rotate around}}{\begin{bmatrix} \sqrt{3}/2 & .5 & 0 \\ -.5 & \sqrt{3}/2 & 0 \\ 0 & 0 & 1 \end{bmatrix}}} \underset{\text{by } -p}{\overset{\text{Translate}}{\begin{bmatrix} 1 & 0 & 2 \\ 0 & 1 & -6 \\ 0 & 0 & 1 \end{bmatrix}}}$$

$$= \begin{bmatrix} \sqrt{3}/2 & .5 & \sqrt{3}-5 \\ -.5 & \sqrt{3}/2 & -3\sqrt{3}+5 \\ 0 & 0 & 1 \end{bmatrix}$$

CHAPTER 3 SUPPLEMENTARY EXERCISES

1. Assume that the matrices mentioned in the statements below have appropriate sizes. Mark each statement True or False. Justify each answer.

___ a. If A and B are $m \times n$, then both AB^T and A^TB are defined.

___ b. If $AB = C$ and C has 2 columns, then A has 2 columns.

___ c. Left-multiplying a matrix B by a diagonal matrix A scales the rows of B.

___ d. If $BC = BD$, then $C = D$.

___ e. If $AC = 0$, then either $A = 0$ or $C = 0$.

___ f. If A and B are $n \times n$, then $(A+B)(A-B) = A^2 - B^2$.

___ g. An elementary $n \times n$ matrix has either n or $n+1$ nonzero entries.

___ h. The transpose of an elementary matrix is an elementary matrix.

___ i. An elementary matrix must be square.

___ j. Every square matrix is a product of elementary matrices.

___ k. If A is a 3×3 matrix with three pivot positions, there exist elementary matrices $E_1, \ldots, E_p$, such that $E_p \cdots E_1 A = I$.

___ l. If $AB = I$, then A is invertible.

___ m. If A and B are square and invertible, then AB is invertible, and $(AB)^{-1} = A^{-1}B^{-1}$.

___ n. If $AB = BA$ and if A is invertible, then $A^{-1}B = BA^{-1}$.

___ o. If A is invertible and $r \neq 0$, then $(rA)^{-1} = rA^{-1}$.

___ p. If A is a 3×3 matrix and the equation $A\mathbf{x} = \begin{bmatrix} 1 \\ 0 \\ 0 \end{bmatrix}$ has a unique solution, then A is invertible.

2. Find the matrix C whose inverse is $C^{-1} = \begin{bmatrix} 4 & 5 \\ 6 & 7 \end{bmatrix}$.

3. Let $A = \begin{bmatrix} 0 & 0 & 0 \\ 1 & 0 & 0 \\ 0 & 1 & 0 \end{bmatrix}$. Show that $A^3 = 0$. Use matrix algebra to compute the product $(I - A)(I + A + A^2)$.

4. Suppose $A^n = 0$ for some $n > 1$. Find an inverse for $I - A$.

5. Suppose an $n \times n$ matrix A satisfies the equation $A^2 - 2A + I = 0$. Show that $A^3 = 3A - 2I$ and $A^4 = 4A - 3I$.

6. Let $A = \begin{bmatrix} 1 & 0 \\ 0 & -1 \end{bmatrix}$, $B = \begin{bmatrix} 0 & 1 \\ 1 & 0 \end{bmatrix}$. These are *Pauli spin matrices* used in the study of electron spin in quantum mechanics. Show that $A^2 = I$, $B^2 = I$, and $AB = -BA$. Matrices such that $AB = -BA$ are said to *anticommute*.

7. Let $A = \begin{bmatrix} 1 & 3 & 8 \\ 2 & 4 & 11 \\ 1 & 2 & 5 \end{bmatrix}$, $B = \begin{bmatrix} -3 & 5 \\ 1 & 5 \\ 3 & 4 \end{bmatrix}$. Compute $A^{-1}B$ without computing A^{-1}. [*Hint*: $A^{-1}B$ is the solution of the equation $AX = B$.]

8. Find a matrix A such that the transformation $\mathbf{x} \mapsto A\mathbf{x}$ takes $\begin{bmatrix} 1 \\ 3 \end{bmatrix}$ and $\begin{bmatrix} 2 \\ 7 \end{bmatrix}$ into $\begin{bmatrix} 1 \\ 1 \end{bmatrix}$ and $\begin{bmatrix} 3 \\ 1 \end{bmatrix}$, respectively. [*Hint*: Write a matrix equation involving A and solve for A.]

9. Suppose $C = E_3E_2E_1B$, where E_1, E_2, E_3 are elementary matrices. Explain why C is row equivalent to B.

10. Suppose that A is invertible. Explain why A^TA is also invertible. Then show that $A^{-1} = (A^TA)^{-1}A^T$.

11. Let $x_1, \ldots, x_n$ be fixed numbers. The matrix below, called a *Vandermonde* matrix, arises in applications such as signal processing, error-correcting codes, and polynomial interpolation.

$$V = \begin{bmatrix} 1 & x_1 & x_1^2 & \cdots & x_1^{n-1} \\ 1 & x_2 & x_2^2 & \cdots & x_2^{n-1} \\ \vdots & \vdots & \vdots & & \vdots \\ 1 & x_n & x_n^2 & \cdots & x_n^{n-1} \end{bmatrix}$$

Given a $\mathbf{y} = (y_1, \ldots, y_n)$ in $\mathbb{R}^n$, suppose that $\mathbf{c} = (c_0, \ldots, c_{n-1})$ is a vector in $\mathbb{R}^n$ that satisfies $V\mathbf{c} = \mathbf{y}$, and define the polynomial

$$p(t) = c_0 + c_1t + c_2t^2 + \cdots + c_{n-1}t^{n-1}$$

a. Show that $p(x_1) = y_1, \ldots, p(x_n) = y_n$. We call $p(t)$ an *interpolating polynomial for the points* $(x_1, y_1), \ldots, (x_n, y_n)$ because the graph of $p(t)$ passes through the points.

b. Suppose that $x_1, \ldots, x_n$ are distinct numbers. Show that the columns of V are linearly independent. [*Hint*: How many zeros can a polynomial of degree $n - 1$ have?]

c. Prove: "If $x_1, \ldots, x_n$ are distinct numbers, and $y_1, \ldots, y_n$ are arbitrary numbers, then there is an interpolating polynomial of degree $\leq n-1$ for $(x_1, y_1), \ldots, (x_n, y_n)$."

12. Let $A = LU$, where L is an invertible lower triangular matrix and U is upper triangular. Explain why the first column of A is a multiple of the first column of L. How is the second column of A related to the columns of L?

13. Given $\mathbf{u}$ in $\mathbb{R}^n$ with $\mathbf{u}^T\mathbf{u} = 1$, let $P = \mathbf{u}\mathbf{u}^T$ (an outer product) and $Q = I - 2P$. Verify the statements:
a. $P^2 = P$ b. $P^T = P$ c. $Q^2 = I$

The transformation $\mathbf{x} \mapsto P\mathbf{x}$ is called a *projection*, and $\mathbf{x} \mapsto Q\mathbf{x}$ is called a *Householder reflection*. Such reflections are used in computer programs to create multiple zeros in a vector (usually a column of a matrix).

14. Let $\mathbf{u} = \begin{bmatrix} 0 \\ 0 \\ 1 \end{bmatrix}$ and $\mathbf{x} = \begin{bmatrix} 1 \\ 5 \\ 3 \end{bmatrix}$. Determine P and Q as in Exercise 13 and compute $P\mathbf{x}$ and $Q\mathbf{x}$. The figure shows that $Q\mathbf{x}$ is the reflection of $\mathbf{x}$ in the x_1x_2-plane.

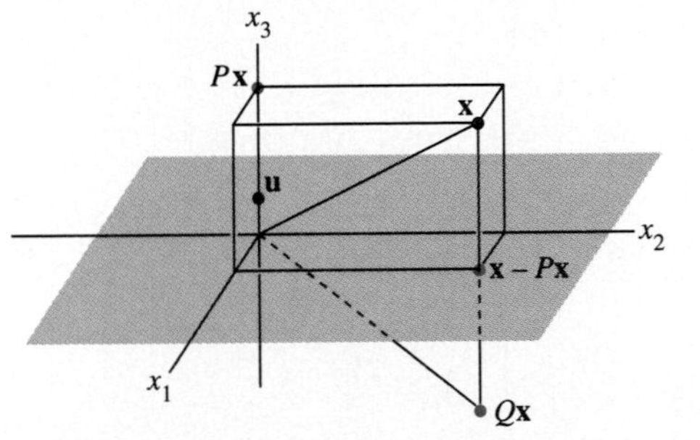

A Householder reflection in the plane $x_3 = 0$.

15. Suppose A is a 3×4 matrix and there exists a 4×3 matrix C such that $AC = I_3$ (the 3×3 identity matrix). Let $\mathbf{b}$ be an arbitrary vector in $\mathbb{R}^3$. Produce a solution of $A\mathbf{x} = \mathbf{b}$.

16. Suppose A is a 5×3 matrix and there exists a 3×5 matrix C such that $CA = I_3$. Suppose further that for some given $\mathbf{b}$ in $\mathbb{R}^5$, the equation $A\mathbf{x} = \mathbf{b}$ has at least one solution. Show that this solution is unique.

4

Determinants

Introductory Example: Determinants in Analytic Geometry

A determinant is a number that is assigned to a square array of numbers in a certain way. This idea was considered as early as 1683 by the Japanese mathematician Seki Takakazu and independently in 1693 by the German mathematician Gottfried Leibnitz (one of the inventors of calculus), about one hundred sixty years before a separate theory of matrices developed.

For the next one hundred twenty years, determinants were studied mainly in connection with systems of linear equations such as

$$\begin{aligned} a_1x + b_1y + c_1z &= 0 \\ a_2x + b_2y + c_2z &= 0 \\ a_3x + b_3y + c_3z &= 0 \end{aligned}$$

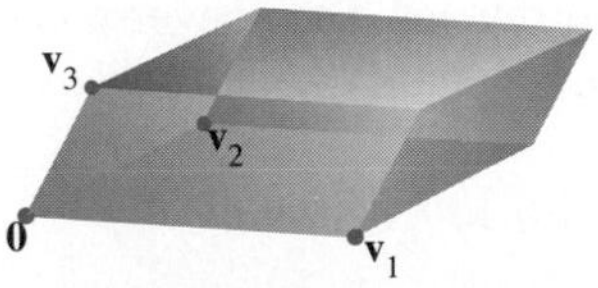

FIGURE 1 The parallelepiped determined by $\mathbf{v}_1$, $\mathbf{v}_2$ and $\mathbf{v}_3$.

Then in 1812, Augustin-Louis Cauchy published a paper in which he used determinants to give formulas for the volumes of certain solid polyhedra. Let $\mathbf{v}_1 = (a_1, b_1, c_1)$, $\mathbf{v}_2 = (a_2, b_2, c_2)$, and $\mathbf{v}_3 = (a_3, b_3, c_3)$, and consider the "crystal" or parallelepiped in Fig. 1. Cauchy showed that the volume of this crystal is the absolute value of the determinant associated with the system shown above.

Cauchy's use of determinants in analytic geometry sparked an intense interest in applications of determinants that lasted for about one hundred years. A *summary* of what was known by the early 1900s filled a four-volume treatise by Thomas Muir.

In Cauchy's day, when life was simple and matrices were small, determinants played a major role in analytic geometry and other parts of mathematics. Today, determinants are of little numerical value in the large-scale matrix computations that arise so often. Nevertheless, determinantal formulas still give important information about matrices, and a knowledge of determinants is useful in some applications of linear algebra.

We have three goals in this chapter: to prove an invertibility criterion for a square matrix A that involves the entries of A rather than its columns, to give formulas for A^{-1} and $A^{-1}\mathbf{b}$ that are used in theoretical applications, and to derive the geometric interpretation of determinants described in the chapter introduction. The first goal is reached in Section 4.2 and the other two in Section 4.3.

4.1 INTRODUCTION TO DETERMINANTS

Let us watch what happens when an invertible 3×3 matrix is row reduced. Consider $A = [a_{ij}]$ with $a_{11} \neq 0$. If we multiply the second and third rows of A by a_{11} and then subtract appropriate multiples of the first row from the other two rows, we find that A is row equivalent to the following two matrices:

$$\begin{bmatrix} a_{11} & a_{12} & a_{13} \\ a_{11}a_{21} & a_{11}a_{22} & a_{11}a_{23} \\ a_{11}a_{31} & a_{11}a_{32} & a_{11}a_{33} \end{bmatrix} \sim \begin{bmatrix} a_{11} & a_{12} & a_{13} \\ 0 & a_{11}a_{22} - a_{12}a_{21} & a_{11}a_{23} - a_{13}a_{21} \\ 0 & a_{11}a_{32} - a_{12}a_{31} & a_{11}a_{33} - a_{13}a_{31} \end{bmatrix} \qquad (1)$$

Since A is invertible, either the $(2, 2)$-entry or the $(3, 2)$-entry on the right in (1) is nonzero. Let us suppose that the $(2, 2)$-entry is nonzero. (Otherwise, we can make a row interchange before proceeding.) Multiply row 3 by $a_{11}a_{22} - a_{12}a_{21}$, and then to the new row 3 add $-(a_{11}a_{32} - a_{12}a_{31})$ times row 2. This will show that

$$A \sim \begin{bmatrix} a_{11} & a_{12} & a_{13} \\ 0 & a_{11}a_{22} - a_{12}a_{21} & a_{11}a_{23} - a_{13}a_{21} \\ 0 & 0 & a_{11}\Delta \end{bmatrix}$$

where

$$\Delta = a_{11}a_{22}a_{33} + a_{12}a_{23}a_{31} + a_{13}a_{21}a_{32} - a_{11}a_{23}a_{32} - a_{12}a_{21}a_{33} - a_{13}a_{22}a_{31} \qquad (2)$$

Since A is invertible, Δ must be nonzero. We call Δ in (2) the **determinant** of the 3×3 matrix A. If a_{11} or $a_{11}a_{22} - a_{12}a_{21}$ is zero, analogous row operations would lead to a triangular echelon form with a multiple of Δ in the lower-right corner. In any case, an invertible 3×3 matrix must have a nonzero determinant. The converse is true, too. In fact we shall prove in the next section that an $n\times n$ matrix is invertible if and only if its determinant is nonzero.

Recall that the determinant of a 2×2 matrix, $A = [a_{ij}]$, is the number

$$\det A = a_{11}a_{22} - a_{12}a_{21}$$

For a 1×1 matrix, say $A = [a_{11}]$, we define $\det A = a_{11}$. To generalize the definition of the determinant to larger matrices, we'll use 2×2 determinants to rewrite the 3×3 determinant Δ described above. Since the terms in Δ can be grouped as $(a_{11}a_{22}a_{33} - a_{11}a_{23}a_{32}) - (a_{12}a_{21}a_{33} - a_{12}a_{23}a_{31}) + (a_{13}a_{21}a_{32} - a_{13}a_{22}a_{31})$,

$$\Delta = a_{11}\cdot\det\begin{bmatrix} a_{22} & a_{23} \\ a_{32} & a_{33}\end{bmatrix} - a_{12}\cdot\det\begin{bmatrix} a_{21} & a_{23} \\ a_{31} & a_{33}\end{bmatrix} + a_{13}\cdot\det\begin{bmatrix} a_{21} & a_{22} \\ a_{31} & a_{32}\end{bmatrix}$$

For brevity, we write

$$\Delta = a_{11}\cdot\det A_{11} - a_{12}\cdot\det A_{12} + a_{13}\cdot\det A_{13} \tag{3}$$

where A_{11}, A_{12}, and A_{13} are obtained from A by deleting the first row and one of the three columns. For any matrix A, let A_{ij} denote the submatrix formed by deleting the ith row and jth column of A. For instance, if

$$A = \begin{bmatrix} 1 & -2 & 5 & 0 \\ 2 & 0 & 4 & -1 \\ 3 & 1 & 0 & 7 \\ 0 & 4 & -2 & 0 \end{bmatrix}$$

then A_{32} is obtained by crossing out row 3 and column 2,

$$\begin{bmatrix} 1 & -2 & 5 & 0 \\ 2 & 0 & 4 & -1 \\ 3 & 1 & 0 & 7 \\ 0 & 4 & -2 & 0 \end{bmatrix}$$

so that

$$A_{32} = \begin{bmatrix} 1 & 5 & 0 \\ 2 & 4 & -1 \\ 0 & -2 & 0 \end{bmatrix}$$

We can now give a *recursive* definition of a determinant. When $n = 3$, $\det A$ is defined using determinants of the 2×2 submatrices A_{1j}, as in (3) above. When $n = 4$, $\det A$ uses determinants of the 3×3 submatrices A_{1j}. In general, an $n\times n$ determinant is defined by determinants of $(n-1)\times(n-1)$ submatrices.

DEFINITION

For $n \geq 2$, the **determinant** of an $n\times n$ matrix $A = [a_{ij}]$ is the sum of n terms of the form $\pm a_{1j}\det A_{1j}$, with plus and minus signs alternating, where the entries $a_{11}, a_{12}, \ldots, a_{1n}$ are from the first row of A. In symbols,

$$\begin{aligned}\det A &= a_{11}\det A_{11} - a_{12}\det A_{12} + \cdots + (-1)^{1+n}a_{1n}\det A_{1n} \\ &= \sum_{j=1}^{n}(-1)^{1+j}a_{1j}\det A_{1j}\end{aligned}$$

EXAMPLE 1 Compute the determinant of

$$A = \begin{bmatrix} 1 & 5 & 0 \\ 2 & 4 & -1 \\ 0 & -2 & 0 \end{bmatrix}$$

Solution

$$\begin{aligned}\det A &= a_{11}\det A_{11} - a_{12}\det A_{12} + a_{13}\det A_{13}\\ &= 1\cdot\det\begin{bmatrix} 4 & -1\\ -2 & 0\end{bmatrix} - 5\cdot\det\begin{bmatrix} 2 & -1\\ 0 & 0\end{bmatrix} + 0\cdot\det\begin{bmatrix} 2 & 4\\ 0 & -2\end{bmatrix}\\ &= 1(0-2) - 5(0-0) + 0(-4-0)\\ &= -2\end{aligned}$$

Another common notation for the determinant of a matrix uses a pair of vertical lines in place of brackets. Thus the calculation in Example 1 may be written as

$$\det A = 1\begin{vmatrix} 4 & -1\\ -2 & 0\end{vmatrix} - 5\begin{vmatrix} 2 & -1\\ 0 & 0\end{vmatrix} + 0\begin{vmatrix} 2 & 4\\ 0 & -2\end{vmatrix} = \cdots = -2$$

To state the next theorem, it is convenient to write the definition of $\det A$ in a slightly different form. Given $A = [a_{ij}]$, the **(i, j)-cofactor** of A is the number C_{ij} given by

$$C_{ij} = (-1)^{i+j}\det A_{ij} \tag{4}$$

Then

$$\det A = a_{11}C_{11} + a_{12}C_{12} + \cdots + a_{1n}C_{1n}$$

This formula is called the **cofactor expansion along the first row** of A. We omit the proof of the following fundamental theorem because the proof would require a lengthy digression.

THEOREM 1

The determinant of an $n\times n$ matrix A may be computed by a cofactor expansion along any row or down any column. The expansion across the ith row using the cofactors in (4) is

$$\det A = a_{i1}C_{i1} + a_{i2}C_{i2} + \cdots + a_{in}C_{in}$$

The cofactor expansion down the jth column is

$$\det A = a_{1j}C_{1j} + a_{2j}C_{2j} + \cdots + a_{nj}C_{nj}$$

The plus or minus sign in the (i, j)-cofactor depends on the position of a_{ij} in the matrix, regardless of the sign of a_{ij} itself. The factor $(-1)^{i+j}$ determines the following checkerboard pattern of signs:

$$\begin{bmatrix} + & - & + & \cdots\\ - & + & - & \\ + & - & + & \\ \vdots & & & \ddots\end{bmatrix}$$

EXAMPLE 2 Use a cofactor expansion across the third row to compute $\det A$, where

$$A = \begin{bmatrix} 1 & 5 & 0\\ 2 & 4 & -1\\ 0 & -2 & 0\end{bmatrix}$$

Solution

$$\begin{aligned}\det A &= a_{31}C_{31} + a_{32}C_{32} + a_{33}C_{33} \\ &= (-1)^{3+1}a_{31}\det A_{31} + (-1)^{3+2}a_{32}\det A_{32} + (-1)^{3+3}a_{33}\det A_{33} \\ &= 0\begin{vmatrix} 5 & 0 \\ 4 & -1 \end{vmatrix} - (-2)\begin{vmatrix} 1 & 0 \\ 2 & -1 \end{vmatrix} + 0\begin{vmatrix} 1 & 5 \\ 2 & 4 \end{vmatrix} \\ &= 0 + 2(-1) + 0 = -2\end{aligned}$$

Theorem 1 is helpful for computing the determinant of a matrix that contains many zeros. For example, if a row is mostly zeros, then the cofactor expansion across that row has many terms that are zero, and the cofactors in those terms need not be calculated. The same approach works with a column that contains many zeros.

EXAMPLE 3 Compute $\det A$, where

$$A = \begin{bmatrix} 3 & -7 & 8 & 9 & -6 \\ 0 & 2 & -5 & 7 & 3 \\ 0 & 0 & 1 & 5 & 0 \\ 0 & 0 & 2 & 4 & -1 \\ 0 & 0 & 0 & -2 & 0 \end{bmatrix}$$

Solution The cofactor expansion down the first column of A has all terms equal to zero except the first. Thus

$$\det A = 3\cdot\begin{vmatrix} 2 & -5 & 7 & 3 \\ 0 & 1 & 5 & 0 \\ 0 & 2 & 4 & -1 \\ 0 & 0 & -2 & 0 \end{vmatrix} - 0\cdot C_{21} + 0\cdot C_{31} - 0\cdot C_{41} + 0\cdot C_{51}$$

Henceforth we shall omit the zero terms in the cofactor expansion. Next, expand this 4×4 determinant down the first column, in order to take advantage of the zeros there. We have

$$\det A = 3\cdot2\cdot\begin{vmatrix} 1 & 5 & 0 \\ 2 & 4 & -1 \\ 0 & -2 & 0 \end{vmatrix}$$

This 3×3 determinant was computed in Example 1 and found to equal -2. Hence $\det A = 3\cdot2\cdot(-2) = -12$.

The matrix in Example 3 was nearly triangular. The method in that example is easily adapted to prove the following theorem.

THEOREM 2

If A is a triangular matrix, then $\det A$ is the product of the entries on the main diagonal of A.

The strategy in Example 3 of looking for zeros works extremely well when an entire row or column consists of zeros. In such a case, the cofactor expansion along such a row or column is a sum of zeros! So the determinant is zero. Unfortunately, most cofactor expansions are not so quickly evaluated.

Numerical Note

By today's standards, a 25×25 matrix is small. Yet it would be impossible to calculate a 25×25 determinant by cofactor expansion. In general, a cofactor expansion requires over $n!$ multiplications, and $25!$ is approximately 1.5×10^{25}.

If a supercomputer could make one trillion multiplications per second, it would have to run for over 500,000 years to compute a 25×25 determinant by this method. Fortunately, there are faster methods, as we'll soon discover.

Exercises 19–40 explore important properties of determinants, mostly for the 2×2 case. The results from Exercises 33–36 will be used in the next section to derive analogous properties for $n\times n$ matrices.

PRACTICE PROBLEM

Compute $\begin{vmatrix} 5 & -7 & 2 & 2 \\ 0 & 3 & 0 & -4 \\ -5 & -8 & 0 & 3 \\ 0 & 5 & 0 & -6 \end{vmatrix}$.

4.1 EXERCISES

Compute the determinants in Exercises 1–8 using a cofactor expansion across the first row. In Exercises 1–4, also compute the determinant by a cofactor expansion down the second column.

1. $\begin{vmatrix} 3 & 0 & 4 \\ 2 & 3 & 2 \\ 0 & 5 & -1 \end{vmatrix}$

2. $\begin{vmatrix} 0 & 5 & 1 \\ 4 & -3 & 0 \\ 2 & 4 & 1 \end{vmatrix}$

3. $\begin{vmatrix} 2 & -4 & 3 \\ 3 & 1 & 2 \\ 1 & 4 & -1 \end{vmatrix}$

4. $\begin{vmatrix} 1 & 3 & 5 \\ 2 & 1 & 1 \\ 3 & 4 & 2 \end{vmatrix}$

5. $\begin{vmatrix} 2 & 3 & -4 \\ 4 & 0 & 5 \\ 5 & 1 & 6 \end{vmatrix}$

6. $\begin{vmatrix} 5 & -2 & 4 \\ 0 & 3 & -5 \\ 2 & -4 & 7 \end{vmatrix}$

7. $\begin{vmatrix} 4 & 3 & 0 \\ 6 & 5 & 2 \\ 9 & 7 & 3 \end{vmatrix}$

8. $\begin{vmatrix} 8 & 1 & 6 \\ 4 & 0 & 3 \\ 3 & -2 & 5 \end{vmatrix}$

Compute the determinants in Exercises 9–14 by cofactor expansions. At each step, choose a row or column that involves the least amount of computation.

9. $\begin{vmatrix} 6 & 0 & 0 & 5 \\ 1 & 7 & 2 & -5 \\ 2 & 0 & 0 & 0 \\ 8 & 3 & 1 & 8 \end{vmatrix}$

10. $\begin{vmatrix} 1 & -2 & 5 & 2 \\ 0 & 0 & 3 & 0 \\ 2 & -6 & -7 & 5 \\ 5 & 0 & 4 & 4 \end{vmatrix}$

11. $\begin{vmatrix} 3 & 5 & -8 & 4 \\ 0 & -2 & 3 & -7 \\ 0 & 0 & 1 & 5 \\ 0 & 0 & 0 & 2 \end{vmatrix}$

12. $\begin{vmatrix} 4 & 0 & 0 & 0 \\ 7 & -1 & 0 & 0 \\ 2 & 6 & 3 & 0 \\ 5 & -8 & 4 & -3 \end{vmatrix}$

13. $\begin{vmatrix} 4 & 0 & -7 & 3 & -5 \\ 0 & 0 & 2 & 0 & 0 \\ 7 & 3 & -6 & 4 & -8 \\ 5 & 0 & 5 & 2 & -3 \\ 0 & 0 & 9 & -1 & 2 \end{vmatrix}$

14. $\begin{vmatrix} 6 & 3 & 2 & 4 & 0 \\ 9 & 0 & -4 & 1 & 0 \\ 8 & -5 & 6 & 7 & 1 \\ 3 & 0 & 0 & 0 & 0 \\ 4 & 2 & 3 & 2 & 0 \end{vmatrix}$

The expansion of a 3×3 determinant can be remembered by the following device. Write a second copy of the first two columns to the right of the matrix, and compute the determinant by multiplying entries on six diagonals:

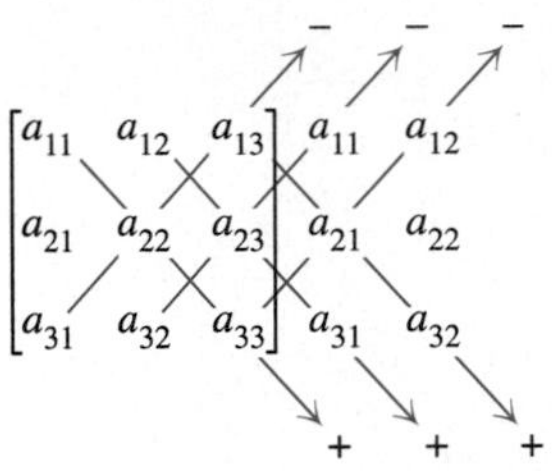

Add downward diagonal products and subtract the upward products. Use this method to compute the determinants in Exercises 15–18. *Warning: This trick does not generalize in any reasonable way to 4×4 or larger matrices.*

15. $\begin{vmatrix} 3 & 0 & 4 \\ 2 & 3 & 2 \\ 0 & 5 & -1 \end{vmatrix}$ **16.** $\begin{vmatrix} 0 & 5 & 1 \\ 4 & -3 & 0 \\ 2 & 4 & 1 \end{vmatrix}$

17. $\begin{vmatrix} 2 & -4 & 3 \\ 3 & 1 & 2 \\ 1 & 4 & -1 \end{vmatrix}$ **18.** $\begin{vmatrix} 1 & 3 & 5 \\ 2 & 1 & 1 \\ 3 & 4 & 2 \end{vmatrix}$

In Exercises 19–24, explore the effect of an elementary row operation on the determinant of a matrix. In each case, state the row operation and describe how it affects the determinant.

19. $\begin{bmatrix} a & b \\ c & d \end{bmatrix}, \begin{bmatrix} c & d \\ a & b \end{bmatrix}$

20. $\begin{bmatrix} a & b & c \\ 3 & 2 & 2 \\ 6 & 5 & 6 \end{bmatrix}, \begin{bmatrix} 3 & 2 & 2 \\ a & b & c \\ 6 & 5 & 6 \end{bmatrix}$

21. $\begin{bmatrix} 3 & 4 \\ 5 & 6 \end{bmatrix}, \begin{bmatrix} 3 & 4 \\ 5+3k & 6+4k \end{bmatrix}$

22. $\begin{bmatrix} a & b \\ c & d \end{bmatrix}, \begin{bmatrix} a+kc & b+kd \\ c & d \end{bmatrix}$

23. $\begin{bmatrix} 1 & 1 & 1 \\ -3 & 8 & -4 \\ 2 & -3 & 2 \end{bmatrix}, \begin{bmatrix} k & k & k \\ -3 & 8 & -4 \\ 2 & -3 & 2 \end{bmatrix}$

24. $\begin{bmatrix} a & b \\ c & d \end{bmatrix}, \begin{bmatrix} a & b \\ kc & kd \end{bmatrix}$

Compute the determinants of the elementary matrices given in Exercises 25–30. (See Section 3.2.)

25. $\begin{bmatrix} 1 & 0 & 0 \\ 0 & 1 & 0 \\ 0 & k & 1 \end{bmatrix}$ **26.** $\begin{bmatrix} 1 & 0 & 0 \\ 0 & 1 & 0 \\ k & 0 & 1 \end{bmatrix}$

27. $\begin{bmatrix} k & 0 & 0 \\ 0 & 1 & 0 \\ 0 & 0 & 1 \end{bmatrix}$ **28.** $\begin{bmatrix} 1 & 0 & 0 \\ 0 & k & 0 \\ 0 & 0 & 1 \end{bmatrix}$

29. $\begin{bmatrix} 0 & 1 & 0 \\ 1 & 0 & 0 \\ 0 & 0 & 1 \end{bmatrix}$ **30.** $\begin{bmatrix} 0 & 0 & 1 \\ 0 & 1 & 0 \\ 1 & 0 & 0 \end{bmatrix}$

Use Exercises 25–30 to answer the questions in Exercises 31 and 32. Give reasons for your answers.

31. What is the determinant of an elementary row replacement matrix?

32. What is the determinant of an elementary scaling matrix with k on the diagonal?

In Exercises 33–36, verify that $\det EA = (\det E)(\det A)$, where E is the elementary matrix shown and $A = \begin{bmatrix} a & b \\ c & d \end{bmatrix}$.

33. $\begin{bmatrix} 0 & 1 \\ 1 & 0 \end{bmatrix}$ **34.** $\begin{bmatrix} 1 & 0 \\ 0 & k \end{bmatrix}$

35. $\begin{bmatrix} 1 & k \\ 0 & 1 \end{bmatrix}$ **36.** $\begin{bmatrix} 1 & 0 \\ k & 1 \end{bmatrix}$

37. Let $A = \begin{bmatrix} 3 & 1 \\ 4 & 2 \end{bmatrix}$. Write $5A$. Is $\det 5A = 5 \det A$?

38. Let $A = \begin{bmatrix} a & b \\ c & d \end{bmatrix}$ and k be a scalar. Find a formula that relates $\det kA$ to k and $\det A$.

39. Let $\mathbf{u} = \begin{bmatrix} 3 \\ 0 \end{bmatrix}$ and $\mathbf{v} = \begin{bmatrix} 1 \\ 2 \end{bmatrix}$. Compute the area of the parallelogram determined by $\mathbf{u}$, $\mathbf{v}$, $\mathbf{u}+\mathbf{v}$, and $\mathbf{0}$, and compute the determinant of $[\,\mathbf{u} \;\; \mathbf{v}\,]$. How do they compare? Replace the first entry of $\mathbf{v}$ by an arbitrary number x, and repeat the problem. Draw a picture and explain what you find.

40. Let $\mathbf{u} = \begin{bmatrix} a \\ b \end{bmatrix}$ and $\mathbf{v} = \begin{bmatrix} c \\ 0 \end{bmatrix}$, where a, b, c are positive (for simplicity). Compute the area of the parallelogram determined by $\mathbf{u}$, $\mathbf{v}$, $\mathbf{u}+\mathbf{v}$, and $\mathbf{0}$, and compute the determinants of the matrices $[\,\mathbf{u} \;\; \mathbf{v}\,]$ and $[\,\mathbf{v} \;\; \mathbf{u}\,]$. Draw a picture and explain what you find.

SOLUTION TO PRACTICE PROBLEM

Take advantage of the zeros. Begin with a cofactor expansion down the third column to obtain a 3×3 matrix, which may be evaluated by an expansion down its first column.

$$\begin{vmatrix} 5 & -7 & 2 & 2 \\ 0 & 3 & 0 & -4 \\ -5 & -8 & 0 & 3 \\ 0 & 5 & 0 & -6 \end{vmatrix} = 2\begin{vmatrix} 0 & 3 & -4 \\ -5 & -8 & 3 \\ 0 & 5 & -6 \end{vmatrix}$$

$$= 2\cdot(-1)(-5)\begin{vmatrix} 3 & -4 \\ 5 & -6 \end{vmatrix} = 20$$

The -1 in the next to last calculation came from the position of the -5 in the 3×3 determinant.

4.2 PROPERTIES OF DETERMINANTS

The secret of determinants lies in how they change when row operations are performed. The following theorem generalizes the results of Exercises 19–24 in Section 4.1. The proof is at the end of this section.

THEOREM 3

Row Operations

Let A be a square matrix.

a. If a multiple of one row of A is added to another to produce a matrix B, then $\det B = \det A$.

b. If two rows of A are interchanged to produce B, then $\det B = -\det A$.

c. If one row of A is multiplied by k to produce B, then $\det B = k\cdot\det A$.

The following examples show how to use Theorem 3 to find determinants efficiently.

EXAMPLE 1 Compute $\det A$, where $A = \begin{bmatrix} 1 & -4 & 2 \\ -2 & 8 & -9 \\ -1 & 7 & 0 \end{bmatrix}$.

Solution The strategy is to reduce A to echelon form and then to use the fact that the determinant of a triangular matrix is the product of the diagonal entries. The first two row replacements in column 1 do not change the determinant:

$$\det A = \begin{vmatrix} 1 & -4 & 2 \\ -2 & 8 & -9 \\ -1 & 7 & 0 \end{vmatrix} = \begin{vmatrix} 1 & -4 & 2 \\ 0 & 0 & -5 \\ -1 & 7 & 0 \end{vmatrix} = \begin{vmatrix} 1 & -4 & 2 \\ 0 & 0 & -5 \\ 0 & 3 & 2 \end{vmatrix}$$

An interchange of rows 2 and 3 reverses the sign of the determinant, so

$$\det A = -\begin{vmatrix} 1 & -4 & 2 \\ 0 & 3 & 2 \\ 0 & 0 & -5 \end{vmatrix} = -(1)(3)(-5) = 15$$

A common use of Theorem 3(c) in hand calculations is to *factor out a common multiple of one row* of a matrix. For instance,

$$\begin{vmatrix} * & * & * \\ 5k & -2k & 3k \\ * & * & * \end{vmatrix} = k\begin{vmatrix} * & * & * \\ 5 & -2 & 3 \\ * & * & * \end{vmatrix}$$

where the starred entries are unchanged. We use this step in the next example.

EXAMPLE 2 Compute $\det A$, where $A = \begin{bmatrix} 2 & -8 & 6 & 8 \\ 3 & -9 & 5 & 10 \\ -3 & 0 & 1 & -2 \\ 1 & -4 & 0 & 6 \end{bmatrix}$.

Solution To simplify the arithmetic, we want a 1 in the upper-left corner. We could interchange rows 1 and 4. Instead, we factor out a 2 from the top row, and then proceed with row replacements in the first column:

$$\det A = 2\begin{vmatrix} 1 & -4 & 3 & 4 \\ 3 & -9 & 5 & 10 \\ -3 & 0 & 1 & -2 \\ 1 & -4 & 0 & 6 \end{vmatrix} = 2\begin{vmatrix} 1 & -4 & 3 & 4 \\ 0 & 3 & -4 & -2 \\ 0 & -12 & 10 & 10 \\ 0 & 0 & -3 & 2 \end{vmatrix}$$

Next, we could factor out another 2 from row 3, or use the 3 in the second column as a pivot. We choose the latter operation, adding 4 times row 2 to row 3:

$$\det A = 2\begin{vmatrix} 1 & -4 & 3 & 4 \\ 0 & 3 & -4 & -2 \\ 0 & 0 & -6 & 2 \\ 0 & 0 & -3 & 2 \end{vmatrix}$$

Finally, adding $-1/2$ times row 3 to row 4, and computing the "triangular" determinant, we find that

$$\det A = 2\begin{vmatrix} 1 & -4 & 3 & 4 \\ 0 & 3 & -4 & -2 \\ 0 & 0 & -6 & 2 \\ 0 & 0 & 0 & 1 \end{vmatrix} = 2\cdot(1)(3)(-6)(1) = -36$$

$$U = \begin{bmatrix} \blacksquare & * & * & * \\ 0 & \blacksquare & * & * \\ 0 & 0 & \blacksquare & * \\ 0 & 0 & 0 & \blacksquare \end{bmatrix}$$
$\det U \neq 0$

$$U = \begin{bmatrix} \blacksquare & * & * & * \\ 0 & \blacksquare & * & * \\ 0 & 0 & 0 & \blacksquare \\ 0 & 0 & 0 & 0 \end{bmatrix}$$
$\det U = 0$

FIGURE 1 Typical echelon forms.

Suppose that a square matrix A has been reduced to an echelon form U by row replacements and row interchanges. (This is always possible. See the row reduction algorithm of Section 1.2.) If there are r interchanges, then Theorem 3 shows that

$$\det A = (-1)^r \det U$$

Furthermore, all of the pivots are still visible in U (because they have not been scaled to 1's). If A is invertible, then the pivots in U are on the diagonal (since A is row equivalent to the identity matrix). In this case, $\det U$ is the product of the pivots. If A is not invertible, then U has a row of zeros and $\det U = 0$. See Fig. 1. Thus we have the formula:

$$\det A = \begin{cases} (-1)^r \cdot \begin{pmatrix} \text{product} \\ \text{of pivots} \end{pmatrix}, & \text{when } A \text{ is invertible,} \\ 0 \quad , & \text{when } A \text{ is not invertible} \end{cases} \tag{1}$$

It is interesting to note that although the echelon form is not unique (because it is not completely row reduced), and the pivots are not unique, the *product* of the pivots *is* unique, except for a possible minus sign.

Formula (1) not only gives a very concrete interpretation of what a determinant is, but also proves the main theorem of this section:

THEOREM 4

A square matrix A is invertible if and only if $\det A \neq 0$.

Theorem 4 adds the statement "$\det A \neq 0$" to the Invertible Matrix Theorem. A useful corollary is that $\det A = 0$ if the rows or columns of A are linearly dependent. In practice, linear dependence is obvious only when two rows or two columns are the same or a row or column is zero.

EXAMPLE 3 Compute $\det A$, where $A = \begin{bmatrix} 3 & -1 & 2 & -5 \\ 0 & 5 & -3 & -6 \\ -6 & 7 & -7 & 4 \\ -5 & -8 & 0 & 9 \end{bmatrix}$.

Solution Add 2 times row 1 to row 3 to obtain

$$\det A = \det \begin{bmatrix} 3 & -1 & 2 & -5 \\ 0 & 5 & -3 & -6 \\ 0 & 5 & -3 & -6 \\ -5 & -8 & 0 & 9 \end{bmatrix} = 0$$

because the second and third rows of the second matrix are equal.

Numerical Notes

1. Most computer programs that compute $\det A$ for a general matrix A use the method of formula (1) above.
2. It can be shown that evaluation of an $n \times n$ determinant using row operations requires $(n^3 + 2n - 3)/3$ multiplications and divisions (ignoring other operations). Any modern microcomputer can calculate a 25×25 determinant in a fraction of a second, since less than 5300 such operations are required.

Computers can also handle large "sparse" matrices, with special routines that take advantage of the presence of many zeros. Of course, zero entries can speed hand computations, too. The calculations in the next example combine the power of row operations with the strategy from Section 4.1 of using zero entries in cofactor expansions.

EXAMPLE 4 Compute $\det A$, where $A = \begin{bmatrix} 0 & 1 & 2 & -1 \\ 2 & 5 & -7 & 3 \\ 0 & 3 & 6 & 2 \\ -2 & -5 & 4 & -2 \end{bmatrix}$.

Solution A good way to begin is to use the 2 in column 1 as a pivot, eliminating the -2 below it. Then use a cofactor expansion to reduce the size of the determinant, followed by another row replacement operation. Thus

$$\det A = \begin{vmatrix} 0 & 1 & 2 & -1 \\ 2 & 5 & -7 & 3 \\ 0 & 3 & 6 & 2 \\ 0 & 0 & -3 & 1 \end{vmatrix} = -2 \begin{vmatrix} 1 & 2 & -1 \\ 3 & 6 & 2 \\ 0 & -3 & 1 \end{vmatrix} = -2 \begin{vmatrix} 1 & 2 & -1 \\ 0 & 0 & 5 \\ 0 & -3 & 1 \end{vmatrix}$$

We could now interchange rows 2 and 3 to get a triangular determinant. Instead, we make a cofactor expansion down the first column:

$$\det A = (-2)(1) \begin{vmatrix} 0 & 5 \\ -3 & 1 \end{vmatrix} = -2 \cdot (15) = -30$$

Column Operations

We can perform operations on the columns of a matrix in a way analogous to the row operations we have considered. The next theorem shows that column operations have the same effects on determinants as row operations.

THEOREM 5

If A is an $n \times n$ matrix, then $\det A^T = \det A$.

Proof The theorem is obvious for $n = 1$. Suppose the theorem is true for $k \times k$ determinants and let $n = k + 1$. Then the cofactor of a_{1j} in A equals the cofactor of a_{j1} in A^T, because the cofactors involve $k \times k$ determinants. Hence the cofactor expansion of $\det A$ along the first *row* equals the cofactor expansion of $\det A^T$ down the first *column*. That is, A and A^T have equal determinants. Thus the theorem is true for $n = 1$, and the truth of the theorem for one value of n implies its truth for the next value of n. By the principle of induction, the theorem is true for all $n \geq 1$. ∎

Because of Theorem 5, each statement in Theorem 3 is true when the word *row* is replaced everywhere by *column*. To verify this property, one merely applies the original Theorem 3 to A^T. A row operation on A^T amounts to a column operation on A.

Column operations are useful for both theoretical purposes and hand computations. However, for simplicity we'll perform only row operations in numerical calculations.

Determinants and Matrix Products

The proof of the following useful theorem is at the end of the section. Applications are in the exercises.

THEOREM 6

If A and B are $n \times n$ matrices, then $\det AB = (\det A)(\det B)$.

EXAMPLE 5 Verify Theorem 6 for $A = \begin{bmatrix} 6 & 1 \\ 3 & 2 \end{bmatrix}$ and $B = \begin{bmatrix} 4 & 3 \\ 1 & 2 \end{bmatrix}$.

Solution

$$AB = \begin{bmatrix} 6 & 1 \\ 3 & 2 \end{bmatrix} \begin{bmatrix} 4 & 3 \\ 1 & 2 \end{bmatrix} = \begin{bmatrix} 25 & 20 \\ 14 & 13 \end{bmatrix}$$

and

$$\det AB = 25 \cdot 13 - 20 \cdot 14 = 325 - 280 = 45$$

Since $\det A = 9$ and $\det B = 5$,

$$(\det A)(\det B) = 9 \cdot 5 = 45 = \det AB$$

∎

Warning: A common misconception is that Theorem 6 has an analogue for *sums* of matrices. However, $\det(A + B)$ is *not* equal to $\det A + \det B$, in general.

A Linearity Property of the Determinant Function

For an $n \times n$ matrix A, we may consider $\det A$ as a function of the n column vectors in A. We will show that if all columns except one are held fixed, then $\det A$ is a *linear function* of that one (vector) variable.

Suppose that the jth column of A is allowed to vary, and write

$$A = [\,\mathbf{a}_1 \quad \cdots \quad \mathbf{a}_{j-1} \quad \mathbf{x} \quad \mathbf{a}_{j+1} \quad \cdots \quad \mathbf{a}_n\,]$$

Define a transformation T from $\mathbb{R}^n$ to $\mathbb{R}$ by

$$T(\mathbf{x}) = \det[\,\mathbf{a}_1 \quad \cdots \quad \mathbf{a}_{j-1} \quad \mathbf{x} \quad \mathbf{a}_{j+1} \quad \cdots \quad \mathbf{a}_n\,]$$

Then,

$$T(k\mathbf{x}) = kT(\mathbf{x}) \quad \text{for all scalars } k \text{ and all } \mathbf{x} \text{ in } \mathbb{R}^n \tag{2}$$

$$T(\mathbf{u}+\mathbf{v}) = T(\mathbf{u}) + T(\mathbf{v}) \quad \text{for all } \mathbf{u}, \mathbf{v} \text{ in } \mathbb{R}^n \tag{3}$$

Property (2) is Theorem 3(c) applied to the columns of A. A proof of (3) follows from a cofactor expansion of $\det A$ down the jth column. (See Exercises 39–41.) This (multi-) linearity property of the determinant turns out to have many useful consequences that are studied in more advanced courses.

Proofs of Theorems 3 and 6

It is convenient to prove Theorem 3 when it is stated in terms of the elementary matrices discussed in Section 3.2. Given a matrix A, we shall say that an elementary matrix E is a *row replacement (matrix)* if EA is obtained from A by adding a multiple of one row to another row; E is an *interchange* if EA is obtained by interchanging two rows of A; and E is *a scale by k* if EA is obtained by multiplying a row of A by a nonzero scalar k. With this terminology, Theorem 3 can be reformulated as follows:

If A is an $n \times n$ matrix and E is an $n \times n$ elementary matrix, then

$$\det EA = (\det E)(\det A)$$

where

$$\det E = \begin{cases} 1 & \text{if } E \text{ is a row replacement} \\ -1 & \text{if } E \text{ is an interchange} \\ r & \text{if } E \text{ is a scale by } r \end{cases}$$

Proof of Theorem 3 The proof is by induction on the size of A. The case of a 2×2 matrix was verified in Exercises 33–36 of Section 4.1. Suppose that the theorem has been verified for determinants of $k \times k$ matrices, and let $n = k+1$ and A be $n \times n$. The action of E on A involves either two rows or only one row. So we may expand $\det EA$ along a row that is unchanged by the action of E, say, row i. Let A_{ij} (respectively, B_{ij}) be the matrix obtained by deleting row i and column j from A (respectively, EA). Then the rows of B_{ij} are obtained from the rows of A_{ij} by the same type of elementary row operation as E performs on A. Since these submatrices are only $k \times k$, the induction assumption implies that

$$\det B_{ij} = \alpha \cdot \det A_{ij}$$

where $\alpha = 1, -1$, or r, depending on the nature of E. The cofactor expansion across row i is

$$\begin{aligned} \det EA &= a_{i1}(-1)^{i+1}\det B_{i1} + \cdots + a_{in}(-1)^{i+n}\det B_{in} \\ &= \alpha a_{i1}(-1)^{i+1}\det A_{i1} + \cdots + \alpha a_{in}(-1)^{i+n}\det A_{in} \\ &= \alpha \cdot \det A \end{aligned}$$

In particular, taking $A = I_n$, we see that $\det E = 1, -1$, or r, depending on the nature of E. Thus the theorem is true for $n = 2$, and the truth of the theorem for one value of n implies its truth for the next value of n. By the principle of induction, the theorem must be true for $n \geq 2$. The theorem is trivially true for $n = 1$. ∎

Proof of Theorem 6 If A is not invertible, then neither is AB, by Exercise 25 in Section 3.3. In this case, $\det AB = (\det A)(\det B)$, because both sides are zero, by Theorem 4. If A is invertible, then by the Invertible Matrix Theorem, A is a product of elementary matrices, say,

$$A = E_p E_{p-1} \cdots E_1$$

For brevity, write $|A|$ for $\det A$. Then repeated application of Theorem 3, as rephrased above, shows that

$$\begin{aligned} |AB| &= |E_p \cdots E_1 B| = |E_p||E_{p-1} \cdots E_1 B| = \cdots \\ &= |E_p| \cdots |E_1||B| = \cdots = |E_p \cdots E_1||B| \\ &= |A||B| \end{aligned}$$

∎

PRACTICE PROBLEMS

1. Compute $\begin{vmatrix} 1 & -3 & 1 & -2 \\ 2 & -5 & -1 & -2 \\ 0 & -4 & 5 & 1 \\ -3 & 10 & -6 & 8 \end{vmatrix}$ in as few steps as possible.

2. Use a determinant to decide if $\mathbf{v}_1, \mathbf{v}_2, \mathbf{v}_3$ are linearly independent, when

$$\mathbf{v}_1 = \begin{bmatrix} 5 \\ -7 \\ 9 \end{bmatrix}, \quad \mathbf{v}_2 = \begin{bmatrix} -3 \\ 3 \\ -5 \end{bmatrix}, \quad \mathbf{v}_3 = \begin{bmatrix} 2 \\ -7 \\ 5 \end{bmatrix}$$

4.2 EXERCISES

Each equation in Exercises 1–4 illustrates a property of determinants. State the property.

1. $\begin{vmatrix} 0 & 5 & -2 \\ 1 & -3 & 6 \\ 4 & -1 & 8 \end{vmatrix} = -\begin{vmatrix} 1 & -3 & 6 \\ 0 & 5 & -2 \\ 4 & -1 & 8 \end{vmatrix}$

2. $\begin{vmatrix} 2 & -6 & 4 \\ 3 & 5 & -2 \\ 1 & 6 & 3 \end{vmatrix} = 2\begin{vmatrix} 1 & -3 & 2 \\ 3 & 5 & -2 \\ 1 & 6 & 3 \end{vmatrix}$

3. $\begin{vmatrix} 1 & 3 & -4 \\ 2 & 0 & -3 \\ 5 & -4 & 7 \end{vmatrix} = \begin{vmatrix} 1 & 3 & -4 \\ 0 & -6 & 5 \\ 5 & -4 & 7 \end{vmatrix}$

4. $\begin{vmatrix} 1 & 2 & 3 \\ 0 & 5 & -4 \\ 3 & 7 & 4 \end{vmatrix} = \begin{vmatrix} 1 & 2 & 3 \\ 0 & 5 & -4 \\ 0 & 1 & -5 \end{vmatrix}$

Find the determinants in Exercises 5–10 by row reduction to echelon form.

5. $\begin{vmatrix} 1 & 5 & -6 \\ -1 & -4 & 4 \\ -2 & -7 & 9 \end{vmatrix}$

6. $\begin{vmatrix} 1 & 5 & -3 \\ 3 & -3 & 3 \\ 2 & 13 & -7 \end{vmatrix}$

7. $\begin{vmatrix} 1 & 3 & 0 & 2 \\ -2 & -5 & 7 & 4 \\ 3 & 5 & 2 & 1 \\ 1 & -1 & 2 & -3 \end{vmatrix}$

8. $\begin{vmatrix} 1 & 3 & 3 & -4 \\ 0 & 1 & 2 & -5 \\ 2 & 5 & 4 & -3 \\ -3 & -7 & -5 & 2 \end{vmatrix}$

9. $\begin{vmatrix} 1 & -1 & -3 & 0 \\ 0 & 1 & 5 & 4 \\ -1 & 2 & 8 & 5 \\ 3 & -1 & -2 & 3 \end{vmatrix}$

10. $\begin{vmatrix} 1 & 3 & -1 & 0 & -2 \\ 0 & 2 & -4 & -1 & -6 \\ -2 & -6 & 2 & 3 & 9 \\ 3 & 7 & -3 & 8 & -7 \\ 3 & 5 & 5 & 2 & 7 \end{vmatrix}$

Combine the methods of row reduction and cofactor expansion to compute the determinants in Exercises 11–14.

11. $\begin{vmatrix} 2 & 5 & -3 & -1 \\ 3 & 0 & 1 & -3 \\ -6 & 0 & -4 & 9 \\ 4 & 10 & -4 & -1 \end{vmatrix}$ **12.** $\begin{vmatrix} -1 & 2 & 3 & 0 \\ 3 & 4 & 3 & 0 \\ 5 & 4 & 6 & 6 \\ 4 & 2 & 4 & 3 \end{vmatrix}$

13. $\begin{vmatrix} 2 & 5 & 4 & 1 \\ 4 & 7 & 6 & 2 \\ 6 & -2 & -4 & 0 \\ -6 & 7 & 7 & 0 \end{vmatrix}$ **14.** $\begin{vmatrix} -3 & -2 & 1 & -4 \\ 1 & 3 & 0 & -3 \\ -3 & 4 & -2 & 8 \\ 3 & -4 & 0 & 4 \end{vmatrix}$

Find the determinants in Exercises 15–20, where
$\begin{vmatrix} a & b & c \\ d & e & f \\ g & h & i \end{vmatrix} = 7.$

15. $\begin{vmatrix} a & b & c \\ d & e & f \\ 5g & 5h & 5i \end{vmatrix}$

16. $\begin{vmatrix} a+d & b+e & c+f \\ d & e & f \\ g & h & i \end{vmatrix}$

17. $\begin{vmatrix} a & b & c \\ g & h & i \\ d & e & f \end{vmatrix}$ **18.** $\begin{vmatrix} g & h & i \\ a & b & c \\ d & e & f \end{vmatrix}$

19. $\begin{vmatrix} a & b & c \\ 2d+a & 2e+b & 2f+c \\ g & h & i \end{vmatrix}$

20. $\begin{vmatrix} a & b & c \\ 3d & 3e & 3f \\ g & h & i \end{vmatrix}$

Use determinants to find out which of the following matrices are invertible.

21. $\begin{bmatrix} 2 & 3 & 0 \\ 1 & 3 & 4 \\ 1 & 2 & 1 \end{bmatrix}$ **22.** $\begin{bmatrix} 5 & 0 & -1 \\ 1 & -3 & -2 \\ 0 & 5 & 3 \end{bmatrix}$

23. $\begin{bmatrix} 2 & 0 & 0 & 8 \\ 1 & -7 & -5 & 0 \\ 3 & 8 & 6 & 0 \\ 0 & 7 & 5 & 4 \end{bmatrix}$

Use determinants to decide which of the following sets of vectors are linearly independent.

24. $\begin{bmatrix} 4 \\ 6 \\ -7 \end{bmatrix}, \begin{bmatrix} -7 \\ 0 \\ 2 \end{bmatrix}, \begin{bmatrix} -3 \\ -5 \\ 6 \end{bmatrix}$ **25.** $\begin{bmatrix} 7 \\ -4 \\ -6 \end{bmatrix}, \begin{bmatrix} -8 \\ 5 \\ 7 \end{bmatrix}, \begin{bmatrix} 7 \\ 0 \\ -5 \end{bmatrix}$

26. $\begin{bmatrix} 3 \\ 5 \\ -6 \\ 4 \end{bmatrix}, \begin{bmatrix} 2 \\ -6 \\ 0 \\ 7 \end{bmatrix}, \begin{bmatrix} -2 \\ -1 \\ 3 \\ 0 \end{bmatrix}, \begin{bmatrix} 0 \\ 0 \\ 0 \\ -3 \end{bmatrix}$

27. Compute $\det B^5$, where $B = \begin{bmatrix} 1 & 0 & 1 \\ 1 & 1 & 2 \\ 1 & 2 & 1 \end{bmatrix}$.

28. Use Theorem 3 (but not Theorem 4) to show that if two rows of a square matrix A are equal, then $\det A = 0$. The same is true for columns. Why?

In Exercises 29–34, mention an appropriate theorem in your explanation.

29. Let A be an invertible matrix. Show that

$$\det A^{-1} = \frac{1}{\det A}$$

30. Find a formula for $\det(rA)$ when A is an $n \times n$ matrix.

31. Let A and B be square matrices. Show that, even though AB and BA may not be equal, it is always true that $\det AB = \det BA$.

32. Let A and P be square matrices, with P invertible. Show that $\det(PAP^{-1}) = \det A$.

33. Let U be a square matrix such that $U^TU = I$. Show that $\det U = \pm 1$.

34. Suppose that A is a square matrix such that $\det A^4 = 0$. Explain why A cannot be invertible.

Verify that $\det AB = (\det A)(\det B)$ for the matrices in Exercises 35 and 36. (Do not use Theorem 6.)

35. $A = \begin{bmatrix} 3 & 0 \\ 6 & 1 \end{bmatrix}, B = \begin{bmatrix} 2 & 0 \\ 5 & 4 \end{bmatrix}$

36. $A = \begin{bmatrix} 3 & 6 \\ -1 & -2 \end{bmatrix}, B = \begin{bmatrix} 4 & 2 \\ -1 & -1 \end{bmatrix}$

37. Let A and B be 3×3 matrices, with $\det A = 4$ and $\det B = -3$. Use properties of determinants (in the text and in the exercises above) to compute:

a. $\det AB$ b. $\det 5A$ c. $\det B^T$
d. $\det A^{-1}$ e. $\det A^3$

38. Let A and B be 4×4 matrices, with $\det A = -1$ and $\det B = 2$. Compute:

a. $\det AB$ b. $\det B^5$ c. $\det 2A$
d. $\det A^T A$ e. $\det B^{-1}AB$

39. Verify that $\det A = \det B + \det C$, where

$$A = \begin{bmatrix} a+e & b+f \\ c & d \end{bmatrix},\ B = \begin{bmatrix} a & b \\ c & d \end{bmatrix},\ C = \begin{bmatrix} e & f \\ c & d \end{bmatrix}$$

40. Let $A = \begin{bmatrix} 1 & 0 \\ 0 & 1 \end{bmatrix}$ and $B = \begin{bmatrix} a & b \\ c & d \end{bmatrix}$. Show that $\det(A+B) = \det A + \det B$ if and only if $a + d = 0$.

41. Verify that $\det A = \det B + \det C$, where

$$A = \begin{bmatrix} a_{11} & a_{12} & u_1 + v_1 \\ a_{21} & a_{22} & u_2 + v_2 \\ a_{31} & a_{32} & u_3 + v_3 \end{bmatrix},$$

$$B = \begin{bmatrix} a_{11} & a_{12} & u_1 \\ a_{21} & a_{22} & u_2 \\ a_{31} & a_{32} & u_3 \end{bmatrix},\ C = \begin{bmatrix} a_{11} & a_{12} & v_1 \\ a_{21} & a_{22} & v_2 \\ a_{31} & a_{32} & v_3 \end{bmatrix}$$

Note, however, that A is *not* the same as $B + C$.

42. Right-multiplication by an elementary matrix E affects the *columns* of A in the same way that left-multiplication affects the *rows*. Use Theorems 5 and 3 and the obvious fact that E^T is another elementary matrix to show that

$$\det AE = (\det E)(\det A)$$

Do not use Theorem 6.

SOLUTIONS TO PRACTICE PROBLEMS

1. Perform row replacements to create zeros in the first column and then create a row of zeros.

$$\begin{vmatrix} 1 & -3 & 1 & -2 \\ 2 & -5 & -1 & -2 \\ 0 & -4 & 5 & 1 \\ -3 & 10 & -6 & 8 \end{vmatrix} = \begin{vmatrix} 1 & -3 & 1 & -2 \\ 0 & 1 & -3 & 2 \\ 0 & -4 & 5 & 1 \\ 0 & 1 & -3 & 2 \end{vmatrix} = \begin{vmatrix} 1 & -3 & 1 & -2 \\ 0 & 1 & -3 & 2 \\ 0 & -4 & 5 & 1 \\ 0 & 0 & 0 & 0 \end{vmatrix} = 0$$

2. $$\det[\,\mathbf{v}_1\ \ \mathbf{v}_2\ \ \mathbf{v}_3\,] = \begin{vmatrix} 5 & -3 & 2 \\ -7 & 3 & -7 \\ 9 & -5 & 5 \end{vmatrix} = \begin{vmatrix} 5 & -3 & 2 \\ -2 & 0 & -5 \\ 9 & -5 & 5 \end{vmatrix} \quad \text{(Row 1 added to row 2)}$$

$$= -(-3)\begin{vmatrix} -2 & -5 \\ 9 & 5 \end{vmatrix} - (-5)\begin{vmatrix} 5 & 2 \\ -2 & -5 \end{vmatrix} \quad \text{(Cofactors of column 2)}$$

$$= 3 \cdot (35) + 5 \cdot (-21) = 0$$

By Theorem 4, the matrix $[\,\mathbf{v}_1\ \ \mathbf{v}_2\ \ \mathbf{v}_3\,]$ is not invertible. The columns are linearly dependent, by the Invertible Matrix Theorem.

4.3 CRAMER'S RULE, VOLUME, AND LINEAR TRANSFORMATIONS

This section applies the theory of the preceding sections to obtain important theoretical formulas and a geometric interpretation of the determinant.

Cramer's Rule

Cramer's Rule is needed in a variety of theoretical calculations. For instance, it can be used to study how the solution of $A\mathbf{x} = \mathbf{b}$ is affected by changes in the entries of $\mathbf{b}$. However, the formula is inefficient for hand calculations, except for 2×2 or perhaps 3×3 matrices.

For any $n \times n$ matrix A and any $\mathbf{b}$ in $\mathbb{R}^n$, let $A_i(\mathbf{b})$ be the matrix obtained from A by replacing column i by the vector $\mathbf{b}$.

$$A_i(\mathbf{b}) = [\,\mathbf{a}_1 \quad \cdots \quad \underset{\substack{\uparrow \\ \text{col i}}}{\mathbf{b}} \quad \cdots \quad \mathbf{a}_n\,]$$

THEOREM 7

Cramer's Rule

Let A be an invertible $n \times n$ matrix. For any $\mathbf{b}$ in $\mathbb{R}^n$, the unique solution $\mathbf{x}$ of $A\mathbf{x} = \mathbf{b}$ has entries given by

$$x_i = \frac{\det A_i(\mathbf{b})}{\det A}, \qquad i = 1, 2, \ldots, n \tag{1}$$

Proof Denote the columns of A by $\mathbf{a}_1, \ldots, \mathbf{a}_n$ and the columns of the $n \times n$ identity matrix I by $\mathbf{e}_1, \ldots, \mathbf{e}_n$. If $A\mathbf{x} = \mathbf{b}$, the definition of matrix multiplication shows that

$$\begin{aligned} A \cdot I_i(\mathbf{x}) &= A\,[\,\mathbf{e}_1 \quad \cdots \quad \mathbf{x} \quad \cdots \quad \mathbf{e}_n\,] = [\,A\mathbf{e}_1 \quad \cdots \quad A\mathbf{x} \quad \cdots \quad A\mathbf{e}_n\,] \\ &= [\,\mathbf{a}_1 \quad \cdots \quad \mathbf{b} \quad \cdots \quad \mathbf{a}_n\,] = A_i(\mathbf{b}) \end{aligned}$$

By the multiplication property for determinants,

$$(\det A)(\det I_i(\mathbf{x})) = \det A_i(\mathbf{b})$$

The second determinant on the left is simply x_i. (Make a cofactor expansion along the ith row.) Hence $(\det A) \cdot x_i = \det A_i(\mathbf{b})$. This proves (1) because A is invertible and $\det A \neq 0$. ∎

EXAMPLE 1 Use Cramer's rule to solve the system

$$\begin{aligned} 3x_1 - 2x_2 &= 6 \\ -5x_1 + 4x_2 &= 8 \end{aligned}$$

Solution View the system as $A\mathbf{x} = \mathbf{b}$. Using the notation introduced above,

$$A = \begin{bmatrix} 3 & -2 \\ -5 & 4 \end{bmatrix}, \quad A_1(\mathbf{b}) = \begin{bmatrix} 6 & -2 \\ 8 & 4 \end{bmatrix}, \quad A_2(\mathbf{b}) = \begin{bmatrix} 3 & 6 \\ -5 & 8 \end{bmatrix}$$

Since $\det A = 2$, the system has a unique solution. By Cramer's rule,

$$\begin{aligned} x_1 &= \frac{\det A_1(\mathbf{b})}{\det A} = \frac{24 + 16}{2} = 20 \\ x_2 &= \frac{\det A_2(\mathbf{b})}{\det A} = \frac{24 + 30}{2} = 27 \end{aligned}$$

∎

Application to Engineering

A number of important engineering problems, particularly in electrical engineering and control theory, can be analyzed by *Laplace transforms*. This approach converts an appropriate system of linear differential equations into a system of linear algebraic equations whose coefficients involve a parameter. The next example illustrates the type of algebraic system that may arise.

EXAMPLE 2 Consider the following system in which s is an unspecified parameter. Determine the values of s for which the system has a unique solution, and use Cramer's rule to describe the solution.

$$\begin{aligned} 3sx_1 - 2x_2 &= 4 \\ -6x_1 + sx_2 &= 1 \end{aligned}$$

Solution View the system as $A\mathbf{x} = \mathbf{b}$. Then

$$A = \begin{bmatrix} 3s & -2 \\ -6 & s \end{bmatrix}, \quad A_1(\mathbf{b}) = \begin{bmatrix} 4 & -2 \\ 1 & s \end{bmatrix}, \quad A_2(\mathbf{b}) = \begin{bmatrix} 3s & 4 \\ -6 & 1 \end{bmatrix}$$

Since

$$\det A = 3s^2 - 12 = 3(s+2)(s-2)$$

the system has a unique solution precisely when $s \neq \pm 2$. For such an s, the solution is $[\,x_1 \quad x_2\,]^T$, where

$$\begin{aligned} x_1 &= \frac{\det A_1(\mathbf{b})}{\det A} = \frac{4s+2}{3(s+2)(s-2)} \\ x_2 &= \frac{\det A_2(\mathbf{b})}{\det A} = \frac{3s+24}{3(s+2)(s-2)} = \frac{s+8}{(s+2)(s-2)} \end{aligned}$$

A Formula for A^{-1}

Cramer's rule leads easily to a general formula for the inverse of an $n \times n$ matrix A. The jth column of A^{-1} is a vector $\mathbf{x}$ that satisfies

$$A\mathbf{x} = \mathbf{e}_j$$

where $\mathbf{e}_j$ is the jth column of the identity matrix, and the ith entry of $\mathbf{x}$ is the (i, j)-entry of A^{-1}. By Cramer's rule,

$$\{(i, j)\text{-entry of } A^{-1}\} = x_i = \frac{\det A_i(\mathbf{e}_j)}{\det A} \tag{2}$$

Recall that A_{ji} denotes the submatrix of A formed by deleting row j and column i. A cofactor expansion down column i of $A_i(\mathbf{e}_j)$ shows that

$$\det A_i(\mathbf{e}_j) = (-1)^{i+j} \det A_{ji} = C_{ji} \tag{3}$$

where C_{ji} is a cofactor of A. By (2), the (i, j)-entry of A^{-1} is the cofactor C_{ji} divided by $\det A$. [Notice that the subscripts on C_{ji} are the reverse of (i, j).] Thus

$$A^{-1} = \frac{1}{\det A}\begin{bmatrix} C_{11} & C_{21} & \cdots & C_{n1} \\ C_{12} & C_{22} & \cdots & C_{n2} \\ \vdots & \vdots & & \vdots \\ C_{1n} & C_{2n} & \cdots & C_{nn} \end{bmatrix} \tag{4}$$

The matrix of cofactors on the right side of (4) is called the **adjugate** (or **classical adjoint**) of A, denoted by adj A. (The term *adjoint* also has another meaning in advanced texts on linear transformations.) The next theorem simply restates (4).

THEOREM 8

An Inverse Formula

Let A be an invertible $n \times n$ matrix. Then

$$A^{-1} = \frac{1}{\det A}\,\text{adj}\,A$$

EXAMPLE 3 Find the inverse of the matrix $A = \begin{bmatrix} 2 & 1 & 3 \\ 1 & -1 & 1 \\ 1 & 4 & -2 \end{bmatrix}$.

Solution The nine cofactors are

$$C_{11} = +\begin{vmatrix} -1 & 1 \\ 4 & -2 \end{vmatrix} = -2, \quad C_{12} = -\begin{vmatrix} 1 & 1 \\ 1 & -2 \end{vmatrix} = 3, \quad C_{13} = +\begin{vmatrix} 1 & -1 \\ 1 & 4 \end{vmatrix} = 5$$

$$C_{21} = -\begin{vmatrix} 1 & 3 \\ 4 & -2 \end{vmatrix} = 14, \quad C_{22} = +\begin{vmatrix} 2 & 3 \\ 1 & -2 \end{vmatrix} = -7, \quad C_{23} = -\begin{vmatrix} 2 & 1 \\ 1 & 4 \end{vmatrix} = -7$$

$$C_{31} = +\begin{vmatrix} 1 & 3 \\ -1 & 1 \end{vmatrix} = 4, \quad C_{32} = -\begin{vmatrix} 2 & 3 \\ 1 & 1 \end{vmatrix} = 1, \quad C_{33} = +\begin{vmatrix} 2 & 1 \\ 1 & -1 \end{vmatrix} = -3$$

The adjugate matrix is the *transpose* of the matrix of cofactors. [For instance, C_{12} goes in the (2,1) position.] Thus

$$\text{adj}\,A = \begin{bmatrix} -2 & 14 & 4 \\ 3 & -7 & 1 \\ 5 & -7 & -3 \end{bmatrix}$$

We could compute $\det A$ directly, but the following computation provides a check on the calculations above *and* produces $\det A$:

$$(\text{adj}\,A)\cdot A = \begin{bmatrix} -2 & 14 & 4 \\ 3 & -7 & 1 \\ 5 & -7 & -3 \end{bmatrix}\begin{bmatrix} 2 & 1 & 3 \\ 1 & -1 & 1 \\ 1 & 4 & -2 \end{bmatrix} = \begin{bmatrix} 14 & 0 & 0 \\ 0 & 14 & 0 \\ 0 & 0 & 14 \end{bmatrix} = 14I$$

Since $(\text{adj } A)A = 14I$, Theorem 8 shows that $\det A = 14$ and

$$A^{-1} = \frac{1}{14}\begin{bmatrix} -2 & 14 & 4 \\ 3 & -7 & 1 \\ 5 & -7 & -3 \end{bmatrix} = \begin{bmatrix} -2/14 & 14/14 & 4/14 \\ 3/14 & -7/14 & 1/14 \\ 5/14 & -7/14 & -3/14 \end{bmatrix}$$

Theorem 8 is useful mainly for theoretical calculations. The formula for A^{-1} permits one to deduce properties of the inverse without actually calculating it. Except in special cases the algorithm in Section 3.2 gives a much better way to compute A^{-1}, if the inverse is really needed.

Determinants as Area or Volume

In the next application, we verify the geometric interpretation of determinants described in the chapter introduction. Although a general discussion of length and distance in $\mathbb{R}^n$ will not be given until Chapter 6, we assume here that the usual Euclidean concepts of length, area, and volume are already understood for $\mathbb{R}^2$ and $\mathbb{R}^3$.

THEOREM 9

If A is a 2×2 matrix, the area of the parallelogram determined by the columns of A is $|\det A|$. If A is a 3×3 matrix, the volume of the parallelepiped determined by the columns of A is $|\det A|$.

Proof The theorem is obviously true for any 2×2 diagonal matrix:

$$\left|\det\begin{bmatrix} a & 0 \\ 0 & d \end{bmatrix}\right| = |ad| = \left\{\begin{matrix}\text{area of} \\ \text{rectangle}\end{matrix}\right\}$$

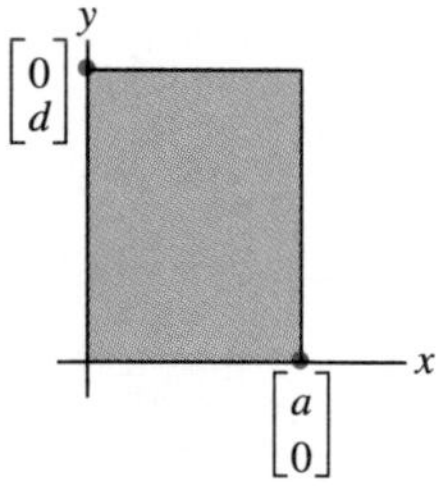

FIGURE 1
Area $= |ad|$.

See Fig. 1. It will suffice to show that any 2×2 matrix $A = [\mathbf{a}_1 \quad \mathbf{a}_2]$ can be transformed into a diagonal matrix in a way that changes neither the area of the associated parallelogram nor $|\det A|$. From Section 4.2, we know that the absolute value of the determinant is unchanged when two columns are interchanged or a multiple of one column is added to another. And it is easy to see that such operations suffice to transform A into a diagonal matrix. Column interchanges do not change the parallelogram at all. So it suffices to prove the following simple geometric observation that applies to vectors in $\mathbb{R}^2$ or $\mathbb{R}^3$:

Let $\mathbf{a}_1$ and $\mathbf{a}_2$ be nonzero vectors. Then for any scalar c, the area of the parallelogram determined by $\mathbf{a}_1$ and $\mathbf{a}_2$ equals the area of the parallelogram determined by $\mathbf{a}_1$ and $\mathbf{a}_2 + c\mathbf{a}_1$.

To prove this statement, we may assume that $\mathbf{a}_2$ is not a multiple of $\mathbf{a}_1$, for otherwise the two parallelograms would be degenerate and have zero area. If L is the line through $\mathbf{0}$ and $\mathbf{a}_1$, then $\mathbf{a}_2 + L$ is the line through $\mathbf{a}_2$ parallel to L, and $\mathbf{a}_2 + c\mathbf{a}_1$ is on this line. See Fig. 2. The points $\mathbf{a}_2$ and $\mathbf{a}_2 + c\mathbf{a}_1$ have the same perpendicular distance

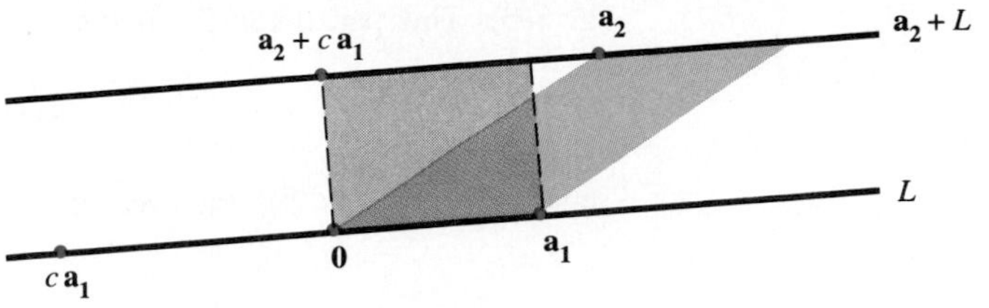

FIGURE 2 Two parallelograms of equal area.

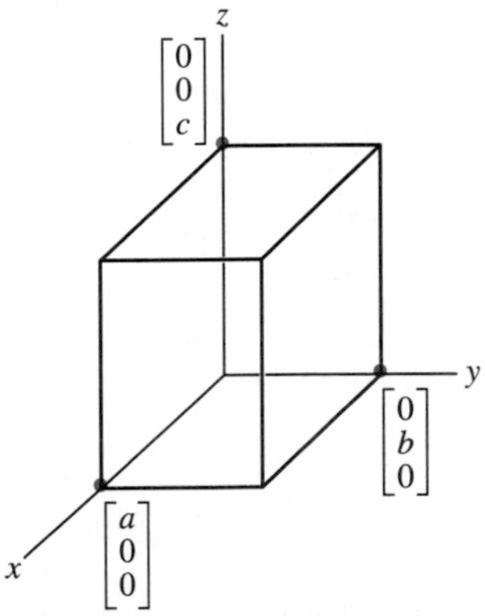

FIGURE 3 Volume $= |abc|$.

to L. Hence the two parallelograms in Fig. 2 have the same area, since they share the base from $\mathbf{0}$ to $\mathbf{a}_1$. This completes the proof for $\mathbb{R}^2$.

The proof for $\mathbb{R}^3$ is similar. The theorem is obviously true for a 3×3 diagonal matrix. See Fig. 3. And any 3×3 matrix A can be transformed into a diagonal matrix with column operations that do not change $|\det A|$. (Think about doing row operations on A^T.) So it suffices to show that these operations do not affect the volume of the parallelepiped determined by the columns of A.

A parallelepiped is shown in Fig. 4 as a shaded box with two sloping sides. Its volume is the area of the base in the plane Span$\{\mathbf{a}_1, \mathbf{a}_3\}$ times the altitude of $\mathbf{a}_2$ above Span$\{\mathbf{a}_1, \mathbf{a}_3\}$. Any vector $\mathbf{a}_2 + c\mathbf{a}_1$ has the same altitude because $\mathbf{a}_2 + c\mathbf{a}_1$ lies in the plane $\mathbf{a}_2$ + Span$\{\mathbf{a}_1, \mathbf{a}_3\}$, which is parallel to Span$\{\mathbf{a}_1, \mathbf{a}_3\}$. Hence the volume of the parallelepiped is unchanged when $[\,\mathbf{a}_1 \quad \mathbf{a}_2 \quad \mathbf{a}_3\,]$ is changed to $[\,\mathbf{a}_1 \quad \mathbf{a}_2 + c\mathbf{a}_1 \quad \mathbf{a}_3\,]$. Thus a column replacement operation does not affect the volume of the parallelepiped. Since column interchanges have no effect on the volume, the proof is complete. ∎

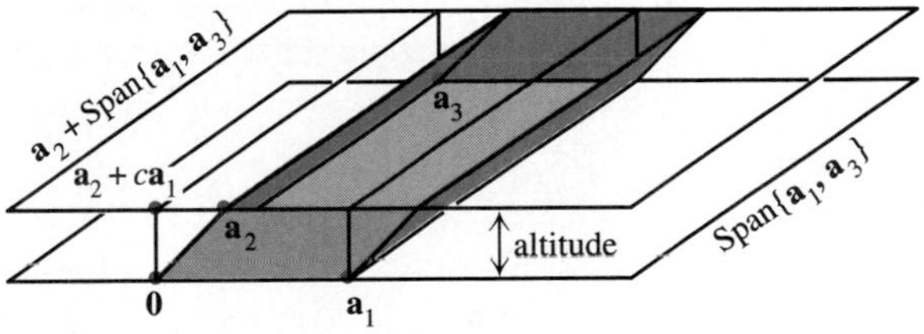

FIGURE 4 Two parallelepipeds of equal volume.

EXAMPLE 4 Calculate the area of the parallelogram determined by the points $(-2, -2)$, $(0, 3)$, $(4, -1)$, and $(6, 4)$. See Fig. 5(a).

Solution First translate the parallelogram to one having the origin as a vertex. For example, subtract the vertex $(-2, -2)$ from each of the four vertices. The new parallelogram has the same area, and its vertices are $(0, 0)$, $(2, 5)$, $(6, 1)$, and $(8, 6)$. See

Fig. 5(b). This parallelogram is determined by the columns of

$$A = \begin{bmatrix} 2 & 6 \\ 5 & 1 \end{bmatrix}$$

Since $|\det A| = |-28|$, the area of the parallelogram is 28. ∎

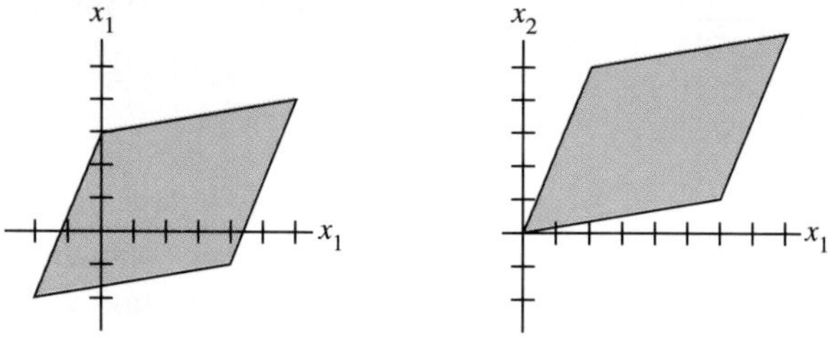

(a) (b)

FIGURE 5 Translating a parallelogram does not change its area.

Linear Transformations

Determinants may be used to describe an important geometric property of linear transformations in the plane and in $\mathbb{R}^3$. If T is a linear transformation and S is a set in the domain of T, let $T(S)$ denote the set of images of points in S. We are interested in how the area (or volume) of $T(S)$ compares with the area (or volume) of the original set S.

THEOREM 10

Let $T: \mathbb{R}^2 \to \mathbb{R}^2$ be the linear transformation determined by a 2×2 matrix A. If S is a parallelogram in $\mathbb{R}^2$, then

$$\{\text{area of } T(S)\} = |\det A|\cdot\{\text{area of } S\} \tag{5}$$

If T is determined by a 3×3 matrix A, and if S is a parallelepiped in $\mathbb{R}^3$, then

$$\{\text{volume of } T(S)\} = |\det A|\cdot\{\text{volume of } S\} \tag{6}$$

Proof Consider the 2×2 case, with $A = [\,\mathbf{a}_1 \;\; \mathbf{a}_2\,]$. A parallelogram at the origin in $\mathbb{R}^2$ determined by vectors $\mathbf{b}_1$ and $\mathbf{b}_2$ has the form

$$S = \{s_1\mathbf{b}_1 + s_2\mathbf{b}_2 : 0 \le s_1 \le 1,\;\; 0 \le s_2 \le 1\}$$

The image of S under T consists of points of the form

$$\begin{aligned} T(s_1\mathbf{b}_1 + s_2\mathbf{b}_2) &= s_1T(\mathbf{b}_1) + s_2T(\mathbf{b}_2) \\ &= s_1A\mathbf{b}_1 + s_2A\mathbf{b}_2 \end{aligned}$$

where $0 \le s_1 \le 1, 0 \le s_2 \le 1$. It follows that $T(S)$ is the parallelogram determined by the columns of the matrix $[\,A\mathbf{b}_1 \;\; A\mathbf{b}_2\,]$. This matrix may be written as AB, where

$B = [\,\mathbf{b}_1 \quad \mathbf{b}_2\,]$. By Theorem 9 and the product theorem for determinants,

$$\begin{aligned}\{\text{area of } T(S)\} &= |\det AB| = |\det A|\cdot|\det B| \\ &= |\det A|\cdot\{\text{area of } S\}\end{aligned} \tag{7}$$

An arbitrary parallelogram has the form $\mathbf{p} + S$, where S is a parallelogram at the origin, as above. It is easy to see that T transforms $\mathbf{p} + S$ into $T(\mathbf{p}) + T(\mathbf{S})$. (See Exercise 26.) Since translation does not affect the area of a set,

$$\begin{aligned}\{\text{area of } T(\mathbf{p} + S)\} &= \{\text{area of } T(\mathbf{p}) + T(S)\} \\ &= \{\text{area of } T(S)\} && \text{Translation} \\ &= |\det A|\cdot\{\text{area of } S\} && \text{By (7)} \\ &= |\det A|\cdot\{\text{area of } \mathbf{p} + S\} && \text{Translation}\end{aligned}$$

This shows that (5) holds for all parallelograms in $\mathbb{R}^2$. The proof of (6) for the 3×3 case is analogous. ∎

When we attempt to generalize Theorem 10 to a region in $\mathbb{R}^2$ or $\mathbb{R}^3$ that is not bounded by straight lines or planes, we must face the problem of how to define and compute its area. This is a question studied in calculus, and we shall only outline the basic idea for $\mathbb{R}^2$. If R is a planar region that has a finite area, then R may be approximated by a grid of small squares that lie inside R. By making the squares sufficiently small, the area of R may be approximated as closely as desired by the sum of the areas of the small squares. See Fig. 6.

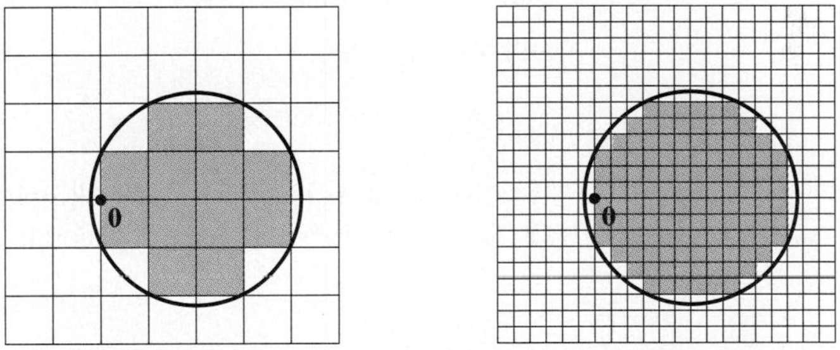

FIGURE 6 Approximating a planar region by squares. The approximation improves as the grid becomes finer.

If T is a linear transformation associated with a 2×2 matrix A, then the image of R under T is approximated by the images of the small squares inside R. The proof of Theorem 10 shows that each such image is a parallelogram whose area is $|\det A|$ times the area of the square. If R' is the union of the squares inside R, then the area of $T(R')$ is $|\det A|$ times the area of R'. See Fig. 7. Also, the area of $T(R')$ is close to the area of $T(R)$. An argument involving a limiting process may be given to justify the following generalization of Theorem 10.

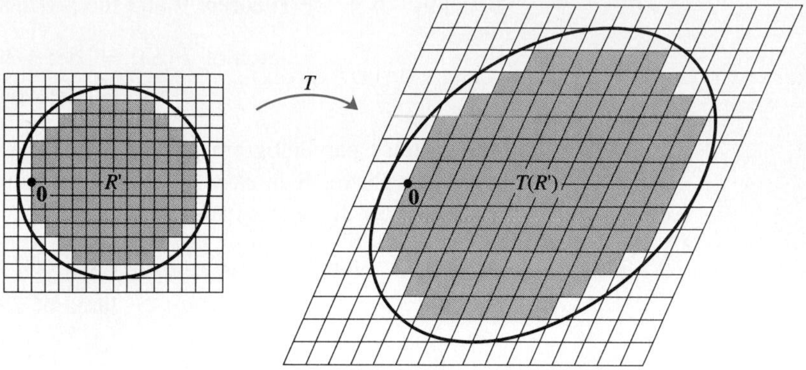

FIGURE 7 Approximating $T(R)$ by a union of parallelograms.

> The conclusions of Theorem 10 hold whenever S is a region in $\mathbb{R}^2$ with finite area or a region in $\mathbb{R}^3$ with finite volume.

EXAMPLE 5 Let a and b be positive numbers. Find the area of the region E bounded by the ellipse whose equation is

$$\frac{x_1^2}{a^2} + \frac{x_2^2}{b^2} = 1$$

Solution We claim that E is the image of the unit disk D under the linear transformation T determined by the matrix $A = \begin{bmatrix} a & 0 \\ 0 & b \end{bmatrix}$, because if $\mathbf{u} = \begin{bmatrix} u_1 \\ u_2 \end{bmatrix}$, $\mathbf{x} = \begin{bmatrix} x_1 \\ x_2 \end{bmatrix}$, and $\mathbf{x} = A\mathbf{u}$, then

$$u_1 = \frac{x_1}{a} \quad \text{and} \quad u_2 = \frac{x_2}{b}$$

It follows that $\mathbf{u}$ is in the unit disk, with $u_1^2 + u_2^2 \leq 1$, if and only if $\mathbf{x}$ is in E, with $(x_1/a)^2 + (x_2/b)^2 \leq 1$. By the generalization of Theorem 10,

$$\begin{aligned} \{\text{area of ellipse }\} &= \{\text{area of } T(D)\} \\ &= |\det A| \cdot \{\text{area of } D\} \\ &= ab \cdot \pi (1)^2 = \pi ab \end{aligned}$$

PRACTICE PROBLEM

Let S be the parallelogram determined by the vectors $\mathbf{b}_1 = \begin{bmatrix} 1 \\ 3 \end{bmatrix}$ and $\mathbf{b}_2 = \begin{bmatrix} 5 \\ 1 \end{bmatrix}$, and let $A = \begin{bmatrix} 1 & -.1 \\ 0 & 2 \end{bmatrix}$. Compute the area of the image of S under the mapping $\mathbf{x} \mapsto A\mathbf{x}$.

4.3 EXERCISES

Use Cramer's rule to compute the solutions of the systems in Exercises 1–6.

1. $\begin{aligned} 5x_1 + 7x_2 &= 3 \\ 2x_1 + 4x_2 &= 1 \end{aligned}$

2. $\begin{aligned} 4x_1 + x_2 &= 6 \\ 5x_1 + 2x_2 &= 7 \end{aligned}$

3. $\begin{aligned} 3x_1 - 2x_2 &= 7 \\ -5x_1 + 6x_2 &= -5 \end{aligned}$

4. $\begin{aligned} -5x_1 + 3x_2 &= 9 \\ 3x_1 - x_2 &= -5 \end{aligned}$

5. $\begin{aligned} 2x_1 + x_2 \qquad &= 7 \\ -3x_1 \qquad + x_3 &= -8 \\ x_2 + 2x_3 &= -3 \end{aligned}$

6. $\begin{aligned} 2x_1 + x_2 + x_3 &= 4 \\ -x_1 \qquad + 2x_3 &= 2 \\ 3x_1 + x_2 + 3x_3 &= -2 \end{aligned}$

In Exercises 7–10, determine the values of the parameter s for which the system has a unique solution, and describe the solution.

7. $\begin{aligned} 6sx_1 + 4x_2 &= 5 \\ 9x_1 + 2sx_2 &= -2 \end{aligned}$

8. $\begin{aligned} 3sx_1 - 5x_2 &= 3 \\ 9x_1 + 5sx_2 &= 2 \end{aligned}$

9. $\begin{aligned} sx_1 - 2sx_2 &= -1 \\ 3x_1 + 6sx_2 &= 4 \end{aligned}$

10. $\begin{aligned} 2sx_1 + x_2 &= 1 \\ 3sx_1 + 6sx_2 &= 2 \end{aligned}$

In Exercises 11–16, compute the adjugate of the given matrix, and then use Theorem 8 to give the inverse of the matrix.

11. $\begin{bmatrix} 0 & -2 & -1 \\ 3 & 0 & 0 \\ -1 & 1 & 1 \end{bmatrix}$

12. $\begin{bmatrix} 1 & 1 & 3 \\ 2 & -2 & 1 \\ 0 & 1 & 0 \end{bmatrix}$

13. $\begin{bmatrix} 3 & 5 & 4 \\ 1 & 0 & 1 \\ 2 & 1 & 1 \end{bmatrix}$

14. $\begin{bmatrix} 3 & 6 & 7 \\ 0 & 2 & 1 \\ 2 & 3 & 4 \end{bmatrix}$

15. $\begin{bmatrix} 3 & 0 & 0 \\ -1 & 1 & 0 \\ -2 & 3 & 2 \end{bmatrix}$

16. $\begin{bmatrix} 1 & 2 & 4 \\ 0 & -3 & 1 \\ 0 & 0 & 3 \end{bmatrix}$

17. Show that if A is 2×2, then Theorem 8 gives the same formula for A^{-1} as that given by Theorem 4 in Section 3.2.

18. Suppose that all the entries in A are integers and $\det A = 1$. Explain why all the entries in A^{-1} are integers.

Find the area of the parallelogram whose vertices are listed in Exercises 19–22.

19. $(0, 0), (5, 2), (6, 4), (11, 6)$

20. $(0, 0), (-1, 3), (4, -5), (3, -2)$

21. $(-1, 0), (0, 5), (1, -4), (2, 1)$

22. $(0, -2), (6, -1), (-3, 1), (3, 2)$

23. Find the volume of the parallelepiped with one vertex at the origin and adjacent vertices at $(1, 0, -2)$, $(1, 2, 4)$, $(7, 1, 0)$.

24. Find the volume of the parallelepiped with one vertex at the origin and adjacent vertices at $(1, 4, 0)$, $(-2, -5, 2)$, $(-1, 2, -1)$.

25. Use the concept of volume to explain why the determinant of a 3×3 matrix A is zero if and only if A is not invertible. Do not appeal to Theorem 4 in Section 4.2. [*Hint*: Think about the columns of A.]

26. Let $T: \mathbb{R}^m \to \mathbb{R}^n$ be a linear transformation, and let $\mathbf{p}$ be a vector and S a set in $\mathbb{R}^m$. Show that the image of $\mathbf{p} + S$ under T is the translated set $T(\mathbf{p}) + T(S)$ in $\mathbb{R}^n$.

27. Let S be the parallelogram determined by the vectors $\mathbf{b}_1 = \begin{bmatrix} -2 \\ 3 \end{bmatrix}$ and $\mathbf{b}_2 = \begin{bmatrix} -2 \\ 5 \end{bmatrix}$, and let $A = \begin{bmatrix} 6 & -2 \\ -3 & 2 \end{bmatrix}$. Compute the area of the image of S under the mapping $\mathbf{x} \mapsto A\mathbf{x}$.

28. Repeat Exercise 27 with $\mathbf{b}_1 = \begin{bmatrix} 4 \\ -7 \end{bmatrix}$, $\mathbf{b}_2 = \begin{bmatrix} 0 \\ 1 \end{bmatrix}$, and $A = \begin{bmatrix} 7 & 2 \\ 1 & 1 \end{bmatrix}$.

29. Find a formula for the area of the triangle whose vertices are $\mathbf{0}$, $\mathbf{v}_1$, and $\mathbf{v}_2$ in $\mathbb{R}^2$.

30. Let R be the triangle with vertices at (x_1, y_1), (x_2, y_2), and (x_3, y_3). Show that

$$\{\text{area of triangle}\} = \tfrac{1}{2}\left|\det \begin{bmatrix} x_1 & y_1 & 1 \\ x_2 & y_2 & 1 \\ x_3 & y_3 & 1 \end{bmatrix}\right|.$$

[*Hint*: Translate R to the origin by subtracting one of the vertices, and use Exercise 29.]

31. Let $T: \mathbb{R}^3 \to \mathbb{R}^3$ be the linear transformation determined by the matrix $A = \begin{bmatrix} a & 0 & 0 \\ 0 & b & 0 \\ 0 & 0 & c \end{bmatrix}$, where a, b, c are positive numbers. Let S be the unit ball, whose bounding surface has the equation $x_1^2 + x_2^2 + x_3^2 = 1$.

a. Show that $T(S)$ is bounded by the ellipsoid with the equation

$$\frac{x_1^2}{a^2} + \frac{x_2^2}{b^2} + \frac{x_3^2}{c^2} = 1$$

b. Use the fact that the volume of the unit ball is $4\pi/3$ to determine the volume of the region bounded by the ellipsoid in part (a).

32. Let S be the tetrahedron in $\mathbb{R}^3$ with vertices at the vectors $\mathbf{0}$, $\mathbf{e}_1$, $\mathbf{e}_2$, and $\mathbf{e}_3$, and let S' be the tetrahedron with vertices at vectors $\mathbf{0}$, $\mathbf{v}_1$, $\mathbf{v}_2$, and $\mathbf{v}_3$. See the accompanying figure.

a. Describe a linear transformation that maps S onto S'.

b. Find a formula for the volume of the tetrahedron S' using the fact that

$$\{\text{volume of } S\} = (1/3)\{\text{area of base}\}\cdot\{\text{height}\}$$

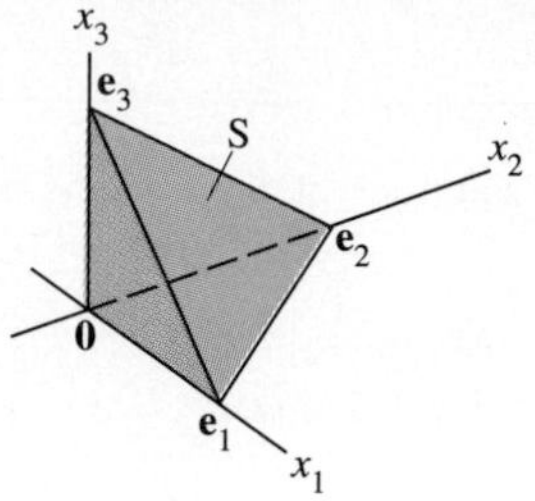

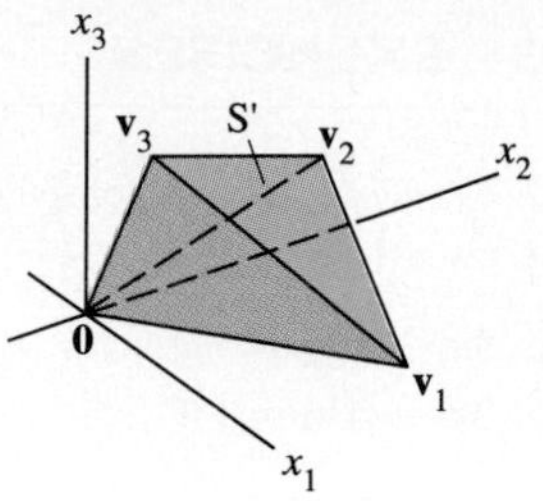

SOLUTION TO PRACTICE PROBLEM

The area of S is $\left|\det\begin{bmatrix}1 & 5\\ 3 & 1\end{bmatrix}\right| = 14$, and $\det A = 2$. By Theorem 10, the area of the image of S under the mapping $\mathbf{x} \mapsto A\mathbf{x}$ is

$$|\det A|\cdot\{\text{area of } S\} = 2\cdot 14 = 28$$

CHAPTER 4 SUPPLEMENTARY EXERCISES

1. Mark each statement True or False. Justify each answer.

___ a. If A is a 2×2 matrix with a zero determinant, then one column of A is a multiple of the other.

___ b. If two rows of a 3×3 matrix A are the same, then $\det A = 0$.

___ c. If A is a 3×3 matrix, then $\det 5A = 5\det A$.

___ d. If A and B are $n\times n$ matrices, with $\det A = 2$ and $\det B = 3$, then $\det(A+B) = 5$.

___ e. If A is $n\times n$ and $\det A = 2$, then $\det A^3 = 6$.

___ f. If B is produced by interchanging two rows of A, then $\det B = \det A$.

___ g. If B is produced by multiplying row 3 of A by 5, then $\det B = 5\cdot\det A$.

___ h. If B is formed by adding to one row of A a linear combination of the other rows, then $\det B = \det A$.

___ i. $\det A^T = -\det A$.

___ j. $\det(-A) = -\det A$.

___ k. $\det A^TA \geq 0$.

___ l. Any system of n linear equations in n variables can be solved by Cramer's rule.

___ m. If $\mathbf{u}$ and $\mathbf{v}$ are in $\mathbb{R}^2$ and $\det[\mathbf{u}\ \ \mathbf{v}] = 10$, then the area of the triangle in the plane with vertices at $\mathbf{0}$, $\mathbf{u}$, and $\mathbf{v}$ is 10.

___ n. If $A^3 = 0$, then $\det A = 0$.

___ o. If A is invertible, then $\det A^{-1} = \det A$.

___ p. If A is invertible, then $(\det A)(\det A^{-1}) = 1$.

Use row operations to show that the determinants in Exercises 2–4 are all zero.

2. $\begin{vmatrix}12 & 13 & 14\\ 15 & 16 & 17\\ 18 & 19 & 20\end{vmatrix}$

3. $\begin{vmatrix}1 & a & b+c\\ 1 & b & a+c\\ 1 & c & a+b\end{vmatrix}$

4. $\begin{vmatrix}a & b & c\\ a+x & b+x & c+x\\ a+y & b+y & c+y\end{vmatrix}$

Compute the determinants in Exercises 5 and 6.

5. $\begin{vmatrix}9 & 1 & 9 & 9 & 9\\ 9 & 0 & 9 & 9 & 2\\ 4 & 0 & 0 & 5 & 0\\ 9 & 0 & 3 & 9 & 0\\ 6 & 0 & 0 & 7 & 0\end{vmatrix}$

6. $\begin{vmatrix}4 & 8 & 8 & 8 & 5\\ 0 & 1 & 0 & 0 & 0\\ 6 & 8 & 8 & 8 & 7\\ 0 & 8 & 8 & 3 & 0\\ 0 & 8 & 2 & 0 & 0\end{vmatrix}$

7. Show that the equation of the line in $\mathbb{R}^2$ through distinct points (x_1, y_1) and (x_2, y_2) may be written as

$$\det\begin{bmatrix} 1 & x & y \\ 1 & x_1 & y_1 \\ 1 & x_2 & y_2 \end{bmatrix} = 0$$

8. Find a 3×3 determinant equation similar to that in Exercise 7 that describes the equation of the line through (x_1, y_1) with slope m.

Exercises 9 and 10 concern determinants of the following *Vandermonde matrices.*

$$T = \begin{bmatrix} 1 & a & a^2 \\ 1 & b & b^2 \\ 1 & c & c^2 \end{bmatrix}, \quad V(t) = \begin{bmatrix} 1 & t & t^2 & t^3 \\ 1 & x_1 & x_1^2 & x_1^3 \\ 1 & x_2 & x_2^2 & x_2^3 \\ 1 & x_3 & x_3^2 & x_3^3 \end{bmatrix}$$

9. Use row operations to show that

$$\det T = (b-a)(c-a)(c-b)$$

10. Let $f(t) = \det V$, with $\mathbf{x}_1, \mathbf{x}_2, \mathbf{x}_3$ all distinct. Explain why $f(t)$ is a cubic polynomial; show that the coefficient of t^3 is nonzero; and find three points on the graph of f.

11. Determine the area of the parallelogram determined by the points $(1, 4)$, $(-1, 5)$, $(3, 9)$, and $(5, 8)$. How can you tell the quadrilateral determined by the points is actually a parallelogram?

12. Use the concept of area of a parallelogram to write a statement about a 2×2 matrix A that is true if and only if A is invertible.

13. Show that if A is invertible, then adj A is invertible, and

$$(\text{adj } A)^{-1} = \frac{1}{\det A} A$$

[*Hint*: Given matrices B and C, what calculation(s) would show that C is the inverse of B?]

14. Let A, B, C, D, I be $n\times n$ matrices. Use the definition or properties of a determinant to justify the following formulas. Part (c) is useful in applications of eigenvalues (Chapter 6).

a. $\det\begin{bmatrix} A & 0 \\ 0 & I \end{bmatrix} = \det A$ b. $\det\begin{bmatrix} I & 0 \\ C & D \end{bmatrix} = \det D$

c. $\det\begin{bmatrix} A & 0 \\ C & D \end{bmatrix} = (\det A)(\det D) = \det\begin{bmatrix} A & B \\ 0 & D \end{bmatrix}$

15. Let A, B, C, D be $n\times n$ matrices with A invertible.

a. Find matrices X and Y to produce the block LU factorization $\begin{bmatrix} A & B \\ C & D \end{bmatrix} = \begin{bmatrix} I & 0 \\ X & I \end{bmatrix}\begin{bmatrix} A & B \\ 0 & Y \end{bmatrix}$ and then show that

$$\det\begin{bmatrix} A & B \\ C & D \end{bmatrix} = (\det A)\cdot\det(D - CA^{-1}B)$$

b. Show if $AC = CA$, then

$$\det\begin{bmatrix} A & B \\ C & D \end{bmatrix} = \det(AD - CB)$$

5

Vector Spaces

Introductory Example: Space Flight and Control Systems

Twelve stories high and weighing 75 tons, the US *Columbia* rose majestically off the launching pad on a cool Palm Sunday morning in April 1981. A product of ten years' intensive research and development, the first U.S. space shuttle was a triumph of control systems engineering design, involving many branches of engineering—aeronautical, chemical, electrical, hydraulic, and mechanical.

The space shuttle's control systems are absolutely critical for flight. Because the shuttle is an unstable airframe, it requires constant computer monitoring during atmospheric flight. The flight control system sends a stream of commands to aerodynamic control surfaces and 44 small thruster jets. Figure 1 shows a typical closed-loop feedback system that controls the pitch of the shuttle during flight. (The pitch is the elevation angle of the nose cone.) The junction symbols $\otimes$ show where signals from various sensors are added to the computer signals flowing along the top of the figure.

Mathematically, the input and output signals to an engineering system are functions. It is important in applications that these functions can be added, as in Fig. 1, and multiplied by scalars. These two operations on functions have algebraic properties that are completely analogous to the operation of adding vectors in $\mathbb{R}^n$ and multiplying a vector by a scalar, as we shall see in Sections 5.1 and 5.8. For this reason, the set of all possible inputs (functions) is called a *vector space*. The mathematical foundation for systems engineering rests on vector spaces of functions, and we need to extend the theory of vectors in $\mathbb{R}^n$ to include such functions. Later on, we will see how other vector spaces arise in engineering, physics, and statistics.

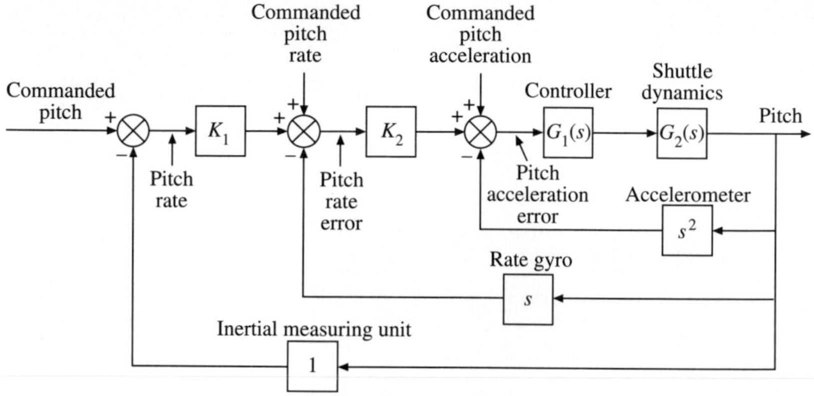

FIGURE 1 Pitch control system for the space shuttle. (Source: *Control Systems Engineering*, by Norman S. Nise, Benjamin-Cummings Publishing, 1992, p. 274. Simplified drawing based on *Space Shuttle GN&C Operations Manual,* Rockwell International, 1988.)

The mathematical seeds planted in Chapters 1 through 3 germinate and begin to blossom in this chapter. The beauty and power of linear algebra will be seen more clearly when we view $\mathbb{R}^n$ as only one of a variety of vector spaces that arise naturally in applied problems. We will find that a study of vector spaces is not much different from a study of $\mathbb{R}^n$ itself, because we can use our geometric experience with $\mathbb{R}^2$ and $\mathbb{R}^3$ to visualize many general concepts.

Beginning with basic definitions in Section 5.1, the general vector space framework develops gradually throughout the chapter. A goal of Sections 5.3 to 5.5 is to demonstrate how closely other vector spaces resemble $\mathbb{R}^n$. Section 5.6 on rank is one of the high points of the chapter, using vector space terminology to tie together important facts about rectangular matrices. Section 5.8 applies the theory of the chapter to discrete signals and difference equations used in digital control systems such as in the space shuttle. Markov chains, in Section 5.9, provide a change of pace from the more theoretical sections of the chapter and make good examples for concepts to be introduced in Chapter 6.

5.1 VECTOR SPACES AND SUBSPACES

Much of the theory in Chapters 2 and 3 rested on certain simple and obvious properties of $\mathbb{R}^n$, listed in Section 2.1. As we shall see, many other mathematical systems have the same properties. The specific properties of interest are listed in the following definition.

DEFINITION

A **vector space** is a nonempty set V of objects, called *vectors*, on which are defined two operations, called *addition* and *multiplication by scalars* (real numbers), subject to the ten axioms (or rules) listed below.[1] The axioms must hold for all vectors $\mathbf{u}$, $\mathbf{v}$, and $\mathbf{w}$ in V and for all scalars c and d.

1. The sum of $\mathbf{u}$ and $\mathbf{v}$, denoted by $\mathbf{u}+\mathbf{v}$, is in V.
2. $\mathbf{u}+\mathbf{v}=\mathbf{v}+\mathbf{u}$.
3. $(\mathbf{u}+\mathbf{v})+\mathbf{w}=\mathbf{u}+(\mathbf{v}+\mathbf{w})$.
4. There is a **zero** vector $\mathbf{0}$ in V such that $\mathbf{u}+\mathbf{0}=\mathbf{u}$.
5. For each $\mathbf{u}$ in V there is a vector $-\mathbf{u}$ in V such that $\mathbf{u}+(-\mathbf{u})=\mathbf{0}$.
6. The scalar multiple of $\mathbf{u}$ by c, denoted by $c\mathbf{u}$, is in V.
7. $c(\mathbf{u}+\mathbf{v})=c\mathbf{u}+c\mathbf{v}$.
8. $(c+d)\mathbf{u}=c\mathbf{u}+d\mathbf{u}$.
9. $c(d\mathbf{u})=(cd)\mathbf{u}$.
10. $1\mathbf{u}=\mathbf{u}$.

Using only these axioms, one can show that the zero vector in Axiom 4 is unique, and the vector $-\mathbf{u}$, called the **negative** of $\mathbf{u}$, in Axiom 5 is unique for each $\mathbf{u}$ in V. See Exercises 23 and 24. Proofs of the following simple facts are also outlined in the exercises:

For each $\mathbf{u}$ in V and scalar c,

$$0\mathbf{u}=\mathbf{0} \tag{1}$$

$$c\mathbf{0}=\mathbf{0} \tag{2}$$

$$-\mathbf{u}=(-1)\mathbf{u} \tag{3}$$

EXAMPLE 1 The spaces $\mathbb{R}^n$, where $n \geq 1$, are the premier examples of vector spaces. The geometric intuition developed for $\mathbb{R}^3$ will help us understand and visualize many concepts throughout the chapter.

EXAMPLE 2 Let V be the set of all arrows (directed line segments) in three-dimensional space, with two arrows regarded as equal if they have the same length and point in the same direction. Define addition by the parallelogram rule (from Section 2.1), and for each $\mathbf{v}$ in V, define $c\mathbf{v}$ to be the arrow whose length is $|c|$ times the length of $\mathbf{v}$, pointing in the same direction as $\mathbf{v}$ if $c \geq 0$ and otherwise pointing

[1] Technically, V is a *real vector space*. All of the theory in this chapter also holds for a *complex vector space* in which the scalars are complex numbers. We will look at this briefly in Chapter 6. Until then, all scalars are assumed to be real.

in the opposite direction. (See Fig. 1.) Show that V is a vector space. This space is a common model in physical problems for various forces.

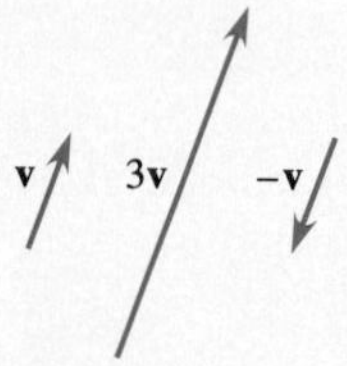

FIGURE 1

Solution The definition of V is geometric, using concepts of length and direction. No xyz-coordinate system is involved. An arrow of zero length is a single point and represents the zero vector. The negative of $\mathbf{v}$ is $(-1)\mathbf{v}$. So Axioms 1, 4, 5, 6, and 10 are evident. The rest are verified by geometry. For instance, see Figs. 2 and 3. ∎

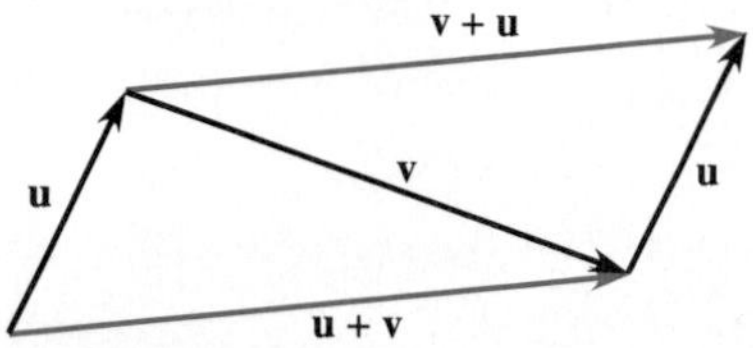

FIGURE 2 $\mathbf{u} + \mathbf{v} = \mathbf{v} + \mathbf{u}$.

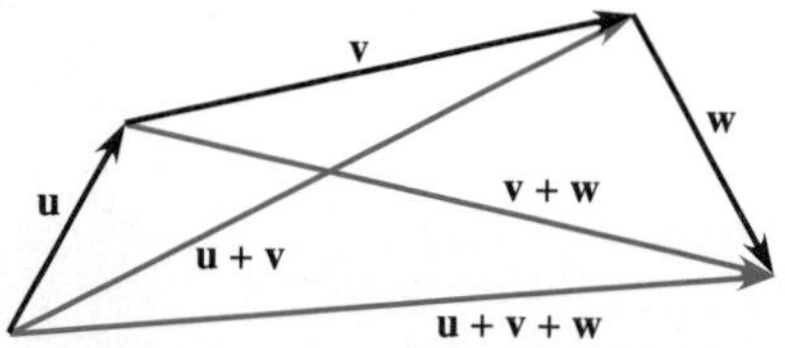

FIGURE 3 $(\mathbf{u}+\mathbf{v})+\mathbf{w} = \mathbf{u}+(\mathbf{v}+\mathbf{w})$.

EXAMPLE 3 Let $\mathbb{S}$ be the space of all doubly infinite sequences of numbers (usually written in a row rather than a column):

$$\{y_k\} = (\ldots, y_{-2}, y_{-1}, y_0, y_1, y_2, \ldots)$$

If $\{z_k\}$ is another element of $\mathbb{S}$, then the sum $\{y_k\} + \{z_k\}$ is the sequence $\{y_k + z_k\}$ formed by adding corresponding terms of $\{y_k\}$ and $\{z_k\}$. The scalar multiple $c\{y_k\}$ is the sequence $\{cy_k\}$. The vector space axioms are verified in the same way as for $\mathbb{R}^n$.

Elements of $\mathbb{S}$ arise in engineering, for example, whenever a signal is measured (or "sampled") at discrete times. A signal might be electrical, mechanical, optical, and so on. The major control systems for the space shuttle, mentioned in the chapter introduction, use discrete, or "digital," signals. For convenience, we will call $\mathbb{S}$ the space of (discrete-time) **signals**. A signal may be visualized by a graph as in Fig. 4. ∎

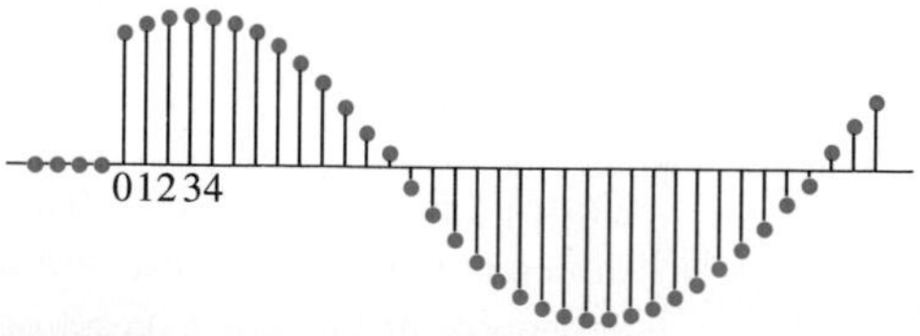

FIGURE 4 A discrete-time signal.

EXAMPLE 4 For $n \geq 0$, the set $\mathbb{P}_n$ of all polynomials of degree at most n is the set of all polynomials of the form

$$\mathbf{p}(t) = a_0 + a_1 t + a_2 t^2 + \cdots + a_n t^n \tag{4}$$

where the coefficients $a_0, \ldots, a_n$ and the variable t are real numbers. The *degree* of $\mathbf{p}$ is the highest power of t in (4) whose coefficient is not zero. If $\mathbf{p}(t) = a_0 \neq 0$, the degree of $\mathbf{p}$ is zero. If all the coefficients are zero, $\mathbf{p}$ is called the zero polynomial, and its degree is not defined.

If $\mathbf{p}$ is given by (4) and if $\mathbf{q}(t) = b_0 + b_1 t + \cdots + b_n t^n$, then the sum $\mathbf{p} + \mathbf{q}$ is defined in the obvious way by

$$\begin{aligned}(\mathbf{p}+\mathbf{q})(t) &= \mathbf{p}(t) + \mathbf{q}(t) \\ &= (a_0 + b_0) + (a_1 + b_1)t + \cdots + (a_n + b_n)t^n\end{aligned}$$

The scalar multiple $c\mathbf{p}$ is the polynomial defined by

$$(c\mathbf{p})(t) = c\mathbf{p}(t) = ca_0 + (ca_1)t + \cdots + (ca_n)t^n$$

These definitions satisfy Axioms 1 and 6 because $\mathbf{p} + \mathbf{q}$ and $c\mathbf{p}$ are polynomials of degree less than or equal to n. Axioms 2, 3, and 7 to 10 are easily verified from properties of the real numbers. Clearly, the zero polynomial acts as the zero vector in Axiom 4. Finally, $(-1)\mathbf{p}$ acts as the negative of $\mathbf{p}$, so Axiom 5 is satisfied. Thus $\mathbb{P}_n$ is a vector space.

EXAMPLE 5 Let V be the set of all real-valued functions defined on a set $\mathbb{D}$. (Typically, $\mathbb{D}$ is the set of real numbers or some interval on the real line.) Functions are added in the usual way: $\mathbf{f} + \mathbf{g}$ is the function whose value at t in the domain $\mathbb{D}$ is $\mathbf{f}(t) + \mathbf{g}(t)$. Likewise, for a scalar c and an $\mathbf{f}$ in V, the scalar multiple $c\mathbf{f}$ is the function whose value at t is $c\mathbf{f}(t)$. For instance, if $\mathbb{D} = \mathbb{R}$, $\mathbf{f}(t) = 1 + \sin 2t$, and $\mathbf{g}(t) = 2 + .5t$, then

$$(\mathbf{f}+\mathbf{g})(t) = 3 + \sin 2t + .5t \quad \text{and} \quad (2\mathbf{g})(t) = 4 + t$$

See Fig. 5. Two functions in V are equal if and only if their values are equal for every t in $\mathbb{D}$. Hence the zero vector in V is the function that is identically zero, $\mathbf{f}(t) = 0$ for all t, and the negative of $\mathbf{f}$ is $(-1)\mathbf{f}$. Axioms 1 and 6 are obviously true, and the other axioms are easily verified using properties of the real numbers.

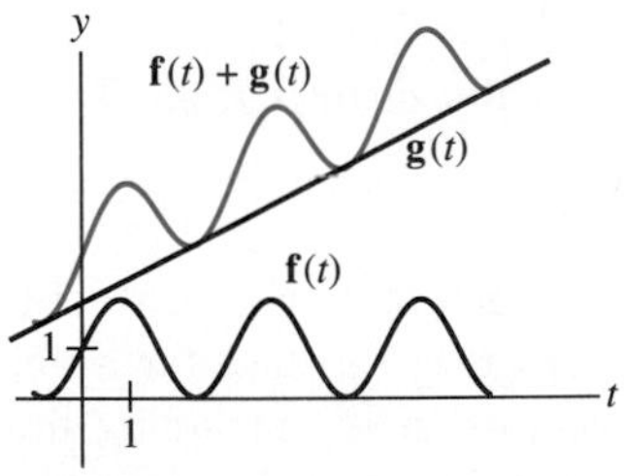

FIGURE 5

Subspaces

In many problems, a vector space consists of an appropriate subset of vectors from some larger vector space. Each polynomial in $\mathbb{P}_3$, for example, is in the vector space V of all functions defined on the real numbers. That is, $\mathbb{P}_3$ is a *subset* of V. Moreover, $\mathbb{P}_3$ is a vector space "inside" the larger space V, and the vector space operations in $\mathbb{P}_3$ are just the ordinary operations on the vectors (functions) in V.

DEFINITION

A **subspace** of a vector space V is a subset H of V such that H is itself a vector space under the same operations of addition and scalar multiplication that are already defined on V.

EXAMPLE 6 The set consisting of only the zero vector in a vector space V is a subspace of V, called the **zero subspace** and written as $\{\mathbf{0}\}$.

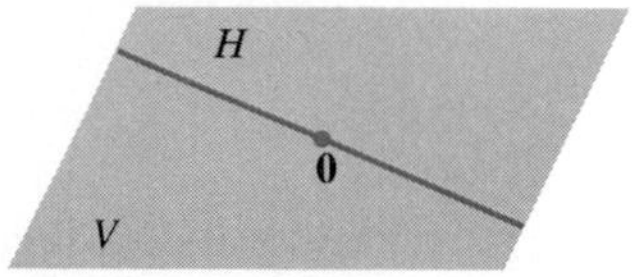

FIGURE 6 A subspace of V.

Every vector space is a subspace (of itself and possibly other larger spaces), and every subspace is a vector space. The term *subspace* is used when at least two vector spaces are in mind, with one inside the other, and the phrase *subspace of V* identifies V as the larger space. (See Fig. 6.)

EXAMPLE 7 Let $\mathbb{P}$ be the set of all polynomials with real coefficients, with operations in $\mathbb{P}$ defined as for functions. Then $\mathbb{P}$ is a subspace of the space of all real-valued functions defined on $\mathbb{R}$. Also, for each $n \geq 0$, $\mathbb{P}_n$ is a subspace of $\mathbb{P}$, because $\mathbb{P}_n$ is obviously a subset of $\mathbb{P}$, addition and scalar multiplication in $\mathbb{P}_n$ are the same as for elements of $\mathbb{P}$, and $\mathbb{P}_n$ is itself a vector space.

EXAMPLE 8 The vector space $\mathbb{R}^2$ is *not* a subspace of $\mathbb{R}^3$ because $\mathbb{R}^2$ is not even a subset of $\mathbb{R}^3$. (The vectors in $\mathbb{R}^3$ all have three entries, whereas the vectors in $\mathbb{R}^2$ have only two.) The set

$$H = \left\{ \begin{bmatrix} s \\ t \\ 0 \end{bmatrix} : s \text{ and } t \text{ are real} \right\}$$

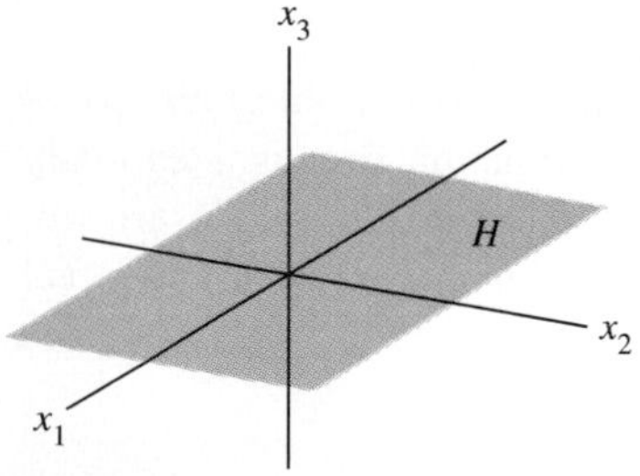

FIGURE 7 A plane as a subspace of $\mathbb{R}^3$.

is a subset of $\mathbb{R}^3$ that "acts" like $\mathbb{R}^2$, although it is logically distinct from $\mathbb{R}^2$. See Fig. 7. Show that H is a subspace of $\mathbb{R}^3$.

Solution Axiom 1 is satisfied because the sum of two vectors with 0 in the third entry is again a vector with 0 in the third entry. Axiom 6 is satisfied for a similar reason. Axioms 2, 3, and 7–10 are true for any vectors in $\mathbb{R}^3$, including those in H. The zero vector is obviously in H, so Axiom 4 is satisfied. Also, given $\mathbf{u} = (s, t, 0)$ in H, the vector $-\mathbf{u} = (-s, -t, 0)$ is also in H, so Axiom 5 is satisfied. Thus H is a vector space using the operations in $\mathbb{R}^3$, and hence H is a subspace of $\mathbb{R}^3$.

As mentioned in Example 8, many of the vector space properties of $\mathbb{R}^3$ are inherited by any subset of $\mathbb{R}^3$. The next theorem says that, in general, we only need to check three conditions to verify that a given subset is a subspace.

THEOREM 1 Subspace Test

A subset H of a vector space V is a subspace of V if and only if the following conditions are all satisfied:

a. The zero vector of V is in H.[2]
b. If $\mathbf{u}$ and $\mathbf{v}$ are in H, then $\mathbf{u}+\mathbf{v}$ is in H.
c. If $\mathbf{u}$ is in H and c is any scalar, then $c\mathbf{u}$ is in H.

Proof If H is a subspace of V, then it is a vector space and hence satisfies all ten vector space axioms, including those listed in the theorem. Conversely, suppose that H satisfies the three conditions above. By condition (a), Axiom 4 is satisfied. Axioms 2, 3, and 7–10 are automatically satisfied because they apply to all elements of V, including those that are in H. If $\mathbf{u}$ is in H, then $(-1)\mathbf{u}$ is in H, by condition (c). Since $(-1)\mathbf{u} = -\mathbf{u}$ by property (3) established above, Axiom 5 is satisfied. The only other axioms are Axioms 1 and 6, and these are conditions (b) and (c). So H is a vector space under the operations defined on V. This proves that H is a subspace of V. ∎

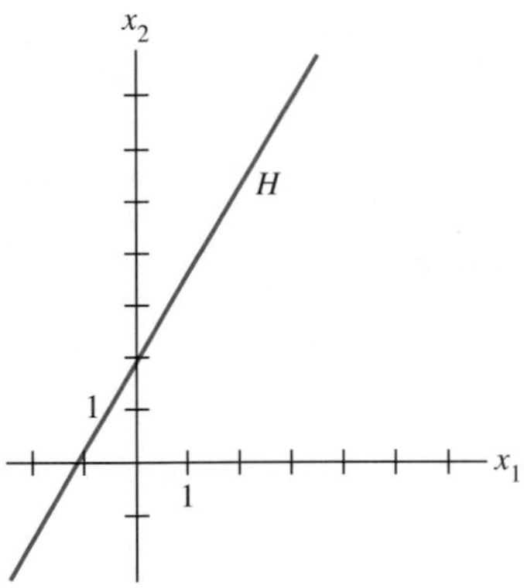

FIGURE 8 A line that is not a vector space.

EXAMPLE 9 Let H be the set of all points in $\mathbb{R}^2$ of the form $(3s,\ 2+5s)$. Determine if H is a subspace of $\mathbb{R}^2$.

Solution The zero vector of $\mathbb{R}^2$ is not in H. For if $(3s,\ 2+5s)$ were zero for some s, then both $3s$ and $2+5s$ would be zero, which is impossible. Thus H is not a subspace of $\mathbb{R}^2$. In fact, it is easy to verify that *none* of the three conditions of the subspace test are satisfied. See Fig. 8. ∎

A Subspace Spanned by a Set

The next example illustrates one of the most common ways of describing a subspace. As in Chapter 2, we use the term **linear combination** for any sum of scalar multiples of vectors. Given a set of vectors in V—say, $S = \{\mathbf{v}_1, \dots, \mathbf{v}_p\}$—we write Span $\{\mathbf{v}_1, \dots, \mathbf{v}_p\}$ or simply Span S for the set of all vectors that can be written as a linear combination of $\mathbf{v}_1, \dots, \mathbf{v}_p$.

EXAMPLE 10 Given $\mathbf{v}_1$ and $\mathbf{v}_2$ in a vector space V, let $H = \text{Span}\,\{\mathbf{v}_1, \mathbf{v}_2\}$. Show that H is a subspace of V.

[2]Some texts replace condition (a) in Theorem 1 by the assumption that H is nonempty. Then condition (a) could be deduced from (c) and property (1) above. But the best way to test for a subspace is to look first for the zero vector. If $\mathbf{0}$ is in H, then conditions (b) and (c) should be checked. If $\mathbf{0}$ is *not* in H, then H cannot be a subspace and the other conditions need not be checked.

Solution The zero vector is in H, since $\mathbf{0} = 0\mathbf{v}_1 + 0\mathbf{v}_2$. Take two arbitrary vectors in H, say,

$$\mathbf{u} = s_1\mathbf{v}_1 + s_2\mathbf{v}_2 \quad \text{and} \quad \mathbf{w} = t_1\mathbf{v}_1 + t_2\mathbf{v}_2$$

By Axioms 2, 3, and 8,

$$\begin{aligned}\mathbf{u} + \mathbf{w} &= (s_1\mathbf{v}_1 + s_2\mathbf{v}_2) + (t_1\mathbf{v}_1 + t_2\mathbf{v}_2) \\ &= (s_1 + t_1)\mathbf{v}_1 + (s_2 + t_2)\mathbf{v}_2\end{aligned}$$

So $\mathbf{u} + \mathbf{w}$ is in H. Furthermore, if c is any scalar, then by Axioms 7 and 9,

$$c\mathbf{u} = c(s_1\mathbf{v}_1 + s_2\mathbf{v}_2) = (cs_1)\mathbf{v}_1 + (cs_2)\mathbf{v}_2$$

which shows that $c\mathbf{u}$ is in H. By the subspace test, H is a subspace of V.

In Section 5.5 we shall prove that every nonzero subspace of $\mathbb{R}^3$, other than $\mathbb{R}^3$ itself, is either Span $\{\mathbf{v}_1, \mathbf{v}_2\}$ for some linearly independent $\mathbf{v}_1$ and $\mathbf{v}_2$ or Span $\{\mathbf{v}\}$ for $\mathbf{v} \neq \mathbf{0}$. In the first case the subspace is a plane through the origin and in the second case a line through the origin. It is helpful to keep these geometric pictures in mind, even for an abstract vector space.

The argument in Example 10 can easily be generalized to prove the following theorem.

THEOREM 2

Given $\mathbf{v}_1, \ldots, \mathbf{v}_p$ in a vector space V, the set Span $\{\mathbf{v}_1, \ldots, \mathbf{v}_p\}$ is a subspace of V.

We call Span $\{\mathbf{v}_1, \ldots, \mathbf{v}_p\}$ **the subspace spanned** (or **generated**) **by** $\{\mathbf{v}_1, \ldots, \mathbf{v}_p\}$. Given any subspace H of V, a **spanning set** for H is a set $\{\mathbf{v}_1, \ldots, \mathbf{v}_p\}$ in H such that H = Span $\{\mathbf{v}_1, \ldots, \mathbf{v}_p\}$.

The next example shows how to use Theorem 2.

EXAMPLE 11 Let H be the set of all vectors of the form $(a - 3b, b - a, a, b)$, where a and b are arbitrary scalars. That is, let $H = \{(a - 3b, b - a, a, b) : a \text{ and } b \text{ in } \mathbb{R}\}$. Show that H is a subspace of $\mathbb{R}^4$.

Solution Write the vectors in H as column vectors. Then an arbitrary vector in H has the form

$$\begin{bmatrix} a - 3b \\ b - a \\ a \\ b \end{bmatrix} = a\underset{\substack{\uparrow \\ \mathbf{v}_1}}{\begin{bmatrix} 1 \\ -1 \\ 1 \\ 0 \end{bmatrix}} + b\underset{\substack{\uparrow \\ \mathbf{v}_2}}{\begin{bmatrix} -3 \\ 1 \\ 0 \\ 1 \end{bmatrix}}$$

This calculation shows that $H = \text{Span}\{\mathbf{v}_1, \mathbf{v}_2\}$, where $\mathbf{v}_1$ and $\mathbf{v}_2$ are the vectors indicated above. Thus H is a subspace of $\mathbb{R}^4$ by Theorem 2.

Example 11 illustrates a useful technique of expressing a given subspace H as the set of linear combinations of some small collection of vectors. If $H = \text{Span}\{\mathbf{v}_1, \dots, \mathbf{v}_p\}$, we can think of the vectors $\mathbf{v}_1, \dots, \mathbf{v}_p$ in the spanning set as "handles" that allow us to hold on to the subspace H. Calculations with the infinitely many vectors in H are often reduced to operations with the finite number of vectors in the spanning set.

EXAMPLE 12 For what value(s) of h will $\mathbf{y}$ be in the subspace of $\mathbb{R}^3$ spanned by $\mathbf{v}_1, \mathbf{v}_2, \mathbf{v}_3$, if

$$\mathbf{v}_1 = \begin{bmatrix} 1 \\ -1 \\ -2 \end{bmatrix}, \quad \mathbf{v}_2 = \begin{bmatrix} 5 \\ -4 \\ -7 \end{bmatrix}, \quad \mathbf{v}_3 = \begin{bmatrix} -3 \\ 1 \\ 0 \end{bmatrix}, \quad \text{and} \quad \mathbf{y} = \begin{bmatrix} -4 \\ 3 \\ h \end{bmatrix}$$

Solution This question is Practice Problem 2 in Section 2.1, written here with the term *subspace* rather than $\text{Span}\{\mathbf{v}_1, \mathbf{v}_2, \mathbf{v}_3\}$. The solution there shows that $\mathbf{y}$ is in $\text{Span}\{\mathbf{v}_1, \mathbf{v}_2, \mathbf{v}_3\}$ if and only if $h = 5$. That solution is worth reviewing now, along with Exercises 15–24 in Section 2.1.

Although many vector spaces in this chapter will be subspaces of $\mathbb{R}^n$, it is important to keep in mind that the abstract theory applies to other vector spaces as well. Vector spaces of functions arise in many applications, and they will receive more attention later.

PRACTICE PROBLEMS

1. Show that the set H in Example 9 is not a vector space, by showing that it is not closed under scalar multiplication; that is, Axiom 6 fails to be true. Find a specific vector $\mathbf{u}$ in H and a scalar c such that $c\mathbf{u}$ is not in H.
2. Let $W = \text{Span}\{\mathbf{v}_1, \dots, \mathbf{v}_p\}$, where $\mathbf{v}_1, \dots, \mathbf{v}_p$ are in a vector space V. Show that $\mathbf{v}_k$ is in W for $1 \le k \le$ p. [*Hint:* First write an equation that shows that $\mathbf{v}_1$ is in W. Then adjust your notation for the general case.]

5.1 EXERCISES

1. Let V be the first quadrant in the xy-plane; that is, let

$$V = \left\{ \begin{bmatrix} x \\ y \end{bmatrix} : x \ge 0, y \ge 0 \right\}$$

a. If $\mathbf{u}$ and $\mathbf{v}$ are in V, is $\mathbf{u} + \mathbf{v}$ in V? Why?

b. Find a specific vector $\mathbf{u}$ in V and a specific scalar c such that $c\mathbf{u}$ is *not* in V. (This is enough to show that V is *not* a vector space.)

2. Let W be the union of the first and third quadrants in the xy-plane. That is, let $W = \left\{ \begin{bmatrix} x \\ y \end{bmatrix} : xy \geq 0 \right\}$.
   a. If $\mathbf{u}$ is in W and c is any scalar, is $c\mathbf{u}$ in W? Why?
   b. Find specific vectors $\mathbf{u}$ and $\mathbf{v}$ in W such that $\mathbf{u}+\mathbf{v}$ is not in W. This is enough to show that W is *not* a vector space.
3. Let H be the set of points inside and on the unit circle in the xy-plane. That is, let $H = \left\{ \begin{bmatrix} x \\ y \end{bmatrix} : x^2 + y^2 \leq 1 \right\}$. Find a specific example—two vectors or a vector and a scalar—to show that H is not a subspace of $\mathbb{R}^2$.
4. Let $H = \left\{ \begin{bmatrix} x \\ y \end{bmatrix} : y \geq x^2 \right\}$. Find a specific example to show that H is not a subspace of $\mathbb{R}^2$.

In Exercises 5–8, determine if the given set is a subspace of $\mathbb{P}_n$ for an appropriate value of n.

5. All polynomials of the form $\mathbf{p}(t) = at^2$, where a is in $\mathbb{R}$.
6. All polynomials of the form $\mathbf{p}(t) = a + t^2$, where a is in $\mathbb{R}$.
7. All polynomials of degree at most 3, with integers as coefficients.
8. All polynomials in $\mathbb{P}_n$ such that $\mathbf{p}(0) = 0$.
9. Let H be the set of all vectors of the form $\begin{bmatrix} s \\ 3s \\ 2s \end{bmatrix}$. Find a vector $\mathbf{v}$ in $\mathbb{R}^3$ such that $H = \text{Span}\,\{\mathbf{v}\}$. Why does this show that H is a subspace of $\mathbb{R}^3$? (Mention a theorem.)
10. Let H be the set of all vectors of the form $\begin{bmatrix} 2t \\ 0 \\ -t \end{bmatrix}$. Show that H is a subspace of $\mathbb{R}^3$. (Use the method of Exercise 9.)
11. Let W be the set of all vectors of the form $\begin{bmatrix} 5b + 2c \\ b \\ c \end{bmatrix}$, where b and c are arbitrary. Find vectors $\mathbf{u}$ and $\mathbf{v}$ such that $W = \text{Span}\,\{\mathbf{u}, \mathbf{v}\}$. Why does this show that W is a subspace of $\mathbb{R}^3$?
12. Let W be the set of all vectors of the form $\begin{bmatrix} s + 3t \\ s - t \\ 2s - t \\ 4t \end{bmatrix}$. Show that W is a subspace of $\mathbb{R}^4$. (Use the method of Exercise 11.)
13. Let $\mathbf{v}_1 = \begin{bmatrix} 1 \\ 0 \\ -1 \end{bmatrix}$, $\mathbf{v}_2 = \begin{bmatrix} 2 \\ 1 \\ 3 \end{bmatrix}$, $\mathbf{v}_3 = \begin{bmatrix} 4 \\ 2 \\ 6 \end{bmatrix}$, and $\mathbf{w} = \begin{bmatrix} 3 \\ 1 \\ 2 \end{bmatrix}$.
   a. Is $\mathbf{w}$ in $\{\mathbf{v}_1, \mathbf{v}_2, \mathbf{v}_3\}$? How many vectors are in $\{\mathbf{v}_1, \mathbf{v}_2, \mathbf{v}_3\}$?
   b. How many vectors are in Span $\{\mathbf{v}_1, \mathbf{v}_2, \mathbf{v}_3\}$?
   c. Is $\mathbf{w}$ in the subspace spanned by $\{\mathbf{v}_1, \mathbf{v}_2, \mathbf{v}_3\}$?
14. Let $\mathbf{v}_1, \mathbf{v}_2, \mathbf{v}_3$ be as in Exercise 13, and let $\mathbf{w} = \begin{bmatrix} 8 \\ 4 \\ 7 \end{bmatrix}$. Is $\mathbf{w}$ in the subspace spanned by $\{\mathbf{v}_1, \mathbf{v}_2, \mathbf{v}_3\}$?

In Exercises 15–18, let W be the set of all vectors of the form shown, where a, b, and c represent arbitrary real numbers. In each case, either find a set S of vectors that spans W or give an example to show that W is *not* a vector space.

15. $\begin{bmatrix} 3a + b \\ 4 \\ a - 5b \end{bmatrix}$
16. $\begin{bmatrix} -a + 1 \\ a - 6b \\ 2b + a \end{bmatrix}$
17. $\begin{bmatrix} a - b \\ b - c \\ c - a \\ b \end{bmatrix}$
18. $\begin{bmatrix} 4a + 3b \\ 0 \\ a + b + c \\ c - 2a \end{bmatrix}$
19. If a mass m is placed at the end of a spring, and if the mass is pulled downward and released, the mass-spring system will begin to oscillate. The displacement y of the mass from its resting position is given by a function of the form

$$y(t) = c_1 \cos \omega t + c_2 \sin \omega t \qquad (5)$$

where ω is a constant that depends on the spring and the mass. Show that the set of all functions described in (5) is a vector space.

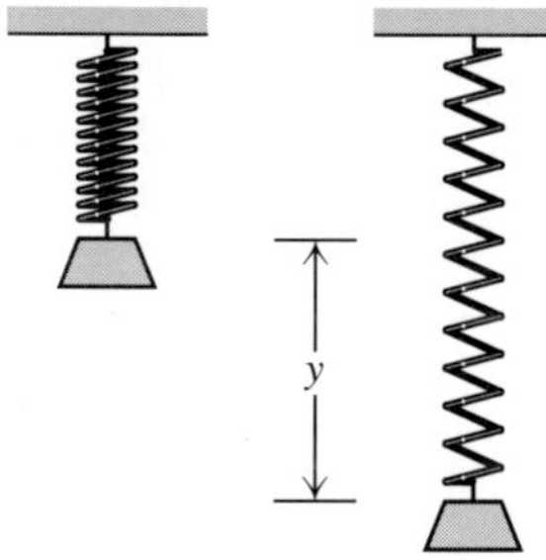

20. The set of all continuous real-valued functions defined on a closed interval $[a, b]$ in $\mathbb{R}$ is denoted by $C[a, b]$. This set is a subspace of the vector space of all real-valued functions defined on $[a, b]$.
   a. What facts about continuous functions should be proved in order to demonstrate that $C[a, b]$ is indeed a subspace as claimed? (These facts are usually discussed in a calculus class.)
   b. Show that $\{\mathbf{f} \text{ in } C[a, b] : \mathbf{f}(a) = \mathbf{f}(b)\}$ is a subspace of $C[a, b]$.

For fixed positive integers m and n, the set $M_{m \times n}$ of all $m \times n$ matrices is a vector space, under the usual operations of addition of matrices and multiplication by real scalars.

21. Determine if the set H of all matrices of the form $\begin{bmatrix} a & b \\ 0 & d \end{bmatrix}$ is a subspace of $M_{2\times 2}$.

22. Let F be a fixed 3×2 matrix, and let H be the set of all matrices A in $M_{2\times 4}$ with the property that $FA = 0$ (the zero matrix in $M_{3\times 4}$). Determine if H is a subspace of $M_{2\times 4}$.

Exercises 23–27 show how the axioms for a vector space V may be used to prove the elementary properties described after the definition of a vector space. Fill in the blanks with the appropriate axiom numbers. You may assume, from Axioms 2, 4, and 5, that $\mathbf{0}+\mathbf{u}=\mathbf{u}$ and $-\mathbf{u}+\mathbf{u}=\mathbf{0}$ for all $\mathbf{u}$.

23. Complete the following proof that the zero vector is unique. Suppose that $\mathbf{w}$ in V has the property that $\mathbf{u}+\mathbf{w}=\mathbf{w}+\mathbf{u}=\mathbf{u}$ for all $\mathbf{u}$ in V. In particular, $\mathbf{0}+\mathbf{w}=\mathbf{0}$. But $\mathbf{0}+\mathbf{w}=\mathbf{w}$, by Axiom ______. Hence $\mathbf{w}=\mathbf{0}+\mathbf{w}=\mathbf{0}$.

24. Complete the following proof that $-\mathbf{u}$ is the *unique vector* in V such that $\mathbf{u}+(-\mathbf{u})=\mathbf{0}$.

Suppose that $\mathbf{w}$ satisfies $\mathbf{u}+\mathbf{w}=\mathbf{0}$. Adding $-\mathbf{u}$ to both sides, we have

$(-\mathbf{u})+[\mathbf{u}+\mathbf{w}]=(-\mathbf{u})+\mathbf{0}$

$[(-\mathbf{u})+\mathbf{u}]+\mathbf{w}=(-\mathbf{u})+\mathbf{0}$, by Axiom ______ (a)

$\mathbf{0}+\mathbf{w}=(-\mathbf{u})+\mathbf{0}$, by Axiom ______ (b)

$\mathbf{w}=-\mathbf{u}$, by Axiom ______ (c)

25. Fill in the missing axiom numbers in the following proof that $0\mathbf{u}=\mathbf{0}$ for every $\mathbf{u}$ in V.

$0\mathbf{u}=(0+0)\mathbf{u}=0\mathbf{u}+0\mathbf{u}$ by Axiom ______ (a)

Add the negative of $0\mathbf{u}$ to both sides:

$0\mathbf{u}+(-0\mathbf{u})=[0\mathbf{u}+0\mathbf{u}]+(-0\mathbf{u})$

$0\mathbf{u}+(-0\mathbf{u})=0\mathbf{u}+[0\mathbf{u}+(-0\mathbf{u})]$, by Axiom ______ (b)

$\mathbf{0}=0\mathbf{u}+\mathbf{0}$, by Axiom ______ (c)

$\mathbf{0}=0\mathbf{u}$, by Axiom ______ (d)

26. Fill in the missing axiom numbers in the following proof that $c\mathbf{0}=\mathbf{0}$ for every scalar c.

$c\mathbf{0}=c(\mathbf{0}+\mathbf{0})$, by Axiom ______ (a)

$=c\mathbf{0}+c\mathbf{0}$, by Axiom ______ (b)

Add the negative of $c\mathbf{0}$ to both sides:

$c\mathbf{0}+(-c\mathbf{0})=[c\mathbf{0}+c\mathbf{0}]+(-c\mathbf{0})$

$c\mathbf{0}+(-c\mathbf{0})=c\mathbf{0}+[c\mathbf{0}+(-c\mathbf{0})]$, by Axiom ______ (c)

$\mathbf{0}=c\mathbf{0}+\mathbf{0}$, by Axiom ______ (d)

$\mathbf{0}=c\mathbf{0}$, by Axiom ______ (e)

27. Prove that $(-1)\mathbf{u}=-\mathbf{u}$. [*Hint*: Show that $\mathbf{u}+(-1)\mathbf{u}=\mathbf{0}$. Use some axioms and the results of Exercises 25 and 24.]

28. Suppose that $c\mathbf{u}=\mathbf{0}$ for some nonzero scalar c. Show that $\mathbf{u}=\mathbf{0}$. Mention the axioms or properties you use.

29. Let $\mathbf{u}$ and $\mathbf{v}$ be vectors in a vector space V, and let H be any subspace of V that contains both $\mathbf{u}$ and $\mathbf{v}$. Explain why H also contains Span $\{\mathbf{u}, \mathbf{v}\}$. This shows that Span $\{\mathbf{u}, \mathbf{v}\}$ is the smallest subspace of V that contains both $\mathbf{u}$ and $\mathbf{v}$.

30. Let H and K be subspaces of a vector space V. The **intersection** of H and K, written as $H \cap K$, is the set of $\mathbf{v}$ in V that belong to both H and K. Show that $H \cap K$ is a subspace of V. Give an example in $\mathbb{R}^2$ to show that the union of two subspaces is not in general a subspace.

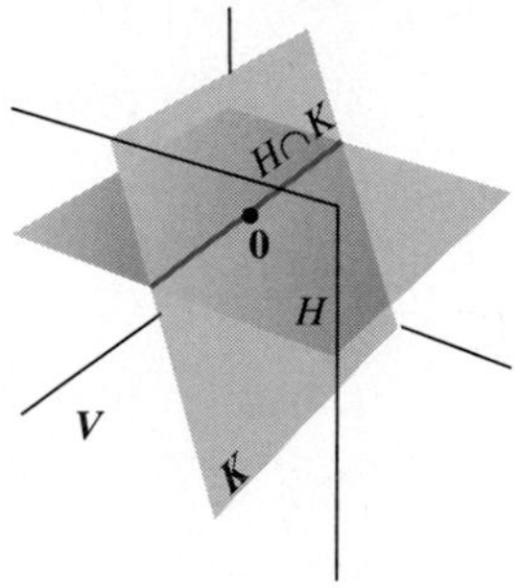

SOLUTIONS TO PRACTICE PROBLEMS

1. Take any $\mathbf{u}$ in H—say, $\mathbf{u}=\begin{bmatrix} 3 \\ 7 \end{bmatrix}$—and take any $c \neq 1$—say, $c=2$. Then $c\mathbf{u}=\begin{bmatrix} 6 \\ 14 \end{bmatrix}$. If this is in V, then there is some s such that

$$\begin{bmatrix} 3s \\ 2+5s \end{bmatrix}=\begin{bmatrix} 6 \\ 14 \end{bmatrix}$$

That is, $s = 2$ and $s = 12/5$, which is impossible. So $2\mathbf{u}$ is not in H and H is not a vector space.

2. $\mathbf{v}_1 = 1\mathbf{v}_1 + 0\mathbf{v}_2 + \cdots + 0\mathbf{v}_p$. This expresses $\mathbf{v}_1$ as a linear combination of $\mathbf{v}_1, \ldots, \mathbf{v}_p$, so $\mathbf{v}_1$ is in W. In general, $\mathbf{v}_k$ is in W because

$$\mathbf{v}_k = 0\mathbf{v}_1 + \cdots + 0\mathbf{v}_{k-1} + 1\mathbf{v}_k + 0\mathbf{v}_{k+1} + \cdots + 0\mathbf{v}_p$$

5.2 NULL SPACES, COLUMN SPACES, AND LINEAR TRANSFORMATIONS

In applications of linear algebra, subspaces of $\mathbb{R}^n$ usually arise in one of two ways: (1) as the set of all solutions to a system of homogeneous linear equations or (2) as the set of all linear combinations of certain specified vectors. In this section, we compare and contrast these two descriptions of subspaces, allowing us to practice using the concept of a subspace. Actually, as you will soon discover, we have been working with subspaces ever since Section 2.1. The main new feature here is the terminology. The section concludes with a discussion of the kernel and range of a linear transformation.

The Null Space of a Matrix

Consider the following system of homogeneous equations:

$$\begin{aligned} x_1 - 3x_2 - 2x_3 &= 0 \\ -5x_1 + 9x_2 + x_3 &= 0 \end{aligned} \tag{1}$$

In matrix form, this system is written as $A\mathbf{x} = \mathbf{0}$, where

$$A = \begin{bmatrix} 1 & -3 & -2 \\ -5 & 9 & 1 \end{bmatrix} \tag{2}$$

Recall that the set of all $\mathbf{x}$ that satisfy (1) is called the **solution set** of the system (1). Often it is convenient to relate this set directly to the matrix A and the equation $A\mathbf{x} = \mathbf{0}$. We call the set of $\mathbf{x}$ that satisfy $A\mathbf{x} = \mathbf{0}$ the **null space** of the matrix A.

DEFINITION

Given an $m \times n$ matrix A, the **null space** of A is the set Nul A of all solutions to the homogeneous equation $A\mathbf{x} = \mathbf{0}$. In set notation,

$$\text{Nul } A = \{\mathbf{x} : \mathbf{x} \text{ is in } \mathbb{R}^n \text{ and } A\mathbf{x} = \mathbf{0}\}$$

A more dynamic description of Nul A is the set of all $\mathbf{x}$ in $\mathbb{R}^n$ that are mapped into the zero vector of $\mathbb{R}^m$ via the linear transformation $\mathbf{x} \mapsto A\mathbf{x}$. See Fig. 1.

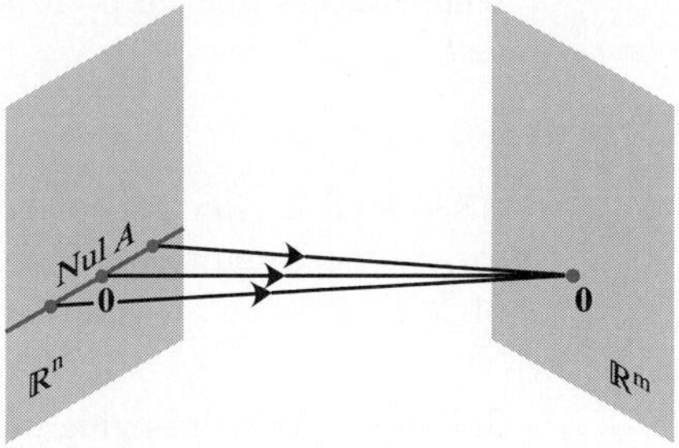

FIGURE 1

EXAMPLE 1 Let A be as in (2), and let $\mathbf{u} = \begin{bmatrix} 5 \\ 3 \\ -2 \end{bmatrix}$. Determine if $\mathbf{u}$ belongs to the null space of A.

Solution To test if $\mathbf{u}$ satisfies $A\mathbf{u} = \mathbf{0}$, simply compute

$$A\mathbf{u} = \begin{bmatrix} 1 & -3 & -2 \\ -5 & 9 & 1 \end{bmatrix} \begin{bmatrix} 5 \\ 3 \\ -2 \end{bmatrix} = \begin{bmatrix} 5 - 9 + 4 \\ -25 + 27 - 2 \end{bmatrix} = \begin{bmatrix} 0 \\ 0 \end{bmatrix}$$

Thus $\mathbf{u}$ is in Nul A.

The term *space* in *null space* is appropriate because the null space of a matrix is a vector space, as we see in the next theorem.

THEOREM 3

The null space of an $m \times n$ matrix A is a subspace of $\mathbb{R}^n$. Equivalently, the set of all solutions to a system $A\mathbf{x} = \mathbf{0}$ of m homogeneous linear equations in n unknowns is a subspace of $\mathbb{R}^n$.

Proof Certainly Nul A is a subset of $\mathbb{R}^n$ because A has n columns. We must show that Nul A satisfies the three conditions of the subspace test (Theorem 1). Of course, $\mathbf{0}$ is in Nul A. To verify the second condition, let $\mathbf{u}$ and $\mathbf{v}$ represent any two vectors in Nul A. Then

$$A\mathbf{u} = \mathbf{0} \quad \text{and} \quad A\mathbf{v} = \mathbf{0}$$

To show that $\mathbf{u} + \mathbf{v}$ is in Nul A, we must show that $A(\mathbf{u} + \mathbf{v}) = \mathbf{0}$. Using a property of matrix multiplication, we find that

$$A(\mathbf{u} + \mathbf{v}) = A\mathbf{u} + A\mathbf{v} = \mathbf{0} + \mathbf{0} = \mathbf{0}$$

Thus $\mathbf{u} + \mathbf{v}$ is in Nul A. Finally, if c is any scalar, then

$$A(c\mathbf{u}) = c(A\mathbf{u}) = c(\mathbf{0}) = \mathbf{0}$$

which shows that $c\mathbf{u}$ is in Nul A. Thus Nul A is a subspace of $\mathbb{R}^n$, by the subspace test. ∎

EXAMPLE 2 Let H be the set of all vectors in $\mathbb{R}^4$ whose coordinates a, b, c, d satisfy the equations $a - 2b + 5c = d$ and $c - a = b$. Show that H is a subspace of $\mathbb{R}^4$.

Solution By rearranging the equations that describe the elements of H, we see that H is the set of all solutions of the following system of homogeneous linear equations:

$$\begin{aligned} a - 2b + 5c - d &= 0 \\ -a - b + c \qquad &= 0 \end{aligned}$$

By Theorem 3, H is a subspace of $\mathbb{R}^4$. ∎

It is important that the linear equations defining the set H are homogeneous. Otherwise, the set of solutions will definitely *not* be a subspace. Also, in extreme cases, the set of solutions could be empty.

EXAMPLE 3 Let H be the set of all solutions of the system

$$\begin{aligned} x_1 + x_2 - 2x_3 &= 4 \\ 3x_1 - x_2 + 6x_3 &= 0 \end{aligned}$$

Explain why H is not a subspace of $\mathbb{R}^3$.

Solution H fails the Subspace Test because the zero vector is not in H. ∎

An Explicit Description of Nul *A*

There is no obvious relation between vectors in Nul A and the entries in A. We say that Nul A is defined *implicitly*, because it is defined by a condition that must be checked. No explicit list or description of the elements in Nul A is given. However, when we *solve the equation* $A\mathbf{x} = \mathbf{0}$, we obtain an *explicit* description of Nul A. Let us review this procedure from Section 2.3.

EXAMPLE 4 Find a spanning set for the null space of the matrix

$$A = \begin{bmatrix} -3 & 6 & -1 & 1 & -7 \\ 1 & -2 & 2 & 3 & -1 \\ 2 & -4 & 5 & 8 & -4 \end{bmatrix}$$

Solution The first step is to find the general solution of $A\mathbf{x} = \mathbf{0}$ in terms of free variables. Row reduce the augmented matrix $[\,A \quad \mathbf{0}\,]$ to *reduced* echelon form and obtain

$$\begin{bmatrix} 1 & -2 & 0 & -1 & 3 & 0 \\ 0 & 0 & 1 & 2 & -2 & 0 \\ 0 & 0 & 0 & 0 & 0 & 0 \end{bmatrix}, \qquad \begin{aligned} x_1 - 2x_2 \qquad - x_4 + 3x_5 &= 0 \\ x_3 + 2x_4 - 2x_5 &= 0 \\ 0 &= 0 \end{aligned}$$

The general solution is $x_1 = 2x_2 + x_4 - 3x_5$, $x_3 = -2x_4 + 2x_5$, with x_2, x_4, and x_5 free. Next, decompose the vector giving the general solution into a linear combination of vectors where *the weights are the free variables*. That is,

$$\begin{bmatrix} x_1 \\ x_2 \\ x_3 \\ x_4 \\ x_5 \end{bmatrix} = \begin{bmatrix} 2x_2 + x_4 - 3x_5 \\ x_2 \\ -2x_4 + 2x_5 \\ x_4 \\ x_5 \end{bmatrix} = x_2 \underset{\uparrow \atop \mathbf{u}}{\begin{bmatrix} 2 \\ 1 \\ 0 \\ 0 \\ 0 \end{bmatrix}} + x_4 \underset{\uparrow \atop \mathbf{v}}{\begin{bmatrix} 1 \\ 0 \\ -2 \\ 1 \\ 0 \end{bmatrix}} + x_5 \underset{\uparrow \atop \mathbf{w}}{\begin{bmatrix} -3 \\ 0 \\ 2 \\ 0 \\ 1 \end{bmatrix}}$$

$$= x_2\mathbf{u} + x_4\mathbf{v} + x_5\mathbf{w} \tag{3}$$

Every linear combination of **u**, **v**, and **w** is an element of Nul A. Thus $\{\mathbf{u}, \mathbf{v}, \mathbf{w}\}$ is a spanning set for Nul A. ∎

Two points should be made about the solution in Example 4 that will apply to all problems of this type. We will use these facts later.

1. The spanning set produced by the method in Example 4 is automatically linearly independent because the free variables are the weights on the spanning vectors. For instance, (3) shows that $\mathbf{0} = x_2\mathbf{u} + x_4\mathbf{v} + x_5\mathbf{w}$ only if the weights x_2, x_4, and x_5 are all zero.
2. The number of vectors in the spanning set for Nul A will equal the number of free variables in the equation $A\mathbf{x} = \mathbf{0}$.

The Column Space of a Matrix

Another important subspace associated with a matrix is its column space. Unlike the null space, the column space is defined explicitly via linear combinations.

DEFINITION

Given an $m \times n$ matrix A, the **column space** of A is the set Col A of all linear combinations of the columns of A. In set notation,

$$\text{Col } A = \{\mathbf{b} : \mathbf{b} \text{ is in } \mathbb{R}^m \text{ and } \mathbf{b} = A\mathbf{x} \quad \text{for some } \mathbf{x} \text{ in } \mathbb{R}^n\} \tag{4}$$

The description (4) is true because a vector **b** is a linear combination of the columns of A if and only if **b** may be written in the form $A\mathbf{x}$, where **x** is a vector whose entries are the weights of the linear combination. The notation $A\mathbf{x}$ for a vector in Col A shows that Col A is the *range* of the linear transformation $\mathbf{x} \mapsto A\mathbf{x}$. We shall return to this point of view at the end of the section.

THEOREM 4

The column space of an $m \times n$ matrix A is a subspace of $\mathbb{R}^m$.

Proof If the columns of an $m \times n$ matrix A are denoted by $\mathbf{a}_1, \ldots, \mathbf{a}_n$, then Col A is just another name or notation for Span $\{\mathbf{a}_1, \ldots, \mathbf{a}_n\}$. This set is a vector space, by Theorem 2 in Section 5.1. It is a subspace of $\mathbb{R}^m$ because the columns of A each have m entries. ∎

EXAMPLE 5 Show that the following set W is a subspace by finding a matrix A such that $W = \text{Col } A$.

$$W = \left\{ \begin{bmatrix} 6a - b \\ a + b \\ -7a \end{bmatrix} : a, b \text{ in } \mathbb{R} \right\}$$

Solution First, write W as a set of linear combinations.

$$W = \left\{ a \begin{bmatrix} 6 \\ 1 \\ -7 \end{bmatrix} + b \begin{bmatrix} -1 \\ 1 \\ 0 \end{bmatrix} : a, b \text{ in } \mathbb{R} \right\} = \text{Span}\left\{ \begin{bmatrix} 6 \\ 1 \\ -7 \end{bmatrix}, \begin{bmatrix} -1 \\ 1 \\ 0 \end{bmatrix} \right\}$$

Second, use the vectors in the spanning set as the columns of A. Let $A = \begin{bmatrix} 6 & -1 \\ 1 & 1 \\ -7 & 0 \end{bmatrix}$.

Then $W = \text{Col } A$, as desired. ∎

Recall from Theorem 2 in Section 2.2 that the columns of A span $\mathbb{R}^n$ if and only if the equation $A\mathbf{x} = \mathbf{b}$ is consistent for all $\mathbf{b}$. We can restate this fact as follows:

If A is an $m \times n$ matrix, then Col $A = \mathbb{R}^m$ if and only if the equation $A\mathbf{x} = \mathbf{b}$ is consistent for every $\mathbf{b}$ in $\mathbb{R}^m$.

The Contrast Between Nul *A* and Col *A*

It is natural to wonder how the null space and column space of a matrix are related. In fact, the two spaces are quite dissimilar, as the three examples below will show. Nevertheless, there is a surprising connection between the null space and column space that we will examine in Section 5.6, after we have more theory available.

EXAMPLE 6 Let

$$A = \begin{bmatrix} 2 & 4 & -2 & 1 \\ -2 & -5 & 7 & 3 \\ 3 & 7 & -8 & 6 \end{bmatrix}$$

a. If the column space of A is a subspace of $\mathbb{R}^k$, what is k?

b. If the null space of A is a subspace of $\mathbb{R}^k$, what is k?

Solution

a. The columns of A each have three entries, so Col A is a subspace of $\mathbb{R}^k$, where $k = 3$.

b. A vector $\mathbf{x}$ such that $A\mathbf{x}$ is defined must have four entries, so Nul A is a subspace of $\mathbb{R}^k$, where $k = 4$. ∎

When a matrix is not square, as in Example 6, the vectors in Nul A and Col A live in entirely different "universes." For example, we have discussed no algebraic operations that connect vectors in $\mathbb{R}^3$ with vectors in $\mathbb{R}^4$. Thus we are not likely to find any relation between individual vectors in Nul A and Col A.

EXAMPLE 7 With A as in Example 6, find a nonzero vector in Col A and a nonzero vector in Nul A.

Solution It is easy to find a vector in Col A. Any column of A will do, say, $\begin{bmatrix} 2 \\ -2 \\ 3 \end{bmatrix}$.

To find a nonzero vector in Nul A, we have to do some work. We row reduce the augmented matrix $[\,A \quad \mathbf{0}\,]$ to obtain

$$[\,A \quad \mathbf{0}\,] \sim \begin{bmatrix} 1 & 0 & 9 & 0 & 0 \\ 0 & 1 & -5 & 0 & 0 \\ 0 & 0 & 0 & 1 & 0 \end{bmatrix}$$

Thus if $\mathbf{x}$ satisfies $A\mathbf{x} = \mathbf{0}$, then $x_1 = -9x_3$, $x_2 = 5x_3$, $x_4 = 0$, and x_3 is free. Assigning a nonzero value to x_3—say, $x_3 = 1$—we obtain a vector in Nul A, namely, $\mathbf{x} = (-9, 5, 1, 0)$. ∎

EXAMPLE 8 With A as in Example 6, let $\mathbf{u} = \begin{bmatrix} 3 \\ -2 \\ -1 \\ 0 \end{bmatrix}$ and $\mathbf{v} = \begin{bmatrix} 3 \\ -1 \\ 3 \end{bmatrix}$.

a. Determine if $\mathbf{u}$ is in Nul A. Could $\mathbf{u}$ be in Col A?

b. Determine if $\mathbf{v}$ is in Col A. Could $\mathbf{v}$ be in Nul A?

Solution

a. An explicit description of Nul A is not needed here. Simply compute the product $A\mathbf{u}$.

$$A\mathbf{u} = \begin{bmatrix} 2 & 4 & -2 & 1 \\ -2 & -5 & 7 & 3 \\ 3 & 7 & -8 & 6 \end{bmatrix} \begin{bmatrix} 3 \\ -2 \\ -1 \\ 0 \end{bmatrix} = \begin{bmatrix} 0 \\ -3 \\ 3 \end{bmatrix} \neq \begin{bmatrix} 0 \\ 0 \\ 0 \end{bmatrix}$$

Obviously, $\mathbf{u}$ is *not* a solution of $A\mathbf{x} = 0$, so $\mathbf{u}$ is not in Nul A. Also, with four coordinates, $\mathbf{u}$ could not possibly be in Col A, since Col A is a subspace of $\mathbb{R}^3$.

b. Reduce $[\,A \quad \mathbf{v}\,]$ to an echelon form.

$$[\,A \quad \mathbf{v}\,] = \begin{bmatrix} 2 & 4 & -2 & 1 & 3 \\ -2 & -5 & 7 & 3 & -1 \\ 3 & 7 & -8 & 6 & 3 \end{bmatrix} \sim \begin{bmatrix} 2 & 4 & -2 & 1 & 3 \\ 0 & 1 & -5 & -4 & -2 \\ 0 & 0 & 0 & 17 & 1 \end{bmatrix}$$

At this point, it is clear that the equation $A\mathbf{x} = \mathbf{v}$ is consistent, so $\mathbf{v}$ is in Col A. With only three coordinates, $\mathbf{v}$ could not possibly be in Nul A, since Nul A is a subspace of $\mathbb{R}^4$. ■

The following table summarizes what we have learned about Nul A and Col A. Item 8 is a restatement of Theorems 9 and 10 in Section 2.6.

Contrast Between Nul A and Col A for an $m \times n$ Matrix A

Nul A	Col A
1. Nul A is a subspace of $\mathbb{R}^n$.	1. Col A is a subspace of $\mathbb{R}^m$.
2. Nul A is implicitly defined; that is, you are given only a condition ($A\mathbf{x} = \mathbf{0}$) that vectors in Nul A must satisfy.	2. Col A is explicitly defined; that is, you are told how to build vectors in Col A.
3. It takes time to find vectors in Nul A. Row operations on $[\,A \quad \mathbf{0}\,]$ are required.	3. It is easy to find vectors in Col A. The columns of A are displayed; others are formed from them.
4. There is no obvious relation between Nul A and the entries in A.	4. There is an obvious relation between Col A and the entries in A, since each column of A is in Col A.
5. A typical vector $\mathbf{v}$ in Nul A has the property that $A\mathbf{v} = \mathbf{0}$.	5. A typical vector $\mathbf{v}$ in Col A has the property that the equation $A\mathbf{x} = \mathbf{v}$ is consistent.
6. Given a specific vector $\mathbf{v}$, it is easy to tell if $\mathbf{v}$ is in Nul A. Just compute $A\mathbf{v}$.	6. Given a specific vector $\mathbf{v}$, it may take time to tell if $\mathbf{v}$ is in Col A. Row operations on $[\,A \quad \mathbf{v}\,]$ are required.
7. Nul $A = \{\mathbf{0}\}$ if and only if the equation $A\mathbf{x} = \mathbf{0}$ has only the trivial solution.	7. Col $A = \mathbb{R}^m$ if and only if the equation $A\mathbf{x} = \mathbf{b}$ has a solution for every $\mathbf{b}$ in $\mathbb{R}^m$.
8. Nul $A = \{\mathbf{0}\}$ if and only if the linear transformation $\mathbf{x} \mapsto A\mathbf{x}$ is one-to-one.	8. Col $A = \mathbb{R}^m$ if and only if the linear transformation $\mathbf{x} \mapsto A\mathbf{x}$ maps $\mathbb{R}^n$ *onto* $\mathbb{R}^m$.

Kernel and Range of a Linear Transformation

Subspaces of vector spaces other than $\mathbb{R}^n$ are often described in terms of a linear transformation instead of a matrix. To make this precise, we generalize the definition given in Section 2.5.

DEFINITION

A **linear transformation** T from a vector space V into a vector space W is a rule that assigns to each vector $\mathbf{x}$ in V a unique vector $T(\mathbf{x})$ in W, such that

(i) $T(\mathbf{u} + \mathbf{v}) = T(\mathbf{u}) + T(\mathbf{v})$ for all $\mathbf{u}, \mathbf{v}$ in V, and

(ii) $T(c\mathbf{u}) = cT(\mathbf{u})$ for all $\mathbf{u}$ in V and all scalars c.

The **kernel** (or **null space**) of such a T is the set of all $\mathbf{u}$ in V such that $T(\mathbf{u}) = \mathbf{0}$ (the zero vector in W). The **range** of T is the set of all vectors in W of the form $T(\mathbf{x})$ for some $\mathbf{x}$ in V. If T happens to arise as a matrix transformation—say, $T(\mathbf{x}) = A\mathbf{x}$ for some matrix A—then the kernel and the range of T are just the null space and the column space of A, as defined earlier.

It is not difficult to show that the kernel of T is a subspace of V. The proof is essentially the same as the one for Theorem 3. Also, the range of T is a subspace of W. See Fig. 2 and Exercise 32.

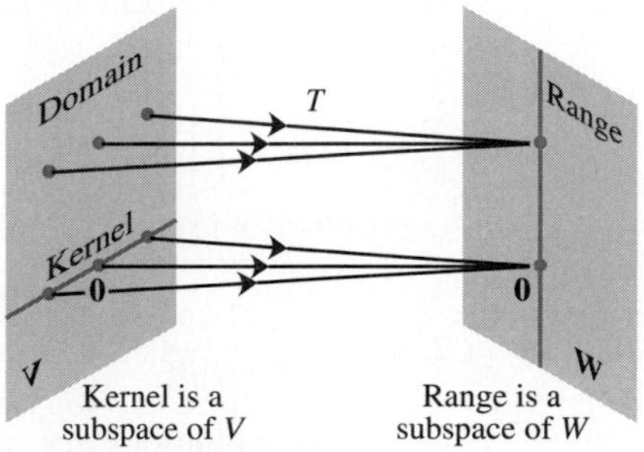

FIGURE 2 Subspaces associated with a linear transformation.

In applications, a subspace usually arises as either the kernel or the range of an appropriate linear transformation. For instance, the set of all solutions of a homogeneous linear differential equation turns out to be the kernel of a linear transformation. Typically, such a linear transformation is described in terms of one or more derivatives of a function. To explain this in any detail would take us too far afield at this point. So we present only two examples. The first explains why the operation of differentiation is a linear transformation.

EXAMPLE 9 (Calculus required) Let V be the vector space of all real-valued functions f defined on an interval $[a, b]$ with the property that they are differentiable and their derivatives are continuous functions on $[a, b]$. Let W be the vector space of all continuous functions on $[a, b]$, and let $D: V \to W$ be the transformation that changes f in V into its derivative f'. In calculus, two simple differentiation rules are

$$D(f + g) = D(f) + D(g) \qquad \text{and} \qquad D(cf) = cD(f)$$

That is, D is a linear transformation. It can be shown that the kernel of D is the set of constant functions on $[a, b]$ and the range of D is the set W of all continuous functions on $[a, b]$.

EXAMPLE 10 (Calculus required) The differential equation

$$y'' + \omega y = 0 \tag{5}$$

where ω is a constant, is used to describe a variety of physical systems, such as the vibration of a weighted spring, the movement of a pendulum, and the voltage in an inductance-capacitance electrical circuit. The set of solutions of (5) is precisely the kernel of the linear transformation that maps a function $y = f(t)$ into the function $f''(t) + \omega f(t)$. Finding an explicit description of this vector space is a problem in differential equations. The solution set turns out to be the space described in Exercise 19 of Section 5.1. ∎

PRACTICE PROBLEMS

1. Let $W = \left\{ \begin{bmatrix} a \\ b \\ c \end{bmatrix} : a - 3b - c = 0 \right\}$. Show that W is a subspace of $\mathbb{R}^3$ in two different ways. (Use two theorems.)

2. Let $A = \begin{bmatrix} 7 & -3 & 5 \\ -4 & 1 & -5 \\ -5 & 2 & -4 \end{bmatrix}$, $\mathbf{v} = \begin{bmatrix} 2 \\ 1 \\ -1 \end{bmatrix}$, and $\mathbf{w} = \begin{bmatrix} 7 \\ 6 \\ -3 \end{bmatrix}$. Suppose you know that the equations $A\mathbf{x} = \mathbf{v}$ and $A\mathbf{x} = \mathbf{w}$ are both consistent. What can you say about the equation $A\mathbf{x} = \mathbf{v} + \mathbf{w}$?

5.2 EXERCISES

1. Determine if $\begin{bmatrix} 1 \\ 3 \\ -4 \end{bmatrix}$ is in Nul A, where

$$A = \begin{bmatrix} 3 & -5 & -3 \\ 6 & -2 & 0 \\ -8 & 4 & 1 \end{bmatrix}.$$

2. Determine if $\mathbf{w} = \begin{bmatrix} 5 \\ -3 \\ 2 \end{bmatrix}$ is in Nul A, where

$$A = \begin{bmatrix} 5 & 21 & 19 \\ 13 & 23 & 2 \\ 8 & 14 & 1 \end{bmatrix}.$$

In Exercises 3–6, find an explicit description of Nul A, by listing vectors that span the null space.

3. $A = \begin{bmatrix} 1 & 3 & 5 & 0 \\ 0 & 1 & 4 & -2 \end{bmatrix}$

4. $A = \begin{bmatrix} 1 & -6 & 4 & 0 \\ 0 & 0 & 2 & 0 \end{bmatrix}$

5. $A = \begin{bmatrix} 1 & -2 & 0 & 4 & 0 \\ 0 & 0 & 1 & -9 & 0 \\ 0 & 0 & 0 & 0 & 1 \end{bmatrix}$

6. $A = \begin{bmatrix} 1 & 5 & -4 & -3 & 1 \\ 0 & 1 & -2 & 1 & 0 \\ 0 & 0 & 0 & 0 & 0 \end{bmatrix}$

In Exercises 7–18, either use an appropriate theorem to show that the given set, W, is a vector space, or find a specific example to the contrary.

7. $\left\{ \begin{bmatrix} a \\ b \\ c \end{bmatrix} : a + b + c = 2 \right\}$

8. $\left\{ \begin{bmatrix} a \\ b \\ c \end{bmatrix} : a = 0,\, b + c = 0 \right\}$

9. $\left\{ \begin{bmatrix} r \\ s \\ t \end{bmatrix} : r + 2s = 3t \right\}$

10. $\left\{ \begin{bmatrix} r \\ s \\ t \end{bmatrix} : 5r - 1 = s + 2t \right\}$

11. $\left\{ \begin{bmatrix} a \\ b \\ c \\ d \end{bmatrix} : \begin{matrix} a - 2b = 4c \\ 2a = c + 3d \end{matrix} \right\}$

12. $\left\{ \begin{bmatrix} a \\ b \\ c \\ d \end{bmatrix} : \begin{array}{l} a + 3b = c \\ b + c + a = d \end{array} \right\}$

13. $\left\{ \begin{bmatrix} a \\ b \\ 2a - b \end{bmatrix} : a, b \text{ real numbers} \right\}$

14. $\left\{ \begin{bmatrix} a \\ 2 \\ 3a \end{bmatrix} : a \text{ real} \right\}$

15. $\left\{ \begin{bmatrix} b - 2d \\ 5 + d \\ b + 3d \\ d \end{bmatrix} : b, d \text{ real} \right\}$

16. $\left\{ \begin{bmatrix} b - 5d \\ 2b \\ 2d + 1 \\ d \end{bmatrix} : b, d \text{ real} \right\}$

17. $\left\{ \begin{bmatrix} c - 6d \\ d \\ c \end{bmatrix} : c, d \text{ real} \right\}$

18. $\left\{ \begin{bmatrix} -a + 2b \\ a - 2b \\ 3a - 6b \end{bmatrix} : a, b \text{ real} \right\}$

In Exercises 19 and 20, find A such that the given set is Col A.

19. $\left\{ \begin{bmatrix} 2s + 3t \\ r + s - 2t \\ 4r + s \\ 3r - s - t \end{bmatrix} : r, s, t \text{ real} \right\}$

20. $\left\{ \begin{bmatrix} b - c \\ 2b + c + d \\ 5c - 4d \\ d \end{bmatrix} : b, c, d \text{ real} \right\}$

For the matrices in Exercises 21–24, (a) find k such that Nul A is a subspace of $\mathbb{R}^k$, and (b) find k such that Col A is a subspace of $\mathbb{R}^k$.

21. $A = \begin{bmatrix} 2 & -6 \\ -1 & 3 \\ -4 & 12 \\ 3 & -9 \end{bmatrix}$

22. $A = [1 \ \ -3 \ \ 9 \ \ 0 \ \ -5]$

23. $A = \begin{bmatrix} 4 & 5 & -2 & 6 & 0 \\ 1 & 1 & 0 & 1 & 0 \end{bmatrix}$

24. $A = \begin{bmatrix} 7 & -2 & 0 \\ -2 & 0 & -5 \\ 0 & -5 & 7 \\ -5 & 7 & -2 \end{bmatrix}$

25. With A as in Exercise 21, find a nonzero vector in Nul A and a nonzero vector in Col A.

26. With A as in Exercise 3, find a nonzero vector in Nul A and a nonzero vector in Col A.

27. Let $A = \begin{bmatrix} -6 & 12 \\ -3 & 6 \end{bmatrix}$ and $\mathbf{w} = \begin{bmatrix} 2 \\ 1 \end{bmatrix}$. Determine if $\mathbf{w}$ is in Col A. Is $\mathbf{w}$ in Nul A?

28. Let $A = \begin{bmatrix} -8 & -2 & -9 \\ 6 & 4 & 8 \\ 4 & 0 & 4 \end{bmatrix}$ and $\mathbf{w} = \begin{bmatrix} 2 \\ 1 \\ -2 \end{bmatrix}$. Determine if $\mathbf{w}$ is in Col A. Is $\mathbf{w}$ in Nul A?

29. It can be shown that a solution of the system below is $x_1 = 3$, $x_2 = 2$, and $x_3 = -1$. Use this fact and the theory from this section to explain why another solution is $x_1 = 30$, $x_2 = 20$, and $x_3 = -10$. (Observe how the solutions are related, but make no other calculations.)

$$\begin{aligned} x_1 - 3x_2 - 3x_3 &= 0 \\ -2x_1 + 4x_2 + 2x_3 &= 0 \\ -x_1 + 5x_2 + 7x_3 &= 0 \end{aligned}$$

30. Consider the following two systems of equations:

$$\begin{aligned} 5x_1 + x_2 - 3x_3 &= 0 \\ -9x_1 + 2x_2 + 5x_3 &= 1 \\ 4x_1 + x_2 - 6x_3 &= 9 \end{aligned} \qquad \begin{aligned} 5x_1 + x_2 - 3x_3 &= 0 \\ -9x_1 + 2x_2 + 5x_3 &= 5 \\ 4x_1 + x_2 - 6x_3 &= 45 \end{aligned}$$

It can be shown that the first system has a solution. Use this fact and the theory from this section to explain why the second system must also have a solution. (Make no row operations.)

31. Use the subspace test to prove Theorem 4 as follows: Given an $m \times n$ matrix A, an element in Col A has the form $A\mathbf{x}$ for some $\mathbf{x}$ in $\mathbb{R}^n$. Let $A\mathbf{x}$ and $A\mathbf{w}$ represent any two vectors in Col A.

a. Explain why the zero vector is in Col A.

b. Show that the vector $A\mathbf{x} + A\mathbf{w}$ is in Col A.

c. Given a scalar c, show that $c(A\mathbf{x})$ is in Col A.

32. Let $T : V \rightarrow W$ be a linear transformation from a vector space V into a vector space W. Use the subspace test to prove that the range of T is a subspace of W. [Typical elements of the range have the form $T(\mathbf{x})$ and $T(\mathbf{w})$ for some $\mathbf{x}, \mathbf{w}$ in V.]

33. Define $T : \mathbb{P}_2 \to \mathbb{R}^2$ by $T(\mathbf{p}) = \begin{bmatrix} \mathbf{p}(0) \\ \mathbf{p}(1) \end{bmatrix}$. For instance, if $\mathbf{p}(t) = 3 + 5t + 7t^2$, then $T(\mathbf{p}) = \begin{bmatrix} 3 \\ 15 \end{bmatrix}$.

a. Show that T is a linear transformation. [*Hint*: For arbitrary polynomials $\mathbf{p}, \mathbf{q}$ in $\mathbb{P}_2$, compute $T(\mathbf{p} + \mathbf{q})$ and $T(c\mathbf{p})$.]

b. Find a polynomial $\mathbf{p}$ in $\mathbb{P}_2$ that spans the kernel of T, and describe the range of T.

34. Define a linear transformation $T : \mathbb{P}_2 \to \mathbb{R}^2$ by $T(\mathbf{p}) = \begin{bmatrix} \mathbf{p}(0) \\ \mathbf{p}(0) \end{bmatrix}$. Find polynomials $\mathbf{p}_1$ and $\mathbf{p}_2$ in $\mathbb{P}_2$ that span the kernel of T, and describe the range of T.

35. Let $M_{2\times 2}$ be the vector space of all 2×2 matrices, and define $T : M_{2\times 2} \to M_{2\times 2}$ by $T(A) = A + A^T$, where $A = \begin{bmatrix} a & b \\ c & d \end{bmatrix}$.

a. Show that T is a linear transformation.

b. Let B be any element of $M_{2\times 2}$ such that $B^T = B$. Find an A in $M_{2\times 2}$ such that $T(A) = B$.

c. Show that the range of T is the set of B in $M_{2\times 2}$ with the property that $B^T = B$.

d. Describe the kernel of T.

36. (Calculus required) Define $T : C[0, 1] \to C[0, 1]$ as follows: For $\mathbf{f}$ in $C[0, 1]$, let $T(\mathbf{f})$ be the antiderivative $\mathbf{F}$ of $\mathbf{f}$ such that $\mathbf{F}(0) = 0$. Show that T is a linear transformation, and describe the kernel of T.

37. Let V and W be vector spaces and let $T : V \to W$ be a linear transformation. Given a subspace U of V, let $T(U)$ denote the set of all images of the form $T(\mathbf{x})$, where $\mathbf{x}$ is in U. Show that $T(U)$ is a subspace of W.

38. Given $T : V \to W$ as in Exercise 37, and given a subspace Z of W, let U be the set of all $\mathbf{x}$ in V such that $T(\mathbf{x})$ is in Z. Show that U is a subspace of V.

SOLUTIONS TO PRACTICE PROBLEMS

1. *First method:* W is a subspace of $\mathbb{R}^3$ by Theorem 3 because W is the set of all solutions to a system of homogeneous linear equations (where the system has only one equation). Equivalently, W is the null space of the 1×3 matrix $A = [\,1 \quad -3 \quad -1\,]$.

Second method: Solve the equation $a - 3b - c = 0$ for the leading variable a in terms of the free variables b and c. Any solution has the form $\begin{bmatrix} 3b + c \\ b \\ c \end{bmatrix}$, where b and c are arbitrary, and

$$\begin{bmatrix} 3b + c \\ b \\ c \end{bmatrix} = b \begin{bmatrix} 3 \\ 1 \\ 0 \end{bmatrix} + c \begin{bmatrix} 1 \\ 0 \\ 1 \end{bmatrix}$$

This calculation shows that $W = \text{Span}\,\{\mathbf{v}_1, \mathbf{v}_2\}$, for

$$\mathbf{v}_1 = \begin{bmatrix} 3 \\ 1 \\ 0 \end{bmatrix}, \qquad \mathbf{v}_2 = \begin{bmatrix} 1 \\ 0 \\ 1 \end{bmatrix}$$

Thus W is a subspace of $\mathbb{R}^3$ by Theorem 2. We could also solve the equation $a - 3b - c = 0$ for b or c and get alternative descriptions of W as the set of linear combinations of two vectors.

2. Both $\mathbf{v}$ and $\mathbf{w}$ are in Col A. Since Col A is a vector space, $\mathbf{v} + \mathbf{w}$ must be in Col A. That is, the equation $A\mathbf{x} = \mathbf{v} + \mathbf{w}$ is consistent.

5.3 LINEARLY INDEPENDENT SETS; BASES

In this section we identify and study the subsets that span a vector space V or a subspace H as "efficiently" as possible. The key idea is that of linear independence, defined as in $\mathbb{R}^n$.

A set of vectors $\{\mathbf{v}_1, \ldots, \mathbf{v}_p\}$ in V is said to be **linearly independent** if the vector equation

$$c_1\mathbf{v}_1 + c_2\mathbf{v}_2 + \cdots + c_p\mathbf{v}_p = \mathbf{0} \tag{1}$$

has *only* the trivial solution, $c_1 = 0, \ldots, c_p = 0$. [1]

The set $\{\mathbf{v}_1, \ldots, \mathbf{v}_p\}$ is said to be **linearly dependent** if (1) has a nontrivial solution, that is, if there are some weights, $c_1, \ldots, c_p$, *not all zero*, such that (1) holds. In such a case, (1) is called a **linear dependence relation** among $\mathbf{v}_1, \ldots, \mathbf{v}_p$.

It is easily seen that a set containing a single vector $\mathbf{v}$ is linearly independent if and only if $\mathbf{v} \neq \mathbf{0}$. Also, just as in $\mathbb{R}^n$, a set of two vectors is linearly dependent if and only if one of the vectors is a multiple of the other. And any set containing the zero vector is linearly dependent. The following theorem is proved in the same way as the corresponding fact about sets in $\mathbb{R}^n$.

THEOREM 5

A set $\{\mathbf{v}_1, \ldots, \mathbf{v}_p\}$ of two or more vectors, with $\mathbf{v}_1 \neq \mathbf{0}$, is linearly dependent if and only if some $\mathbf{v}_j$ (with $j > 1$) is a linear combination of the preceding vectors, $\mathbf{v}_1, \ldots \mathbf{v}_{j-1}$.

The main difference between linear dependence in $\mathbb{R}^n$ and in a general vector space is that when the vectors are not n-tuples, the homogeneous equation (1) usually cannot be written as a system of n linear equations. That is, the vectors cannot be made into the columns of a matrix A in order to study the equation $A\mathbf{x} = \mathbf{0}$. We must rely instead on the definition of linear dependence and on Theorem 5.

EXAMPLE 1 Let $\mathbf{p}_1(t) = 1$, $\mathbf{p}_2(t) = t$, and $\mathbf{p}_3(t) = 4 - t$. Then $\{\mathbf{p}_1, \mathbf{p}_2, \mathbf{p}_3\}$ is linearly dependent in $\mathbb{P}$ because $\mathbf{p}_3 = 4\mathbf{p}_1 - \mathbf{p}_2$.

EXAMPLE 2 The set $\{\sin t, \cos t\}$ is linearly independent in $C[0, 1]$ because $\sin t$ and $\cos t$ are not multiples of one another *as vectors in* $C[0, 1]$. That is, there is no scalar c such that $\cos t = c \cdot \sin t$ for all t in [0,1]. (Look at the graphs of $\sin t$ and $\cos t$.) However, $\{\sin t \cos t, \sin 2t\}$ is linearly dependent because of the identity: $\sin 2t = 2 \sin t \cos t$, for all t.

[1] It is convenient to use $c_1, \ldots, c_p$ in (1) for the scalars instead of $x_1, \ldots, x_p$, as we did in Chapter 2.

DEFINITION

Let H be a subspace of a vector space V. A set of vectors $\mathcal{B} = \{\mathbf{b}_1, \dots, \mathbf{b}_p\}$ in V is a **basis** for H if

(i) $\mathcal{B}$ is a linearly independent set, and

(ii) the subspace spanned by $\mathcal{B}$ coincides with H; that is,

$$H = \text{Span}\{\mathbf{b}_1, \dots, \mathbf{b}_p\}$$

The definition of a basis applies to the case when $H = V$, because any vector space is a subspace of itself. Thus a basis of V is a linearly independent set that spans V. Observe that when $H \neq V$, condition (ii) includes the requirement that each of the vectors $\mathbf{b}_1, \dots, \mathbf{b}_p$ must belong to H, because Span $\{\mathbf{b}_1, \dots, \mathbf{b}_p\}$ contains $\mathbf{b}_1, \dots, \mathbf{b}_p$, as we saw in Section 5.1.

EXAMPLE 3 Let A be an invertible $n \times n$ matrix, say, $A = [\,\mathbf{a}_1 \;\; \cdots \;\; \mathbf{a}_n\,]$. Then the columns of A form a basis for $\mathbb{R}^n$ because they are linearly independent and they span $\mathbb{R}^n$, by the Invertible Matrix Theorem.

EXAMPLE 4 Let $\mathbf{e}_1, \dots, \mathbf{e}_n$ be the columns of the $n \times n$ identity matrix, I_n. That is,

$$\mathbf{e}_1 = \begin{bmatrix} 1 \\ 0 \\ \vdots \\ 0 \end{bmatrix}, \quad \mathbf{e}_2 = \begin{bmatrix} 0 \\ 1 \\ \vdots \\ 0 \end{bmatrix}, \quad \dots, \quad \mathbf{e}_n = \begin{bmatrix} 0 \\ \vdots \\ 0 \\ 1 \end{bmatrix}$$

The set $\{\mathbf{e}_1, \dots, \mathbf{e}_n\}$ is called the **standard basis** for $\mathbb{R}^n$ (Fig. 1).

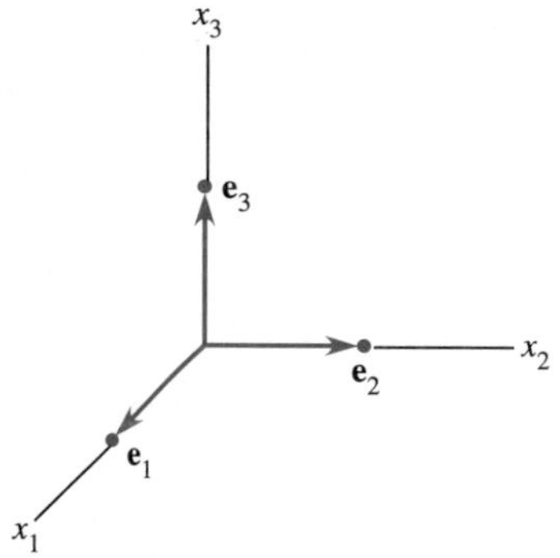

FIGURE 1 The standard basis for $\mathbb{R}^3$.

EXAMPLE 5 Let $\mathbf{v}_1 = \begin{bmatrix} 3 \\ 0 \\ -6 \end{bmatrix}$, $\mathbf{v}_2 = \begin{bmatrix} -4 \\ 1 \\ 7 \end{bmatrix}$, and $\mathbf{v}_3 = \begin{bmatrix} -2 \\ 1 \\ 5 \end{bmatrix}$. Determine if $\{\mathbf{v}_1, \mathbf{v}_2, \mathbf{v}_3\}$ is a basis for $\mathbb{R}^3$.

Solution Since there are exactly three vectors here in $\mathbb{R}^3$, we can use any of several methods to determine if the matrix $A = [\,\mathbf{v}_1 \;\; \mathbf{v}_2 \;\; \mathbf{v}_3\,]$ is invertible. For instance, a simple computation shows that $\det A = 6 \neq 0$. Thus A is invertible. As in Example 3, the columns of A form a basis for $\mathbb{R}^3$.

EXAMPLE 6 Let $S = \{1, t, t^2, \dots, t^n\}$. Verify that S is a basis for $\mathbb{P}_n$. This basis is called the **standard basis** for $\mathbb{P}_n$.

Solution Certainly S spans $\mathbb{P}_n$. To show that S is linearly independent, suppose that $c_0, \dots, c_n$ satisfy

$$c_0 \cdot 1 + c_1 t + c_2 t^2 + \cdots + c_n t^n = \mathbf{0}(t) \tag{2}$$

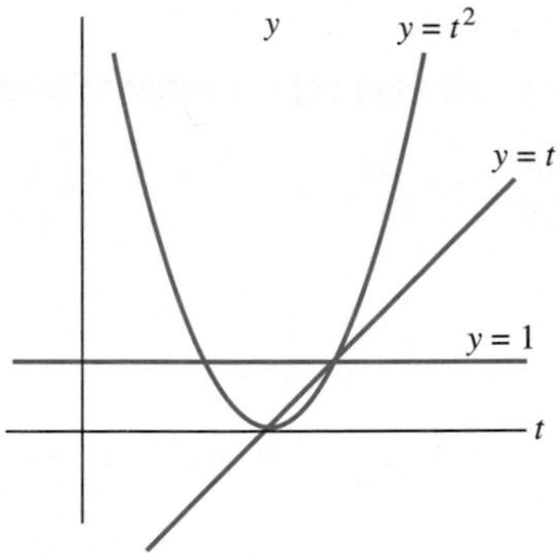

FIGURE 2 The standard basis for $\mathbb{P}_2$.

This equality means that the polynomial on the left has the same values as the zero polynomial on the right. A fundamental theorem in algebra says that the only polynomial in $\mathbb{P}_n$ with more than n zeros is the zero polynomial. That is, (2) holds for all t only if $c_0 = \cdots = c_n = 0$. This proves that S is linearly independent and hence is a basis for $\mathbb{P}_n$. See Fig. 2. ▮

Problems involving linear independence and spanning in $\mathbb{P}_n$ are handled best by a technique to be discussed in Section 5.4.

The Spanning Set Theorem

As we shall see, a basis is an "efficient" spanning set that contains no unnecessary vectors. In fact, a basis can be constructed from a spanning set by discarding unneeded vectors.

EXAMPLE 7 Let $\mathbf{v}_1 = \begin{bmatrix} 1 \\ -2 \\ -3 \end{bmatrix}$, $\mathbf{v}_2 = \begin{bmatrix} -3 \\ 5 \\ 7 \end{bmatrix}$, $\mathbf{v}_3 = \begin{bmatrix} -4 \\ 5 \\ 6 \end{bmatrix}$, and $H = \text{Span}\,\{\mathbf{v}_1, \mathbf{v}_2, \mathbf{v}_3\}$. Note that $\mathbf{v}_3 = 5\mathbf{v}_1 + 3\mathbf{v}_2$, and show that $\text{Span}\,\{\mathbf{v}_1, \mathbf{v}_2, \mathbf{v}_3\} = \text{Span}\,\{\mathbf{v}_1, \mathbf{v}_2\}$. Then find a basis for the subspace H.

Solution Certainly, every vector in $\text{Span}\,\{\mathbf{v}_1, \mathbf{v}_2\}$ belongs to H because

$$c_1\mathbf{v}_1 + c_2\mathbf{v}_2 = c_1\mathbf{v}_1 + c_2\mathbf{v}_2 + 0\mathbf{v}_3$$

Now let $\mathbf{x}$ be any vector in H, say, $\mathbf{x} = c_1\mathbf{v}_1 + c_2\mathbf{v}_2 + c_3\mathbf{v}_3$. Since $\mathbf{v}_3 = 5\mathbf{v}_1 + 3\mathbf{v}_2$, we may substitute

$$\begin{aligned} \mathbf{x} &= c_1\mathbf{v}_1 + c_2\mathbf{v}_2 + c_3(5\mathbf{v}_1 + 3\mathbf{v}_2) \\ &= (c_1 + 5c_3)\mathbf{v}_1 + (c_2 + 3c_3)\mathbf{v}_2 \end{aligned}$$

Thus $\mathbf{x}$ is in $\text{Span}\,\{\mathbf{v}_1, \mathbf{v}_2\}$, so every vector in H already belongs to $\text{Span}\,\{\mathbf{v}_1, \mathbf{v}_2\}$. We conclude that H and $\text{Span}\,\{\mathbf{v}_1, \mathbf{v}_2\}$ are actually the same set of vectors. It follows that $\{\mathbf{v}_1, \mathbf{v}_2\}$ is a basis of H since $\{\mathbf{v}_1, \mathbf{v}_2\}$ is obviously linearly independent. ▮

The next theorem generalizes Example 7.

THEOREM 6

The Spanning Set Theorem

Let $S = \{\mathbf{v}_1, \ldots, \mathbf{v}_p\}$ be a set in V and let $H = \text{Span}\,\{\mathbf{v}_1, \ldots, \mathbf{v}_p\}$.

a. If one of the vectors in S—say, $\mathbf{v}_k$—is a linear combination of the remaining vectors in S, then the set formed from S by removing $\mathbf{v}_k$ still spans H.

b. If $H \neq \{\mathbf{0}\}$, some subset of S is a basis for H.

Proof

a. By rearranging the list of vectors in S, if necessary, we may suppose that $\mathbf{v}_p$ is a linear combination of $\mathbf{v}_1, \ldots, \mathbf{v}_{p-1}$, say,

$$\mathbf{v}_p = a_1\mathbf{v}_1 + \cdots + a_{p-1}\mathbf{v}_{p-1} \tag{3}$$

Given any $\mathbf{x}$ in H, we may write

$$\mathbf{x} = c_1\mathbf{v}_1 + \cdots + c_{p-1}\mathbf{v}_{p-1} + c_p\mathbf{v}_p \tag{4}$$

for suitable scalars $c_1, \ldots, c_p$. Substituting the expression for $\mathbf{v}_p$ from (3) into (4), it is easy to see that $\mathbf{x}$ is a linear combination of $\mathbf{v}_1, \ldots, \mathbf{v}_{p-1}$. Thus $\{\mathbf{v}_1, \ldots, \mathbf{v}_{p-1}\}$ spans H, because $\mathbf{x}$ was an arbitrary element of H.

b. If the original spanning set S is linearly independent, then it is already a basis for H. Otherwise, one of the vectors in S depends on the others and may be deleted, by part (a). As long as there are two or more vectors in the spanning set, we may repeat this process until the spanning set is linearly independent and hence is a basis for H. If the spanning set is eventually reduced to one vector, that vector will be nonzero (and hence linearly independent) because $H \neq \{\mathbf{0}\}$. ∎

Bases for Nul *A* and Col *A*

We already know how to find vectors that span the null space of a matrix A. The discussion in Section 5.2 pointed out that our method always produces a linearly independent set. Thus the method produces a *basis* for Nul A.

The next two examples describe a simple algorithm for finding a basis for the column space.

EXAMPLE 8 Find a basis for Col B, where

$$B = [\mathbf{b}_1 \quad \mathbf{b}_2 \quad \cdots \quad \mathbf{b}_5] = \begin{bmatrix} 1 & 4 & 0 & 2 & 0 \\ 0 & 0 & 1 & -1 & 0 \\ 0 & 0 & 0 & 0 & 1 \\ 0 & 0 & 0 & 0 & 0 \end{bmatrix}$$

Solution Obviously, each nonpivot column of B is a linear combination of the pivot columns. In fact, $\mathbf{b}_2 = 4\mathbf{b}_1$ and $\mathbf{b}_4 = 2\mathbf{b}_1 - \mathbf{b}_3$. By the Spanning Set Theorem, we may discard $\mathbf{b}_2$ and $\mathbf{b}_4$ and $\{\mathbf{b}_1, \mathbf{b}_3, \mathbf{b}_5\}$ will still span Col B. Let

$$S = \{\mathbf{b}_1, \mathbf{b}_3, \mathbf{b}_5\} = \left\{ \begin{bmatrix} 1 \\ 0 \\ 0 \\ 0 \end{bmatrix}, \begin{bmatrix} 0 \\ 1 \\ 0 \\ 0 \end{bmatrix}, \begin{bmatrix} 0 \\ 0 \\ 1 \\ 0 \end{bmatrix} \right\}$$

It is clear that no vector in S is a linear combination of the vectors that precede it, and $\mathbf{b}_1 \neq \mathbf{0}$. By Theorem 5, S is linearly independent, and hence S is a basis for Col B. ∎

What about a matrix A that is *not* in reduced echelon form? Recall that any linear dependence relationship among the columns of A may be expressed in the form

$A\mathbf{x} = \mathbf{0}$, where $\mathbf{x}$ is a column of weights. (If some columns are not involved in a particular dependence relation, then their weights are zero.) When A is row reduced to a matrix B, the columns of B are often totally different from the columns of A. However, the equations $A\mathbf{x} = \mathbf{0}$ and $B\mathbf{x} = \mathbf{0}$ have exactly the same set of solutions. That is, the columns of A have *exactly the same linear dependence relationships* as the columns of B.

Elementary row operations on a matrix do not affect the linear dependence relations among the columns of the matrix.

EXAMPLE 9 It can be shown that the matrix

$$A = [\,\mathbf{a}_1 \quad \mathbf{a}_2 \quad \cdots \quad \mathbf{a}_5\,] = \begin{bmatrix} 1 & 4 & 0 & 2 & -1 \\ 3 & 12 & 1 & 5 & 5 \\ 2 & 8 & 1 & 3 & 2 \\ 5 & 20 & 2 & 8 & 8 \end{bmatrix}$$

is row equivalent to the matrix B in Example 8. Find a basis for Col A.

Solution In Example 8 we saw that

$$\mathbf{b}_2 = 4\mathbf{b}_1 \qquad \text{and} \qquad \mathbf{b}_4 = 2\mathbf{b}_1 - \mathbf{b}_3$$

so we can expect that

$$\mathbf{a}_2 = 4\mathbf{a}_1 \qquad \text{and} \qquad \mathbf{a}_4 = 2\mathbf{a}_1 - \mathbf{a}_3$$

Check that this is indeed the case! Thus we may discard $\mathbf{a}_2$ and $\mathbf{a}_4$ when selecting a minimal spanning set for Col A. In fact, $\{\mathbf{a}_1, \mathbf{a}_3, \mathbf{a}_5\}$ must be linearly independent because any linear dependence relationship among $\mathbf{a}_1, \mathbf{a}_3, \mathbf{a}_5$ would imply a linear dependence relationship among $\mathbf{b}_1, \mathbf{b}_3, \mathbf{b}_5$. But we know that $\{\mathbf{b}_1, \mathbf{b}_3, \mathbf{b}_5\}$ is a linearly independent set. Thus $\{\mathbf{a}_1, \mathbf{a}_3, \mathbf{a}_5\}$ is a basis for Col A. The columns we have used for this basis are the pivot columns of A.

Examples 8 and 9 illustrate the following useful fact.

THEOREM 7

The pivot columns of a matrix A form a basis for Col A.

Proof The general proof uses the arguments discussed above. Let B be the reduced echelon form of A. The set of pivot columns of B is linearly independent, for no vector in the set is a linear combination of the vectors that precede it. Since A is row equivalent to B, the pivot columns of A are linearly independent, too, because any linear dependence relation among the columns of A would correspond to a linear dependence relation among the columns of B. For this same reason, every nonpivot column of A is a linear combination of the pivot columns of A. Thus the nonpivot columns of A may be discarded from the spanning set for Col A, by the Spanning Set Theorem. This leaves the pivot columns of A as a basis for Col A. ∎

Warning: Be careful to use *pivot columns of* A *itself* for the basis of Col A. The columns of an echelon form B are often not in the column space of A. For instance, the columns of the B in Example 8 all have zeros in their last entries, so they cannot span the column space of the A in Example 9.

Two Views of a Basis

When using the Spanning Set Theorem, the deletion of vectors from a spanning set must stop when the set becomes linearly independent. If an additional vector is deleted, it will not be a linear combination of the remaining vectors and hence the smaller set will no longer span V. Thus a basis is a spanning set that is as small as possible.

A basis is also a linearly independent set that is as large as possible. If S is a basis for V, and if S is enlarged by one vector—say, $\mathbf{w}$—then the new set cannot be linearly independent, because S spans V, and $\mathbf{w}$ is therefore a linear combination of the elements in S.

EXAMPLE 10 The following three sets in $\mathbb{R}^3$ show how a linearly independent set can be enlarged to a basis and how further enlargement destroys the linear independence of the set. Also, a spanning set can be shrunk to a basis, but further shrinking destroys the spanning property.

$$\left\{\begin{bmatrix}1\\0\\0\end{bmatrix},\begin{bmatrix}2\\3\\0\end{bmatrix}\right\} \qquad \left\{\begin{bmatrix}1\\0\\0\end{bmatrix},\begin{bmatrix}2\\3\\0\end{bmatrix},\begin{bmatrix}4\\5\\6\end{bmatrix}\right\} \qquad \left\{\begin{bmatrix}1\\0\\0\end{bmatrix},\begin{bmatrix}2\\3\\0\end{bmatrix},\begin{bmatrix}4\\5\\6\end{bmatrix},\begin{bmatrix}7\\8\\9\end{bmatrix}\right\}$$

Linearly independent but does not span $\mathbb{R}^3$ — A basis for $\mathbb{R}^3$ — Spans $\mathbb{R}^3$ but is linearly dependent

∎

PRACTICE PROBLEMS

1. Let $\mathbf{v}_1 = \begin{bmatrix}1\\-2\\3\end{bmatrix}$, $\mathbf{v}_2 = \begin{bmatrix}-2\\7\\-9\end{bmatrix}$. Determine if $\{\mathbf{v}_1, \mathbf{v}_2\}$ is a basis for $\mathbb{R}^3$. Is $\{\mathbf{v}_1, \mathbf{v}_2\}$ a basis for $\mathbb{R}^2$?

2. Let $\mathbf{v}_1 = \begin{bmatrix}1\\-3\\4\end{bmatrix}$, $\mathbf{v}_2 = \begin{bmatrix}6\\2\\-1\end{bmatrix}$, $\mathbf{v}_3 = \begin{bmatrix}2\\-2\\3\end{bmatrix}$, $\mathbf{v}_4 = \begin{bmatrix}-4\\-8\\9\end{bmatrix}$. Find a basis for the subspace W spanned by $\{\mathbf{v}_1, \mathbf{v}_2, \mathbf{v}_3, \mathbf{v}_4\}$.

3. Let $\mathbf{v}_1 = \begin{bmatrix} 1 \\ 0 \\ 0 \end{bmatrix}$, $\mathbf{v}_2 = \begin{bmatrix} 0 \\ 1 \\ 0 \end{bmatrix}$, and $H = \left\{ \begin{bmatrix} s \\ s \\ 0 \end{bmatrix} : s \text{ in } \mathbb{R} \right\}$. Then every vector in H is a linear combination of $\mathbf{v}_1$ and $\mathbf{v}_2$ because

$$\begin{bmatrix} s \\ s \\ 0 \end{bmatrix} = s \begin{bmatrix} 1 \\ 0 \\ 0 \end{bmatrix} + s \begin{bmatrix} 0 \\ 1 \\ 0 \end{bmatrix}$$

Is $\{\mathbf{v}_1, \mathbf{v}_2\}$ a basis for H?

5.3 EXERCISES

Determine which sets in Exercises 1–12 are bases for $\mathbb{R}^2$ or $\mathbb{R}^3$. Of the sets that are *not* bases, determine which ones are linearly independent and which ones span $\mathbb{R}^2$ or $\mathbb{R}^3$. Justify your answers.

1. $\begin{bmatrix} 3 \\ 2 \end{bmatrix}, \begin{bmatrix} -7 \\ 5 \end{bmatrix}$

2. $\begin{bmatrix} 4 \\ 0 \end{bmatrix}, \begin{bmatrix} -1 \\ 1 \end{bmatrix}, \begin{bmatrix} 3 \\ -5 \end{bmatrix}$

3. $\begin{bmatrix} 1 \\ -3 \end{bmatrix}, \begin{bmatrix} -4 \\ 12 \end{bmatrix}, \begin{bmatrix} 2 \\ -6 \end{bmatrix}$

4. $\begin{bmatrix} -4 \\ 6 \end{bmatrix}, \begin{bmatrix} 6 \\ -9 \end{bmatrix}$

5. $\begin{bmatrix} 1 \\ 0 \\ 0 \end{bmatrix}, \begin{bmatrix} 1 \\ 1 \\ 0 \end{bmatrix}, \begin{bmatrix} 1 \\ 1 \\ 1 \end{bmatrix}$

6. $\begin{bmatrix} 1 \\ 0 \\ 1 \end{bmatrix}, \begin{bmatrix} 0 \\ 0 \\ 0 \end{bmatrix}, \begin{bmatrix} 0 \\ 1 \\ 0 \end{bmatrix}$

7. $\begin{bmatrix} 1 \\ 0 \\ -2 \end{bmatrix}, \begin{bmatrix} 3 \\ 2 \\ -4 \end{bmatrix}, \begin{bmatrix} -3 \\ -5 \\ 1 \end{bmatrix}$

8. $\begin{bmatrix} 2 \\ -2 \\ 1 \end{bmatrix}, \begin{bmatrix} 1 \\ -3 \\ 2 \end{bmatrix}, \begin{bmatrix} -7 \\ 5 \\ 4 \end{bmatrix}$

9. $\begin{bmatrix} 1 \\ -3 \\ 0 \end{bmatrix}, \begin{bmatrix} -2 \\ 9 \\ 0 \end{bmatrix}, \begin{bmatrix} 0 \\ 0 \\ 0 \end{bmatrix}, \begin{bmatrix} 0 \\ -3 \\ 5 \end{bmatrix}$

10. $\begin{bmatrix} 1 \\ 2 \\ -3 \end{bmatrix}, \begin{bmatrix} -4 \\ -5 \\ 6 \end{bmatrix}$

11. $\begin{bmatrix} -2 \\ 3 \\ 0 \end{bmatrix}, \begin{bmatrix} 6 \\ -1 \\ 5 \end{bmatrix}$

12. $\begin{bmatrix} 1 \\ -4 \\ 3 \end{bmatrix}, \begin{bmatrix} 0 \\ 3 \\ -1 \end{bmatrix}, \begin{bmatrix} 3 \\ -5 \\ 4 \end{bmatrix}, \begin{bmatrix} 0 \\ 2 \\ -2 \end{bmatrix}$

Find bases for the null spaces of the matrices given in Exercises 13 and 14. Refer to the remarks that follow Example 4 in Section 5.2.

13. $\begin{bmatrix} 1 & 0 & -3 & 2 \\ 0 & 1 & -5 & 4 \\ 3 & -2 & 1 & -2 \end{bmatrix}$

14. $\begin{bmatrix} 1 & 0 & -5 & 1 & 4 \\ -2 & 1 & 6 & -2 & -2 \\ 0 & 2 & -8 & 1 & 9 \end{bmatrix}$

15. Find a basis for the set of vectors in $\mathbb{R}^3$ in the plane $x + 2y + z = 0$. [*Hint*: Think of the equation as a "system" of homogeneous equations.]

16. Find a basis for the set of vectors in $\mathbb{R}^2$ on the line $y = 5x$.

In Exercises 17 and 18, assume that A is row equivalent to B. Find bases for Nul A and Col A.

17. $A = \begin{bmatrix} -2 & 4 & -2 & -4 \\ 2 & -6 & -3 & 1 \\ -3 & 8 & 2 & -3 \end{bmatrix}$, $B = \begin{bmatrix} 1 & 0 & 6 & 5 \\ 0 & 2 & 5 & 3 \\ 0 & 0 & 0 & 0 \end{bmatrix}$

18. $A = \begin{bmatrix} 1 & 2 & -5 & 11 & -3 \\ 2 & 4 & -5 & 15 & 2 \\ 1 & 2 & 0 & 4 & 5 \\ 3 & 6 & -5 & 19 & -2 \end{bmatrix}$,

$B = \begin{bmatrix} 1 & 2 & 0 & 4 & 5 \\ 0 & 0 & 5 & -7 & 8 \\ 0 & 0 & 0 & 0 & -9 \\ 0 & 0 & 0 & 0 & 0 \end{bmatrix}$

In Exercises 19 and 20, find a basis of Span $\{\mathbf{v}_1, \ldots, \mathbf{v}_5\}$.

19. $\mathbf{v}_1 = \begin{bmatrix} 1 \\ 0 \\ -3 \\ 2 \end{bmatrix}$, $\mathbf{v}_2 = \begin{bmatrix} 0 \\ 1 \\ 2 \\ -3 \end{bmatrix}$, $\mathbf{v}_3 = \begin{bmatrix} -3 \\ -4 \\ 1 \\ 6 \end{bmatrix}$,

$\mathbf{v}_4 = \begin{bmatrix} 1 \\ -3 \\ -8 \\ 7 \end{bmatrix}$, $\mathbf{v}_5 = \begin{bmatrix} 2 \\ 1 \\ -6 \\ 9 \end{bmatrix}$

20. $\mathbf{v}_1 = \begin{bmatrix} 1 \\ 0 \\ 0 \\ 1 \end{bmatrix}$, $\mathbf{v}_2 = \begin{bmatrix} -2 \\ 1 \\ -1 \\ 1 \end{bmatrix}$, $\mathbf{v}_3 = \begin{bmatrix} 6 \\ -1 \\ 2 \\ -1 \end{bmatrix}$,

$$\mathbf{v}_4 = \begin{bmatrix} 5 \\ -3 \\ 3 \\ -4 \end{bmatrix}, \quad \mathbf{v}_5 = \begin{bmatrix} 0 \\ 3 \\ -1 \\ 1 \end{bmatrix}$$

21. Let $\mathbf{v}_1 = \begin{bmatrix} 4 \\ -3 \\ 7 \end{bmatrix}, \mathbf{v}_2 = \begin{bmatrix} 1 \\ 9 \\ -2 \end{bmatrix}, \mathbf{v}_3 = \begin{bmatrix} 7 \\ 11 \\ 6 \end{bmatrix}$, and $H = \text{Span}\{\mathbf{v}_1, \mathbf{v}_2, \mathbf{v}_3\}$. It may be verified that $4\mathbf{v}_1 + 5\mathbf{v}_2 - 3\mathbf{v}_3 = \mathbf{0}$. Use this information to find a basis for H. There is more than one answer.

22. Let $\mathbf{v}_1 = \begin{bmatrix} 7 \\ 4 \\ -9 \\ -5 \end{bmatrix}, \mathbf{v}_2 = \begin{bmatrix} 4 \\ -7 \\ 2 \\ 5 \end{bmatrix}, \mathbf{v}_3 = \begin{bmatrix} 1 \\ -5 \\ 3 \\ 4 \end{bmatrix}$. It may be verified that $\mathbf{v}_1 - 3\mathbf{v}_2 + 5\mathbf{v}_3 = \mathbf{0}$. Use this information to find a basis for $H = \text{Span}\{\mathbf{v}_1, \mathbf{v}_2, \mathbf{v}_3\}$.

23. Suppose $\mathbb{R}^4 = \text{Span}\{\mathbf{v}_1, \ldots, \mathbf{v}_4\}$. Explain why $\{\mathbf{v}_1, \ldots, \mathbf{v}_4\}$ is a basis for $\mathbb{R}^4$.

24. Let $\mathcal{B} = \{\mathbf{v}_1, \ldots, \mathbf{v}_n\}$ be a linearly independent set in $\mathbb{R}^n$. Explain why $\mathcal{B}$ must be a basis for $\mathbb{R}^n$.

25. Let $\mathbf{v}_1 = \begin{bmatrix} 1 \\ 0 \\ 1 \end{bmatrix}, \mathbf{v}_2 = \begin{bmatrix} 0 \\ 1 \\ 1 \end{bmatrix}, \mathbf{v}_3 = \begin{bmatrix} 0 \\ 1 \\ 0 \end{bmatrix}$, and let H be the set of vectors in $\mathbb{R}^3$ whose second and third entries are equal. Then every vector in H has a unique expansion as a linear combination of $\mathbf{v}_1, \mathbf{v}_2, \mathbf{v}_3$, because

$$\begin{bmatrix} s \\ t \\ t \end{bmatrix} = s\begin{bmatrix} 1 \\ 0 \\ 1 \end{bmatrix} + (t - s)\begin{bmatrix} 0 \\ 1 \\ 1 \end{bmatrix} + s\begin{bmatrix} 0 \\ 1 \\ 0 \end{bmatrix}$$

for any s and t. Is $\{\mathbf{v}_1, \mathbf{v}_2, \mathbf{v}_3\}$ a basis for H? Why or why not?

26. In the vector space of all real-valued functions, find a basis for the subspace spanned by $\{\sin t, \sin 2t, \sin t \cos t\}$.

27. Let V be the vector space of functions that describe the vibration of a mass-spring system. (Refer to Exercise 19 in Section 5.1.) Find a basis for V.

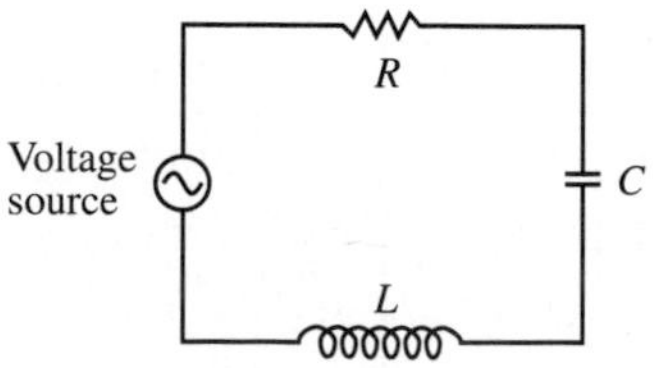

28. (*RLC* Circuit) The circuit in the figure consists of a resistor (R ohms), an inductor (L henrys), a capacitor (C farads), and an initial voltage source. Let $b = R/(2L)$, and suppose that R, L, C have been selected so that b also equals $1/\sqrt{LC}$. (This is done, for instance, when the circuit is used in a voltmeter.) Let $v(t)$ be the voltage (in volts) at time t, measured across the capacitor. It can be shown that v is in the null space H of the linear transformation that maps $v(t)$ into $L\,v''(t) + R\,v'(t) + (1/C)\,v(t)$, and H consists of all functions of the form $v(t) = e^{-bt}(c_1 + c_2 t)$ Find a basis for H.

Exercises 29 and 30 show that every basis for $\mathbb{R}^n$ must contain exactly n vectors.

29. Let $S = \{\mathbf{v}_1, \ldots, \mathbf{v}_k\}$ be a set of k vectors in $\mathbb{R}^n$, with $k < n$. Use a theorem from Section 2.2 to explain why S cannot be a basis for $\mathbb{R}^n$.

30. Let $S = \{\mathbf{v}_1, \ldots, \mathbf{v}_k\}$ be a set of k vectors in $\mathbb{R}^n$, with $k > n$. Use a theorem from Chapter 2 to explain why S cannot be a basis for $\mathbb{R}^n$.

Exercises 31 and 32 reveal an important connection between linear independence and linear transformations and provide practice using the definition of linear dependence. Let V and W be vector spaces, let $T : V \to W$ be a linear transformation, and let $\{\mathbf{v}_1, \ldots, \mathbf{v}_p\}$ be a subset of V.

31. Show that if $\{\mathbf{v}_1, \ldots, \mathbf{v}_p\}$ is linearly dependent in V, then the set of images, $\{T(\mathbf{v}_1), \ldots, T(\mathbf{v}_p)\}$, is linearly dependent in W. This fact shows that if a linear transformation maps a set $\{\mathbf{v}_1, \ldots, \mathbf{v}_p\}$ into a linearly *independent* set $\{T(\mathbf{v}_1), \ldots, T(\mathbf{v}_p)\}$, then the original set is linearly independent, too (because it cannot be linearly dependent).

32. Suppose that T is a one-to-one transformation, so that an equation $T(\mathbf{u}) = T(\mathbf{v})$ always implies $\mathbf{u} = \mathbf{v}$. Show that if the set of images $\{T(\mathbf{v}_1), \ldots, T(\mathbf{v}_p)\}$ is linearly dependent, then $\{\mathbf{v}_1, \ldots, \mathbf{v}_p\}$ is linearly dependent. This fact shows that *a one-to-one linear transformation maps a linearly independent set onto a linearly independent set* (because in this case the set of images cannot be linearly dependent).

SOLUTIONS TO PRACTICE PROBLEMS

1. Let $A = [\,\mathbf{v}_1 \quad \mathbf{v}_2\,]$. Row operations show that

$$A = \begin{bmatrix} 1 & -2 \\ -2 & 7 \\ 3 & -9 \end{bmatrix} \sim \begin{bmatrix} 1 & -2 \\ 0 & 3 \\ 0 & 0 \end{bmatrix}$$

Not every row of A contains a pivot position. So the columns of A do not span $\mathbb{R}^3$, by Theorem 2 in Section 2.2. Hence $\{\mathbf{v}_1, \mathbf{v}_2\}$ is not a basis for $\mathbb{R}^3$. Since $\mathbf{v}_1$ and $\mathbf{v}_2$ are not in $\mathbb{R}^2$, they cannot possibly be a basis for $\mathbb{R}^2$. However, since $\mathbf{v}_1$ and $\mathbf{v}_2$ are obviously linearly independent, they are a basis for a subspace of $\mathbb{R}^3$, namely, Span $\{\mathbf{v}_1, \mathbf{v}_2\}$.

2. Set up a matrix A whose column space is the space spanned by $\{\mathbf{v}_1, \mathbf{v}_2, \mathbf{v}_3, \mathbf{v}_4\}$, and then row reduce A to find its pivot columns.

$$A = \begin{bmatrix} 1 & 6 & 2 & -4 \\ -3 & 2 & -2 & -8 \\ 4 & -1 & 3 & 9 \end{bmatrix} \sim \begin{bmatrix} 1 & 6 & 2 & -4 \\ 0 & 20 & 4 & -20 \\ 0 & -25 & -5 & 25 \end{bmatrix} \sim \begin{bmatrix} 1 & 6 & 2 & -4 \\ 0 & 5 & 1 & -5 \\ 0 & 0 & 0 & 0 \end{bmatrix}$$

The first two columns of A are the pivot columns and hence form a basis of Col $A = W$. Hence $\{\mathbf{v}_1, \mathbf{v}_2\}$ is a basis for W. Note that the reduced echelon form of A is not needed in order to locate the pivot columns.

3. Neither $\mathbf{v}_1$ nor $\mathbf{v}_2$ is in H, so $\{\mathbf{v}_1, \mathbf{v}_2\}$ cannot be a basis for H. In fact, $\{\mathbf{v}_1, \mathbf{v}_2\}$ is a basis for the *plane* of all vectors of the form $(c_1, c_2, 0)$, but H is only a *line*.

5.4 COORDINATE SYSTEMS

An important reason for specifying a basis $\mathcal{B}$ for a vector space V is to impose a "coordinate system" on V. In this section we shall show that if $\mathcal{B}$ contains n vectors, then the coordinate system will make V act like $\mathbb{R}^n$. If V is already $\mathbb{R}^n$ itself, then $\mathcal{B}$ will determine a coordinate system that gives a new "view" of V.

The existence of coordinate systems rests on the following fundamental result.

THEOREM 8

The Unique Representation Theorem

Let $\mathcal{B} = \{\mathbf{b}_1, \ldots, \mathbf{b}_n\}$ be a basis for a vector space V. Then for each $\mathbf{x}$ in V, there exists a unique set of scalars $c_1, \ldots, c_n$ such that

$$\mathbf{x} = c_1\mathbf{b}_1 + \cdots + c_n\mathbf{b}_n \qquad (1)$$

Proof Since $\mathcal{B}$ spans V, there exist scalars such that (1) holds. Suppose $\mathbf{x}$ also has the representation

$$\mathbf{x} = d_1\mathbf{b}_1 + \cdots + d_n\mathbf{b}_n$$

for scalars $d_1, \dots, d_n$. Then, subtracting, we have

$$\mathbf{0} = \mathbf{x} - \mathbf{x} = (c_1 - d_1)\mathbf{b}_1 + \cdots + (c_n - d_n)\mathbf{b}_n \tag{2}$$

Since $\mathcal{B}$ is linearly independent, the weights in (2) must all be zero. That is, $c_j = d_j$ for $1 \le j \le n$. ∎

DEFINITION

Suppose the set $\mathcal{B} = \{\mathbf{b}_1, \dots, \mathbf{b}_n\}$ is a basis for V and $\mathbf{x}$ is in V. The **coordinates of x relative to the basis $\mathcal{B}$** (or the **$\mathcal{B}$-coordinates of x**) are the weights $c_1, \dots, c_n$ such that $\mathbf{x} = c_1\mathbf{b}_1 + \cdots + c_n\mathbf{b}_n$.

If $c_1, \dots, c_n$ are the $\mathcal{B}$-coordinates of $\mathbf{x}$, then the vector in $\mathbb{R}^n$

$$[\mathbf{x}]_{\mathcal{B}} = \begin{bmatrix} c_1 \\ \vdots \\ c_n \end{bmatrix}$$

is called the **coordinate vector of x (relative to $\mathcal{B}$)**, or the **$\mathcal{B}$-coordinate vector** of **x**. The mapping $\mathbf{x} \mapsto [\mathbf{x}]_{\mathcal{B}}$ is called the **coordinate mapping (determined by $\mathcal{B}$)**.[1]

EXAMPLE 1 Consider a basis $\mathcal{B} = \{\mathbf{b}_1, \mathbf{b}_2\}$ for $\mathbb{R}^2$, where $\mathbf{b}_1 = \begin{bmatrix} 1 \\ 0 \end{bmatrix}$, and $\mathbf{b}_2 = \begin{bmatrix} 1 \\ 2 \end{bmatrix}$. Suppose an $\mathbf{x}$ in $\mathbb{R}^2$ has the coordinate vector $[\mathbf{x}]_{\mathcal{B}} = \begin{bmatrix} -2 \\ 3 \end{bmatrix}$. Find $\mathbf{x}$.

Solution The $\mathcal{B}$-coordinates of $\mathbf{x}$ tell how to build $\mathbf{x}$ from the vectors in $\mathcal{B}$. That is,

$$\mathbf{x} = (-2)\mathbf{b}_1 + 3\mathbf{b}_2 = (-2)\begin{bmatrix} 1 \\ 0 \end{bmatrix} + 3\begin{bmatrix} 1 \\ 2 \end{bmatrix} = \begin{bmatrix} 1 \\ 6 \end{bmatrix}$$

∎

EXAMPLE 2 The entries in the vector $\mathbf{x} = \begin{bmatrix} 1 \\ 6 \end{bmatrix}$ are the coordinates of $\mathbf{x}$ relative to the *standard basis* $\mathcal{E} = \{\mathbf{e}_1, \mathbf{e}_2\}$, since

$$\begin{bmatrix} 1 \\ 6 \end{bmatrix} = 1\cdot\begin{bmatrix} 1 \\ 0 \end{bmatrix} + 6\cdot\begin{bmatrix} 0 \\ 1 \end{bmatrix} = 1\cdot\mathbf{e}_1 + 6\cdot\mathbf{e}_2$$

If $\mathcal{E} = \{\mathbf{e}_1, \mathbf{e}_2\}$, then $[\mathbf{x}]_{\mathcal{E}} = \mathbf{x}$.

∎

[1]Whenever we discuss coordinate vectors, we assume that $\mathcal{B}$ is an *ordered basis* whose vectors are listed in some fixed preassigned order. This property makes the definition of $[\mathbf{x}]_{\mathcal{B}}$ unambiguous.

A Graphical Interpretation of Coordinates

A coordinate system on a set consists of a one-to-one mapping of the points in the set into $\mathbb{R}^n$. For example, ordinary graph paper provides a coordinate system for the plane when one selects perpendicular axes and a unit of measurement on each axis. Figure 1 shows the standard basis $\{\mathbf{e}_1, \mathbf{e}_2\}$, the vectors $\mathbf{b}_1 (= \mathbf{e}_1)$ and $\mathbf{b}_2$ from Example 1, and the vector $\mathbf{x} = \begin{bmatrix} 1 \\ 6 \end{bmatrix}$. The coordinates 1 and 6 give the location of $\mathbf{x}$ relative to the standard basis: 1 unit in the $\mathbf{e}_1$ direction and 6 units in the $\mathbf{e}_2$ direction.

Figure 2 shows the vectors $\mathbf{b}_1, \mathbf{b}_2$, and $\mathbf{x}$ from Fig. 1. (Geometrically, the three vectors lie on a vertical line in both figures.) However, the standard coordinate grid was erased and replaced by a grid especially adapted to the basis $\mathcal{B}$ in Example 1. The coordinate vector $[\mathbf{x}]_{\mathcal{B}} = \begin{bmatrix} -2 \\ 3 \end{bmatrix}$ gives the location of $\mathbf{x}$ on this new coordinate system: -2 units in the $\mathbf{b}_1$ direction and 3 units in the $\mathbf{b}_2$ direction.

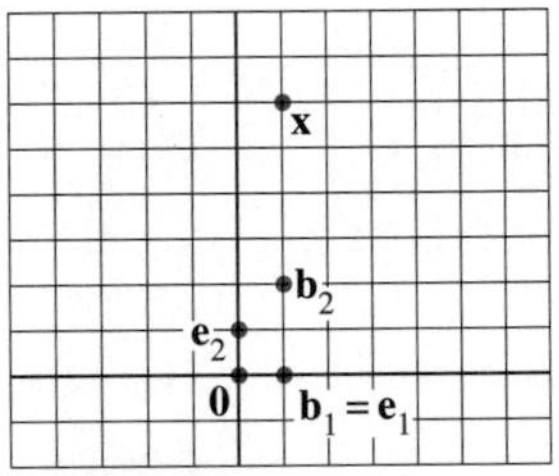

FIGURE 1 Standard graph paper.

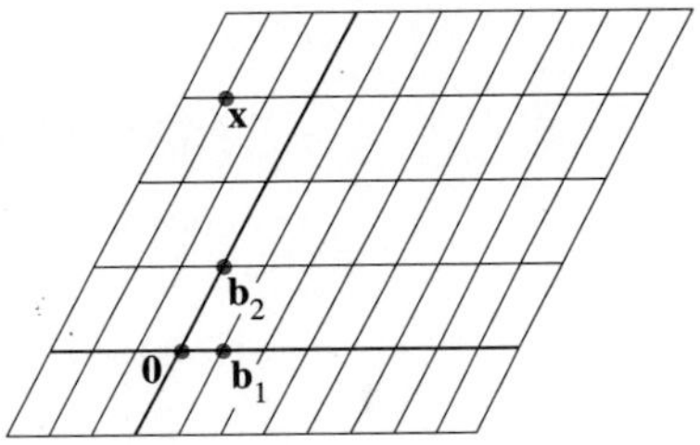

FIGURE 2 $\mathcal{B}$-graph paper.

EXAMPLE 3 In crystallography, the description of a crystal lattice is aided by choosing a basis $\{\mathbf{u}, \mathbf{v}, \mathbf{w}\}$ for $\mathbb{R}^3$ that corresponds to three adjacent edges of one "unit cell" of the crystal. An entire lattice is constructed by stacking together many copies of one cell. There are fourteen basic types of unit cells; three are displayed in Fig. 3.[2]

The coordinates of atoms within the crystal are given relative to the basis for the lattice. For instance,

$$\begin{bmatrix} 1/2 \\ 1/2 \\ 1 \end{bmatrix}$$

identifies the top face-centered atom in the cell in Fig. 3(b).

[2]See *The Science and Engineering of Materials,* Alt. Ed., by Donald R. Askeland (Boston: Prindle, Weber & Schmidt, 1985), p. 36.

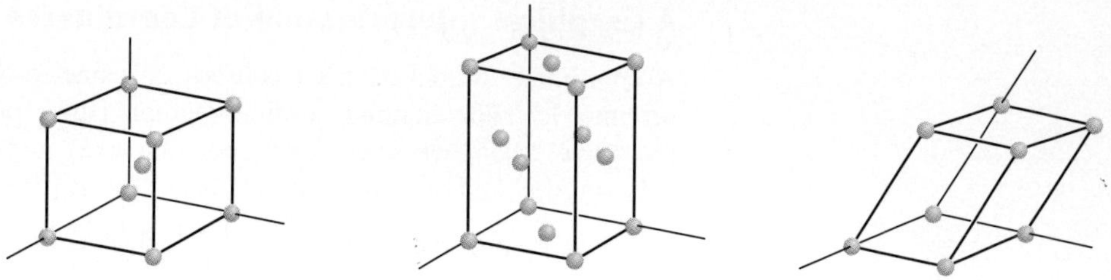

(a) Body-centered cubic

(b) Face-centered orthorhombic

(c) Simple monoclinic

FIGURE 3 Examples of unit cells.

Coordinates in $\mathbb{R}^n$

When a basis $\mathcal{B}$ for $\mathbb{R}^n$ is fixed, the $\mathcal{B}$-coordinate vector of a specified $\mathbf{x}$ is easily found, as in the next example.

EXAMPLE 4 Let $\mathbf{b}_1 = \begin{bmatrix} 2 \\ 1 \end{bmatrix}$, $\mathbf{b}_2 = \begin{bmatrix} -1 \\ 1 \end{bmatrix}$, $\mathbf{x} = \begin{bmatrix} 4 \\ 5 \end{bmatrix}$, and $\mathcal{B} = \{\mathbf{b}_1, \mathbf{b}_2\}$. Find the coordinate vector $[\mathbf{x}]_\mathcal{B}$ of $\mathbf{x}$ relative to $\mathcal{B}$.

Solution The $\mathcal{B}$-coordinates c_1, c_2 of $\mathbf{x}$ satisfy

$$c_1 \underset{\mathbf{b}_1}{\begin{bmatrix} 2 \\ 1 \end{bmatrix}} + c_2 \underset{\mathbf{b}_2}{\begin{bmatrix} -1 \\ 1 \end{bmatrix}} = \underset{\mathbf{x}}{\begin{bmatrix} 4 \\ 5 \end{bmatrix}}$$

or

$$\begin{bmatrix} \underset{\mathbf{b}_1}{\begin{matrix} 2 \\ 1 \end{matrix}} & \underset{\mathbf{b}_2}{\begin{matrix} -1 \\ 1 \end{matrix}} \end{bmatrix} \begin{bmatrix} c_1 \\ c_2 \end{bmatrix} = \underset{\mathbf{x}}{\begin{bmatrix} 4 \\ 5 \end{bmatrix}} \tag{3}$$

This equation may be solved by row operations on an augmented matrix or by using the inverse of the matrix on the left. In any case, the solution is $c_1 = 3$, $c_2 = 2$. Thus $\mathbf{x} = 3\mathbf{b}_1 + 2\mathbf{b}_2$ and

$$[\mathbf{x}]_\mathcal{B} = \begin{bmatrix} c_1 \\ c_2 \end{bmatrix} = \begin{bmatrix} 3 \\ 2 \end{bmatrix}$$

See Fig. 4.

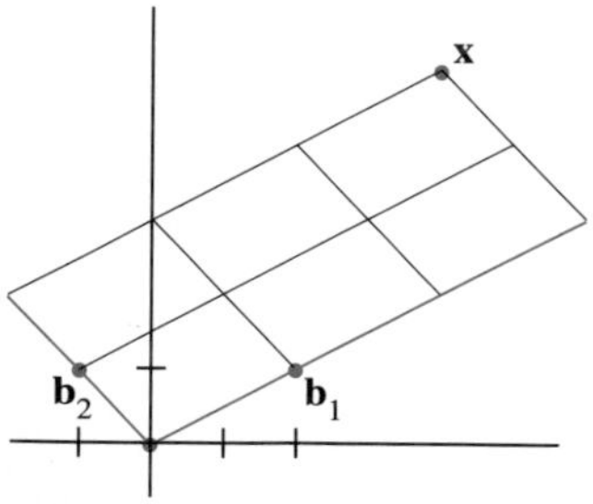

FIGURE 4 The $\mathcal{B}$-coordinate vector of $\mathbf{x}$ is $(3, 2)$.

The matrix in (3) changes the $\mathcal{B}$-coordinates of a vector $\mathbf{x}$ into the standard coordinates for $\mathbf{x}$. An analogous change of coordinates can be carried out in $\mathbb{R}^n$ for a basis $\mathcal{B} = \{\mathbf{b}_1, \dots, \mathbf{b}_n\}$. Let

$$P_\mathcal{B} = [\, \mathbf{b}_1 \quad \mathbf{b}_2 \quad \cdots \quad \mathbf{b}_n \,]$$

Then the vector equation

$$\mathbf{x} = c_1\mathbf{b}_1 + c_2\mathbf{b}_2 + \cdots + c_n\mathbf{b}_n$$

is equivalent to

$$\boxed{\mathbf{x} = P_{\mathcal{B}}[\mathbf{x}]_{\mathcal{B}}} \tag{4}$$

We call $P_{\mathcal{B}}$ the **change-of-coordinates matrix** from $\mathcal{B}$ to the standard basis in $\mathbb{R}^n$. Left-multiplication by $P_{\mathcal{B}}$ transforms the coordinate vector $[\mathbf{x}]_{\mathcal{B}}$ into $\mathbf{x}$. The change-of-coordinates equation (4) is important and will be needed at several points in Chapters 6 and 8.

Since the columns of $P_{\mathcal{B}}$ form a basis for $\mathbb{R}^n$, $P_{\mathcal{B}}$ is invertible (by the Invertible Matrix Theorem). Left-multiplication by $P_{\mathcal{B}}^{-1}$ converts $\mathbf{x}$ into its $\mathcal{B}$-coordinate vector:

$$P_{\mathcal{B}}^{-1}\mathbf{x} = [\mathbf{x}]_{\mathcal{B}}$$

The correspondence $\mathbf{x} \mapsto [\mathbf{x}]_{\mathcal{B}}$, produced here by $P_{\mathcal{B}}^{-1}$, is the coordinate mapping mentioned earlier. Since $P_{\mathcal{B}}^{-1}$ is an invertible matrix, the coordinate mapping is a one-to-one linear transformation from $\mathbb{R}^n$ onto $\mathbb{R}^n$, by the Invertible Matrix Theorem. (See also Theorem 10 in Section 2.6.) This property of the coordinate mapping is also true in a general vector space that has a basis, as we shall see.

The Coordinate Mapping

Choosing an ordered basis $\mathcal{B} = \{\mathbf{b}_1, \ldots, \mathbf{b}_n\}$ for a vector space V introduces a coordinate system in V. The coordinate mapping $\mathbf{x} \mapsto [\mathbf{x}]_{\mathcal{B}}$ connects the possibly unfamiliar space V to the familiar space $\mathbb{R}^n$. See Fig. 5. Points in V can be identified now by their new "names."

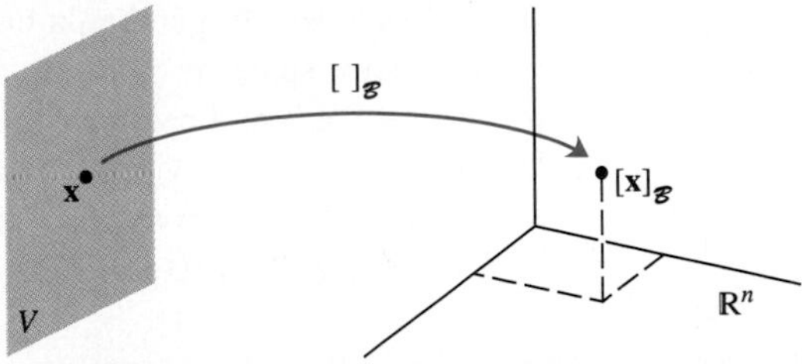

FIGURE 5 The coordinate mapping from V onto $\mathbb{R}^n$.

THEOREM 9

Let $\mathcal{B} = \{\mathbf{b}_1, \ldots, \mathbf{b}_n\}$ be an ordered basis for a vector space V. Then the coordinate mapping $\mathbf{x} \mapsto [\mathbf{x}]_{\mathcal{B}}$ is a one-to-one linear transformation from V onto $\mathbb{R}^n$.

Proof Take two typical vectors in V, say,

$$\mathbf{u} = c_1\mathbf{b}_1 + \cdots + c_n\mathbf{b}_n$$
$$\mathbf{w} = d_1\mathbf{b}_1 + \cdots + d_n\mathbf{b}_n$$

Then, using vector operations,

$$\mathbf{u}+\mathbf{w} = (c_1 + d_1)\mathbf{b}_1 + \cdots + (c_n + d_n)\mathbf{b}_n$$

It follows that

$$[\mathbf{u}+\mathbf{w}]_{\mathcal{B}} = \begin{bmatrix} c_1 + d_1 \\ \vdots \\ c_n + d_n \end{bmatrix} = \begin{bmatrix} c_1 \\ \vdots \\ c_n \end{bmatrix} + \begin{bmatrix} d_1 \\ \vdots \\ d_n \end{bmatrix} = [\mathbf{u}]_{\mathcal{B}} + [\mathbf{w}]_{\mathcal{B}}$$

Thus the coordinate mapping preserves addition. If r is any scalar, then

$$r\mathbf{u} = r(c_1\mathbf{b}_1 + \cdots + c_n\mathbf{b}_n) = (rc_1)\mathbf{b}_1 + \cdots + (rc_n)\mathbf{b}_n$$

So

$$[r\mathbf{u}]_{\mathcal{B}} = \begin{bmatrix} rc_1 \\ \vdots \\ rc_n \end{bmatrix} = r\begin{bmatrix} c_1 \\ \vdots \\ c_n \end{bmatrix} = r[\mathbf{u}]_{\mathcal{B}}$$

Thus the coordinate mapping also preserves scalar multiplication and hence is a linear transformation. See Exercises 23 and 24 for the verification that the coordinate mapping is one-to-one and maps V onto $\mathbb{R}^n$. ∎

The linearity of the coordinate mapping extends to linear combinations, just as in Section 2.5. If $\mathbf{u}_1, \ldots, \mathbf{u}_p$ are in V and if $c_1, \ldots, c_p$ are scalars, then

$$[c_1\mathbf{u}_1 + \cdots + c_p\mathbf{u}_p]_{\mathcal{B}} = c_1[\mathbf{u}_1]_{\mathcal{B}} + \cdots + c_p[\mathbf{u}_p]_{\mathcal{B}} \tag{5}$$

In words, (5) says that the $\mathcal{B}$-coordinate vector of a linear combination of $\mathbf{u}_1, \ldots, \mathbf{u}_p$ is the *same* linear combination of their coordinate vectors.

The coordinate mapping in Theorem 9 is an important example of an *isomorphism* from V onto $\mathbb{R}^n$. In general, a one-to-one linear transformation from a vector space V onto a vector space W is called an **isomorphism** from V onto W (*iso* from the Greek for "the same," and *morph* from the Greek for "form" or "structure"). The notation and terminology for V and W may differ, but the two spaces are indistinguishable as vector spaces. *Every vector space calculation in* V *is accurately reproduced in* W, *and vice-versa.* See Exercises 25 and 26.

EXAMPLE 5 Let $\mathcal{B}$ be the standard basis of the space $\mathbb{P}_3$ of polynomials; that is, let $\mathcal{B} = \{1, t, t^2, t^3\}$. A typical element $\mathbf{p}$ of $\mathbb{P}_3$ has the form

$$\mathbf{p}(t) = a_0 + a_1t + a_2t^2 + a_3t^3$$

Since $\mathbf{p}$ is already displayed as a linear combination of the standard basis vectors, we conclude that

$$[\mathbf{p}]_{\mathcal{B}} = \begin{bmatrix} a_0 \\ a_1 \\ a_2 \\ a_3 \end{bmatrix}$$

Thus the coordinate mapping $\mathbf{p} \mapsto [\mathbf{p}]_{\mathcal{B}}$ is an isomorphism from $\mathbb{P}_3$ onto $\mathbb{R}^4$. All vector space operations in $\mathbb{P}_3$ correspond to operations in $\mathbb{R}^4$. ∎

If we think of $\mathbb{P}_3$ and $\mathbb{R}^4$ as displays on two computer screens that are connected via the coordinate mapping, then every vector space operation in $\mathbb{P}_3$ on one screen is exactly duplicated by a corresponding vector operation in $\mathbb{R}^4$ on the other screen. The vectors on the $\mathbb{P}_3$ screen look different from those on the $\mathbb{R}^4$ screen, but they "act" as vectors in exactly the same way. See Fig. 6.

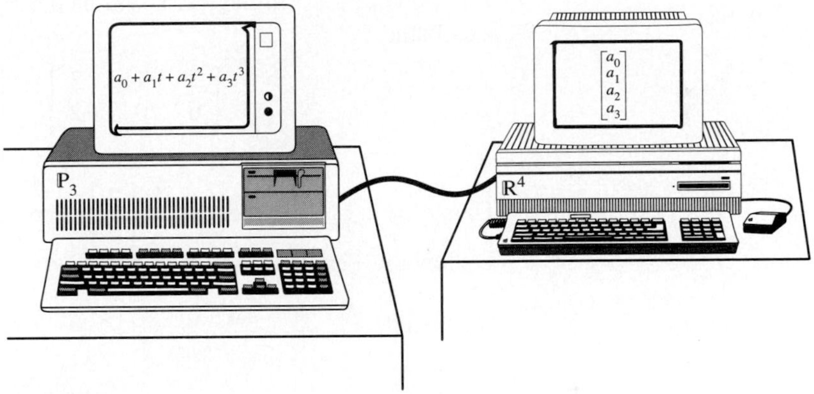

FIGURE 6 The space $\mathbb{P}_3$ is isomorphic to $\mathbb{R}^4$.

EXAMPLE 6 Use coordinate vectors to verify that the polynomials $1+2t^2$, $4+t+5t^2$, and $3+2t$ are linearly dependent in $\mathbb{P}_2$.

Solution The coordinate mapping from Example 5 produces the coordinate vectors $(1, 0, 2)$, $(4, 1, 5)$, and $(3, 2, 0)$, respectively. Writing these vectors as the *columns* of a matrix A, we can determine their independence by row reducing the augmented matrix for $A\mathbf{x} = \mathbf{0}$:

$$\begin{bmatrix} 1 & 4 & 3 & 0 \\ 0 & 1 & 2 & 0 \\ 2 & 5 & 0 & 0 \end{bmatrix} \sim \begin{bmatrix} 1 & 4 & 3 & 0 \\ 0 & 1 & 2 & 0 \\ 0 & 0 & 0 & 0 \end{bmatrix}$$

The columns of A are linearly dependent, so the corresponding polynomials are linearly dependent. In fact, it is easy to check that column 3 of A is 2 times column 2 minus 5 times column 1. The corresponding relation for the polynomials is

$$3 + 2t = 2(4 + t + 5t^2) - 5(1 + 2t^2)$$

∎

The final example concerns a plane in $\mathbb{R}^3$ that is isomorphic to $\mathbb{R}^2$.

EXAMPLE 7 Let $\mathbf{v}_1 = \begin{bmatrix} 3 \\ 6 \\ 2 \end{bmatrix}$, $\mathbf{v}_2 = \begin{bmatrix} -1 \\ 0 \\ 1 \end{bmatrix}$, $\mathbf{x} = \begin{bmatrix} 3 \\ 12 \\ 7 \end{bmatrix}$, and $\mathcal{B} = \{\mathbf{v}_1, \mathbf{v}_2\}$. Then $\mathcal{B}$ is a basis for $H = \text{Span}\{\mathbf{v}_1, \mathbf{v}_2\}$. Determine if $\mathbf{x}$ is in H, and if it is, find the coordinate vector of $\mathbf{x}$ relative to $\mathcal{B}$.

Solution If $\mathbf{x}$ is in H, then the following vector equation is consistent.

$$c_1 \begin{bmatrix} 3 \\ 6 \\ 2 \end{bmatrix} + c_2 \begin{bmatrix} -1 \\ 0 \\ 1 \end{bmatrix} = \begin{bmatrix} 3 \\ 12 \\ 7 \end{bmatrix}$$

The scalars, c_1, c_2, if they exist, will be the $\mathcal{B}$-coordinates of $\mathbf{x}$. Using row operations, we obtain

$$\begin{bmatrix} 3 & -1 & 3 \\ 6 & 0 & 12 \\ 2 & 1 & 7 \end{bmatrix} \sim \begin{bmatrix} 1 & 0 & 2 \\ 0 & 1 & 3 \\ 0 & 0 & 0 \end{bmatrix}$$

Thus $c_1 = 2$, $c_2 = 3$, and $[\mathbf{x}]_{\mathcal{B}} = \begin{bmatrix} 2 \\ 3 \end{bmatrix}$. The coordinate system on H determined by $\mathcal{B}$ is shown in Fig. 7.

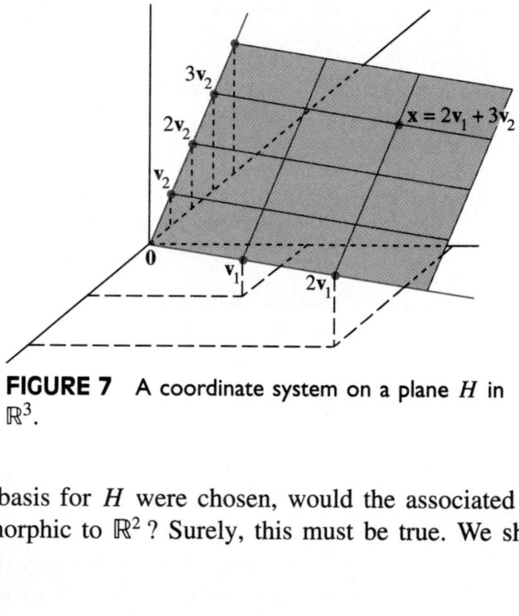

FIGURE 7 A coordinate system on a plane H in $\mathbb{R}^3$.

If a different basis for H were chosen, would the associated coordinate system also make H isomorphic to $\mathbb{R}^2$? Surely, this must be true. We shall prove it in the next section.

PRACTICE PROBLEMS

1. Let $\mathbf{b}_1 = \begin{bmatrix} 1 \\ 0 \\ 0 \end{bmatrix}$, $\mathbf{b}_2 = \begin{bmatrix} -3 \\ 4 \\ 0 \end{bmatrix}$, $\mathbf{b}_3 = \begin{bmatrix} 3 \\ -6 \\ 3 \end{bmatrix}$, and $\mathbf{x} = \begin{bmatrix} -8 \\ 2 \\ 3 \end{bmatrix}$.

a. Show that the set $\mathcal{B} = \{\mathbf{b}_1, \mathbf{b}_2, \mathbf{b}_3\}$ is a basis of $\mathbb{R}^3$.

b. Find the change-of-coordinates matrix from $\mathcal{B}$ to the standard basis.

c. Write the equation that relates $\mathbf{x}$ in $\mathbb{R}^3$ to $[\mathbf{x}]_{\mathcal{B}}$.

d. Find $[\mathbf{x}]_{\mathcal{B}}$, for the $\mathbf{x}$ given above.

2. The set $\mathcal{B} = \{1 + t,\ 1 + t^2,\ t + t^2\}$ is a basis for $\mathbb{P}_2$. Find the coordinate vector of $\mathbf{p}(t) = 6 + 3t - t^2$ relative to $\mathcal{B}$.

5.4 EXERCISES

In Exercises 1–4, find the vector $\mathbf{x}$ determined by the given coordinate vector $[\mathbf{x}]_{\mathcal{B}}$ and the given basis $\mathcal{B}$.

1. $\mathcal{B} = \left\{ \begin{bmatrix} 3 \\ -5 \end{bmatrix}, \begin{bmatrix} -4 \\ 6 \end{bmatrix} \right\}, [\mathbf{x}]_{\mathcal{B}} = \begin{bmatrix} 5 \\ 3 \end{bmatrix}$

2. $\mathcal{B} = \left\{ \begin{bmatrix} 4 \\ 5 \end{bmatrix}, \begin{bmatrix} 6 \\ 7 \end{bmatrix} \right\}, [\mathbf{x}]_{\mathcal{B}} = \begin{bmatrix} 8 \\ -5 \end{bmatrix}$

3. $\mathcal{B} = \left\{ \begin{bmatrix} 1 \\ -4 \\ 3 \end{bmatrix}, \begin{bmatrix} 5 \\ 2 \\ -2 \end{bmatrix}, \begin{bmatrix} 4 \\ -7 \\ 0 \end{bmatrix} \right\}, [\mathbf{x}]_{\mathcal{B}} = \begin{bmatrix} 3 \\ 0 \\ -1 \end{bmatrix}$

4. $\mathcal{B} = \left\{ \begin{bmatrix} -1 \\ 2 \\ 0 \end{bmatrix}, \begin{bmatrix} 3 \\ -5 \\ 2 \end{bmatrix}, \begin{bmatrix} 4 \\ -7 \\ 3 \end{bmatrix} \right\}, [\mathbf{x}]_{\mathcal{B}} = \begin{bmatrix} -4 \\ 8 \\ -7 \end{bmatrix}$

In Exercises 5–8, find the coordinate vector $[\mathbf{x}]_{\mathcal{B}}$ of $\mathbf{x}$ relative to the given basis $\mathcal{B} = \{\mathbf{b}_1, \dots, \mathbf{b}_n\}$.

5. $\mathbf{b}_1 = \begin{bmatrix} 1 \\ -3 \end{bmatrix}, \mathbf{b}_2 = \begin{bmatrix} 2 \\ -5 \end{bmatrix}, \mathbf{x} = \begin{bmatrix} -2 \\ 1 \end{bmatrix}$

6. $\mathbf{b}_1 = \begin{bmatrix} 1 \\ -2 \end{bmatrix}, \mathbf{b}_2 = \begin{bmatrix} 5 \\ -6 \end{bmatrix}, \mathbf{x} = \begin{bmatrix} 4 \\ 0 \end{bmatrix}$

7. $\mathbf{b}_1 = \begin{bmatrix} 1 \\ -1 \\ -3 \end{bmatrix}, \mathbf{b}_2 = \begin{bmatrix} -3 \\ 4 \\ 9 \end{bmatrix}, \mathbf{b}_3 = \begin{bmatrix} 2 \\ -2 \\ 4 \end{bmatrix}, \mathbf{x} = \begin{bmatrix} 8 \\ -9 \\ 6 \end{bmatrix}$

8. $\mathbf{b}_1 = \begin{bmatrix} 1 \\ 0 \\ 3 \end{bmatrix}, \mathbf{b}_2 = \begin{bmatrix} 2 \\ 1 \\ 8 \end{bmatrix}, \mathbf{b}_3 = \begin{bmatrix} 1 \\ -1 \\ 2 \end{bmatrix}, \mathbf{x} = \begin{bmatrix} 3 \\ -5 \\ 4 \end{bmatrix}$

In Exercises 9 and 10, find the change-of-coordinates matrix from $\mathcal{B}$ to the standard basis in $\mathbb{R}^n$.

9. $\mathcal{B} = \left\{ \begin{bmatrix} 2 \\ -9 \end{bmatrix}, \begin{bmatrix} 1 \\ 8 \end{bmatrix} \right\}$

10. $\mathcal{B} = \left\{ \begin{bmatrix} 3 \\ -1 \\ 4 \end{bmatrix}, \begin{bmatrix} 2 \\ 0 \\ -5 \end{bmatrix}, \begin{bmatrix} 8 \\ -2 \\ 7 \end{bmatrix} \right\}$

In Exercises 11 and 12, use an inverse matrix to find $[\mathbf{x}]_{\mathcal{B}}$ for the given $\mathbf{x}$ and $\mathcal{B}$.

11. $\mathcal{B} = \left\{ \begin{bmatrix} 3 \\ -5 \end{bmatrix}, \begin{bmatrix} -4 \\ 6 \end{bmatrix} \right\}, \mathbf{x} = \begin{bmatrix} 2 \\ -6 \end{bmatrix}$

12. $\mathcal{B} = \left\{ \begin{bmatrix} 4 \\ 5 \end{bmatrix}, \begin{bmatrix} 6 \\ 7 \end{bmatrix} \right\}, \mathbf{x} = \begin{bmatrix} 2 \\ 0 \end{bmatrix}$

13. The set $\mathcal{B} = \{1 + t^2,\ t + t^2,\ 1 + 2t + t^2\}$ is a basis for $\mathbb{P}_2$. Find the coordinate vector of $\mathbf{p}(t) = 1 + 4t + 7t^2$ relative to $\mathcal{B}$.

14. The set $\mathcal{B} = \{1 - t^2,\ t - t^2,\ 2 - 2t + t^2\}$ is a basis for $\mathbb{P}_2$. Find the coordinate vector of $\mathbf{p}(t) = 3 + t - 6t^2$ relative to $\mathcal{B}$.

Exercises 15 and 16 concern the crystal lattice for titanium, which has the hexagonal structure shown on the left in the accompanying figure. The vectors $\begin{bmatrix} 2.6 \\ -1.5 \\ 0 \end{bmatrix}, \begin{bmatrix} 0 \\ 3 \\ 0 \end{bmatrix}, \begin{bmatrix} 0 \\ 0 \\ 4.8 \end{bmatrix}$ in $\mathbb{R}^3$ form a basis for the unit cell shown on the right. The numbers here are Ångstrom units (1 Å $= 10^{-8}$cm). In alloys of titanium, some additional atoms may be in the unit cell at the "octahedral" and "tetrahedral" sites (so named because of the geometric objects formed by atoms at these locations).

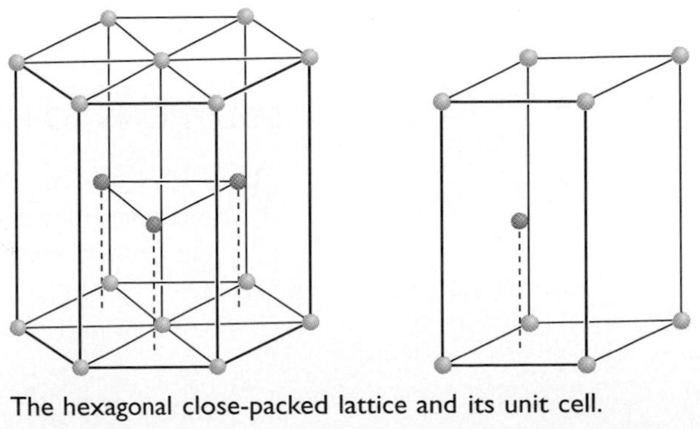

The hexagonal close-packed lattice and its unit cell.

15. One of the octahedral sites is $\begin{bmatrix} 1/2 \\ 1/4 \\ 1/6 \end{bmatrix}$, relative to the lattice basis. Determine the coordinates of this site relative to the standard basis of $\mathbb{R}^3$.

16. One of the tetrahedral sites is $\begin{bmatrix} 1/2 \\ 1/2 \\ 1/3 \end{bmatrix}$. Determine the coordinates of the site relative to the standard basis of $\mathbb{R}^3$.

17. The set $\mathbf{v}_1 = \begin{bmatrix} 1 \\ -3 \end{bmatrix}, \mathbf{v}_2 = \begin{bmatrix} 2 \\ -8 \end{bmatrix}, \mathbf{v}_3 = \begin{bmatrix} -3 \\ 7 \end{bmatrix}$ spans $\mathbb{R}^2$ but is not a basis. Find two different ways to express $\begin{bmatrix} 1 \\ 1 \end{bmatrix}$ as a linear combination of $\mathbf{v}_1, \mathbf{v}_2, \mathbf{v}_3$.

18. The set $\mathbf{v}_1 = \begin{bmatrix} 1 \\ 3 \end{bmatrix}, \mathbf{v}_2 = \begin{bmatrix} 3 \\ 8 \end{bmatrix}, \mathbf{v}_3 = \begin{bmatrix} 2 \\ 5 \end{bmatrix}$ spans $\mathbb{R}^2$ but is not a basis. Find two different ways to express $\begin{bmatrix} 1 \\ 1 \end{bmatrix}$ as a linear combination of $\mathbf{v}_1, \mathbf{v}_2, \mathbf{v}_3$.

19. Let S be a finite set in a vector space V with the property that every $\mathbf{x}$ in V has a unique representation as a linear combination of elements of S. Show that S is a basis of V.

20. Suppose that $\{\mathbf{v}_1, \dots, \mathbf{v}_4\}$ is a linearly dependent spanning set for a vector space V. Show that each $\mathbf{w}$ in V may be expressed in more than one way as a linear combination of $\mathbf{v}_1, \dots, \mathbf{v}_4$. [*Hint*: Let $\mathbf{w} = k_1\mathbf{v}_1 + \cdots + k_4\mathbf{v}_4$ be an arbitrary vector in V. Use the linear dependence of $\{\mathbf{v}_1, \dots, \mathbf{v}_4\}$ to produce another representation of $\mathbf{w}$ as a linear combination of $\mathbf{v}_1, \dots, \mathbf{v}_4$.]

21. Let $\mathcal{B} = \left\{\begin{bmatrix} 1 \\ -4 \end{bmatrix}, \begin{bmatrix} -2 \\ 9 \end{bmatrix}\right\}$. Since the coordinate mapping determined by $\mathcal{B}$ is a linear transformation from $\mathbb{R}^2$ into $\mathbb{R}^2$, this mapping must be implemented by some 2×2 matrix A. Find it. [*Hint*: Multiplication by A should transform a vector $\mathbf{x}$ into its coordinate vector $[\mathbf{x}]_{\mathcal{B}}$.]

22. Let $\mathcal{B} = \{\mathbf{b}_1, \dots, \mathbf{b}_n\}$ be a basis for $\mathbb{R}^n$. Produce a description of an $n \times n$ matrix A that implements the coordinate mapping $\mathbf{x} \mapsto [\mathbf{x}]_{\mathcal{B}}$. (See Exercise 21.)

Exercises 23–26 concern a vector space V, an ordered basis $\mathcal{B} = \{\mathbf{b}_1, \dots, \mathbf{b}_n\}$, and the coordinate mapping $\mathbf{x} \mapsto [\mathbf{x}]_{\mathcal{B}}$.

23. Show that the coordinate mapping is one-to-one. [Suppose that $[\mathbf{u}]_{\mathcal{B}} = [\mathbf{w}]_{\mathcal{B}}$ for some $\mathbf{u}$ and $\mathbf{w}$ in V, and show that $\mathbf{u} = \mathbf{w}$.]

24. Show that the coordinate mapping is **onto** $\mathbb{R}^n$. That is, given any $\mathbf{y}$ in $\mathbb{R}^n$, with entries $y_1, \dots, y_n$, produce a $\mathbf{u}$ in V such that $[\mathbf{u}]_{\mathcal{B}} = \mathbf{y}$.

25. Show that a subset $\{\mathbf{u}_1, \dots, \mathbf{u}_p\}$ in V is linearly independent if and only if the set of coordinate vectors $\{[\mathbf{u}_1]_{\mathcal{B}}, \dots, [\mathbf{u}_p]_{\mathcal{B}}\}$ is linearly independent in $\mathbb{R}^n$. *Hint*: Since the coordinate mapping is one-to-one, the following equations have the same solutions, $c_1, \dots, c_p$,

$$c_1\mathbf{u}_1 + \cdots + c_p\mathbf{u}_p = \mathbf{0} \qquad \text{The zero vector in } V$$

$$[c_1\mathbf{u}_1 + \cdots + c_p\mathbf{u}_p]_{\mathcal{B}} = [\mathbf{0}]_{\mathcal{B}} \qquad \text{The zero vector in } \mathbb{R}^n$$

26. Given vectors $\mathbf{u}_1, \dots, \mathbf{u}_p$, and $\mathbf{w}$ in V, show that $\mathbf{w}$ is a linear combination of $\mathbf{u}_1, \dots, \mathbf{u}_p$ if and only if $[\mathbf{w}]_{\mathcal{B}}$ is a linear combination of the coordinate vectors $[\mathbf{u}_1]_{\mathcal{B}}, \dots, [\mathbf{u}_p]_{\mathcal{B}}$.

In Exercises 27–30, use coordinate vectors to test the linear independence of the sets of polynomials.

27. $1 + 2t, 3 - t, -1 + 3t^2$

28. $1 - 2t^2 - 3t^3, t + t^3, 1 + 3t - 2t^2$

29. $1 + t^3, 3 + t - 2t^2, -t + 3t^2 - t^3$

30. $(1 - t)^3, (2 - 3t)^2, 3t^2 - 4t^3$

SOLUTIONS TO PRACTICE PROBLEMS

1. a. It is evident that the matrix $P_{\mathcal{B}} = [\mathbf{b}_1 \ \ \mathbf{b}_2 \ \ \mathbf{b}_3]$ is row equivalent to the identity matrix. By the Invertible Matrix Theorem, $P_{\mathcal{B}}$ is invertible and its columns form a basis for $\mathbb{R}^3$.

b. From part (a), the change-of-coordinates matrix is $P_{\mathcal{B}} = \begin{bmatrix} 1 & -3 & 3 \\ 0 & 4 & -6 \\ 0 & 0 & 3 \end{bmatrix}$.

c. $\mathbf{x} = P_{\mathcal{B}}[\mathbf{x}]_{\mathcal{B}}$

d. To solve part (c), it is probably easier to row reduce an augmented matrix instead of computing $P_{\mathcal{B}}^{-1}$. We have

$$\underset{P_{\mathcal{B}}\qquad\qquad \mathbf{x}}{\begin{bmatrix} 1 & -3 & 3 & -8 \\ 0 & 4 & -6 & 2 \\ 0 & 0 & 3 & 3 \end{bmatrix}} \sim \underset{I\qquad\qquad [x]_{\mathcal{B}}}{\begin{bmatrix} 1 & 0 & 0 & -5 \\ 0 & 1 & 0 & 2 \\ 0 & 0 & 1 & 1 \end{bmatrix}}$$

Hence

$$[\mathbf{x}]_{\mathcal{B}} = \begin{bmatrix} -5 \\ 2 \\ 1 \end{bmatrix}$$

2. The coordinates of $\mathbf{p}(t) = 6 + 3t - t^2$ with respect to $\mathcal{B}$ satisfy

$$c_1(1 + t) + c_2(1 + t^2) + c_3(t + t^2) = 6 + 3t - t^2$$

Equating coefficients of like powers of t, we have

$$\begin{aligned} c_1 + c_2 \qquad &= 6 \\ c_1 \qquad + c_3 &= 3 \\ c_2 + c_3 &= -1 \end{aligned}$$

Solving, we find that $c_1 = 5$, $c_2 = 1$, $c_3 = -2$, and $[\mathbf{p}]_{\mathcal{B}} = \begin{bmatrix} 5 \\ 1 \\ -2 \end{bmatrix}$.

5.5 THE DIMENSION OF A VECTOR SPACE

Recall that a vector space V with a basis $\mathcal{B}$ containing n vectors is isomorphic to $\mathbb{R}^n$. In this section, we show that this number n is an intrinsic property (called the dimension) of the space V that does not depend on the particular choice of basis. The discussion of dimension will give additional insight into properties of bases.

The first theorem generalizes a well-known result about the vector space $\mathbb{R}^n$.

THEOREM 10

If a vector space V has a basis $\mathcal{B} = \{\mathbf{b}_1, \ldots, \mathbf{b}_n\}$, then any set in V containing more than n vectors must be linearly dependent.

Proof Let $\{\mathbf{u}_1, \ldots, \mathbf{u}_p\}$ be a set in V with more than n vectors. The coordinate vectors $[\mathbf{u}_1]_{\mathcal{B}}, \ldots, [\mathbf{u}_p]_{\mathcal{B}}$ form a linearly dependent set in $\mathbb{R}^n$, because there are more vectors (p) than entries (n) in the vectors. So there exist scalars $c_1, \ldots, c_p$, not all zero, such that

$$c_1[\mathbf{u}_1]_{\mathcal{B}} + \cdots + c_p[\mathbf{u}_p]_{\mathcal{B}} = \begin{bmatrix} 0 \\ \vdots \\ 0 \end{bmatrix} \qquad \text{The zero vector in } \mathbb{R}^n$$

Since the coordinate mapping is a linear transformation,

$$[c_1\mathbf{u}_1 + \cdots + c_p\mathbf{u}_p]_{\mathcal{B}} = \begin{bmatrix} 0 \\ \vdots \\ 0 \end{bmatrix}$$

The zero vector on the right contains the n weights needed to build the vector $c_1\mathbf{u}_1 + \cdots + c_p\mathbf{u}_p$ from the basis vectors in $\mathcal{B}$. That is, $c_1\mathbf{u}_1 + \cdots + c_p\mathbf{u}_p = 0\cdot\mathbf{b}_1 + \cdots + 0\cdot\mathbf{b}_n = \mathbf{0}$. Since the c_i are not all zero, $\{\mathbf{u}_1, \ldots, \mathbf{u}_p\}$ is linearly dependent.[1] ∎

THEOREM 11

If a vector space V has a basis of n vectors, then every basis of V must consist of exactly n vectors.

Proof Let $\mathcal{B}_1$ be a basis of n vectors and let $\mathcal{B}_2$ be any other basis (of V). Since $\mathcal{B}_1$ is a basis and $\mathcal{B}_2$ is linearly independent, $\mathcal{B}_2$ has no more than n vectors, by Theorem 10. Also, since $\mathcal{B}_2$ is a basis and $\mathcal{B}_1$ is linearly independent, $\mathcal{B}_2$ has at least n vectors. Thus $\mathcal{B}_2$ consists of exactly n vectors. ∎

If a nonzero vector space V is spanned by a finite set S, then a subset of S is a basis for V, by the Spanning Set Theorem. In this case, Theorem 11 insures that the following definition makes sense.

DEFINITION

If V is spanned by a finite set, then V is said to be **finite-dimensional**, and the **dimension** of V, written as $\dim V$, is the number of vectors in a basis for V. The dimension of the zero vector space $\{\mathbf{0}\}$ is defined to be zero. If V is not spanned by a finite set, then V is said to be **infinite-dimensional**.

EXAMPLE 1 The standard basis for $\mathbb{R}^n$ contains n vectors, so $\dim \mathbb{R}^n = n$. The standard polynomial basis $\{1, t, t^2\}$ shows that $\dim \mathbb{P}_2 = 3$. In general, $\dim \mathbb{P}_n = n+1$. The space $\mathbb{P}$ of all polynomials is infinite-dimensional (Exercise 25). ∎

EXAMPLE 2 Let $H = \text{Span}\{\mathbf{v}_1, \mathbf{v}_2\}$, where $\mathbf{v}_1 = \begin{bmatrix} 3 \\ 6 \\ 2 \end{bmatrix}$ and $\mathbf{v}_2 = \begin{bmatrix} -1 \\ 0 \\ 1 \end{bmatrix}$. Then H is the plane studied in Example 7 of Section 5.4. A basis for H is $\{\mathbf{v}_1, \mathbf{v}_2\}$,

[1]Theorem 10 also applies to infinite sets in V. An infinite set is said to be linearly dependent if some finite subset is linearly dependent; otherwise, the set is linearly independent. If S is an infinite set in V, take any subset $\{\mathbf{u}_1, \ldots, \mathbf{u}_p\}$ of S, with $p > n$. The proof above shows that this subset is linearly dependent, and hence so is S.

since $\mathbf{v}_1$ and $\mathbf{v}_2$ are not multiples and hence are linearly independent. Thus $\dim H = 2$.

EXAMPLE 3 Find the dimension of the subspace

$$H = \left\{ \begin{bmatrix} a - 3b + 6c \\ 5a + 4d \\ b - 2c - d \\ 5d \end{bmatrix} : a, b, c, d \text{ in } \mathbb{R} \right\}$$

Solution It is easy to see that H is the set of all linear combinations of the vectors

$$\mathbf{v}_1 = \begin{bmatrix} 1 \\ 5 \\ 0 \\ 0 \end{bmatrix}, \quad \mathbf{v}_2 = \begin{bmatrix} -3 \\ 0 \\ 1 \\ 0 \end{bmatrix}, \quad \mathbf{v}_3 = \begin{bmatrix} 6 \\ 0 \\ -2 \\ 0 \end{bmatrix}, \quad \mathbf{v}_4 = \begin{bmatrix} 0 \\ 4 \\ -1 \\ 5 \end{bmatrix}$$

Clearly, $\mathbf{v}_1 \neq \mathbf{0}$, $\mathbf{v}_2$ is not a multiple of $\mathbf{v}_1$, but $\mathbf{v}_3$ is a multiple of $\mathbf{v}_2$. By the Spanning Set Theorem, we may discard $\mathbf{v}_3$ and still have a set that spans H. Finally, $\mathbf{v}_4$ is not a linear combination of $\mathbf{v}_1$ and $\mathbf{v}_2$. So $\{\mathbf{v}_1, \mathbf{v}_2, \mathbf{v}_4\}$ is linearly independent (by Theorem 5 in Section 5.3) and hence is a basis for H. Thus $\dim H = 3$.

EXAMPLE 4 The subspaces of $\mathbb{R}^3$ may be classified by dimension. See Fig. 1.

0-dimensional subspaces. Only the zero subspace.

1-dimensional subspaces. Any subspace spanned by a single nonzero vector. Such subspaces are lines through the origin.

2-dimensional subspaces. Any subspace spanned by two linearly independent vectors. Such subspaces are planes through the origin.

3-dimensional subspaces. Only $\mathbb{R}^3$ itself. Any three linearly independent vectors in $\mathbb{R}^3$ span all of $\mathbb{R}^3$, by the Invertible Matrix Theorem.

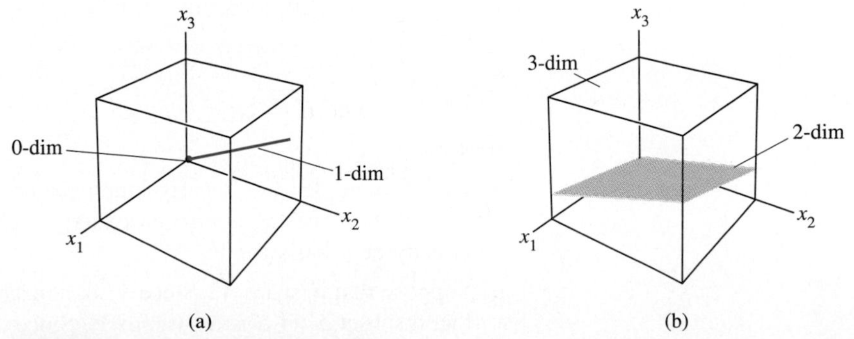

FIGURE 1 Sample subspaces of $\mathbb{R}^3$.

Subspaces of a Finite-Dimensional Space

The next theorem is a natural counterpart to the Spanning Set Theorem.

THEOREM 12

Let H be a subspace of a finite-dimensional vector space V. Any linearly independent set in H can be expanded, if necessary, to a basis for H. Also, H is finite-dimensional and

$$\dim H \leq \dim V$$

Proof If $H = \{\mathbf{0}\}$, then certainly $\dim H = 0 \leq \dim V$. Otherwise, let $S = \{\mathbf{u}_1, \ldots, \mathbf{u}_k\}$ be any linearly independent set in H. If S spans H, then S is a basis for H. Otherwise, there is some $\mathbf{u}_{k+1}$ in H that is not in Span S. But then $\{\mathbf{u}_1, \ldots, \mathbf{u}_k, \mathbf{u}_{k+1}\}$ will be linearly independent, because no vector in the set can be a linear combination of vectors that precede it (by Theorem 5).

As long as the new set does not span H, we can continue this process of expanding S to a larger linearly independent set in H. But the number of vectors in a linearly independent expansion of S can never exceed the dimension of V, by Theorem 10. So eventually the expansion of S will span H and hence will be a basis for H, and $\dim H \leq \dim V$. ∎

When the dimension of a vector space or subspace is known, the search for a basis is simplified by the next theorem. It shows that if a set has the right number of elements, then the subspace test is reduced to showing either that the set is linearly independent or that it spans the space. The theorem is of critical importance in numerous applied problems (involving differential equations or difference equations, for example) where linear independence is much easier to verify than spanning.

THEOREM 13

Let V be an n-dimensional vector space, $n \geq 1$, and let S be a subset of V that contains exactly n elements.

a. If S is linearly independent, then S is a basis for V.
b. If S spans V, then S is a basis for V.

Proof

a. By Theorem 12, the linearly independent set S may be extended to a basis for V. But that basis must contain exactly n elements, since $\dim V = n$. So S must already be a basis for V.
b. Suppose that S spans V. Since V is nonzero, the Spanning Set Theorem implies that a subset S' of S is a basis of V. Since $\dim V = n$, S' must contain n vectors. Hence $S = S'$. ∎

The Dimensions of Nul A and Col A

Since the pivot columns of a matrix A form a basis for Col A, we know the dimension of Col A as soon as we know the pivot columns. The dimension of Nul A might seem to require more work, since finding a basis for Nul A usually takes more time than a basis for Col A. But there is a shortcut!

Let A be an $m \times n$ matrix, and suppose that the equation $A\mathbf{x} = \mathbf{0}$ has k free variables. From Section 5.2, we know that the standard method of finding a spanning set for Nul A will produce exactly k linearly independent vectors—say, $\mathbf{u}_1, \ldots, \mathbf{u}_k$—one for each free variable. So $\{\mathbf{u}_1, \ldots, \mathbf{u}_k\}$ is a basis for Nul A, and the number of free variables determines the size of the basis. Let us summarize these facts for future reference.

> The dimension of Nul A is the number of free variables in the equation $A\mathbf{x} = \mathbf{0}$, and the dimension of Col A is the number of pivot columns in A.

EXAMPLE 5 Find the dimensions of the null space and column space of

$$A = \begin{bmatrix} -3 & 6 & -1 & 1 & -7 \\ 1 & -2 & 2 & 3 & -1 \\ 2 & -4 & 5 & 8 & -4 \end{bmatrix}$$

Solution Row reduce the augmented matrix $[\,A \quad \mathbf{0}\,]$ to echelon form and obtain

$$\begin{bmatrix} 1 & -2 & 2 & 3 & -1 & 0 \\ 0 & 0 & 1 & 2 & -2 & 0 \\ 0 & 0 & 0 & 0 & 0 & 0 \end{bmatrix}$$

There are three free variables—x_2, x_4, and x_5. Hence the dimension of Nul A is 3. Also, dim Col $A = 2$ because A has two pivot columns.

PRACTICE PROBLEMS

Decide whether each statement is true or false, and give a reason for each answer. Here V is a nonzero finite-dimensional vector space.

1. If dim $V = p$ and if S is a linearly dependent subset of V, then S contains more than p vectors.
2. If S spans V and if T is a subset of V that contains more vectors than S, then T is linearly dependent.

5.5 EXERCISES

For each subspace in Exercises 1–8, (a) find a basis and (b) state the dimension.

1. $\left\{ \begin{bmatrix} s - 2t \\ s + t \\ 3t \end{bmatrix} : s, t \text{ in } \mathbb{R} \right\}$

2. $\left\{ \begin{bmatrix} 4s \\ -3s \\ -t \end{bmatrix} : s, t \text{ in } \mathbb{R} \right\}$

3. $\left\{ \begin{bmatrix} 2c \\ a-b \\ b-3c \\ a+2b \end{bmatrix} : a, b, c \text{ in } \mathbb{R} \right\}$

4. $\left\{ \begin{bmatrix} a+b \\ 2a \\ 3a-b \\ -b \end{bmatrix} : a, b \text{ in } \mathbb{R} \right\}$

5. $\left\{ \begin{bmatrix} a-4b-2c \\ 2a+5b-4c \\ -a+2c \\ -3a+7b+6c \end{bmatrix} : a, b, c \text{ in } \mathbb{R} \right\}$

6. $\left\{ \begin{bmatrix} 3a+6b-c \\ 6a-2b-2c \\ -9a+5b+3c \\ -3a+b+c \end{bmatrix} : a, b, c \text{ in } \mathbb{R} \right\}$

7. $\{(a, b, c) : a - 3b + c = 0, b - 2c = 0, 2b - c = 0\}$

8. $\{(a, b, c, d) : a - 3b + c = 0\}$

9. Find the dimension of the subspace of all vectors in $\mathbb{R}^3$ whose first and third entries are equal.

10. Find the dimension of the subspace H of $\mathbb{R}^2$ spanned by $\begin{bmatrix} 2 \\ -5 \end{bmatrix}, \begin{bmatrix} -4 \\ 10 \end{bmatrix}, \begin{bmatrix} -3 \\ 6 \end{bmatrix}$.

In Exercises 11 and 12, find the dimension of the subspace spanned by the given vectors.

11. $\begin{bmatrix} 1 \\ 0 \\ 2 \end{bmatrix}, \begin{bmatrix} 3 \\ 1 \\ 1 \end{bmatrix}, \begin{bmatrix} 9 \\ 4 \\ -2 \end{bmatrix}, \begin{bmatrix} -7 \\ -3 \\ 1 \end{bmatrix}$

12. $\begin{bmatrix} 1 \\ -2 \\ 0 \end{bmatrix}, \begin{bmatrix} -3 \\ 4 \\ 1 \end{bmatrix}, \begin{bmatrix} -8 \\ 6 \\ 5 \end{bmatrix}, \begin{bmatrix} -3 \\ 0 \\ 7 \end{bmatrix}$

Determine the dimensions of Nul A and Col A for the matrices shown in Exercises 13–18.

13. $A = \begin{bmatrix} 1 & -6 & 9 & 0 & -2 \\ 0 & 1 & 2 & -4 & 5 \\ 0 & 0 & 0 & 5 & 1 \\ 0 & 0 & 0 & 0 & 0 \end{bmatrix}$

14. $A = \begin{bmatrix} 1 & 3 & -4 & 2 & -1 & 6 \\ 0 & 0 & 1 & -3 & 7 & 0 \\ 0 & 0 & 0 & 1 & 4 & -3 \\ 0 & 0 & 0 & 0 & 0 & 0 \end{bmatrix}$

15. $A = \begin{bmatrix} 1 & 0 & 9 & 5 \\ 0 & 0 & 1 & -4 \end{bmatrix}$

16. $A = \begin{bmatrix} 3 & 4 \\ -6 & 10 \end{bmatrix}$

17. $A = \begin{bmatrix} 1 & -1 & 0 \\ 0 & 4 & 7 \\ 0 & 0 & 5 \end{bmatrix}$

18. $A = \begin{bmatrix} 1 & 4 & -1 \\ 0 & 7 & 0 \\ 0 & 0 & 0 \end{bmatrix}$

19. The first four Hermite polynomials are $1, 2t, -2 + 4t^2$, and $-12t + 8t^3$. These polynomials arise naturally in the study of certain important differential equations in mathematical physics.[2] Show that the first four Hermite polynomials form a basis of $\mathbb{P}_3$.

20. The first four Laguerre polynomials are $1, 1 - t, 2 - 4t + t^2$, and $6 - 18t + 9t^2 - t^3$. Show that these polynomials form a basis of $\mathbb{P}_3$.

21. Let $\mathcal{B}$ be the basis of $\mathbb{P}_3$ consisting of the Hermite polynomials in Exercise 19, and let $\mathbf{p}(t) = 7 - 12t - 8t^2 + 12t^3$. Find the coordinate vector of $\mathbf{p}$ relative to $\mathcal{B}$.

22. Let $\mathcal{B}$ be the basis of $\mathbb{P}_2$ consisting of the first three Laguerre polynomials listed in Exercise 20, and let $\mathbf{p}(t) = 7 - 8t + 3t^2$. Find the coordinate vector of $\mathbf{p}$ relative to $\mathcal{B}$.

23. Let S be a subset of an n-dimensional vector space V, and suppose that S contains fewer than n vectors. Explain why S cannot span V.

24. Let H be an n-dimensional subspace of an n-dimensional vector space V. Show that $H = V$.

25. Explain why the space $\mathbb{P}$ of all polynomials is an infinite-dimensional space.

26. Show that the space $C(\mathbb{R})$ of all continuous functions defined on the real line is an infinite-dimensional space.

Decide whether the statements in Exercises 27–32 are true or false. Give a reason for each answer. In each case, V is a finite-dimensional vector space, and the vectors listed belong to V.

27. If there exists a set $\{\mathbf{v}_1, \dots, \mathbf{v}_p\}$ that spans V, then $\dim V \le p$.

28. If there exists a linearly dependent set $\{\mathbf{v}_1, \dots, \mathbf{v}_p\}$ in V, then $\dim V \le p$.

29. If there exists a linearly independent set $\{\mathbf{v}_1, \dots, \mathbf{v}_p\}$ in V, then $\dim V \ge p$.

30. If every set of p elements in V fails to span V, then $\dim V > p$.

31. If $\dim V = p$, then there exists a spanning set of $p + 1$ vectors in V.

[2]See *Introduction to Functional Analysis*, 2d ed., by A.E. Taylor and David C. Lay (New York: John Wiley & Sons, 1980), pp. 92–93. Other sets of polynomials are discussed there, too.

32. If $\dim V = p$, then every set of $p - 1$ vectors is linearly independent.

Exercises 33 and 34 concern finite-dimensional vector spaces V and W, and a linear transformation $T : V \to W$.

33. Let H be a subspace of V and let $T(H)$ be the set of images of vectors in H. Then $T(H)$ is a subspace of W, by Exercise 37 in Section 5.2. Prove that $\dim T(H) \leq \dim H$.

34. Let H be a subspace of V and suppose that T is a one-to-one (linear) mapping of V into W. Prove that $\dim T(H) = \dim H$. If T happens to be a one-to-one mapping of V *onto* W, then $\dim V = \dim W$. Isomorphic finite-dimensional vector spaces have the same dimension.

SOLUTIONS TO PRACTICE PROBLEMS

1. False. Consider the set $\{\mathbf{0}\}$.
2. True. By the Spanning Set Theorem, S contains a basis for V; call that basis S'. Then T will contain more vectors than S'. By Theorem 10, T is linearly dependent.

5.6 RANK

With the aid of vector space concepts, this section takes a look *inside* a matrix and reveals several interesting and useful relationships hidden in its rows and columns.

For instance, imagine placing 2000 random numbers into a 40×50 matrix A and then determining both the maximum number of linearly independent columns in A and the maximum number of linearly independent columns in A^T (rows in A). Remarkably, the two numbers are the same. As we shall soon see, their common value is the *rank* of the matrix. To explain why, we need to examine the subspace spanned by the rows of A.

The Row Space

If A is an $m \times n$ matrix, each row of A has n entries and thus may be identified with a vector in $\mathbb{R}^n$. The set of all linear combinations of the row vectors is called the **row space** of A and is denoted by Row A. Each row has n entries, so Row A is a subspace of $\mathbb{R}^n$. Since the rows of A are identified with the columns of A^T, we could also write Col A^T in place of Row A.

EXAMPLE 1 Let

$$A = \begin{bmatrix} -2 & -5 & 8 & 0 & -17 \\ 1 & 3 & -5 & 1 & 5 \\ 3 & 11 & -19 & 7 & 1 \\ 1 & 7 & -13 & 5 & -3 \end{bmatrix} \quad \text{and} \quad \begin{aligned} \mathbf{r}_1 &= (-2, -5, 8, 0, -17) \\ \mathbf{r}_2 &= (1, 3, -5, 1, 5) \\ \mathbf{r}_3 &= (3, 11, -19, 7, 1) \\ \mathbf{r}_4 &= (1, 7, -13, 5, -3) \end{aligned}$$

The row space of A is the subspace of $\mathbb{R}^5$ spanned by $\{\mathbf{r}_1, \mathbf{r}_2, \mathbf{r}_3, \mathbf{r}_4\}$. That is, Row A = Span $\{\mathbf{r}_1, \mathbf{r}_2, \mathbf{r}_3, \mathbf{r}_4\}$. It is natural to write row vectors horizontally; however, they could also be written as column vectors if that were more convenient. ∎

If we knew some linear dependence relations among the rows of the A in Example 1, we could use the Spanning Set Theorem to shrink the spanning set to a basis. Unfortunately, row operations on A will not give us that information, because row operations change the row dependence relations. But row reducing A is certainly worthwhile, as the next theorem shows!

THEOREM 14

If two matrices A and B are row equivalent, then their row spaces are the same. If B is in echelon form, the nonzero rows of B form a basis for the row space of A as well as B.

Proof If B is obtained from A by row operations, the rows of B are linear combinations of the rows of A. It follows that any linear combination of the rows of B is automatically a linear combination of the rows of A. Thus the row space of B is contained in the row space of A. Since row operations are reversible, the same argument shows that the row space of A is a subset of the row space of B. So the two row spaces are the same. If B is in echelon form, its nonzero rows are linearly independent because no nonzero row is a linear combination of the nonzero rows below it. Thus the nonzero rows of B form a basis of the (common) row space of B and A. ∎

The main result of this section involves the three spaces: Row A, Col A, and Nul A. The following example prepares the way for this result and shows how *one* sequence of row operations on A leads to bases for all three spaces.

EXAMPLE 2 Find bases for the row space, the column space, and the null space of the matrix

$$A = \begin{bmatrix} -2 & -5 & 8 & 0 & -17 \\ 1 & 3 & -5 & 1 & 5 \\ 3 & 11 & -19 & 7 & 1 \\ 1 & 7 & -13 & 5 & -3 \end{bmatrix}$$

Solution To find bases for the row space and the column space, row reduce A to an echelon form:

$$A \sim B = \begin{bmatrix} 1 & 3 & -5 & 1 & 5 \\ 0 & 1 & -2 & 2 & -7 \\ 0 & 0 & 0 & -4 & 20 \\ 0 & 0 & 0 & 0 & 0 \end{bmatrix}$$

By Theorem 14, the first three rows of B form a basis for the row space of A (as well as the row space of B). Thus

$$\text{Basis for Row } A = \{(1, 3, -5, 1, 5), (0, 1, -2, 2, -7), (0, 0, 0, -4, 20)\}$$

For the column space, observe from B that the pivots are in columns 1, 2, and 4. Hence columns 1, 2, and 4 of A (not B) form a basis for Col A:

$$\text{Basis for Col } A = \left\{ \begin{bmatrix} -2 \\ 1 \\ 3 \\ 1 \end{bmatrix}, \begin{bmatrix} -5 \\ 3 \\ 11 \\ 7 \end{bmatrix}, \begin{bmatrix} 0 \\ 1 \\ 7 \\ 5 \end{bmatrix} \right\}$$

Notice that any echelon form of A provides (in its nonzero rows) a basis for Row A and also identifies the pivot columns of A for Col A. However, for Nul A, we need the *reduced echelon form*. Further row operations on B yield

$$A \sim B \sim C = \begin{bmatrix} 1 & 0 & 1 & 0 & 1 \\ 0 & 1 & -2 & 0 & 3 \\ 0 & 0 & 0 & 1 & -5 \\ 0 & 0 & 0 & 0 & 0 \end{bmatrix}$$

The equation $A\mathbf{x} = \mathbf{0}$ is equivalent to $C\mathbf{x} = \mathbf{0}$, that is,

$$\begin{aligned} x_1 + \qquad x_3 \qquad\quad + \ x_5 &= 0 \\ x_2 - 2x_3 \qquad\quad + 3x_5 &= 0 \\ x_4 - 5x_5 &= 0 \end{aligned}$$

So $x_1 = -x_3 - x_5$, $x_2 = 2x_3 - 3x_5$, $x_4 = 5x_5$, with x_3 and x_5 free variables. The usual calculations (discussed in Section 5.2) show that

$$\text{Basis for Nul } A = \left\{ \begin{bmatrix} -1 \\ 2 \\ 1 \\ 0 \\ 0 \end{bmatrix}, \begin{bmatrix} -1 \\ -3 \\ 0 \\ 5 \\ 1 \end{bmatrix} \right\}$$

Observe that, unlike the basis for Col A, the bases for Row A and Nul A have no simple connection with the entries in A itself.[1]

∎

Warning: Although the first three rows of B in Example 2 are linearly independent, it is wrong to conclude that the first three rows of A are linearly independent. (In fact, the third row of A is 2 times the first row plus 7 times the second row.) Row operations do *not* preserve the linear dependence relations among the *rows* of a matrix.

[1]It is possible to find a basis for the row space Row A that uses rows of A. First form A^T and then row reduce until the pivot columns of A^T are found. These pivot columns of A^T are rows of A, and they form a basis for the row space of A.

The Rank Theorem

The next theorem describes fundamental relations between the dimensions of Col A, Row A, and Nul A.

DEFINITION

The **rank** of A is the dimension of the column space of A.

Since Row A is the same as Col A^T, the dimension of the row space of A is the rank of A^T. The dimension of the null space is sometimes called the **nullity** of A, though we shall not use the term.

An alert reader may have already discovered part or all of the next theorem while working the exercises in Section 5.5 or reading Example 2 above.

THEOREM 15

The Rank Theorem

The dimensions of the column space and the row space of an $m \times n$ matrix A are equal. This common dimension, the rank of A, also equals the number of pivot positions in A and satisfies the equation

$$\text{rank}\, A + \dim \text{Nul}\, A = n$$

Proof By Theorem 7 in Section 5.3, rank A is the number of pivot columns in A. Equivalently, rank A is the number of pivot positions in an echelon form B of A. Furthermore, since B has a nonzero row for each pivot, and since these rows form a basis for the row space of A, the rank of A is also the dimension of the row space.

From Section 5.5, the dimension of Nul A equals the number of free variables in the equation $A\mathbf{x} = \mathbf{0}$. Expressed another way, the dimension of Nul A is the number of columns of A that are *not* pivot columns. (It is the number of these columns, not the columns themselves, that is related to Nul A.) Obviously,

$$\left\{\begin{matrix}\text{number of}\\ \text{pivot columns}\end{matrix}\right\} + \left\{\begin{matrix}\text{number of}\\ \text{nonpivot columns}\end{matrix}\right\} = \left\{\begin{matrix}\text{number of}\\ \text{columns}\end{matrix}\right\}$$

This proves the theorem. ∎

The ideas behind Theorem 15 are visible in the calculations in Example 2. The three pivot positions in the echelon form B determine the basic variables and identify the basis vectors for Col A and those for Row A.

EXAMPLE 3

a. If A is a 7×9 matrix with a two-dimensional null space, what is the rank of A?

b. Could a 6×9 matrix have a two-dimensional null space?

Solution

a. Since A has 9 columns, $(\text{rank } A) + 2 = 9$, and hence $\text{rank } A = 7$.

b. If a 6×9 matrix, call it B, had a two-dimensional null space, it would have to have rank 7, by the Rank Theorem. But the columns of B are vectors in $\mathbb{R}^6$, and so the dimension of Col B cannot exceed 6; that is, rank B cannot exceed 6. Thus dim Nul B is at least 3, since B has 9 columns.

The next example provides a nice way to visualize the subspaces we have been studying. In Chapter 7, we will learn that Row A and Nul A have only the zero vector in common and are actually "perpendicular" to each other. The same fact will apply to Row A^T (= Col A) and Nul A^T. So the figure in Example 4 creates a good mental image for the general case. (The value of studying A^T along with A is demonstrated in Exercise 29.)

EXAMPLE 4 Let $A = \begin{bmatrix} 3 & 0 & -1 \\ 3 & 0 & -1 \\ 4 & 0 & 5 \end{bmatrix}$. It is readily checked that Nul A is the x_2-axis, Row A is the x_1x_3-plane, Col A is the plane whose equation is $x_1 - x_2 = 0$, and Nul A^T is the set of all multiples of $(1, -1, 0)$. Figure 1 shows Nul A and Row A in the domain of the linear transformation $\mathbf{x} \mapsto A\mathbf{x}$; the range of this mapping, Col A, is shown in a separate copy of $\mathbb{R}^3$, along with Nul A^T.

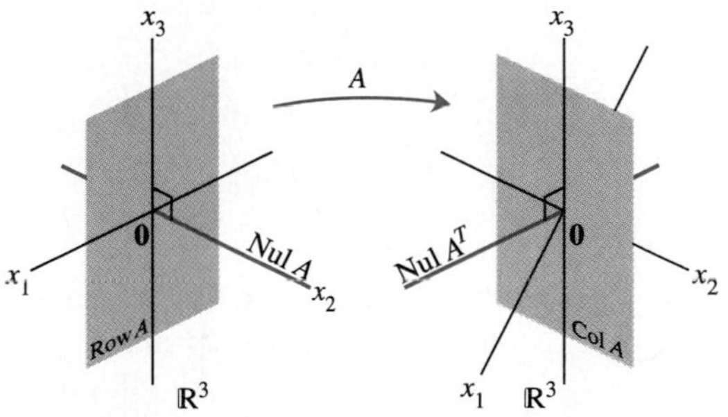

FIGURE 1 Subspaces associated with a matrix A.

Applications to Systems of Equations

The Rank Theorem is a powerful tool for processing information about systems of linear equations. The next example simulates the way a real-life problem using linear equations might be stated, without explicit mention of linear algebra terms such as matrix, subspace, and dimension.

EXAMPLE 5 A scientist has found two solutions to a homogeneous system of 40 equations in 42 variables. The two solutions are not multiples, and all other solutions can be constructed by adding together appropriate multiples of these two solutions. Can the scientist be *certain* that an associated nonhomogeneous system (with the same coefficients) has a solution?

Solution Yes. Let A be the 40×42 coefficient matrix of the system. The given information implies that the two solutions are linearly independent and span Nul A. So dim Nul $A = 2$. By the Rank Theorem, dim Col $A = 42 - 2 = 40$. Since $\mathbb{R}^{40}$ is the only subspace of $\mathbb{R}^{40}$ whose dimension is 40, Col A must be all of $\mathbb{R}^{40}$. This means that every nonhomogeneous equation $A\mathbf{x} = \mathbf{b}$ has a solution.

Rank and the Invertible Matrix Theorem

The various vector space concepts associated with a matrix provide several more statements for the Invertible Matrix Theorem. We list only the new statements here, but we reference them so they follow the statements in the original Invertible Matrix Theorem in Section 3.3.

THEOREM

The Invertible Matrix Theorem (continued)

Let A be an $n \times n$ matrix. Then the following statements are each equivalent to the statement that A is an invertible matrix:

i. The columns of A form a basis of $\mathbb{R}^n$
j. Col $A = \mathbb{R}^n$
k. dim Col $A = n$
l. rank $A = n$
m. Nul $A = \{\mathbf{0}\}$
n. dim Nul $A = 0$

Proof Statement (i) is logically equivalent to statements (d′) and (e′) regarding linear independence and spanning. The other statements above are linked into the theorem by the following chain of almost trivial implications:

$$(e) \Rightarrow (j) \Rightarrow (k) \Rightarrow (l) \Rightarrow (n) \Rightarrow (m) \Rightarrow (d)$$

Only the implication (l) $\Rightarrow$ (n) bears comment. It follows from the Rank Theorem because A is $n \times n$. Statements (d) and (e) are already known to be equivalent, so the chain is a circle of implications.

We have refrained from adding to the Invertible Matrix Theorem obvious statements about the row space of A, because the row space is the column space of A^T. Recall from (h) of the Invertible Matrix Theorem that A is invertible if and only if A^T is invertible. Hence every statement in the Invertible Matrix Theorem may also be stated for A^T. To do so would double the length of the theorem and produce a list of over 30 statements!

6. If a 6×3 matrix A has rank 3, find dim Nul A, dim Row A, and rank A^T.

7. Suppose that a 4×7 matrix A has four pivot columns. Is Col $A=\mathbb{R}^4$? Is Nul $A=\mathbb{R}^3$? Explain your answers.

8. Suppose that a 5×6 matrix A has four pivot columns. What is dim Nul A? Is Col $A=\mathbb{R}^4$? Why or why not?

9. If the null space of a 5×6 matrix A is 4-dimensional, what is the dimension of the column space of A?

10. If the null space of a 7×6 matrix A is 5-dimensional, what is the dimension of the column space of A?

11. If the null space of an 8×5 matrix A is 2-dimensional, what is the dimension of the row space of A?

12. If the null space of a 5×6 matrix A is 4-dimensional, what is the dimension of the row space of A?

13. If A is a 7×5 matrix, what is the largest possible rank of A? If A is a 5×7 matrix, what is the largest possible rank of A? Explain your answers.

14. If A is a 4×3 matrix, what is the largest possible dimension of the row space of A? If A is a 3×4 matrix, what is the largest possible dimension of the row space of A? Explain.

15. If A is a 6×8 matrix, what is the smallest possible dimension of Nul A?

16. If A is a 6×4 matrix, what is the smallest possible dimension of Nul A?

17. If A is a 5×7 matrix with all zero entries, find dim Nul A.

18. If A is a 5×7 matrix, what is the smallest possible rank of A?

19. Suppose that the solutions of a homogeneous system of five linear equations in six unknowns are all multiples of one nonzero solution. Will the system necessarily have a solution for every possible choice of constants on the right sides of the equations? Explain.

20. Suppose that a nonhomogeneous system of six linear equations in eight unknowns has a solution, with two free variables. Is it possible to change some constants on the equations' right sides to make the new system inconsistent? Explain.

21. Suppose a nonhomogeneous system of nine linear equations in ten unknowns has a solution for all possible constants on the right sides of the equations. Is it possible to find two nonzero solutions of the associated homogeneous system that are *not* multiples of each other? Discuss.

22. Is it possible that all solutions of a homogeneous system of ten linear equations in twelve variables are multiples of one fixed nonzero solution? Discuss.

23. A homogeneous system of twelve linear equations in eight unknowns has two fixed solutions that are not multiples of each other, and all other solutions are linear combinations of these two solutions. Can the set of all solutions be described with fewer than twelve homogeneous linear equations? If so, how many? Discuss.

24. Is it possible for a nonhomogeneous system of seven equations in six unknowns to have a unique solution for some right-hand side of constants? Is it possible for such a system to have a unique solution for every right-hand side? Explain.

25. A scientist solves a nonhomogeneous system of ten linear equations in twelve unknowns and finds that the general solution involves three free parameters. Can the scientist be certain that, if the right sides of the equations are changed, the new nonhomogeneous system will have a solution? Discuss.

26. In statistical theory, a common requirement is that a matrix be of *full rank*. That is, the rank should be as large as possible. Explain why an $m\times n$ matrix with more rows than columns has full rank if and only if its columns are linearly independent.

Exercises 27–29 concern an $m\times n$ matrix A and what are often called the *fundamental subspaces* determined by A.

27. Which of the subspaces Row A, Col A, Nul A, Row A^T, Col A^T, and Nul A^T are in $\mathbb{R}^m$ and which are in $\mathbb{R}^n$? How many distinct subspaces are in this list?

28. Justify the following equalities:

a. dim Row A + dim Nul $A = n$ Number of columns of A

b. dim Col A + dim Nul $A^T = m$ Number of rows of A

29. Use Exercise 28 to explain why the equation $A\mathbf{x}=\mathbf{b}$ has a solution for all b in $\mathbb{R}^m$ if and only if the equation $A^T\mathbf{x}=\mathbf{0}$ has only the trivial solution.

30. Suppose A is $m\times n$ and $\mathbf{b}$ is in $\mathbb{R}^m$. What has to be true about the two numbers rank $[\,A \quad \mathbf{b}\,]$ and rank A for the equation $A\mathbf{x}=\mathbf{b}$ to be consistent?

Rank 1 matrices are important in some computer algorithms and several theoretical contexts, including the singular value decomposition in Chapter 8. It can be shown that an $m\times n$ matrix A has rank 1 if and only if it is an outer product; that is, $A=\mathbf{u}\mathbf{v}^T$ for some $\mathbf{u}$ in $\mathbb{R}^m$ and $\mathbf{v}$ in $\mathbb{R}^n$. Exercises 31–33 suggest why this property is true.

31. Verify that rank $\mathbf{u}\mathbf{v}^T=1$ if $\mathbf{u}=\begin{bmatrix}2\\-3\\5\end{bmatrix}$ and $\mathbf{v}=\begin{bmatrix}a\\b\\c\end{bmatrix}$.

32. Let $\mathbf{u}=\begin{bmatrix}1\\2\end{bmatrix}$. Find $\mathbf{v}$ in $\mathbb{R}^3$ such that $\begin{bmatrix}1&-3&4\\2&-6&8\end{bmatrix}=\mathbf{u}\mathbf{v}^T$.

Numerical Note

Unless exact arithmetic is performed on a matrix whose entries are specified exactly, row operations can change the apparent rank of a matrix. For instance, if the value of x in the matrix $\begin{bmatrix} 5 & 7 \\ 5 & x \end{bmatrix}$ is not stored exactly as 7 in a computer, then the rank may be 1 or 2, depending on whether the computer treats $x - 7$ as zero.

In practical applications, the effective rank of a matrix A is often determined from the singular value decomposition of A, to be discussed in Section 8.4.

PRACTICE PROBLEMS

The matrices below are row equivalent.

$$A = \begin{bmatrix} 2 & -1 & 1 & -6 & 8 \\ 1 & -2 & -4 & 3 & -2 \\ -7 & 8 & 10 & 3 & -10 \\ 4 & -5 & -7 & 0 & 4 \end{bmatrix}, \quad B = \begin{bmatrix} 1 & -2 & -4 & 3 & -2 \\ 0 & 3 & 9 & -12 & 12 \\ 0 & 0 & 0 & 0 & 0 \\ 0 & 0 & 0 & 0 & 0 \end{bmatrix}$$

1. Find rank A and dim Nul A.
2. Find bases for Col A and Row A.
3. What is the next step to perform if one wants to find a basis for Nul A?
4. How many pivot columns are in a row echelon form of A^T?

5.6 EXERCISES

In Exercises 1–4, assume that the matrix A is row equivalent to B. Without calculations, list rank A and dim Nul A. Then find bases for Col A, Row A, and Nul A.

1. $A = \begin{bmatrix} 1 & -4 & 9 & -7 \\ -1 & 2 & -4 & 1 \\ 5 & -6 & 10 & 7 \end{bmatrix}, B = \begin{bmatrix} 1 & 0 & -1 & 5 \\ 0 & -2 & 5 & 6 \\ 0 & 0 & 0 & 0 \end{bmatrix}$

2. $A = \begin{bmatrix} 1 & -3 & 4 & -1 & 9 \\ -2 & 6 & -6 & -1 & -10 \\ -3 & 9 & -6 & -6 & -3 \\ 3 & -9 & 4 & 9 & 0 \end{bmatrix},$

$B = \begin{bmatrix} 1 & -3 & 0 & 5 & -7 \\ 0 & 0 & 2 & -3 & 8 \\ 0 & 0 & 0 & 0 & 5 \\ 0 & 0 & 0 & 0 & 0 \end{bmatrix}$

3. $A = \begin{bmatrix} 2 & -3 & 6 & 2 & 5 \\ -2 & 3 & -3 & -3 & -4 \\ 4 & -6 & 9 & 5 & 9 \\ -2 & 3 & 3 & -4 & 1 \end{bmatrix},$

$B = \begin{bmatrix} 2 & -3 & 6 & 2 & 5 \\ 0 & 0 & 3 & -1 & 1 \\ 0 & 0 & 0 & 1 & 3 \\ 0 & 0 & 0 & 0 & 0 \end{bmatrix}$

4. $A = \begin{bmatrix} 1 & 1 & -3 & 7 & 9 & -9 \\ 1 & 2 & -4 & 10 & 13 & -12 \\ 1 & -1 & -1 & 1 & 1 & -3 \\ 1 & -3 & 1 & -5 & -7 & 3 \\ 1 & -2 & 0 & 0 & -5 & -4 \end{bmatrix},$

$B = \begin{bmatrix} 1 & 1 & -3 & 7 & 9 & -9 \\ 0 & 1 & -1 & 3 & 4 & -3 \\ 0 & 0 & 0 & 1 & -1 & -2 \\ 0 & 0 & 0 & 0 & 0 & 0 \\ 0 & 0 & 0 & 0 & 0 & 0 \end{bmatrix}$

5. If a 3×8 matrix A has rank 3, find dim Nul A, dim Row A, and rank A^T.

33. Let A be any 2×3 matrix such that rank $A = 1$, let $\mathbf{u}$ be the first column of A, and suppose that $\mathbf{u} \neq \mathbf{0}$. Explain why there is a vector $\mathbf{v}$ in $\mathbb{R}^3$ such that $A = \mathbf{u}\mathbf{v}^T$. How could this construction be modified if the first column of A were zero?

34. Let A be an $m \times n$ matrix of rank r, and let U be an echelon form of A. Explain why there exists an invertible matrix E such that $A = EU$, and use this factorization to write A as the sum of r rank 1 matrices. [*Hint*: See Theorem 10 in Section 3.4.]

SOLUTIONS TO PRACTICE PROBLEMS

1. A has two pivot columns, so rank $A = 2$. Since A has 5 columns altogether, $\dim \text{Nul } A = 5 - 2 = 3$.

2. The pivot columns of A are the first two columns. So a basis for Col A is

$$\{\mathbf{a}_1, \mathbf{a}_2\} = \left\{ \begin{bmatrix} 2 \\ 1 \\ -7 \\ 4 \end{bmatrix}, \begin{bmatrix} -1 \\ -2 \\ 8 \\ -5 \end{bmatrix} \right\}$$

The nonzero rows of B form a basis for Row A, namely, $\{(1, -2, -4, 3, -2), (0, 3, 9, -12, 12)\}$. In this particular example, it happens that any two rows of A form a basis for the row space, because the row space is 2-dimensional and none of the rows of A is a multiple of another row. In general, the nonzero rows of an echelon form of A should be used as a basis for Row A, not the rows of A itself.

3. For Nul A, the next step is to perform row operations on B to obtain the reduced echelon form of A.

4. Rank A^T = rank A, by the Rank Theorem, because Col A^T = Row A. So A^T has two pivot positions.

5.7 CHANGE OF BASIS

When a basis $\mathcal{B}$ is chosen for an n-dimensional vector space V, the associated coordinate mapping onto $\mathbb{R}^n$ provides a coordinate system for V. Each $\mathbf{x}$ in V is identified uniquely by its $\mathcal{B}$-coordinate vector $[\mathbf{x}]_{\mathcal{B}}$.[1]

In some applications, a problem is described initially using a basis $\mathcal{B}$, but the problem's solution is aided by changing $\mathcal{B}$ to a new basis $\mathcal{C}$. (Examples will be given in Chapters 6 and 8.) Each vector is assigned a new $\mathcal{C}$-coordinate vector. In this section, we study how $[\mathbf{x}]_{\mathcal{C}}$ and $[\mathbf{x}]_{\mathcal{B}}$ are related for each $\mathbf{x}$ in V.

To visualize the problem, consider the two coordinate systems in Fig. 1. In Fig. 1(a), $\mathbf{x} = 3\mathbf{b}_1 + \mathbf{b}_2$, while in Fig. 1(b), the same $\mathbf{x}$ is shown as $\mathbf{x} = 6\mathbf{c}_1 + 4\mathbf{c}_2$. That is,

$$[\mathbf{x}]_{\mathcal{B}} = \begin{bmatrix} 3 \\ 1 \end{bmatrix} \quad \text{and} \quad [\mathbf{x}]_{\mathcal{C}} = \begin{bmatrix} 6 \\ 4 \end{bmatrix}$$

[1] Think of $[\mathbf{x}]_{\mathcal{B}}$ as a "name" for $\mathbf{x}$ that lists the weights used to build $\mathbf{x}$ as a linear combination of the basis vectors in $\mathcal{B}$.

Our problem is to find the connection between the two coordinate vectors. Example 1 shows how to do this, provided we know how $\mathbf{b}_1$ and $\mathbf{b}_2$ are formed from $\mathbf{c}_1$ and $\mathbf{c}_2$.

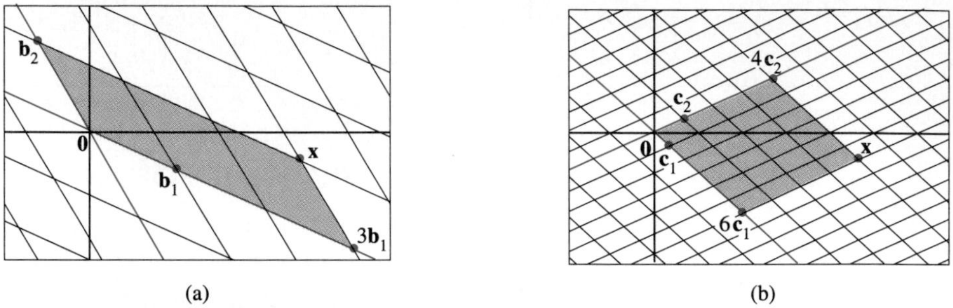

FIGURE 1 Two coordinate systems for the same vector space.

EXAMPLE 1 Consider two bases $\mathcal{B} = \{\mathbf{b}_1, \mathbf{b}_2\}$ and $\mathcal{C} = \{\mathbf{c}_1, \mathbf{c}_2\}$ for a vector space V, such that

$$\mathbf{b}_1 = 4\mathbf{c}_1 + \mathbf{c}_2 \quad \text{and} \quad \mathbf{b}_2 = -6\mathbf{c}_1 + \mathbf{c}_2 \tag{1}$$

Suppose that

$$\mathbf{x} = 3\mathbf{b}_1 + \mathbf{b}_2 \tag{2}$$

That is, suppose that $[\mathbf{x}]_{\mathcal{B}} = \begin{bmatrix} 3 \\ 1 \end{bmatrix}$. Find $[\mathbf{x}]_{\mathcal{C}}$.

Solution Apply the coordinate mapping determined by $\mathcal{C}$ to $\mathbf{x}$ in (2). Since the coordinate mapping is a linear transformation,

$$\begin{aligned} [\mathbf{x}]_{\mathcal{C}} &= [3\mathbf{b}_1 + \mathbf{b}_2]_{\mathcal{C}} \\ &= 3[\mathbf{b}_1]_{\mathcal{C}} + [\mathbf{b}_2]_{\mathcal{C}} \end{aligned}$$

We can write this vector equation as a matrix equation, using the vectors in the linear combination as the columns of a matrix:

$$[\mathbf{x}]_{\mathcal{C}} = \begin{bmatrix} [\mathbf{b}_1]_{\mathcal{C}} & [\mathbf{b}_2]_{\mathcal{C}} \end{bmatrix} \begin{bmatrix} 3 \\ 1 \end{bmatrix} \tag{3}$$

This formula gives $[\mathbf{x}]_{\mathcal{C}}$, once we know the columns of the matrix. From (1),

$$[\mathbf{b}_1]_{\mathcal{C}} = \begin{bmatrix} 4 \\ 1 \end{bmatrix} \quad \text{and} \quad [\mathbf{b}_2]_{\mathcal{C}} = \begin{bmatrix} -6 \\ 1 \end{bmatrix}$$

Thus (3) provides the solution:

$$[\mathbf{x}]_{\mathcal{C}} = \begin{bmatrix} 4 & -6 \\ 1 & 1 \end{bmatrix} \begin{bmatrix} 3 \\ 1 \end{bmatrix} = \begin{bmatrix} 6 \\ 4 \end{bmatrix}$$

The $\mathcal{C}$-coordinates of $\mathbf{x}$ match those of the $\mathbf{x}$ in Fig. 1.

The argument used to derive formula (3) is easily generalized to yield the following result. See Exercise 13.

THEOREM 16

Let $\mathcal{B} = \{\mathbf{b}_1, \ldots, \mathbf{b}_n\}$ and $\mathcal{C} = \{\mathbf{c}_1, \ldots, \mathbf{c}_n\}$ be bases of a vector space V. Then there is an $n \times n$ matrix $\underset{\mathcal{C}\leftarrow\mathcal{B}}{P}$ such that

$$[\mathbf{x}]_{\mathcal{C}} = \underset{\mathcal{C}\leftarrow\mathcal{B}}{P}[\mathbf{x}]_{\mathcal{B}} \tag{4}$$

The columns of $\underset{\mathcal{C}\leftarrow\mathcal{B}}{P}$ are the $\mathcal{C}$-coordinate vectors of the vectors in the basis $\mathcal{B}$. That is,

$$\underset{\mathcal{C}\leftarrow\mathcal{B}}{P} = \begin{bmatrix} [\mathbf{b}_1]_{\mathcal{C}} & [\mathbf{b}_2]_{\mathcal{C}} & \cdots & [\mathbf{b}_n]_{\mathcal{C}} \end{bmatrix}$$

The matrix $\underset{\mathcal{C}\leftarrow\mathcal{B}}{P}$ in Theorem 16 is called the **change-of-coordinates matrix from $\mathcal{B}$ to $\mathcal{C}$**. Multiplication by $\underset{\mathcal{C}\leftarrow\mathcal{B}}{P}$ converts $\mathcal{B}$-coordinates into $\mathcal{C}$-coordinates.[2] Figure 2 illustrates the change-of-coordinates equation (4).

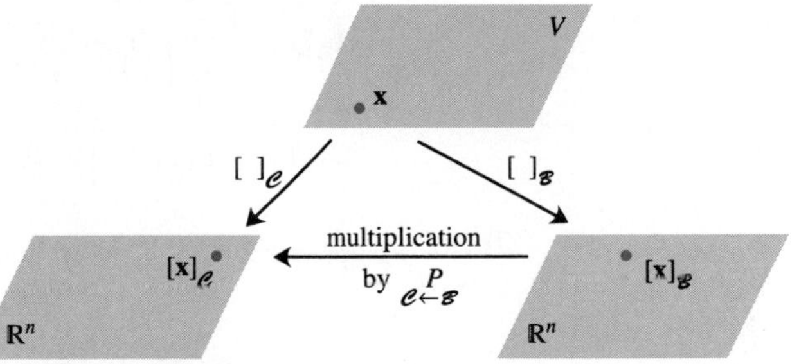

FIGURE 2 Two coordinate systems for V.

The columns of $\underset{\mathcal{C}\leftarrow\mathcal{B}}{P}$ are linearly independent because they are the coordinate vectors of the linearly independent set $\mathcal{B}$. (See Exercise 25 in Section 5.4.) It follows that $\underset{\mathcal{C}\leftarrow\mathcal{B}}{P}$ is invertible. Left-multiplying both sides of (4) by $(\underset{\mathcal{C}\leftarrow\mathcal{B}}{P})^{-1}$, we obtain

$$(\underset{\mathcal{C}\leftarrow\mathcal{B}}{P})^{-1}[\mathbf{x}]_{\mathcal{C}} = [\mathbf{x}]_{\mathcal{B}}$$

Thus $(\underset{\mathcal{C}\leftarrow\mathcal{B}}{P})^{-1}$ is the matrix that converts $\mathcal{C}$-coordinates into $\mathcal{B}$-coordinates. That is,

$$(\underset{\mathcal{C}\leftarrow\mathcal{B}}{P})^{-1} = \underset{\mathcal{B}\leftarrow\mathcal{C}}{P} \tag{5}$$

[2]To remember how to construct the matrix, think of $\underset{\mathcal{C}\leftarrow\mathcal{B}}{P}[\mathbf{x}]_{\mathcal{B}}$ as a linear combination of the columns of $\underset{\mathcal{C}\leftarrow\mathcal{B}}{P}$. The matrix-vector product is a $\mathcal{C}$-coordinate vector, so the columns of $\underset{\mathcal{C}\leftarrow\mathcal{B}}{P}$ should be $\mathcal{C}$-coordinate vectors, too.

Change of Basis in $\mathbb{R}^n$

If $\mathcal{B} = \{\mathbf{b}_1, \dots, \mathbf{b}_n\}$ and $\mathcal{E}$ is the *standard basis* $\{\mathbf{e}_1, \dots, \mathbf{e}_n\}$ in $\mathbb{R}^n$, then $[\mathbf{b}_1]_{\mathcal{E}} = \mathbf{b}_1$, and likewise for the other vectors in $\mathcal{B}$. In this case, $\underset{\mathcal{E}\leftarrow\mathcal{B}}{P}$ is the same as the change-of-coordinates matrix $P_{\mathcal{B}}$ introduced in Section 5.4, namely,

$$P_{\mathcal{B}} = [\,\mathbf{b}_1 \quad \mathbf{b}_2 \quad \cdots \quad \mathbf{b}_n\,]$$

To change coordinates between two nonstandard bases in $\mathbb{R}^n$, we need Theorem 16. The theorem shows that to solve the change-of-basis problem, we need the coordinate vectors of the old basis relative to the new basis.

EXAMPLE 2 Let $\mathbf{b}_1 = \begin{bmatrix} -9 \\ 1 \end{bmatrix}$, $\mathbf{b}_2 = \begin{bmatrix} -5 \\ -1 \end{bmatrix}$, $\mathbf{c}_1 = \begin{bmatrix} 1 \\ -4 \end{bmatrix}$, $\mathbf{c}_2 = \begin{bmatrix} 3 \\ -5 \end{bmatrix}$, and consider the bases for $\mathbb{R}^2$ given by $\mathcal{B} = \{\mathbf{b}_1, \mathbf{b}_2\}$ and $\mathcal{C} = \{\mathbf{c}_1, \mathbf{c}_2\}$. Find the change-of-coordinates matrix from $\mathcal{B}$ to $\mathcal{C}$.

Solution The matrix $\underset{\mathcal{C}\leftarrow\mathcal{B}}{P}$ involves the $\mathcal{C}$-coordinate vectors of $\mathbf{b}_1$ and $\mathbf{b}_2$. Let $[\mathbf{b}_1]_{\mathcal{C}} = \begin{bmatrix} x_1 \\ x_2 \end{bmatrix}$ and $[\mathbf{b}_2]_{\mathcal{C}} = \begin{bmatrix} y_1 \\ y_2 \end{bmatrix}$. Then, by definition,

$$[\,\mathbf{c}_1 \quad \mathbf{c}_2\,]\begin{bmatrix} x_1 \\ x_2 \end{bmatrix} = \mathbf{b}_1 \qquad \text{and} \qquad [\,\mathbf{c}_1 \quad \mathbf{c}_2\,]\begin{bmatrix} y_1 \\ y_2 \end{bmatrix} = \mathbf{b}_2$$

To solve both systems simultaneously, augment the coefficient matrix with $\mathbf{b}_1$ *and* $\mathbf{b}_2$, and row reduce:

$$[\,\mathbf{c}_1 \quad \mathbf{c}_2 \mid \mathbf{b}_1 \quad \mathbf{b}_2\,] = \left[\begin{array}{rr|rr} 1 & 3 & -9 & -5 \\ -4 & -5 & 1 & -1 \end{array}\right] \sim \left[\begin{array}{rr|rr} 1 & 0 & 6 & 4 \\ 0 & 1 & -5 & -3 \end{array}\right] \tag{6}$$

Thus

$$[\mathbf{b}_1]_{\mathcal{C}} = \begin{bmatrix} 6 \\ -5 \end{bmatrix} \qquad \text{and} \qquad [\mathbf{b}_2]_{\mathcal{C}} = \begin{bmatrix} 4 \\ -3 \end{bmatrix}$$

The desired change-of-coordinates matrix is therefore

$$\underset{\mathcal{C}\leftarrow\mathcal{B}}{P} = [\,[\mathbf{b}_1]_{\mathcal{C}} \quad [\mathbf{b}_2]_{\mathcal{C}}\,] = \begin{bmatrix} 6 & 4 \\ -5 & -3 \end{bmatrix}$$

Observe that the matrix $\underset{\mathcal{C}\leftarrow\mathcal{B}}{P}$ in Example 2 already appeared in (6). This is not surprising because the first column of $\underset{\mathcal{C}\leftarrow\mathcal{B}}{P}$ results from row reducing $[\,\mathbf{c}_1 \quad \mathbf{c}_2 \mid \mathbf{b}_1\,]$ to $[\,I \mid [\mathbf{b}_1]_{\mathcal{C}}\,]$, and similarly for the second column of $\underset{\mathcal{C}\leftarrow\mathcal{B}}{P}$. Thus

$$\boxed{[\,\mathbf{c}_1 \quad \mathbf{c}_2 \mid \mathbf{b}_1 \quad \mathbf{b}_2\,] \sim [\,I \mid \underset{\mathcal{C}\leftarrow\mathcal{B}}{P}\,]}$$

An analogous procedure works for finding the change-of-coordinates matrix between any two bases in $\mathbb{R}^n$.

EXAMPLE 3 Let $\mathbf{b}_1 = \begin{bmatrix} 1 \\ -3 \end{bmatrix}$, $\mathbf{b}_2 = \begin{bmatrix} -2 \\ 4 \end{bmatrix}$, $\mathbf{c}_1 = \begin{bmatrix} -7 \\ 9 \end{bmatrix}$, $\mathbf{c}_2 = \begin{bmatrix} -5 \\ 7 \end{bmatrix}$, and consider the bases for $\mathbb{R}^2$ given by $\mathcal{B} = \{\mathbf{b}_1, \mathbf{b}_2\}$ and $\mathcal{C} = \{\mathbf{c}_1, \mathbf{c}_2\}$.

a. Find the change-of-coordinates matrix from $\mathcal{C}$ to $\mathcal{B}$.

b. Find the change-of-coordinates matrix from $\mathcal{B}$ to $\mathcal{C}$.

Solution

a. Notice that $\underset{\mathcal{B}\leftarrow\mathcal{C}}{P}$ is needed rather than $\underset{\mathcal{C}\leftarrow\mathcal{B}}{P}$, and compute

$$[\,\mathbf{b}_1 \quad \mathbf{b}_2 \;\vdots\; \mathbf{c}_1 \quad \mathbf{c}_2\,] = \left[\begin{array}{rr:rr} 1 & -2 & -7 & -5 \\ -3 & 4 & 9 & 7 \end{array}\right] \sim \left[\begin{array}{rr:rr} 1 & 0 & 5 & 3 \\ 0 & 1 & 6 & 4 \end{array}\right]$$

So

$$\underset{\mathcal{B}\leftarrow\mathcal{C}}{P} = \begin{bmatrix} 5 & 3 \\ 6 & 4 \end{bmatrix}$$

b. By part (a) and property (5) above (with $\mathcal{B}$ and $\mathcal{C}$ interchanged),

$$\underset{\mathcal{C}\leftarrow\mathcal{B}}{P} = (\underset{\mathcal{B}\leftarrow\mathcal{C}}{P})^{-1} = \frac{1}{2}\begin{bmatrix} 4 & -3 \\ -6 & 5 \end{bmatrix} = \begin{bmatrix} 2 & -3/2 \\ -3 & 5/2 \end{bmatrix}$$

PRACTICE PROBLEMS

1. Let $\mathcal{F} = \{\mathbf{f}_1, \mathbf{f}_2\}$ and $\mathcal{G} = \{\mathbf{g}_1, \mathbf{g}_2\}$ be bases for a vector space V, and let P be a matrix whose columns are $[\mathbf{f}_1]_{\mathcal{G}}$ and $[\mathbf{f}_2]_{\mathcal{G}}$. Which of the following equations is satisfied by P for all $\mathbf{v}$ in V?

   (i) $[\mathbf{v}]_{\mathcal{F}} = P[\mathbf{v}]_{\mathcal{G}}$ (ii) $[\mathbf{v}]_{\mathcal{G}} = P[\mathbf{v}]_{\mathcal{F}}$

2. Let $\mathcal{B}$ and $\mathcal{C}$ be as in Example 1. Use the results of that example to find the change-of-coordinates matrix from $\mathcal{C}$ to $\mathcal{B}$.

5.7 EXERCISES

1. Let $\mathcal{B} = \{\mathbf{b}_1, \mathbf{b}_2\}$ and $\mathcal{C} = \{\mathbf{c}_1, \mathbf{c}_2\}$ be bases for a vector space V, and suppose that $\mathbf{b}_1 = 6\mathbf{c}_1 - 2\mathbf{c}_2$ and $\mathbf{b}_2 = 9\mathbf{c}_1 - 4\mathbf{c}_2$.
   a. Find the change-of-coordinates matrix from $\mathcal{B}$ to $\mathcal{C}$.
   b. Find $[\mathbf{x}]_{\mathcal{C}}$ for $\mathbf{x} = -3\mathbf{b}_1 + 2\mathbf{b}_2$. Use part (a).

2. Let $\mathcal{B} = \{\mathbf{b}_1, \mathbf{b}_2\}$ and $\mathcal{C} = \{\mathbf{c}_1, \mathbf{c}_2\}$ be bases for a vector space V, and suppose that $\mathbf{b}_1 = -\mathbf{c}_1 + 4\mathbf{c}_2$ and $\mathbf{b}_2 = 5\mathbf{c}_1 - 3\mathbf{c}_2$.
   a. Find the change-of-coordinates matrix from $\mathcal{B}$ to $\mathcal{C}$.
   b. Find $[\mathbf{x}]_{\mathcal{C}}$ for $\mathbf{x} = 5\mathbf{b}_1 + 3\mathbf{b}_2$.

3. Let $\mathcal{U} = \{\mathbf{u}_1, \mathbf{u}_2\}$ and $\mathcal{W} = \{\mathbf{w}_1, \mathbf{w}_2\}$ be bases for V, and let P be a matrix whose columns are $[\mathbf{u}_1]_{\mathcal{W}}$ and $[\mathbf{u}_2]_{\mathcal{W}}$. Which

of the following equations is satisfied by P for all $\mathbf{x}$ in V?

(i) $[\mathbf{x}]_{\mathcal{U}} = P[\mathbf{x}]_{\mathcal{W}}$ (ii) $[\mathbf{x}]_{\mathcal{W}} = P[\mathbf{x}]_{\mathcal{U}}$

4. Let $\mathcal{A} = \{\mathbf{a}_1, \mathbf{a}_2, \mathbf{a}_3\}$ and $\mathcal{D} = \{\mathbf{d}_1, \mathbf{d}_2, \mathbf{d}_3\}$ be bases for V, and let $P = \begin{bmatrix} [\mathbf{d}_1]_{\mathcal{A}} & [\mathbf{d}_2]_{\mathcal{A}} & [\mathbf{d}_3]_{\mathcal{A}} \end{bmatrix}$. Which of the following equations is satisfied by P for all $\mathbf{x}$ in V?

(i) $[\mathbf{x}]_{\mathcal{A}} = P[\mathbf{x}]_{\mathcal{D}}$ (ii) $[\mathbf{x}]_{\mathcal{D}} = P[\mathbf{x}]_{\mathcal{A}}$

5. Let $\mathcal{A} = \{\mathbf{a}_1, \mathbf{a}_2, \mathbf{a}_3\}$ and $\mathcal{B} = \{\mathbf{b}_1, \mathbf{b}_2, \mathbf{b}_3\}$ be bases for a vector space V, and suppose that $\mathbf{a}_1 = 4\mathbf{b}_1 - \mathbf{b}_2$, $\mathbf{a}_2 = -\mathbf{b}_1 + \mathbf{b}_2 + \mathbf{b}_3$, and $\mathbf{a}_3 = \mathbf{b}_2 - 2\mathbf{b}_3$.

a. Find the change-of-coordinates matrix from $\mathcal{A}$ to $\mathcal{B}$.

b. Find $[\mathbf{x}]_{\mathcal{B}}$ for $\mathbf{x} = 3\mathbf{a}_1 + 4\mathbf{a}_2 + \mathbf{a}_3$.

6. Let $\mathcal{D} = \{\mathbf{d}_1, \mathbf{d}_2, \mathbf{d}_3\}$ and $\mathcal{F} = \{\mathbf{f}_1, \mathbf{f}_2, \mathbf{f}_3\}$ be bases for a vector space V, and suppose that $\mathbf{f}_1 = 2\mathbf{d}_1 - \mathbf{d}_2 + \mathbf{d}_3$, $\mathbf{f}_2 = 3\mathbf{d}_2 + \mathbf{d}_3$, and $\mathbf{f}_3 = -3\mathbf{d}_1 + 2\mathbf{d}_3$.

a. Find the change-of-coordinates matrix from $\mathcal{F}$ to $\mathcal{D}$.

b. Find $[\mathbf{x}]_{\mathcal{D}}$ for $\mathbf{x} = \mathbf{f}_1 - 2\mathbf{f}_2 + 2\mathbf{f}_3$.

In Exercises 7–10, let $\mathcal{B} = \{\mathbf{b}_1, \mathbf{b}_2\}$ and $\mathcal{C} = \{\mathbf{c}_1, \mathbf{c}_2\}$ be bases for $\mathbb{R}^2$. In each exercise, find the change-of-coordinates matrix from $\mathcal{B}$ to $\mathcal{C}$, and the change-of-coordinates matrix from $\mathcal{C}$ to $\mathcal{B}$.

7. $\mathbf{b}_1 = \begin{bmatrix} 7 \\ 5 \end{bmatrix}, \mathbf{b}_2 = \begin{bmatrix} -3 \\ -1 \end{bmatrix}, \mathbf{c}_1 = \begin{bmatrix} 1 \\ -5 \end{bmatrix}, \mathbf{c}_2 = \begin{bmatrix} -2 \\ 2 \end{bmatrix}$

8. $\mathbf{b}_1 = \begin{bmatrix} -1 \\ 8 \end{bmatrix}, \mathbf{b}_2 = \begin{bmatrix} 1 \\ -5 \end{bmatrix}, \mathbf{c}_1 = \begin{bmatrix} 1 \\ 4 \end{bmatrix}, \mathbf{c}_2 = \begin{bmatrix} 1 \\ 1 \end{bmatrix}$

9. $\mathbf{b}_1 = \begin{bmatrix} -6 \\ -1 \end{bmatrix}, \mathbf{b}_2 = \begin{bmatrix} 2 \\ 0 \end{bmatrix}, \mathbf{c}_1 = \begin{bmatrix} 2 \\ -1 \end{bmatrix}, \mathbf{c}_2 = \begin{bmatrix} 6 \\ -2 \end{bmatrix}$

10. $\mathbf{b}_1 = \begin{bmatrix} 7 \\ -2 \end{bmatrix}, \mathbf{b}_2 = \begin{bmatrix} 2 \\ -1 \end{bmatrix}, \mathbf{c}_1 = \begin{bmatrix} 4 \\ 1 \end{bmatrix}, \mathbf{c}_2 = \begin{bmatrix} 5 \\ 2 \end{bmatrix}$

11. In $\mathbb{P}_2$, find the change-of-coordinates matrix from the basis $\mathcal{B} = \{1 - 2t + t^2, 3 - 5t + 4t^2, 2t + 3t^2\}$ to the standard basis $\mathcal{C} = \{1, t, t^2\}$. Then find the $\mathcal{B}$-coordinate vector for $-1 + 2t$.

12. In $\mathbb{P}_2$, find the change-of-coordinates matrix from the basis $\mathcal{B} = \{1 - 3t^2, 2 + t - 5t^2, 1 + 2t\}$ to the standard basis. Then write t^2 as a linear combination of the polynomials in $\mathcal{B}$.

13. Complete the proof of Theorem 16 by filling in justifications for each step shown below.
Given $\mathbf{v}$ in V, we may write

$$\mathbf{v} = x_1\mathbf{b}_1 + x_2\mathbf{b}_2 + \cdots + x_n\mathbf{b}_n$$

for some scalars $x_1, \ldots, x_n$, because ___(a)___. Applying the coordinate mapping determined by the basis $\mathcal{C}$, we have

$$[\mathbf{v}]_{\mathcal{C}} = x_1[\mathbf{b}_1]_{\mathcal{C}} + x_2[\mathbf{b}_2]_{\mathcal{C}} + \cdots + x_n[\mathbf{b}_n]_{\mathcal{C}}$$

because ___(b)___. We may write this equation in the form

$$[\mathbf{v}]_{\mathcal{C}} = \begin{bmatrix} [\mathbf{b}_1]_{\mathcal{C}} & [\mathbf{b}_2]_{\mathcal{C}} & \cdots & [\mathbf{b}_n]_{\mathcal{C}} \end{bmatrix} \begin{bmatrix} x_1 \\ \vdots \\ x_n \end{bmatrix} \quad (7)$$

by the definition of ___(c)___. This proves Theorem 16 because the vector on the right side of (7) is ___(d)___.

SOLUTIONS TO PRACTICE PROBLEMS

1. Since the columns of P are $\mathcal{G}$-coordinate vectors, a vector of the form $P\mathbf{x}$ must be a $\mathcal{G}$-coordinate vector. Thus P satisfies equation (ii).

2. The coordinate vectors found in Example 1 show that

$$\underset{C \leftarrow B}{P} = \begin{bmatrix} [\mathbf{b}_1]_{\mathcal{C}} & [\mathbf{b}_2]_{\mathcal{C}} \end{bmatrix} = \begin{bmatrix} 4 & -6 \\ 1 & 1 \end{bmatrix}$$

Hence

$$\underset{B \leftarrow C}{P} = (\underset{C \leftarrow B}{P})^{-1} = \frac{1}{10}\begin{bmatrix} 1 & 6 \\ -1 & 4 \end{bmatrix} = \begin{bmatrix} .1 & .6 \\ -.1 & .4 \end{bmatrix}$$

5.8 APPLICATIONS TO DIFFERENCE EQUATIONS

Now that powerful computers are widely available, more and more scientific and engineering problems are being treated in a way that uses discrete, or "digital," data rather than continuous data. Difference equations are often the appropriate tool to analyze such data. Even when a differential equation is used to model a continuous process, a numerical solution is often produced from a related difference equation.

This section highlights some fundamental properties of linear difference equations that are explained best using linear algebra.

Discrete-Time Signals

The vector space $\mathbb{S}$ of discrete-time signals was introduced in Section 5.1. A **signal** in $\mathbb{S}$ is a function defined only on the integers and is visualized as a sequence of numbers, say, $\{y_k\}$. Figure 1 shows three typical signals whose general terms are $(.7)^k$, 1^k, and $(-1)^k$, respectively.

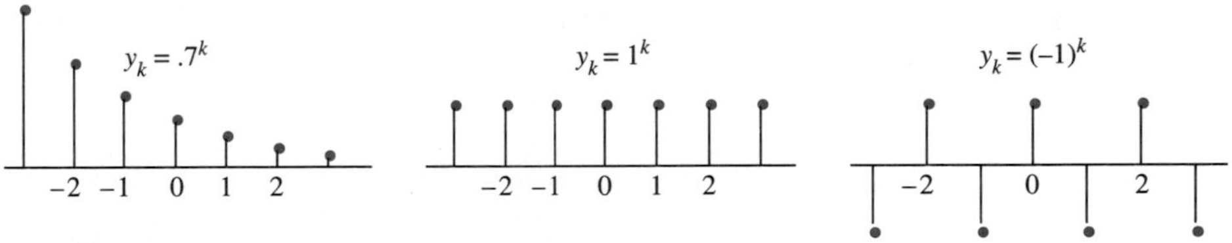

FIGURE 1 Three signals in $\mathbb{S}$.

Digital signals obviously arise in electrical and control systems engineering, but discrete-data sequences are also generated in biology, physics, economics, demography, and many other areas, wherever a process is measured, or *sampled*, at discrete time intervals. When a process begins at a specific time, it is sometimes convenient to write a signal as a sequence of the form $(y_0, y_1, y_2, \ldots)$. The terms y_k for $k < 0$ either are assumed to be zero or are simply omitted.

EXAMPLE 1 The crystal clear sounds from a compact disc player are produced from music that has been sampled at the rate of 44,100 times per second. See Fig. 2. At each measurement, the amplitude of the music signal is recorded as a number, say y_k. The original music is composed of many different sounds of varying frequencies, yet the sequence $\{y_k\}$ contains enough information to reproduce all of the frequencies in the sound up to about 20,000 cycles per second, higher than the human ear can sense. ∎

Linear Independence in the Space $\mathbb{S}$ of Signals

To simplify notation, we consider a set of only three signals in $\mathbb{S}$, say, $\{u_k\}$, $\{v_k\}$, and $\{w_k\}$. They are linearly independent precisely when the equation

$$c_1u_k + c_2v_k + c_3w_k = 0 \quad \text{for all } k \tag{1}$$

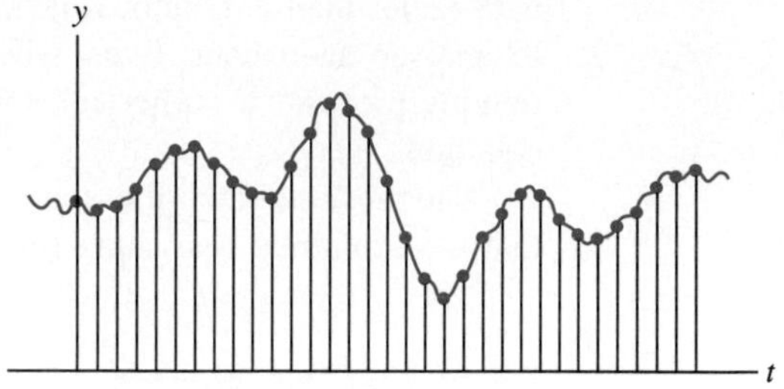

FIGURE 2 Sampled data from a music signal.

implies that $c_1 = c_2 = c_3 = 0$. The phrase "for all k" means for all integers—positive, negative, and zero. One could also consider signals that start with $k = 0$, for example, in which case "for all k" would mean for all integers $k \geq 0$.

Suppose c_1, c_2, c_3 satisfy (1). Then the equation in (1) holds for any three consecutive values of k, say, $k, k+1$, and $k+2$. Thus (1) implies that

$$c_1 u_{k+1} + c_2 v_{k+1} + c_3 w_{k+1} = 0 \quad \text{for all } k$$

and

$$c_1 u_{k+2} + c_2 v_{k+2} + c_3 w_{k+2} = 0 \quad \text{for all } k$$

Hence c_1, c_2, c_3 satisfy

$$\begin{bmatrix} u_k & v_k & w_k \\ u_{k+1} & v_{k+1} & w_{k+1} \\ u_{k+2} & v_{k+2} & w_{k+2} \end{bmatrix} \begin{bmatrix} c_1 \\ c_2 \\ c_3 \end{bmatrix} = \begin{bmatrix} 0 \\ 0 \\ 0 \end{bmatrix} \quad \text{for all } k \tag{2}$$

The coefficient matrix in this system is called the **Casorati matrix** of the signals, and the determinant of the matrix is called the **Casoratian** of $\{u_k\}$, $\{v_k\}$, and $\{w_k\}$. If for at least one value of k the Casorati matrix is invertible, then (2) will imply that $c_1 = c_2 = c_3 = 0$, which will prove that the three signals are linearly independent.

EXAMPLE 2 Verify that 1^k, $(-2)^k$, and 3^k are linearly independent signals.

Solution The Casorati matrix is

$$\begin{bmatrix} 1^k & (-2)^k & 3^k \\ 1^{k+1} & (-2)^{k+1} & 3^{k+1} \\ 1^{k+2} & (-2)^{k+2} & 3^{k+2} \end{bmatrix}$$

Row operations can show fairly easily that this matrix is always invertible. However, it is faster to substitute a value for k—say, $k = 0$—and row reduce the numerical matrix:

$$\begin{bmatrix} 1 & 1 & 1 \\ 1 & -2 & 3 \\ 1 & 4 & 9 \end{bmatrix} \sim \begin{bmatrix} 1 & 1 & 1 \\ 0 & -3 & 2 \\ 0 & 3 & 8 \end{bmatrix} \sim \begin{bmatrix} 1 & 1 & 1 \\ 0 & -3 & 2 \\ 0 & 0 & 10 \end{bmatrix}$$

The Casorati matrix is invertible for $k = 0$. So 1^k, $(-2)^k$, and 3^k are linearly independent. ∎

If a Casorati matrix is not invertible, the associated signals being tested may or may not be linearly dependent. (See Exercise 33.) However, it can be shown that if the signals are all solutions of the *same* homogeneous difference equation (described below), then either the Casorati matrix is invertible for all k and the signals are linearly independent, or else for all k the Casorati matrix is not invertible and the signals are linearly dependent. A nice proof using linear transformations is in the Study Guide.

Linear Difference Equations

Given scalars $a_0, \ldots, a_n$, with a_0 and a_n nonzero, and given a signal $\{z_k\}$, the equation

$$a_0 y_{k+n} + a_1 y_{k+n-1} + \cdots + a_{n-1} y_{k+1} + a_n y_k = z_k \quad \text{for all } k \tag{3}$$

is called a **linear difference equation** (or **linear recurrence relation) of order n.** For simplicity, a_0 is often taken equal to 1. If $\{z_k\}$ is the zero sequence, the equation is **homogeneous**; otherwise, the equation is **nonhomogeneous**.

EXAMPLE 3 In digital signal processing, a difference equation such as (3) above describes a **linear filter**, and $a_0, \ldots, a_n$ are called the **filter coefficients**. If $\{y_k\}$ is treated as the input and $\{z_k\}$ the output, then the solutions of the associated homogeneous equation are the signals that are filtered *out* and transformed into the zero signal. Let us feed two different signals into the filter

$$.35 y_{k+2} + .5 y_{k+1} + .35 y_k = z_k$$

Here .35 is an abbreviation for $\sqrt{2}/4$. The first signal is created by sampling the continuous signal $y = \cos(\pi t/4)$ at integer values of t, as in Fig. 3(a). The discrete signal is

$$\{y_k\} = \{\ldots, \cos(0), \cos(\pi/4), \cos(2\pi/4), \cos(3\pi/4), \ldots\}$$

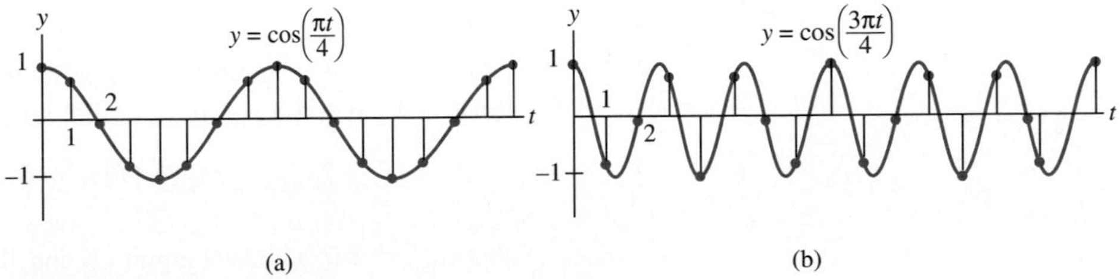

FIGURE 3 Discrete signals with different frequencies.

For simplicity, write $\pm .7$ in place of $\pm\sqrt{2}/2$, so that

$$\{y_k\} = \{\ldots, \underset{\substack{\uparrow \\ k=0}}{1}, .7, 0, -.7, -1, -.7, 0, .7, 1, .7, 0, \ldots\}$$

Table 1 shows a calculation of the output sequence $\{z_k\}$, where .35(.7) is an abbreviation for $(\sqrt{2}/4)(\sqrt{2}/2) = .25$. The output is $\{y_k\}$, shifted by one term.

TABLE 1 Computing the Output of a Filter

k	y_k	y_{k+1}	y_{k+2}	$.35y_k$	$+.5y_{k+1}$	$+.35y_{k+2}$	$=$	z_k
0	1	.7	0	.35(1)	+.5(.7)	+.35(0)	=	.7
1	.7	0	−.7	.35(.7)	+.5(0)	+.35(−.7)	=	0
2	0	−.7	−1	.35(0)	+.5(−.7)	+.35(−1)	=	−.7
3	−.7	−1	−.7	.35(−.7)	+.5(−1)	+.35(−.7)	=	−1
4	−1	−.7	0	.35(−1)	+.5(−.7)	+.35(0)	=	−.7
5	−.7	0	.7	.35(−.7)	+.5(0)	+.35(.7)	=	0
⋮	⋮							⋮

A different input signal is produced from the higher frequency signal $y = \cos(3\pi t/4)$, shown in Fig. 3(b). Sampling at the same rate as before produces a new input sequence:

$$\{w_k\} = \{\ldots,\ \underset{\substack{\uparrow \\ k=0}}{1},\ -.7,\ 0,\ .7,\ -1,\ .7,\ 0,\ -.7,\ 1,\ -.7,\ 0, \ldots\}$$

When $\{w_k\}$ is fed into the filter, the output is the zero sequence. The filter, called a *low-pass filter*, lets $\{y_k\}$ pass through, but stops the higher frequency $\{w_k\}$.

In many applications, a sequence $\{z_k\}$ is specified for the right side of a difference equation (3), and a $\{y_k\}$ that satisfies (3) is called a **solution** of the equation. The next example shows how to find solutions for a homogeneous equation.

EXAMPLE 4 Solutions of a homogeneous difference equation often have the form $y_k = r^k$ for some r. Find some solutions of the equation

$$y_{k+3} - 2y_{k+2} - 5y_{k+1} + 6y_k = 0 \quad \text{for all } k \tag{4}$$

Solution Substitute r^k for y_k in the equation and factor the left side:

$$r^{k+3} - 2r^{k+2} - 5r^{k+1} + 6r^k = 0 \tag{5}$$

$$r^k(r^3 - 2r^2 - 5r + 6) = 0$$

$$r^k(r-1)(r+2)(r-3) = 0 \tag{6}$$

Since (5) is equivalent to (6), r^k satisfies the difference equation (4) if and only if r satisfies (6). Thus 1^k, $(-2)^k$, and 3^k are all solutions of (4). For instance, to verify that 3^k is a solution of (4), compute

$$\begin{aligned}3^{k+3} &- 2\cdot 3^{k+2} - 5\cdot 3^{k+1} + 6\cdot 3^k \\ &= 3^k(27 - 18 - 15 + 6) = 0 \quad \text{for all } k\end{aligned}$$

In general, a nonzero signal r^k satisfies the homogeneous difference equation

$$y_{k+n} + a_1 y_{k+n-1} + \cdots + a_{n-1} y_{k+1} + a_n y_k = 0 \quad \text{for all } k$$

if and only if r is a root of the **auxiliary equation**

$$r^n + a_1 r^{n-1} + \cdots + a_{n-1} r + a_n = 0$$

We will not consider the case when r is a repeated root of the auxiliary equation. When the auxiliary equation has a *complex root*, the difference equation has solutions of the form $s^k \cos k\omega$ and $s^k \sin k\omega$, for constants s and ω. This happened in Example 3.

Solution Sets of Linear Difference Equations

Given $a_1, \ldots, a_n$, consider the mapping $T : \mathbb{S} \to \mathbb{S}$ that transforms a signal $\{y_k\}$ into a signal $\{w_k\}$ given by

$$w_k = y_{k+n} + a_1 y_{k+n-1} + \cdots + a_{n-1} y_{k+1} + a_n y_k$$

It is readily checked that T is a *linear* transformation. This implies that the solution set of the homogeneous equation

$$y_{k+n} + a_1 y_{k+n-1} + \cdots + a_{n-1} y_{k+1} + a_n y_k = 0 \quad \text{for all } k$$

is the null space of T (the set of signals that T maps into the zero signal) and hence the solution set is a *subspace* of $\mathbb{S}$. Any linear combination of solutions is again a solution.

The next theorem, a simple but basic result, will lead to more information about the solution sets of difference equations.

THEOREM 17

If $a_n \neq 0$ and if $\{z_k\}$ is given, the equation

$$y_{k+n} + a_1 y_{k+n-1} + \cdots + a_{n-1} y_{k+1} + a_n y_k = z_k \quad \text{for all } k \tag{7}$$

has a unique solution whenever $y_0, \ldots, y_{n-1}$ are specified.

Proof If $y_0, \ldots, y_{n-1}$ are specified, use (7) to *define*

$$y_n = z_0 - [a_1 y_{n-1} + \cdots + a_{n-1} y_1 + a_n y_0]$$

And now that $y_1, \ldots, y_n$ are specified, use (7) to define y_{n+1}. In general, use the *recursion relation*

$$y_{n+k} = z_k - [a_1 y_{k+n-1} + \cdots + a_n y_k] \tag{8}$$

to define y_{n+k} for $k \geq 0$. To define y_k for $k < 0$, use the recursion relation

$$y_k = \frac{1}{a_n} z_k - \frac{1}{a_n} [y_{k+n} + a_1 y_{k+n-1} + \cdots + a_{n-1} y_{k+1}] \tag{9}$$

This produces a signal that satisfies (7). Conversely, any signal that satisfies (7) for all k certainly satisfies (8) and (9), so the solution of (7) is unique. ∎

THEOREM 18

The set H of all solutions of the nth order homogeneous linear difference equation

$$y_{k+n} + a_1 y_{k+n-1} + \cdots + a_{n-1} y_{k+1} + a_n y_k = 0 \quad \text{for all } k \tag{10}$$

is an n-dimensional vector space.

Proof We explained earlier why H is a subspace of $\mathbb{S}$. For $\{y_k\}$ in H, let $F\{y_k\}$ be the vector in $\mathbb{R}^n$ given by $(y_0, y_1, \ldots, y_{n-1})$. It is readily verified that $F: H \to \mathbb{R}^n$ is a linear transformation. Given any vector $(y_0, y_1, \ldots, y_{n-1})$ in $\mathbb{R}^n$, Theorem 17 says that there is a unique signal $\{y_k\}$ in H such that $F\{y_k\} = (y_0, y_1, \ldots, y_{n-1})$. This means that F is a one-to-one linear transformation of H onto $\mathbb{R}^n$; that is, F is an isomorphism. Thus $\dim H = \dim \mathbb{R}^n = n$. (See Exercise 34 in Section 5.5.) ∎

EXAMPLE 5 Find a basis for the set of all solutions to the difference equation

$$y_{k+3} - 2y_{k+2} - 5y_{k+1} + 6y_k = 0 \quad \text{for all } k$$

Solution Our work in linear algebra really pays off now! We know from Examples 2 and 4 that 1^k, $(-2)^k$, and 3^k are linearly independent solutions. In general, it can be difficult to verify directly that a set of signals *spans* the solution space. But that is no problem here because of two key theorems—Theorem 18, which shows that the solution space is exactly three-dimensional, and Theorem 13, in Section 5.5, which says that a linearly independent set of n vectors in an n-dimensional space is automatically a basis. So $1^k, (-2)^k$, and 3^k form a basis for the solution space. ∎

The standard way to describe the "general solution" of (10) is to exhibit a basis for the subspace of all solutions. Such a basis is usually called a **fundamental set of solutions** of (10). In practice, if we can find n linearly independent signals that satisfy (10), they will automatically span the n-dimensional solution space, as we saw in the example above.

Nonhomogeneous Equations

The general solution of the nonhomogeneous difference equation

$$y_{k+n} + a_1 y_{k+n-1} + \cdots + a_{n-1} y_{k+1} + a_n y_k = z_k \quad \text{for all } k \tag{11}$$

may be written as one particular solution of (11) plus an arbitrary linear combination of a fundamental set of solutions of the corresponding homogeneous equation (10). This fact is analogous to the result in Section 2.3 about how the solution sets of $A\mathbf{x} = \mathbf{b}$ and $A\mathbf{x} = \mathbf{0}$ are parallel. Both results have the same explanation: The mapping $\mathbf{x} \mapsto A\mathbf{x}$ is linear, and the mapping that transforms the signal $\{y_k\}$ into the signal $\{z_k\}$ in (11) is linear. See Exercise 35.

EXAMPLE 6 Verify that the signal $y_k = k^2$ satisfies the difference equation

$$y_{k+2} - 4y_{k+1} + 3y_k = -4k \quad \text{for all } k \tag{12}$$

Then find a description of all solutions of this equation.

Solution Substitute k^2 for y_k in the left side of (12):

$$\begin{aligned} &(k+2)^2 - 4(k+1)^2 + 3k^2 \\ &\quad = (k^2 + 4k + 4) - 4(k^2 + 2k + 1) + 3k^2 \\ &\quad = -4k \end{aligned}$$

So k^2 is indeed a solution of (12). The next step is to solve the homogeneous equation

$$y_{k+2} - 4y_{k+1} + 3y_k = 0 \tag{13}$$

The auxiliary equation is

$$r^2 - 4r + 3 = (r-1)(r-3) = 0$$

The roots are $r = 1, 3$. So two solutions of the homogeneous difference equation are 1^k and 3^k. They are obviously not multiples of each other, so they are linearly independent signals. (The Casorati test could have been used, too.) By Theorem 18, the solution space is two-dimensional, so 3^k and 1^k form a basis for the set of solutions of (13). Translating that set by a particular solution of the nonhomogeneous equation (12), we obtain the general solution of 12:

$$k^2 + c_1 1^k + c_2 3^k, \quad \text{or} \quad k^2 + c_1 + c_2 3^k$$

Figure 4 gives a geometric visualization of the two solution sets. Each point in the figure corresponds to one signal in $\mathbb{S}$.

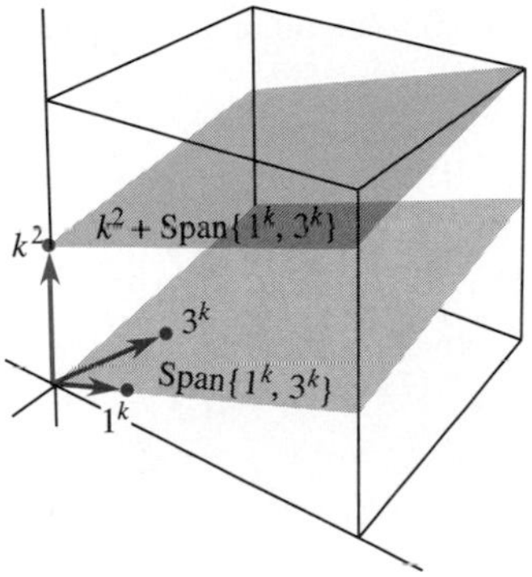

FIGURE 4 Solution sets of difference equations (12) and (13).

Reduction to Systems of First Order Equations

A modern way to study a homogeneous nth order linear difference equation is to replace it by an equivalent system of first-order difference equations, written in the form

$$\mathbf{x}_{k+1} = A\mathbf{x}_k \quad \text{for } k = 0, 1, 2, \ldots$$

where the vectors $\mathbf{x}_k$ are in $\mathbb{R}^n$ and A is an $n \times n$ matrix.

A simple example of such a (vector-valued) difference equation was already studied in Section 2.7. Further examples will be covered in Sections 5.9 and 6.6.

EXAMPLE 7 Write the following difference equation as a first-order system:

$$y_{k+3} - 2y_{k+2} - 5y_{k+1} + 6y_k = 0 \quad \text{for all } k$$

Solution For each k, set

$$\mathbf{x}_k = \begin{bmatrix} y_k \\ y_{k+1} \\ y_{k+2} \end{bmatrix}$$

The difference equation says that $y_{k+3} = -6y_k + 5y_{k+1} + 2y_{k+2}$, so

$$\mathbf{x}_{k+1} = \begin{bmatrix} y_{k+1} \\ y_{k+2} \\ y_{k+3} \end{bmatrix} = \begin{bmatrix} 0 & + & y_{k+1} & + & 0 \\ 0 & + & 0 & + & y_{k+2} \\ -6y_k & + & 5y_{k+1} & + & 2y_{k+2} \end{bmatrix} = \begin{bmatrix} 0 & 1 & 0 \\ 0 & 0 & 1 \\ -6 & 5 & 2 \end{bmatrix} \begin{bmatrix} y_k \\ y_{k+1} \\ y_{k+2} \end{bmatrix}$$

That is,

$$\mathbf{x}_{k+1} = A\mathbf{x}_k \quad \text{for all } k, \quad \text{where} \quad A = \begin{bmatrix} 0 & 1 & 0 \\ 0 & 0 & 1 \\ -6 & 5 & 2 \end{bmatrix}$$

In general, the equation

$$y_{k+n} + a_1 y_{k+n-1} + \cdots + a_{n-1} y_{k+1} + a_n y_k = 0 \quad \text{for all } k$$

may be rewritten as $\mathbf{x}_{k+1} = A\mathbf{x}_k$ for all k, where

$$\mathbf{x}_k = \begin{bmatrix} y_k \\ y_{k+1} \\ \vdots \\ y_{k+n-1} \end{bmatrix}, \qquad A = \begin{bmatrix} 0 & 1 & 0 & & 0 \\ 0 & 0 & 1 & & 0 \\ \vdots & & & \ddots & \vdots \\ 0 & 0 & 0 & & 1 \\ -a_n & -a_{n-1} & -a_{n-2} & \cdots & -a_1 \end{bmatrix}$$

Further Reading

Hamming, R.W. *Digital Filters*, 2d ed. Englewood Cliffs, N.J.: Prentice-Hall, 1983, pp. 1–37.

Mickens, Ronald E. *Difference Equations*, 2d ed. New York: Van Nostrand Reinhold, 1990, pp. 88–141.

Oppenheim, Alan V., and Alan S. Willsky. *Signals and Systems*. Englewood Cliffs, N.J.: Prentice-Hall, 1983, pp. 1–16, 26–45.

PRACTICE PROBLEM

It can be shown that the signals 2^k, $3^k \sin \frac{k\pi}{2}$, and $3^k \cos \frac{k\pi}{2}$ are solutions of

$$y_{k+3} - 2y_{k+2} + 9y_{k+1} - 18y_k = 0$$

Show that these signals form a basis for the set of all solutions of the difference equation.

5.8 EXERCISES

Verify that the signals in Exercises 1 and 2 are solutions of the accompanying difference equation.

1. $2^k, (-4)^k$; $y_{k+2} + 2y_{k+1} - 8y_k = 0$
2. $3^k, (-3)^k$; $y_{k+2} - 9y_k = 0$

Show that the signals in Exercises 3–6 form a basis for the solution set of the accompanying difference equation.

3. The signals and equation in Exercise 1
4. The signals and equation in Exercise 2
5. $(-3)^k, k(-3)^k$; $y_{k+2} + 6y_{k+1} + 9y_k = 0$
6. $5^k \cos \frac{k\pi}{2}, 5^k \sin \frac{k\pi}{2}$; $y_{k+2} + 25y_k = 0$

In Exercises 7–12, assume that the signals listed are solutions of the given difference equation. Determine if the signals form a basis for the solution space of the equation.

7. $1^k, 2^k, (-2)^k$; $y_{k+3} - y_{k+2} - 4y_{k+1} + 4y_k = 0$
8. $2^k, 4^k, (-5)^k$; $y_{k+3} - y_{k+2} - 22y_{k+1} + 40y_k = 0$
9. $1^k, 3^k \cos \frac{k\pi}{2}, 3^k \sin \frac{k\pi}{2}$; $y_{k+3} - y_{k+2} + 9y_{k+1} - 9y_k = 0$
10. $(-1)^k, k(-1)^k, 5^k$; $y_{k+3} - 3y_{k+2} - 9y_{k+1} - 5y_k = 0$
11. $(-1)^k, 3^k$; $y_{k+3} + y_{k+2} - 9y_{k+1} - 9y_k = 0$
12. $1^k, (-1)^k$; $y_{k+4} - 2y_{k+2} + y_k = 0$

In Exercises 13–16, find a basis for the solution space of the difference equation.

13. $y_{k+2} - y_{k+1} + \frac{2}{9}y_k = 0$
14. $y_{k+2} - 7y_{k+1} + 12y_k = 0$
15. $y_{k+2} - 25y_k = 0$
16. $16y_{k+2} + 8y_{k+1} - 3y_k = 0$

Exercises 17 and 18 concern a simple model of the national economy described by the difference equation

$$Y_{k+2} - a(1+b)Y_{k+1} + abY_k = 1 \qquad (14)$$

Here Y_k is the total national income during year k, a is a constant less than 1, called the *marginal propensity to consume*, and b is a positive *constant of adjustment* that describes how changes in consumer spending affect the annual rate of private investment.[1]

17. Find the general solution of (14) when $a = .9$ and $b = \frac{4}{9}$. (*Note*: First find a particular solution of the form $Y_k = T$, where T is a constant, called the equilibrium level of national income.) What happens to Y_k as k increases?
18. Find the general solution of (14) when $a = .9$ and $b = .5$.

A lightweight cantilevered beam is supported at N points spaced 10 feet apart, and a weight of 500 lb. is placed at the end of the beam, 10 feet from the first support, as in the figure. Let y_k be the bending moment at the kth support. Then $y_1 = 5000$ ft-lb. Suppose the beam is rigidly attached at the Nth support and the bending moment there is zero. In between, the moments satisfy the *three-moment equation*

$$y_{k+2} + 4y_{k+1} + y_k = 0 \qquad \text{for } k = 1, 2, \ldots, N-2 \qquad (15)$$

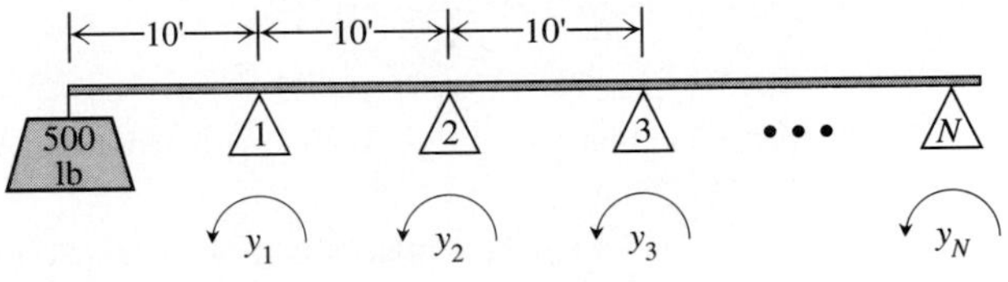

Bending moments on a cantilevered beam.

19. Find the general solution of difference equation (15).
20. Find the particular solution of (15) that satisfies the *boundary conditions* $y_1 = 5000$ and $y_N = 0$. (The answer involves N.)
21. When a signal is produced from a sequence of measurements made on a process (a chemical reaction, a flow of heat through a tube, a moving robot arm, etc.), the signal usually contains random *noise* produced by measurement errors. A standard method of preprocessing the data to reduce the noise is to smooth or filter the data. One simple filter is a *moving average* that replaces each y_k by its average with the two adjacent values:

$$\tfrac{1}{3}y_{k+1} + \tfrac{1}{3}y_k + \tfrac{1}{3}y_{k-1} = z_k \qquad \text{for } k = 1, 2, \ldots$$

Suppose a signal y_k, for $k = 0, \ldots, 14$, is

9, 5, 7, 3, 2, 4, 6, 5, 7, 6, 8, 10, 9, 5, 7

Use the filter to compute $z_1, \ldots, z_{13}$. Make a broken-line

[1]For example, see *Discrete Dynamical Systems*, by James T. Sandefur (Oxford: Clarenden Press, 1990), pp. 267–276. The original *accelerator-multiplier model* is due to the economist P.A. Samuelson.

graph that superimposes the original signal and the smoothed signal.

22. Let $\{y_k\}$ be the sequence produced by sampling the continuous signal $2\cos\frac{\pi t}{4} + \cos\frac{3\pi t}{4}$ at $t = 0, 1, 2, \ldots$, as shown in the figure. The values of y_k, beginning with $k = 0$, are

$3, .7, 0, -.7, -3, -.7, 0, .7, 3, .7, 0, \ldots$

where .7 is an abbreviation for $\sqrt{2}/2$.

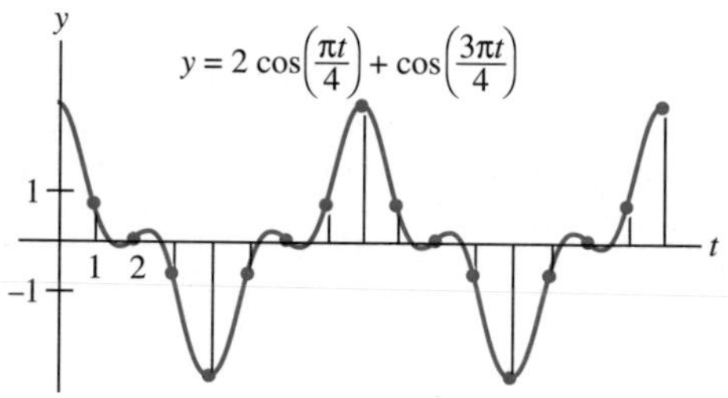

Sampled data from $2\cos\frac{\pi t}{4} + \cos\frac{3\pi t}{4}$.

a. Compute the output signal $\{z_k\}$ when $\{y_k\}$ is fed into the filter in Example 3.

b. Explain how and why the output in part (a) is related to the calculations in Example 3.

Exercises 23 and 24 refer to a difference equation of the form $y_{k+1} - ay_k = b$, for suitable constants a and b.

23. A loan of \$10,000 has an interest rate of 1% per month and a monthly payment of \$450. The loan is made at month $k = 0$, and the first payment is made one month later, at $k = 1$. For $k = 0, 1, 2, \ldots$, let y_k be the unpaid balance of the loan just after the kth monthly payment. Thus

$$y_1 = 10{,}000 + (.01)10{,}000 - 450$$

New balance due — Balance — Interest added — Payment

Write a difference equation satisfied by $\{y_k\}$.

24. At time $k = 0$, an initial investment of \$1000 is made into a savings account that pays 6% interest per year compounded monthly. (The interest rate per month is .005.) Each month after the initial investment, an additional \$200 is added to the account. For $k = 0, 1, 2, \ldots$, let y_k be the amount in the account at time k, just after a deposit has been made. Write a difference equation satisfied by $\{y_k\}$.

In Exercises 25–28, show that the given signal is a solution of the difference equation. Then find the general solution of that difference equation.

25. $y_k = k^2$; $y_{k+2} + 3y_{k+1} - 4y_k = 10k + 7$

26. $y_k = 1 + k$; $y_{k+2} - 8y_{k+1} + 15y_k = 8k + 2$

27. $y_k = 2 - 2k$; $y_{k+2} - \frac{9}{2}y_{k+1} + 2y_k = 3k + 2$

28. $y_k = 2k - 4$; $y_{k+2} + \frac{3}{2}y_{k+1} - y_k = 1 + 3k$

Write the difference equations in Exercises 29 and 30 as first-order systems, $\mathbf{x}_{k+1} = A\mathbf{x}_k$, for all k.

29. $y_{k+4} - 6y_{k+3} + 8y_{k+2} + 6y_{k+1} - 9y_k = 0$

30. $y_{k+3} - \frac{3}{4}y_{k+2} + \frac{1}{16}y_k = 0$

31. Is the following difference equation of order 3? Explain.

$$y_{k+3} + 5y_{k+2} + 6y_{k+1} = 0$$

32. What is the order of the following difference equation? Explain your answer.

$$y_{k+3} + a_1 y_{k+2} + a_2 y_{k+1} + a_3 y_k = 0$$

33. Let $y_k = k^2$ and $z_k = 2k|k|$. Are the signals $\{y_k\}$ and $\{z_k\}$ linearly independent? Evaluate the associated Casorati matrix $C(k)$ for $k = 0$, $k = -1$, and $k = -2$, and discuss your results.

34. Let f, g, h be linearly independent functions defined for all real numbers, and construct three signals by sampling the values of the functions at the integers:

$$u_k = f(k), \qquad v_k = g(k), \qquad w_k = h(k)$$

Must the signals be linearly independent in $\mathbb{S}$? Discuss.

35. Let a and b be nonzero numbers. Show that the mapping T defined by

$$T\{y_k\} = y_{k+2} + ay_{k+1} + by_k$$

is a linear transformation from $\mathbb{S}$ into $\mathbb{S}$.

36. Let V be a vector space and let $T : V \to V$ be a linear transformation. Given $\mathbf{z}$ in V, suppose that $\mathbf{x}_p$ in V satisfies $T(\mathbf{x}_p) = \mathbf{z}$, and let $\mathbf{u}$ be any vector in the null space of T. Show that $\mathbf{u} + \mathbf{x}_p$ satisfies the nonhomogeneous equation $T(\mathbf{x}) = \mathbf{z}$.

SOLUTION TO PRACTICE PROBLEM

Examine the Casorati matrix:

$$C(k) = \begin{bmatrix} 2^k & 3^k \sin\frac{k\pi}{2} & 3^k \cos\frac{k\pi}{2} \\ 2^{k+1} & 3^{k+1}\sin\frac{(k+1)\pi}{2} & 3^{k+1}\cos\frac{(k+1)\pi}{2} \\ 2^{k+2} & 3^{k+2}\sin\frac{(k+2)\pi}{2} & 3^{k+2}\cos\frac{(k+2)\pi}{2} \end{bmatrix}$$

Set $k = 0$ and row reduce the matrix to verify that it has three pivot positions and hence is invertible:

$$C(0) = \begin{bmatrix} 1 & 0 & 1 \\ 2 & 3 & 0 \\ 4 & 0 & -9 \end{bmatrix} \sim \begin{bmatrix} 1 & 0 & 1 \\ 0 & 3 & -2 \\ 0 & 0 & -13 \end{bmatrix}$$

The Casorati matrix is invertible at $k = 0$, so the signals are linearly independent. Since there are three signals, and the solution space H of the difference equation has dimension 3, by Theorem 18, these signals form a basis for H.

5.9 APPLICATIONS TO MARKOV CHAINS

The Markov chains described in this section are used as mathematical models of a wide variety of situations in biology, business, chemistry, engineering, physics, and elsewhere. In each case, the model is used to describe an experiment or measurement that is performed many times in the same way, where the outcome of each trial of the experiment falls into one of several specified possible outcomes, and where the outcome of one trial depends only on the immediately preceding trial.

For example, if the population of a city and its suburbs were measured each year, then a vector such as

$$\mathbf{v}_0 = \begin{bmatrix} .60 \\ .40 \end{bmatrix} \tag{1}$$

could indicate that 60% of the population lives in the city and 40% in the suburbs. The decimals in $\mathbf{v}_0$ add up to 1 because they account for the entire population of the region. Percentages are more convenient for our purposes here than population totals.

A vector with nonnegative entries that add up to one is called a **probability vector**. A **stochastic matrix** is a square matrix whose columns are probability vectors. A **Markov chain** is a sequence of probability vectors $\mathbf{v}_0, \mathbf{v}_1, \mathbf{v}_2, \ldots$, together with a stochastic matrix P, such that

$$\mathbf{v}_1 = P\mathbf{v}_0, \qquad \mathbf{v}_2 = P\mathbf{v}_1, \qquad \mathbf{v}_3 = P\mathbf{v}_2, \qquad \ldots$$

Thus the Markov chain is described by the first-order difference equation

$$\mathbf{v}_{k+1} = P\mathbf{v}_k \quad \text{for } k = 0, 1, 2, \ldots$$

When a Markov chain of vectors in $\mathbb{R}^n$ describes a system or a sequence of experiments, the entries in $\mathbf{v}_k$ list the probabilities that the system is in each of n possible states, or the probabilities that the outcome of the experiment is one of n possible outcomes. For this reason, $\mathbf{v}_k$ is often called a **state vector**.

EXAMPLE 1 In Section 2.7 we examined a model for population movement between a city and its suburbs. See Fig. 1. The annual migration between these two parts of the metropolitan region was governed by the *migration matrix* M:

$$\begin{array}{c} \text{From:} \\ \begin{array}{cc} \text{City} & \text{Suburbs} \end{array} \quad \text{To:} \end{array}$$
$$M = \begin{bmatrix} .95 & .03 \\ .05 & .97 \end{bmatrix} \begin{array}{l} \text{City} \\ \text{Suburbs} \end{array}$$

That is, each year 5% of the city population moves to the suburbs, and 3% of the suburban population moves to the city. The columns of M are probability vectors, so M is a stochastic matrix. Suppose that the 1990 population of the region is 600,000 in the city and 400,000 in the suburbs. Then the initial distribution of the population in the region is given by $\mathbf{v}_0$ in (1) above. What is the distribution of the population in 1991? In 1992?

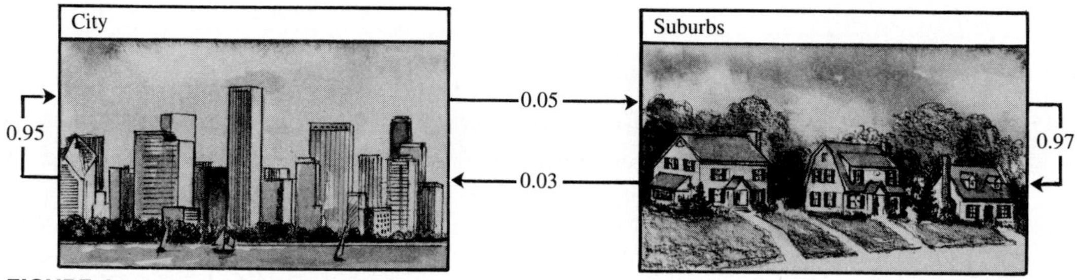

FIGURE 1 Annual percentage migration between city and suburbs.

Solution In Example 2 of Section 2.7, we saw that after one year, the population vector $\begin{bmatrix} 600,000 \\ 400,000 \end{bmatrix}$ changed to

$$\begin{bmatrix} .95 & .03 \\ .05 & .97 \end{bmatrix} \begin{bmatrix} 600,000 \\ 400,000 \end{bmatrix} = \begin{bmatrix} 582,000 \\ 418,000 \end{bmatrix}$$

If we divide both sides of this equation by the total population of 1 million, and use the fact that $kM\mathbf{x} = M(k\mathbf{x})$, we find that

$$\begin{bmatrix} .95 & .03 \\ .05 & .97 \end{bmatrix} \begin{bmatrix} .600 \\ .400 \end{bmatrix} = \begin{bmatrix} .582 \\ .418 \end{bmatrix}$$

The vector $\mathbf{v}_1 = \begin{bmatrix} .582 \\ .418 \end{bmatrix}$ gives the population distribution in 1991. That is, 58.2% of the region lived in the city and 41.8% lived in the suburbs. Similarly, the population distribution in 1992 is described by a vector $\mathbf{v}_2$, where

$$\mathbf{v}_2 = M\mathbf{v}_1 = \begin{bmatrix} .95 & .03 \\ .05 & .97 \end{bmatrix} \begin{bmatrix} .582 \\ .418 \end{bmatrix} = \begin{bmatrix} .565 \\ .435 \end{bmatrix}$$

EXAMPLE 2 Suppose that the voting results of a congressional election at a certain voting precinct are represented by a vector $\mathbf{v}$ in $\mathbb{R}^3$:

$$\mathbf{v} = \begin{bmatrix} \%\text{ voting Democratic } (D) \\ \%\text{ voting Republican } (R) \\ \%\text{ voting Libertarian } (L) \end{bmatrix}$$

Suppose that we record the outcome of the congressional election every two years by a vector of this type and that the outcome of one election depends only on the results of the preceding election. Then the sequence of vectors that describe the votes every two years may be a Markov chain. As an example of a stochastic matrix P for this chain, we take

$$\begin{array}{c} \text{From:} \\ \begin{array}{ccc} \text{D} & \text{R} & \text{L} \end{array} \end{array} \quad \text{To:}$$

$$P = \begin{bmatrix} .70 & .10 & .30 \\ .20 & .80 & .30 \\ .10 & .10 & .40 \end{bmatrix} \begin{matrix} \text{D} \\ \text{R} \\ \text{L} \end{matrix}$$

The entries in the first column labeled "D" describe what the persons voting Democratic in one election will do in the next election. Here we have supposed that 70% will vote "D" again in the next election, 20% will vote "R," and 10% will vote "L." A similar interpretation holds for the other columns of P. A diagram for this matrix is shown in Fig. 2.

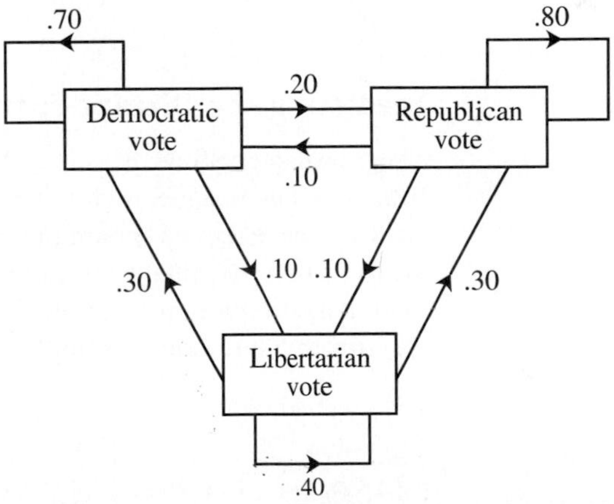

FIGURE 2 Voting changes from one election to the next.

If the "transition" percentages remain constant over many years from one election to the next, then the sequence of vectors that give the voting outcomes forms a Markov chain. Suppose that in one election, the outcome is given by

$$\mathbf{v}_0 = \begin{bmatrix} .55 \\ .40 \\ .05 \end{bmatrix}$$

Determine the likely outcome of the next election and the likely outcome of the election after that.

Solution The outcome of the next election is described by the state vector $\mathbf{v}_1$ and the election after that by $\mathbf{v}_2$, where

$$\mathbf{v}_1 = P\mathbf{v}_0 = \begin{bmatrix} .70 & .10 & .30 \\ .20 & .80 & .30 \\ .10 & .10 & .40 \end{bmatrix} \begin{bmatrix} .55 \\ .40 \\ .05 \end{bmatrix} = \begin{bmatrix} .440 \\ .445 \\ .115 \end{bmatrix}, \quad \begin{array}{l} 44\% \text{ will vote D.} \\ 44.5\% \text{ will vote R.} \\ 11.5\% \text{ will vote L.} \end{array}$$

$$\mathbf{v}_2 = P\mathbf{v}_1 = \begin{bmatrix} .70 & .10 & .30 \\ .20 & .80 & .30 \\ .10 & .10 & .40 \end{bmatrix} \begin{bmatrix} .440 \\ .445 \\ .115 \end{bmatrix} = \begin{bmatrix} .3870 \\ .4785 \\ .1345 \end{bmatrix}, \quad \begin{array}{l} 38.7\% \text{ will vote D.} \\ 47.8\% \text{ will vote R.} \\ 13.5\% \text{ will vote L.} \end{array}$$

To understand why $\mathbf{v}_1$ does indeed give the outcome of the next election, suppose that 1000 persons voted in the "first" election, with 550 voting "D," 400 voting "R," and 50 voting "L." (See the percentages in $\mathbf{v}_0$.) In the next election, 70% of the 550 will vote "D" again, 10% of the 400 will switch from "R" to "D," and 30% of the 50 will switch from "L" to "D." Thus the total "D" vote will be

$$.70(550) + .10(400) + .30(50) = 385 + 40 + 15 = 440 \tag{2}$$

Thus 44% of the vote next time will be for the "D" candidate. The calculation in (2) is essentially the same as that used to compute the first entry in $\mathbf{v}_1$. Analogous calculations could be made for the other entries in $\mathbf{v}_1$, for the entries in $\mathbf{v}_2$, and so on.

Predicting the Distant Future

The most interesting aspect of Markov chains is the study of a chain's long-term behavior. For instance, what can be said in Example 2 about the voting after many elections have passed (assuming that the given stochastic matrix continues to describe the transition percentages from one election to the next)? Or, what happens to the population distribution in Example 1 "in the long run"? Before answering these questions, we turn to a numerical example.

EXAMPLE 3 Let $P = \begin{bmatrix} .5 & .2 & .3 \\ .3 & .8 & .3 \\ .2 & 0 & .4 \end{bmatrix}$ and $\mathbf{v}_0 = \begin{bmatrix} 1 \\ 0 \\ 0 \end{bmatrix}$. Consider a system whose state is described by the Markov chain $\mathbf{v}_{k+1} = P\mathbf{v}_k$, for $k = 0, 1, \ldots$. What happens to the system as time passes? Compute the state vectors $\mathbf{v}_1, \ldots, \mathbf{v}_{15}$ to find out.

Solution The entries in the vectors that follow have been rounded to four significant figures.

$$\mathbf{v}_1 = P\mathbf{v}_0 = \begin{bmatrix} .5 & .2 & .3 \\ .3 & .8 & .3 \\ .2 & 0 & .4 \end{bmatrix} \begin{bmatrix} 1 \\ 0 \\ 0 \end{bmatrix} = \begin{bmatrix} .5 \\ .3 \\ .2 \end{bmatrix}$$

$$\mathbf{v}_2 = P\mathbf{v}_1 = \begin{bmatrix} .5 & .2 & .3 \\ .3 & .8 & .3 \\ .2 & 0 & .4 \end{bmatrix} \begin{bmatrix} .5 \\ .3 \\ .2 \end{bmatrix} = \begin{bmatrix} .37 \\ .45 \\ .18 \end{bmatrix}$$

$$\mathbf{v}_3 = P\mathbf{v}_2 = \begin{bmatrix} .5 & .2 & .3 \\ .3 & .8 & .3 \\ .2 & 0 & .4 \end{bmatrix} \begin{bmatrix} .37 \\ .45 \\ .18 \end{bmatrix} = \begin{bmatrix} .329 \\ .525 \\ .146 \end{bmatrix}$$

Continuing in this manner, we have

$$\mathbf{v}_4 = \begin{bmatrix} .3133 \\ .5625 \\ .1242 \end{bmatrix}, \quad \mathbf{v}_5 = \begin{bmatrix} .3064 \\ .5813 \\ .1123 \end{bmatrix}, \quad \mathbf{v}_6 = \begin{bmatrix} .3032 \\ .5906 \\ .1062 \end{bmatrix}, \quad \mathbf{v}_7 = \begin{bmatrix} .3016 \\ .5953 \\ .1031 \end{bmatrix}$$

$$\mathbf{v}_8 = \begin{bmatrix} .3008 \\ .5977 \\ .1015 \end{bmatrix}, \quad \mathbf{v}_9 = \begin{bmatrix} .3004 \\ .5988 \\ .1008 \end{bmatrix}, \quad \mathbf{v}_{10} = \begin{bmatrix} .3002 \\ .5994 \\ .1004 \end{bmatrix}, \quad \mathbf{v}_{11} = \begin{bmatrix} .3001 \\ .5997 \\ .1002 \end{bmatrix}$$

$$\mathbf{v}_{12} = \begin{bmatrix} .30005 \\ .59985 \\ .10010 \end{bmatrix}, \quad \mathbf{v}_{13} = \begin{bmatrix} .30002 \\ .59993 \\ .10005 \end{bmatrix}, \quad \mathbf{v}_{14} = \begin{bmatrix} .30001 \\ .59996 \\ .10003 \end{bmatrix}, \quad \mathbf{v}_{15} = \begin{bmatrix} .30001 \\ .59998 \\ .10001 \end{bmatrix}$$

These vectors seem to be approaching $\mathbf{q} = \begin{bmatrix} .3 \\ .6 \\ .1 \end{bmatrix}$. The probabilities are hardly changing from one value of k to the next. Observe that the following calculation is exact (with no rounding error):

$$P\mathbf{q} = \begin{bmatrix} .5 & .2 & .3 \\ .3 & .8 & .3 \\ .2 & 0 & .4 \end{bmatrix} \begin{bmatrix} .3 \\ .6 \\ .1 \end{bmatrix} = \begin{bmatrix} .15 + .12 + .03 \\ .09 + .48 + .03 \\ .06 + 0 + .04 \end{bmatrix} = \begin{bmatrix} .30 \\ .60 \\ .10 \end{bmatrix} = \mathbf{q}$$

When the system is in state $\mathbf{q}$, there is no change in the system from one measurement to the next. ∎

Steady-State Vectors

If P is a stochastic matrix, then a **steady-state vector** (or **equilibrium vector**) for P is a probability vector $\mathbf{q}$ such that

$$P\mathbf{q} = \mathbf{q}$$

It can be shown that every stochastic matrix has a steady-state vector. In Example 3 above, $\mathbf{q}$ is a steady-state vector for P.

EXAMPLE 4 The probability vector $\mathbf{q} = \begin{bmatrix} .375 \\ .625 \end{bmatrix}$ is a steady-state vector for the population migration matrix M in Example 1, because

$$M\mathbf{q} = \begin{bmatrix} .95 & .03 \\ .05 & .97 \end{bmatrix} \begin{bmatrix} .375 \\ .625 \end{bmatrix} = \begin{bmatrix} .35625 + .01875 \\ .01875 + .60625 \end{bmatrix} = \begin{bmatrix} .375 \\ .625 \end{bmatrix} = \mathbf{q}$$

∎

If the total population of the metropolitan region in Example 1 is 1 million, then the **q** from Example 4 would correspond to having 375,000 persons in the city and 625,000 in the suburbs. At the end of one year, the migration *out of* the city would be (.05)(375,000) = 18,750 persons, and the migration *into* the city from the suburbs would be (.03)(625,000) = 18,750 persons. As a result, the population in the city would remain the same. Similarly, the suburban population would be stable.

The next example shows how to *find* a steady-state vector.

EXAMPLE 5 Let $P = \begin{bmatrix} .6 & .3 \\ .4 & .7 \end{bmatrix}$. Find a steady-state vector for P.

Solution First, solve the equation $P\mathbf{x} = \mathbf{x}$.

$$P\mathbf{x} - \mathbf{x} = \mathbf{0}$$

$$P\mathbf{x} - I\mathbf{x} = \mathbf{0} \quad \text{(Recall from Section 2.2 that } Ix = x.\text{)}$$

$$(P - I)\mathbf{x} = \mathbf{0}$$

For P as above,

$$P - I = \begin{bmatrix} .6 & .3 \\ .4 & .7 \end{bmatrix} - \begin{bmatrix} 1 & 0 \\ 0 & 1 \end{bmatrix} = \begin{bmatrix} -.4 & .3 \\ .4 & -.3 \end{bmatrix}$$

To find all solutions of $(P - I)\mathbf{x} = \mathbf{0}$, row reduce the augmented matrix

$$\begin{bmatrix} -.4 & .3 & 0 \\ .4 & -.3 & 0 \end{bmatrix} \sim \begin{bmatrix} -.4 & .3 & 0 \\ 0 & 0 & 0 \end{bmatrix} \sim \begin{bmatrix} 1 & -3/4 & 0 \\ 0 & 0 & 0 \end{bmatrix}$$

Then $x_1 = \frac{3}{4}x_2$ and x_2 is free. The general solution is $x_2 \begin{bmatrix} 3/4 \\ 1 \end{bmatrix}$.

Next, choose a simple basis for the solution space. One obvious choice is $\begin{bmatrix} 3/4 \\ 1 \end{bmatrix}$ but a better choice with no fractions is $\mathbf{w} = \begin{bmatrix} 3 \\ 4 \end{bmatrix}$ (corresponding to $x_2 = 4$).

Finally, find a probability vector in the set of all solutions of $P\mathbf{x} = \mathbf{x}$. This process is easy, since every solution is a multiple of the **w** above. Divide **w** by the sum of its entries and obtain

$$\mathbf{q} = \begin{bmatrix} 3/7 \\ 4/7 \end{bmatrix}$$

As a check, compute

$$P\mathbf{q} = \begin{bmatrix} 6/10 & 3/10 \\ 4/10 & 7/10 \end{bmatrix} \begin{bmatrix} 3/7 \\ 4/7 \end{bmatrix} = \begin{bmatrix} 18/70 + 12/70 \\ 12/70 + 28/70 \end{bmatrix} = \begin{bmatrix} 30/70 \\ 40/70 \end{bmatrix} = \mathbf{q}$$

The next theorem shows that what happened in Example 3 is typical of many stochastic matrices. We say that a stochastic matrix is **regular** if some matrix power

P^k contains only strictly positive entries. For the P in Example 3, we have

$$P^2 = \begin{bmatrix} .37 & .26 & .33 \\ .45 & .70 & .45 \\ .18 & .04 & .22 \end{bmatrix}$$

Since every entry in P^2 is strictly positive, P is a regular stochastic matrix.

Also, we say that a sequence of vectors $\{\mathbf{v}_k : k = 1, 2, \ldots\}$ **converges** to a vector $\mathbf{q}$ as $k \to \infty$ if the entries in the $\mathbf{v}_k$ can be made as close as desired to the corresponding entries in $\mathbf{q}$ by taking k sufficiently large.

THEOREM 19

If P is an $n \times n$ regular stochastic matrix, then P has a unique steady-state vector $\mathbf{q}$. Further, if $\mathbf{v}_0$ is any initial state and $\mathbf{v}_{k+1} = P\mathbf{v}_k$ for $k = 0, 1, 2, \ldots$, then the Markov chain $\{\mathbf{v}_k\}$ converges to $\mathbf{q}$ as $k \to \infty$.

This theorem is proved in standard texts on Markov chains. The amazing part of the theorem is that the initial state has no effect on the long-term behavior of the Markov chain.

EXAMPLE 6 In Example 2, what percentage of the voters are likely to vote for the Republican candidate in some election many years from now, assuming that the election outcomes form a Markov chain?

Solution The *wrong* approach is to pick some initial vector $\mathbf{v}_0$ and compute $\mathbf{v}_1, \ldots, \mathbf{v}_k$ for some large value of k. You have no way of knowing how many vectors to compute, and you cannot be sure of the limiting values of the entries in the $\mathbf{v}_k$.

The correct approach is to compute the steady-state vector and then appeal to Theorem 19. Given P as in Example 2, form $P - I$ by subtracting 1 from each diagonal entry in P. Then row reduce the augmented matrix:

$$[\,(P - I) \quad \mathbf{0}\,] = \begin{bmatrix} -.3 & .1 & .3 & 0 \\ .2 & -.2 & .3 & 0 \\ .1 & .1 & -.6 & 0 \end{bmatrix}$$

Recall from earlier work with decimals that the arithmetic is simplified by multiplying each row by 10.[1]

$$\begin{bmatrix} -3 & 1 & 3 & 0 \\ 2 & -2 & 3 & 0 \\ 1 & 1 & -6 & 0 \end{bmatrix} \sim \begin{bmatrix} 1 & 0 & -9/4 & 0 \\ 0 & 1 & -15/4 & 0 \\ 0 & 0 & 0 & 0 \end{bmatrix}$$

The general solution of $(P - I)\mathbf{x} = \mathbf{0}$ is $x_1 = \frac{9}{4}x_3$, $x_2 = \frac{15}{4}x_3$, and x_3 is free. Choosing $x_3 = 4$, we obtain a basis for the solution space whose entries are integers, and from

[1] *Warning*: Don't multiply only P by 10. Instead, multiply the augmented matrix for equation $(P - I)\mathbf{x} = \mathbf{0}$ by 10.

this we easily find the steady-state vector whose entries sum to 1:

$$\mathbf{w} = \begin{bmatrix} 9 \\ 15 \\ 4 \end{bmatrix}, \qquad \text{and} \qquad \mathbf{q} = \begin{bmatrix} 9/28 \\ 15/28 \\ 4/28 \end{bmatrix} \approx \begin{bmatrix} .32 \\ .54 \\ .14 \end{bmatrix}$$

The entries in $\mathbf{q}$ describe the distribution of votes at an election to be held many years from now (assuming the stochastic matrix continues to describe the changes from one election to the next). Thus, eventually, about 54% of the vote will be for the Republican candidate. ∎

Numerical Note

You may have noticed that if $\mathbf{v}_{k+1} = P\mathbf{v}_k$ for $k = 0, 1, \ldots,$ then

$$\mathbf{v}_2 = P\mathbf{v}_1 = P(P\mathbf{v}_0) = P^2\mathbf{v}_0,$$

and, in general,

$$\mathbf{v}_k = P^k\mathbf{v}_0 \quad \text{for } k = 0, 1, \ldots$$

This fact is mainly useful for theoretical purposes. To compute a specific vector such as $\mathbf{v}_3$, it is faster to compute $\mathbf{v}_1$, $\mathbf{v}_2$, and then $\mathbf{v}_3$, rather than to compute P^2, P^3, and then $P^3\mathbf{v}_0$.

PRACTICE PROBLEMS

1. Suppose that the residents of a metropolitan region move according to the probabilities in the migration matrix of Example 1 and that a resident is chosen "at random." Then a state vector for a certain year may be interpreted as giving the probabilities that the person is a city resident or a suburban resident at that time.

   a. Suppose that the person chosen is a city resident now, so that $\mathbf{v}_0 = \begin{bmatrix} 1 \\ 0 \end{bmatrix}$. What is the likelihood that the person will live in the suburbs next year?

   b. What is the likelihood that the person will be living in the suburbs in two years?

2. Let $P = \begin{bmatrix} .6 & .2 \\ .4 & .8 \end{bmatrix}$ and $\mathbf{q} = \begin{bmatrix} .3 \\ .7 \end{bmatrix}$. Is $\mathbf{q}$ a steady-state vector for P?

3. What percentage of the population in Example 1 will live in the suburbs after many years?

5.9 EXERCISES

1. A small remote village receives radio broadcasts from two radio stations, a news station and a music station. Of the listeners who are tuned to the news station, 70% will remain listening to the news after the station break that occurs each

half hour, while 30% will switch to the music station at the station break. Of the listeners who are tuned to the music station, 60% will switch to the news station at the station break, while 40% will remain listening to the music. Suppose that at 8:15 A.M., everyone is listening to the news.

a. Give the stochastic matrix that describes how the radio listeners tend to change stations at each station break. Label the rows and columns.

b. Give the initial state vector.

c. What percent of the listeners will be listening to the music station at 9:25 A.M. (after the station breaks at 8:30 and 9:00 A.M.)?

2. On any given day, a student is either healthy or ill. Of the students who are healthy today, 95% will be healthy tomorrow. Of the students who are ill today, 55% will still be ill tomorrow.

a. What is the stochastic matrix for this situation?

b. Suppose that on Monday 20% of the students are ill. What fraction or percentage of the students are likely to be ill on Tuesday? On Wednesday?

c. If a student is well today, what is the probability that he or she will be well two days from now?

3. A laboratory animal may eat any one of three foods each day. Laboratory records show that if the animal chooses one food on one trial, it will choose the same food on the next trial with probability 50%, and it will choose the other foods on the next trial with equal probabilities of 25%.

a. What is the stochastic matrix for this situation?

b. If the animal chooses food #1 on an initial trial, what is the probability that it will choose food #2 on the second trial after the initial trial?

4. The weather in Columbus is either good, indifferent, or bad on any given day. If the weather is good today, there is a 60% chance the weather will be good tomorrow, a 30% chance the weather will be indifferent, and a 10% chance the weather will be bad. If the weather is indifferent today, it will be good tomorrow with probability .40 and indifferent with probability .30. Finally, if the weather is bad today, it will be good tomorrow with probability .40 and indifferent with probability .50.

a. What is the stochastic matrix for this situation?

b. Suppose that today there is a 50% chance of good weather and a 50% chance of indifferent weather. What are the chances of bad weather tomorrow?

c. Suppose that the predicted weather for Monday is 40% indifferent weather and 60% bad weather. What are the chances for good weather on Wednesday?

In Exercises 5–8, find the steady-state vector.

5. $\begin{bmatrix} .1 & .6 \\ .9 & .4 \end{bmatrix}$

6. $\begin{bmatrix} .8 & .5 \\ .2 & .5 \end{bmatrix}$

7. $\begin{bmatrix} .7 & .1 & .1 \\ .2 & .8 & .2 \\ .1 & .1 & .7 \end{bmatrix}$

8. $\begin{bmatrix} .7 & .2 & .2 \\ 0 & .2 & .4 \\ .3 & .6 & .4 \end{bmatrix}$

9. Determine if $P = \begin{bmatrix} .2 & 1 \\ .8 & 0 \end{bmatrix}$ is a regular stochastic matrix.

10. Determine if $P = \begin{bmatrix} 1 & .2 \\ 0 & .8 \end{bmatrix}$ is a regular stochastic matrix.

11. a. Find the steady-state vector for the Markov chain in Exercise 1.

b. At some time late in the day, what fraction of the listeners will be listening to the news?

12. a. Find the steady-state vector for the Markov chain in Exercise 2.

b. What is the probability that after many days a specific person is ill? Does it matter if that person is ill today?

13. Refer to Exercise 3. Which food will the animal prefer after many trials?

14. Refer to Exercise 4. In the long run, how likely is it for the weather in Columbus to be good on a given day?

15. The Demographic Research Unit of the California State Department of Finance supplied data for the following migration matrix which describes the movement of the United States population during 1989. In 1989, about 11.7% of the total population lived in California. What percentage of the total population would eventually live in California if the listed migration probabilities were to remain constant over many years?

From: CA	Rest of U.S.	To:
.9821	.0029	California
.0179	.9971	Rest of U.S.

16. In Detroit, Hertz Rent A Car has a fleet of about 2000 cars. The pattern of rental and return locations is given by the fractions in the table below. On a typical day, about how many cars will be rented or ready to rent from the Downtown location?

Cars Rented From: City Airport	Down-town	Metro Airport	Returned To:
.90	.01	.09	City Airport
.01	.90	.01	Downtown
.09	.09	.90	Metro Airport

17. Let P be an $n \times n$ stochastic matrix. The following argument shows that the equation $P\mathbf{x} = \mathbf{x}$ has a nontrivial solution. (In fact, a steady-state solution exists with nonnegative entries. A proof is given in some advanced texts.) Justify each assertion below. (Mention a theorem when appropriate.)

    a. If all the other rows of $P - I$ are added to the bottom row, the result is a row of zeros.

    b. The rows of $P - I$ are linearly dependent.

    c. The dimension of the row space of $P - I$ is less than n.

    d. $P - I$ has a nontrivial null space.

18. Show that every 2×2 stochastic matrix has at least one steady-state vector. Any such matrix may be written in the form $P = \begin{bmatrix} 1-\alpha & \beta \\ \alpha & 1-\beta \end{bmatrix}$, where α and β are constants between 0 and 1. (There are two linearly independent steady-state vectors if $\alpha = \beta = 0$. Otherwise, there is only one.)

19. Let S be the $1 \times n$ row matrix with a 1 in each column,

    $S = [1 \quad 1 \quad \cdots \quad 1]$

    a. Explain why a vector $\mathbf{v}$ in $\mathbb{R}^n$ is a probability vector if and only if its entries are nonnegative and $S\mathbf{v} = 1$. (A 1×1 matrix such as the product $S\mathbf{v}$ is usually written without the matrix bracket symbols.)

    b. Let P be an $n \times n$ stochastic matrix. Explain why $SP = S$.

    c. Let P be an $n \times n$ stochastic matrix and let $\mathbf{v}$ be a probability vector. Show that $P\mathbf{v}$ is also a probability vector.

20. Use Exercise 19 to show that if P is an $n \times n$ stochastic matrix, then so is P^2.

SOLUTIONS TO PRACTICE PROBLEMS

1. a. Since 5% of the city residents will move to the suburbs within one year, there is a 5% chance of choosing such a person. Without further knowledge about the person, we say that there is a 5% chance the person will move to the suburbs. This fact is contained in the second entry of the state vector $\mathbf{v}_1$, where

$$\mathbf{v}_1 = M\mathbf{v}_0 = \begin{bmatrix} .95 & .03 \\ .05 & .97 \end{bmatrix} \begin{bmatrix} 1 \\ 0 \end{bmatrix} = \begin{bmatrix} .95 \\ .05 \end{bmatrix}$$

   b. The likelihood the person is living in the suburbs after two years is 9.6%, because

$$\mathbf{v}_2 = M\mathbf{v}_1 = \begin{bmatrix} .95 & .03 \\ .05 & .97 \end{bmatrix} \begin{bmatrix} .95 \\ .05 \end{bmatrix} = \begin{bmatrix} .904 \\ .096 \end{bmatrix}$$

2. The steady-state vector satisfies $P\mathbf{x} = \mathbf{x}$. Since

$$P\mathbf{q} = \begin{bmatrix} .6 & .2 \\ .4 & .8 \end{bmatrix} \begin{bmatrix} .3 \\ .7 \end{bmatrix} = \begin{bmatrix} .32 \\ .68 \end{bmatrix} \neq \mathbf{q}$$

we conclude that $\mathbf{q}$ is *not* the steady-state vector for P.

3. The P in Example 1 is a regular stochastic matrix because its entries are all strictly positive. So we may use Theorem 19. We already know the steady-state vector from Example 4. Thus the population distribution vectors $\mathbf{v}_k$ converge to

$$\mathbf{q} = \begin{bmatrix} .375 \\ .625 \end{bmatrix}$$

Eventually 62.5% of the population will live in the suburbs.

CHAPTER 5 SUPPLEMENTARY EXERCISES

1. Mark each statement as True or False. Justify each answer. In parts (a)–(f), $\mathbf{v}_1, \ldots, \mathbf{v}_p$ are vectors in a nonzero finite-dimensional vector space V, and $S = \{\mathbf{v}_1, \ldots, \mathbf{v}_p\}$.

____ a. The set of all linear combinations of $\mathbf{v}_1, \ldots, \mathbf{v}_p$ is a vector space.

____ b. If $\{\mathbf{v}_1, \ldots, \mathbf{v}_{p-1}\}$ spans V, then S spans V.

____ c. If $\{\mathbf{v}_1, \ldots, \mathbf{v}_{p-1}\}$ is linearly independent, then so is S.

____ d. If S is linearly independent, then S is a basis for V.

____ e. If Span $S = V$, then some subset of S is a basis for V.

____ f. If dim $V = p$ and Span $S = V$, then S cannot be linearly dependent.

____ g. A plane in $\mathbb{R}^3$ is a two-dimensional subspace.

____ h. The nonpivot columns of a matrix are always linearly dependent.

____ i. Row operations on a matrix A can change the linear dependence relations among the rows of A.

____ j. Row operations on a matrix can change the null space.

____ k. The rank of a matrix equals the number of nonzero rows.

____ l. If an $m \times n$ matrix A is row equivalent to an echelon matrix U, and if U has k nonzero rows, then the dimension of the solution space of $A\mathbf{x} = \mathbf{0}$ is $m - k$.

____ m. If B is obtained from a matrix A by several elementary row operations, then rank B = rank A.

____ n. If A is $m \times n$ and rank $A = m$, then the linear transformation $\mathbf{x} \mapsto A\mathbf{x}$ is one-to-one.

____ o. If A is $m \times n$ and the linear transformation $\mathbf{x} \mapsto A\mathbf{x}$ is onto, then rank $A = m$.

____ p. A change-of-coordinates matrix is always invertible.

____ q. If $\mathcal{B} = \{\mathbf{b}_1, \ldots, \mathbf{b}_n\}$ and $\mathcal{C} = \{\mathbf{c}_1, \ldots, \mathbf{c}_n\}$ are bases for a vector space V, then the jth column of the change-of-coordinates matrix $\underset{\mathcal{C} \leftarrow \mathcal{B}}{P}$ is the coordinate vector $[\mathbf{c}_j]_{\mathcal{B}}$.

2. Find a basis for the set of all vectors of the form

$$\begin{bmatrix} a - 2b + 5c \\ 2a + 5b - 8c \\ -a - 4b + 7c \\ 3a + b + c \end{bmatrix} \quad \text{(Be careful.)}$$

3. Let $\mathbf{u}_1 = \begin{bmatrix} -2 \\ 4 \\ -6 \end{bmatrix}$, $\mathbf{u}_2 = \begin{bmatrix} 1 \\ 2 \\ -5 \end{bmatrix}$, $\mathbf{b} = \begin{bmatrix} b_1 \\ b_2 \\ b_3 \end{bmatrix}$, and $W =$ Span $\{\mathbf{u}_1, \mathbf{u}_2\}$. Find an *implicit* description of W; that is, find a set of one or more homogeneous equations that characterize the points of W. [*Hint*: When is $\mathbf{b}$ in W?]

4. Suppose $\mathbf{p}_1, \mathbf{p}_2, \mathbf{p}_3, \mathbf{p}_4$ are specific polynomials that span a two-dimensional subspace H of $\mathbb{P}_5$. Describe how one can find a basis for H by examining the four polynomials and making almost no computations.

5. What would you have to know about the solution set of a homogeneous system of 18 linear equations in 20 variables in order to know that every associated nonhomogeneous equation has a solution? Discuss.

6. Let H be an n-dimensional subspace of an n-dimensional vector space V. Explain why $H = V$.

7. Let S be a maximal linearly independent subset of a vector space V. That is, S has the property that if a vector not in S is adjoined to S, then the new set will no longer be linearly independent. Prove that S must be a basis for V. [*Hint*: What if S were linearly independent but not a basis of V?]

8. Let S be a finite minimal spanning set of a vector space V. That is, S has the property that if a vector is removed from S, then the new set will no longer span V. Prove that S must be a basis for V.

Exercises 9–12 develop properties of rank that are sometimes needed in applications. Assume the matrix A is $m \times n$.

9. Show that if P is an invertible $m \times m$ matrix, then rank PA = rank A. [*Hint*: Explain why P is a product of elementary matrices, and show that PA is row equivalent to A.]

10. Show that if Q is invertible, then rank AQ = rank A. [*Hint*: Use Exercise 9 to study rank $(AQ)^T$.]

11. a. Show that if B is $n \times p$, then rank $AB \leq$ rank A. [*Hint*: Explain why every vector in the column space of AB is in the column space of A.]

b. Show that if B is $n \times p$, then rank $AB \leq$ rank B. [*Hint*: Use part (a) to study rank $(AB)^T$.]

12. A **submatrix** of a matrix A is any matrix that results from deleting some (or no) rows and/or columns of A. It can be shown that A has rank r if and only if A contains an invertible $r \times r$ submatrix and no larger square submatrix is invertible. Demonstrate part of this statement by explaining (a) why an $m \times n$ matrix A of rank r has an $m \times r$ submatrix A_1 of rank r, and (b) why A_1 has an invertible $r \times r$ submatrix A_2.

The concept of rank plays an important role in the design of engineering control systems, such as the space shuttle system mentioned in the chapter's introductory example. A *state-space model* of a control system includes a difference equation of the form

$$\mathbf{x}_{k+1} = A\mathbf{x}_k + B\mathbf{u}_k \qquad \text{for } k = 0, 1, \ldots$$

where A is $n \times n$, B is $n \times m$, $\{\mathbf{x}_k\}$ is a sequence of "state vectors" in $\mathbb{R}^n$ that describe the state of the system at discrete times, and $\{\mathbf{u}_k\}$ is a *control* or *input* sequence. The pair (A, B) is said to be **controllable** if

$$\text{rank } [\, B \quad AB \quad A^2B \quad \cdots \quad A^{n-1}B \,] = n$$

If (A, B) is controllable, then the system can be controlled or driven to any specified state $\mathbf{x}$ in at most n steps, simply by choosing an appropriate control sequence. Determine if the matrix pairs in Exercises 13 and 14 are controllable.

13. $A = \begin{bmatrix} .9 & 1 & 0 \\ 0 & -.9 & 0 \\ 0 & 0 & .5 \end{bmatrix}, \quad B = \begin{bmatrix} 0 \\ 1 \\ 1 \end{bmatrix}$

14. $A = \begin{bmatrix} .8 & -.3 & 0 \\ .2 & .5 & 1 \\ 0 & 0 & -.5 \end{bmatrix}, \quad B = \begin{bmatrix} 1 \\ 1 \\ 0 \end{bmatrix}$

6

Eigenvalues and Eigenvectors

Introductory Example: Dynamical Systems and Spotted Owls

In 1990 the northern spotted owl became the center of a nationwide controversy over the use and misuse of the majestic forests in the Pacific Northwest. Environmentalists convinced the federal government that the owl was threatened with extinction if logging continued in the old-growth forests (with trees over 200 years old), where the owls prefer to live. The timber industry, anticipating the loss of 30,000 to 100,000 jobs as a result of new government restrictions on logging, argued that the owl should not be classified as a "threatened species" and cited a number of published scientific reports to support its case.[1]

Caught in the crossfire of the two lobbying groups, mathematical ecologists intensified their drive to understand the population dynamics of the spotted owl. The life cycle of a spotted owl divides naturally into three stages: juvenile (up to 1 year old), subadult (1 to 2 years), and adult (over 2 years). The owl mates for life during the subadult and adult stages, begins to breed as an adult, and lives for up to 20 years. Each owl pair requires about 1000 hectares (4 square miles) for its own home territory. A critical time in the life cycle is when the juveniles leave the nest. To survive and become a subadult, a juvenile must successfully find a new home range (and usually a mate).

A first step in studying the population dynamics is to model the population at yearly intervals, at times denoted by $k = 0, 1, 2, \ldots$. Usually, one assumes that there

[1]"The Great Spotted Owl War," *Reader's Digest*, November 1992, pp. 91–95.

is a 1:1 ratio of males to females in each life stage and counts only the females. The population at year k can be described by a vector $\mathbf{x}_k = (j_k, s_k, a_k)$, where j_k, s_k, and a_k are the numbers of females in the juvenile, subadult, and adult stages, respectively.

Using actual field data from demographic studies, R. Lamberson and co-workers considered the following *stage-matrix model*:[2]

$$\begin{bmatrix} j_{k+1} \\ s_{k+1} \\ a_{k+1} \end{bmatrix} = \begin{bmatrix} 0 & 0 & .33 \\ .18 & 0 & 0 \\ 0 & .71 & .94 \end{bmatrix} \begin{bmatrix} j_k \\ s_k \\ a_k \end{bmatrix}$$

Here the number of new juvenile females in year $k+1$ is .33 times the number of adult females in year k (based on the average birth rate per owl pair). Also, 18% of the juveniles survive to become subadults, and 71% of the subadults and 94% of the adults survive to be counted as adults.

The stage-matrix model is a difference equation of the form $\mathbf{x}_{k+1} = A\mathbf{x}_k$. Such an equation is often called a **dynamical system** (or a **discrete linear dynamical system**) because it describes the changes in a system as time passes.

The 18% juvenile survival rate in the Lamberson stage matrix is the entry affected most by the amount of old-growth forest available. Actually, 60% of the juveniles normally survive to leave the nest, but in the Willow Creek region of California studied by Lamberson and his colleagues, only 30% of the juveniles that left the nest were able to find new home ranges. The rest perished during the search process.

A significant reason for the failure of owls to find new home ranges is the increasing fragmentation of old-growth timber stands due to clear-cutting of scattered areas on the old-growth land. When an owl leaves the protective canopy of the forest and crosses a clear-cut area, the risk of attack by predators increases dramatically. Section 6.6 will show that the model described above predicts the eventual demise of the spotted owl, but that if 50% of the juveniles that survive to leave the nest also find new home ranges, then the owl population will thrive.

The goal of this chapter is to dissect the action of a linear transformation $\mathbf{x} \mapsto A\mathbf{x}$ into elements that are easily visualized. Except for a brief digression in Section 6.4, all matrices in the chapter are square. The main applications described here are to discrete dynamical systems, such as described in the chapter's introductory example. However, the basic concepts—eigenvectors and eigenvalues—are useful throughout pure and applied mathematics, and they appear in settings far more general than we consider here. Eigenvalues are also used to study differential equations and *continuous* dynamical systems, they provide critical information in engineering design, and they arise naturally in fields such as physics and chemistry.

---

[2] R. H. Lamberson, R. McKelvey, B.R. Noon, and C. Voss, "A Dynamic Analysis of the Viability of the Northern Spotted Owl in a Fragmented Forest Environment," *Conservation Biology* 6 (1992): 505–512. Also, a private communication from Professor Lamberson, 1993.

6.1 EIGENVECTORS AND EIGENVALUES

Although a transformation $\mathbf{x} \mapsto A\mathbf{x}$ may move vectors in a variety of directions, it often happens that there are special vectors on which the action of A is quite simple.

EXAMPLE 1 Let $A = \begin{bmatrix} 3 & -2 \\ 1 & 0 \end{bmatrix}$, $\mathbf{u} = \begin{bmatrix} -1 \\ 1 \end{bmatrix}$, and $\mathbf{v} = \begin{bmatrix} 2 \\ 1 \end{bmatrix}$. The images of $\mathbf{u}$ and $\mathbf{v}$ under multiplication by A are shown in Fig. 1. In fact, $A\mathbf{v}$ is just $2\mathbf{v}$. So A only "stretches," or dilates, $\mathbf{v}$.

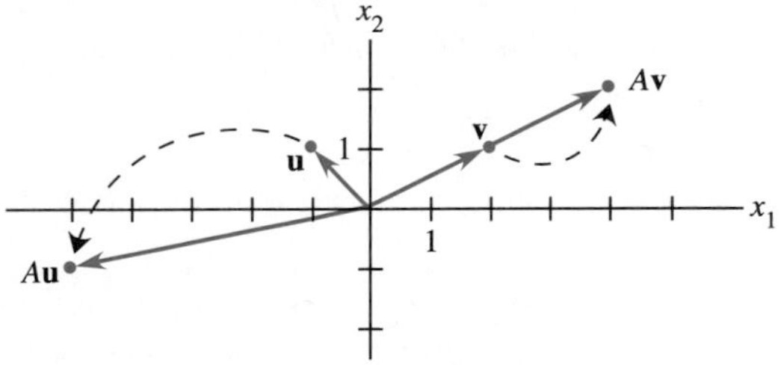

FIGURE 1 Effects of multiplication by A.

As another example, readers of Section 5.9 will recall that if A is a stochastic matrix, then the steady-state vector $\mathbf{q}$ for A satisfies the equation $A\mathbf{x} = \mathbf{x}$. That is, $A\mathbf{q} = 1 \cdot \mathbf{q}$.

In this section, we study equations such as

$$A\mathbf{x} = 2\mathbf{x} \quad \text{or} \quad A\mathbf{x} = -4\mathbf{x}$$

and we look for vectors that are transformed by A into a scalar multiple of themselves.

DEFINITION

An **eigenvector** of an $n \times n$ matrix A is a nonzero vector $\mathbf{x}$ such that $A\mathbf{x} = \lambda\mathbf{x}$ for some scalar λ. A scalar λ is called an **eigenvalue** of A if there is a nontrivial solution $\mathbf{x}$ of $A\mathbf{x} = \lambda\mathbf{x}$; such an $\mathbf{x}$ is called an *eigenvector corresponding to* λ.

It is easy to determine if a given vector is an eigenvector of a matrix. It is also easy to decide if a specified scalar is an eigenvalue.

EXAMPLE 2 Let $A = \begin{bmatrix} 1 & 6 \\ 5 & 2 \end{bmatrix}$, $\mathbf{u} = \begin{bmatrix} 6 \\ -5 \end{bmatrix}$, and $\mathbf{v} = \begin{bmatrix} 3 \\ -2 \end{bmatrix}$. Are $\mathbf{u}$ and $\mathbf{v}$ eigenvectors of A?

Solution

$$A\mathbf{u} = \begin{bmatrix} 1 & 6 \\ 5 & 2 \end{bmatrix} \begin{bmatrix} 6 \\ -5 \end{bmatrix} = \begin{bmatrix} -24 \\ 20 \end{bmatrix} = -4 \begin{bmatrix} 6 \\ -5 \end{bmatrix} = -4\mathbf{u}$$

$$A\mathbf{v} = \begin{bmatrix} 1 & 6 \\ 5 & 2 \end{bmatrix} \begin{bmatrix} 3 \\ -2 \end{bmatrix} = \begin{bmatrix} -9 \\ 11 \end{bmatrix} \neq \lambda \begin{bmatrix} 3 \\ -2 \end{bmatrix}$$

Thus $\mathbf{u}$ is an eigenvector corresponding to an eigenvalue -4, but $\mathbf{v}$ is not an eigenvector of A, because $A\mathbf{v}$ is not a multiple of $\mathbf{v}$.

EXAMPLE 3 Show that 7 is an eigenvalue of the A in Example 2, and find the corresponding eigenvectors.

Solution The scalar 7 is an eigenvalue of A if and only if the equation

$$A\mathbf{x} = 7\mathbf{x} \tag{1}$$

has a nontrivial solution. But (1) is equivalent to $A\mathbf{x} - 7\mathbf{x} = \mathbf{0}$, or

$$(A - 7I)\mathbf{x} = \mathbf{0} \tag{2}$$

To solve this homogeneous equation, form the matrix

$$A - 7I = \begin{bmatrix} 1 & 6 \\ 5 & 2 \end{bmatrix} - \begin{bmatrix} 7 & 0 \\ 0 & 7 \end{bmatrix} = \begin{bmatrix} -6 & 6 \\ 5 & -5 \end{bmatrix}$$

The columns of $A - 7I$ are obviously linearly dependent, so (2) has nontrivial solutions. Thus 7 *is* an eigenvalue of A. To find the corresponding eigenvectors, use row operations:

$$\begin{bmatrix} -6 & 6 & 0 \\ 5 & -5 & 0 \end{bmatrix} \sim \begin{bmatrix} 1 & -1 & 0 \\ 0 & 0 & 0 \end{bmatrix}$$

The general solution has the form $x_2 \begin{bmatrix} 1 \\ 1 \end{bmatrix}$. Each vector of this form with $x_2 \neq 0$ is an eigenvector corresponding to $\lambda = 7$.

The equivalence of Eqs. (1) and (2) obviously holds for any λ in place of $\lambda = 7$. Thus λ is an eigenvalue of A if and only if the equation

$$(A - \lambda I)\mathbf{x} = \mathbf{0} \tag{3}$$

has a nontrivial solution. The set of *all* solutions of (3) is just the null space of the matrix $A - \lambda I$. So this set is a *subspace* of $\mathbb{R}^n$ and is called the **eigenspace** of A corresponding to λ. The eigenspace consists of the zero vector and all the eigenvectors corresponding to λ.

Example 3 shows that for the A in Example 2, the eigenspace corresponding to $\lambda = 7$ consists of *all* multiples of (1, 1), which is the line through (1, 1) and the origin. From Example 2, one can check that the eigenspace corresponding to $\lambda = -4$ is the line through $(6, -5)$. These eigenspaces are shown in Fig. 2, along with eigenvectors $(1, 1)$ and $(3/2, -5/4)$ and the geometric action of the transformation $\mathbf{x} \mapsto A\mathbf{x}$ on each eigenspace.

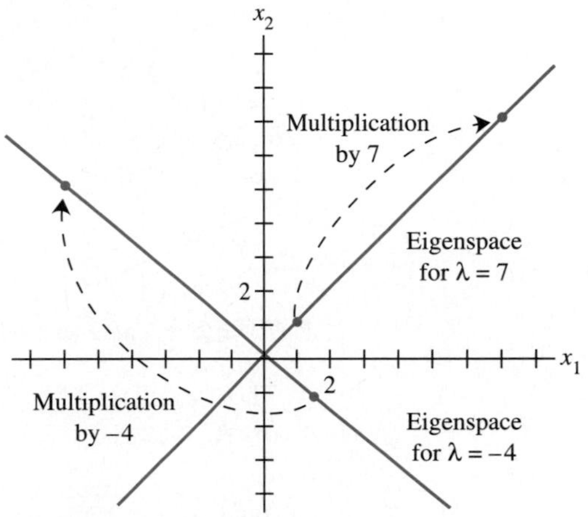

FIGURE 2 Eigenspaces for $\lambda = -4$ and $\lambda = 7$.

EXAMPLE 4 Let $A = \begin{bmatrix} 4 & -1 & 6 \\ 2 & 1 & 6 \\ 2 & -1 & 8 \end{bmatrix}$. An eigenvalue of A is 2. Find a basis for the corresponding eigenspace.

Solution Form

$$A - 2I = \begin{bmatrix} 4 & -1 & 6 \\ 2 & 1 & 6 \\ 2 & -1 & 8 \end{bmatrix} - \begin{bmatrix} 2 & 0 & 0 \\ 0 & 2 & 0 \\ 0 & 0 & 2 \end{bmatrix} = \begin{bmatrix} 2 & -1 & 6 \\ 2 & -1 & 6 \\ 2 & -1 & 6 \end{bmatrix}$$

and row reduce the augmented matrix for $(A - 2I)\mathbf{x} = \mathbf{0}$:

$$\begin{bmatrix} 2 & -1 & 6 & 0 \\ 2 & -1 & 6 & 0 \\ 2 & -1 & 6 & 0 \end{bmatrix} \sim \begin{bmatrix} 2 & -1 & 6 & 0 \\ 0 & 0 & 0 & 0 \\ 0 & 0 & 0 & 0 \end{bmatrix}$$

At this point we are confident that 2 is indeed an eigenvalue of A because the equation $(A - 2I)\mathbf{x} = \mathbf{0}$ has free variables. The general solution is

$$\begin{bmatrix} x_1 \\ x_2 \\ x_3 \end{bmatrix} = x_2 \begin{bmatrix} 1/2 \\ 1 \\ 0 \end{bmatrix} + x_3 \begin{bmatrix} -3 \\ 0 \\ 1 \end{bmatrix}, \qquad x_2 \text{ and } x_3 \text{ free}$$

The eigenspace, shown in Fig. 3, is a two-dimensional subspace of $\mathbb{R}^3$. A basis is

$$\left\{ \begin{bmatrix} 1 \\ 2 \\ 0 \end{bmatrix}, \begin{bmatrix} -3 \\ 0 \\ 1 \end{bmatrix} \right\}$$

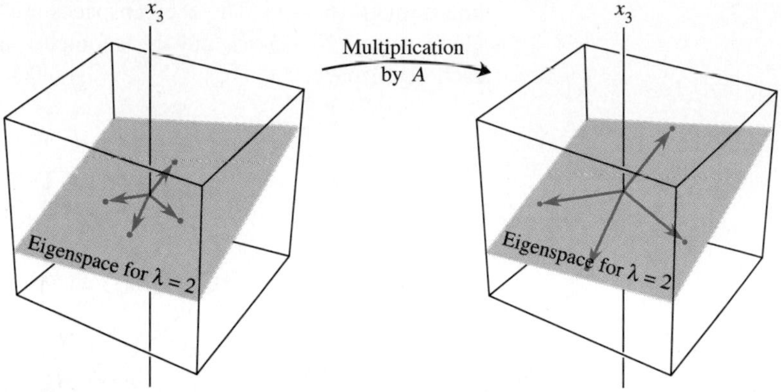

FIGURE 3 A acts as a dilation on the eigenspace.

Numerical Note

When both eigenvalues and eigenvectors are unknown, solving the equation $A\mathbf{x} = \lambda\mathbf{x}$ can be extremely difficult or even impossible. There are numerical algorithms for computing approximations to eigenvalues and eigenvectors, but the effectiveness of an algorithm depends on the type of matrix being studied. No one method is completely satisfactory, although there are computer programs today that will compute eigenvalues and eigenvectors to any desired degree of accuracy for matrices that are not too large. Acceptable sizes of matrices, however, are increasing each year as computing power and software improve.

The following theorem describes one of the few special cases in which eigenvalues can be found precisely. Calculation of eigenvalues will also be discussed in the next section.

THEOREM 1

Let A be a triangular matrix. Then the eigenvalues of A are the entries on its main diagonal.

Proof For simplicity, consider the 3×3 case. If A is upper triangular, then $A - \lambda I$ has the form

$$A - \lambda I = \begin{bmatrix} a_{11} & a_{12} & a_{13} \\ 0 & a_{22} & a_{23} \\ 0 & 0 & a_{33} \end{bmatrix} - \begin{bmatrix} \lambda & 0 & 0 \\ 0 & \lambda & 0 \\ 0 & 0 & \lambda \end{bmatrix}$$

$$= \begin{bmatrix} a_{11} - \lambda & a_{12} & a_{13} \\ 0 & a_{22} - \lambda & a_{23} \\ 0 & 0 & a_{33} - \lambda \end{bmatrix}$$

The scalar λ is an eigenvalue of A if and only if the equation $(A - \lambda I)\mathbf{x} = \mathbf{0}$ has a nontrivial solution, that is, if and only if the equation has a free variable. Because of the zero entries in $A - \lambda I$, it is easy to see that $(A - \lambda I)\mathbf{x} = \mathbf{0}$ has a free variable if and only if at least one of the entries on the diagonal of $A - \lambda I$ is zero. This happens if and only if λ equals one of the entries a_{11}, a_{22}, a_{33} in A. For the case when A is lower triangular, see Exercise 28. ∎

EXAMPLE 5 Let $A = \begin{bmatrix} 3 & 6 & -8 \\ 0 & 0 & 6 \\ 0 & 0 & 2 \end{bmatrix}$ and $B = \begin{bmatrix} 4 & 0 & 0 \\ -2 & 1 & 0 \\ 5 & 3 & 4 \end{bmatrix}$. The eigenvalues of A are 3, 0, and 2. The eigenvalues of B are 4 and 1. ∎

What does it mean for a matrix A to have an eigenvalue 0, such as in Example 5? This happens if and only if the equation

$$A\mathbf{x} = 0\mathbf{x} \tag{4}$$

has a nontrivial solution. But (4) is equivalent to $A\mathbf{x} = \mathbf{0}$, which has a nontrivial solution if and only if A is not invertible. Thus 0 *is an eigenvalue of* A *if and only if* A *is not invertible*. This observation leads to the final statement for the Invertible Matrix Theorem. The other statements were given in Sections 3.3 and 5.6.

THEOREM

The Invertible Matrix Theorem (concluded)

Let A be an $n \times n$ matrix. Then A is invertible if and only if:

o. The number 0 is *not* an eigenvalue of A.

The following important theorem will be needed later. Its proof illustrates a typical calculation with eigenvectors.

THEOREM 2

If $\mathbf{v}_1, \ldots, \mathbf{v}_r$ are eigenvectors that correspond to distinct eigenvalues $\lambda_1, \ldots, \lambda_r$ of an $n \times n$ matrix A then the set $\{\mathbf{v}_1, \ldots, \mathbf{v}_r\}$ is linearly independent.

Proof If $\{\mathbf{v}_1, \ldots, \mathbf{v}_r\}$ is linearly dependent, then there is a least index p such that $\mathbf{v}_{p+1}$ is a linear combination of the preceding (linearly independent) vectors, and there exist scalars $c_1, \ldots, c_p$ such that

$$c_1\mathbf{v}_1 + \cdots + c_p\mathbf{v}_p = \mathbf{v}_{p+1} \tag{5}$$

Multiplying both sides of (5) by A and using the fact that $A\mathbf{v}_k = \lambda_k\mathbf{v}_k$ for each k, we obtain

$$\begin{aligned} c_1A\mathbf{v}_1 + \cdots + c_pA\mathbf{v}_p &= A\mathbf{v}_{p+1} \\ c_1\lambda_1\mathbf{v}_1 + \cdots + c_p\lambda_p\mathbf{v}_p &= \lambda_{p+1}\mathbf{v}_{p+1} \end{aligned} \tag{6}$$

Multiplying both sides of (5) by λ_{p+1} and subtracting the result from (6), we have

$$c_1(\lambda_1 - \lambda_{p+1})\mathbf{v}_1 + \cdots + c_p(\lambda_p - \lambda_{p+1})\mathbf{v}_p = \mathbf{0} \tag{7}$$

Since $\{\mathbf{v}_1, \ldots, \mathbf{v}_p\}$ is linearly independent, the weights in (7) are all zero. But none of the factors $\lambda_i - \lambda_{p+1}$ are zero, because the eigenvalues are distinct. Hence $c_i = 0$ for $i = 1, \ldots, p$. But then (5) says that $\mathbf{v}_{p+1} = \mathbf{0}$, which is impossible. Hence $\{\mathbf{v}_1, \ldots, \mathbf{v}_r\}$ cannot be linearly dependent and therefore must be linearly independent. ∎

Eigenvectors and Difference Equations

We conclude the section by showing how to construct solutions of the first-order difference equation:

$$\mathbf{x}_{k+1} = A\mathbf{x}_k \qquad (k = 0, 1, 2, \ldots) \tag{8}$$

If A is an $n \times n$ matrix, then (8) is a *recursive* description of a sequence $\{\mathbf{x}_k\}$ in $\mathbb{R}^n$. A **solution** of (8) is an explicit description of $\{\mathbf{x}_k\}$ whose formula for each $\mathbf{x}_k$ does not depend directly on A or on the preceding terms in the sequence other than the initial term $\mathbf{x}_0$.

The simplest way to build a solution of (8) is to take an eigenvector $\mathbf{x}_0$ and its corresponding eigenvalue λ and let

$$\mathbf{x}_k = \lambda^k \mathbf{x}_0 \quad (k = 1, 2, \ldots) \tag{9}$$

This sequence works, because

$$\begin{aligned} A\mathbf{x}_k &= A(\lambda^k \mathbf{x}_0) = \lambda^k (A\mathbf{x}_0) \\ &= \lambda^k (\lambda \mathbf{x}_0) = \lambda^{k+1} \mathbf{x}_0 \\ &= \mathbf{x}_{k+1} \end{aligned}$$

Linear combinations of solutions of the form (9) are solutions, too! See Exercise 31.

PRACTICE PROBLEMS

1. Is 5 an eigenvalue of $A = \begin{bmatrix} 6 & -3 & 1 \\ 3 & 0 & 5 \\ 2 & 2 & 6 \end{bmatrix}$?
2. If $\mathbf{x}$ is an eigenvector for A corresponding to λ, what is $A^3\mathbf{x}$?

6.1 EXERCISES

1. Is $\lambda = 2$ an eigenvalue of $\begin{bmatrix} 3 & 2 \\ 3 & 8 \end{bmatrix}$?
2. Is $\lambda = -2$ an eigenvalue of $\begin{bmatrix} 7 & 3 \\ 3 & -1 \end{bmatrix}$?
3. Is $\begin{bmatrix} 1 \\ 4 \end{bmatrix}$ an eigenvector of $\begin{bmatrix} -3 & 1 \\ -3 & 8 \end{bmatrix}$? If so, find the eigenvalue.
4. Is $\begin{bmatrix} 3 \\ 2 \end{bmatrix}$ an eigenvector of $\begin{bmatrix} 5 & -3 \\ -4 & 9 \end{bmatrix}$? If so, find the eigenvalue.
5. Is $\begin{bmatrix} 4 \\ -3 \\ 1 \end{bmatrix}$ an eigenvector of $\begin{bmatrix} 3 & 7 & 9 \\ -4 & -5 & 1 \\ 2 & 4 & 4 \end{bmatrix}$? If so, find the eigenvalue.
6. Is $\begin{bmatrix} 1 \\ -2 \\ 1 \end{bmatrix}$ an eigenvector of $\begin{bmatrix} 3 & 6 & 7 \\ 3 & 3 & 7 \\ 5 & 6 & 5 \end{bmatrix}$? If so, find the eigenvalue.

7. Is $\lambda = 4$ an eigenvalue of $\begin{bmatrix} 3 & 0 & -1 \\ 2 & 3 & 1 \\ -3 & 4 & 5 \end{bmatrix}$? If so, find one corresponding eigenvector.

8. Is $\lambda = 3$ an eigenvalue of $\begin{bmatrix} 1 & 2 & 2 \\ 3 & -2 & 1 \\ 0 & 1 & 1 \end{bmatrix}$? If so, find one corresponding eigenvector.

In Exercises 9–16, find a basis for the eigenspace corresponding to each listed eigenvalue.

9. $A = \begin{bmatrix} 5 & 0 \\ 2 & 1 \end{bmatrix}, \lambda = 1, 5$

10. $A = \begin{bmatrix} 10 & -9 \\ 4 & -2 \end{bmatrix}, \lambda = 4$

11. $A = \begin{bmatrix} 4 & -2 \\ -3 & 9 \end{bmatrix}, \lambda = 10$

12. $A = \begin{bmatrix} 7 & 4 \\ -3 & -1 \end{bmatrix}, \lambda = 1, 5$

13. $A = \begin{bmatrix} 4 & 0 & 1 \\ -2 & 1 & 0 \\ -2 & 0 & 1 \end{bmatrix}, \lambda = 1, 2, 3$

14. $A = \begin{bmatrix} 1 & 0 & -1 \\ 1 & -3 & 0 \\ 4 & -13 & 1 \end{bmatrix}, \lambda = -2$

15. $A = \begin{bmatrix} 4 & 2 & 3 \\ -1 & 1 & -3 \\ 2 & 4 & 9 \end{bmatrix}, \lambda = 3$

16. $A = \begin{bmatrix} 3 & 0 & 2 & 0 \\ 1 & 3 & 1 & 0 \\ 0 & 1 & 1 & 0 \\ 0 & 0 & 0 & 4 \end{bmatrix}, \lambda = 4$

Find the eigenvalues of the matrices in Exercises 17–20.

17. $\begin{bmatrix} 7 & 0 & 0 \\ 8 & -4 & 0 \\ 1 & 5 & 2 \end{bmatrix}$

18. $\begin{bmatrix} 3 & -1 & -1 \\ 0 & 3 & 6 \\ 0 & 0 & 4 \end{bmatrix}$

19. $\begin{bmatrix} 0 & 0 & 0 \\ 0 & 2 & 5 \\ 0 & 0 & -1 \end{bmatrix}$

20. $\begin{bmatrix} 4 & 0 & 0 \\ 0 & 0 & 0 \\ 1 & 0 & -3 \end{bmatrix}$

21. Without calculation, find one eigenvalue of $A = \begin{bmatrix} 1 & 2 & 3 \\ 1 & 2 & 3 \\ 1 & 2 & 3 \end{bmatrix}$.

22. Without calculation, find one eigenvalue and two linearly independent eigenvectors of $A = \begin{bmatrix} 5 & 5 & 5 \\ 5 & 5 & 5 \\ 5 & 5 & 5 \end{bmatrix}$.

23. Explain why a 2×2 matrix can have at most two distinct eigenvalues. Explain why an $n \times n$ matrix can have at most n distinct eigenvalues.

24. Construct an example of a 2×2 matrix with only one distinct eigenvalue.

25. Let λ be an eigenvalue of an invertible matrix A. Show that λ^{-1} is an eigenvalue of A^{-1}. [*Hint*: Suppose a nonzero $\mathbf{x}$ satisfies $A\mathbf{x} = \lambda\mathbf{x}$.]

26. Show that if A^2 is the zero matrix, then the only eigenvalue of A is 0.

27. Show that A and A^T have the same eigenvalues. [*Hint*: Find out how $A - \lambda I$ and $A^T - \lambda I$ are related; then explain why $A - \lambda I$ is invertible if and only if $A^T - \lambda I$ is invertible.]

28. Use Exercise 27 to complete the proof of Theorem 1 for the case when A is lower triangular.

29. Consider an $n \times n$ matrix A with the property that the row sums all equal the same number s. Show that s is an eigenvalue of A. [*Hint*: Find an eigenvector.]

30. Consider an $n \times n$ matrix A with the property that the column sums all equal the same number s. Show that s is an eigenvalue of A. [*Hint*: Use Exercises 27 and 29.]

31. Let $\mathbf{u}$ and $\mathbf{v}$ be eigenvectors of a matrix A, with corresponding eigenvalues λ and μ, and let c_1 and c_2 be scalars. Define

$$\mathbf{x}_k = c_1\lambda^k\mathbf{u} + c_2\mu^k\mathbf{v} \quad (k = 0, 1, 2, \ldots)$$

a. What is $\mathbf{x}_{k+1}$, by definition?

b. Compute $A\mathbf{x}_k$ from the formula for $\mathbf{x}_k$, and show that $A\mathbf{x}_k = \mathbf{x}_{k+1}$. This calculation will prove that the sequence $\{\mathbf{x}_k\}$ defined above satisfies the difference equation $\mathbf{x}_{k+1} = A\mathbf{x}_k$ $(k = 0, 1, 2, \ldots)$.

32. Describe how you might try to build a solution of a difference equation $\mathbf{x}_{k+1} = A\mathbf{x}_k$ $(k = 0, 1, 2, \ldots)$ if you were given the initial $\mathbf{x}_0$ and this vector did not happen to be an eigenvector of A. [*Hint*: How might you relate $\mathbf{x}_0$ to eigenvectors of A?]

SOLUTIONS TO PRACTICE PROBLEMS

1. The number 5 is an eigenvalue of A if and only if the equation $(A - 5I)\mathbf{x} = \mathbf{0}$ has a nontrivial solution. Form

$$A - 5I = \begin{bmatrix} 6 & -3 & 1 \\ 3 & 0 & 5 \\ 2 & 2 & 6 \end{bmatrix} - \begin{bmatrix} 5 & 0 & 0 \\ 0 & 5 & 0 \\ 0 & 0 & 5 \end{bmatrix} = \begin{bmatrix} 1 & -3 & 1 \\ 3 & -5 & 5 \\ 2 & 2 & 1 \end{bmatrix}$$

and row reduce the augmented matrix:

$$\begin{bmatrix} 1 & -3 & 1 & 0 \\ 3 & -5 & 5 & 0 \\ 2 & 2 & 1 & 0 \end{bmatrix} \sim \begin{bmatrix} 1 & -3 & 1 & 0 \\ 0 & 4 & 2 & 0 \\ 0 & 8 & -1 & 0 \end{bmatrix} \sim \begin{bmatrix} 1 & -3 & 1 & 0 \\ 0 & 4 & 2 & 0 \\ 0 & 0 & -5 & 0 \end{bmatrix}$$

At this point it is clear that the homogeneous system has no free variables. Thus $A - 5I$ is an invertible matrix, which means that 5 is *not* an eigenvalue of A.

2. If $\mathbf{x}$ is an eigenvector for A corresponding to λ, then $A\mathbf{x} = \lambda\mathbf{x}$ and so

$$A^2\mathbf{x} = A(\lambda\mathbf{x}) = \lambda A\mathbf{x} = \lambda^2\mathbf{x}$$

Again, $A^3\mathbf{x} = A(A^2\mathbf{x}) = A(\lambda^2\mathbf{x}) = \lambda^2 A\mathbf{x} = \lambda^3\mathbf{x}$. The general pattern, $A^k\mathbf{x} = \lambda^k\mathbf{x}$, is easily proved by induction.

6.2 THE CHARACTERISTIC EQUATION

Useful information about the eigenvalues of a square matrix A is encoded in a special scalar equation called the characteristic equation of A. A simple example will lead to the general case.

EXAMPLE 1 Find the eigenvalues of $A = \begin{bmatrix} 2 & 3 \\ 3 & -6 \end{bmatrix}$.

Solution We must find all scalars λ such that the matrix equation

$$(A - \lambda I)\mathbf{x} = \mathbf{0}$$

has a nontrivial solution. By the Invertible Matrix Theorem, this problem is equivalent to finding all λ such that the matrix $A - \lambda I$ is *not* invertible, where

$$A - \lambda I = \begin{bmatrix} 2 & 3 \\ 3 & -6 \end{bmatrix} - \begin{bmatrix} \lambda & 0 \\ 0 & \lambda \end{bmatrix} = \begin{bmatrix} 2-\lambda & 3 \\ 3 & -6-\lambda \end{bmatrix}$$

By Theorem 4 in Section 3.2, this matrix fails to be invertible precisely when its determinant is zero. So the eigenvalues of A are the solutions of the equation

$$\det(A - \lambda I) = \det\begin{bmatrix} 2-\lambda & 3 \\ 3 & -6-\lambda \end{bmatrix} = 0$$

Recall that

$$\det\begin{bmatrix} a & b \\ c & d \end{bmatrix} = ad - bc$$

So

$$\begin{aligned}\det(A - \lambda I) &= (2 - \lambda)(-6 - \lambda) - (3)(3) \\ &= -12 + 6\lambda - 2\lambda + \lambda^2 - 9 \\ &= \lambda^2 + 4\lambda - 21\end{aligned}$$

Setting $\lambda^2 + 4\lambda - 21 = 0$, we have $(\lambda - 3)(\lambda + 7) = 0$, so the eigenvalues of A are 3 and -7. ∎

The determinant in Example 1 transformed the matrix equation $(A - \lambda I)\mathbf{x} = \mathbf{0}$, which involves *two* unknowns (λ and $\mathbf{x}$), into the scalar equation $\lambda^2 + 4\lambda - 21 = 0$, which involves only one unknown. The same idea works for $n \times n$ matrices. However, before turning to larger matrices, we summarize the properties of determinants needed to study eigenvalues.

Determinants

Let A be an $n \times n$ matrix, U be any echelon form obtained from A by row replacements and row interchanges (without scaling), and r be the number of such row interchanges. Then the **determinant** of A, written as $\det A$, is $(-1)^r$ times the product of the diagonal entries $u_{11}, \ldots, u_{nn}$ in U. If A is invertible, then $u_{11}, \ldots, u_{nn}$ are all *pivots*. Otherwise, at least u_{nn} is zero and the product $u_{11} \cdots u_{nn}$ is zero. Thus[1]

$$\det A = \begin{cases} (-1)^r \cdot \begin{pmatrix} \text{product of} \\ \text{pivots in } U \end{pmatrix}, & \text{when } A \text{ is invertible} \\ 0 & \text{when } A \text{ is not invertible} \end{cases} \qquad (1)$$

If A is a 3×3 matrix, then $|\det A|$ turns out to be the *volume* of the parallelepiped determined by the columns $\mathbf{a}_1, \mathbf{a}_2, \mathbf{a}_3$ of A, as in Fig. 1. (See Section 4.3 for details.)

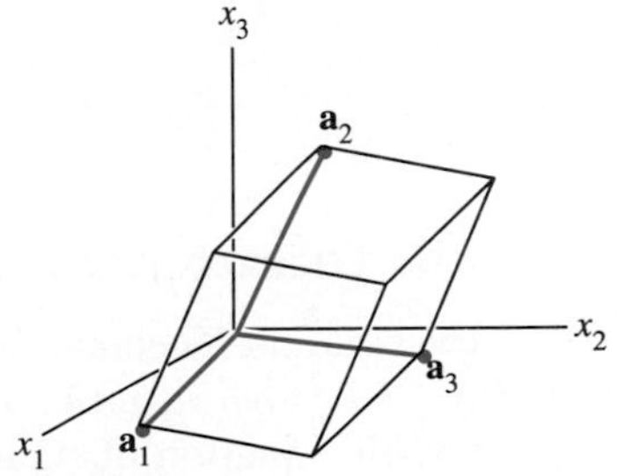

FIGURE 1

[1]Formula (1) was derived in Section 4.2. Readers who have not studied Chapter 4 may use this formula as the definition of $\det A$. It is a remarkable and nontrivial fact that any echelon form U obtained from A (without scaling) gives the same value for $\det A$.

EXAMPLE 2 Compute $\det A$ for $A = \begin{bmatrix} 1 & 5 & 0 \\ 2 & 4 & -1 \\ 0 & -2 & 0 \end{bmatrix}$.

Solution The following row reduction uses one row interchange:

$$A \sim \begin{bmatrix} 1 & 5 & 0 \\ 0 & -6 & -1 \\ 0 & -2 & 0 \end{bmatrix} \sim \begin{bmatrix} 1 & 5 & 0 \\ 0 & -2 & 0 \\ 0 & -6 & -1 \end{bmatrix} \sim \begin{bmatrix} 1 & 5 & 0 \\ 0 & -2 & 0 \\ 0 & 0 & -1 \end{bmatrix} = U_1$$

So $\det A$ equals $(-1)^1(1)(-2)(-1) = -2$. The following alternative row reduction avoids the row interchange and produces a different echelon form. The last step adds $-1/3$ times row 2 to row 3:

$$A \sim \begin{bmatrix} 1 & 5 & 0 \\ 0 & -6 & -1 \\ 0 & -2 & 0 \end{bmatrix} \sim \begin{bmatrix} 1 & 5 & 0 \\ 0 & -6 & -1 \\ 0 & 0 & 1/3 \end{bmatrix} = U_2$$

This time $\det A$ is $(-1)^0(1)(-6)(1/3) = -2$, the same as before.

The next theorem lists facts needed from Section 4.2. Parts (a) and (d), of course, follow immediately from (1) above.

THEOREM 3 **Properties of Determinants.**

Let A and B be $n \times n$ matrices.

a. A is invertible if and only if $\det A \neq 0$.
b. $\det AB = (\det A)(\det B)$.
c. $\det A^T = \det A$.
d. If A is triangular, then $\det A$ is the product of the entries on the main diagonal of A.
e. A row replacement operation on A does not change the determinant. A row interchange changes the sign of the determinant. A row scaling also scales the determinant by the same scalar factor.

The Characteristic Equation

By virtue of Theorem 3(a), we can use a determinant to determine when a matrix $A - \lambda I$ is *not* invertible. The scalar equation $\det(A - \lambda I) = 0$ is called the **characteristic equation** of A, and the argument in Example 1 justifies the following fact.

A scalar λ is an eigenvalue of an $n \times n$ matrix A if and only if λ satisfies the characteristic equation

$$\det(A - \lambda I) = 0$$

EXAMPLE 3 Find the characteristic equation of

$$A = \begin{bmatrix} 5 & -2 & 6 & -1 \\ 0 & 3 & -8 & 0 \\ 0 & 0 & 5 & 4 \\ 0 & 0 & 0 & 1 \end{bmatrix}$$

Solution Form $A - \lambda I$, and use Theorem 3(d):

$$\det(A - \lambda I) = \det \begin{bmatrix} 5-\lambda & -2 & 6 & -1 \\ 0 & 3-\lambda & -8 & 0 \\ 0 & 0 & 5-\lambda & 4 \\ 0 & 0 & 0 & 1-\lambda \end{bmatrix}$$
$$= (5-\lambda)(3-\lambda)(5-\lambda)(1-\lambda)$$

The characteristic equation is

$$(5-\lambda)^2(3-\lambda)(1-\lambda) = 0$$

or

$$(\lambda-5)^2(\lambda-3)(\lambda-1) = 0$$

Expanding the product, we can also write

$$\lambda^4 - 14\lambda^3 + 68\lambda^2 - 130\lambda + 75 = 0$$

In Examples 1 and 3, $\det(A - \lambda I)$ is a polynomial in λ. It can be shown that if A is an $n \times n$ matrix, then $\det(A - \lambda I)$ is a polynomial of degree n called the **characteristic polynomial** of A.

The eigenvalue 5 in Example 3 is said to have *multiplicity* 2 because $(\lambda - 5)$ occurs two times as a factor of the characteristic polynomial. In general, the **(algebraic) multiplicity** of an eigenvalue λ is its multiplicity as a root of the characteristic equation.

EXAMPLE 4 The characteristic polynomial of a 6×6 matrix is $\lambda^6 - 4\lambda^5 - 12\lambda^4$. Find the eigenvalues and their multiplicities.

Solution Factor the polynomial

$$\lambda^6 - 4\lambda^5 - 12\lambda^4 = \lambda^4(\lambda^2 - 4\lambda - 12) = \lambda^4(\lambda-6)(\lambda+2)$$

The eigenvalues are 0 (multiplicity 4), 6 (multiplicity 1), and −2 (multiplicity 1).

We could also list the eigenvalues in Example 4 as 0, 0, 0, 0, 6, and −2, so that the eigenvalues are repeated according to their multiplicities.

Because the characteristic equation for an $n \times n$ matrix involves an nth degree polynomial, the equation has exactly n roots, counting multiplicities, provided complex roots are allowed. Such complex roots, called *complex eigenvalues*, will be discussed in Section 6.5. Until then, we consider only real eigenvalues, and scalars will continue to be real numbers.

The characteristic equation is important for theoretical purposes. In practical work, however, eigenvalues of any matrix larger than 2×2 should be found by a computer, unless the matrix is triangular or has other special properties. Although a 3×3 characteristic polynomial is easy to compute by hand, factoring it can be difficult (unless the matrix is carefully chosen). See the Numerical Notes below.

Similarity

The next theorem illustrates one use of the characteristic polynomial, and it provides the foundation for several iterative methods that *approximate* eigenvalues. If A and B are $n\times n$ matrices, then A **is similar to** B if there is an invertible matrix P such that $P^{-1}AP = B$, or equivalently, $A = PBP^{-1}$. Writing Q for P^{-1}, we have $Q^{-1}BQ = A$. So B is also similar to A, and we say simply that A and B **are similar**. Changing A into $P^{-1}AP$ is called a **similarity transformation**.

THEOREM 4

If $n\times n$ matrices A and B are similar, then they have the same characteristic polynomial and hence the same eigenvalues.

Proof If $B = P^{-1}AP$, then

$$B - \lambda I = P^{-1}AP - \lambda P^{-1}P = P^{-1}(AP - \lambda P) = P^{-1}(A - \lambda I)P$$

Using the multiplicative property (b) of Theorem 3, we compute

$$\begin{aligned} \det(B - \lambda I) &= \det[P^{-1}(A - \lambda I)P] \\ &= \det(P^{-1})\cdot\det(A - \lambda I)\cdot\det(P) \end{aligned} \tag{2}$$

Since $\det(P^{-1})\cdot\det(P) = \det(P^{-1}P) = \det I = 1$, we see from (2) that $\det(B - \lambda I) = \det(A - \lambda I)$. ▮

Warning: Similarity is not the same as row equivalence. (If A is row equivalent to B, then $B = EA$ for some invertible matrix E.) Row operations on a matrix usually change its eigenvalues.

Application to Dynamical Systems

Eigenvalues and eigenvectors hold the key to the discrete evolution of a dynamical system, as mentioned in the chapter introduction.

EXAMPLE 5 Let $A = \begin{bmatrix} .95 & .03 \\ .05 & .97 \end{bmatrix}$. Analyze the long-term behavior of the dynamical system defined by $\mathbf{x}_{k+1} = A\mathbf{x}_k$ $(k = 0, 1, 2, \ldots)$, with $\mathbf{x}_0 = \begin{bmatrix} .6 \\ .4 \end{bmatrix}$.

Solution The first step is to find the eigenvalues of A and a basis for each eigenspace. The characteristic equation for A is

$$0 = \det\begin{bmatrix} .95-\lambda & .03 \\ .05 & .97-\lambda \end{bmatrix} = (.95-\lambda)(.97-\lambda) - (.03)(.05)$$
$$= \lambda^2 - 1.92\lambda + .92$$

By the quadratic formula

$$\lambda = \frac{1.92 \pm \sqrt{(1.92)^2 - 4(.92)}}{2} = \frac{1.92 \pm \sqrt{.0064}}{2}$$
$$= \frac{1.92 \pm .08}{2} = 1 \quad \text{or} \quad .92$$

It is readily checked that eigenvectors corresponding to $\lambda = 1$ and $\lambda = .92$ are multiples of

$$\mathbf{u}_1 = \begin{bmatrix} .375 \\ .625 \end{bmatrix} \quad \text{and} \quad \mathbf{u}_2 = \begin{bmatrix} 1 \\ -1 \end{bmatrix}$$

respectively.

The next step is to write the given $\mathbf{x}_0$ in terms of $\mathbf{u}_1$ and $\mathbf{u}_2$. This can be done because $\{\mathbf{u}_1, \mathbf{u}_2\}$ is obviously a basis for $\mathbb{R}^2$. (Why?) So there exist weights c_1 and c_2 such that

$$\mathbf{x}_0 = c_1\mathbf{u}_1 + c_2\mathbf{u}_2 = [\,\mathbf{u}_1 \quad \mathbf{u}_2\,]\begin{bmatrix} c_1 \\ c_2 \end{bmatrix} \tag{3}$$

In fact,

$$\begin{bmatrix} c_1 \\ c_2 \end{bmatrix} = [\mathbf{u}_1 \quad \mathbf{u}_2]^{-1}\mathbf{x}_0 = \begin{bmatrix} .375 & 1 \\ .625 & -1 \end{bmatrix}^{-1}\begin{bmatrix} .60 \\ .40 \end{bmatrix}$$
$$= \frac{1}{-1}\begin{bmatrix} -1 & -1 \\ -.625 & .375 \end{bmatrix}\begin{bmatrix} .60 \\ .40 \end{bmatrix} = \begin{bmatrix} 1.000 \\ .225 \end{bmatrix} \tag{4}$$

Because $\mathbf{u}_1$ and $\mathbf{u}_2$ in (3) are eigenvectors of A, with $A\mathbf{u}_1 = \mathbf{u}_1$ and $A\mathbf{u}_2 = (.92)\mathbf{u}_2$, we easily compute each $\mathbf{x}_k$:

$$\mathbf{x}_1 = A\mathbf{x}_0 = c_1A\mathbf{u}_1 + c_2A\mathbf{u}_2 \qquad \text{Using linearity of } \mathbf{x} \mapsto A\mathbf{x}$$
$$= c_1\mathbf{u}_1 + c_2(.92)\mathbf{u}_2 \qquad \mathbf{u}_1 \text{ and } \mathbf{u}_2 \text{ are eigenvectors.}$$
$$\mathbf{x}_2 = A\mathbf{x}_1 = c_1A\mathbf{u}_1 + c_2(.92)A\mathbf{u}_2$$
$$= c_1\mathbf{u}_1 + c_2(.92)^2\mathbf{u}_2$$

and so on. In general,

$$\mathbf{x}_k = c_1\mathbf{u}_1 + c_2(.92)^k\mathbf{u}_2 \qquad (k = 0, 1, 2, \ldots)$$

Using c_1 and c_2 from (4),

$$\mathbf{x}_k = \begin{bmatrix} .375 \\ .625 \end{bmatrix} + .225(.92)^k\begin{bmatrix} 1 \\ -1 \end{bmatrix} \qquad (k = 0, 1, 2, \ldots) \tag{5}$$

This explicit formula for $\mathbf{x}_k$ gives the solution of the difference equation $\mathbf{x}_{k+1} = A\mathbf{x}_k$. As $k \to \infty$, $(.92)^k$ tends to zero and $\mathbf{x}_k$ tends to $\begin{bmatrix} .325 \\ .625 \end{bmatrix} = \mathbf{u}_1$.

The calculations in Example 5 have an interesting application to a Markov chain in Section 5.9. Persons who read that section may recognize that the A in Example 5 above is the same as the migration matrix M in Section 5.9, $\mathbf{x}_0$ is the initial population distribution between city and suburbs, and $\mathbf{x}_k$ represents the population distribution after k years.

Theorem 19 in Section 5.9 stated that for a matrix such as A, the sequence $\mathbf{x}_k$ tends to a "steady-state" vector. Now we know *why* the $\mathbf{x}_k$ behave this way, at least for the migration matrix. The steady-state vector is $\mathbf{u}_1$ (since $A\mathbf{u}_1 = \mathbf{u}_1$), and formula (5) for $\mathbf{x}_k$ shows precisely why $\mathbf{x}_k \to \mathbf{u}_1$.

Numerical Notes

1. Computer software such as Mathematica and Maple can use symbolic calculations to find the characteristic polynomial of a moderate-sized matrix. But there is no formula or finite algorithm to solve the characteristic equation of a general $n \times n$ matrix for $n \geq 5$.
2. The best numerical methods for finding eigenvalues avoid the characteristic polynomial entirely. In fact, MATLAB finds the characteristic polynomial of a matrix A by first computing the eigenvalues $\lambda_1, \ldots, \lambda_n$ of A and then expanding the product $(\lambda - \lambda_1)(\lambda - \lambda_2) \cdots (\lambda - \lambda_n)$.
3. Several common algorithms for estimating the eigenvalues of a matrix A are based on Theorem 4. The powerful *QR algorithm* is discussed in the exercises. Another technique, called *Jacobi's method*, works when $A = A^T$, and computes a sequence of matrices of the form

$$A_1 = A \quad \text{and} \quad A_{k+1} = P_k^{-1} A_k P_k \quad (\text{for } k = 1, 2, \ldots)$$

Each matrix in the sequence is similar to A and so has the same eigenvalues as A. The nondiagonal entries of A_{k+1} tend to zero as k increases, and the diagonal entries tend to approach the eigenvalues of A.

4. Other methods of estimating eigenvalues are discussed in Section 6.7.

PRACTICE PROBLEM

Find the characteristic equation and eigenvalues of $A = \begin{bmatrix} 1 & -4 \\ 4 & 2 \end{bmatrix}$.

6.2 EXERCISES

Find the characteristic polynomial and the eigenvalues of the matrices in Exercises 1–8.

1. $\begin{bmatrix} 2 & 7 \\ 7 & 2 \end{bmatrix}$

2. $\begin{bmatrix} 5 & 3 \\ 3 & 5 \end{bmatrix}$

3. $\begin{bmatrix} 3 & -2 \\ 1 & -1 \end{bmatrix}$

4. $\begin{bmatrix} 5 & -3 \\ -4 & 3 \end{bmatrix}$

5. $\begin{bmatrix} 2 & 1 \\ -1 & 4 \end{bmatrix}$

6. $\begin{bmatrix} 3 & -4 \\ 4 & 8 \end{bmatrix}$

7. $\begin{bmatrix} 5 & 3 \\ -4 & 4 \end{bmatrix}$

8. $\begin{bmatrix} 7 & -2 \\ 2 & 3 \end{bmatrix}$

Exercises 9–14 require techniques from Section 4.1. Find the characteristic polynomial of each matrix, using either a cofactor expansion or the special formula for 3×3 determinants described prior to Exercises 15–18 in Section 4.1. [*Note*: Finding the characteristic polynomial of a 3×3 matrix is not easy to do with just row operations, because the variable λ is involved.]

9. $\begin{bmatrix} 1 & 0 & -1 \\ 2 & 3 & -1 \\ 0 & 6 & 0 \end{bmatrix}$

10. $\begin{bmatrix} 0 & 3 & 1 \\ 3 & 0 & 2 \\ 1 & 2 & 0 \end{bmatrix}$

11. $\begin{bmatrix} 4 & 0 & 0 \\ 5 & 3 & 2 \\ -2 & 0 & 2 \end{bmatrix}$

12. $\begin{bmatrix} -1 & 0 & 1 \\ -3 & 4 & 1 \\ 0 & 0 & 2 \end{bmatrix}$

13. $\begin{bmatrix} 6 & -2 & 0 \\ -2 & 9 & 0 \\ 5 & 8 & 3 \end{bmatrix}$

14. $\begin{bmatrix} 5 & -2 & 3 \\ 0 & 1 & 0 \\ 6 & 7 & -2 \end{bmatrix}$

For the matrices in Exercises 15–17, list the eigenvalues, repeated according to their multiplicities.

15. $\begin{bmatrix} 4 & -7 & 0 & 2 \\ 0 & 3 & -4 & 6 \\ 0 & 0 & 3 & -8 \\ 0 & 0 & 0 & 1 \end{bmatrix}$

16. $\begin{bmatrix} 5 & 0 & 0 & 0 \\ 8 & -4 & 0 & 0 \\ 0 & 7 & 1 & 0 \\ 1 & -5 & 2 & 1 \end{bmatrix}$

17. $\begin{bmatrix} 3 & 0 & 0 & 0 & 0 \\ -5 & 1 & 0 & 0 & 0 \\ 3 & 8 & 0 & 0 & 0 \\ 0 & -7 & 2 & 1 & 0 \\ -4 & 1 & 9 & -2 & 3 \end{bmatrix}$

18. It can be shown that the algebraic multiplicity of an eigenvalue λ is always greater than or equal to the dimension of the eigenspace corresponding to λ. Find h in the matrix A below such that the eigenspace for $\lambda = 5$ is two-dimensional:

$$A = \begin{bmatrix} 5 & -2 & 6 & -1 \\ 0 & 3 & h & 0 \\ 0 & 0 & 5 & 4 \\ 0 & 0 & 0 & 1 \end{bmatrix}$$

19. Let A be an $n\times n$ matrix and suppose that A has n real eigenvalues, $\lambda_1, \dots, \lambda_n$, repeated according to multiplicities, so that

$$\det(A - \lambda I) = (\lambda_1 - \lambda)(\lambda_2 - \lambda)\cdots(\lambda_n - \lambda)$$

Explain why $\det A$ is the product of the n eigenvalues of A. (This result is true for any square matrix when complex eigenvalues are considered.)

20. Use a property of determinants to show that A and A^T have the same characteristic polynomial.

A widely used method for estimating eigenvalues of a general A is the *QR algorithm*. Under suitable conditions, this algorithm produces a sequence of matrices, all similar to A, that become almost upper triangular, and the diagonal entries approach the eigenvalues of A. The main idea is to factor A (or another matrix similar to A) in the form $A = Q_1R_1$, where $Q_1^T = Q_1^{-1}$ and R_1 is upper triangular. The factors are interchanged to form $A_1 = R_1Q_1$, which is again factored as $A_1 = Q_2R_2$; then $A_2 = R_2Q_2$, and so on. The similarity of $A, A_1, \dots$, follows from the more general result in Exercise 21.

21. Show that if $A = QR$ with Q invertible, then A is similar to $A_1 = RQ$.

22. Show that if A and B are similar, then $\det A = \det B$.

23. Let $A = \begin{bmatrix} .6 & .3 \\ .4 & .7 \end{bmatrix}$, $\mathbf{u}_1 = \begin{bmatrix} 3/7 \\ 4/7 \end{bmatrix}$, $\mathbf{v}_0 = \begin{bmatrix} .5 \\ .5 \end{bmatrix}$. [*Note*: A is the stochastic matrix studied in Example 5 of Section 5.9.]

a. Find a basis for $\mathbb{R}^2$ consisting of $\mathbf{u}_1$ and another eigenvector of A.

b. Write $\mathbf{v}_0$ as a linear combination of the vectors in part (a).

c. For $k = 1, 2, \dots$, define $\mathbf{v}_k = A^k\mathbf{v}_0$. Show that $\mathbf{v}_k \to \mathbf{u}_1$ as k increases.

24. Let $A = \begin{bmatrix} a & b \\ c & d \end{bmatrix}$. Use formula (1) for a determinant (given in this section) to show that $\det A = ad - bc$. Consider two cases: $a \neq 0$ and $a = 0$.

25. Let $A = \begin{bmatrix} .5 & .2 & .3 \\ .3 & .8 & .3 \\ .2 & 0 & .4 \end{bmatrix}$, $\mathbf{u}_1 = \begin{bmatrix} .3 \\ .6 \\ .1 \end{bmatrix}$, $\mathbf{u}_2 = \begin{bmatrix} 1 \\ -3 \\ 2 \end{bmatrix}$,

$\mathbf{u}_3 = \begin{bmatrix} -1 \\ 0 \\ 1 \end{bmatrix}$, $\mathbf{w} = \begin{bmatrix} 1 \\ 1 \\ 1 \end{bmatrix}$.

a. Show that $\mathbf{u}_1, \mathbf{u}_2, \mathbf{u}_3$ are eigenvectors of A. [*Note*: A is the stochastic matrix studied in Example 3 of Section 5.9.]

b. Let $\mathbf{v}_0$ be any vector in $\mathbb{R}^3$ with nonnegative entries whose sum is 1. (In Section 5.9, $\mathbf{v}_0$ was called a probability vector.) Explain why there are constants c_1, c_2, c_3 such that $\mathbf{v}_0 = c_1\mathbf{u}_1 + c_2\mathbf{u}_2 + c_3\mathbf{u}_3$. Compute $\mathbf{w}^T\mathbf{v}_0$, and deduce that $c_1 = 1$.

c. For $k = 1, 2, \ldots,$ define $\mathbf{v}_k = A^k\mathbf{v}_0$, with $\mathbf{v}_0$ as in part (b). Show that $\mathbf{v}_k \to \mathbf{u}_1$ as k increases.

SOLUTION TO PRACTICE PROBLEM

The characteristic equation is

$$0 = \det(A - \lambda I) = \det\begin{bmatrix} 1-\lambda & -4 \\ 4 & 2-\lambda \end{bmatrix}$$

$$= (1-\lambda)(2-\lambda) - (-4)(4) = \lambda^2 - 3\lambda + 18$$

When we attempt to solve this, we find that

$$\lambda = \frac{3 \pm \sqrt{(-3)^2 - 4(18)}}{2} = \frac{3 \pm \sqrt{-63}}{2}$$

It is clear that the characteristic equation has no real solutions, so A has no real eigenvalues. A is acting on the real vector space $\mathbb{R}^2$, and there is no nonzero vector $\mathbf{v}$ in $\mathbb{R}^2$ such that $A\mathbf{v} = \lambda\mathbf{v}$ for some scalar λ.

6.3 DIAGONALIZATION

In many cases, the eigenvalue-eigenvector information contained within a matrix A can be displayed in a useful factorization of the form $A = PDP^{-1}$. In this section, the factorization enables us to compute A^k quickly for large values of k, a fundamental idea in several applications of linear algebra. Later, in Section 6.6, the factorization will be used to analyze (and *decouple*) a dynamical system.

The "D" in the factorization stands for *diagonal*. Powers of such a D are trivial to compute.

EXAMPLE 1 If $D = \begin{bmatrix} 5 & 0 \\ 0 & 3 \end{bmatrix}$, then $D^2 = \begin{bmatrix} 5 & 0 \\ 0 & 3 \end{bmatrix}\begin{bmatrix} 5 & 0 \\ 0 & 3 \end{bmatrix} = \begin{bmatrix} 5^2 & 0 \\ 0 & 3^2 \end{bmatrix}$ and

$$D^3 = DD^2 = \begin{bmatrix} 5 & 0 \\ 0 & 3 \end{bmatrix}\begin{bmatrix} 5^2 & 0 \\ 0 & 3^2 \end{bmatrix} = \begin{bmatrix} 5^3 & 0 \\ 0 & 3^3 \end{bmatrix}$$

In general,

$$D^k = \begin{bmatrix} 5^k & 0 \\ 0 & 3^k \end{bmatrix} \quad \text{for } k \geq 1$$

If $A = PDP^{-1}$ for some invertible P and diagonal D, then A^k is also easy to compute, as the next example shows.

EXAMPLE 2 Let $A = \begin{bmatrix} 7 & 2 \\ -4 & 1 \end{bmatrix}$. Find a formula for A^k, given that $A = PDP^{-1}$, where

$$P = \begin{bmatrix} 1 & 1 \\ -1 & -2 \end{bmatrix} \quad \text{and} \quad D = \begin{bmatrix} 5 & 0 \\ 0 & 3 \end{bmatrix}$$

Solution The standard formula for the inverse of a 2×2 matrix yields

$$P^{-1} = \begin{bmatrix} 2 & 1 \\ -1 & -1 \end{bmatrix}$$

Then, by associativity of matrix multiplication,

$$A^2 = (PDP^{-1})(PDP^{-1}) = PD\underbrace{(P^{-1}P)}_{I}DP^{-1} = PDDP^{-1}$$

$$= PD^2P^{-1} = \begin{bmatrix} 1 & 1 \\ -1 & -2 \end{bmatrix} \begin{bmatrix} 5^2 & 0 \\ 0 & 3^2 \end{bmatrix} \begin{bmatrix} 2 & 1 \\ -1 & -1 \end{bmatrix}$$

Again,

$$A^3 = (PDP^{-1})A^2 = (PD\underbrace{P^{-1})P}_{I}D^2P^{-1} = PDD^2P^{-1} = PD^3P^{-1}$$

In general, for $k \geq 1$,

$$A^k = PD^kP^{-1} = \begin{bmatrix} 1 & 1 \\ -1 & -2 \end{bmatrix} \begin{bmatrix} 5^k & 0 \\ 0 & 3^k \end{bmatrix} \begin{bmatrix} 2 & 1 \\ -1 & -1 \end{bmatrix}$$

$$= \begin{bmatrix} 2 \cdot 5^k - 3^k & 5^k - 3^k \\ 2 \cdot 3^k - 2 \cdot 5^k & 2 \cdot 3^k - 5^k \end{bmatrix}$$

A square matrix A is said to be **diagonalizable** if A is similar to a diagonal matrix, that is, if $A = PDP^{-1}$ for some invertible matrix P and some diagonal matrix D. The next theorem gives a characterization of diagonalizable matrices and tells how to construct a suitable factorization.

THEOREM 5

The Diagonalization Theorem

An $n \times n$ matrix A is diagonalizable if and only if A has n linearly independent eigenvectors.

If $A = PDP^{-1}$ where D is diagonal, then the diagonal entries of D are eigenvalues of A and the columns of P are the corresponding eigenvectors.

In other words, A is diagonalizable if and only if there are enough eigenvectors to form a basis of $\mathbb{R}^n$. We call such a basis an **eigenvector basis**.

Proof First, observe that if P is any $n\times n$ matrix with columns $\mathbf{u}_1, \ldots, \mathbf{u}_n$, and if D is any diagonal matrix with diagonal entries $\lambda_1, \ldots, \lambda_n$, then

$$AP = A[\,\mathbf{u}_1 \quad \mathbf{u}_2 \quad \cdots \quad \mathbf{u}_n\,] = [\,A\mathbf{u}_1 \quad A\mathbf{u}_2 \quad \cdots \quad A\mathbf{u}_n\,] \tag{1}$$

while

$$PD = P\begin{bmatrix} \lambda_1 & 0 & \cdots & 0 \\ 0 & \lambda_2 & \cdots & 0 \\ \vdots & \vdots & & \vdots \\ 0 & 0 & \cdots & \lambda_n \end{bmatrix} = [\,\lambda_1\mathbf{u}_1 \quad \lambda_2\mathbf{u}_2 \quad \cdots \quad \lambda_n\mathbf{u}_n\,] \tag{2}$$

Suppose now that A is diagonalizable and $A = PDP^{-1}$. Then right-multiplying this relation by P, we have $AP = PD$. In this case, (1) and (2) imply that

$$[\,A\mathbf{u}_1 \quad A\mathbf{u}_2 \quad \cdots \quad A\mathbf{u}_n\,] = [\,\lambda_1\mathbf{u}_1 \quad \lambda_2\mathbf{u}_2 \quad \cdots \quad \lambda_n\mathbf{u}_n\,] \tag{3}$$

Equating columns, we find that

$$A\mathbf{u}_1 = \lambda_1\mathbf{u}_1, \quad A\mathbf{u}_2 = \lambda_2\mathbf{u}_2, \quad \ldots, \quad A\mathbf{u}_n = \lambda_n\mathbf{u}_n \tag{4}$$

Since P is invertible, its columns $\mathbf{u}_1, \ldots, \mathbf{u}_n$ must be linearly independent. Also, since these columns are nonzero, (4) shows that $\lambda_1, \ldots, \lambda_n$ are eigenvalues and $\mathbf{u}_1, \ldots, \mathbf{u}_n$ are corresponding eigenvectors. This proves the second statement of the theorem and half of the first statement.

Finally, given any n eigenvectors $\mathbf{u}_1, \ldots, \mathbf{u}_n$, we may use them to construct the columns of P and use corresponding eigenvalues $\lambda_1, \ldots, \lambda_n$ to construct D. By (1)–(3), we have $AP = PD$. This is true without any condition on the eigenvectors. If, in fact, the eigenvectors are linearly independent, then P will be invertible (by the Invertible Matrix Theorem), and we may solve $AP = PD$ to get $A = PDP^{-1}$. ∎

Diagonalizing Matrices

EXAMPLE 3 Diagonalize the following matrix, if possible.

$$A = \begin{bmatrix} 1 & 3 & 3 \\ -3 & -5 & -3 \\ 3 & 3 & 1 \end{bmatrix}$$

That is, find an invertible matrix P and a diagonal matrix D such that $A = PDP^{-1}$.

Solution There are four steps to implement the description in Theorem 5.

Step 1. Find the eigenvalues of *A*. As mentioned in Section 6.2, the mechanics of this step are appropriate for a computer when the matrix is larger than 2×2. To avoid unnecessary distractions, the text will usually supply information needed for this step. In the present case, the characteristic equation turns out to involve a cubic polynomial that can be factored:

$$\begin{aligned} 0 = \det(A - \lambda I) &= -\lambda^3 - 3\lambda^2 + 4 \\ &= -(\lambda - 1)(\lambda + 2)^2 \end{aligned}$$

The eigenvalues are $\lambda = 1$ and $\lambda = -2$.

Step 2. Find three linearly independent eigenvectors of A. *Three* vectors are needed because A is a 3×3 matrix. This is the critical step. If it fails, then Theorem 5 says that A cannot be diagonalized. The method of Section 6.1 produces a basis for each eigenspace:

$$\text{Basis for } \lambda = 1: \quad \mathbf{u}_1 = \begin{bmatrix} 1 \\ -1 \\ 1 \end{bmatrix}$$

$$\text{Basis for } \lambda = -2: \quad \mathbf{u}_2 = \begin{bmatrix} -1 \\ 1 \\ 0 \end{bmatrix} \quad \text{and} \quad \mathbf{u}_3 = \begin{bmatrix} -1 \\ 0 \\ 1 \end{bmatrix}$$

You may check that $\{\mathbf{u}_1, \mathbf{u}_2, \mathbf{u}_3\}$ is a linearly independent set.

Step 3. Construct P from the vectors in step 2. The order of the vectors is unimportant. Using the order chosen in step 2, form

$$P = [\,\mathbf{u}_1 \quad \mathbf{u}_2 \quad \mathbf{u}_3\,] = \begin{bmatrix} 1 & -1 & -1 \\ -1 & 1 & 0 \\ 1 & 0 & 1 \end{bmatrix}$$

Step 4. Construct D from the corresponding eigenvalues. In this step it is essential that the order of the eigenvalues matches the order chosen for the columns of P. Use the eigenvalue $\lambda = -2$ twice, once for each of the eigenvectors corresponding to $\lambda = -2$:

$$D = \begin{bmatrix} 1 & 0 & 0 \\ 0 & -2 & 0 \\ 0 & 0 & -2 \end{bmatrix}$$

It is a good idea to check that P and D really work. To avoid computing P^{-1}, simply verify that $AP = PD$. This is equivalent to $A = PDP^{-1}$ when P is invertible. (However, be sure that P is invertible!) We compute

$$AP = \begin{bmatrix} 1 & 3 & 3 \\ -3 & -5 & -3 \\ 3 & 3 & 1 \end{bmatrix} \begin{bmatrix} 1 & -1 & -1 \\ -1 & 1 & 0 \\ 1 & 0 & 1 \end{bmatrix} = \begin{bmatrix} 1 & 2 & 2 \\ -1 & -2 & 0 \\ 1 & 0 & -2 \end{bmatrix}$$

$$PD = \begin{bmatrix} 1 & -1 & -1 \\ -1 & 1 & 0 \\ 1 & 0 & 1 \end{bmatrix} \begin{bmatrix} 1 & 0 & 0 \\ 0 & -2 & 0 \\ 0 & 0 & -2 \end{bmatrix} = \begin{bmatrix} 1 & 2 & 2 \\ -1 & -2 & 0 \\ 1 & 0 & -2 \end{bmatrix}$$

∎

EXAMPLE 4 Diagonalize the following matrix, if possible.

$$A = \begin{bmatrix} 2 & 4 & 3 \\ -4 & -6 & -3 \\ 3 & 3 & 1 \end{bmatrix}$$

Solution The characteristic equation of A turns out to be exactly the same as that in Example 3:

$$0 = \det(A - \lambda I) = -\lambda^3 - 3\lambda^2 + 4 = -(\lambda - 1)(\lambda + 2)^2$$

The eigenvalues are $\lambda = 1$ and $\lambda = -2$. However, when we look for eigenvectors, we find that each eigenspace is only one-dimensional.

$$\text{Basis for } \lambda = 1: \quad \mathbf{u}_1 = \begin{bmatrix} 1 \\ -1 \\ 1 \end{bmatrix}$$

$$\text{Basis for } \lambda = -2: \quad \mathbf{u}_2 = \begin{bmatrix} -1 \\ 1 \\ 0 \end{bmatrix}$$

There are no other eigenvalues, and every eigenvector of A is a multiple of either $\mathbf{u}_1$ or $\mathbf{u}_2$. Hence it is impossible to construct a basis of $\mathbb{R}^3$ using eigenvectors of A. By Theorem 5, A is *not* diagonalizable.

The following theorem provides a *sufficient* condition for a matrix to be diagonalizable.

THEOREM 6

If an $n \times n$ matrix A has n distinct eigenvalues, then A is diagonalizable.

Proof Let $\mathbf{v}_1, \ldots, \mathbf{v}_n$ be eigenvectors corresponding to the n distinct eigenvalues of A. Then $\{\mathbf{v}_1, \ldots, \mathbf{v}_n\}$ is linearly independent, by Theorem 2 in Section 6.1. Hence A is diagonalizable, by Theorem 5. ∎

It is not *necessary* for an $n \times n$ matrix to have n distinct eigenvalues in order to be diagonalizable. The 3×3 matrix in Example 3 is diagonalizable even though it has only two distinct eigenvalues.

EXAMPLE 5 Determine if the following matrix is diagonalizable.

$$A = \begin{bmatrix} 5 & -8 & 1 \\ 0 & 0 & 7 \\ 0 & 0 & -2 \end{bmatrix}$$

Solution This is easy! Since the matrix is triangular, its eigenvalues are obviously 5, 0, and -2. Since A is a 3×3 matrix with three distinct eigenvalues, A is diagonalizable. ∎

Matrices Whose Eigenvalues Are Not Distinct

If an $n\times n$ matrix A has n distinct eigenvalues, with corresponding eigenvectors $\mathbf{v}_1, \ldots, \mathbf{v}_n$, and if $P = [\mathbf{v}_1 \ \cdots \ \mathbf{v}_n]$, then P is automatically invertible because its columns are linearly independent, by Theorem 2. When A is diagonalizable but has fewer than n distinct eigenvalues, it is still possible to build P in a way that makes P automatically invertible, as the next theorem shows.

THEOREM 7

Let A be an $n\times n$ matrix whose distinct eigenvalues are $\lambda_1, \ldots, \lambda_p$. For $k = 1, \ldots, p$, let $\mathcal{B}_k$ be a basis for the eigenspace corresponding to λ_k. Let $\mathcal{B}$ be the total collection of vectors that belong to the sets $\mathcal{B}_1, \ldots, \mathcal{B}_p$. That is,

$$\mathcal{B} = \mathcal{B}_1 \cup \mathcal{B}_2 \cup \cdots \cup \mathcal{B}_p$$

Then $\mathcal{B}$ is a linearly independent set of vectors in $\mathbb{R}^n$, and A is diagonalizable if and only if $\mathcal{B}$ contains n vectors.

Proof We consider only the case when A has three distinct eigenvalues, λ_1, λ_2, and λ_3. Suppose that bases are found for the eigenspaces as follows.

Basis for Eigenspace	Corresponding to
$\mathcal{B}_1 = \{\mathbf{u}_1, \ldots, \mathbf{u}_i\}$	λ_1
$\mathcal{B}_2 = \{\mathbf{v}_1, \ldots, \mathbf{v}_j\}$	λ_2
$\mathcal{B}_3 = \{\mathbf{w}_1, \ldots, \mathbf{w}_k\}$	λ_3

To show that $\mathcal{B}_1 \cup \mathcal{B}_2 \cup \mathcal{B}_3$ is a linearly independent set, suppose that there are weights such that

$$\underbrace{a_1\mathbf{u}_1 + \cdots + a_i\mathbf{u}_i}_{\mathbf{x}} + \underbrace{b_1\mathbf{v}_1 + \cdots + b_j\mathbf{v}_j}_{\mathbf{y}} + \underbrace{c_1\mathbf{w}_1 + \cdots + c_k\mathbf{w}_k}_{\mathbf{z}} = \mathbf{0}$$

Combine parts of the sum as shown into vectors $\mathbf{x}, \mathbf{y}, \mathbf{z}$ that belong to the eigenspaces for $\lambda_1, \lambda_2, \lambda_3$, respectively. Since the three eigenvalues are distinct, the linear dependence relation $\mathbf{x} + \mathbf{y} + \mathbf{z} = \mathbf{0}$ implies that all three eigenvectors $\mathbf{x}, \mathbf{y}, \mathbf{z}$ are zero, by Theorem 2 in Section 6.1. But then the equation

$$a_1\mathbf{u}_1 + \cdots + a_i\mathbf{u}_i = \mathbf{x} = \mathbf{0}$$

implies that $a_1 = \cdots = a_i = 0$, because $\mathcal{B}_1$ is a linearly independent set. Similarly, the b's and c's are all zero. Thus the set

$$\mathcal{B} = \{\mathbf{u}_1, \dots, \mathbf{u}_i; \mathbf{v}_1, \dots, \mathbf{v}_j; \mathbf{w}_1, \dots, \mathbf{w}_k\}$$

is linearly independent. If there are n eigenvectors in $\mathcal{B}$, then A is diagonalizable, by Theorem 5. Conversely, if A is diagonalizable, then there are n linearly independent eigenvectors, and they may be grouped according to which eigenvalues they belong. ∎

EXAMPLE 6 Diagonalize the following matrix, if possible.

$$A = \begin{bmatrix} 5 & 0 & 0 & 0 \\ 0 & 5 & 0 & 0 \\ 1 & 4 & -3 & 0 \\ -1 & -2 & 0 & -3 \end{bmatrix}$$

Solution Since A is a triangular matrix, the eigenvalues are 5 and -3. Using the method of Section 6.1, we find a basis for each eigenspace.

$$\text{Basis for } \lambda = 5: \quad \mathbf{u}_1 = \begin{bmatrix} -8 \\ 4 \\ 1 \\ 0 \end{bmatrix} \quad \text{and} \quad \mathbf{u}_2 = \begin{bmatrix} -16 \\ 4 \\ 0 \\ 1 \end{bmatrix}$$

$$\text{Basis for } \lambda = -3: \quad \mathbf{u}_3 = \begin{bmatrix} 0 \\ 0 \\ 1 \\ 0 \end{bmatrix} \quad \text{and} \quad \mathbf{u}_4 = \begin{bmatrix} 0 \\ 0 \\ 0 \\ 1 \end{bmatrix}$$

The set $\{\mathbf{u}_1, \dots, \mathbf{u}_4\}$ is linearly independent, by Theorem 7. So the matrix $P = [\,\mathbf{u}_1 \ \cdots \ \mathbf{u}_4\,]$ is invertible, and $A = PDP^{-1}$, where

$$P = \begin{bmatrix} -8 & -16 & 0 & 0 \\ 4 & 4 & 0 & 0 \\ 1 & 0 & 1 & 0 \\ 0 & 1 & 0 & 1 \end{bmatrix} \quad \text{and} \quad D = \begin{bmatrix} 5 & 0 & 0 & 0 \\ 0 & 5 & 0 & 0 \\ 0 & 0 & -3 & 0 \\ 0 & 0 & 0 & -3 \end{bmatrix}$$

∎

PRACTICE PROBLEMS

1. Compute A^8 where $A = \begin{bmatrix} 4 & -3 \\ 2 & -1 \end{bmatrix}$.
2. Let $A = \begin{bmatrix} -3 & 12 \\ -2 & 7 \end{bmatrix}$, $\mathbf{u}_1 = \begin{bmatrix} 3 \\ 1 \end{bmatrix}$, and $\mathbf{u}_2 = \begin{bmatrix} 2 \\ 1 \end{bmatrix}$. Suppose you are told that $\mathbf{u}_1$ and $\mathbf{u}_2$ are eigenvectors of A. Use this information to diagonalize A.
3. Let A be a 4×4 matrix with eigenvalues 5, 3, and -2, and suppose that you know the eigenspace for $\lambda = 3$ is two-dimensional. Do you have enough information to determine if A is diagonalizable?

6.3 EXERCISES

In Exercises 1 and 2, let $A = PDP^{-1}$ and compute A^4.

1. $P = \begin{bmatrix} 5 & 7 \\ 2 & 3 \end{bmatrix}$, $D = \begin{bmatrix} 2 & 0 \\ 0 & 1 \end{bmatrix}$

2. $P = \begin{bmatrix} 2 & -3 \\ -3 & 5 \end{bmatrix}$, $D = \begin{bmatrix} 1 & 0 \\ 0 & 1/2 \end{bmatrix}$

In Exercises 3 and 4, use the factorization $A = PDP^{-1}$ to compute A^k, where k represents an arbitrary positive integer.

3. $\begin{bmatrix} a & 0 \\ 3(a-b) & b \end{bmatrix} = \begin{bmatrix} 1 & 0 \\ 3 & 1 \end{bmatrix}\begin{bmatrix} a & 0 \\ 0 & b \end{bmatrix}\begin{bmatrix} 1 & 0 \\ -3 & 1 \end{bmatrix}$

4. $\begin{bmatrix} -2 & 12 \\ -1 & 5 \end{bmatrix} = \begin{bmatrix} 3 & 4 \\ 1 & 1 \end{bmatrix}\begin{bmatrix} 2 & 0 \\ 0 & 1 \end{bmatrix}\begin{bmatrix} -1 & 4 \\ 1 & -3 \end{bmatrix}$

In Exercises 5 and 6, the matrix A is factored in the form PDP^{-1}. Use the Diagonalization Theorem to find the eigenvalues of A and a basis for each eigenspace.

5. $\begin{bmatrix} 2 & 2 & 1 \\ 1 & 3 & 1 \\ 1 & 2 & 2 \end{bmatrix} =$
$\begin{bmatrix} 1 & 1 & 2 \\ 1 & 0 & -1 \\ 1 & -1 & 0 \end{bmatrix}\begin{bmatrix} 5 & 0 & 0 \\ 0 & 1 & 0 \\ 0 & 0 & 1 \end{bmatrix}\begin{bmatrix} 1/4 & 1/2 & 1/4 \\ 1/4 & 1/2 & -3/4 \\ 1/4 & -1/2 & 1/4 \end{bmatrix}$

6. $\begin{bmatrix} 4 & 0 & -2 \\ 2 & 5 & 4 \\ 0 & 0 & 5 \end{bmatrix} =$
$\begin{bmatrix} -2 & 0 & -1 \\ 0 & 1 & 2 \\ 1 & 0 & 0 \end{bmatrix}\begin{bmatrix} 5 & 0 & 0 \\ 0 & 5 & 0 \\ 0 & 0 & 4 \end{bmatrix}\begin{bmatrix} 0 & 0 & 1 \\ 2 & 1 & 4 \\ -1 & 0 & -2 \end{bmatrix}$

Diagonalize the matrices in Exercises 7–20, if possible. The eigenvalues for Exercises 11–16 are: (11) $\lambda = 1, 2, 3$; (12) $\lambda = 2, 8$; (13) $\lambda = 5, 1$; (14) $\lambda = 5, 4$; (15) $\lambda = 3, 1$; and (16) $\lambda = 2, 1$.

7. $\begin{bmatrix} 1 & 0 \\ 6 & -1 \end{bmatrix}$

8. $\begin{bmatrix} 5 & 1 \\ 0 & 5 \end{bmatrix}$

9. $\begin{bmatrix} 3 & -1 \\ 1 & 5 \end{bmatrix}$

10. $\begin{bmatrix} 2 & 3 \\ 4 & 1 \end{bmatrix}$

11. $\begin{bmatrix} -1 & 4 & -2 \\ -3 & 4 & 0 \\ -3 & 1 & 3 \end{bmatrix}$

12. $\begin{bmatrix} 4 & 2 & 2 \\ 2 & 4 & 2 \\ 2 & 2 & 4 \end{bmatrix}$

13. $\begin{bmatrix} 2 & 2 & -1 \\ 1 & 3 & -1 \\ -1 & -2 & 2 \end{bmatrix}$

14. $\begin{bmatrix} 4 & 0 & -2 \\ 2 & 5 & 4 \\ 0 & 0 & 5 \end{bmatrix}$

15. $\begin{bmatrix} 7 & 4 & 16 \\ 2 & 5 & 8 \\ -2 & -2 & -5 \end{bmatrix}$

16. $\begin{bmatrix} 0 & -4 & -6 \\ -1 & 0 & -3 \\ 1 & 2 & 5 \end{bmatrix}$

17. $\begin{bmatrix} 4 & 0 & 0 \\ 1 & 4 & 0 \\ 0 & 0 & 5 \end{bmatrix}$

18. $\begin{bmatrix} 0 & 0 & 0 \\ 0 & 0 & 0 \\ 3 & 0 & 5 \end{bmatrix}$

19. $\begin{bmatrix} 5 & -3 & 0 & 9 \\ 0 & 3 & 1 & -2 \\ 0 & 0 & 2 & 0 \\ 0 & 0 & 0 & 2 \end{bmatrix}$

20. $\begin{bmatrix} 4 & 0 & 0 & 0 \\ 0 & 4 & 0 & 0 \\ 0 & 0 & 2 & 0 \\ 1 & 0 & 0 & 2 \end{bmatrix}$

21. A is a 5×5 matrix with two eigenvalues. One eigenspace is three-dimensional and the other eigenspace is two-dimensional. Is A diagonalizable? Why?

22. A is a 3×3 matrix with two eigenvalues. Each eigenspace is one-dimensional. Is A diagonalizable? Why?

23. A is a 4×4 matrix with three eigenvalues. One eigenspace is one-dimensional, and one of the other eigenspaces is two-dimensional. Is it possible that A is *not* diagonalizable? Justify your answer.

24. A is a 7×7 matrix with three eigenvalues. One eigenspace is two-dimensional, and one of the other eigenspaces is three-dimensional. Is it possible that A is *not* diagonalizable? Justify your answer.

25. Show that if A is both diagonalizable and invertible, then so is A^{-1}.

26. Show that if A has n linearly independent eigenvectors, then so does A^T. [*Hint*: Use Theorem 5.]

27. A factorization $A = PDP^{-1}$ is not unique. Demonstrate this for the matrix A in Example 2. With $D_1 = \begin{bmatrix} 3 & 0 \\ 0 & 5 \end{bmatrix}$, use the information in Example 2 to find a matrix P_1 such that $A = P_1D_1P_1^{-1}$.

28. With A and D as in Example 2, find an invertible P_2 unequal to the P in Example 2, given that $A = P_2DP_2^{-1}$.

SOLUTIONS TO PRACTICE PROBLEMS

1. $\det(A - \lambda I) = \lambda^2 - 3\lambda + 2 = (\lambda - 2)(\lambda - 1)$. The eigenvalues are 2 and 1, and corresponding eigenvectors are $\mathbf{u}_1 = \begin{bmatrix} 3 \\ 2 \end{bmatrix}$ and $\mathbf{u}_2 = \begin{bmatrix} 1 \\ 1 \end{bmatrix}$. Next, form

$$P = \begin{bmatrix} 3 & 1 \\ 2 & 1 \end{bmatrix}, \qquad D = \begin{bmatrix} 2 & 0 \\ 0 & 1 \end{bmatrix}, \qquad \text{and} \qquad P^{-1} = \begin{bmatrix} 1 & -1 \\ -2 & 3 \end{bmatrix}$$

Since $A = PDP^{-1}$,

$$A^8 = PD^8P^{-1} = \begin{bmatrix} 3 & 1 \\ 2 & 1 \end{bmatrix} \begin{bmatrix} 2^8 & 0 \\ 0 & 1^8 \end{bmatrix} \begin{bmatrix} 1 & -1 \\ -2 & 3 \end{bmatrix}$$
$$= \begin{bmatrix} 3 & 1 \\ 2 & 1 \end{bmatrix} \begin{bmatrix} 256 & 0 \\ 0 & 1 \end{bmatrix} \begin{bmatrix} 1 & -1 \\ -2 & 3 \end{bmatrix} = \begin{bmatrix} 766 & -765 \\ 510 & -509 \end{bmatrix}$$

2. Compute $A\mathbf{u}_1 = \begin{bmatrix} -3 & 12 \\ -2 & 7 \end{bmatrix} \begin{bmatrix} 3 \\ 1 \end{bmatrix} = \begin{bmatrix} 3 \\ 1 \end{bmatrix} = 1 \cdot \mathbf{u}_1$, and

$$A\mathbf{u}_2 = \begin{bmatrix} -3 & 12 \\ -2 & 7 \end{bmatrix} \begin{bmatrix} 2 \\ 1 \end{bmatrix} = \begin{bmatrix} 6 \\ 3 \end{bmatrix} = 3 \cdot \mathbf{u}_2$$

Clearly, $\mathbf{u}_1$ and $\mathbf{u}_2$ are eigenvectors for the eigenvalues 1 and 3, respectively. Thus

$$A = PDP^{-1}, \quad \text{where} \quad P = \begin{bmatrix} 3 & 2 \\ 1 & 1 \end{bmatrix} \quad \text{and} \quad D = \begin{bmatrix} 1 & 0 \\ 0 & 3 \end{bmatrix}$$

3. Yes, A is diagonalizable. There is a basis $\{\mathbf{u}_1, \mathbf{u}_2\}$ for the eigenspace corresponding to $\lambda = 3$. In addition, there will be at least one eigenvector for $\lambda = 5$ and one for $\lambda = -2$. Call them $\mathbf{u}_3$ and $\mathbf{u}_4$. Then $\{\mathbf{u}_1, \ldots, \mathbf{u}_4\}$ is linearly independent and A is diagonalizable, by Theorem 7. There can be no additional eigenvectors that are linearly independent from $\mathbf{u}_1, \ldots, \mathbf{u}_4$, because the vectors are all in $\mathbb{R}^4$. Hence the eigenspaces for $\lambda = 5$ and $\lambda = -2$ are both one-dimensional.

6.4 EIGENVECTORS AND LINEAR TRANSFORMATIONS

The goal of this section is to understand the matrix factorization $A = PDP^{-1}$ as a statement about linear transformations. We shall see that the transformation $\mathbf{x} \mapsto A\mathbf{x}$ is essentially the same as the very simple mapping $\mathbf{u} \mapsto D\mathbf{u}$, when viewed from the proper perspective. A similar interpretation will apply to A and D even when D is not a diagonal matrix.

Recall from Section 2.6 that any linear transformation T from $\mathbb{R}^n$ to $\mathbb{R}^m$ may be implemented via left-multiplication by a matrix A, called the *standard matrix* of T. Now we need the same sort of representation for any linear transformation between two finite-dimensional vector spaces.

The Matrix of a Linear Transformation

Let V be an n-dimensional vector space, W an m-dimensional vector space, and T any linear transformation from V to W. To associate a matrix with T, we choose (ordered) bases $\mathcal{B}$ and $\mathcal{C}$ for V and W, respectively.

Given any $\mathbf{x}$ in V, the coordinate vector $[\mathbf{x}]_{\mathcal{B}}$ is in $\mathbb{R}^n$ and the coordinate vector of its image, $[T(\mathbf{x})]_{\mathcal{C}}$, is in $\mathbb{R}^m$, as shown in Fig. 1.

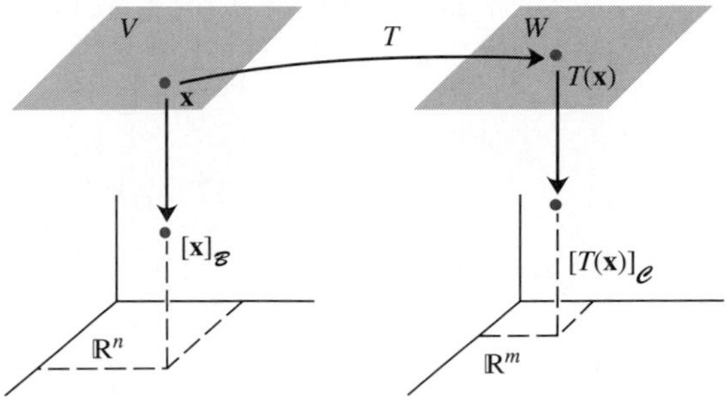

FIGURE 1 A linear transformation from V to W.

The connection between $[\mathbf{x}]_{\mathcal{B}}$ and $[T(\mathbf{x})]_{\mathcal{C}}$ is easy to find. Let $\{\mathbf{b}_1, \ldots, \mathbf{b}_n\}$ be the basis $\mathcal{B}$ for V. If $\mathbf{x} = r_1\mathbf{b}_1 + \cdots + r_n\mathbf{b}_n$, then

$$[\mathbf{x}]_{\mathcal{B}} = \begin{bmatrix} r_1 \\ \vdots \\ r_n \end{bmatrix}$$

and

$$T(\mathbf{x}) = T(r_1\mathbf{b}_1 + \cdots + r_n\mathbf{b}_n) = r_1T(\mathbf{b}_1) + \cdots + r_nT(\mathbf{b}_n) \tag{1}$$

because T is linear. Using the basis $\mathcal{C}$ in W, we can rewrite (1) in terms of $\mathcal{C}$-coordinate vectors:

$$[T(\mathbf{x})]_{\mathcal{C}} = r_1[T(\mathbf{b}_1)]_{\mathcal{C}} + \cdots + r_n[T(\mathbf{b}_n)]_{\mathcal{C}} \tag{2}$$

Since $\mathcal{C}$-coordinate vectors are in $\mathbb{R}^m$, the vector equation (2) may be written as a matrix equation, namely,

$$[T(\mathbf{x})]_{\mathcal{C}} = M[\mathbf{x}]_{\mathcal{B}} \tag{3}$$

where

$$M = \big[[T(\mathbf{b}_1)]_{\mathcal{C}} \quad [T(\mathbf{b}_2)]_{\mathcal{C}} \quad \cdots \quad [T(\mathbf{b}_n)]_{\mathcal{C}}\big] \tag{4}$$

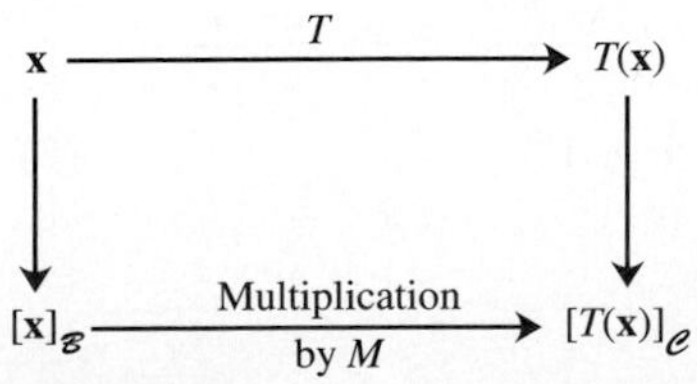

FIGURE 2

The matrix M is a matrix representation of T, called the **matrix for T relative to the bases $\mathcal{B}$ and $\mathcal{C}$**. See Fig. 2

Equation (3) says that, as far as coordinate vectors are concerned, the action of T on $\mathbf{x}$ may be viewed as left-multiplication by M.

EXAMPLE 1 Suppose that $\mathcal{B} = \{\mathbf{b}_1, \mathbf{b}_2\}$ is a basis for V and $\mathcal{C} = \{\mathbf{c}_1, \mathbf{c}_2, \mathbf{c}_3\}$ is a basis for W. Let $T: V \to W$ be a linear transformation with the property that

$$T(\mathbf{b}_1) = 3\mathbf{c}_1 - 2\mathbf{c}_2 + 5\mathbf{c}_3 \quad \text{and} \quad T(\mathbf{b}_2) = 4\mathbf{c}_1 + 7\mathbf{c}_2 - \mathbf{c}_3$$

Find the matrix M for T relative to $\mathcal{B}$ and $\mathcal{C}$.

Solution The $\mathcal{C}$-coordinate vectors of the *images* of $\mathbf{b}_1$ and $\mathbf{b}_2$ are

$$[T(\mathbf{b}_1)]_{\mathcal{C}} = \begin{bmatrix} 3 \\ -2 \\ 5 \end{bmatrix} \quad \text{and} \quad [T(\mathbf{b}_2)]_{\mathcal{C}} = \begin{bmatrix} 4 \\ 7 \\ -1 \end{bmatrix}$$

Hence,

$$M = \begin{bmatrix} 3 & 4 \\ -2 & 7 \\ 5 & -1 \end{bmatrix}$$

If $\mathcal{B}$ and $\mathcal{C}$ are bases for the same space V and if T is the identity transformation $T(\mathbf{x}) = \mathbf{x}$ for $\mathbf{x}$ in V, then the matrix M in (4) is just a change-of-coordinates matrix (see Section 5.7).

Linear Transformations from V into V

In the common case when W is the same as V and the basis $\mathcal{C}$ is the same as $\mathcal{B}$, the matrix M in (4) is called the **matrix for T relative to $\mathcal{B}$**, or simply the **$\mathcal{B}$-matrix** for T, and is denoted by $[T]_{\mathcal{B}}$. See Fig. 3.

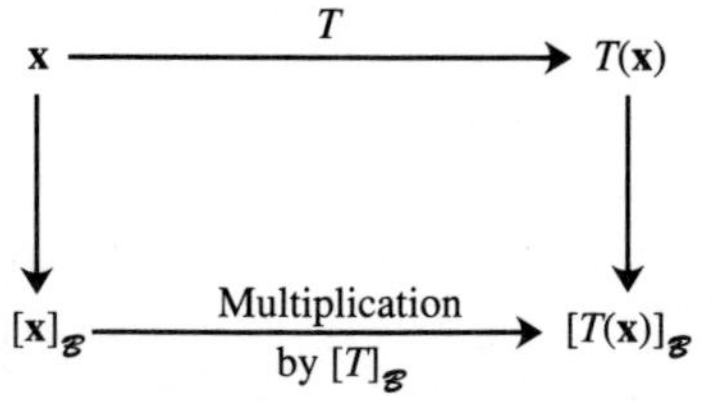

FIGURE 3

The $\mathcal{B}$-matrix of $T: V \to V$ satisfies

$$[T(\mathbf{x})]_{\mathcal{B}} = [T]_{\mathcal{B}}[\mathbf{x}]_{\mathcal{B}}, \quad \text{for all } \mathbf{x} \text{ in } V \tag{5}$$

EXAMPLE 2 The mapping $T: \mathbb{P}_2 \to \mathbb{P}_2$ defined by

$$T(a_0 + a_1 t + a_2 t^2) = a_1 + 2a_2 t$$

is a linear transformation. (Calculus students will recognize T as the differentiation operator.)

a. Find the $\mathcal{B}$-matrix for T, when $\mathcal{B}$ is the basis $\{1, t, t^2\}$.
b. Verify that $[T(\mathbf{p})]_{\mathcal{B}} = [T]_{\mathcal{B}}[\mathbf{p}]_{\mathcal{B}}$ for each $\mathbf{p}$ in $\mathbb{P}_2$.

Solution

a. Compute the images of the basis vectors:

$$T(1) = 0 \quad \text{The zero polynomial}$$
$$T(t) = 1 \quad \text{The polynomial whose value is always 1}$$
$$T(t^2) = 2t$$

Then write the $\mathcal{B}$-coordinate vectors of $T(1)$, $T(t)$, and $T(t^2)$ (which are found by inspection in this example) and place them together as the matrix for T:

$$[T(1)]_{\mathcal{B}} = \begin{bmatrix} 0 \\ 0 \\ 0 \end{bmatrix}, \quad [T(t)]_{\mathcal{B}} = \begin{bmatrix} 1 \\ 0 \\ 0 \end{bmatrix}, \quad [T(t^2)]_{\mathcal{B}} = \begin{bmatrix} 0 \\ 2 \\ 0 \end{bmatrix}$$

$$[T]_{\mathcal{B}} = \begin{bmatrix} 0 & 1 & 0 \\ 0 & 0 & 2 \\ 0 & 0 & 0 \end{bmatrix}$$

b. For a general $\mathbf{p}(t) = a_0 + a_1 t + a_2 t^2$, we have

$$[T(\mathbf{p})]_{\mathcal{B}} = [a_1 + 2a_2 t]_{\mathcal{B}} = \begin{bmatrix} a_1 \\ 2a_2 \\ 0 \end{bmatrix} = \begin{bmatrix} 0 & 1 & 0 \\ 0 & 0 & 2 \\ 0 & 0 & 0 \end{bmatrix} \begin{bmatrix} a_0 \\ a_1 \\ a_2 \end{bmatrix} = [T]_{\mathcal{B}}[\mathbf{p}]_{\mathcal{B}}$$

See Fig. 4. ∎

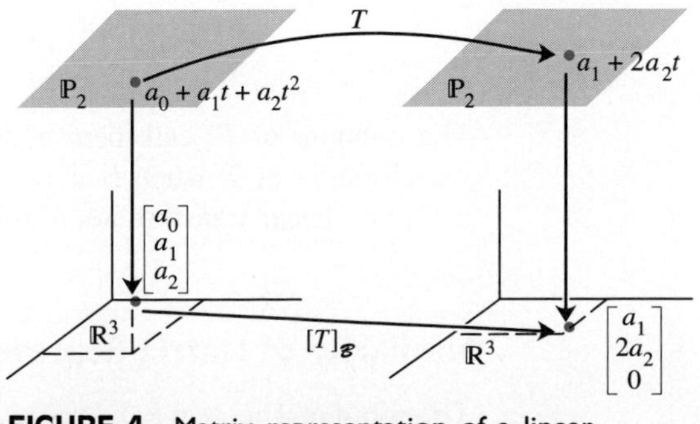

FIGURE 4 Matrix representation of a linear transformation.

Linear Transformations on $\mathbb{R}^n$

In an applied problem involving $\mathbb{R}^n$, a linear transformation T usually appears first as a matrix transformation, $\mathbf{x} \mapsto A\mathbf{x}$. If A is diagonalizable, then there is a basis $\mathcal{B}$ for $\mathbb{R}^n$ consisting of eigenvectors of A. Theorem 8 below shows that, in this case, the $\mathcal{B}$-matrix of T is diagonal. Diagonalizing A amounts to finding a diagonal matrix representation of $\mathbf{x} \mapsto A\mathbf{x}$.

THEOREM 8 Diagonal Matrix Representation

Suppose $A = PDP^{-1}$, where D is a diagonal $n \times n$ matrix. If $\mathcal{B}$ is the basis for $\mathbb{R}^n$ formed from the columns of P, then D is the $\mathcal{B}$-matrix of the transformation $\mathbf{x} \mapsto A\mathbf{x}$.

Proof Denote the columns of P by $\mathbf{b}_1, \dots, \mathbf{b}_n$, so that $\mathcal{B} = \{\mathbf{b}_1, \dots, \mathbf{b}_n\}$ and $P = [\,\mathbf{b}_1 \;\cdots\; \mathbf{b}_n\,]$. In this case P is the change-of-coordinates matrix $P_{\mathcal{B}}$ discussed in Section 5.4, where

$$P[\mathbf{x}]_{\mathcal{B}} = \mathbf{x} \quad \text{and} \quad [\mathbf{x}]_{\mathcal{B}} = P^{-1}\mathbf{x}$$

If $T(\mathbf{x}) = A\mathbf{x}$ for $\mathbf{x}$ in $\mathbb{R}^n$, then

$$\begin{aligned}
[T]_{\mathcal{B}} &= [\,[T(\mathbf{b}_1)]_{\mathcal{B}} \;\cdots\; [T(\mathbf{b}_n)]_{\mathcal{B}}\,] && \text{Definition of } [T]_{\mathcal{B}} \\
&= [\,[A\mathbf{b}_1]_{\mathcal{B}} \;\cdots\; [A\mathbf{b}_n]_{\mathcal{B}}\,] && \text{Since } T(\mathbf{x}) = A\mathbf{x} \\
&= [\,P^{-1}A\mathbf{b}_1 \;\cdots\; P^{-1}A\mathbf{b}_n\,] && \text{Change of coordinates} \\
&= P^{-1}A\,[\,\mathbf{b}_1 \;\cdots\; \mathbf{b}_n\,] && \text{Matrix multiplication} \\
&= P^{-1}AP && (6)
\end{aligned}$$

Since $A = PDP^{-1}$, we have $[T]_{\mathcal{B}} = P^{-1}AP = D$. ∎

EXAMPLE 3 Define $T : \mathbb{R}^2 \to \mathbb{R}^2$ by $T(\mathbf{x}) = A\mathbf{x}$, where $A = \begin{bmatrix} 7 & 2 \\ -4 & 1 \end{bmatrix}$. Find a basis $\mathcal{B}$ for $\mathbb{R}^2$ with the property that the $\mathcal{B}$-matrix of T is a diagonal matrix.

Solution From Example 2 in Section 6.3, we know that $A = PDP^{-1}$, where

$$P = \begin{bmatrix} 1 & 1 \\ -1 & -2 \end{bmatrix} \quad \text{and} \quad D = \begin{bmatrix} 5 & 0 \\ 0 & 3 \end{bmatrix}$$

The columns of P, call them $\mathbf{b}_1$ and $\mathbf{b}_2$, are eigenvectors of A. By Theorem 8, D is the $\mathcal{B}$-matrix of T when $\mathcal{B} = \{\mathbf{b}_1, \mathbf{b}_2\}$. The mappings $\mathbf{x} \mapsto A\mathbf{x}$ and $\mathbf{u} \mapsto D\mathbf{u}$ describe the same linear transformation, relative to different bases. ∎

Similarity of Matrix Representations

The proof of Theorem 8 did not use the fact that D was diagonal. Hence, if A is similar to a matrix C, with $A = PCP^{-1}$, then C is the $\mathcal{B}$-matrix of the transformation $\mathbf{x} \mapsto A\mathbf{x}$

when the basis $\mathcal{B}$ is formed from the columns of P. The factorization $A = PCP^{-1}$ is shown in Fig. 5.

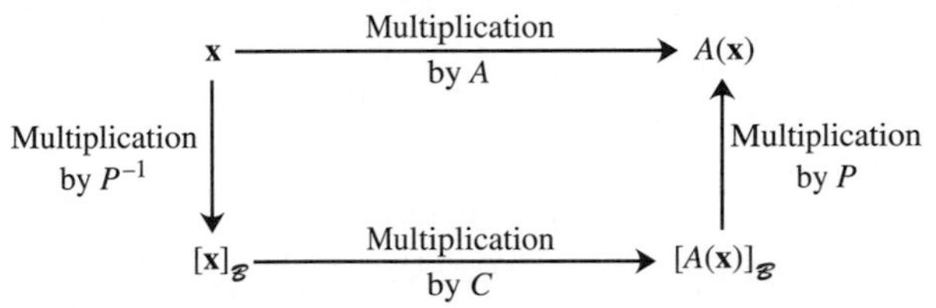

FIGURE 5 Similarity of two matrix representations: $A = PCP^{-1}$.

Conversely, if $T : \mathbb{R}^n \to \mathbb{R}^n$ is defined by $T(\mathbf{x}) = A\mathbf{x}$, and if $\mathcal{B}$ is any basis for $\mathbb{R}^n$, then the $\mathcal{B}$-matrix of T is similar to A. In fact, the calculations in (6) show that if P is the matrix whose columns come from the vectors in $\mathcal{B}$, then $[T]_{\mathcal{B}} = P^{-1}AP$. Thus, the set of all matrices similar to a matrix A coincides with the set of all matrix representations of the transformation $\mathbf{x} \mapsto A\mathbf{x}$.

Numerical Note

An efficient way to compute a $\mathcal{B}$-matrix $P^{-1}AP$ is to compute AP and then to row reduce the augmented matrix $[\,P \quad AP\,]$ to $[\,I \quad P^{-1}AP\,]$. A separate computation of P^{-1} is unnecessary. See Exercise 9 in Section 3.2.

PRACTICE PROBLEMS

1. Find $T(a_0 + a_1t + a_2t^2)$, if T is a linear transformation from $\mathbb{P}_2$ to $\mathbb{P}_2$ whose matrix relative to $\mathcal{B} = \{1, t, t^2\}$ is

$$[T]_{\mathcal{B}} = \begin{bmatrix} 3 & 4 & 0 \\ 0 & 5 & -1 \\ 1 & -2 & 7 \end{bmatrix}$$

2. Let A, B, C be $n \times n$ matrices. The text has shown that if A is similar to B, then B is similar to A. This property, together with the statements below, shows that "similar to" is an *equivalence relation*. (Row equivalence is another example of an equivalence relation.) Verify parts (a) and (b).

   a. A is similar to A.

   b. If A is similar to B and B is similar to C, then A is similar to C.

6.4 EXERCISES

1. Let $\mathcal{B} = \{\mathbf{b}_1, \mathbf{b}_2, \mathbf{b}_3\}$ and $\mathcal{D} = \{\mathbf{d}_1, \mathbf{d}_2\}$ be bases for vector spaces V and W, respectively. Let $T: V \to W$ be a linear transformation with the property that

$$T(\mathbf{b}_1) = 3\mathbf{d}_1 - 5\mathbf{d}_2, \quad T(\mathbf{b}_2) = -\mathbf{d}_1 + 6\mathbf{d}_2, \quad T(\mathbf{b}_3) = 4\mathbf{d}_2$$

Find the matrix for T relative to $\mathcal{B}$ and $\mathcal{D}$.

2. Let $\mathcal{D} = \{\mathbf{d}_1, \mathbf{d}_2\}$ and $\mathcal{B} = \{\mathbf{b}_1, \mathbf{b}_2\}$ be bases for vector spaces V and W, respectively. Let $T: V \to W$ be a linear transformation with the property that

$$T(\mathbf{d}_1) = 2\mathbf{b}_1 - 3\mathbf{b}_2, \qquad T(\mathbf{d}_2) = -4\mathbf{b}_1 + 5\mathbf{b}_2$$

Find the matrix for T relative to $\mathcal{D}$ and $\mathcal{B}$.

3. Let $\mathcal{E} = \{\mathbf{e}_1, \mathbf{e}_2, \mathbf{e}_3\}$ be the standard basis for $\mathbb{R}^3$, $\mathcal{B} = \{\mathbf{b}_1, \mathbf{b}_2, \mathbf{b}_3\}$ be a basis for a vector space V, and $T: \mathbb{R}^3 \to V$ be a linear transformation with the property that

$$T(x_1, x_2, x_3) = (x_3 - x_2)\mathbf{b}_1 - (x_1 + x_3)\mathbf{b}_2 + (x_1 - x_2)\mathbf{b}_3$$

a. Compute $T(\mathbf{e}_1)$, $T(\mathbf{e}_2)$, and $T(\mathbf{e}_3)$.

b. Compute $[T(\mathbf{e}_1)]_{\mathcal{B}}$, $[T(\mathbf{e}_2)]_{\mathcal{B}}$, and $[T(\mathbf{e}_3)]_{\mathcal{B}}$.

c. Find the matrix for T relative to $\mathcal{E}$ and $\mathcal{B}$.

4. Let $\mathcal{B} = \{\mathbf{b}_1, \mathbf{b}_2, \mathbf{b}_3\}$ be a basis for a vector space V and $T: V \to \mathbb{R}^2$ be a linear transformation with the property that

$$T(x_1\mathbf{b}_1 + x_2\mathbf{b}_2 + x_3\mathbf{b}_3) = \begin{bmatrix} 2x_1 - 4x_2 + 5x_3 \\ -x_2 + 3x_3 \end{bmatrix}$$

Find the matrix for T relative to $\mathcal{B}$ and the standard basis for $\mathbb{R}^2$.

5. Let $T: \mathbb{P}_2 \to \mathbb{P}_3$ be the transformation that maps a polynomial $\mathbf{p}(t)$ into the polynomial $(t + 5)\mathbf{p}(t)$.

a. Find the image of $\mathbf{p}(t) = 2 - t + t^2$.

b. Show that T is a linear transformation.

c. Find the matrix for T relative to the bases $\{1, t, t^2\}$ and $\{1, t, t^2, t^3\}$.

6. Let $T: \mathbb{P}_2 \to \mathbb{P}_4$ be the transformation that maps a polynomial $\mathbf{p}(t)$ into the polynomial $\mathbf{p}(t) + t^2\mathbf{p}(t)$.

a. Find the image of $\mathbf{p}(t) = 2 - t + t^2$.

b. Show that T is a linear transformation.

c. Find the matrix for T relative to the bases $\{1, t, t^2\}$ and $\{1, t, t^2, t^3, t^4\}$.

7. Assume that the mapping $T: \mathbb{P}_2 \to \mathbb{P}_2$ defined by

$$T(a_0 + a_1t + a_2t^2) = 3a_0 + (5a_0 - 2a_1)t + (4a_1 + a_2)t^2$$

is linear. Find the matrix representation of T relative to the basis $\mathcal{B} = \{1, t, t^2\}$.

8. Let $\mathcal{B} = \{\mathbf{b}_1, \mathbf{b}_2, \mathbf{b}_3\}$ be a basis for a vector space V. Find $T(3\mathbf{b}_1 - 4\mathbf{b}_2)$, if T is a linear transformation from V to V whose matrix relative to $\mathcal{B}$ is

$$[T]_{\mathcal{B}} = \begin{bmatrix} 0 & -6 & 1 \\ 0 & 5 & -1 \\ 1 & -2 & 7 \end{bmatrix}$$

9. Define $T: \mathbb{P}_2 \to \mathbb{R}^3$ as shown below.

$$T(\mathbf{p}) = \begin{bmatrix} \mathbf{p}(-1) \\ \mathbf{p}(0) \\ \mathbf{p}(1) \end{bmatrix}$$

a. Find the image under T of $\mathbf{p}(t) = 5 + 3t$.

b. Show that T is a linear transformation.

c. Find the matrix for T relative to the basis $\{1, t, t^2\}$ for $\mathbb{P}_2$ and the standard basis for $\mathbb{R}^3$.

10. Define $T: \mathbb{P}_3 \to \mathbb{R}^4$ as shown below.

$$T(\mathbf{p}) = \begin{bmatrix} \mathbf{p}(-3) \\ \mathbf{p}(-1) \\ \mathbf{p}(1) \\ \mathbf{p}(3) \end{bmatrix}$$

a. Show that T is a linear transformation.

b. Find the matrix for T relative to the basis $\{1, t, t^2, t^3\}$ for $\mathbb{P}_2$ and the standard basis for $\mathbb{R}^4$.

In Exercises 11 and 12, find the $\mathcal{B}$-matrix of the transformation $\mathbf{x} \mapsto A\mathbf{x}$, when $\mathcal{B} = \{\mathbf{b}_1, \mathbf{b}_2\}$.

11. $A = \begin{bmatrix} 3 & 4 \\ -1 & -1 \end{bmatrix}$, $\mathbf{b}_1 = \begin{bmatrix} 2 \\ -1 \end{bmatrix}$, $\mathbf{b}_2 = \begin{bmatrix} 1 \\ 2 \end{bmatrix}$

12. $A = \begin{bmatrix} -1 & 4 \\ -2 & 3 \end{bmatrix}$, $\mathbf{b}_1 = \begin{bmatrix} 3 \\ 2 \end{bmatrix}$, $\mathbf{b}_2 = \begin{bmatrix} -1 \\ 1 \end{bmatrix}$

In Exercises 13–16, define $T: \mathbb{R}^2 \to \mathbb{R}^2$ by $T(\mathbf{x}) = A\mathbf{x}$. Find a basis $\mathcal{B}$ for $\mathbb{R}^2$ with the property that $[T]_{\mathcal{B}}$ is diagonal.

13. $A = \begin{bmatrix} 0 & 1 \\ -3 & 4 \end{bmatrix}$

14. $A = \begin{bmatrix} 5 & -3 \\ -7 & 1 \end{bmatrix}$

15. $A = \begin{bmatrix} 4 & -2 \\ -1 & 3 \end{bmatrix}$

16. $A = \begin{bmatrix} 4 & 6 \\ -1 & -1 \end{bmatrix}$

17. Let $A = \begin{bmatrix} 1 & 1 \\ -1 & 3 \end{bmatrix}$ and $\mathcal{B} = \{\mathbf{b}_1, \mathbf{b}_2\}$, for $\mathbf{b}_1 = \begin{bmatrix} 1 \\ 1 \end{bmatrix}$, $\mathbf{b}_2 = \begin{bmatrix} 5 \\ 4 \end{bmatrix}$. Define $T: \mathbb{R}^2 \to \mathbb{R}^2$ by $T(\mathbf{x}) = A\mathbf{x}$.

a. Verify that $\mathbf{b}_1$ is an eigenvector of A but that A is not diagonalizable.

b. Find the $\mathcal{B}$-matrix for T.

18. Define $T: \mathbb{R}^3 \to \mathbb{R}^3$ by $T(\mathbf{x}) = A\mathbf{x}$, where A is a 3×3 matrix with eigenvalues 5 and -2. Does there exist a basis $\mathcal{B}$ for $\mathbb{R}^3$ such that the $\mathcal{B}$-matrix for T is a diagonal matrix? Discuss.

Verify the statements in Exercises 19–26. Here $A, B, \ldots,$ represent $n \times n$ matrices.

19. If A is invertible and similar to B, then B is invertible and A^{-1} is similar to B^{-1}. [*Hint*: $P^{-1}AP = B$ for some invertible P. Explain why B is invertible. Then find an invertible Q such that $Q^{-1}A^{-1}Q = B^{-1}$.]

20. If A is similar to B, then A^2 is similar to B^2.

21. If B is similar to A and C is similar to A, then B is similar to C. [*Hint*: By hypothesis, there exist invertible P and Q such that $P^{-1}BP = A$ and $Q^{-1}CQ = A$.]

22. If A is diagonalizable and B is similar to A, then B is also diagonalizable.

23. If $B = P^{-1}AP$ and $\mathbf{x}$ is an eigenvector of A corresponding to an eigenvalue λ, then $P^{-1}\mathbf{x}$ is an eigenvector of B corresponding also to λ.

24. If A and B are similar, then they have the same rank. [*Hint*: Refer to Supplementary Exercises 9 and 10 for Chapter 5.]

25. The *trace* of a square matrix A is the sum of the diagonal entries in A and is denoted by $\operatorname{tr} A$. It can be verified that $\operatorname{tr}(FG) = \operatorname{tr}(GF)$ for any two $n \times n$ matrices F and G. Show that if A and B are similar, then $\operatorname{tr} A = \operatorname{tr} B$. What can you say about $\operatorname{tr} A$ if A is diagonalizable?

26. If A is diagonalizable, then A and A^T are similar.

27. Let V be $\mathbb{R}^n$ with a basis $\mathcal{B} = \{\mathbf{b}_1, \ldots, \mathbf{b}_n\}$, let W be $\mathbb{R}^n$ with the standard basis, denoted here by $\mathcal{E}$, and consider the identity transformation $I: \mathbb{R}^n \to \mathbb{R}^n$, where $I(\mathbf{x}) = \mathbf{x}$. Find the matrix for I relative to $\mathcal{B}$ and $\mathcal{E}$. What was this matrix called in Section 5.4?

28. Let V be a vector space with a basis $\mathcal{B} = \{\mathbf{b}_1, \ldots, \mathbf{b}_n\}$, W be the space V with a basis $\mathcal{C} = \{\mathbf{c}_1, \ldots, \mathbf{c}_n\}$, and I be the identity transformation $I: V \to W$. Find the matrix for I relative to $\mathcal{B}$ and $\mathcal{C}$. What was this matrix called in Section 5.7?

29. Let V be a vector space with a basis $\mathcal{B} = \{\mathbf{b}_1, \ldots, \mathbf{b}_n\}$. Find the $\mathcal{B}$-matrix of the identity transformation $I: V \to V$.

SOLUTIONS TO PRACTICE PROBLEMS

1. Let $\mathbf{p}(t) = a_0 + a_1 t + a_2 t^2$ and compute

$$[T(\mathbf{p})]_{\mathcal{B}} = [T]_{\mathcal{B}}[\mathbf{p}]_{\mathcal{B}} = \begin{bmatrix} 3 & 4 & 0 \\ 0 & 5 & -1 \\ 1 & -2 & 7 \end{bmatrix} \begin{bmatrix} a_0 \\ a_1 \\ a_2 \end{bmatrix} = \begin{bmatrix} 3a_0 + 4a_1 \\ 5a_1 - a_2 \\ a_0 - 2a_1 + 7a_2 \end{bmatrix}$$

So $T(\mathbf{p}) = (3a_0 + 4a_1) + (5a_1 - a_2)t + (a_0 - 2a_1 + 7a_2)t^2$.

2. a. $A = (I)^{-1}AI$, so A is similar to A.

b. By hypothesis, there exist invertible matrices P and Q with the property that $B = P^{-1}AP$ and $C = Q^{-1}BQ$. Substituting, and using a fact about the inverse of a product, we have

$$C = Q^{-1}BQ = Q^{-1}(P^{-1}AP)Q = (PQ)^{-1}A(PQ)$$

This equation has the proper form to show that A is similar to C.

6.5 COMPLEX EIGENVALUES

Since the characteristic equation of an $n \times n$ matrix involves a polynomial of degree n, the equation always has exactly n roots, counting multiplicities, *provided that possibly complex roots are included.* In this section we show that if the characteristic equation of a matrix A has some complex roots, then these roots provide critical information about A. The key is to let A act on the space $\mathbb{C}^n$ of n-tuples of complex numbers.[1]

[1]Refer to Appendix B for a brief discussion of complex numbers. Matrix algebra and concepts about vector spaces studied for real vector spaces carry over to the case with complex entries and scalars. In particular, $A(c\mathbf{x} + d\mathbf{y}) = cA\mathbf{x} + dA\mathbf{y}$, for A an $m \times n$ matrix with complex entries, $\mathbf{x}, \mathbf{y}$ in $\mathbb{C}^n$ and c, d in $\mathbb{C}$.

Our interest in $\mathbb{C}^n$ does not arise from a desire to "generalize" the results of the earlier chapters, although that would in fact open up significant new applications of linear algebra.[2] Rather, our study of complex eigenvalues is essential in order to uncover "hidden" information about certain matrices with real entries that arise in a variety of real-life problems. Such problems include many real dynamical systems that involve periodic motion, vibration, or some type of rotation in space.

The matrix eigenvalue-eigenvector theory already developed for $\mathbb{R}^n$ applies equally well to $\mathbb{C}^n$. So a complex scalar λ satisfies $\det(A - \lambda I) = 0$ if and only if there is a nonzero vector $\mathbf{x}$ in $\mathbb{C}^n$ such that $A\mathbf{x} = \lambda\mathbf{x}$. We call λ a **(complex) eigenvalue** and $\mathbf{x}$ a **(complex) eigenvector** corresponding to λ.

EXAMPLE 1 If $A = \begin{bmatrix} 0 & -1 \\ 1 & 0 \end{bmatrix}$, then the linear transformation $\mathbf{x} \mapsto A\mathbf{x}$ on $\mathbb{R}^2$ rotates the plane counterclockwise through a quarter-turn. The action of A is periodic, since after four quarter-turns, a vector is back where it started. Obviously, no nonzero vector is mapped into a multiple of itself, so A has no eigenvectors in $\mathbb{R}^2$ and hence no real eigenvalues. In fact, the characteristic equation of A is

$$\lambda^2 + 1 = 0$$

The only roots are complex: $\lambda = i$ and $\lambda = -i$. However, if we permit A to act on $\mathbb{C}^2$, then it is readily seen that

$$\begin{bmatrix} 0 & -1 \\ 1 & 0 \end{bmatrix}\begin{bmatrix} 1 \\ -i \end{bmatrix} = \begin{bmatrix} i \\ 1 \end{bmatrix} = i\begin{bmatrix} 1 \\ -i \end{bmatrix}$$

$$\begin{bmatrix} 0 & -1 \\ 1 & 0 \end{bmatrix}\begin{bmatrix} 1 \\ i \end{bmatrix} = \begin{bmatrix} -i \\ 1 \end{bmatrix} = -i\begin{bmatrix} 1 \\ i \end{bmatrix}$$

Thus i and $-i$ are eigenvalues, with $\begin{bmatrix} 1 \\ -i \end{bmatrix}$ and $\begin{bmatrix} 1 \\ i \end{bmatrix}$ as corresponding eigenvectors. (A method for *finding* complex eigenvectors is discussed in Example 2.)

The main focus of this section will be on the matrix in the next example.

EXAMPLE 2 Let $A = \begin{bmatrix} .5 & -.6 \\ .75 & 1.1 \end{bmatrix}$. Find the eigenvalues of A, and find a basis for each eigenspace.

Solution The characteristic equation of A is

$$\begin{aligned} 0 = \det\begin{bmatrix} .5 - \lambda & -.6 \\ .75 & 1.1 - \lambda \end{bmatrix} &= (.5 - \lambda)(1.1 - \lambda) - (-.6)(.75) \\ &= \lambda^2 - 1.6\lambda + 1 \end{aligned}$$

[2] A second course in linear algebra often discusses such topics. They are of particular importance in electrical engineering.

From the quadratic formula, $\lambda = \frac{1}{2}[1.6 \pm \sqrt{(-1.6)^2 - 4}] = .8 \pm .6i$. For the eigenvalue $\lambda = .8 - .6i$, we study

$$A - (.8 - .6i)I = \begin{bmatrix} .5 & -.6 \\ .75 & 1.1 \end{bmatrix} - \begin{bmatrix} .8 - .6i & 0 \\ 0 & .8 - .6i \end{bmatrix}$$

$$= \begin{bmatrix} -.3 + .6i & -.6 \\ .75 & .3 + .6i \end{bmatrix} \tag{1}$$

Row reduction of the usual augmented matrix is quite unpleasant by hand because of the complex arithmetic. However, here is a nice observation that really simplifies matters: Since $.8 - .6i$ is an eigenvalue, we know that the system

$$\begin{aligned} (-.3 + .6i)x_1 - \qquad .6x_2 &= 0 \\ .75x_1 + (.3 + .6i)x_2 &= 0 \end{aligned} \tag{2}$$

has a nontrivial solution (with x_1 and x_2 possibly complex numbers). Therefore, *both equations in (2) determine the same relationship between* x_1 *and* x_2*, and either equation may be used to express one variable in terms of the other.*[3]

The second equation in (2) leads to

$$\begin{aligned} .75x_1 &= (-.3 - .6i)x_2 \\ x_1 &= (-.4 - .8i)x_2 \end{aligned}$$

Taking $x_2 = 5$ to eliminate the decimals, we have $x_1 = -2 - 4i$. A basis for the eigenspace corresponding to $\lambda = .8 - .6i$ is

$$\mathbf{v}_1 = \begin{bmatrix} -2 - 4i \\ 5 \end{bmatrix}$$

Analogous calculations for $\lambda = .8 + .6i$ produce the eigenvector

$$\mathbf{v}_2 = \begin{bmatrix} -2 + 4i \\ 5 \end{bmatrix}$$

As a sample check on our work, we compute

$$A\mathbf{v}_2 = \begin{bmatrix} .5 & -.6 \\ .75 & 1.1 \end{bmatrix} \begin{bmatrix} -2 + 4i \\ 5 \end{bmatrix} = \begin{bmatrix} -4 + 2i \\ 4 + 3i \end{bmatrix} = (.8 + .6i)\mathbf{v}_2$$

Surprisingly, the matrix A in Example 2 determines a transformation $\mathbf{x} \mapsto A\mathbf{x}$ that is essentially a rotation. This fact becomes evident when appropriate points are plotted.

EXAMPLE 3 One way to see how multiplication by the A in Example 2 affects points is to plot an arbitrary initial point—say, $\mathbf{x}_0 = (2, 0)$—and then to plot successive im-

[3]Another way to see this is to realize that the matrix in (1) is not invertible, so its rows are linearly dependent (as vectors in $\mathbb{C}^2$), and hence one row is a (complex) multiple of the other.

ages of this point under repeated multiplications by A. That is, plot

$$\mathbf{x}_1 = A\mathbf{x}_0 = \begin{bmatrix} .5 & -.6 \\ .75 & 1.1 \end{bmatrix}\begin{bmatrix} 2 \\ 0 \end{bmatrix} = \begin{bmatrix} 1.0 \\ 1.5 \end{bmatrix}$$

$$\mathbf{x}_2 = A\mathbf{x}_1 = \begin{bmatrix} .5 & -.6 \\ .75 & 1.1 \end{bmatrix}\begin{bmatrix} 1.0 \\ 1.5 \end{bmatrix} = \begin{bmatrix} -.4 \\ 2.4 \end{bmatrix}$$

$$\mathbf{x}_3 = A\mathbf{x}_2, \ldots$$

Figure 1 shows $\mathbf{x}_0, \ldots, \mathbf{x}_8$ as heavy dots. The smaller dots are the locations of $\mathbf{x}_9, \ldots, \mathbf{x}_{100}$. The sequence lies along an elliptical orbit. ■

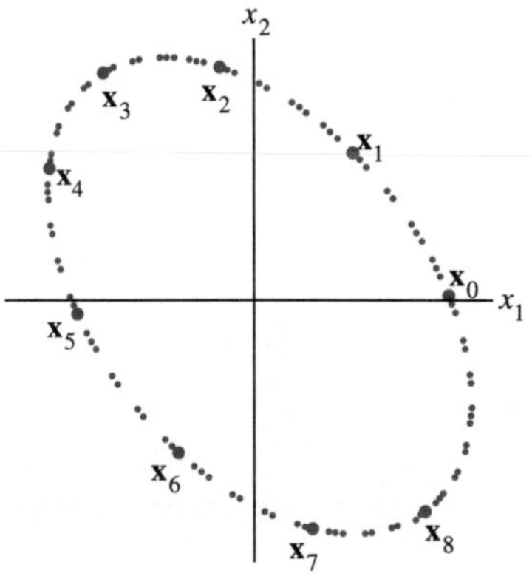

FIGURE 1 Iterates of a point $\mathbf{x}_0$ under the action of a matrix with a complex eigenvalue.

Of course, Fig. 1 does not explain *why* the rotation occurs. The secret to the rotation is hidden in the real and imaginary parts of a complex eigenvector.

Real and Imaginary Parts of Vectors

The complex conjugate of a complex vector $\mathbf{x}$ in $\mathbb{C}^n$ is the vector $\overline{\mathbf{x}}$ in $\mathbb{C}^n$ whose entries are the complex conjugates of the entries in $\mathbf{x}$. The **real** and **imaginary parts** of a complex vector $\mathbf{x}$ are the vectors $\operatorname{Re}\mathbf{x}$ and $\operatorname{Im}\mathbf{x}$ formed from the real and imaginary parts of the entries of $\mathbf{x}$.

EXAMPLE 4 If $\mathbf{x} = \begin{bmatrix} 3-i \\ i \\ 2+5i \end{bmatrix} = \begin{bmatrix} 3 \\ 0 \\ 2 \end{bmatrix} + i\begin{bmatrix} -1 \\ 1 \\ 5 \end{bmatrix}$, then

$$\operatorname{Re}\mathbf{x} = \begin{bmatrix} 3 \\ 0 \\ 2 \end{bmatrix}, \quad \operatorname{Im}\mathbf{x} = \begin{bmatrix} -1 \\ 1 \\ 5 \end{bmatrix}, \quad \text{and} \quad \overline{\mathbf{x}} = \begin{bmatrix} 3 \\ 0 \\ 2 \end{bmatrix} - i\begin{bmatrix} -1 \\ 1 \\ 5 \end{bmatrix} = \begin{bmatrix} 3+i \\ -i \\ 2-5i \end{bmatrix}$$ ■

If B is an $m \times n$ matrix with possibly complex entries, then $\bar{B}$ denotes the matrix whose entries are the complex conjugates of the entries in B. Properties of conjugates for complex numbers carry over to complex matrix algebra:

$$\overline{r\mathbf{x}} = \bar{r}\bar{\mathbf{x}}, \quad \overline{B\mathbf{x}} = \bar{B}\bar{\mathbf{x}}, \quad \overline{BC} = \bar{B}\bar{C}, \quad \text{and} \quad \overline{rB} = \bar{r}\bar{B}$$

Eigenvalues and Eigenvectors of a Real Matrix That Acts on $\mathbb{C}^n$

Let A be an $n \times n$ matrix whose entries are real. Then $\overline{A\mathbf{x}} = \bar{A}\bar{\mathbf{x}} = A\bar{\mathbf{x}}$. If λ is an eigenvalue of A with $\mathbf{x}$ a corresponding eigenvector in $\mathbb{C}^n$, then

$$A\bar{\mathbf{x}} = \overline{A\mathbf{x}} = \overline{\lambda\mathbf{x}} = \bar{\lambda}\bar{\mathbf{x}}$$

Hence $\bar{\lambda}$ is also an eigenvalue of A, with $\bar{\mathbf{x}}$ a corresponding eigenvector. This shows that *when* A *is real, its complex eigenvalues occur in conjugate pairs.* (Here and elsewhere, we use the term *complex eigenvalue* to refer to an eigenvalue $\lambda = a + bi$ with $b \neq 0$.)

EXAMPLE 5 The eigenvalues of the real matrix in Example 2 are complex conjugates, namely, $.8 - .6i$ and $.8 + .6i$. The corresponding eigenvectors found in Example 2 are also conjugates:

$$\mathbf{v}_1 = \begin{bmatrix} -2 - 4i \\ 5 \end{bmatrix} \quad \text{and} \quad \mathbf{v}_2 = \begin{bmatrix} -2 + 4i \\ 5 \end{bmatrix} = \bar{\mathbf{v}}_1$$

As we shall see, the next example provides the basic "building block" for all real 2×2 matrices with complex eigenvalues.

EXAMPLE 6 If $C = \begin{bmatrix} a & -b \\ b & a \end{bmatrix}$, where a and b are real and not both zero, then the eigenvalues of C are $\lambda = a \pm bi$. (See the Practice Problem.) Also, if $r = |\lambda| = \sqrt{a^2 + b^2}$, then

$$C = r\begin{bmatrix} a/r & -b/r \\ b/r & a/r \end{bmatrix} = \begin{bmatrix} r & 0 \\ 0 & r \end{bmatrix}\begin{bmatrix} \cos\varphi & -\sin\varphi \\ \sin\varphi & \cos\varphi \end{bmatrix}$$

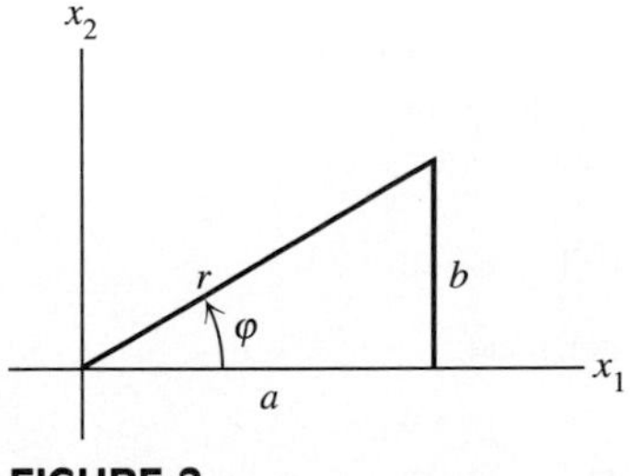

FIGURE 2

where φ is the angle between the positive x-axis and the ray from (0, 0) through (a, b). See Fig. 2 and Appendix B. The angle φ is called the *argument* of $\lambda = a + bi$. Thus the transformation $\mathbf{x} \mapsto C\mathbf{x}$ may be viewed as the composition of a rotation through the angle φ and a scaling by $|\lambda|$ (see Fig. 3).

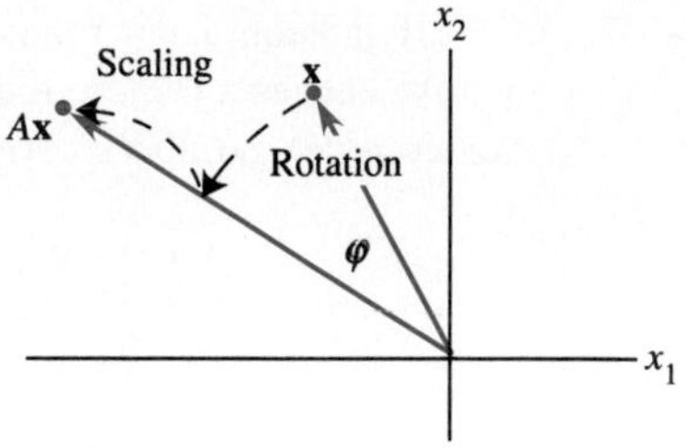

FIGURE 3 A rotation followed by a scaling.

Finally, we are ready to uncover the rotation that is hidden within a real matrix having a complex eigenvalue.

EXAMPLE 7 Let $A = \begin{bmatrix} .5 & -.6 \\ .75 & 1.1 \end{bmatrix}$, $\lambda = .8 - .6i$, and $\mathbf{v}_1 = \begin{bmatrix} -2-4i \\ 5 \end{bmatrix}$, as in Example 2. Also, let P be the 2×2 real matrix

$$P = [\operatorname{Re}\mathbf{v}_1 \quad \operatorname{Im}\mathbf{v}_1] = \begin{bmatrix} -2 & -4 \\ 5 & 0 \end{bmatrix}$$

and let

$$C = P^{-1}AP = \frac{1}{20}\begin{bmatrix} 0 & 4 \\ -5 & -2 \end{bmatrix}\begin{bmatrix} .5 & -.6 \\ .75 & 1.1 \end{bmatrix}\begin{bmatrix} -2 & -4 \\ 5 & 0 \end{bmatrix} = \begin{bmatrix} .8 & -.6 \\ .6 & .8 \end{bmatrix}$$

By Example 6, C is a pure rotation because $|\lambda|^2 = (.8)^2 + (.6)^2 = 1$. From $C = P^{-1}AP$, we obtain

$$A = PCP^{-1} = P\begin{bmatrix} .8 & -.6 \\ .6 & .8 \end{bmatrix}P^{-1}$$

Here is the rotation "inside" A! The matrix P provides a change of variable, say, $\mathbf{x} = P\mathbf{u}$. The action of A amounts to a change of variable from $\mathbf{x}$ to $\mathbf{u}$, followed by a rotation and then a return to the original variable. See Fig. 4.

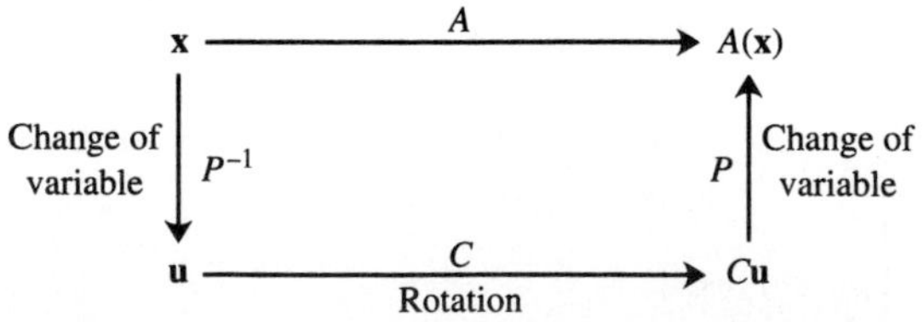

FIGURE 4 Rotation due to a complex eigenvalue.

The next theorem shows that the calculations in Example 7 can be carried out for any 2×2 real matrix A having a complex eigenvalue λ. The proof uses the fact that if the entries in A are real, then $A(\operatorname{Re}\mathbf{x}) = \operatorname{Re} A\mathbf{x}$ and $A(\operatorname{Im}\mathbf{x}) = \operatorname{Im} A\mathbf{x}$ (see Exercises 25 and 26). The details are omitted.

THEOREM 9

Let A be a real 2×2 matrix with a complex eigenvalue $\lambda = a - bi$ $(b \neq 0)$ and associated eigenvector $\mathbf{v}$ in $\mathbb{C}^2$. Then

$$A = PCP^{-1}, \quad \text{where} \quad P = [\operatorname{Re}\mathbf{v} \quad \operatorname{Im}\mathbf{v}] \quad \text{and} \quad C = \begin{bmatrix} a & -b \\ b & a \end{bmatrix}$$

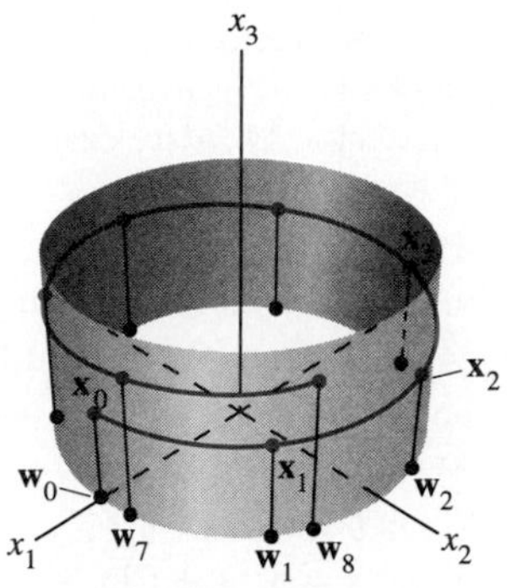

FIGURE 5 Iterates of two points under the action of a 3×3 matrix with a complex eigenvalue.

The phenomenon displayed in Example 7 persists in higher dimensions. For instance, if A is a 3×3 matrix with a complex eigenvalue, then there is a plane in $\mathbb{R}^3$ on which A acts as a rotation (possibly combined with scaling). Every vector in that plane is rotated into another point on the same plane. We say that the plane is **invariant** under A.

EXAMPLE 8 The matrix $A = \begin{bmatrix} .8 & -.6 & 0 \\ .6 & .8 & 0 \\ 0 & 0 & 1.07 \end{bmatrix}$ has eigenvalues $.8 \pm .6i$ and 1.07. Any vector in the x_1x_2-plane (with third coordinate 0) is rotated by A into another point in the plane. Any vector not in the plane has its x_3-coordinate multiplied by 1.07. The iterates of the points $\mathbf{w}_0 = (2, 0, 0)$ and $\mathbf{x}_0 = (2, 0, 1)$ under multiplication by A are shown in Fig. 5.

PRACTICE PROBLEM

Show that if a and b are real, then the eigenvalues of $A = \begin{bmatrix} a & -b \\ b & a \end{bmatrix}$ are $a \pm bi$, with corresponding eigenvectors $\begin{bmatrix} 1 \\ -i \end{bmatrix}$ and $\begin{bmatrix} 1 \\ i \end{bmatrix}$.

6.5 EXERCISES

Let each matrix in Exercises 1–6 act on $\mathbb{C}^2$. Find the eigenvalues and a basis for each eigenspace in $\mathbb{C}^2$.

1. $\begin{bmatrix} 1 & -2 \\ 1 & 3 \end{bmatrix}$
2. $\begin{bmatrix} 5 & -5 \\ 1 & 1 \end{bmatrix}$
3. $\begin{bmatrix} 1 & 5 \\ -2 & 3 \end{bmatrix}$
4. $\begin{bmatrix} 5 & -2 \\ 1 & 3 \end{bmatrix}$
5. $\begin{bmatrix} 0 & 1 \\ -8 & 4 \end{bmatrix}$
6. $\begin{bmatrix} 4 & 3 \\ -3 & 4 \end{bmatrix}$

In Exercises 7–12, use Example 6 to list the eigenvalues of A. In each case, the transformation $\mathbf{x} \mapsto A\mathbf{x}$ is the composition of a rotation followed by a scaling. Give the angle φ of the rotation, where $-\pi < \varphi \leq \pi$, and give the scale factor r.

7. $\begin{bmatrix} \sqrt{3} & -1 \\ 1 & \sqrt{3} \end{bmatrix}$
8. $\begin{bmatrix} \sqrt{3} & 3 \\ -3 & \sqrt{3} \end{bmatrix}$
9. $\begin{bmatrix} -\sqrt{3}/2 & 1/2 \\ -1/2 & -\sqrt{3}/2 \end{bmatrix}$
10. $\begin{bmatrix} -5 & -5 \\ 5 & -5 \end{bmatrix}$
11. $\begin{bmatrix} .1 & .1 \\ -.1 & .1 \end{bmatrix}$
12. $\begin{bmatrix} 0 & .3 \\ -.3 & 0 \end{bmatrix}$

In Exercises 13–20, find an invertible matrix P and a matrix C of the form $\begin{bmatrix} a & -b \\ b & a \end{bmatrix}$ such that the given matrix has the form $A = PCP^{-1}$. For Exercises 13–16, use information from Exercises 1–4.

13. $\begin{bmatrix} 1 & -2 \\ 1 & 3 \end{bmatrix}$
14. $\begin{bmatrix} 5 & -5 \\ 1 & 1 \end{bmatrix}$

15. $\begin{bmatrix} 1 & 5 \\ -2 & 3 \end{bmatrix}$

16. $\begin{bmatrix} 5 & -2 \\ 1 & 3 \end{bmatrix}$

17. $\begin{bmatrix} 1 & -.8 \\ 4 & -2.2 \end{bmatrix}$

18. $\begin{bmatrix} 1 & -1 \\ .4 & .6 \end{bmatrix}$

19. $\begin{bmatrix} 1.52 & -.7 \\ .56 & .4 \end{bmatrix}$

20. $\begin{bmatrix} -1.64 & -2.4 \\ 1.92 & 2.2 \end{bmatrix}$

21. In Example 2, solve the first equation in (2) for x_2 in terms of x_1, and from that produce the eigenvector $\mathbf{y} = \begin{bmatrix} 2 \\ -1+2i \end{bmatrix}$ for the matrix A. Show that this $\mathbf{y}$ is a (complex) multiple of the vector $\mathbf{v}_1$ used in Example 2.

22. Let A be a complex (or real) $n \times n$ matrix and let $\mathbf{x}$ in $\mathbb{C}^n$ be an eigenvector corresponding to an eigenvalue λ in $\mathbb{C}$. Show that for each nonzero complex scalar μ, the vector $\mu\mathbf{x}$ is an eigenvector of A.

Chapter 8 will focus on matrices A with the property that $A^T = A$. Exercises 23 and 24 show that every eigenvalue of such a matrix is necessarily real.

23. Let A be an $n \times n$ real matrix with the property that $A^T = A$, let $\mathbf{x}$ be any vector in $\mathbb{C}^n$, and let $q = \overline{\mathbf{x}}^T A\mathbf{x}$. The equalities below show that q is a real number by verifying that $\overline{q} = q$. Give a reason for each step.

$$\overline{q} = \overline{\overline{\mathbf{x}}^T A\mathbf{x}} = \mathbf{x}^T \overline{A\mathbf{x}} = \mathbf{x}^T A\overline{\mathbf{x}} = (\mathbf{x}^T A\overline{\mathbf{x}})^T = \overline{\mathbf{x}}^T A^T \mathbf{x} = q$$
$$\text{(a)} \quad \text{(b)} \quad \text{(c)} \quad \text{(d)} \quad \text{(e)}$$

24. Let A be an $n \times n$ real matrix with the property that $A^T = A$. Show that if $A\mathbf{x} = \lambda\mathbf{x}$ for some nonzero vector $\mathbf{x}$ in $\mathbb{C}^n$, then, in fact, λ is real and the real part of $\mathbf{x}$ is an eigenvector of A. [*Hint*: Compute $\overline{\mathbf{x}}^T A\mathbf{x}$ and use Exercise 23. Also, examine the real and imaginary parts of $A\mathbf{x}$.]

25. Let A be a real $n \times n$ matrix and let $\mathbf{x}$ be a vector in $\mathbb{C}^n$. Show that $\text{Re}(A\mathbf{x}) = A(\text{Re}\,\mathbf{x})$ and $\text{Im}(A\mathbf{x}) = A(\text{Im}\,\mathbf{x})$. [*Hint*: If $\mathbf{y}$ is in $\mathbb{C}^n$, then $\text{Re}\,\mathbf{y} = (\mathbf{y} + \overline{\mathbf{y}})/2$ and $\text{Im}\,\mathbf{y} = (\mathbf{y} - \overline{\mathbf{y}})/(2i)$.]

26. Let A be a real 2×2 matrix with a complex eigenvalue $\lambda = a - bi$ $(b \neq 0)$ and associated eigenvector $\mathbf{v}$ in $\mathbb{C}^2$.

a. Show that $A(\text{Re}\,\mathbf{v}) = a\,\text{Re}\,\mathbf{v} + b\,\text{Im}\,\mathbf{v}$ and $A(\text{Im}\,\mathbf{v}) = -b\,\text{Re}\,\mathbf{v} + a\,\text{Im}\,\mathbf{v}$. [*Hint*: Write $\mathbf{v} = \text{Re}\,\mathbf{v} + i\,\text{Im}\,\mathbf{v}$ and compute $A\mathbf{v}$.]

b. Verify that if P and C are given as in Theorem 9, then $AP = PC$.

SOLUTION TO PRACTICE PROBLEM

Remember that it is easy to test whether a vector is an eigenvector. There is no need to examine the characteristic equation. Compute

$$A\mathbf{x} = \begin{bmatrix} a & -b \\ b & a \end{bmatrix}\begin{bmatrix} 1 \\ -i \end{bmatrix} = \begin{bmatrix} a+bi \\ b-ai \end{bmatrix} = (a+bi)\begin{bmatrix} 1 \\ -i \end{bmatrix}$$

Thus $\begin{bmatrix} 1 \\ -i \end{bmatrix}$ is an eigenvector corresponding to $\lambda = a + bi$. From the discussion in this section, $\begin{bmatrix} 1 \\ i \end{bmatrix}$ must be an eigenvector corresponding to $\overline{\lambda} = a - bi$.

6.6 APPLICATIONS TO DYNAMICAL SYSTEMS

Eigenvalues and eigenvectors provide the key to understanding the long-term behavior, or *evolution*, of a dynamical system described by a difference equation $\mathbf{x}_{k+1} = A\mathbf{x}_k$. Such an equation was used to model population movement in Section 2.7, various Markov chains in Section 5.9, and the spotted owl population in the introductory example for this chapter. The vectors $\mathbf{x}_k$ give information about the system as time (denoted by k) passes. In the spotted owl example, for instance, $\mathbf{x}_k$ listed the number of owls in three age classes at time k.

The applications in this section focus on ecological problems because they are easier to state and explain than, say, problems in physics or engineering. However, dynamical systems arise in many scientific fields. For instance, standard undergraduate courses in control systems discuss several aspects of dynamical systems. The modern *state-space* design method in such courses relies heavily on matrix algebra.[1] The *steady-state response* of a control system is the engineering equivalent of what we call here the "long-term behavior" of the dynamical system $\mathbf{x}_{k+1} = A\mathbf{x}_k$.

Until Example 6, we assume that A is diagonalizable, with n linearly independent eigenvectors, $\mathbf{v}_1, \ldots, \mathbf{v}_n$, and corresponding eigenvalues, $\lambda_1, \ldots, \lambda_n$. For convenience, assume the eigenvectors are arranged so that $|\lambda_1| \geq |\lambda_2| \geq \cdots \geq |\lambda_n|$. Since $\{\mathbf{v}_1, \ldots, \mathbf{v}_n\}$ is a basis for $\mathbb{R}^n$, any initial vector $\mathbf{x}_0$ may be written uniquely as

$$\mathbf{x}_0 = c_1\mathbf{v}_1 + \cdots + c_n\mathbf{v}_n \tag{1}$$

This *eigenvector decomposition* of $\mathbf{x}_0$ determines what happens to the sequence $\{\mathbf{x}_k\}$. The next calculation generalizes the simple case examined in Example 5 of Section 6.2. Since the $\mathbf{v}_i$ are eigenvectors,

$$\begin{aligned}\mathbf{x}_1 = A\mathbf{x}_0 &= c_1A\mathbf{v}_1 + \cdots + c_nA\mathbf{v}_n \\ &= c_1\lambda_1\mathbf{v}_1 + \cdots + c_n\lambda_n\mathbf{v}_n\end{aligned}$$

In general,

$$\mathbf{x}_k = c_1(\lambda_1)^k\mathbf{v}_1 + \cdots + c_n(\lambda_n)^k\mathbf{v}_n \quad (k = 0, 1, 2, \ldots) \tag{2}$$

The examples that follow illustrate what can happen in (2) as $k \to \infty$.

A Predator–Prey System

Deep in the redwood forests of California, dusky-footed wood rats provide up to 80% of the diet for the spotted owl, the main predator of the wood rat. Example 1 uses a linear dynamical system to model the physical system of the owls and the rats. (The numbers in the example are somewhat contrived to simplify the calculations.)

EXAMPLE 1 Denote the owl and wood rat populations at time k by $\mathbf{x}_k = \begin{bmatrix} O_k \\ R_k \end{bmatrix}$, where k is the time in months, O_k is the number of owls in the region studied, and R_k is the number of rats (measured in thousands). Suppose that

$$\begin{aligned} O_{k+1} &= (.5)O_k + (.4)R_k \\ R_{k+1} &= -p\cdot O_k + (1.1)R_k \end{aligned} \tag{3}$$

where p is a positive parameter to be specified. The $(.5)O_k$ in the first equation says that with no wood rats for food, only half of the owls will survive each month, while the $(1.1)R_k$ in the second equation says that with no owls as predators, the

[1] See G.F. Franklin, J.D. Powell, and A. Emami-Naeimi, *Feedback Control of Dynamic Systems*, 2d ed. (Reading, Mass.: Addison-Wesley, 1991). This undergraduate text has a nice introduction to dynamic models (Chapter 2). State-space design is covered in Chapters 6 and 8.

rats will grow by 10% per month. If rats are plentiful, the $(.4)R_k$ will tend to make the owl population rise, while the negative term $-p \cdot O_k$ measures the deaths of rats due to predation by owls. Determine the evolution of this system when the predation parameter p is .104.

Solution When $p = .104$, the eigenvalues of A turn out to be $\lambda_1 = 1.02$ and $\lambda_2 = .58$. Corresponding eigenvectors are

$$\mathbf{v}_1 = \begin{bmatrix} 10 \\ 13 \end{bmatrix}, \quad \mathbf{v}_2 = \begin{bmatrix} 5 \\ 1 \end{bmatrix}$$

An initial $\mathbf{x}_0$ may be written as $\mathbf{x}_0 = c_1\mathbf{v}_1 + c_2\mathbf{v}_2$. Then, for $k \geq 0$,

$$\begin{aligned} \mathbf{x}_k &= c_1(1.02)^k\mathbf{v}_1 + c_2(.58)^k\mathbf{v}_2 \\ &= c_1(1.02)^k \begin{bmatrix} 10 \\ 13 \end{bmatrix} + c_2(.58)^k \begin{bmatrix} 5 \\ 1 \end{bmatrix} \end{aligned}$$

As $k \to \infty$, $(.58)^k$ rapidly approaches zero. Assume $c_1 \neq 0$. Then, for all sufficiently large k, $\mathbf{x}_k$ is approximately the same as $c_1(1.02)^k\mathbf{v}_2$, and we write

$$\mathbf{x}_k \approx c_1(1.02)^k \begin{bmatrix} 10 \\ 13 \end{bmatrix} \tag{4}$$

The approximation in (4) improves as k increases, and so for large k,

$$\mathbf{x}_{k+1} \approx c_1(1.02)^{k+1} \begin{bmatrix} 10 \\ 13 \end{bmatrix} = (1.02)c_1(1.02)^k \begin{bmatrix} 10 \\ 13 \end{bmatrix} \approx 1.02\mathbf{x}_k \tag{5}$$

The approximation in (5) says that eventually both entries of $\mathbf{x}_k$ (the numbers of owls and rats) grow by a factor of almost 1.02 each month, a 2% monthly growth rate. By (4), $\mathbf{x}_k$ is approximately a multiple of (10, 13), so the entries in $\mathbf{x}_k$ are nearly in the same ratio as 10 to 13. That is, for every 10 owls there are about 13 thousand rats. ∎

Example 1 illustrates two general facts about a dynamical system $\mathbf{x}_{k+1} = A\mathbf{x}_k$ in which A is $n \times n$, its eigenvalues satisfy $|\lambda_1| \geq 1$ and $1 > |\lambda_j|$ for $j = 2, \ldots, n$, and $\mathbf{v}_1$ is an eigenvector corresponding to λ_1. If $\mathbf{x}_0$ is given by (1), with $c_1 \neq 0$, then for all sufficiently large k,

$$\mathbf{x}_{k+1} \approx \lambda_1\mathbf{x}_k \tag{6}$$

and

$$\mathbf{x}_k \approx c_1(\lambda_1)^k\mathbf{v}_1 \tag{7}$$

The approximations in (6) and (7) can be made as close as desired by taking k sufficiently large. By (6), the $\mathbf{x}_k$ eventually grow almost by a factor of λ_1 each time, so λ_1 determines the eventual growth rate of the system. Also, by (7), the ratio of any two entries in $\mathbf{x}_k$ (for large k) is nearly the same as the ratio of the corresponding entries in $\mathbf{v}_1$. The case when $\lambda_1 = 1$ is illustrated by Example 5 in Section 6.2.

Graphical Description of Solutions

When A is 2×2, algebraic calculations can be supplemented by a geometric description of a system's evolution. We can view the equation $\mathbf{x}_{k+1} = A\mathbf{x}_k$ as a description of what happens to an initial point $\mathbf{x}_0$ in $\mathbb{R}^2$ as it is transformed repeatedly by the mapping $\mathbf{x} \mapsto A\mathbf{x}$. The graph of $\mathbf{x}_0, \mathbf{x}_1, \ldots$ is called a **trajectory** of the dynamical system.

EXAMPLE 2 Plot several trajectories of the dynamical system $\mathbf{x}_{k+1} = A\mathbf{x}_k$, when

$$A = \begin{bmatrix} .80 & 0 \\ 0 & .64 \end{bmatrix}$$

Solution The eigenvalues of A are .8 and .64, with eigenvectors $\mathbf{v}_1 = \begin{bmatrix} 1 \\ 0 \end{bmatrix}$ and $\mathbf{v}_2 = \begin{bmatrix} 0 \\ 1 \end{bmatrix}$. If $\mathbf{x}_0 = c_1\mathbf{v}_1 + c_2\mathbf{v}_2$, then

$$\mathbf{x}_k = c_1(.8)^k \begin{bmatrix} 1 \\ 0 \end{bmatrix} + c_2(.64)^k \begin{bmatrix} 0 \\ 1 \end{bmatrix}$$

Of course, $\mathbf{x}_k$ tends to $\mathbf{0}$ because $(.8)^k$ and $(.64)^k$ both approach 0 as $k \to \infty$. But *the way* $\mathbf{x}_k$ goes toward $\mathbf{0}$ is interesting. Figure 1 shows the first few terms of several trajectories that begin at points on the boundary of the box with corners at $(\pm 3, \pm 3)$. The points on a trajectory are connected by a thin curve, to make the trajectory easier to see. ∎

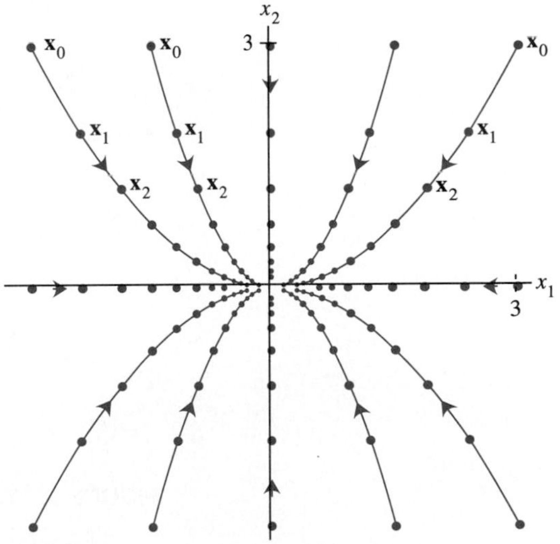

FIGURE 1 The origin as an attractor.

In Example 2, the origin is called an **attractor** of the dynamical system because both eigenvalues are less than 1 in magnitude. All trajectories tend toward $\mathbf{0}$. The direction of greatest attraction is along the line through **0** and the eigenvector for the eigenvalue of smaller magnitude.

In the next example, both eigenvalues of A are larger than 1 in magnitude, and **0** is called a **repellor** of the dynamical system. All solutions of $\mathbf{x}_{k+1} = A\mathbf{x}_k$ except the (constant) zero solution are unbounded and tend away from the origin.[2]

EXAMPLE 3 Plot several typical solutions of the equation $\mathbf{x}_{k+1} = A\mathbf{x}_k$, where

$$A = \begin{bmatrix} 1.44 & 0 \\ 0 & 1.2 \end{bmatrix}$$

Solution The eigenvalues of A are 1.44 and 1.2. If $\mathbf{x}_0 = \begin{bmatrix} c_1 \\ c_2 \end{bmatrix}$, then

$$\mathbf{x}_k = c_1(1.44)^k \begin{bmatrix} 1 \\ 0 \end{bmatrix} + c_2(1.2)^k \begin{bmatrix} 0 \\ 1 \end{bmatrix}$$

Both terms grow in size, but the first term grows faster. So the direction of greatest repulsion is the line through **0** and the eigenvector for the eigenvalue of larger magnitude. Figure 2 shows several trajectories that begin at points quite close to **0**.

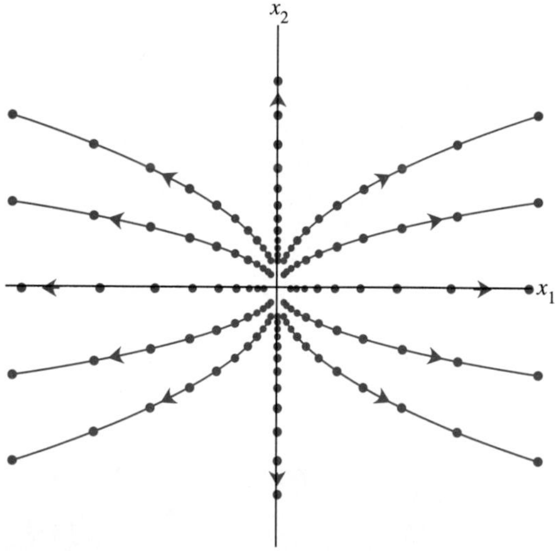

FIGURE 2 The origin as a repellor.

[2]The origin is the only possible attractor or repellor in a *linear* dynamical system, but there can be multiple attractors and repellors in a more general dynamical system for which the mapping $\mathbf{x}_k \mapsto \mathbf{x}_{k+1}$ is not linear. In such a system, attractors and repellors are defined in terms of the eigenvalues of a special matrix (with variable entries) called the *Jacobian matrix* of the system.

In the next example, $\mathbf{0}$ is called a **saddle point** because one eigenvalue is greater than 1 in magnitude and one is less than 1 in magnitude. The origin attracts solutions from some directions and repels them in other directions.

EXAMPLE 4 Plot several typical solutions of the equation $\mathbf{y}_{k+1} = D\mathbf{y}_k$, where

$$D = \begin{bmatrix} 2.0 & 0 \\ 0 & 0.5 \end{bmatrix}$$

(We write D and $\mathbf{y}$ here instead of A and $\mathbf{x}$ because this example will be used later.) Show that a solution $\{\mathbf{y}_k\}$ is unbounded if its initial point is not on the x_2-axis.

Solution The eigenvalues of D are 2 and .5. If $\mathbf{y}_0 = \begin{bmatrix} c_1 \\ c_2 \end{bmatrix}$, then

$$\mathbf{y}_k = c_1 2^k \begin{bmatrix} 1 \\ 0 \end{bmatrix} + c_2(.5)^k \begin{bmatrix} 0 \\ 1 \end{bmatrix} \tag{8}$$

If $\mathbf{y}_0$ is on the x_2-axis, then $c_1 = 0$ and $\mathbf{y}_k \to \mathbf{0}$ as $k \to \infty$. But if $\mathbf{y}_0$ is not on the x_2-axis, then the first term in the sum for $\mathbf{y}_k$ becomes arbitrarily large, and so $\{\mathbf{y}_k\}$ is unbounded. Figure 3 shows ten trajectories that begin near or on the x_2-axis.

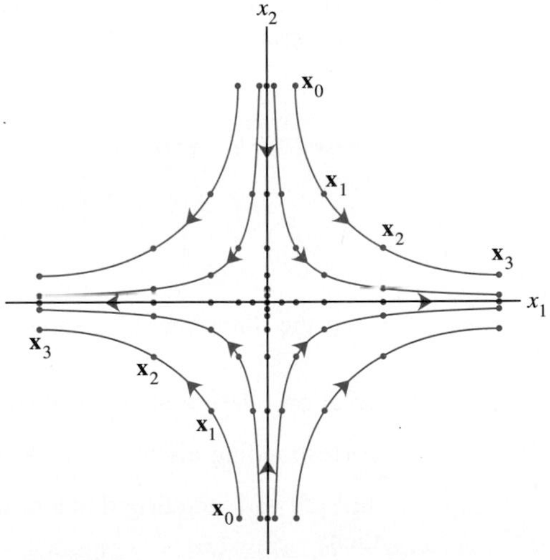

FIGURE 3 The origin as a saddle point.

Change of Variable

The preceding three examples involved diagonal matrices. To handle the nondiagonal case, we return for a moment to the $n \times n$ case in which eigenvectors of A form a basis $\{\mathbf{v}_1, \ldots, \mathbf{v}_n\}$ for $\mathbb{R}^n$. Let $P = [\,\mathbf{v}_1 \;\; \cdots \;\; \mathbf{v}_n\,]$, and let D be the diagonal matrix with the corresponding eigenvalues on the diagonal. Given a sequence $\{\mathbf{x}_k\}$ satisfying

$\mathbf{x}_{k+1} = A\mathbf{x}_k$, define a new sequence $\{\mathbf{y}_k\}$ by

$$\mathbf{y}_k = P^{-1}\mathbf{x}_k, \quad \text{or equivalently,} \quad \mathbf{x}_k = P\mathbf{y}_k$$

Substituting these relations into the equation $\mathbf{x}_{k+1} = A\mathbf{x}_k$, and using the fact that $A = PDP^{-1}$, we find that

$$P\mathbf{y}_{k+1} = AP\mathbf{y}_k = (PDP^{-1})P\mathbf{y}_k = PD\mathbf{y}_k$$

Left-multiplying both sides by P^{-1}, we obtain

$$\mathbf{y}_{k+1} = D\mathbf{y}_k$$

If we write $\mathbf{y}_k$ as $\mathbf{y}(k)$ and denote the entries in $\mathbf{y}(k)$ by $y_1(k), \dots, y_n(k)$, then

$$\begin{bmatrix} y_1(k+1) \\ \vdots \\ y_n(k+1) \end{bmatrix} = \begin{bmatrix} \lambda_1 & 0 & \cdots & 0 \\ 0 & \lambda_2 & & \vdots \\ \vdots & & \ddots & 0 \\ 0 & \cdots & 0 & \lambda_n \end{bmatrix} \begin{bmatrix} y_1(k) \\ \vdots \\ y_n(k) \end{bmatrix}$$

The change of variable from $\mathbf{x}_k$ to $\mathbf{y}_k$ has *decoupled* the system of difference equations. The evolution of $y_1(k)$, for example, is unaffected by what happens to $y_2(k), \dots, y_n(k)$, because $y_1(k+1) = \lambda_1 \cdot y_1(k)$ for each k.

The equation $\mathbf{x}_k = P\mathbf{y}_k$ says that $\mathbf{y}_k$ is the coordinate vector of $\mathbf{x}_k$ with respect to the eigenvector basis $\{\mathbf{v}_1, \dots, \mathbf{v}_n\}$. We can decouple the system $\mathbf{x}_{k+1} = A\mathbf{x}_k$ by making calculations in the new eigenvector coordinate system. When $n = 2$, this amounts to using graph paper with axes in the directions of the two eigenvectors.

EXAMPLE 5 Show that the origin is a saddle point for solutions of $\mathbf{x}_{k+1} = A\mathbf{x}_k$, where

$$A = \begin{bmatrix} 1.25 & -.75 \\ -.75 & 1.25 \end{bmatrix}$$

Find the directions of greatest attraction and greatest repulsion.

Solution Using standard techniques, we find that A has eigenvalues 2 and .5, with corresponding eigenvectors $\mathbf{v}_1 = \begin{bmatrix} 1 \\ -1 \end{bmatrix}$ and $\mathbf{v}_2 = \begin{bmatrix} 1 \\ 1 \end{bmatrix}$, respectively. Since $|2| > 1$ and $|.5| < 1$, the origin is a saddle point of the dynamical system. If $\mathbf{x}_0 = c_1\mathbf{v}_1 + c_2\mathbf{v}_2$, then

$$\mathbf{x}_k = c_1 2^k \mathbf{v}_1 + c_2(.5)^k \mathbf{v}_2 \tag{9}$$

This equation looks just like (8) in Example 4, with $\mathbf{v}_1$ and $\mathbf{v}_2$ in place of the standard basis.

On graph paper, draw axes through $\mathbf{v}_1$ and $\mathbf{v}_2$. See Fig. 4. Movement along these axes corresponds to movement along the standard axes in Fig. 3. In Fig. 4, the direction of greatest *repulsion* is the line through $\mathbf{v}_1$, the eigenvector whose eigenvalue is greater than 1. If $\mathbf{x}_0$ is on this line, the c_2 in (9) is zero and $\mathbf{x}_k$ moves quickly away from $\mathbf{0}$. The direction of greatest *attraction* is determined by the eigenvector $\mathbf{v}_2$ whose eigenvalue is less than 1.

A number of trajectories are shown in Fig. 4. When this graph is viewed in terms of the eigenvector axes, the picture "looks" essentially the same as that in Fig. 3.

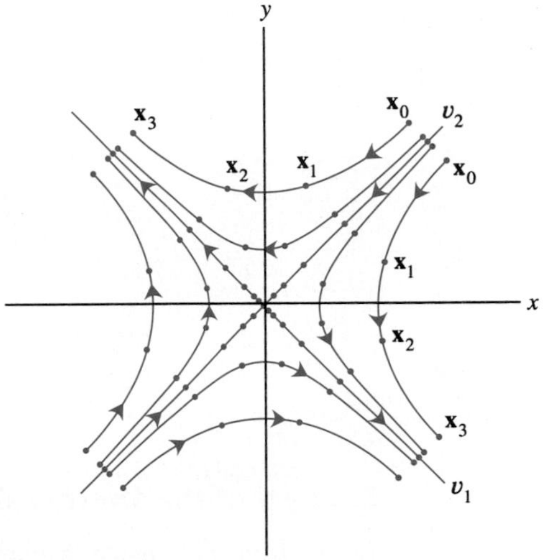

FIGURE 4 The origin as a saddle point.

Complex Eigenvalues

When a 2×2 matrix A has complex eigenvalues, A is not diagonalizable (when acting on $\mathbb{R}^n$), but the dynamical system $\mathbf{x}_{k+1} = A\mathbf{x}_k$ is easy to describe. Example 3 of Section 6.5 illustrated the case in which the eigenvalues have absolute value 1. The iterates of a point $\mathbf{x}_0$ spiraled around the origin along an elliptical trajectory.

If A has two complex eigenvalues whose absolute value is greater than 1, then $\mathbf{0}$ is a repellor and iterates of $\mathbf{x}_0$ will spiral outward around the origin. If the absolute values of the complex eigenvalues are less than 1, the origin is an attractor and the iterates of $\mathbf{x}_0$ spiral inward toward the origin, as in the following example.

EXAMPLE 6 It may be verified that the matrix

$$A = \begin{bmatrix} .8 & .5 \\ -.1 & 1.0 \end{bmatrix}$$

has eigenvalues $.9 \pm .2i$, with eigenvectors $\begin{bmatrix} 1 \mp 2i \\ 1 \end{bmatrix}$. Figure 5 shows three trajectories of the system $\mathbf{x}_{k+1} = A\mathbf{x}_k$, with initial vectors $\begin{bmatrix} 0 \\ 2.5 \end{bmatrix}$, $\begin{bmatrix} 3 \\ 0 \end{bmatrix}$, and $\begin{bmatrix} 0 \\ -2.5 \end{bmatrix}$.

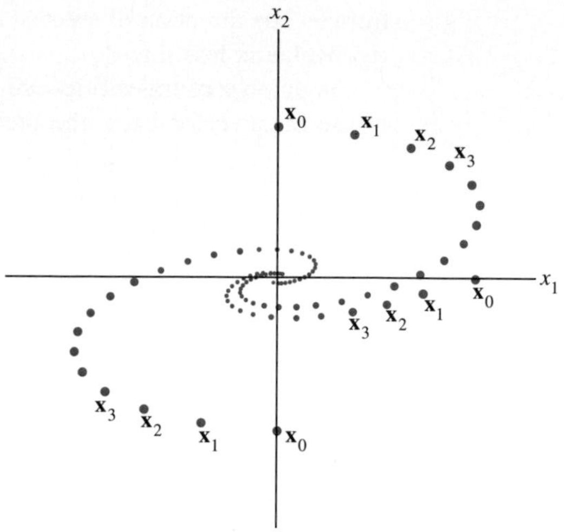

FIGURE 5 Rotation associated with complex eigenvalues.

Survival of the Spotted Owls

Recall from the chapter's introductory example that the spotted owl population in the Willow Creek area of California was modeled by a dynamical system $\mathbf{x}_{k+1} = A\mathbf{x}_k$ in which the entries in $\mathbf{x}_k = (j_k, s_k, a_k)$ listed the numbers of females (at time k) in the juvenile, subadult, and adult life stages, respectively, and A is the stage-matrix

$$A = \begin{bmatrix} 0 & 0 & .33 \\ .18 & 0 & 0 \\ 0 & .71 & .94 \end{bmatrix} \tag{10}$$

MATLAB shows that the eigenvalues of A are approximately $\lambda_1 = .98$, $\lambda_2 = -.02 + .21i$, and $\lambda_3 = -.02 - .21i$. Observe that all three eigenvalues are less than 1 in magnitude, because $|\lambda_2|^2 = |\lambda_3|^2 = (-.02)^2 + (.21)^2 = .0445$.

For the moment, let A act on the complex vector space $\mathbb{C}^3$. Then, because A has three distinct eigenvalues, the three corresponding eigenvectors are linearly independent and form a basis for $\mathbb{C}^3$. Denote the eigenvectors by $\mathbf{v}_1, \mathbf{v}_2$, and $\mathbf{v}_3$. Then the general solution of $\mathbf{x}_{k+1} = A\mathbf{x}_k$ (using vectors in $\mathbb{C}^3$) has the form

$$\mathbf{x}_k = c_1(\lambda_1)^k\mathbf{v}_1 + c_2(\lambda_2)^k\mathbf{v}_2 + c_3(\lambda_3)^k\mathbf{v}_3 \tag{11}$$

If $\mathbf{x}_0$ is a real initial vector, then $\mathbf{x}_1 = A\mathbf{x}_0$ is real because A is real. Similarly, the equation $\mathbf{x}_{k+1} = A\mathbf{x}_k$ shows that each $\mathbf{x}_k$ on the left of (11) is real, even though it is expressed as a sum of complex vectors. However, each term on the right of (11) is approaching the zero vector, because the eigenvalues are all less than 1 in magnitude. Therefore the real sequence $\mathbf{x}_k$ approaches the zero vector, too. Sadly, this model thus predicts that the spotted owls will eventually all perish.

Is there hope for the spotted owls? Recall from the chapter introductory example that the 18% entry in the matrix A in (10) comes from the fact that although 60% of the juvenile owls live long enough to leave the nest and search for a new home territory, only 30% of that group survive the search and find a new home range. Search survival is strongly influenced by the number of clear-cut areas in the forest which make the search more difficult and dangerous.

Some owl populations live in areas with few or no clear-cut areas. It may be that a larger percentage of the juvenile owls there survive and find a new home range. Of course, the problem of the owls is more complex than we have described, but the final example provides a happy ending to the story.

EXAMPLE 7 Suppose the search survival rate of the juvenile owls is 50%, so the (2, 1)-entry in the stage-matrix A in (10) is .3 instead of .18. What does the stage-matrix model predict about this spotted owl population?

Solution Now the eigenvalues of A turn out to be approximately $\lambda_1 = 1.01$, $\lambda_2 = -.03 + .26i$, and $\lambda_3 = -.03 - .26i$. An eigenvector for λ_1 is approximately $\mathbf{v}_1 = (10, 3, 31)$. Let $\mathbf{v}_2$ and $\mathbf{v}_3$ be (complex) eigenvectors for λ_2 and λ_3. In this case, (11) becomes

$$\mathbf{x}_k = c_1(1.01)^k\mathbf{v}_1 + c_2(-.03 + .26i)^k\mathbf{v}_2 + c_3(-.03 - .26i)^k\mathbf{v}_3$$

As $k \to \infty$, the second two vectors tend to zero. So $\mathbf{x}_k$ becomes more and more like the (real) vector $c_1(1.01)^k\mathbf{v}_1$. The approximations in (6) and (7), following Example 1, apply here. Thus the long-term growth rate of the owl population will be 1.01, and the population will grow slowly. The eigenvector $\mathbf{v}_1$ describes the eventual distribution of the owls by life stages: For every 31 adults, there will be about 10 juveniles and 3 subadults. ∎

Further Reading

Franklin, G.F., J.D. Powell, and M.L. Workman. *Digital Control of Dynamic Systems*, 2d ed. Reading, Mass.: Addison-Wesley, 1990.

Sandefur, James T. *Discrete Dynamical Systems—Theory and Applications*. Oxford: Clarendon Press, 1990.

Tuchinsky, Philip. *Management of a Buffalo Herd*, UMAP Module 207. Lexington, Mass.: COMAP, 1980.

PRACTICE PROBLEMS

1. The matrix A below has eigenvalues 1, 2/3, and 1/3, with corresponding eigenvectors $\mathbf{v}_1, \mathbf{v}_2, \mathbf{v}_3$:

$$A = \frac{1}{9}\begin{bmatrix} 7 & -2 & 0 \\ -2 & 6 & 2 \\ 0 & 2 & 5 \end{bmatrix}, \quad \mathbf{v}_1 = \begin{bmatrix} -2 \\ 2 \\ 1 \end{bmatrix}, \quad \mathbf{v}_2 = \begin{bmatrix} 2 \\ 1 \\ 2 \end{bmatrix}, \quad \mathbf{v}_3 = \begin{bmatrix} 1 \\ 2 \\ -2 \end{bmatrix}$$

Find the general solution of the equation $\mathbf{x}_{k+1} = A\mathbf{x}_k$, if $\mathbf{x}_0 = \begin{bmatrix} 1 \\ 11 \\ -2 \end{bmatrix}$.

2. What happens to the sequence $\{\mathbf{x}_k\}$ in Practice Problem 1 as $k \to \infty$?

6.6 EXERCISES

1. Let A be a 2×2 matrix with eigenvalues 3 and 1/3, and corresponding eigenvectors $\mathbf{v}_1 = \begin{bmatrix} 1 \\ 1 \end{bmatrix}$ and $\mathbf{v}_2 = \begin{bmatrix} -1 \\ 1 \end{bmatrix}$. Let $\{\mathbf{x}_k\}$ be a solution of the difference equation $\mathbf{x}_{k+1} = A\mathbf{x}_k$, $\mathbf{x}_0 = \begin{bmatrix} 9 \\ 1 \end{bmatrix}$.
   a. Compute $\mathbf{x}_1 = A\mathbf{x}_0$. [*Hint*: You do not need to know A itself.]
   b. Find a formula for $\mathbf{x}_k$ involving k and the eigenvectors $\mathbf{v}_1$ and $\mathbf{v}_2$.

2. Suppose that the eigenvalues of a 3×3 matrix A are 3, 4/5, 3/5, with corresponding eigenvectors $\begin{bmatrix} 1 \\ 0 \\ -3 \end{bmatrix}$, $\begin{bmatrix} 2 \\ 1 \\ -5 \end{bmatrix}$, $\begin{bmatrix} -3 \\ -3 \\ 7 \end{bmatrix}$. Let $\mathbf{x}_0 = \begin{bmatrix} -2 \\ -5 \\ 3 \end{bmatrix}$. Find the solution of the equation $\mathbf{x}_{k+1} = A\mathbf{x}_k$ for the specified $\mathbf{x}_0$, and describe what happens as $k \to \infty$.

3. Determine the evolution of the dynamical system in Example 1 when the predation parameter p is .2 in (3). (Give a formula for $\mathbf{x}_k$.) Does the owl population grow or decline? What about the wood rat population?

4. Determine a value of the predation parameter for the predator–prey model in Example 1 that leads to constant levels of the owl and wood rat populations. What is the ratio between the sizes of the population in this case? The *equilibrium* between the two populations is unstable, in the sense that a minor change in any parameter of the model (such as birth rate or predation rate) will correspond to a population that is either increasing or decreasing.

5. In old-growth forests of Douglas fir, the spotted owl dines mainly on flying squirrels. Suppose the predator–prey matrix for these two populations is $A = \begin{bmatrix} .4 & .3 \\ -p & 1.2 \end{bmatrix}$. Show that if the predation parameter p is .325, both populations grow. Estimate the long-term growth rate and the eventual ratio of owls to flying squirrels.

6. Show that if the predation parameter in Exercise 5 is .5, both the owls and the squirrels eventually perish. What value of p corresponds to a system in which both populations remain constant? What are the relative population sizes in this case?

7. Let A have the properties described in Exercise 1.
   a. Is the origin an attractor, a repellor, or a saddle point of the dynamical system $\mathbf{x}_{k+1} = A\mathbf{x}_k$?
   b. Find the directions of greatest attraction and/or repulsion for this dynamical system.
   c. Make a graphical description of the system, showing the directions of greatest attraction or repulsion. Include a rough sketch of several typical trajectories (without computing specific points).

8. Determine the nature of the origin for the dynamical system $\mathbf{x}_{k+1} = A\mathbf{x}_k$ (attractor, repellor, saddle point), if A has the properties described in Exercise 2. Find the directions of greatest attraction or repulsion.

In Exercises 9–14, classify the origin as an attractor, repellor, or saddle point of the dynamical system $\mathbf{x}_{k+1} = A\mathbf{x}_k$. Find the directions of greatest attraction and/or repulsion.

9. $A = \begin{bmatrix} 1.7 & -.3 \\ -1.2 & .8 \end{bmatrix}$

10. $A = \begin{bmatrix} .3 & .4 \\ -.3 & 1.1 \end{bmatrix}$

11. $A = \begin{bmatrix} .4 & .5 \\ -.4 & 1.3 \end{bmatrix}$

12. $A = \begin{bmatrix} .5 & .6 \\ -.3 & 1.4 \end{bmatrix}$

13. $A = \begin{bmatrix} .8 & .3 \\ -.4 & 1.5 \end{bmatrix}$

14. $A = \begin{bmatrix} 1.7 & .6 \\ -.4 & .7 \end{bmatrix}$

15. The Markov chain in Exercise 8 of Section 5.9 is a dynamical system, $\mathbf{v}_{k+1} = P\mathbf{v}_k$, and the eigenvalues of P are 1, .5, and −.2. Find a formula for $\mathbf{v}_k$ when $\mathbf{v}_0 = (1, 0, 0)$. [*Hint*: One eigenvector, (.4, .2, .4), was already found in that exercise.]

16. Use MATLAB to produce the general solution of the dynamical system $\mathbf{x}_{k+1} = A\mathbf{x}_k$, when A is the stochastic matrix for the Hertz Rent A Car model in Exercise 16 of Section 5.9.

17. Construct a stage-matrix model for an animal species that has two life stages: juvenile (up to 1 year old) and adult. Suppose that the female adults give birth each year to an average of 1.6 female juveniles. Each year, 30% of the juveniles survive to become adults and 80% of the adults survive. For $k \geq 0$, let $\mathbf{x}_k = (j_k, a_k)$, where the entries in $\mathbf{x}_k$ are the numbers of female juveniles and female adults in year k.

a. Construct the stage-matrix A such that $\mathbf{x}_{k+1} = A\mathbf{x}_k$ for $k \geq 0$.

b. Show that the population is growing, compute the eventual growth rate of the population, and give the eventual ratio of juveniles to adults.

18. A herd of American buffalo (bison) can be modeled by a stage matrix similar to that for the spotted owls. The females can be divided into calves (up to 1 year old), yearlings (1 to 2 years), and adults. Suppose that an average of 42 female calves are born each year per 100 adult females. (Only adults produce offspring.) Each year, about 60% of the calves survive, 75% of the yearlings survive, and 95% of the adults survive. For $k \geq 0$, let $\mathbf{x}_k = (c_k, y_k, a_k)$, where the entries in $\mathbf{x}_k$ are the numbers of females in each life stage at year k.

a. Construct the stage-matrix A for the buffalo herd, such that $\mathbf{x}_{k+1} = A\mathbf{x}_k$ for $k \geq 0$.

b. (MATLAB) Show that the buffalo herd is growing, determine the expected growth rate after many years, and give the expected numbers of calves and yearlings present per 100 adults.

SOLUTIONS TO PRACTICE PROBLEMS

1. The first step is to write $\mathbf{x}_0$ as a linear combination of $\mathbf{v}_1, \mathbf{v}_2, \mathbf{v}_3$. Row reduction of $[\mathbf{v}_1 \quad \mathbf{v}_2 \quad \mathbf{v}_3 \quad \mathbf{x}_0]$ produces the weights $c_1 = 2$, $c_2 = 1$, $c_3 = 3$, so that

$$\mathbf{x}_0 = 2\mathbf{v}_1 + 1\mathbf{v}_2 + 3\mathbf{v}_3$$

Since the eigenvalues are 1, $\frac{2}{3}$, and $\frac{1}{3}$, the general solution is

$$\begin{aligned}\mathbf{x}_k &= (2\cdot 1^k)\mathbf{v}_1 + (1\cdot(\tfrac{2}{3})^k)\mathbf{v}_2 + (3\cdot(\tfrac{1}{3})^k)\mathbf{v}_3 \\ &= 2\begin{bmatrix}-2\\2\\1\end{bmatrix} + (\tfrac{2}{3})^k\begin{bmatrix}2\\1\\2\end{bmatrix} + 3\cdot(\tfrac{1}{3})^k\begin{bmatrix}1\\2\\-2\end{bmatrix}\end{aligned} \tag{12}$$

2. As $k \to \infty$, the second and third terms in (12) tend to the zero vector, and

$$\mathbf{x}_k = 2\mathbf{v}_1 + (\tfrac{2}{3})^k\mathbf{v}_2 + 3(\tfrac{1}{3})^k\mathbf{v}_3 \to 2\mathbf{v}_1 = \begin{bmatrix}-4\\4\\2\end{bmatrix}$$

6.7 ITERATIVE ESTIMATES FOR EIGENVALUES

In scientific applications of linear algebra, eigenvalues seldom are known precisely. Fortunately, a close numerical approximation is usually quite satisfactory. In fact, some applications require only a rough approximation to the largest eigenvalue. The first algorithm described below will work well for this case. Also, it provides a foundation for a more powerful method that can give fast estimates for other eigenvalues as well.

The Power Method

The power method applies to an $n \times n$ matrix A with a **strictly dominant eigenvalue** λ_1, which means that λ_1 must be larger in absolute value than all the other eigenvalues. In this case, the power method produces a scalar sequence that approaches λ_1 and a vector sequence that approaches a corresponding eigenvector. The background for the method will rest on the eigenvector decomposition used at the beginning of Section 6.6.

Assume for simplicity that A is diagonalizable and $\mathbb{R}^n$ has a basis of eigenvectors $\mathbf{v}_1, \ldots, \mathbf{v}_n$, arranged so their corresponding eigenvalues $\lambda_1, \ldots, \lambda_n$ decrease in size, with the strictly dominant eigenvalue first. That is,

$$|\lambda_1| > |\lambda_2| \geq |\lambda_3| \geq \cdots \geq |\lambda_n| \tag{1}$$

↑ Strictly larger

As we saw in (2) of Section 6.6, if $\mathbf{x}$ in $\mathbb{R}^n$ is written as $\mathbf{x} = c_1\mathbf{v}_1 + \cdots + c_n\mathbf{v}_n$, then

$$A^k\mathbf{x} = c_1(\lambda_1)^k\mathbf{v}_1 + c_2(\lambda_2)^k\mathbf{v}_2 + \cdots + c_n(\lambda_n)^k\mathbf{v}_n \quad (k = 1, 2, \ldots)$$

Assume $c_1 \neq 0$. Then, dividing by $(\lambda_1)^k$,

$$\frac{1}{(\lambda_1)^k}A^k\mathbf{x} = c_1\mathbf{v}_1 + c_2\left(\frac{\lambda_2}{\lambda_1}\right)^k\mathbf{v}_2 + \cdots + c_n\left(\frac{\lambda_n}{\lambda_1}\right)^k\mathbf{v}_n \quad (k = 1, 2, \ldots) \tag{2}$$

From (1), the fractions $\lambda_2/\lambda_1, \ldots, \lambda_n/\lambda_1$ are all less than 1 in magnitude and so their powers go to zero. Hence

$$(\lambda_1)^{-k}A^k\mathbf{x} \to c_1\mathbf{v}_1 \quad \text{as } k \to \infty \tag{3}$$

Thus for large k, a scalar multiple of $A^k\mathbf{x}$ determines almost the same *direction* as the eigenvector $c_1\mathbf{v}_1$. Since positive scalar multiples do not change the direction of a vector, $A^k\mathbf{x}$ itself points almost in the same direction as $\mathbf{v}_1$ or $-\mathbf{v}_1$, provided $c_1 \neq 0$.

EXAMPLE 1 Let $A = \begin{bmatrix} 1.8 & .8 \\ .2 & 1.2 \end{bmatrix}$, $\mathbf{v}_1 = \begin{bmatrix} 4 \\ 1 \end{bmatrix}$, and $\mathbf{x} = \begin{bmatrix} -.5 \\ 1 \end{bmatrix}$. Then A has eigenvalues 2 and 1, and the eigenspace for $\lambda_1 = 2$ is the line through $\mathbf{0}$ and $\mathbf{v}_1$. For $k = 0, \ldots, 8$, compute $A^k\mathbf{x}$ and construct the line through $\mathbf{0}$ and $A^k\mathbf{x}$. What happens as k increases?

Solution The first three calculations are

$$A\mathbf{x} = \begin{bmatrix} 1.8 & .8 \\ .2 & 1.2 \end{bmatrix}\begin{bmatrix} -.5 \\ 1 \end{bmatrix} = \begin{bmatrix} -.1 \\ 1.1 \end{bmatrix}$$

$$A^2\mathbf{x} = A(A\mathbf{x}) = \begin{bmatrix} 1.8 & .8 \\ .2 & 1.2 \end{bmatrix}\begin{bmatrix} -.1 \\ 1.1 \end{bmatrix} = \begin{bmatrix} .7 \\ 1.3 \end{bmatrix}$$

$$A^3\mathbf{x} = A(A^2\mathbf{x}) = \begin{bmatrix} 1.8 & .8 \\ .2 & 1.2 \end{bmatrix}\begin{bmatrix} .7 \\ 1.3 \end{bmatrix} = \begin{bmatrix} 2.3 \\ 1.7 \end{bmatrix}$$

Analogous calculations complete Table 1.

TABLE 1 Iterates of a Vector

k	0	1	2	3	4	5	6	7	8
$A^k\mathbf{x}$	$\begin{bmatrix} -.5 \\ 1 \end{bmatrix}$	$\begin{bmatrix} -.1 \\ 1.1 \end{bmatrix}$	$\begin{bmatrix} .7 \\ 1.3 \end{bmatrix}$	$\begin{bmatrix} 2.3 \\ 1.7 \end{bmatrix}$	$\begin{bmatrix} 5.5 \\ 2.5 \end{bmatrix}$	$\begin{bmatrix} 11.9 \\ 4.1 \end{bmatrix}$	$\begin{bmatrix} 24.7 \\ 7.3 \end{bmatrix}$	$\begin{bmatrix} 50.3 \\ 13.7 \end{bmatrix}$	$\begin{bmatrix} 101.5 \\ 26.5 \end{bmatrix}$

The vectors $\mathbf{x}$, $A\mathbf{x}$, ..., $A^4\mathbf{x}$ are shown in Fig. 1. The other vectors are growing too long to display. However, line segments are drawn showing the directions of those vectors. In fact, the directions of the vectors are what we really want to see, not the vectors themselves. The lines seem to be approaching the line representing the eigenspace spanned by $\mathbf{v}_1$. More precisely, the angle between the line (subspace) determined by $A^k\mathbf{x}$ and the line (eigenspace) determined by $\mathbf{v}_1$ goes to zero as $k \to \infty$. ∎

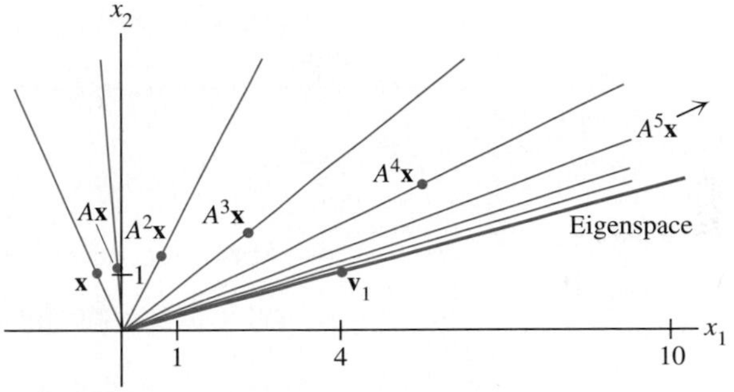

FIGURE 1 Directions determined by $\mathbf{x}, A\mathbf{x}, A^2\mathbf{x}, \ldots, A^7\mathbf{x}$.

The vectors $(\lambda_1)^{-k}A^k\mathbf{x}$ in (3) are scaled to make them converge to $c_1\mathbf{v}_1$, provided $c_1 \neq 0$. We cannot scale $A^k\mathbf{x}$ in this way because we do not know λ_1. But we can scale each $A^k\mathbf{x}$ to make its largest entry a 1. It turns out that the resulting sequence $\{\mathbf{x}_k\}$ will converge to a multiple of $\mathbf{v}_1$ whose largest entry is 1. Figure 2 shows the scaled sequence for Example 1. The eigenvalue λ_1 can be estimated from the sequence $\{\mathbf{x}_k\}$, too. When $\mathbf{x}_k$ is close to an eigenvector for λ_1, the vector $A\mathbf{x}_k$ will be close to $\lambda_1\mathbf{x}_k$, with each entry in $A\mathbf{x}_k$ approximately λ_1 times the corresponding entry in $\mathbf{x}_k$. Because the largest entry in $\mathbf{x}_k$ is 1, the largest entry in $A\mathbf{x}_k$ will be close to λ_1. (Careful proofs of these statements are omitted.)

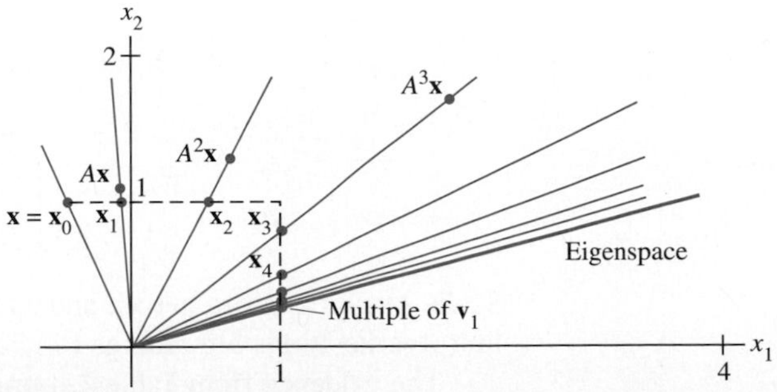

FIGURE 2 Scaled multiples of $\mathbf{x}, A\mathbf{x}, A^2\mathbf{x}, \ldots, A^7\mathbf{x}$.

The Power Method for Estimating a Strictly Dominant Eigenvalue

1. Select an initial vector $\mathbf{x}_0$ whose largest entry is a 1.
2. For $k = 0, 1, \ldots,$
   a. Compute $A\mathbf{x}_k$.
   b. Let μ_k be an entry in $A\mathbf{x}_k$ whose absolute value is as large as possible.
   c. Compute $\mathbf{x}_{k+1} = (1/\mu_k)A\mathbf{x}_k$.
3. For almost all choices of $\mathbf{x}_0$, the sequence $\{\mu_k\}$ approaches the dominant eigenvalue, and the sequence $\{\mathbf{x}_k\}$ approaches a corresponding eigenvector.

EXAMPLE 2 Apply the power method to $A = \begin{bmatrix} 6 & 5 \\ 1 & 2 \end{bmatrix}$ with $\mathbf{x}_0 = \begin{bmatrix} 0 \\ 1 \end{bmatrix}$. Stop when $k = 5$, and estimate the dominant eigenvalue and a corresponding eigenvector of A.

Solution Calculations in this example and the next were made with MATLAB, which computes with 16-digit accuracy, although we show only a few significant figures here. To begin, we compute $A\mathbf{x}_0$ and identify the largest entry μ_0 in $A\mathbf{x}_0$:

$$A\mathbf{x}_0 = \begin{bmatrix} 6 & 5 \\ 1 & 2 \end{bmatrix}\begin{bmatrix} 0 \\ 1 \end{bmatrix} = \begin{bmatrix} 5 \\ 2 \end{bmatrix}, \qquad \mu_0 = 5$$

Scale $A\mathbf{x}_0$ by $1/\mu_0$ to get $\mathbf{x}_1$, compute $A\mathbf{x}_1$, and identify the largest entry in $A\mathbf{x}_1$:

$$\mathbf{x}_1 = \frac{1}{\mu_0}A\mathbf{x}_0 = \frac{1}{5}\begin{bmatrix} 5 \\ 2 \end{bmatrix} = \begin{bmatrix} 1 \\ .4 \end{bmatrix}$$

$$A\mathbf{x}_1 = \begin{bmatrix} 6 & 5 \\ 1 & 2 \end{bmatrix}\begin{bmatrix} 1 \\ .4 \end{bmatrix} = \begin{bmatrix} 8 \\ 1.8 \end{bmatrix}, \qquad \mu_1 = 8$$

Scale $A\mathbf{x}_1$ by $1/\mu_1$ to get $\mathbf{x}_2$, compute $A\mathbf{x}_2$, and identify the largest entry in $A\mathbf{x}_2$:

$$\mathbf{x}_2 = \frac{1}{\mu_1}A\mathbf{x}_1 = \frac{1}{8}\begin{bmatrix} 8 \\ 1.8 \end{bmatrix} = \begin{bmatrix} 1 \\ .225 \end{bmatrix}$$

$$A\mathbf{x}_2 = \begin{bmatrix} 6 & 5 \\ 1 & 2 \end{bmatrix}\begin{bmatrix} 1 \\ .225 \end{bmatrix} = \begin{bmatrix} 7.125 \\ 1.450 \end{bmatrix}, \qquad \mu_2 = 7.125$$

Scale $A\mathbf{x}_2$ by $1/\mu_2$ to get $\mathbf{x}_3$, and so on. The results of MATLAB calculations for the first five iterations are arranged in Table 2.

The evidence from Table 2 strongly suggests that $\{\mathbf{x}_k\}$ approaches (1, .2) and $\{\mu_k\}$ approaches 7. If so, then (1, .2) is an eigenvector and 7 is the dominant eigenvalue.

This is easily verified by computing

$$A\begin{bmatrix}1\\.2\end{bmatrix}=\begin{bmatrix}6&5\\1&2\end{bmatrix}\begin{bmatrix}1\\.2\end{bmatrix}=\begin{bmatrix}7\\1.4\end{bmatrix}=7\begin{bmatrix}1\\.2\end{bmatrix}$$

∎

TABLE 2 The Power Method

k	0	1	2	3	4	5
$\mathbf{x}_k$	$\begin{bmatrix}0\\1\end{bmatrix}$	$\begin{bmatrix}1\\.4\end{bmatrix}$	$\begin{bmatrix}1\\.225\end{bmatrix}$	$\begin{bmatrix}1\\.2035\end{bmatrix}$	$\begin{bmatrix}1\\.2005\end{bmatrix}$	$\begin{bmatrix}1\\.20007\end{bmatrix}$
$A\mathbf{x}_k$	$\begin{bmatrix}5\\2\end{bmatrix}$	$\begin{bmatrix}8\\1.8\end{bmatrix}$	$\begin{bmatrix}7.125\\1.450\end{bmatrix}$	$\begin{bmatrix}7.0175\\1.4070\end{bmatrix}$	$\begin{bmatrix}7.0025\\1.4010\end{bmatrix}$	$\begin{bmatrix}7.00036\\1.40014\end{bmatrix}$
μ_k	5	8	7.125	7.0175	7.0025	7.00036

The sequence $\{\mu_k\}$ in Example 2 converged quickly to $\lambda_1 = 7$ because the second eigenvalue of A was much smaller. (In fact, $\lambda_2 = 1$.) In general, the rate of convergence depends on the ratio $|\lambda_2/\lambda_1|$, because the vector $c_2(\lambda_2/\lambda_1)^k\mathbf{v}_2$ in (2) is the main source of error when using a scaled version of $A^k\mathbf{x}$ as an estimate of $c_1\mathbf{v}_1$.(The other fractions λ_j/λ_1 are likely to be smaller.) If $|\lambda_2/\lambda_1|$ is close to 1, then $\{\mu_k\}$ and $\{\mathbf{x}_k\}$ can converge very slowly, and other approximation methods may be preferred.

There is a slight chance with the power method that a random choice of initial vector $\mathbf{x}$ will have no component in the $\mathbf{v}_1$ direction (when $c_1 = 0$). But computer rounding errors during the calculations of the $\mathbf{x}_k$ are likely to create a vector with at least a small component in the direction of $\mathbf{v}_1$. If that occurs, the $\mathbf{x}_k$ will start to converge to a multiple of $\mathbf{v}_1$.

The Inverse Power Method

This method provides an approximation for *any* eigenvalue, provided a good initial estimate α of the eigenvalue λ is known. In this case, we let $B = (A-\alpha I)^{-1}$ and apply the power method to B. It can be shown that if the eigenvalues of A are $\lambda_1, \dots, \lambda_n$, then the eigenvalues of B are

$$\frac{1}{\lambda_1-\alpha},\quad \frac{1}{\lambda_2-\alpha},\quad \dots,\quad \frac{1}{\lambda_n-\alpha}$$

and the corresponding eigenvectors are the same as those for A. (See Exercises 15 and 16.)

Suppose, for example, that α is closer to λ_2 than to the other eigenvalues of A. Then $1/(\lambda_2-\alpha)$ will be a strictly dominant eigenvalue of B. If α is really close to λ_2, then $1/(\lambda_2-\alpha)$ is *much* larger than the other eigenvalues of B, and the inverse power method produces a very rapid approximation to λ_2 for almost all choices of $\mathbf{x}_0$. The following algorithm gives the details.

Notice that B, or rather $(A-\alpha I)^{-1}$, does not appear in the algorithm. Instead of computing $(A-\alpha I)^{-1}\mathbf{x}_k$ to get the next vector in the sequence, it is better to *solve* the equation $(A - \alpha I)\mathbf{y}_k = \mathbf{x}_k$ for $\mathbf{y}_k$ (and then scale $\mathbf{y}_k$ to produce $\mathbf{x}_{k+1}$). Since this equation for $\mathbf{y}_k$ must be solved for each k, an LU factorization of $A - \alpha I$ will speed up the process.

The Inverse Power Method for Estimating an Eigenvalue λ of A

1. Select an initial estimate α sufficiently close to λ.
2. Select an initial vector $\mathbf{x}_0$ whose largest entry is a 1.
3. For $k = 0, 1, \ldots,$
   a. Solve $(A - \alpha I)\mathbf{y}_k = \mathbf{x}_k$ for $\mathbf{y}_k$.
   b. Let μ_k be an entry in $\mathbf{y}_k$ whose absolute value is as large as possible.
   c. Compute $\nu_k = \alpha + (1/\mu_k)$.
   d. Compute $\mathbf{x}_{k+1} = (1/\mu_k)\mathbf{y}_k$.
4. For almost all choices of $\mathbf{x}_0$, the sequence $\{\nu_k\}$ approaches the eigenvalue λ of A, and the sequence $\{\mathbf{x}_k\}$ approaches a corresponding eigenvector.

EXAMPLE 3 It is not uncommon in some applications to need to know the smallest eigenvalue of a matrix A and to have at hand rough estimates of the eigenvalues. Suppose 21, 3.3, and 1.9 are estimates for the eigenvalues of the matrix A below. Find the smallest eigenvalue, accurate to six decimal places.

$$A = \begin{bmatrix} 10 & -8 & -4 \\ -8 & 13 & 4 \\ -4 & 5 & 4 \end{bmatrix}$$

Solution The two smallest eigenvalues seem close together, so we use the inverse power method for $A - 1.9I$. Results of a MATLAB calculation are shown in Table 3. Here $\mathbf{x}_0$ was chosen arbitrarily, $\mathbf{y}_k = (A - 1.9I)^{-1}\mathbf{x}_k$, μ_k is the largest entry in $\mathbf{y}_k$, $\nu_k = 1.9 + 1/\mu_k$, and $\mathbf{x}_{k+1} = (1/\mu_k)\mathbf{y}_k$. As it turns out, the initial eigenvalue estimate was fairly good, and the inverse power sequence converged quickly. The exact eigenvalue is 2. ∎

TABLE 3 The Inverse Power Method

k	0	1	2	3	4
$\mathbf{x}_k$	$\begin{bmatrix} 1 \\ 1 \\ 1 \end{bmatrix}$	$\begin{bmatrix} .5736 \\ .0646 \\ 1 \end{bmatrix}$	$\begin{bmatrix} .5054 \\ .0045 \\ 1 \end{bmatrix}$	$\begin{bmatrix} .5004 \\ .0003 \\ 1 \end{bmatrix}$	$\begin{bmatrix} .50003 \\ .00002 \\ 1 \end{bmatrix}$
$\mathbf{y}_k$	$\begin{bmatrix} 4.45 \\ .50 \\ 7.76 \end{bmatrix}$	$\begin{bmatrix} 5.0131 \\ .0442 \\ 9.9197 \end{bmatrix}$	$\begin{bmatrix} 5.0012 \\ .0031 \\ 9.9949 \end{bmatrix}$	$\begin{bmatrix} 5.0001 \\ .0002 \\ 9.9996 \end{bmatrix}$	$\begin{bmatrix} 5.000006 \\ .000015 \\ 9.999975 \end{bmatrix}$
μ_k	7.76	9.9197	9.9949	9.9996	9.999975
ν_k	2.03	2.0008	2.00005	2.000004	2.0000003

If an estimate for the smallest eigenvalue of a matrix is not available, one can simply take $\alpha = 0$ in the inverse power method. This choice of α works reasonably well if the smallest eigenvalue is much closer to zero than to the other eigenvalues.

The two algorithms presented in this section are practical tools for many simple situations, and they provide an introduction to the problem of eigenvalue estimation. A more robust and widely used iterative method is the QR algorithm. For instance, it is the heart of the MATLAB command "eig(A)," which rapidly computes eigenvalues and eigenvectors of A. A brief description of the QR algorithm was given in the exercises for Section 6.2. Further details are in most modern numerical analysis texts.

PRACTICE PROBLEM

How can you tell if a given vector $\mathbf{x}$ is a good approximation to an eigenvector of a matrix A; if it is, how would you estimate the corresponding eigenvalue? Experiment with

$$A = \begin{bmatrix} 5 & 8 & 4 \\ 8 & 3 & -1 \\ 4 & -1 & 2 \end{bmatrix} \quad \text{and} \quad \mathbf{x} = \begin{bmatrix} 1.0 \\ -4.3 \\ 8.1 \end{bmatrix}$$

6.7 EXERCISES

In Exercises 1–4, the matrix A is followed by a sequence $\{\mathbf{x}_k\}$ produced by the power method. Use these data to estimate the largest eigenvalue of A, and give a corresponding eigenvector.

1. $A = \begin{bmatrix} 4 & 3 \\ 1 & 2 \end{bmatrix}$;

$$\begin{bmatrix} 1 \\ 0 \end{bmatrix}, \begin{bmatrix} 1 \\ .25 \end{bmatrix}, \begin{bmatrix} 1 \\ .3158 \end{bmatrix}, \begin{bmatrix} 1 \\ .3298 \end{bmatrix}, \begin{bmatrix} 1 \\ .3326 \end{bmatrix}$$

2. $A = \begin{bmatrix} 1.8 & -.8 \\ -3.2 & 4.2 \end{bmatrix}$;

$$\begin{bmatrix} 1 \\ 0 \end{bmatrix}, \begin{bmatrix} -.5625 \\ 1 \end{bmatrix}, \begin{bmatrix} -.3021 \\ 1 \end{bmatrix}, \begin{bmatrix} -.2601 \\ 1 \end{bmatrix}, \begin{bmatrix} -.2520 \\ 1 \end{bmatrix}$$

3. $A = \begin{bmatrix} .5 & .2 \\ .4 & .7 \end{bmatrix}$;

$$\begin{bmatrix} 1 \\ 0 \end{bmatrix}, \begin{bmatrix} 1 \\ .8 \end{bmatrix}, \begin{bmatrix} .6875 \\ 1 \end{bmatrix}, \begin{bmatrix} .5577 \\ 1 \end{bmatrix}, \begin{bmatrix} .5188 \\ 1 \end{bmatrix}$$

4. $A = \begin{bmatrix} 4.1 & -6 \\ 3 & -4.4 \end{bmatrix}$;

$$\begin{bmatrix} 1 \\ 1 \end{bmatrix}, \begin{bmatrix} 1 \\ .7368 \end{bmatrix}, \begin{bmatrix} 1 \\ .7541 \end{bmatrix}, \begin{bmatrix} 1 \\ .7490 \end{bmatrix}, \begin{bmatrix} 1 \\ .7502 \end{bmatrix}$$

5. Let $A = \begin{bmatrix} 15 & 16 \\ -20 & -21 \end{bmatrix}$. The vectors $\mathbf{x}, \ldots, A^5\mathbf{x}$ are $\begin{bmatrix} 1 \\ 1 \end{bmatrix}$,

$$\begin{bmatrix} 31 \\ -41 \end{bmatrix}, \begin{bmatrix} -191 \\ 241 \end{bmatrix}, \begin{bmatrix} 991 \\ -1241 \end{bmatrix}, \begin{bmatrix} -4991 \\ 6241 \end{bmatrix}, \begin{bmatrix} 24991 \\ -31241 \end{bmatrix}.$$

Find a vector with a 1 in the second entry that is close to an eigenvector of A. Use four decimal places. Check your estimate and give an estimate for the dominant eigenvalue of A.

6. Let $A = \begin{bmatrix} -2 & -3 \\ 6 & 7 \end{bmatrix}$. Repeat Exercise 5, using the following sequence $\mathbf{x}, A\mathbf{x}, \ldots, A^5\mathbf{x}$.

$$\begin{bmatrix} 1 \\ 1 \end{bmatrix}, \begin{bmatrix} -5 \\ 13 \end{bmatrix}, \begin{bmatrix} -29 \\ 61 \end{bmatrix}, \begin{bmatrix} -125 \\ 253 \end{bmatrix}, \begin{bmatrix} -509 \\ 1021 \end{bmatrix}, \begin{bmatrix} -2045 \\ 4093 \end{bmatrix}$$

Exercises 7–12 and 17–20 require MATLAB or other computational aid. In Exercises 7 and 8, use the power method with the $\mathbf{x}_0$ given. List $\{\mathbf{x}_k\}$ and $\{\mu_k\}$ for $k = 1, \ldots, 5$. In Exercises 9 and 10, list μ_5 and μ_6.

7. $A = \begin{bmatrix} 6 & 7 \\ 8 & 5 \end{bmatrix}, \mathbf{x}_0 = \begin{bmatrix} 1 \\ 0 \end{bmatrix}$

8. $A = \begin{bmatrix} 2 & 1 \\ 4 & 5 \end{bmatrix}, \mathbf{x}_0 = \begin{bmatrix} 1 \\ 0 \end{bmatrix}$

9. $A = \begin{bmatrix} 8 & 0 & 12 \\ 1 & -2 & 1 \\ 0 & 3 & 0 \end{bmatrix}, \mathbf{x}_0 = \begin{bmatrix} 1 \\ 0 \\ 0 \end{bmatrix}$

10. $A = \begin{bmatrix} 1 & 2 & -2 \\ 1 & 1 & 9 \\ 0 & 1 & 9 \end{bmatrix}$, $\mathbf{x}_0 = \begin{bmatrix} 1 \\ 0 \\ 0 \end{bmatrix}$

Another estimate can be made for an eigenvalue when an approximate eigenvector is available. Observe that if $A\mathbf{x} = \lambda\mathbf{x}$, then $\mathbf{x}^T A\mathbf{x} = \mathbf{x}^T(\lambda\mathbf{x}) = \lambda(\mathbf{x}^T\mathbf{x})$, and the **Rayleigh quotient**

$$R(\mathbf{x}) = \frac{\mathbf{x}^T A\mathbf{x}}{\mathbf{x}^T\mathbf{x}}$$

equals λ. If $\mathbf{x}$ is close to an eigenvector for λ, then this quotient is close to λ. When A is a symmetric matrix ($A^T = A$), the Rayleigh quotient $R(\mathbf{x}_k) = (\mathbf{x}_k^T A\mathbf{x}_k)/(\mathbf{x}_k^T\mathbf{x}_k)$ will have roughly twice as many digits of accuracy as the scaling factor μ_k in the power method. Verify this increased accuracy in Exercises 11 and 12 by computing μ_k and $R(\mathbf{x}_k)$ for $k = 1, \ldots, 4$.

11. $A = \begin{bmatrix} 5 & 2 \\ 2 & 2 \end{bmatrix}$, $\mathbf{x}_0 = \begin{bmatrix} 1 \\ 0 \end{bmatrix}$

12. $A = \begin{bmatrix} -3 & 2 \\ 2 & 0 \end{bmatrix}$, $\mathbf{x}_0 = \begin{bmatrix} 1 \\ 0 \end{bmatrix}$

Exercises 13 and 14 apply to a 3×3 matrix A whose eigenvalues are estimated to be 4, −4, and 3.

13. If the eigenvalues close to 4 and −4 are known to have different absolute values, will the power method work? Is it likely to be useful?

14. Suppose the eigenvalues close to 4 and −4 are known to have exactly the same absolute value. Describe how one might obtain a sequence that estimates the eigenvalue close to 4.

15. Suppose $A\mathbf{x} = \lambda\mathbf{x}$ with $\mathbf{x} \neq \mathbf{0}$. Let α be a scalar different from the eigenvalues of A, and let $B = (A - \alpha I)^{-1}$. Subtract $\alpha\mathbf{x}$ from both sides of the equation $A\mathbf{x} = \lambda\mathbf{x}$, and use algebra to show that $1/(\lambda - \alpha)$ is an eigenvalue of B, with $\mathbf{x}$ a corresponding eigenvector.

16. Suppose μ is an eigenvalue of the B in Exercise 15, and that $\mathbf{x}$ is a corresponding eigenvector, so that $(A-\alpha I)^{-1}\mathbf{x} = \mu\mathbf{x}$. Use this equation to find an eigenvalue of A in terms of μ and α.

17. Use the inverse power method to estimate the middle eigenvalue of the A in Example 3, with accuracy to four decimal places. Set $\mathbf{x}_0 = (1, 0, 0)$.

18. Let A be as in Exercise 9. Use the inverse power method with $\mathbf{x}_0 = (1, 0, 0)$ to estimate the eigenvalue of A near $\alpha = -1.4$, and obtain an accuracy to four decimal places.

In Exercises 19 and 20, find (a) the largest eigenvalue, and (b) the smallest eigenvalue. In each case, set $\mathbf{x}_0 = (1, 0, 0, 0)$ and carry out approximations until the approximating sequence seems accurate to four decimal places. Include the approximate eigenvector.

19. $A = \begin{bmatrix} 10 & 7 & 8 & 7 \\ 7 & 5 & 6 & 5 \\ 8 & 6 & 10 & 9 \\ 7 & 5 & 9 & 10 \end{bmatrix}$

20. $A = \begin{bmatrix} 1 & 2 & 3 & 2 \\ 2 & 12 & 13 & 11 \\ -2 & 3 & 0 & 2 \\ 4 & 5 & 7 & 2 \end{bmatrix}$

21. A common misconception is that if A has a strictly dominant eigenvalue, then for any sufficiently large value of k the vector $A^k\mathbf{x}$ is approximately equal to an eigenvector of A. For the three matrices below, study what happens to $A^k\mathbf{x}$ when $\mathbf{x} = (.5, .5)$, and try to draw general conclusions (for a 2×2 matrix).

a. $A = \begin{bmatrix} .8 & 0 \\ 0 & .2 \end{bmatrix}$ b. $A = \begin{bmatrix} 1 & 0 \\ 0 & .8 \end{bmatrix}$

c. $A = \begin{bmatrix} 8 & 0 \\ 0 & 2 \end{bmatrix}$

SOLUTION TO PRACTICE PROBLEM

For the given A and $\mathbf{x}$,

$$A\mathbf{x} = \begin{bmatrix} 5 & 8 & 4 \\ 8 & 3 & -1 \\ 4 & -1 & 2 \end{bmatrix}\begin{bmatrix} 1.00 \\ -4.30 \\ 8.10 \end{bmatrix} = \begin{bmatrix} 3.00 \\ -13.00 \\ 24.50 \end{bmatrix}$$

If $A\mathbf{x}$ is nearly a multiple of $\mathbf{x}$, then the ratios of corresponding entries in the two vectors should be nearly constant. So compute:

{entry in $A\mathbf{x}$} ÷	{entry in $\mathbf{x}$} =	{ratio}
3.00	1.00	3.000
−13.00	−4.30	3.023
24.50	8.10	3.025

Each entry in $A\mathbf{x}$ is about 3 times the corresponding entry in $\mathbf{x}$, so $\mathbf{x}$ is close to an eigenvector. Any of the ratios above is an estimate for the eigenvalue. (To five decimal places, the eigenvalue is 3.02409.)

CHAPTER 6 SUPPLEMENTARY EXERCISES

Throughout these supplementary exercises, A and B represent square matrices of appropriate sizes.

1. Mark each statement as True or False. Justify each answer.

____ a. If A is invertible and 1 is an eigenvalue for A, then 1 is also an eigenvalue for A^{-1}.

____ b. If A is row equivalent to the identity matrix I, then A is diagonalizable.

____ c. If A contains a row or column of zeros, then 0 is an eigenvalue of A.

____ d. There exists a 2×2 matrix that has no eigenvectors in $\mathbb{R}^2$.

____ e. Eigenvalues must be nonzero scalars.

____ f. Eigenvectors must be nonzero vectors.

____ g. Two distinct eigenvectors are linearly independent.

____ h. Two eigenvectors corresponding to the same eigenvalue are always linearly dependent.

____ i. Similar matrices always have exactly the same eigenvalues.

____ j. Similar matrices always have exactly the same eigenvectors.

____ k. The sum of two eigenvectors of a matrix A is also an eigenvector of A.

____ l. The eigenvalues of an upper triangular matrix A are the nonzero entries on the diagonal of A.

____ m. A and A^T have the same eigenvalues, counting multiplicities.

____ n. If a 5×5 matrix A has fewer than 5 distinct eigenvalues, then A is not diagonalizable.

____ o. If A is diagonalizable, then the columns of A are linearly independent.

____ p. A nonzero eigenvector cannot correspond to two different eigenvalues of A.

____ q. A square matrix A is invertible if and only if there is a coordinate system in which the transformation $\mathbf{x} \mapsto A\mathbf{x}$ is represented by a diagonal matrix.

2. Show that if $\mathbf{x}$ is an eigenvector of the matrix product AB and $B\mathbf{x} \neq \mathbf{0}$, then $B\mathbf{x}$ is an eigenvector of BA.

3. Suppose $\mathbf{x}$ is an eigenvector of A corresponding to an eigenvalue λ.

a. Show that $\mathbf{x}$ is an eigenvector of $5I - A$. What is the corresponding eigenvalue?

b. Show that $\mathbf{x}$ is an eigenvector of $5I - 3A + A^2$. What is the corresponding eigenvalue?

4. If $p(t) = c_0 + c_1 t + c_2 t^2 + \cdots + c_n t^n$, define $p(A)$ to be the matrix formed by replacing each power of t in $p(t)$ by the corresponding power of A (with $A^0 = I$). That is,

$$p(A) = c_0 I + c_1 A + c_2 A^2 + \cdots + c_n A^n$$

Show that if λ is an eigenvalue of A, then one eigenvalue of $p(A)$ is $p(\lambda)$.

5. Suppose $A = PDP^{-1}$ where P is 2×2 and $D = \begin{bmatrix} 2 & 0 \\ 0 & 7 \end{bmatrix}$.

a. Let $B = 5I - 3A + A^2$. Show that B is diagonalizable by finding a suitable factorization of B.

b. Given $p(t)$ and $p(A)$ as in Exercise 4, show that $p(A)$ is diagonalizable.

6. Suppose A is diagonalizable and that $p(t)$ is the characteristic polynomial of A. Define $p(A)$ as in Exercise 4, and show that $p(A)$ is the zero matrix. This fact, which also is true for *any* square matrix, is called the *Cayley–Hamilton theorem.*

7. Show that $I - A$ is invertible when all the eigenvalues of A are less than 1 in magnitude. [*Hint*: What would be true if $I - A$ were not invertible?]

8. Show that if A is diagonalizable, with all eigenvalues less than 1 in magnitude, then A^k tends to the zero matrix as

$k \to \infty$. [*Hint*: Consider $A^k\mathbf{x}$ where $\mathbf{x}$ represents any one of the columns of I.]

9. Let $\mathbf{u}$ be an eigenvector of A corresponding to an eigenvalue λ, and let H be the line in $\mathbb{R}^n$ through $\mathbf{u}$ and the origin.

a. Explain why H is invariant under A in the sense that $A\mathbf{x}$ is in H whenever $\mathbf{x}$ is in H.

b. Let K be a one-dimensional subspace of $\mathbb{R}^n$ that is invariant under A. Explain why K contains an eigenvector of A.

10. Let $G = \begin{bmatrix} A & X \\ 0 & B \end{bmatrix}$. Use the definition in Section 6.2 for $\det G$ to explain why $\det G = (\det A)(\det B)$. From this deduce that the characteristic polynomial of G is the product of the characteristic polynomials of A and B.

Use Exercise 10 to find the eigenvalues of the matrices:

11. $A = \begin{bmatrix} 3 & -2 & 8 \\ 0 & 5 & -2 \\ 0 & -4 & 3 \end{bmatrix}$

12. $A = \begin{bmatrix} 1 & 5 & -6 & -7 \\ 2 & 4 & 5 & 2 \\ 0 & 0 & -7 & -4 \\ 0 & 0 & 3 & 1 \end{bmatrix}$

13. Let $A = \begin{bmatrix} .4 & -.3 \\ .4 & 1.2 \end{bmatrix}$. Explain why A^k approaches $\begin{bmatrix} -.5 & -.75 \\ 1.0 & 1.50 \end{bmatrix}$ as $k \to \infty$.

Exercises 14–18 concern the polynomial

$$p(t) = a_0 + a_1 t + \cdots + a_{n-1}t^{n-1} + t^n$$

and an $n \times n$ matrix C_p called the **companion matrix** of p:

$$C_p = \begin{bmatrix} 0 & 1 & 0 & \cdots & 0 \\ 0 & 0 & 1 & & 0 \\ \vdots & & & & \vdots \\ 0 & 0 & 0 & & 1 \\ -a_0 & -a_1 & -a_2 & \cdots & -a_{n-1} \end{bmatrix}$$

14. Write the companion matrix C_p for $p(t) = 6 - 5t + t^2$, and then find the characteristic polynomial of C_p.

15. Let $p(t) = (t-2)(t-3)(t-4) = -24 + 26t - 9t^2 + t^3$. Write the companion matrix for $p(t)$, and use techniques from Chapter 4 to find its characteristic polynomial.

16. Use mathematical induction to prove that

$$\begin{aligned} \det(C_p - \lambda I) &= (-1)^n(a_0 + a_1\lambda + \cdots + a_{n-1}\lambda^{n-1} + \lambda^n) \\ &= (-1)^n p(\lambda) \end{aligned}$$

[*Hint*: Expanding by cofactors down the first column, show that $\det(C_p - \lambda I)$ has the form $(-\lambda)B + (-1)^n a_0$, where B is a certain polynomial (by the induction assumption).]

17. Let $p(t) = a_0 + a_1 t + a_2 t^2 + t^3$, and let λ be a zero of p.

a. Write the companion matrix for p.

b. Explain why $\lambda^3 = -a_0 - a_1\lambda - a_2\lambda^2$, and show that $(1, \lambda, \lambda^2)$ is an eigenvector of the companion matrix for p.

18. Let p be the polynomial in Exercise 17, and suppose that p has distinct roots λ_1, λ_2, and λ_3. Let V be the Vandermonde matrix

$$V = \begin{bmatrix} 1 & 1 & 1 \\ \lambda_1 & \lambda_2 & \lambda_3 \\ \lambda_1^2 & \lambda_2^2 & \lambda_3^2 \end{bmatrix}$$

(The transpose of V was considered in Supplementary Exercise 11 in Chapter 3.) Use Exercise 17 and a theorem from this chapter to deduce that V is invertible (but do not compute V^{-1}). Then explain why $V^{-1}C_pV$ is a diagonal matrix.

19. The MATLAB command "roots(p)" computes the roots of a polynomial $p(t) = a_0 + \cdots + a_{n-1}t^{n-1} + t^n$. Read a MATLAB manual, and then describe the basic idea behind the algorithm for the "roots" command.

7

Orthogonality and Least-Squares

Introductory Example: Readjusting the North American Datum

Imagine starting a massive project that you estimate will take ten years and require the efforts of scores of people to construct and solve a 1,800,000 by 900,000 system of linear equations. That is exactly what the National Geodetic Survey did in 1974, when it set out to update the North American Datum (NAD)—a network of 268,000 carefully surveyed and marked reference points that span the entire North American continent above the Isthmus of Panama, together with Greenland, Hawaii, the Virgin Islands, Puerto Rico, and other Caribbean islands.

The recorded latitudes and longitudes in the NAD must be determined to within a few centimeters because they form the basis for all surveys, maps, legal property boundaries, state and regional land-use plans, and layouts of civil engineering projects such as highways and public utility lines. More than 200,000 new points had been added to an old set of measurements since the last adjustment of the geodetic reference points, in 1927. Errors had gradually accumulated over the years, and in some places the earth itself had moved—up to 5 centimeters per year. By 1970, there was an urgent need to completely overhaul the system, and plans were made to determine a new set of coordinates for the reference points.

Measurement data collected over a period of 140 years had to be converted to computer-readable form, and the data itself had to be standardized. (For instance, mathematical models of the earth's crustal motion were used to update measurements made years ago along the San Andreas fault in California.) After that, measurements had to be cross-checked to identify errors arising from either the original data or the data entered into the computer. The final calculations involved about 1.8 million observations, each weighted according to its relative accuracy and each giving rise to one equation.

The system of equations for the NAD had no solution in the ordinary sense, but rather had a *least-squares solution*, which assigned latitudes and longitudes to the reference points in a way that corresponded best to the 1.8 million observations. The least-squares solution was found by solving a related linear system of so-called *normal equations*, which involved 928,735 equations in 928,735 variables!

Because the normal equations were too large for existing computers, they were broken down into smaller systems by a technique called *Helmert blocking*, which recursively partitioned the coefficient matrix into smaller and smaller blocks. The smallest blocks provided equations for geographically contiguous blocks of 500 to 2000 reference points in the NAD. Figure 1 shows how the United States was subdivided for this Helmert blocking. Solutions of the smaller systems were used after several intermediate steps to produce the final values for all 928,735 variables.[1]

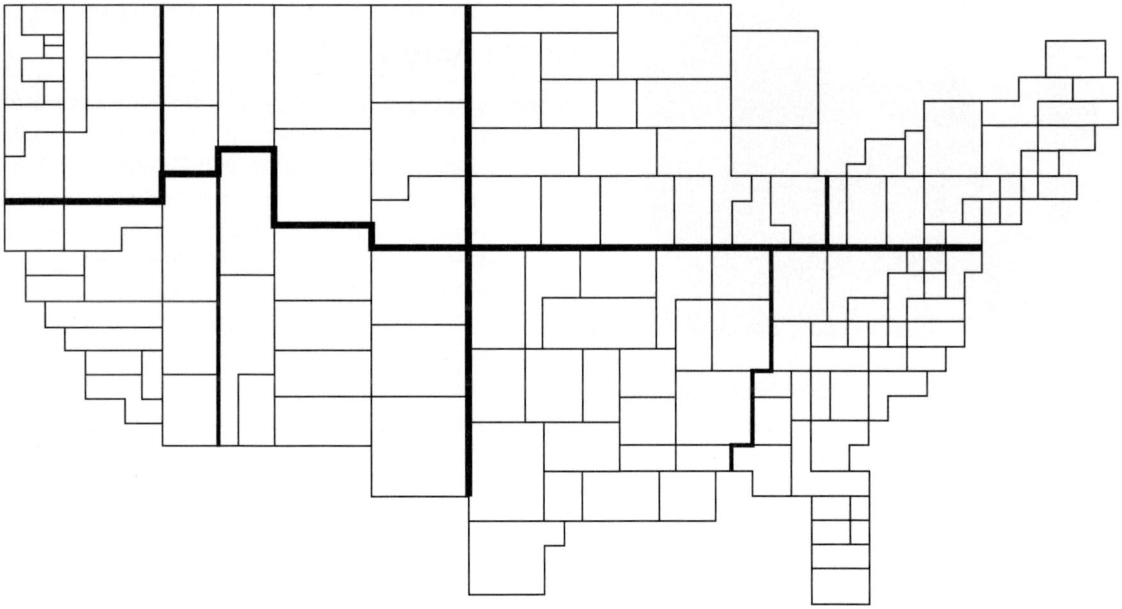

FIGURE 1 Helmert block boundaries for contiguous United States.

The database for the NAD readjustment was completed in 1983. Three years later, after extensive analysis and over 940 hours of computer processing time, the largest least-squares problem ever attempted was solved.

[1]A mathematical discussion of the Helmert blocking strategy, along with details about the entire NAD project, appears in *North American Datum of 1983*, Charles R. Schwarz (ed.), National Geodetic Survey, National Oceanic and Atmospheric Administration (NOAA) Professional Paper NOS 2, 1989.

A linear system $A\mathbf{x} = \mathbf{b}$ that arises from experimental data frequently has no solution, just as in the introductory example. Often an acceptable substitute for a solution is a vector $\hat{\mathbf{x}}$ that makes the distance between $A\hat{\mathbf{x}}$ and $\mathbf{b}$ as small as possible. The definition of distance, given in Section 7.1, involves a sum of squares, and the desired $\hat{\mathbf{x}}$ is called a *least-squares solution* of $A\mathbf{x} = \mathbf{b}$. Sections 7.1 to 7.3 develop the fundamental concepts of orthogonality and orthogonal projections, which are used in Section 7.5 to find $\hat{\mathbf{x}}$.

Section 7.4 provides another opportunity to see orthogonal projections at work, creating a matrix factorization widely used in numerical linear algebra. The remaining sections examine some of the many least-squares problems that arise in applications, including those in vector spaces more general than $\mathbb{R}^n$. In all cases, however, the scalars are real numbers.

7.1 INNER PRODUCT, LENGTH, AND ORTHOGONALITY

Geometric concepts of length, distance, and perpendicularity, which are well known for $\mathbb{R}^2$ and $\mathbb{R}^3$, are defined here for $\mathbb{R}^n$. These concepts provide powerful geometric tools for solving many applied problems, including the least-squares problems mentioned above. All three notions are defined in terms of the inner product of two vectors.

The Inner Product

If $\mathbf{u}$ and $\mathbf{v}$ are vectors in $\mathbb{R}^n$, then we regard $\mathbf{u}$ and $\mathbf{v}$ as $n \times 1$ matrices. The transpose $\mathbf{u}^T$ is a $1 \times n$ matrix, and the matrix product $\mathbf{u}^T\mathbf{v}$ is a 1×1 matrix, which we write as a single real number (a scalar) without brackets. The number $\mathbf{u}^T\mathbf{v}$ is called the **inner product** of $\mathbf{u}$ and $\mathbf{v}$, and often it is written as $\mathbf{u} \cdot \mathbf{v}$. This inner product, mentioned in the exercises for Section 3.1, is also referred to as a **dot product**. If

$$\mathbf{u} = \begin{bmatrix} u_1 \\ u_2 \\ \vdots \\ u_n \end{bmatrix}, \qquad \mathbf{v} = \begin{bmatrix} v_1 \\ v_2 \\ \vdots \\ v_n \end{bmatrix}$$

then the inner product of $\mathbf{u}$ and $\mathbf{v}$ is

$$\mathbf{u} \cdot \mathbf{v} = \mathbf{u}^T\mathbf{v} = [\, u_1 \quad u_2 \quad \cdots \quad u_n \,] \begin{bmatrix} v_1 \\ v_2 \\ \vdots \\ v_n \end{bmatrix} = u_1v_1 + u_2v_2 + \cdots + u_nv_n$$

EXAMPLE 1 Compute $\mathbf{u} \cdot \mathbf{v}$ and $\mathbf{v} \cdot \mathbf{u}$ when $\mathbf{u} = \begin{bmatrix} 2 \\ -5 \\ -1 \end{bmatrix}$ and $\mathbf{v} = \begin{bmatrix} 3 \\ 2 \\ -3 \end{bmatrix}$.

Solution $\mathbf{u} \cdot \mathbf{v} = \mathbf{u}^T\mathbf{v} = [\,2 \quad -5 \quad -1\,] \begin{bmatrix} 3 \\ 2 \\ -3 \end{bmatrix} = (2)(3) + (-5)(2) + (-1)(-3) = -1$

$$\mathbf{v} \cdot \mathbf{u} = \mathbf{v}^T\mathbf{u} = [\,3 \quad 2 \quad -3\,] \begin{bmatrix} 2 \\ -5 \\ -1 \end{bmatrix} = (3)(2) + (2)(-5) + (-3)(-1) = -1$$

It is clear from the calculations in Example 1 why $\mathbf{u} \cdot \mathbf{v} = \mathbf{v} \cdot \mathbf{u}$. This commutativity of the inner product holds in general. The following properties of the inner product are easily deduced from properties of the transpose operation in Section 3.1. (See Exercises 17 and 18.)

THEOREM 1

Let $\mathbf{u}$, $\mathbf{v}$, and $\mathbf{w}$ be vectors in $\mathbb{R}^n$, and let c be a scalar. Then

a. $\mathbf{u} \cdot \mathbf{v} = \mathbf{v} \cdot \mathbf{u}$

b. $(\mathbf{u} + \mathbf{v}) \cdot \mathbf{w} = \mathbf{u} \cdot \mathbf{w} + \mathbf{v} \cdot \mathbf{w}$

c. $(c\mathbf{u}) \cdot \mathbf{v} = c(\mathbf{u} \cdot \mathbf{v}) = \mathbf{u} \cdot (c\mathbf{v})$

d. $\mathbf{u} \cdot \mathbf{u} \geq 0$, and $\mathbf{u} \cdot \mathbf{u} = 0$ if and only if $\mathbf{u} = \mathbf{0}$.

Properties (b) and (c) can be combined several times to produce the following useful rule:

$$(c_1\mathbf{u}_1 + \cdots + c_p\mathbf{u}_p) \cdot \mathbf{w} = c_1(\mathbf{u}_1 \cdot \mathbf{w}) + \cdots + c_p(\mathbf{u}_p \cdot \mathbf{w})$$

The Length of a Vector

If $\mathbf{v}$ is in $\mathbb{R}^n$, with entries $v_1, \ldots, v_n$, then the square root of $\mathbf{v} \cdot \mathbf{v}$ is defined because $\mathbf{v} \cdot \mathbf{v}$ is nonnegative.

DEFINITION

The **length** (or **norm**) of $\mathbf{v}$ is the nonnegative scalar $\|\mathbf{v}\|$ defined by

$$\|\mathbf{v}\| = \sqrt{\mathbf{v} \cdot \mathbf{v}} = \sqrt{v_1^2 + v_2^2 + \cdots + v_n^2}, \quad \text{and} \quad \|\mathbf{v}\|^2 = \mathbf{v} \cdot \mathbf{v}$$

Suppose that $\mathbf{v}$ is in $\mathbb{R}^2$, say, $\mathbf{v} = \begin{bmatrix} v_1 \\ v_2 \end{bmatrix}$. If we identify $\mathbf{v}$ with a geometric point in the plane, as usual, then $\|\mathbf{v}\|$ coincides with the usual notion of the length of the line segment from the origin to $\mathbf{v}$. This follows from the Pythagorean theorem applied to a triangle such as the one in Fig. 1.

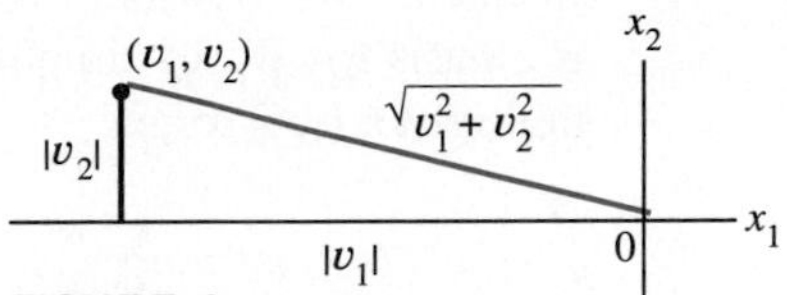

FIGURE 1 Interpretation of $\|\mathbf{v}\|$ as length.

A similar calculation with the diagonal of a rectangular box shows that the definition of length of a vector $\mathbf{v}$ in $\mathbb{R}^3$ coincides with the usual notion of length.

For any scalar c, the length of $c\mathbf{v}$ is $|c|$ times the length of $\mathbf{v}$. That is

$$\|c\mathbf{v}\| = |c|\,\|\mathbf{v}\|$$

(To see this, compute $\|c\mathbf{v}\|^2 = (c\mathbf{v})\cdot(c\mathbf{v}) = c^2\mathbf{v}\cdot\mathbf{v} = c^2\|\mathbf{v}\|^2$ and take square roots.)

A vector whose length is 1 is called a **unit vector**. If we *divide* a nonzero vector $\mathbf{v}$ by its length—that is, multiply by $1/\|\mathbf{v}\|$—we obtain a unit vector $\mathbf{u}$ because the length of $\mathbf{u}$ is $(1/\|\mathbf{v}\|)\|\mathbf{v}\|$. The process of creating $\mathbf{u}$ from $\mathbf{v}$ is sometimes called **normalizing** $\mathbf{v}$, and we say that $\mathbf{u}$ is *in the same direction* as $\mathbf{v}$.

Several examples that follow use the space-saving notation for (column) vectors.

EXAMPLE 2 Let $\mathbf{v} = (1, -2, 2, 0)$. Find a unit vector $\mathbf{u}$ in the same direction as $\mathbf{v}$.

Solution First compute the length of $\mathbf{v}$:

$$\|\mathbf{v}\|^2 = \mathbf{v}\cdot\mathbf{v} = (1)^2 + (-2)^2 + (2)^2 + (0)^2 = 9$$
$$\|\mathbf{v}\| = \sqrt{9} = 3$$

Then multiply $\mathbf{v}$ by $1/\|\mathbf{v}\|$ to obtain

$$\mathbf{u} = \frac{1}{\|\mathbf{v}\|}\mathbf{v} = \frac{1}{3}\mathbf{v} = \frac{1}{3}\begin{bmatrix} 1 \\ -2 \\ 2 \\ 0 \end{bmatrix} = \begin{bmatrix} 1/3 \\ -2/3 \\ 2/3 \\ 0 \end{bmatrix}$$

To check that $\|\mathbf{u}\| = 1$, it suffices to show that $\|\mathbf{u}\|^2 = 1$.

$$\|\mathbf{u}\|^2 = \mathbf{u}\cdot\mathbf{u} = (\tfrac{1}{3})^2 + (-\tfrac{2}{3})^2 + (\tfrac{2}{3})^2 + (0)^2$$
$$= \tfrac{1}{9} + \tfrac{4}{9} + \tfrac{4}{9} + 0 = 1$$

EXAMPLE 3 Let W be the subspace of $\mathbb{R}^2$ spanned by $\mathbf{x} = (\frac{2}{3}, 1)$. Find a unit vector $\mathbf{z}$ that is a basis for W.

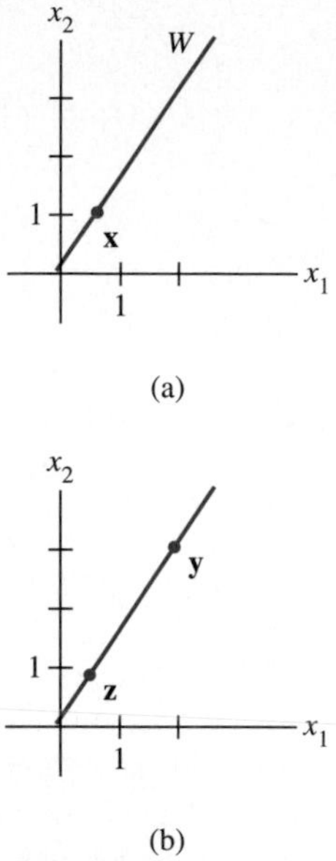

FIGURE 2 Normalizing a vector to produce a unit vector.

Solution W consists of all multiples of **x**, as in Fig. 2(a). Any nonzero vector in W is a basis for W. To simplify the calculation, "scale" **x** to eliminate fractions. That is, multiply **x** by 3 to get

$$\mathbf{y} = \begin{bmatrix} 2 \\ 3 \end{bmatrix}$$

Now compute $\|\mathbf{y}\|^2 = 2^2 + 3^2 = 13$, $\|\mathbf{y}\| = \sqrt{13}$, and normalize **y** to get

$$\mathbf{z} = \frac{1}{\sqrt{13}} \begin{bmatrix} 2 \\ 3 \end{bmatrix} = \begin{bmatrix} 2/\sqrt{13} \\ 3/\sqrt{13} \end{bmatrix}$$

See Fig. 2(b). ∎

Distance in $\mathbb{R}^n$

We are ready now to describe how close one vector is to another. Recall that if a and b are real numbers, the distance on the number line between a and b is the number $|a - b|$. Two examples are shown in Fig. 3. This definition of distance in $\mathbb{R}$ has a direct analogue in $\mathbb{R}^n$.

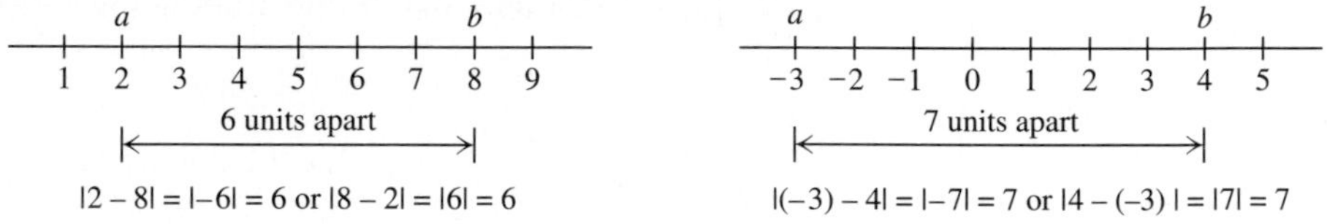

FIGURE 3 Distances in $\mathbb{R}$.

DEFINITION

For **u** and **v** in $\mathbb{R}^n$, the **distance between u and v**, written as dist(**u**, **v**), is the length of the vector $\mathbf{u} - \mathbf{v}$. That is,

$$\text{dist}(\mathbf{u}, \mathbf{v}) = \|\mathbf{u} - \mathbf{v}\|$$

In $\mathbb{R}^2$ and $\mathbb{R}^3$, this definition of distance coincides with the usual formulas for the Euclidean distance between two points, as the next two examples show.

EXAMPLE 4 Compute the distance between the vectors $\mathbf{u} = (7, 1)$ and $\mathbf{v} = (3, 2)$.

Solution Calculate

$$\mathbf{u} - \mathbf{v} = \begin{bmatrix} 7 \\ 1 \end{bmatrix} - \begin{bmatrix} 3 \\ 2 \end{bmatrix} = \begin{bmatrix} 4 \\ -1 \end{bmatrix}$$

$$\|\mathbf{u} - \mathbf{v}\| = \sqrt{4^2 + (-1)^2} = \sqrt{17}$$

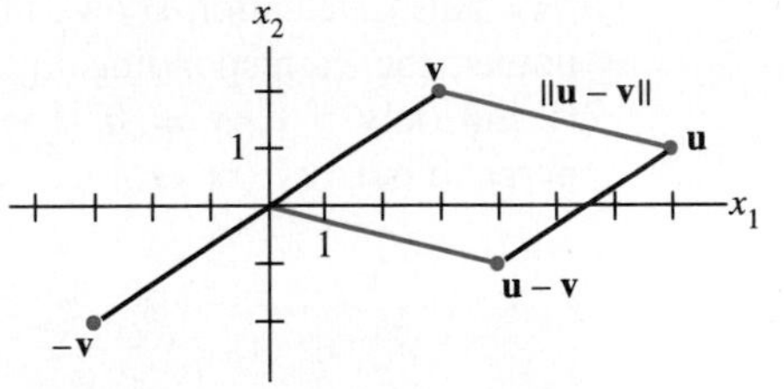

FIGURE 4 The distance between **u** and **v**.

The vectors **u**, **v** and **u** − **v** are shown in Fig. 4. When the vector **u** − **v** is added to **v** the result is **u**. Notice that the parallelogram in Fig. 4 shows that the distance from **v** to **u** is the same as the distance from **0** to **u** − **v**.

EXAMPLE 5 If $\mathbf{u} = (u_1, u_2, u_3)$ and $\mathbf{v} = (v_1, v_2, v_3)$, then

$$\begin{aligned}\operatorname{dist}(\mathbf{u}, \mathbf{v}) &= \|\mathbf{u} - \mathbf{v}\| = \sqrt{(\mathbf{u} - \mathbf{v})\cdot(\mathbf{u} - \mathbf{v})} \\ &= \sqrt{(u_1 - v_1)^2 + (u_2 - v_2)^2 + (u_3 - v_3)^2}\end{aligned}$$

Orthogonal Vectors

The rest of the chapter depends on the fact that the concept of perpendicular lines in ordinary Euclidean geometry has an analogue in $\mathbb{R}^n$.

Consider $\mathbb{R}^2$ or $\mathbb{R}^3$ and two lines through the origin determined by vectors **u** and **v**. The two lines shown in Fig. 5 are geometrically perpendicular if and only if the line through **u** is the perpendicular bisector of the line segment from −**v** to **v**. This is the same as requiring the squares of the distances from **u** to −**v** and from **u** to **v** to be equal. Now

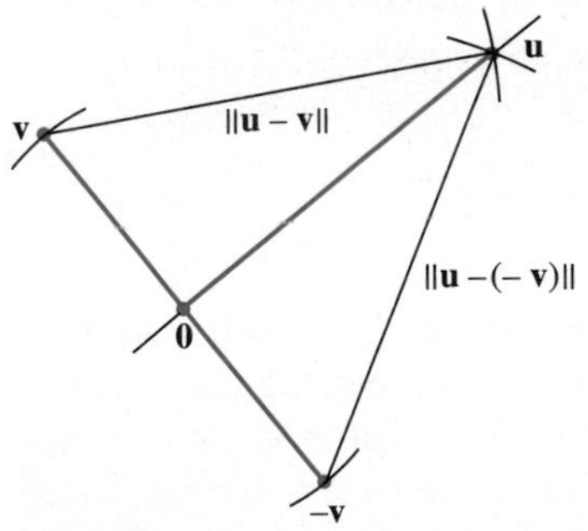

FIGURE 5

$$\begin{aligned}[\operatorname{dist}(\mathbf{u}, -\mathbf{v})]^2 &= \|\mathbf{u} - (-\mathbf{v})\|^2 = \|\mathbf{u} + \mathbf{v}\|^2 \\ &= (\mathbf{u} + \mathbf{v})\cdot(\mathbf{u} + \mathbf{v}) \\ &= \mathbf{u}\cdot(\mathbf{u} + \mathbf{v}) + \mathbf{v}\cdot(\mathbf{u} + \mathbf{v}) && \text{Theorem 1(b)} \\ &= \mathbf{u}\cdot\mathbf{u} + \mathbf{u}\cdot\mathbf{v} + \mathbf{v}\cdot\mathbf{u} + \mathbf{v}\cdot\mathbf{v} && \text{Theorem 1(a), (b)} \\ &= \|\mathbf{u}\|^2 + \|\mathbf{v}\|^2 + 2\mathbf{u}\cdot\mathbf{v} && \text{Theorem 1(a)} \quad (1)\end{aligned}$$

The same calculations with **v** and −**v** interchanged show that

$$\begin{aligned}[\operatorname{dist}(\mathbf{u}, \mathbf{v})]^2 &= \|\mathbf{u}\|^2 + \|-\mathbf{v}\|^2 + 2\mathbf{u}\cdot(-\mathbf{v}) \\ &= \|\mathbf{u}\|^2 + \|\mathbf{v}\|^2 - 2\mathbf{u}\cdot\mathbf{v}\end{aligned}$$

The two squared distances are equal if and only if $2\mathbf{u}\cdot\mathbf{v} = -2\mathbf{u}\cdot\mathbf{v}$, which happens if and only if $\mathbf{u}\cdot\mathbf{v} = 0$.

This calculation shows that when vectors $\mathbf{u}$ and $\mathbf{v}$ are identified with geometric points, the corresponding lines through the points and the origin are perpendicular if and only if $\mathbf{u} \cdot \mathbf{v} = 0$. The following definition generalizes to $\mathbb{R}^n$ this notion of perpendicularity (or *orthogonality*, as it is commonly called in linear algebra).

DEFINITION

Two vectors $\mathbf{u}$ and $\mathbf{v}$ in $\mathbb{R}^n$ are **orthogonal** (to each other) if $\mathbf{u} \cdot \mathbf{v} = 0$.

Observe that the zero vector is orthogonal to every vector in $\mathbb{R}^n$ because $\mathbf{0}^T\mathbf{v} = 0$ for all $\mathbf{v}$.

A key fact about orthogonal vectors is given in the following theorem. The proof follows immediately from the calculation in (1) above and the definition of orthogonality. The right triangle shown in Fig. 6 provides a visualization of the lengths that appear in the theorem.

THEOREM 2

The Pythagorean Theorem

Two vectors $\mathbf{u}$ and $\mathbf{v}$ are orthogonal if and only if $\|\mathbf{u}+\mathbf{v}\|^2 = \|\mathbf{u}\|^2 + \|\mathbf{v}\|^2$.

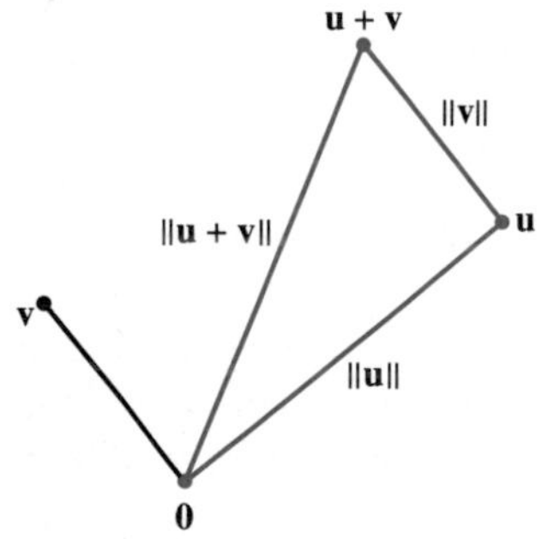

FIGURE 6

Orthogonal Complements

To provide practice using inner products, we introduce a concept now that will be of use in Section 7.3 and elsewhere in the chapter. If a vector $\mathbf{z}$ is orthogonal to every vector in a subspace W of $\mathbb{R}^n$, then $\mathbf{z}$ is said to be **orthogonal to** W. The set of all vectors $\mathbf{z}$ that are orthogonal to W is called the **orthogonal complement** of W and is denoted by $W^\perp$. (Read $W^\perp$ as "W perpendicular" or simply "W perp.")

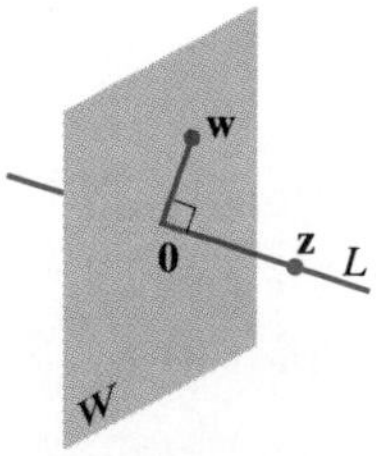

FIGURE 7 A plane and line through $\mathbf{0}$ as orthogonal complements.

EXAMPLE 6 Let W be a plane through the origin in $\mathbb{R}^3$, and let L be the line through the origin and perpendicular to W. If $\mathbf{z}$ is on L, and $\mathbf{w}$ is in W, then the line segment from $\mathbf{0}$ to $\mathbf{z}$ is perpendicular to the line segment from $\mathbf{0}$ to $\mathbf{w}$; that is, $\mathbf{z} \cdot \mathbf{w} = 0$. See Fig. 7. So each vector on L is orthogonal to every $\mathbf{w}$ in W. In fact, L consists of *all* vectors that are orthogonal to the $\mathbf{w}$'s in W, and W consists of all vectors orthogonal to the $\mathbf{z}$'s in L. That is,

$$L = W^\perp \quad \text{and} \quad W = L^\perp$$

The following two facts about $W^\perp$, with W a subspace of $\mathbb{R}^n$, are needed later in the chapter. Proofs are suggested in Exercises 29 and 30. Exercises 27–31 provide excellent practice using properties of the inner product.

1. A vector $\mathbf{x}$ is in $W^{\perp}$ if and only if $\mathbf{x}$ is orthogonal to every vector in a set that spans W.
2. $W^{\perp}$ is a subspace of $\mathbb{R}^n$.

The next theorem and Exercise 31 verify the claims made in Section 5.6 concerning the subspaces shown in Fig. 8. (Also see Exercise 28 in Section 5.6.)

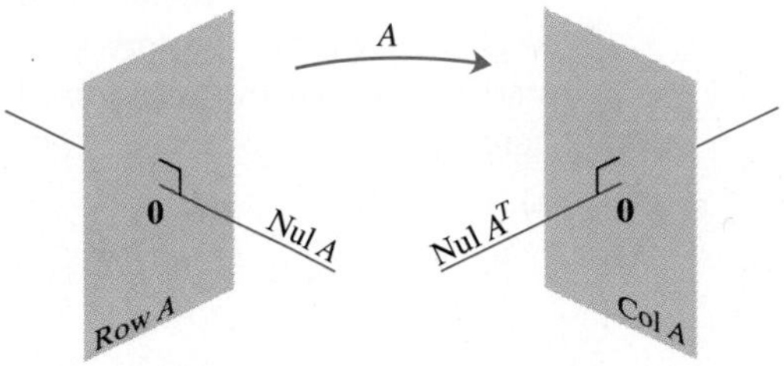

FIGURE 8 The fundamental subspaces of an $m \times n$ matrix A.

THEOREM 3

Let A be an $m \times n$ matrix. Then the orthogonal complement of the row space of A is the nullspace of A, and the orthogonal complement of the column space of A is the nullspace of A^T:

$$(\text{Row } A)^{\perp} = \text{Nul } A, \quad (\text{Col } A)^{\perp} = \text{Nul } A^T$$

Proof The row–column rule for computing $A\mathbf{x}$ shows that if $\mathbf{x}$ is in Nul A, then $\mathbf{x}$ is orthogonal to each row of A (with the rows treated as vectors in $\mathbb{R}^n$). Since the rows of A span the row space, $\mathbf{x}$ is orthogonal to Row A. Conversely, if $\mathbf{x}$ is orthogonal to Row A, then $\mathbf{x}$ is certainly orthogonal to the rows of A, and hence $A\mathbf{x} = \mathbf{0}$. This proves the first statement. The second statement follows from the first by replacing A with A^T and using the fact that Col A = Row A^T. ∎

Angles in $\mathbb{R}^2$ and $\mathbb{R}^3$ (Optional)

If $\mathbf{u}$ and $\mathbf{v}$ are nonzero vectors in either $\mathbb{R}^2$ or $\mathbb{R}^3$, then there is a nice connection between their inner product and the angle ϑ between the two line segments from the origin to the points identified with $\mathbf{u}$ and $\mathbf{v}$. The formula is

$$\mathbf{u} \cdot \mathbf{v} = \|\mathbf{u}\| \, \|\mathbf{v}\| \cos \vartheta \tag{2}$$

To verify this formula for vectors in $\mathbb{R}^2$, consider the triangle shown in Fig. 9, with sides of length $\|\mathbf{u}\|$, $\|\mathbf{v}\|$, and $\|\mathbf{u} - \mathbf{v}\|$. By the law of cosines,

$$\|\mathbf{u} - \mathbf{v}\|^2 = \|\mathbf{u}\|^2 + \|\mathbf{v}\|^2 - 2\|\mathbf{u}\|\,\|\mathbf{v}\| \cos \vartheta$$

which may be rearranged to produce

$$\begin{aligned}\|\mathbf{u}\|\,\|\mathbf{v}\|\cos\vartheta &= \frac{1}{2}\left[\|\mathbf{u}\|^2+\|\mathbf{v}\|^2-\|\mathbf{u}-\mathbf{v}\|^2\right]\\ &= \frac{1}{2}\left[u_1^2+u_2^2+v_1^2+v_2^2-(u_1-v_1)^2-(u_2-v_2)^2\right]\\ &= u_1v_1+u_2v_2\\ &= \mathbf{u}\cdot\mathbf{v}\end{aligned}$$

The verification for $\mathbb{R}^3$ is similar. When $n > 3$, formula (2) may be used to *define* the angle between two vectors in $\mathbb{R}^n$. In statistics, for instance, this angle measures what statisticians call the *covariance* of certain vectors. We shall not pursue these ideas here.

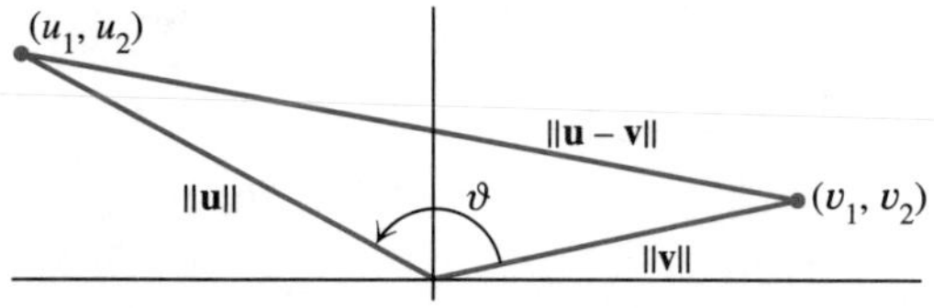

FIGURE 9 The angle between two vectors.

PRACTICE PROBLEMS

Let $\mathbf{a} = \begin{bmatrix}-2\\1\end{bmatrix}$, $\mathbf{b} = \begin{bmatrix}-3\\1\end{bmatrix}$, $\mathbf{c} = \begin{bmatrix}4/3\\-1\\2/3\end{bmatrix}$, and $\mathbf{d} = \begin{bmatrix}5\\6\\-1\end{bmatrix}$.

1. Compute $\dfrac{\mathbf{a}\cdot\mathbf{b}}{\mathbf{a}\cdot\mathbf{a}}$ and $\left(\dfrac{\mathbf{a}\cdot\mathbf{b}}{\mathbf{a}\cdot\mathbf{a}}\right)\mathbf{a}$.
2. Find a unit vector **u** in the direction of **c**.
3. Show that **d** is orthogonal to **c**.
4. Use the results of Practice Problems 2 and 3 to explain why **d** must be orthogonal to the unit vector **u**.

7.1 EXERCISES

Compute the quantities in Exercises 1–10 using the vectors

$\mathbf{u} = \begin{bmatrix}-1\\2\end{bmatrix}$, $\mathbf{v} = \begin{bmatrix}4\\6\end{bmatrix}$, $\mathbf{w} = \begin{bmatrix}3\\-1\\-5\end{bmatrix}$, $\mathbf{x} = \begin{bmatrix}6\\-2\\3\end{bmatrix}$

1. $\mathbf{u}\cdot\mathbf{u}$, $\mathbf{v}\cdot\mathbf{u}$, and $\dfrac{\mathbf{v}\cdot\mathbf{u}}{\mathbf{u}\cdot\mathbf{u}}$

2. $\mathbf{w}\cdot\mathbf{w}$, $\mathbf{x}\cdot\mathbf{w}$, and $\dfrac{\mathbf{x}\cdot\mathbf{w}}{\mathbf{w}\cdot\mathbf{w}}$

3. $\dfrac{1}{\mathbf{w}\cdot\mathbf{w}}\mathbf{w}$

4. $\dfrac{1}{\mathbf{u}\cdot\mathbf{u}}\mathbf{u}$

5. $\left(\dfrac{\mathbf{u}\cdot\mathbf{v}}{\mathbf{v}\cdot\mathbf{v}}\right)\mathbf{v}$

6. $\left(\dfrac{\mathbf{x}\cdot\mathbf{w}}{\mathbf{x}\cdot\mathbf{x}}\right)\mathbf{x}$

7. $\|\mathbf{u}\|$

8. $\|\mathbf{v}\|$

9. $\|\mathbf{w}\|$

10. $\|\mathbf{x}\|$

In Exercises 11–14, find a unit vector in the direction of the given vector.

11. $\begin{bmatrix} -30 \\ 40 \end{bmatrix}$

12. $\begin{bmatrix} -6 \\ 4 \\ -3 \end{bmatrix}$

13. $\begin{bmatrix} 7/4 \\ 1/2 \\ 1 \end{bmatrix}$

14. $\begin{bmatrix} 8/3 \\ 2 \end{bmatrix}$

15. Find the distance between $\mathbf{x} = \begin{bmatrix} 10 \\ -3 \end{bmatrix}$ and $\mathbf{y} = \begin{bmatrix} -1 \\ -5 \end{bmatrix}$.

16. Find the distance between $\mathbf{u} = \begin{bmatrix} 0 \\ -5 \\ 2 \end{bmatrix}$ and $\mathbf{z} = \begin{bmatrix} -4 \\ -1 \\ 8 \end{bmatrix}$.

17. Use the transpose definition of the inner product to verify parts (b) and (c) of Theorem 1. Mention the appropriate parts of a theorem from Chapter 3.

18. Let $\mathbf{u} = (u_1, u_2, u_3)$. Explain why $\mathbf{u} \cdot \mathbf{u} \geq 0$. When is $\mathbf{u} \cdot \mathbf{u} = 0$?

Determine which pairs of vectors in Exercises 19–22 are orthogonal.

19. $\mathbf{a} = \begin{bmatrix} 8 \\ -5 \end{bmatrix}, \mathbf{b} = \begin{bmatrix} -2 \\ -3 \end{bmatrix}$

20. $\mathbf{u} = \begin{bmatrix} 12 \\ 3 \\ -5 \end{bmatrix}, \mathbf{v} = \begin{bmatrix} 2 \\ -3 \\ 3 \end{bmatrix}$

21. $\mathbf{u} = \begin{bmatrix} 3 \\ 2 \\ -5 \\ 0 \end{bmatrix}, \mathbf{v} = \begin{bmatrix} -4 \\ 1 \\ -2 \\ 6 \end{bmatrix}$

22. $\mathbf{y} = \begin{bmatrix} -3 \\ 7 \\ 4 \\ 0 \end{bmatrix}, \mathbf{z} = \begin{bmatrix} 1 \\ -8 \\ 15 \\ -7 \end{bmatrix}$

23. Let $\mathbf{u} = \begin{bmatrix} 2 \\ -5 \\ -1 \end{bmatrix}$ and $\mathbf{v} = \begin{bmatrix} -7 \\ -4 \\ 6 \end{bmatrix}$. Compute and compare $\mathbf{u} \cdot \mathbf{v}$, $\|\mathbf{u}\|^2$, $\|\mathbf{v}\|^2$, and $\|\mathbf{u}+\mathbf{v}\|^2$. Do not use the Pythagorean theorem.

24. Verify the *parallelogram law* for vectors $\mathbf{u}$ and $\mathbf{v}$ in $\mathbb{R}^n$:

$$\|\mathbf{u}+\mathbf{v}\|^2 + \|\mathbf{u}-\mathbf{v}\|^2 = 2\|\mathbf{u}\|^2 + 2\|\mathbf{v}\|^2$$

25. Let $\mathbf{v} = \begin{bmatrix} a \\ b \end{bmatrix}$. Describe the set H of vectors $\begin{bmatrix} x \\ y \end{bmatrix}$ that are orthogonal to $\mathbf{v}$. [*Hint*: If $\mathbf{v} = \mathbf{0}$, then H is $\mathbb{R}^2$. If $\mathbf{v} \neq \mathbf{0}$, find a basis for H by inspection.]

26. Let $\mathbf{u} = \begin{bmatrix} 5 \\ -6 \\ 7 \end{bmatrix}$, and let W be the set of all $\mathbf{x}$ in $\mathbb{R}^3$ such that $\mathbf{u} \cdot \mathbf{x} = 0$. What theorem in Chapter 5 can be used to show that W is a subspace of $\mathbb{R}^3$? Describe W in geometric language.

27. Suppose that a vector $\mathbf{y}$ is orthogonal to vectors $\mathbf{u}$ and $\mathbf{v}$. Show that $\mathbf{y}$ is orthogonal to the vector $\mathbf{u} + \mathbf{v}$.

28. Suppose that $\mathbf{y}$ is orthogonal to $\mathbf{u}$ and $\mathbf{v}$. Show that $\mathbf{y}$ is orthogonal to every $\mathbf{w}$ in Span$\{\mathbf{u}, \mathbf{v}\}$. [*Hint*: An arbitrary $\mathbf{w}$ in Span$\{\mathbf{u}, \mathbf{v}\}$ has the form $\mathbf{w} = c_1\mathbf{u} + c_2\mathbf{v}$. Show that $\mathbf{y}$ is orthogonal to such a $\mathbf{w}$.]

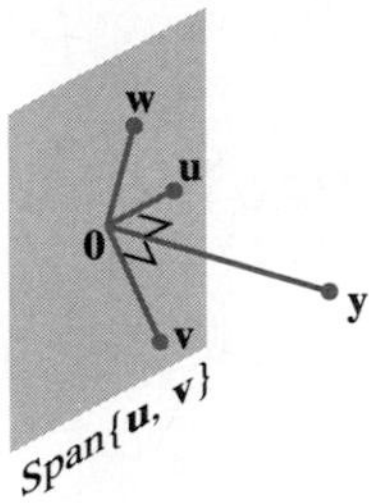

29. Let $W = \text{Span}\{\mathbf{v}_1, \ldots, \mathbf{v}_p\}$. Show that if $\mathbf{x}$ is orthogonal to each $\mathbf{v}_j$, for $1 \leq j \leq p$, then $\mathbf{x}$ is orthogonal to every vector in W.

30. Let W be a subspace of $\mathbb{R}^n$, and let $W^\perp$ be the set of all vectors orthogonal to W. Show that $W^\perp$ is a subspace of $\mathbb{R}^n$ using the following steps.

a. Take $\mathbf{z}$ in $W^\perp$ and let $\mathbf{u}$ represent any element of W. Then $\mathbf{z} \cdot \mathbf{u} = 0$. Take any scalar c and show that $c\mathbf{z}$ is orthogonal to $\mathbf{u}$. (Since $\mathbf{u}$ was an arbitrary element of W, this will show that $c\mathbf{z}$ is in $W^\perp$.)

b. Take $\mathbf{z}_1$ and $\mathbf{z}_2$ in $W^\perp$, and let $\mathbf{u}$ be any element of W. Show that $\mathbf{z}_1 + \mathbf{z}_2$ is orthogonal to $\mathbf{u}$. What can you conclude about $\mathbf{z}_1 + \mathbf{z}_2$? Why?

c. Finish the proof that $W^\perp$ is a subspace of $\mathbb{R}$.

31. Show that if $\mathbf{x}$ is in both W and $W^\perp$, then $\mathbf{x} = \mathbf{0}$.

SOLUTIONS TO PRACTICE PROBLEMS

1. $\mathbf{a} \cdot \mathbf{b} = 7, \mathbf{a} \cdot \mathbf{a} = 5$. Hence $\dfrac{\mathbf{a} \cdot \mathbf{b}}{\mathbf{a} \cdot \mathbf{a}} = \dfrac{7}{5}$, and $\left(\dfrac{\mathbf{a} \cdot \mathbf{b}}{\mathbf{a} \cdot \mathbf{a}}\right)\mathbf{a} = \dfrac{7}{5}\mathbf{a} = \begin{bmatrix} -14/5 \\ 7/5 \end{bmatrix}$.

2. Scale **c**, multiplying by 3 to get $\mathbf{y} = \begin{bmatrix} 4 \\ -3 \\ 2 \end{bmatrix}$. Compute $\|\mathbf{y}\|^2 = 29$ and $\|\mathbf{y}\| = \sqrt{29}$.

The unit vector in the direction of both **c** and **y** is $\mathbf{u} = \dfrac{1}{\|\mathbf{y}\|}\mathbf{y} = \begin{bmatrix} 4/\sqrt{29} \\ -3/\sqrt{29} \\ 2/\sqrt{29} \end{bmatrix}$.

3. **d** is orthogonal to **c**, because

$$\mathbf{d}\cdot\mathbf{c} = \begin{bmatrix} 5 \\ 6 \\ -1 \end{bmatrix} \cdot \begin{bmatrix} 4/3 \\ -1 \\ 2/3 \end{bmatrix} = \frac{20}{3} - 6 - \frac{2}{3} = 0$$

4. **d** is orthogonal to **u** because **u** has the form $k\mathbf{c}$ for some k, and

$$\mathbf{d}\cdot\mathbf{u} = \mathbf{d}\cdot(k\mathbf{c}) = k(\mathbf{d}\cdot\mathbf{c}) = k(0) = 0$$

7.2 ORTHOGONAL SETS

A set of vectors $\{\mathbf{u}_1, \ldots, \mathbf{u}_p\}$ in $\mathbb{R}^n$ is said to be an **orthogonal set** if each pair of distinct vectors from the set is orthogonal, that is, if $\mathbf{u}_i \cdot \mathbf{u}_j = 0$ whenever $i \neq j$.

EXAMPLE 1 Show that $\{\mathbf{u}_1, \mathbf{u}_2, \mathbf{u}_3\}$ is an orthogonal set, where

$$\mathbf{u}_1 = \begin{bmatrix} 3 \\ 1 \\ 1 \end{bmatrix}, \quad \mathbf{u}_2 = \begin{bmatrix} -1 \\ 2 \\ 1 \end{bmatrix}, \quad \mathbf{u}_3 = \begin{bmatrix} -1/2 \\ -2 \\ 7/2 \end{bmatrix}$$

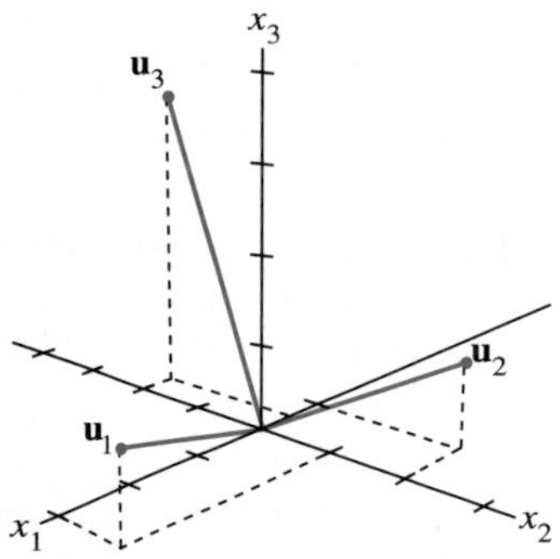

FIGURE 1

Solution Consider the three possible pairs of distinct vectors, namely, $\{\mathbf{u}_1, \mathbf{u}_2\}$, $\{\mathbf{u}_1, \mathbf{u}_3\}$, and $\{\mathbf{u}_2, \mathbf{u}_3\}$.

$$\mathbf{u}_1 \cdot \mathbf{u}_2 = 3(-1) + 1(2) + 1(1) = 0$$
$$\mathbf{u}_1 \cdot \mathbf{u}_3 = 3\left(-\tfrac{1}{2}\right) + 1(-2) + 1\left(\tfrac{7}{2}\right) = 0$$
$$\mathbf{u}_2 \cdot \mathbf{u}_3 = -1\left(-\tfrac{1}{2}\right) + 2(-2) + 1\left(\tfrac{7}{2}\right) = 0$$

Each pair of distinct vectors is orthogonal, and so $\{\mathbf{u}_1, \mathbf{u}_2, \mathbf{u}_3\}$ is an orthogonal set. See Fig. 1.

THEOREM 4

If $S = \{\mathbf{u}_1, \ldots, \mathbf{u}_p\}$ is an orthogonal set of nonzero vectors in $\mathbb{R}^n$, then S is linearly independent and hence is a basis for the subspace spanned by S.

Proof If $\mathbf{0} = c_1\mathbf{u}_1 + \cdots + c_p\mathbf{u}_p$ for some scalars $c_1, \ldots, c_p$, then

$$\begin{aligned} 0 = \mathbf{0}\cdot\mathbf{u}_1 &= (c_1\mathbf{u}_1 + c_2\mathbf{u}_2 + \cdots + c_p\mathbf{u}_p)\cdot\mathbf{u}_1 \\ &= (c_1\mathbf{u}_1)\cdot\mathbf{u}_1 + (c_2\mathbf{u}_2)\cdot\mathbf{u}_1 + \cdots + (c_p\mathbf{u}_p)\cdot\mathbf{u}_1 \end{aligned}$$

$$= c_1(\mathbf{u}_1 \cdot \mathbf{u}_1) + c_2(\mathbf{u}_2 \cdot \mathbf{u}_1) + \cdots + c_p(\mathbf{u}_p \cdot \mathbf{u}_1)$$
$$= c_1(\mathbf{u}_1 \cdot \mathbf{u}_1)$$

because $\mathbf{u}_1$ is orthogonal to $\mathbf{u}_2, \ldots, \mathbf{u}_p$. Since $\mathbf{u}_1$ is nonzero, $\mathbf{u}_1 \cdot \mathbf{u}_1$ is not zero and so $c_1 = 0$. Similarly, $c_2, \ldots, c_p$ must be zero. Thus S is linearly independent. ∎

Let S be an orthogonal set of nonzero vectors in $\mathbb{R}^n$, and let W be the subspace spanned by S. Then S is called an **orthogonal basis** for W because it is both an orthogonal set and a basis for W. If there are n vectors in S, then $W = \mathbb{R}^n$ (by Theorem 13 in Section 5.5) and S is an orthogonal basis for $\mathbb{R}^n$. The next theorem suggests why an orthogonal basis is much nicer than other bases: The weights in a linear combination can be computed very quickly.

THEOREM 5

Let $\{\mathbf{u}_1, \ldots, \mathbf{u}_p\}$ be an orthogonal basis for a subspace W of $\mathbb{R}^n$. Then each $\mathbf{y}$ in W has a unique representation as a linear combination of $\mathbf{u}_1, \ldots, \mathbf{u}_p$. In fact, if

$$\mathbf{y} = c_1\mathbf{u}_1 + \cdots + c_p\mathbf{u}_p$$

then

$$c_j = \frac{\mathbf{y} \cdot \mathbf{u}_j}{\mathbf{u}_j \cdot \mathbf{u}_j} \qquad (j = 1, \ldots, p)$$

Proof As in the preceding proof, the orthogonality of $\{\mathbf{u}_1, \ldots, \mathbf{u}_p\}$ shows that

$$\mathbf{y} \cdot \mathbf{u}_1 = (c_1\mathbf{u}_1 + c_2\mathbf{u}_2 + \cdots + c_p\mathbf{u}_p) \cdot \mathbf{u}_1 = c_1(\mathbf{u}_1 \cdot \mathbf{u}_1)$$

Since $\mathbf{u}_1 \cdot \mathbf{u}_1$ is not zero, the equation above may be solved for c_1. To find c_j for $j = 2, \ldots, p$, compute $\mathbf{y} \cdot \mathbf{u}_j$ and solve for c_j. ∎

EXAMPLE 2 The set $S = \{\mathbf{u}_1, \mathbf{u}_2, \mathbf{u}_3\}$ in Example 1 is an orthogonal basis for $\mathbb{R}^3$. Express the vector $\mathbf{y} = \begin{bmatrix} 6 \\ 1 \\ -8 \end{bmatrix}$ as a linear combination of the vectors in S.

Solution Compute

$$\begin{aligned} \mathbf{y} \cdot \mathbf{u}_1 &= 11, & \mathbf{y} \cdot \mathbf{u}_2 &= -12, & \mathbf{y} \cdot \mathbf{u}_3 &= -33 \\ \mathbf{u}_1 \cdot \mathbf{u}_1 &= 11, & \mathbf{u}_2 \cdot \mathbf{u}_2 &= 6, & \mathbf{u}_3 \cdot \mathbf{u}_3 &= 33/2 \end{aligned}$$

By Theorem 5,

$$\begin{aligned} \mathbf{y} &= \frac{\mathbf{y} \cdot \mathbf{u}_1}{\mathbf{u}_1 \cdot \mathbf{u}_1}\mathbf{u}_1 + \frac{\mathbf{y} \cdot \mathbf{u}_2}{\mathbf{u}_2 \cdot \mathbf{u}_2}\mathbf{u}_2 + \frac{\mathbf{y} \cdot \mathbf{u}_3}{\mathbf{u}_3 \cdot \mathbf{u}_3}\mathbf{u}_3 \\ &= \frac{11}{11}\mathbf{u}_1 + \frac{-12}{6}\mathbf{u}_2 + \frac{-33}{33/2}\mathbf{u}_3 \\ &= \mathbf{u}_1 - 2\mathbf{u}_2 - 2\mathbf{u}_3 \end{aligned}$$

∎

Notice how easy it is to compute the weights needed to build $\mathbf{y}$ from an orthogonal basis. If the basis were not orthogonal, it would be necessary to solve a system of linear equations to find the weights, as in Chapter 2.

Orthonormal Sets

A set $\{\mathbf{u}_1, \ldots, \mathbf{u}_p\}$ is an **orthonormal set** if it is an orthogonal set of unit vectors. If W is the subspace spanned by such a set, then $\{\mathbf{u}_1, \ldots, \mathbf{u}_p\}$ is an **orthonormal basis** for W, since the set is automatically linearly independent, by Theorem 4.

The simplest example of an orthonormal set is the standard basis $\{\mathbf{e}_1, \ldots, \mathbf{e}_n\}$ for $\mathbb{R}^n$. Any subset of $\{\mathbf{e}_1, \ldots, \mathbf{e}_n\}$ is orthonormal, too. Here is a more complicated example.

EXAMPLE 3 Show that $\{\mathbf{v}_1, \mathbf{v}_2, \mathbf{v}_3\}$ is an orthonormal basis of $\mathbb{R}^3$, where

$$\mathbf{v}_1 = \begin{bmatrix} 3/\sqrt{11} \\ 1/\sqrt{11} \\ 1/\sqrt{11} \end{bmatrix}, \quad \mathbf{v}_2 = \begin{bmatrix} -1/\sqrt{6} \\ 2/\sqrt{6} \\ 1/\sqrt{6} \end{bmatrix}, \quad \mathbf{v}_3 = \begin{bmatrix} -1/\sqrt{66} \\ -4/\sqrt{66} \\ 7/\sqrt{66} \end{bmatrix}$$

Solution Compute

$$\begin{aligned}
\mathbf{v}_1 \cdot \mathbf{v}_2 &= -3/\sqrt{66} + 2/\sqrt{66} + 1/\sqrt{66} = 0 \\
\mathbf{v}_1 \cdot \mathbf{v}_3 &= -3/\sqrt{726} - 4/\sqrt{726} + 7/\sqrt{726} = 0 \\
\mathbf{v}_2 \cdot \mathbf{v}_3 &= 1/\sqrt{396} - 8/\sqrt{396} + 7/\sqrt{396} = 0
\end{aligned}$$

Thus $\{\mathbf{v}_1, \mathbf{v}_2, \mathbf{v}_3\}$ is an orthogonal set. Also,

$$\begin{aligned}
\mathbf{v}_1 \cdot \mathbf{v}_1 &= 9/11 + 1/11 + 1/11 = 1 \\
\mathbf{v}_2 \cdot \mathbf{v}_2 &= 1/6 + 4/6 + 1/6 = 1 \\
\mathbf{v}_3 \cdot \mathbf{v}_3 &= 1/66 + 16/66 + 49/66 = 1
\end{aligned}$$

which shows that $\mathbf{v}_1$, $\mathbf{v}_2$, and $\mathbf{v}_3$ are unit vectors. Thus $\{\mathbf{v}_1, \mathbf{v}_2, \mathbf{v}_3\}$ is an orthonormal set. Since the set is linearly independent, its three vectors form a basis for $\mathbb{R}^3$. See Fig. 2.

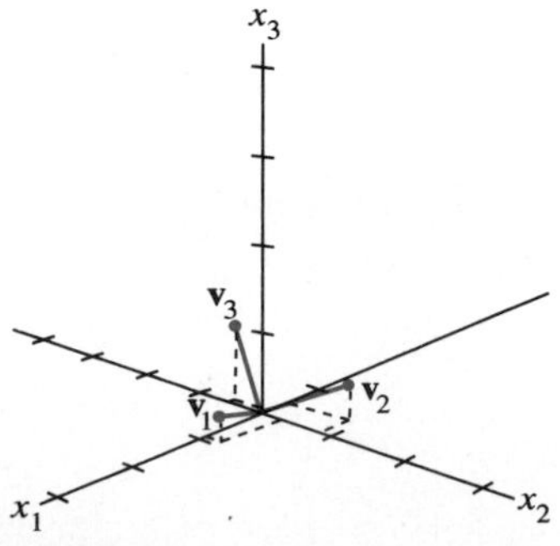

FIGURE 2

When the vectors in an orthogonal set are "normalized" to have unit length, the new vectors will still be orthogonal, and hence the new set will be an orthonormal set. See Exercise 24. It is easy to check that the vectors in Example 3 are simply the unit vectors in the directions of the vectors in Example 1.

Matrices whose columns form an orthonormal set are important in applications and in computer algorithms for matrix computations. Their main properties are given in Theorems 6 and 7.

THEOREM 6

An $m \times n$ matrix U has orthonormal columns if and only if $U^TU = I$.

Proof To simplify notation, we suppose that U has only three columns, each a vector in $\mathbb{R}^m$. The proof of the general case is essentially the same. Let $U = [\,\mathbf{u}_1 \quad \mathbf{u}_2 \quad \mathbf{u}_3\,]$ and compute

$$U^TU = \begin{bmatrix} \mathbf{u}_1^T \\ \mathbf{u}_2^T \\ \mathbf{u}_3^T \end{bmatrix} [\,\mathbf{u}_1 \quad \mathbf{u}_2 \quad \mathbf{u}_3\,] = \begin{bmatrix} \mathbf{u}_1^T\mathbf{u}_1 & \mathbf{u}_1^T\mathbf{u}_2 & \mathbf{u}_1^T\mathbf{u}_3 \\ \mathbf{u}_2^T\mathbf{u}_1 & \mathbf{u}_2^T\mathbf{u}_2 & \mathbf{u}_2^T\mathbf{u}_3 \\ \mathbf{u}_3^T\mathbf{u}_1 & \mathbf{u}_3^T\mathbf{u}_2 & \mathbf{u}_3^T\mathbf{u}_3 \end{bmatrix} \tag{1}$$

The entries in the matrix at the right are inner products, using transpose notation. The columns of U are orthogonal if and only if

$$\mathbf{u}_1^T\mathbf{u}_2 = \mathbf{u}_2^T\mathbf{u}_1 = 0, \quad \mathbf{u}_1^T\mathbf{u}_3 = \mathbf{u}_3^T\mathbf{u}_1 = 0, \quad \mathbf{u}_2^T\mathbf{u}_3 = \mathbf{u}_3^T\mathbf{u}_2 = 0 \tag{2}$$

The columns of U all have unit length if and only if

$$\mathbf{u}_1^T\mathbf{u}_1 = 1, \quad \mathbf{u}_2^T\mathbf{u}_2 = 1, \quad \mathbf{u}_3^T\mathbf{u}_3 = 1 \tag{3}$$

The theorem follows immediately from (1)–(3). ∎

THEOREM 7

Let U be an $m \times n$ matrix with orthonormal columns, and let $\mathbf{x}$ and $\mathbf{y}$ be in $\mathbb{R}^n$. Then

a. $\|U\mathbf{x}\| = \|\mathbf{x}\|$
b. $(U\mathbf{x}) \cdot (U\mathbf{y}) = \mathbf{x} \cdot \mathbf{y}$
c. $(U\mathbf{x}) \cdot (U\mathbf{y}) = 0$ if and only if $\mathbf{x} \cdot \mathbf{y} = 0$.

Properties (a) and (c) say that the linear mapping $\mathbf{x} \mapsto U\mathbf{x}$ preserves lengths and orthogonality. This property is crucial for many computer algorithms. See Exercises 25 and 26 for the proof.

EXAMPLE 4 Let $U = \begin{bmatrix} 1/\sqrt{2} & 2/3 \\ 1/\sqrt{2} & -2/3 \\ 0 & 1/3 \end{bmatrix}$ and $\mathbf{x} = \begin{bmatrix} \sqrt{2} \\ 3 \end{bmatrix}$. Notice that U has orthonormal columns and

$$U^TU = \begin{bmatrix} 1/\sqrt{2} & 1/\sqrt{2} & 0 \\ 2/3 & -2/3 & 1/3 \end{bmatrix} \begin{bmatrix} 1/\sqrt{2} & 2/3 \\ 1/\sqrt{2} & -2/3 \\ 0 & 1/3 \end{bmatrix} = \begin{bmatrix} 1 & 0 \\ 0 & 1 \end{bmatrix}$$

Verify that $\|U\mathbf{x}\| = \|\mathbf{x}\|$.

Solution

$$U\mathbf{x} = \begin{bmatrix} 1/\sqrt{2} & 2/3 \\ 1/\sqrt{2} & -2/3 \\ 0 & 1/3 \end{bmatrix} \begin{bmatrix} \sqrt{2} \\ 3 \end{bmatrix} = \begin{bmatrix} 3 \\ -1 \\ 1 \end{bmatrix}$$

$$\|U\mathbf{x}\| = \sqrt{9+1+1} = \sqrt{11}$$

$$\|\mathbf{x}\| = \sqrt{2+9} = \sqrt{11}$$

Theorems 5 and 6 are particularly useful when applied to *square* matrices. An **orthogonal matrix** is a square invertible matrix U such that $U^{-1} = U^T$. By Theorem 6, such a matrix has orthonormal columns.[1] It is easy to see that any *square* matrix with orthonormal columns is an orthogonal matrix. Surprisingly, such a matrix must have orthonormal *rows*, too. See Exercises 27 and 28. Orthogonal matrices will be used extensively in Chapter 8.

EXAMPLE 5 The matrix

$$U = \begin{bmatrix} 3/\sqrt{11} & -1/\sqrt{6} & -1/\sqrt{66} \\ 1/\sqrt{11} & 2/\sqrt{6} & -4/\sqrt{66} \\ 1/\sqrt{11} & 1/\sqrt{6} & 7/\sqrt{66} \end{bmatrix}$$

is an orthogonal matrix because it is square and its columns are orthonormal, by Example 3.

We turn next to a construction that will become a key step in many calculations involving orthogonality, and it will lead to a geometric interpretation of Theorem 5.

An Orthogonal Projection

Given nonzero vectors $\mathbf{u}$ and $\mathbf{y}$ in $\mathbb{R}^n$, consider the problem of decomposing $\mathbf{y}$ into the sum of two vectors, one a multiple of $\mathbf{u}$ and the other orthogonal to $\mathbf{u}$. We wish to write

$$\mathbf{y} = \hat{\mathbf{y}} + \mathbf{z} \tag{4}$$

[1] A better name might be *orthonormal matrix*, a term found in some statistics texts. However, *orthogonal matrix* is the standard term in linear algebra.

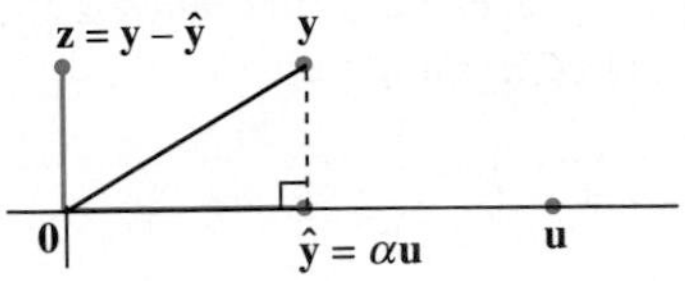

FIGURE 3 Finding α to make $\mathbf{y} - \hat{\mathbf{y}}$ orthogonal to $\mathbf{u}$.

where $\hat{\mathbf{y}} = \alpha\mathbf{u}$ for some scalar α and $\mathbf{z}$ is some vector orthogonal to $\mathbf{u}$. See Fig. 3. Given any scalar α, let $\mathbf{z} = \mathbf{y} - \alpha\mathbf{u}$, so that (4) is satisfied. Then $\mathbf{y} - \hat{\mathbf{y}}$ is orthogonal to $\mathbf{u}$ if and only if

$$0 = (\mathbf{y} - \alpha\mathbf{u}) \cdot \mathbf{u} = \mathbf{y} \cdot \mathbf{u} - (\alpha\mathbf{u}) \cdot \mathbf{u} = \mathbf{y} \cdot \mathbf{u} - \alpha(\mathbf{u} \cdot \mathbf{u})$$

That is, (4) is satisfied with $\mathbf{z}$ orthogonal to $\mathbf{u}$ if and only $\alpha = \dfrac{\mathbf{y} \cdot \mathbf{u}}{\mathbf{u} \cdot \mathbf{u}}$ and $\hat{\mathbf{y}} = \dfrac{\mathbf{y} \cdot \mathbf{u}}{\mathbf{u} \cdot \mathbf{u}}\mathbf{u}$. The following terminology will be useful later.

$$\hat{\mathbf{y}} = \frac{\mathbf{y} \cdot \mathbf{u}}{\mathbf{u} \cdot \mathbf{u}}\mathbf{u} \quad \text{is the } \textbf{orthogonal projection of y onto u} \tag{5}$$

and

$$\mathbf{z} = \mathbf{y} - \frac{\mathbf{y} \cdot \mathbf{u}}{\mathbf{u} \cdot \mathbf{u}}\mathbf{u} \quad \text{is the } \textbf{component of y orthogonal to u}$$

If c is any nonzero scalar and if $\mathbf{u}$ is replaced by $c\mathbf{u}$ in the definition of $\hat{\mathbf{y}}$, then the orthogonal projection of $\mathbf{y}$ onto $c\mathbf{u}$ is exactly the same as the orthogonal projection of $\mathbf{y}$ onto $\mathbf{u}$ (Exercise 23). Hence this projection is determined by the *subspace* Span $\{\mathbf{u}\}$, and we may call $\hat{\mathbf{y}}$ the **orthogonal projection onto** Span $\{\mathbf{u}\}$.

EXAMPLE 6 Let $\mathbf{y} = \begin{bmatrix} 7 \\ 6 \end{bmatrix}$ and $\mathbf{u} = \begin{bmatrix} 4 \\ 2 \end{bmatrix}$. Find the orthogonal projection of $\mathbf{y}$ onto $\mathbf{u}$. Then write $\mathbf{y}$ as the sum of two orthogonal vectors, one in Span $\{\mathbf{u}\}$ and one orthogonal to $\mathbf{u}$.

Solution Compute

$$\mathbf{y} \cdot \mathbf{u} = \begin{bmatrix} 7 \\ 6 \end{bmatrix} \cdot \begin{bmatrix} 4 \\ 2 \end{bmatrix} = 40$$

$$\mathbf{u} \cdot \mathbf{u} = \begin{bmatrix} 4 \\ 2 \end{bmatrix} \cdot \begin{bmatrix} 4 \\ 2 \end{bmatrix} = 20$$

The orthogonal projection of $\mathbf{y}$ onto $\mathbf{u}$ is

$$\hat{\mathbf{y}} = \frac{\mathbf{y} \cdot \mathbf{u}}{\mathbf{u} \cdot \mathbf{u}}\mathbf{u} = \frac{40}{20}\mathbf{u} = 2\begin{bmatrix} 4 \\ 2 \end{bmatrix} = \begin{bmatrix} 8 \\ 4 \end{bmatrix}$$

and the component of $\mathbf{y}$ orthogonal to $\mathbf{u}$ is

$$\mathbf{y} - \hat{\mathbf{y}} = \begin{bmatrix} 7 \\ 6 \end{bmatrix} - \begin{bmatrix} 8 \\ 4 \end{bmatrix} = \begin{bmatrix} -1 \\ 2 \end{bmatrix}$$

The sum of these two vectors is $\mathbf{y}$. That is,

$$\underset{\substack{\uparrow \\ \mathrm{y}}}{\begin{bmatrix} 7 \\ 6 \end{bmatrix}} = \underset{\substack{\uparrow \\ \hat{\mathrm{y}}}}{\begin{bmatrix} 8 \\ 4 \end{bmatrix}} + \underset{\substack{\uparrow \\ (\mathrm{y} - \hat{\mathrm{y}})}}{\begin{bmatrix} -1 \\ 2 \end{bmatrix}}$$

This decomposition of $\mathbf{y}$ is illustrated in Fig. 4. *Note*: If the calculations above are correct, then $\{\hat{\mathbf{y}}, \mathbf{y} - \hat{\mathbf{y}}\}$ will be an orthogonal set. As a check, compute

$$\hat{\mathbf{y}} \cdot (\mathbf{y} - \hat{\mathbf{y}}) = \begin{bmatrix} 8 \\ 4 \end{bmatrix} \cdot \begin{bmatrix} -1 \\ 2 \end{bmatrix} = -8 + 8 = 0$$

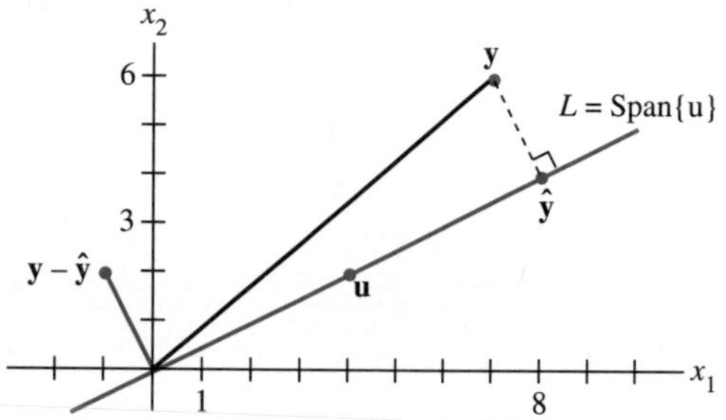

FIGURE 4 The orthogonal projection of $\mathbf{y}$ onto a line through the origin.

Since the line segment in Fig. 4 between $\mathbf{y}$ and $\hat{\mathbf{y}}$ is perpendicular to L, by construction of $\hat{\mathbf{y}}$, the point identified with $\hat{\mathbf{y}}$ is the closest point of L to $\mathbf{y}$. (This can be proved from geometry. We will assume this now for $\mathbb{R}^2$ and prove it for $\mathbb{R}^n$ in Section 7.3.)

EXAMPLE 7 Find the distance in Fig. 4 from $\mathbf{y}$ to L.

Solution The distance from $\mathbf{y}$ to L is the length of the perpendicular line segment from $\mathbf{y}$ to the orthogonal projection $\hat{\mathbf{y}}$. This length equals the length of $\mathbf{y} - \hat{\mathbf{y}}$. Thus the distance is

$$\|\mathbf{y} - \hat{\mathbf{y}}\| = \sqrt{(-1)^2 + 2^2} = \sqrt{5}$$

We conclude this section with two remarks that relate orthogonal projections to Theorem 5 and to an important problem in physics.

A Geometric Interpretation of Theorem 5

The formula for the orthogonal projection $\hat{\mathbf{y}}$ in (5) has the same appearance as each of the terms in Theorem 5. Thus Theorem 5 decomposes a vector $\mathbf{y}$ into a sum of orthogonal projections onto one-dimensional subspaces.

It is easy to visualize the case in which $W = \mathbb{R}^2 = \text{Span}\{\mathbf{u}_1, \mathbf{u}_2\}$, with $\mathbf{u}_1$ and $\mathbf{u}_2$ orthogonal. Any $\mathbf{y}$ in $\mathbb{R}^2$ can be written in the form

$$\mathbf{y} = \frac{\mathbf{y} \cdot \mathbf{u}_1}{\mathbf{u}_1 \cdot \mathbf{u}_1}\mathbf{u}_1 + \frac{\mathbf{y} \cdot \mathbf{u}_2}{\mathbf{u}_2 \cdot \mathbf{u}_2}\mathbf{u}_2 \tag{6}$$

The first term in (6) is the projection of $\mathbf{y}$ onto the subspace spanned by $\mathbf{u}_1$ (the line through $\mathbf{u}_1$ and the origin), and the second term is the projection of $\mathbf{y}$ onto the subspace spanned by $\mathbf{u}_2$. Thus (6) expresses $\mathbf{y}$ as the sum of its projections onto the (orthogonal) axes determined by $\mathbf{u}_1$ and $\mathbf{u}_2$. See Fig. 5.

Theorem 5 decomposes each $\mathbf{y}$ in Span$\{\mathbf{u}_1, \ldots, \mathbf{u}_p\}$ into the sum of p projections onto one-dimensional subspaces.

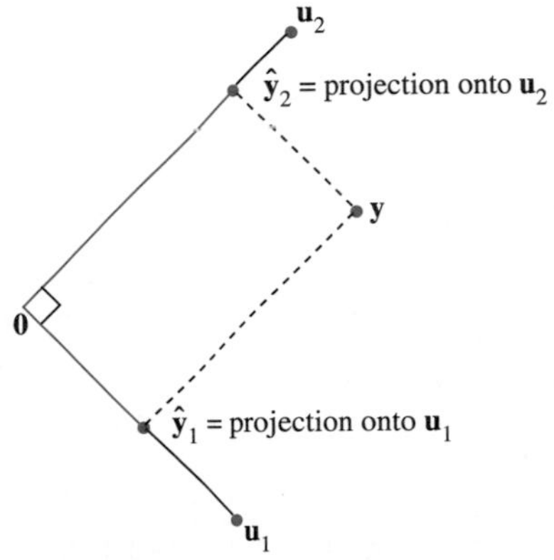

FIGURE 5 A vector decomposed into the sum of two projections.

Decomposing a Force into Component Forces

A common problem in physics is to study the effect of some sort of force on an object. By choosing an appropriate coordinate system, the force is represented by a vector $\mathbf{y}$ in $\mathbb{R}^2$ or $\mathbb{R}^3$. Often the problem involves some particular direction of interest, which is represented by another vector $\mathbf{u}$. For instance, if the object is moving in a straight line when the force is applied, the vector $\mathbf{u}$ might point in the direction of movement, as in Fig. 6. A key step in the problem is to decompose the force into a component in the direction of $\mathbf{u}$ and a component orthogonal to $\mathbf{u}$. The calculations would be analogous to those made in Example 6 above.

FIGURE 6

PRACTICE PROBLEMS

1. Let $\mathbf{u}_1 = \begin{bmatrix} -1/\sqrt{5} \\ 2/\sqrt{5} \end{bmatrix}$, $\mathbf{u}_2 = \begin{bmatrix} 2/\sqrt{5} \\ 1/\sqrt{5} \end{bmatrix}$. Show that $\{\mathbf{u}_1, \mathbf{u}_2\}$ is an orthonormal basis for $\mathbb{R}^2$.
2. Let $\mathbf{y}$ and L be as in Example 6. Compute the orthogonal projection $\hat{\mathbf{y}}$ of $\mathbf{y}$ onto L using $\mathbf{u} = \begin{bmatrix} 2 \\ 1 \end{bmatrix}$ instead of the $\mathbf{u}$ in Example 6.
3. Let U and $\mathbf{x}$ be as in Example 4, and let $\mathbf{y} = \begin{bmatrix} -3\sqrt{2} \\ 6 \end{bmatrix}$. Verify that $U\mathbf{x} \cdot U\mathbf{y} = \mathbf{x} \cdot \mathbf{y}$.

7.2 EXERCISES

In Exercises 1–6, determine which sets of vectors are orthogonal.

1. $\begin{bmatrix} -1 \\ 4 \\ -3 \end{bmatrix}, \begin{bmatrix} 5 \\ 2 \\ 1 \end{bmatrix}, \begin{bmatrix} 3 \\ -4 \\ -7 \end{bmatrix}$

2. $\begin{bmatrix} 1 \\ -2 \\ 1 \end{bmatrix}, \begin{bmatrix} 0 \\ 1 \\ 2 \end{bmatrix}, \begin{bmatrix} -5 \\ -2 \\ 1 \end{bmatrix}$

3. $\begin{bmatrix} 2 \\ -7 \\ -1 \end{bmatrix}, \begin{bmatrix} -6 \\ -3 \\ 9 \end{bmatrix}, \begin{bmatrix} 3 \\ 1 \\ -1 \end{bmatrix}$

4. $\begin{bmatrix} 2 \\ -5 \\ -3 \end{bmatrix}, \begin{bmatrix} 0 \\ 0 \\ 0 \end{bmatrix}, \begin{bmatrix} 4 \\ -2 \\ 6 \end{bmatrix}$

5. $\begin{bmatrix} 3 \\ -2 \\ 1 \\ 3 \end{bmatrix}, \begin{bmatrix} -1 \\ 3 \\ -3 \\ 4 \end{bmatrix}, \begin{bmatrix} 3 \\ 8 \\ 7 \\ 0 \end{bmatrix}$

6. $\begin{bmatrix} 5 \\ -4 \\ 0 \\ 3 \end{bmatrix}, \begin{bmatrix} -4 \\ 1 \\ -3 \\ 8 \end{bmatrix}, \begin{bmatrix} 3 \\ 3 \\ 5 \\ -1 \end{bmatrix}$

In Exercises 7–10, show that $\{\mathbf{u}_1, \mathbf{u}_2\}$ or $\{\mathbf{u}_1, \mathbf{u}_2, \mathbf{u}_3\}$ is an orthogonal basis for $\mathbb{R}^2$ or $\mathbb{R}^3$, respectively. Then express $\mathbf{x}$ as a linear combination of the $\mathbf{u}$'s.

7. $\mathbf{u}_1 = \begin{bmatrix} 2 \\ -3 \end{bmatrix}$, $\mathbf{u}_2 = \begin{bmatrix} 6 \\ 4 \end{bmatrix}$, $\mathbf{x} = \begin{bmatrix} 9 \\ -7 \end{bmatrix}$

8. $\mathbf{u}_1 = \begin{bmatrix} 3 \\ 1 \end{bmatrix}$, $\mathbf{u}_2 = \begin{bmatrix} -2 \\ 6 \end{bmatrix}$, $\mathbf{x} = \begin{bmatrix} -6 \\ 3 \end{bmatrix}$

9. $\mathbf{u}_1 = \begin{bmatrix} 1 \\ 0 \\ 1 \end{bmatrix}$, $\mathbf{u}_2 = \begin{bmatrix} -1 \\ 4 \\ 1 \end{bmatrix}$, $\mathbf{u}_3 = \begin{bmatrix} 2 \\ 1 \\ -2 \end{bmatrix}$, and $\mathbf{x} = \begin{bmatrix} 8 \\ -4 \\ -3 \end{bmatrix}$

10. $\mathbf{u}_1 = \begin{bmatrix} 3 \\ -3 \\ 0 \end{bmatrix}$, $\mathbf{u}_2 = \begin{bmatrix} 2 \\ 2 \\ -1 \end{bmatrix}$, $\mathbf{u}_3 = \begin{bmatrix} 1 \\ 1 \\ 4 \end{bmatrix}$, and $\mathbf{x} = \begin{bmatrix} 5 \\ -3 \\ 1 \end{bmatrix}$

In Exercises 11–16, determine which sets of vectors are orthonormal. If a set is only orthogonal, normalize the vectors to produce an orthonormal set.

11. $\begin{bmatrix} 1/3 \\ 1/3 \\ 1/3 \end{bmatrix}, \begin{bmatrix} -1/2 \\ 0 \\ 1/2 \end{bmatrix}$

12. $\begin{bmatrix} 0 \\ 1 \\ 0 \end{bmatrix}, \begin{bmatrix} 0 \\ -1 \\ 0 \end{bmatrix}$

13. $\begin{bmatrix} -.6 \\ .8 \end{bmatrix}, \begin{bmatrix} .8 \\ .6 \end{bmatrix}$

14. $\begin{bmatrix} -2/3 \\ 1/3 \\ 2/3 \end{bmatrix}, \begin{bmatrix} 1/3 \\ 2/3 \\ 0 \end{bmatrix}$

15. $\begin{bmatrix} 1/\sqrt{10} \\ 3/\sqrt{20} \\ 3/\sqrt{20} \end{bmatrix}, \begin{bmatrix} 3/\sqrt{10} \\ -1/\sqrt{20} \\ -1/\sqrt{20} \end{bmatrix}, \begin{bmatrix} 0 \\ -1/\sqrt{2} \\ 1/\sqrt{2} \end{bmatrix}$

16. $\begin{bmatrix} 1/\sqrt{18} \\ 4/\sqrt{18} \\ 1/\sqrt{18} \end{bmatrix}, \begin{bmatrix} 1/\sqrt{2} \\ 0 \\ -1/\sqrt{2} \end{bmatrix}, \begin{bmatrix} -2/3 \\ 1/3 \\ -2/3 \end{bmatrix}$

17. Compute the orthogonal projection of $\begin{bmatrix} 1 \\ 7 \end{bmatrix}$ onto the line through $\begin{bmatrix} -4 \\ 2 \end{bmatrix}$ and the origin.

18. Compute the orthogonal projection of $\begin{bmatrix} 1 \\ -1 \end{bmatrix}$ onto the line through $\begin{bmatrix} -1 \\ 3 \end{bmatrix}$ and the origin.

19. Let $\mathbf{y} = \begin{bmatrix} 2 \\ 3 \end{bmatrix}$ and $\mathbf{u} = \begin{bmatrix} 4 \\ -7 \end{bmatrix}$. Write $\mathbf{y}$ as the sum of two orthogonal vectors, one in Span $\{\mathbf{u}\}$ and one orthogonal to $\mathbf{u}$.

20. Let $\mathbf{y} = \begin{bmatrix} 2 \\ 6 \end{bmatrix}$ and $\mathbf{u} = \begin{bmatrix} 7 \\ 1 \end{bmatrix}$. Write $\mathbf{y}$ as the sum of a vector in Span $\{\mathbf{u}\}$ and a vector orthogonal to $\mathbf{u}$.

21. Let $\mathbf{y} = \begin{bmatrix} 3 \\ 1 \end{bmatrix}$ and $\mathbf{u} = \begin{bmatrix} 8 \\ 6 \end{bmatrix}$. Compute the distance from $\mathbf{y}$ to the line through $\mathbf{u}$ and the origin.

22. Let $\mathbf{y} = \begin{bmatrix} -3 \\ 9 \end{bmatrix}$ and $\mathbf{u} = \begin{bmatrix} 1 \\ 2 \end{bmatrix}$. Compute the distance from $\mathbf{y}$ to the line through $\mathbf{u}$ and the origin.

23. Show that the orthogonal projection of a vector $\mathbf{y}$ onto a line

L through the origin in $\mathbb{R}^2$ does not depend on the choice of the nonzero $\mathbf{u}$ in L used in the formula for $\hat{\mathbf{y}}$. To do this, suppose that $\mathbf{y}$ and $\mathbf{u}$ are given and that $\hat{\mathbf{y}}$ has been computed by formula (5). Replace $\mathbf{u}$ in that formula by $c\mathbf{u}$, where c is an unspecified nonzero scalar. Show that the new formula gives the same $\hat{\mathbf{y}}$.

24. Let $\{\mathbf{v}_1, \mathbf{v}_2\}$ be an orthogonal set of nonzero vectors and c_1, c_2 be any nonzero scalars. Show that $\{c_1\mathbf{v}_1, c_2\mathbf{v}_2\}$ is also an orthogonal set. Since orthogonality of a set is defined in terms of pairs of vectors, this shows that if the vectors in an orthogonal set are normalized, the new set will still be orthogonal.

25. Prove Theorem 7(a). [*Hint*: Compute $\|U\mathbf{x}\|^2$.]

26. Prove Theorem 7(b). Part (c) follows immediately from (b).

27. Let U be a square matrix with orthonormal columns. Explain why U is invertible. (Mention the theorems you use.)

28. Let U be an $n \times n$ orthogonal matrix. Show that the rows of U form an orthonormal basis of $\mathbb{R}^n$.

29. Let U and V be orthogonal matrices. Explain why UV is an orthogonal matrix. [That is, explain why UV is invertible and its inverse is $(UV)^T$.]

30. Let U be an orthogonal matrix, and construct V by interchanging some of the columns of U. Explain why V is orthogonal.

SOLUTIONS TO PRACTICE PROBLEMS

1. The vectors are orthogonal because

$$\mathbf{u}_1 \cdot \mathbf{u}_2 = -2/5 + 2/5 = 0$$

They are unit vectors because

$$\|\mathbf{u}_1\|^2 = (-1/\sqrt{5})^2 + (2/\sqrt{5})^2 = 1/5 + 4/5 = 1$$
$$\|\mathbf{u}_2\|^2 = (2/\sqrt{5})^2 + (1/\sqrt{5})^2 = 4/5 + 1/5 = 1$$

In particular, the set $\{\mathbf{u}_1, \mathbf{u}_2\}$ is linearly independent and hence is a basis for $\mathbb{R}^2$ since there are two vectors in the set.

2. When $\mathbf{y} = \begin{bmatrix} 7 \\ 6 \end{bmatrix}$ and $\mathbf{u} = \begin{bmatrix} 2 \\ 1 \end{bmatrix}$,

$$\hat{\mathbf{y}} = \frac{\mathbf{y} \cdot \mathbf{u}}{\mathbf{u} \cdot \mathbf{u}}\mathbf{u} = \frac{20}{5}\begin{bmatrix} 2 \\ 1 \end{bmatrix} = 4\begin{bmatrix} 2 \\ 1 \end{bmatrix} = \begin{bmatrix} 8 \\ 4 \end{bmatrix}$$

This is the same $\hat{\mathbf{y}}$ found in Example 6. The orthogonal projection does not seem to depend on the $\mathbf{u}$ chosen on the line. See Exercise 23.

3.

$$U\mathbf{y} = \begin{bmatrix} 1/\sqrt{2} & 2/3 \\ 1/\sqrt{2} & -2/3 \\ 0 & 1/3 \end{bmatrix}\begin{bmatrix} -3\sqrt{2} \\ 6 \end{bmatrix} = \begin{bmatrix} 1 \\ -7 \\ 2 \end{bmatrix}$$

Also, from Example 4, $\mathbf{x} = \begin{bmatrix} \sqrt{2} \\ 3 \end{bmatrix}$ and $U\mathbf{x} = \begin{bmatrix} 3 \\ -1 \\ 1 \end{bmatrix}$. Hence

$$U\mathbf{x} \cdot U\mathbf{y} = 3 + 7 + 2 = 12, \text{ and } \mathbf{x} \cdot \mathbf{y} = -6 + 18 = 12$$

7.3 ORTHOGONAL PROJECTIONS

The orthogonal projection of a point in $\mathbb{R}^2$ onto a line through the origin has an important analogue in $\mathbb{R}^n$. Given a vector $\mathbf{y}$ and a subspace W in $\mathbb{R}^n$, there is a vector $\hat{\mathbf{y}}$ in W such that (1) $\hat{\mathbf{y}}$ is the unique vector in W for which $\mathbf{y} - \hat{\mathbf{y}}$ is orthogonal to W, and (2) $\hat{\mathbf{y}}$ is the unique vector in W closest to $\mathbf{y}$. See Fig. 1.

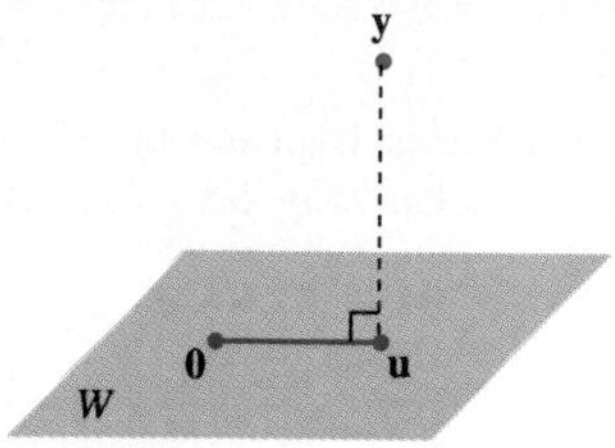

FIGURE 1

To prepare for the first theorem, we observe that whenever a vector $\mathbf{y}$ is written as a linear combination of vectors $\mathbf{u}_1, \ldots, \mathbf{u}_n$ in a basis of $\mathbb{R}^n$, the terms in the sum for $\mathbf{y}$ can be grouped into two parts so that $\mathbf{y}$ can be written as

$$\mathbf{y} = \mathbf{z}_1 + \mathbf{z}_2$$

where $\mathbf{z}_1$ is a linear combination of some of the $\mathbf{u}_i$ and $\mathbf{z}_2$ is a linear combination of the rest of the $\mathbf{u}_i$. This idea is particularly useful when $\{\mathbf{u}_1, \ldots, \mathbf{u}_n\}$ is an orthogonal basis. Recall from Section 7.1 that $W^\perp$ denotes the set of all vectors orthogonal to a set W.

EXAMPLE 1 Let $\{\mathbf{u}_1, \ldots, \mathbf{u}_5\}$ be an orthogonal basis for $\mathbb{R}^5$ and let

$$\mathbf{y} = c_1\mathbf{u}_1 + \cdots + c_5\mathbf{u}_5$$

Consider the subspace $W = \text{Span}\{\mathbf{u}_1, \mathbf{u}_2\}$, and write $\mathbf{y}$ as the sum of a vector $\mathbf{z}_1$ in W and a vector $\mathbf{z}_2$ in $W^\perp$.

Solution Write

$$\mathbf{y} = \underbrace{c_1\mathbf{u}_1 + c_2\mathbf{u}_2}_{\mathbf{z}_1} + \underbrace{c_3\mathbf{u}_3 + c_4\mathbf{u}_4 + c_5\mathbf{u}_5}_{\mathbf{z}_2}$$

where

$$\mathbf{z}_1 = c_1\mathbf{u}_1 + c_2\mathbf{u}_2 \quad \text{is in Span}\{\mathbf{u}_1, \mathbf{u}_2\}\text{, and}$$
$$\mathbf{z}_2 = c_3\mathbf{u}_3 + c_4\mathbf{u}_4 + c_5\mathbf{u}_5 \quad \text{is in Span}\{\mathbf{u}_3, \mathbf{u}_4, \mathbf{u}_5\}.$$

To show that $\mathbf{z}_2$ is in $W^\perp$, it suffices to show that $\mathbf{z}_2$ is orthogonal to the vectors in the basis $\{\mathbf{u}_1, \mathbf{u}_2\}$ for W. (See Section 7.1.) Using properties of the inner product, compute

$$\begin{aligned}\mathbf{z}_2 \cdot \mathbf{u}_1 &= (c_3\mathbf{u}_3 + c_4\mathbf{u}_4 + c_5\mathbf{u}_5) \cdot \mathbf{u}_1 \\ &= c_3\mathbf{u}_3 \cdot \mathbf{u}_1 + c_4\mathbf{u}_4 \cdot \mathbf{u}_1 + c_5\mathbf{u}_5 \cdot \mathbf{u}_1 \\ &= 0\end{aligned}$$

because $\mathbf{u}_1$ is orthogonal to $\mathbf{u}_3$, $\mathbf{u}_4$, and $\mathbf{u}_5$. A similar calculation shows that $\mathbf{z}_2 \cdot \mathbf{u}_2 = 0$. Thus $\mathbf{z}_2$ is in $W^\perp$.

The next theorem shows that the decomposition $\mathbf{y} = \mathbf{z}_1 + \mathbf{z}_2$ in Example 1 may be computed without having an orthogonal basis for $\mathbb{R}^n$. It is enough to have an orthogonal basis only for W.

THEOREM 8 The Orthogonal Decomposition Theorem

Let W be a subspace of $\mathbb{R}^n$ that has an orthogonal basis. Then each $\mathbf{y}$ in $\mathbb{R}^n$ can be written uniquely in the form

$$\mathbf{y} = \hat{\mathbf{y}} + \mathbf{z} \tag{1}$$

where $\hat{\mathbf{y}}$ is in W and $\mathbf{z}$ is in $W^{\perp}$. In fact, if $\{\mathbf{u}_1, \dots, \mathbf{u}_p\}$ is any orthogonal basis of W, then

$$\hat{\mathbf{y}} = \frac{\mathbf{y} \cdot \mathbf{u}_1}{\mathbf{u}_1 \cdot \mathbf{u}_1}\mathbf{u}_1 + \cdots + \frac{\mathbf{y} \cdot \mathbf{u}_p}{\mathbf{u}_p \cdot \mathbf{u}_p}\mathbf{u}_p \tag{2}$$

and $\mathbf{z} = \mathbf{y} - \hat{\mathbf{y}}$.

The vector $\hat{\mathbf{y}}$ in (1) is called the **orthogonal projection of y onto** W and often is written as $\text{proj}_W \mathbf{y}$. See Fig. 2. When W is a one-dimensional subspace, the formula for $\hat{\mathbf{y}}$ matches the formula given in Section 7.2.

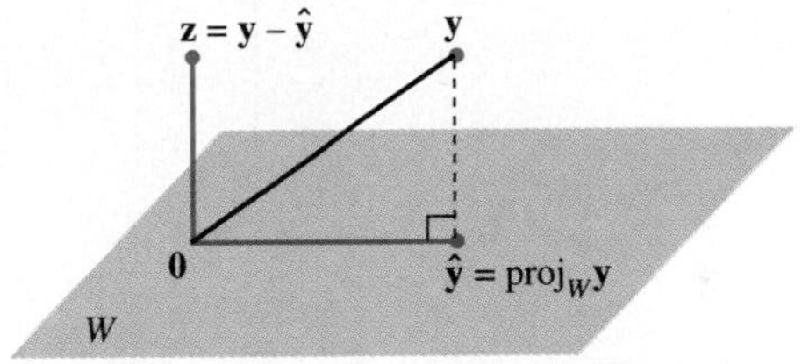

FIGURE 2 The orthogonal projection of $\mathbf{y}$ onto W.

Proof Let $\{\mathbf{u}_1, \dots, \mathbf{u}_p\}$ be an orthogonal basis of W, and define $\hat{\mathbf{y}}$ by (2). Clearly, $\hat{\mathbf{y}}$ is in W because $\hat{\mathbf{y}}$ is a linear combination of the basis $\mathbf{u}_1, \dots, \mathbf{u}_p$. Let $\mathbf{z} = \mathbf{y} - \hat{\mathbf{y}}$. Since $\mathbf{u}_1$ is orthogonal to $\mathbf{u}_2, \dots, \mathbf{u}_p$, it follows from (2) that

$$\begin{aligned}\mathbf{z} \cdot \mathbf{u}_1 = (\mathbf{y} - \hat{\mathbf{y}}) \cdot \mathbf{u}_1 &= \mathbf{y} \cdot \mathbf{u}_1 - \left[\frac{\mathbf{y} \cdot \mathbf{u}_1}{\mathbf{u}_1 \cdot \mathbf{u}_1}\right]\mathbf{u}_1 \cdot \mathbf{u}_1 - 0 - \cdots - 0 \\ &= \mathbf{y} \cdot \mathbf{u}_1 - \mathbf{y} \cdot \mathbf{u}_1 = 0\end{aligned}$$

Thus $\mathbf{z}$ is orthogonal to $\mathbf{u}_1$. Similarly, $\mathbf{z}$ is orthogonal to each $\mathbf{u}_j$ in the basis for W. Hence $\mathbf{z}$ is orthogonal to every vector in W. That is, $\mathbf{z}$ is in $W^{\perp}$.

To show that the decomposition in (1) is unique, suppose that $\mathbf{y}$ can also be written as $\mathbf{y} = \hat{\mathbf{y}}_1 + \mathbf{z}_1$, with $\hat{\mathbf{y}}_1$ in W and $\mathbf{z}_1$ in $W^{\perp}$. Then $\hat{\mathbf{y}} + \mathbf{z} = \hat{\mathbf{y}}_1 + \mathbf{z}_1$ (since both sides equal $\mathbf{y}$), and so

$$\hat{\mathbf{y}} - \hat{\mathbf{y}}_1 = \mathbf{z}_1 - \mathbf{z}$$

This equality shows that the vector $\mathbf{v} = \hat{\mathbf{y}} - \hat{\mathbf{y}}_1$ is in W and in $W^{\perp}$ (because $\mathbf{z}_1$ and $\mathbf{z}$ are both in $W^{\perp}$, and $W^{\perp}$ is a subspace). Hence $\mathbf{v} \cdot \mathbf{v} = 0$, which shows that $\mathbf{v} = \mathbf{0}$. This proves that $\hat{\mathbf{y}} = \hat{\mathbf{y}}_1$, and also $\mathbf{z}_1 = \mathbf{z}$.

We began with any orthogonal basis for W and used (2) to produce a $\hat{\mathbf{y}}$ with the desired properties. The uniqueness of the decomposition (1) shows that $\hat{\mathbf{y}}$ depends only on W and not on the particular basis used in (2). ∎

Theorem 8 actually applies to *every* subspace of $\mathbb{R}^n$ because every subspace of $\mathbb{R}^n$ possesses an orthogonal basis, as we shall see in the next section.

EXAMPLE 2 Let $\mathbf{u}_1 = \begin{bmatrix} 2 \\ 5 \\ -1 \end{bmatrix}$, $\mathbf{u}_2 = \begin{bmatrix} -2 \\ 1 \\ 1 \end{bmatrix}$, and $\mathbf{y} = \begin{bmatrix} 1 \\ 2 \\ 3 \end{bmatrix}$. Observe that $\{\mathbf{u}_1, \mathbf{u}_2\}$ is an orthogonal basis for $W = \text{Span}\{\mathbf{u}_1, \mathbf{u}_2\}$. Write $\mathbf{y}$ as the sum of a vector in W and a vector orthogonal to W.

Solution The orthogonal projection of $\mathbf{y}$ onto W is

$$\begin{aligned} \hat{\mathbf{y}} &= \frac{\mathbf{y} \cdot \mathbf{u}_1}{\mathbf{u}_1 \cdot \mathbf{u}_1}\mathbf{u}_1 + \frac{\mathbf{y} \cdot \mathbf{u}_2}{\mathbf{u}_2 \cdot \mathbf{u}_2}\mathbf{u}_2 \\ &= \frac{9}{30}\begin{bmatrix} 2 \\ 5 \\ -1 \end{bmatrix} + \frac{3}{6}\begin{bmatrix} -2 \\ 1 \\ 1 \end{bmatrix} = \frac{9}{30}\begin{bmatrix} 2 \\ 5 \\ -1 \end{bmatrix} + \frac{15}{30}\begin{bmatrix} -2 \\ 1 \\ 1 \end{bmatrix} = \begin{bmatrix} -2/5 \\ 2 \\ 1/5 \end{bmatrix} \end{aligned}$$

Also

$$\mathbf{y} - \hat{\mathbf{y}} = \begin{bmatrix} 1 \\ 2 \\ 3 \end{bmatrix} - \begin{bmatrix} -2/5 \\ 2 \\ 1/5 \end{bmatrix} = \begin{bmatrix} 7/5 \\ 0 \\ 14/5 \end{bmatrix}$$

Theorem 8 ensures that $\mathbf{y} - \hat{\mathbf{y}}$ is in $W^\perp$. To check the calculations, however, it is a good idea to verify that $\mathbf{y} - \hat{\mathbf{y}}$ is orthogonal to both $\mathbf{u}_1$ and $\mathbf{u}_2$ and hence to all of W. The desired decomposition of $\mathbf{y}$ is

$$\mathbf{y} = \begin{bmatrix} 1 \\ 2 \\ 3 \end{bmatrix} = \begin{bmatrix} -2/5 \\ 2 \\ 1/5 \end{bmatrix} + \begin{bmatrix} 7/5 \\ 0 \\ 14/5 \end{bmatrix}$$

∎

A Geometric Interpretation of the Orthogonal Projection

When W is a one-dimensional subspace, formula (2) for $\text{proj}_W \mathbf{y}$ contains just one term. Thus, when $\dim W > 1$, each term in (2) is itself an orthogonal projection of $\mathbf{y}$ onto a one-dimensional subspace spanned by one of the $\mathbf{u}$'s in the basis for W. Figure 3 illustrates this when W is a subspace of $\mathbb{R}^3$ spanned by $\mathbf{u}_1$ and $\mathbf{u}_2$. Here $\hat{\mathbf{y}}_1$ and $\hat{\mathbf{y}}_2$ denote the projections of $\mathbf{y}$ onto the lines spanned by $\mathbf{u}_1$ and $\mathbf{u}_2$, respectively. The orthogonal projection $\hat{\mathbf{y}}$ of $\mathbf{y}$ onto W is the sum of the projections of $\mathbf{y}$ onto one-dimensional subspaces. The vector $\hat{\mathbf{y}}$ in Fig. 3 corresponds to the vector $\mathbf{y}$ in Fig. 5 of Section 7.2 because now it is $\hat{\mathbf{y}}$ that is in W.

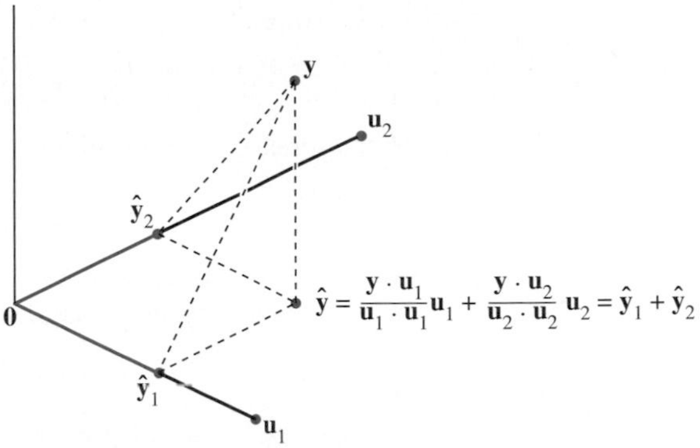

FIGURE 3 The orthogonal projection of $\mathbf{y}$ is the sum of its projections onto one-dimensional subspaces.

Properties of Orthogonal Projections

If $\{\mathbf{u}_1, \ldots, \mathbf{u}_p\}$ is an orthogonal basis for W and if $\mathbf{y}$ happens to be in W, then the formula for $\text{proj}_W\,\mathbf{y}$ is exactly the same as the representation of $\mathbf{y}$ given in Theorem 5 in Section 7.2. In this case, $\text{proj}_W\,\mathbf{y} = \mathbf{y}$.

> If $\mathbf{y}$ is in $W = \text{Span}\{\mathbf{u}_1 \ldots, \mathbf{u}_p\}$, then $\text{proj}_W\mathbf{y} = \mathbf{y}$.

This fact also follows from the next theorem.

THEOREM 9 The Best Approximation Theorem

> Let W be a subspace of $\mathbb{R}^n$, $\mathbf{y}$ be any vector in $\mathbb{R}^n$, and $\hat{\mathbf{y}}$ be the orthogonal projection of $\mathbf{y}$ onto W determined by an orthogonal basis of W. Then $\hat{\mathbf{y}}$ is the closest point in W to $\mathbf{y}$, in the sense that
>
> $$\|\mathbf{y} - \hat{\mathbf{y}}\| < \|\mathbf{y} - \mathbf{v}\| \tag{3}$$
>
> for all $\mathbf{v}$ in W distinct from $\hat{\mathbf{y}}$.

The vector $\hat{\mathbf{y}}$ in Theorem 9 is called **the best approximation to y by elements of** W. In later sections we shall examine problems where a given $\mathbf{y}$ must be replaced or "approximated" by a vector $\mathbf{v}$ in some fixed subspace W. The distance from $\mathbf{y}$ to $\mathbf{v}$, given by $\|\mathbf{y} - \mathbf{v}\|$, can be regarded as the "error" of using $\mathbf{v}$ in place of $\mathbf{y}$. Theorem 9 says that this error is minimized when $\mathbf{v} = \hat{\mathbf{y}}$.

Equation (3) leads to a new proof that $\hat{\mathbf{y}}$ does not depend on the particular orthogonal basis used to compute it. If a different orthogonal basis for W were used to construct an orthogonal projection of $\mathbf{y}$, then this projection would also be the closest point in W to $\mathbf{y}$, namely, $\hat{\mathbf{y}}$.

Proof Take $\mathbf{v}$ in W distinct from $\hat{\mathbf{y}}$. See Fig. 4. Then $\mathbf{v} - \hat{\mathbf{y}}$ is in W. By the Orthogonal Decomposition Theorem, $\mathbf{y} - \hat{\mathbf{y}}$ is orthogonal to W. In particular, $\mathbf{y} - \hat{\mathbf{y}}$ is orthogonal to $\mathbf{v} - \hat{\mathbf{y}}$. Since

$$\mathbf{y} - \mathbf{v} = (\mathbf{y} - \hat{\mathbf{y}}) + (\hat{\mathbf{y}} - \mathbf{v})$$

the Pythagorean Theorem gives

$$\|\mathbf{y} - \mathbf{v}\|^2 = \|\mathbf{y} - \hat{\mathbf{y}}\|^2 + \|\hat{\mathbf{y}} - \mathbf{v}\|^2$$

(See the colored "right triangle" in Fig. 4.) Now $\|\hat{\mathbf{y}} - \mathbf{v}\|^2 > 0$ because $\hat{\mathbf{y}} - \mathbf{v} \neq \mathbf{0}$, and so the inequality in (3) is clear. ∎

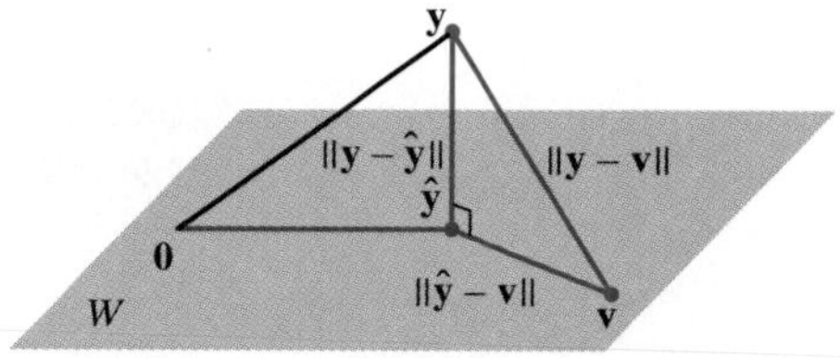

FIGURE 4 The orthogonal projection of **y** onto W is the closest point in W to **y**.

EXAMPLE 3 If $\mathbf{u}_1 = \begin{bmatrix} 2 \\ 5 \\ -1 \end{bmatrix}$, $\mathbf{u}_2 = \begin{bmatrix} -2 \\ 1 \\ 1 \end{bmatrix}$, $\mathbf{y} = \begin{bmatrix} 1 \\ 2 \\ 3 \end{bmatrix}$, and $W = \text{Span}\{\mathbf{u}_1, \mathbf{u}_2\}$, as in Example 2, then the closest point in W to $\mathbf{y}$ is

$$\hat{\mathbf{y}} = \frac{\mathbf{y} \cdot \mathbf{u}_1}{\mathbf{u}_1 \cdot \mathbf{u}_1}\mathbf{u}_1 + \frac{\mathbf{y} \cdot \mathbf{u}_2}{\mathbf{u}_2 \cdot \mathbf{u}_2}\mathbf{u}_2 = \begin{bmatrix} -2/5 \\ 2 \\ 1/5 \end{bmatrix}$$

∎

EXAMPLE 4 The distance from a point $\mathbf{y}$ in $\mathbb{R}^n$ to a subspace W is defined as the distance from $\mathbf{y}$ to the nearest point in W. Find the distance from $\mathbf{y}$ to $W = \text{Span}\{\mathbf{u}_1, \mathbf{u}_2\}$, where

$$\mathbf{y} = \begin{bmatrix} -1 \\ -5 \\ 10 \end{bmatrix}, \quad \mathbf{u}_1 = \begin{bmatrix} 5 \\ -2 \\ 1 \end{bmatrix}, \quad \mathbf{u}_2 = \begin{bmatrix} 1 \\ 2 \\ -1 \end{bmatrix}$$

Solution By the Best Approximation Theorem, the distance from $\mathbf{y}$ to W is $\|\mathbf{y} - \hat{\mathbf{y}}\|$, where $\hat{\mathbf{y}} = \text{proj}_W \mathbf{y}$. Since $\{\mathbf{u}_1, \mathbf{u}_2\}$ is an orthogonal basis for W, we have

$$\hat{\mathbf{y}} = \frac{15}{30}\mathbf{u}_1 + \frac{-21}{6}\mathbf{u}_2 = \frac{1}{2}\begin{bmatrix} 5 \\ -2 \\ 1 \end{bmatrix} - \frac{7}{2}\begin{bmatrix} 1 \\ 2 \\ -1 \end{bmatrix} = \begin{bmatrix} -1 \\ -8 \\ 4 \end{bmatrix}$$

$$\mathbf{y} - \hat{\mathbf{y}} = \begin{bmatrix} -1 \\ -5 \\ 10 \end{bmatrix} - \begin{bmatrix} -1 \\ -8 \\ 4 \end{bmatrix} = \begin{bmatrix} 0 \\ 3 \\ 6 \end{bmatrix}$$

$$\|\mathbf{y} - \hat{\mathbf{y}}\|^2 = 3^2 + 6^2 = 45$$

The distance from $\mathbf{y}$ to W is $\sqrt{45} = 3\sqrt{5}$.

The final theorem of the section shows how formula (2) for $\text{proj}_W \mathbf{y}$ is simplified when the basis for W is an orthonormal set.

THEOREM 10

If $\{\mathbf{u}_1, \ldots, \mathbf{u}_p\}$ is an orthonormal basis for a subspace W of $\mathbb{R}^n$, then

$$\text{proj}_W \mathbf{y} = (\mathbf{y} \cdot \mathbf{u}_1)\mathbf{u}_1 + (\mathbf{y} \cdot \mathbf{u}_2)\mathbf{u}_2 + \cdots + (\mathbf{y} \cdot \mathbf{u}_p)\mathbf{u}_p \tag{4}$$

If $U = [\,\mathbf{u}_1 \quad \mathbf{u}_2 \quad \cdots \quad \mathbf{u}_p\,]$, then

$$\text{proj}_W \mathbf{y} = UU^T\mathbf{y} \quad \text{for all } \mathbf{y} \text{ in } \mathbb{R}^n \tag{5}$$

Proof Formula (4) follows immediately from (2). Also, (4) shows that $\text{proj}_W \mathbf{y}$ is a linear combination of the columns of U using the weights $\mathbf{y} \cdot \mathbf{u}_1$, $\mathbf{y} \cdot \mathbf{u}_2, \ldots, \mathbf{y} \cdot \mathbf{u}_p$. The weights may be written as $\mathbf{u}_1^T\mathbf{y}, \mathbf{u}_2^T\mathbf{y}, \ldots, \mathbf{u}_p^T\mathbf{y}$, showing that they are the entries in $U^T\mathbf{y}$ and justifying (5). ∎

Suppose that U is $n \times p$ with orthonormal columns, and let W be the column space of U. Then

$$U^TU\mathbf{x} = I_p\mathbf{x} = \mathbf{x} \quad \text{for all } \mathbf{x} \text{ in } \mathbf{R}^p \qquad \text{Theorem 6}$$
$$UU^T\mathbf{y} = \text{proj}_W \mathbf{y} \quad \text{for all } \mathbf{y} \text{ in } \mathbf{R}^n \qquad \text{Theorem 10}$$

If U is an $n \times n$ (square) matrix with orthonormal columns, then U is an *orthogonal* matrix, the column space W is all of $\mathbb{R}^n$, and $UU^T\mathbf{y} = I\mathbf{y} = \mathbf{y}$ for all $\mathbf{y}$ in $\mathbb{R}^n$.

Although formula (4) is important for theoretical purposes, in practice it usually involves calculations with square roots of numbers (in the entries of the $\mathbf{u}_i$). Formula (2) is recommended for hand calculations.

PRACTICE PROBLEM

Let $\mathbf{u}_1 = \begin{bmatrix} -7 \\ 1 \\ 4 \end{bmatrix}$, $\mathbf{u}_2 = \begin{bmatrix} -1 \\ 1 \\ -2 \end{bmatrix}$, $\mathbf{y} = \begin{bmatrix} -9 \\ 1 \\ 6 \end{bmatrix}$, and $W = \text{Span}\{\mathbf{u}_1, \mathbf{u}_2\}$. Use the fact that $\mathbf{u}_1$ and $\mathbf{u}_2$ are orthogonal to compute $\text{proj}_W \mathbf{y}$.

7.3 EXERCISES

In Exercises 1 and 2, you may assume that $\{\mathbf{u}_1, \ldots, \mathbf{u}_4\}$ is an orthogonal basis for $\mathbb{R}^4$.

1. $\mathbf{u}_1 = \begin{bmatrix} 0 \\ 1 \\ -4 \\ -1 \end{bmatrix}$, $\mathbf{u}_2 = \begin{bmatrix} 3 \\ 5 \\ 1 \\ 1 \end{bmatrix}$, $\mathbf{u}_3 = \begin{bmatrix} 1 \\ 0 \\ 1 \\ -4 \end{bmatrix}$, $\mathbf{u}_4 = \begin{bmatrix} 5 \\ -3 \\ -1 \\ 1 \end{bmatrix}$,

$\mathbf{x} = \begin{bmatrix} 10 \\ -8 \\ 2 \\ 0 \end{bmatrix}$. Write $\mathbf{x}$ as the sum of two vectors, one in Span $\{\mathbf{u}_1, \mathbf{u}_2, \mathbf{u}_3\}$ and the other in Span $\{\mathbf{u}_4\}$.

2. $\mathbf{u}_1 = \begin{bmatrix} 1 \\ 2 \\ 1 \\ 1 \end{bmatrix}$, $\mathbf{u}_2 = \begin{bmatrix} -2 \\ 1 \\ -1 \\ 1 \end{bmatrix}$, $\mathbf{u}_3 = \begin{bmatrix} 1 \\ 1 \\ -2 \\ -1 \end{bmatrix}$, $\mathbf{u}_4 = \begin{bmatrix} -1 \\ 1 \\ 1 \\ -2 \end{bmatrix}$,

$\mathbf{v} = \begin{bmatrix} 4 \\ 5 \\ -3 \\ 3 \end{bmatrix}$. Write $\mathbf{v}$ as the sum of two vectors, one in Span $\{\mathbf{u}_1\}$ and the other in Span $\{\mathbf{u}_2, \mathbf{u}_3, \mathbf{u}_4\}$.

In Exercises 3–6, find the orthogonal projection of $\mathbf{y}$ onto the subspace spanned by the orthogonal vectors $\mathbf{u}_1$ and $\mathbf{u}_2$.

3. $\mathbf{y} = \begin{bmatrix} -1 \\ 4 \\ 3 \end{bmatrix}$, $\mathbf{u}_1 = \begin{bmatrix} 1 \\ 1 \\ 0 \end{bmatrix}$, $\mathbf{u}_2 = \begin{bmatrix} -1 \\ 1 \\ 0 \end{bmatrix}$

4. $\mathbf{y} = \begin{bmatrix} 6 \\ 3 \\ -2 \end{bmatrix}$, $\mathbf{u}_1 = \begin{bmatrix} 3 \\ 4 \\ 0 \end{bmatrix}$, $\mathbf{u}_2 = \begin{bmatrix} -4 \\ 3 \\ 0 \end{bmatrix}$

5. $\mathbf{y} = \begin{bmatrix} -1 \\ 2 \\ 6 \end{bmatrix}$, $\mathbf{u}_1 = \begin{bmatrix} 3 \\ -1 \\ 2 \end{bmatrix}$, $\mathbf{u}_2 = \begin{bmatrix} 1 \\ -1 \\ -2 \end{bmatrix}$

6. $\mathbf{y} = \begin{bmatrix} 6 \\ 4 \\ 1 \end{bmatrix}$, $\mathbf{u}_1 = \begin{bmatrix} -4 \\ -1 \\ 1 \end{bmatrix}$, $\mathbf{u}_2 = \begin{bmatrix} 0 \\ 1 \\ 1 \end{bmatrix}$

In Exercises 7–10, let W be the subspace spanned by the $\mathbf{u}$'s, and write $\mathbf{y}$ as the sum of a vector in W and a vector orthogonal to W.

7. $\mathbf{y} = \begin{bmatrix} 1 \\ 3 \\ 5 \end{bmatrix}$, $\mathbf{u}_1 = \begin{bmatrix} 1 \\ 3 \\ -2 \end{bmatrix}$, $\mathbf{u}_2 = \begin{bmatrix} 5 \\ 1 \\ 4 \end{bmatrix}$

8. $\mathbf{y} = \begin{bmatrix} -1 \\ 4 \\ 3 \end{bmatrix}$, $\mathbf{u}_1 = \begin{bmatrix} 1 \\ 1 \\ 1 \end{bmatrix}$, $\mathbf{u}_2 = \begin{bmatrix} -1 \\ 3 \\ -2 \end{bmatrix}$

9. $\mathbf{y} = \begin{bmatrix} 4 \\ 3 \\ 3 \\ -1 \end{bmatrix}$, $\mathbf{u}_1 = \begin{bmatrix} 1 \\ 1 \\ 0 \\ 1 \end{bmatrix}$, $\mathbf{u}_2 = \begin{bmatrix} -1 \\ 3 \\ 1 \\ -2 \end{bmatrix}$, $\mathbf{u}_3 = \begin{bmatrix} -1 \\ 0 \\ 1 \\ 1 \end{bmatrix}$

10. $\mathbf{y} = \begin{bmatrix} 3 \\ 4 \\ 5 \\ 6 \end{bmatrix}$, $\mathbf{u}_1 = \begin{bmatrix} 1 \\ 1 \\ 0 \\ -1 \end{bmatrix}$, $\mathbf{u}_2 = \begin{bmatrix} 1 \\ 0 \\ 1 \\ 1 \end{bmatrix}$, $\mathbf{u}_3 = \begin{bmatrix} 0 \\ -1 \\ 1 \\ -1 \end{bmatrix}$

In Exercises 11 and 12, find the closest point to $\mathbf{y}$ in the subspace W spanned by $\mathbf{v}_1$ and $\mathbf{v}_2$.

11. $\mathbf{y} = \begin{bmatrix} 3 \\ 1 \\ 5 \\ 1 \end{bmatrix}$, $\mathbf{v}_1 = \begin{bmatrix} 3 \\ 1 \\ -1 \\ 1 \end{bmatrix}$, $\mathbf{v}_2 = \begin{bmatrix} 1 \\ -1 \\ 1 \\ -1 \end{bmatrix}$

12. $\mathbf{y} = \begin{bmatrix} 3 \\ -1 \\ 1 \\ 13 \end{bmatrix}$, $\mathbf{v}_1 = \begin{bmatrix} 1 \\ -2 \\ -1 \\ 2 \end{bmatrix}$, $\mathbf{v}_2 = \begin{bmatrix} -4 \\ 1 \\ 0 \\ 3 \end{bmatrix}$

In Exercises 13 and 14, find the best approximation to $\mathbf{z}$ by vectors of the form $c_1\mathbf{v}_1 + c_2\mathbf{v}_2$.

13. $\mathbf{z} = \begin{bmatrix} 3 \\ -7 \\ 2 \\ 3 \end{bmatrix}$, $\mathbf{v}_1 = \begin{bmatrix} 2 \\ -1 \\ -3 \\ 1 \end{bmatrix}$, $\mathbf{v}_2 = \begin{bmatrix} 1 \\ 1 \\ 0 \\ -1 \end{bmatrix}$

14. $\mathbf{z} = \begin{bmatrix} 2 \\ 4 \\ 0 \\ -1 \end{bmatrix}$, $\mathbf{v}_1 = \begin{bmatrix} 2 \\ 0 \\ -1 \\ -3 \end{bmatrix}$, $\mathbf{v}_2 = \begin{bmatrix} 5 \\ -2 \\ 4 \\ 2 \end{bmatrix}$

15. Let $\mathbf{y} = \begin{bmatrix} 5 \\ -9 \\ 5 \end{bmatrix}$, $\mathbf{u}_1 = \begin{bmatrix} -3 \\ -5 \\ 1 \end{bmatrix}$, $\mathbf{u}_2 = \begin{bmatrix} -3 \\ 2 \\ 1 \end{bmatrix}$. Find the distance from $\mathbf{y}$ to the plane in $\mathbb{R}^3$ spanned by $\mathbf{u}_1$ and $\mathbf{u}_2$.

16. Let $\mathbf{y}$, $\mathbf{v}_1$, and $\mathbf{v}_2$ be as in Exercise 12. Find the distance from $\mathbf{y}$ to the subspace of $\mathbb{R}^4$ spanned by $\mathbf{v}_1$ and $\mathbf{v}_2$.

17. Let $\mathbf{y} = \begin{bmatrix} 4 \\ 8 \\ 1 \end{bmatrix}$, $\mathbf{u}_1 = \begin{bmatrix} 2/3 \\ 1/3 \\ 2/3 \end{bmatrix}$, $\mathbf{u}_2 = \begin{bmatrix} -2/3 \\ 2/3 \\ 1/3 \end{bmatrix}$, and $W =$ Span $\{\mathbf{u}_1, \mathbf{u}_2\}$.

a. Let $U = [\,\mathbf{u}_1 \quad \mathbf{u}_2\,]$. Compute U^TU and UU^T.

b. Compute $\text{proj}_W\,\mathbf{y}$ and $(UU^T)\mathbf{y}$

18. Let $\mathbf{y} = \begin{bmatrix} 7 \\ 9 \end{bmatrix}$, $\mathbf{u}_1 = \begin{bmatrix} 1/\sqrt{10} \\ -3/\sqrt{10} \end{bmatrix}$, and $W =$ Span $\{\mathbf{u}_1\}$.

a. Let U be the 2×1 matrix whose only column is $\mathbf{u}_1$. Compute U^TU and UU^T.

b. Compute $\text{proj}_W\,\mathbf{y}$ and $(UU^T)\mathbf{y}$.

19. Let $\mathbf{u}_1 = \begin{bmatrix} 1 \\ 1 \\ -2 \end{bmatrix}$, $\mathbf{u}_2 = \begin{bmatrix} 5 \\ -1 \\ 2 \end{bmatrix}$, and $\mathbf{u}_3 = \begin{bmatrix} 0 \\ 0 \\ 1 \end{bmatrix}$. Note that $\mathbf{u}_1$ and $\mathbf{u}_2$ are orthogonal but that $\mathbf{u}_3$ is not orthogonal to $\mathbf{u}_1$ or $\mathbf{u}_2$. It can be shown that $\mathbf{u}_3$ is not in the subspace W spanned by $\mathbf{u}_1$ and $\mathbf{u}_2$. Use this fact to construct a vector $\mathbf{v}$ in $\mathbb{R}^3$ that is orthogonal to $\mathbf{u}_1$ and $\mathbf{u}_2$.

20. Let $\mathbf{u}_1$ and $\mathbf{u}_2$ be as in Exercise 19, and let $\mathbf{u}_4 = \begin{bmatrix} 0 \\ 1 \\ 0 \end{bmatrix}$. It can be shown that $\mathbf{u}_4$ is not in the subspace W spanned by $\mathbf{u}_1$ and $\mathbf{u}_2$. Use this fact to construct a vector $\mathbf{v}$ in $\mathbb{R}^3$ that is orthogonal to $\mathbf{u}_1$ and $\mathbf{u}_2$.

21. Let A be an $m \times n$ matrix. Prove that every vector $\mathbf{x}$ in $\mathbb{R}^n$ can be written in the form $\mathbf{x} = \mathbf{p} + \mathbf{u}$, where $\mathbf{p}$ is in Row A and $\mathbf{u}$ is in Nul A. Also, show that if the equation $A\mathbf{x} = \mathbf{b}$ is consistent, then there is a unique $\mathbf{p}$ in Row A such that $A\mathbf{p} = \mathbf{b}$.

22. Let W be a subspace of $\mathbb{R}^n$ with an orthogonal basis $\{\mathbf{w}_1, \ldots, \mathbf{w}_p\}$ and let $\{\mathbf{v}_1, \ldots, \mathbf{v}_q\}$ be an orthogonal basis for $W^\perp$.

a. Explain why $\{\mathbf{w}_1, \ldots, \mathbf{w}_p, \mathbf{v}_1, \ldots, \mathbf{v}_q\}$ is an orthogonal set.

b. Explain why the set in part (a) spans $\mathbb{R}^n$.

c. Show that $\dim W + \dim W^\perp = n$.

SOLUTION TO PRACTICE PROBLEM

Compute

$$\text{proj}_W \mathbf{y} = \frac{\mathbf{y} \cdot \mathbf{u}_1}{\mathbf{u}_1 \cdot \mathbf{u}_1}\mathbf{u}_1 + \frac{\mathbf{y} \cdot \mathbf{u}_2}{\mathbf{u}_2 \cdot \mathbf{u}_2}\mathbf{u}_2 = \frac{88}{66}\mathbf{u}_1 + \frac{-2}{6}\mathbf{u}_2$$
$$= \frac{4}{3}\begin{bmatrix} -7 \\ 1 \\ 4 \end{bmatrix} - \frac{1}{3}\begin{bmatrix} -1 \\ 1 \\ -2 \end{bmatrix} = \begin{bmatrix} -9 \\ 1 \\ 6 \end{bmatrix} = \mathbf{y}$$

In this case $\mathbf{y}$ happens to be a linear combination of $\mathbf{u}_1$ and $\mathbf{u}_2$, so $\mathbf{y}$ is in W. The closest point in W to $\mathbf{y}$ is $\mathbf{y}$ itself.

7.4 THE GRAM–SCHMIDT PROCESS

The Gram–Schmidt process is a simple algorithm for producing an orthogonal or orthonormal basis for any subspace of $\mathbb{R}^n$. The first two examples of the process are aimed at hand calculation.

EXAMPLE 1 Let $W = \text{Span}\{\mathbf{x}_1, \mathbf{x}_2\}$, where $\mathbf{x}_1 = \begin{bmatrix} 3 \\ 6 \\ 0 \end{bmatrix}$ and $\mathbf{x}_2 = \begin{bmatrix} 1 \\ 2 \\ 2 \end{bmatrix}$. Construct an orthogonal basis $\{\mathbf{v}_1, \mathbf{v}_2\}$ for W.

Solution The subspace W is shown in Fig. 1, along with $\mathbf{x}_1, \mathbf{x}_2$, and the projection $\mathbf{p}$ of $\mathbf{x}_2$ onto $\mathbf{x}_1$. The component of $\mathbf{x}_2$ orthogonal to $\mathbf{x}_1$ is $\mathbf{x}_2 - \mathbf{p}$, which is in W because it is formed from $\mathbf{x}_2$ and a multiple of $\mathbf{x}_1$. Let $\mathbf{v}_1 = \mathbf{x}_1$ and

$$\mathbf{v}_2 = \mathbf{x}_2 - \mathbf{p} = \mathbf{x}_2 - \frac{\mathbf{x}_2 \cdot \mathbf{x}_1}{\mathbf{x}_1 \cdot \mathbf{x}_1}\mathbf{x}_1$$
$$= \begin{bmatrix} 1 \\ 2 \\ 2 \end{bmatrix} - \frac{15}{45}\begin{bmatrix} 3 \\ 6 \\ 0 \end{bmatrix} = \begin{bmatrix} 0 \\ 0 \\ 2 \end{bmatrix}$$

Then $\{\mathbf{v}_1, \mathbf{v}_2\}$ is an orthogonal set of nonzero vectors in W. Since $\dim W = 2$, $\{\mathbf{v}_1, \mathbf{v}_2\}$ is a basis for W. ∎

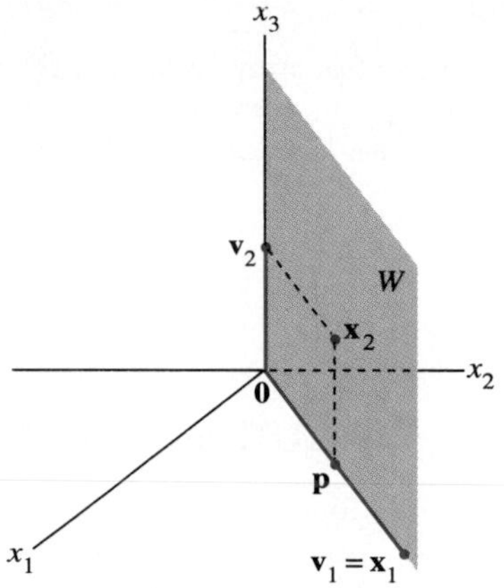

FIGURE 1 Construction of an orthogonal basis $\{\mathbf{v}_1, \mathbf{v}_2\}$.

The next example fully illustrates the Gram–Schmidt process. Study it carefully.

EXAMPLE 2 Let $\mathbf{x}_1 = \begin{bmatrix} 1 \\ 1 \\ 1 \\ 1 \end{bmatrix}$, $\mathbf{x}_2 = \begin{bmatrix} 0 \\ 1 \\ 1 \\ 1 \end{bmatrix}$, $\mathbf{x}_3 = \begin{bmatrix} 0 \\ 0 \\ 1 \\ 1 \end{bmatrix}$. Then $\{\mathbf{x}_1, \mathbf{x}_2, \mathbf{x}_3\}$ is clearly linearly independent and thus is a basis for a subspace W of $\mathbb{R}^4$. Construct an orthogonal basis for W.

Solution **Step 1.** Let $\mathbf{v}_1 = \mathbf{x}_1$ and $W_1 = \text{Span}\{\mathbf{x}_1\} = \text{Span}\{\mathbf{v}_1\}$.

Step 2. Let $\mathbf{v}_2$ be the vector produced by subtracting from $\mathbf{x}_2$ its projection onto the subspace W_1. That is, let

$$\begin{aligned} \mathbf{v}_2 &= \mathbf{x}_2 - \text{proj}_{W_1} \mathbf{x}_2 \\ &= \mathbf{x}_2 - \frac{\mathbf{x}_2 \cdot \mathbf{v}_1}{\mathbf{v}_1 \cdot \mathbf{v}_1} \mathbf{v}_1 \text{ (since } \mathbf{v}_1 = \mathbf{x}_1) \\ &= \begin{bmatrix} 0 \\ 1 \\ 1 \\ 1 \end{bmatrix} - \frac{3}{4} \begin{bmatrix} 1 \\ 1 \\ 1 \\ 1 \end{bmatrix} = \begin{bmatrix} -3/4 \\ 1/4 \\ 1/4 \\ 1/4 \end{bmatrix} \end{aligned}$$

As in Example 1, $\mathbf{v}_2$ is the component of $\mathbf{x}_2$ orthogonal to $\mathbf{x}_1$ and $\{\mathbf{v}_1, \mathbf{v}_2\}$ is an orthogonal basis for the subspace W_2 spanned by $\mathbf{x}_1$ and $\mathbf{x}_2$.

Step 2′ (optional). If appropriate, scale $\mathbf{v}_2$ to simplify later computations. Since $\mathbf{v}_2$ has fractional entries, it is convenient to scale it by a factor of 4 and replace $\{\mathbf{v}_1, \mathbf{v}_2\}$

by the orthogonal basis

$$\mathbf{v}_1 = \begin{bmatrix} 1 \\ 1 \\ 1 \\ 1 \end{bmatrix}, \quad \mathbf{v}_2' = \begin{bmatrix} -3 \\ 1 \\ 1 \\ 1 \end{bmatrix}$$

Step 3. Let $\mathbf{v}_3$ be the vector produced by subtracting from $\mathbf{x}_3$ its projection onto the subspace W_2. Use the orthogonal basis $\{\mathbf{v}_1, \mathbf{v}_2'\}$ to compute the projection onto W_2:

$$\text{proj}_{W_2}\mathbf{x}_3 = \underbrace{\frac{\mathbf{x}_3 \cdot \mathbf{v}_1}{\mathbf{v}_1 \cdot \mathbf{v}_1}\mathbf{v}_1}_{\text{Projection of } \mathbf{x}_3 \text{ onto } \mathbf{v}_1} + \underbrace{\frac{\mathbf{x}_3 \cdot \mathbf{v}_2'}{\mathbf{v}_2' \cdot \mathbf{v}_2'}\mathbf{v}_2'}_{\text{Projection of } \mathbf{x}_3 \text{ onto } \mathbf{v}_2'}$$

$$= \frac{2}{4}\begin{bmatrix} 1 \\ 1 \\ 1 \\ 1 \end{bmatrix} + \frac{2}{12}\begin{bmatrix} -3 \\ 1 \\ 1 \\ 1 \end{bmatrix} = \begin{bmatrix} 0 \\ 2/3 \\ 2/3 \\ 2/3 \end{bmatrix}$$

Then $\mathbf{v}_3$ is the component of $\mathbf{x}_3$ orthogonal to W_2, namely,

$$\mathbf{v}_3 = \mathbf{x}_3 - \text{proj}_{W_2}\mathbf{x}_3 = \begin{bmatrix} 0 \\ 0 \\ 1 \\ 1 \end{bmatrix} - \begin{bmatrix} 0 \\ 2/3 \\ 2/3 \\ 2/3 \end{bmatrix} = \begin{bmatrix} 0 \\ -2/3 \\ 1/3 \\ 1/3 \end{bmatrix}$$

See Fig. 2 for a diagram of this construction. Observe that $\mathbf{v}_3$ is in W, because $\mathbf{x}_3$ and $\text{proj}_{W_2}\mathbf{x}_3$ are both in W. Thus $\{\mathbf{v}_1, \mathbf{v}_2', \mathbf{v}_3\}$ is an orthogonal set of nonzero vectors (and hence a linearly independent set) in W. Obviously, W is three-dimensional since it was defined by a basis of three vectors. Hence, by Theorem 13 in Section 5.5, $\{\mathbf{v}_1, \mathbf{v}_2', \mathbf{v}_3\}$ is an orthogonal basis for W.

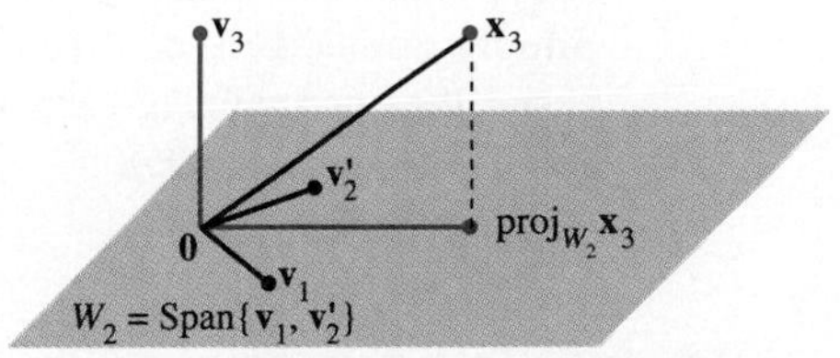

FIGURE 2 The construction of $\mathbf{v}_3$ from $\mathbf{x}_3$ and W_2.

The proof of the next theorem shows that this strategy really works. Scaling of vectors is not mentioned because it is used only to simplify hand calculations.

THEOREM 11

The Gram–Schmidt Process

Given a basis $\{\mathbf{x}_1, \ldots, \mathbf{x}_p\}$ for a subspace W of $\mathbb{R}^n$, define

$$\begin{aligned}
\mathbf{v}_1 &= \mathbf{x}_1 \\
\mathbf{v}_2 &= \mathbf{x}_2 - \frac{\mathbf{x}_2 \cdot \mathbf{v}_1}{\mathbf{v}_1 \cdot \mathbf{v}_1}\mathbf{v}_1 \\
\mathbf{v}_3 &= \mathbf{x}_3 - \frac{\mathbf{x}_3 \cdot \mathbf{v}_1}{\mathbf{v}_1 \cdot \mathbf{v}_1}\mathbf{v}_1 - \frac{\mathbf{x}_3 \cdot \mathbf{v}_2}{\mathbf{v}_2 \cdot \mathbf{v}_2}\mathbf{v}_2 \\
&\vdots \\
\mathbf{v}_p &= \mathbf{x}_p - \frac{\mathbf{x}_p \cdot \mathbf{v}_1}{\mathbf{v}_1 \cdot \mathbf{v}_1}\mathbf{v}_1 - \frac{\mathbf{x}_p \cdot \mathbf{v}_2}{\mathbf{v}_2 \cdot \mathbf{v}_2}\mathbf{v}_2 - \cdots - \frac{\mathbf{x}_p \cdot \mathbf{v}_{p-1}}{\mathbf{v}_{p-1} \cdot \mathbf{v}_{p-1}}\mathbf{v}_{p-1}
\end{aligned}$$

Then $\{\mathbf{v}_1, \ldots, \mathbf{v}_p\}$ is an orthogonal basis for W. In addition

$$\text{Span}\{\mathbf{v}_1, \ldots, \mathbf{v}_k\} = \text{Span}\{\mathbf{x}_1, \ldots, \mathbf{x}_k\} \quad \text{for } 1 \le k \le p \tag{2}$$

Proof For $1 \le k \le p$, let $W_k = \text{Span}\{\mathbf{x}_1, \ldots, \mathbf{x}_k\}$. Set $\mathbf{v}_1 = \mathbf{x}_1$, so that $\text{Span}\{\mathbf{v}_1\} = \text{Span}\{\mathbf{x}_1\}$. Suppose that for some k we have constructed $\mathbf{v}_1, \ldots, \mathbf{v}_k$ so that $\{\mathbf{v}_1, \ldots, \mathbf{v}_k\}$ is an orthogonal basis for W_k. Define

$$\mathbf{v}_{k+1} = \mathbf{x}_{k+1} - \text{proj}_{W_k}\mathbf{x}_{k+1}$$

Note that $\text{proj}_{W_k}\mathbf{x}_{k+1}$ is in W_k and hence also in W_{k+1}. Since $\mathbf{x}_{k+1}$ is in W_{k+1}, so is $\mathbf{v}_{k+1}$. Furthermore, $\mathbf{v}_{k+1} \neq \mathbf{0}$ because $\mathbf{x}_{k+1}$ is not in $W_k = \text{Span}\{\mathbf{x}_1, \ldots, \mathbf{x}_k\}$. Hence $\{\mathbf{v}_1, \ldots, \mathbf{v}_{k+1}\}$ is an orthogonal set of nonzero vectors in the $(k+1)$-dimensional space W_{k+1}. By Theorem 13 in Section 5.5, this set is an orthogonal basis for W_{k+1}. Hence $W_{k+1} = \text{Span}\{\mathbf{v}_1, \ldots, \mathbf{v}_{k+1}\}$. After p steps, the process stops. ∎

Orthonormal Bases

An orthonormal basis is constructed easily from an orthogonal basis $\{\mathbf{v}_1, \ldots, \mathbf{v}_p\}$: Simply normalize (i.e., "scale") all the $\mathbf{v}_k$. When working problems by hand, this is easier than normalizing each $\mathbf{v}_k$ as soon as it is found (because it avoids unnecessary writing of square roots).

EXAMPLE 3 In Example 1, we constructed the orthogonal basis

$$\mathbf{v}_1 = \begin{bmatrix} 3 \\ 6 \\ 0 \end{bmatrix}, \quad \mathbf{v}_2 = \begin{bmatrix} 0 \\ 0 \\ 2 \end{bmatrix}$$

An orthonormal basis is

$$\mathbf{u}_1 = \frac{1}{\|\mathbf{v}_1\|}\mathbf{v}_1 = \frac{1}{\sqrt{45}}\begin{bmatrix} 3 \\ 6 \\ 0 \end{bmatrix} = \begin{bmatrix} 1/\sqrt{5} \\ 2/\sqrt{5} \\ 0 \end{bmatrix}$$

$$\mathbf{u}_2 = \frac{1}{\|\mathbf{v}_2\|}\mathbf{v}_2 = \begin{bmatrix} 0 \\ 0 \\ 1 \end{bmatrix}$$

QR Factorization of Matrices

If $\mathbf{x}_1, \ldots, \mathbf{x}_n$ are the columns of an $m \times n$ matrix A, then applying the Gram–Schmidt process (with normalizations) to $\mathbf{x}_1, \ldots, \mathbf{x}_n$ amounts to *factoring* A as described in the next theorem. This factorization is widely used in computer algorithms for various computations, such as solving equations (discussed in Section 7.5) and finding eigenvalues (mentioned in the exercises for Section 6.2).

THEOREM 12

The QR Factorization

If A is an $m \times n$ matrix with linearly independent columns, then A may be factored as $A = QR$, where Q is an $m \times n$ matrix whose columns form an orthonormal basis for Col A and R is an $n \times n$ upper triangular invertible matrix with positive entries on its diagonal.

Proof The columns of A form a basis $\{\mathbf{x}_1, \ldots, \mathbf{x}_n\}$ for Col A. Construct an orthonormal basis $\{\mathbf{v}_1, \ldots, \mathbf{v}_n\}$ for W = Col A with property (1) in Theorem 11. This basis may be constructed by the Gram–Schmidt process or some other means. Let

$$Q = [\,\mathbf{v}_1 \quad \mathbf{v}_2 \quad \cdots \quad \mathbf{v}_n\,]$$

For $k = 1, \ldots, n$, $\mathbf{x}_k$ is in Span$\{\mathbf{x}_1, \ldots, \mathbf{x}_k\}$ = Span$\{\mathbf{v}_1, \ldots, \mathbf{v}_k\}$. So there are constants, $r_{1k}, \ldots, r_{kk}$, such that

$$\mathbf{x}_k = r_{1k}\mathbf{v}_1 + \cdots + r_{kk}\mathbf{v}_k + 0\cdot\mathbf{v}_{k+1} + \cdots + 0\cdot\mathbf{v}_n$$

We may assume that $r_{kk} \geq 0$. (If $r_{kk} < 0$, multiply both r_{kk} and $\mathbf{v}_k$ by -1.) This shows that $\mathbf{x}_k$ is a linear combination of the columns of Q using as weights the entries in the vector

$$\mathbf{r}_k = \begin{bmatrix} r_{1k} \\ \vdots \\ r_{kk} \\ 0 \\ \vdots \\ 0 \end{bmatrix}$$

That is, $\mathbf{x}_k = Q\mathbf{r}_k$ for $k = 1, \ldots, n$. Let $R = [\,\mathbf{r}_1 \;\; \cdots \;\; \mathbf{r}_n\,]$. Then

$$A = [\,\mathbf{x}_1 \;\; \cdots \;\; \mathbf{x}_n\,] = [\,Q\mathbf{r}_1 \;\; \cdots \;\; Q\mathbf{r}_n\,] = QR$$

The fact that R is invertible follows easily from the fact that the columns of A are linearly independent (Exercise 17). Since R is clearly upper triangular, its nonnegative diagonal entries must be positive. ∎

EXAMPLE 4 Find a QR factorization of $A = \begin{bmatrix} 1 & 0 & 0 \\ 1 & 1 & 0 \\ 1 & 1 & 1 \\ 1 & 1 & 1 \end{bmatrix}$.

Solution The columns of A are the vectors $\mathbf{x}_1, \mathbf{x}_2, \mathbf{x}_3$ in Example 2. An orthogonal basis for Col $A = \text{Span}\{\mathbf{x}_1, \mathbf{x}_2, \mathbf{x}_3\}$ was found in that example:

$$\mathbf{v}_1 = \begin{bmatrix} 1 \\ 1 \\ 1 \\ 1 \end{bmatrix}, \quad \mathbf{v}_2' = \begin{bmatrix} -3 \\ 1 \\ 1 \\ 1 \end{bmatrix}, \quad \mathbf{v}_3 = \begin{bmatrix} 0 \\ -2/3 \\ 1/3 \\ 1/3 \end{bmatrix}$$

Scale $\mathbf{v}_3$ by letting $\mathbf{v}_3' = 3\mathbf{v}_3$. Then normalize the three vectors to obtain $\mathbf{u}_1, \mathbf{u}_2, \mathbf{u}_3$, and use these vectors as the columns of Q:

$$Q = \begin{bmatrix} 1/2 & -3/\sqrt{12} & 0 \\ 1/2 & 1/\sqrt{12} & -2/\sqrt{6} \\ 1/2 & 1/\sqrt{12} & 1/\sqrt{6} \\ 1/2 & 1/\sqrt{12} & 1/\sqrt{6} \end{bmatrix}$$

By construction, the first k columns of Q are an orthonormal basis of Span$\{\mathbf{x}_1, \ldots, \mathbf{x}_k\}$. From the proof of Theorem 12, $A = QR$ for some R. To find R, observe that $Q^TQ = I$, because the columns of Q are orthonormal. Hence

$$Q^TA = Q^T(QR) = IR = R$$

Thus we may compute

$$R = \begin{bmatrix} 1/2 & 1/2 & 1/2 & 1/2 \\ -3/\sqrt{12} & 1/\sqrt{12} & 1/\sqrt{12} & 1/\sqrt{12} \\ 0 & -2/\sqrt{6} & 1/\sqrt{6} & 1/\sqrt{6} \end{bmatrix} \begin{bmatrix} 1 & 0 & 0 \\ 1 & 1 & 0 \\ 1 & 1 & 1 \\ 1 & 1 & 1 \end{bmatrix}$$

$$= \begin{bmatrix} 2 & 3/2 & 1 \\ 0 & 3/\sqrt{12} & 2/\sqrt{12} \\ 0 & 0 & 2/\sqrt{6} \end{bmatrix}$$

∎

Numerical Notes

1. When the Gram–Schmidt process is run on a computer, roundoff error can build up as the vectors $\mathbf{u}_k$ are calculated, one by one. For j and k large but unequal, the scalar products $\mathbf{u}_j^T\mathbf{u}_k$ may not be sufficiently close to zero. This loss of orthogonality can be reduced substantially by rearranging the order of the calculations.[1]
2. To produce a QR factorization of a matrix A, a computer program usually left-multiplies A by a sequence of orthogonal matrices until A is transformed into an upper triangular matrix. This construction is analogous to the left-multiplication by elementary matrices that produces an LU factorization of A.

PRACTICE PROBLEM

Let $W = \text{Span}\{\mathbf{x}_1, \mathbf{x}_2\}$, where $\mathbf{x}_1 = \begin{bmatrix} 1 \\ 1 \\ 1 \end{bmatrix}$ and $\mathbf{x}_2 = \begin{bmatrix} 1/3 \\ 1/3 \\ -2/3 \end{bmatrix}$. Construct an orthonormal basis for W.

7.4 EXERCISES

In Exercises 1–6, the given set is a basis for a subspace W. Use the Gram–Schmidt process to produce an orthogonal basis for W.

1. $\begin{bmatrix} 3 \\ 0 \\ -1 \end{bmatrix}, \begin{bmatrix} 8 \\ 5 \\ -6 \end{bmatrix}$

2. $\begin{bmatrix} 0 \\ 4 \\ 2 \end{bmatrix}, \begin{bmatrix} 5 \\ 6 \\ -7 \end{bmatrix}$

3. $\begin{bmatrix} 2 \\ -5 \\ 1 \end{bmatrix}, \begin{bmatrix} 4 \\ -1 \\ 2 \end{bmatrix}$

4. $\begin{bmatrix} 3 \\ -4 \\ 5 \end{bmatrix}, \begin{bmatrix} -3 \\ 14 \\ -7 \end{bmatrix}$

5. $\begin{bmatrix} 1 \\ -4 \\ 0 \\ 1 \end{bmatrix}, \begin{bmatrix} 7 \\ -7 \\ -4 \\ 1 \end{bmatrix}$

6. $\begin{bmatrix} 3 \\ -1 \\ 2 \\ -1 \end{bmatrix}, \begin{bmatrix} -5 \\ 9 \\ -9 \\ 3 \end{bmatrix}$

7. Find an orthonormal basis of the subspace spanned by the vectors in Exercise 3.

8. Find an orthonormal basis of the subspace spanned by the vectors in Exercise 4.

Find an orthogonal basis for the column spaces of the matrices in Exercises 9–12.

9. $\begin{bmatrix} 3 & -5 & 1 \\ 1 & 1 & 1 \\ -1 & 5 & -2 \\ 3 & -7 & 8 \end{bmatrix}$

10. $\begin{bmatrix} -1 & 6 & 6 \\ 3 & -8 & 3 \\ 1 & -2 & 6 \\ 1 & -4 & -3 \end{bmatrix}$

11. $\begin{bmatrix} 1 & 2 & 5 \\ -1 & 1 & -4 \\ -1 & 4 & -3 \\ 1 & -4 & 7 \\ 1 & 2 & 1 \end{bmatrix}$

12. $\begin{bmatrix} 1 & 3 & 5 \\ -1 & -3 & 1 \\ 0 & 2 & 3 \\ 1 & 5 & 2 \\ 1 & 5 & 8 \end{bmatrix}$

In Exercises 13 and 14, the columns of Q were obtained by applying the Gram–Schmidt process to the columns of A. Find an upper triangular matrix R such that $A = QR$. Check your work.

[1] See *Fundamentals of Matrix Computations*, by David S. Watkins (New York: John Wiley & Sons, 1991) pp. 167–180.

13. $A = \begin{bmatrix} 5 & 9 \\ 1 & 7 \\ -3 & -5 \\ 1 & 5 \end{bmatrix}, Q = \begin{bmatrix} 5/6 & -1/6 \\ 1/6 & 5/6 \\ -3/6 & 1/6 \\ 1/6 & 3/6 \end{bmatrix}$

14. $A = \begin{bmatrix} -2 & 3 \\ 5 & 7 \\ 2 & -2 \\ 4 & 6 \end{bmatrix}, Q = \begin{bmatrix} -2/7 & 5/7 \\ 5/7 & 2/7 \\ 2/7 & -4/7 \\ 4/7 & 2/7 \end{bmatrix}$

15. Find a QR factorization of the matrix in Exercise 11.

16. Find a QR factorization of the matrix in Exercise 12.

17. Suppose that $A = QR$, where Q is $m \times n$ and R is $n \times n$. Show that if the columns of A are linearly independent, then R must be invertible. [*Hint*: Study the equation $R\mathbf{x} = \mathbf{0}$, and use the fact that $A = QR$.]

18. Suppose that $A = QR$, where R is an invertible matrix. Show that A and Q have the same column space. [*Hint*: Given $\mathbf{y}$ in Col A, show that $\mathbf{y} = Q\mathbf{x}$ for some $\mathbf{x}$. Also, given $\mathbf{y}$ in Col Q, show that $y = A\mathbf{x}$ for some $\mathbf{x}$.]

19. (Modified QR factorization). Given $A = QR$ as in Theorem 12, describe how to find an orthogonal $m \times m$ (square) matrix Q_1 and an invertible $n \times n$ upper triangular matrix R such that

$$A = Q_1 \begin{bmatrix} R \\ 0 \end{bmatrix}$$

where the zero matrix has $m - n$ rows and n columns.

SOLUTION TO PRACTICE PROBLEM

Let $\mathbf{v}_1 = \mathbf{x}_1 = \begin{bmatrix} 1 \\ 1 \\ 1 \end{bmatrix}$ and $\mathbf{v}_2 = \mathbf{x}_2 - \dfrac{\mathbf{x}_2 \cdot \mathbf{v}_1}{\mathbf{v}_1 \cdot \mathbf{v}_1}\mathbf{v}_1 = \mathbf{x}_2 - 0\mathbf{v}_1 = \mathbf{x}_2$. Obviously, $\{\mathbf{x}_1, \mathbf{x}_2\}$ was already orthogonal. All that is needed is to normalize the vectors. Let

$$\mathbf{u}_1 = \frac{1}{\|\mathbf{v}_1\|}\mathbf{v}_1 = \frac{1}{\sqrt{3}}\begin{bmatrix} 1 \\ 1 \\ 1 \end{bmatrix} = \begin{bmatrix} 1/\sqrt{3} \\ 1/\sqrt{3} \\ 1/\sqrt{3} \end{bmatrix}$$

Instead of normalizing $\mathbf{v}_2$ directly, normalize $\mathbf{v}_2' = 3\mathbf{v}_2$ instead:

$$\mathbf{u}_2 = \frac{1}{\|\mathbf{v}_2'\|}\mathbf{v}_2' = \frac{1}{\sqrt{1^2 + 1^2 + (-2)^2}}\begin{bmatrix} 1 \\ 1 \\ -2 \end{bmatrix} = \begin{bmatrix} 1/\sqrt{6} \\ 1/\sqrt{6} \\ -2/\sqrt{6} \end{bmatrix}$$

Then $\{\mathbf{u}_1, \mathbf{u}_2\}$ is an orthonormal basis for W.

7.5 LEAST-SQUARES PROBLEMS

The chapter's introductory example described a massive problem $A\mathbf{x} = \mathbf{b}$ that had no solution. Inconsistent systems arise often in applications, though usually not with such an enormous coefficient matrix. When a solution is demanded and none exists, the best one can do is to find an $\mathbf{x}$ that makes $A\mathbf{x}$ as close as possible to $\mathbf{b}$.

Think of $A\mathbf{x}$ as an *approximation* to $\mathbf{b}$. The smaller the distance between $\mathbf{b}$ and $A\mathbf{x}$, given by $\|\mathbf{b} - A\mathbf{x}\|$, the better the approximation. The **general least-squares problem** is to find an $\mathbf{x}$ that makes $\|\mathbf{b} - A\mathbf{x}\|$ as small as possible. The term *least-squares* arises from the fact that $\|\mathbf{b} - A\mathbf{x}\|$ is the square root of a sum of squares.

DEFINITION

If A is $m \times n$ and $\mathbf{b}$ is in $\mathbb{R}^m$, a **least-squares solution** of $A\mathbf{x} = \mathbf{b}$ is an $\hat{\mathbf{x}}$ in $\mathbb{R}^n$ such that

$$\|\mathbf{b} - A\hat{\mathbf{x}}\| \leq \|\mathbf{b} - A\mathbf{x}\|$$

for all $\mathbf{x}$ in $\mathbb{R}^n$.

The most important aspect of the least squares problem is that no matter what $\mathbf{x}$ we select, the vector $A\mathbf{x}$ will necessarily be in the column space, Col A. So we seek an $\mathbf{x}$ that makes $A\mathbf{x}$ the closest point in Col A to $\mathbf{b}$. See Fig. 1. (Of course, if $\mathbf{b}$ happens to be in Col A, then $\mathbf{b}$ *is* $A\mathbf{x}$ for some $\mathbf{x}$ and such an $\mathbf{x}$ is a "least-squares solution.")

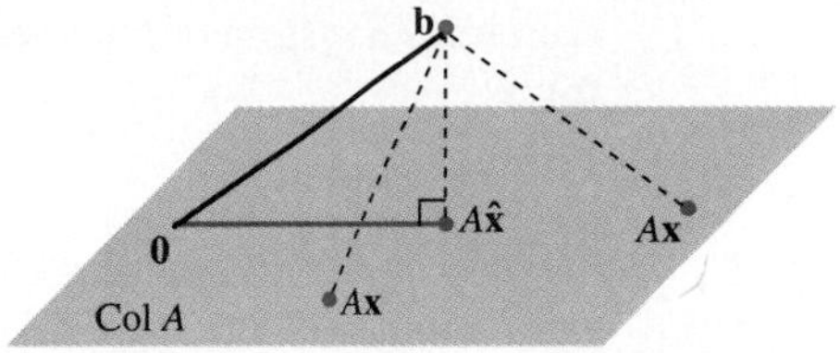

FIGURE 1 $\mathbf{b}$ is closer to $A\hat{\mathbf{x}}$ than to $A\mathbf{x}$ for other $\mathbf{x}$.

Solution of the General Least-Squares Problem

Given A and $\mathbf{b}$ as above, apply the Best Approximation Theorem in Section 7.3 to the subspace Col A. Let

$$\hat{\mathbf{b}} = \text{proj}_{\text{Col } A}\,\mathbf{b}$$

Because $\hat{\mathbf{b}}$ is in the column space of A, the equation $A\mathbf{x} = \hat{\mathbf{b}}$ *is* consistent, and there is an $\hat{\mathbf{x}}$ in $\mathbb{R}^n$ such that

$$A\hat{\mathbf{x}} = \hat{\mathbf{b}} \tag{1}$$

Since $\hat{\mathbf{b}}$ is the closest point in Col A to $\mathbf{b}$, a vector $\hat{\mathbf{x}}$ is a least-squares solution of $A\mathbf{x} = \mathbf{b}$ if and only if $\hat{\mathbf{x}}$ satisfies (1). Such an $\hat{\mathbf{x}}$ in $\mathbb{R}^n$ is a list of weights that will build $\hat{\mathbf{b}}$ out of the columns of A. See Fig. 2. (There will be many solutions of (1) if the equation has free variables.)

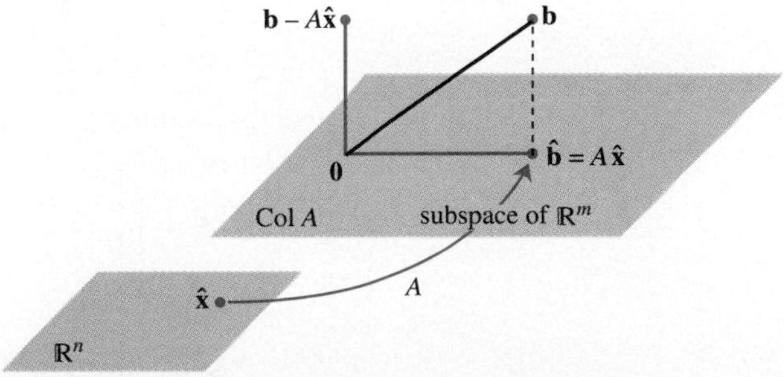

FIGURE 2 The least-squares solution $\hat{\mathbf{x}}$ is in $\mathbb{R}^n$.

Suppose that $\hat{\mathbf{x}}$ satisfies $A\hat{\mathbf{x}} = \hat{\mathbf{b}}$. By the Orthogonal Decomposition Theorem in Section 7.3, the projection $\hat{\mathbf{b}}$ has the property that $\mathbf{b} - \hat{\mathbf{b}}$ is orthogonal to Col A, so $\mathbf{b} - A\hat{\mathbf{x}}$ is orthogonal to each column of A. If $\mathbf{a}_j$ is any column of A, then $\mathbf{a}_j \cdot (\mathbf{b} - A\hat{\mathbf{x}}) = 0$ and $\mathbf{a}_j^T(\mathbf{b} - A\hat{\mathbf{x}}) = 0$. Since each $\mathbf{a}_j^T$ is a row of A^T,

$$A^T(\mathbf{b} - A\hat{\mathbf{x}}) = \mathbf{0} \tag{2}$$

$$A^T\mathbf{b} - A^TA\hat{\mathbf{x}} = \mathbf{0}$$

$$A^TA\hat{\mathbf{x}} = A^T\mathbf{b} \tag{3}$$

[Equation (2) also follows from Theorem 3 in Section 7.1.] The matrix equation (3) represents a system of linear equations commonly referred to as the **normal equations for $\hat{\mathbf{x}}$**.

THEOREM 13

The set of least-squares solutions of $A\mathbf{x} = \mathbf{b}$ coincides with the nonempty set of solutions of the normal equations $A^TA\hat{\mathbf{x}} = A^T\mathbf{b}$.

Proof We have already shown that the set of least-squares solutions is nonempty and any such $\hat{\mathbf{x}}$ satisfies the normal equations. Conversely, suppose that $\hat{\mathbf{x}}$ satisfies $A^TA\hat{\mathbf{x}} = A^T\mathbf{b}$. Then $\hat{\mathbf{x}}$ satisfies (2) above, which shows that $\mathbf{b} - A\hat{\mathbf{x}}$ is orthogonal to the rows of A^T and hence is orthogonal to the columns of A. Since the columns of A span Col A, the vector $\mathbf{b} - A\hat{\mathbf{x}}$ is orthogonal to all of Col A. Hence the equation

$$\mathbf{b} = A\hat{\mathbf{x}} + (\mathbf{b} - A\hat{\mathbf{x}})$$

is a decomposition of $\mathbf{b}$ into the sum of a vector in Col A and a vector orthogonal to Col A. By the uniqueness of the orthogonal decomposition, $A\hat{\mathbf{x}}$ must be the orthogonal projection of $\mathbf{b}$ onto Col A. That is, $A\hat{\mathbf{x}} = \hat{\mathbf{b}}$ and $\hat{\mathbf{x}}$ is a least-squares solution. ∎

EXAMPLE 1 Find a least-squares solution of the inconsistent system $A\mathbf{x} = \mathbf{b}$ for

$$A = \begin{bmatrix} 4 & 0 \\ 0 & 2 \\ 1 & 1 \end{bmatrix}, \quad \mathbf{b} = \begin{bmatrix} 2 \\ 0 \\ 11 \end{bmatrix}$$

Solution To use (3), compute:

$$A^TA = \begin{bmatrix} 4 & 0 & 1 \\ 0 & 2 & 1 \end{bmatrix}\begin{bmatrix} 4 & 0 \\ 0 & 2 \\ 1 & 1 \end{bmatrix} = \begin{bmatrix} 17 & 1 \\ 1 & 5 \end{bmatrix}$$

$$A^T\mathbf{b} = \begin{bmatrix} 4 & 0 & 1 \\ 0 & 2 & 1 \end{bmatrix}\begin{bmatrix} 2 \\ 0 \\ 11 \end{bmatrix} = \begin{bmatrix} 19 \\ 11 \end{bmatrix}$$

Then the equation $A^TA\hat{\mathbf{x}} = A^T\mathbf{b}$ becomes

$$\begin{bmatrix} 17 & 1 \\ 1 & 5 \end{bmatrix}\begin{bmatrix} x_1 \\ x_2 \end{bmatrix} = \begin{bmatrix} 19 \\ 11 \end{bmatrix}$$

Row operations can be used to solve this system, but since A^TA is invertible and 2×2, it is probably faster to compute

$$(A^TA)^{-1} = \frac{1}{84}\begin{bmatrix} 5 & -1 \\ -1 & 17 \end{bmatrix}$$

and then to solve $(A^TA)\hat{\mathbf{x}} = A^T\mathbf{b}$ as

$$\begin{aligned}\hat{\mathbf{x}} &= (A^TA)^{-1}A^T\mathbf{b} \\ &= \frac{1}{84}\begin{bmatrix} 5 & -1 \\ -1 & 17 \end{bmatrix}\begin{bmatrix} 19 \\ 11 \end{bmatrix} = \frac{1}{84}\begin{bmatrix} 84 \\ 168 \end{bmatrix} = \begin{bmatrix} 1 \\ 2 \end{bmatrix}\end{aligned}$$

In many calculations, A^TA is invertible, but this is not always the case. The next example involves a matrix of the sort that appears in what are called *analysis of variance* problems in statistics.

EXAMPLE 2 Find a least-squares solution of $A\mathbf{x} = \mathbf{b}$ for

$$A = \begin{bmatrix} 1 & 1 & 0 & 0 \\ 1 & 1 & 0 & 0 \\ 1 & 0 & 1 & 0 \\ 1 & 0 & 1 & 0 \\ 1 & 0 & 0 & 1 \\ 1 & 0 & 0 & 1 \end{bmatrix}, \quad \mathbf{b} = \begin{bmatrix} -3 \\ -1 \\ 0 \\ 2 \\ 5 \\ 1 \end{bmatrix}$$

Solution Compute

$$A^TA = \begin{bmatrix} 1 & 1 & 1 & 1 & 1 & 1 \\ 1 & 1 & 0 & 0 & 0 & 0 \\ 0 & 0 & 1 & 1 & 0 & 0 \\ 0 & 0 & 0 & 0 & 1 & 1 \end{bmatrix}\begin{bmatrix} 1 & 1 & 0 & 0 \\ 1 & 1 & 0 & 0 \\ 1 & 0 & 1 & 0 \\ 1 & 0 & 1 & 0 \\ 1 & 0 & 0 & 1 \\ 1 & 0 & 0 & 1 \end{bmatrix} = \begin{bmatrix} 6 & 2 & 2 & 2 \\ 2 & 2 & 0 & 0 \\ 2 & 0 & 2 & 0 \\ 2 & 0 & 0 & 2 \end{bmatrix}$$

$$A^T\mathbf{b} = \begin{bmatrix} 1 & 1 & 1 & 1 & 1 & 1 \\ 1 & 1 & 0 & 0 & 0 & 0 \\ 0 & 0 & 1 & 1 & 0 & 0 \\ 0 & 0 & 0 & 0 & 1 & 1 \end{bmatrix}\begin{bmatrix} -3 \\ -1 \\ 0 \\ 2 \\ 5 \\ 1 \end{bmatrix} = \begin{bmatrix} 4 \\ -4 \\ 2 \\ 6 \end{bmatrix}$$

The augmented matrix for $A^TA\hat{\mathbf{x}} = A^T\mathbf{b}$ is

$$\begin{bmatrix} 6 & 2 & 2 & 2 & 4 \\ 2 & 2 & 0 & 0 & -4 \\ 2 & 0 & 2 & 0 & 2 \\ 2 & 0 & 0 & 2 & 6 \end{bmatrix} \sim \begin{bmatrix} 1 & 0 & 0 & 1 & 3 \\ 0 & 1 & 0 & -1 & -5 \\ 0 & 0 & 1 & -1 & -2 \\ 0 & 0 & 0 & 0 & 0 \end{bmatrix}$$

The general solution is $x_1 = 3 - x_4$, $x_2 = -5 + x_4$, $x_3 = -2 + x_4$, and x_4 is free. So the general least-squares solution of $A\mathbf{x} = \mathbf{b}$ has the form

$$\hat{\mathbf{x}} = \begin{bmatrix} 3 \\ -5 \\ -2 \\ 0 \end{bmatrix} + x_4 \begin{bmatrix} -1 \\ 1 \\ 1 \\ 1 \end{bmatrix}$$

The next theorem gives a useful criterion for when there is only one least-squares solution of $A\mathbf{x} = \mathbf{b}$. (Of course, the orthogonal projection $\hat{\mathbf{b}}$ is always unique.)

THEOREM 14

The matrix A^TA is invertible if and only if the columns of A are linearly independent. In this case, the equation $A\mathbf{x} = \mathbf{b}$ has only one least-squares solution $\hat{\mathbf{x}}$, and it is given by

$$\hat{\mathbf{x}} = (A^TA)^{-1}A^T\mathbf{b} \tag{4}$$

The main elements of a proof of Theorem 14 are outlined in Exercises 17–19, which also review concepts from Chapter 5. Formula (4) for $\hat{\mathbf{x}}$ is useful mainly for theoretical purposes and for hand calculations when A^TA is a 2×2 invertible matrix.

When a least-squares solution $\hat{\mathbf{x}}$ is used to produce $A\hat{\mathbf{x}}$ as an approximation to $\mathbf{b}$, the distance from $\mathbf{b}$ to $A\hat{\mathbf{x}}$ is called the **least-squares error** of this approximation.

EXAMPLE 3 Given A and $\mathbf{b}$ as in Example 1, determine the least-squares error in the least-squares solution of $A\mathbf{x} = \mathbf{b}$.

Solution From Example 1,

$$\mathbf{b} = \begin{bmatrix} 2 \\ 0 \\ 11 \end{bmatrix} \quad \text{and} \quad A\hat{\mathbf{x}} = \begin{bmatrix} 4 & 0 \\ 0 & 2 \\ 1 & 1 \end{bmatrix}\begin{bmatrix} 1 \\ 2 \end{bmatrix} = \begin{bmatrix} 4 \\ 4 \\ 3 \end{bmatrix}$$

Hence

$$\mathbf{b} - A\hat{\mathbf{x}} = \begin{bmatrix} 2 \\ 0 \\ 11 \end{bmatrix} - \begin{bmatrix} 4 \\ 4 \\ 3 \end{bmatrix} = \begin{bmatrix} -2 \\ -4 \\ 8 \end{bmatrix}$$

and

$$\|\mathbf{b} - A\hat{\mathbf{x}}\| = \sqrt{(-2)^2 + (-4)^2 + 8^2} = \sqrt{84}$$

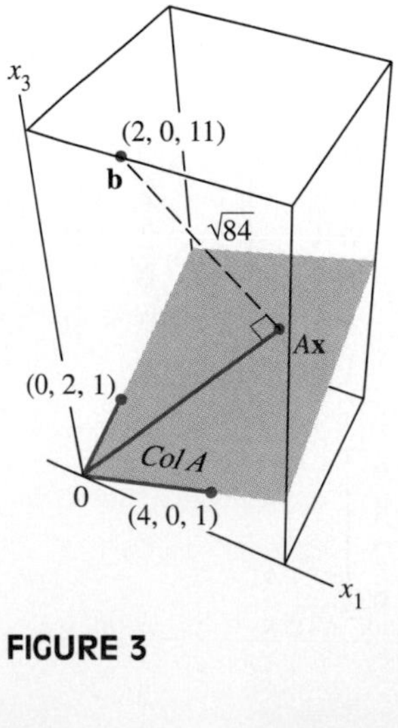

FIGURE 3

The least-squares error is $\sqrt{84}$. For any $\mathbf{x}$ in $\mathbb{R}^2$, the distance between $\mathbf{b}$ and the vector $A\mathbf{x}$ will be at least $\sqrt{84}$. See Fig. 3. Note that the least-squares solution $\hat{\mathbf{x}}$ itself does not appear in the figure.

Alternative Calculations of Least-Squares Solutions

The next example shows how to find a least-squares solution of $A\mathbf{x} = \mathbf{b}$ when the columns of A are orthogonal. Such matrices often arise in linear regression problems, discussed in the next section.

EXAMPLE 4 Find a least-squares solution of $A\mathbf{x} = \mathbf{b}$ for

$$A = \begin{bmatrix} 1 & -6 \\ 1 & -2 \\ 1 & 1 \\ 1 & 7 \end{bmatrix}, \quad \mathbf{b} = \begin{bmatrix} -1 \\ 2 \\ 1 \\ 6 \end{bmatrix}$$

Solution Because the columns $\mathbf{a}_1$ and $\mathbf{a}_2$ of A are orthogonal, the orthogonal projection of $\mathbf{b}$ onto Col A is given by

$$\hat{\mathbf{b}} = \frac{\mathbf{b} \cdot \mathbf{a}_1}{\mathbf{a}_1 \cdot \mathbf{a}_1} \mathbf{a}_1 + \frac{\mathbf{b} \cdot \mathbf{a}_2}{\mathbf{a}_2 \cdot \mathbf{a}_2} \mathbf{a}_2 = \frac{8}{4} \mathbf{a}_1 + \frac{45}{90} \mathbf{a}_2 \tag{5}$$

$$= \begin{bmatrix} 2 \\ 2 \\ 2 \\ 2 \end{bmatrix} + \begin{bmatrix} -3 \\ -1 \\ 1/2 \\ 7/2 \end{bmatrix} = \begin{bmatrix} -1 \\ 1 \\ 5/2 \\ 11/2 \end{bmatrix}$$

Now that $\hat{\mathbf{b}}$ is known, we can solve $A\hat{\mathbf{x}} = \hat{\mathbf{b}}$. But this is trivial, since we already know what weights to place on the columns of A to produce $\hat{\mathbf{b}}$. It is clear from (5) that

$$\hat{\mathbf{x}} = \begin{bmatrix} 8/4 \\ 45/90 \end{bmatrix} = \begin{bmatrix} 2 \\ 1/2 \end{bmatrix}$$

In some cases, the normal equations for a least-squares problem can be *ill-conditioned*; that is, small errors in the calculations of the entries of A^TA can sometimes cause relatively large errors in the solution $\hat{\mathbf{x}}$. If the columns of A are linearly independent, the least-squares solution often can be computed more reliably through a QR factorization of A (described in Section 7.4).[1]

[1] The QR method is compared with the standard normal equation method in G. Golub and C. Van Loan, *Matrix Computations*, 2nd ed. (Baltimore: Johns Hopkins Press, 1989), pp. 230–231.

THEOREM 15

Given an $m \times n$ matrix A with linearly independent columns, let $A = QR$ be a QR factorization of A as in Theorem 12. Then for each $\mathbf{b}$ in $\mathbb{R}^m$, the equation $A\mathbf{x} = \mathbf{b}$ has a unique least-squares solution, given by

$$\hat{\mathbf{x}} = R^{-1}Q^T\mathbf{b} \tag{6}$$

Proof Let $\hat{\mathbf{x}} = R^{-1}Q^T\mathbf{b}$. Then

$$A\hat{\mathbf{x}} = QR\hat{\mathbf{x}} = QRR^{-1}Q^T\mathbf{b} = QQ^T\mathbf{b}$$

By Theorem 12, the columns of Q form an orthonormal basis for Col A. Hence by Theorem 10, $QQ^T\mathbf{b}$ is the orthogonal projection $\hat{\mathbf{b}}$ of $\mathbf{b}$ onto Col A. Then $A\hat{\mathbf{x}} = \hat{\mathbf{b}}$, which shows that $\hat{\mathbf{x}}$ is a least-squares solution of $A\mathbf{x} = \mathbf{b}$. The uniqueness of $\hat{\mathbf{x}}$ follows from Theorem 14. ∎

Numerical Note

Since the R in Theorem 15 is upper triangular, the $\hat{\mathbf{x}}$ should be calculated from the equation

$$R\hat{\mathbf{x}} = Q^T\mathbf{b} \tag{7}$$

It is much faster to solve (7) by back-substitution or row operations than to compute R^{-1} and use (6).

EXAMPLE 5 Find the least-squares solution of $A\mathbf{x} = \mathbf{b}$ for

$$A = \begin{bmatrix} 1 & 3 & 5 \\ 1 & 1 & 0 \\ 1 & 1 & 2 \\ 1 & 3 & 3 \end{bmatrix}, \quad \mathbf{b} = \begin{bmatrix} 3 \\ 5 \\ 7 \\ -3 \end{bmatrix}$$

Solution The QR factorization of A may be obtained as in Section 7.4.

$$A = QR = \begin{bmatrix} 1/2 & 1/2 & 1/2 \\ 1/2 & -1/2 & -1/2 \\ 1/2 & -1/2 & 1/2 \\ 1/2 & 1/2 & -1/2 \end{bmatrix} \begin{bmatrix} 2 & 4 & 5 \\ 0 & 2 & 3 \\ 0 & 0 & 2 \end{bmatrix}$$

Then

$$Q^T\mathbf{b} = \begin{bmatrix} 1/2 & 1/2 & 1/2 & 1/2 \\ 1/2 & -1/2 & -1/2 & 1/2 \\ 1/2 & -1/2 & 1/2 & -1/2 \end{bmatrix} \begin{bmatrix} 3 \\ 5 \\ 7 \\ -3 \end{bmatrix} = \begin{bmatrix} 6 \\ -6 \\ 4 \end{bmatrix}$$

The least-squares solution $\hat{\mathbf{x}}$ satisfies $R\hat{\mathbf{x}} = Q^T\mathbf{b}$; that is,

$$\begin{bmatrix} 2 & 4 & 5 \\ 0 & 2 & 3 \\ 0 & 0 & 2 \end{bmatrix} \begin{bmatrix} x_1 \\ x_2 \\ x_3 \end{bmatrix} = \begin{bmatrix} 6 \\ -6 \\ 4 \end{bmatrix}$$

This equation is solved easily and yields $\hat{\mathbf{x}} = \begin{bmatrix} 10 \\ -6 \\ 2 \end{bmatrix}$.

PRACTICE PROBLEMS

1. Let $A = \begin{bmatrix} 1 & -3 & -3 \\ 1 & 5 & 1 \\ 1 & 7 & 2 \end{bmatrix}$ and $\mathbf{b} = \begin{bmatrix} 5 \\ -3 \\ -5 \end{bmatrix}$. Find a least-squares solution of $A\mathbf{x} = \mathbf{b}$, and compute the associated least-squares error.
2. What can you say about the least-squares solution of $A\mathbf{x} = \mathbf{b}$ when $\mathbf{b}$ is orthogonal to the columns of A?

7.5 EXERCISES

In Exercises 1–4, find a least-squares solution of $A\mathbf{x} = \mathbf{b}$ by (a) constructing the normal equations for $\hat{\mathbf{x}}$ and (b) solving for $\hat{\mathbf{x}}$.

1. $A = \begin{bmatrix} -1 & 2 \\ 2 & -3 \\ -1 & 3 \end{bmatrix}$, $\mathbf{b} = \begin{bmatrix} 4 \\ 1 \\ 2 \end{bmatrix}$

2. $A = \begin{bmatrix} 2 & 1 \\ -2 & 0 \\ 2 & 3 \end{bmatrix}$, $\mathbf{b} = \begin{bmatrix} -5 \\ 8 \\ 1 \end{bmatrix}$

3. $A = \begin{bmatrix} 1 & -2 \\ -1 & 2 \\ 0 & 3 \\ 2 & 5 \end{bmatrix}$, $\mathbf{b} = \begin{bmatrix} 3 \\ 1 \\ -4 \\ 2 \end{bmatrix}$

4. $A = \begin{bmatrix} 1 & 3 \\ 1 & -1 \\ 1 & 1 \end{bmatrix}$, $\mathbf{b} = \begin{bmatrix} 5 \\ 1 \\ 0 \end{bmatrix}$

In Exercises 5 and 6, describe all least-squares solutions of the equation $A\mathbf{x} = \mathbf{b}$.

5. $A = \begin{bmatrix} 1 & 1 & 0 \\ 1 & 1 & 0 \\ 1 & 0 & 1 \\ 1 & 0 & 1 \end{bmatrix}$, $\mathbf{b} = \begin{bmatrix} 1 \\ 3 \\ 8 \\ 2 \end{bmatrix}$

6. $A = \begin{bmatrix} 1 & 1 & 0 \\ 1 & 1 & 0 \\ 1 & 1 & 0 \\ 1 & 0 & 1 \\ 1 & 0 & 1 \\ 1 & 0 & 1 \end{bmatrix}$, $\mathbf{b} = \begin{bmatrix} 7 \\ 2 \\ 3 \\ 6 \\ 5 \\ 4 \end{bmatrix}$

7. Compute the least-squares error associated with the least-squares solution found in Exercise 3.

8. Compute the least-squares error associated with the least-squares solution found in Exercise 4.

In Exercises 9–12, find (a) the orthogonal projection of $\mathbf{b}$ onto Col A and (b) a least-squares solution of $A\mathbf{x} = \mathbf{b}$.

9. $A = \begin{bmatrix} 1 & 5 \\ 3 & 1 \\ -2 & 4 \end{bmatrix}$, $\mathbf{b} = \begin{bmatrix} 4 \\ -2 \\ -3 \end{bmatrix}$

10. $A = \begin{bmatrix} 1 & 2 \\ -1 & 4 \\ 1 & 2 \end{bmatrix}$, $\mathbf{b} = \begin{bmatrix} 3 \\ -1 \\ 5 \end{bmatrix}$

11. $A = \begin{bmatrix} 4 & 0 & 1 \\ 1 & -5 & 1 \\ 6 & 1 & 0 \\ 1 & -1 & -5 \end{bmatrix}$, $\mathbf{b} = \begin{bmatrix} 9 \\ 0 \\ 0 \\ 0 \end{bmatrix}$

12. $A = \begin{bmatrix} 1 & 1 & 0 \\ 1 & 0 & -1 \\ 0 & 1 & 1 \\ -1 & 1 & -1 \end{bmatrix}$, $\mathbf{b} = \begin{bmatrix} 2 \\ 5 \\ 6 \\ 6 \end{bmatrix}$

13. Let $A = \begin{bmatrix} 3 & 4 \\ -2 & 1 \\ 3 & 4 \end{bmatrix}$, $\mathbf{b} = \begin{bmatrix} 11 \\ -9 \\ 5 \end{bmatrix}$, $\mathbf{u} = \begin{bmatrix} 5 \\ -1 \end{bmatrix}$, and $\mathbf{v} = \begin{bmatrix} 5 \\ -2 \end{bmatrix}$. Compute $A\mathbf{u}$ and $A\mathbf{v}$, and compare them with $\mathbf{b}$. Could $\mathbf{u}$ possibly be a least-squares solution of $A\mathbf{x} = \mathbf{b}$? (Answer this without computing a least-squares solution.)

14. Let $A = \begin{bmatrix} 2 & 1 \\ -3 & -4 \\ 3 & 2 \end{bmatrix}$, $\mathbf{b} = \begin{bmatrix} 5 \\ 4 \\ 4 \end{bmatrix}$, $\mathbf{u} = \begin{bmatrix} 4 \\ -5 \end{bmatrix}$, and $\mathbf{v} = \begin{bmatrix} 6 \\ -5 \end{bmatrix}$. Compute $A\mathbf{u}$ and $A\mathbf{v}$, and compare them with $\mathbf{b}$. Is it possible that at least one of $\mathbf{u}$ or $\mathbf{v}$ could be a least-squares solution of $A\mathbf{x} = \mathbf{b}$? (Answer this without computing a least-squares solution.)

In Exercises 15 and 16, use the factorization $A = QR$ to find the least-squares solution of $A\mathbf{x} = \mathbf{b}$.

15. $A = \begin{bmatrix} 2 & 3 \\ 2 & 4 \\ 1 & 1 \end{bmatrix}$, $Q = \begin{bmatrix} 2/3 & 1/3 \\ 2/3 & -2/3 \\ 1/3 & 2/3 \end{bmatrix}$, $R = \begin{bmatrix} 3 & 5 \\ 0 & -1 \end{bmatrix}$, and $\mathbf{b} = \begin{bmatrix} 7 \\ 3 \\ 1 \end{bmatrix}$.

16. $A = \begin{bmatrix} 1 & -1 \\ 1 & 4 \\ 1 & -1 \\ 1 & 4 \end{bmatrix}$, $Q = \begin{bmatrix} 1/2 & -1/2 \\ 1/2 & 1/2 \\ 1/2 & -1/2 \\ 1/2 & 1/2 \end{bmatrix}$, $R = \begin{bmatrix} 2 & 3 \\ 0 & 5 \end{bmatrix}$, and $\mathbf{b} = \begin{bmatrix} -1 \\ 6 \\ 5 \\ 7 \end{bmatrix}$.

17. Let A be an $m \times n$ matrix. Use the steps below to show that a vector $\mathbf{x}$ in $\mathbb{R}^n$ satisfies $A\mathbf{x} = \mathbf{0}$ if and only if $A^TA\mathbf{x} = \mathbf{0}$. This will show that Nul A = Nul A^TA.

a. Show that if $A\mathbf{x} = \mathbf{0}$, then $A^TA\mathbf{x} = \mathbf{0}$.

b. Suppose that $A^TA\mathbf{x} = \mathbf{0}$. Explain why $\mathbf{x}^TA^TA\mathbf{x} = \mathbf{0}$, and use this to show that $\|A\mathbf{x}\|^2 = 0$, which will show that $A\mathbf{x} = \mathbf{0}$.

18. Let A be an $m \times n$ matrix such that A^TA is invertible. Show that the columns of A are linearly independent. [*Careful*: You may not assume that A is invertible; it may not even be square.]

19. Let A be an $m \times n$ matrix whose columns are linearly independent. [*Careful*: A need not be square.]

a. Use Exercise 17 to show that A^TA is an invertible matrix.

b. Explain why A must have at least as many rows as columns.

c. Determine the rank of A.

20. Use Exercise 17 to show that rank A^TA = rank A. [*Hint*: How many columns does A^TA have? How is this connected with the rank of A^TA?]

21. Suppose that A is $m \times n$ with linearly independent columns and $\mathbf{b}$ is in $\mathbb{R}^m$. Use the normal equations to produce a formula for $\hat{\mathbf{b}}$, the projection of $\mathbf{b}$ onto Col A. [*Hint*: Find $\hat{\mathbf{x}}$ first. The formula does not require an orthogonal basis for Col A.]

22. Find a formula for the least-squares solution of $A\mathbf{x} = \mathbf{b}$ when the columns of A are orthonormal.

23. Describe all least-squares solutions of the system

$$x + y = 2$$
$$x + y = 4$$

24. (MATLAB) Example 3 in Section 5.8 displayed a low-pass linear filter that changed a signal $\{y_k\}$ into $\{y_{k+1}\}$ and changed a higher-frequency signal $\{w_k\}$ into the zero signal, where $y_k = \cos(\pi k/4)$ and $w_k = \cos(3\pi k/4)$. The following calculations will design a filter with approximately those properties. The filter equation is

$$a_0 y_{k+2} + a_1 y_{k+1} + a_2 y_k = z_k \quad \text{for all } k \tag{8}$$

Because the signals are periodic, with period 8, it suffices to study Eq. (8) for $k = 0, \ldots, 7$. The action on the two signals described above translates into two sets of eight equations:

$$\begin{array}{c} k=0 \\ k=1 \\ \vdots \\ \\ \\ \\ \\ k=7 \end{array} \overset{\begin{array}{ccc} y_{k+2} & y_{k+1} & y_k \end{array}}{\begin{bmatrix} 0 & .7 & 1 \\ -.7 & 0 & .7 \\ -1 & -.7 & 0 \\ -.7 & -1 & -.7 \\ 0 & -.7 & -1 \\ .7 & 0 & -.7 \\ 1 & .7 & 0 \\ .7 & 1 & .7 \end{bmatrix}} \begin{bmatrix} a_0 \\ a_1 \\ a_2 \end{bmatrix} = \overset{y_{k+1}}{\begin{bmatrix} .7 \\ 0 \\ -.7 \\ -1 \\ -.7 \\ 0 \\ .7 \\ 1 \end{bmatrix}};$$

$$\overset{\begin{array}{ccc} w_{k+2} & w_{k+1} & w_k \end{array}}{\begin{bmatrix} 0 & -.7 & 1 \\ .7 & 0 & -.7 \\ -1 & .7 & 0 \\ .7 & -1 & .7 \\ 0 & .7 & -1 \\ -.7 & 0 & .7 \\ 1 & -.7 & 0 \\ -.7 & 1 & -.7 \end{bmatrix}} \begin{bmatrix} a_0 \\ a_1 \\ a_2 \end{bmatrix} = \begin{bmatrix} 0 \\ 0 \\ 0 \\ 0 \\ 0 \\ 0 \\ 0 \\ 0 \end{bmatrix}$$

Write an equation $A\mathbf{x} = \mathbf{b}$, where A is a 16×3 matrix formed from the two coefficient matrices above and $\mathbf{b}$ in $\mathbb{R}^{16}$ is formed from the two right sides of the equations. Find a_0, a_1, a_2 given by the least-squares solution of $A\mathbf{x} = \mathbf{b}$. (The .7 in the data above was used as an approximation for $\sqrt{2}/2$, to illustrate how a typical computation in an applied problem might proceed. If .707 were used instead, the resulting filter coefficients would agree to at least seven decimal places with $\sqrt{2}/4$, $1/2$, and $\sqrt{2}/4$, the values produced by exact arithmetic calculations.)

SOLUTIONS TO PRACTICE PROBLEMS

1. First, compute

$$A^TA = \begin{bmatrix} 1 & 1 & 1 \\ -3 & 5 & 7 \\ -3 & 1 & 2 \end{bmatrix}\begin{bmatrix} 1 & -3 & -3 \\ 1 & 5 & 1 \\ 1 & 7 & 2 \end{bmatrix} = \begin{bmatrix} 3 & 9 & 0 \\ 9 & 83 & 28 \\ 0 & 28 & 14 \end{bmatrix}$$

$$A^T\mathbf{b} = \begin{bmatrix} 1 & 1 & 1 \\ -3 & 5 & 7 \\ -3 & 1 & 2 \end{bmatrix}\begin{bmatrix} 5 \\ -3 \\ -5 \end{bmatrix} = \begin{bmatrix} -3 \\ -65 \\ -28 \end{bmatrix}$$

Next, row reduce the augmented matrix for the normal equations, $A^TA\mathbf{x} = A^T\mathbf{b}$:

$$\begin{bmatrix} 3 & 9 & 0 & -3 \\ 9 & 83 & 28 & -65 \\ 0 & 28 & 14 & -28 \end{bmatrix} \sim \begin{bmatrix} 1 & 3 & 0 & -1 \\ 0 & 56 & 28 & -56 \\ 0 & 28 & 14 & -28 \end{bmatrix} \sim \cdots$$

$$\sim \begin{bmatrix} 1 & 0 & -3/2 & 2 \\ 0 & 1 & 1/2 & -1 \\ 0 & 0 & 0 & 0 \end{bmatrix}$$

The general least-squares solution is $x_1 = 2 + \frac{3}{2}x_3$, $x_2 = -1 - \frac{1}{2}x_3$, with x_3 free. For one specific solution, take $x_3 = 0$ (for example), and get

$$\hat{\mathbf{x}} = \begin{bmatrix} 2 \\ -1 \\ 0 \end{bmatrix}$$

To find the least-squares error, compute

$$\hat{\mathbf{b}} = A\hat{\mathbf{x}} = \begin{bmatrix} 1 & -3 & -3 \\ 1 & 5 & 1 \\ 1 & 7 & 2 \end{bmatrix}\begin{bmatrix} 2 \\ -1 \\ 0 \end{bmatrix} = \begin{bmatrix} 5 \\ -3 \\ -5 \end{bmatrix}$$

It turns out that $\hat{\mathbf{b}} = \mathbf{b}$, so $\|\mathbf{b} - \hat{\mathbf{b}}\| = 0$. The least-squares error is zero because $\mathbf{b}$ happens to be in Col A.

2. If $\mathbf{b}$ is orthogonal to the columns of A, then the projection of $\mathbf{b}$ onto the column space of A is $\mathbf{0}$. In this case a least-squares solution $\hat{\mathbf{x}}$ of $A\mathbf{x} = \mathbf{b}$ will satisfy $A\hat{\mathbf{x}} = \mathbf{0}$.

7.6 APPLICATIONS TO LINEAR MODELS

One task in science and engineering is to analyze and understand relationships among several quantities that vary. This section describes a variety of situations in which data are used to build or verify a formula that predicts the value of one variable as a function of other variables. In each case, the problem will amount to solving a least-squares problem.

For easy application of the discussion to real problems that readers may encounter later in their careers, we choose notation that is commonly used in the statistical analysis of scientific and engineering data. Instead of $A\mathbf{x} = \mathbf{b}$, we write $X\boldsymbol{\beta} = \mathbf{y}$ and refer to X as the **design matrix**, $\boldsymbol{\beta}$ the **parameter vector**, and $\mathbf{y}$ the **observation vector**.

Least-Squares Lines

The simplest relation between two variables x and y is the linear equation $y = \beta_0 + \beta_1 x$.[1] Experimental data often produce points $(x_1, y_1), \ldots, (x_n, y_n)$ that when graphed seem to lie close to a line. We want to determine the parameters β_0 and β_1 that make the line as "close" to the points as possible.

Suppose β_0 and β_1 are fixed, and consider the line $y = \beta_0 + \beta_1 x$ in Fig. 1. Corresponding to each data point (x_j, y_j) there is a point $(x_j, \beta_0 + \beta_1 x_j)$ on the line with the same x-coordinate. We call y_j the *observed* value of y and $\beta_0 + \beta_1 x_j$ the *predicted* y-value (determined by the line). The difference between an observed y-value and a predicted y-value is called a *residual.*

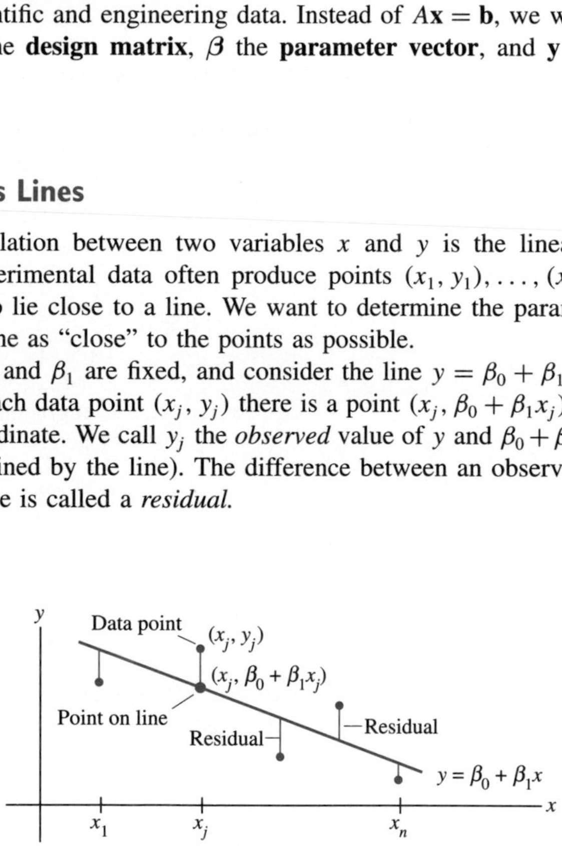

FIGURE 1 Fitting a line to experimental data.

There are several ways to measure how "close" the line is to the data. The usual choice (primarily because the mathematical calculations are simple) is to add the squares of the residuals. The **least-squares line** is the line $y = \beta_0 + \beta_1 x$ that minimizes the sum of the squares of the residuals. The coefficients β_0, β_1 of this line are called (linear) **regression coefficients**.

[1] This notation is commonly used for least-squares lines instead of $y = mx + b$.

If the data points were on the line, the parameters β_0 and β_1 would satisfy the equations

Predicted y-value		Observed y-value
$\beta_0 + \beta_1 x_1$	$=$	y_1
$\beta_0 + \beta_1 x_2$	$=$	y_2
$\vdots$		$\vdots$
$\beta_0 + \beta_1 x_n$	$=$	y_n

We may write this system as

$$X\boldsymbol{\beta} = \mathbf{y}, \quad \text{where } X = \begin{bmatrix} 1 & x_1 \\ 1 & x_2 \\ \vdots & \vdots \\ 1 & x_n \end{bmatrix}, \quad \boldsymbol{\beta} = \begin{bmatrix} \beta_0 \\ \beta_1 \end{bmatrix}, \quad \mathbf{y} = \begin{bmatrix} y_1 \\ y_2 \\ \vdots \\ y_n \end{bmatrix} \tag{1}$$

Of course, if the data points don't lie on a line, then there are no parameters β_0, β_1 for which the predicted y-values in $X\boldsymbol{\beta}$ equal the observed y-values in $\mathbf{y}$, and $X\boldsymbol{\beta} = \mathbf{y}$ has no solution. This is a least-squares problem, $A\mathbf{x} = \mathbf{b}$, with different notation!

The square of the distance between $X\boldsymbol{\beta}$ and $\mathbf{y}$ is precisely the sum of the squares of the residuals. The $\boldsymbol{\beta}$ that minimizes this sum also minimizes the distance between $X\boldsymbol{\beta}$ and $\mathbf{y}$. *Computing the least-squares solution of $X\boldsymbol{\beta} = \mathbf{y}$ is equivalent to finding the $\boldsymbol{\beta}$ that determines the least-squares line in Fig. 1.*

EXAMPLE 1 Find the equation $y = \beta_0 + \beta_1 x$ of the least-squares line that best fits the data points (2, 1), (5, 2), (7, 3), (8, 3).

Solution Use the x-coordinates of the data to build the matrix X in (1) and the y-coordinates to build the vector $\mathbf{y}$:

$$X = \begin{bmatrix} 1 & 2 \\ 1 & 5 \\ 1 & 7 \\ 1 & 8 \end{bmatrix}, \quad \mathbf{y} = \begin{bmatrix} 1 \\ 2 \\ 3 \\ 3 \end{bmatrix}$$

For the least-squares solution of $X\boldsymbol{\beta} = \mathbf{y}$, we compute the normal equations, which become (with the new notation)

$$X^T X \hat{\boldsymbol{\beta}} = X^T \mathbf{y}$$

We have

$$X^T X = \begin{bmatrix} 1 & 1 & 1 & 1 \\ 2 & 5 & 7 & 8 \end{bmatrix} \begin{bmatrix} 1 & 2 \\ 1 & 5 \\ 1 & 7 \\ 1 & 8 \end{bmatrix} = \begin{bmatrix} 4 & 22 \\ 22 & 142 \end{bmatrix}$$

$$X^T \mathbf{y} = \begin{bmatrix} 1 & 1 & 1 & 1 \\ 2 & 5 & 7 & 8 \end{bmatrix} \begin{bmatrix} 1 \\ 2 \\ 3 \\ 3 \end{bmatrix} = \begin{bmatrix} 9 \\ 57 \end{bmatrix}$$

The normal equations are

$$\begin{bmatrix} 4 & 22 \\ 22 & 142 \end{bmatrix} \begin{bmatrix} \beta_0 \\ \beta_1 \end{bmatrix} = \begin{bmatrix} 9 \\ 57 \end{bmatrix}$$

Hence

$$\begin{bmatrix} \beta_0 \\ \beta_1 \end{bmatrix} = \begin{bmatrix} 4 & 22 \\ 22 & 142 \end{bmatrix}^{-1} \begin{bmatrix} 9 \\ 57 \end{bmatrix} = \frac{1}{84} \begin{bmatrix} 142 & -22 \\ -22 & 4 \end{bmatrix} \begin{bmatrix} 9 \\ 57 \end{bmatrix} = \frac{1}{84} \begin{bmatrix} 24 \\ 30 \end{bmatrix} = \begin{bmatrix} 2/7 \\ 5/14 \end{bmatrix}$$

Thus the least-squares line has the equation

$$y = \frac{2}{7} + \frac{5}{14} x$$

See Fig. 2. ∎

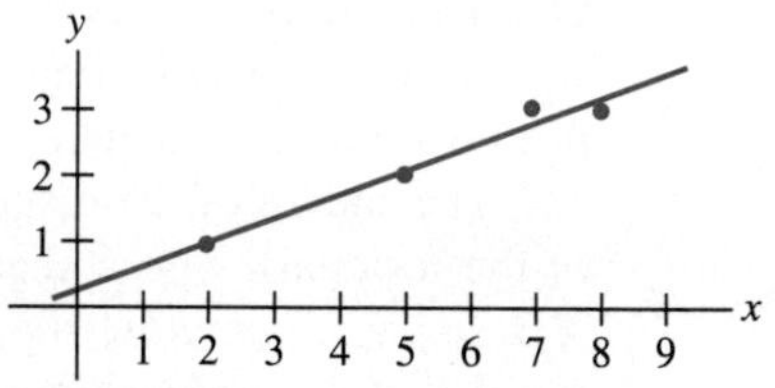

FIGURE 2 The least-squares line $y = \frac{2}{7} + \frac{5}{14}x$.

A common practice before computing a least-squares line is to compute the average $\overline{x}$ of the original x-values and form a new variable $x^* = x - \overline{x}$. The new x-data are said to be in **mean-deviation form**. In this case the two columns of the design matrix will be orthogonal. Solution of the normal equations is simplified, just as in Example 4 of Section 7.5. See Exercises 17 and 18.

The General Linear Model

In some applications it is necessary to fit data points with something other than a straight line. In the examples that follow, the matrix equation is still $X\boldsymbol{\beta} = \mathbf{y}$, but the specific form of X changes from one problem to the next. Statisticians usually introduce a **residual vector** $\boldsymbol{\epsilon}$, defined by $\boldsymbol{\epsilon} = \mathbf{y} - X\boldsymbol{\beta}$, and write

$$\mathbf{y} = X\boldsymbol{\beta} + \boldsymbol{\epsilon}$$

Any equation of this form is referred to as a **linear model**. Once X and $\mathbf{y}$ are determined, the goal is to minimize the length of $\boldsymbol{\epsilon}$, which amounts to finding a least-squares solution of $X\boldsymbol{\beta} = \mathbf{y}$. In each case, the least-squares solution $\hat{\boldsymbol{\beta}}$ is a solution of the normal equations

$$X^T X \hat{\boldsymbol{\beta}} = X^T \mathbf{y}$$

Least-Squares Fitting of Other Curves

When data points $(x_1, y_1), \ldots, (x_n, y_n)$ on a "scatter plot" do not lie close to any line, it may be appropriate to postulate some other functional relationship between x and y.

The next three examples show how to fit data by curves that have the general form

$$y = \beta_0 f_0(x) + \beta_1 f_1(x) + \cdots + \beta_k f_k(x) \qquad (2)$$

where the $f_0, \ldots, f_k$ are known functions and the $\beta_0, \ldots, \beta_k$ are parameters that must be determined. As we shall see, Eq. (2) describes a linear model because it is linear in the unknown parameters.

For a particular value of x, (2) gives a predicted or "fitted" value of y. The difference between the observed value and the predicted value is the residual. The parameters $\beta_0, \ldots, \beta_k$ must be determined so as to minimize the sum of the squares of the residuals.

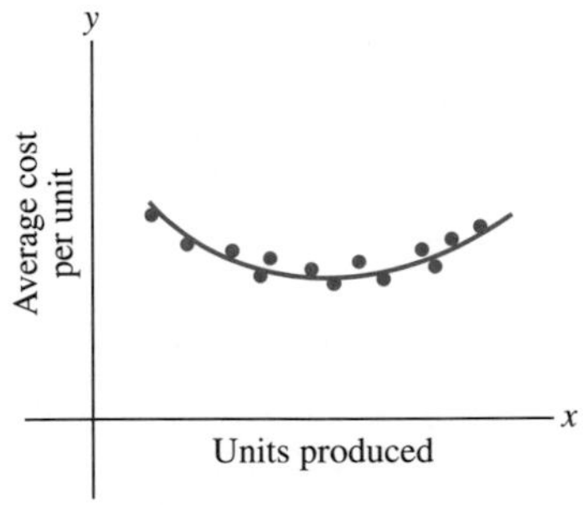

FIGURE 3 Average cost curve.

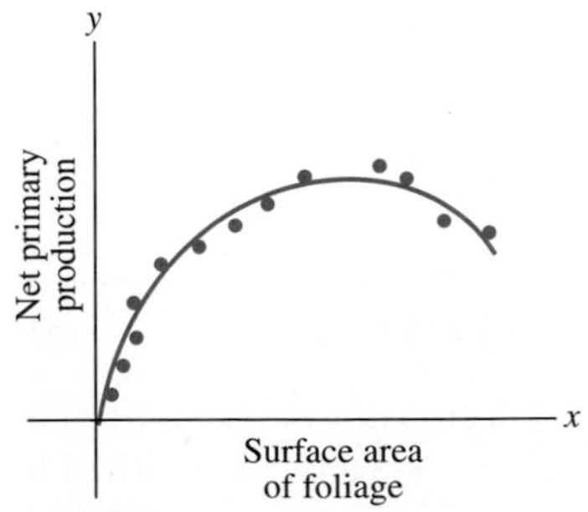

FIGURE 4 Production of nutrients.

EXAMPLE 2 Suppose data points $(x_1, y_1), \ldots, (x_n, y_n)$ appear to lie along some sort of parabola instead of a straight line. For instance, if the x-coordinate denotes the production level for a company, and y denotes the average cost per unit of operating at a level of x units per day, then a typical average cost curve looks like a parabola that opens upward (Fig. 3). In ecology, a parabolic curve that opens downward is used to model the net primary production of nutrients in a plant, as a function of the surface area of the foliage (Fig. 4). Suppose we wish to approximate the data by an equation of the form

$$y = \beta_0 + \beta_1 x + \beta_2 x^2 \qquad (3)$$

Describe the linear model that produces a "least-squares fit" of the data by Eq. (3).

Solution Equation (3) describes the ideal relationship. Suppose that the actual values of the parameters are $\beta_0, \beta_1, \beta_2$. Then the coordinates of the first data point (x_1, y_1) will satisfy an equation of the form

$$y_1 = \beta_0 + \beta_1 x_1 + \beta_2 x_1^2 + \epsilon_1$$

where ϵ_1 is the residual error between the observed value y_1 and the predicted y-value $\beta_0 + \beta_1 x_1 + \beta_2 x_1^2$. Let us make a similar equation for each of the data points.

$$\begin{aligned} y_1 &= \beta_0 + \beta_1 x_1 + \beta_2 x_1^2 + \epsilon_1 \\ y_2 &= \beta_0 + \beta_1 x_2 + \beta_2 x_2^2 + \epsilon_2 \\ &\vdots \qquad\qquad \vdots \\ y_n &= \beta_0 + \beta_1 x_n + \beta_2 x_n^2 + \epsilon_n \end{aligned}$$

It is a simple matter to write this system of equations in the form $\mathbf{y} = X\boldsymbol{\beta} + \boldsymbol{\epsilon}$. We find X by inspecting the first few rows of the system and looking for the pattern.

$$\begin{bmatrix} y_1 \\ y_2 \\ \vdots \\ y_n \end{bmatrix} = \begin{bmatrix} 1 & x_1 & x_1^2 \\ 1 & x_2 & x_2^2 \\ \vdots & \vdots & \vdots \\ 1 & x_n & x_n^2 \end{bmatrix} \begin{bmatrix} \beta_0 \\ \beta_1 \\ \beta_2 \end{bmatrix} + \begin{bmatrix} \epsilon_1 \\ \epsilon_2 \\ \vdots \\ \epsilon_n \end{bmatrix}$$

$$\mathbf{y} \quad = \quad X \quad\quad \boldsymbol{\beta} \quad + \quad \boldsymbol{\epsilon}$$

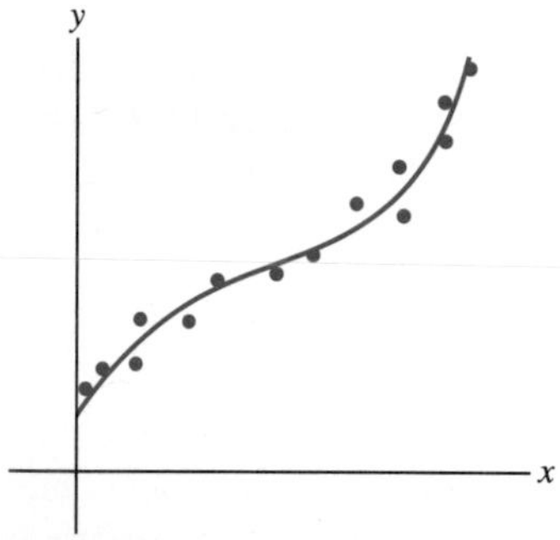

FIGURE 5 Data points along a cubic curve.

EXAMPLE 3 If data points tend to follow a pattern such as in Fig. 5, then an appropriate model might be an equation of the form

$$y = \beta_0 + \beta_1 x + \beta_2 x^2 + \beta_3 x^3$$

Such data, for instance, could come from a company's total costs, as a function of the level of production. Describe the linear model that gives a least-squares fit of this type to data $(x_1, y_1), \ldots, (x_n, y_n)$.

Solution By an analysis similar to that in Example 2, we obtain

Observation vector; Design matrix; Parameter vector; Residual vector

$$\mathbf{y} = \begin{bmatrix} y_1 \\ y_2 \\ \vdots \\ y_n \end{bmatrix}, \quad X = \begin{bmatrix} 1 & x_1 & x_1^2 & x_1^3 \\ 1 & x_2 & x_2^2 & x_2^3 \\ \vdots & \vdots & \vdots & \vdots \\ 1 & x_n & x_n^2 & x_n^3 \end{bmatrix}, \quad \boldsymbol{\beta} = \begin{bmatrix} \beta_0 \\ \beta_1 \\ \beta_2 \\ \beta_3 \end{bmatrix}, \quad \boldsymbol{\epsilon} = \begin{bmatrix} \epsilon_1 \\ \epsilon_2 \\ \vdots \\ \epsilon_n \end{bmatrix}$$

Multiple Regression

Suppose an experiment involves two independent variables—say, u and v—and one dependent variable, y. A simple equation to predict y from u and v has the form

$$y = \beta_0 + \beta_1 u + \beta_2 v \tag{4}$$

A more general prediction equation might have the form

$$y = \beta_0 + \beta_1 u + \beta_2 v + \beta_3 u^2 + \beta_4 uv + \beta_5 v^2 \tag{5}$$

This equation is used in geology, for instance, to model erosion surfaces, glacial cirques, soil pH, and other quantities. In such cases, the least-squares fit is called a *trend surface*.

Both (4) and (5) lead to a linear model because they are linear in the unknown parameters (even though u and v are multiplied). In general, a linear model will arise whenever y is to be predicted by an equation of the form

$$y = \beta_0 f_0(u, v) + \beta_1 f_1(u, v) + \cdots + \beta_k f_k(u, v)$$

where the $f_0, \dots, f_k$ are any sort of known functions and where $\beta_0, \dots, \beta_k$ are unknown weights.

EXAMPLE 4 In geography, local models of terrain are constructed from data $(u_1, v_1, y_1), \dots, (u_n, v_n, y_n)$, where u_j, v_j, and y_j are latitude, longitude, and altitude, respectively. Describe the linear model that gives a least-squares fit to such data by using the form of Eq. (4). The solution is called the least-squares plane. See Fig. 6.

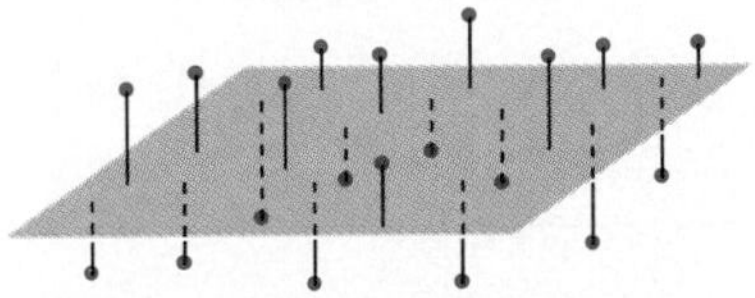

FIGURE 6 A least-squares plane.

Solution We expect the data to satisfy the following equations:

$$\begin{aligned} y_1 &= \beta_0 + \beta_1 u_1 + \beta_2 v_1 + \epsilon_1 \\ y_2 &= \beta_0 + \beta_1 u_2 + \beta_2 v_2 + \epsilon_2 \\ &\vdots \\ y_n &= \beta_0 + \beta_1 u_n + \beta_2 v_n + \epsilon_n \end{aligned}$$

This system has the matrix form $\mathbf{y} = X\boldsymbol{\beta} + \boldsymbol{\epsilon}$, where

$$\underset{\text{Observation vector}}{\mathbf{y} = \begin{bmatrix} y_1 \\ y_2 \\ \vdots \\ y_n \end{bmatrix}}, \quad \underset{\text{Design matrix}}{X = \begin{bmatrix} 1 & u_1 & v_1 \\ 1 & u_2 & v_2 \\ \vdots & \vdots & \vdots \\ 1 & u_n & v_n \end{bmatrix}}, \quad \underset{\text{Parameter vector}}{\boldsymbol{\beta} = \begin{bmatrix} \beta_0 \\ \beta_1 \\ \beta_2 \end{bmatrix}}, \quad \underset{\text{Residual vector}}{\boldsymbol{\epsilon} = \begin{bmatrix} \epsilon_1 \\ \epsilon_2 \\ \vdots \\ \epsilon_n \end{bmatrix}}$$

Example 4 shows that the linear model for multiple regression has the same abstract form as the model for the simple regression in the earlier examples. Linear algebra gives us the power to understand the general principle behind all the linear models. Once X is defined properly, the normal equations for $\boldsymbol{\beta}$ have the same matrix form, no matter how many variables are involved. Thus, for any linear model where X^TX is invertible, the least-squares $\hat{\boldsymbol{\beta}}$ is given by $(X^TX)^{-1}X^T\mathbf{y}$.

Further Reading

W.C. Krumbein and F.A. Graybill, *An Introduction to Statistical Models in Geology*, New York: McGraw-Hill, 1965.

David J. Unwin, *An Introduction to Trend Surface Analysis*, Concepts and Techniques in Modern Geography, No. 5, Norwich, England: Geo Books, 1975.

PRACTICE PROBLEM

When the monthly sales of a product are subject to seasonal fluctuations, a curve that approximates the sales data might have the form

$$y = \beta_0 + \beta_1 x + \beta_2 \sin(2\pi x/12)$$

where x is the time in months. The term $\beta_0 + \beta_1 x$ gives the basic sales trend, and the sine term reflects the seasonal changes in sales. Give the design matrix and the parameter vector for the linear model that leads to a least-squares fit of the equation above. Assume that the data are $(x_1, y_1), \ldots, (x_n, y_n)$.

7.6 EXERCISES

In Exercises 1–4, find the equation $y = \beta_0 + \beta_1 x$ of the least-squares line that best fits the given data points.

1. $(0, 1), (1, 1), (2, 2), (3, 2)$
2. $(1, 0), (2, 1), (4, 2), (5, 3)$
3. $(-1, 0), (0, 1), (1, 2), (2, 4)$
4. $(2, 3), (3, 2), (5, 1), (6, 0)$
5. Let X be the design matrix used to find the least-squares line to fit data $(x_1, y_1), \ldots, (x_n, y_n)$. Use a theorem in Section 7.5 to show that the normal equations have a unique solution if and only if the data include at least two data points with different x-coordinates.
6. Let X be the design matrix in Example 2 corresponding to a least-squares fit of a parabola to data $(x_1, y_1), \ldots, (x_n, y_n)$. Suppose that x_1, x_2, x_3 are distinct. Explain why there is only one parabola that fits the data best, in a least-squares sense. (See Exercise 5.)
7. A certain experiment produces data (1, 1.8), (2, 2.7), (3, 3.4), (4, 3.8), and (5, 3.9). Describe the model that produces a least-squares fit of these points by a function of the form

   $$y = \beta_1 x + \beta_2 x^2$$

   Such a function might arise, for example, as the revenue from the sale of x units of a product, when the amount offered for sale affects the price to be set for the product. Give the design matrix, the observation vector, and the unknown parameter vector. (Optional: Use MATLAB to estimate β_1 and β_2.)
8. A simple curve that often makes a good model for the variable costs of a company, as a function of the sales level x, has the form

   $$y = \beta_1 x + \beta_2 x^2 + \beta_3 x^3$$

   There is no constant term because fixed costs are not included. Give the design matrix and the parameter vector for the linear model that leads to a least-squares fit of the equation above, with data $(x_1, y_1), \ldots, (x_n, y_n)$.
9. A certain experiment produces the data (1, 7.9), (2, 5.4), and (3, −.9). Describe the model that produces a least-squares fit of these points by a function of the form

   $$y = A\cos x + B\sin x$$

10. Suppose radioactive substances A and B have decay constants of .02 and .07, respectively. If a mixture of these two substances at time $t = 0$ contains M_A grams of A and M_B grams of B, then a model for the total amount y of the mixture present at time t is

    $$y = M_A e^{-.02t} + M_B e^{-.07t}$$

    Suppose the initial amounts M_A, M_B are unknown, but a scientist is able to measure the total amount present at several times and records the following points (t_i, y_i) : (10, 21.34), (11, 20.68), and (12, 20.05). Describe a linear model that may be used to estimate M_A and M_B. (Optional: Use MATLAB to estimate the values of M_A and M_B.)
11. (MATLAB) According to Kepler's first law, a comet should have an elliptic, parabolic, or hyperbolic orbit (with gravitational attractions from the planets ignored). In suitable polar coordinates, the position (r, ϑ) of a comet satisfies an equation of the form

    $$r = \beta + e(r\cdot\cos\vartheta)$$

    where β is a constant and e is the *eccentricity* of the orbit, with $e < 1$ for an ellipse, $e = 1$ for a parabola, and $e > 1$ for a hyperbola. Suppose that observations of a newly discovered comet provide the data below. Determine the type of orbit and predict where the comet will be when $\vartheta = 4.6$ (radians).[2]

ϑ	.88	1.10	1.42	1.77	2.14
r	3.00	2.30	1.65	1.25	1.01

Halley's Comet last appeared in 1986 and will reappear in 2061.

12. (MATLAB) A healthy child's systolic blood pressure p (in *mm* of mercury) and weight w (in pounds) are approximately related by the equation

$$\beta_0 + \beta_1 \ln w = p$$

Use the following experimental data to estimate the systolic blood pressure of a healthy child weighing 100 pounds.

w	44	61	82	113	131
$\ln w$	3.78	4.11	4.41	4.73	4.87
p	91	98	103	110	112

13. Given the design matrix $X = \begin{bmatrix} 1 & -1 \\ 1 & 3 \\ 1 & 6 \\ 1 & 12 \end{bmatrix}$, apply the Gram–Schmidt process to the columns of X to produce a new matrix of the form $[\,\mathbf{1}\quad \mathbf{v}\,]$. How are the entries in $\mathbf{v}$ related to the entries in $\mathbf{x}$?

14. Let $\overline{x} = \frac{1}{n}(x_1 + \cdots + x_n)$ and $\overline{y} = \frac{1}{n}(y_1 + \cdots + y_n)$. Show that the least-squares line for the data $(x_1, y_1), \ldots, (x_n, y_n)$ must pass through $(\overline{x}, \overline{y})$. That is, show that $\overline{x}$ and $\overline{y}$ satisfy the linear equation $\overline{y} = \hat{\beta}_0 + \hat{\beta}_1\overline{x}$. [*Hint*: Derive this equation from the vector equation $\mathbf{y} = X\hat{\boldsymbol{\beta}} + \boldsymbol{\epsilon}$. Denote the first column of X by $\mathbf{1}$. Use the fact that the residual vector $\boldsymbol{\epsilon}$ is orthogonal to the column space of X and hence is orthogonal to $\mathbf{1}$.]

Given data for a least-squares problem, $(x_1, y_1), \ldots, (x_n, y_n)$, the following abbreviations are helpful:

$$\Sigma x = \textstyle\sum_{i=1}^n x_i, \quad \Sigma x^2 = \sum_{i=1}^n x_i^2,$$
$$\Sigma y = \textstyle\sum_{i=1}^n y_i, \quad \Sigma xy = \sum_{i=1}^n x_i y_i$$

The normal equations for a least-squares line $y = \hat{\beta}_0 + \hat{\beta}_1 x$ may be written in the form

$$\begin{aligned} n\hat{\beta}_0 + \hat{\beta}_1 \Sigma x &= \Sigma y \\ \hat{\beta}_0 \Sigma x + \hat{\beta}_1 \Sigma x^2 &= \Sigma xy \end{aligned} \qquad (6)$$

15. Derive the normal equations (6) from the matrix form given in this section.

16. Use a matrix inverse to solve the system of equations in (6) and thereby obtain formulas for $\hat{\beta}_0$ and $\hat{\beta}_1$ that appear in most statistics texts.

17. a. Rewrite the data in Example 1 with new x-coordinates in mean deviation form. Let X be the associated design matrix. Why are the columns of X orthogonal?

b. Write the normal equations for the data in part (a), and solve them to find the least-squares line, $y = \beta_0 + \beta_1 x^*$, where $x^* = x - 5.5$.

18. Suppose that the x-coordinates of the data $(x_1, y_1), \ldots, (x_n, y_n)$ are in mean deviation form, so that $\sum x_i = 0$. Show that if X is the design matrix for the least-squares line in this case, then X^TX is a diagonal matrix.

Exercises 19 and 20 involve a design matrix X with two or more columns and $\hat{\boldsymbol{\beta}}$ a least-squares solution of $\mathbf{y} = X\boldsymbol{\beta}$. Consider the following numbers.

(i) $\|X\hat{\boldsymbol{\beta}}\|^2$—the sum of the squares of the "regression term." Denote this number by SS(R).

(ii) $\|\mathbf{y} - X\hat{\boldsymbol{\beta}}\|^2$—the sum of the squares for error term. Denote this number by SS(E), the "least-squares error."

(iii) $\|\mathbf{y}\|^2$—the "total" sum of the squares of the y-values. Denote this number by SS(T).

Every statistics text that discusses regression and the linear model $\mathbf{y} = X\boldsymbol{\beta} + \boldsymbol{\epsilon}$ introduces these numbers, though terminology and

[2]The basic idea of least-squares fitting of data is due to K.F. Gauss (and, independently, to A. Legendre), whose initial rise to fame occurred in 1801 when he used the method to determine the path of the asteroid *Ceres.* Forty days after the asteroid was discovered, it disappeared behind the sun. Gauss predicted it would appear ten months later and he gave its location. The accuracy of the prediction astonished the European scientific community.

notation vary somewhat. To simplify matters, assume that the mean of the y-values is zero. In this case SS(T) is proportional to what is called the *variance* of the set of y-values.

19. Justify the equation SS(T) = SS(R) + SS(E). [*Hint*: Use a theorem, and explain why the hypotheses of the theorem are satisfied.] This equation is extremely important in statistics, both in regression theory and in the analysis of variance.

20. Show that $\|X\hat{\beta}\|^2 = \hat{\beta}^T X^T \mathbf{y}$. [*Hint*: Rewrite the left side and use the fact that $\hat{\beta}$ satisfies the normal equations.] This formula for SS(R) is used in statistics. From this and from Exercise 19, obtain the standard formula for the least-squares error:

$$\text{SS(E)} = \mathbf{y}^T\mathbf{y} - \hat{\beta}^T X^T \mathbf{y}$$

SOLUTION TO PRACTICE PROBLEM

We must construct X and β so that the kth row of $X\beta$ is the predicted y-value that corresponds to the data point (x_k, y_k), namely,

$$\beta_0 + \beta_1 x_k + \beta_2 \sin(2\pi x_k/12)$$

It should be clear that

$$X = \begin{bmatrix} 1 & x_1 & \sin(2\pi x_1/12) \\ \vdots & \vdots & \vdots \\ 1 & x_n & \sin(2\pi x_n/12) \end{bmatrix}, \quad \beta = \begin{bmatrix} \beta_0 \\ \beta_1 \\ \beta_2 \end{bmatrix}$$

7.7 INNER PRODUCT SPACES

Notions of length, distance, and orthogonality are often important in applications involving a vector space. For $\mathbb{R}^n$, these concepts were based on the properties of the inner product listed in Theorem 1 of Section 7.1. For other spaces, we need analogues of the inner product with the same properties. The conclusions of Theorem 1 now become *axioms* in the following definition.

DEFINITION

An **inner product** on a vector space V is a function that, to each pair of vectors $\mathbf{u}$ and $\mathbf{v}$ in V, associates a real number $\langle \mathbf{u}, \mathbf{v} \rangle$ and satisfies the following axioms, for all $\mathbf{u}, \mathbf{v}, \mathbf{w}$ in V and all scalars c:

i. $\langle \mathbf{u}, \mathbf{v} \rangle = \langle \mathbf{v}, \mathbf{u} \rangle$

ii. $\langle \mathbf{u} + \mathbf{v}, \mathbf{w} \rangle = \langle \mathbf{u}, \mathbf{w} \rangle + \langle \mathbf{v}, \mathbf{w} \rangle$

iii. $\langle c\mathbf{u}, \mathbf{v} \rangle = c\langle \mathbf{u}, \mathbf{v} \rangle$

iv. $\langle \mathbf{u}, \mathbf{u} \rangle \geq 0$ and $\langle \mathbf{u}, \mathbf{u} \rangle = 0$ if and only if $\mathbf{u} = \mathbf{0}$

A vector space with an inner product is called an **inner product space**.

The vector space $\mathbb{R}^n$ with the standard inner product is an inner product space, and nearly everything discussed in this chapter for $\mathbb{R}^n$ carries over to inner product spaces. The examples in this section and the next lay the foundation for a variety of applications treated in courses in engineering, physics, mathematics, and statistics.

EXAMPLE 1 Fix any two positive numbers—say, 4 and 5—and for vectors $\mathbf{u} = (u_1, u_2)$ and $\mathbf{v} = (v_1, v_2)$ in $\mathbb{R}^2$, set

$$\langle \mathbf{u}, \mathbf{v} \rangle = 4u_1v_1 + 5u_2v_2 \tag{1}$$

Show that (1) defines an inner product.

Solution Certainly axiom (i) is satisfied, since $\langle \mathbf{u}, \mathbf{v} \rangle = 4u_1v_1 + 5u_2v_2 = 4v_1u_1 + 5v_2u_2 = \langle \mathbf{v}, \mathbf{u} \rangle$. If $\mathbf{w} = (w_1, w_2)$, then

$$\begin{aligned} \langle \mathbf{u} + \mathbf{v}, \mathbf{w} \rangle &= 4(u_1 + v_1)w_1 + 5(u_2 + v_2)w_2 \\ &= 4u_1w_1 + 5u_2w_2 + 4v_1w_1 + 5v_2w_2 \\ &= \langle \mathbf{u}, \mathbf{w} \rangle + \langle \mathbf{v}, \mathbf{w} \rangle \end{aligned}$$

This verifies (ii). For (iii), we have

$$\langle c\mathbf{u}, \mathbf{v} \rangle = 4(cu_1)v_1 + 5(cu_2)v_2 = c(4u_1v_1 + 5u_2v_2) = c\langle \mathbf{u}, \mathbf{v} \rangle$$

For (iv), observe that $\langle \mathbf{u}, \mathbf{u} \rangle = 4u_1^2 + 5u_2^2 \geq 0$, and $4u_1^2 + 5u_2^2 = 0$ only if $u_1 = u_2 = 0$, that is, if $\mathbf{u} = \mathbf{0}$. Clearly, $\langle \mathbf{0}, \mathbf{0} \rangle = 0$. So (1) defines an inner product on $\mathbb{R}^2$.

Inner products similar to (1) can be defined on $\mathbb{R}^n$. They arise naturally in connection with "weighted least-squares problems," in which weights are assigned to the various entries in the sum for the inner product in such a way that more importance is given to the more reliable measurements.

From now on, when an inner product space involves polynomials or other functions, we shall write the functions in the familiar way, rather than use the boldface type for vectors. Nevertheless, it is important to remember that each function *is* a vector when it is treated as an element of a vector space.

EXAMPLE 2 Let $t_0, \cdots, t_n$ be distinct real numbers. For p and q in $\mathbb{P}_n$, define

$$\langle p, q \rangle = p(t_0)q(t_0) + p(t_1)q(t_1) + \cdots + p(t_n)q(t_n) \tag{2}$$

Inner product axioms (i) through (iii) are readily checked. For (iv), observe that

$$\langle p, p \rangle = [p(t_0)]^2 + [p(t_1)]^2 + \cdots + [p(t_n)]^2 \geq 0$$

Clearly, $\langle \mathbf{0}, \mathbf{0} \rangle = 0$. (We still use a boldface zero for the zero polynomial, the zero vector in $\mathbb{P}_n$.) If $\langle p, p \rangle = 0$, then p must vanish at $n+1$ points: $t_0, \ldots, t_n$. This is possible only if p is the zero polynomial, because the degree of p is less than $n+1$. Thus (2) defines an inner product on $\mathbb{P}_n$.

EXAMPLE 3 Let V be $\mathbb{P}_2$, with the inner product from Example 2, where $t_0 = 0$, $t_1 = \frac{1}{2}$, and $t_2 = 1$. Let $p(t) = 12t^2$ and $q(t) = 2t - 1$. Compute $\langle p, q\rangle$ and $\langle q, q\rangle$.

Solution

$$\begin{aligned}\langle p, q\rangle &= p(0)q(0) + p(\tfrac{1}{2})q(\tfrac{1}{2}) + p(1)q(1)\\ &= (0)(-1) + (3)(0) + (12)(1) = 12\\ \langle q, q\rangle &= [q(0)]^2 + [q(\tfrac{1}{2})]^2 + [q(1)]^2\\ &= (-1)^2 + (0)^2 + (1)^2 = 2\end{aligned}$$

Lengths, Distances, and Orthogonality

Let V be an inner product space, with the inner product denoted by $\langle \mathbf{u}, \mathbf{v}\rangle$. Just as in $\mathbb{R}^n$, we define the **length** or **norm** of a vector $\mathbf{v}$ to be the scalar

$$\|\mathbf{v}\| = \sqrt{\langle \mathbf{v}, \mathbf{v}\rangle}$$

Equivalently, $\|\mathbf{v}\|^2 = \langle \mathbf{v}, \mathbf{v}\rangle$. (This definition makes sense because $\langle \mathbf{v}, \mathbf{v}\rangle \geq 0$, but the definition *does not* say that $\langle \mathbf{v}, \mathbf{v}\rangle$ is a "sum of squares," because $\mathbf{v}$ need not be an element of $\mathbb{R}^n$.)

A **unit vector** is one whose length is 1. The **distance between u and v** is $\|\mathbf{u}-\mathbf{v}\|$. Vectors $\mathbf{u}$ and $\mathbf{v}$ are **orthogonal** if $\langle \mathbf{u}, \mathbf{v}\rangle = 0$.

EXAMPLE 4 Let $\mathbb{P}_2$ have the inner product (2) of Example 3. Compute the lengths of the vectors $p(t) = 12t^2$ and $q(t) = 2t - 1$.

Solution

$$\begin{aligned}\|p\|^2 &= \langle p, p\rangle = [p(0)]^2 + [p(\tfrac{1}{2})]^2 + [p(1)]^2\\ &= 0 + [3]^2 + [12]^2 = 153\\ \|p\| &= \sqrt{153}\end{aligned}$$

In Example 3, we found that $\langle q, q\rangle = 2$. Hence $\|q\| = \sqrt{2}$.

The Gram–Schmidt Process

The existence of orthogonal bases for finite-dimensional subspaces of an inner product space may be established by the Gram–Schmidt process, just as in $\mathbb{R}^n$. Certain orthogonal bases that arise frequently in applications may be constructed by this process.

The orthogonal projection of a vector onto a subspace W with an orthogonal basis may be constructed as usual. The projection does not depend on the choice of orthogonal basis, and it has the properties described in the Orthogonal Decomposition Theorem and the Best Approximation Theorem.

EXAMPLE 5 Let V be $\mathbb{P}_4$ with the inner product in Example 2, involving evaluation of polynomials at -2, -1, 0, 1, and 2, and view $\mathbb{P}_2$ as a subspace of V. Produce an orthogonal basis for $\mathbb{P}_2$ by applying the Gram–Schmidt process to the polynomials $1, t$, and t^2.

Solution The inner product depends only on the values of the polynomials at $-2, \ldots, 2$, so we list the values of each polynomial as a vector in $\mathbb{R}^5$, underneath the name of the polynomial:

$$\begin{array}{lccc} \text{Polynomial:} & 1 & t & t^2 \\ \text{Vector of values:} & \begin{bmatrix} 1 \\ 1 \\ 1 \\ 1 \\ 1 \end{bmatrix}, & \begin{bmatrix} -2 \\ -1 \\ 0 \\ 1 \\ 2 \end{bmatrix}, & \begin{bmatrix} 4 \\ 1 \\ 0 \\ 1 \\ 4 \end{bmatrix} \end{array}$$

The inner product of two polynomials in V equals the (standard) inner product of the corresponding vectors in $\mathbb{R}^5$. Obviously, t is orthogonal to the constant function 1. So take $p_0(t) = 1$ and $p_1(t) = t$. For p_2, use the vectors in $\mathbb{R}^5$ to compute the projection of t^2 onto Span$\{p_0, p_1\}$:

$$\begin{aligned} \langle t^2, p_0 \rangle &= \langle t^2, 1 \rangle = 4 + 1 + 0 + 1 + 4 = 10 \\ \langle p_0, p_0 \rangle &= 5 \\ \langle t^2, p_1 \rangle &= \langle t^2, t \rangle = -8 + (-1) + 0 + 1 + 8 = 0 \end{aligned}$$

The orthogonal projection of t^2 onto Span$\{1, t\}$ is $\frac{10}{5} p_0 + 0 p_1$. Thus

$$p_2(t) = t^2 - 2p_0(t) = t^2 - 2$$

An orthogonal basis for the subspace $\mathbb{P}_2$ of V is:

$$\begin{array}{lccc} \text{Polynomial:} & p_0 & p_1 & p_2 \\ \text{Vector of values:} & \begin{bmatrix} 1 \\ 1 \\ 1 \\ 1 \\ 1 \end{bmatrix}, & \begin{bmatrix} -2 \\ -1 \\ 0 \\ 1 \\ 2 \end{bmatrix}, & \begin{bmatrix} 2 \\ -1 \\ -2 \\ -1 \\ 2 \end{bmatrix} \end{array} \qquad (3)$$

Best Approximation in Inner Product Spaces

A common problem in applied mathematics involves a vector space V whose elements are functions. The problem is to approximate a function f in V by a function g from a specified subspace W of V. The "closeness" of the approximation of f depends on the way $\|f - g\|$ is defined. We shall consider only the case in which the distance between f and g is determined by an inner product. In this case, the *best approximation to f by functions in W* is the orthogonal projection of f onto the subspace W.

EXAMPLE 6 Let V be $\mathbb{P}_4$ with the inner product in Example 5, and let p_0, p_1, and p_2 be the orthogonal basis found in Example 5 for the subspace $\mathbb{P}_2$. Find the best approximation to $p(t) = 5 - (1/2)t^4$ by polynomials in $\mathbb{P}_2$.

Solution The values of p_0, p_1, and p_2 at the numbers $-2, -1, 0, 1$, and 2 are listed in $\mathbb{R}^5$ vectors in (3) above. The corresponding values for p are $-3, 9/2, 5, 9/2$, and -3. We compute

$$\langle p, p_0\rangle = 8, \qquad \langle p, p_1\rangle = 0, \quad \langle p, p_2\rangle = -31$$
$$\langle p_0, p_0\rangle = 5, \qquad \langle p_2, p_2\rangle = 14$$

Then the best approximation in V to p by polynomials in $\mathbb{P}_2$ is

$$\begin{aligned}\hat{p} = \text{proj}_{\mathbb{P}_2} p &= \frac{\langle p, p_0\rangle}{\langle p_0, p_0\rangle} p_0 + \frac{\langle p, p_1\rangle}{\langle p_1, p_1\rangle} p_1 + \frac{\langle p, p_2\rangle}{\langle p_2, p_2\rangle} p_2 \\ &= \frac{8}{5} p_0 + \frac{-31}{14} p_2 = \frac{8}{5} - \frac{31}{14}(t^2 - 2)\end{aligned}$$

This polynomial is the closest to p of all polynomials in $\mathbb{P}_2$, when the distance between polynomials is measured only at $-2, -1, 0, 1$, and 2. See Fig. 1.

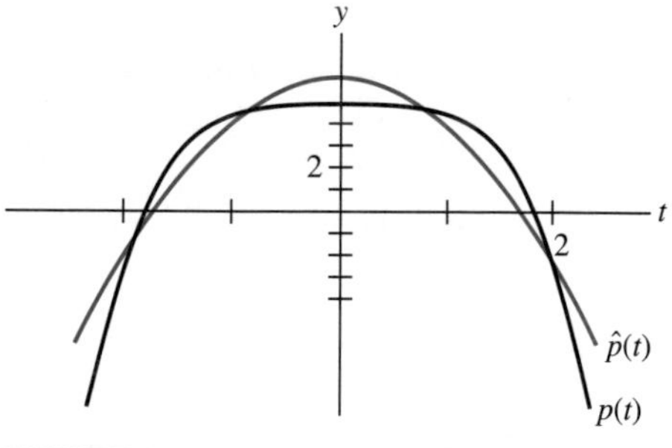

FIGURE 1

The polynomials p_0, p_1, and p_2 in Examples 5 and 6 belong to a whole class of polynomials that are referred to in statistics as "orthogonal polynomials."[1] The orthogonality refers to the type of inner product described in Example 2.

[1]See *Statistics and Experimental Design in Engineering and the Physical Sciences*, by Norman L. Johnson and Fred C. Leone (New York: John Wiley & Sons, 1964), pp. 424–436. Tables on pp. 430–431 from this source list "Orthogonal Polynomials," which are simply the values of the polynomials at numbers such as $-2, -1, 0, 1$, and 2.

Two Inequalities

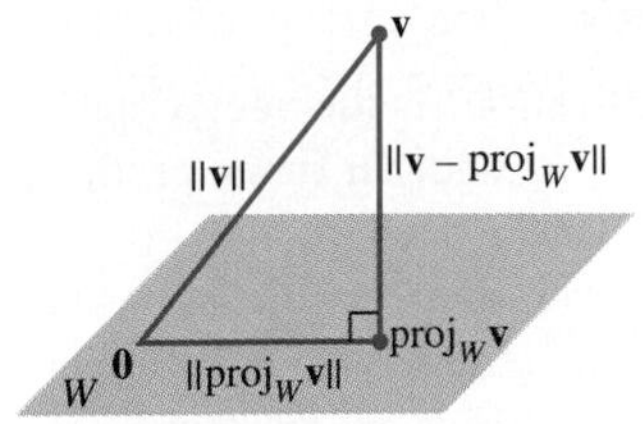

FIGURE 2 The hypotenuse is the longest side.

Given a vector **v** in an inner product space V and given a finite-dimensional subspace W, we may apply the Pythagorean Theorem to the orthogonal decomposition of **v** with respect to W and obtain

$$\|\mathbf{v}\|^2 = \|\text{proj}_W \mathbf{v}\|^2 + \|\mathbf{v} - \text{proj}_W \mathbf{v}\|^2$$

See Fig. 2. In particular, this shows that the norm of the projection of **v** onto W does not exceed the norm of **v** itself. This simple observation leads to the following important inequality.

THEOREM 16

The Cauchy–Schwarz Inequality

For all **u**, **v** in V,

$$|\langle \mathbf{u}, \mathbf{v}\rangle| \leq \|\mathbf{u}\|\,\|\mathbf{v}\| \tag{4}$$

Proof If $\mathbf{u} = \mathbf{0}$, then both sides of (4) are zero and hence (4) is true in this case. (See Practice Problem 1.) If $\mathbf{u} \neq 0$, let W be the subspace spanned by **u**. Recall that $\|c\mathbf{u}\| = |c|\,\|\mathbf{u}\|$ for any scalar c. Thus

$$\|\text{proj}_W \mathbf{v}\| = \left\| \frac{\langle \mathbf{v}, \mathbf{u}\rangle}{\langle \mathbf{u}, \mathbf{u}\rangle}\mathbf{u} \right\| = \frac{|\langle \mathbf{v}, \mathbf{u}\rangle|}{|\langle \mathbf{u}, \mathbf{u}\rangle|}\|\mathbf{u}\| = \frac{|\langle \mathbf{v}, \mathbf{u}\rangle|}{\|\mathbf{u}\|^2}\|\mathbf{u}\| = \frac{|\langle \mathbf{u}, \mathbf{v}\rangle|}{\|\mathbf{u}\|}$$

Since $\|\text{proj}_W \mathbf{v}\| \leq \|\mathbf{v}\|$, we have $\dfrac{|\langle \mathbf{u}, \mathbf{v}\rangle|}{\|\mathbf{u}\|} \leq \|\mathbf{v}\|$, which gives (4). ∎

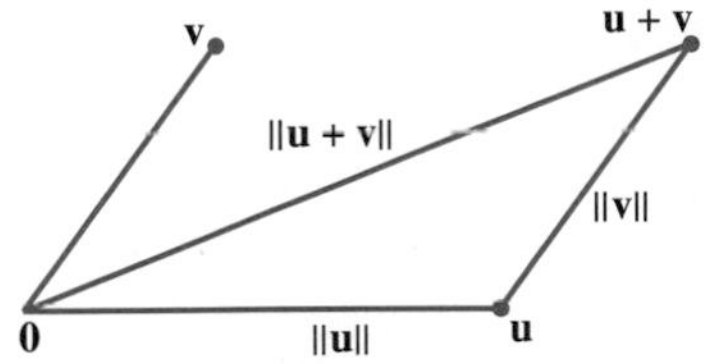

FIGURE 3 The lengths of the sides of a triangle.

The Cauchy–Schwarz inequality is useful in many branches of mathematics. A few simple applications are in the exercises. Our main need for it here is to prove another fundamental inequality involving norms of vectors. See Fig. 3.

THEOREM 17

The Triangle Inequality

For all **u**, **v** in V,

$$\|\mathbf{u} + \mathbf{v}\| \leq \|\mathbf{u}\| + \|\mathbf{v}\|$$

Proof

$$\begin{aligned} \|\mathbf{u} + \mathbf{v}\|^2 &= \langle \mathbf{u} + \mathbf{v}, \mathbf{u} + \mathbf{v}\rangle = \langle \mathbf{u}, \mathbf{u}\rangle + 2\langle \mathbf{u}, \mathbf{v}\rangle + \langle \mathbf{v}, \mathbf{v}\rangle \\ &\leq \|\mathbf{u}\|^2 + 2|\langle \mathbf{u}, \mathbf{v}\rangle| + \|\mathbf{v}\|^2 \\ &\leq \|\mathbf{u}\|^2 + 2\|\mathbf{u}\|\,\|\mathbf{v}\| + \|\mathbf{v}\|^2 \qquad \text{Cauchy–Schwarz} \\ &= (\|\mathbf{u}\| + \|\mathbf{v}\|)^2 \end{aligned}$$

The triangle inequality follows immediately by taking square roots of both sides. ∎

An Inner-Product For $C[a,b]$ (Calculus required)

Probably the most widely used inner product space for applications is the vector space $C[a, b]$ of all continuous functions on an interval $a \leq t \leq b$, with an inner product we shall describe.

We begin by considering a polynomial p and any integer n larger than or equal to the degree of p. Then p is in $\mathbb{P}_n$, and we may compute a "length" for p using the inner product of Example 2 involving evaluation at $n+1$ points in $[a, b]$. However, this length of p captures the behavior at only those $n+1$ points. Since p is in $\mathbb{P}_n$ for all large n, we could use a much larger n, with many more points for the "evaluation" inner product. See Fig. 4.

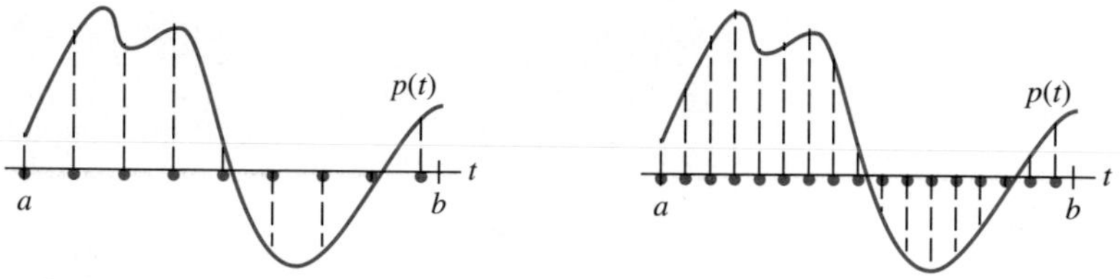

FIGURE 4 Using different numbers of evaluation points in $[a, b]$ to compute $\|p\|^2$.

Let us partition $[a, b]$ into $n+1$ subintervals of length $\Delta t = (b-a)/(n+1)$, and let $t_0, \ldots, t_n$ be arbitrary points in these subintervals.

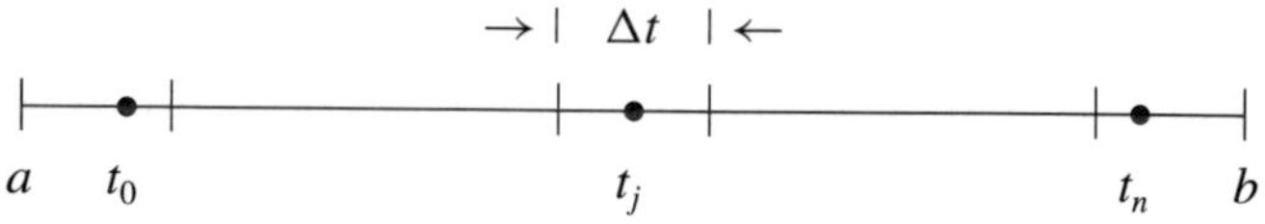

If n is large, the inner product on $\mathbb{P}_n$ determined by $t_0, \ldots, t_n$ will tend to give a large value to $\langle p, p \rangle$, so let us scale it down and divide by $n+1$. Observe that $1/(n+1) = \Delta t/(b-a)$, and define

$$\langle p, q \rangle = \frac{1}{n+1} \sum_{j=0}^{n} p(t_j)q(t_j) = \frac{1}{b-a} \left[\sum_{j=0}^{n} p(t_j)q(t_j)\Delta t \right]$$

Now, let n increase without bound. Since polynomials p and q are continuous functions, the expression in brackets is a Riemann sum that approaches a definite integral, and we are led to consider the *average value of* $p(t)q(t)$ on the interval $[a, b]$:

$$\frac{1}{b-a} \int_a^b p(t)q(t)\,dt$$

This quantity is defined for polynomials of any degree (in fact for all continuous functions), and it has all the properties of an inner product, as the next example shows. The scale factor $1/(b-a)$ in front is inessential and is often omitted for simplicity.

EXAMPLE 7 For f, g in $C[a, b]$, set

$$\langle f, g\rangle = \int_a^b f(t)g(t)\,dt \tag{5}$$

Show that (5) defines an inner product on $C[a, b]$.

Solution Inner product axioms (i)–(iii) follow from elementary properties of definite integrals. For axiom (iv), observe that

$$\langle f, f\rangle = \int_a^b [f(t)]^2\,dt \geq 0$$

The function $[f(t)]^2$ is continuous and nonnegative on $[a, b]$. If the definite integral of $[f(t)]^2$ is zero, then $[f(t)]^2$ must be identically zero, by a theorem in advanced calculus, in which case f is the zero function. Thus $\langle f, f\rangle = 0$ implies that f is the zero function on $[a, b]$. So (5) defines an inner product on $C[a, b]$. ∎

EXAMPLE 8 Let V be the space $C[0, 1]$ with the inner product of Example 7, and let W be the subspace spanned by the polynomials $p_1(t) = 1$, $p_2(t) = 2t - 1$, and $p_3(t) = 12t^2$. Use the Gram–Schmidt process to find an orthogonal basis for W.

Solution Let $q_1 = p_1$, and compute

$$\langle p_2, q_1\rangle = \int_0^1 (2t-1)(1)\,dt = (t^2 - t)\Big|_0^1 = 0$$

So p_2 is already orthogonal to q_1, and we can take $q_2 = p_2$. For the projection of p_3 onto $W_2 = \text{Span}\{q_1, q_2\}$, we compute

$$\langle p_3, q_1\rangle = \int_0^1 12t^2 \cdot 1\,dt = 4t^3\Big|_0^1 = 4$$

$$\langle q_1, q_1\rangle = \int_0^1 1 \cdot 1\,dt = t\Big|_0^1 = 1$$

$$\langle p_3, q_2\rangle = \int_0^1 12t^2(2t-1)\,dt = \int_0^1 (24t^3 - 12t^2)\,dt = 2$$

$$\langle q_2, q_2\rangle = \int_0^1 (2t-1)^2\,dt = \frac{1}{6}(2t-1)^3\Big|_0^1 = \frac{1}{3}$$

Then

$$\text{proj}_{W_2} p_3 = \frac{\langle p_3, q_1\rangle}{\langle q_1, q_1\rangle} q_1 + \frac{\langle p_3, q_2\rangle}{\langle q_2, q_2\rangle} q_2 = \frac{4}{1} q_1 + \frac{2}{1/3} q_2 = 4q_1 + 6q_2$$

and

$$q_3 = p_3 - \text{proj}_{W_2} p_3 = p_3 - 4q_1 - 6q_2$$

As a function, $q_3(t) = 12t^2 - 4 - 6(2t - 1) = 12t^2 - 12t + 2$. The orientation basis for the subspace W is $\{q_1, q_2, q_3\}$.

PRACTICE PROBLEMS

Use the inner product axioms to verify the following statements.

1. $\langle \mathbf{v}, \mathbf{0} \rangle = \langle \mathbf{0}, \mathbf{v} \rangle = 0$.
2. $\langle \mathbf{u}, \mathbf{v} + \mathbf{w} \rangle = \langle \mathbf{u}, \mathbf{v} \rangle + \langle \mathbf{u}, \mathbf{w} \rangle$.

7.7 EXERCISES

1. Let $\mathbb{R}^2$ have the inner product of Example 1, $\mathbf{x} = (1, 1)$, and $\mathbf{y} = (5, -1)$.

a. Find $\|\mathbf{x}\|$ and $\|\mathbf{y}\|$.

b. Describe all vectors (z_1, z_2) that are orthogonal to $\mathbf{y}$.

2. Let $\mathbb{R}^2$ have the inner product of Example 1. Show that the Cauchy–Schwarz inequality holds for $\mathbf{x} = (3, -2)$ and $\mathbf{y} = (-2, 1)$. [*Suggestion*: Study $|\langle \mathbf{x}, \mathbf{y} \rangle|^2$.]

Exercises 3–8 refer to $\mathbb{P}_2$ with the inner product given by evaluation at -1, 0, and 1. (See Example 2.)

3. Compute $\langle p, q \rangle$, where $p(t) = 4 + t$, $q(t) = 5 - 4t^2$.

4. Compute $\langle p, q \rangle$, where $p(t) = 3t - t^2$, $q(t) = 3 + 2t^2$.

5. Compute $\|p\|$ and $\|q\|$, for p and q in Exercise 3.

6. Compute $\|p\|$ and $\|q\|$, for p and q in Exercise 4.

7. Compute the orthogonal projection of q onto the subspace spanned by p, for p and q in Exercise 3.

8. Compute the orthogonal projection of q onto the subspace spanned by p, for p and q in Exercise 4.

9. Let $\mathbb{P}_3$ have the inner product given by evaluation at -3, -1, 1, and 3. Let $p_0(t) = 1$, $p_1(t) = t$ and $p_2(t) = t^2$.

a. Compute the orthogonal projection of p_2 onto the subspace spanned by p_0 and p_1.

b. Find a polynomial q that is orthogonal to p_0 and p_1, such that $\{p_0, p_1, q\}$ is an orthogonal basis for Span$\{p_0, p_1, p_2\}$. Scale the polynomial q so that its vector of values at $(-3, -1, 1, 3)$ is $(1, -1, -1, 1)$.

10. Let $\mathbb{P}_3$ have the inner product as in Exercise 9 and p_0, p_1, and q be the polynomials described there. Find the best approximation to $p(t) = t^3$ by polynomials in Span$\{p_0, p_1, q\}$.

11. Let p_0, p_1, p_2 be the orthogonal polynomials described in Example 5, where the inner product on $\mathbb{P}_4$ is given by evaluation at -2, -1, 0, 1, and 2. Find the orthogonal projection of t^3 onto Span$\{p_0, p_1, p_2\}$.

12. Find a polynomial p_3 such that $\{p_0, p_1, p_2, p_3\}$ (see Exercise 11) is an orthogonal basis for the subspace $\mathbb{P}_3$ of $\mathbb{P}_4$. Scale the polynomial p_3 so that its vector of values is $(-1, 2, 0, -2, 1)$.

13. Let A be any invertible $n \times n$ matrix. Show that for $\mathbf{u}$, $\mathbf{v}$ in $\mathbb{R}^n$, the formula $\langle \mathbf{u}, \mathbf{v} \rangle = (A\mathbf{u}) \cdot (A\mathbf{v}) = (A\mathbf{u})^T(A\mathbf{v})$ defines an inner product on $\mathbb{R}^n$.

14. Let T be a one-to-one linear transformation from a vector space V into $\mathbb{R}^n$. Show that for $\mathbf{u}$, $\mathbf{v}$ in V, the formula $\langle \mathbf{u}, \mathbf{v} \rangle = T(\mathbf{u}) \cdot T(\mathbf{v})$ defines an inner product on V.

Use the inner product axioms and other results of this section to verify the statements in Exercises 15–18.

15. $\langle \mathbf{u}, c\mathbf{v} \rangle = c\langle \mathbf{u}, \mathbf{v} \rangle$ for all scalars c.

16. If $\{\mathbf{u}, \mathbf{v}\}$ is an orthonormal set in V, then $\|\mathbf{u} - \mathbf{v}\| = \sqrt{2}$.

17. $\langle \mathbf{u}, \mathbf{v} \rangle = \frac{1}{4}\|\mathbf{u} + \mathbf{v}\|^2 - \frac{1}{4}\|\mathbf{u} - \mathbf{v}\|^2$.

18. $\|\mathbf{u} + \mathbf{v}\|^2 + \|\mathbf{u} - \mathbf{v}\|^2 = 2\|\mathbf{u}\|^2 + 2\|\mathbf{v}\|^2$.

19. Given $a \geq 0$ and $b \geq 0$, let $\mathbf{u} = \begin{bmatrix} \sqrt{a} \\ \sqrt{b} \end{bmatrix}$ and $\mathbf{v} = \begin{bmatrix} \sqrt{b} \\ \sqrt{a} \end{bmatrix}$. Use the Cauchy–Schwarz inequality to compare the geometric mean $\sqrt{ab}$ with the arithmetic mean $(a + b)/2$.

20. Let $\mathbf{u} = \begin{bmatrix} a \\ b \end{bmatrix}$ and $\mathbf{v} = \begin{bmatrix} 1 \\ 1 \end{bmatrix}$. Use the Cauchy–Schwarz inequality to show that

$$\left(\frac{a+b}{2}\right)^2 \leq \frac{a^2+b^2}{2}$$

Exercises 21–24 refer to $V = C[0, 1]$, with the inner product given by an integral, as in Example 7.

21. Compute $\langle f, g\rangle$, where $f(t) = 1 - 3t^2$ and $g(t) = t - t^3$.

22. Compute $\langle f, g\rangle$, where $f(t) = 5t - 3$ and $g(t) = t^3 - t^2$.

23. Compute $\|f\|$ for f in Exercise 21.

24. Compute $\|g\|$ for g in Exercise 22.

25. Let V be the space $C[-1, 1]$ with the inner product of Example 7. Find an orthogonal basis for the subspace spanned by the polynomials $1, t$, and t^2. The polynomials in this basis are called *Legendre polynomials*.

26. Let V be the space $C[-2, 2]$ with the inner product of Example 7. Find an orthogonal basis for the subspace spanned by the polynomials $1, t$, and t^2.

SOLUTIONS TO PRACTICE PROBLEMS

1. By axiom (i), $\langle \mathbf{v}, \mathbf{0}\rangle = \langle \mathbf{0}, \mathbf{v}\rangle$. Then $\langle \mathbf{0}, \mathbf{v}\rangle = \langle 0\mathbf{v}, \mathbf{v}\rangle = 0\langle \mathbf{v}, \mathbf{v}\rangle$, by axiom (iii), so $\langle \mathbf{0}, \mathbf{v}\rangle = 0$.
2. By axioms (i), (ii), and then (i) again, $\langle \mathbf{u}, \mathbf{v}+\mathbf{w}\rangle = \langle \mathbf{v}+\mathbf{w}, \mathbf{u}\rangle = \langle \mathbf{v}, \mathbf{u}\rangle + \langle \mathbf{w}, \mathbf{u}\rangle = \langle \mathbf{u}, \mathbf{v}\rangle + \langle \mathbf{u}, \mathbf{w}\rangle$.

7.8 APPLICATIONS OF INNER PRODUCT SPACES

The examples in this section suggest how the inner product spaces defined in Section 7.7 arise in practical problems. The first example is connected with the massive least-squares problem of updating the North American Datum, described in the chapter's introductory example.

Weighted Least-Squares

Let $\mathbf{y}$ be a vector of n observations, $y_1, \ldots, y_n$, and suppose that we wish to approximate $\mathbf{y}$ by a vector $\hat{\mathbf{y}}$ that belongs to some specified subspace of $\mathbb{R}^n$. (In Section 7.5, $\hat{\mathbf{y}}$ was written as $A\mathbf{x}$ so that $\hat{\mathbf{y}}$ was in the column space of A.) Denote the entries in $\hat{\mathbf{y}}$ by $\hat{y}_1, \ldots, \hat{y}_n$. Then the *sum of the squares for error*, or SS(E), in approximating $\mathbf{y}$ by $\hat{\mathbf{y}}$ is

$$\text{SS(E)} = (y_1 - \hat{y}_1)^2 + \cdots + (y_n - \hat{y}_n)^2 \tag{1}$$

This is simply $\|\mathbf{y} - \hat{\mathbf{y}}\|^2$, using the standard length in $\mathbb{R}^n$.

Now suppose that the measurements that produced the entries in $\mathbf{y}$ are not equally reliable. (This was the case, for instance, for the North American Datum, since measurements were made over a period of 140 years. As another example, the entries in $\mathbf{y}$ might be computed from various samples of measurements, with unequal sample sizes.) Then it becomes appropriate to weight the squared errors in (1) in such a way that more importance is assigned to the more reliable measurements.[1] If the weights are denoted by $w_1^2, \ldots, w_n^2$, then the weighted sum of the squares for error is

$$\text{Weighted SS(E)} = w_1^2(y_1 - \hat{y}_1)^2 + \cdots + w_n^2(y_n - \hat{y}_n)^2 \tag{2}$$

This is the square of the length of $\mathbf{y} - \hat{\mathbf{y}}$, where the length is derived from an inner product analogous to that in Example 1 of Section 7.7, namely,

$$\langle \mathbf{x}, \mathbf{y} \rangle = w_1^2 x_1 y_1 + \cdots + w_n^2 x_n y_n$$

It is sometimes convenient to transform a weighted least-squares problem into an equivalent ordinary least-squares problem. Let W be the diagonal matrix with $w_1, \ldots, w_n$ on its diagonal, so that

$$W\mathbf{y} = \begin{bmatrix} w_1 & 0 & \cdots & 0 \\ 0 & w_2 & & \\ \vdots & & \ddots & \vdots \\ 0 & & \cdots & w_n \end{bmatrix} \begin{bmatrix} y_1 \\ y_2 \\ \vdots \\ y_n \end{bmatrix} = \begin{bmatrix} w_1 y_1 \\ w_2 y_2 \\ \vdots \\ w_n y_n \end{bmatrix}$$

with a similar expression for $W\hat{\mathbf{y}}$. Observe that the jth term in (2) may be written as

$$w_j^2(y_j - \hat{y}_j)^2 = (w_j y_j - w_j \hat{y}_j)^2$$

It follows that the weighted SS(E) in (2) is the square of the ordinary length in $\mathbb{R}^n$ of $W\mathbf{y} - W\hat{\mathbf{y}}$, which we write as $\|W\mathbf{y} - W\hat{\mathbf{y}}\|^2$.

Now suppose that the approximating vector $\hat{\mathbf{y}}$ is to be constructed from the columns of a matrix A. Then we seek an $\hat{\mathbf{x}}$ that makes $A\hat{\mathbf{x}} = \hat{\mathbf{y}}$ as close to $\mathbf{y}$ as possible. However, the measure of closeness is the weighted error,

$$\|W\mathbf{y} - W\hat{\mathbf{y}}\|^2 = \|W\mathbf{y} - WA\hat{\mathbf{x}}\|^2$$

Thus $\hat{\mathbf{x}}$ is the (ordinary) least-squares solution of the equation

$$WA\mathbf{x} = W\mathbf{y}$$

The normal equation for the least-squares solution is

$$(WA)^T WA\hat{\mathbf{x}} = (WA)^T W\mathbf{y}$$

EXAMPLE 1 Find the least squares line $y = \beta_0 + \beta_1 x$ that best fits the data $(-2, 3)$, $(-1, 5)$, $(0, 5)$, $(1, 4)$, $(2, 3)$. Suppose that the errors in measuring the y-values of the last two data points are greater than for the other points. Weight these data half as much as the rest of the data.

[1] Note for readers with a background in statistics: Suppose that the errors in measuring the y_i are independent random variables with means equal to zero and variances of $\sigma_1^2, \ldots, \sigma_n^2$. Then the appropriate weights in (2) are $w_i^2 = 1/\sigma_i^2$. The larger the variance of the error, the smaller the weight.

Solution As in Section 7.6, write X for the matrix A and $\boldsymbol{\beta}$ for the vector $\mathbf{x}$, and obtain

$$X = \begin{bmatrix} 1 & -2 \\ 1 & -1 \\ 1 & 0 \\ 1 & 1 \\ 1 & 2 \end{bmatrix}, \quad \boldsymbol{\beta} = \begin{bmatrix} \beta_0 \\ \beta_1 \end{bmatrix}, \quad \mathbf{y} = \begin{bmatrix} 3 \\ 5 \\ 5 \\ 4 \\ 3 \end{bmatrix}$$

For a weighting matrix, choose W with diagonal entries 2, 2, 2, 1, and 1. Left-multiplication by W scales the rows of X and $\mathbf{y}$:

$$WX = \begin{bmatrix} 2 & -4 \\ 2 & -2 \\ 2 & 0 \\ 1 & 1 \\ 1 & 2 \end{bmatrix}, \quad W\mathbf{y} = \begin{bmatrix} 6 \\ 10 \\ 10 \\ 4 \\ 3 \end{bmatrix}$$

For the normal equation, compute

$$(WX)^T WX = \begin{bmatrix} 14 & -9 \\ -9 & 25 \end{bmatrix} \quad \text{and} \quad (WX)^T W\mathbf{y} = \begin{bmatrix} 59 \\ -34 \end{bmatrix}$$

and solve

$$\begin{bmatrix} 14 & -9 \\ -9 & 25 \end{bmatrix} \begin{bmatrix} \beta_0 \\ \beta_1 \end{bmatrix} = \begin{bmatrix} 59 \\ -34 \end{bmatrix}$$

The solution of the normal equation is (to two significant digits) $\beta_0 = 4.3$ and $\beta_1 = .20$. The desired line is

$$y = 4.3 + .20x$$

In contrast, the ordinary least-squares line for these data is

$$y = 4.0 - .10x$$

Both lines are displayed in Fig. 1.

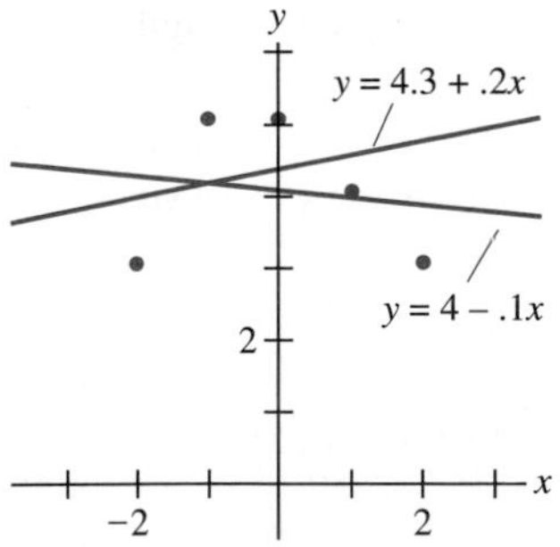

FIGURE 1 Weighted and ordinary least-squares lines.

Trend Analysis of Data

Let $f(t)$ represent an unknown function whose values are known (perhaps only approximately) at $t_0, \ldots, t_n$. If there is a "linear trend" in the data $f(t_0), \ldots, f(t_n)$, then we may expect to approximate the values of f by a function of the form $\beta_0 + \beta_1 t$. If there is a "quadratic trend" to the data, then we would try a function of the form $\beta_0 + \beta_1 t + \beta_2 t^2$. This was discussed in Section 7.6, from a different point of view.

In some statistical problems it is important to be able to separate the linear trend from the quadratic trend (and possibly cubic or higher order trends). For instance, suppose engineers are analyzing the performance of a new car, and $f(t)$ represents the distance between the car at time t and some reference point. If the car is traveling at constant velocity, then the graph of $f(t)$ should be a straight line whose slope is the car's velocity. If the gas pedal is suddenly pressed to the floor, the graph of $f(t)$ will change to include a quadratic term and possibly a cubic term (due to the acceleration). To analyze the ability of the car to pass another car, for example, engineers may want to separate the quadratic and cubic components from the linear term.

If the function is approximated by a curve of the form $y = \beta_0 + \beta_1 t + \beta_2 t^2$, the coefficient β_2 may not give the desired information about the quadratic trend in the data because it may not be "independent" in a statistical sense from the other β_i. To make what is known as a **trend analysis** of the data, we introduce an inner product on the space $\mathbb{P}_n$ analogous to that given in Example 2 of Section 7.7. For p, q in $\mathbb{P}_n$, define

$$\langle p, q\rangle = p(t_0)q(t_0) + \cdots + p(t_n)q(t_n)$$

In practice, statisticians seldom need to consider trends in data of degree higher than cubic or quartic. So let p_0, p_1, p_2, p_3 denote an orthogonal basis of the subspace $\mathbb{P}_3$ of $\mathbb{P}_n$, obtained by applying the Gram–Schmidt process to the polynomials $1, t, t^2$ and t^3. By Supplementary Exercise 11 in Chapter 3, there is a polynomial g in $\mathbb{P}_{n-1}$ whose values at $t_1, \dots, t_n$ coincide with those of the unknown function f. Let $\hat{g}$ be the orthogonal projection (with respect to the given inner product) of g onto $\mathbb{P}_3$, say,

$$\hat{g} = c_0 p_0 + c_1 p_1 + c_2 p_2 + c_3 p_3$$

Then $\hat{g}$ is called a cubic **trend function**, and $c_0, \dots, c_3$ are the **trend coefficients** of the data. The coefficient c_1 measures the linear trend, c_2 the quadratic trend, and c_3 the cubic trend. It turns out that if the data have certain properties, these coefficients are statistically independent.

Since $p_0, \dots, p_3$ are orthogonal, the trend coefficients may be computed one at a time, independently of one another. (Recall that $c_i = \langle g, p_i\rangle / \langle p_i, p_i\rangle$.) We can ignore p_3 and c_3 if we only want the quadratic trend. And if, for example, we needed to determine the quartic trend, we would only have to find (via Gram–Schmidt) a polynomial p_4 in $\mathbb{P}_4$ that is orthogonal to $\mathbb{P}_3$ and compute $\langle g, p_4\rangle / \langle p_4, p_4\rangle$.

EXAMPLE 2 The simplest and most common use of trend analysis occurs when the points $t_1, \dots, t_n$ may be adjusted so that they are evenly spaced and sum to zero. Fit a quadratic trend function to the data $(-2, 3)$, $(-1, 5)$, $(0, 5)$, $(1, 4)$, and $(2, 3)$.

Solution The t-coordinates are suitably scaled to use the orthogonal polynomials found in Example 5 of Section 7.7. We have

$$\begin{array}{lcccc} \text{Polynomial:} & p_0 & p_1 & p_2 & \text{Data: } g \\ \text{Vector of values:} & \begin{bmatrix} 1 \\ 1 \\ 1 \\ 1 \\ 1 \end{bmatrix}, & \begin{bmatrix} -2 \\ -1 \\ 0 \\ 1 \\ 2 \end{bmatrix}, & \begin{bmatrix} 2 \\ -1 \\ -2 \\ -1 \\ 2 \end{bmatrix}, & \begin{bmatrix} 3 \\ 5 \\ 5 \\ 4 \\ 3 \end{bmatrix} \end{array}$$

The calculations involve only these vectors, not the specific formulas for the orthogonal polynomials: The best approximation to the data by polynomials in $\mathbb{P}_2$ is the

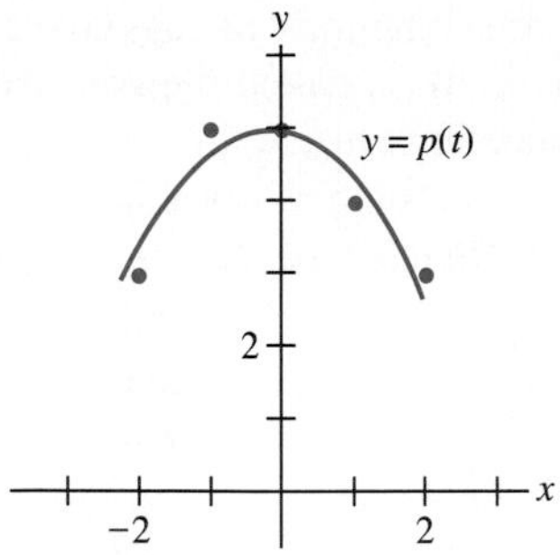

FIGURE 2 Approximation by a quadratic trend function.

orthogonal projection given by

$$\hat{p} = \frac{\langle g, p_0\rangle}{\langle p_0, p_0\rangle} p_0 + \frac{\langle g, p_1\rangle}{\langle p_1, p_1\rangle} p_1 + \frac{\langle g, p_2\rangle}{\langle p_2, p_2\rangle} p_2$$
$$= \frac{20}{5} p_0 - \frac{1}{10} p_1 + \frac{-7}{14} p_2$$

and

$$\hat{p}(t) = 4 - .1t - .5(t^2 - 2) \tag{3}$$

Since the coefficient of p_2 is not extremely small, it would be reasonable to conclude that the trend is at least quadratic. This is confirmed by the graph in Fig. 2.

Fourier Series (Calculus required)

Continuous functions are often approximated by some linear combination of sine and cosine functions. For instance, the continuous function might represent a sound wave, an electric signal of some type, or the movement of a vibrating mechanical system.

For simplicity, we consider functions on $0 \le t \le 2\pi$. It turns out that any function in $C[0, 2\pi]$ may be approximated as closely as desired by a function of the form

$$\frac{a_0}{2} + a_1 \cos t + \cdots + a_n \cos nt + b_1 \sin t + \cdots + b_n \sin nt \tag{4}$$

The function (4) is called a **trigonometric polynomial**. If a_n and b_n are not both zero, the polynomial is said to be of **order n**. The connection between trigonometric polynomials and other functions in $C[0, 2\pi]$ depends on the fact that for any $n > 1$, the set

$$\{1, \cos t, \cos 2t, \ldots, \cos nt, \sin t, \sin 2t, \ldots, \sin nt\} \tag{5}$$

is orthogonal with respect to the inner product

$$\langle f, g\rangle = \int_0^{2\pi} f(t)g(t)\,dt \tag{6}$$

This orthogonality is verified in the following example and in Exercises 5 and 6.

EXAMPLE 3 Let $C[0, 2\pi]$ have the inner product (6) and let m and n be unequal positive integers. Show that $\cos mt$ and $\cos nt$ are orthogonal.

Solution We use a trigonometric identity. When $m \ne n$,

$$\langle \cos mt, \cos nt\rangle = \int_0^{2\pi} \cos mt \cos nt\,dt$$
$$= \frac{1}{2}\int_0^{2\pi} [\cos\,(m+n)t + \cos\,(m-n)t]\,dt$$
$$= \frac{1}{2}\left[\frac{\sin(m+n)t}{m+n} + \frac{\sin(m-n)t}{m-n}\right]\Bigg|_0^{2\pi} = 0$$

Let W be the subspace of $C[0, 2\pi]$ spanned by the functions in (5). Given f in $C[0, 2\pi]$, the best approximation to f by functions in W is called the **nth order Fourier approximation** to f on $[0, 2\pi]$. Since the functions in (5) are orthogonal, the best approximation is given by the orthogonal projection onto W. In this case the coefficients a_k and b_k in (4) are called the **Fourier coefficients** of f. The standard formula for an orthogonal projection shows that

$$a_k = \frac{\langle f, \cos kt\rangle}{\langle \cos kt, \cos kt\rangle}, \quad b_k = \frac{\langle f, \sin kt\rangle}{\langle \sin kt, \sin kt\rangle}, \quad k \geq 1$$

In Exercise 7, you are asked to show that $\langle \cos kt, \cos kt\rangle = \pi$ and $\langle \sin kt, \sin kt\rangle = \pi$. Thus

$$a_k = \frac{1}{\pi}\int_0^{2\pi} f(t)\cos kt\, dt, \quad b_k = \frac{1}{\pi}\int_0^{2\pi} f(t)\sin kt\, dt \tag{7}$$

The coefficient of the (constant) function 1 in the orthogonal projection is readily seen to be

$$\frac{\langle f, 1\rangle}{\langle 1, 1\rangle} = \frac{1}{2\pi}\int_0^{2\pi} f(t)\cdot 1\, dt = \frac{1}{2}\left[\frac{1}{\pi}\int_0^{2\pi} f(t)\cos(0\cdot t)\, dt\right] = \frac{a_0}{2}$$

where a_0 is defined by (7) for $k = 0$. This explains why the constant term in (4) is written as $a_0/2$.

EXAMPLE 4 Find the nth-order Fourier approximation to the function $f(t) = t$ on the interval $[0, 2\pi]$.

Solution We compute

$$\frac{a_0}{2} = \frac{1}{2}\cdot\frac{1}{\pi}\int_0^{2\pi} t\, dt = \frac{1}{2\pi}\left[\frac{1}{2}t^2\Big|_0^{2\pi}\right] = \pi$$

and for $k > 0$, using integration by parts,

$$a_k = \frac{1}{\pi}\int_0^{2\pi} t\cos kt\, dt = \frac{1}{\pi}\left[\frac{1}{k^2}\cos kt + \frac{t}{k}\sin kt\right]_0^{2\pi} = 0$$

$$b_k = \frac{1}{\pi}\int_0^{2\pi} t\sin kt\, dt = \frac{1}{\pi}\left[\frac{1}{k^2}\sin kt - \frac{t}{k}\cos kt\right]_0^{2\pi} = -\frac{2}{k}$$

Thus the nth-Fourier approximation of $f(t) = t$ is

$$\pi - 2\sin t - \sin 2t - \frac{2}{3}\sin 3t - \cdots - \frac{2}{n}\sin nt$$

Figure 3 shows the third- and fourth-order Fourier approximations of f.

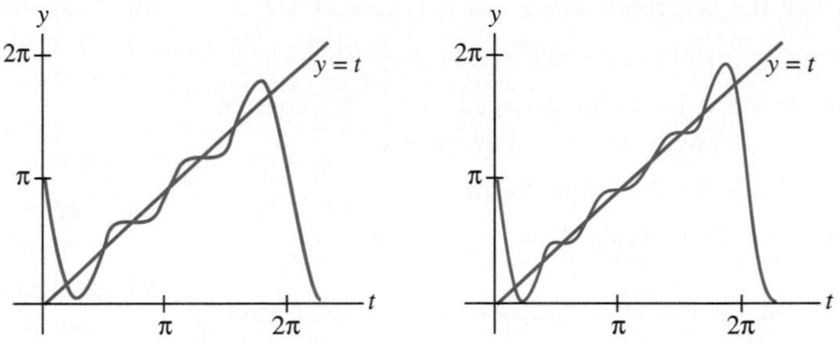

(a) Third order (b) Fourth order

FIGURE 3 Fourier approximations of the function $f(t) = t$.

The norm of the difference between f and a Fourier approximation is called the **mean square error** in the approximation. (The term *mean* refers to the fact that the norm is determined by an integral.) It can be shown that the mean square error approaches zero as the order of the Fourier approximation increases. For this reason, it is common to write

$$f(t) = \frac{a_0}{2} + \sum_{m=1}^{\infty} (a_m \cos mt + b_m \sin mt)$$

This expression for $f(t)$ is called the **Fourier series** for f on $[0, 2\pi]$. The term $a_m \cos mt$, for example, is the projection of f onto the one-dimensional subspace spanned by $\cos mt$.

PRACTICE PROBLEMS

1. Let $q_1(t) = 1, q_2(t) = t$, and $q_3(t) = 3t^2 - 4$. Verify that $\{q_1, q_2, q_3\}$ is an orthogonal set in $C[-2, 2]$ with the inner product of Example 7 in Section 7.7 (integration from -2 to 2).
2. Find the first-order and third-order Fourier approximations to

$$f(t) = 3 - 2\sin t + 5\sin 2t - 6\cos 2t$$

7.8 EXERCISES

1. Find the least-squares line $y = \beta_0 + \beta_1 x$ that best fits the data $(-2, 0), (-1, 0), (0, 2), (1, 4), (2, 4)$, assuming that the first and last data points are less reliable. Weight them half as much as the three interior points.
2. Suppose that in a weighted least-squares problem 5 out of 25 data points have a y-measurement that is less reliable than the others, and they are to be weighted half as much as the other 20 points. One method is to weight the 20 points by a factor of 1 and the other 5 by a factor of $\frac{1}{2}$. A second method is to weight the 20 points by a factor of 2 and the other 5 by a factor of 1. Do the two methods produce different results? Explain.
3. Fit a cubic trend function to the data in Example 2. The orthogonal cubic polynomial is $p_3(t) = \frac{5}{6}t^3 - \frac{17}{6}t$.
4. To make a trend analysis of six evenly spaced data points, one needs orthogonal polynomials with respect to evaluation at the points $t = -5, -3, -1, 1, 3$, and 5.

a. Show that the first three orthogonal polynomials are

$$p_0(t) = 1, \quad p_1(t) = t, \quad \text{and} \quad p_2(t) = \tfrac{3}{8}t^2 - \tfrac{35}{8}$$

(The polynomial p_2 has been scaled so that its values at the evaluation points are small integers.)

b. Fit a quadratic trend function to the data

$$(-5, 1), (-3, 1), (-1, 4), (1, 4), (3, 6), (5, 8)$$

In Exercises 5–14, the space is $C[0, 2\pi]$ with the inner product (6).

5. Show that $\sin mt$ and $\sin nt$ are orthogonal when $m \neq n$.

6. Show that $\sin mt$ and $\cos nt$ are orthogonal for all positive integers m and n.

7. Show that $\|\cos kt\|^2 = \pi$ and $\|\sin kt\|^2 = \pi$ for $k > 0$.

8. Find the third-order Fourier approximation to $f(t) = t - 1$.

9. Find the third-order Fourier approximation to $f(t) = 2\pi - t$.

10. Find the third-order Fourier approximation to the *square wave function*, $f(t) = 1$ for $0 \le t < \pi$ and $f(t) = -1$ for $\pi \le t < 2\pi$.

11. Find the third-order Fourier approximation to $\sin^2 t$, without performing any integration calculations.

12. Find the third-order Fourier approximation to $\cos^3 t$, without performing any integration calculations.

13. Explain why a Fourier coefficient of the sum of two functions is the sum of the corresponding Fourier coefficients of the two functions.

14. Suppose the first few Fourier coefficients of some function f in $C[0, 2\pi]$ are a_0, a_1, a_2, and b_1, b_2, b_3. Which of the following trigonometric polynomials is closer to f? Defend your answer.

$$g(t) = \frac{a_0}{2} + a_1 \cos t + a_2 \cos 2t + b_1 \sin t$$

$$h(t) = \frac{a_0}{2} + a_1 \cos t + a_2 \cos 2t + b_1 \sin t + b_2 \sin 2t$$

SOLUTIONS TO PRACTICE PROBLEMS

1. Compute

$$< q_1, q_2 > \; = \int_{-2}^{2} 1 \cdot t \, dt = \frac{1}{2}t^2 \Big|_{-2}^{2} = 0$$

$$< q_1, q_3 > \; = \int_{-2}^{2} 1 \cdot (3t^2 - 4) \, dt = (t^3 - 4t) \Big|_{-2}^{2} = 0$$

$$< q_2, q_3 > \; = \int_{-2}^{2} t \cdot (3t^2 - 4) \, dt = \left(\frac{3}{4}t^4 - 2t^2\right) \Big|_{-2}^{2} = 0$$

2. The third-order Fourier approximation to $f(t)$ is the best approximation in $C[0, 2\pi]$ to $f(t)$ by functions (vectors) in the subspace spanned by 1, $\cos t$, $\cos 2t$, $\cos 3t$, $\sin t$, $\sin 2t$, and $\sin 3t$. But $f(t)$ is obviously *in* this subspace, so f is its own best approximation.

$$f(t) = 3 - 2 \sin t + 5 \sin 2t - 6 \cos 2t$$

For the first-order approximation, the closest function to f in the subspace $W = \text{Span}\{1, \cos t, \sin t\}$ is $3 - 2 \sin t$. The other two terms in the formula for $f(t)$ are orthogonal to the functions in W, so they contribute nothing to the integrals that give the Fourier coefficients for a first-order approximation.

CHAPTER 7 SUPPLEMENTARY EXERCISES

1. The following statements refer to vectors in $\mathbb{R}^n$ (or $\mathbb{R}^m$) with the standard inner product. Mark each statement True or False. Justify each answer.

____ a. The length of every vector is a positive number.

____ b. A vector $\mathbf{v}$ and its negative $-\mathbf{v}$ have equal lengths.

____ c. The distance between $\mathbf{u}$ and $\mathbf{v}$ is $\|\mathbf{u}-\mathbf{v}\|$.

____ d. If r is any scalar, then $\|r\mathbf{v}\| = r\|\mathbf{v}\|$.

____ e. If two vectors are orthogonal, they are linearly independent.

____ f. If $\mathbf{x}$ is orthogonal to both $\mathbf{u}$ and $\mathbf{v}$, then $\mathbf{x}$ must be orthogonal to $\mathbf{u}-\mathbf{v}$.

____ g. If $\|\mathbf{u}+\mathbf{v}\|^2 = \|\mathbf{u}\|^2+\|\mathbf{v}\|^2$, then $\mathbf{u}$ and $\mathbf{v}$ are orthogonal.

____ h. If $\|\mathbf{u}-\mathbf{v}\|^2 = \|\mathbf{u}\|^2+\|\mathbf{v}\|^2$, then $\mathbf{u}$ and $\mathbf{v}$ are orthogonal.

____ i. The orthogonal projection of $\mathbf{y}$ onto $\mathbf{u}$ is a scalar multiple of $\mathbf{y}$.

____ j. If a vector $\mathbf{y}$ coincides with its orthogonal projection onto a subspace W, then $\mathbf{y}$ is in W.

____ k. The set of all vectors in $\mathbb{R}^n$ orthogonal to one fixed vector is a subspace of $\mathbb{R}^n$.

____ l. If W is a subspace of $\mathbb{R}^n$, then W and $W^\perp$ have no vectors in common.

____m. If $\{\mathbf{v}_1, \mathbf{v}_2, \mathbf{v}_3\}$ is an orthogonal set and if c_1, c_2, c_3 are scalars, then $\{c_1\mathbf{v}_1, c_2\mathbf{v}_2, c_3\mathbf{v}_3\}$ is an orthogonal set.

____ n. If a matrix U has orthonormal columns, then $UU^T = I$.

____ o. A square matrix with orthogonal columns is an orthogonal matrix.

____ p. If a square matrix has orthonormal columns, then it also has orthonormal rows.

____ q. If W is a subspace, then $\|\text{proj}_W\,\mathbf{v}\|^2+\|\mathbf{v}-\text{proj}_W\,\mathbf{v}\|^2 = \|\mathbf{v}\|^2$.

____ r. A least-squares solution of $A\mathbf{x} = \mathbf{b}$ is the vector $A\hat{\mathbf{x}}$ in Col A closest to $\mathbf{b}$, so that $\|\mathbf{b} - A\hat{\mathbf{x}}\| \le \|\mathbf{b} - A\mathbf{x}\|$ for all $\mathbf{x}$.

____ s. The normal equations for a least-squares solution of $A\mathbf{x} = \mathbf{b}$ are given by $\hat{\mathbf{x}} = (A^TA)^{-1}A^T\mathbf{b}$.

2. Let $\{\mathbf{v}_1, \ldots, \mathbf{v}_p\}$ be an orthonormal set. Verify the following equality by induction, beginning with $p = 2$. If $\mathbf{x} = c_1\mathbf{v}_1 + \cdots + c_p\mathbf{v}_p$, then

$$\|\mathbf{x}\|^2 = |c_1|^2 + \cdots + |c_p|^2$$

3. Let $\{\mathbf{v}_1, \ldots, \mathbf{v}_p\}$ be an orthonormal set in $\mathbb{R}^n$. Verify the following inequality, called *Bessel's inequality*, which is true for each $\mathbf{x}$ in $\mathbb{R}^n$:

$$\|\mathbf{x}\|^2 \ge |\mathbf{x}\cdot\mathbf{v}_1|^2 + |\mathbf{x}\cdot\mathbf{v}_2|^2 + \cdots + |\mathbf{x}\cdot\mathbf{v}_p|^2$$

4. Let U be an $n\times n$ orthogonal matrix. Show that if $\{\mathbf{v}_1, \ldots, \mathbf{v}_n\}$ is an orthonormal basis for $\mathbb{R}^n$, then so is $\{U\mathbf{v}_1, \ldots, U\mathbf{v}_n\}$.

5. Show that if an $n\times n$ matrix U satisfies $(U\mathbf{x})\cdot(U\mathbf{y}) = \mathbf{x}\cdot\mathbf{y}$ for all $\mathbf{x}$ and $\mathbf{y}$ in $\mathbb{R}^n$, then U is an orthogonal matrix.

6. Show that if U is an orthogonal matrix, then any real eigenvalue of U must be ± 1.

7. A *Householder matrix*, or an *elementary reflector*, has the form $Q = I - 2\mathbf{u}\mathbf{u}^T$ where $\mathbf{u}$ is a unit vector. (See Exercise 13 in the Supplementary Exercises for Chapter 3.) Show that Q is an orthogonal matrix.

Elementary reflectors are often used in computer programs to produce a QR factorization of a matrix A. If A has linearly independent columns, then left-multiplication by a sequence of elementary reflectors can produce an upper triangular matrix.

8. Let $\mathbf{u}$ and $\mathbf{v}$ be linearly independent vectors in $\mathbb{R}^n$ that are *not* orthogonal. Describe how to find the best approximation to $\mathbf{z}$ in $\mathbb{R}^n$ by vectors of the form $x_1\mathbf{u} + x_2\mathbf{v}$ without first constructing an orthogonal basis for Span$\{\mathbf{u}, \mathbf{v}\}$.

9. Suppose the columns of A are linearly independent. Determine what happens to the least-squares solution $\hat{\mathbf{x}}$ of $A\mathbf{x} = \mathbf{b}$ when $\mathbf{b}$ is replaced by $c\mathbf{b}$ for some nonzero scalar c.

10. If a, b, c are distinct numbers, then the following system is inconsistent because the graphs of the equations are parallel planes. Show that the set of all least-squares solutions of the system is precisely the plane whose equation is $x-2y+5z = (a+b+c)/3$.

$$x - 2y + 5z = a$$
$$x - 2y + 5z = b$$
$$x - 2y + 5z = c$$

11. Use the steps below to prove the following relations among the four fundamental subspaces of an $m\times n$ matrix A.

$$\text{Row } A = (\text{Nul } A)^\perp, \quad \text{Col } A = (\text{Nul } A^T)^\perp$$

a. Show that Row A is contained in $(\text{Nul } A)^\perp$. (Show that if $\mathbf{x}$ is in Row A, then $\mathbf{x}$ is orthogonal to every $\mathbf{u}$ in Nul A.)

b. Suppose rank $A = r$. Find dim Nul A and $\dim(\text{Nul } A)^\perp$, and then from (a) deduce that Row $A = (\text{Nul } A)^\perp$. [*Hint:* Study the exercises for Section 7.3.]

c. Explain why Col $A = (\text{Nul } A^T)^\perp$.

12. Explain why an equation $A\mathbf{x} = \mathbf{b}$ has a solution if and only if $\mathbf{b}$ is orthogonal to all solutions of the equation $A^T\mathbf{x} = \mathbf{0}$.

Exercises 13 and 14 concern the (real) *Schur factorization* of an $n \times n$ matrix A in the form $A = URU^T$, where U is an orthogonal matrix and R is an $n \times n$ upper triangular matrix.[1]

13. Show that if A admits a (real) Schur factorization, $A = URU^T$, then A has n real eigenvalues, counting multiplicities.

14. Let A be an $n \times n$ matrix with n real eigenvalues, counting multiplicities, denoted by $\lambda_1, \ldots, \lambda_n$. It can be shown that A admits a (real) Schur factorization. Parts (a) and (b) show the key ideas in the proof. The rest of the proof amounts to repeating (a) and (b) for successively smaller matrices, and then piecing together the results.

a. Let $\mathbf{u}_1$ be a unit eigenvector corresponding to λ_1, let $\mathbf{u}_2, \ldots, \mathbf{u}_n$ be any other vectors such that $\{\mathbf{u}_1, \ldots, \mathbf{u}_n\}$ is an orthonormal basis for $\mathbb{R}^n$, and then let $U = [\,\mathbf{u}_1 \;\; \mathbf{u}_2 \;\; \cdots \;\; \mathbf{u}_n\,]$. Show that the first column of U^TAU is $\lambda_1\mathbf{e}_1$, where $\mathbf{e}_1$ is the first column of the $n \times n$ identity matrix.

b. Part (a) implies that U^TAU has the form shown below. Explain why the eigenvalues of A_1 are $\lambda_2, \ldots, \lambda_n$. [*Hint*: See the Supplementary Exercises for Chapter 6.]

$$U^TAU = \begin{bmatrix} \lambda_1 & * & * & * & * \\ 0 & & & & \\ \vdots & & & A_1 & \\ 0 & & & & \end{bmatrix}$$

[1] If complex numbers are allowed, *every* $n \times n$ matrix A admits a (complex) Schur factorization, $A = URU^{-1}$, where R is upper triangular and U^{-1} is the *conjugate* transpose of U. This very useful fact is discussed in *Matrix Analysis*, by Roger A. Horn and Charles A. Johnson, Cambridge University Press, Cambridge, 1985, pp. 79–100.

8

Symmetric Matrices and Quadratic Forms

Introductory Example: Multichannel Image Processing

Around the world in little more than 80 *minutes*, the two Landsat satellites streak silently across the sky in near polar orbits, recording images of terrain and coastline, in swaths 185 kilometers wide. Every 16 days each satellite passes over almost every square kilometer of the earth's surface, so any location can be monitored every 8 days.

The Landsat images are useful for many purposes. Developers and urban planners use them to study the rate and direction of urban growth, industrial development, and other changes in land usage. Rural countries can analyze soil moisture, classify the vegetation in remote regions, and locate inland lakes and streams. Governments can detect and assess damage from natural disasters, such as forest fires, lava flows, floods, and hurricanes. Environmental agencies can identify pollution from smoke stacks and measure water temperatures in lakes and rivers near power plants.

Sensors aboard the satellite acquire seven simultaneous images of any region on earth to be studied. The sensors record energy from separate wavelength bands—three in the visible light spectrum and four in infrared and thermal bands. Each image is digitized and stored as a rectangular array of numbers, each number indicating the signal intensity at a corresponding small point (or *pixel*) on the image. Each of the seven images is one channel of a *multichannel* or *multispectral image*.

The seven Landsat images of one fixed region typically contain much redundant information, since some features will appear in several images. Yet other features, because of their color or temperature, may reflect light that is recorded by only one or two sensors. One goal of multichannel image processing is to view the data in a way that extracts information better than studying each image separately.

Principal component analysis is an effective way to suppress redundant information and provide in only one or two composite images most of the information from the initial data. Roughly speaking, the goal is to find a special linear combination of the images, that is, a list of weights that at each pixel combine all seven corresponding image values into one new value. The weights are chosen in a way that makes the range of light intensities or *scene variance* in the composite image (called the *first principal component*) greater than that in any of the original images. Additional *component* images also can be constructed, by criteria that will be explained in Section 8.5.

Principal component analysis is illustrated in the photos below, taken over Railroad Valley, Nevada. Images from three Landsat spectral bands are shown in (a)–(c). The total information in the three bands is rearranged in the three principal component images in (d)–(f). The first component (d) displays (or "explains") *93.5%* of the scene variance present in the initial data. In this way, the three-channel initial data have been reduced to one-channel data, with a loss in some sense of only *6.5%* of the scene variance.

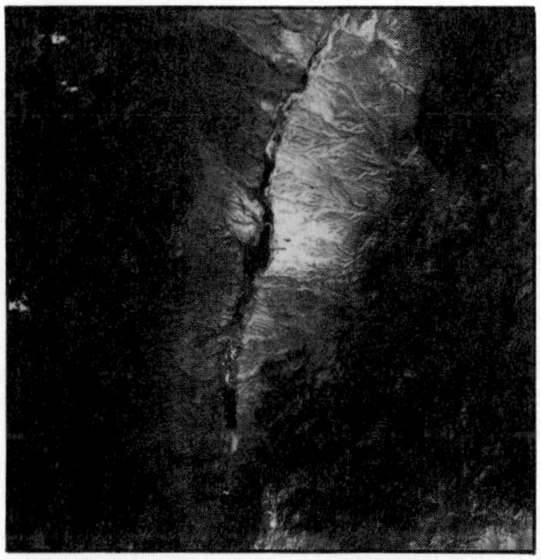

(a) Spectral band 1: Visible blue.

(b) Spectral band 4: Near infrared.

(c) Spectral band 7: Mid infrared.

(d) Principal component 1: 93.5%.

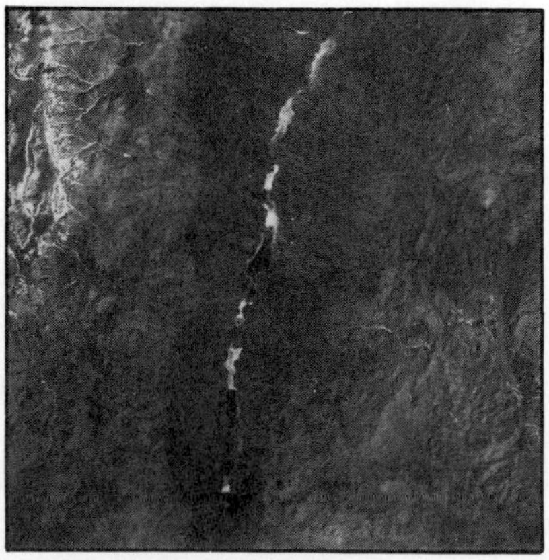

(e) Principal Component 2: 5.3%.

(f) Principal component 3: 1.2%.

Earth Satellite Corporation of Rockville, Maryland, which kindly supplied the photos shown here, is experimenting with images from 224 separate spectral bands. Principal component analysis, essential for such massive data sets, typically reduces the data to about 15 usable principal components.

Symmetric matrices arise more often in applications, in one way or another, than any other major class of matrices. The theory is rich and beautiful, depending in an essential way on both the diagonalization technique from Chapter 6 and the orthogonality from Chapter 7. The diagonalization of a symmetric matrix, described in Section 8.1, is the foundation for the discussion in Sections 8.2 and 8.3 concerning quadratic forms. Section 8.3, in turn, is needed for the final two sections on the singular value decomposition and on the image processing described in the introductory example. Throughout the chapter, all vectors and matrices have real entries.

8.1 DIAGONALIZATION OF SYMMETRIC MATRICES

A **symmetric** matrix is a matrix A such that $A^T = A$. Such a matrix is necessarily square. Its main diagonal entries are arbitrary, but its other entries occur in pairs—on opposite sides of the main diagonal.

EXAMPLE 1 Of the following matrices, only the first three are symmetric:

$$\text{Symmetric:}\quad \begin{bmatrix} 1 & 0 \\ 0 & -3 \end{bmatrix}, \quad \begin{bmatrix} 0 & -1 & 0 \\ -1 & 5 & 8 \\ 0 & 8 & -7 \end{bmatrix}, \quad \begin{bmatrix} a & b & c \\ b & d & e \\ c & e & f \end{bmatrix}$$

$$\text{Nonsymmetric:}\quad \begin{bmatrix} 1 & -3 \\ 3 & 0 \end{bmatrix}, \quad \begin{bmatrix} 1 & -4 & 0 \\ -6 & 1 & -4 \\ 0 & -6 & 1 \end{bmatrix}, \quad \begin{bmatrix} 5 & 4 & 3 & 2 \\ 4 & 3 & 2 & 1 \\ 3 & 2 & 1 & 0 \end{bmatrix}$$

To begin the study of symmetric matrices, it is helpful to review the diagonalization process of Section 6.3.

EXAMPLE 2 If possible, diagonalize the matrix $A = \begin{bmatrix} 6 & -2 & -1 \\ -2 & 6 & -1 \\ -1 & -1 & 5 \end{bmatrix}$.

Solution The characteristic equation of A is

$$0 = -\lambda^3 + 17\lambda^2 - 90\lambda + 144 = -(\lambda - 8)(\lambda - 6)(\lambda - 3)$$

Standard calculations produce a basis for each eigenspace:

$$\lambda = 8: \quad \mathbf{u}_1 = \begin{bmatrix} -1 \\ 1 \\ 0 \end{bmatrix}; \qquad \lambda = 6: \quad \mathbf{u}_2 = \begin{bmatrix} -1 \\ -1 \\ 2 \end{bmatrix}; \qquad \lambda = 3: \quad \mathbf{u}_3 = \begin{bmatrix} 1 \\ 1 \\ 1 \end{bmatrix}$$

These three vectors form a basis for $\mathbb{R}^3$, and we could use them as the columns for a matrix P that diagonalizes A. However, it is easy to see that $\{\mathbf{u}_1, \mathbf{u}_2, \mathbf{u}_3\}$ is an *orthogonal set*; and P will be easier to use if its columns are orthonormal. Since a nonzero multiple of an eigenvector is still an eigenvector, we can normalize $\mathbf{u}_1$, $\mathbf{u}_2$, and $\mathbf{u}_3$ to produce the unit eigenvectors

$$\mathbf{v}_1 = \begin{bmatrix} -1/\sqrt{2} \\ 1/\sqrt{2} \\ 0 \end{bmatrix}, \quad \mathbf{v}_2 = \begin{bmatrix} -1/\sqrt{6} \\ -1/\sqrt{6} \\ 2/\sqrt{6} \end{bmatrix}, \quad \mathbf{v}_3 = \begin{bmatrix} 1/\sqrt{3} \\ 1/\sqrt{3} \\ 1/\sqrt{3} \end{bmatrix}$$

Let

$$P = \begin{bmatrix} -1/\sqrt{2} & -1/\sqrt{6} & 1/\sqrt{3} \\ 1/\sqrt{2} & -1/\sqrt{6} & 1/\sqrt{3} \\ 0 & 2/\sqrt{6} & 1/\sqrt{3} \end{bmatrix}, \quad D = \begin{bmatrix} 8 & 0 & 0 \\ 0 & 6 & 0 \\ 0 & 0 & 3 \end{bmatrix}$$

Then $A = PDP^{-1}$, as usual. But this time, since P is square and has orthonormal columns, P is an *orthogonal* matrix, and P^{-1} is simply P^T. (See Section 7.2.)

Theorem 1 explains why the eigenvectors in Example 2 are orthogonal—they correspond to distinct eigenvalues.

THEOREM 1

If A is symmetric, then any two eigenvectors from different eigenspaces are orthogonal.

Proof Let $\mathbf{u}_1$ and $\mathbf{u}_2$ be eigenvectors that correspond to distinct eigenvalues, say, λ_1 and λ_2. To show that $\mathbf{u}_1 \cdot \mathbf{u}_2 = 0$, we compute

$$\begin{aligned} \lambda_1\mathbf{u}_1 \cdot \mathbf{u}_2 &= (\lambda_1\mathbf{u}_1)^T\mathbf{u}_2 = (A\mathbf{u}_1)^T\mathbf{u}_2 && \text{Since } \mathbf{u}_1 \text{ is an eigenvector} \\ &= (\mathbf{u}_1^T A^T)\mathbf{u}_2 = \mathbf{u}_1^T(A\mathbf{u}_2) && \text{Since } A^T = A \\ &= \mathbf{u}_1^T(\lambda_2\mathbf{u}_2) && \text{Since } \mathbf{u}_2 \text{ is an eigenvector} \\ &= \lambda_2\mathbf{u}_1^T\mathbf{u}_2 = \lambda_2\mathbf{u}_1 \cdot \mathbf{u}_2 \end{aligned}$$

Hence $(\lambda_1 - \lambda_2)\mathbf{u}_1 \cdot \mathbf{u}_2 = 0$. But $\lambda_1 - \lambda_2 \neq 0$, so $\mathbf{u}_1 \cdot \mathbf{u}_2 = 0$.

The special type of diagonalization in Example 2 is crucial for the theory of symmetric matrices. A matrix A is said to be **orthogonally diagonalizable** if there are an orthogonal matrix P (with $P^{-1} = P^T$) and a diagonal matrix D such that

$$A = PDP^T = PDP^{-1} \tag{1}$$

To orthogonally diagonalize an $n \times n$ matrix, we must be able to find n linearly independent and orthonormal eigenvectors. When is this possible? If A *is* orthogonally diagonalizable as in (1), then

$$A^T = (PDP^T)^T = P^{TT}D^TP^T = PDP^T = A$$

Thus A is symmetric! Theorem 2 shows that, conversely, every symmetric matrix is orthogonally diagonalizable. The proof is much harder and is omitted; the main idea for a proof will be given after Theorem 3.

THEOREM 2

An $n \times n$ matrix A is orthogonally diagonalizable if and only if A is a symmetric matrix.

This theorem is rather amazing, because our experience in Chapter 6 would suggest that it is usually impossible to tell when a matrix is diagonalizable. But this is not the case for symmetric matrices.

The next example shows how to handle a matrix whose eigenvalues are not all distinct.

EXAMPLE 3 Orthogonally diagonalize the matrix $A = \begin{bmatrix} 3 & -2 & 4 \\ -2 & 6 & 2 \\ 4 & 2 & 3 \end{bmatrix}$ whose characteristic equation is

$$0 = -\lambda^3 + 12\lambda^2 - 21\lambda - 98 = -(\lambda - 7)^2(\lambda + 2)$$

Solution The usual calculations produce bases for the eigenspaces:

$$\lambda = 7: \quad \mathbf{u}_1 = \begin{bmatrix} 1 \\ 0 \\ 1 \end{bmatrix}, \quad \mathbf{u}_2 = \begin{bmatrix} -1/2 \\ 1 \\ 0 \end{bmatrix}; \qquad \lambda = -2: \quad \mathbf{u}_3 = \begin{bmatrix} -1 \\ -1/2 \\ 1 \end{bmatrix}$$

Although $\mathbf{u}_1$ and $\mathbf{u}_2$ are linearly independent, they are not orthogonal. Recall from Section 7.2 that the projection of $\mathbf{u}_2$ onto $\mathbf{u}_1$ is $\dfrac{\mathbf{u}_2 \cdot \mathbf{u}_1}{\mathbf{u}_1 \cdot \mathbf{u}_1}\mathbf{u}_1$, and the component of $\mathbf{u}_2$ orthogonal to $\mathbf{u}_1$ is

$$\mathbf{z}_2 = \mathbf{u}_2 - \frac{\mathbf{u}_2 \cdot \mathbf{u}_1}{\mathbf{u}_1 \cdot \mathbf{u}_1}\mathbf{u}_1 = \begin{bmatrix} -1/2 \\ 1 \\ 0 \end{bmatrix} - \frac{-1/2}{2}\begin{bmatrix} 1 \\ 0 \\ 1 \end{bmatrix} = \begin{bmatrix} -1/4 \\ 1 \\ 1/4 \end{bmatrix}$$

Then $\{\mathbf{u}_1, \mathbf{z}_2\}$ is an orthogonal set in the eigenspace for $\lambda = 7$. (Note that $\mathbf{z}_2$ is a linear combination of the eigenvectors $\mathbf{u}_1$ and $\mathbf{u}_2$, so $\mathbf{z}_2$ is in the eigenspace. This construction of $\mathbf{z}_2$ is just the Gram–Schmidt process of Section 7.4.) Since the eigenspace is two-dimensional (with basis $\mathbf{u}_1, \mathbf{u}_2$), the orthogonal set $\{\mathbf{u}_1, \mathbf{z}_2\}$ is an *orthogonal basis* for the eigenspace.

Normalizing $\mathbf{u}_1$ and $\mathbf{z}_2$, we obtain the following orthonormal basis for the eigenspace for $\lambda = 7$:

$$\mathbf{v}_1 = \begin{bmatrix} 1/\sqrt{2} \\ 0 \\ 1/\sqrt{2} \end{bmatrix}, \qquad \mathbf{v}_2 = \begin{bmatrix} -1/\sqrt{18} \\ 4/\sqrt{18} \\ 1/\sqrt{18} \end{bmatrix}$$

An orthonormal basis for the eigenspace for $\lambda = -2$ is

$$\mathbf{v}_3 = \frac{1}{\|2\mathbf{u}_3\|}2\mathbf{u}_3 = \frac{1}{3}\begin{bmatrix} -2 \\ -1 \\ 2 \end{bmatrix} = \begin{bmatrix} -2/3 \\ -1/3 \\ 2/3 \end{bmatrix}$$

By Theorem 1, $\mathbf{v}_3$ is orthogonal to the other eigenvectors $\mathbf{v}_1$ and $\mathbf{v}_2$. Hence $\{\mathbf{v}_1, \mathbf{v}_2, \mathbf{v}_3\}$ is an orthonormal set. Let

$$P = [\,\mathbf{v}_1 \quad \mathbf{v}_2 \quad \mathbf{v}_3\,] = \begin{bmatrix} 1/\sqrt{2} & -1/\sqrt{18} & -2/3 \\ 0 & 4/\sqrt{18} & -1/3 \\ 1/\sqrt{2} & 1/\sqrt{18} & 2/3 \end{bmatrix}, \qquad D = \begin{bmatrix} 7 & 0 & 0 \\ 0 & 7 & 0 \\ 0 & 0 & -2 \end{bmatrix}$$

Then P orthogonally diagonalizes A, and $A = PDP^{-1}$.

In Example 3, the eigenvalue 7 has multiplicity two and the eigenspace is two-dimensional. This fact is not accidental, as the next theorem shows.

The Spectral Theorem

The set of eigenvalues of a matrix A is sometimes called the *spectrum* of A, and the following description of the eigenvalues is called a *spectral theorem.*

THEOREM 3

The Spectral Theorem for Symmetric Matrices

An $n \times n$ symmetric matrix A has the following properties:

a. A has n real eigenvalues, counting multiplicities.

b. If λ is an eigenvalue of A with multiplicity k, then the eigenspace for λ is k-dimensional.

c. The eigenspaces are mutually orthogonal, in the sense that eigenvectors corresponding to different eigenvalues are orthogonal.

d. A is orthogonally diagonalizable.

Part (a) follows from Exercise 24 of Section 6.5. Part (b) follows easily from part (d). (See Exercise 31.) Part (c) is Theorem 1. Because of (a), a proof of (d) can be given using the Schur factorization discussed in Supplementary Exercise 14 in Chapter 7. The details are omitted. However, see Exercise 32.

Spectral Decomposition

Suppose that $A = PDP^{-1}$, where the columns of P are orthonormal eigenvectors $\mathbf{v}_1, \ldots, \mathbf{v}_n$ of A and the corresponding eigenvalues $\lambda_1, \ldots, \lambda_n$ are in the diagonal matrix D. Then, since $P^{-1} = P^T$,

$$A = PDP^T = [\mathbf{v}_1 \quad \cdots \quad \mathbf{v}_n] \begin{bmatrix} \lambda_1 & & 0 \\ & \ddots & \\ 0 & & \lambda_n \end{bmatrix} \begin{bmatrix} \mathbf{v}_1^T \\ \vdots \\ \mathbf{v}_n^T \end{bmatrix}$$

$$= [\lambda_1 \mathbf{v}_1 \quad \cdots \quad \lambda_n \mathbf{v}_n] \begin{bmatrix} \mathbf{v}_1^T \\ \vdots \\ \mathbf{v}_n^T \end{bmatrix}$$

Using the column–row expansion of a product (Theorem 10 in Section 3.4), we can write

$$A = \lambda_1 \mathbf{v}_1 \mathbf{v}_1^T + \lambda_2 \mathbf{v}_2 \mathbf{v}_2^T + \cdots + \lambda_n \mathbf{v}_n \mathbf{v}_n^T \tag{2}$$

This representation of A is called a **spectral decomposition** of A because it breaks up A into pieces determined by the spectrum (eigenvalues) of A. Each term in (2) is an $n \times n$ matrix of rank 1. For example, every column of $\lambda_1 \mathbf{v}_1 \mathbf{v}_1^T$ is a multiple of $\mathbf{v}_1$. Furthermore, each matrix $\mathbf{v}_j \mathbf{v}_j^T$ is a **projection matrix** in the sense that for each $\mathbf{x}$ in $\mathbb{R}^n$, the vector $(\mathbf{v}_j \mathbf{v}_j^T)\mathbf{x}$ is the orthogonal projection of $\mathbf{x}$ onto the subspace spanned by $\mathbf{v}_j$. See Exercise 33.

EXAMPLE 4 Construct a spectral decomposition of the matrix A that has the orthogonal diagonalization

$$A = \begin{bmatrix} 7 & 2 \\ 2 & 4 \end{bmatrix} = \begin{bmatrix} 2/\sqrt{5} & -1/\sqrt{5} \\ 1/\sqrt{5} & 2/\sqrt{5} \end{bmatrix} \begin{bmatrix} 8 & 0 \\ 0 & 3 \end{bmatrix} \begin{bmatrix} 2/\sqrt{5} & 1/\sqrt{5} \\ -1/\sqrt{5} & 2/\sqrt{5} \end{bmatrix}$$

Solution Denote the columns of P by $\mathbf{v}_1$ and $\mathbf{v}_2$. Then

$$A = 8\mathbf{v}_1 \mathbf{v}_1^T + 3\mathbf{v}_2 \mathbf{v}_2^T$$

To verify this decomposition of A, compute

$$\mathbf{v}_1 \mathbf{v}_1^T = \begin{bmatrix} 2/\sqrt{5} \\ 1/\sqrt{5} \end{bmatrix} [2/\sqrt{5} \quad 1/\sqrt{5}] = \begin{bmatrix} 4/5 & 2/5 \\ 2/5 & 1/5 \end{bmatrix}$$

$$\mathbf{v}_2 \mathbf{v}_2^T = \begin{bmatrix} -1/\sqrt{5} \\ 2/\sqrt{5} \end{bmatrix} [-1/\sqrt{5} \quad 2/\sqrt{5}] = \begin{bmatrix} 1/5 & -2/5 \\ -2/5 & 4/5 \end{bmatrix}$$

and

$$8\mathbf{v}_1 \mathbf{v}_1^T + 3\mathbf{v}_2 \mathbf{v}_2^T = \begin{bmatrix} 32/5 & 16/5 \\ 16/5 & 8/5 \end{bmatrix} + \begin{bmatrix} 3/5 & -6/5 \\ -6/5 & 12/5 \end{bmatrix} = \begin{bmatrix} 7 & 2 \\ 2 & 4 \end{bmatrix} = A$$

PRACTICE PROBLEMS

1. Show that if A is a symmetric matrix, then A^2 is symmetric.
2. Show that if A is orthogonally diagonalizable, then so is A^2.

8.1 EXERCISES

Determine which of the matrices in Exercises 1–6 are symmetric.

1. $\begin{bmatrix} 3 & 5 \\ 5 & -7 \end{bmatrix}$

2. $\begin{bmatrix} -3 & 5 \\ -5 & 3 \end{bmatrix}$

3. $\begin{bmatrix} 2 & 2 \\ 4 & 4 \end{bmatrix}$

4. $\begin{bmatrix} 0 & 8 & 3 \\ 8 & 0 & -2 \\ 3 & -2 & 0 \end{bmatrix}$

5. $\begin{bmatrix} -6 & 2 & 0 \\ 0 & -6 & 2 \\ 0 & 0 & -6 \end{bmatrix}$

6. $\begin{bmatrix} 1 & 2 & 1 & 2 \\ 2 & 1 & 2 & 1 \\ 1 & 2 & 1 & 2 \end{bmatrix}$

Determine which of the matrices in Exercises 7–12 are orthogonal. If orthogonal, find the inverse.

7. $\begin{bmatrix} .6 & .8 \\ .8 & -.6 \end{bmatrix}$

8. $\begin{bmatrix} 1/\sqrt{2} & -1/\sqrt{2} \\ 1/\sqrt{2} & 1/\sqrt{2} \end{bmatrix}$

9. $\begin{bmatrix} -5 & 2 \\ 2 & 5 \end{bmatrix}$

10. $\begin{bmatrix} -1 & 2 & 2 \\ 2 & -1 & 2 \\ 2 & 2 & -1 \end{bmatrix}$

11. $\begin{bmatrix} 2/3 & 2/3 & 1/3 \\ 0 & 1/\sqrt{5} & -2/\sqrt{5} \\ \sqrt{5}/3 & -4/\sqrt{45} & -2/\sqrt{45} \end{bmatrix}$

12. $\begin{bmatrix} .5 & .5 & -.5 & -.5 \\ -.5 & .5 & -.5 & .5 \\ .5 & .5 & .5 & .5 \\ -.5 & .5 & .5 & -.5 \end{bmatrix}$

Orthogonally diagonalize the matrices in Exercises 13–24, giving an orthogonal matrix P and a diagonal matrix D. To save you time, the eigenvalues in Exercises 17–24 are: (17) 5, 2, −2; (18) 25, 3, −50; (19) 7, 4, 1; (20) 13, 7, 1; (21) 5, 2; (22) 10, 1; (23) 3, 1; and (24) 2, 0.

13. $\begin{bmatrix} 3 & 1 \\ 1 & 3 \end{bmatrix}$

14. $\begin{bmatrix} 1 & 5 \\ 5 & 1 \end{bmatrix}$

15. $\begin{bmatrix} 16 & -4 \\ -4 & 1 \end{bmatrix}$

16. $\begin{bmatrix} -7 & 24 \\ 24 & 7 \end{bmatrix}$

17. $\begin{bmatrix} 1 & 1 & 3 \\ 1 & 3 & 1 \\ 3 & 1 & 1 \end{bmatrix}$

18. $\begin{bmatrix} -2 & -36 & 0 \\ -36 & -23 & 0 \\ 0 & 0 & 3 \end{bmatrix}$

19. $\begin{bmatrix} 3 & 2 & 0 \\ 2 & 4 & 2 \\ 0 & 2 & 5 \end{bmatrix}$

20. $\begin{bmatrix} 7 & -4 & 4 \\ -4 & 5 & 0 \\ 4 & 0 & 9 \end{bmatrix}$

21. $\begin{bmatrix} 3 & 1 & 1 \\ 1 & 3 & 1 \\ 1 & 1 & 3 \end{bmatrix}$

22. $\begin{bmatrix} 5 & -4 & -2 \\ -4 & 5 & 2 \\ -2 & 2 & 2 \end{bmatrix}$

23. $\begin{bmatrix} 2 & 0 & 1 & 0 \\ 0 & 2 & 0 & 1 \\ 1 & 0 & 2 & 0 \\ 0 & 1 & 0 & 2 \end{bmatrix}$

24. $\begin{bmatrix} 2 & 0 & 0 & 0 \\ 0 & 1 & 0 & 1 \\ 0 & 0 & 2 & 0 \\ 0 & 1 & 0 & 1 \end{bmatrix}$

25. Suppose that A is invertible and orthogonally diagonalizable. Explain why A^{-1} is also orthogonally diagonalizable.

26. Suppose that A and B are both orthogonally diagonalizable and $AB = BA$. Explain why AB is also orthogonally diagonalizable.

27. Construct a spectral decomposition of A in Example 2.

28. Construct a spectral decomposition of A in Example 3.

29. Suppose A is a 6×6 symmetric matrix of rank 4. Explain why A has exactly four nonzero eigenvalues, counting multiplicities. [*Hint*: Use the Rank Theorem.]

30. Show that if A is an $n \times n$ symmetric matrix, then $A\mathbf{x} \cdot \mathbf{y} = \mathbf{x} \cdot A\mathbf{y}$ for all $\mathbf{x}, \mathbf{y}$ in $\mathbb{R}^n$.

31. Let $A = PDP^{-1}$, where P is orthogonal and D is diagonal, and let λ be an eigenvalue of A of multiplicity k. Then λ appears k times on the diagonal of D. Explain why the dimension of the eigenspace for λ is k.

32. Suppose $A = PRP^{-1}$, where P is orthogonal and R is upper triangular. Show that if A is symmetric, then R is symmetric and hence is actually a diagonal matrix.

33. Let $\mathbf{v}$ be a unit vector in $\mathbb{R}^n$ and let $B = \mathbf{v}\mathbf{v}^T$.
    a. Given any $\mathbf{x}$ in $\mathbb{R}^n$, compute $B\mathbf{x}$ and show that $B\mathbf{x}$ is the orthogonal projection onto $\mathbf{v}$, as described in Section 7.2.
    b. Show that B is a symmetric matrix and $B^2 = B$.

34. Let B be an $n \times n$ symmetric matrix such that $B^2 = B$. Any such matrix is called a **projection matrix** (or an **orthogonal projection matrix**). Given any $\mathbf{y}$ in $\mathbb{R}^n$, let $\hat{\mathbf{y}} = B\mathbf{y}$ and $\mathbf{z} = \mathbf{y} - \hat{\mathbf{y}}$.
    a. Show that $\mathbf{z}$ is orthogonal to $\hat{\mathbf{y}}$.
    b. Let W be the column space of B. Show that $\mathbf{y}$ is the sum of a vector in W and a vector in $W^{\perp}$. Why does this prove that $B\mathbf{y}$ is the orthogonal projection of $\mathbf{y}$ onto the column space of B?

SOLUTIONS TO PRACTICE PROBLEMS

1. $(A^2)^T = (AA)^T = A^T A^T$, by a property of transposes. By hypothesis, $A^T = A$. So $(A^2)^T = AA = A^2$, which shows that A^2 is symmetric.
2. If A is orthogonally diagonalizable, then A is symmetric, by Theorem 2. By Practice Problem 1, A^2 is symmetric and hence is orthogonally diagonalizable (Theorem 2).

8.2 QUADRATIC FORMS

Until now, our attention in this text has focused on linear equations, except for the sums of squares we encountered in Chapter 7 when computing $\mathbf{x}^T\mathbf{x}$. Such sums and more general expressions, called *quadratic forms*, occur frequently in applications of linear algebra to engineering (in design criteria and optimization) and signal processing (as output noise power). They also arise, for example, in physics (as potential and kinetic energy), differential geometry (as normal curvature of surfaces), economics (as utility functions), and statistics (in confidence ellipsoids). Some of the mathematical background for such applications flows easily from our work on symmetric matrices.

A **quadratic form** on $\mathbb{R}^n$ is a function Q defined on $\mathbb{R}^n$ whose value at a vector $\mathbf{x}$ in $\mathbb{R}^n$ can be computed by an expression of the form $Q(\mathbf{x}) = \mathbf{x}^T A\mathbf{x}$, where A is an $n \times n$ symmetric matrix. The matrix A is called the **matrix of the quadratic form**.

The simplest example of a quadratic form is $Q(\mathbf{x}) = \mathbf{x}^T I\mathbf{x} = \|\mathbf{x}\|^2$. Examples 1 and 2 show the connection between any symmetric matrix A and the quadratic form $\mathbf{x}^T A\mathbf{x}$.

EXAMPLE 1 Let $\mathbf{x} = \begin{bmatrix} x_1 \\ x_2 \end{bmatrix}$. Compute $\mathbf{x}^T A\mathbf{x}$ for the following matrices:

a. $A = \begin{bmatrix} 4 & 0 \\ 0 & 3 \end{bmatrix}$ b. $A = \begin{bmatrix} 3 & -2 \\ -2 & 7 \end{bmatrix}$

Solution

a. $\mathbf{x}^T A\mathbf{x} = [\,x_1 \quad x_2\,]\begin{bmatrix} 4 & 0 \\ 0 & 3 \end{bmatrix}\begin{bmatrix} x_1 \\ x_2 \end{bmatrix} = [\,x_1 \quad x_2\,]\begin{bmatrix} 4x_1 \\ 3x_2 \end{bmatrix} = 4x_1^2 + 3x_2^2.$

b. There are two -2 entries in A. Watch how they enter the calculations. The $(1, 2)$-entry in A is in boldface type.

$$\begin{aligned} \mathbf{x}^T A\mathbf{x} &= [\,x_1 \quad x_2\,]\begin{bmatrix} 3 & \mathbf{-2} \\ -2 & 7 \end{bmatrix}\begin{bmatrix} x_1 \\ x_2 \end{bmatrix} = [\,x_1 \quad x_2\,]\begin{bmatrix} 3x_1 - \mathbf{2}x_2 \\ -2x_1 + 7x_2 \end{bmatrix} \\ &= x_1(3x_1 - \mathbf{2}x_2) + x_2(-2x_1 + 7x_2) \\ &= 3x_1^2 - \mathbf{2}x_1x_2 - 2x_2x_1 + 7x_2^2 \\ &= 3x_1^2 - 4x_1x_2 + 7x_2^2 \end{aligned}$$

The presence of $-4x_1x_2$ in the quadratic form in Example 1(b) is due to the -2 entries off the diagonal in the matrix A. In contrast, the quadratic form associated with the diagonal matrix A in Example 1(a) has no x_1x_2 *cross-product* term.

EXAMPLE 2 For $\mathbf{x}$ in $\mathbb{R}^3$, let $Q(\mathbf{x}) = 5x_1^2 + 3x_2^2 + 2x_3^2 - x_1x_2 + 8x_2x_3$. Write this quadratic form as $\mathbf{x}^TA\mathbf{x}$.

Solution The coefficients of x_1^2, x_2^2, x_3^2 go on the diagonal of A. To make A symmetric, the coefficient of x_ix_j for $i \neq j$ must be split evenly between the (i, j)- and (j, i)-entries in A. The coefficient of x_1x_3 is 0. It is readily checked that

$$Q(\mathbf{x}) = \mathbf{x}^TA\mathbf{x} = [\,x_1 \quad x_2 \quad x_3\,]\begin{bmatrix} 5 & -1/2 & 0 \\ -1/2 & 3 & 4 \\ 0 & 4 & 2 \end{bmatrix}\begin{bmatrix} x_1 \\ x_2 \\ x_3 \end{bmatrix}$$

EXAMPLE 3 Let $Q(\mathbf{x}) = x_1^2 - 8x_1x_2 - 5x_2^2$. Compute the value of $Q(\mathbf{x})$ for $\mathbf{x} = \begin{bmatrix} -3 \\ 1 \end{bmatrix}, \begin{bmatrix} 2 \\ -2 \end{bmatrix}$, and $\begin{bmatrix} 1 \\ -3 \end{bmatrix}$.

Solution

$$Q(-3, 1) = (-3)^2 - 8(-3)(1) - 5(1)^2 = 28$$
$$Q(2, -2) = (2)^2 - 8(2)(-2) - 5(-2)^2 = 16$$
$$Q(1, -3) = (1)^2 - 8(1)(-3) - 5(-3)^2 = -20$$

In some cases, quadratic forms are easier to use when they have no cross-product terms—that is, when the matrix of the quadratic form is a diagonal matrix. Fortunately, the cross-product term can be eliminated by making a suitable change of variable.

Change of Variable in a Quadratic Form

If $\mathbf{x}$ represents a variable vector in $\mathbb{R}^n$, then a **change of variable** is an equation of the form

$$\mathbf{x} = P\mathbf{u}, \quad \text{or equivalently,} \quad \mathbf{u} = P^{-1}\mathbf{x} \tag{1}$$

where P is an invertible matrix and $\mathbf{u}$ is a new variable vector in $\mathbb{R}^n$. Here $\mathbf{u}$ is the coordinate vector of $\mathbf{x}$ relative to the basis of $\mathbb{R}^n$ determined by the columns of P. (See Section 5.4.)

If the change of variable (1) is made in a quadratic form $\mathbf{x}^TA\mathbf{x}$, then

$$\mathbf{x}^TA\mathbf{x} = (P\mathbf{u})^TA(P\mathbf{u}) = \mathbf{u}^TP^TAP\mathbf{u} = \mathbf{u}^T(P^TAP)\mathbf{u} \tag{2}$$

and the new matrix of the quadratic form is P^TAP. If P *orthogonally* diagonalizes A, then $P^T = P^{-1}$ and $P^TAP = P^{-1}AP = D$. The matrix of the new quadratic form is diagonal! That is the strategy of the next example.

EXAMPLE 4 Make a change of variable that transforms the quadratic form in Example 3 into a quadratic form with no cross-product term.

Solution The matrix of the quadratic form in Example 3 is

$$A = \begin{bmatrix} 1 & -4 \\ -4 & -5 \end{bmatrix}$$

The first step is to orthogonally diagonalize A. Its eigenvalues turn out to be $\lambda = 3$ and $\lambda = -7$. Associated unit eigenvectors are

$$\lambda = 3: \quad \begin{bmatrix} 2/\sqrt{5} \\ -1/\sqrt{5} \end{bmatrix}; \qquad \lambda = -7: \quad \begin{bmatrix} 1/\sqrt{5} \\ 2/\sqrt{5} \end{bmatrix}$$

These vectors are automatically orthogonal (because they correspond to distinct eigenvalues) and so provide an orthonormal basis for $\mathbb{R}^2$. Let

$$P = \begin{bmatrix} 2/\sqrt{5} & 1/\sqrt{5} \\ -1/\sqrt{5} & 2/\sqrt{5} \end{bmatrix}, \qquad D = \begin{bmatrix} 3 & 0 \\ 0 & -7 \end{bmatrix}$$

Then $A = PDP^{-1}$, and $D = P^{-1}AP = P^TAP$, as pointed out earlier. A suitable change of variable is

$$\mathbf{x} = P\mathbf{u}, \qquad \text{where } \mathbf{x} = \begin{bmatrix} x_1 \\ x_2 \end{bmatrix} \quad \text{and} \quad \mathbf{u} = \begin{bmatrix} u_1 \\ u_2 \end{bmatrix}$$

Then

$$\begin{aligned} x_1^2 - 8x_1x_2 - 5x_2^2 &= \mathbf{x}^TA\mathbf{x} = (P\mathbf{u})^TA(P\mathbf{u}) \\ &= \mathbf{u}^TP^TAP\mathbf{u} = \mathbf{u}^TD\mathbf{u} \\ &= 3u_1^2 - 7u_2^2 \end{aligned}$$

To illustrate the meaning of the equality of quadratic forms in Example 4, we may compute $Q(\mathbf{x})$ for $\mathbf{x} = (2, -2)$ using the new quadratic form. First, since $\mathbf{x} = P\mathbf{u}$, we have

$$\mathbf{u} = P^{-1}\mathbf{x} = P^T\mathbf{x}$$

so

$$\mathbf{u} = \begin{bmatrix} 2/\sqrt{5} & -1/\sqrt{5} \\ 1/\sqrt{5} & 2/\sqrt{5} \end{bmatrix} \begin{bmatrix} 2 \\ -2 \end{bmatrix} = \begin{bmatrix} 6/\sqrt{5} \\ -2/\sqrt{5} \end{bmatrix}$$

Hence

$$\begin{aligned} 3u_1^2 - 7u_2^2 &= 3(6/\sqrt{5})^2 - 7(-2/\sqrt{5})^2 = 3(36/5) - 7(4/5) \\ &= 80/5 = 16 \end{aligned}$$

This is the value of $Q(\mathbf{x})$ in Example 3 when $\mathbf{x} = (2, -2)$. See Fig. 1.

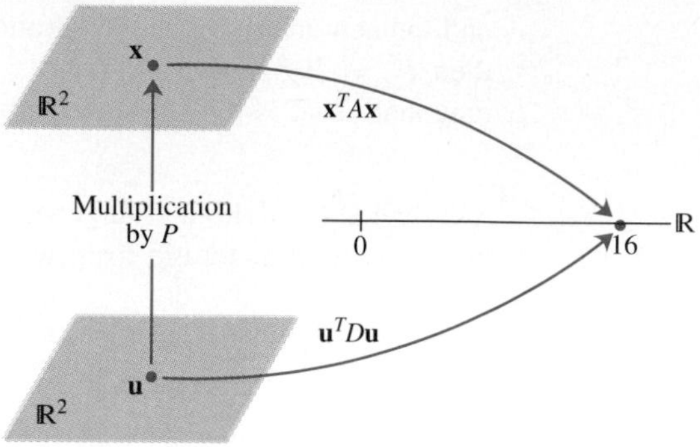

FIGURE 1 Change of variable in $\mathbf{x}^T A\mathbf{x}$.

Example 4 illustrates the following theorem. The proof of the theorem was essentially given before Example 4.

THEOREM 4

The Principal Axes Theorem

Let A be an $n \times n$ symmetric matrix. Then there is an orthogonal change of variable, $\mathbf{x} = P\mathbf{u}$, that transforms the quadratic form $\mathbf{x}^T A\mathbf{x}$ into a quadratic form $\mathbf{u}^T D\mathbf{u}$ with no cross-product term.

The columns of P in the theorem are called the **principal axes** of the quadratic form $\mathbf{x}^T A\mathbf{x}$. The vector $\mathbf{u}$ is the coordinate vector of $\mathbf{x}$ relative to the orthonormal basis of $\mathbb{R}^n$ given by these principal axes.

A Geometric View of Principal Axes

Suppose that $Q(\mathbf{x}) = \mathbf{x}^T A\mathbf{x}$, where A is an invertible 2×2 symmetric matrix, and let c be a constant. It can be shown that the set of all $\mathbf{x}$ in $\mathbb{R}^2$ that satisfy

$$\mathbf{x}^T A\mathbf{x} = c \tag{3}$$

either corresponds to an ellipse (or circle), a hyperbola, two intersecting lines, a single point, or contains no points at all. If A is a diagonal matrix, the graph is in *standard position*, such as in Fig. 2. If A is not a diagonal matrix, the graph of (3) is rotated out of standard position, as in Fig. 3. Finding the *principal axes* (determined by the eigenvectors of A) amounts to finding a new coordinate system with respect to which the graph is in standard position.

The hyperbola in Fig. 3(b) is the graph of the equation $\mathbf{x}^T A\mathbf{x} = 16$, where A is the matrix in Example 4. The positive u_1-axis in Fig. 3(b) is in the direction of the first column of the P in Example 4, and the positive u_2-axis is in the direction of the second column of P.

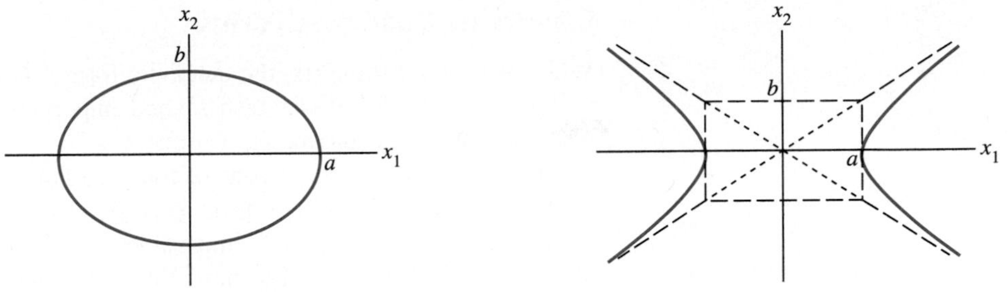

$\dfrac{x_1^2}{a^2} + \dfrac{x_2^2}{b^2} = 1,\ a > b > 0$

ellipse

$\dfrac{x_1^2}{a^2} - \dfrac{x_2^2}{b^2} = 1,\ a > b > 0$

hyperbola

FIGURE 2 An ellipse and a hyperbola in standard position.

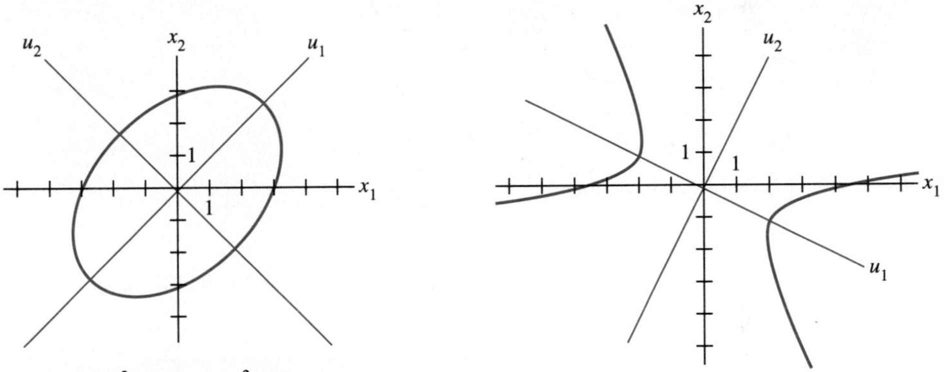

(a) $5x_1^2 - 4x_1x_2 + 5x_2^2 = 48$

(b) $x_1^2 - 8x_1x_2 - 5x_2^2 = 16$

FIGURE 3 An ellipse and a hyperbola *not* in standard position.

EXAMPLE 5 The ellipse in Fig. 3(a) is the graph of the equation $5x_1^2 - 4x_1x_2 + 5x_2^2 = 48$. Find a change of variable that removes the cross-product term from the equation.

Solution The matrix of the quadratic form is $A = \begin{bmatrix} 5 & -2 \\ -2 & 5 \end{bmatrix}$. The eigenvalues of A turn out to be 3 and 7, with corresponding unit eigenvectors

$$\mathbf{v}_1 = \begin{bmatrix} 1/\sqrt{2} \\ 1/\sqrt{2} \end{bmatrix}, \qquad \mathbf{v}_2 = \begin{bmatrix} -1/\sqrt{2} \\ 1/\sqrt{2} \end{bmatrix}$$

Let $P = [\,\mathbf{v}_1 \quad \mathbf{v}_2\,] = \begin{bmatrix} 1/\sqrt{2} & -1/\sqrt{2} \\ 1/\sqrt{2} & 1/\sqrt{2} \end{bmatrix}$. Then P orthogonally diagonalizes A, so the change of variable $\mathbf{x} = P\mathbf{u}$ produces the quadratic form $\mathbf{u}^T D\mathbf{u} = 3u_1^2 + 7u_2^2$. The new axes for this change of variable are shown in Fig. 3(a).

Classifying Quadratic Forms

When A is an $n \times n$ matrix, the quadratic form $Q(\mathbf{x}) = \mathbf{x}^T A\mathbf{x}$ is a real-valued function with domain $\mathbb{R}^n$. We distinguish several important classes of quadratic forms by the type of *values* they assume for various $\mathbf{x}$'s.

Figure 4 displays the graphs of four quadratic forms. For each point $\mathbf{x} = (x_1, x_2)$ in the domain of a quadratic form Q, a point (x_1, x_2, z) is plotted, where $z = Q(\mathbf{x})$. Notice that except at $\mathbf{x} = \mathbf{0}$, the values of $Q(\mathbf{x})$ are all positive in Fig. 4(a) and all negative in Fig. 4(d). The horizontal cross sections of the graphs are ellipses in Figs. 4(a) and 4(d), and hyperbolas in 4(c).

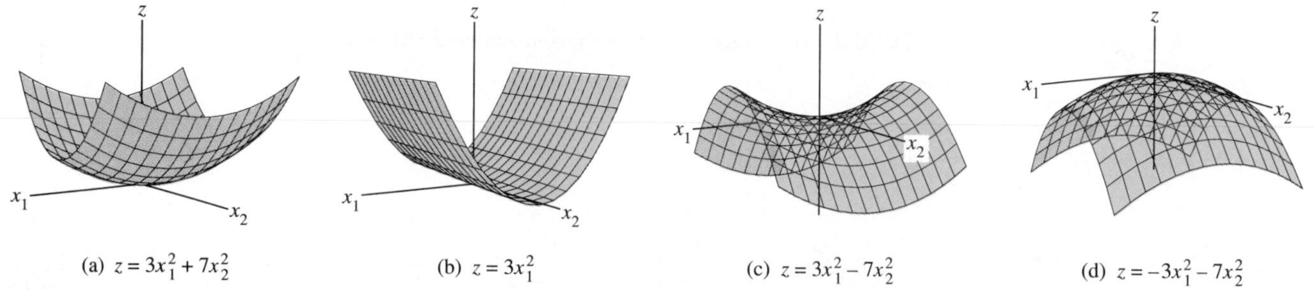

FIGURE 4 Graphs of quadratic forms.

The simple 2×2 examples in Fig. 4 illustrate the following definitions.

DEFINITION

A quadratic form Q is

a. **positive definite** if $Q(\mathbf{x}) > 0$ for all $\mathbf{x} \neq \mathbf{0}$,
b. **negative definite** if $Q(\mathbf{x}) < 0$ for all $\mathbf{x} \neq \mathbf{0}$,
c. **indefinite** if $Q(\mathbf{x})$ assumes both positive and negative values.

Also, Q is said to be **positive semidefinite** if $Q(\mathbf{x}) \geq 0$ for all $\mathbf{x}$, and Q is **negative semidefinite** if $Q(\mathbf{x}) \leq 0$ for all $\mathbf{x}$. The quadratic forms in parts (a) and (b) of Fig. 4 are both positive semidefinite.

Theorem 5 characterizes some quadratic forms in terms of eigenvalues.

THEOREM 5

Quadratic Forms and Eigenvalues

Let A be an $n \times n$ symmetric matrix. Then a quadratic form $\mathbf{x}^T A\mathbf{x}$ is

a. positive definite if and only if the eigenvalues of A are all positive,
b. negative definite if and only if the eigenvalues of A are all negative,
c. indefinite if and only if A has both positive and negative eigenvalues.

Proof By the Principal Axes Theorem, there exists an orthogonal change of variable $\mathbf{x} = P\mathbf{u}$ such that

$$Q(\mathbf{x}) = \mathbf{x}^T A\mathbf{x} = \mathbf{u}^T D\mathbf{u} = \lambda_1 u_1^2 + \lambda_2 u_2^2 + \cdots + \lambda_n u_n^2 \tag{4}$$

where $\lambda_1, \ldots, \lambda_n$ are the eigenvalues of A. Since P is invertible, there is a one-to-one correspondence between all nonzero $\mathbf{x}$ and all nonzero $\mathbf{u}$. Thus the values of $Q(\mathbf{x})$ for $\mathbf{x} \neq \mathbf{0}$ coincide with the values of the expression on the right side of (4), which is obviously controlled by the signs of the eigenvalues $\lambda_1, \ldots, \lambda_n$, in the three ways described in the theorem. ▮

EXAMPLE 6 Is $Q(\mathbf{x}) = 3x_1^2 + 2x_2^2 + x_3^2 + 4x_1x_2 + 4x_2x_3$ positive definite?

Solution Because of all the plus signs, the form "looks" positive definite. But the matrix of the form is

$$A = \begin{bmatrix} 3 & 2 & 0 \\ 2 & 2 & 2 \\ 0 & 2 & 1 \end{bmatrix}$$

and the eigenvalues of A turn out to be 5, 2, and -1. So Q is an indefinite quadratic form, not positive definite. ▮

The classification of a quadratic form is often carried over to the matrix of the form. Thus a **positive definite matrix** A is a *symmetric* matrix for which the quadratic form $\mathbf{x}^T A\mathbf{x}$ is positive definite. Other terms, such as **positive semidefinite matrix**, are defined analogously.

Numerical Note

A fast way to determine whether a symmetric matrix A is positive definite is to attempt to factor A in the form $A = R^T R$, where R is upper triangular with positive diagonal entries. (A slightly modified algorithm for an LU factorization is one approach.) Such a *Cholesky factorization* is possible if and only if A is positive definite. See Supplementary Exercise 7.

PRACTICE PROBLEM

Describe a positive semidefinite matrix A in terms of its eigenvalues.

8.2 EXERCISES

1. Compute the quadratic form $\mathbf{x}^T A\mathbf{x}$, when $A = \begin{bmatrix} 5 & 1/3 \\ 1/3 & 1 \end{bmatrix}$ and

a. $\mathbf{x} = \begin{bmatrix} x_1 \\ x_2 \end{bmatrix}$ b. $\mathbf{x} = \begin{bmatrix} 6 \\ 1 \end{bmatrix}$ c. $\mathbf{x} = \begin{bmatrix} 1 \\ 3 \end{bmatrix}$

2. Compute the quadratic form $\mathbf{x}^T A\mathbf{x}$, for $A = \begin{bmatrix} 4 & 3 & 0 \\ 3 & 2 & 1 \\ 0 & 1 & 1 \end{bmatrix}$ and

a. $\mathbf{x} = \begin{bmatrix} x_1 \\ x_2 \\ x_3 \end{bmatrix}$ b. $\mathbf{x} = \begin{bmatrix} 2 \\ -1 \\ 5 \end{bmatrix}$ c. $\mathbf{x} = \begin{bmatrix} 1/\sqrt{3} \\ 1/\sqrt{3} \\ 1/\sqrt{3} \end{bmatrix}$

3. Find the matrix of the quadratic form. Assume $\mathbf{x}$ is in $\mathbb{R}^2$.

a. $10x_1^2 - 6x_1x_2 - 3x_2^2$ b. $5x_1^2 + 3x_1x_2$

4. Find the matrix of the quadratic form. Assume $\mathbf{x}$ is in $\mathbb{R}^2$.

a. $20x_1^2 + 15x_1x_2 - 10x_2^2$ b. x_1x_2

5. Find the matrix of the quadratic form. Assume $\mathbf{x}$ is in $\mathbb{R}^3$.

a. $8x_1^2 + 7x_2^2 - 3x_3^2 - 6x_1x_2 + 4x_1x_3 - 2x_2x_3$

b. $4x_1x_2 + 6x_1x_3 - 8x_2x_3$

6. Find the matrix of the quadratic form. Assume $\mathbf{x}$ is in $\mathbb{R}^3$.

a. $5x_1^2 - x_2^2 + 7x_3^2 + 5x_1x_2 - 3x_1x_3$

b. $x_3^2 - 4x_1x_2 + 4x_2x_3$

7. Make a change of variable, $\mathbf{x} = P\mathbf{u}$, that transforms the quadratic form $x_1^2 + 10x_1x_2 + x_2^2$ into a quadratic form with no cross-product term. Give P and the new quadratic form.

8. Let A be the matrix of the quadratic form

$9x_1^2 + 7x_2^2 + 11x_3^2 - 8x_1x_2 + 8x_1x_3$

It can be shown that the eigenvalues of A are 3, 9, and 15. Find an orthogonal matrix P such that the change of variable $\mathbf{x} = P\mathbf{u}$ transforms $\mathbf{x}^TA\mathbf{x}$ into a quadratic form with no cross-product term. Give P and the new quadratic form.

Classify the quadratic forms in Exercises 9–14. Then make a change of variable, $\mathbf{x} = P\mathbf{u}$, that transforms the quadratic form into one with no cross-product term. Write the new quadratic form.

9. $3x_1^2 - 4x_1x_2 + 6x_2^2$ **10.** $9x_1^2 - 8x_1x_2 + 3x_2^2$

11. $2x_1^2 + 10x_1x_2 + 2x_2^2$ **12.** $-5x_1^2 + 4x_1x_2 - 2x_1^2$

13. $x_1^2 - 6x_1x_2 + 9x_2^2$ **14.** $8x_1^2 + 6x_1x_2$

15. What is the largest possible value of the quadratic form $5x_1^2 + 8x_2^2$ if $\mathbf{x} = (x_1, x_2)$ and $\mathbf{x}^T\mathbf{x} = 1$, that is, if $x_1^2 + x_2^2 = 1$? (Try some examples of $\mathbf{x}$.)

16. What is the largest value of the quadratic form $5x_1^2 - 3x_2^2$ if $\mathbf{x}^T\mathbf{x} = 1$?

Exercises 17 and 18 show how to classify a quadratic form $Q(\mathbf{x}) = \mathbf{x}^TA\mathbf{x}$, when $A = \begin{bmatrix} a & b \\ b & d \end{bmatrix}$ and $\det A \neq 0$, without finding the eigenvalues of A.

17. If λ_1 and λ_2 are the eigenvalues of A, then the characteristic polynomial of A can be written in two ways: $\det(A - \lambda I)$ and $(\lambda - \lambda_1)(\lambda - \lambda_2)$. Use this fact to show that $\lambda_1 + \lambda_2 = a + d$ (the diagonal entries of A) and $\lambda_1\lambda_2 = \det A$.

18. Verify the following statements.

a. Q is positive definite if $\det A > 0$ and $a > 0$.

b. Q is negative definite if $\det A > 0$ and $a < 0$.

c. Q is indefinite if $\det A < 0$.

19. Suppose $A = B^TB$, where B is an $n \times n$ matrix.

a. Show that A is symmetric and positive semidefinite.

b. Show that if B is invertible, then A is positive definite.

20. Show that if an $n \times n$ matrix A is positive definite, then there exists a positive definite matrix B such that $A = B^TB$. [*Hint*: Write $A = PDP^T$, with $P^T = P^{-1}$. Produce a matrix C such that $D = C^TC$, and let $B = PCP^T$. Show that B works.]

21. Let A and B be symmetric $n \times n$ matrices whose eigenvalues are all positive. Show that the eigenvalues of $A + B$ are all positive. [*Hint*: Consider quadratic forms.]

22. Let A be an $n \times n$ invertible symmetric matrix. Show that if the quadratic form $\mathbf{x}^TA\mathbf{x}$ is positive definite, then so is the quadratic form $\mathbf{x}^TA^{-1}\mathbf{x}$. [*Hint*: Consider eigenvalues.]

SOLUTION TO PRACTICE PROBLEM

Make an orthogonal change of variable $\mathbf{x} = P\mathbf{u}$, and write

$$\mathbf{x}^TA\mathbf{x} = \mathbf{u}^TD\mathbf{u} = \lambda_1u_1^2 + \lambda_2u_2^2 + \cdots + \lambda_nu_n^2$$

as in (4). If an eigenvalue—say, λ_i—were negative, then $\mathbf{x}^TA\mathbf{x}$ would be negative for the $\mathbf{x}$ corresponding to $\mathbf{u} = \mathbf{e}_i$ (the ith column of I_n). So the eigenvalues of a positive semidefinite quadratic form must all be nonnegative. Conversely, if the eigenvalues are nonnegative, the expansion above shows that $\mathbf{x}^TA\mathbf{x}$ must be positive semidefinite.

8.3 CONSTRAINED OPTIMIZATION

Engineers, economists, scientists, and mathematicians often need to find the maximum or minimum value of a quadratic form $Q(\mathbf{x})$ for $\mathbf{x}$ in some specified set. Typically, the problem can be arranged so that $\mathbf{x}$ varies over the set of unit vectors. As we shall see, this *constrained optimization problem* has an interesting and elegant solution. Example 6 below and the discussion in Section 8.5 illustrate how such problems arise in practice.

The requirement that a vector $\mathbf{x}$ in $\mathbb{R}^n$ be a unit vector may be stated in several equivalent ways:

$$\|\mathbf{x}\| = 1, \qquad \|\mathbf{x}\|^2 = 1, \qquad \mathbf{x}^T\mathbf{x} = 1$$

and

$$x_1^2 + x_2^2 + \cdots + x_n^2 = 1 \tag{1}$$

To save space we shall use $\mathbf{x}^T\mathbf{x} = 1$, but the expanded version (1) is commonly used in applications.

When a quadratic form Q has no cross-product terms, it is easy to find the maximum and minimum of $Q(\mathbf{x})$ for $\mathbf{x}^T\mathbf{x} = 1$.

EXAMPLE 1 Find the maximum and minimum values of $Q(\mathbf{x}) = 9x_1^2 + 4x_2^2 + 3x_3^2$ subject to the constraint $\mathbf{x}^T\mathbf{x} = 1$.

Solution Since x_2^2 and x_3^2 are nonnegative, note that

$$4x_2^2 \le 9x_2^2 \qquad \text{and} \qquad 3x_3^2 \le 9x_3^2$$

and hence

$$\begin{aligned} Q(\mathbf{x}) &= 9x_1^2 + 4x_2^2 + 3x_3^2 \\ &\le 9x_1^2 + 9x_2^2 + 9x_3^2 \\ &= 9(x_1^2 + x_2^2 + x_3^2) \\ &= 9 \end{aligned}$$

whenever $x_1^2 + x_2^2 + x_3^2 = 1$. So the maximum value of $Q(\mathbf{x})$ cannot exceed 9 when $\mathbf{x}$ is a unit vector. Furthermore, $Q(\mathbf{x}) = 9$ when $\mathbf{x} = (1, 0, 0)$. Thus 9 is the maximum value of $Q(\mathbf{x})$ for $\mathbf{x}^T\mathbf{x} = 1$.

To find the minimum value of $Q(\mathbf{x})$, observe that

$$9x_1^2 \ge 3x_1^2, \qquad 4x_2^2 \ge 3x_2^2$$

and hence

$$Q(\mathbf{x}) \ge 3x_1^2 + 3x_2^2 + 3x_3^2 = 3(x_1^2 + x_2^2 + x_3^2) = 3$$

whenever $x_1^2 + x_2^2 + x_3^2 = 1$. Also, $Q(\mathbf{x}) = 3$ when $x_1 = 0$, $x_2 = 0$, and $x_3 = 1$. So 3 is the minimum value of $Q(\mathbf{x})$ when $\mathbf{x}^T\mathbf{x} = 1$.

It is easy to see in Example 1 that the matrix of the quadratic form Q has eigenvalues 9, 4, and 3 and that the largest and smallest eigenvalues equal, respectively, the (constrained) maximum and minimum of $Q(\mathbf{x})$. The same holds true for any quadratic form, as we shall see.

EXAMPLE 2 Let $A = \begin{bmatrix} 3 & 0 \\ 0 & 7 \end{bmatrix}$, and for $\mathbf{x}$ in $\mathbb{R}^2$ let $Q(\mathbf{x}) = \mathbf{x}^T A\mathbf{x}$. Figure 1 displays the graph of Q. Figure 2 shows only the portion of the graph for $|x_1| \le 1$ and $|x_2| \le 1$. In Fig. 2 the intersection of the cylinder with the surface is the set of points (x_1, x_2, z) such that $z = Q(x_1, x_2)$ and $x_1^2 + x_2^2 = 1$. The "heights" of these points are the constrained values of $Q(\mathbf{x})$. Geometrically, the constrained optimization problem is to locate the highest and lowest points on the intersection curve.

The two highest points on the curve are 7 units above the x_1x_2-plane, occurring where $x_1 = 0$ and $x_2 = \pm 1$. These points correspond to the eigenvalue 7 of A and the eigenvectors $\mathbf{x} = (0, 1)$ and $-\mathbf{x} = (0, -1)$. Similarly, the two lowest points on the curve are 3 units above the x_1x_2-plane. They correspond to the eigenvalue 3 and the eigenvectors $(1, 0)$ and $(-1, 0)$.

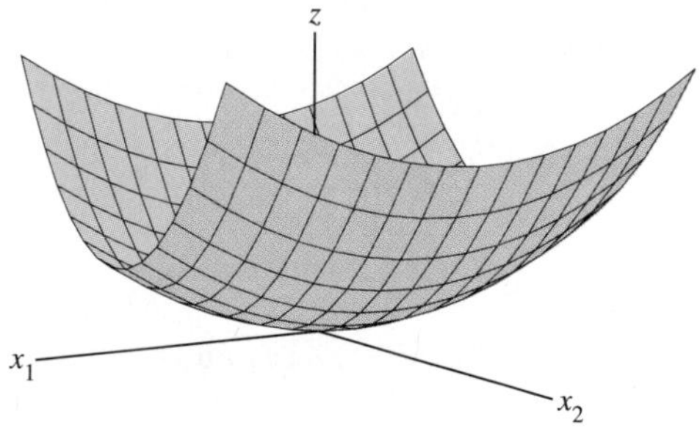

FIGURE 1 $z = 3x_1^2 + 7x_2^2$.

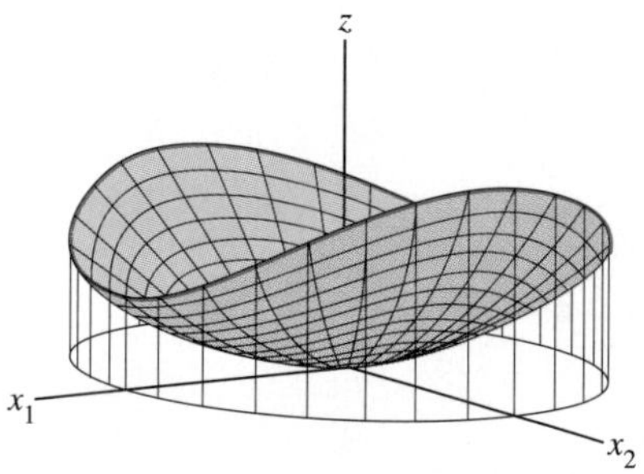

FIGURE 2 The intersection of $z = 3x_1^2 + 7x_2^2$ and the cylinder $x_1^2 + x_2^2 = 1$.

Every point on the intersection curve in Fig. 2 has a z-coordinate between 3 and 7, and for any number t between 3 and 7 there is a unit vector $\mathbf{x}$ such that $Q(\mathbf{x}) = t$. In other words, the set of all possible values of $\mathbf{x}^T A\mathbf{x}$, for $\|\mathbf{x}\| = 1$, is the closed interval $3 \le t \le 7$.

It can be shown that for any symmetric matrix A, the set of all possible values of $\mathbf{x}^T A\mathbf{x}$, for $\|\mathbf{x}\| = 1$, is a closed interval on the real axis. (See Exercise 13.) Denote the left and right endpoints of this interval by m and M, respectively. That is, let

$$m = \min\{\mathbf{x}^T A\mathbf{x} : \|\mathbf{x}\| = 1\}, \quad M = \max\{\mathbf{x}^T A\mathbf{x} : \|\mathbf{x}\| = 1\} \tag{2}$$

Exercise 12 asks you to prove that if λ is an eigenvalue of A, then $m \le \lambda \le M$.

The next theorem says that m and M are themselves eigenvalues of A, just as in Example 2.[1]

THEOREM 6

> Let A be a symmetric matrix, and define m and M as in (2). Then M is the largest eigenvalue λ_1 of A and m is the smallest eigenvalue of A. The value of $\mathbf{x}^T A\mathbf{x}$ is M when $\mathbf{x}$ is a unit eigenvector $\mathbf{v}_1$ corresponding to M. The value of $\mathbf{x}^T A\mathbf{x}$ is m when $\mathbf{x}$ is a unit eigenvector corresponding to m.

Proof Orthogonally diagonalize A as PDP^{-1}. We know that

$$\mathbf{x}^T A\mathbf{x} = \mathbf{y}^T D\mathbf{y} \quad \text{when } \mathbf{x} = P\mathbf{y} \tag{3}$$

Also,

$$\|\mathbf{x}\| = \|P\mathbf{y}\| = \|\mathbf{y}\| \text{ for all } \mathbf{y}$$

because $P^T P = I$, and $\|P\mathbf{y}\|^2 = (P\mathbf{y})^T(P\mathbf{y}) = \mathbf{y}^T P^T P\mathbf{y} = \mathbf{y}^T\mathbf{y} = \|\mathbf{y}\|^2$. In particular, $\|\mathbf{y}\| = 1$ if and only if $\|\mathbf{x}\| = 1$. Thus $\mathbf{x}^T A\mathbf{x}$ and $\mathbf{y}^T D\mathbf{y}$ assume the same set of values as $\mathbf{x}$ and $\mathbf{y}$ range over the set of all unit vectors.

To simplify notation, we shall suppose that A is a 3×3 matrix with eigenvalues $a \geq b \geq c$. Arrange the (eigenvector) columns of P so that $P = [\,\mathbf{v}_1 \;\; \mathbf{v}_2 \;\; \mathbf{v}_3\,]$ and

$$D = \begin{bmatrix} a & 0 & 0 \\ 0 & b & 0 \\ 0 & 0 & c \end{bmatrix}$$

Given any unit vector $\mathbf{y}$ in $\mathbb{R}^3$ with coordinates y_1, y_2, y_3, observe that

$$\begin{aligned} ay_1^2 &= ay_1^2 \\ by_2^2 &\leq ay_2^2 \\ cy_3^2 &\leq ay_3^2 \end{aligned}$$

Adding these inequalities, we have

$$\begin{aligned} \mathbf{y}^T D\mathbf{y} &= ay_1^2 + by_2^2 + cy_3^2 \\ &\leq ay_1^2 + ay_2^2 + ay_3^2 \\ &= a(y_1^2 + y_2^2 + y_3^2) \\ &= a\|\mathbf{y}\|^2 = a \end{aligned}$$

Thus $M \leq a$, by definition of M. However, $\mathbf{y}^T D\mathbf{y} = a$ when $\mathbf{y} = \mathbf{e}_1 = (1, 0, 0)$, so in fact $M = a$. By (3), the $\mathbf{x}$ that corresponds to $\mathbf{y} = \mathbf{e}_1$ is the eigenvector $\mathbf{v}_1$ of A, because

$$\mathbf{x} = P\mathbf{e}_1 = [\,\mathbf{v}_1 \;\; \mathbf{v}_2 \;\; \mathbf{v}_3\,]\begin{bmatrix} 1 \\ 0 \\ 0 \end{bmatrix} = \mathbf{v}_1$$

---

[1] The use of *minimum* and *maximum* in (2), and *smallest* and *largest* in the theorem, refers to the natural ordering of the real numbers, not to magnitudes.

Thus $M = a = \mathbf{e}_1^T D\mathbf{e}_1 = \mathbf{v}_1^T A\mathbf{v}_1$, which proves the statement about M. A similar argument shows that m is the smallest eigenvalue, c, and this value of $\mathbf{x}^T A\mathbf{x}$ is attained when $\mathbf{x} = P\mathbf{e}_3 = \mathbf{v}_3$. ▮

EXAMPLE 3 Let $A = \begin{bmatrix} 3 & 2 & 1 \\ 2 & 3 & 1 \\ 1 & 1 & 4 \end{bmatrix}$. Find the maximum value of the quadratic form $\mathbf{x}^T A\mathbf{x}$ subject to the constraint $\mathbf{x}^T\mathbf{x} = 1$, and find a unit vector at which this maximum value is attained.

Solution By Theorem 6, we seek the largest eigenvalue of A. The characteristic equation turns out to be

$$0 = -\lambda^3 + 10\lambda^2 - 27\lambda + 18 = -(\lambda - 6)(\lambda - 3)(\lambda - 1)$$

Clearly, the largest eigenvalue is 6.

The constrained maximum of $\mathbf{x}^T A\mathbf{x}$ is attained when $\mathbf{x}$ is a unit eigenvector for $\lambda = 6$. Solving $(A - 6I)\mathbf{x} = 0$, we find an eigenvector $\begin{bmatrix} 1 \\ 1 \\ 1 \end{bmatrix}$ and $\mathbf{v}_1 = \begin{bmatrix} 1/\sqrt{3} \\ 1/\sqrt{3} \\ 1/\sqrt{3} \end{bmatrix}$. ▮

In later applications, we will need to consider values of $\mathbf{x}^T A\mathbf{x}$ when $\mathbf{x}$ not only is a unit vector but also is orthogonal to the eigenvector $\mathbf{v}_1$ mentioned in Theorem 6. This case is treated in the next theorem.

THEOREM 7

Let A, λ_1, and $\mathbf{v}_1$ be as in Theorem 6. Then the maximum value of $\mathbf{x}^T A\mathbf{x}$ subject to the constraints

$$\mathbf{x}^T\mathbf{x} = 1, \quad \mathbf{x}^T\mathbf{v}_1 = 0$$

is the second largest eigenvalue, λ_2, and this maximum is attained when $\mathbf{x}$ is an eigenvector $\mathbf{v}_2$ corresponding to λ_2.

Theorem 7 may be proved by an argument similar to the one above in which the theorem is reduced to the case where the matrix of the quadratic form is diagonal. The next example gives an idea of the proof for the case of a diagonal matrix.

EXAMPLE 4 Find the maximum value of $9x_1^2 + 4x_2^2 + 3x_3^2$ subject to the constraints $\mathbf{x}^T\mathbf{x} = 1$ and $\mathbf{x}^T\mathbf{v}_1 = 0$, where $\mathbf{v}_1 = (1, 0, 0)$. Note that $\mathbf{v}_1$ is a unit eigenvector corresponding to the largest eigenvalue $\lambda = 9$ of the matrix of the quadratic form.

Solution If the coordinates of $\mathbf{x}$ are x_1, x_2, x_3, then the constraint $\mathbf{x}^T\mathbf{v}_1 = 0$ means simply that $x_1 = 0$. For such a unit vector, $x_2^2 + x_3^2 = 1$, and

$$\begin{aligned} 9x_1^2 + 4x_2^2 + 3x_3^2 &= 4x_2^2 + 3x_3^2 \\ &\leq 4x_2^2 + 4x_3^2 \\ &= 4(x_2^2 + x_3^2) \\ &= 4 \end{aligned}$$

Thus the constrained maximum of the quadratic form does not exceed 4. And this value is attained for $\mathbf{x} = (0, 1, 0)$, which is an eigenvector for the second largest eigenvalue of the matrix of the quadratic form.

EXAMPLE 5 Let A be the matrix in Example 3 and let $\mathbf{v}_1$ be a unit eigenvector corresponding to the largest eigenvalue of A. Find the maximum value of $\mathbf{x}^TA\mathbf{x}$ subject to the conditions

$$\mathbf{x}^T\mathbf{x} = 1, \qquad \mathbf{x}^T\mathbf{v}_1 = 0 \tag{4}$$

Solution From Example 3, the second largest eigenvalue of A is $\lambda = 3$. Solve $(A - 3I)\mathbf{x} = \mathbf{0}$ to find an eigenvector, and normalize it to obtain

$$\mathbf{v}_2 = \begin{bmatrix} 1/\sqrt{6} \\ 1/\sqrt{6} \\ -2/\sqrt{6} \end{bmatrix}$$

The vector $\mathbf{v}_2$ is automatically orthogonal to $\mathbf{v}_1$ because the vectors correspond to different eigenvalues. Thus the maximum of $\mathbf{x}^TA\mathbf{x}$ subject to the constraints in (4) is 3, attained when $\mathbf{x} = \mathbf{v}_2$.

The next theorem generalizes Theorem 7 and, together with Theorem 6, gives a useful characterization of *all* the eigenvalues of A. The proof is omitted.

THEOREM 8

Let A be a symmetric $n \times n$ matrix with an orthogonal diagonalization $A = PDP^{-1}$, where the entries on the diagonal of D are arranged so that $\lambda_1 \geq \lambda_2 \geq \cdots \geq \lambda_n$, and where the columns of P are corresponding unit eigenvectors $\mathbf{v}_1, \ldots, \mathbf{v}_n$. Then for $k = 2, \ldots, n$, the maximum value of $\mathbf{x}^TA\mathbf{x}$ subject to the constraints

$$\mathbf{x}^T\mathbf{x} = 1, \quad \mathbf{x}^T\mathbf{v}_1 = 0, \quad \ldots, \quad \mathbf{x}^T\mathbf{v}_{k-1} = 0$$

is the eigenvalue λ_k, and this maximum is attained at $\mathbf{x} = \mathbf{v}_k$.

Theorem 8 will be helpful in Sections 8.4 and 8.5. The following application requires only Theorem 6.

EXAMPLE 6 During the next year, a county government is planning to repair x hundred miles of public roads and bridges and to improve y hundred acres of parks and recreation areas. The county must decide how to allocate its resources (funds, equipment, labor, etc.) between these two projects. If it is more cost-effective to work simultaneously on both projects rather than to work on only one, then x and y might satisfy a *budget constraint* such as

$$4x^2 + 9y^2 \leq 36$$

See Fig. 3. Each point (x, y) in the shaded *feasible set* represents a possible public works schedule for the year. The points on the budget constraint curve, $4x^2 + 9y^2 = 36$, use the maximum amounts of resources available.

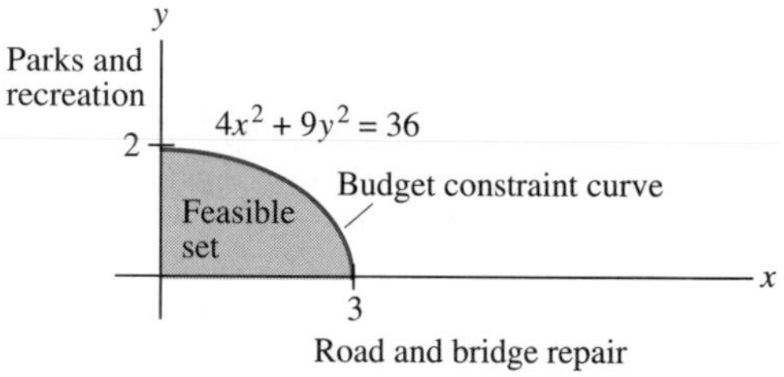

FIGURE 3 Public works schedules.

In choosing its public works schedule, the county wants to consider the opinions of the county residents. To measure the value or *utility* that the residents would assign to the various work schedules (x, y), economists sometimes use a function such as

$$q(x, y) = xy$$

The set of points (x, y) at which $q(x, y)$ is a constant is called an *indifference curve*. Three such curves are shown in Fig. 4. Points along an indifference curve correspond to alternatives that county residents as a group would find equally valuable.[2] Find the public works schedule that will maximize the utility function q.

Solution The budget constraint curve does not describe a set of unit vectors, but a change of variable can fix that problem. Rewrite the constraint equation in the form

$$\left(\frac{x}{3}\right)^2 + \left(\frac{y}{2}\right)^2 = 1$$

and define

$$x_1 = \frac{x}{3}, \quad x_2 = \frac{y}{2}, \quad \text{that is,} \quad x = 3x_1 \quad \text{and} \quad y = 2x_2$$

Then the budget constraint curve becomes

$$x_1^2 + x_2^2 = 1$$

[2]Indifference curves are discussed in Michael D. Intriligator, *Econometric Models, Techniques, and Applications* (Englewood Cliffs, N.J.: Prentice-Hall, 1978), pp. 206–209.

and the utility function becomes $q(3x_1, 2x_2) = (3x_1)(2x_2) = 6x_1x_2$. Let $\mathbf{x} = \begin{bmatrix} x_1 \\ x_2 \end{bmatrix}$. Then the problem is to maximize $Q(\mathbf{x}) = 6x_1x_2$ subject to $\mathbf{x}^T\mathbf{x} = 1$. Note that $Q(\mathbf{x}) = \mathbf{x}^T A\mathbf{x}$, where

$$A = \begin{bmatrix} 0 & 3 \\ 3 & 0 \end{bmatrix}$$

The eigenvalues of A are ± 3, with eigenvectors $\begin{bmatrix} 1/\sqrt{2} \\ 1/\sqrt{2} \end{bmatrix}$ for $\lambda = 3$ and $\begin{bmatrix} -1/\sqrt{2} \\ 1/\sqrt{2} \end{bmatrix}$ for $\lambda = -3$. Thus the maximum value of $Q(\mathbf{x}) = q(x_1, x_2)$ is 3, attained when $x_1 = 1/\sqrt{2}$ and $x_2 = 1/\sqrt{2}$.

In terms of the original variables, the optimum public works schedule is $x = 3x_1 = 3/\sqrt{2} \approx 2.1$ hundred miles of roads and $y = 2x_2 = \sqrt{2} \approx 1.4$ hundred acres of parks and recreational areas. The optimum public works schedule is the point where the budget constraint curve and the indifference curve $q(x, y) = 3$ just meet. Points (x, y) with a higher utility lie on indifference curves that do not touch the budget constraint curve. See Fig. 4. ∎

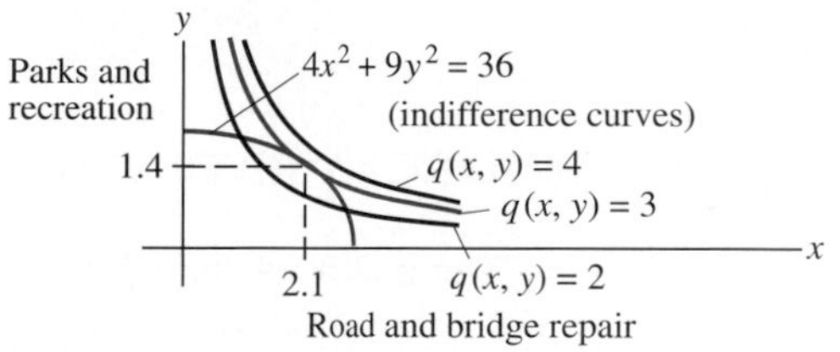

FIGURE 4 The optimum public works schedule is (2.1, 1.4).

PRACTICE PROBLEMS

1. Let $Q(\mathbf{x}) = 3x_1^2 + 3x_2^2 + 2x_1x_2$. Find a change of variable that transforms Q into a quadratic form with no cross-product term, and give the new quadratic form.
2. With Q as in Problem 1, find the maximum value of $Q(\mathbf{x})$ subject to the constraint $\mathbf{x}^T\mathbf{x} = 1$, and find a unit vector at which the maximum is attained.

8.3 EXERCISES

In Exercises 1 and 2, find the change of variable $\mathbf{x} = P\mathbf{y}$ that transforms the quadratic form $\mathbf{x}^T A\mathbf{x}$ into $\mathbf{y}^T D\mathbf{y}$ as shown.

1. $5x_1^2 + 6x_2^2 + 7x_3^2 + 4x_1x_2 - 4x_2x_3 = 9y_1^2 + 6y_2^2 + 3y_3^2$

2. $3x_1^2 + 2x_2^2 + 2x_3^2 + 2x_1x_2 + 2x_1x_3 + 4x_2x_3 = 5y_1^2 + 2y_2^2$
[*Hint*: $\mathbf{x}$ and $\mathbf{y}$ must have the same number of coordinates, so the quadratic form shown here must have a coefficient of zero for y_3^2.]

In Exercises 3–6, find (a) the maximum value of $Q(\mathbf{x})$ subject to the constraint $\mathbf{x}^T\mathbf{x} = 1$ and (b) a unit vector $\mathbf{v}$ where this maximum is attained. (c) Find the maximum of $Q(\mathbf{x})$ subject to the constraints $\mathbf{x}^T\mathbf{x} = 1$ and $\mathbf{x}^T\mathbf{v} = 0$.

3. $Q(\mathbf{x}) = 5x_1^2 + 6x_2^2 + 7x_3^2 + 4x_1x_2 - 4x_2x_3$ (See Exercise 1.)

4. $Q(\mathbf{x}) = 3x_1^2 + 2x_2^2 + 2x_3^2 + 2x_1x_2 + 2x_1x_3 + 4x_2x_3$ (See Exercise 2.)

5. $Q(\mathbf{x}) = 5x_1^2 + 5x_2^2 - 4x_1x_2$

6. $Q(\mathbf{x}) = 7x_1^2 + 3x_2^2 + 3x_1x_2$

7. Let $Q(\mathbf{x}) = -2x_1^2 - x_2^2 + 4x_1x_2 + 4x_2x_3$. Find a unit vector $\mathbf{x}$ in $\mathbb{R}^3$ at which $Q(\mathbf{x})$ is maximized, subject to $\mathbf{x}^T\mathbf{x} = 1$. [*Hint*: The eigenvalues of the matrix of the form Q are 2, −1, and −4.]

8. Let $Q(\mathbf{x}) = 7x_1^2 + x_2^2 + 7x_3^2 - 8x_1x_2 - 4x_1x_3 - 8x_2x_3$. Find a unit vector $\mathbf{x}$ in $\mathbb{R}^3$ at which $Q(\mathbf{x})$ is maximized, subject to $\mathbf{x}^T\mathbf{x} = 1$. [*Hint*: The eigenvalues of the matrix of the form Q are 9 and −3.]

9. Find the maximum value of $Q(\mathbf{x}) = 7x_1^2 + 3x_2^2 - 2x_1x_2$, subject to the constraint $x_1^2 + x_2^2 = 1$. (Do not go on to find the vector where the maximum is attained.)

10. Find the maximum value of $Q(\mathbf{x}) = -3x_1^2 + 5x_2^2 - 2x_1x_2$, subject to the constraint $x_1^2 + x_2^2 = 1$. (Do not go on to find the vector where the maximum is attained.)

11. Suppose that $\mathbf{x}$ is a unit eigenvector of a symmetric matrix A corresponding to an eigenvalue 3. What is the value of $\mathbf{x}^TA\mathbf{x}$?

12. Let λ be any eigenvalue of a symmetric matrix A. Show that $m \leq \lambda \leq M$, where m and M are defined as in (2). [*Hint*: Find an $\mathbf{x}$ such that $\lambda = \mathbf{x}^TA\mathbf{x}$.]

13. Let A be an $n \times n$ symmetric matrix, let M and m denote the maximum and minimum values of the quadratic form $\mathbf{x}^TA\mathbf{x}$, and denote corresponding unit eigenvectors by $\mathbf{v}_1$ and $\mathbf{v}_n$. The following calculations show that given any number t between M and m, there is a unit vector $\mathbf{x}$ such that $t = \mathbf{x}^TA\mathbf{x}$. Verify that $t = (1-\alpha)M + \alpha m$ for some number α between 0 and 1. Then let $\mathbf{x} = \sqrt{1-\alpha}\,\mathbf{v}_1 + \sqrt{\alpha}\,\mathbf{v}_n$, and show that $\mathbf{x}^T\mathbf{x} = 1$ and $\mathbf{x}^TA\mathbf{x} = t$.

SOLUTIONS TO PRACTICE PROBLEMS

1. The matrix of the quadratic form is $A = \begin{bmatrix} 3 & 1 \\ 1 & 3 \end{bmatrix}$. It is easy to find the eigenvalues, 4 and 2, and corresponding unit eigenvectors, $\begin{bmatrix} 1/\sqrt{2} \\ 1/\sqrt{2} \end{bmatrix}$ and $\begin{bmatrix} -1/\sqrt{2} \\ 1/\sqrt{2} \end{bmatrix}$. So the desired change of variable is $\mathbf{x} = P\mathbf{u}$, where $P = \begin{bmatrix} 1/\sqrt{2} & -1/\sqrt{2} \\ 1/\sqrt{2} & 1/\sqrt{2} \end{bmatrix}$. A common error here is to forget to normalize the eigenvectors. The new quadratic form is $\mathbf{u}^TD\mathbf{u} = 4u_1^2 + 2u_2^2$.

2. The maximum of $Q(\mathbf{x})$ for $\mathbf{x}$ a unit vector is 4, and the maximum is attained at the unit eigenvector $\begin{bmatrix} 1/\sqrt{2} \\ 1/\sqrt{2} \end{bmatrix}$. A common incorrect answer is $\begin{bmatrix} 1 \\ 0 \end{bmatrix}$. This vector maximizes the quadratic form $\mathbf{u}^TD\mathbf{u}$ instead of $Q(\mathbf{x})$.

8.4 THE SINGULAR VALUE DECOMPOSITION

The diagonalization theorems in Sections 6.3 and 8.1 play a part in many interesting applications. Unfortunately, as we know, not all matrices can be factored as $A = PDP^{-1}$ with D diagonal. However, a factorization $A = QDP^{-1}$ *is* possible for any $m \times n$ matrix A! A special factorization of this type, the *singular value decomposition*, is one of the most useful matrix factorizations in applied linear algebra.

The singular value decomposition is based on the following property of the ordinary diagonalization that can be imitated for rectangular matrices: The absolute values of the eigenvalues of a symmetric matrix A measure the amounts that A stretches or shrinks certain vectors (the eigenvectors). If $A\mathbf{x} = \lambda\mathbf{x}$ and $\|\mathbf{x}\| = 1$, then

$$\|A\mathbf{x}\| = \|\lambda\mathbf{x}\| = |\lambda|\,\|\mathbf{x}\| = |\lambda| \tag{1}$$

If λ_1 is the eigenvalue with the greatest magnitude, then a corresponding unit eigenvector $\mathbf{v}_1$ identifies a direction in which the stretching effect of A is greatest. That is, the length of $A\mathbf{x}$ is maximized when $\mathbf{x} = \mathbf{v}_1$, and $\|A\mathbf{v}_1\| = |\lambda_1|$, by (1). This description of $\mathbf{v}_1$ and $|\lambda_1|$ has an analogue for rectangular matrices that will lead to the singular value decomposition.

EXAMPLE 1 If $A = \begin{bmatrix} 4 & 11 & 14 \\ 8 & 7 & -2 \end{bmatrix}$, then the linear transformation $\mathbf{x} \mapsto A\mathbf{x}$ maps the unit sphere $\{\mathbf{x} : \|\mathbf{x}\| = 1\}$ in $\mathbb{R}^3$ onto an ellipse in $\mathbb{R}^2$, shown in Fig. 1. Find a unit vector $\mathbf{x}$ at which the length $\|A\mathbf{x}\|$ is maximized, and compute this maximum length.

Solution The quantity $\|A\mathbf{x}\|^2$ is maximized at the same $\mathbf{x}$ that maximizes $\|A\mathbf{x}\|$, and $\|A\mathbf{x}\|^2$ is easier to study. Observe that

$$\|A\mathbf{x}\|^2 = (A\mathbf{x})^T(A\mathbf{x}) = \mathbf{x}^T A^T A\mathbf{x} = \mathbf{x}^T(A^T A)\mathbf{x}$$

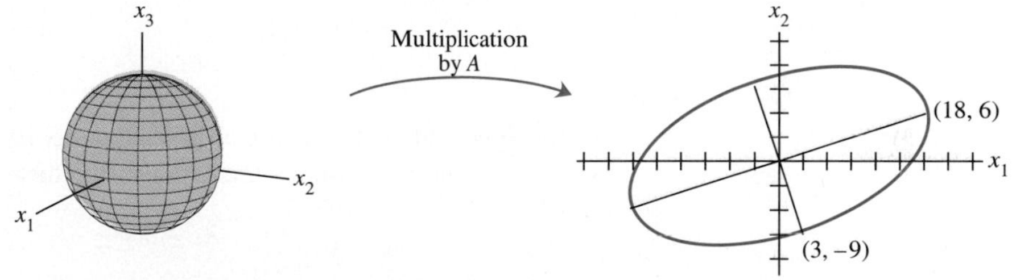

FIGURE 1 A transformation from $\mathbb{R}^3$ to $\mathbb{R}^2$.

Also, $A^T A$ is a symmetric matrix, since $(A^T A)^T = A^T A^{TT} = A^T A$. So the problem now is to maximize the quadratic form $\mathbf{x}^T(A^T A)\mathbf{x}$ subject to the constraint $\|\mathbf{x}\| = 1$. That's a problem from Section 8.3, and we know the solution. By Theorem 6, the maximum value is the largest eigenvalue λ_1 of $A^T A$. Also, the maximum value is attained at a unit eigenvector of $A^T A$ corresponding to λ_1.

We compute

$$A^T A = \begin{bmatrix} 4 & 8 \\ 11 & 7 \\ 14 & -2 \end{bmatrix} \begin{bmatrix} 4 & 11 & 14 \\ 8 & 7 & -2 \end{bmatrix} = \begin{bmatrix} 80 & 100 & 40 \\ 100 & 170 & 140 \\ 40 & 140 & 200 \end{bmatrix}$$

The eigenvalues of $A^T A$ are $\lambda_1 = 360$, $\lambda_2 = 90$, and $\lambda_3 = 0$. Corresponding unit eigenvectors are, respectively,

$$\mathbf{v}_1 = \begin{bmatrix} 1/3 \\ 2/3 \\ 2/3 \end{bmatrix}, \quad \mathbf{v}_2 = \begin{bmatrix} -2/3 \\ -1/3 \\ 2/3 \end{bmatrix}, \quad \mathbf{v}_3 = \begin{bmatrix} 2/3 \\ -2/3 \\ 1/3 \end{bmatrix}$$

The maximum value of $\|A\mathbf{x}\|^2$ is 360, attained when $\mathbf{x}$ is the unit vector $\mathbf{v}_1$. The vector $A\mathbf{v}_1$ is a point on the ellipse in Fig. 1 farthest from the origin, namely,

$$A\mathbf{v}_1 = \begin{bmatrix} 4 & 11 & 14 \\ 8 & 7 & -2 \end{bmatrix} \begin{bmatrix} 1/3 \\ 2/3 \\ 2/3 \end{bmatrix} = \begin{bmatrix} 18 \\ 6 \end{bmatrix}$$

For $\|\mathbf{x}\| = 1$, the maximum value of $\|A\mathbf{x}\|$ is $\|A\mathbf{v}_1\| = \sqrt{360} = 6\sqrt{10}$.

Example 1 suggests that the effect of A on the unit sphere in $\mathbb{R}^3$ is related to the quadratic form $\mathbf{x}^T(A^TA)\mathbf{x}$. In fact, the entire geometric behavior of the transformation $\mathbf{x} \mapsto A\mathbf{x}$ is captured by this quadratic form, as we shall see.

The Singular Values of an $m \times n$ Matrix

Let A be an $m \times n$ matrix. Then A^TA is symmetric and can be orthogonally diagonalized. Let $\{\mathbf{v}_1, \dots, \mathbf{v}_n\}$ be an orthonormal basis for $\mathbb{R}^n$ consisting of eigenvectors of A^TA, and let $\lambda_1, \dots, \lambda_n$ be the associated eigenvalues of A^TA. Then, for $1 \leq i \leq n$,

$$\begin{aligned} \|A\mathbf{v}_i\|^2 &= (A\mathbf{v}_i)^T A\mathbf{v}_i = \mathbf{v}_i^T A^T A\mathbf{v}_i \\ &= \mathbf{v}_i^T(\lambda_i \mathbf{v}_i) && \text{Since } \mathbf{v}_i \text{ is an eigenvector of } A^TA \\ &= \lambda_i && \text{Since } \mathbf{v}_i \text{ is a unit vector} \end{aligned} \tag{2}$$

So the eigenvalues of A^TA are all nonnegative. By renumbering, if necessary, we may assume that the eigenvalues are arranged so that

$$\lambda_1 \geq \lambda_2 \geq \cdots \lambda_n \geq 0$$

The **singular values** of A are the square roots of the eigenvalues of A^TA, denoted by $\sigma_1, \dots, \sigma_n$, and they are arranged in decreasing order. That is, $\sigma_i = \sqrt{\lambda_i}$ for $1 \leq i \leq n$. By (2), the singular values of A are the lengths of the vectors $A\mathbf{v}_1, \dots, A\mathbf{v}_n$.

EXAMPLE 2 Let A be the matrix in Example 1. Since the eigenvalues of A^TA are 360, 90, and 0, the singular values of A are

$$\sigma_1 = \sqrt{360} = 6\sqrt{10}, \quad \sigma_2 = \sqrt{90} = 3\sqrt{10}, \quad \sigma_3 = 0$$

From Example 1, the first singular value of A is the maximum of $\|A\mathbf{x}\|$ over all unit vectors, and the maximum is attained at the unit eigenvector $\mathbf{v}_1$. From Theorem 7 in Section 8.3, we can see that the second singular value of A is the maximum of $\|A\mathbf{x}\|$ over all unit vectors that are *orthogonal to* $\mathbf{v}_1$, and this maximum is attained at the second unit eigenvector, $\mathbf{v}_2$ (Exercise 21). For the $\mathbf{v}_2$ in Example 1,

$$A\mathbf{v}_2 = \begin{bmatrix} 4 & 11 & 14 \\ 8 & 7 & -2 \end{bmatrix} \begin{bmatrix} -2/3 \\ -1/3 \\ 2/3 \end{bmatrix} = \begin{bmatrix} 3 \\ -9 \end{bmatrix}$$

This point is on the minor axis of the ellipse in Fig. 1. The first two singular values of A are the lengths of the major and minor semiaxes of the ellipse. ∎

An important property of the singular values is that they give information about the rank of A.

THEOREM 9

If an $m \times n$ matrix A has r nonzero singular values, $\sigma_1 \geq \sigma_2 \geq \cdots \geq \sigma_r > 0$ with $\sigma_{r+1} = \cdots = \sigma_n = 0$, then rank $A = r$.

Proof Let $\{\mathbf{v}_1, \dots, \mathbf{v}_n\}$ be an orthonormal basis of $\mathbb{R}^n$ of eigenvectors of A^TA, ordered so that the corresponding eigenvalues of A^TA satisfy $\lambda_1 \geq \cdots \geq \lambda_n$. Then for $i \neq j$,

$$(A\mathbf{v}_i)^T(A\mathbf{v}_j) = \mathbf{v}_i^T A^T A \mathbf{v}_j = \mathbf{v}_i^T(\lambda_j \mathbf{v}_j) = 0$$

since $\mathbf{v}_i$ and $\lambda_j \mathbf{v}_j$ are orthogonal. Thus $\{A\mathbf{v}_1, \dots, A\mathbf{v}_n\}$ is an orthogonal set. Let r be the number of nonzero singular values of A; that is, r is the number of nonzero eigenvalues of A^TA. From (2), we see that $A\mathbf{v}_i \neq \mathbf{0}$ if and only if $1 \leq i \leq r$. Then $\{A\mathbf{v}_1, \dots, A\mathbf{v}_r\}$ is linearly independent and clearly is in Col A. Furthermore, for any $\mathbf{y}$ in Col A—say, $\mathbf{y} = A\mathbf{x}$—we may write $\mathbf{x} = c_1\mathbf{v}_1 + \cdots + c_n\mathbf{v}_n$, and

$$\begin{aligned} \mathbf{y} = A\mathbf{x} &= c_1 A\mathbf{v}_1 + \cdots + c_r A\mathbf{v}_r + c_{r+1}A\mathbf{v}_{r+1} + \cdots + c_n A\mathbf{v}_n \\ &= c_1 A\mathbf{v}_1 + \cdots + c_r A\mathbf{v}_r + \mathbf{0} + \cdots + \mathbf{0} \end{aligned}$$

Thus $\mathbf{y}$ is in Span $\{A\mathbf{v}_1, \dots, A\mathbf{v}_r\}$, which shows that $\{A\mathbf{v}_1, \dots, A\mathbf{v}_r\}$ is an (orthogonal) basis for Col A. Hence rank $A = r$. ∎

Numerical Note

In some cases the rank of A may be very sensitive to small changes in the entries of A. The obvious method of counting the number of pivot columns in A does not work well if A is row reduced by a computer. Roundoff error often creates an echelon form with full rank.

In practice, the most reliable way to estimate the rank of a large matrix A is to count the number of nonzero singular values. In this case, extremely small nonzero singular values are assumed to be zero for all practical purposes, and the *effective rank* of the matrix is the number obtained by counting the remaining nonzero singular values.[1]

[1] In general, rank estimation is not a simple problem. For a discussion of the subtle issues involved, see Philip E. Gill, Walter Murray, and Margaret H. Wright, *Numerical Linear Algebra and Optimization*, vol. 1 (Redwood City, Calif.: Addison-Wesley, 1991) Sec. 5.8.

The Singular Value Decomposition

The decomposition of A involves an $m \times n$ "diagonal" matrix Σ of the form

$$\Sigma = \begin{bmatrix} D & 0 \\ 0 & 0 \end{bmatrix} \begin{matrix} \\ \leftarrow m - r \text{ rows} \end{matrix} \qquad (3)$$
$$\uparrow\!\!\_\_\ n - r \text{ columns}$$

where D is an $r \times r$ diagonal matrix for some r not exceeding the smaller of m and n. (If r equals m or n or both, some or all of the zero matrices will not appear.)

THEOREM 10 The Singular Value Decomposition

Let A be an $m \times n$ matrix with rank r. Then there exists an $m \times n$ matrix Σ as in (3), where the diagonal entries in D are the first r singular values of A, $\sigma_1 \geq \sigma_2 \geq \cdots \geq \sigma_r > 0$, and there exist an $m \times m$ orthogonal matrix U and an $n \times n$ orthogonal matrix V such that

$$A = U \Sigma V^T$$

Any factorization $A = U\Sigma V^T$, with U and V orthogonal and Σ as in (3), is called a **singular value decomposition (SVD)** of A. The matrices U and V are not unique, but the diagonal entries of Σ are necessarily the singular values of A. See Exercise 17. The columns of U in such a decomposition are called **left singular vectors** of A, and the columns of V are called **right singular vectors** of A.

Proof Let λ_i and $\mathbf{v}_i$ be as in the proof of Theorem 9. Then $\sigma_i = \sqrt{\lambda_i} = \|A\mathbf{v}_i\| > 0$ for $1 \leq i \leq r$, and $\{A\mathbf{v}_1, \ldots, A\mathbf{v}_r\}$ is an orthogonal basis for Col A. For $1 \leq i \leq r$, define

$$\mathbf{u}_i = \frac{1}{\|A\mathbf{v}_i\|} A\mathbf{v}_i = \frac{1}{\sigma_i} A\mathbf{v}_i$$

so that

$$A\mathbf{v}_i = \sigma_i \mathbf{u}_i \qquad (1 \leq i \leq r) \qquad (4)$$

Then $\{\mathbf{u}_1, \ldots, \mathbf{u}_r\}$ is an orthonormal basis of Col A. Extend this set to an orthonormal basis $\{\mathbf{u}_1, \ldots, \mathbf{u}_m\}$ of $\mathbb{R}^m$, and let

$$U = [\,\mathbf{u}_1 \quad \mathbf{u}_2 \quad \cdots \quad \mathbf{u}_m\,] \qquad \text{and} \qquad V = [\,\mathbf{v}_1 \quad \mathbf{v}_2 \quad \cdots \quad \mathbf{v}_n\,]$$

Then U and V are orthogonal matrices. Also, from (4),

$$AV = [\,A\mathbf{v}_1 \quad \cdots \quad A\mathbf{v}_r \quad \mathbf{0} \quad \cdots \quad \mathbf{0}\,] = [\,\sigma_1\mathbf{u}_1 \quad \cdots \quad \sigma_r\mathbf{u}_r \quad \mathbf{0} \quad \cdots \quad \mathbf{0}\,]$$

Let D be the diagonal matrix with diagonal entries $\sigma_1, \ldots, \sigma_r$, and let Σ be as in (3) above. Then

$$U\Sigma = [\,\mathbf{u}_1 \quad \mathbf{u}_2 \quad \cdots \quad \mathbf{u}_m\,]\left[\begin{array}{cccc|c} \sigma_1 & & & 0 & \\ & \sigma_2 & & & 0 \\ & & \ddots & & \\ 0 & & & \sigma_r & \\ \hline & & 0 & & 0 \end{array}\right]$$

$$= [\,\sigma_1\mathbf{u}_1 \quad \cdots \quad \sigma_r\mathbf{u}_r \quad \mathbf{0} \quad \cdots \quad \mathbf{0}\,]$$

$$= AV$$

Since V is an orthogonal matrix, $U\Sigma V^T = AVV^T = A$. ∎

EXAMPLE 3 Find a singular value decomposition of $A = \begin{bmatrix} 4 & 11 & 14 \\ 8 & 7 & -2 \end{bmatrix}$.

Solution From Example 1, we can use $\mathbf{v}_1$, $\mathbf{v}_2$, and $\mathbf{v}_3$ as the right singular vectors of A. Using the calculations of $A\mathbf{v}_1$ and $A\mathbf{v}_2$ from Examples 1 and 2, we set

$$\mathbf{u}_1 = \frac{1}{\sigma_1}A\mathbf{v}_1 = \frac{1}{6\sqrt{10}}\begin{bmatrix} 18 \\ 6 \end{bmatrix} = \begin{bmatrix} 3/\sqrt{10} \\ 1/\sqrt{10} \end{bmatrix}$$

$$\mathbf{u}_2 = \frac{1}{\sigma_2}A\mathbf{v}_2 = \frac{1}{3\sqrt{10}}\begin{bmatrix} 3 \\ -9 \end{bmatrix} = \begin{bmatrix} 1/\sqrt{10} \\ -3/\sqrt{10} \end{bmatrix}$$

Then $\{\mathbf{u}_1, \mathbf{u}_2\}$ is a basis for $\mathbb{R}^2$. Let $U = [\,\mathbf{u}_1 \quad \mathbf{u}_2\,]$, $V = [\,\mathbf{v}_1 \quad \mathbf{v}_2 \quad \mathbf{v}_3\,]$, and

$$D = \begin{bmatrix} 6\sqrt{10} & 0 \\ 0 & 3\sqrt{10} \end{bmatrix}, \qquad \Sigma = \begin{bmatrix} 6\sqrt{10} & 0 & 0 \\ 0 & 3\sqrt{10} & 0 \end{bmatrix}$$

Then

$$A = \underset{U}{\begin{bmatrix} 3/\sqrt{10} & 1/\sqrt{10} \\ 1/\sqrt{10} & -3/\sqrt{10} \end{bmatrix}} \underset{\Sigma}{\begin{bmatrix} 6\sqrt{10} & 0 & 0 \\ 0 & 3\sqrt{10} & 0 \end{bmatrix}} \underset{V^T}{\begin{bmatrix} 1/3 & 2/3 & 2/3 \\ -2/3 & -1/3 & 2/3 \\ 2/3 & -2/3 & 1/3 \end{bmatrix}}$$

∎

EXAMPLE 4 Find a singular value decomposition of $A = \begin{bmatrix} 1 & -1 \\ -2 & 2 \\ 2 & -2 \end{bmatrix}$.

Solution First, compute $A^TA = \begin{bmatrix} 9 & -9 \\ -9 & 9 \end{bmatrix}$. The eigenvalues of A^TA are 18 and 0, with corresponding unit eigenvectors

$$\mathbf{v}_1 = \begin{bmatrix} 1/\sqrt{2} \\ -1/\sqrt{2} \end{bmatrix}, \quad \mathbf{v}_2 = \begin{bmatrix} 1/\sqrt{2} \\ 1/\sqrt{2} \end{bmatrix}$$

Next,

$$A\mathbf{v}_1 = \begin{bmatrix} 2/\sqrt{2} \\ -4/\sqrt{2} \\ 4/\sqrt{2} \end{bmatrix}, \quad \sigma_1 = \|A\mathbf{v}_1\| = \sqrt{18} = 3\sqrt{2}$$

and

$$\mathbf{u}_1 = \frac{1}{3\sqrt{2}}A\mathbf{v}_1 = \begin{bmatrix} 1/3 \\ -2/3 \\ 2/3 \end{bmatrix}$$

Also, $A\mathbf{v}_2 = \mathbf{0}$, since $\mathbf{v}_2$ corresponds to the zero eigenvalue of A^TA.

The next step is to extend the set $\{\mathbf{u}_1\}$ to a basis for $\mathbb{R}^3$. We need two orthonormal vectors that are orthogonal to $\mathbf{u}_1$. Each vector must satisfy $\mathbf{u}_1^T\mathbf{x} = 0$, which is equivalent to the equation $x_1 - 2x_2 + 2x_3 = 0$. A basis for the solution set of this equation is

$$\mathbf{w}_1 = \begin{bmatrix} 2 \\ 1 \\ 0 \end{bmatrix}, \quad \mathbf{w}_2 = \begin{bmatrix} -2 \\ 0 \\ 1 \end{bmatrix}$$

(Check that $\mathbf{w}_1$ and $\mathbf{w}_2$ are orthogonal to $\mathbf{u}_1$.) Applying the Gram–Schmidt process to $\{\mathbf{w}_1, \mathbf{w}_2\}$, we obtain

$$\mathbf{u}_2 = \begin{bmatrix} 2/\sqrt{5} \\ 1/\sqrt{5} \\ 0 \end{bmatrix}, \quad \mathbf{u}_3 = \begin{bmatrix} -2/\sqrt{45} \\ 4/\sqrt{45} \\ 5/\sqrt{45} \end{bmatrix}$$

Finally, if $U = [\,\mathbf{u}_1 \;\; \mathbf{u}_2 \;\; \mathbf{u}_3\,]$, $V = [\,\mathbf{v}_1 \;\; \mathbf{v}_2\,]$, and $\Sigma = \begin{bmatrix} 3\sqrt{2} & 0 \\ 0 & 0 \\ 0 & 0 \end{bmatrix}$, then

$$A = \begin{bmatrix} 1 & -1 \\ -2 & 2 \\ 2 & -2 \end{bmatrix} = \begin{bmatrix} 1/3 & 2/\sqrt{5} & -2/\sqrt{45} \\ -2/3 & 1/\sqrt{5} & 4/\sqrt{45} \\ 2/3 & 0 & 5/\sqrt{45} \end{bmatrix} \begin{bmatrix} 3\sqrt{2} & 0 \\ 0 & 0 \\ 0 & 0 \end{bmatrix} \begin{bmatrix} 1/\sqrt{2} & -1/\sqrt{2} \\ 1/\sqrt{2} & 1/\sqrt{2} \end{bmatrix}$$

Applications of the Singular Value Decomposition

The SVD is often used to estimate the rank of a matrix, as noted above. Several other numerical applications are described briefly below, and an application to image processing is presented in Section 8.5.

EXAMPLE 5 *(The condition number)* Most numerical calculations involving an equation $A\mathbf{x} = \mathbf{b}$ are as reliable as possible when the SVD of A is used. The two orthogonal matrices U and V do not affect lengths of vectors or angles between vectors (Theorem 7 in Section 7.2). Any possible instabilities in numerical calculations are identified in Σ. If the singular values of A are extremely large or small, roundoff errors are almost inevitable, but an error analysis is aided by knowing the entries in Σ and V.

If σ_r is the smallest nonzero singular number of A, then the quotient σ_1/σ_r is called the **condition number** of A. This number is used to estimate the sensitivity of a computed solution of $A\mathbf{x} = \mathbf{b}$ to changes (or errors) in the entries of A and $\mathbf{b}$.

EXAMPLE 6 *(Bases for fundamental subspaces)* Given an $m \times n$ matrix A, let $\mathbf{u}_1, \ldots, \mathbf{u}_n$ be the left singular vectors, $\mathbf{v}_1, \ldots, \mathbf{v}_m$ the right singular vectors, and $\sigma_1, \ldots, \sigma_n$ the singular values, and let r be the rank of A. The proof of Theorem 9 showed that

$$\{\mathbf{u}_1, \ldots, \mathbf{u}_r\} \text{ is an orthonormal basis for Col } A \tag{5}$$

Recall from Theorem 3 in Section 7.1 that $(\text{Col } A)^{\perp} = \text{Nul } A^T$. Hence

$$\{\mathbf{u}_{r+1}, \ldots, \mathbf{u}_m\} \text{ is an orthonormal basis for Nul } A^T \tag{6}$$

Since $A\mathbf{v}_i = \sigma_i\mathbf{u}_i$ for $1 \le i \le r$, and σ_i is 0 if and only if $i > r$, we conclude that

$$\{\mathbf{v}_{r+1}, \ldots, \mathbf{v}_n\} \text{ is an orthonormal basis for Nul } A \tag{7}$$

From (5) and (6), the orthogonal complement of Nul A^T is Col A. Interchanging A and A^T, we have $(\text{Nul } A)^{\perp} = \text{Col } A^T = \text{Row } A$. Hence, from (7),

$$\{\mathbf{v}_1, \ldots, \mathbf{v}_r\} \text{ is an orthonormal basis for Row } A \tag{8}$$

Explicit orthonormal bases for the four fundamental subspaces of A are useful in some calculations, particularly in constrained optimization problems.

EXAMPLE 7 *(Reduced SVD and the pseudoinverse of A)* When Σ contains rows or columns of zeros, a more compact decomposition of A is possible. Using the notation established above, let $r = \text{rank } A$ and partition U and V into submatrices whose first blocks contain r columns:

$$U = [\,U_r \quad U_{m-r}\,], \quad \text{where } U_r = [\,\mathbf{u}_1 \quad \cdots \quad \mathbf{u}_r\,]$$
$$V = [\,V_r \quad V_{n-r}\,], \quad \text{where } V_r = [\,\mathbf{v}_1 \quad \cdots \quad \mathbf{v}_r\,]$$

Then U_r is $m \times r$ and V_r is $n \times r$. (To simplify notation, we consider U_{m-r} or V_{n-r} even though one of them may have no columns.) Then partitioned matrix multiplication shows that

$$A = [\,U_r \quad U_{m-r}\,]\begin{bmatrix} D & 0 \\ 0 & 0 \end{bmatrix}\begin{bmatrix} V_r^T \\ V_{n-r}^T \end{bmatrix} = U_r D V_r^T \tag{9}$$

This factorization of A is called a **reduced singular value decomposition** of A. Since the diagonal entries in D are nonzero, we can form the following matrix, called the **pseudoinverse** (also, the **Moore-Penrose inverse**) of A:

$$A^+ = V_r D^{-1} U_r^T \tag{10}$$

Supplementary Exercises 12–14 at the end of the chapter explore some of the properties of the reduced singular value decomposition and the pseudoinverse.

EXAMPLE 8 *(Least-squares solution)* Given the equation $A\mathbf{x} = \mathbf{b}$, use the pseudoinverse of A in (10) to define

$$\hat{\mathbf{x}} = A^{+}\mathbf{b} = V_r D^{-1} U_r^T \mathbf{b}$$

Then, from the SVD in (9),

$$\begin{aligned} A\hat{\mathbf{x}} &= (U_r D V_r^T)(V_r D^{-1} U_r^T \mathbf{b}) \\ &= U_r D D^{-1} U_r^T \mathbf{b} \qquad \text{Because } V_r^T V_r = I_r \\ &= U_r U_r^T \mathbf{b} \end{aligned}$$

It follows from (5) that $U_r U_r^T \mathbf{b}$ is the orthogonal projection $\hat{\mathbf{b}}$ of $\mathbf{b}$ onto Col A. (See Theorem 10 in Section 7.3.) Thus $\hat{\mathbf{x}}$ is a least-squares solution of $A\mathbf{x} = \mathbf{b}$. In fact, this $\hat{\mathbf{x}}$ has the smallest length among all least-squares solutions of $A\mathbf{x} = \mathbf{b}$. See Supplementary Exercise 14.

Numerical Note

Examples 1–4 and the exercises illustrate the concept of singular values and suggest how to perform calculations by hand. In practice, the computation of A^TA should be avoided, since any errors in the entries of A are squared in the entries of A^TA. There exist fast iterative methods that produce the singular values and singular vectors of A accurately to many decimal places.

Further Reading

Horn, Roger A., and Charles R. Johnson. *Matrix Analysis*, vol. 1, Cambridge: Cambridge University Press, 1985, pp. 414–445.

Long, Cliff. "Visualization of Matrix Singular Value Decomposition." *Mathematics Magazine* 56 (1983), pp. 161–167.

Strang, Gilbert. *Linear Algebra and Its Applications*, 3rd ed. San Diego: Harcourt Brace Jovanovich, 1988, pp. 442–452.

Watkins, David S. *Fundamentals of Matrix Computations.* New York: Wiley, 1991, pp. 390–398, 409–421.

PRACTICE PROBLEM

Given a singular value decomposition, $A = U\Sigma V^T$, find an SVD for A^T. How are the singular values of A and A^T related?

8.4 EXERCISES

Find the singular values of the matrices in Exercises 1–4.

1. $\begin{bmatrix} 1 & 0 \\ 0 & -3 \end{bmatrix}$

2. $\begin{bmatrix} -5 & 0 \\ 0 & 0 \end{bmatrix}$

3. $\begin{bmatrix} \sqrt{6} & 1 \\ 0 & \sqrt{6} \end{bmatrix}$

4. $\begin{bmatrix} \sqrt{3} & 2 \\ 0 & \sqrt{3} \end{bmatrix}$

Find an SVD of each matrix in Exercises 5–12. [*Hints*: In Exercise 11, one choice for U is $\begin{bmatrix} -1/3 & 2/3 & 2/3 \\ 2/3 & -1/3 & 2/3 \\ 2/3 & 2/3 & -1/3 \end{bmatrix}$

In Exercise 12, one column of U can be $\begin{bmatrix} 1/\sqrt{6} \\ -2/\sqrt{6} \\ 1/\sqrt{6} \end{bmatrix}$.]

5. $\begin{bmatrix} -3 & 0 \\ 0 & 0 \end{bmatrix}$ **6.** $\begin{bmatrix} -2 & 0 \\ 0 & -1 \end{bmatrix}$

7. $\begin{bmatrix} 2 & -1 \\ 2 & 2 \end{bmatrix}$ **8.** $\begin{bmatrix} 2 & 3 \\ 0 & 2 \end{bmatrix}$

9. $\begin{bmatrix} 7 & 1 \\ 0 & 0 \\ 5 & 5 \end{bmatrix}$ **10.** $\begin{bmatrix} 4 & -2 \\ 2 & -1 \\ 0 & 0 \end{bmatrix}$

11. $\begin{bmatrix} -3 & 1 \\ 6 & -2 \\ 6 & -2 \end{bmatrix}$ **12.** $\begin{bmatrix} 1 & 1 \\ 0 & 1 \\ -1 & 1 \end{bmatrix}$

13. Find the SVD of $A = \begin{bmatrix} 3 & 2 & 2 \\ 2 & 3 & -2 \end{bmatrix}$. [*Hint*: Work with A^T.]

In Exercises 14–18, A is an $m \times n$ matrix with a singular value decomposition $A = U\Sigma V^T$. Justify each answer.

14. Suppose A is square and invertible. Find a singular value decomposition for A^{-1}.

15. Let $A = U\Sigma V^T$, where U is an $m \times m$ orthogonal matrix, Σ is an $m \times n$ "diagonal" matrix, and V is an $n \times n$ orthogonal matrix. Show that the columns of V are eigenvectors of A^TA, the columns of U are eigenvectors of AA^T, and the diagonal entries of Σ are the singular values of A. [*Hint*: Compute A^TA.]

16. Show that if A is square, then $|\det A|$ is the product of the singular values of A.

17. Show that if P is an orthogonal $m \times m$ matrix, then PA has the same singular values as A.

18. Show that if A is $n \times n$ and positive definite, then the singular values of A are the same as the eigenvalues of A.

19. Let A be an $m \times n$ matrix with nonzero singular values $\sigma_1, \ldots, \sigma_r$, left singular vectors $\mathbf{u}_1, \ldots, \mathbf{u}_m$, and right singular vectors $\mathbf{v}_1, \ldots, \mathbf{v}_n$. Show that

$$A = \sigma_1\mathbf{u}_1\mathbf{v}_1^T + \sigma_2\mathbf{u}_2\mathbf{v}_2^T + \cdots + \sigma_r\mathbf{u}_r\mathbf{v}_r^T$$

20. Using the notation of Exercise 19, show that $A^T\mathbf{u}_j = \sigma_j\mathbf{v}_j$ for $1 \le j \le r = \text{rank } A$.

21. Justify the statement in Example 2 that the second singular value of a matrix A is the maximum of $\|A\mathbf{x}\|$ as $\mathbf{x}$ varies over all unit vectors orthogonal to $\mathbf{v}_1$, with $\mathbf{v}_1$ a right singular vector corresponding to the first singular value of A.

22. Let A be an $m \times n$ matrix with singular values $\sigma_1, \ldots, \sigma_n$, and right singular vectors $\mathbf{v}_1, \ldots, \mathbf{v}_n$. Give a description of σ_k, for $2 \le k \le n$, as the maximum of $\|A\mathbf{x}\|$ as $\mathbf{x}$ varies over a suitable set. Justify your description.

23. Let $T: \mathbb{R}^n \to \mathbb{R}^m$ be a linear transformation. Describe how to find a basis $\mathcal{B}$ for $\mathbb{R}^n$ and a basis $\mathcal{C}$ for $\mathbb{R}^m$ such that the matrix for T relative to $\mathcal{B}$ and $\mathcal{C}$ is an $m \times n$ "diagonal" matrix.

SOLUTION TO PRACTICE PROBLEM

If $A = U\Sigma V^T$, where Σ is $m \times n$, then $A^T = (V^T)^T\Sigma^TU^T = V\Sigma^TU^T$. This is an SVD for A^T because V and U are orthogonal matrices and Σ^T is an $n \times m$ "diagonal" matrix. Since Σ and Σ^T have the same nonzero diagonal entries, A and A^T have the same nonzero singular values. [*Note*: If A is $2 \times n$, then AA^T is only 2×2 and its eigenvalues may be easier to compute (by hand) than the eigenvalues of A^TA].

8.5 APPLICATIONS TO IMAGE PROCESSING AND STATISTICS

The satellite photographs in the chapter's introduction provide an example of multidimensional or *multivariate* data—information organized so that each datum in the data set is identified with a point (vector) in $\mathbb{R}^n$. The main goal of this section is to explain a technique, called *principal component analysis*, used to analyze such multivariate data. The calculations will illustrate the use of orthogonal diagonalization and the singular value decomposition.

Principal component analysis can be applied to any data that consist of lists of measurements made on a collection of objects or individuals. For instance, consider a chemical process that produces a plastic material. To monitor the process, 300 samples are taken of the material produced and each sample is subjected to a battery of eight tests, such as melting point, density, ductility, tensile strength, and so on. The laboratory report for each sample is a vector in $\mathbb{R}^8$, and the set of such vectors forms an 8×300 matrix, called the **matrix of observations**.

Loosely speaking, we can say that the process control data are eight-dimensional. The next two examples describe data that can be visualized graphically.

EXAMPLE 1 An example of two-dimensional data is given by a set of weights and heights of N college students. Let $\mathbf{X}_j$ denote the **observation vector** in $\mathbb{R}^2$ that lists the weight and height of the jth student. If w denotes weight and h height, then the matrix of observations has the form

$$\begin{bmatrix} w_1 & w_2 & \cdots & w_N \\ h_1 & h_2 & \cdots & h_N \end{bmatrix}$$
$$\begin{matrix} \uparrow & \uparrow & & \uparrow \\ \mathbf{X}_1 & \mathbf{X}_2 & & \mathbf{X}_N \end{matrix}$$

The set of observation vectors can be visualized as a two-dimensional *scatter plot*. See Fig. 1.

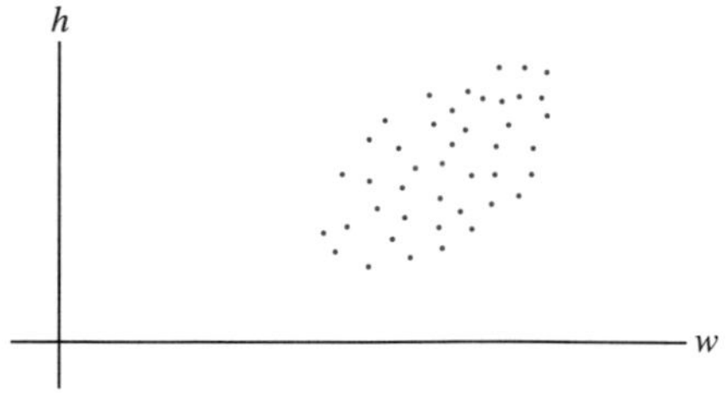

FIGURE 1 A scatter plot of observation vectors $\mathbf{X}_1, \ldots, \mathbf{X}_N$.

EXAMPLE 2 The first three photographs of Railroad Valley, Nevada, shown in the chapter introduction, can be viewed as *one* image of the region, with *three spectral components*, because simultaneous measurements of the region were made at three separate wavelengths. Each photograph gives different information about the same physical region. For instance, the first pixel in the upper-left corner of each photograph corresponds to the same place on the ground (about 30 meters by 30 meters). To each pixel there corresponds an observation vector in $\mathbb{R}^3$ that lists the signal intensities for that pixel in the three spectral bands.

Typically, the image is 2000×2000 pixels, so there are 4 million pixels in the image. The data for the image form a matrix with 3 rows and 4 million columns

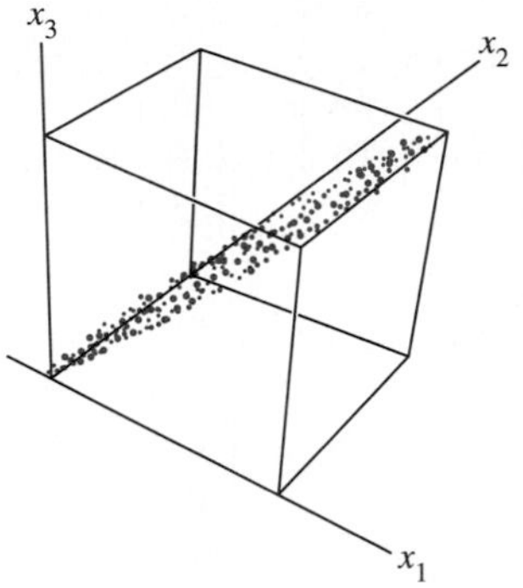

FIGURE 2 A scatter plot of spectral data for a photograph.

(with columns arranged in any convenient order). In this case, the "multidimensional" character of the data refers to the three *spectral* dimensions rather than the two *spatial* dimensions that naturally belong to any photograph. The data can be visualized as a cluster of 4 million points in $\mathbb{R}^3$, perhaps as in Fig. 2. ∎

Mean and Covariance

To prepare for principal component analysis, let $[\mathbf{X}_1 \ \cdots \ \mathbf{X}_N]$ be a $p \times N$ matrix of observations, such as described above. The **sample mean**, $\mathbf{M}$, of the observation vectors $\mathbf{X}_1, \ldots, \mathbf{X}_N$ is given by

$$\mathbf{M} = \frac{1}{N}(\mathbf{X}_1 + \cdots + \mathbf{X}_N)$$

For the data in Fig. 1, the sample mean is the point in the "center" of the scatter plot. For $k = 1, \ldots, N$, let

$$\hat{\mathbf{X}}_k = \mathbf{X}_k - \mathbf{M}$$

The columns of the $p \times N$ matrix

$$B = [\hat{\mathbf{X}}_1 \ \hat{\mathbf{X}}_2 \ \cdots \ \hat{\mathbf{X}}_N]$$

have a zero sample mean, and B is said to be in **mean-deviation form**. When the sample mean is subtracted from the data in Fig. 1, the resulting scatter plot has the form in Fig. 3.

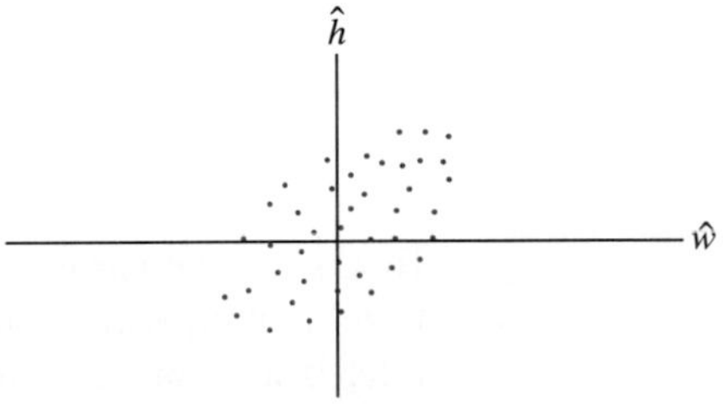

FIGURE 3 Weight–height data in mean-deviation form.

The **(sample) covariance matrix** is the $p \times p$ matrix S defined by

$$S = \frac{1}{N-1}BB^T$$

Since any matrix of the form BB^T is positive semidefinite, so is S. (See Exercise 10.)

EXAMPLE 3 Three measurements are made on each of four individuals in a random sample from a population. The observation vectors are

$$\mathbf{X}_1 = \begin{bmatrix} 1 \\ 2 \\ 1 \end{bmatrix}, \quad \mathbf{X}_2 = \begin{bmatrix} 4 \\ 2 \\ 13 \end{bmatrix}, \quad \mathbf{X}_3 = \begin{bmatrix} 7 \\ 8 \\ 1 \end{bmatrix}, \quad \mathbf{X}_4 = \begin{bmatrix} 8 \\ 4 \\ 5 \end{bmatrix}$$

Compute the sample mean and the covariance matrix.

Solution The sample mean is

$$\mathbf{M} = \frac{1}{4}\left(\begin{bmatrix}1\\2\\1\end{bmatrix} + \begin{bmatrix}4\\2\\13\end{bmatrix} + \begin{bmatrix}7\\8\\1\end{bmatrix} + \begin{bmatrix}8\\4\\5\end{bmatrix}\right) = \frac{1}{4}\begin{bmatrix}20\\16\\20\end{bmatrix} = \begin{bmatrix}5\\4\\5\end{bmatrix}$$

Subtracting the sample mean from $\mathbf{X}_1, \ldots, \mathbf{X}_4$, we obtain

$$\hat{\mathbf{X}}_1 = \begin{bmatrix}-4\\-2\\-4\end{bmatrix}, \quad \hat{\mathbf{X}}_2 = \begin{bmatrix}-1\\-2\\8\end{bmatrix}, \quad \hat{\mathbf{X}}_3 = \begin{bmatrix}2\\4\\-4\end{bmatrix}, \quad \hat{\mathbf{X}}_4 = \begin{bmatrix}3\\0\\0\end{bmatrix}$$

and

$$B = \begin{bmatrix}-4 & -1 & 2 & 3\\-2 & -2 & 4 & 0\\-4 & 8 & -4 & 0\end{bmatrix}$$

The sample covariance matrix is

$$S = \frac{1}{3}\begin{bmatrix}-4 & -1 & 2 & 3\\-2 & -2 & 4 & 0\\-4 & 8 & -4 & 0\end{bmatrix}\begin{bmatrix}-4 & -2 & -4\\-1 & -2 & 8\\2 & 4 & -4\\3 & 0 & 0\end{bmatrix}$$

$$= \frac{1}{3}\begin{bmatrix}30 & 18 & 0\\18 & 24 & -24\\0 & -24 & 96\end{bmatrix} = \begin{bmatrix}10 & 6 & 0\\6 & 8 & -8\\0 & -8 & 32\end{bmatrix}$$

To discuss the entries in $S = [s_{ij}]$, let $\mathbf{X}$ represent a vector that varies over the set of observation vectors and denote the coordinates of $\mathbf{X}$ by $x_1, \ldots, x_p$. Then x_1, for example, is a scalar that varies over the set of first coordinates of $\mathbf{X}_1, \ldots, \mathbf{X}_N$. For $j = 1, \ldots, p$, the diagonal entry s_{jj} in S is called the **variance** of x_j.

The variance of x_j measures the spread of the values of x_j. (See Exercise 13.) In Example 3, the variance of x_1 is 10 and the variance of x_3 is 32. The fact that 32 is more than 10 means that the set of third entries in the response vectors contains a wider spread of values than the set of first entries.

The **total variance** of the data is the sum of the variances on the diagonal of S. In general, the sum of the diagonal entries of a square matrix S is called the **trace** of the matrix, written $\operatorname{tr}(S)$. Thus

$$\{\text{total variance}\} = \operatorname{tr}(S)$$

The entry s_{ij} in S for $i \neq j$ is called the **covariance** of x_i and x_j. Observe that in Example 3, the covariance between x_1 and x_3 is 0 because the (1, 3)-entry in S is zero. Statisticians say that x_1 and x_3 are **uncorrelated**. Analysis of the multivariate data in $\mathbf{X}_1, \ldots, \mathbf{X}_N$ is greatly simplified when most or all of the variables $x_1, \ldots, x_p$ are uncorrelated, that is, when the covariance matrix of $\mathbf{X}_1, \ldots, \mathbf{X}_N$ is diagonal or nearly diagonal.

Principal Component Analysis

For simplicity, assume that the matrix $[\mathbf{X}_1 \ \cdots \ \mathbf{X}_N]$ is already in mean-deviation form. The goal of principal component analysis is to find an orthogonal $p \times p$ matrix $P = [\mathbf{v}_1 \ \cdots \ \mathbf{v}_p]$ that determines a change of variable, $\mathbf{X} = P\mathbf{U}$, or

$$\begin{bmatrix} x_1 \\ x_2 \\ \vdots \\ x_p \end{bmatrix} = [\mathbf{v}_1 \ \ \mathbf{v}_2 \ \ \cdots \ \ \mathbf{v}_p] \begin{bmatrix} u_1 \\ u_2 \\ \vdots \\ u_p \end{bmatrix}$$

with the property that the new variables $u_1, \ldots, u_p$ are uncorrelated and are arranged in order of decreasing variance.

The orthogonal change of variable $\mathbf{X} = P\mathbf{U}$ means that each observation vector $\mathbf{X}_k$ receives a "new name," $\mathbf{U}_k$, such that $\mathbf{X}_k = P\mathbf{U}_k$. Notice that $\mathbf{U}_k$ is the coordinate vector of $\mathbf{X}_k$ with respect to the columns of P, and $\mathbf{U}_k = P^{-1}\mathbf{X}_k = P^T\mathbf{X}_k$ for $k = 1, \ldots, N$.

It is not difficult to verify that for any orthogonal P, the covariance matrix of $\mathbf{U}_1, \ldots, \mathbf{U}_N$ is P^TSP (Exercise 11). So the desired orthogonal matrix P is one that makes P^TSP diagonal. Let D be a diagonal matrix with the eigenvalues $\lambda_1, \ldots, \lambda_p$ of S on the diagonal, arranged so that $\lambda_1 \geq \lambda_2 \geq \cdots \lambda_p \geq 0$, and let P be an orthogonal matrix whose columns are the corresponding unit eigenvectors $\mathbf{v}_1, \ldots, \mathbf{v}_p$. Then $S = PDP^T$ and $P^TSP = D$.

The unit eigenvectors $\mathbf{v}_1, \ldots, \mathbf{v}_p$ of the covariance matrix S are called the **principal components** of the data (in the matrix of observations). The **first principal component** is the eigenvector corresponding to the largest eigenvalue of S, the **second principal component** is the eigenvector corresponding to the second largest eigenvalue, and so on.

The first principal component $\mathbf{v}_1$ determines the new variable u_1 in the following way. Let $c_1, \ldots, c_p$ be the entries in $\mathbf{v}_1$. Since $\mathbf{v}_1^T$ is the first row of P^T, the equation $\mathbf{U} = P^T\mathbf{X}$ shows that

$$u_1 = \mathbf{v}_1^T\mathbf{X} = c_1x_1 + c_2x_2 + \cdots + c_px_p$$

Thus u_1 is a linear combination of the original variables $x_1, \ldots, x_p$, using the entries in the eigenvector $\mathbf{v}_1$ as weights. In a similar fashion, $\mathbf{v}_2$ determines the variable u_2, and so on.

EXAMPLE 4 The initial data for the multispectral image of Railroad Valley (Example 2) consisted of 4 million vectors in $\mathbb{R}^3$. The associated covariance matrix[1] is

$$S = \begin{bmatrix} 2382.78 & 2611.84 & 2136.20 \\ 2611.84 & 3106.47 & 2553.90 \\ 2136.20 & 2553.90 & 2650.71 \end{bmatrix}$$

[1]Data for Example 4 and Exercises 5 and 6 were provided by Earth Satellite Corporation, Rockville, Maryland.

Find the principal components of the data, and list the new variable determined by the first principal component.

Solution The eigenvalues of S and the associated principal components (the unit eigenvectors) are

$$\lambda_1 = 7614.23 \qquad \lambda_2 = 427.63 \qquad \lambda_3 = 98.10$$

$$\mathbf{v}_1 = \begin{bmatrix} .5417 \\ .6295 \\ .5570 \end{bmatrix}, \quad \mathbf{v}_2 = \begin{bmatrix} -.4894 \\ -.3026 \\ .8179 \end{bmatrix}, \quad \mathbf{v}_3 = \begin{bmatrix} .6834 \\ -.7157 \\ .1441 \end{bmatrix}$$

Using two decimal places for simplicity, the variable for the first principal component is

$$u_1 = .54x_1 + .63x_2 + .56x_3$$

This equation was used to create photograph (d) in the chapter introduction. The variables x_1, x_2, x_3 are the signal intensities in the three spectral bands. The values of x_1, converted to a "gray scale" between black and white, produced photograph (a). Similarly, the values of x_2 and x_3 produced photographs (b) and (c), respectively. At each pixel in (d), the gray scale value is computed from u_1, a weighted linear combination of x_1, x_2, x_3. In this sense, photograph (d) "displays" the first principal component of the data.

In Example 4, the covariance matrix for the transformed data, using variables u_1, u_2, u_3, is

$$D = \begin{bmatrix} 7614.23 & 0 & 0 \\ 0 & 427.63 & 0 \\ 0 & 0 & 98.10 \end{bmatrix}$$

Although D is obviously simpler than the original covariance matrix S, the merit of constructing the new variables is not yet apparent. However, the variances of the variables u_1, u_2, u_3 appear on the diagonal of D, and obviously the first variance in D is much larger than the other two. As we shall see, this fact will permit us to view the data as essentially one-dimensional rather than three-dimensional.

Reducing the Dimension of Multivariate Data

Principal component analysis is potentially valuable for applications in which most of the variation or dynamic range in the data is due to variations in *only a few* of the new variables, $u_1, \ldots, u_p$.

It can be shown that an orthogonal change of variables, $\mathbf{U} = P\mathbf{X}$, does not change the total variance of the data. (Roughly speaking, this is true because left-multiplication by P does not change the lengths of vectors or the angles between them. See Exercise 12.) This means that if $S = PDP^T$, then

$$\begin{Bmatrix} \text{total variance} \\ \text{of } x_1, \dots, x_p \end{Bmatrix} = \begin{Bmatrix} \text{total variance} \\ \text{of } u_1, \dots, u_p \end{Bmatrix} = \operatorname{tr}(D) = \lambda_1 + \cdots + \lambda_p$$

The variance of u_j is λ_j, and the quotient $\lambda_j/\operatorname{tr}(S)$ measures the fraction of the total variance that is "explained" or "captured" by u_j.

EXAMPLE 5 Compute the various percentages of variance of the Railroad Valley multispectral data that are displayed in the principal component photographs, (d)–(f), shown in the chapter introduction.

Solution The total variance of the data is

$$\operatorname{tr}(D) = 7614.23 + 427.63 + 98.10 = 8139.96$$

[Verify that this number also equals $\operatorname{tr}(S)$.] The percentages of the total variance explained by the principal components are

First component	Second component	Third component
$\dfrac{7614.23}{8139.36} = 93.5\%$	$\dfrac{427.63}{8139.36} = 5.3\%$	$\dfrac{98.10}{8139.36} = 1.2\%$

In a sense, 93.5% of the information collected by Landsat for the Railroad Valley region is displayed in photograph (d), with 5.3% in (e) and only 1.2% remaining for (f).

The calculations in Example 5 show that the data have practically no variance in the third (new) coordinate. The values of u_3 are all close to zero. Geometrically, the data points lie nearly in the plane $u_3 = 0$, and their locations can be determined fairly accurately by knowing only the values of u_1 and u_2. In fact, u_2 also has relatively small variance, which means that the points lie approximately along a line and the data are essentially one-dimensional. See Fig. 2, in which the data resemble a popsicle stick.

Characterizations of Principal Component Variables

If $u_1, \dots, u_p$ arise from a principal component analysis of a $p \times N$ matrix of observations, then the variance of u_1 is as large as possible in the following sense: If $\mathbf{v}$ is any unit vector and if $u = \mathbf{v}^T\mathbf{X}$, then the variance of the values of u as $\mathbf{X}$ varies over the original data $\mathbf{X}_1, \dots, \mathbf{X}_N$ turns out to be $\mathbf{v}^TS\mathbf{v}$. By Theorem 8 in Section 8.3, the maximum value of $\mathbf{v}^TS\mathbf{v}$, over all unit vectors $\mathbf{v}$, is the largest eigenvalue λ_1 of S, and this variance is attained when $\mathbf{v}$ is the corresponding eigenvector $\mathbf{v}_1$. In the same way, Theorem 8 shows that u_2 has maximum possible variance among all variables $u = \mathbf{v}^T\mathbf{X}$ that are *uncorrelated* with u_1. Likewise, u_3 has maximum possible variance among all variables uncorrelated with both u_1 and u_2, and so on.

Numerical Note

The singular value decomposition is the main tool for performing principal component analysis in practical applications. If B is a $p \times N$ matrix of observations in mean-deviation form, and if $A = (1/\sqrt{N-1})B^T$, then A^TA is the covariance matrix, S. The squares of the singular values of A are the p eigenvalues of S, and the right singular vectors of A are the principal components of the data.

As mentioned in Section 8.4, iterative calculation of the SVD for A is faster and more accurate than an eigenvalue decomposition of S. This is particularly true, for instance, in the hyperspectral image processing (with $p = 224$) mentioned in the chapter introduction. Principal component analysis is completed in seconds on specialized workstations.

Further Reading

Lillesand, Thomas M., and Ralph W. Kiefer. *Remote Sensing and Image Interpretation*, 2nd ed. New York: John Wiley, 1987, pp. 655–661.

PRACTICE PROBLEMS

The following table lists the weights and heights of five boys:

Boy	#1	#2	#3	#4	#5
Weight (lbs)	120	125	125	135	145
Height (in)	61	60	64	68	72

1. Find the covariance matrix for the data.
2. Make a principal component analysis of the data to find a single *size index* that explains most of the variation in the data.

8.5 EXERCISES

In Exercises 1 and 2, convert the matrix of observations to mean-deviation form and construct the sample covariance matrix.

1. $\begin{bmatrix} 19 & 22 & 6 & 3 & 2 & 20 \\ 12 & 6 & 9 & 15 & 13 & 5 \end{bmatrix}$

2. $\begin{bmatrix} 1 & 5 & 2 & 6 & 7 & 3 \\ 3 & 11 & 6 & 8 & 15 & 11 \end{bmatrix}$

3. Find the principal components of the data for Exercise 1.

4. Find the principal components of the data for Exercise 2.

5. (MATLAB) A Landsat image with three spectral components was made of Homestead Air Force Base in Florida (after the base was hit by hurricane Andrew in 1992). The covariance matrix of the data is shown below. Find the first principal component of the data, and compute the percentage of the total variance that is contained in this component.

$$S = \begin{bmatrix} 164.12 & 32.73 & 81.04 \\ 32.73 & 539.44 & 249.13 \\ 81.04 & 249.13 & 189.11 \end{bmatrix}$$

6. (MATLAB) The covariance matrix below was obtained from a Landsat image of the Columbia River in Washington, using data from three spectral bands. Let x_1, x_2, x_3 denote the spectral components of each pixel in the image. Find a new variable of the form $u_1 = c_1x_1 + c_2x_2 + c_3x_3$ that has maximum possible variance, subject to the constraint that

$c_1^2 + c_2^2 + c_3^2 = 1$. What percentage of the total variance in the data is explained by u_1?

$$S = \begin{bmatrix} 29.64 & 18.38 & 5.00 \\ 18.38 & 20.82 & 14.06 \\ 5.00 & 14.06 & 29.21 \end{bmatrix}$$

7. Let x_1, x_2 denote the variables for the two-dimensional data in Exercise 1. Find a new variable u_1 of the form $u_1 = c_1x_1 + c_2x_2$, with $c_1^2 + c_2^2 = 1$, such that u_1 has maximum possible variance over the given data. How much of the variance in the data is explained by u_1?

8. Repeat Exercise 7 for the data in Exercise 2.

9. Suppose that three tests are administered to a random sample of college students. Let $\mathbf{X}_1, \ldots, \mathbf{X}_n$ be observation vectors in $\mathbb{R}^3$ that list the three scores of each student, and for $j = 1, 2, 3$ let x_j denote a student's score on the jth exam. Suppose the covariance matrix of the data is

$$S = \begin{bmatrix} 5 & 2 & 0 \\ 2 & 6 & 2 \\ 0 & 2 & 7 \end{bmatrix}$$

Let y be an "index" of student performance, with $y = c_1x_1 + c_2x_2 + c_3x_3$ and $c_1^2 + c_2^2 + c_3^2 = 1$. Choose c_1, c_2, c_3 so that the variance of y over the data set is as large as possible. [*Hint*: The eigenvalues of the sample covariance matrix are $\lambda = 3, 6$, and 9.]

10. Let B be a $p \times N$ matrix. Show that BB^T is symmetric and positive semidefinite.

11. Given multivariate data $\mathbf{X}_1, \ldots, \mathbf{X}_N$ (in $\mathbb{R}^p$) in mean-deviation form, let P be a $p \times p$ matrix, and define $\mathbf{U}_k = P^T\mathbf{X}_k$ for $k = 1, \ldots, N$.

a. Show that $\mathbf{U}_1, \ldots, \mathbf{U}_N$ are in mean-deviation form. [*Hint*: Let $\mathbf{w}$ be the vector in $\mathbb{R}^N$ with a 1 in each entry. Then $[\,\mathbf{X}_1 \ \cdots \ \mathbf{X}_N\,]\mathbf{w} = \mathbf{0}$ (the zero vector in $\mathbb{R}^p$).]

b. Show that if the covariance matrix of $\mathbf{X}_1, \ldots, \mathbf{X}_N$ is S, then the covariance matrix of $\mathbf{U}_1, \ldots, \mathbf{U}_N$ is P^TSP.

12. Let $\mathbf{X}$ denote a vector that varies over the columns of a $p \times N$ matrix of observations, and let P be a $p \times p$ orthogonal matrix. Show that the change of variable $\mathbf{U} = P\mathbf{X}$ does not change the total variance of the data. [*Hint*: By Exercise 11, it suffices to show that $\operatorname{tr}(P^TSP) = \operatorname{tr}(S)$. Use a property of the trace mentioned in Exercise 25 in Section 6.4.]

13. The sample covariance matrix is a generalization of a formula for the variance of a sample of N scalar measurements, say, $t_1, \ldots, t_N$. If m is the average of $t_1, \ldots, t_N$, then the *sample variance* is given by

$$\frac{1}{N-1}\sum_{k=1}^{N}(t_k - m)^2 \qquad (1)$$

Show how the sample covariance matrix, S, defined prior to Example 3, may be written in a form similar to (1). [*Hint*: Use partitioned matrix multiplication to write S as $1/(N-1)$ times the sum of N matrices of size $p \times p$. For $1 \le k \le N$, write $\mathbf{X}_k - \mathbf{M}$ in place of $\hat{\mathbf{X}}_k$.]

SOLUTIONS TO PRACTICE PROBLEMS

1. First arrange the data in mean-deviation form. The sample mean vector is easily seen to be $\mathbf{M} = \begin{bmatrix} 130 \\ 65 \end{bmatrix}$. Subtract $\mathbf{M}$ from the observation vectors (the columns in the table) to obtain

$$B = \begin{bmatrix} -10 & -5 & -5 & 5 & 15 \\ -4 & -5 & -1 & 3 & 7 \end{bmatrix}$$

Then the sample covariance matrix is

$$S = \frac{1}{5-1}\begin{bmatrix} -10 & -5 & -5 & 5 & 15 \\ -4 & -5 & -1 & 3 & 7 \end{bmatrix}\begin{bmatrix} -10 & -4 \\ -5 & -5 \\ -5 & -1 \\ 5 & 3 \\ 15 & 7 \end{bmatrix}$$

$$= \frac{1}{4}\begin{bmatrix} 400 & 190 \\ 190 & 100 \end{bmatrix} = \begin{bmatrix} 100.0 & 47.5 \\ 47.5 & 25.0 \end{bmatrix}$$

2. The eigenvalues of S are (to two decimal places)

$$\lambda_1 = 123.02 \text{ and } \lambda_2 = 1.98$$

The unit eigenvector corresponding to λ_1 is $\mathbf{v} = \begin{bmatrix} .900 \\ .436 \end{bmatrix}$. (Since S is 2×2, the computations can be done by hand if MATLAB is not available.) For the *size index*, set

$$y = .900\hat{w} + .436\hat{h}$$

where $\hat{w}$ and $\hat{h}$ are weight and height, respectively, in mean-deviation form. The variance of this index over the data set is 123.02. Because the total variance is $\text{tr}(S) = 100 + 25 = 125$, the size index accounts for practically all (98.4%) of the variance of the data.

The original data for Practice Problem 1 and the line determined by the first principal component $\mathbf{v}$ are shown in the accompanying figure. It can be shown that the line is the best approximation to the data, in the sense that the sum of the squares of the *orthogonal* distances to the line is minimized. In fact, principal component analysis is equivalent to what is termed *orthogonal regression*, but that is a story for another day. Perhaps we'll meet again.

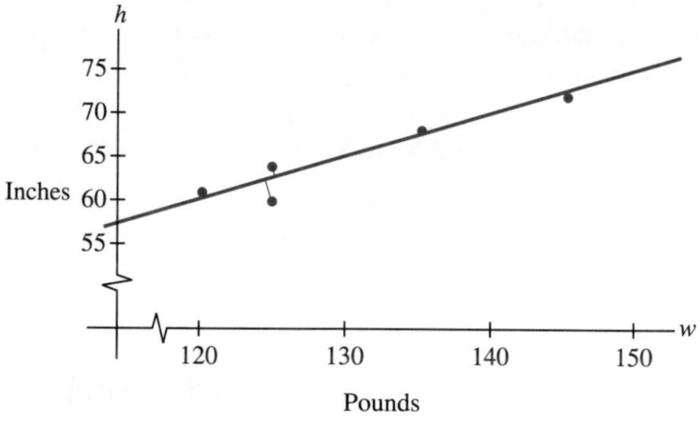

An orthogonal regression line determined by the first principal component of the data.

CHAPTER 8 SUPPLEMENTARY EXERCISES

1. Mark each statement True or False. Justify each answer. In each part, A represents an $n\times n$ matrix.

___ a. If A is orthogonally diagonalizable, A is symmetric.

___ b. If A is an orthogonal matrix, then A is symmetric.

___ c. If A is an orthogonal matrix, then $\|A\mathbf{x}\| = \|\mathbf{x}\|$ for all $\mathbf{x}$ in $\mathbb{R}^n$.

___ d. The principal axes of a quadratic form $\mathbf{x}^T A\mathbf{x}$ can be the columns of any matrix P that diagonalizes A.

___ e. If P is $n\times n$ with orthogonal columns, then $P^T = P^{-1}$.

___ f. If every coefficient in a quadratic form is positive, then the quadratic form is positive definite.

___ g. If $\mathbf{x}^T A\mathbf{x} > 0$, then the quadratic form $\mathbf{x}^T A\mathbf{x}$ is positive definite.

___ h. A suitable change of variable will change any quadratic form into one with no cross-product term.

___ i. The largest value of a quadratic form $\mathbf{x}^T A\mathbf{x}$ is the largest entry on the diagonal of A.

___ j. The maximum value of a positive definite quadratic form $\mathbf{x}^T A\mathbf{x}$ is the largest eigenvalue of A.

_____ k. A positive definite quadratic form can be changed into a negative definite form by a suitable change of variable $\mathbf{x} = P\mathbf{u}$, for some orthogonal matrix P.

_____ l. An indefinite quadratic form is one whose eigenvalues are not definite.

_____ m. If P is an $n \times n$ orthogonal matrix, then the change of variable $\mathbf{x} = P\mathbf{u}$ transforms $\mathbf{x}^T A\mathbf{x}$ into a quadratic form whose matrix is $P^{-1}AP$.

_____ n. If U is $m \times n$ with orthogonal columns, then $UU^T\mathbf{x}$ is the orthogonal projection of $\mathbf{x}$ onto Col U.

_____ o. If B is $m \times n$ and $\mathbf{x}$ is a unit vector in $\mathbb{R}^n$, then $\|B\mathbf{x}\| \leq \sigma_1$, where σ_1 is the first singular value of B.

_____ p. A singular value decomposition of an $m \times n$ matrix B can be written as $B = P\Sigma Q$, where P is an $m \times m$ orthogonal matrix, Q is an $n \times n$ orthogonal matrix, and Σ is an $m \times n$ "diagonal" matrix.

_____ q. If A is $n \times n$, then A and A^TA have the same singular values.

2. Let $\{\mathbf{v}_1, \ldots, \mathbf{v}_n\}$ be an orthonormal basis for $\mathbb{R}^n$, and let $\lambda_1, \ldots, \lambda_n$ be any real scalars. Define

$$A = \lambda_1\mathbf{v}_1\mathbf{v}_1^T + \cdots + \lambda_n\mathbf{v}_n\mathbf{v}_n^T$$

a. Show that A is symmetric.

b. Show that $\lambda_1, \ldots, \lambda_n$ are the eigenvalues of A.

3. Let A be an $n \times n$ symmetric matrix of rank r. Explain why the spectral decomposition of A represents A as the sum of r rank 1 matrices.

4. Let A be an $n \times n$ symmetric matrix.

a. Show that Nul $A = (\text{Col } A)^\perp$. [*Hint*: See Section 7.1.]

b. Show that each $\mathbf{y}$ in $\mathbb{R}^n$ can be written in the form $\mathbf{y} = \hat{\mathbf{y}} + \mathbf{z}$, with $\hat{\mathbf{y}}$ in Col A and $\mathbf{z}$ in Nul A.

5. Show that if $\mathbf{v}$ is an eigenvector of an $n \times n$ matrix A and $\mathbf{v}$ corresponds to a nonzero eigenvalue of A, then $\mathbf{v}$ is in Col A. [*Hint*: Use the definition of an eigenvector.]

6. Let A be an $n \times n$ symmetric matrix. Use Exercise 5 and an eigenvector basis for $\mathbb{R}^n$ to give a second proof of the decomposition in Exercise 4(b).

7. Prove that an $n \times n$ matrix A is positive definite if and only if A admits a *Cholesky factorization*, namely, $A = R^TR$ for some invertible upper triangular matrix R whose diagonal entries are all positive. [*Hint*: Use a QR factorization and Exercise 20 from Section 8.2.]

8. Use Exercise 7 to show that if A is positive definite, then A has an LU factorization, $A = LU$, where U has positive pivots on its diagonal. (The converse is true, too.)

If A is $m \times n$, then the matrix $G = A^TA$ is called the *Gram matrix* of A. In this case, the entries of G are the inner products of the columns of A.

9. Show that the Gram matrix of any matrix A is positive semidefinite, with the same rank as A. (See the Exercises in Section 7.5.)

10. Show that if an $n \times n$ matrix G is positive semidefinite and has rank r, then G is the Gram matrix of some $r \times n$ matrix A. This is a called a *rank-revealing factorization* of G. [*Hint*: Consider the spectral decomposition of G, and first write G as BB^T for an $n \times r$ matrix B.]

11. Prove that any $n \times n$ matrix A admits a *polar decomposition* of the form $A = PQ$, where P is an $n \times n$ positive semidefinite matrix with the same rank as A and Q is an $n \times n$ orthogonal matrix. [*Hint*: Use a singular value decomposition, $A = U\Sigma V^T$, and observe that $A = (U\Sigma U^T)(UV^T)$.] This decomposition is used, for instance, in mechanical engineering to model the deformation of a material. The matrix P describes the stretching or compression of the material (in the directions of the eigenvectors of P) and Q describes the rotation of the material in space.

Exercises 12–14 concern an $m \times n$ matrix A with a reduced singular value decomposition, $A = U_rDV_r^T$, and the pseudoinverse $A^+ = V_rD^{-1}U_r^T$.

12. Verify the properties of A^+:

a. For each $\mathbf{y}$ in $\mathbb{R}^m$, $AA^+\mathbf{y}$ is the orthogonal projection of $\mathbf{y}$ onto Col A.

b. For each $\mathbf{x}$ in $\mathbb{R}^n$, $A^+A\mathbf{x}$ is the orthogonal projection of $\mathbf{x}$ onto Row A.

c. $AA^+A = A$ and $A^+AA^+ = A^+$.

13. Suppose the equation $A\mathbf{x} = \mathbf{b}$ is consistent and let $\mathbf{x}^+ = A^+\mathbf{b}$. By Exercise 21 in Section 7.3, there is exactly one vector $\mathbf{p}$ in Row A such that $A\mathbf{p} = \mathbf{b}$. The following steps prove that $\mathbf{x}^+ = \mathbf{p}$ and $\mathbf{x}^+$ is the *minimum length solution* of $A\mathbf{x} = \mathbf{b}$.

a. Show that $\mathbf{x}^+$ is a solution of $A\mathbf{x} = \mathbf{b}$ and $\mathbf{x}^+$ is in Row A. [*Hint*: Write $\mathbf{b}$ as $A\mathbf{x}$ for some $\mathbf{x}$, and use Exercise 12.]

b. Show that if $\mathbf{x}$ is any solution of $A\mathbf{x} = \mathbf{b}$, then $\|\mathbf{x}^+\| \leq \|\mathbf{x}\|$, with equality only if $\mathbf{x} = \mathbf{x}^+$.

14. Given any $\mathbf{b}$ in $\mathbb{R}^m$, adapt Exercise 13 to show that $A^+\mathbf{b}$ is the *least-squares solution of minimum length.* [*Hint*: Consider the equation $A\mathbf{x} = \hat{\mathbf{b}}$, where $\hat{\mathbf{b}}$ is the orthogonal projection of $\mathbf{b}$ onto Col A.]

Appendix A

Uniqueness of the Reduced Echelon Form

THEOREM

Uniqueness of the Reduced Echelon Form

Each $m \times n$ matrix A is row equivalent to a unique reduced echelon matrix U.

Proof The proof uses the idea from Section 5.3 that the columns of row-equivalent matrices have exactly the same linear dependence relations.

The row reduction algorithm shows that there exists at least one such matrix U. Suppose that A is row equivalent to matrices U and V in reduced echelon form. The leftmost nonzero entry in a row of U is a "leading 1." Call the location of such a leading 1 a pivot position, and call the column that contains it a pivot column. (This definition uses only the echelon nature of U and V and does not assume the uniqueness of the reduced echelon form.)

The pivot columns of U and V are precisely the nonzero columns that are *not* linearly dependent on the columns to their left. (This condition is satisfied automatically by a *first* column if it is nonzero.) Since U and V are row equivalent (both being row equivalent to A), their columns have the same linear dependence relations. Hence, the pivot columns of U and V appear in the same locations. If there are r such columns, then since U and V are in reduced echelon form, their pivot columns are the first r columns of the $m \times m$ identity matrix. Thus, *corresponding pivot columns of U and V are equal.*

Finally, consider any nonpivot column of U, say column j. This column is either zero or a linear combination of the pivot columns to its left (because those pivot columns are a basis for the space spanned by the columns to the left of column j). Either case can be expressed by writing $U\mathbf{x} = \mathbf{0}$ for some $\mathbf{x}$ whose jth entry is 1. Then $V\mathbf{x} = \mathbf{0}$, too, which says that column j of V is either zero or the *same* linear combination of the pivot columns of V to *its* left. Since corresponding pivot columns of U and V are equal, columns j of U and V are also equal. This holds for all nonpivot columns, so $V = U$, which proves that U is unique. ∎

Appendix B

Complex Numbers

A **complex number** is an expression z of the form

$$z = a + bi$$

where a and b are real numbers and i is a formal symbol satisfying the relation $i^2 = -1$. We call a the **real part** of z and b the **imaginary part** of z. Two complex numbers are considered equal if and only if their real and imaginary parts are equal.

For example, $z = 5 + (-2)i$ is a complex number whose real part is 5 and imaginary part is -2. For simplicity, we may write $z = 5 - 2i$.

A real number a is considered as a special type of complex number, by identifying a with $a + 0i$. Furthermore, arithmetic operations on real numbers may be extended to the set of complex numbers.

The **complex number system**, denoted by $\mathbb{C}$, is the set of all complex numbers, together with the following operations of addition and multiplication:

$$(a + bi) + (c + di) = (a + c) + (b + d)i \tag{1}$$

$$(a + bi)(c + di) = (ac - bd) + (ad + bc)i \tag{2}$$

These rules reduce to ordinary addition and multiplication of real numbers when b and d are zero in (1) and (2). It is readily checked that the usual laws of arithmetic for $\mathbb{R}$ also hold for $\mathbb{C}$. For this reason, multiplication is usually computed by algebraic expansion, as in the following example.

EXAMPLE 1

$$\begin{aligned}(5 - 2i)(3 + 4i) &= 15 + 20i - 6i - 8i^2 \\ &= 15 + 14i - 8(-1) \\ &= 23 + 14i\end{aligned}$$

That is, multiply each term of $5 - 2i$ by each term of $3 + 4i$, use $i^2 = -1$, and write the result in the form $a + bi$.

Subtraction of complex numbers z_1 and z_2 is defined by

$$z_1 - z_2 = z_1 + (-1)z_2$$

In particular, we write $-z$ in place of $(-1)z$.

The **conjugate** of $z = a+bi$ is the complex number $\overline{z}$ (read as "z bar"), defined by

$$\overline{z} = a - bi$$

Obtain $\overline{z}$ from z by reversing the sign of the imaginary part.

EXAMPLE 2 The conjugate of $-3 + 4i$ is $-3 - 4i$; write $\overline{-3+4i} = -3 - 4i$.

Observe that if $z = a + bi$, then

$$z\overline{z} = (a + bi)(a - bi) = a^2 - abi + bai - b^2i^2 = a^2 + b^2 \tag{3}$$

Since $z\overline{z}$ is real and nonnegative, it has a square root. The **absolute value** (or **modulus**) of z is the real number $|z|$ defined by

$$|z| = \sqrt{z\overline{z}} = \sqrt{a^2 + b^2}$$

If z is a real number, then $z = a + 0i$, and $|z| = \sqrt{a^2}$, which equals the ordinary absolute value of a.

Some useful properties of conjugates and absolute value are listed below; w and z denote complex numbers.

1. $\overline{z} = z$ if and only if z is a real number.
2. $\overline{w + z} = \overline{w} + \overline{z}$.
3. $\overline{wz} = \overline{w}\overline{z}$; in particular, $\overline{rz} = r\overline{z}$ if r is a real number.
4. $z\overline{z} = |z|^2 \geq 0$.
5. $|wz| = |w|\,|z|$.
6. $|w + z| \leq |w| + |z|$.

If $z \neq 0$, then $|z| > 0$ and z has a multiplicative inverse, denoted by $1/z$ or z^{-1} and given by

$$\frac{1}{z} = z^{-1} = \frac{\overline{z}}{|z|^2}$$

Of course, a quotient w/z simply means $w \cdot (1/z)$.

EXAMPLE 3 Let $w = 3 + 4i$ and $z = 5 - 2i$. Compute

a. $z\bar{z}$ b. $|z|$ c. $\dfrac{w}{z}$

Solution

a. Using (3), $z\bar{z} = 5^2 + (-2)^2 = 25 + 4 = 29$
b. $|z| = \sqrt{z\bar{z}} = \sqrt{29}$
c. To compute w/z, multiply both the numerator and denominator by $\bar{z}$, the conjugate of the denominator. Because of (3), this eliminates the i in the denominator:

$$\begin{aligned} \frac{w}{z} &= \frac{3+4i}{5-2i} = \frac{3+4i}{5-2i} \cdot \frac{5+2i}{5+2i} \\ &= \frac{15+6i+20i-8}{5^2+(-2)^2} = \frac{7+26i}{29} \\ &= \frac{7}{29} + \frac{26}{29}i \end{aligned}$$

Geometric Interpretation

Each complex number $z = a + bi$ corresponds to a point (a, b) in the plane $\mathbb{R}^2$, as in Fig. 1. The horizontal axis is called the **real axis** because the points $(a, 0)$ on it correspond to the real numbers. The vertical axis is the **imaginary axis** because the points $(0, b)$ on it correspond to the **pure imaginary numbers** of the form $0 + bi$, or simply bi.

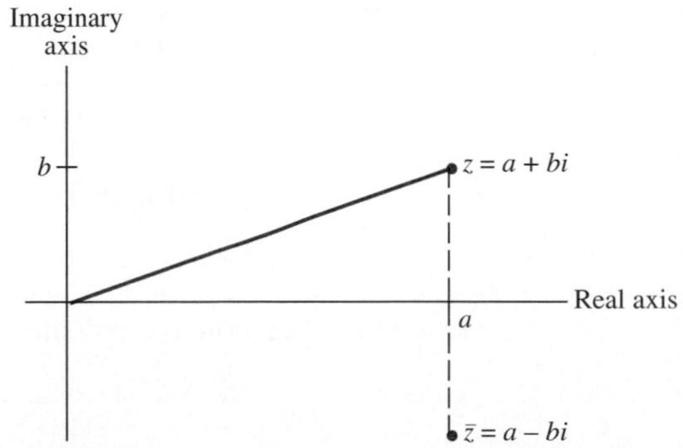

FIGURE 1 The complex conjugate is a mirror image.

The conjugate of z is the mirror image of z in the real axis. The absolute value of z is the distance from (a, b) to the origin. Addition of complex numbers $z = a + bi$ and $w = c + di$ corresponds to vector addition of (a, b) and (c, d) in $\mathbb{R}^2$, as in Fig. 2.

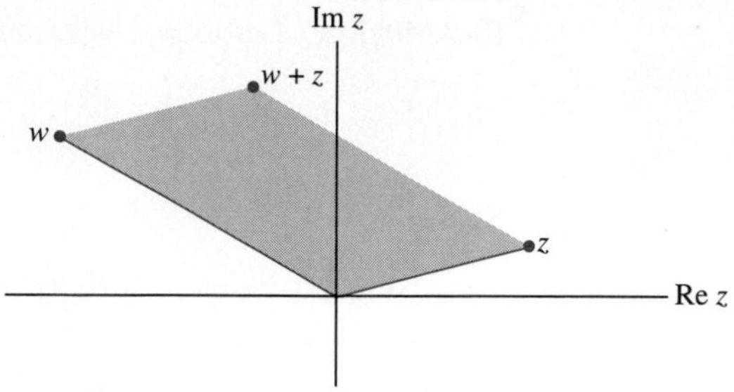

FIGURE 2 Addition of complex numbers.

To give a graphical representation of complex multiplication, we use **polar coordinates** in $\mathbb{R}^2$. Given a nonzero complex number $z = a + bi$, let ϑ be the angle between the positive real axis and the point (a, b), as in Fig. 3 where $-\pi < \vartheta \leq \pi$. The angle ϑ is called the **argument** of z; we write $\vartheta = \arg z$. From trigonometry,

$$a = |z| \cos \vartheta, \qquad b = |z| \sin \vartheta$$

and so

$$z = a + bi = |z|(\cos \vartheta + i \sin \vartheta)$$

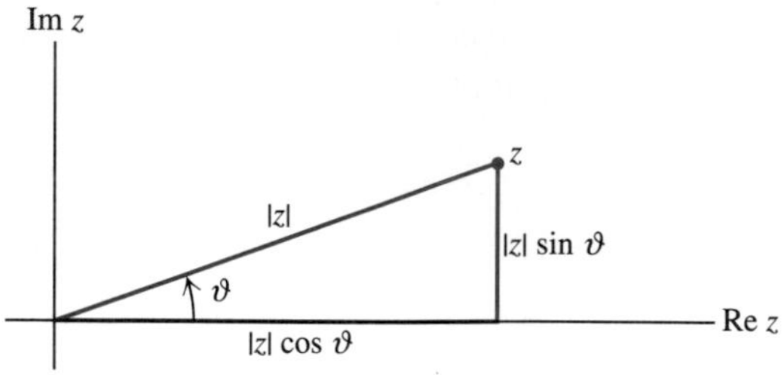

FIGURE 3 Polar coordinates of z.

If w is another nonzero complex number, say,

$$w = |w|(\cos \phi + i \sin \phi)$$

then using standard trigonometric identities for the sine and cosine of the sum of two angles, one can verify that

$$wz = |w||z|[\cos(\phi + \vartheta) + i \sin(\phi + \vartheta)] \tag{4}$$

See Fig. 4. A similar formula may be written for quotients in polar form. The formulas for products and quotients may be stated in words as follows.

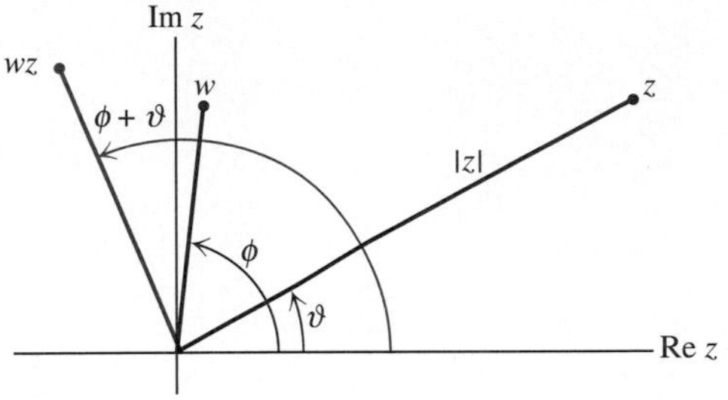

FIGURE 4 Multiplication with polar coordinates.

> The product of two nonzero complex numbers is given in polar form by the product of their absolute values and the sum of their arguments. The quotient of two nonzero complex numbers is given by the quotient of their absolute values and the difference of their arguments.

EXAMPLE 4

a. When w has absolute value 1, then $w = \cos\phi + i\sin\phi$, where ϕ is the argument of w. Multiplication of any nonzero number z by w simply rotates z through the angle ϕ.

b. The argument of i itself is $\pi/2$ radians, so multiplication of z by i rotates z through an angle of $\pi/2$ radians. For example, $3 + i$ is rotated into $(3 + i)i = -1 + 3i$.

Powers of a Complex Number

Formula (4) applies when $z = w = r(\cos\vartheta + i\sin\vartheta)$. In this case $z^2 = r^2(\cos 2\vartheta + i\sin 2\vartheta)$, and

$$\begin{aligned} z^3 = z\cdot z^2 &= r(\cos\vartheta + i\sin\vartheta)\cdot r^2(\cos 2\vartheta + i\sin 2\vartheta) \\ &= r^3(\cos 3\vartheta + i\sin 3\vartheta) \end{aligned}$$

In general, for any positive integer k,

$$z^k = r^k(\cos k\vartheta + i\sin k\vartheta)$$

This fact is known as *De Moivre's theorem.*

Complex Numbers and $\mathbb{R}^2$

Although the elements of $\mathbb{R}^2$ and $\mathbb{C}$ are in one-to-one correspondence, and the operations of addition are essentially the same, there is a logical distinction between $\mathbb{R}^2$ and $\mathbb{C}$. In $\mathbb{R}^2$ we can only multiply a vector by a real scalar, whereas in $\mathbb{C}$ we may multiply any two complex numbers to obtain a third complex number. (The dot product in $\mathbb{R}^2$ doesn't count, because it produces a scalar, not an element of $\mathbb{R}^2$.) We use scalar notation for elements in $\mathbb{C}$ to emphasize this distinction.

Glossary

A

adjugate (or **classical adjoint**): The matrix adj A formed from a square matrix A by replacing the (i, j)-entry of A by the (i, j)-cofactor, for all i and j, and then transposing the resulting matrix.

affine transformation: A mapping $T: \mathbb{R}^n \to \mathbb{R}^m$ of the form $T(\mathbf{x}) = A\mathbf{x} + \mathbf{b}$, with A an $m \times n$ matrix and $\mathbf{b}$ in $\mathbb{R}^m$.

algebraic multiplicity: The multiplicity of an eigenvalue as a root of the characteristic equation.

angle (between nonzero vectors $\mathbf{u}$ and $\mathbf{v}$ in $\mathbb{R}^2$ or $\mathbb{R}^3$): The angle ϑ between the two directed line segments from the origin to the points $\mathbf{u}$ and $\mathbf{v}$. Related to the scalar product by: $\mathbf{u} \cdot \mathbf{v} = \|\mathbf{u}\| \, \|\mathbf{v}\| \cos \vartheta$.

associative law of multiplication: $A(BC) = (AB)C$, for all A, B, C.

attractor (of a dynamical system $\mathbf{x}_{k+1} = A\mathbf{x}_k$): The origin of $\mathbb{R}^n$ when all eigenvalues of A are less than 1 in magnitude. All trajectories tend toward $\mathbf{0}$.

augmented matrix: A matrix made up of a coefficient matrix for a linear system and one or more columns to the right. Each extra column contains the constants from the right side of a system with the given coefficient matrix.

auxiliary equation: A polynomial equation in a variable r, created from the coefficients of a homogeneous difference equation.

B

back-substitution (with matrix notation): The backward phase of row reduction of an augmented matrix that transforms an echelon matrix into a reduced echelon matrix; used to find the solution(s) of a system of linear equations.

backward phase (of row reduction): The last part of the algorithm that reduces a matrix in echelon form to a reduced echelon form.

basic variable: A variable in a linear system that corresponds to a pivot column in the coefficient matrix.

basis (for a subspace H): A set $\mathcal{B} = \{\mathbf{v}_1, \ldots, \mathbf{v}_p\}$ in V such that (i) $\mathcal{B}$ is a linearly independent set and (ii) the subspace spanned by $\mathcal{B}$ coincides with H, that is, $H = \text{Span}\,\{\mathbf{v}_1, \ldots, \mathbf{v}_p\}$.

$\mathcal{B}$-coordinates of $\mathbf{x}$: *See* coordinates of $\mathbf{x}$ relative to the basis $\mathcal{B}$.

best approximation: The closest point in a given subspace to a given vector.

block diagonal (matrix): A partitioned matrix $A = [A_{ij}]$ such that each block A_{ij} is a zero matrix for $i \neq j$.

block matrix: *See* partitioned matrix.

block matrix multiplication: The row–column multiplication of partitioned matrices as if the block entries were scalars.

block upper triangular (matrix): A partitioned matrix $A = [A_{ij}]$ such that each block A_{ij} is a zero matrix for $i > j$.

$\mathcal{B}$-matrix (for T): A matrix $[T]_{\mathcal{B}}$ for a linear transformation $T: V \to V$ relative to a basis $\mathcal{B}$ for V, with the property that $[T(\mathbf{x})]_{\mathcal{B}} = [T]_{\mathcal{B}} [\mathbf{x}]_{\mathcal{B}}$ for all $\mathbf{x}$ in V.

C

Cauchy–Schwarz inequality: $|\langle \mathbf{u}, \mathbf{v} \rangle| \leq \|\mathbf{u}\| \cdot \|\mathbf{v}\|$ for all $\mathbf{u}, \mathbf{v}$.

change of basis: *See* change-of-coordinates matrix.

change-of-coordinates matrix (from a basis $\mathcal{B}$ to a basis $\mathcal{C}$): A matrix $\underset{\mathcal{C}\leftarrow\mathcal{B}}{P}$ that transforms $\mathcal{B}$-coordinate vectors into $\mathcal{C}$-coordinate vectors: $[\mathbf{x}]_{\mathcal{C}} = \underset{\mathcal{C}\leftarrow\mathcal{B}}{P}[\mathbf{x}]_{\mathcal{B}}$. If $\mathcal{C}$ is the standard basis for $\mathbb{R}^n$, then $\underset{\mathcal{C}\leftarrow\mathcal{B}}{P}$ is sometimes written as $P_{\mathcal{B}}$.

characteristic equation (of A): $\det(A - \lambda I) = 0$.

characteristic polynomial (of A): $\det(A - \lambda I)$ or, in some texts, $\det(\lambda I - A)$.

Cholesky factorization: A factorization $A = R^TR$, where R is an invertible upper triangular matrix whose diagonal entries are all positive.

coefficient matrix: A matrix whose entries are the coefficients of a system.

cofactor: A number $C_{ij} = (-1)^{i+j}\det A_{ij}$, called the (i, j)-cofactor of A, where A_{ij} is the submatrix formed by deleting the ith row and the jth column of A.

cofactor expansion: A formula for $\det A$ using cofactors associated with one row or one column, such as for row 1:

$$\det A = a_{11}C_{11} + \cdots + a_{1n}C_{1n}$$

collinear (vectors): Two or more vectors (points) that lie on the same line through the origin.

column–row expansion: The expression of a product AB as a sum of outer products: $\text{col}_1(A)\text{row}_1(B) + \cdots + \text{col}_n(A)\text{row}_n(B)$, where n is the number of columns of A.

column space (of an $m\times n$ matrix A): The set Col A of all linear combinations of the columns of A. That is, $\text{Col } A = \{\mathbf{y} : \mathbf{y} = A\mathbf{x} \text{ for some } \mathbf{x} \text{ in } \mathbb{R}^n\}$.

column sum: The sum of the entries in a column of a matrix.

column vector: A matrix with only one column, or a single column of a matrix that has several columns.

commuting matrices: Two matrices A and B such that $AB = BA$.

companion matrix: A special form of matrix whose characteristic polynomial is $(-1)^n p(\lambda)$ when $p(\lambda)$ is a specified polynomial whose leading term is λ^n.

complex eigenvalue: A nonreal root of the characteristic equation of an $n\times n$ matrix A, when A is allowed to act on the complex vector space $\mathbb{C}^n$.

complex eigenvector: A nonzero vector $\mathbf{x}$ in $\mathbb{C}^n$ such that $A\mathbf{x} = \lambda\mathbf{x}$, where A is an $n\times n$ matrix and λ is a complex eigenvalue.

component of y orthogonal to u (for $\mathbf{u} \neq \mathbf{0}$): The vector

$$\mathbf{y} - \frac{\mathbf{y}\cdot\mathbf{u}}{\mathbf{u}\cdot\mathbf{u}}\mathbf{u}.$$

composition of linear transformations: A mapping produced by applying two or more linear transformations in succession. If the transformations are matrix transformations, say left-multiplication by B followed by left-multiplication by A, then the composition is the mapping $\mathbf{x} \mapsto A(B\mathbf{x})$.

condition number (of A): The quotient σ_1/σ_r, where σ_1 is the largest singular value of A and σ_r is the smallest nonzero singular value.

conformable for block multiplication: Two partitioned matrices A and B such that the block product AB is defined: The column partition of A must match the row partition of B.

consistent linear system: A linear system with at least one solution.

constrained optimization: The problem of maximizing a quantity such as $\mathbf{x}^TA\mathbf{x}$ or $\|A\mathbf{x}\|$ when $\mathbf{x}$ is subject to one or more constraints, such as $\mathbf{x}^T\mathbf{x} = 1$ or $\mathbf{x}^T\mathbf{v} = 0$.

consumption matrix: A matrix in the Leontief input–output model whose columns are the unit consumption vectors for the various sectors of an economy.

contraction: A mapping $\mathbf{x} \mapsto r\mathbf{x}$ for some scalar r, with $0 \le r \le 1$.

controllable (pair of matrices): A matrix pair (A,B) where A is $n\times n$, B has n rows, and $\text{rank}\,[B \;\; AB \;\; A^2B \;\; \cdots \;\; A^{n-1}B] = n$. Related to a state-space model of a control system and the difference equation $\mathbf{x}_{k+1} = A\mathbf{x}_k + B\mathbf{u}_k$ $(k = 0, 1, \ldots)$.

convergent (sequence of vectors): A sequence $\{\mathbf{x}_k\}$ such that the entries in $\mathbf{x}_k$ can be made as close as desired to the entries in some fixed vector for all k sufficiently large.

coordinate mapping (determined by an ordered basis $\mathcal{B}$ in a vector space V): A mapping that associates to each $\mathbf{x}$ in V its coordinate vector $[\mathbf{x}]_{\mathcal{B}}$.

coordinates of x relative to the basis $\mathcal{B} = \{\mathbf{b}_1, \ldots, \mathbf{b}_n\}$: The weights $c_1, \ldots, c_n$ in the equation $\mathbf{x} = c_1\mathbf{b}_1 + \cdots + c_n\mathbf{b}_n$.

coordinate vector of x relative to $\mathcal{B}$: The vector $[\mathbf{x}]_{\mathcal{B}}$ whose entries are the coordinates of $\mathbf{x}$ relative to the basis $\mathcal{B}$.

covariance (of variables x_i and x_j, for $i \neq j$): The entry s_{ij} in the covariance matrix S for a matrix of observations, where x_i and x_j vary over the ith and jth coordinates, respectively, of the observation vectors.

covariance matrix (or **sample covariance matrix**): The $p\times p$ matrix S defined by $S = (N-1)^{-1}BB^T$, where B is a $p\times N$ matrix of observations in mean-deviation form.

Cramer's Rule: A formula for each entry in the solution $\mathbf{x}$ of the equation $A\mathbf{x} = \mathbf{b}$ when A is an invertible matrix.

cross-product term: A term cx_ix_j in a quadratic form, with $i \neq j$.

D

decoupled system: A difference equation $\mathbf{y}_{k+1} = A\mathbf{y}_k$ where A is a diagonal matrix. The discrete evolution of a particular entry in $\mathbf{y}_k$ (as a function of k) is unaffected by what happens to the other entries as $k \to \infty$.

design matrix: The matrix X in the linear model $\mathbf{y} = \mathbf{X}\beta + \boldsymbol{\varepsilon}$, where the columns of X are determined in some way by the observed values of some independent variables.

determinant (of a square matrix A): The number det A defined inductively by a cofactor expansion along the first row of A. Also, $(-1)^r$ times the product of the diagonal entries in any echelon form U obtained from A by row replacements and r row interchanges (but no scaling operations).

diagonal entries (in a matrix): Entries having equal row and column indices.

diagonalizable (matrix): A matrix that may be written in factored form as PDP^{-1}, where D is a diagonal matrix and P is an invertible matrix.

diagonal matrix: A square matrix whose entries *not* on the main diagonal are all zero.

difference equation (or **linear recurrence relation**): An equation of the form $\mathbf{x}_{k+1} = A\mathbf{x}_k$ $(k = 0, 1, 2, \ldots)$ whose solution is a sequence of vectors, $\mathbf{x}_0, \mathbf{x}_1, \ldots$.

dilation: A mapping $\mathbf{x} \mapsto r\mathbf{x}$ for some scalar r, with $1 < r$.

dimension (of a vector space V): The number of vectors in a basis for V, written as dim V. The dimension of the zero space is 0.

discrete linear dynamical system (or briefly, a **dynamical system**): A difference equation of the form $\mathbf{x}_{k+1} = A\mathbf{x}_k$ that describes the changes in a system (usually a physical system) as time passes. The physical system is measured at discrete times, when $k = 0, 1, 2, \ldots$, and the **state** of the system at time k is a vector $\mathbf{x}_k$ whose entries provide certain facts of interest about the system.

distance between u and v: The length of the vector $\mathbf{u} - \mathbf{v}$, denoted by dist $(\mathbf{u}, \mathbf{v})$.

distance to a subspace: The distance from a given point (vector) $\mathbf{v}$ to the nearest point in the subspace.

distributive laws: (left) $A(B + C) = AB + AC$, and (right) $(B + C)A = BA + CA$, for all A, B, C.

domain (of a transformation T): The set of all vectors $\mathbf{x}$ for which $T(\mathbf{x})$ is defined.

dot product: *See* inner product.

dynamical system: *See* discrete linear dynamical system.

E

echelon form (or **row echelon form,** of a matrix): An echelon matrix that is row equivalent to the given matrix.

echelon matrix (or **row echelon matrix**): A rectangular matrix that has three properties: (1) All nonzero rows are above each row of all zeros. (2) The leading entry in each row is in a column to the right of any leading entry in a row above it. (3) All entries in a column below a leading entry are zero.

eigenspace (of A corresponding to λ): The set of *all* solutions of $A\mathbf{x} = \lambda\mathbf{x}$, where λ is an eigenvalue of A. Consists of the zero vector and all eigenvectors corresponding to λ.

eigenvalue (of A): A scalar λ such that the equation $A\mathbf{x} = \lambda\mathbf{x}$ has a solution for some nonzero vector $\mathbf{x}$.

eigenvector (of A): A *nonzero* vector $\mathbf{x}$ such that $A\mathbf{x} = \lambda\mathbf{x}$ for some scalar λ.

eigenvector basis: A basis consisting entirely of eigenvectors of a given matrix.

eigenvector decomposition (of $\mathbf{x}$): An equation, $\mathbf{x} = c_1\mathbf{v}_1 + \cdots + c_n\mathbf{v}_n$, expressing $\mathbf{x}$ as a linear combination of eigenvectors of a matrix.

elementary matrix: An invertible matrix that results by performing one elementary row operation on an identity matrix.

elementary row operations: (1) (Replacement) Replace one row by the sum of itself and a multiple of another row. (2) Interchange two rows. (3) (Scaling) Multiply all entries in a row by a nonzero constant.

equal vectors: Vectors in $\mathbb{R}^n$ whose corresponding entries are the same.

equilibrium prices: A set of prices for the total output of the various sectors in an economy, such that the income of each sector exactly balances its expenses.

equilibrium vector: *See* steady-state vector.

equivalent (linear) systems: Linear systems with the same solution set.

exchange model: *See* Leontief exchange model.

existence question: Asks, "Does a solution to the system exist?" That is, "Is the system consistent?" Also, "Does a solution of $A\mathbf{x} = \mathbf{b}$ exist for *all* possible $\mathbf{b}$?"

expansion by cofactors: *See* cofactor expansion.

explicit description (of a subspace W of $\mathbb{R}^n$): A parametric representation of W as the set of all linear combinations of a set of specified vectors.

F

factorization (of A): An equation that expresses A as a product of two or more matrices.

final demand vector (or **bill of final demands**): The vector $\mathbf{d}$ in the Leontief input-output model that lists the dollar value of the goods and services demanded from the various sectors by the nonproductive part of the economy. The vector $\mathbf{d}$ can represent consumer demand, government consumption, surplus production, exports, or other external demand.

finite-dimensional (vector space): A vector space that is spanned by a finite set of vectors.

flexibility matrix: A matrix whose jth column gives the deflections of an elastic beam at specified points when a unit force is applied at the jth point on the beam.

forward phase (of row reduction): The first part of the algorithm that reduces a matrix to echelon form.

Fourier approximation (of order n): The closest point in the subspace of nth-order trigonometric polynomials to a given function in $C[0, 2\pi]$.

Fourier coefficients: The weights used to make a trigonometric polynomial as a Fourier approximation to a function.

Fourier series: An infinite series that converges to a function in the inner product space $C[0, 2\pi]$, with the inner product given by a definite integral.

free variable: Any variable in a linear system that is not a basic variable.

full rank (matrix): An $m \times n$ matrix whose rank is the smaller of m and n.

fundamental set of solutions: A basis for the set of solutions of a homogeneous linear difference equation.

fundamental subspaces (of A): The null space and the column space of A, and the null space and the column space of A^T, with Col A^T commonly called the row space of A.

G

Gaussian elimination: *See* row reduction algorithm.

Gauss–Seidel algorithm: An iterative method that produces a sequence of vectors that in certain cases converges to a solution of an equation $A\mathbf{x} = \mathbf{b}$; based on the decomposition $A = M - N$, with M the lower triangular part of A.

general least-squares problem: Given an $m \times n$ matrix A and a vector $\mathbf{b}$ in $\mathbb{R}^m$, find $\hat{\mathbf{x}}$ in $\mathbb{R}^n$ such that $\| \mathbf{b} - A\hat{\mathbf{x}} \| \le \| \mathbf{b} - A\mathbf{x} \|$ for all $\mathbf{x}$ in $\mathbb{R}^n$.

general solution (of a linear system): A parametric description of a solution set that expresses the basic variables in terms of the free variables (the parameters), if any. After Chapter 1, the parametric description is written in vector form.

Givens rotation: A linear transformation from $\mathbb{R}^n$ to $\mathbb{R}^n$ used in computer programs to create zero entries in a vector (usually a column of a matrix).

Gram matrix (of A): The matrix A^TA.

Gram–Schmidt process: An algorithm for producing an orthogonal or orthonormal basis for a subspace that is spanned by a given set of vectors.

H

homogeneous coordinates: In $\mathbb{R}^3$, the representation of (x,y,z) as (X,Y,Z,H) for any $H \neq 0$, where $x = X/H$, $y = Y/H$, and $z = Z/H$. In $\mathbb{R}^2$, H is usually taken as 1, and the homogeneous coordinates of (x,y) are written as $(x,y,1)$.

homogeneous equation: An equation of the form $A\mathbf{x} = \mathbf{0}$, possibly written as a vector equation or as a system of linear equations.

Householder reflection: A transformation $\mathbf{x} \mapsto Q\mathbf{x}$, where $Q = I - 2\mathbf{u}\mathbf{u}^T$ and $\mathbf{u}$ is a unit vector ($\mathbf{u}^T\mathbf{u} = 1$).

I

identity matrix (denoted by I or I_n): A matrix with ones on the diagonal and zeros elsewhere.

image (of a vector $\mathbf{x}$ under a transformation T): The vector $T(\mathbf{x})$ assigned to $\mathbf{x}$ by T.

implicit description (of a subspace W of $\mathbb{R}^n$): A set of one or more homogeneous equations that characterize the points of W.

Im x: The vector in $\mathbb{R}^n$ formed from the imaginary parts of the entries of a vector $\mathbf{x}$ in $\mathbb{C}^n$.

inconsistent linear system: A linear system with no solution.

indefinite matrix: A symmetric matrix A such that $\mathbf{x}^TA\mathbf{x}$ assumes both positive and negative values.

indefinite quadratic form: A quadratic form Q such that $Q(\mathbf{x})$ assumes both positive and negative values.

infinite-dimensional (vector space): A nonzero vector space V that has no finite basis.

inner product: The scalar $\mathbf{u}^T\mathbf{v}$, usually written as $\mathbf{u} \cdot \mathbf{v}$, where $\mathbf{u}$ and $\mathbf{v}$ are vectors in $\mathbb{R}^n$ viewed as $n \times 1$ matrices. Also called the **dot product** of **u** and **v**. In general, a function on a vector space that assigns to each pair of vectors **u** and **v** a number $\langle \mathbf{u},\mathbf{v} \rangle$, subject to certain axioms. See Section 7.7.

inner product space: A vector space on which is defined an inner product.

input–output matrix: *See* consumption matrix.

input–output model: *See* Leontief input–output model.

intermediate demands: Demands for goods or services that will be consumed in the process of producing other goods and services for consumers. If **x** is the production level and C is the consumption matrix, then $C\mathbf{x}$ lists the intermediate demands.

interpolating polynomial: A polynomial whose graph passes through every point in a set of data points in $\mathbb{R}^2$.

invariant subspace (for A): A subspace H such that $A\mathbf{x}$ is in H whenever **x** is in H.

inverse (of an $n \times n$ matrix A): An $n \times n$ matrix A^{-1} such that $AA^{-1} = A^{-1}A = I_n$.

inverse power method: An algorithm for estimating an eigenvalue λ of a square matrix, when a good initial estimate of λ is available.

invertible linear transformation: A linear transformation $T:\mathbb{R}^n \to \mathbb{R}^n$ such that there exists a function $S:\mathbb{R}^n \to \mathbb{R}^n$ satisfying both $T(S(\mathbf{x})) = \mathbf{x}$ and $S(T(\mathbf{x})) = \mathbf{x}$ for all **x** in $\mathbb{R}^n$.

invertible matrix: A square matrix that possesses an inverse.

isomorphic vector spaces: Two vector spaces V and W for which there is a one-to-one linear transformation T that maps V onto W.

isomorphism: A one-to-one linear mapping from one vector space onto another.

J

Jacobi's method: An iterative method that produces a sequence of vectors that in certain cases converges to a solution of an equation $A\mathbf{x} = \mathbf{b}$; based on the decomposition $A = M - N$, with M the diagonal matrix formed from the diagonal entries in A.

K

kernel (of a linear transformation $T:V \to W$): The set of **x** in V such that $T(\mathbf{x}) = \mathbf{0}$.

Kirchhoff's laws: (1) (**current law**) The current flow into a node equals the current flow out of the node. (2) (**voltage law**) The algebraic sum of the RI voltage drops in one direction around a loop equals the algebraic sum of the voltage sources in the same direction around the loop.

L

ladder network: An electrical network assembled by connecting in series two or more electrical circuits.

leading entry: The leftmost nonzero entry in a row of a matrix.

least-squares error: The distance from **b** to $A\hat{\mathbf{x}}$, $\| \mathbf{b} - A\hat{\mathbf{x}} \|$, when **x** is a least-squares solution of $A\mathbf{x} = \mathbf{b}$.

least-squares line: The line $y = \hat{\beta}_0 + \hat{\beta}_1 x$ that minimizes the least-squares error in the equation $\mathbf{y} = X\boldsymbol{\beta} + \boldsymbol{\epsilon}$.

least-squares solution (of $A\mathbf{x} = \mathbf{b}$): A vector $\hat{\mathbf{x}}$ such that $\| \mathbf{b} - A\hat{\mathbf{x}} \| \leq \| \mathbf{b} - A\mathbf{x} \|$ for all **x** in $\mathbb{R}^n$.

left inverse (of A): Any rectangular matrix C such that $CA = I$.

left-multiplication (by A): Multiplication of a vector or matrix on the left by A.

left singular vectors (of A): The columns of U in the singular value decomposition $A = U\Sigma V^T$.

length (or **norm**, of **v**): The scalar $\| \mathbf{v} \| = \sqrt{\mathbf{v} \cdot \mathbf{v}} = \sqrt{\langle \mathbf{v},\mathbf{v} \rangle}$.

Leontief exchange (or **closed**) **model**: A model of an economy where inputs and outputs are fixed, and where a set of prices for the outputs of the sectors is sought such that the income of each sector equals its expenditures. This "equilibrium" condition is expressed as a system of linear equations, with the prices as the unknowns. Each column of the input–output matrix sums to one, and the entries in each column give the fractions of that sector's output that go to the various sectors.

Leontief input-output model (or **Leontief production equation**): The equation $\mathbf{x} = C\mathbf{x} + \mathbf{d}$, where **x** is production, **d** is final demand, and C is the consumption (or input–output) matrix.

linear combination: A sum of scalar multiples of vectors. The scalars are called the *weights*.

linear dependence relation: A homogeneous vector equation where the weights are all specified and at least one weight is nonzero.

linear equation (in the variables $x_1,\ldots,x_n$): An equation that may be written in the form $a_1x_1 + a_2x_2 + \cdots + a_nx_n = b$, where b and the coefficients $a_1,\ldots,a_n$ are real numbers.

linear filter: A linear difference equation used to transform discrete-time signals.

linearly dependent (vectors): A set $\{\mathbf{v}_1,\ldots,\mathbf{v}_p\}$ with the property that there exist weights $c_1,\ldots,c_p$, not all zero, such that $c_1\mathbf{v}_1 + \cdots + c_p\mathbf{v}_p = \mathbf{0}$. That is, the vector equation $c_1\mathbf{v}_1 + c_2\mathbf{v}_2 + \cdots + c_p\mathbf{v}_p = \mathbf{0}$ has a *nontrivial* solution.

linearly independent (vectors): A set $\{\mathbf{v}_1,\ldots,\mathbf{v}_p\}$ with the property that the vector equation $c_1\mathbf{v}_1 + c_2\mathbf{v}_2 + \cdots + c_p\mathbf{v}_p = \mathbf{0}$ has *only* the trivial solution, $c_1 = \cdots = c_p = 0$.

linear model (in statistics): Any equation of the form $\mathbf{y} = X\boldsymbol{\beta} + \boldsymbol{\varepsilon}$, where X and $\mathbf{y}$ are known and $\boldsymbol{\beta}$ is to be chosen to minimize the length of the **residual vector**, $\boldsymbol{\varepsilon}$.

linear system: A collection of one or more linear equations involving the same set of variables, say, $x_1,\ldots,x_n$.

linear transformation T (from a vector space V into a vector space W): A rule T that to each vector $\mathbf{x}$ in V assigns a unique vector $T(\mathbf{x})$ in W, such that (i) $T(\mathbf{u} + \mathbf{v}) = T(\mathbf{u}) + T(\mathbf{v})$ for all $\mathbf{u},\mathbf{v}$ in V, and (ii) $T(c\mathbf{u}) = cT(\mathbf{u})$ for all $\mathbf{u}$ in V and all scalars c. Notation: $T: V \to W$; also, $\mathbf{x} \mapsto A\mathbf{x}$ when $T:\mathbb{R}^n \to \mathbb{R}^m$ and A is the standard matrix for T.

line through p parallel to a: The set $\{\mathbf{p} + t\mathbf{a} : t \text{ in } \mathbb{R}\}$.

lower triangular matrix: A matrix with zeros above the main diagonal.

lower triangular part (of A): A lower triangular matrix whose entries on the main diagonal and below agree with those in A.

LU factorization: The representation of a matrix A in the form $A = LU$ where L is a square lower triangular matrix with ones on the diagonal (a unit lower triangular matrix) and U is upper triangular.

M

magnitude (of a vector): *See* norm.

main diagonal (of a matrix): The entries with equal row and column indices.

mapping: *See* transformation.

Markov chain: A sequence of probability vectors $\mathbf{v}_0$, $\mathbf{v}_1$, $\mathbf{v}_2,\ldots$, together with a stochastic matrix P such that $\mathbf{v}_{k+1} = P\mathbf{v}_k$ for $k = 0, 1, 2,\ldots$.

matrix: A rectangular array of numbers.

matrix equation: An equation that involves at least one matrix; for instance, $A\mathbf{x} = \mathbf{b}$.

matrix for T relative to bases $\mathcal{B}$ and $\mathcal{C}$: A matrix M for a linear transformation $T:V\to W$ with the property that $[T(\mathbf{x})]_{\mathcal{C}} = M[\mathbf{x}]_{\mathcal{B}}$ for all $\mathbf{x}$ in V, where $\mathcal{B}$ is a basis for V and $\mathcal{C}$ is a basis for W. When $W = V$ and $\mathcal{C} = \mathcal{B}$, the matrix M is called the $\mathcal{B}$-matrix for T and is denoted by $[T]_{\mathcal{B}}$.

matrix of observations: A $p \times N$ matrix whose columns are observation vectors, each column listing p measurements made on an individual or object in a specified population or set.

matrix transformation: A mapping $\mathbf{x} \mapsto A\mathbf{x}$, where A is an $m \times n$ matrix and $\mathbf{x}$ represents any vector in $\mathbb{R}^n$.

maximal linearly independent set (in V): A linearly independent set $\mathcal{B}$ in V such that if a vector $\mathbf{v}$ in V but not in $\mathcal{B}$ is added to $\mathcal{B}$, then the new set is linearly dependent.

mean-deviation form (of a matrix of observations): A matrix whose row vectors are in mean-deviation form. For each row, the entries sum to zero.

mean-deviation form (of a vector): A vector whose entries sum to zero.

mean square error: The error of an approximation in an inner product space, where the inner product is defined by a definite integral.

migration matrix: A matrix that gives the percentage movement between different locations, from one period to the next.

minimal spanning set (for a subspace H): A set $\mathcal{B}$ that spans H and has the property that if one of the elements of $\mathcal{B}$ is removed from $\mathcal{B}$, then the new set does not span H.

$m \times n$ matrix: A matrix with m rows and n columns.

Moore–Penrose inverse: *See* pseudoinverse.

multiple regression: A linear model involving several independent variables and one dependent variable.

N

negative definite matrix: A symmetric matrix A such that $\mathbf{x}^TA\mathbf{x} < 0$ for all $\mathbf{x} \neq \mathbf{0}$.

negative definite quadratic form: A quadratic form Q such that $Q(\mathbf{x}) < 0$ for all $\mathbf{x} \neq \mathbf{0}$.

negative semidefinite matrix: A symmetric matrix A such that $\mathbf{x}^T A\mathbf{x} \leq 0$ for all $\mathbf{x}$.

negative semidefinite quadratic form: A quadratic form Q such that $Q(\mathbf{x}) \leq 0$ for all $\mathbf{x}$.

network: A set of points called *junctions* or *nodes*, with lines or arcs called *branches* between some or all of the junctions. The direction of flow in each branch is indicated, and the flow amount (or rate) is either shown or denoted by a variable.

nonhomogeneous equation: An equation of the form $A\mathbf{x} = \mathbf{b}$ with $\mathbf{b} \neq \mathbf{0}$, possibly written as a vector equation or as a system of linear equations.

nonsingular (matrix): An invertible matrix.

nontrivial solution: A nonzero solution of a homogeneous equation or system of homogeneous equations.

nonzero (matrix or vector): A matrix (with possibly only one row or column) that contains at least one nonzero entry.

norm (or **length**, of $\mathbf{v}$): The scalar $\|\mathbf{v}\| = \sqrt{\mathbf{v} \cdot \mathbf{v}} = \sqrt{\langle \mathbf{v}, \mathbf{v} \rangle}$.

normal equations: The system of equations represented by $A^T A\hat{\mathbf{x}} = A^T\mathbf{b}$, whose solution yields all least-squares solutions of $A\mathbf{x} = \mathbf{b}$. In statistics, a common notation is $X^T X\boldsymbol{\beta} = X^T\mathbf{y}$.

normalizing (a vector $\mathbf{v}$): The process of creating a unit vector $\mathbf{u}$ that is a positive multiple of $\mathbf{v}$.

null space (of an $m \times n$ matrix A): The set Nul A of all solutions to the homogeneous equation $A\mathbf{x} = \mathbf{0}$. Nul $A = \{\mathbf{x} : \mathbf{x}$ is in $\mathbb{R}^n$ and $A\mathbf{x} = \mathbf{0}\}$.

O

observation vector: The vector $\mathbf{y}$ in the linear model $\mathbf{y} = X\boldsymbol{\beta} + \boldsymbol{\varepsilon}$, where the entries in y are the observed values of a dependent variable.

one-to-one (mapping): A mapping $T:\mathbb{R}^n \to \mathbb{R}^m$ such that each $\mathbf{b}$ in R^m is the image of *at most* one $\mathbf{x}$ in $\mathbb{R}^n$.

onto (mapping): A mapping $T:\mathbb{R}^n \to \mathbb{R}^m$ such that each $\mathbf{b}$ in R^m is the image of *at least* one $\mathbf{x}$ in $\mathbb{R}^n$.

ordered basis: A basis whose vectors are listed in some fixed preassigned order. A basis is assumed to be ordered whenever coordinate vectors are discussed.

origin: The zero vector.

orthogonal basis: A basis that is also an orthogonal set.

orthogonal complement (of W): The set $W^\perp$ of all vectors orthogonal to W.

orthogonal decomposition: The representation of a vector $\mathbf{y}$ as the sum of two vectors, one in a specified subspace W and the other in $W^\perp$. In general, a decomposition $\mathbf{y} = c_1\mathbf{u}_1 + \cdots + c_p\mathbf{u}_p$, where $\{\mathbf{u}_1,\ldots,\mathbf{u}_p\}$ is an orthogonal basis for a subspace that contains $\mathbf{y}$.

orthogonally diagonalizable (matrix): A matrix A that admits a factorization, $A = PDP^{-1}$, with P an orthogonal matrix ($P^{-1} = P^T$) and D diagonal.

orthogonal matrix: A square invertible matrix U such that $U^{-1} = U^T$.

orthogonal projection of y onto u (or onto the line through $\mathbf{u}$ and the origin for $\mathbf{u} \neq \mathbf{0}$): The vector $\hat{\mathbf{y}}$ defined by $\hat{\mathbf{y}} = \dfrac{\mathbf{y} \cdot \mathbf{u}}{\mathbf{u} \cdot \mathbf{u}}\mathbf{u}$.

orthogonal projection of y onto *W*: The unique vector $\hat{\mathbf{y}}$ in W such that $\mathbf{y} - \hat{\mathbf{y}}$ is orthogonal to W. Notation: $\hat{\mathbf{y}} = \text{proj}_W\mathbf{y}$.

orthogonal set: A set S of vectors such that $\mathbf{u} \cdot \mathbf{v} = 0$ for each distinct pair $\mathbf{u},\mathbf{v}$ in S.

orthogonal to *W*: Orthogonal to every vector in W.

orthonormal basis: A basis that is an orthogonal set of unit vectors.

orthonormal set: An orthogonal set of unit vectors.

outer product: A matrix product $\mathbf{u}\mathbf{v}^T$ where $\mathbf{u}$ and $\mathbf{v}$ are vectors in $\mathbb{R}^n$ viewed as $n \times 1$ matrices. (The transpose symbol is on the "outside" of the symbols $\mathbf{u}$ and $\mathbf{v}$.)

overdetermined system: A system of equations with more equations than unknowns.

P

parallelogram rule for addition: A geometric interpretation of the sum of two vectors $\mathbf{u},\mathbf{v}$ as the diagonal of the parallelogram determined by $\mathbf{u}$, $\mathbf{v}$, and $\mathbf{0}$.

parameter vector: The unknown vector $\boldsymbol{\beta}$ in the linear model $\mathbf{y} = X\boldsymbol{\beta} + \boldsymbol{\varepsilon}$.

parametric equation of a line: An equation of the form $\mathbf{x} = \mathbf{p} + t\mathbf{a}$, where t is a parameter.

parametric equation of a plane: An equation of the form $\mathbf{x} = \mathbf{p} + c\mathbf{u} + d\mathbf{v}$, where c and d are parameters.

partitioned matrix (or **block matrix**): A matrix whose entries are themselves matrices of appropriate sizes.

permuted lower triangular matrix: A matrix such that a permutation of its rows will form a lower triangular matrix.

permuted LU factorization: The representation of a matrix A in the form $A = LU$ where L is a square matrix such that a permutation of its rows will form a unit lower triangular matrix, and U is upper triangular.

pivot: A nonzero number that either is used in a pivot position to create zeros through row operations or is changed into a leading 1, which in turn is used to create zeros.

pivot column: A column that contains a pivot position.

pivot position: A position that will contain a leading entry when the matrix is reduced to echelon form.

polar decomposition (of A): A factorization $A = PQ$, where P is an $n \times n$ positive semidefinite matrix with the same rank as A, and Q is an $n \times n$ orthogonal matrix.

positive definite matrix: A symmetric matrix A such that $\mathbf{x}^T A \mathbf{x} > 0$ for all $\mathbf{x} \neq \mathbf{0}$.

positive definite quadratic form: A quadratic form Q such that $Q(\mathbf{x}) > 0$ for all $\mathbf{x} \neq \mathbf{0}$.

positive semidefinite matrix: A symmetric matrix A such that $\mathbf{x}^T A \mathbf{x} \geq 0$ for all $\mathbf{x}$.

positive semidefinite quadratic form: A quadratic form Q such that $Q(\mathbf{x}) \geq 0$ for all $\mathbf{x}$.

power method: An algorithm for estimating a (strictly) dominant eigenvalue of a square matrix.

principal axes (of a quadratic form $\mathbf{x}^T A \mathbf{x}$): The orthonormal columns of an orthogonal matrix P such that $P^{-1}AP$ is diagonal. (These columns are unit eigenvectors of A.) Usually the columns of P are ordered in such a way that the corresponding eigenvalues of A are arranged in decreasing order of magnitude.

principal components (of the data in a matrix of observations B): The unit eigenvectors of a sample covariance matrix S for B, with the eigenvectors arranged so that the corresponding eigenvalues of S decrease in magnitude. If B is in mean-deviation form, then the principal components are the right singular vectors in a singular value decomposition of B^T.

probability vector: A vector in $\mathbb{R}^n$ whose entries are nonnegative and sum to one.

product $A\mathbf{x}$: The linear combination of the columns of A using the entries in $\mathbf{x}$ as weights.

production vector: The vector in the Leontief input–output model that lists the amounts that are to be produced by the various sectors of an economy.

projection matrix (or **orthogonal projection matrix**): A symmetric matrix B such that $B^2 = B$. A simple example is $B = \mathbf{v}\mathbf{v}^T$, where $\mathbf{v}$ is a unit vector.

proper subspace: Any subspace of a vector space V other than V itself.

pseudoinverse (of A): The matrix $VD^{-1}U^T$, when UDV^T is a reduced singular value decomposition of A.

Q

quadratic form: A function Q defined for $\mathbf{x}$ in $\mathbb{R}^n$ by $Q(\mathbf{x}) = \mathbf{x}^T A \mathbf{x}$ where A is an $n \times n$ symmetric matrix (called the **matrix of the quadratic form**).

QR factorization: A factorization of an $m \times n$ matrix A with linearly independent columns, $A = QR$, where Q is an $m \times n$ matrix whose columns form an orthonormal basis for Col A, and R is an $n \times n$ upper triangular invertible matrix.

R

range (of a linear transformation T): The set of all vectors of the form $T(\mathbf{x})$ for some $\mathbf{x}$ in the domain of T.

rank (of a matrix A): The dimension of the column space of A, denoted by rank A.

Rayleigh quotient: $R(\mathbf{x}) = (\mathbf{x}^T A \mathbf{x})/(\mathbf{x}^T \mathbf{x})$. An estimate of an eigenvalue of A (usually a symmetric matrix).

recurrence relation: *See* difference equation.

reduced echelon form (or **reduced row echelon form,** of a matrix): A reduced echelon matrix that is row equivalent to the given matrix.

reduced echelon matrix: A rectangular matrix in echelon form that has these additional properties: The leading entry in each nonzero row is 1, and each leading 1 is the only nonzero entry in its column.

reduced singular value decomposition: A factorization $A = UDV^T$, for an $m \times n$ matrix A of rank r, where U is $m \times r$ with orthonormal columns, D is $r \times r$ with the r nonzero singular values of A on its diagonal, and V is $n \times r$ with orthonormal columns.

regression coefficients: The coefficients β_0 and β_1 in the least-squares line $y = \beta_0 + \beta_1 x$.

regular stochastic matrix: A stochastic matrix P such that some matrix power P^k contains only strictly positive entries.

repellor (of a dynamical system $\mathbf{x}_{k+1} = A\mathbf{x}_k$): The origin in $\mathbb{R}^n$ when all eigenvalues of A are greater than 1 in magnitude. All trajectories except the constant $\mathbf{0}$ sequence tend away from $\mathbf{0}$.

residual vector: The quantity $\boldsymbol{\varepsilon}$ that appears in the general linear model: $\mathbf{y} = X\boldsymbol{\beta} + \boldsymbol{\varepsilon}$; that is, $\boldsymbol{\varepsilon} = \mathbf{y} - X\boldsymbol{\beta}$, the difference between the observed values and the predicted values (of y).

Re $\mathbf{x}$: The vector in $\mathbb{R}^n$ formed from the real parts of the entries of a vector $\mathbf{x}$ in $\mathbb{C}^n$.

right inverse (of A): Any rectangular matrix C such that $AC = I$.

right singular vectors (of A): The columns of V in the singular value decomposition $A = U\Sigma V^T$.

row–column rule: The rule for computing a product AB in which the (i, j)-entry of AB is the sum of the products of corresponding entries from row i of A and column j of B.

row equivalent (matrices): Two matrices for which there exists a (finite) sequence of row operations that transforms one matrix into the other.

row reduced (matrix): A matrix that has been transformed by elementary row operations into a matrix in echelon form.

row reduction algorithm: A systematic method using elementary row operations that reduces a matrix to echelon form or reduced echelon form.

row replacement: An elementary row operation that replaces one row of a matrix by the sum of the row and a multiple of another row.

row space (of a matrix A): The set Row A of all linear combinations of the vectors formed from the rows of A; also denoted by Col A^T.

row sum: The sum of the entries in a row of a matrix.

row vector: A matrix with only one row, or a single row of a matrix that has several rows.

rule for computing $A\mathbf{x}$: The ith entry of $A\mathbf{x}$ as the sum of the products of corresponding entries from row i of A and from the vector $\mathbf{x}$.

S

saddle point (of a dynamical system $\mathbf{x}_{k+1} = A\mathbf{x}_k$): The origin in $\mathbb{R}^n$ when some eigenvalue of A is greater than 1 in magnitude and some eigenvalue is less than 1 in magnitude. Some points $\mathbf{x}$ are attracted to $\mathbf{0}$ and some are repelled away from $\mathbf{0}$.

same direction (as a vector $\mathbf{v}$): A vector that is a positive multiple of $\mathbf{v}$.

sample mean: The average $\mathbf{M}$ of a set of vectors, $\mathbf{X}_1, \ldots, \mathbf{X}_N$, given by $\mathbf{M} = (1/N)(\mathbf{X}_1 + \cdots + \mathbf{X}_N)$.

scalar: A (real) number used to multiply a vector or matrix.

scalar multiple of u by c: The vector $c\mathbf{u}$ obtained by multiplying each entry in $\mathbf{u}$ by c.

scale (a vector): Multiply a vector (or a row or column of a matrix) by a nonzero scalar.

Schur complement: A certain matrix formed from the blocks of a 2×2 partitioned matrix $A = [A_{ij}]$. If A_{11} is invertible, its Schur complement is given by $A_{22} - A_{21}A_{11}^{-1}A_{12}$. If A_{22} is invertible, its Schur complement is given by $A_{11} - A_{12}A_{22}^{-1}A_{21}$.

Schur factorization (of A, for real scalars): A factorization $A = URU^T$ of an $n\times n$ matrix A having n real eigenvalues, where U is an $n\times n$ orthogonal matrix and R is an upper triangular matrix.

set spanned by $\{\mathbf{v}_1, \ldots, \mathbf{v}_p\}$: The set Span $\{\mathbf{v}_1, \ldots, \mathbf{v}_p\}$.

signal (or **discrete-time signal**): A doubly infinite sequence of numbers, $\{y_k\}$; a function defined on the integers; belongs to the vector space $\mathbb{S}$.

similar (matrices): Matrices A and B such that $P^{-1}AP = B$, or equivalently, $A = PBP^{-1}$, for some invertible matrix P.

similarity transformation: A transformation of a matrix, $A \mapsto P^{-1}AP$.

singular (matrix): A square matrix that has no inverse.

singular value decomposition (of an $m\times n$ matrix A): $A = U\Sigma V^T$, where U is an $m\times m$ orthogonal matrix, V is an $n\times n$ orthogonal matrix, and Σ is an $m\times n$ matrix with nonnegative entries on the main diagonal (arranged in decreasing order of magnitude) and zeros elsewhere. If rank $A = r$, then Σ has exactly r positive entries (the nonzero singular values of A) on the diagonal.

singular values (of A): The (positive) square roots of the eigenvalues of A^TA, arranged in decreasing order of magnitude.

size (of a matrix): Two numbers, written in the form $m\times n$, that specify the number of rows (m) and columns (n) in the matrix.

solution (of a linear system): A list $(s_1, s_2, \ldots, s_n)$ of numbers that makes each equation in the system into a true statement when the values $s_1, \ldots, s_n$ are substituted for $x_1, \ldots, x_n$, respectively.

solution set: The set of all possible solutions of a linear system.

Span $\{\mathbf{v}_1, \ldots, \mathbf{v}_p\}$: The set of all linear combinations of $\mathbf{v}_1, \ldots, \mathbf{v}_p$. Also, the *subspace spanned* (or *generated*) by $\mathbf{v}_1, \ldots, \mathbf{v}_p$.

spanning set (for a subspace H): Any set $\{\mathbf{v}_1, \ldots, \mathbf{v}_p\}$ in H such that $H = $ Span $\{\mathbf{v}_1, \ldots, \mathbf{v}_p\}$.

spectral decomposition (of A): A representation $A = \lambda_1\mathbf{v}_1\mathbf{v}_1^T + \cdots + \lambda_n\mathbf{v}_n\mathbf{v}_n^T$, where $\{\mathbf{v}_1, \ldots, \mathbf{v}_n\}$ is an orthonormal basis of eigenvectors of A, and $\lambda_1, \ldots, \lambda_n$ are eigenvalues of A.

stage-matrix model: A difference equation $\mathbf{x}_{k+1} = A\mathbf{x}_k$ where $\mathbf{x}_k$ lists the number of females in a population at time k, with the females classified by various stages of development (such as juvenile, subadult, and adult).

standard basis: The basis $\mathscr{E} = \{\mathbf{e}_1, \ldots, \mathbf{e}_n\}$ for $\mathbb{R}^n$ consisting of the columns of the $n \times n$ identity matrix, or the basis $\{1, t, \ldots, t^n\}$ for $\mathbb{P}_n$.

standard matrix (for a linear transformation T): The matrix A such that $T(\mathbf{x}) = A\mathbf{x}$ for all $\mathbf{x}$ in the domain of T.

standard position: The position of the graph of an equation $\mathbf{x}^T A\mathbf{x} = c$ when A is a diagonal matrix.

state vector: A probability vector. In general, a vector that describes the "state" of a physical system, often in connection with a difference equation $\mathbf{x}_{k+1} = A\mathbf{x}_k$.

steady-state vector (for a stochastic matrix P): A probability vector $\mathbf{v}$ such that $P\mathbf{v} = \mathbf{v}$.

stiffness matrix: The inverse of a flexibility matrix. The jth column of a stiffness matrix gives the loads that must be applied at specified points on an elastic beam in order to produce a unit deflection at the jth point on the beam.

stochastic matrix: A square matrix whose columns are probability vectors.

strictly diagonally dominant (matrix): A matrix with the property that the absolute value of each diagonal entry exceeds the *sum* of the absolute values of the other entries in the same row.

strictly dominant eigenvalue: An eigenvalue λ_1 of a matrix A with the property that $|\lambda_1| > |\lambda_k|$ for all other eigenvalues λ_k of A.

submatrix (of A): Any matrix obtained by deleting some rows and/or columns of A; also, A itself.

subspace: A subset H of some vector space V such that H is itself a vector space under the operations of vector addition and scalar multiplication defined on V.

subspace test: Three conditions that are necessary and sufficient for a subset of a vector space V to be a subspace of V. See Theorem 1 in Section 5.1.

symmetric matrix: A matrix A such that $A^T = A$.

system of linear equations (or a **linear system**): A collection of one or more linear equations involving the same set of variables, say, $x_1, \ldots, x_n$.

T

total variance: The trace of the covariance matrix S of a matrix of observations.

trace (of a square matrix A): The sum of the diagonal entries in A, denoted by tr A.

trajectory: The graph of a solution $\{\mathbf{x}_0, \mathbf{x}_1, \mathbf{x}_2, \ldots\}$ of a dynamical system $\mathbf{x}_{k+1} = A\mathbf{x}_k$, often connected by a thin curve, to make the trajectory easier to see.

transfer matrix: A matrix A associated with an electrical circuit having input and output terminals, such that the output vector is A times the input vector.

transformation (or **function** or **mapping**) T from $\mathbb{R}^n$ to $\mathbb{R}^m$: A rule that assigns to each vector $\mathbf{x}$ in $\mathbb{R}^n$ a unique vector $T(\mathbf{x})$ in $\mathbb{R}^m$. Notation: $T: \mathbb{R}^n \to \mathbb{R}^m$. Also, $T: V \to W$ denotes a rule that assigns to each $\mathbf{x}$ in V a unique vector $T(\mathbf{x})$ in W.

translation (by a vector $\mathbf{p}$): The operation of adding $\mathbf{p}$ to a vector or to each vector in a given set.

transpose (of A): An $n \times m$ matrix A^T whose columns are the corresponding rows of the $m \times n$ matrix A.

trend analysis: The use of orthogonal polynomials to fit data, with the inner product given by evaluation at a finite set of points.

triangle inequality: $\|\mathbf{u} + \mathbf{v}\| \leq \|\mathbf{u}\| + \|\mathbf{v}\|$ for all $\mathbf{u}, \mathbf{v}$.

trigonometric polynomial: A linear combination of the constant function 1 and sine and cosine functions such as $\cos nt$ and $\sin nt$.

trivial solution: The solution $\mathbf{x} = \mathbf{0}$ of a homogeneous equation $A\mathbf{x} = \mathbf{0}$.

U

uncorrelated variables: Any two variables x_i and x_j (with $i \neq j$) that range over the ith and jth coordinates of the observation vectors in an observation matrix, such that the covariance s_{ij} is zero.

underdetermined system: A system of equations with fewer equations than unknowns.

uniqueness question: Asks, "If a solution of a system exists, is it unique; that is, is it the only one?"

unit consumption vector: A column vector in the Leontief input–output model that lists the inputs a sector needs for each unit of its output; a column of the consumption matrix.

unit lower triangular matrix: A square lower triangular matrix with ones on the main diagonal.

unit vector: A vector $\mathbf{v}$ such that $\|\mathbf{v}\| = 1$.

upper triangular matrix: A matrix U with zeros below the diagonal entries $u_{11}, u_{22}, \ldots$.

V

Vandermonde matrix: an $n \times n$ matrix V or its transpose, when V has the form

$$V = \begin{bmatrix} 1 & x_1 & x_1^2 & \cdots & x_1^{n-1} \\ 1 & x_2 & x_2^2 & \cdots & x_2^{n-1} \\ \cdot & \cdot & \cdot & & \cdot \\ \cdot & \cdot & \cdot & & \cdot \\ \cdot & \cdot & \cdot & & \cdot \\ 1 & x_n & x_n^2 & \cdots & x_n^{n-1} \end{bmatrix}$$

variance (of a variable x_j): The diagonal entry s_{jj} in the covariance matrix S for a matrix of observations, where x_j varies over the jth coordinates of the observation vectors.

vector: A list of numbers; a matrix with only one column. In general, any element of a vector space.

vector addition: Adding vectors by adding corresponding entries.

vector equation: An equation involving a linear combination of vectors with undetermined weights.

vector space: A set of objects, called vectors, on which two operations are defined, called addition and multiplication by scalars (real numbers). Ten axioms must be satisfied. See the first definition in Section 5.1.

vector subtraction: Computing $\mathbf{u} + (-1)\mathbf{v}$ and writing the result as $\mathbf{u} - \mathbf{v}$.

W

weighted least squares: Least-squares problems with a weighted inner product such as $\langle \mathbf{x},\mathbf{y} \rangle = w_1^2 x_1 y_1 + \cdots + w_n^2 x_n y_n$.

weights: The scalars used in a linear combination.

Z

zero subspace: The subspace $\{\mathbf{0}\}$ consisting of only the zero vector.

zero vector: The unique vector, denoted by $\mathbf{0}$, such that $\mathbf{u} + \mathbf{0} = \mathbf{u}$ for all $\mathbf{u}$. In $\mathbb{R}^n$, $\mathbf{0}$ is the vector whose entries are all zero.

ANSWERS TO ODD-NUMBERED EXERCISES

CHAPTER 1

Section 1.1, page 10

1. $(-10, 2)$ **3.** Inconsistent

5. Interchange rows 2 and 3.

7. Either interchange rows 3 and 4, or multiply row 3 by 1/2.

9. $(-5, 5, 3)$ **11.** Inconsistent **13.** $(8, 13, 10, 4)$

15. $(18, -5, 4)$ **17.** $(2, 1, -1)$ **19.** Inconsistent

Note: The matrices you obtain in Exercises 21–26 may differ from the ones listed here. But your conclusions about the consistency of the systems should be the same as the answers given here.

21. Row equivalent to $\begin{bmatrix} 1 & -5 & -4 & 0 \\ 0 & 1 & 2 & -3 \\ 0 & 0 & 3 & -5 \end{bmatrix}$, hence consistent.

23. Row equivalent to $\begin{bmatrix} 1 & 3 & -1 & 2 \\ 0 & 1 & -2 & 4 \\ 0 & 0 & 8 & -3 \end{bmatrix}$, hence consistent.

25. Row equivalent to $\begin{bmatrix} 1 & 0 & 0 & -2 & -3 \\ 0 & 1 & 1 & 0 & 0 \\ 0 & 0 & 1 & 3 & -4 \\ 0 & 0 & 0 & 0 & -5 \end{bmatrix}$, hence inconsistent.

27. $h = 5/2$ **29.** $h \neq -1/2$

31. Multiply row 2 by 1/2; multiply row 2 by 2.

33. Add -2 times row 2 to row 3; add 2 times row 2 to row 3.

Section 1.2, page 22

1. Reduced echelon: a, b; only echelon: c

3. Reduced echelon: c; only echelon: a, b

5. a. $\begin{bmatrix} 1 & 0 & 0 \\ 0 & 1 & 0 \\ 0 & 0 & 1 \end{bmatrix}$; pivot cols 1, 2, 3

b. $\begin{bmatrix} 1 & 0 & -1 & -2 \\ 0 & 1 & 2 & 3 \\ 0 & 0 & 0 & 0 \end{bmatrix}$; pivot cols 1, 2

c. $\begin{bmatrix} 1 & 3 & 0 & 0 & 3 \\ 0 & 0 & 1 & 0 & 0 \\ 0 & 0 & 0 & 1 & 1/3 \\ 0 & 0 & 0 & 0 & 0 \end{bmatrix}$; pivot cols 1, 3, 4

7. $\begin{cases} x_1 = -3 \\ x_2 \text{ is free} \\ x_3 = 4 \end{cases}$ **9.** $\begin{cases} x_1 = 4 - 4x_3 \\ x_2 = 3 - 2x_3 \\ x_3 \text{ is free} \end{cases}$

11. $\begin{cases} x_1 = -7 - 4x_2 \\ x_2 \text{ is free} \\ x_3 = 5 \end{cases}$ **13.** $\begin{cases} x_1 = \frac{3}{2} + 2x_2 \\ x_2 \text{ is free} \end{cases}$

15. Inconsistent **17.** Inconsistent

19. $\begin{cases} x_1 = -1 - x_5 \\ x_2 = 1 + 3x_5 \\ x_3 \text{ is free} \\ x_4 = -4 - 5x_5 \\ x_5 \text{ is free} \end{cases}$ 21. $\begin{cases} x_1 = 2x_3 \\ x_2 = -8 - 6x_3 \\ x_3 \text{ is free} \\ x_4 = -5 \\ x_5 = 0 \end{cases}$

23. Any h 25. $h \neq 4$

27. **a.** $h = -6$, and $k \neq 2$
b. $h \neq -6$ **c.** $h = -6$, and $k = 2$

29. The system is inconsistent because the pivot in column 5 means that there is a row of the form $[\,0 \quad 0 \quad 0 \quad 0 \quad 1\,]$. Since the matrix is the *augmented* matrix for a system, Theorem 2 shows that the system has no solution.

31. An underdetermined system always has more variables than equations. There cannot be more basic variables than there are equations, so there must be at least one free variable. Such a variable may be assigned infinitely many different values. If the system is consistent, each different value of a free variable will produce a different solution.

33. *Hint*: What do pivot columns in a coefficient matrix have to do with free variables in the system of equations?

Warning: Although the Study Guide has complete solutions for *every* odd-numbered exercise whose answer here is only a "Hint," you *must* really try to work the solution yourself. Otherwise, you will not benefit from the exercise.

Section 1.3, page 31

1. $\begin{cases} x_1 = 20 - x_3 \\ x_2 = 60 + x_3 \\ x_3 \text{ is free} \\ x_4 = 60 \end{cases}$. The largest value of x_3 is 20.

3. **a.** $\begin{cases} x_1 = -40 + x_3 \\ x_2 = 10 + x_3 \\ x_3 \text{ is free} \\ x_4 = 50 + x_6 \\ x_5 = 60 + x_6 \\ x_6 \text{ is free} \end{cases}$ **b.** $\begin{cases} x_2 = 50 \\ x_3 = 40 \\ x_4 = 50 \\ x_5 = 60 \end{cases}$

5. $5I + 7I = 12 + 6$
$I = 1.5$ amps

7. $\begin{aligned} I_1 - I_2 + I_3 &= 0 \\ 6I_1 + 2I_2 \qquad &= 0 \\ 2I_2 + 3I_3 &= 18 \end{aligned}$ $\begin{cases} I_1 = -1 \text{ amp} \\ I_2 = 3 \text{ amps} \\ I_3 = 4 \text{ amps} \end{cases}$

9. $\begin{aligned} I_1 + I_2 - I_3 &= 0 \\ 5I_1 - 5I_2 \qquad &= 5 \\ 5I_2 + 5I_3 &= 35 \end{aligned}$ $\begin{cases} I_1 = 3 \text{ amps} \\ I_2 = 2 \text{ amps} \\ I_3 = 5 \text{ amps} \end{cases}$

11. $p_{\text{Goods}} = \frac{7}{8} p_{\text{Services}}$, where p_{Services} is free. A typical solution would be $p_{\text{Services}} = 80$ and $p_{\text{Goods}} = 70$.

13. **a.**

Distribution of Output			
Chemicals	Fuels	Machinery	Purchased by
.2	.8	.4	Chemicals
.3	.1	.4	Fuels
.5	.1	.2	Machinery

b. $\begin{bmatrix} .8 & -.8 & -.4 & 0 \\ -.3 & .9 & -.4 & 0 \\ -.5 & -.1 & .8 & 0 \end{bmatrix}$

c. $p_{\text{Chemicals}} = 141.7$, $p_{\text{Fuels}} = 91.7$, $p_{\text{Machinery}} = 100$. To two significant figures:

$$p_{\text{Chemicals}} = 140, \quad p_{\text{Fuels}} = 92, \quad p_{\text{Machinery}} = 100$$

Supplementary Exercises, page 34

1. **a.** T **b.** F **c.** F **d.** T **e.** F **f.** T **g.** F **h.** T **i.** F **j.** T **k.** F **l.** T **m.** F **n.** F **o.** T

2. If $a = 0$ and $b \neq 0$, the solution set is empty, because $0x = 0 \neq b$. If $a \neq 0$, then $x = b/a$; the solution is unique. If $a = 0$ and $b = 0$, the equation $0x = 0$ has infinitely many solutions.

3. **a.** A system of three equations with infinitely many solutions
b. A system of three equations with a unique solution
c. A system of three equations with no solution

4. A system of two linear equations in three variables is represented by two planes. Either these planes are distinct and parallel, or they intersect in a line, or they coincide. In the first case, the solution set is empty. In the other cases, the solution set contains infinitely many solutions.

5. A matrix in echelon form is also in reduced echelon form if and only if each pivot column contains 1 in the pivot position and zeros elsewhere.

6. An echelon form of an augmented matrix provides answers to existence and uniqueness questions. A reduced echelon form of an augmented matrix provides the solution to a system of equations, if a solution exists.

7. If the coefficient matrix has a pivot position in every row, then there is a pivot position in the bottom row and there is no room for a pivot in the augmented column. So the system is consistent, by Theorem 2.

8. Since there are three pivots (one in each row), the augmented matrix must reduce to the form

$$\begin{bmatrix} 1 & 0 & 0 & * \\ 0 & 1 & 0 & * \\ 0 & 0 & 1 & * \end{bmatrix}$$

Clearly, a solution exists and is unique.

9. a. The solution set: (i) is empty if $h = 8$ and $k \neq 5/4$; (ii) contains a unique solution if $h \neq 8$; and (iii) contains infinitely many solutions if $h = 8$ and $k = 5/4$.
b. The solution set: (i) is empty if $2h + k = 0$; (ii) contains a unique solution if $2h + k \neq 0$; and (iii) cannot contain infinitely many solutions.

10. a. An echelon form of the augmented matrix is

$$\begin{bmatrix} 2 & -1 & h \\ 0 & -1 & k+3h \end{bmatrix}$$

This cannot have a pivot in the augmented column, so the system is consistent for all h and k.
b. An echelon form of the augmented matrix is

$$\begin{bmatrix} 2 & -1 & h \\ 0 & 0 & k+3h \end{bmatrix}$$

If $k + 3h \neq 0$, there is a pivot in the augmented column and the system is inconsistent. The system is consistent if and only if $k + 3h - 0$.

11. a. $2g + h + k = 0$ **b.** $-5g + 4h + k = 0$

12. a. $x_1 = 5/7 \approx .7143$; $x_2 = 2/7 \approx .2857$
b. $x_1 = 10x_3$; $x_2 = 2x_3$; x_3 is free

13. $p(t) = 7 + 6t - t^2$ **14.** $15.2 - 16.3t + 6.3t^2 - .7t^3$

CHAPTER 2

Section 2.1, page 46

1. $\begin{bmatrix} 5 \\ 1 \end{bmatrix}, \begin{bmatrix} -1 \\ 4 \end{bmatrix}$

3.

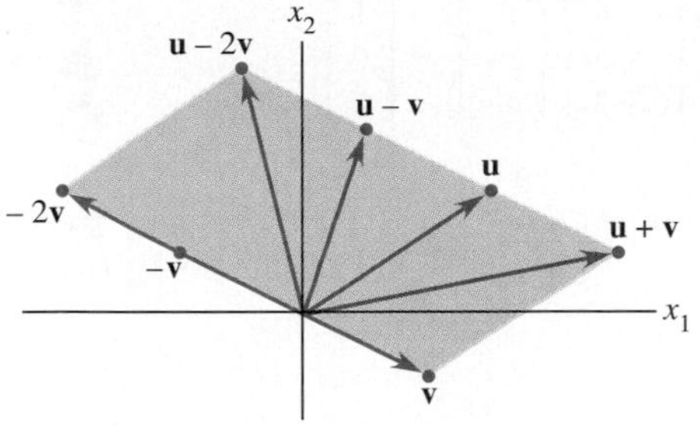

5. $\mathbf{a} = -\frac{5}{4}\mathbf{b} - \frac{3}{2}\mathbf{c}$ **7.** $s = 5, t = 3$ **9.** $\begin{bmatrix} 6 \\ 6 \\ -6 \end{bmatrix}$

11.
$$\begin{aligned} 3x_1 - 2x_2 &= 8 \\ x_1 \quad\quad &= -6 \\ -5x_1 + 4x_2 &= 3 \end{aligned}$$

13. $x_1 \begin{bmatrix} 2 \\ 1 \\ 0 \end{bmatrix} + x_2 \begin{bmatrix} -1 \\ -8 \\ 4 \end{bmatrix} + x_3 \begin{bmatrix} 5 \\ 2 \\ -4 \end{bmatrix} = \begin{bmatrix} 3 \\ 5 \\ 5 \end{bmatrix}$

15. Yes **17.** No **19.** No **21.** $h = 3$

23. *Hint*: Show that $\begin{bmatrix} 2 & 2 & h \\ -1 & 1 & k \end{bmatrix}$ is consistent for all h and k. Explain what this calculation shows about Span$\{\mathbf{u}, \mathbf{v}\}$.

25. a. No, three **b.** Yes, infinitely many
c. $\mathbf{a}_1 = 1\cdot\mathbf{a}_1 + 0\cdot\mathbf{a}_2 + 0\cdot\mathbf{a}_3$

27. a. $5\mathbf{v}_1$ is 5 days' output of mine 1.
b. The total output is $x_1\mathbf{v}_1 + x_2\mathbf{v}_2$, so x_1 and x_2 should satisfy

$$x_1\mathbf{v}_1 + x_2\mathbf{v}_2 = \begin{bmatrix} 150 \\ 2825 \end{bmatrix}$$

29. $(1.3, .9, 0)$

Section 2.2, page 54

1. $A\mathbf{x} = 5\begin{bmatrix} 2 \\ 3 \end{bmatrix} - 3\begin{bmatrix} 4 \\ 5 \end{bmatrix} = \begin{bmatrix} 10 \\ 15 \end{bmatrix} + \begin{bmatrix} -12 \\ -15 \end{bmatrix} = \begin{bmatrix} -2 \\ 0 \end{bmatrix}$,
and $A\mathbf{x} = \begin{bmatrix} 2\cdot5 + 4\cdot(-3) \\ 3\cdot5 + 5\cdot(-3) \end{bmatrix} = \begin{bmatrix} -2 \\ 0 \end{bmatrix}$. Show your work here and for Exercises 2–6, but thereafter perform the calculations mentally.

3. $A\mathbf{x} = 1\cdot\begin{bmatrix} 5 \\ -4 \end{bmatrix} + 1\cdot\begin{bmatrix} 2 \\ 4 \end{bmatrix} + 1\cdot\begin{bmatrix} 1 \\ 7 \end{bmatrix} = \begin{bmatrix} 8 \\ 7 \end{bmatrix}$, and
$A\mathbf{x} = \begin{bmatrix} 5\cdot1 + 2\cdot1 + 1\cdot1 \\ -4\cdot1 + 4\cdot1 + 7\cdot1 \end{bmatrix} = \begin{bmatrix} 8 \\ 7 \end{bmatrix}$

5. The product is not defined.

7. $\begin{bmatrix} 3 & -1 & 4 \\ -4 & 1 & -5 \\ 0 & 1 & -3 \end{bmatrix}\begin{bmatrix} x_1 \\ x_2 \\ x_3 \end{bmatrix} = \begin{bmatrix} 1 \\ 0 \\ 6 \end{bmatrix}$

9. $x_1\begin{bmatrix} 2 \\ 0 \\ -3 \end{bmatrix} + x_2\begin{bmatrix} 4 \\ 1 \\ -5 \end{bmatrix} + x_3\begin{bmatrix} -6 \\ 3 \\ 7 \end{bmatrix} = \begin{bmatrix} 2 \\ 5 \\ -3 \end{bmatrix}$

11. $\mathbf{x} = \begin{bmatrix} 0 \\ 2 \\ 1 \end{bmatrix}$

13. $2\begin{bmatrix} 4 \\ -7 \end{bmatrix} + 6\begin{bmatrix} -2 \\ 1 \end{bmatrix} - 1\begin{bmatrix} -5 \\ -8 \end{bmatrix} + 0\begin{bmatrix} 9 \\ -3 \end{bmatrix} = \begin{bmatrix} 1 \\ 0 \end{bmatrix}$

15. $\begin{bmatrix} -4 & 3 \\ 1 & -5 \\ 4 & 2 \end{bmatrix}\begin{bmatrix} x_1 \\ x_2 \end{bmatrix} = \begin{bmatrix} -2 \\ 0 \\ 3 \end{bmatrix}$ **17.** Yes

19. The equation $A\mathbf{x} = \mathbf{b}$ is not consistent unless $2b_1 + b_2 = 0$. The set of $\mathbf{b}$ for which the equation *is* consistent is a line through the origin: $x_2 = -2x_1$.

21. 3 rows **23.** No **25.** Yes **27.** No

29. $c_1 = -1$, $c_2 = 4$, $c_3 = 2$

31. $A(\mathbf{u}+\mathbf{v}) = \begin{bmatrix} 5 & 1 & -3 \\ 7 & -2 & 1 \end{bmatrix}\begin{bmatrix} -1 \\ 4 \\ 3 \end{bmatrix} = \begin{bmatrix} -10 \\ -12 \end{bmatrix}$,

$A\mathbf{u} + A\mathbf{v} = \begin{bmatrix} -1 \\ 4 \end{bmatrix} + \begin{bmatrix} -9 \\ -16 \end{bmatrix} = \begin{bmatrix} -10 \\ -12 \end{bmatrix}$

33. Use the fact that $A(\mathbf{x}_1 + \mathbf{x}_2) = A\mathbf{x}_1 + A\mathbf{x}_2$, so that $A(\mathbf{x}_1 + \mathbf{x}_2) = \mathbf{y}_1 + \mathbf{y}_2 = \mathbf{w}$.

35. *Hint*: Use a theorem from this section.

Section 2.3, page 61

1. $\mathbf{x} = \mathbf{a} + t\mathbf{b}$, or $\begin{bmatrix} x_1 \\ x_2 \end{bmatrix} = \begin{bmatrix} 3 \\ -8 \end{bmatrix} + t\begin{bmatrix} -1 \\ 5 \end{bmatrix}$, or

$\begin{cases} \mathbf{x}_1 = 3 - t \\ \mathbf{x}_2 = -8 + 5t \end{cases}$

3. $\begin{bmatrix} x_1 \\ x_2 \end{bmatrix} = \begin{bmatrix} -1 \\ 4 \end{bmatrix} + t\begin{bmatrix} 1 \\ 3 \end{bmatrix}$, or $\begin{cases} \mathbf{x}_1 = -1 + t \\ \mathbf{x}_2 = 4 + 3t \end{cases}$

5. No **7.** Yes, there are at most two basic variables.

9. $x_3\begin{bmatrix} 5 \\ 1 \\ 1 \end{bmatrix}$ **11.** $x_2\begin{bmatrix} 2 \\ 1 \\ 0 \\ 0 \end{bmatrix} + x_4\begin{bmatrix} -5/3 \\ 0 \\ 2/3 \\ 1 \end{bmatrix}$

13. $x_2\begin{bmatrix} 5 \\ 1 \\ 0 \\ 0 \\ 0 \\ 0 \end{bmatrix} + x_3\begin{bmatrix} 0 \\ 0 \\ 1 \\ 0 \\ 0 \\ 0 \end{bmatrix} + x_6\begin{bmatrix} -2 \\ 0 \\ 0 \\ 3 \\ -5 \\ 1 \end{bmatrix}$

15. $x_2\begin{bmatrix} 4 \\ 1 \\ 0 \end{bmatrix} + x_3\begin{bmatrix} -3 \\ 0 \\ 1 \end{bmatrix}$

17. The solution set is the line through $\begin{bmatrix} 4 \\ -1 \\ 0 \end{bmatrix}$ parallel to $\begin{bmatrix} -3 \\ 6 \\ 1 \end{bmatrix}$.

19. $\begin{bmatrix} 7 \\ 4 \\ 0 \end{bmatrix} + x_3\begin{bmatrix} 5 \\ 1 \\ 1 \end{bmatrix}$. The solution set is the line through $\begin{bmatrix} 7 \\ 4 \\ 0 \end{bmatrix}$, parallel to the line that is the solution set of the homogeneous system in Exercise 9.

21. Let $\mathbf{p} = \begin{bmatrix} 7 \\ 0 \\ 0 \end{bmatrix}$, $\mathbf{u} = \begin{bmatrix} 4 \\ 1 \\ 0 \end{bmatrix}$, $\mathbf{v} = \begin{bmatrix} -3 \\ 0 \\ 1 \end{bmatrix}$. The solution set of the homogeneous equation is the plane Span $\{\mathbf{u}, \mathbf{v}\}$ spanned by $\mathbf{u}$ and $\mathbf{v}$. The solution set of the nonhomogeneous equation is the translated plane $\mathbf{p}$ + Span $\{\mathbf{u}, \mathbf{v}\}$, which passes through $\mathbf{p}$.

23. $A\mathbf{w} = A(\mathbf{u}+\mathbf{v}) = A\mathbf{u} + A\mathbf{v} = \mathbf{0} + \mathbf{0} = \mathbf{0}$, by Theorem 3.

25. **a.** $A\mathbf{w} = A(\mathbf{p} + \mathbf{v}_h) = A\mathbf{p} + A\mathbf{v}_h = \mathbf{b} + \mathbf{0} = \mathbf{b}$
b. $A\mathbf{v}_h = A(\mathbf{w} - \mathbf{p}) = A\mathbf{w} - A\mathbf{p} = \mathbf{b} - \mathbf{b} = \mathbf{0}$

27. The solution set is all of $\mathbb{R}^3$.

29. **a.** No **b.** Yes **31.** **a.** No **b.** No

33. One answer: $\mathbf{x} = \begin{bmatrix} -2 \\ 1 \end{bmatrix}$

Section 2.4, page 69

1. Lin. indep. **3.** Lin. dep. **5.** Lin. indep.

7. Lin. dep. **9.** Lin. indep. **11.** Lin. dep.

13. **a.** No h **b.** All h **15.** $h = -7$ **17.** All h

19. Lin. dep. **21.** Lin. dep. **23.** Lin. indep.

25. A: any 3×2 matrix with nonzero columns that are not multiples of each other; B: any 3×2 matrix with one column a multiple of the other.

27. $\mathbf{x} = \begin{bmatrix} 1 \\ 1 \\ -1 \end{bmatrix}$ **29.** True, by Theorem 5

31. True, because there are more vectors than entries in each vector.

33. True. A linear dependence relation among $\mathbf{v}_1, \mathbf{v}_2, \mathbf{v}_3$ may be extended to a linear dependence relation among $\mathbf{v}_1, \mathbf{v}_2, \mathbf{v}_3, \mathbf{v}_4$ by placing a zero weight on $\mathbf{v}_4$.

35. 5 pivot columns

37. *Hint*: Consider one appropriate equation.

Section 2.5, page 77

1. $\begin{bmatrix} 3 \\ 15 \end{bmatrix}, \begin{bmatrix} -12 \\ -3 \end{bmatrix}$ **3.** $\begin{bmatrix} 4 \\ 3 \\ 4 \end{bmatrix}$, yes **5.** $\begin{bmatrix} -4 \\ 1 \\ 0 \end{bmatrix}$, no

7. $a = 5, b = 7$ **9.** $x_3 \begin{bmatrix} 5 \\ -3 \\ 1 \\ 0 \end{bmatrix} + x_4 \begin{bmatrix} -3 \\ 2 \\ 0 \\ 1 \end{bmatrix}$ **11.** No

13. b. A reflection through the origin

15. A contraction

17. A reflection through the line $x_1 = x_2$

19. $\begin{bmatrix} 4 \\ 0 \end{bmatrix}, \begin{bmatrix} 3 \\ -12 \end{bmatrix}, \begin{bmatrix} 7 \\ -12 \end{bmatrix}$ **21.** $\begin{bmatrix} 9 \\ 7 \end{bmatrix}, \begin{bmatrix} 3x_1 - 2x_2 \\ -5x_1 + 7x_2 \end{bmatrix}$

23. *Hint*: Use the parametric equation of a line, which describes a typical point on the line through $\mathbf{p}$ in the direction of $\mathbf{v}$.

25. *Hint*: Since $\{\mathbf{v}_1, \mathbf{v}_2, \mathbf{v}_3\}$ is linearly dependent, you can write a certain equation and work with it.

27. a. Let $f(x) = mx$. For x, y in $\mathbb{R}$ and any scalars c, d,

$$\begin{aligned} f(cx + dy) &= m(cx + dy) = mcx + mdy \\ &= c(mx) + d(my) \\ &= c \cdot f(x) + d \cdot f(y) \end{aligned}$$

b. $f(0) = m(0) + b = b \neq 0$ **c.** The graph of f is a line.

29. One possibility: $T(0, 0) = (0, 4, 0) \neq (0, 0, 0)$; that is, T does not map the zero vector into the zero vector.

Section 2.6, page 84

1. $\begin{bmatrix} 4 & -5 \\ -1 & 3 \\ 2 & -6 \end{bmatrix}$ **3.** $\begin{bmatrix} 1 & -2 & 3 \\ 4 & 9 & -8 \end{bmatrix}$ **5.** $\begin{bmatrix} -1 & 0 \\ 0 & -1 \end{bmatrix}$

7. $\begin{bmatrix} 1 & 0 \\ 0 & -1 \end{bmatrix}$ **9.** $\begin{bmatrix} 0 & -1 \\ -1 & 0 \end{bmatrix}$ **11.** $\begin{bmatrix} 1 & 0 & 0 \\ 0 & 1 & 0 \\ 0 & 0 & 0 \end{bmatrix}$

13. $\begin{bmatrix} 1 & 0 \\ 2 & 1 \end{bmatrix}$ **15.** $\begin{bmatrix} 0 & 2 & -1 \\ 1 & 1 & -1 \\ 1 & 0 & 0 \end{bmatrix}$ **17.** $\begin{bmatrix} 0 & 0 & 1 \\ 0 & 1 & 0 \\ 1 & 0 & 0 \end{bmatrix}$

19. $\begin{bmatrix} 0 & 3 & -1 \\ 1 & 4 & 1 \end{bmatrix}$ **21.** $\begin{bmatrix} 1 & 1 & 0 & 0 \\ 0 & 1 & 1 & 0 \\ 0 & 0 & 1 & 1 \\ 0 & 0 & 0 & 0 \end{bmatrix}$

23. $\begin{bmatrix} -3 \\ 1 \end{bmatrix}$ **25.** No **27.** Yes

29. Not one-to-one, not onto $\mathbb{R}^4$

31. n. See Study Guide for an explanation.

33. *Hint*: If $\mathbf{e}_j$ is the jth column of the identity matrix, then $B\mathbf{e}_j$ is the jth column of B.

35. *Hint*: Either $m < n$ or $m > n$ is impossible. Decide which.

Section 2.7, page 90

1. a. $x_1 \begin{bmatrix} 110 \\ 4 \\ 20 \\ 2 \end{bmatrix} + x_2 \begin{bmatrix} 130 \\ 3 \\ 18 \\ 5 \end{bmatrix} = \begin{bmatrix} 295 \\ 9 \\ 48 \\ 8 \end{bmatrix}$, where x_1 is the number of servings of Cheerios and x_2 is the number of servings of 100% Natural Cereal.
b. 3/2 serving of Cheerios together with 1 serving of 100% Natural Cereal

3. $\begin{bmatrix} 36 & 51 & 13 & 80 \\ 52 & 34 & 74 & 0 \\ 0 & 7 & 1.1 & 3.4 \\ 1.26 & .19 & .8 & .18 \end{bmatrix} \begin{bmatrix} x_1 \\ x_2 \\ x_3 \\ x_4 \end{bmatrix} = \begin{bmatrix} 33 \\ 45 \\ 3 \\ .8 \end{bmatrix}$, where $x_1, \ldots, x_4$, represent the number of units (100 g) of nonfat milk, soy flour, whey, and soy protein, respectively, to be used in the mixture. The solution is $x_1 = .64, x_2 = .54, x_3 = -.09, x_4 = -.21$. This solution is not feasible, because negative amounts of whey and isolated soy protein are impossible.

5. a. $\mathbf{x}_{k+1} = M\mathbf{x}_k$, for $k = 0, 1, 2, \ldots,$ where $M = \begin{bmatrix} .96 & .03 \\ .04 & .97 \end{bmatrix}$, and $\mathbf{x}_0 = \begin{bmatrix} 600{,}000 \\ 400{,}000 \end{bmatrix}$
b. The population in 1992 (when $k = 2$) is $\mathbf{x}_2 = \begin{bmatrix} 576{,}840 \\ 423{,}160 \end{bmatrix}$.

7. a. $M = \begin{bmatrix} .98285 & .002576 \\ .01715 & .997424 \end{bmatrix}$

b. $\mathbf{x}_{10} = \begin{bmatrix} 30{,}215{,}000 \\ 218{,}495{,}000 \end{bmatrix}$ To the nearest thousand

c. 12.15% in California in 2000, and 87.85% elsewhere in U.S.

9. a. The population of the city decreases. After 7 years, the populations are about equal, but the city population continues to decline. The decrease each year seems to grow smaller. After 20 years, there are only 417,000 persons in the city. (*Note*: 417,456, rounded to the nearest thousand.)

b. The population of the city increases, but not very fast. After 20 years, the population has grown from 350,000 to 370,000 persons. (*Note*: 370,283, rounded to the nearest thousand.)

Supplementary Exercises, page 92

1. a. T **b.** F **c.** F **d.** T **e.** F **f.** F **g.** F **h.** F **i.** F **j.** F **k.** F **l.** T **m.** T **n.** T **o.** T

2. a. Let $\mathbf{v}_1 = \begin{bmatrix} 3 \\ -6 \end{bmatrix}$, $\mathbf{v}_2 = \begin{bmatrix} -1 \\ 3 \end{bmatrix}$, $\mathbf{v}_3 = \begin{bmatrix} 2 \\ -7 \end{bmatrix}$, and $\mathbf{b} = \begin{bmatrix} 1 \\ 5 \end{bmatrix}$. "Determine if $\mathbf{b}$ is a linear combination of $\mathbf{v}_1, \mathbf{v}_2, \mathbf{v}_3$." Or, "Determine if $\mathbf{b}$ is in Span $\{\mathbf{v}_1, \mathbf{v}_2, \mathbf{v}_3\}$." Solution: Yes, $\mathbf{b}$ is a linear combination of $\mathbf{v}_1, \mathbf{v}_2, \mathbf{v}_3$.

b. Let $A = \begin{bmatrix} 3 & -1 & 2 \\ -6 & 3 & -7 \end{bmatrix}$. "Determine if $\mathbf{b}$ is in the set spanned by the columns of A."

c. Define $T(\mathbf{x}) = A\mathbf{x}$. "Determine if $\mathbf{b}$ is in the range of T."

3. a. Let $\mathbf{v}_1 = \begin{bmatrix} 1 \\ -5 \\ 3 \end{bmatrix}$, $\mathbf{v}_2 = \begin{bmatrix} -2 \\ 3 \\ 1 \end{bmatrix}$, and $\mathbf{b} = \begin{bmatrix} b_1 \\ b_2 \\ b_3 \end{bmatrix}$.

Determine if Span $\{\mathbf{v}_1, \mathbf{v}_2\} = \mathbb{R}^3$. Solution: No.

b. Let $A = \begin{bmatrix} 1 & -2 \\ -5 & 3 \\ 3 & 1 \end{bmatrix}$. Determine if the columns of A span $\mathbb{R}^3$.

c. Define $T(\mathbf{x}) = A\mathbf{x}$. Determine if T maps $\mathbb{R}^2$ onto $\mathbb{R}^3$.

4. By Theorem 2 in Section 2.2, A must have a pivot in each of its 3 rows. Since A has 3 columns, each column must be a pivot column. So the equation $A\mathbf{x} = \mathbf{0}$ can have no free variables, and the columns of A are linearly independent. By Theorem 10 in Section 2.6, the transformation $\mathbf{x} \mapsto A\mathbf{x}$ is one-to-one.

5. If $T(\mathbf{u}) = \mathbf{v}$, then since T is linear,

$$T(-\mathbf{u}) = T((-1)\mathbf{u}) = (-1)T(\mathbf{u}) = -\mathbf{v}$$

6. Write $A = [\,\mathbf{v}_4 \;\; \mathbf{v}_3 \;\; \mathbf{v}_2 \;\; \mathbf{v}_1\,]$. The pattern of zero entries in the vectors makes it obvious that $\mathbf{v}_1$ is not zero, $\mathbf{v}_2$ is not a multiple of $\mathbf{v}_1$, $\mathbf{v}_3$ is not a linear combination of $\mathbf{v}_1$ and $\mathbf{v}_2$, and $\mathbf{v}_4$ is not a linear combination of $\mathbf{v}_1, \mathbf{v}_2, \mathbf{v}_3$. By Theorem 5 in Section 2.4, $\{\mathbf{v}_1, \mathbf{v}_2, \mathbf{v}_3, \mathbf{v}_4\}$ is linearly independent. So the columns of A are linearly independent.

7. *Hint*: First write a parametric equation of the line.

8. $A = \begin{bmatrix} 1 & 0 & 0 \\ 0 & -1 & 0 \\ 0 & 0 & 1 \end{bmatrix}$ **9.** $a = 4/5, b = -3/5$

10. $a = 1/\sqrt{5}, b = -2/\sqrt{5}$

CHAPTER 3

Section 3.1, page 105

1. $\begin{bmatrix} -14 & 0 & 2 \\ 2 & -10 & -4 \end{bmatrix}$ **3.** $\begin{bmatrix} -15 & 4 & 3 \\ 7 & -13 & -4 \end{bmatrix}$

5. Not defined **7.** $\begin{bmatrix} -7 & 4 \\ -4 & 0 \end{bmatrix}$

9. $\begin{bmatrix} -1 & 1 \\ -3 & 5 \end{bmatrix}, \begin{bmatrix} 12 & -3 \\ 9 & -6 \end{bmatrix}$ **11.** $\begin{bmatrix} 5 & 0 \\ 4 & -4 \\ -3 & -7 \end{bmatrix}$ **13.** 5×7

15. $(CD)E$ takes 12 multiplications; $C(DE)$ takes 8. Both $= \begin{bmatrix} -61 \\ -28 \end{bmatrix}$.

17. $AB = AC = \begin{bmatrix} 7 & -2 \\ 21 & -6 \end{bmatrix}$

19. AD is obtained by multiplying the columns of A by 2, 3, and 4, respectively. DA is obtained by multiplying the rows of A by 2, 3, and 4, respectively. Any diagonal matrix of the form λI, where λ is a scalar, will commute with A.

21. The first two columns of AB are $A\mathbf{b}_1$ and $A\mathbf{b}_2$. They are equal, since $\mathbf{b}_1$ and $\mathbf{b}_2$ are equal.

23. The third column of AB is the sum of the first two columns of AB. Here's why. Denote the first three columns of B by $\mathbf{b}_1, \mathbf{b}_2, \mathbf{b}_3$. If $\mathbf{b}_3 = \mathbf{b}_1 + \mathbf{b}_2$, then the third column of AB is $A\mathbf{b}_3 = A\mathbf{b}_1 + A\mathbf{b}_2$, by a property of matrix-vector multiplication.

25. The columns of A are linearly dependent. Why?

27. $A^T = \begin{bmatrix} 1 & -3 \\ 2 & 4 \end{bmatrix}$, $B^T = \begin{bmatrix} -8 & -7 \\ 4 & 5 \end{bmatrix}$, $A^T + B^T = \begin{bmatrix} -7 & -10 \\ 6 & 9 \end{bmatrix}$, $(A+B)^T = \begin{bmatrix} -7 & 6 \\ -10 & 9 \end{bmatrix}^T = \begin{bmatrix} -7 & -10 \\ 6 & 9 \end{bmatrix}$

29. $AB = \begin{bmatrix} -22 & 14 \\ -4 & 8 \end{bmatrix}$, $(AB)^T = \begin{bmatrix} -22 & -4 \\ 14 & 8 \end{bmatrix}$,

$A^T B^T = \begin{bmatrix} -20 & -22 \\ 0 & 6 \end{bmatrix}$, $B^T A^T = \begin{bmatrix} -22 & -4 \\ 14 & 8 \end{bmatrix}$

31. $\mathbf{u}^T\mathbf{v} = [\,-2 \quad 3 \quad -4\,]\begin{bmatrix} a \\ b \\ c \end{bmatrix} = -2a + 3b - 4c$,

$\mathbf{v}^T\mathbf{u} = -2a + 3b - 4c$

$\mathbf{u}\mathbf{v}^T = \begin{bmatrix} -2 \\ 3 \\ -4 \end{bmatrix}[\,a \quad b \quad c\,] = \begin{bmatrix} -2a & -2b & -2c \\ 3a & 3b & 3c \\ -4a & -4b & -4c \end{bmatrix}$

$\mathbf{v}\mathbf{u}^T = \begin{bmatrix} a \\ b \\ c \end{bmatrix}[\,-2 \quad 3 \quad -4\,] = \begin{bmatrix} -2a & 3a & -4a \\ -2b & 3b & -4b \\ -2c & 3c & -4c \end{bmatrix}$

33. AB is 5×5, BA is 2×2, $(AB)^T$ is 5×5, $(BA)^T$ is 2×2, $A^T B^T$ is 2×2, $B^T A^T$ is 5×5. $(AB)^T$ cannot equal $A^T B^T$ because they are different sizes.

35. *Hint*: Let r be a scalar, and denote the jth columns of A and B by $\mathbf{a}_j$ and $\mathbf{b}_j$, respectively. Show that the jth columns of $r(A+B)$ and $rA + rB$ are equal.

37. *Hint*: Show that the (i, j)-entry of $A(B+C)$, given in the statement of the exercise, equals the (i, j)-entry of $AB + AC$.

39. *Hint*: Use the row–column rule to write the (i, j)-entry of each matrix in Theorem 2(d).

41. *Hint*: Let $\mathbf{e}_j$ and $\mathbf{a}_j$ denote the jth columns of I_n and A, respectively, and use the definition of matrix multiplication.

43. *Hint*: Denote the jth column of B by $\mathbf{b}_j$, and consider the jth row of $(AB)^T$. Use a property of matrix multiplication that describes the rows of a product.

Section 3.2, page 114

1. $\begin{bmatrix} 3 & 8 \\ 1 & 3 \end{bmatrix}$ **3.** $\begin{bmatrix} -13/3 & -7/3 \\ -2 & -1 \end{bmatrix}$ **5.** $\mathbf{x} = \begin{bmatrix} 31 \\ 11 \end{bmatrix}$

7. a and **b**: $\begin{bmatrix} 13 \\ -4 \end{bmatrix}, \begin{bmatrix} -6 \\ 2 \end{bmatrix}, \begin{bmatrix} 7 \\ -2 \end{bmatrix}, \begin{bmatrix} -3 \\ 2 \end{bmatrix}$.

9. a. The proof can be modeled after the proof of Theorem 5.
b. *Hint:* Write $B = [\,\mathbf{b}_1 \quad \cdots \quad \mathbf{b}_p\,]$. Another idea that works is to consider a sequence of elementary matrices that reduces A to I via left-multiplication, and examine what that sequence does to B.

11. Suppose that $\mathbf{x}$ satisfies $A\mathbf{x} = \mathbf{0}$. Since A is invertible, Theorem 5 implies that $\mathbf{x} = A^{-1}\mathbf{0} = \mathbf{0}$.

13. $AB = AC \Rightarrow A^{-1}AB = A^{-1}AC \Rightarrow IB = IC \Rightarrow B = C$. No. In general, B and C may be different, if A is not invertible.

15. $D = C^{-1}B^{-1}A^{-1}$

17. $A = BCB^{-1}$ (In general, $BCB^{-1} \neq C$.)

19. $X = CB - A$

21. *Hint*: Consider the vector $\begin{bmatrix} -b \\ a \end{bmatrix}$ and use the fact that $ad - bc = 0$. Also consider the case when $a = b = 0$.

23. Interchanges the corresponding two rows of A; yes

25. Multiplies the third row of A by 5; yes

27. $E = \begin{bmatrix} 1 & 0 & 0 & 0 \\ 0 & 1 & 0 & 0 \\ 0 & 0 & 1 & 0 \\ 0 & -3 & 0 & 1 \end{bmatrix}$; $EA = \begin{bmatrix} 1 & 0 & 0 & 0 \\ 2 & 1 & 0 & 0 \\ 3 & 2 & 1 & 0 \\ -2 & 0 & 2 & 1 \end{bmatrix}$,

which results from adding $-3\cdot\text{row}_2(A)$ to $\text{row}_4(A)$. E would have the same effect on any 4×4 matrix.

29. $\begin{bmatrix} -9 & 2 \\ 5 & -1 \end{bmatrix}$ **31.** $\begin{bmatrix} 6 & 10 & -5 \\ -6 & -9 & 5 \\ -1 & -2 & 1 \end{bmatrix}$

33. $\begin{bmatrix} 8 & -24 & 7 \\ -2 & 7 & -2 \\ 1 & -3 & 1 \end{bmatrix}$ **35.** $\begin{bmatrix} 5 \\ -8 \\ 5 \end{bmatrix}$

37. .21, .26, and .17 inch.

39. If A were invertible, then the equation $CA = I$ would imply that $CAA^{-1} = IA^{-1}$, and $C = A^{-1}$, in which case AC would be I. However, A cannot be invertible, because

$$AC = \begin{bmatrix} 7 & 6 & -3 \\ -4 & -3 & 2 \\ 6 & 6 & -2 \end{bmatrix}$$

Section 3.3, page 120

To save space in the answers, we use IMT to denote the Invertible Matrix Theorem (Theorem 8).

1. No, by the IMT. The columns are linearly dependent, since they are multiples. Another reason is that the determinant is zero.

3. No, by the IMT. The columns are linearly dependent, since they include the zero vector.

5. Yes, by the IMT. The matrix is row equivalent to $\begin{bmatrix} 1 & -7 & 5 \\ 0 & 3 & -6 \\ 0 & 0 & -5 \end{bmatrix}$ and hence has 3 pivot columns.

7. No, by the IMT. The matrix is row equivalent to $\begin{bmatrix} 1 & 0 & 3 \\ 0 & 3 & 4 \\ 0 & 0 & 0 \end{bmatrix}$ and hence is *not* row equivalent to I.

9. Yes, by the IMT. The matrix is row equivalent to $\begin{bmatrix} 1 & 3 & 0 & -1 \\ 0 & 1 & -2 & -1 \\ 0 & 0 & 3 & 0 \\ 0 & 0 & 0 & -4 \end{bmatrix}$ and hence has 4 pivot columns.

11. Yes, after a few row operations, one sees that the matrix has 4 pivot columns.

13. A square upper triangular matrix is invertible if and only if the entries on the diagonal are nonzero. The same holds true for a square lower triangular matrix.

15. G is not invertible because statement (b) of the IMT is false. So statement (d′) is false, too. The columns of G are linearly dependent.

17. Statement (d′) of the IMT is true, so (e′) is true, too. The equation $P\mathbf{x} = \mathbf{b}$ has a unique solution for all $\mathbf{b}$ in $\mathbb{R}^5$.

19. Statement (e) of the IMT is false, so (d) is false, too. The equation $B\mathbf{x} = \mathbf{0}$ has a nontrivial solution.

21. *Hint*: Use a theorem in Section 3.2.

23. *Hint*: Use the IMT first.

25. *Hint*: Define $C = B(AB)^{-1}$ and compute AC. Unfortunately, by itself this computation does not prove that A is invertible. Why not?

27. *Hint*: To show that T is one-to-one, suppose that $T(\mathbf{u}) = T(\mathbf{v})$ for some vectors $\mathbf{u}$ and $\mathbf{v}$ in $\mathbb{R}^n$, and deduce that $\mathbf{u} = \mathbf{v}$. To show that T is onto, take $\mathbf{y}$ in $\mathbb{R}^n$ and use S to produce an $\mathbf{x}$ such that $T(\mathbf{x}) = \mathbf{y}$. Use Eqs. (1) and (2) for these arguments. A second explanation can be given using Theorem 9 together with a theorem from Section 2.6.

29. $T^{-1}(\mathbf{x}) = B\mathbf{x}$, where $B = \begin{bmatrix} 7 & 9 \\ 4 & 5 \end{bmatrix}$. What theorem justifies this?

31. The goal is to show that $S(\mathbf{v})$ and $U(\mathbf{v})$ are equal for all $\mathbf{v}$ in $\mathbb{R}^n$, which will show that S and V are equal as functions. Use the hint already given in the exercise.

Section 3.4, page 126

1. $\begin{bmatrix} A & B \\ EA + C & EB + D \end{bmatrix}$ **3.** $\begin{bmatrix} C & D \\ A & B \end{bmatrix}$

5. $X = -CA^{-1}$, $Y = D - CA^{-1}B$

7. $X = -A_{21}A_{11}^{-1}$, $Y = -A_{31}A_{11}^{-1}$, $B_{22} = A_{22} - A_{21}A_{11}^{-1}A_{12}$

9. $\begin{bmatrix} I & -A & -B \\ 0 & I & 0 \\ 0 & 0 & I \end{bmatrix}$ **11.** $[A \quad B]\begin{bmatrix} \mathbf{u} \\ \mathbf{v} \end{bmatrix} = \mathbf{y}$

13. The calculations in Example 5 showed that if A is invertible, then both A_{11} and A_{22} are invertible. Conversely, suppose A_{11} and A_{22} are both invertible, and define B to be the matrix that Example 5 says should be the inverse of A. Verify that $AB = I$. Why does this imply that A is invertible?

15. $G_{k+1} = [X_k \quad \mathbf{x}_{k+1}]\begin{bmatrix} X_k^T \\ \mathbf{x}_{k+1}^T \end{bmatrix} = X_kX_k^T + \mathbf{x}_{k+1}\mathbf{x}_{k+1}^T = G_k + \mathbf{x}_{k+1}\mathbf{x}_{k+1}^T$. Only the outer product matrix $\mathbf{x}_{k+1}\mathbf{x}_{k+1}^T$ needs to be computed (and then added to G_k).

17. $W(s) = I_m - C(A - sI_n)^{-1}B$. This is the Schur complement of $A - sI_n$ in the system matrix.

19. If A and B are $(k+1)\times(k+1)$ and lower triangular, then we may write $A = \begin{bmatrix} a & \mathbf{0}^T \\ \mathbf{x} & A_1 \end{bmatrix}$ and $B = \begin{bmatrix} b & \mathbf{0}^T \\ \mathbf{y} & B_1 \end{bmatrix}$, where A_1 and B_1 are $k\times k$ and lower triangular, $\mathbf{x}$ and $\mathbf{y}$ are in $\mathbb{R}^n$, and a and b are suitable scalars. Assume that the product of any $k\times k$ lower triangular matrices is lower triangular, and compute the product AB. What do you conclude?

Section 3.5, page 134

1. $L\mathbf{y} = \mathbf{b} \Rightarrow \mathbf{y} = \begin{bmatrix} -7 \\ -2 \\ 6 \end{bmatrix}$, $U\mathbf{x} = \mathbf{y} \Rightarrow \mathbf{x} = \begin{bmatrix} 3 \\ 4 \\ -6 \end{bmatrix}$

3. $\mathbf{y} = \begin{bmatrix} 1 \\ 3 \\ 3 \end{bmatrix}$, $\mathbf{x} = \begin{bmatrix} -1 \\ 3 \\ 3 \end{bmatrix}$ **5.** $\mathbf{y} = \begin{bmatrix} 1 \\ 5 \\ 1 \\ -3 \end{bmatrix}$, $\mathbf{x} = \begin{bmatrix} -2 \\ -1 \\ 2 \\ -3 \end{bmatrix}$

7. $LU = \begin{bmatrix} 1 & 0 \\ -3/2 & 1 \end{bmatrix}\begin{bmatrix} 2 & 5 \\ 0 & 7/2 \end{bmatrix}$

9. $\begin{bmatrix} 1 & 0 & 0 \\ -1 & 1 & 0 \\ 3 & 2/3 & 1 \end{bmatrix}\begin{bmatrix} 3 & -1 & 2 \\ 0 & -3 & 12 \\ 0 & 0 & -8 \end{bmatrix}$

11. $\begin{bmatrix} 1 & 0 & 0 \\ 2 & 1 & 0 \\ -1/3 & 1 & 1 \end{bmatrix}\begin{bmatrix} 3 & -6 & 3 \\ 0 & 5 & -4 \\ 0 & 0 & 5 \end{bmatrix}$

13. $\begin{bmatrix} 1 & 0 & 0 & 0 \\ -1 & 1 & 0 & 0 \\ 4 & 5 & 1 & 0 \\ -2 & -1 & 0 & 1 \end{bmatrix} \begin{bmatrix} 1 & 3 & -5 & -3 \\ 0 & -2 & 3 & 1 \\ 0 & 0 & 0 & 0 \\ 0 & 0 & 0 & 0 \end{bmatrix}$

15. $\begin{bmatrix} 1 & 0 & 0 \\ 3 & 1 & 0 \\ -1/2 & -2 & 1 \end{bmatrix} \begin{bmatrix} 2 & -4 & 4 & -2 \\ 0 & 3 & -5 & 3 \\ 0 & 0 & 0 & 5 \end{bmatrix}$

17. $U^{-1} = \begin{bmatrix} 1/4 & 3/8 & 1/4 \\ 0 & -1/2 & 1/2 \\ 0 & 0 & 1/2 \end{bmatrix}, L^{-1} = \begin{bmatrix} 1 & 0 & 0 \\ 1 & 1 & 0 \\ -2 & 0 & 1 \end{bmatrix},$

$A^{-1} = \begin{bmatrix} 1/8 & 3/8 & 1/4 \\ -3/2 & -1/2 & 1/2 \\ -1 & 0 & 1/2 \end{bmatrix}$

19. *Hint*: Think about row reducing $[\,A \quad I\,]$.

21. *Hint*: Represent the row operations by a sequence of elementary matrices.

23. a. Denote the rows of D as transposes of column vectors. Then partitioned matrix multiplication yields

$$A = CD = [\,\mathbf{c}_1 \quad \cdots \quad \mathbf{c}_4\,] \begin{bmatrix} \mathbf{v}_1^T \\ \vdots \\ \mathbf{v}_4^T \end{bmatrix} = \mathbf{c}_1\mathbf{v}_1^T + \cdots + \mathbf{c}_4\mathbf{v}_4^T$$

b. A has 40,000 entries. Since C has 1600 entries and D has 400 entries, together they occupy only 5% of the memory needed to store A.

25. Explain why U, D, and V^T are invertible. Then use a theorem on the inverse of a product of invertible matrices.

27. a.

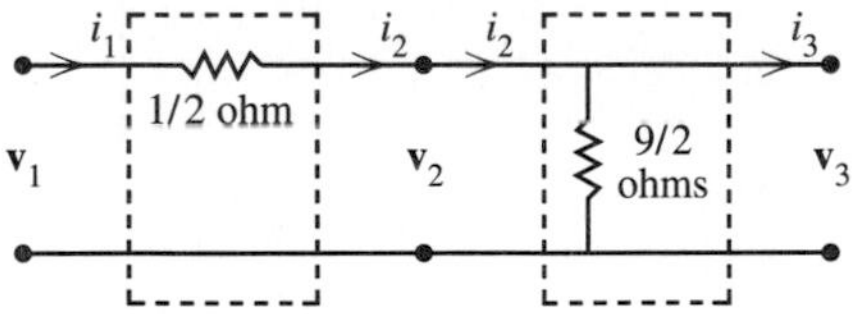

b.

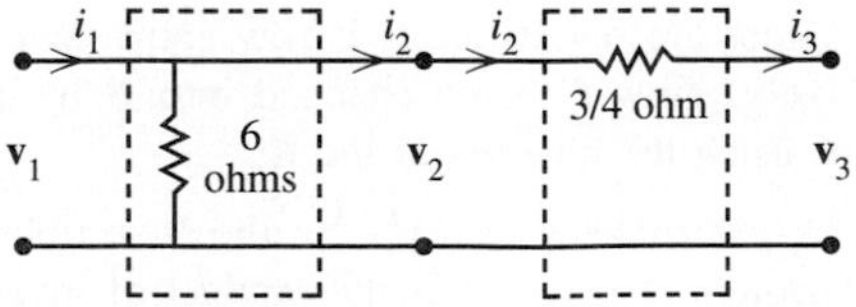

29. a. $\begin{bmatrix} 1 + R_2/R_1 & -R_2 \\ -1/R_1 - R_2/(R_1R_3) - 1/R_3 & 1 + R_2/R_3 \end{bmatrix}$

b. $A = \begin{bmatrix} 1 & 0 \\ -1/6 & 1 \end{bmatrix} \begin{bmatrix} 1 & -12 \\ 0 & 1 \end{bmatrix} \begin{bmatrix} 1 & 0 \\ -1/36 & 1 \end{bmatrix}$

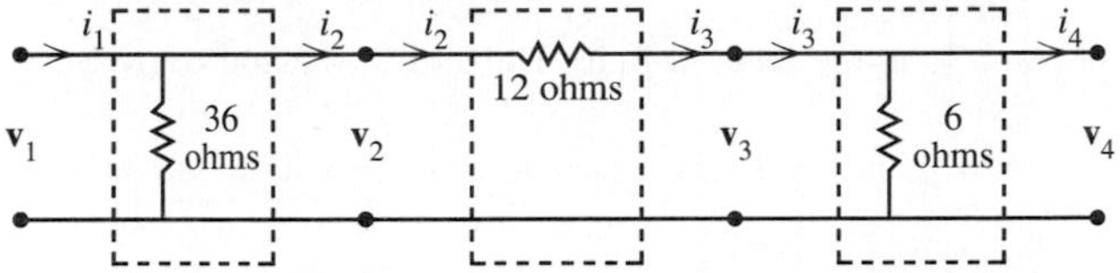

Section 3.6, page 141

The answers here were computed by MATLAB in double precision (about 16 significant digits) and reported in the "short format" of about 5 significant digits.

1. $\mathbf{x}^{(1)} = \begin{bmatrix} 1.75 \\ -1.4 \end{bmatrix}, \mathbf{x}^{(2)} = \begin{bmatrix} 2.1 \\ -1.05 \end{bmatrix}, \mathbf{x}^{(3)} = \begin{bmatrix} 2.0125 \\ -.98 \end{bmatrix},$

$\ldots, \mathbf{x}^{(6)} = \begin{bmatrix} 2.0003 \\ -1.0001 \end{bmatrix}$

3. $\mathbf{x}^{(1)} = \begin{bmatrix} 3.6667 \\ -3. \\ 2.4286 \end{bmatrix}, \mathbf{x}^{(2)} = \begin{bmatrix} 4.6667 \\ -2.7619 \\ 3.7143 \end{bmatrix},$

$\mathbf{x}^{(3)} = \begin{bmatrix} 4.5873 \\ -2.4476 \\ 3.6122 \end{bmatrix}, \ldots, \mathbf{x}^{(9)} = \begin{bmatrix} 4.4999 \\ -2.5001 \\ 3.4999 \end{bmatrix}$

5. $\mathbf{x}^{(1)} = \begin{bmatrix} 1.75 \\ -1.05 \end{bmatrix}, \mathbf{x}^{(2)} = \begin{bmatrix} 2.0125 \\ -.9975 \end{bmatrix}, \ldots,$

$\mathbf{x}^{(4)} = \begin{bmatrix} 2.0000 \\ -1.0000 \end{bmatrix}$. Jacobi took 6 iterations for about the same accuracy.

7. $\mathbf{x}^{(1)} = \begin{bmatrix} 3.6667 \\ -3.7333 \\ 4.0286 \end{bmatrix}, \mathbf{x}^{(2)} = \begin{bmatrix} 4.9111 \\ -2.3708 \\ 3.4446 \end{bmatrix}, \ldots,$

$\mathbf{x}^{(6)} = \begin{bmatrix} 4.5000 \\ -2.5000 \\ 3.5000 \end{bmatrix}$. Jacobi took 9 iterations for about the same accuracy.

9. Only (b) is strictly diagonally dominant.

11. $\mathbf{x}^{(1)} = \begin{bmatrix} 2 \\ 4 \end{bmatrix}, \mathbf{x}^{(2)} = \begin{bmatrix} -10 \\ -56 \end{bmatrix}, \mathbf{x}^{(3)} = \begin{bmatrix} 170 \\ 844 \end{bmatrix}$. With the two equations interchanged, Gauss–Seidel needs only 4 iterations to produce $\mathbf{x}^{(4)} = \begin{bmatrix} 1.2500 \\ .2500 \end{bmatrix}$.

13. Gauss–Seidel produces $\mathbf{x}^{(21)} = \begin{bmatrix} 6.000 \\ 7.000 \end{bmatrix}$, accurate to 3 decimal places. *Note*: $\mathbf{x}^{(20)} = \begin{bmatrix} 5.9995 \\ 6.9994 \end{bmatrix}$, which rounds to 3-place accuracy.

15. The Gauss–Seidel iterates oscillate between $\begin{bmatrix} 6 \\ 3 \\ 1 \end{bmatrix}$ and $\begin{bmatrix} 5 \\ 2 \\ 0 \end{bmatrix}$, so the method fails. The Jacobi method converges slowly, but finally becomes accurate to within .001 at

$$\mathbf{x}^{(151)} = \begin{bmatrix} 5.4991 \\ 2.4995 \\ 0.5002 \end{bmatrix}.$$

17. a. $M = I$, $N = C$, and $A = I - C$; and $\mathbf{d}$ in (7) is $\mathbf{b}$ in (1).
b. $\mathbf{x}^{(2)} = C\mathbf{x}^{(1)} + \mathbf{d} = C(C\mathbf{x}^{(0)} + \mathbf{d}) + \mathbf{d} = \mathbf{d} + C\mathbf{d}$
c. *Hint*: The statement is true for $k = 1$ and $k = 2$. Suppose that for some k, the following statement is true:

$$\mathbf{x}^{(k)} = \mathbf{d} + C\mathbf{d} + C^2\mathbf{d} + \cdots + C^{k-1}\mathbf{d}$$

Use this and the recursion relation to show that the formula for $\mathbf{x}^{(k+1)}$ is also true.

Section 3.7, page 147

1. $C = \begin{bmatrix} .10 & .60 & .60 \\ .30 & .20 & 0 \\ .30 & .10 & .10 \end{bmatrix}$,

$\{\text{intermediate demand}\} = \begin{bmatrix} 60 \\ 20 \\ 10 \end{bmatrix}$

3. $\mathbf{x} = \begin{bmatrix} 40 \\ 15 \\ 15 \end{bmatrix}$ **5.** $\mathbf{x} = \begin{bmatrix} 110 \\ 120 \end{bmatrix}$

7. a. $\begin{bmatrix} 1.6 \\ 1.2 \end{bmatrix}$ **b.** $\begin{bmatrix} 111.6 \\ 121.2 \end{bmatrix}$ **9.** $\mathbf{x} = \begin{bmatrix} 82.8 \\ 131.0 \\ 110.3 \end{bmatrix}$

11. *Hint*: Use properties of transposes to obtain $\mathbf{p}^T = \mathbf{p}^T C + \mathbf{v}^T$, so that $\mathbf{p}^T\mathbf{x} = (\mathbf{p}^T C + \mathbf{v}^T)\mathbf{x} = \mathbf{p}^T C\mathbf{x} + \mathbf{v}^T\mathbf{x}$. Now compute $\mathbf{p}^T\mathbf{x}$ from the production equation.

Section 3.8, page 156

1. $\begin{bmatrix} 1 & .25 & 0 \\ 0 & 1 & 0 \\ 0 & 0 & 1 \end{bmatrix}$ **3.** $\begin{bmatrix} \sqrt{2}/2 & -\sqrt{2}/2 & \sqrt{2} \\ \sqrt{2}/2 & \sqrt{2}/2 & 2\sqrt{2} \\ 0 & 0 & 1 \end{bmatrix}$

5. $\begin{bmatrix} \sqrt{3}/2 & 1/2 & 0 \\ 1/2 & -\sqrt{3}/2 & 0 \\ 0 & 0 & 1 \end{bmatrix}$

7. $\begin{bmatrix} 1/2 & -\sqrt{3}/2 & 3+4\sqrt{3} \\ \sqrt{3}/2 & 1/2 & 4-3\sqrt{3} \\ 0 & 0 & 1 \end{bmatrix}$. See the Practice Problem.

9. $A(BD)$ requires 1600 multiplications. $(AB)D$ requires 808 multiplications.

11. Use the fact that $\sec\varphi - \tan\varphi\sin\varphi = \dfrac{1}{\cos\varphi} - \dfrac{\sin^2\varphi}{\cos\varphi} = \cos\varphi$.

13. $\begin{bmatrix} A & \mathbf{p} \\ 0 & 1 \end{bmatrix} = \begin{bmatrix} I & \mathbf{p} \\ 0 & 1 \end{bmatrix}\begin{bmatrix} A & 0 \\ 0 & 1 \end{bmatrix}$. First apply the linear transformation A and then translate by $\mathbf{p}$.

15. (12, −6, 3) **17.** $\begin{bmatrix} 1 & 0 & 0 & 0 \\ 0 & 1/2 & -\sqrt{3}/2 & 0 \\ 0 & \sqrt{3}/2 & 1/2 & 0 \\ 0 & 0 & 0 & 1 \end{bmatrix}$

19. The triangle with vertices at (7, 2, 0), (7.5, 5, 0), (5, 5, 0)

Supplementary Exercises, page 158

1. a. T **b.** F **c.** T **d.** F **e.** F **f.** F **g.** T **h.** T **i.** T **j.** F **k.** T **l.** F **m.** F **n.** T **o.** F **p.** T

2. $\dfrac{1}{-2}\begin{bmatrix} 7 & -5 \\ -6 & 4 \end{bmatrix} = \begin{bmatrix} -7/2 & 5/2 \\ 3 & -2 \end{bmatrix}$

3. I **4.** $I + A + A^2 + \cdots + A^{n-1}$

5. $A^2 = 2A - I$. Multiply by A: $A^3 = 2A^2 - A$. Substitute $A^2 = 2A - I$: $A^3 = 2(2A - I) - A = 3A - 2I$. Multiply by A: $A^4 = A(3A - 2I) = 3A^2 - 2A$. Substitute $A^2 = 2A - I$ again: $A^4 = 3(2A - I) - 2A = 4A - 3I$.

7. See Exercise 9 in Section 3.2. Row reduction of $[\,A \quad B\,]$ to $[\,I \quad A^{-1}B\,]$ yields $A^{-1}B = \begin{bmatrix} 10 & -1 \\ 9 & 10 \\ -5 & -3 \end{bmatrix}$.

8. $A = \begin{bmatrix} 1 & 3 \\ 1 & 1 \end{bmatrix}\begin{bmatrix} 7 & -2 \\ -3 & 1 \end{bmatrix} = \begin{bmatrix} -2 & 1 \\ 4 & -1 \end{bmatrix}$

9. Left-multiplication by an elementary matrix produces an elementary row operation: $B \sim E_1B \sim E_2E_1B \sim E_3E_2E_1B = C$, so B is row equivalent to C. Since row operations are reversible, C is row equivalent to B. (Alternatively, show C being changed into B by row operations using the inverses of the E_i.)

10. Since A is invertible, so is A^T, by the Invertible Matrix Theorem. Then A^TA is the product of invertible matrices and so is invertible. Thus, the formula $(A^TA)^{-1}A^T$ makes sense. By Theorem 6 in Section 3.2, $(A^TA)^{-1}\cdot A^T = A^{-1}(A^T)^{-1}\cdot A^T = A^{-1}\cdot I = A^{-1}$.

11. a. $p(x_i) = c_0 + c_1 x_i + \cdots + c_{n-1}x_i^{n-1} = \text{row}_i(V)\cdot\begin{bmatrix} c_0 \\ \vdots \\ c_{n-1}\end{bmatrix} = \text{row}_i(V\mathbf{c}) = y_i$

b. If $V\mathbf{c} = \mathbf{0}$, then the entries in $\mathbf{c}$ are the coefficients of a polynomial whose value at $x_1, \ldots, x_n$ is zero. A nonzero polynomial of degree $n-1$ cannot have n zeros, so the polynomial must be identically zero. That is, the entries in $\mathbf{c}$ must all be zero. This shows that the columns of V are linearly independent.

c. Assuming that $x_1, \ldots, x_n$ are distinct, we know from (b) that the columns of V are linearly independent. By the Invertible Matrix Theorem, V is invertible and its columns span $\mathbb{R}^n$. So for every $\mathbf{y} = (y_1, \ldots, y_n)$ in $\mathbb{R}^n$, there is a polynomial $p(t)$ whose coefficients are in $\mathbf{c}$ such that $V\mathbf{c} = \mathbf{y}$. By (a), $p(t)$ is an interpolating polynomial for $(x_1, y_1), \ldots, (x_n, y_n)$.

12. If $A = LU$, then $\text{col}_1(A) = L\cdot\text{col}_1(U)$. Since $\text{col}_1(U)$ has zeros in every entry except possibly the first, $L\cdot\text{col}_1(U)$ is a linear combination of the columns of L in which all weights except possibly the first are zero. So $\text{col}_1(A)$ is a multiple of the first column of L. Similarly, $\text{col}_2(A) = L\cdot\text{col}_2(U)$, which is a linear combination of the columns of L using the first two entries in $\text{col}_2(U)$ as weights [because the other entries in $\text{col}_2(U)$ are zero]. Thus, $\text{col}_2(A)$ is a linear combination of the first two columns of L.

13. a. $P^2 = (\mathbf{u}\mathbf{u}^T)(\mathbf{u}\mathbf{u}^T) = \mathbf{u}(\mathbf{u}^T\mathbf{u})\mathbf{u}^T = \mathbf{u}(1)\mathbf{u}^T = P$
b. $P^T = (\mathbf{u}\mathbf{u}^T)^T = \mathbf{u}^{TT}\mathbf{u}^T = \mathbf{u}\mathbf{u}^T = P$
c. $Q^2 = (I - 2P)(I - 2P) = I - 2P - 2PI + 2P(2P)$
$= I - 4P + 4P^2 = I$, because of part (a).

14. $P\mathbf{x} = \begin{bmatrix} 0 \\ 0 \\ 3\end{bmatrix}$, $Q\mathbf{x} = \begin{bmatrix} 1 \\ 5 \\ -3\end{bmatrix}$

15. Take $\mathbf{x} = C\mathbf{b}$. Then $A\mathbf{x} = A(C\mathbf{b}) = AC\mathbf{b} = I\mathbf{b} = \mathbf{b}$.

16. Suppose $\mathbf{x}$ satisfies $A\mathbf{x} = \mathbf{b}$. Then $C(A\mathbf{x}) = C\mathbf{b}$ and $CA\mathbf{x} = C\mathbf{b}$. Since $CA = I$, we conclude that $\mathbf{x}$ must be $C\mathbf{b}$, which shows that $C\mathbf{b}$ is the only solution of $A\mathbf{x} = \mathbf{b}$.

CHAPTER 4

Section 4.1, page 166

1. 1 **3.** −5 **5.** −23 **7.** 4

9. 10. Start with row 3.

11. −12. Start with column 1 or row 4.

13. 6. Start with row 2 or column 2. **15.** 1 **17.** −5

19. $ad - bc$, $cb - da$. Interchanging two rows changes the sign of the determinant.

21. -2, $(18 + 12k) - (20 + 12k) = -2$. A row replacement does not change the value of a determinant.

23. -5, $k(4) - k(2) + k(-7) = -5k$. Scaling a row by a constant k multiplies the determinant by k.

25. 1 **27.** k **29.** −1

31. 1. The matrix is upper or lower triangular, with only 1's on the diagonal. The determinant is the product of the diagonal entries.

33. $\det EA = \det\begin{bmatrix} c & d \\ a & b\end{bmatrix} = cb - ad = (-1)(ad - bc) = (\det E)(\det A)$

35. $\det EA = \det\begin{bmatrix} a + kc & b + kd \\ c & d\end{bmatrix}$
$= (a + kc)d - (b + kd)c$
$= ad + kcd - bc - kdc = (+1)(ad - bc)$
$= (\det E)(\det A)$

37. $5A = \begin{bmatrix} 15 & 5 \\ 20 & 10\end{bmatrix}$, no

39. The area of the parallelogram and the determinant of $[\mathbf{u}\ \ \mathbf{v}]$ both equal 6. If $\mathbf{v} = \begin{bmatrix} x \\ 2\end{bmatrix}$ for any x, the area is still 6. In each case the base of the parallelogram is unchanged, and the altitude remains 2 because the second entry of $\mathbf{v}$ is always 2.

Section 4.2, page 174

1. Interchanging two rows reverses the sign of the determinant.

3. A replacement operation does not change the determinant.

5. 3 **7.** 0 **9.** 3 **11.** 120 **13.** 6 **15.** 35

17. −7 **19.** 14 **21.** Invertible **23.** Not invertible

25. Linearly independent **27.** −32

29. *Hint*: Show that $(\det A)(\det A^{-1}) = 1$.

31. *Hint*: Use Theorem 6.

33. *Hint*: Use Theorem 6 and another theorem.

35. $\det AB = \det\begin{bmatrix} 6 & 0 \\ 17 & 4\end{bmatrix} = 24$; $(\det A)(\det B) = 3\cdot 8 = 24$

37. a. −12 **b.** 500 **c.** −3 **d.** 1/4 **e.** 64

39. $\det A = (a+e)d - (b+f)c = ad + ed - bc - fc$
$= ad - bc + ed - fc = \det B + \det C$

41. *Hint*: Compute $\det A$ by a cofactor expansion down column 3.

Section 4.3, page 185

1. $\begin{bmatrix} 5/6 \\ -1/6 \end{bmatrix}$ **3.** $\begin{bmatrix} 4 \\ 5/2 \end{bmatrix}$ **5.** $\begin{bmatrix} 3/2 \\ 4 \\ -7/2 \end{bmatrix}$

7. $s \neq \pm\sqrt{3}$; $x_1 = \dfrac{5s+4}{6(s^2-3)}$, $x_2 = \dfrac{-4s-15}{4(s^2-3)}$

9. $s \neq 0, -1$; $x_1 = \dfrac{1}{3(s+1)}$, $x_2 = \dfrac{4s+3}{6s(s+1)}$

11. $\text{adj } A = \begin{bmatrix} 0 & 1 & 0 \\ -3 & -1 & -3 \\ 3 & 2 & 6 \end{bmatrix}$, $A^{-1} = \frac{1}{3}\begin{bmatrix} 0 & 1 & 0 \\ -3 & -1 & -3 \\ 3 & 2 & 6 \end{bmatrix}$

13. $\text{adj } A = \begin{bmatrix} -1 & -1 & 5 \\ 1 & -5 & 1 \\ 1 & 7 & -5 \end{bmatrix}$, $A^{-1} = \frac{1}{6}\begin{bmatrix} -1 & -1 & 5 \\ 1 & -5 & 1 \\ 1 & 7 & -5 \end{bmatrix}$

15. $\text{adj } A = \begin{bmatrix} 2 & 0 & 0 \\ 2 & 6 & 0 \\ -1 & -9 & 3 \end{bmatrix}$, $A^{-1} = \frac{1}{6}\begin{bmatrix} 2 & 0 & 0 \\ 2 & 6 & 0 \\ -1 & -9 & 3 \end{bmatrix}$

17. If $A = \begin{bmatrix} a & b \\ c & d \end{bmatrix}$, then $C_{11} = d$, $C_{12} = -c$, $C_{21} = -b$, $C_{22} = a$. The adjugate matrix is the transpose of cofactors:

$$\text{adj } A = \begin{bmatrix} d & -b \\ -c & a \end{bmatrix}$$

Following Theorem 8, divide by $\det A$; this produces the formula from Section 3.2.

19. 8 **21.** 14 **23.** 22

25. A 3×3 matrix A is not invertible if and only if its columns are linearly dependent (by the Invertible Matrix Theorem). This happens if and only if one of the columns is in a plane containing the other two columns, which is equivalent to the condition that the parallelepiped determined by these columns has zero volume, which in turn is equivalent to the condition that $\det A = 0$.

27. 24 **29.** $\frac{1}{2}|\det[\,\mathbf{v}_1 \quad \mathbf{v}_2\,]|$

31. a. See Example 6. **b.** $4\pi abc/3$

Supplementary Exercises, page 186

1. a. T **b.** T **c.** F **d.** F **e.** F **f.** F **g.** T **h.** T **i.** F **j.** F **k.** T **l.** F **m.** F **n.** T **o.** F **p.** T

The solutions of Exercises 2, 3, and 4 are all based on the fact that if a matrix contains two rows (or two columns) that are multiples of each other, then the determinant of the matrix is zero, by Theorem 4, because the matrix cannot be invertible.

2. $\begin{vmatrix} 12 & 13 & 14 \\ 15 & 16 & 17 \\ 18 & 19 & 20 \end{vmatrix} = \begin{vmatrix} 12 & 13 & 14 \\ 3 & 3 & 3 \\ 6 & 6 & 6 \end{vmatrix} = 0$

3. Make two row replacement operations and then factor out a common multiple in row 2 and a common multiple in row 3.

$$\begin{vmatrix} 1 & a & b+c \\ 1 & b & a+c \\ 1 & c & a+b \end{vmatrix} = \begin{vmatrix} 1 & a & b+c \\ 0 & b-a & a-b \\ 0 & c-a & a-c \end{vmatrix}$$
$$= (b-a)(c-a)\begin{vmatrix} 1 & a & b+c \\ 0 & 1 & -1 \\ 0 & 1 & -1 \end{vmatrix} = 0$$

4. $\begin{vmatrix} a & b & c \\ a+x & b+x & c+x \\ a+y & b+y & c+y \end{vmatrix} = \begin{vmatrix} a & b & c \\ x & x & x \\ y & y & y \end{vmatrix} =$

$$xy\begin{vmatrix} a & b & c \\ 1 & 1 & 1 \\ 1 & 1 & 1 \end{vmatrix} = 0$$

5. -12 **6.** 12

7. When the determinant is expanded by cofactors of the first row, the equation has the form

$$a + bx + cy = 0$$

where at least one of b and c is not zero. This is the equation of a line. It is clear that (x_1, y_1) and (x_2, y_2) are on the line, because when the coordinates of one of the points are substituted for x and y, two rows of the determinant are equal and so the determinant is zero.

8. $\det\begin{bmatrix} 1 & x & y \\ 1 & x_1 & y_1 \\ 0 & 1 & m \end{bmatrix} = 0$. When the determinant is expanded by cofactors of the first row, the equation has the form $1 \cdot (mx_1 - y_1) - x(m) + y \cdot 1 = 0$, which can be rewritten as $y - y_1 = m(x - x_1)$.

9. Note that $T \sim \begin{bmatrix} 1 & a & a^2 \\ 0 & b-a & b^2-a^2 \\ 0 & c-a & c^2-a^2 \end{bmatrix}$. Hence, using Theorem 3,

$$\det T = (b-a)(c-a) \cdot \det\begin{bmatrix} 1 & a & a^2 \\ 0 & 1 & b+a \\ 0 & 1 & c+a \end{bmatrix}$$

$$= (b-a)(c-a)\cdot\det\begin{bmatrix}1 & a & a^2\\ 0 & 1 & b+a\\ 0 & 0 & c-b\end{bmatrix}$$
$$= (b-a)(c-a)(c-b)$$

10. An expansion of the determinant along the top row of V shows that $f(t)$ has the form

$$f(t) = c_0 + c_1 t + c_2 t^2 + c_3 t^3$$

where, by Exercise 9,

$$c_3 = \det\begin{bmatrix}1 & x_1 & x_1^2\\ 1 & x_2 & x_2^2\\ 1 & x_3 & x_3^2\end{bmatrix}$$
$$= (x_2-x_1)(x_3-x_1)(x_3-x_2) \neq 0$$

So $f(t)$ is a cubic polynomial in t. The points $(x_1, 0)$, $(x_2, 0)$, and $(x_3, 0)$ are on the graph of f, because when x_1, x_2, or x_3 are substituted for t in V, the matrix V will have two rows the same and hence have a zero determinant. That is, $f(x_i) = 0$ for $i = 1, 2, 3$.

11. 12. If one vertex is subtracted from all four vertices, and if the new vertices are $\mathbf{0}$, $\mathbf{v}_1$, $\mathbf{v}_2$, and $\mathbf{v}_3$, then the translated figure (and hence the original figure) will be a parallelogram if and only if one of $\mathbf{v}_1, \mathbf{v}_2, \mathbf{v}_3$ is the sum of the other two vectors.

12. A 2×2 matrix A is invertible if and only if the parallelogram determined by the columns of A has nonzero area.

13. $(\text{adj } A)\cdot\dfrac{1}{\det A}A = A^{-1}A$, by the inverse formula

$= I$

By the Invertible Matrix Theorem, adj A is invertible and the matrix on the right is the inverse.

14. a. An expansion by cofactors along the last row shows that for $1 \le k \le n$,

$$\det\begin{bmatrix}A & 0\\ 0 & I_k\end{bmatrix} = 0 + \cdots + 0 + (-1)^{2n+2k}\cdot 1\cdot\det\begin{bmatrix}A & 0\\ 0 & I_{k-1}\end{bmatrix}$$

When $k = 1$, we interpret I_0 as having *no* rows or columns. Chaining these equalities together,

$$\det\begin{bmatrix}A & 0\\ 0 & I_n\end{bmatrix} = \cdots = \det\begin{bmatrix}A & 0\\ 0 & I_2\end{bmatrix} = \det\begin{bmatrix}A & 0\\ 0 & 1\end{bmatrix}$$
$$= \det A$$

b. An expansion by cofactors along the first row shows that for $1 \le k \le n$,

$$\det\begin{bmatrix}I_k & 0\\ C_k & D\end{bmatrix} = 1\cdot\det\begin{bmatrix}I_{k-1} & 0\\ C_{k-1} & D\end{bmatrix} + 0 + \cdots + 0$$

where $C_n = C$ and C_{k-1} is formed by deleting the first column of C_k. Chaining these equalities together, as in (a), produces the desired equation.

c. Observe that $\begin{bmatrix}A & 0\\ C & D\end{bmatrix} = \begin{bmatrix}A & 0\\ 0 & I\end{bmatrix}\begin{bmatrix}I & 0\\ C & D\end{bmatrix}$.

From the multiplicative property of determinants and parts (a) and (b),

$$\det\begin{bmatrix}A & 0\\ C & D\end{bmatrix} = \det\begin{bmatrix}A & 0\\ 0 & I\end{bmatrix}\cdot\det\begin{bmatrix}I & 0\\ C & D\end{bmatrix}$$
$$= (\det A)(\det D)$$

We have proved that *the determinant of a* 2×2 *block lower triangular matrix is the product of the determinants of the diagonal entries* (assuming square diagonal entries). The second part of (c) follows from the first part and the fact that the determinant of a matrix equals the determinant of its transpose:

$$\det\begin{bmatrix}A & B\\ 0 & D\end{bmatrix} = \det\begin{bmatrix}A & B\\ 0 & D\end{bmatrix}^T = \det\begin{bmatrix}A^T & 0\\ B^T & D^T\end{bmatrix}$$
$$= (\det A^T)(\det D^T) = (\det A)(\det D)$$

15. a. $X = CA^{-1}$, $Y = D - CA^{-1}B$. Now use Exercise 14(c).

b. From part (a), and the multiplicative property of determinants,

$$\det\begin{bmatrix}A & B\\ C & D\end{bmatrix} = \det[A(D - CA^{-1}B)]$$
$$= \det[AD - ACA^{-1}B]$$
$$= \det(AD - CAA^{-1}B) \qquad \text{Since } CA = AC$$
$$= \det(AD - CB) \qquad \text{Since } AA^{-1} = I$$

CHAPTER 5

Section 5.1, page 197

1. a. $\mathbf{u} + \mathbf{v}$ is in V because its entries will both be nonnegative.

b. Example: if $\mathbf{u} = \begin{bmatrix}2\\2\end{bmatrix}$ and $c = -1$, then $\mathbf{u}$ is in V, but $c\mathbf{u}$ is not in V.

3. *Example*: If $\mathbf{u} = \begin{bmatrix}.5\\.5\end{bmatrix}$ and $c = 4$, then $\mathbf{u}$ is in H, but $c\mathbf{u}$ is not in H.

5. Yes

7. No, the set is not closed under multiplication by scalars that are not integers.

9. $H = \text{Span}\{\mathbf{v}\}$, where $\mathbf{v} = \begin{bmatrix} 1 \\ 3 \\ 2 \end{bmatrix}$. By Theorem 2, H is a subspace of $\mathbb{R}^3$.

11. $W = \text{Span}\{\mathbf{u}, \mathbf{v}\}$, where $\mathbf{u} = \begin{bmatrix} 5 \\ 1 \\ 0 \end{bmatrix}$, $\mathbf{v} = \begin{bmatrix} 2 \\ 0 \\ 1 \end{bmatrix}$. By Theorem 2, W is a subspace of $\mathbb{R}^3$.

13. **a.** There are only three vectors in $\{\mathbf{v}_1, \mathbf{v}_2, \mathbf{v}_3\}$, and $\mathbf{w}$ is not one of them.
b. There are infinitely many vectors in $\text{Span}\{\mathbf{v}_1, \mathbf{v}_2, \mathbf{v}_3\}$.
c. $\mathbf{w}$ is in $\text{Span}\{\mathbf{v}_1, \mathbf{v}_2, \mathbf{v}_3\}$.

15. Not a vector space because the zero vector is not in W

17. $S = \left\{ \begin{bmatrix} 1 \\ 0 \\ -1 \\ 0 \end{bmatrix}, \begin{bmatrix} -1 \\ 1 \\ 0 \\ 1 \end{bmatrix}, \begin{bmatrix} 0 \\ -1 \\ 1 \\ 0 \end{bmatrix} \right\}$

19. *Hint*: Use a theorem from this section.
Warning: Although the Study Guide has complete solutions for *every* odd-numbered exercise whose answer here is only a "Hint," you *must* really try to work the solution yourself. Otherwise, you will not benefit from the exercise.

21. Yes. The conditions of the Subspace Test are obviously satisfied: The zero matrix is in H, the sum of two upper triangular matrices is upper triangular, and any scalar multiple of an upper triangular matrix is again upper triangular.

23. 4 **25.** **a.** 8 **b.** 3 **c.** 5 **d.** 4

27.
$$\begin{aligned} \mathbf{u} + (-1)\mathbf{u} &= 1\mathbf{u} + (-1)\mathbf{u} && \text{By Axiom 10} \\ &= [1 + (-1)]\mathbf{u} && \text{By Axiom 8} \\ &= 0\mathbf{u} = \mathbf{0} && \text{By Exercise 25} \end{aligned}$$

From Exercise 24 it follows that $(-1)\mathbf{u} = -\mathbf{u}$.

29. Any subspace H that contains $\mathbf{u}$ and $\mathbf{v}$ must also contain all scalar multiples of $\mathbf{u}$ and $\mathbf{v}$ and hence must contain all sums of scalar multiples of $\mathbf{u}$ and $\mathbf{v}$. Thus H must contain $\text{Span}\{\mathbf{u}, \mathbf{v}\}$.

Section 5.2, page 208

1. $\begin{bmatrix} 3 & -5 & -3 \\ 6 & -2 & 0 \\ -8 & 4 & 1 \end{bmatrix} \begin{bmatrix} 1 \\ 3 \\ -4 \end{bmatrix} = \begin{bmatrix} 0 \\ 0 \\ 0 \end{bmatrix}$, so $\mathbf{w}$ is in Nul A.

3. $\begin{bmatrix} 7 \\ -4 \\ 1 \\ 0 \end{bmatrix}, \begin{bmatrix} -6 \\ 2 \\ 0 \\ 1 \end{bmatrix}$ **5.** $\begin{bmatrix} 2 \\ 1 \\ 0 \\ 0 \\ 0 \end{bmatrix}, \begin{bmatrix} -4 \\ 0 \\ 9 \\ 1 \\ 0 \end{bmatrix}$

7. W is not a subspace because $\mathbf{0}$ is not in W.

9. W is a subspace of $\mathbb{R}^3$ by Theorem 3, because W is the set of solutions of the "system" $r + 2s - 3t = 0$.

11. W is a subspace of $\mathbb{R}^4$, because W is the set of solutions of the system

$$\begin{aligned} a - 2b - 4c &= 0 \\ 2a - c - 3d &= 0 \end{aligned}$$

13. W is a subspace of $\mathbb{R}^3$ by Theorem 2 because

$$W = \text{Span}\left\{ \begin{bmatrix} 1 \\ 0 \\ 2 \end{bmatrix}, \begin{bmatrix} 0 \\ 1 \\ -1 \end{bmatrix} \right\}.$$

15. W is not a subspace because $\mathbf{0}$ is not in W.

17. $W = \text{Col}\,A$ for $A = \begin{bmatrix} 1 & -6 \\ 0 & 1 \\ 1 & 0 \end{bmatrix}$, so W is a vector space by Theorem 4.

19. $\begin{bmatrix} 0 & 2 & 3 \\ 1 & 1 & -2 \\ 4 & 1 & 0 \\ 3 & -1 & -1 \end{bmatrix}$ **21.** **a.** 2 **b.** 4 **23.** **a.** 5 **b.** 2

25. $\begin{bmatrix} 3 \\ 1 \end{bmatrix}$ in Nul A, $\begin{bmatrix} 2 \\ -1 \\ -4 \\ 3 \end{bmatrix}$ in Col A. Other answers possible.

27. $\mathbf{w}$ is in both Nul A and Col A.

29. Let $\mathbf{x} = \begin{bmatrix} 3 \\ 2 \\ -1 \end{bmatrix}$ and $A = \begin{bmatrix} 1 & -3 & -3 \\ -2 & 4 & 2 \\ -1 & 5 & 7 \end{bmatrix}$. Then $\mathbf{x}$ is in Nul A. Since Nul A is a subspace of $\mathbb{R}^3$, $10\mathbf{x}$ is in Nul A.

31. **a.** $A\mathbf{0} = \mathbf{0}$, so the zero vector is in Col A.
b. By a property of matrix multiplication, $A\mathbf{x} + A\mathbf{w} = A(\mathbf{x} + \mathbf{w})$, which shows that $A\mathbf{x} + A\mathbf{w}$ is a linear combination of the columns of A and hence is in Col A.
c. $c(A\mathbf{x}) = A(c\mathbf{x})$, which shows that $c(A\mathbf{x})$ is in Col A for all scalars c.

33. **a.** For arbitrary polynomials $\mathbf{p}, \mathbf{q}$ in $\mathbb{P}_2$ and any scalar c,

$$T(\mathbf{p}+\mathbf{q}) = \begin{bmatrix} (\mathbf{p}+\mathbf{q})(0) \\ (\mathbf{p}+\mathbf{q})(1) \end{bmatrix} = \begin{bmatrix} \mathbf{p}(0)+\mathbf{q}(0) \\ \mathbf{p}(1)+\mathbf{q}(1) \end{bmatrix}$$
$$= \begin{bmatrix} \mathbf{p}(0) \\ \mathbf{p}(1) \end{bmatrix} + \begin{bmatrix} \mathbf{q}(0) \\ \mathbf{q}(1) \end{bmatrix} = T(\mathbf{p}) + T(\mathbf{q})$$
$$T(c\mathbf{p}) = \begin{bmatrix} c\mathbf{p}(0) \\ c\mathbf{p}(1) \end{bmatrix} = c\begin{bmatrix} \mathbf{p}(0) \\ \mathbf{p}(1) \end{bmatrix} = cT(\mathbf{p})$$

So T is a linear transformation from $\mathbb{P}_2$ into $\mathbb{P}_2$.
b. Any quadratic polynomial that vanishes at 0 and 1 must be a multiple of $\mathbf{p}(t) = t(t-1)$. The range of T is $\mathbb{R}^2$.

35. **a.** For A, B in $M_{2\times 2}$ and any scalar c,

$$\begin{aligned} T(A+B) &= (A+B) + (A+B)^T \\ &= A + B + A^T + B^T \quad \text{Property of transposes} \\ &= (A+A^T) + (B+B^T) = T(A) + T(B) \\ T(cA) &= (cA) + (cA)^T = cA + cA^T \\ &= c(A+A^T) = cT(A) \end{aligned}$$

So T is a linear transformation from $M_{2\times 2}$ into $M_{2\times 2}$.
b. If B is any element in $M_{2\times 2}$ with the property that $B^T = B$, and if $A = \frac{1}{2}B$, then

$$T(A) = \tfrac{1}{2}B + (\tfrac{1}{2}B)^T = \tfrac{1}{2}B + \tfrac{1}{2}B = B$$

c. Part (b) showed that the range of T contains all B such that $B^T = B$. So it suffices to show that any B in the range of T has this property. If $B = T(A)$, then by properties of transposes,

$$B^T = (A+A^T)^T = A^T + A^{TT} = A^T + A = B$$

d. The kernel of T is $\left\{\begin{bmatrix} 0 & b \\ -b & 0 \end{bmatrix} : b \text{ real}\right\}$.

37. *Hint*: Typical elements of $T(U)$ have the form $T(\mathbf{u}_1)$ and $T(\mathbf{u}_2)$, where $\mathbf{u}_1, \mathbf{u}_2$ are in U. Use the Subspace Test.

Section 5.3, page 217

1. Yes, the columns of the square matrix $\begin{bmatrix} 3 & -7 \\ 2 & 5 \end{bmatrix}$ are linearly independent, so they also span $\mathbb{R}^2$, by the Invertible Matrix Theorem. Hence the columns form a basis for $\mathbb{R}^2$.

3. No, the set is linearly dependent because there are more vectors than entries in the vectors. Also, the three vectors are multiples; hence they span only a line through the origin. Alternatively, compute $\begin{bmatrix} 1 & -4 & 2 \\ -3 & 12 & -6 \end{bmatrix} \sim \begin{bmatrix} 1 & -4 & 2 \\ 0 & 0 & 0 \end{bmatrix}$. This matrix fails to have a pivot in each row, so its columns do not span $\mathbb{R}^2$.

5. Yes, the 3×3 matrix $A = \begin{bmatrix} 1 & 1 & 1 \\ 0 & 1 & 1 \\ 0 & 0 & 1 \end{bmatrix}$ has 3 pivot positions. By the Invertible Matrix Theorem, A is invertible and its columns form a basis for $\mathbb{R}^3$. (See Example 3.)

7. No. The vectors are linearly dependent and do not span $\mathbb{R}^3$.

9. No, the set is linearly dependent because the zero vector is in the set. However, $\begin{bmatrix} 1 & -2 & 0 & 0 \\ -3 & 9 & 0 & -3 \\ 0 & 0 & 0 & 5 \end{bmatrix} \sim \begin{bmatrix} 1 & -2 & 0 & 0 \\ 0 & 3 & 0 & -3 \\ 0 & 0 & 0 & 5 \end{bmatrix}$. The matrix has pivots in each row and hence its columns span $\mathbb{R}^3$.

11. No, the vectors are linearly independent because they are not multiples, but they do not span $\mathbb{R}^3$. The matrix $\begin{bmatrix} -2 & 6 \\ 3 & -1 \\ 0 & 5 \end{bmatrix}$ can have at most two pivots since it has only two columns. So there will not be a pivot in each row.

13. $\begin{bmatrix} 3 \\ 5 \\ 1 \\ 0 \end{bmatrix}, \begin{bmatrix} -2 \\ -4 \\ 0 \\ 1 \end{bmatrix}$ **15.** $\begin{bmatrix} -2 \\ 1 \\ 0 \end{bmatrix}, \begin{bmatrix} -1 \\ 0 \\ 1 \end{bmatrix}$

17. Basis for Nul A: $\begin{bmatrix} -6 \\ -5/2 \\ 1 \\ 0 \end{bmatrix}, \begin{bmatrix} -5 \\ -3/2 \\ 0 \\ 1 \end{bmatrix}$;

Basis for Col A: $\begin{bmatrix} -2 \\ 2 \\ -3 \end{bmatrix}, \begin{bmatrix} 4 \\ -6 \\ 8 \end{bmatrix}$

19. $\mathbf{v}_1, \mathbf{v}_2, \mathbf{v}_4$

21. The three simplest answers are $\{\mathbf{v}_1, \mathbf{v}_2\}$ or $\{\mathbf{v}_1, \mathbf{v}_3\}$ or $\{\mathbf{v}_2, \mathbf{v}_3\}$. Other answers are possible.

23. *Hint*: Use the Invertible Matrix Theorem.

25. No. (Why is the set not a basis for H?)

27. $\{\cos \omega t, \sin \omega t\}$

29. Let A be the $n\times k$ matrix $[\,\mathbf{v}_1 \ \cdots \ \mathbf{v}_k\,]$. Since A has fewer columns than rows, there cannot be a pivot position in each row of A. By Theorem 2 in Section 2.2, the columns of A do not span $\mathbb{R}^n$ and hence are not a basis for $\mathbb{R}^n$.

31. *Hint*: If $\{\mathbf{v}_1, \dots, \mathbf{v}_p\}$ is linearly dependent, then there exist $c_1, \dots, c_p$, not all zero, such that $c_1\mathbf{v}_1 + \cdots + c_p\mathbf{v}_p = \mathbf{0}$. Use this equation.

Section 5.4, page 227

1. $\begin{bmatrix} 3 \\ -7 \end{bmatrix}$ **3.** $\begin{bmatrix} -1 \\ -5 \\ 9 \end{bmatrix}$ **5.** $\begin{bmatrix} 8 \\ -5 \end{bmatrix}$ **7.** $\begin{bmatrix} -1 \\ -1 \\ 3 \end{bmatrix}$

9. $\begin{bmatrix} 2 & 1 \\ -9 & 8 \end{bmatrix}$ **11.** $\begin{bmatrix} 6 \\ 4 \end{bmatrix}$ **13.** $\begin{bmatrix} 2 \\ 6 \\ -1 \end{bmatrix}$ **15.** $\begin{bmatrix} 1.3 \\ 0 \\ 0.8 \end{bmatrix}$

17. $\begin{bmatrix} 1 \\ 1 \end{bmatrix} = 5\mathbf{v}_1 - 2\mathbf{v}_2 = 10\mathbf{v}_1 - 3\mathbf{v}_2 + \mathbf{v}_3$, (infinitely many answers)

19. *Hint*: By hypothesis, the zero vector has a unique representation as a linear combination of elements of S.

21. $\begin{bmatrix} 9 & 2 \\ 4 & 1 \end{bmatrix}$

23. *Hint*: Suppose that $[\mathbf{u}]_{\mathcal{B}} = [\mathbf{w}]_{\mathcal{B}}$ for some $\mathbf{u}$ and $\mathbf{w}$ in V, and denote the entries in $[\mathbf{u}]_{\mathcal{B}}$ by $c_1, \dots, c_n$. Use the definition of $[\mathbf{u}]_{\mathcal{B}}$.

25. One possible approach: First, show that if $\mathbf{u}_1, \dots, \mathbf{u}_p$ are linearly *dependent*, then $[\mathbf{u}_1]_{\mathcal{B}}, \dots, [\mathbf{u}_p]_{\mathcal{B}}$ are linearly dependent. Second, show that if $[\mathbf{u}_1]_{\mathcal{B}}, \dots, [\mathbf{u}_p]_{\mathcal{B}}$ are linearly dependent, then $\mathbf{u}_1, \dots, \mathbf{u}_p$ are linearly *dependent*. Use the two equations displayed in the exercise. A slightly different proof is given in the Study Guide.

27. Linearly independent. Why?

29. Linearly independent. Why?

Section 5.5, page 233

1. $\begin{bmatrix} 1 \\ 1 \\ 0 \end{bmatrix}, \begin{bmatrix} -2 \\ 1 \\ 3 \end{bmatrix}$; dim = 2

3. $\begin{bmatrix} 0 \\ 1 \\ 0 \\ 1 \end{bmatrix}, \begin{bmatrix} 0 \\ -1 \\ 1 \\ 2 \end{bmatrix}, \begin{bmatrix} 2 \\ 0 \\ -3 \\ 0 \end{bmatrix}$; dim = 3

5. $\begin{bmatrix} 1 \\ 2 \\ -1 \\ -3 \end{bmatrix}, \begin{bmatrix} -4 \\ 5 \\ 0 \\ 7 \end{bmatrix}$; dim = 2 **7.** No basis; dim = 0

9. 2 **11.** 2 **13.** 2, 3 **15.** 2, 2 **17.** 0, 3

19. *Hint*: You only need to show that the first four Hermite polynomials are linearly independent. Why?

21. $[\mathbf{p}]_{\mathcal{B}} = (3, 3, -2, \frac{3}{2})$

23. *Hint*: Suppose S does span V, and use the Spanning Set Theorem. This leads to a contradiction, which shows that spanning hypothesis is false.

25. *Hint*: Use the fact that each $\mathbb{P}_n$ is a subspace of $\mathbb{P}$.

27. True. Why? **29.** True. Why? **31.** True. Why?

33. *Hint*: Since H is a subspace of a finite-dimensional space, H is finite-dimensional and hence has a basis, say, $\mathbf{v}_1, \dots, \mathbf{v}_p$. First show that $\{T(\mathbf{v}_1), \dots, T(\mathbf{v}_p)\}$ spans $T(H)$. [Assume $H \neq \{0\}$.]

Section 5.6, page 241

1. rank $A = 2$; dim Nul $A = 2$;

Basis for Col A: $\begin{bmatrix} 1 \\ -1 \\ 5 \end{bmatrix}, \begin{bmatrix} -4 \\ 2 \\ -6 \end{bmatrix}$

Basis for Row A: $(1, 0, -1, 5), (0, -2, 5, 6)$;

Nul A: $\begin{bmatrix} 1 \\ 5/2 \\ 1 \\ 0 \end{bmatrix}, \begin{bmatrix} -5 \\ 3 \\ 0 \\ 1 \end{bmatrix}$

3. rank $A = 3$; dim Nul $A = 2$;

Basis for Col A: $\begin{bmatrix} 2 \\ -2 \\ 4 \\ -2 \end{bmatrix}, \begin{bmatrix} 6 \\ -3 \\ 9 \\ 3 \end{bmatrix}, \begin{bmatrix} 2 \\ -3 \\ 5 \\ -4 \end{bmatrix}$

Basis for Row A: $(2, -3, 6, 2, 5), (0, 0, 3, -1, 1), (0, 0, 0, 1, 3)$

Basis for Nul A: $\begin{bmatrix} 3/2 \\ 1 \\ 0 \\ 0 \\ 0 \end{bmatrix}, \begin{bmatrix} 9/2 \\ 0 \\ -4/3 \\ -3 \\ 1 \end{bmatrix}$

5. 5, 3, 3

7. Yes, no. Since Col A is a four-dimensional subspace of $\mathbb{R}^4$, it coincides with $\mathbb{R}^4$. It is impossible for Nul A to be $\mathbb{R}^3$, because the vectors in Nul A have 7 entries. Nul A is a three-dimensional subspace of $\mathbb{R}^7$, by the Rank Theorem.

9. 2 **11.** 3 **13.** 5, 5 **15.** 2 **17.** 7 **19.** Yes

21. No

23. Yes. Only six homogeneous linear equations are necessary.

25. No

27. Row A and Nul A are in $\mathbb{R}^n$; Col A and Nul A^T are in $\mathbb{R}^m$. There are only four distinct subspaces, because Row A^T = Col A and Col A^T = Row A.

29. Recall that dim Col $A = m$ precisely when Col $A = \mathbb{R}^m$, or equivalently, when the equation $A\mathbf{x} = \mathbf{b}$ is consistent for all $\mathbf{b}$. By Exercise 28(b), dim Col $A = m$ precisely when dim Nul $A^T = 0$, or equivalently, when the equation $A^T\mathbf{x} = \mathbf{0}$ has only the trivial solution.

31. $\mathbf{u}\mathbf{v}^T = \begin{bmatrix} 2a & 2b & 2c \\ -3a & -3b & -3c \\ 5a & 5b & 5c \end{bmatrix}$. The columns are all multiples of $\mathbf{u}$, so Col $\mathbf{u}\mathbf{v}^T$ is one-dimensional.

33. *Hint*: Let $A = [\,\mathbf{u} \quad \mathbf{u}_2 \quad \mathbf{u}_3\,]$. If $\mathbf{u} \neq \mathbf{0}$, then $\mathbf{u}$ is a basis for Col A. Why?

Section 5.7, page 247

1. a. $\begin{bmatrix} 6 & 9 \\ -2 & -4 \end{bmatrix}$ **b.** $\begin{bmatrix} 0 \\ -2 \end{bmatrix}$ **3.** (ii)

5. a. $\begin{bmatrix} 4 & -1 & 0 \\ -1 & 1 & 1 \\ 0 & 1 & -2 \end{bmatrix}$ **b.** $\begin{bmatrix} 8 \\ 2 \\ 2 \end{bmatrix}$

7. $\underset{\mathcal{C}\leftarrow\mathcal{B}}{P} = \begin{bmatrix} -3 & 1 \\ -5 & 2 \end{bmatrix}$, $\underset{\mathcal{B}\leftarrow\mathcal{C}}{P} = \begin{bmatrix} -2 & 1 \\ -5 & 3 \end{bmatrix}$

9. $\underset{\mathcal{C}\leftarrow\mathcal{B}}{P} = \begin{bmatrix} 9 & -2 \\ -4 & 1 \end{bmatrix}$, $\underset{\mathcal{B}\leftarrow\mathcal{C}}{P} = \begin{bmatrix} 1 & 2 \\ 4 & 9 \end{bmatrix}$

11. $\underset{\mathcal{C}\leftarrow\mathcal{B}}{P} = \begin{bmatrix} 1 & 3 & 0 \\ -2 & -5 & 2 \\ 1 & 4 & 3 \end{bmatrix}$, $[-1+2t]_{\mathcal{B}} = \begin{bmatrix} 5 \\ -2 \\ 1 \end{bmatrix}$

13. a. $\mathcal{B}$ is a basis for V.
b. The coordinate mapping is a linear transformation.
c. The product of a matrix and a vector.
d. The coordinate vector of $\mathbf{v}$ relative to $\mathcal{B}$.

Section 5.8, page 257

1. If $y_k = 2^k$, then $y_{k+1} = 2^{k+1}$ and $y_{k+2} = 2^{k+2}$. Substituting these formulas into the left side of the equation,

$$\begin{aligned} y_{k+2} + 2y_{k+1} - 8y_k &= 2^{k+2} + 2\cdot 2^{k+1} - 8\cdot 2^k \\ &= 2^k(2^2 + 2\cdot 2 - 8) \\ &= 2^k(0) = 0 \qquad \text{for all } k \end{aligned}$$

Since the difference equation holds for all k, 2^k is a solution. A similar calculation works for $y_k = (-4)^k$.

3. The signals 2^k and $(-4)^k$ are linearly independent because neither is a multiple of the other. For instance, there is no scalar c such that $2^k = c(-4)^k$ for *all* k. By Theorem 18, the solution set H of the difference equation in Exercise 1 is two-dimensional. By Theorem 13 in Section 5.5, the two linearly independent signals 2^k and $(-4)^k$ form a basis for H.

5. If $y_k = (-3)^k$, then

$$\begin{aligned} y_{k+2} + 6y_{k+1} + 9y_k &= (-3)^{k+2} + 6(-3)^{k+1} + 9(-3)^k \\ &= (-3)^k[(-3)^2 + 6(-3) + 9] \\ &= (-3)^k(0) = 0 \qquad \text{for all } k \end{aligned}$$

Similarly, if $y_k = k(-3)^k$, then

$$\begin{aligned} &y_{k+2} + 6y_{k+1} + 9y_k \\ &= (k+2)(-3)^{k+2} + 6(k+1)(-3)^{k+1} + 9k(-3)^k \\ &= (-3)^k[(k+2)(-3)^2 + 6(k+1)(-3) + 9k] \\ &= (-3)^k[9k + 18 - 18k - 18 + 9k] \\ &= (-3)^k(0) \qquad \text{for all } k \end{aligned}$$

Thus, both $(-3)^k$ and $k(-3)^k$ are in the solution space H of the difference equation. Also, there is no scalar c such that $k(-3)^k = c(-3)^k$ *for all* k, because c must be chosen independently of k. Likewise, there is no scalar c such that $(-3) = ck(-3)^k$ for all k. So the two signals are linearly independent. Since dim $H = 2$, the signals form a basis for H, by Theorem 13.

7. Yes **9.** Yes

11. No, two signals cannot span the three-dimensional solution space.

13. $(\frac{1}{3})^k$, $(\frac{2}{3})^k$ **15.** 5^k, $(-5)^k$

17. $Y_k = c_1(.8)^k + c_2(.5)^k + 10$

19. $y_k = c_1(-2+\sqrt{3})^k + c_2(-2-\sqrt{3})^k$

21. 7, 5, 4, 3, 4, 5, 6, 6, 7, 8, 9, 8, 7; see figure below.

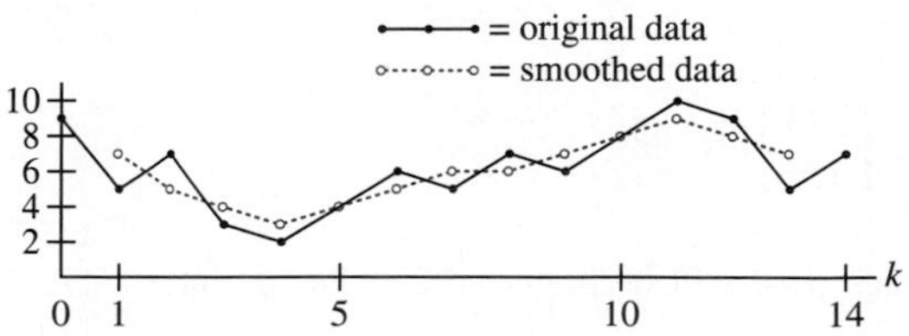

23. $y_{k+1} - 1.01y_k = -450, \qquad y_0 = 10{,}000$

25. $k^2 + c_1 \cdot (-4)^k + c_2$

27. $2 - 2k + c_1 4^k + c_2 \cdot 2^{-k}$

29. $\mathbf{x}_{k+1} = A\mathbf{x}_k$, where

$$A = \begin{bmatrix} 0 & 1 & 0 & 0 \\ 0 & 0 & 1 & 0 \\ 0 & 0 & 0 & 1 \\ 9 & -6 & -8 & 6 \end{bmatrix}, \mathbf{x} = \begin{bmatrix} y_k \\ y_{k+1} \\ y_{k+2} \\ y_{k+3} \end{bmatrix}$$

31. The equation holds for all k, so it holds with k replaced by $k-1$, which transforms the equation into

$$y_{k+2} + 5y_{k+1} + 6y_k = 0 \qquad \text{for all } k$$

The equation is of order 2.

33. For all k, the Casorati matrix $C(k)$ is not invertible. In this case, the Casorati matrix gives no information about the linear independence/dependence of the set of signals. In fact, the two signals are not multiples of each other, so they are linearly independent.

35. *Hint*: Verify the two properties that define a linear transformation. For $\{y_k\}$ and $\{z_k\}$ in $\mathbb{S}$, study $T(\{y_k\}+\{z_k\})$. Note that if r is any scalar, then the kth term of $r\{y_k\}$ is ry_k; so

$$T(r\{y_k\}) = ry_{k+2} + a(ry_{k+1}) + b(ry_k)$$

Section 5.9, page 266

1. a. From: N, M; To: News, Music

$$\begin{bmatrix} .7 & .6 \\ .3 & .4 \end{bmatrix}$$

b. $\begin{bmatrix} 1 \\ 0 \end{bmatrix}$ **c.** 33%

3. a. From: 1, 2, 3; To: 1, 2, 3

$$\begin{bmatrix} .5 & .25 & .25 \\ .25 & .5 & .25 \\ .25 & .25 & .5 \end{bmatrix}$$

b. .3125

5. $\begin{bmatrix} .4 \\ .6 \end{bmatrix}$

7. $\begin{bmatrix} 1/4 \\ 1/2 \\ 1/4 \end{bmatrix}$

9. Yes, because P^2 has all positive entries

11. a. $\begin{bmatrix} 2/3 \\ 1/3 \end{bmatrix}$ **b.** 2/3

13. Each food will be preferred equally, because $\begin{bmatrix} 1/3 \\ 1/3 \\ 1/3 \end{bmatrix}$ is the steady-state vector.

15. About 13.9% of the United States population

17. a. The entries in a column of P sum to 1. A column in the matrix $P - I$ has the same entries as in P except that one of the entries is decreased by 1. Hence each column sum is 0.
b. By (a), the bottom row of $P - I$ is the negative of the sum of the other rows.
c. By (b) and the Spanning Set Theorem, the bottom row of $P - I$ may be removed and the remaining $(n-1)$ rows will still span the row space. Alternatively, use (a) and the fact that row operations do not change the row space. Let A be the matrix obtained from $P - I$ by adding to the bottom row all the other rows. By (a), the row space is spanned by the first $(n-1)$ rows of A.
d. By the Rank Theorem and (c), the dimension of the column space of $P - I$ is less than n, and hence the null space is nontrivial. Instead of the rank theorem, you may use the Invertible Matrix Theorem, since $P - I$ is a square matrix.

19. a. The product $S\mathbf{v}$ equals the sum of the entries in $\mathbf{v}$. For a probability vector this sum must be 1.
b. $P = [\,\mathbf{p}_1 \;\; \mathbf{p}_2 \;\; \cdots \;\; \mathbf{p}_n\,]$, where the $\mathbf{p}_i$ are probability vectors. By matrix multiplication and part (a),

$$SP = [\,S\mathbf{p}_1 \;\; S\mathbf{p}_2 \;\; \cdots \;\; S\mathbf{p}_n\,] = [\,1 \;\; 1 \;\; \cdots \;\; 1\,] = S$$

c. By part (b), $S(P\mathbf{v}) = (SP)\mathbf{v} = S\mathbf{v} = 1$. Also, the entries in $P\mathbf{v}$ are nonnegative. Hence, by (a), $P\mathbf{v}$ is a probability vector.

Supplementary Exercises, page 269

1. a. T **b.** T **c.** F **d.** F **e.** T **f.** T **g.** F **h.** F **i.** T **j.** F **k.** F **l.** F **m.** T **n.** F **o.** T **p.** T **q.** F

2. Any two of the three: $\begin{bmatrix} 1 \\ 2 \\ -1 \\ 3 \end{bmatrix}, \begin{bmatrix} -2 \\ 5 \\ -4 \\ 1 \end{bmatrix}, \begin{bmatrix} 5 \\ -8 \\ 7 \\ 1 \end{bmatrix}$

3. The set of all (b_1, b_2, b_3) satisfying $b_1 + 2b_2 + b_3 = 0$

4. Choose any two nonzero polynomials that are not multiples. Since they are linearly independent and belong to a two-dimensional space, they will be a basis for H.

5. You would have to know that the solution set of the homogeneous system is spanned by two solutions that are not multiples. In this case, the null space of the 18×20 coefficient matrix A is two-dimensional. By the Rank Theorem, dim Col $A = 20 - 2 = 18$, which means that Col $A = \mathbb{R}^{18}$, because A has 18 rows, and every equation $A\mathbf{x} = \mathbf{b}$ is consistent.

6. The case $n = 0$ is trivial. If $n > 0$, then a basis for H consists of n linearly independent vectors, say $\mathbf{u}_1, \ldots, \mathbf{u}_n$. These vectors remain linearly independent when considered as elements of V. But any n linearly independent vectors in the n-dimensional space V must form a basis for V, by Theorem 13 in Section 5.5. So $\mathbf{u}_1, \ldots, \mathbf{u}_n$ span V. Thus $H = \text{Span}\{\mathbf{u}_1, \ldots, \mathbf{u}_n\} = V$.

7. Let $S = \{\mathbf{v}_1, \ldots, \mathbf{v}_p\}$. If S were linearly independent and not a basis for V, then S would not span V. In this case, there would be a vector $\mathbf{v}_{p+1}$ in V that is not in $\text{Span}\{\mathbf{v}_1, \ldots, \mathbf{v}_p\}$. Let $S' = \{\mathbf{v}_1, \ldots, \mathbf{v}_p, \mathbf{v}_{p+1}\}$. Then S' is linearly independent because none of the vectors in S' is a linear combination of the vectors that precede it. Since S' is larger than S, this would contradict the maximality of S. Hence S must be a basis for V.

8. If S is a finite spanning set for V, then a subset of S, say S', is a basis of V. Since S' must span V, S' cannot be a proper subset of S because of the minimality of S. Thus $S' = S$, which proves that S is a basis of V.

9. *Hint*: Use the Invertible Matrix Theorem, and then see the boxed statement before Example 9 in Section 5.3.

10. Note that $(AQ)^T = Q^T A^T$. Since Q^T is invertible, we may use Exercise 9 to conclude that

$$\text{rank}\,(AQ)^T = \text{rank}\,Q^T A^T = \text{rank}\,A^T$$

Since the ranks of a matrix and its transpose are equal (by the Rank Theorem), $\text{rank}\,AQ = \text{rank}\,A$.

11. a. *Hint*: Use the definition of $A\mathbf{b}_j$, where $\mathbf{b}_j$ is a column of B, and conclude that $\text{Col}\,AB$ is contained in $\text{Col}\,A$. Then consider the dimensions of the two subspaces.
b. From Exercise 11(a):

$$\text{rank}\,AB = \text{rank}\,(AB)^T = \text{rank}\,B^T A^T \le \text{rank}\,B^T$$
$$(AB)^T = \text{rank}\,B$$

12. (The problem tacitly assumes $r > 0$.) If $\text{rank}\,A = r$, then A has a set of r linearly independent columns. Let A_1 be the $m \times r$ matrix formed from these r columns. Then $\text{rank}\,A_1 = r$ because the columns are linearly independent. By the Rank Theorem, $\dim \text{Row}\,A_1 = r$, so there are r linearly independent rows in A_1. Let A_2 be the $r \times r$ submatrix formed from these r rows. Then $\text{rank}\,A_2 = r$ because A_2 has r linearly independent rows. Since A_2 is square, A_2 is invertible, by the Invertible Matrix Theorem.

13. $$[\,B \quad AB \quad A^2B\,] = \begin{bmatrix} 0 & 1 & 0 \\ 1 & -.9 & .81 \\ 1 & .5 & .25 \end{bmatrix} \sim \begin{bmatrix} 1 & 0 & .81 \\ 0 & 1 & 0 \\ 0 & 0 & -.56 \end{bmatrix}.$$

This matrix has rank 3, so the pair (A, B) is controllable.

14. $[\,B \quad AB \quad A^2B\,] = \begin{bmatrix} 1 & .5 & .19 \\ 1 & .7 & .45 \\ 0 & 0 & 0 \end{bmatrix}$. This matrix obviously has rank less than 3, so the pair (A, B) is not controllable.

CHAPTER 6

Section 6.1, page 278

1. Yes **3.** No **5.** Yes, $\lambda = 0$ **7.** Yes, $\begin{bmatrix} 1 \\ 1 \\ -1 \end{bmatrix}$

9. $\lambda = 1$: $\begin{bmatrix} 0 \\ 1 \end{bmatrix}$; $\lambda = 5$: $\begin{bmatrix} 2 \\ 1 \end{bmatrix}$ **11.** $\begin{bmatrix} -1 \\ 3 \end{bmatrix}$

13. $\lambda = 1$: $\begin{bmatrix} 0 \\ 1 \\ 0 \end{bmatrix}$; $\lambda = 2$: $\begin{bmatrix} -1 \\ 2 \\ 2 \end{bmatrix}$; $\lambda = 3$: $\begin{bmatrix} -1 \\ 1 \\ 1 \end{bmatrix}$

15. $\begin{bmatrix} -2 \\ 1 \\ 0 \end{bmatrix}, \begin{bmatrix} -3 \\ 0 \\ 1 \end{bmatrix}$ **17.** 7, −4, 2 **19.** 0, 2, −1

21. 0 **23.** *Hint*: Use Theorem 2.

25. *Hint*: Use the equation $A\mathbf{x} = \lambda\mathbf{x}$ to find an equation involving A^{-1}.

27. *Hint*: For any λ, $(A - \lambda I)^T = A^T - \lambda I$. By a theorem (which one?), $A^T - \lambda I$ is invertible if and only if $A - \lambda I$ is invertible.

29. Let $\mathbf{v}$ be the vector in $\mathbb{R}^n$ whose entries are all 1's. Then $A\mathbf{v} = s\mathbf{v}$.

31. a. $\mathbf{x}_{k+1} = c_1\lambda^{k+1}\mathbf{u} + c_2\mu^{k+1}\mathbf{v}$
b.
$$\begin{aligned} A\mathbf{x}_k &= A(c_1\lambda^k\mathbf{u} + c_2\mu^k\mathbf{v}) \\ &= c_1\lambda^k A\mathbf{u} + c_2\mu^k A\mathbf{v} && \text{Linearity} \\ &= c_1\lambda^k \lambda\mathbf{u} + c_2\mu^k \mu\mathbf{v} && \mathbf{u} \text{ and } \mathbf{v} \text{ are eigenvectors} \\ &= \mathbf{x}_{k+1} \end{aligned}$$

Section 6.2, page 286

1. $\lambda^2 - 4\lambda - 45$; 9, −5 **3.** $\lambda^2 - 2\lambda - 1$; $1 \pm \sqrt{2}$

5. $\lambda^2 - 6\lambda + 9$; 3 **7.** $\lambda^2 - 9\lambda + 32$; no real eigenvalues

9. $-\lambda^3 + 4\lambda^2 - 9\lambda - 6$ **11.** $-\lambda^3 + 9\lambda^2 - 26\lambda + 24$

13. $-\lambda^3 + 18\lambda^2 - 95\lambda + 150$ **15.** 4, 3, 3, 1 **17.** 3, 3, 1, 1, 0

19. *Hint*: The equation given holds for all λ.

21. *Hint*: Find an invertible matrix P so that $P^{-1}AP = RQ$.

23. a. $\{\mathbf{u}_1, \mathbf{u}_2\}$, where $\mathbf{u}_2 = \begin{bmatrix} -1 \\ 1 \end{bmatrix}$ is an eigenvector for $\lambda = .3$

b. $\mathbf{v}_0 = \mathbf{u}_1 - (1/14)\mathbf{u}_2$

c. $\mathbf{v}_k = \mathbf{u}_1 - (1/14)(.3)^k\mathbf{u}_2$. As $k \to \infty$, $(.3)^k \to 0$, and so $\mathbf{v}_k \to \mathbf{u}_1$.

25. a. $A\mathbf{u}_1 = \mathbf{u}_1$, $A\mathbf{u}_2 = .5\mathbf{u}_2$, $A\mathbf{u}_3 = .2\mathbf{u}_3$. The eigenvalues of A are now obvious. You should work on parts (b) and (c) before consulting the Study Guide solutions.

27. One answer is $P_1 = \begin{bmatrix} 1 & 1 \\ -2 & -1 \end{bmatrix}$, whose columns are eigenvectors corresponding to the eigenvalues in D_1.

Section 6.3, page 295

1. $\begin{bmatrix} 226 & -525 \\ 90 & -209 \end{bmatrix}$ **3.** $\begin{bmatrix} a^k & 0 \\ 3(a^k - b^k) & b^k \end{bmatrix}$

5. $\lambda = 5$: $\begin{bmatrix} 1 \\ 1 \\ 1 \end{bmatrix}$; $\lambda = 1$: $\begin{bmatrix} 1 \\ 0 \\ -1 \end{bmatrix}, \begin{bmatrix} 2 \\ -1 \\ 0 \end{bmatrix}$

When an answer involves a diagonalization, $A = PDP^{-1}$, the factors P and D are not unique, so your answer may differ from that given here.

7. $P = \begin{bmatrix} 1 & 0 \\ 3 & 1 \end{bmatrix}$, $D = \begin{bmatrix} 1 & 0 \\ 0 & -1 \end{bmatrix}$ **9.** Not diagonalizable

11. $P = \begin{bmatrix} 1 & 2 & 1 \\ 3 & 3 & 1 \\ 4 & 3 & 1 \end{bmatrix}$, $D = \begin{bmatrix} 3 & 0 & 0 \\ 0 & 2 & 0 \\ 0 & 0 & 1 \end{bmatrix}$

13. $P = \begin{bmatrix} 1 & 2 & 1 \\ 1 & -1 & 0 \\ -1 & 0 & 1 \end{bmatrix}$, $D = \begin{bmatrix} 5 & 0 & 0 \\ 0 & 1 & 0 \\ 0 & 0 & 1 \end{bmatrix}$

15. $P = \begin{bmatrix} -1 & -4 & -2 \\ 1 & 0 & -1 \\ 0 & 1 & 1 \end{bmatrix}$, $D = \begin{bmatrix} 3 & 0 & 0 \\ 0 & 3 & 1 \\ 0 & 0 & 1 \end{bmatrix}$

17. Not diagonalizable

19. $P = \begin{bmatrix} 1 & 3 & -1 & -1 \\ 0 & 2 & -1 & 2 \\ 0 & 0 & 1 & 0 \\ 0 & 0 & 0 & 1 \end{bmatrix}$, $D = \begin{bmatrix} 5 & 0 & 0 & 0 \\ 0 & 3 & 0 & 0 \\ 0 & 0 & 2 & 0 \\ 0 & 0 & 0 & 2 \end{bmatrix}$

21. Yes **23.** No. A must be diagonalizable.

25. *Hint*: Write $A = PDP^{-1}$. Since A is invertible, 0 is not an eigenvalue of A, so D has nonzero entries on its diagonal.

Section 6.4, page 301

1. $\begin{bmatrix} 3 & -1 & 0 \\ -5 & 6 & 4 \end{bmatrix}$

3. a. $T(\mathbf{e}_1) = -\mathbf{b}_2 + \mathbf{b}_3$, $T(\mathbf{e}_2) = -\mathbf{b}_1 - \mathbf{b}_3$, $T(\mathbf{e}_3) = \mathbf{b}_1 - \mathbf{b}_2$

c. $\begin{bmatrix} 0 & -1 & 1 \\ -1 & 0 & -1 \\ 1 & -1 & 0 \end{bmatrix}$ **5. a.** $10 - 3t + 4t^2 + t^3$

b. For any $\mathbf{p}$, $\mathbf{q}$ in $\mathbb{P}_2$ and any scalar c,

$$\begin{aligned} T[\mathbf{p}(t) + \mathbf{q}(t)] &= (t+5)[\mathbf{p}(t) + \mathbf{q}(t)] \\ &= (t+5)\mathbf{p}(t) + (t+5)\mathbf{q}(t) \\ &= T[\mathbf{p}(t)] + T[\mathbf{q}(t)] \end{aligned}$$

$$\begin{aligned} T[c\cdot\mathbf{p}(t)] &= (t+5)[c\cdot\mathbf{p}(t)] = c\cdot(t+5)\mathbf{p}(t) \\ &= c\cdot T[\mathbf{p}(t)] \end{aligned}$$

c. $\begin{bmatrix} 5 & 0 & 0 \\ 1 & 5 & 0 \\ 0 & 1 & 5 \\ 0 & 0 & 1 \end{bmatrix}$ **7.** $\begin{bmatrix} 3 & 0 & 0 \\ 5 & -2 & 0 \\ 0 & 4 & 1 \end{bmatrix}$

9. a. $\begin{bmatrix} 2 \\ 5 \\ 8 \end{bmatrix}$

b. *Hint*: Compute $T(\mathbf{p} + \mathbf{q})$ and $T(c\cdot\mathbf{p})$ for arbitrary $\mathbf{p}$, $\mathbf{q}$ in $\mathbb{P}_3$ and an arbitrary scalar c.

c. $\begin{bmatrix} 1 & -1 & 1 \\ 1 & 0 & 0 \\ 1 & 1 & 1 \end{bmatrix}$ **11.** $\begin{bmatrix} 1 & 5 \\ 0 & 1 \end{bmatrix}$

13. $\mathbf{b}_1 = \begin{bmatrix} 1 \\ 1 \end{bmatrix}$, $\mathbf{b}_2 = \begin{bmatrix} 1 \\ 3 \end{bmatrix}$ **15.** $\mathbf{b}_1 = \begin{bmatrix} -2 \\ 1 \end{bmatrix}$, $\mathbf{b}_2 = \begin{bmatrix} 1 \\ 1 \end{bmatrix}$

17. a. $A\mathbf{b}_1 = 2\mathbf{b}_1$, so $\mathbf{b}_1$ is an eigenvector of A. However, A has only one eigenvalue, $\lambda = 2$, and the eigenspace is only one-dimensional, so A is not diagonalizable.

b. $\begin{bmatrix} 2 & -1 \\ 0 & 2 \end{bmatrix}$

19. *Hint*: By definition, if A is similar to B, there exists an invertible matrix P such that $P^{-1}AP = B$. (See Section 6.2.) Then B is invertible because it is the product of invertible matrices. Use the equation $P^{-1}AP = B$.

21. *Hint*: Use the equations $P^{-1}BP = A$ and $Q^{-1}CQ = A$ to produce a similar equation that relates B and C.

23. *Hint*: Compute $B(P^{-1}\mathbf{x})$.

25. *Hint*: Write $A = PBP^{-1} = (PB)P^{-1}$, and use the trace property. If B is diagonal, how is tr B related to the eigenvalues of A?

27. For each j, $I(\mathbf{b}_j) = \mathbf{b}_j$. Since the standard coordinate vector of any vector in $\mathbb{R}^n$ is just the vector itself, $[I(\mathbf{b}_j)]_{\mathcal{E}} = \mathbf{b}_j$. Thus the matrix for I relative to $\mathcal{B}$ and the standard basis $\mathcal{E}$ is simply $[\mathbf{b}_1 \ \ \mathbf{b}_2 \ \ \cdots \ \ \mathbf{b}_n]$. This matrix is precisely the *change-of-coordinates* matrix $P_{\mathcal{B}}$ defined in Section 5.4.

29. *Hint*: If $\mathcal{B} = \{\mathbf{b}_1, \dots, \mathbf{b}_n\}$, what is the $\mathcal{B}$-coordinate vector of $\mathbf{b}_j$?

Section 6.5, page 309

1. $\lambda = 2+i, \begin{bmatrix} -1+i \\ 1 \end{bmatrix}; \lambda = 2-i, \begin{bmatrix} -1-i \\ 1 \end{bmatrix}$

3. $\lambda = 2+3i, \begin{bmatrix} 1-3i \\ 2 \end{bmatrix}; \lambda = 2-3i, \begin{bmatrix} 1+3i \\ 2 \end{bmatrix}$

5. $\lambda = 2+2i, \begin{bmatrix} 1 \\ 2+2i \end{bmatrix}; \lambda = 2-2i, \begin{bmatrix} 1 \\ 2-2i \end{bmatrix}$

7. $\lambda = \sqrt{3} \pm i$, $\varphi = \pi/6$ radians, $r = 2$

9. $\lambda = -\sqrt{3}/2 \pm (1/2)i$, $\varphi = -5\pi/6$ radians, $r = 1$

11. $\lambda = .1 \pm .1i$, $\varphi = -\pi/4$ radians, $r = \sqrt{2}/10$

In Exercises 13–19, other answers are possible. Any P that makes $P^{-1}AP$ equal to the given C or to C^T is a satisfactory answer. First find P; then compute $P^{-1}AP$.

13. $P = \begin{bmatrix} -1 & -1 \\ 1 & 0 \end{bmatrix}, C = \begin{bmatrix} 2 & -1 \\ 1 & 2 \end{bmatrix}$

15. $P = \begin{bmatrix} 1 & 3 \\ 2 & 0 \end{bmatrix}, C = \begin{bmatrix} 2 & -3 \\ 3 & 2 \end{bmatrix}$

17. $P = \begin{bmatrix} 2 & -1 \\ 5 & 0 \end{bmatrix}, C = \begin{bmatrix} -.6 & -.8 \\ .8 & -.6 \end{bmatrix}$

19. $P = \begin{bmatrix} 2 & -1 \\ 2 & 0 \end{bmatrix}, C = \begin{bmatrix} .96 & -.28 \\ .28 & .96 \end{bmatrix}$

21. $y = \begin{bmatrix} 2 \\ -1+2i \end{bmatrix} = \dfrac{(-1+2i)}{5} \begin{bmatrix} -2-4i \\ 5 \end{bmatrix}$

23. (a) properties of conjugates; (b) $\overline{A\mathbf{x}} = A\overline{\mathbf{x}}$ and A is real; (c) $c^T = c$ when c is a scalar and hence may be viewed as a 1×1 matrix; (d) properties of transposes; (e) $A^T = A$, definition of q

25. *Hint*: Compute Re $(A\mathbf{x})$ and Im $(A\mathbf{x})$, and use the fact that $\overline{A\mathbf{x}} = A\overline{\mathbf{x}}$.

Section 6.6, page 320

1. a. *Hint*: Find c_1, c_2 such that $\mathbf{x}_0 = c_1\mathbf{v}_1 + c_2\mathbf{v}_2$. Use this representation and the fact that $\mathbf{v}_1$ and $\mathbf{v}_2$ are eigenvectors of A to compute $\mathbf{x}_1 = \begin{bmatrix} 49/3 \\ 41/3 \end{bmatrix}$.
b. In general, $\mathbf{x}_k = 5(3)^k\mathbf{v}_1 - 4(\frac{1}{3})^k\mathbf{v}_2$ for $k \geq 0$.

3. When $p = .2$, the eigenvalues of A are .9 and .7, and

$$\mathbf{x}_k = c_1(.9)^k \begin{bmatrix} 1 \\ 1 \end{bmatrix} + c_2(.7)^k \begin{bmatrix} 2 \\ 1 \end{bmatrix} \to 0, \qquad \text{as } k \to \infty$$

The higher predation rate cuts down the owls' food supply, and eventually both predator and prey populations perish.

5. If $p = .325$, the eigenvalues are 1.05 and .55. Since $1.05 > 1$, both populations will grow at 5% per year. An eigenvector for 1.05 is (6, 13), so eventually there will be approximately 6 spotted owls to every 13 (thousand) tree squirrels.

7. a. The origin is a saddle point because A has one eigenvalue larger than 1 and one smaller than 1 (in absolute value).
b. The direction of greatest attraction is given by the eigenvector corresponding to the eigenvalue 1/3, namely, $\mathbf{v}_2$. All vectors that are multiples of $\mathbf{v}_2$ are attracted to the origin. The direction of greatest repulsion is given by the eigenvector $\mathbf{v}_1$. All multiples of $\mathbf{v}_1$ are repelled.
c. See the Study Guide.

9. Saddle point; eigenvalues of A: 2, .5; direction of greatest repulsion: the line through (0, 0) and (−1, 1); direction of greatest attraction: the line through (0, 0) and (1, 4)

11. Attractor; eigenvalues: .9, .8; greatest attraction: line through (0, 0) and (5, 4)

13. Repellor; eigenvalues: 1.2, 1.1; greatest repulsion: line through (0, 0) and (3, 4)

15. $\mathbf{v}_k = \begin{bmatrix} .4 \\ .2 \\ .4 \end{bmatrix} - \frac{6}{7}(.5)^k \begin{bmatrix} -.7 \\ .4 \\ .3 \end{bmatrix} - \frac{1}{7}(-.2)^k \begin{bmatrix} 0 \\ -1 \\ 1 \end{bmatrix}$

17. a. $A = \begin{bmatrix} 0 & 1.6 \\ .3 & .8 \end{bmatrix}$
b. The population is growing because the largest eigenvalue of A is 1.2, which is larger than 1 in magnitude. The eventual growth rate is 1.2, which is 20% growth per year. An eigenvector of (4,3) for $\lambda_1 = 1.2$ shows that there will be 4 juveniles for every 3 adults.

Section 6.7, page 327

1. Eigenvector: $\mathbf{x}_4 = \begin{bmatrix} 1 \\ .3326 \end{bmatrix}$, or $A\mathbf{x}_4 = \begin{bmatrix} 4.9978 \\ 1.6652 \end{bmatrix}$; $\lambda \approx 4.9978$

3. Eigenvector: $\mathbf{x}_4 = \begin{bmatrix} .5188 \\ 1 \end{bmatrix}$, or $A\mathbf{x}_4 = \begin{bmatrix} .4594 \\ .9075 \end{bmatrix}$; $\lambda \approx .9075$

5. $\mathbf{x} = \begin{bmatrix} -.7999 \\ 1 \end{bmatrix}$, $A\mathbf{x} = \begin{bmatrix} 4.0015 \\ -5.0020 \end{bmatrix}$; estimated $\lambda = -5.0020$

7. $\mathbf{x}_k$: $\begin{bmatrix} .75 \\ 1 \end{bmatrix}, \begin{bmatrix} 1 \\ .9565 \end{bmatrix}, \begin{bmatrix} .9932 \\ 1 \end{bmatrix}, \begin{bmatrix} 1 \\ .9990 \end{bmatrix}, \begin{bmatrix} .9998 \\ 1 \end{bmatrix}$; μ_k: 11.5, 12.78, 12.96, 12.9948, 12.9990

9. $\mu_5 = 8.4233$, $\mu_6 = 8.4246$; actual value: 8.42443 (5 places)

11. μ_k : 5.8000, 5.9655, 5.9942, 5.9990 (k = 1,2,3,4); $R(\mathbf{x}_k)$: 5.9655, 5.9990, 5.99997, 5.9999993

13. Yes, but the sequences may converge very slowly.

15. *Hint*: Write $A\mathbf{x} - \alpha\mathbf{x} = (A - \alpha I)\mathbf{x}$, and use the fact that $(A - \alpha I)$ is invertible when α is *not* an eigenvalue of A.

17. $\nu_0 = 3.3384$, $\nu_1 = 3.32119$ (accurate to 4 places with rounding), $\nu_2 = 3.3212209$. Actual: 3.3212201 (accurate to 7 places)

19. a. $\mu_6 = 30.2887 = \mu_7$ to four decimal places. To six places, the largest eigenvalue is 30.288685, with eigenvector (.957629, .688937, 1, .943782).
b. The inverse power method (with $\alpha = 0$) produces $\mu_1^{-1} = .010141$, $\mu_2^{-1} = .010150$. To seven places, the smallest eigenvalue is .0101500, with eigenvector (−.603972, 1, −.251135, .148953). The reason for the rapid convergence is that the next-to-smallest eigenvalue is near .85.

21. a. If the eigenvalues of A are all less than 1 in magnitude, and if $\mathbf{x} \neq \mathbf{0}$, then $A^k\mathbf{x}$ is approximately an eigenvector for large k.
b. If the strictly dominant eigenvalue is 1, and if $\mathbf{x}$ has a component in the direction of the corresponding eigenvector, then $\{A^k\mathbf{x}\}$ will converge to a multiple of that eigenvector.
c. If the eigenvalues of A are all greater than 1 in magnitude, and if $\mathbf{x}$ is not an eigenvector, then the distance from $A^k\mathbf{x}$ to the nearest eigenvector will *increase* as $k \to \infty$.

Supplementary Exercises, page 329

1. a. T **b.** F **c.** T **d.** T **e.** F **f.** T **g.** F **h.** F **i.** T **j.** F **k.** F **l.** F **m.** T **n.** F **o.** F **p.** T **q.** F

2. If $AB\mathbf{x} = \lambda\mathbf{x}$, then $A(B\mathbf{x}) = \lambda\mathbf{x}$ and $BA(B\mathbf{x}) = \lambda(B\mathbf{x})$. This equation says that $B\mathbf{x}$ is an eigenvector of BA, because $B\mathbf{x} \neq \mathbf{0}$.

3. a. $(5I - A)\mathbf{x} = 5\mathbf{x} - A\mathbf{x} = 5\mathbf{x} - \lambda\mathbf{x} = (5 - \lambda)\mathbf{x}$. The eigenvalue is $5 - \lambda$.
b. $(5I - 3A + A^2)\mathbf{x} = 5\mathbf{x} - 3A\mathbf{x} + A(A\mathbf{x}) = 5\mathbf{x} - 3(\lambda\mathbf{x}) + \lambda^2\mathbf{x} = (5 - 3\lambda + \lambda^2)\mathbf{x}$. The eigenvalue is $5 - 3\lambda + \lambda^2$.

4.
$$\begin{aligned} p(A)\mathbf{x} &= (c_0 I + c_1 A + c_2 A^2 + \cdots + c_n A^n)\mathbf{x} \\ &= c_0\mathbf{x} + c_1(A\mathbf{x}) + c_2(A^2\mathbf{x}) + \cdots + c_n(A^n\mathbf{x}) \\ &= c_0\mathbf{x} + c_1\lambda\mathbf{x} + c_2\lambda^2\mathbf{x} + \cdots + c_n\lambda^n\mathbf{x} = p(\lambda)\mathbf{x} \end{aligned}$$

So $p(\lambda)$ is an eigenvalue of $p(A)$.

5. a. If $A = PDP^{-1}$, then $A^k = PD^kP^{-1}$, and

$$\begin{aligned} B = 5I - 3A + A^2 &= 5PD^0P^{-1} - 3PDP^{-1} + PD^2P^{-1} \\ &= P(5I - 3D + D^2)P^{-1} \end{aligned}$$

Since D is diagonal, so is $5I - 3D + D^2$. Thus B is similar to a diagonal matrix.
b.
$$\begin{aligned} p(A) &= c_0 I + c_1 PDP^{-1} + c_2 PD^2P^{-1} + \\ &\quad \cdots + c_n PD^nP^{-1} \\ &= P(c_0 I + c_1 D + c_2 D^2 + \cdots + c_n D^n)P^{-1} \\ &= Pp(D)P^{-1} \end{aligned}$$

This shows that $p(A)$ is diagonalizable, because $p(D)$ is a linear combination of diagonal matrices and hence is diagonal. In fact, because D is diagonal, it is easy to see that

$$p(D) = \begin{bmatrix} p(2) & 0 \\ 0 & p(7) \end{bmatrix}$$

6. If $A = PDP^{-1}$, then $p(A) = Pp(D)P^{-1}$, as shown in Exercise 5. If the (j, j) entry in D is λ, then the (j, j) entry in D^k is λ^k, and so the (j, j) entry in $p(D)$ is $p(\lambda)$. If p is the characteristic polynomial of A, then $p(\lambda) = 0$ for each diagonal entry of D, because these entries in D are the eigenvalues of A. Thus $p(D)$ is the zero matrix. Thus $p(A) = P \cdot 0 \cdot P^{-1} = 0$.

7. If $I - A$ were not invertible, then the equation $(I - A)\mathbf{x} = \mathbf{0}$ would have a nontrivial solution $\mathbf{x}$. Then $\mathbf{x} - A\mathbf{x} = \mathbf{0}$ and $A\mathbf{x} = 1 \cdot \mathbf{x}$, which shows that A would have 1 as an eigenvalue. This cannot happen if all the eigenvalues are less than 1 in magnitude. So $I - A$ must be invertible.

8. *Hint*: Let $\mathbf{e}_j$ be a column of I, write $\mathbf{e}_j$ in terms of a basis for $\mathbb{R}^n$ consisting of eigenvectors of A, and show that $A^k\mathbf{e}_j \to \mathbf{0}$ as $k \to \infty$. Another approach is to use the diagonalization of A to study A^k.

9. a. Take $\mathbf{x}$ in H. Then $\mathbf{x} = c\mathbf{u}$ for some scalar c. So $A\mathbf{x} = A(c\mathbf{u}) = c(A\mathbf{u}) = c(\lambda\mathbf{u}) = (c\lambda)\mathbf{u}$, which shows that $A\mathbf{x}$ is in H.
b. Let $\mathbf{x}$ be a nonzero vector in K. Since K is one-dimensional, K must be the set of all scalar multiples of $\mathbf{x}$. If K is invariant under A, then $A\mathbf{x}$ is in K and hence $A\mathbf{x}$ is a multiple of $\mathbf{x}$. Thus $\mathbf{x}$ is an eigenvector of A.

10. Let U be an echelon form of A and V an echelon form of B, obtained with r and s row interchanges, respectively, and no scaling. Then

$$\det A = (-1)^r \det U \qquad \text{and} \qquad \det B = (-1)^s \det V$$

Using first the row operations that reduce A to U, we can reduce G to a matrix of the form $G' = \begin{bmatrix} U & Y \\ 0 & B \end{bmatrix}$. Then, using the row operations that reduce B to V, we can further reduce G' to $G'' = \begin{bmatrix} U & Y \\ 0 & V \end{bmatrix}$. There will be $(r+s)$ row interchanges, and so

$$\det \begin{bmatrix} A & X \\ 0 & B \end{bmatrix} = (-1)^{r+s} \det \begin{bmatrix} U & Y \\ 0 & V \end{bmatrix}$$

Since $\begin{bmatrix} U & Y \\ 0 & V \end{bmatrix}$ is upper triangular, its determinant is obviously equal to $(\det U)(\det V)$. Thus

$$\det G = (-1)^{r+s}(\det U)(\det V) = (\det A)(\det B)$$

11. 1, 3, 7 **12.** 6, −1, −1, −5

13. The eigenvalues of A are 1 and .6. Use this to factor A and A^k.

$$A = \begin{bmatrix} -1 & -3 \\ 2 & 2 \end{bmatrix}\begin{bmatrix} 1 & 0 \\ 0 & .6 \end{bmatrix}\cdot\frac{1}{4}\begin{bmatrix} 2 & 3 \\ -2 & -1 \end{bmatrix}$$

$$A^k = \begin{bmatrix} -1 & -3 \\ 2 & 2 \end{bmatrix}\begin{bmatrix} 1^k & 0 \\ 0 & .6^k \end{bmatrix}\cdot\frac{1}{4}\begin{bmatrix} 2 & 3 \\ -2 & -1 \end{bmatrix}$$

$$= \frac{1}{4}\begin{bmatrix} -1 & -3 \\ 2 & 2 \end{bmatrix}\begin{bmatrix} 2 & 3 \\ -2\cdot(.6)^k & -(.6)^k \end{bmatrix}$$

$$= \frac{1}{4}\begin{bmatrix} -2+6(.6)^k & -3+3(.6)^k \\ 4-4(.6)^k & -6-2(.6)^k \end{bmatrix}$$

$$\to \frac{1}{4}\begin{bmatrix} -2 & -3 \\ 4 & 6 \end{bmatrix} \qquad \text{as } k \to \infty$$

14. $C_p = \begin{bmatrix} 0 & 1 \\ -6 & 5 \end{bmatrix}$; $\det(C_p - \lambda I) = 6 - 5\lambda + \lambda^2 = p(\lambda)$

15. $C_p = \begin{bmatrix} 0 & 1 & 0 \\ 0 & 0 & 1 \\ 24 & -26 & 9 \end{bmatrix}$;
$\det(C_p - \lambda I) = 24 - 26\lambda + 9\lambda^2 - \lambda^3$

16. If p is a polynomial of order 2, then a calculation such as in Exercise 14 shows that the characteristic polynomial of C_p is $p(\lambda) = (-1)^2 p(\lambda)$, so the result is true for $n = 2$. Suppose the result is true for $n = k$ for some $k \geq 2$, and consider a polynomial p of degree $k+1$. Then expanding $\det(C_p - \lambda I)$ by cofactors down the first column, we have

$$\det(C_p - \lambda I) = (-\lambda)\det\begin{bmatrix} -\lambda & 1 & \cdots & 0 \\ \vdots & & & \vdots \\ 0 & & & 1 \\ -a_1 & -a_2 & \cdots & -a_k - \lambda \end{bmatrix} + (-1)^{k+1}a_0$$

The $k \times k$ matrix shown is $C_q - \lambda I$, where $q(t) = a_1 + a_2 t + \cdots + a_k t^{k-1} + t^k$. By the induction assumption, the determinant of $C_q - \lambda I$ is $(-1)^k q(\lambda)$. Thus

$$\begin{aligned}\det(C_p - \lambda I) &= (-1)^{k+1}a_0 + (-\lambda)(-1)^k q(\lambda) \\ &= (-1)^{k+1}[a_0 + \lambda(a_1 + \cdots + a_k\lambda^{k-1} + \lambda^k)] \\ &= (-1)^{k+1}p(\lambda)\end{aligned}$$

So the formula holds for $n = k+1$ when it holds for $n = k$. By the principle of induction, the formula for $\det(C_p - \lambda I)$ is true for all $n \geq 2$.

17. a. $C_p = \begin{bmatrix} 0 & 1 & 0 \\ 0 & 0 & 1 \\ -a_0 & -a_1 & -a_2 \end{bmatrix}$

b. $C_p\begin{bmatrix} 1 \\ \lambda \\ \lambda^2 \end{bmatrix} = \begin{bmatrix} \lambda \\ \lambda^2 \\ -a_0 - a_1\lambda - a_2\lambda^2 \end{bmatrix} = \begin{bmatrix} \lambda \\ \lambda^2 \\ \lambda^3 \end{bmatrix}$

$= \lambda\begin{bmatrix} 1 \\ \lambda \\ \lambda^2 \end{bmatrix}$. This calculation shows that $(1, \lambda, \lambda^2)$ is an eigenvector of C_p corresponding to the eigenvalue λ.

18. From Exercise 17, the columns of the Vandermonde matrix are eigenvectors of C_p, corresponding to the eigenvalues $\lambda_1, \lambda_2, \lambda_3$ (the roots of the polynomial p). Since these eigenvalues are distinct, the eigenvectors form a linearly independent set, by Theorem 2 in Section 6.1. Thus V has linearly independent columns and hence is invertible, by the Invertible Matrix Theorem. Finally, since the columns of V are eigenvectors of C_p, the proof of the Diagonalization Theorem (Theorem 5 in Section 6.3) shows that $V^{-1}C_pV$ is diagonal.

19. The MATLAB command "roots(p)" requires as input a row vector p whose entries are the coefficients of a polynomial, with the highest-order coefficient listed first. MATLAB constructs a companion matrix C_p whose characteristic polynomial is p, so the roots of p are the eigenvalues of C_p. The numerical values of the eigenvalues (roots) are found by the same QR algorithm used by the command "eig(A)."

CHAPTER 7

Section 7.1, page 340

1. $5, 8, \frac{8}{5}$ **3.** $\begin{bmatrix} 3/35 \\ -1/35 \\ -1/7 \end{bmatrix}$ **5.** $\begin{bmatrix} 8/13 \\ 12/13 \end{bmatrix}$ **7.** $\sqrt{5}$

9. $\sqrt{35}$ **11.** $\begin{bmatrix} -.6 \\ .8 \end{bmatrix}$ **13.** $\begin{bmatrix} 7/\sqrt{69} \\ 2/\sqrt{69} \\ 4/\sqrt{69} \end{bmatrix}$ **15.** $5\sqrt{5}$

17. *Hint*: Use Theorems 3 and 2 from Section 3.1.

19. Not orthogonal **21.** Orthogonal

23. $\mathbf{u}\cdot\mathbf{v} = 0$, $\|\mathbf{u}\|^2 = 30$, $\|\mathbf{v}\|^2 = 101$, $\|\mathbf{u}+\mathbf{v}\|^2 = (-5)^2 + (-9)^2 + 5^2 = 131 = 30 + 101$

25. The set of all multiples of $\begin{bmatrix} -b \\ a \end{bmatrix}$ (when $\mathbf{v} \neq \mathbf{0}$)

27. *Hint*: Use the definition of orthogonality.

29. *Hint*: Consider a typical vector $\mathbf{w} = c_1\mathbf{v}_1 + \cdots + c_p\mathbf{v}_p$ in W.

31. *Hint*: If $\mathbf{x}$ is in $W^\perp$, then $\mathbf{x}$ is orthogonal to every vector in W.

Section 7.2, page 350

1. Not orthogonal **3.** Not orthogonal **5.** Orthogonal

7. Show $\mathbf{u}_1\cdot\mathbf{u}_2 = 0$, mention Theorem 4, and observe that two linearly independent vectors in $\mathbb{R}^2$ form a basis. Then obtain

$$\mathbf{x} = \frac{39}{13}\begin{bmatrix} 2 \\ -3 \end{bmatrix} + \frac{26}{52}\begin{bmatrix} 6 \\ 4 \end{bmatrix} = 3\begin{bmatrix} 2 \\ -3 \end{bmatrix} + \frac{1}{2}\begin{bmatrix} 6 \\ 4 \end{bmatrix}$$

9. Show $\mathbf{u}_1\cdot\mathbf{u}_2 = 0$, $\mathbf{u}_1\cdot\mathbf{u}_3 = 0$, and $\mathbf{u}_2\cdot\mathbf{u}_3 = 0$. Mention Theorem 4, and observe that three linearly independent vectors in $\mathbb{R}^3$ form a basis. Then obtain

$$\mathbf{x} = \tfrac{5}{2}\mathbf{u}_1 - \tfrac{27}{18}\mathbf{u}_2 + \tfrac{18}{9}\mathbf{u}_3 = \tfrac{5}{2}\mathbf{u}_1 - \tfrac{3}{2}\mathbf{u}_2 + 2\mathbf{u}_3$$

11. $\begin{bmatrix} 1/\sqrt{3} \\ 1/\sqrt{3} \\ 1/\sqrt{3} \end{bmatrix}, \begin{bmatrix} -1/\sqrt{2} \\ 0 \\ 1/\sqrt{2} \end{bmatrix}$ **13.** Orthonormal

15. Orthonormal **17.** $\begin{bmatrix} -2 \\ 1 \end{bmatrix}$

19. $\mathbf{y} = \begin{bmatrix} -4/5 \\ 7/5 \end{bmatrix} + \begin{bmatrix} 14/5 \\ 8/5 \end{bmatrix}$

21. $\mathbf{y} - \hat{\mathbf{y}} = \begin{bmatrix} .6 \\ -.8 \end{bmatrix}$, distance $= 1$

23. Suppose $\hat{\mathbf{y}} = \dfrac{\mathbf{y}\cdot\mathbf{u}}{\mathbf{u}\cdot\mathbf{u}}\mathbf{u}$. Replacing $\mathbf{u}$ by $c\mathbf{u}$, where $c \neq 0$,

$$\frac{\mathbf{y}\cdot(c\mathbf{u})}{(c\mathbf{u})\cdot(c\mathbf{u})}(c\mathbf{u}) = \frac{c(\mathbf{y}\cdot\mathbf{u})}{c^2\mathbf{u}\cdot\mathbf{u}}(c)\mathbf{u} = \hat{\mathbf{y}}$$

25. *Hint*: $\|U\mathbf{x}\|^2 = (U\mathbf{x})^T(U\mathbf{x})$.

27. *Hint*: You need two theorems, one of which applies only to *square* matrices.

29. *Hint*: If you have a candidate for an inverse, you can check to see whether the candidate works.

Section 7.3, page 357

1. $\mathbf{x} = -\frac{8}{9}\mathbf{u}_1 - \frac{2}{9}\mathbf{u}_2 + \frac{2}{3}\mathbf{u}_3 + 2\mathbf{u}_4$; $\mathbf{x} = \begin{bmatrix} 0 \\ -2 \\ 4 \\ -2 \end{bmatrix} + \begin{bmatrix} 10 \\ -6 \\ -2 \\ 2 \end{bmatrix}$

3. $\begin{bmatrix} -1 \\ 4 \\ 0 \end{bmatrix}$ **5.** $\begin{bmatrix} -1 \\ 2 \\ 6 \end{bmatrix} = \mathbf{y}$

7. $\mathbf{y} = \begin{bmatrix} 10/3 \\ 2/3 \\ 8/3 \end{bmatrix} + \begin{bmatrix} -7/3 \\ 7/3 \\ 7/3 \end{bmatrix}$

9. $\mathbf{y} = \begin{bmatrix} 2 \\ 4 \\ 0 \\ 0 \end{bmatrix} + \begin{bmatrix} 2 \\ -1 \\ 3 \\ -1 \end{bmatrix}$ **11.** $\begin{bmatrix} 3 \\ -1 \\ 1 \\ -1 \end{bmatrix}$ **13.** $\begin{bmatrix} -1 \\ -3 \\ -2 \\ 3 \end{bmatrix}$

15. $\sqrt{40}$

17. a. $U^TU = \begin{bmatrix} 1 & 0 \\ 0 & 1 \end{bmatrix}$, $UU^T = \begin{bmatrix} 8/9 & -2/9 & 2/9 \\ -2/9 & 5/9 & 4/9 \\ 2/9 & 4/9 & 5/9 \end{bmatrix}$

b. $\text{proj}_W\mathbf{y} = 6\mathbf{u}_1 + 3\mathbf{u}_2 = \begin{bmatrix} 2 \\ 4 \\ 5 \end{bmatrix}$, and $(UU^T)\mathbf{y} = \begin{bmatrix} 2 \\ 4 \\ 5 \end{bmatrix}$

19. Any multiple of $\begin{bmatrix} 0 \\ 2/5 \\ 1/5 \end{bmatrix}$, such as $\begin{bmatrix} 0 \\ 2 \\ 1 \end{bmatrix}$

21. *Hint:* Use Theorem 3 and the Orthogonal Decomposition Theorem. For the uniqueness, suppose $A\mathbf{p} = \mathbf{b}$ and $A\mathbf{p}_1 = \mathbf{b}$, and consider the equations $\mathbf{p} = \mathbf{p}_1 + (\mathbf{p} - \mathbf{p}_1)$ and $\mathbf{p} = \mathbf{p} + \mathbf{0}$.

Section 7.4, page 365

1. $\begin{bmatrix} 3 \\ 0 \\ -1 \end{bmatrix}, \begin{bmatrix} -1 \\ 5 \\ -3 \end{bmatrix}$ **3.** $\begin{bmatrix} 2 \\ -5 \\ 1 \end{bmatrix}, \begin{bmatrix} 3 \\ 3/2 \\ 3/2 \end{bmatrix}$

5. $\begin{bmatrix} 1 \\ -4 \\ 0 \\ 1 \end{bmatrix}, \begin{bmatrix} 5 \\ 1 \\ -4 \\ -1 \end{bmatrix}$ **7.** $\begin{bmatrix} 2/\sqrt{30} \\ -5/\sqrt{30} \\ 1/\sqrt{30} \end{bmatrix}, \begin{bmatrix} 2/\sqrt{6} \\ 1/\sqrt{6} \\ 1/\sqrt{6} \end{bmatrix}$

9. $\begin{bmatrix} 3 \\ 1 \\ -1 \\ 3 \end{bmatrix}, \begin{bmatrix} 1 \\ 3 \\ 3 \\ -1 \end{bmatrix}, \begin{bmatrix} -3 \\ 1 \\ 1 \\ 3 \end{bmatrix}$

11. $\begin{bmatrix} 1 \\ -1 \\ -1 \\ 1 \\ 1 \end{bmatrix}, \begin{bmatrix} 3 \\ 0 \\ 3 \\ -3 \\ 3 \end{bmatrix}, \begin{bmatrix} 2 \\ 0 \\ 2 \\ 2 \\ -2 \end{bmatrix}$

13. $R = \begin{bmatrix} 6 & 12 \\ 0 & 6 \end{bmatrix}$

15. $Q = \begin{bmatrix} 1/\sqrt{5} & 1/2 & 1/2 \\ -1/\sqrt{5} & 0 & 0 \\ -1/\sqrt{5} & 1/2 & 1/2 \\ 1/\sqrt{5} & -1/2 & 1/2 \\ 1/\sqrt{5} & 1/2 & -1/2 \end{bmatrix}$,

$R = \begin{bmatrix} \sqrt{5} & -\sqrt{5} & 4\sqrt{5} \\ 0 & 6 & -2 \\ 0 & 0 & 4 \end{bmatrix}$

17. Suppose $\mathbf{x}$ satisfies $R\mathbf{x} = \mathbf{0}$, then $QR\mathbf{x} = Q\mathbf{0} = \mathbf{0}$, and $A\mathbf{x} = \mathbf{0}$. Since the columns of A are linearly independent, $\mathbf{x}$ must be zero. This fact, in turn, shows that the columns of R are linearly independent. Since R is square, it is invertible, by the Invertible Matrix Theorem.

19. Denote the columns of Q by $\mathbf{q}_1, \ldots, \mathbf{q}_n$. Note that $n \leq m$, because A is $m \times n$ and has linearly independent columns. Use the fact that the columns of Q can be extended to a basis for $\mathbb{R}^m$, say $\{\mathbf{q}_1, \ldots, \mathbf{q}_m\}$. (The Study Guide describes one method.) Let $Q_0 = [\,\mathbf{q}_{n+1} \ \cdots \ \mathbf{q}_m\,]$ and $Q_1 = [\,Q \ \ Q_0\,]$. Then, using partitioned matrix multiplication, $Q_1 \begin{bmatrix} R \\ 0 \end{bmatrix} = QR = A$.

Section 7.5, page 373

1. a. $\begin{bmatrix} 6 & -11 \\ -11 & 22 \end{bmatrix} \begin{bmatrix} x_1 \\ x_2 \end{bmatrix} = \begin{bmatrix} -4 \\ 11 \end{bmatrix}$ **b.** $\hat{\mathbf{x}} = \begin{bmatrix} 3 \\ 2 \end{bmatrix}$

3. a. $\begin{bmatrix} 6 & 6 \\ 6 & 42 \end{bmatrix} \begin{bmatrix} x_1 \\ x_2 \end{bmatrix} = \begin{bmatrix} 6 \\ -6 \end{bmatrix}$ **b.** $\hat{\mathbf{x}} = \begin{bmatrix} 4/3 \\ -1/3 \end{bmatrix}$

5. $\hat{\mathbf{x}} = \begin{bmatrix} 5 \\ -3 \\ 0 \end{bmatrix} + x_3 \begin{bmatrix} -1 \\ 1 \\ 1 \end{bmatrix}$ **7.** $2\sqrt{5}$

9. a. $\begin{bmatrix} 1 \\ 1 \\ 0 \end{bmatrix}$ **b.** $\hat{\mathbf{x}} = \begin{bmatrix} 2/7 \\ 1/7 \end{bmatrix}$

11. a. $\begin{bmatrix} 3 \\ 1 \\ 4 \\ -1 \end{bmatrix}$ **b.** $\hat{\mathbf{x}} = \begin{bmatrix} 2/3 \\ 0 \\ 1/3 \end{bmatrix}$

13. $A\mathbf{u} = \begin{bmatrix} 11 \\ -11 \\ 11 \end{bmatrix}$, $A\mathbf{v} = \begin{bmatrix} 7 \\ -12 \\ 7 \end{bmatrix}$, $\mathbf{b} - A\mathbf{u} = \begin{bmatrix} 0 \\ -2 \\ -6 \end{bmatrix}$,

$\mathbf{b} - A\mathbf{v} = \begin{bmatrix} 4 \\ 3 \\ -2 \end{bmatrix}$. No, $\mathbf{u}$ could not possibly be a least-squares solution of $A\mathbf{x} = \mathbf{b}$. Why?

15. $\hat{\mathbf{x}} = \begin{bmatrix} 4 \\ -1 \end{bmatrix}$

17. a. If $A\mathbf{x} = \mathbf{0}$, then $A^T A\mathbf{x} = A^T\mathbf{0} = \mathbf{0}$. This shows that Nul A is contained in Nul $A^T A$.
b. If $A^T A\mathbf{x} = \mathbf{0}$, then $\mathbf{x}^T A^T A\mathbf{x} = \mathbf{x}^T\mathbf{0} = 0$. So $(A\mathbf{x})^T(A\mathbf{x}) = 0$, which means that $\|A\mathbf{x}\|^2 = 0$, and hence $A\mathbf{x} = \mathbf{0}$. This shows that Nul $A^T A$ is contained in Nul A.

19. *Hint*: For (a), use an important theorem from Chapter 3.

21. By Theorem 14, $\hat{\mathbf{b}} = A\hat{\mathbf{x}} = A(A^T A)^{-1} A^T\mathbf{b}$. The matrix $A(A^T A)^{-1} A^T$ occurs frequently in statistics, where it is sometimes called the *hat-matrix*.

23. The normal equations are $\begin{bmatrix} 2 & 2 \\ 2 & 2 \end{bmatrix} \begin{bmatrix} x \\ y \end{bmatrix} = \begin{bmatrix} 6 \\ 6 \end{bmatrix}$, whose solution is the set of (x, y) such that $x + y = 3$. The solutions correspond to points on the line midway between the lines $x + y = 2$ and $x + y = 4$.

Section 7.6, page 382

1. $y = .4x + .9$ **3.** $y = 1.3x + 1.1$

5. If two data points have different x-coordinates, then the two columns of the design matrix X cannot be multiples of each other and hence are linearly independent. By

Theorem 14 in Section 7.5, the normal equations have a unique solution.

7. $\mathbf{y} = X\boldsymbol{\beta} + \boldsymbol{\epsilon}$, where $\mathbf{y} = \begin{bmatrix} 1.8 \\ 2.7 \\ 3.4 \\ 3.8 \\ 3.9 \end{bmatrix}$, $X = \begin{bmatrix} 1 & 1 \\ 2 & 4 \\ 3 & 9 \\ 4 & 16 \\ 5 & 25 \end{bmatrix}$,

$\boldsymbol{\beta} = \begin{bmatrix} \beta_1 \\ \beta_2 \end{bmatrix}$, $\boldsymbol{\epsilon} = \begin{bmatrix} \epsilon_1 \\ \epsilon_2 \\ \epsilon_3 \\ \epsilon_4 \\ \epsilon_5 \end{bmatrix}$ MATLAB: $\beta_1 = 1.76$, $\beta_2 = -.20$

9. $\mathbf{y} = X\boldsymbol{\beta} + \boldsymbol{\epsilon}$, where $\mathbf{y} = \begin{bmatrix} 7.9 \\ 5.4 \\ -.9 \end{bmatrix}$, $X = \begin{bmatrix} \cos 1 & \sin 1 \\ \cos 2 & \sin 2 \\ \cos 3 & \sin 3 \end{bmatrix}$,

$\boldsymbol{\beta} = \begin{bmatrix} A \\ B \end{bmatrix}$, $\boldsymbol{\epsilon} = \begin{bmatrix} \epsilon_1 \\ \epsilon_2 \\ \epsilon_3 \end{bmatrix}$

11. $\beta = 1.45$ and $e = .811$; the orbit is an ellipse. The equation $r = k/(1 - e\cdot\cos\vartheta)$ produces $r = 1.33$ when $\vartheta = 4.6$.

13. $\mathbf{v} = \begin{bmatrix} -6 \\ -2 \\ 1 \\ 7 \end{bmatrix}$. The entries in $\mathbf{v}$ are formed by subtracting $\overline{x}$ from the corresponding entries in $\mathbf{x}$.

15. *Hint*: Use Eq. (1) to compute X^TX and $X^T\mathbf{y}$.

17. a. The mean of the x-data is $\overline{x} = 5.5$. The data in mean-deviation form are $(-3.5, 1)$, $(-.5, 2)$, $(1.5, 3)$, $(2.5, 3)$. The columns of X are orthogonal because the entries in the second column sum to 1.

b. $\begin{bmatrix} 4 & 0 \\ 0 & 21 \end{bmatrix}\begin{bmatrix} \beta_0 \\ \beta_1 \end{bmatrix} = \begin{bmatrix} 9 \\ 7.5 \end{bmatrix}$,

$y = \frac{9}{4} + \frac{5}{14}x^* = \frac{9}{4} + \frac{5}{14}(x - 5.5)$

19. *Hint*: The equation has a nice geometric interpretation.

Section 7.7, page 392

1. a. 3, $\sqrt{105}$ **b.** All multiples of $\begin{bmatrix} 1 \\ 4 \end{bmatrix}$ **3.** 28

5. $5\sqrt{2}, 3\sqrt{3}$ **7.** $\dfrac{56}{25} + \dfrac{14}{25}t$

9. a. Constant polynomial, $p(t) \equiv 5$
b. $t^2 - 5$ is orthogonal to p_0 and p_1; values: $(4, -4, -4, 4)$; answer: $q(t) = \frac{1}{4}(t^2 - 5)$

11. $\frac{17}{5}t$

13. Verify each of the four axioms. For instance:

$$\begin{aligned}(\text{i})\ \langle \mathbf{u}, \mathbf{v}\rangle &= (A\mathbf{u})\cdot(A\mathbf{v}) && \text{Definition}\\ &= (A\mathbf{v})\cdot(A\mathbf{u}) && \text{Property of the dot product}\\ &= \langle \mathbf{v}, \mathbf{u}\rangle && \text{Definition}\end{aligned}$$

15.
$$\begin{aligned}\langle \mathbf{u}, c\mathbf{v}\rangle &= \langle c\mathbf{v}, \mathbf{u}\rangle && \text{Axiom (i)}\\ &= c\langle \mathbf{v}, \mathbf{u}\rangle && \text{Axiom (iii)}\\ &= c\langle \mathbf{u}, \mathbf{v}\rangle && \text{Axiom (i)}\end{aligned}$$

17. *Hint*: Compute 4 times the right-hand side.

19. $\langle \mathbf{u}, \mathbf{v}\rangle = \sqrt{a}\sqrt{b} + \sqrt{b}\sqrt{a} = 2\sqrt{ab}$, $\|\mathbf{u}\|^2 = (\sqrt{a})^2 + (\sqrt{b})^2 = a + b$, since a and b are nonnegative. So $\|\mathbf{u}\| = \sqrt{a+b}$. Similarly, $\|\mathbf{v}\| = \sqrt{b+a}$. By Cauchy–Schwarz, $2\sqrt{ab} \le \sqrt{a+b}\sqrt{b+a} = a + b$. Hence, $\sqrt{ab} \le \frac{a+b}{2}$.

21. 0 **23.** $2/\sqrt{5}$ **25.** $1, t, 3t^2 - 1$

Section 7.8, page 399

1. $y = 2 + \frac{3}{2}t$

3. $p(t) = 4p_0 - .1p_1 - .5p_2 + .2p_3$
$= 4 - .1t - .5(t^2 - 2) + .2\left(\frac{5}{6}t^3 - \frac{17}{6}t\right)$

(This polynomial happens to fit the data exactly.)

5. Use the identity $\sin mt \sin nt = \frac{1}{2}[\cos(m-n)t - \cos(m+n)t]$.

7. Use the identity $\cos^2 kt = \dfrac{1 + \cos 2kt}{2}$.

9. $\pi + 2\sin t + \sin 2t + \frac{2}{3}\sin 3t$ [*Hint*: Save time by using results from Example 4.]

11. $\frac{1}{2} - \frac{1}{2}\cos 2t$ (Why?)

13. *Hint*: Take functions f and g in $C(0, 2\pi)$, and fix an integer $m \ge 0$. Compute the Fourier coefficient of $f + g$ that involves $\cos mt$, and compute the Fourier coefficient that involves $\sin mt$ $(m > 0)$.

Supplementary Exercises, page 401

1. a. F **b.** T **c.** T **d.** F **e.** F **f.** T **g.** T **h.** T **i.** F **j.** T **k.** T **l.** F **m.** T **n.** F **o.** F **p.** T **q.** T **r.** F **s.** F

2. *Hint*: If $\{\mathbf{v}_1, \mathbf{v}_2\}$ is an orthonormal set and $\mathbf{x} = c_1\mathbf{v}_1 + c_2\mathbf{v}_2$, then the vectors $c_1\mathbf{v}_1$ and $c_2\mathbf{v}_2$ are orthogonal, and

$$\begin{aligned}\|\mathbf{x}\|^2 &= \|c_1\mathbf{v}_1 + c_2\mathbf{v}_2\|^2 = \|c_1\mathbf{v}_1\|^2 + \|c_2\mathbf{v}_2\|^2\\ &= (|c_1|\|\mathbf{v}_1\|)^2 + (|c_2|\|\mathbf{v}_2\|)^2 = |c_1|^2 + |c_2|^2\end{aligned}$$

(Explain why.) So the stated equality holds for $p = 2$. Suppose that the equality holds for $p = k$, with $k \geq 2$, let $\{\mathbf{v}_1, \dots, \mathbf{v}_{k+1}\}$ be an orthonormal set, and consider $\mathbf{x} = c_1\mathbf{v}_1 + \cdots + c_k\mathbf{v}_k + c_{k+1}\mathbf{v}_{k+1} = \mathbf{u}_k + c_{k+1}\mathbf{v}_{k+1}$, where $\mathbf{u}_k = c_1\mathbf{v}_1 + \cdots + c_k\mathbf{v}_k$.

3. Given $\mathbf{x}$ and an orthonormal set $\{\mathbf{v}_1, \dots, \mathbf{v}_p\}$ in $\mathbb{R}^n$, let $\hat{\mathbf{x}}$ be the orthogonal projection of $\mathbf{x}$ onto the subspace spanned by $\mathbf{v}_1, \dots, \mathbf{v}_p$. By Theorem 10 in Section 7.3,

$$\hat{\mathbf{x}} = (\mathbf{x} \cdot \mathbf{v}_1)\mathbf{v}_1 + \cdots + (\mathbf{x} \cdot \mathbf{v}_p)\mathbf{v}_p$$

By Exercise 2, $\|\hat{\mathbf{x}}\|^2 = |\mathbf{x} \cdot \mathbf{v}_1|^2 + \cdots + |\mathbf{x} \cdot \mathbf{v}_p|^2$. Bessel's inequality follows from the fact that $\|\hat{\mathbf{x}}\|^2 \leq \|\mathbf{x}\|^2$, noted before the proof of the Cauchy–Schwarz inequality in Section 7.7.

4. By parts (a) and (c) of Theorem 7 in Section 7.2, $\{U\mathbf{v}_1, \dots, U\mathbf{v}_n\}$ is an orthonormal set in $\mathbb{R}^n$. Since there are n vectors in the set, the set is a basis for $\mathbb{R}^n$.

5. Suppose $(U\mathbf{x}) \cdot (U\mathbf{y}) = \mathbf{x} \cdot \mathbf{y}$ for all $\mathbf{x}, \mathbf{y}$ in $\mathbb{R}^n$, and let $\mathbf{e}_1, \dots, \mathbf{e}_n$ be the standard basis for $\mathbb{R}^n$. For $j = 1, \dots, n$, $U\mathbf{e}_j$ is the jth column of U. Since $\|U\mathbf{e}_j\|^2 = (U\mathbf{e}_j) \cdot (U\mathbf{e}_j) = \mathbf{e}_j \cdot \mathbf{e}_j = 1$, the columns of U are unit vectors; since $(U\mathbf{e}_j) \cdot (U\mathbf{e}_k) = \mathbf{e}_j \cdot \mathbf{e}_k = 0$ for $j \neq k$, the columns are pairwise orthogonal.

6. If $U\mathbf{x} = \lambda\mathbf{x}$ for some $\mathbf{x} \neq \mathbf{0}$, then by Theorem 7(a) in Section 7.2 and by a property of the norm, $\|\mathbf{x}\| = \|U\mathbf{x}\| = \|\lambda\mathbf{x}\| = |\lambda|\|\mathbf{x}\|$, which shows that $|\lambda| = 1$ (because $\|\mathbf{x}\| \neq 0$).

7. *Hint*: Compute Q^TQ, using the fact that $(\mathbf{u}\mathbf{u}^T)^T = \mathbf{u}^{TT}\mathbf{u}^T = \mathbf{u}\mathbf{u}^T$.

8. Let $W = \text{Span}\,\{\mathbf{u}, \mathbf{v}\}$. Given $\mathbf{z}$ in $\mathbb{R}^n$, let $\hat{\mathbf{z}} = \text{proj}_W \mathbf{z}$. Then $\hat{\mathbf{z}}$ is in Col A, where $A = [\,\mathbf{u} \quad \mathbf{v}\,]$, say, $\hat{\mathbf{z}} = A\hat{\mathbf{x}}$ for some $\hat{\mathbf{x}}$ in $\mathbb{R}^2$. So $\hat{\mathbf{x}}$ is a least-squares solution of $A\mathbf{x} = \mathbf{z}$. The normal equations can be solved to produce $\hat{\mathbf{x}}$, and then $\hat{\mathbf{z}}$ is found by computing $A\hat{\mathbf{x}}$.

9. Use Theorem 14 in Section 7.5. If $c \neq 0$, the least-squares solution of $A\mathbf{x} = c\mathbf{b}$ is given by $(A^TA)^{-1}A^T(c\mathbf{b})$, which equals $c(A^TA)^{-1}A^T\mathbf{b}$, by linearity of matrix multiplication. This solution is c times the least-squares solution of $A\mathbf{x} = \mathbf{b}$.

10. *Hint*: Let $\mathbf{x} = \begin{bmatrix} x \\ y \\ z \end{bmatrix}$, $\mathbf{b} = \begin{bmatrix} a \\ b \\ c \end{bmatrix}$, $\mathbf{v} = \begin{bmatrix} 1 \\ -2 \\ 5 \end{bmatrix}$, and $A = \begin{bmatrix} \mathbf{v}^T \\ \mathbf{v}^T \\ \mathbf{v}^T \end{bmatrix} = \begin{bmatrix} 1 & -2 & 5 \\ 1 & -2 & 5 \\ 1 & -2 & 5 \end{bmatrix}$. Then the given set of equations is $A\mathbf{x} = \mathbf{b}$, and the set of all least-squares solutions coincides with the set of solutions of $A^TA\mathbf{x} = A^T\mathbf{b}$ (Theorem 13 in Section 7.5). Study this equation, and use the fact that $(\mathbf{v}\mathbf{v}^T)\mathbf{x} = \mathbf{v}(\mathbf{v}^T\mathbf{x}) = (\mathbf{v}^T\mathbf{x})\mathbf{v}$, because $\mathbf{v}^T\mathbf{x}$ is a scalar.

11. **a.** The row-column calculation of $A\mathbf{u}$ shows that each row of A is orthogonal to every $\mathbf{u}$ in Nul A. So each row of A is in $(\text{Nul}\,A)^\perp$. Since $(\text{Nul}\,A)^\perp$ is a subspace, it must contain all linear combinations of the rows of A; hence $(\text{Nul}\,A)^\perp$ contains Row A.
b. If rank $A = r$, then dim Nul $A = n - r$, by the Rank Theorem. By Exercise 22(c) in Section 7.3,

$$\dim \text{Nul}\,A + \dim\,(\text{Nul}\,A)^\perp = n$$

So $\dim\,(\text{Nul}\,A)^\perp$ must be r. But Row A is an r-dimensional subspace of $(\text{Nul}\,A)^\perp$, by the Rank Theorem and part (a). Therefore, Row A must coincide with $(\text{Nul}\,A)^\perp$.
c. Replace A by A^T in part (b), and conclude that Row A^T coincides with $(\text{Nul}\,A^T)^\perp$. Since Row A^T = Col A, this proves (c).

12. The equation $A\mathbf{x} = \mathbf{b}$ has a solution if and only if $\mathbf{b}$ is in Col A. By Exercise 11(c), $A\mathbf{x} = \mathbf{b}$ has a solution if and only if $\mathbf{b}$ is in $(\text{Nul}\,A^T)^\perp$. But $\mathbf{b}$ is orthogonal to Nul A^T if and only if $\mathbf{b}$ is orthogonal to all solutions of $A^T\mathbf{x} = \mathbf{0}$.

13. If $A = URU^T$ with U orthogonal, then A is similar to R (because U is invertible and $U^T = U^{-1}$) and so A has the same eigenvalues as R (by Theorem 4 in Section 6.2), namely, the n real numbers on the diagonal of R.

14. a. If $U = [\,\mathbf{u}_1 \quad \mathbf{u}_2 \quad \cdots \quad \mathbf{u}_n\,]$, then $AU = [\,\lambda_1\mathbf{u}_1 \quad A\mathbf{u}_2 \quad \cdots \quad A\mathbf{u}_2\,]$. Since $\mathbf{u}_1$ is a unit vector and $\mathbf{u}_2, \dots, \mathbf{u}_n$ are all orthogonal to $\mathbf{u}_1$, the first column of U^TAU is $U^T(\lambda_1\mathbf{u}_1) = \lambda_1 U^T\mathbf{u}_1 = \lambda_1\mathbf{e}_1$.
b. From (a),

$$U^TAU = \begin{bmatrix} \lambda_1 & * & * & * & * \\ 0 & & & & \\ \vdots & & & A_1 & \\ 0 & & & & \end{bmatrix}$$

And from Supplementary Exercise 10 in Chapter 6,

$$\det\,(U^TAU - \lambda I) = \det\,((\lambda_1 - \lambda)I)\det\,(A_1 - \lambda I)$$

This shows that the eigenvalues of U^TAU, namely, $\lambda_1, \dots, \lambda_n$, consist of λ_1 and the eigenvalues of A_1. So the eigenvalues of A_1 are $\lambda_2, \dots, \lambda_n$.

CHAPTER 8

Section 8.1, page 410

1. Symmetric **3.** Not symmetric **5.** Not symmetric

7. Orthogonal, $\begin{bmatrix} .6 & .8 \\ .8 & -.6 \end{bmatrix}$ **9.** Not orthogonal

11. Orthogonal, $\begin{bmatrix} 2/3 & 0 & 5/\sqrt{45} \\ 2/3 & 1/\sqrt{5} & -4/\sqrt{45} \\ 1/3 & -2/\sqrt{5} & -2/\sqrt{45} \end{bmatrix}$

13. $P = \begin{bmatrix} 1/\sqrt{2} & -1/\sqrt{2} \\ 1/\sqrt{2} & 1/\sqrt{2} \end{bmatrix}, D = \begin{bmatrix} 4 & 0 \\ 0 & 2 \end{bmatrix}$

15. $P = \begin{bmatrix} -4/\sqrt{17} & 1/\sqrt{17} \\ 1/\sqrt{17} & 4/\sqrt{17} \end{bmatrix}, D = \begin{bmatrix} 17 & 0 \\ 0 & 0 \end{bmatrix}$

17. $P = \begin{bmatrix} 1/\sqrt{3} & 1/\sqrt{6} & -1/\sqrt{2} \\ 1/\sqrt{3} & -2/\sqrt{6} & 0 \\ 1/\sqrt{3} & 1/\sqrt{6} & 1/\sqrt{2} \end{bmatrix}, D = \begin{bmatrix} 5 & 0 & 0 \\ 0 & 2 & 0 \\ 0 & 0 & -2 \end{bmatrix}$

19. $P = \begin{bmatrix} 1/3 & 2/3 & 2/3 \\ 2/3 & 1/2 & -2/3 \\ 2/3 & -2/3 & 1/3 \end{bmatrix}, D = \begin{bmatrix} 7 & 0 & 0 \\ 0 & 4 & 0 \\ 0 & 0 & 1 \end{bmatrix}$

21. $P = \begin{bmatrix} 1/\sqrt{3} & -1/\sqrt{2} & -1/\sqrt{6} \\ 1/\sqrt{3} & 1/\sqrt{2} & -1/\sqrt{6} \\ 1/\sqrt{3} & 0 & 2/\sqrt{6} \end{bmatrix}, D = \begin{bmatrix} 5 & 0 & 0 \\ 0 & 2 & 0 \\ 0 & 0 & 2 \end{bmatrix}$

23. $P = \begin{bmatrix} 1/\sqrt{2} & 0 & -1/\sqrt{2} & 0 \\ 0 & 1/\sqrt{2} & 0 & -1/\sqrt{2} \\ 1/\sqrt{2} & 0 & 1/\sqrt{2} & 0 \\ 0 & 1/\sqrt{2} & 0 & 1/\sqrt{2} \end{bmatrix},$

$D = \begin{bmatrix} 3 & 0 & 0 & 0 \\ 0 & 3 & 0 & 0 \\ 0 & 0 & 1 & 0 \\ 0 & 0 & 0 & 1 \end{bmatrix}$

25. *Hint*: First, explain why A is symmetric. Then show that A^T is symmetric, too.

27. $A = 8\mathbf{v}_1\mathbf{v}_1^T + 6\mathbf{v}_2\mathbf{v}_2^T + 3\mathbf{v}_3\mathbf{v}_3^T$, where $\mathbf{v}_1 = \begin{bmatrix} -1/\sqrt{2} \\ 1/\sqrt{2} \\ 0 \end{bmatrix}$,

$\mathbf{v}_2 = \begin{bmatrix} -1/\sqrt{6} \\ -1/\sqrt{6} \\ 2/\sqrt{6} \end{bmatrix}$, and $\mathbf{v}_3 = \begin{bmatrix} 1/\sqrt{3} \\ 1/\sqrt{3} \\ 1/\sqrt{3} \end{bmatrix}$

29. Since A is 6×6, it has six eigenvalues, counting multiplicities. By the Rank Theorem, dim Nul $A = 6 -$ rank $A = 2$. So 0 is an eigenvalue of multiplicity exactly 2. The other four eigenvalues of A must be nonzero.

31. The Diagonalization Theorem in Section 6.3 says that the columns of P are (linearly independent) eigenvectors corresponding to the eigenvalues of A listed on the diagonal of D. So P has exactly k columns of eigenvectors corresponding to λ. These k columns form a basis for the eigenspace.

33. *Hint*: $(\mathbf{v}\mathbf{v}^T)\mathbf{x} = \mathbf{v}(\mathbf{v}^T\mathbf{x}) = (\mathbf{v}^T\mathbf{x})\mathbf{v}$, because $\mathbf{v}^T\mathbf{x}$ is a scalar.

Section 8.2, page 417

1. a. $5x_1^2 + \frac{2}{3}x_1x_2 + x_2^2$ **b.** 185 **c.** 16

3. a. $\begin{bmatrix} 10 & -3 \\ -3 & -3 \end{bmatrix}$ **b.** $\begin{bmatrix} 5 & 3/2 \\ 3/2 & 0 \end{bmatrix}$

5. a. $\begin{bmatrix} 8 & -3 & 2 \\ -3 & 7 & -1 \\ 2 & -1 & -3 \end{bmatrix}$ **b.** $\begin{bmatrix} 0 & 2 & 3 \\ 2 & 0 & -4 \\ 3 & -4 & 0 \end{bmatrix}$

7. $\mathbf{x} = P\mathbf{u}$, where $P = \frac{1}{\sqrt{2}}\begin{bmatrix} 1 & -1 \\ 1 & 1 \end{bmatrix}$, $\mathbf{u}^T D\mathbf{u} = 6u_1^2 - 4u_2^2$

9. Positive definite, because eigenvalues are 7 and 2

Change of variable: $\mathbf{x} = P\mathbf{u}$, with $P = \left(\frac{1}{\sqrt{5}}\right)\begin{bmatrix} -1 & 2 \\ 2 & 1 \end{bmatrix}$

New quadratic form: $7u_1^2 + 2u_2^2$

11. Indefinite, because eigenvalues are 7 and -3

Change of variable: $\mathbf{x} = P\mathbf{u}$, with $P = \left(\frac{1}{\sqrt{2}}\right)\begin{bmatrix} 1 & -1 \\ 1 & 1 \end{bmatrix}$

New quadratic form: $7u_1^2 - 3u_2^2$

13. Positive semidefinite, because eigenvalues are 10 and 0

Change of variable: $\mathbf{x} = P\mathbf{u}$, with $P = \left(\frac{1}{\sqrt{10}}\right)\begin{bmatrix} 1 & 3 \\ -3 & 1 \end{bmatrix}$

New quadratic form: $10u_1^2$

15. 8

17. Write the characteristic polynomial in two ways:

$$\det(A - \lambda I) = \det \begin{bmatrix} a - \lambda & b \\ b & d - \lambda \end{bmatrix} = \lambda^2 - (a + d)\lambda + ad - b^2$$

and

$$(\lambda - \lambda_1)(\lambda - \lambda_2) = \lambda^2 - (\lambda_1 + \lambda_2)\lambda + \lambda_1\lambda_2$$

Equate coefficients to obtain $\lambda_1 + \lambda_2 = a + d$ and $\lambda_1\lambda_2 = ad - b^2 = \det A$.

19. a. The matrix B^TB is symmetric because $(B^TB)^T = B^TB^{TT} = B^TB$. Also, $\mathbf{x}^TA\mathbf{x} = \mathbf{x}^TB^TB\mathbf{x} = (B\mathbf{x})^TB\mathbf{x} = \|B\mathbf{x}\|^2 \geq 0$, so $\mathbf{x}^TA\mathbf{x}$ is positive semidefinite.

b. *Hint*: To show that A is positive definite, suppose that $\mathbf{x}^T A\mathbf{x} = 0$ and deduce that $\mathbf{x} = \mathbf{0}$.

21. *Hint*: Show that $A + B$ is symmetric and the quadratic form $\mathbf{x}^T(A + B)\mathbf{x}$ is positive definite.

Section 8.3, page 425

1. $\mathbf{x} = P\mathbf{y}$, where $P = \begin{bmatrix} 1/3 & 2/3 & -2/3 \\ 2/3 & 1/3 & 2/3 \\ -2/3 & 2/3 & 1/3 \end{bmatrix}$

3. a. 9 **b.** $\begin{bmatrix} 1/3 \\ 2/3 \\ -2/3 \end{bmatrix}$ **c.** 6 **5. a.** 7 **b.** $\begin{bmatrix} -1/\sqrt{2} \\ 1/\sqrt{2} \end{bmatrix}$ **c.** 3

7. $\begin{bmatrix} 1/3 \\ 2/3 \\ 2/3 \end{bmatrix}$ **9.** $5 + \sqrt{5}$ **11.** 3

13. *Hint*: If $m = M$, take $\alpha = 0$. Otherwise, let $\alpha = (M - t)/(M - m)$. If $t \ge m$, then $\alpha \le 1$; if $t \le M$, then $\alpha \ge 0$. Verify that α works as advertised, and complete the proof.

Section 8.4, page 434

1. 3, 1 **3.** 3, 2

5. $\begin{bmatrix} -3 & 0 \\ 0 & 0 \end{bmatrix} = \begin{bmatrix} -1 & 0 \\ 0 & 1 \end{bmatrix}\begin{bmatrix} 3 & 0 \\ 0 & 0 \end{bmatrix}\begin{bmatrix} 1 & 0 \\ 0 & 1 \end{bmatrix}$

7. $\begin{bmatrix} 2 & -1 \\ 2 & 2 \end{bmatrix} = \begin{bmatrix} 1/\sqrt{5} & 2/\sqrt{5} \\ 2/\sqrt{5} & -1/\sqrt{5} \end{bmatrix}\begin{bmatrix} 3 & 0 \\ 0 & 2 \end{bmatrix} \cdot \begin{bmatrix} 2/\sqrt{5} & 1/\sqrt{5} \\ 1/\sqrt{5} & -2/\sqrt{5} \end{bmatrix}$

9. $\begin{bmatrix} 7 & 1 \\ 0 & 0 \\ 5 & 5 \end{bmatrix} = \begin{bmatrix} 1/\sqrt{2} & -1/\sqrt{2} & 0 \\ 0 & 0 & 1 \\ 1/\sqrt{2} & 1/\sqrt{2} & 0 \end{bmatrix} \cdot \begin{bmatrix} 3\sqrt{10} & 0 \\ 0 & \sqrt{10} \\ 0 & 0 \end{bmatrix}\begin{bmatrix} 2/\sqrt{5} & 1/\sqrt{5} \\ -1/\sqrt{5} & 2/\sqrt{5} \end{bmatrix}$

11. $\begin{bmatrix} -3 & 1 \\ 6 & -2 \\ 6 & -2 \end{bmatrix} = \begin{bmatrix} -1/3 & 2/3 & 2/3 \\ 2/3 & -1/3 & 2/3 \\ 2/3 & 2/3 & -1/3 \end{bmatrix} \cdot \begin{bmatrix} 3\sqrt{10} & 0 \\ 0 & 0 \\ 0 & 0 \end{bmatrix}\begin{bmatrix} 3/\sqrt{10} & -1/\sqrt{10} \\ 1/\sqrt{10} & 3/\sqrt{10} \end{bmatrix}$

13. $\begin{bmatrix} 3 & 2 & 2 \\ 2 & 3 & -2 \end{bmatrix} = \begin{bmatrix} 1/\sqrt{2} & -1/\sqrt{2} \\ 1/\sqrt{2} & 1/\sqrt{2} \end{bmatrix}\begin{bmatrix} 5 & 0 & 0 \\ 0 & 3 & 0 \end{bmatrix} \cdot \begin{bmatrix} 1/\sqrt{2} & 1/\sqrt{2} & 0 \\ -1/\sqrt{18} & 1/\sqrt{18} & -4/\sqrt{18} \\ -2/3 & 2/3 & 1/3 \end{bmatrix}$

15. *Hint*: Since U and V are orthogonal,

$$A^TA = (U\Sigma V^T)^T U\Sigma V^T = V\Sigma^T U^T U\Sigma V^T = V(\Sigma^T\Sigma)V^{-1}$$

Thus V diagonalizes A^TA. What does this tell you about V?

17. Let $A = U\Sigma V^T$. The matrix PU is orthogonal because it is square and $(PU)^T PU = U^T P^T PU = U^T U = I$. So the equation $PA = (PU)\Sigma V^T$ has the form required for a singular value decomposition. By Exercise 15, the diagonal entries in Σ are the singular values of PA.

19. *Hint*: Use a column–row expansion of $(U\Sigma)V^T$.

21. *Hint*: Use Theorem 7 in Section 8.3.

23. *Hint*: Consider the SVD for the standard matrix of T, say, $A = U\Sigma V^T = U\Sigma V^{-1}$. Let $\mathcal{B} = \{\mathbf{v}_1, \ldots, \mathbf{v}_n\}$ and $\mathcal{C} = \{\mathbf{u}_1, \ldots, \mathbf{u}_m\}$ be bases constructed from the columns of V and U, respectively. Compute the matrix for T relative to $\mathcal{B}$ and $\mathcal{C}$, as in Section 6.4. To do this, you must show that $V^{-1}\mathbf{v}_j = \mathbf{e}_j$, the jth column of I_n.

Section 8.5, page 442

1. $M = \begin{bmatrix} 12 \\ 10 \end{bmatrix}$; $B = \begin{bmatrix} 7 & 10 & -6 & -9 & -10 & 8 \\ 2 & -4 & -1 & 5 & 3 & -5 \end{bmatrix}$; $S = \begin{bmatrix} 86 & -27 \\ -27 & 16 \end{bmatrix}$

3. $\begin{bmatrix} .95 \\ -.32 \end{bmatrix}$ for $\lambda = 95.2$, $\begin{bmatrix} .32 \\ .95 \end{bmatrix}$ for $\lambda = 6.8$

5. (.130, .874, .467), 75.9% of the variance

7. $u_1 = .95x_1 - .32x_2$; u_1 explains 93.3% of the variance.

9. $c_1 = 1/3$, $c_2 = 2/3$, $c_3 = 2/3$

11. a. If $\mathbf{w}$ is the vector in $\mathbb{R}^N$ with a 1 in each entry, then

$$[\,\mathbf{X}_1 \;\cdots\; \mathbf{X}_N\,]\mathbf{w} = \mathbf{X}_1 + \cdots + \mathbf{X}_N = \mathbf{0}$$

because the $\mathbf{X}_k$ are in mean-deviation form. Then

$$[\,\mathbf{U}_1 \;\cdots\; \mathbf{U}_N\,]\mathbf{w} = [\,P^T\mathbf{X}_1 \;\cdots\; P^T\mathbf{X}_N\,]\mathbf{w} \quad \text{By definition}$$
$$= P^T[\,\mathbf{X}_1 \;\cdots\; \mathbf{X}_N\,]\mathbf{w} = P^T\mathbf{0} = \mathbf{0}$$

That is, $\mathbf{U}_1 + \cdots + \mathbf{U}_N = \mathbf{0}$, so the $\mathbf{U}_k$ are in mean-deviation form.

b. *Hint*: Because the $\mathbf{X}_j$ are in mean-deviation form, the covariance matrix of the $\mathbf{X}_j$ is $1/(N-1)\cdot [\,\mathbf{X}_1 \;\cdots\; \mathbf{X}_N\,][\,\mathbf{X}_1 \;\cdots\; \mathbf{X}_N\,]^T$. Compute the covariance matrix of the $\mathbf{U}_j$, using part (a).

13. If $B = [\,\hat{\mathbf{X}}_1 \;\; \cdots \;\; \hat{\mathbf{X}}_N\,] =$ then

$$S = \frac{1}{N-1}BB^T = \frac{1}{N-1}[\,\hat{\mathbf{X}}_1 \;\; \cdots \;\; \hat{\mathbf{X}}_N\,]\begin{bmatrix}\hat{\mathbf{X}}_1^T \\ \vdots \\ \hat{\mathbf{X}}_N^T\end{bmatrix}$$

$$= \frac{1}{N-1}\sum_1^N \hat{\mathbf{X}}_k\hat{\mathbf{X}}_k^T = \frac{1}{N-1}\sum_1^N (\mathbf{X}_k - \mathbf{M})(\mathbf{X}_k^T - \mathbf{M})^T$$

Supplementary Exercises, page 444

1. a. T **b.** F **c.** T **d.** F **e.** F **f.** F **g.** F **h.** T **i.** F **j.** F **k.** F **l.** F **m.** T **n.** T **o.** T **p.** T **q.** F

2. a.
$$\begin{aligned} A^T &= (\lambda_1\mathbf{v}_1\mathbf{v}_1^T)^T + \cdots + (\lambda_n\mathbf{v}_n\mathbf{v}_n^T)^T \\ &= \lambda_1\mathbf{v}_1^{TT}\mathbf{v}_1^T + \cdots + \lambda_n\mathbf{v}_n^{TT}\mathbf{v}_n^T \\ &= \lambda_1\mathbf{v}_1\mathbf{v}_1^T + \cdots + \lambda_n\mathbf{v}_n\mathbf{v}_n^T = A \end{aligned}$$

b.
$$\begin{aligned} A\mathbf{v}_1 &= (\lambda_1\mathbf{v}_1\mathbf{v}_1^T)\mathbf{v}_1 + \cdots + (\lambda_n\mathbf{v}_n\mathbf{v}_n^T)\mathbf{v}_1 \\ &= \lambda_1\mathbf{v}_1, \text{ because } \mathbf{v}_1^T\mathbf{v}_1 = 1 \text{ and } \mathbf{v}_j^T\mathbf{v}_1 = 0 \text{ for } j \neq 1 \end{aligned}$$

Thus λ_1 is an eigenvalue of A. A similar argument shows that for $j = 2, \ldots, n$, λ_j is an eigenvalue of A.

3. If rank $A = r$, then dim Nul $A = n - r$, by the Rank Theorem. So 0 is an eigenvalue of multiplicity $n - r$. Hence, of the n terms in the spectral decomposition of A, exactly $n - r$ are zero. The remaining r terms (corresponding to the nonzero eigenvalues) are all rank 1 matrices, as mentioned in the discussion of the spectral decomposition.

4. a. By Theorem 3 in Section 7.1, Nul $A = (\text{Row } A)^{\perp} = (\text{Col } A^T)^{\perp}$. Since A is symmetric, $(\text{Col } A^T)^{\perp} = (\text{Col } A)^{\perp}$.
b. By the Orthogonal Decomposition Theorem in Section 7.3, each $\mathbf{y}$ in $\mathbb{R}^n$ can be written as $\mathbf{y} = \hat{\mathbf{y}} + \mathbf{z}$, with $\hat{\mathbf{y}}$ in Col A and $\mathbf{z}$ in $(\text{Col } A)^{\perp}$. By part (a), $\mathbf{z}$ is in Nul A.

5. If $A\mathbf{v} = \lambda\mathbf{v}$ for some nonzero λ, then $\mathbf{v} = \lambda^{-1}A\mathbf{v} = A(\lambda^{-1}\mathbf{v})$, which shows that $\mathbf{v}$ is a linear combination of the columns of A.

6. *Hint*: Since A is symmetric, there is an orthonormal eigenvector basis $\{\mathbf{v}_1, \ldots, \mathbf{v}_n\}$ for $\mathbb{R}^n$. If rank $A = r$, then 0 is an eigenvalue with multiplicity $n - r$, and we may assume that $\mathbf{v}_1, \ldots, \mathbf{v}_r$ are the unit eigenvectors corresponding to the remaining r nonzero eigenvalues. (See the solution to Exercise 3.) Given $\mathbf{y}$ in $\mathbb{R}^n$, use this basis to build a decomposition of $\mathbf{y}$.

7. *Hint*: If $A = R^TR$, where R is invertible, then A is positive definite, by Exercise 19 in Section 8.2. Conversely, suppose that A is positive definite. Then by Exercise 20 in Section 8.2, $A = B^TB$ for some positive definite matrix B. Explain why B admits a QR factorization, and use it to create the Cholesky factorization of A.

8. *Hint*: Suppose A is positive definite, and consider a Cholesky factorization, $A = R^TR$. Let D be the diagonal matrix whose diagonal entries are the (positive) entries on the diagonal of R. Then $A = R^TR = (R^TD^{-1})(DR)$. Explain why this is an LU factorization of A.

9. If A is $m \times n$ and $\mathbf{x}$ is in $\mathbb{R}^n$, then $\mathbf{x}^TA^TA\mathbf{x} = (A\mathbf{x})^T(A\mathbf{x}) = \|A\mathbf{x}\|^2 \geq 0$. Thus A^TA is positive semidefinite. By Exercise 20 in Section 7.5, rank $A^TA =$ rank A.

10. If rank $G = r$, then dim Nul $G = n - r$, by the Rank Theorem. Hence 0 is an eigenvalue of multiplicity $n - r$, and the spectral decomposition of G is

$$G = \lambda_1\mathbf{v}_1\mathbf{v}_1^T + \cdots + \lambda_r\mathbf{v}_r\mathbf{v}_r^T$$

Also, $\lambda_1, \ldots, \lambda_r$ are positive because G is positive semidefinite. Thus

$$G = (\sqrt{\lambda}\mathbf{v}_1)(\sqrt{\lambda}\mathbf{v}_1)^T + \cdots + (\sqrt{\lambda}\mathbf{v}_r)(\sqrt{\lambda}\mathbf{v}_r)^T$$

By the column–row expansion of a matrix product, $G = BB^T$, where B is the $n \times r$ matrix:

$$B = [\,\sqrt{\lambda}\mathbf{v}_1 \;\; \cdots \;\; \sqrt{\lambda}\mathbf{v}_r\,]$$

Finally, $G = A^TA$ for $A = B^T$.

11. *Hint*: Write an SVD of A in the form $A = U\Sigma V^T = PQ$, where $P = U\Sigma U^T$ and $Q = UV^T$. Show that P is symmetric and has the same eigenvalues as Σ. Compute Q^TQ and explain why Q is an orthogonal matrix.

12. a. Because the columns of V_r are orthonormal, $AA^+\mathbf{y} = (U_rDV_r^T)(V_rD^{-1}U_r^T)\mathbf{y} = (U_rDD^{-1}U_r^T)\mathbf{y} = U_rU_r^T\mathbf{y}$. Since $U_rU_r^T\mathbf{y}$ is the orthogonal projection onto Col U_r (by Theorem 9 in Section 7.3), and since Col $U_r =$ Col A by (6) in Example 6 from Section 8.4, $AA^+\mathbf{y}$ is the orthogonal projection onto Col A.
b. See the Study Guide.
c. *Hint*: $U_r^TU_r = I$ and $V_r^TV_r = I$.

13. a. If $\mathbf{b} = A\mathbf{x}$, then $\mathbf{x}^+ = A^+\mathbf{b} = A^+A\mathbf{x}$. By Exercise 12(a), $\mathbf{x}^+$ is the orthogonal projection of $\mathbf{x}$ onto Row A. Also, by Exercise 12(c), $A\mathbf{x}^+ = A(A^+A\mathbf{x}) = A\mathbf{x} = \mathbf{b}$.
b. Since $\mathbf{x}^+$ is the orthogonal projection onto Row A, the Pythagorean theorem shows that $\|\mathbf{x}\|^2 = \|\mathbf{x}^+\|^2 + \|\mathbf{x} - \mathbf{x}^+\|^2$. Part (b) follows immediately.

14. The least-squares solutions of $A\mathbf{x} = \mathbf{b}$ are precisely the solutions of $A\mathbf{x} = \hat{\mathbf{b}}$, where $\hat{\mathbf{b}}$ is the orthogonal projection of $\mathbf{b}$ onto Col A. From Exercise 13, the minimum length solution of $A\mathbf{x} = \hat{\mathbf{b}}$ is $A^+\hat{\mathbf{b}}$, so $A^+\hat{\mathbf{b}}$ is the minimum length least-squares solution of $A\mathbf{x} = \mathbf{b}$. However, $\hat{\mathbf{b}} = AA^+\mathbf{b}$, by Exercise 12(a), and hence $A^+\hat{\mathbf{b}} = A^+AA^+\mathbf{b} = A^+\mathbf{b}$, by Exercise 12(c). Thus $A^+\mathbf{b}$ is the minimum length least-squares solution of $A\mathbf{x} = \mathbf{b}$.

ANSWERS TO EVEN-NUMBERED EXERCISES

CHAPTER 1

Section 1.1, page 10

2. $(3, -2)$ **4.** $(12, 3/2)$

6. Add -4 times row 2 to row 3.

8. Either add 2 times row 3 to row 2, or add -3 times row 3 to row 1.

10. $(7, -3, 2)$ **12.** $(0, 0, 0)$ **14.** $(-24, 6, 5, -1)$

16. $(5, 11, -8)$ **18.** Inconsistent **20.** $(-3, -1, 1)$

Note: Other echelon forms are possible in Exercises 21–26, but the pivot positions will be the same.

22. Row equivalent to $\begin{bmatrix} 1 & 2 & -4 & -3 \\ 0 & 1 & -4 & -2 \\ 0 & 0 & 5 & 3 \end{bmatrix}$, hence consistent.

24. Row equivalent to $\begin{bmatrix} 1 & -6 & 0 & 0 & 5 \\ 0 & 1 & -4 & 1 & 0 \\ 0 & 0 & 1 & 5 & 8 \\ 0 & 0 & 0 & 0 & -8 \end{bmatrix}$, hence inconsistent.

26. Row equivalent to $\begin{bmatrix} 1 & 0 & -2 & 0 & -1 \\ 0 & 1 & 0 & -1 & 2 \\ 0 & 0 & 1 & -3/2 & 3 \\ 0 & 0 & 0 & -5 & 15 \end{bmatrix}$, hence consistent.

28. All h **30.** $h = 6$

32. Interchange rows 1 and 2; interchange rows 1 and 2.

34. Add -3 times row 1 to row 3; add 3 times row 1 to row 3.

Section 1.2, page 22

2. Reduced echelon: a, d; only echelon: b

4. Reduced echelon: none; only echelon: b, c

6. a. $\begin{bmatrix} 1 & 0 & 0 \\ 0 & 1 & 0 \\ 0 & 0 & 1 \end{bmatrix}$; pivot cols 1, 2, 3

b. $\begin{bmatrix} 1 & 0 & -1 & -2 \\ 0 & 1 & 2 & 3 \\ 0 & 0 & 0 & 0 \end{bmatrix}$; pivot cols 1, 2

c. $\begin{bmatrix} 1 & 0 & 0 & 0 & -1 \\ 0 & 1 & 0 & 0 & -1 \\ 0 & 0 & 1 & 0 & 1 \\ 0 & 0 & 0 & 1 & 1 \end{bmatrix}$; pivot cols 1, 2, 3, 4

8. $\begin{cases} x_1 = 4 \\ x_2 = 3 \\ x_3 \text{ is free} \end{cases}$ **10.** $\begin{cases} x_1 = -5 - 3x_2 \\ x_2 \text{ is free} \\ x_3 = -4 \end{cases}$

12. $\begin{cases} x_1 = 3 - 3x_3 \\ x_2 = 2 - x_3 \\ x_3 \text{ is free} \end{cases}$ **14.** $\begin{cases} x_1 = -2 \\ x_2 = 3 \end{cases}$

16. $\begin{cases} x_1 = -3 - 8x_4 \\ x_2 = -6 - 4x_4 \\ x_3 = 5 + 7x_4 \\ x_4 \text{ is free} \end{cases}$ **18.** Inconsistent

20. $\begin{cases} x_1 = 3 + 5x_3 \\ x_2 = 6 - 4x_3 + x_4 \\ x_3 \text{ is free} \\ x_4 \text{ is free} \\ x_5 = 0 \end{cases}$

22. $h \neq -12$ **24.** All h

26. a. $h = 3/2$ and $k \neq 2$ **b.** $h \neq 3/2$
c. $h = 3/2$ and $k = 2$

28. Yes

30. Yes; example:
$$\begin{aligned} x_1 + x_2 &= 2 \\ x_1 - x_2 &= 0 \\ 3x_1 + 2x_2 &= 5 \end{aligned}$$

32.
$$\begin{aligned} x_1 + x_2 + x_3 &= 4 \\ 2x_1 + 2x_2 + 2x_3 &= 5 \end{aligned}$$

34. Every column in the augmented matrix except the rightmost column is a pivot column, and the rightmost column is *not* a pivot column.

Section 1.3, page 31

2. a. $\begin{cases} x_1 = 100 + x_3 - x_5 \\ x_2 = 100 - x_3 + x_5 \\ x_3 \text{ is free} \\ x_4 = 60 - x_5 \\ x_5 \text{ is free} \end{cases}$ **b.** $\begin{cases} x_1 = 40 + x_3 \\ x_2 = 160 - x_3 \\ x_3 \text{ is free} \\ x_4 = 0 \\ x_5 = 60 \end{cases}$

c. Minimum value of x_1 is 40.

4. a. $\begin{cases} x_1 = 100 + x_6 \\ x_2 = x_6 \\ x_3 = 50 + x_6 \\ x_4 = -70 + x_6 \\ x_5 = 80 + x_6 \\ x_6 \text{ is free} \end{cases}$ **b.** 70

6. $3I + 5I = 15 + 5,\ I = 2.5$ amps

8.
$$\begin{aligned} I_1 - I_2 + I_3 &= 0 \\ 8I_1 &= 24 \\ 6I_3 &= 24 \end{aligned} \qquad \begin{cases} I_1 = 3 \text{ amps} \\ I_2 = 7 \text{ amps} \\ I_3 = 4 \text{ amps} \end{cases}$$

10.
$$\begin{aligned} I_1 - I_2 + I_3 &= 0 \\ 5I_1 + 5I_2 &= 30 \\ 5I_2 &= 10 \end{aligned} \qquad \begin{cases} I_1 = 4 \text{ amps} \\ I_2 = 2 \text{ amps} \\ I_3 = -2 \text{ amps} \end{cases}$$

12. Take some other value for p_s, say, 200 million dollars. The other equilibrium prices are then $p_c = 188$ million, $p_e = 170$ million. Any constant multiple of these prices is a set of equilibrium prices. Changing the unit of measurement to, say, German marks has the same effect as multiplying all equilibrium prices by a constant. The *ratios* of the prices remain the same, no matter what currency is used.

14. $x_1 = .7869x_3$, $x_2 = .3770x_3$, x_3 is free. The data probably justify only two significant figures, so we can take $x_3 = 100$ and round off the other prices to get $x_1 = 79$ and $x_2 = 38$.

CHAPTER 2

Section 2.1, page 46

2. $\begin{bmatrix} -4 \\ 1 \end{bmatrix}, \begin{bmatrix} 5 \\ 4 \end{bmatrix}$

4.

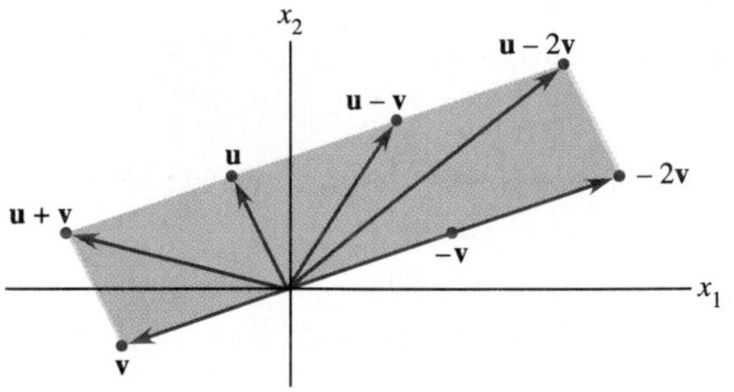

6. $\mathbf{x} = \mathbf{u} + \frac{2}{3}\mathbf{v} - 2\mathbf{w}$ **8.** $s = 2,\ t = -\frac{8}{3}$ **10.** $\begin{bmatrix} -2 \\ 1 \\ 3 \end{bmatrix}$

12.
$$\begin{aligned} 2x_1 - x_2 - 7x_3 &= 0 \\ 3x_1 + 4x_2 + x_3 &= 0 \end{aligned}$$

14. $x_1 \begin{bmatrix} 1 \\ 5 \\ 3 \end{bmatrix} + x_2 \begin{bmatrix} 6 \\ 0 \\ -1 \end{bmatrix} + x_3 \begin{bmatrix} 2 \\ -6 \\ 4 \end{bmatrix} = \begin{bmatrix} 5 \\ 7 \\ -1 \end{bmatrix}$

16. No **18.** Yes **20.** Yes **22.** $h = -2$

24. Let $\mathbf{w} = \begin{bmatrix} h \\ k \end{bmatrix}$. Then $\mathbf{w}$ is in Span $\{\mathbf{u}, \mathbf{v}\}$ if and only if the vector equation $x_1\mathbf{u} + x_2\mathbf{v} = \mathbf{w}$ is consistent. Row reduce the augmented matrix:

$$\begin{bmatrix} 2 & 1 & h \\ -6 & 5 & k \end{bmatrix} \sim \begin{bmatrix} 2 & 1 & h \\ 0 & 8 & k + 3h \end{bmatrix}$$

This system is consistent for all h and k. (See Theorem 2 in Section 1.2.)

26. **a.** Yes **b.** $\mathbf{a}_3 = 0\cdot\mathbf{a}_1 + 0\cdot\mathbf{a}_2 + 1\cdot\mathbf{a}_3$

28. **a.** $27.6x_1 + 30.2x_2$ million Btu

b. $x_1\begin{bmatrix}27.6\\3100\\250\end{bmatrix} + x_2\begin{bmatrix}30.2\\6400\\360\end{bmatrix}$

30. Let $\mathbf{u} = (u_1, \dots, u_n)$, $\mathbf{v} = (v_1, \dots, v_n)$, $\mathbf{w} = (w_1, \dots, w_n)$.

a. For $j = 1, \dots, n$, the jth entry of $(\mathbf{u}+\mathbf{v})+\mathbf{w}$ is $(u_j + v_j) + w_j$. By associativity of addition in $\mathbb{R}$, this entry equals $u_j + (v_j + w_j)$, which is the jth entry of $\mathbf{u}+(\mathbf{v}+\mathbf{w})$. By definition of equality of vectors, $(\mathbf{u}+\mathbf{v})+\mathbf{w}$ equals $\mathbf{u}+(\mathbf{v}+\mathbf{w})$.

b. For $j = 1, \dots, n$, $u_j + (-1)u_j = (-1)u_j + u_j = 0$, by properties of $\mathbb{R}$. By vector equality, $\mathbf{u} + (-1)\mathbf{u} = (-1)\mathbf{u} + \mathbf{u} = \mathbf{0}$.

c. For any scalar c, the jth entry of $c(\mathbf{u}+\mathbf{v})$ is $c(u_j + v_j)$, and the jth entry of $c\mathbf{u} + c\mathbf{v}$ is $cu_j + cv_j$ (by definition of scalar multiplication and vector addition). These entries are equal, by a distributive law in $\mathbb{R}$. So $c(\mathbf{u}+\mathbf{v}) = c\mathbf{u} + c\mathbf{v}$.

d. For scalars c and d, the jth entries of $c(d\mathbf{u})$ and $(cd)\mathbf{u}$ are $c(du_j)$ and $(cd)u_j$, respectively. These entries in $\mathbb{R}$ are equal, so the vectors $c(d\mathbf{u})$ and $(cd)\mathbf{u}$ are equal.

Section 2.2, page 54

2. $A\mathbf{x} = 5\begin{bmatrix}4\\2\\0\end{bmatrix} + 2\begin{bmatrix}1\\-5\\6\end{bmatrix} = \begin{bmatrix}20\\10\\0\end{bmatrix} + \begin{bmatrix}2\\-10\\12\end{bmatrix} = \begin{bmatrix}22\\0\\12\end{bmatrix}$,

and $A\mathbf{x} = \begin{bmatrix}4\cdot5 + 1\cdot2\\2\cdot5 - 5\cdot2\\0\cdot5 + 6\cdot2\end{bmatrix} = \begin{bmatrix}22\\0\\12\end{bmatrix}$

4. The product is not defined.

6. $A\mathbf{x} = r\begin{bmatrix}0\\0\\1\end{bmatrix} + s\begin{bmatrix}0\\1\\0\end{bmatrix} + t\begin{bmatrix}1\\0\\0\end{bmatrix} = \begin{bmatrix}t\\s\\r\end{bmatrix}$, and

$A\mathbf{x} = \begin{bmatrix}0\cdot r + 0\cdot s + 1\cdot t\\0\cdot r + 1\cdot s + 0\cdot t\\1\cdot r + 0\cdot s + 0\cdot t\end{bmatrix} = \begin{bmatrix}t\\s\\r\end{bmatrix}$

8. $\begin{bmatrix}0 & 3 & -2 & 1\\1 & -2 & 6 & 0\\7 & 1 & -5 & -8\end{bmatrix}\begin{bmatrix}x_1\\x_2\\x_3\\x_4\end{bmatrix} = \begin{bmatrix}0\\0\\0\end{bmatrix}$

10. $x_1\begin{bmatrix}0\\1\\-3\end{bmatrix} + x_2\begin{bmatrix}5\\2\\-1\end{bmatrix} + x_3\begin{bmatrix}3\\1\\2\end{bmatrix} = \begin{bmatrix}-1\\0\\1\end{bmatrix}$

12. $\mathbf{x} = \begin{bmatrix}3/5\\-4/5\\1\end{bmatrix}$ **14.** $-3\begin{bmatrix}6\\1\\-5\\9\end{bmatrix} - 7\begin{bmatrix}-2\\3\\4\\-3\end{bmatrix} = \begin{bmatrix}4\\-24\\13\\-6\end{bmatrix}$

16. $\begin{bmatrix}3 & -5 & 0\\1 & 2 & -1\end{bmatrix}\begin{bmatrix}y_1\\y_2\\y_3\end{bmatrix} = \begin{bmatrix}-4\\7\end{bmatrix}$ **18.** No

20. The equation $A\mathbf{x} = \mathbf{b}$ is not consistent unless $-b_1 + 2b_2 + b_3 = 0$. The set of $\mathbf{b}$ such that the equation *is* consistent is a plane through the origin: $-x_1 + 2x_2 + x_3 = 0$.

22. 4 rows. There is one pivot in each of the four pivot columns, and each pivot is in a different row.

24. The columns of A do not span $\mathbb{R}^4$, by Theorem 2, because an echelon form of A has a row of zeros, with pivot positions in only 3 rows.

26. No **28.** Yes

30. $2\begin{bmatrix}3\\8\\4\end{bmatrix} - 5\begin{bmatrix}1\\3\\1\end{bmatrix} = \begin{bmatrix}1\\1\\3\end{bmatrix}$, so $x_1 = 2$, $x_2 = -5$.

32. $5\mathbf{u} = \begin{bmatrix}5\\15\\15\end{bmatrix}$, $A(5\mathbf{u}) = \begin{bmatrix}5 & 1 & -3\\7 & -2 & 1\end{bmatrix}\begin{bmatrix}5\\15\\15\end{bmatrix} = \begin{bmatrix}-5\\20\end{bmatrix}$

$A\mathbf{u} = \begin{bmatrix}5 & 1 & -3\\7 & -2 & 1\end{bmatrix}\begin{bmatrix}1\\3\\3\end{bmatrix} = \begin{bmatrix}-1\\4\end{bmatrix}$, $5(A\mathbf{u}) = \begin{bmatrix}-5\\20\end{bmatrix}$

34. Use the fact that $A(4\mathbf{y}) = 4A\mathbf{y}$. **36.** No, no

Section 2.3, page 61

2. $\mathbf{x} = \mathbf{a} + t\mathbf{b}$,

or $\begin{bmatrix}x_1\\x_2\end{bmatrix} = \begin{bmatrix}-4\\0\end{bmatrix} + t\begin{bmatrix}2\\-3\end{bmatrix}$, or $\begin{cases}x_1 = -4 + 2t\\x_2 = -3t\end{cases}$

4. $\begin{bmatrix}x_1\\x_2\end{bmatrix} = \begin{bmatrix}9\\-5\end{bmatrix} + t\begin{bmatrix}-7\\4\end{bmatrix}$, or $\begin{cases}x_1 = 9 - 7t\\x_2 = -5 + 4t\end{cases}$

6. Yes, there are at most three basic variables. **8.** No

10. $x_3\begin{bmatrix}-3\\5\\1\end{bmatrix}$ **12.** $x_3\begin{bmatrix}-1\\-3\\1\\0\end{bmatrix} + x_4\begin{bmatrix}1/2\\-3/2\\0\\1\end{bmatrix}$

14. $x_2\begin{bmatrix}-6\\1\\0\\0\\0\\0\end{bmatrix} + x_4\begin{bmatrix}-8\\0\\3\\1\\0\\0\end{bmatrix} + x_5\begin{bmatrix}1\\0\\-4\\0\\1\\0\end{bmatrix}$

16. $x_2\begin{bmatrix}5\\1\\0\\0\end{bmatrix}+x_3\begin{bmatrix}0\\0\\1\\0\end{bmatrix}+x_4\begin{bmatrix}-4\\0\\0\\1\end{bmatrix}$

18. The set is a "line" in $\mathbb{R}^4$ through $\begin{bmatrix}7\\-5\\1\\0\end{bmatrix}$ parallel to $\begin{bmatrix}1\\-2\\-3\\1\end{bmatrix}$.

20. $\begin{bmatrix}-8\\4\\0\end{bmatrix}+x_3\begin{bmatrix}-3\\5\\1\end{bmatrix}$. The solution set is a line through $\begin{bmatrix}-8\\4\\0\end{bmatrix}$, parallel to the solution set of the homogeneous equation in Exercise 10.

22. Let $\mathbf{p}=\begin{bmatrix}-1\\0\\0\end{bmatrix}$, $\mathbf{u}=\begin{bmatrix}-3\\1\\0\end{bmatrix}$, $\mathbf{v}=\begin{bmatrix}8\\0\\1\end{bmatrix}$. The solution set of the homogeneous equation is the plane Span $\{\mathbf{u},\mathbf{v}\}$ spanned by $\mathbf{u}$ and $\mathbf{v}$. The solution set of the nonhomogeneous equation is the translated plane $\mathbf{p}$ + Span $\{\mathbf{u},\mathbf{v}\}$, which passes through $\mathbf{p}$.

24. $A\mathbf{w}=A(5\mathbf{u})=5A\mathbf{u}=5\cdot\mathbf{0}=\mathbf{0}$, by Theorem 3.

26. According to Theorem 4, the number of solutions of $A\mathbf{x}=\mathbf{b}$ is the same as the number of vectors $\mathbf{v}_h$ satisfying $A\mathbf{x}=\mathbf{0}$.

28. No, because the "origin" is the vector $\mathbf{0}$, and $A\mathbf{0}=\mathbf{0}\neq\mathbf{b}$.

30. a. Yes **b.** No **32. a.** Yes **b.** Yes

34. One answer: $\mathbf{x}=\begin{bmatrix}-3\\1\end{bmatrix}$

Section 2.4, page 69

2. Lin. dep. **4.** Lin. dep. **6.** Lin. indep.

8. Lin. dep. **10.** Lin. indep. **12.** Lin. dep.

14. a. All h **b.** All h

16. $h=-3$ **18.** All h

20. Lin. indep. **22.** Lin. dep.

24. Lin. dep.

26. A: any 2×2 matrix with nonzero columns that are not multiples of each other; B: any 2×2 matrix with one column a multiple of the other

28. $\mathbf{x}=\begin{bmatrix}1\\2\\-1\end{bmatrix}$ **30.** True, by Theorem 7

32. False. Counterexample:

$\mathbf{v}_1=\begin{bmatrix}1\\1\\1\\1\end{bmatrix}$, $\mathbf{v}_2=\begin{bmatrix}2\\2\\2\\2\end{bmatrix}$, $\mathbf{v}_3=\begin{bmatrix}1\\0\\0\\0\end{bmatrix}$, $\mathbf{v}_4=\begin{bmatrix}3\\3\\3\\3\end{bmatrix}$

34. True. If the equation $x_1\mathbf{v}_1+x_2\mathbf{v}_2+x_3\mathbf{v}_3=\mathbf{0}$ had a nontrivial solution (at least one of x_1, x_2, x_3 nonzero), then so would the equation $x_1\mathbf{v}_1+x_2\mathbf{v}_2+x_3\mathbf{v}_3+0\cdot\mathbf{v}_4=\mathbf{0}$. But that can't happen, because $\{\mathbf{v}_1,\mathbf{v}_2,\mathbf{v}_3,\mathbf{v}_4\}$ is linearly independent. So $\{\mathbf{v}_1,\mathbf{v}_2,\mathbf{v}_3\}$ must be linearly independent.

36. a. n **b.** The columns of A are linearly independent if and only if the equation $A\mathbf{x}=\mathbf{0}$ has only the trivial solution. This happens if and only if $A\mathbf{x}=\mathbf{0}$ has no free variables, which in turn happens if and only if every variable is a basic variable, that is, if and only if every column of A is a pivot column.

38. An $m\times n$ matrix A with n pivot columns has a pivot in each column. So the equation $A\mathbf{x}=\mathbf{b}$ has no free variables. If there is a solution, it must be unique.

Section 2.5, page 77

2. $\begin{bmatrix}2\\0\\-6\end{bmatrix}$, $\begin{bmatrix}10\\-2\\8\end{bmatrix}$ **4.** $\begin{bmatrix}-2\\4\\1\end{bmatrix}$, yes **6.** $\begin{bmatrix}1\\-5\\0\end{bmatrix}$, no

8. 4 rows and 3 columns **10.** $x_3\begin{bmatrix}-1\\4\\1\\0\end{bmatrix}$ **12.** Yes

14. A projection onto the x_2-axis

16. A reflection in the x_2-axis

18. An expansion (scaling) in the x_1-direction (only) by a factor of 2

20. $\begin{bmatrix}21\\-9\\3\end{bmatrix}$, $\begin{bmatrix}-4\\0\\-8\end{bmatrix}$, $\begin{bmatrix}17\\-9\\-5\end{bmatrix}$

22.
$$\begin{aligned}T(x)&=T(x\cdot1)\\&=x\cdot T(1),\quad\text{since } x \text{ is in } \mathbb{R}\\&=x\cdot m=mx\end{aligned}$$

24. a. If $\mathbf{x} = \mathbf{p} + t(\mathbf{q} - \mathbf{p})$ as in Example 2 of Section 2.3, then $\mathbf{x} = \mathbf{p} - t\mathbf{p} + t\mathbf{q}$, and $\mathbf{x} = (1-t)\mathbf{p} + t\mathbf{q}$.
b. By the linearity of T,

$$T((1-t)\mathbf{p} + t\mathbf{q}) = (1-t)T(\mathbf{p}) + tT(\mathbf{q}) \quad \text{for } 0 \le t \le 1$$

If $T(\mathbf{p})$ and $T(\mathbf{q})$ are distinct, the images form the line segment between $T(\mathbf{p})$ and $T(\mathbf{q})$. Otherwise, all the images coincide with one point, $T(\mathbf{p})$.

26. If $\mathbf{x}$ is in the parallelogram determined by $\mathbf{u}$ and $\mathbf{v}$, then $\mathbf{x} = a\mathbf{u} + b\mathbf{v}$, for some a and b between 0 and 1. Using the linearity of T, $T(\mathbf{x}) = T(a\mathbf{u} + b\mathbf{v}) = aT(\mathbf{u}) + bT(\mathbf{v})$. Since $0 \le a, b \le 1$, this formula for $T(\mathbf{x})$ shows that $T(\mathbf{x})$ lies in the parallelogram determined by $T(\mathbf{u})$ and $T(\mathbf{v})$.

28. Take any (x_1, x_2) with $x_2 \ne 0$, and use a negative scalar. For instance, $T(0, 1) = (-2, 3)$, but $T(-1\cdot(0, 1)) = T(0, -1) = (2, 3) \ne (-1)\cdot T(0, 1)$.

30. $T(\mathbf{0}) = A\mathbf{0} + \mathbf{b} = \mathbf{b} \ne \mathbf{0}$, so T cannot be a linear transformation.

Section 2.6, page 84

2. $\begin{bmatrix} 3 & -2 \\ 3 & 5 \end{bmatrix}$ **4.** $\begin{bmatrix} 1 & 3 \\ 2 & -6 \\ 0 & 1 \\ 5 & 0 \end{bmatrix}$ **6.** $\begin{bmatrix} 0 & 1 \\ -1 & 0 \end{bmatrix}$

8. $\begin{bmatrix} 0 & 1 \\ 1 & 0 \end{bmatrix}$ **10.** $\begin{bmatrix} -1 & 0 \\ 0 & -1 \end{bmatrix}$ **12.** $\begin{bmatrix} 0 & 0 & 0 \\ 0 & 1 & 0 \\ 0 & 0 & 1 \end{bmatrix}$

14. $\begin{bmatrix} 1 & -3 \\ 0 & 1 \end{bmatrix}$ **16.** $\begin{bmatrix} 5 & -6 \\ 0 & 1 \\ 2 & -2 \end{bmatrix}$ **18.** $\begin{bmatrix} -1 & 5 \\ 0 & 0 \\ 3 & 1 \\ 1 & 0 \end{bmatrix}$

20. $\begin{bmatrix} 1 & 0 & 0 \\ 4 & 1 & 0 \\ 0 & 0 & 1 \end{bmatrix}$ **22.** $[3 \quad -4 \quad 0 \quad 8]$

24. $\begin{bmatrix} 2 \\ -3 \end{bmatrix}$ **26.** Yes **28.** No

30. One-to-one and onto $\mathbb{R}^3$

32. m. A has m pivot columns if and only if A has a pivot position in each row. By Theorem 2, this happens if and only if the columns of A span $\mathbb{R}^m$, and this in turn happens, by Theorem 10, if and only if T maps $\mathbb{R}^n$ onto $\mathbb{R}^m$.

34. The transformation T maps $\mathbb{R}^n$ *onto* $\mathbb{R}^m$ if and only if for each $\mathbf{y}$ in $\mathbb{R}^m$ *there exists* an $\mathbf{x}$ in $\mathbb{R}^n$ such that $\mathbf{y} = T(\mathbf{x})$.

36. If T is one-to-one, then the columns of its standard matrix A must be linearly independent. Since A is $m \times n$, m must be greater than or equal to n.

Section 2.7, page 90

2. $B = \begin{bmatrix} 110 & 110 \\ 3 & 2 \\ 21 & 25 \\ 3 & 0 \end{bmatrix}$, $u = \begin{bmatrix} 3 \\ 2 \end{bmatrix}$

4. a. $\mathbf{x}_1 \begin{bmatrix} 10 \\ 50 \\ 30 \end{bmatrix} + x_2 \begin{bmatrix} 20 \\ 40 \\ 10 \end{bmatrix} + x_3 \begin{bmatrix} 20 \\ 10 \\ 40 \end{bmatrix} = \begin{bmatrix} 100 \\ 300 \\ 200 \end{bmatrix}$, where x_1, x_2, and x_3 are the number of units of foods 1, 2, and 3, respectively, to be used in the meal.
b. $x_1 = 150/33 \approx 4.55$, $x_2 = 50/33 \approx 1.52$, and $x_3 = 40/33 \approx 1.21$

6. a. $\mathbf{x}_{k+1} = M\mathbf{x}_k + \mathbf{v}$, for $k = 0, 1, 2, \ldots$, where $M = \begin{bmatrix} .94 & .04 \\ .06 & .96 \end{bmatrix}$, $\mathbf{v} = \begin{bmatrix} 10{,}000 \\ 8{,}000 \end{bmatrix}$, and $\mathbf{x}_0 = \begin{bmatrix} 800{,}000 \\ 500{,}000 \end{bmatrix}$
b. The population in 1992 (when $k = 2$) is $\mathbf{x}_2 = \begin{bmatrix} 766{,}520 \\ 569{,}480 \end{bmatrix}$.

8. $\mathbf{x}_0 = \begin{bmatrix} 304 \\ 48 \\ 98 \end{bmatrix}$, $\mathbf{x}_1 \approx \begin{bmatrix} 307 \\ 48 \\ 95 \end{bmatrix}$, $\mathbf{x}_2 = \begin{bmatrix} 310 \\ 48 \\ 92 \end{bmatrix}$

CHAPTER 3

Section 3.1, page 105

2. $\begin{bmatrix} 6 & 4 & 0 \\ 4 & 2 & 2 \end{bmatrix}$ **4.** Not defined **6.** $\begin{bmatrix} 19 & -8 & 1 \\ 4 & -16 & -4 \end{bmatrix}$

8. Not defined **10.** $\begin{bmatrix} 3 & -5 & 3 \\ 5 & 6 & -2 \\ -3 & 2 & -2 \end{bmatrix}$, $\begin{bmatrix} 2 & -5 & 3 \\ 5 & 5 & -2 \\ -3 & 2 & -3 \end{bmatrix}$

12. $\begin{bmatrix} 5 & 5 \\ 15 & -5 \\ 1 & 3 \end{bmatrix}$ **14.** 2 **16.** $k = 9$

18. Example: $\begin{bmatrix} 12 & 3 \\ 4 & 1 \end{bmatrix}$

20. They do.

22. The first and third rows of AB are $\text{row}_1(A)\cdot B$ and $\text{row}_3(A)\cdot B$, respectively. They are equal, since $\text{row}_1(A) = \text{row}_3(A)$.

24. The second column of AB is also all zeros.

26. $\mathbf{b}_1 = \begin{bmatrix} 7 \\ 4 \end{bmatrix}, \mathbf{b}_2 = \begin{bmatrix} -8 \\ -5 \end{bmatrix}$

28. $A\mathbf{u} = \begin{bmatrix} 1 \\ -23 \end{bmatrix}, (A\mathbf{u})^T = [\,1 \quad -23\,], \mathbf{u}^T = [\,5 \quad -2\,],$
$\mathbf{u}^T A^T = [\,1 \quad -23\,]$

30. $(3A)^T = \begin{bmatrix} 3 & 6 \\ -9 & 12 \end{bmatrix}^T = \begin{bmatrix} 3 & -9 \\ 6 & 12 \end{bmatrix} =$
$3\begin{bmatrix} 1 & -3 \\ 2 & 4 \end{bmatrix} = 3A^T$

32. $\mathbf{u}^T\mathbf{v} = (\mathbf{v}^T\mathbf{u})^T = \mathbf{v}^T\mathbf{u}$, because $\mathbf{v}^T\mathbf{u}$ is a 1×1 matrix, which we regard as a scalar; $\mathbf{u}\mathbf{v}^T = (\mathbf{v}\mathbf{u}^T)^T$

34. $AC = \begin{bmatrix} ac & ad+bc \\ 0 & ac \end{bmatrix}, (AC)^T = \begin{bmatrix} ac & 0 \\ ad+bc & ac \end{bmatrix} =$
$A^T C^T$ (in this case)

36. $(r+s)\mathbf{a}_j = r\mathbf{a}_j + s\mathbf{a}_j$ for all j, by vector algebra

38. The (i, j)-entry in $(B+C)A$ is

$$\sum_{k=1}^{m}(b_{ik} + c_{ik})a_{kj} = \sum_{k=1}^{m}(b_{ik}a_{kj} + c_{ik}a_{kj}) = \sum_{k=1}^{m} b_{ik}a_{kj} + \sum_{k=1}^{m} c_{ik}a_{kj}$$

The expression on the right is the (i, j)-entry in $BA+CA$.

40. $I_m A = I_m\,[\,\mathbf{a}_1 \;\cdots\; \mathbf{a}_n\,]$
$= [\,I_m\mathbf{a}_1 \;\cdots\; I_m\mathbf{a}_n\,]$ Matrix multiplication
$= [\,\mathbf{a}_1 \;\cdots\; \mathbf{a}_m\,] = A$

42. The (i, j)-entry of $(A+B)^T$ is the (j, i)-entry of $A+B$, namely, the sum of the (j, i)-entries in A and B, which, in turn, is the sum of the (i, j)-entries in A^T and B^T.

44. $(AB\mathbf{x})^T = \mathbf{x}^T(AB)^T = \mathbf{x}^T B^T A^T$.

Section 3.2, page 114

2. $\begin{bmatrix} 6 & 5 \\ -5 & -4 \end{bmatrix}$ **4.** $\begin{bmatrix} 4 & 9/2 \\ -3 & -7/2 \end{bmatrix}$ **6.** $\begin{bmatrix} 15 \\ 7 \end{bmatrix}$

8. $\begin{bmatrix} 21 \\ -8 \end{bmatrix}, \begin{bmatrix} -29 \\ 11 \end{bmatrix}, \begin{bmatrix} 6 \\ -2 \end{bmatrix}, \begin{bmatrix} -5 \\ 2 \end{bmatrix}$

10. $AC = I \Rightarrow A^{-1}AC = A^{-1}I$ (suppressing parentheses because of associativity) $\Rightarrow IC = A^{-1}$ and $C = A^{-1}$.

12. If A is invertible, then the equation $A\mathbf{x} = \mathbf{0}$ has only the trivial solution, by Theorem 5. It follows that the columns of A are linearly independent, by the definition of $A\mathbf{x}$.

14. $(B-C)A = 0 \Rightarrow (B-C)AA^{-1} = 0A^{-1} \Rightarrow$
$(B-C)I = 0 \Rightarrow B - C = 0 \Rightarrow B = C$.

16. Let $C = AB$. Then $CB^{-1} = ABB^{-1} \Rightarrow CB^{-1} = AI \Rightarrow A = CB^{-1}$. This shows that A is the product of invertible matrices and hence is invertible, by Theorem 6. [*Note*: You cannot use the formula $(AB)^{-1} = B^{-1}A^{-1}$ in the proof, because you cannot assume that A is invertible.]

18. $B = P^{-1}AP$

20. Take transposes in the equations $AA^{-1} = I$ and $A^{-1}A = I$ to obtain

$$(A^{-1})^T A^T = I^T = I \quad \text{and} \quad A^T(A^{-1})^T = I$$

These equations say that A^T is invertible, with inverse $(A^{-1})^T$.

22. $\dfrac{1}{ad-bc}\begin{bmatrix} d & -b \\ -c & a \end{bmatrix}\begin{bmatrix} a & b \\ c & d \end{bmatrix}$
$= \dfrac{1}{ad-bc}\begin{bmatrix} da-bc & db-bd \\ -ca+ac & -cb+ad \end{bmatrix}$
$= \dfrac{1}{ad-bc}\begin{bmatrix} da-bc & 0 \\ 0 & -cb+ad \end{bmatrix} = \begin{bmatrix} 1 & 0 \\ 0 & 1 \end{bmatrix}$

A similar calculation verifies the inverse on the right side.

24. Take $F = E$ from Exercise 23.

26. $F = \begin{bmatrix} 1 & 0 & 0 & 0 \\ 0 & 1 & 0 & 0 \\ 0 & 0 & 1/5 & 0 \\ 0 & 0 & 0 & 1 \end{bmatrix}$

28. $F = \begin{bmatrix} 1 & 0 & 0 & 0 \\ 0 & 1 & 0 & 0 \\ 0 & 0 & 1 & 0 \\ 0 & 3 & 0 & 1 \end{bmatrix}$ **30.** $\begin{bmatrix} -1 & 2 \\ -1/3 & 1 \end{bmatrix}$

32. $\begin{bmatrix} -28 & -13 & 3 \\ 2 & 1 & 0 \\ -7 & -3 & 1 \end{bmatrix}$ **34.** Not invertible **36.** $\begin{bmatrix} -1 \\ 3 \\ -2 \end{bmatrix}$

38. The *stiffness matrix* is $125\begin{bmatrix} 2 & -1 & 0 \\ -1 & 3 & -1 \\ 0 & -1 & 2 \end{bmatrix}$;

$\mathbf{f} = \begin{bmatrix} 20 \\ -10 \\ 0 \end{bmatrix}$ lb.

40. If A were invertible, then the equation $AD = I$ would imply that $A^{-1}AD = A^{-1}I$ and $D = A^{-1}$, in which case DA would be I. However, A cannot be invertible, because

$$DA = \begin{bmatrix} 5/9 & 2/9 & 4/9 \\ 2/9 & 8/9 & -2/9 \\ 4/9 & -2/9 & 5/9 \end{bmatrix} \neq I$$

Section 3.3, page 120

The Invertible Matrix Theorem is abbreviated here by IMT.

2. Yes, by the IMT. The columns are linearly independent since they are not multiples. Also, the determinant is not zero.

4. Yes, by the IMT. The matrix has three pivot columns.

6. No, by the IMT. The matrix is row equivalent to $\begin{bmatrix} 1 & 3 & 4 \\ 0 & 6 & 15 \\ 0 & 0 & 0 \end{bmatrix}$. (Interchange rows 1 and 3 and row reduce.) So the matrix is *not* row equivalent to I.

8. No, by the IMT. The matrix is row equivalent to $\begin{bmatrix} 1 & 4 & 2 \\ 0 & -1 & -1 \\ 0 & 0 & 0 \end{bmatrix}$ and so is *not* row equivalent to I.

10. Yes, by the IMT. The matrix has 4 pivot positions.

12. No, a 4×3 matrix is not invertible.

14. The equation $A\mathbf{x} = \mathbf{0}$ *always* has the trivial solution. This fact tells us *nothing* about the columns of A.

16. H is invertible, by the IMT. So it is *not* possible for an equation $H\mathbf{x} = \mathbf{v}$ to have more than one solution.

18. No, because statement (e″) of the IMT is false.

20. Statement (e′) of the IMT is false, so statement (e″) is false, too. Thus the columns of C do *not* span $\mathbb{R}^n$.

22. If A is invertible, then A^{-1} is invertible, by Theorem 6(a). So the IMT applies to A^{-1}, and the columns of A^{-1} are linearly independent.

24. A is invertible by the IMT, and hence A^T is invertible [by Theorem 6(c) or by the IMT]. Thus the columns of A^T are linearly independent. That is, the rows of A are linearly independent.

26. One method is to let $D = (AB)^{-1}A$ and use part (g) of the IMT. Another is to show that $B\mathbf{x} = \mathbf{0}$ has only the trivial solution and then use the IMT. If $B\mathbf{x} = \mathbf{0}$, then $AB\mathbf{x} = A\mathbf{0} = \mathbf{0}$. Since AB is invertible, $\mathbf{x} = \mathbf{0}$.

28. If T maps $\mathbb{R}^n$ onto $\mathbb{R}^n$, then the columns of its standard matrix A span $\mathbb{R}^n$, by Theorem 10 in Section 2.6. By the IMT, A is invertible. Hence, by Theorem 9, T is invertible.

30. The standard matrix of T is $A = \begin{bmatrix} 6 & -8 \\ -5 & 7 \end{bmatrix}$, which is invertible because $\det A = 2 \neq 0$. By Theorem 9, T is invertible, and

$$T^{-1}(\mathbf{x}) = B\mathbf{x}, \quad \text{where } B = A^{-1} = \tfrac{1}{2}\begin{bmatrix} 7 & 8 \\ 5 & 6 \end{bmatrix}$$

32. Given $\mathbf{u}, \mathbf{v}$ in $\mathbb{R}^n$, let $\mathbf{x} = S(\mathbf{u})$ and $\mathbf{y} = S(\mathbf{v})$. Then $T(\mathbf{x}) = T(S(\mathbf{u})) = \mathbf{u}$ and $T(\mathbf{y}) = T(S(\mathbf{v})) = \mathbf{v}$, by Eq. 2. Hence

$$\begin{aligned} S(\mathbf{u}+\mathbf{v}) &= S(T(\mathbf{x}) + T(\mathbf{y})) & \\ &= S(T(\mathbf{x}+\mathbf{y})) & \text{Because } T \text{ is linear} \\ &= \mathbf{x}+\mathbf{y} & \text{By Eq. (1)} \\ &= S(\mathbf{u}) + S(\mathbf{v}) & \end{aligned}$$

So S preserves sums. For any scalar r,

$$\begin{aligned} S(r\mathbf{u}) &= S(rT(\mathbf{x})) = S(T(r\mathbf{x})) & \text{Because } T \text{ is linear} \\ &= r\mathbf{x} & \text{By Eq. (1)} \\ &= rS(\mathbf{u}) & \end{aligned}$$

So S preserves scalar multiples. Thus S is a linear transformation.

Section 3.4, page 126

2. $\begin{bmatrix} AC & AD \\ BE & BF \end{bmatrix}$ **4.** $\begin{bmatrix} A - XC & B - XD \\ C & D \end{bmatrix}$

6. $X = -B^{-1}A, \quad Y = B^{-1}, \quad Z = C$

8. $X = -A_{11}^{-1}A_{12}, \quad Y = -A_{22}^{-1}A_{23}$

10. $\begin{bmatrix} I & 0 & 0 \\ -C & I & 0 \\ -A + BC & -B & I \end{bmatrix}$

12. Suppose A is invertible, and let $A^{-1} = \begin{bmatrix} D & E \\ F & G \end{bmatrix}$. The equation $AA^{-1} = I$ implies that $BD = I$ and $CG = I$. Since B and C are square, they must be invertible, by the IMT. Conversely, if B and C are invertible, then the matrix $\begin{bmatrix} B^{-1} & 0 \\ 0 & C^{-1} \end{bmatrix}$ is easily seen to be the inverse of A.

14. $X = A_{21}A_{11}^{-1}, \quad Y = A_{11}^{-1}A_{12}$

16. The Schur complement of X^TX is $\mathbf{x}_0^T\mathbf{x}_0 - (\mathbf{x}_0^TX)(X^TX)^{-1}(X^T\mathbf{x}_0) = \mathbf{x}_0^T(I - X(X^TX)^{-1}X^T)\mathbf{x}_0 = \mathbf{x}_0^TM\mathbf{x}_0$.

18. The Schur complement of $A - BC - sI$ is $I + C(A - BC - sI)^{-1}B$. *Note*: The proof that this function actually is the inverse of the $W(s)$ in Exercise 17 involves only matrix algebra, but it is a little tricky. The following algebraic identity is needed:

$$\begin{aligned} CU^{-1}B - CV^{-1}B &= C(U^{-1} - V^{-1})B \\ &= CU^{-1}(V - U)V^{-1}B \end{aligned}$$

for any invertible $n \times n$ matrices U and V and any B and C such that the multiplication is well defined.

20. Let $A = \begin{bmatrix} A_{11} & 0 \\ A_{21} & A_{22} \end{bmatrix}$, with A_{11} and A_{22} square, and suppose that A is invertible. Then A^T is invertible and upper triangular. From Example 5 applied to A^T, we conclude that A_{11}^T and A_{22}^T are invertible, and hence A_{11} and A_{22} are invertible. The analogous formula for A^{-1} is

$$A^{-1} = \begin{bmatrix} A_{11}^{-1} & 0 \\ -A_{22}^{-1}A_{21}A_{11}^{-1} & A_{22}^{-1} \end{bmatrix}$$

The fact that this matrix really is A^{-1} can be verified by direct calculation.

Section 3.5, page 134

2. $L\mathbf{y} = \mathbf{b} \Rightarrow \mathbf{y} = \begin{bmatrix} 2 \\ -2 \\ 2 \end{bmatrix}$, $U\mathbf{x} = \mathbf{y} \Rightarrow \mathbf{x} = \begin{bmatrix} 1/4 \\ 2 \\ 1 \end{bmatrix}$

4. $\mathbf{y} = \begin{bmatrix} 0 \\ -5 \\ -18 \end{bmatrix}$, $\mathbf{x} = \begin{bmatrix} -5 \\ 1 \\ 3 \end{bmatrix}$

6. $\mathbf{y} = \begin{bmatrix} 1 \\ 1 \\ -2 \\ 1 \end{bmatrix}$, $\mathbf{x} = \begin{bmatrix} 3 \\ -2 \\ 1 \\ 1 \end{bmatrix}$

8. $LU = \begin{bmatrix} 1 & 0 \\ 2/3 & 1 \end{bmatrix}\begin{bmatrix} 6 & 9 \\ 0 & -1 \end{bmatrix}$

10. $\begin{bmatrix} 1 & 0 & 0 \\ -2 & 1 & 0 \\ -3 & -5 & 1 \end{bmatrix}\begin{bmatrix} -5 & 3 & 4 \\ 0 & -2 & -1 \\ 0 & 0 & 9 \end{bmatrix}$

12. $\begin{bmatrix} 1 & 0 & 0 \\ 1/2 & 1 & 0 \\ -3 & -2 & 1 \end{bmatrix}\begin{bmatrix} 2 & -4 & 2 \\ 0 & 7 & -5 \\ 0 & 0 & 0 \end{bmatrix}$

14. $\begin{bmatrix} 1 & 0 & 0 & 0 \\ 3 & 1 & 0 & 0 \\ -2 & -1 & 1 & 0 \\ -1 & -2 & 0 & 1 \end{bmatrix}\begin{bmatrix} 1 & 4 & -1 & 5 \\ 0 & -5 & 1 & -6 \\ 0 & 0 & 0 & 0 \\ 0 & 0 & 0 & 0 \end{bmatrix}$

16. $\begin{bmatrix} 1 & 0 & 0 & 0 & 0 \\ -2 & 1 & 0 & 0 & 0 \\ 3/2 & -2 & 1 & 0 & 0 \\ -3 & 2 & 0 & 1 & 0 \\ 4 & -3 & 0 & 0 & 1 \end{bmatrix}\begin{bmatrix} 2 & -6 & 6 \\ 0 & -7 & 5 \\ 0 & 0 & 0 \\ 0 & 0 & 0 \\ 0 & 0 & 0 \end{bmatrix}$

18. $L = \begin{bmatrix} 1 & 0 & 0 \\ -6 & 1 & 0 \\ 1 & -6 & 1 \end{bmatrix}$, $U = \begin{bmatrix} 1 & 2 & 2 \\ 0 & 1 & 0 \\ 0 & 0 & 1 \end{bmatrix}$,

$L^{-1} = \begin{bmatrix} 1 & 0 & 0 \\ 6 & 1 & 0 \\ 35 & 6 & 1 \end{bmatrix}$, $U^{-1} = \begin{bmatrix} 1 & -2 & -2 \\ 0 & 1 & 0 \\ 0 & 0 & 1 \end{bmatrix}$,

and $A^{-1} = U^{-1}L^{-1} = \begin{bmatrix} -81 & -14 & -2 \\ 6 & 1 & 0 \\ 35 & 6 & 1 \end{bmatrix}$

20. Since L is unit lower triangular, it is invertible and may be row reduced to I by adding suitable multiples of a row to the rows below it, beginning with the top row. If elementary matrices $E_1, \ldots, E_p$ implement these row operations, then

$$E_p \cdots E_1 A = (E_p \cdots E_1 L)U = IU = U$$

This shows that A may be row reduced to U using only row-replacement operations.

22. $B = \begin{bmatrix} 1 & 0 & 0 \\ 3 & 1 & 0 \\ 1 & -1 & 1 \\ 2 & 2 & -1 \\ -3 & -3 & 2 \end{bmatrix}$, $C = \begin{bmatrix} 2 & -4 & -2 & 3 \\ 0 & 3 & 1 & -1 \\ 0 & 0 & 0 & 5 \end{bmatrix}$; if $A = LU$, with only 3 nonzero rows in U, use the first three columns of L for B and the top three rows of U for C.

24. Since Q is square and $Q^TQ = I$, Q is invertible and $Q^{-1} = Q^T$, by the Invertible Matrix Theorem. Thus A is the product of invertible matrices and hence is invertible. By Theorem 5, the equation $A\mathbf{x} = \mathbf{b}$ has a unique solution for all $\mathbf{b}$. From $A\mathbf{x} = \mathbf{b}$, we have $QR\mathbf{x} = \mathbf{b}$, $Q^TQR\mathbf{x} = Q^T\mathbf{b}$, $R\mathbf{x} = Q^T\mathbf{b}$, and $\mathbf{x} = R^{-1}Q^T\mathbf{b}$. A good algorithm for finding $\mathbf{b}$ is to compute $Q^T\mathbf{b}$ and then row reduce $[\,R \quad Q^T\mathbf{b}\,]$. (See Exercise 9 in Section 3.2.) The reduction is fast because R is triangular.

26. In general, $A^k = PD^kP^{-1}$, where

$$D^k = \begin{bmatrix} 1 & 0 & 0 \\ 0 & 1/2^k & 0 \\ 0 & 0 & 1/3^k \end{bmatrix}.$$

28. $\begin{bmatrix} 1 & 0 \\ -1/R_3 & 1 \end{bmatrix}\begin{bmatrix} 1 & 0 \\ -1/R_2 & 1 \end{bmatrix}\begin{bmatrix} 1 & 0 \\ -1/R_1 & 1 \end{bmatrix} =$ $\begin{bmatrix} 1 & 0 \\ -(1/R_1 + 1/R_2 + 1/R_3) & 1 \end{bmatrix}$. The single shunt resistance is $\frac{1}{R_1} + \frac{1}{R_2} + \frac{1}{R_3}$.

30. The transfer matrix of the following circuit is

$$\begin{bmatrix} 1 + R_3/R_2 & -R_1 - R_3 - R_1R_3/R_2 \\ -1/R_2 & 1 + R_1/R_2 \end{bmatrix}$$

Set that matrix equal to $A = \begin{bmatrix} 4/3 & -12 \\ -1/4 & 3 \end{bmatrix}$, and solve to find $R_1 = 8$ ohms, $R_2 = 4$ ohms, $R_3 = 4/3$ ohms.

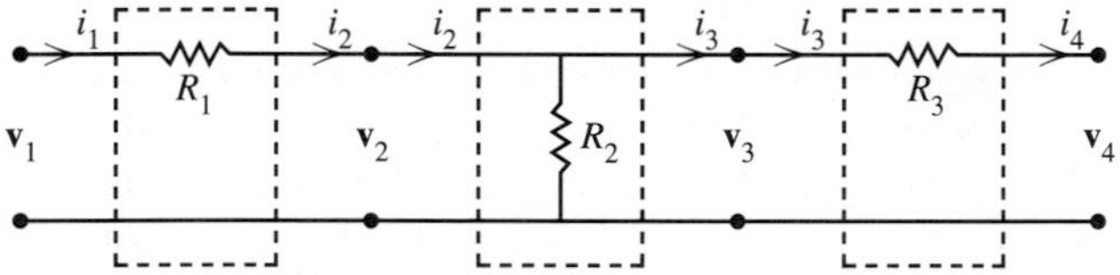

Section 3.6, page 141

The answers here were computed by MATLAB in double precision (about 16 significant digits) and reported in the "short format" of about 5 significant digits.

2. $\mathbf{x}^{(1)} = \begin{bmatrix} 2.5 \\ 5.375 \end{bmatrix}$, $\mathbf{x}^{(2)} = \begin{bmatrix} 3.0375 \\ 5.0625 \end{bmatrix}$, $\mathbf{x}^{(3)} = \begin{bmatrix} 3.0063 \\ 4.9953 \end{bmatrix}$, $\ldots, \mathbf{x}^{(5)} = \begin{bmatrix} 2.9999 \\ 5.0001 \end{bmatrix}$

4. $\mathbf{x}^{(1)} = \begin{bmatrix} 2.98 \\ 1.01 \\ -1.96 \end{bmatrix}$, $\mathbf{x}^{(2)} = \begin{bmatrix} 3.0002 \\ 1.0006 \\ -2.0004 \end{bmatrix}$, $\mathbf{x}^{(3)} = \begin{bmatrix} 3.0000 \\ 1.0000 \\ -2.0000 \end{bmatrix}$

6. $\mathbf{x}^{(1)} = \begin{bmatrix} 2.5 \\ 5.0625 \end{bmatrix}$, $\mathbf{x}^{(2)} = \begin{bmatrix} 3.0063 \\ 4.9992 \end{bmatrix}, \ldots, \mathbf{x}^{(4)} = \begin{bmatrix} 3.0000 \\ 5.0000 \end{bmatrix}$. Jacobi took 5 iterations for about the same accuracy.

8. $\mathbf{x}^{(1)} = \begin{bmatrix} 2.98 \\ 1.0398 \\ -2.0016 \end{bmatrix}$, $\mathbf{x}^{(2)} = \begin{bmatrix} 3.0008 \\ 1.0000 \\ -2.0000 \end{bmatrix}$, $\mathbf{x}^{(3)} = \begin{bmatrix} 3.0000 \\ 1.0000 \\ -2.0000 \end{bmatrix}$. Jacobi also took 3 iterations for about the same accuracy.

10. Only (a) is strictly diagonally dominant.

12. $\mathbf{x}^{(1)} = \begin{bmatrix} -3 \\ -22 \\ -4 \end{bmatrix}$, $\mathbf{x}^{(2)} = \begin{bmatrix} -87 \\ -358 \\ -88 \end{bmatrix}$, $\mathbf{x}^{(3)} = \begin{bmatrix} -1347 \\ -5398 \\ -1348 \end{bmatrix}$.
With the first two equations interchanged, Gauss–Seidel produces $\mathbf{x}^{(6)} = \begin{bmatrix} 3.0000 \\ 2.0000 \\ 2.0000 \end{bmatrix}$.

14. Gauss–Seidel produces $\mathbf{x}^{(18)} = \begin{bmatrix} 10.000 \\ 13.000 \\ -15.000 \end{bmatrix}$, accurate to three decimal places. *Note*: $\mathbf{x}^{(17)} = \begin{bmatrix} 9.9991 \\ 12.9995 \\ -14.9997 \end{bmatrix}$, which rounds to three-place accuracy.

16. The Jacobi method produces a sequence of vectors whose entries grow slowly and do not converge. The Gauss–Seidel method produces $\mathbf{x}^{(13)} = \begin{bmatrix} 3.9998 \\ -1.0009 \\ -2.0005 \end{bmatrix}$, accurate to within .001.

18. a. By definition,

$$M\mathbf{x}^{(k+1)} = N\mathbf{x}^{(k)} + \mathbf{b}$$

Also, since $\mathbf{x}^*$ satisfies $A\mathbf{x}^* = \mathbf{b}$,

$$M\mathbf{x}^* = N\mathbf{x}^* + \mathbf{b}$$

Subtracting, and using a property of matrix multiplication,

$$M(\mathbf{x}^{(k+1)} - \mathbf{x}^*) = N(\mathbf{x}^{(k)} - \mathbf{x}^*)$$

Left-multiplying both sides by M^{-1}, and using the definition of the error vector $\mathbf{e}^{(k)}$,

$$\mathbf{x}^{(k+1)} - \mathbf{x}^* = M^{-1}N(\mathbf{x}^{(k)} - \mathbf{x}^*), \quad \text{and}$$
$$\mathbf{e}^{(k+1)} = M^{-1}N\mathbf{e}^{(k)}$$

b. The statement $\mathbf{e}^{(k)} = (M^{-1}N)^k\mathbf{e}^{(0)}$ is obvious for $k = 0$. Suppose it holds for some k, and apply $M^{-1}N$ to both sides. Then, using part (a), we find that

$$M^{-1}N\mathbf{e}^{(k)} = M^{-1}N(M^{-1}N)^k\mathbf{e}^{(0)}$$

and

$$\mathbf{e}^{(k+1)} = (M^{-1}N)^{k+1}\mathbf{e}^{(0)}$$

Thus, for each $k \geq 0$, the truth of the equation for k implies its truth for $k+1$. By the principle of induction, the equation is true for all integers $k \geq 0$.

Section 3.7, page 147

2. $\begin{bmatrix} 33.33 \\ 35.00 \\ 15.00 \end{bmatrix}$

4. Agriculture is less profitable than manufacturing because it requires more inputs per unit of output. So an 18-unit demand for agriculture produces more intermediate demand than an 18-unit demand for manufacturing.

6. $\begin{bmatrix} 50 \\ 45 \end{bmatrix}$

8. a. Since $\mathbf{x}$ satisfies $(I - C)\mathbf{x} = \mathbf{d}$ and $\Delta\mathbf{x}$ satisfies $(I - C)\Delta\mathbf{x} = \Delta\mathbf{d}$, linearity of matrix multiplication shows that

$$(I - C)(\mathbf{x} + \Delta\mathbf{x}) = (I - C)\mathbf{x} + (I - C)\Delta\mathbf{x} = \mathbf{d} + \Delta\mathbf{d}$$

which means that $\mathbf{x} + \Delta\mathbf{x}$ satisfies the production equation for a demand of $\mathbf{d} + \Delta\mathbf{d}$.
b. If $\Delta\mathbf{x}$ satisfies $(I - C)\Delta\mathbf{x} = \Delta\mathbf{d}$, then $\Delta\mathbf{x} = (I - C)^{-1}\Delta\mathbf{d}$, which is the first column of $(I - C)^{-1}$ in the case when $\Delta\mathbf{d}$ is the first column of I.

10. By the argument in Exercise 8, the effect of raising the demand for the output of one sector of the economy is given by the entries in the corresponding column of $(I - C)^{-1}$. When these entries are all positive, every sector must increase its output by some positive (though possibly small) quantity. So an increase in demand for *any* sector will increase the demand for *every* sector.

12. $D_{m+1} = I + CD_m$

Section 3.8, page 156

2. $\begin{bmatrix} -1 & 0 \\ 0 & 1 \end{bmatrix}\begin{bmatrix} 5 & 2 & 4 \\ 0 & 2 & 3 \end{bmatrix} = \begin{bmatrix} -5 & -2 & -4 \\ 0 & 2 & 3 \end{bmatrix}$

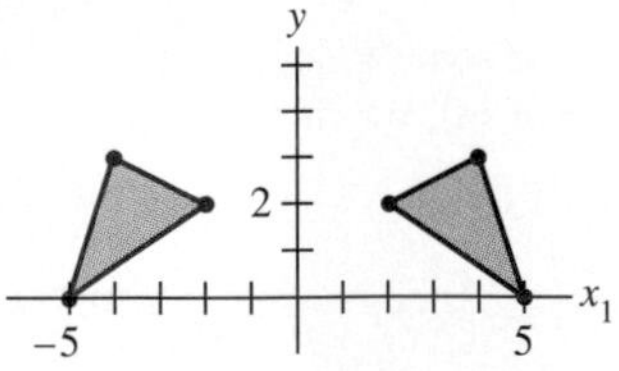

4. $\begin{bmatrix} .8 & 0 & -1.6 \\ 0 & 1.2 & 3.6 \\ 0 & 0 & 1 \end{bmatrix}$ **6.** $\begin{bmatrix} \sqrt{3}/2 & -1/2 & 0 \\ -1/2 & -\sqrt{3}/2 & 0 \\ 0 & 0 & 1 \end{bmatrix}$

8. $\begin{bmatrix} \sqrt{2}/2 & -\sqrt{2}/2 & 3+2\sqrt{2} \\ \sqrt{2}/2 & \sqrt{2}/2 & 7-5\sqrt{2} \\ 0 & 0 & 1 \end{bmatrix}$

10. D commutes with R but not with T; T does not commute with R.

12. Two identities: $\tan\varphi/2 = \frac{1-\cos\varphi}{\sin\varphi} = \frac{\sin\varphi}{1+\cos\varphi}$. The first identity shows that $1 - (\tan\varphi/2)(\sin\varphi) = \cos\varphi$, and hence

$$\begin{bmatrix} 1 & -\tan\varphi/2 & 0 \\ 0 & 1 & 0 \\ 0 & 0 & 1 \end{bmatrix}\begin{bmatrix} 1 & 0 & 0 \\ \sin\varphi & 1 & 0 \\ 0 & 0 & 1 \end{bmatrix} = \begin{bmatrix} \cos\varphi & -\tan\varphi/2 & 0 \\ \sin\varphi & 1 & 0 \\ 0 & 0 & 1 \end{bmatrix}$$

The second identity shows that

$$(\cos\varphi)(-\tan\varphi/2) - \tan\varphi/2 = -(\cos\varphi + 1)(\tan\varphi/2) = -\sin\varphi$$

Hence

$$\begin{bmatrix} \cos\varphi & -\tan\varphi/2 & 0 \\ \sin\varphi & 1 & 0 \\ 0 & 0 & 1 \end{bmatrix}\begin{bmatrix} 1 & -\tan\varphi/2 & 0 \\ 0 & 1 & 0 \\ 0 & 0 & 1 \end{bmatrix} = \begin{bmatrix} \cos\varphi & -\sin\varphi & 0 \\ \sin\varphi & \cos\varphi & 0 \\ 0 & 0 & 1 \end{bmatrix}$$

14. The matrix from Exercise 7 may be written as

$$\begin{bmatrix} 1/2 & -\sqrt{3}/2 & 3+4\sqrt{3} \\ \sqrt{3}/2 & 1/2 & 4-3\sqrt{3} \\ 0 & 0 & 1 \end{bmatrix} = \begin{bmatrix} 1 & 0 & 3+4\sqrt{3} \\ 0 & 1 & 4-3\sqrt{3} \\ 0 & 0 & 1 \end{bmatrix}\begin{bmatrix} 1/2 & -\sqrt{3}/2 & 0 \\ \sqrt{3}/2 & 1/2 & 0 \\ 0 & 0 & 1 \end{bmatrix}$$

This is a rotation through 60° about the origin, followed by a translation by $(3+4\sqrt{3}, 4-3\sqrt{3})$.

16. Both $(1, -2, 3, 4)$ and $(10, -20, 30, 40)$ are homogeneous coordinates for $(1/4, -1/2, 3/4)$ because of the formulas $x = X/H$, $y = Y/H$, and $z = Z/H$.

18. $\begin{bmatrix} \sqrt{3}/2 & 1/2 & 0 & 5 \\ -1/2 & \sqrt{3}/2 & 0 & -2 \\ 0 & 0 & 1 & 1 \\ 0 & 0 & 0 & 1 \end{bmatrix}$

20. The triangle with vertices $(6, 2, 0)$, $(15, 10, 0)$, $(2, 3, 0)$

CHAPTER 4

Section 4.1, page 166

2. 2 **4.** 20 **6.** 1 **8.** −11

10. −6. Start with row 2.

12. 36. Start with row 1 or column 4.

14. 9. Start with row 4 or column 5. **16.** 2 **18.** 20

20. $2a - 6b + 3c$, $-2a + 6b - 3c$. Interchanging two rows reverses the sign of the determinant.

22. $ad - bc$, $(ad + kcd) - (bc + kdc) = ad - bc$; row replacement does not change a determinant.

24. $ad - bc$, $a(kd) - b(kc) = k(ad - bc)$. Scaling a row by k multiplies the determinant by k.

26. 1 **28.** k **30.** -1

32. k; a scaling matrix is diagonal, with k on the diagonal and with 1's as the other diagonal entries. The determinant is the product of the diagonal entries.

34. $\det EA = \begin{bmatrix} a & b \\ kc & kd \end{bmatrix} = akd - bkc = k(ad - bc) = (\det E)(\det A)$

36. $\det EA = \begin{bmatrix} a & b \\ ka + c & kb + d \end{bmatrix} = a(kb + d) - b(ka + c)$
$= akb + ad - bka - bc = (+1)(ad - bc)$
$= (\det E)(\det A)$

38. $\det kA = k^2 \cdot \det A$

40. The area of the parallelogram and the determinant of $[\mathbf{v} \ \ \mathbf{u}]$ are both bc. The determinant of $[\mathbf{u} \ \ \mathbf{v}]$ is $-bc$. Both matrices determine the same parallelogram, with base of length c and height b.

Section 4.2, page 174

2. A constant may be factored out of one row.

4. A row replacement operation does not change the determinant.

6. -18 **8.** 0 **10.** 24 **12.** 114 **14.** 0 **16.** 7

18. 7 **20.** 21 **22.** Not invertible

24. Linearly independent **26.** Linearly dependent

28. If two rows are equal, add (-1) times one row to the other row. This doesn't change the determinant, by Theorem 3, but it produces a row of zeros, and so the determinant is zero. The result about columns can be explained in the same way, or one can use Theorem 5: If A has two identical columns, then A^T has two identical rows. In this case, $\det A^T = 0$. So $\det A = 0$, too, by Theorem 5.

30. $\det(rA) = r^n \cdot \det A$

32. $\det(PAP^{-1}) = (\det P)(\det A)(\det P^{-1})$ By Theorem 6
$= (\det P)(\det A)(\det P)^{-1}$ By Exercise 29
$= \det A$

34. $0 = \det A^4 = (\det A)^4$, by Theorem 6. So $\det A = 0$, which implies that A is not invertible, by Theorem 4.

36. $\det AB = \det \begin{bmatrix} 6 & 0 \\ -2 & 0 \end{bmatrix} = 0$

$(\det A)(\det B) = (-6 + 6)(-4 + 2) = 0$

38. a. -2 **b.** 32 **c.** -16 **d.** 1 **e.** -1

40. $\det(A + B) = \det \begin{bmatrix} 1 + a & b \\ c & 1 + d \end{bmatrix} = 1 + a + d + ad - bc$. Also, $\det A + \det B = 1 + (ad - bc)$. Since $\det(A + B) - (\det A + \det B) = a + d$, we have $\det(A + B) = \det A + \det B$ if and only if $a + d = 0$.

42.

$\det AE = \det(AE)^T$	Theorem 5
$= \det E^T A^T$	Property of matrix multiplication
$= (\det E^T)(\det A^T)$	Theorem 3; E^T is an elementary matrix
$= (\det E)(\det A)$	Theorem 5 used twice

Section 4.3, page 185

2. $\begin{bmatrix} 5/3 \\ -2/3 \end{bmatrix}$ **4.** $\begin{bmatrix} -3/2 \\ 1/2 \end{bmatrix}$ **6.** $\begin{bmatrix} -4 \\ 13 \\ -1 \end{bmatrix}$

8. All real s; $x_1 = \dfrac{3s + 2}{3(s^2 + 3)}$, $x_2 = \dfrac{2s - 9}{5(s^2 + 3)}$

10. $s \neq 0, 1/4$; $x_1 = \dfrac{6s - 2}{3s(4s - 1)}$, $x_2 = \dfrac{1}{3(4s - 1)}$

12. $\text{adj } A = \begin{bmatrix} -1 & 3 & 7 \\ 0 & 0 & 5 \\ 2 & -1 & -4 \end{bmatrix}$, $A^{-1} = \frac{1}{5}\begin{bmatrix} -1 & 3 & 7 \\ 0 & 0 & 5 \\ 2 & -1 & -4 \end{bmatrix}$

14. $\text{adj } A = \begin{bmatrix} 5 & -3 & -8 \\ 2 & -2 & -3 \\ -4 & 3 & 6 \end{bmatrix}$, $A^{-1} = (-1)\begin{bmatrix} 5 & -3 & -8 \\ 2 & -2 & -3 \\ -4 & 3 & 6 \end{bmatrix}$

16. $\text{adj } A = \begin{bmatrix} -9 & -6 & 14 \\ 0 & 3 & -1 \\ 0 & 0 & -3 \end{bmatrix}$, $A^{-1} = -\frac{1}{9}\begin{bmatrix} -9 & -6 & 14 \\ 0 & 3 & -1 \\ 0 & 0 & -3 \end{bmatrix}$

18. Each cofactor in A is an integer because it is just a sum of products of entries of A. Hence all the entries in adj A are integers. Since $\det A = 1$, the inverse formula in Theorem 8 shows that all the entries in A^{-1} are integers.

20. 7 **22.** 21 **24.** 15

26. By definition, $\mathbf{p} + S$ is the set of all vectors of the form $\mathbf{p} + \mathbf{v}$, where $\mathbf{v}$ is in S. Applying T to a typical vector in $\mathbf{p} + S$, we have $T(\mathbf{p} + \mathbf{v}) = T(\mathbf{p}) + T(\mathbf{v})$. (Why?) This vector is in the set denoted by $T(\mathbf{p}) + T(S)$. This proves that T maps the set $\mathbf{p} + S$ into the set $T(\mathbf{p}) + T(S)$.

Conversely, any vector in $T(\mathbf{p}) + T(S)$ has the form $T(\mathbf{p}) + T(\mathbf{v})$ for some $\mathbf{v}$ in S. This vector may be written as $T(\mathbf{p} + \mathbf{v})$. (Why?) This shows that every vector in $T(\mathbf{p}) + T(S)$ is the image under T of some point in $\mathbf{p} + S$.

28. Use Theorem 8. Or, compute the vectors that determine the image, namely, the columns of

$$A[\mathbf{b}_1 \quad \mathbf{b}_2] = \begin{bmatrix} 14 & 2 \\ -3 & 1 \end{bmatrix}$$

The determinant of this matrix is 20.

30. Let $\mathbf{p} = (x_3, y_3)$ and let $R' = R - \mathbf{p}$. The vertices of R' are $\mathbf{v}_1 = (x_1 - x_3, y_1 - y_3)$, $\mathbf{v}_2 = (x_2 - x_3, y_2 - y_3)$, and the origin. Then

$$\begin{aligned} \{\text{area of } R\} &= \{\text{area of } R'\} \\ &= \frac{1}{2}\left\{\begin{matrix}\text{area of parallelogram} \\ \text{determined by } \mathbf{v}_1 \text{ and } \mathbf{v}_2\end{matrix}\right\} \\ &= \frac{1}{2}\left|\det\begin{bmatrix} x_1 - x_3 & x_2 - x_3 \\ y_1 - y_3 & y_2 - y_3 \end{bmatrix}\right| \qquad (1) \end{aligned}$$

Also, using row operations,

$$\det\begin{bmatrix} x_1 & y_1 & 1 \\ x_2 & y_2 & 1 \\ x_3 & y_3 & 1 \end{bmatrix} = \det\begin{bmatrix} x_1 - x_3 & y_1 - y_3 & 0 \\ x_2 - x_3 & y_2 - y_3 & 0 \\ x_3 & y_3 & 1 \end{bmatrix}$$
$$= \det\begin{bmatrix} x_1 - x_3 & y_1 - y_3 \\ x_2 - x_3 & y_2 - y_3 \end{bmatrix} = \det\begin{bmatrix} x_1 - x_3 & x_2 - x_3 \\ y_1 - y_3 & y_2 - y_3 \end{bmatrix}$$

This calculation and (1) give the desired result.

32. From the formula in the exercise,

$$\{\text{volume of } S\} = \tfrac{1}{3}\{\text{area of base}\}\cdot\{\text{height}\} = \tfrac{1}{6}$$

because the vectors $\mathbf{e}_1$, $\mathbf{e}_2$, $\mathbf{e}_3$ have unit length. The tetrahedron S' with vertices at $\mathbf{0}$, $\mathbf{v}_1$, $\mathbf{v}_2$, and $\mathbf{v}_3$ is the image of S under the linear transformation T such that $T(\mathbf{e}_1) = \mathbf{v}_1$, $T(\mathbf{e}_2) = \mathbf{v}_2$, and $T(\mathbf{e}_3) = \mathbf{v}_3$. The standard matrix for T is $A = [\mathbf{v}_1 \quad \mathbf{v}_2 \quad \mathbf{v}_3]$. By Theorem 10,

$$\{\text{volume of } S'\} = |\det A|\cdot\tfrac{1}{6} = \tfrac{1}{6}|\det[\mathbf{v}_1 \quad \mathbf{v}_2 \quad \mathbf{v}_3]|$$

CHAPTER 5

Section 5.1, page 197

2. a. Given $\begin{bmatrix} x \\ y \end{bmatrix}$ in W, the entries x and y have the same sign. If x and y are both multiplied by the same scalar (whether positive or negative), then cx and cy will have the same sign.

b. *Example*: If $\mathbf{u} = \begin{bmatrix} -1 \\ -7 \end{bmatrix}$ and $\mathbf{v} = \begin{bmatrix} 2 \\ 3 \end{bmatrix}$, then $\mathbf{u}$ and $\mathbf{v}$ are in W, but $\mathbf{u} + \mathbf{v}$ is not in W.

4. *Example*: If $\mathbf{u} = \begin{bmatrix} 0 \\ 1 \end{bmatrix}$ and $c = -1$, then $\mathbf{u}$ is in H, but $c\mathbf{u}$ is not in H.

6. No, the zero polynomial is not in the set. **8.** Yes

10. $H = \text{Span}\{\mathbf{v}\}$, where $\mathbf{v} = \begin{bmatrix} 2 \\ 0 \\ -1 \end{bmatrix}$. By Theorem 2, H is a subspace of $\mathbb{R}^3$.

12. $W = \text{Span}\{\mathbf{u}, \mathbf{v}\}$, where $\mathbf{u} = \begin{bmatrix} 1 \\ 1 \\ 2 \\ 0 \end{bmatrix}$, $\mathbf{v} = \begin{bmatrix} 3 \\ -1 \\ -1 \\ 4 \end{bmatrix}$. By Theorem 2, W is a subspace of $\mathbb{R}^4$.

14. No

16. Not a vector space because the zero vector is not in W

18. $S = \left\{\begin{bmatrix} 4 \\ 0 \\ 1 \\ -2 \end{bmatrix}, \begin{bmatrix} 3 \\ 0 \\ 1 \\ 0 \end{bmatrix}, \begin{bmatrix} 0 \\ 0 \\ 1 \\ 1 \end{bmatrix}\right\}$

20. a. The constant function $\mathbf{f}(t) = 0$ is continuous. The sum of two continuous functions is continuous. A constant multiple of a continuous function is continuous.
b. Use the Subspace Test.

22. Yes. See the proof of Theorem 3 in Section 5.2 for a proof that is similar to the one needed here.

24. a. 3 **b.** 5 **c.** 4 **26. a.** 4 **b.** 7 **c.** 3 **d.** 5 **e.** 4

28.
$$\begin{aligned} \mathbf{u} &= 1\cdot\mathbf{u} && \text{Axiom 10} \\ &= c^{-1}c\cdot\mathbf{u} = c^{-1}(c\mathbf{u}) && \text{Axiom 9} \\ &= c^{-1}\mathbf{0} = \mathbf{0} && \text{Property (2)} \end{aligned}$$

30. Both H and K contain the zero vector of V because they are subspaces of V. Hence $\mathbf{0}$ is in $H \cap K$. Take $\mathbf{u}$ and $\mathbf{v}$ in $H \cap K$. Then $\mathbf{u}$ and $\mathbf{v}$ are in both H and K. Since H is a subspace, $\mathbf{u} + \mathbf{v}$ is in H. Likewise, $\mathbf{u} + \mathbf{v}$ is in K. Hence $\mathbf{u} + \mathbf{v}$ is in $H \cap K$. For any scalar c, the vector $c\mathbf{u}$ is in both H and K because they are subspaces. Hence $c\mathbf{u}$ is in $H \cap K$. By the Subspace Test, $H \cap K$ is a subspace.

The union of two subspaces is not in general a subspace. In $\mathbb{R}^2$, let H be the x-axis and K the y-axis. The sum of a nonzero vector in H and a nonzero vector in K is not on either the x-axis or the y-axis. So $H \cup K$ is not closed under vector addition, and $H \cup K$ is not a subspace of $\mathbb{R}^2$.

Section 5.2, page 208

2. $\begin{bmatrix} 5 & 21 & 19 \\ 13 & 23 & 2 \\ 8 & 14 & 1 \end{bmatrix} \begin{bmatrix} 5 \\ -3 \\ 2 \end{bmatrix} = \begin{bmatrix} 0 \\ 0 \\ 0 \end{bmatrix}$, so **w** is in Nul A.

4. $\begin{bmatrix} 6 \\ 1 \\ 0 \\ 0 \end{bmatrix}, \begin{bmatrix} 0 \\ 0 \\ 0 \\ 1 \end{bmatrix}$ **6.** $\begin{bmatrix} -6 \\ 2 \\ 1 \\ 0 \\ 0 \end{bmatrix}, \begin{bmatrix} 8 \\ -1 \\ 0 \\ 1 \\ 0 \end{bmatrix}, \begin{bmatrix} -1 \\ 0 \\ 0 \\ 0 \\ 1 \end{bmatrix}$

8. W is a subspace of $\mathbb{R}^3$ by Theorem 3, because W is the set of solutions of the system

$$\begin{aligned} a \quad\quad &= 0 \\ b + c &= 0 \end{aligned}$$

10. W is not a subspace because $\mathbf{0}$ is not in W.

12. W is a subspace of $\mathbb{R}^4$, because W is the set of solutions of the system

$$\begin{aligned} a + 3b - c \quad\quad &= 0 \\ a + b + c - d &= 0 \end{aligned}$$

14. W is not a subspace because $\mathbf{0}$ is not in W.

16. W is not a subspace because $\mathbf{0}$ is not in W.

18. $W = \text{Col } A$ for $A = \begin{bmatrix} -1 & 2 \\ 1 & -2 \\ 3 & -6 \end{bmatrix}$, so W is a vector space by Theorem 4.

20. $\begin{bmatrix} 1 & -1 & 0 \\ 2 & 1 & 1 \\ 0 & 5 & -4 \\ 0 & 0 & 1 \end{bmatrix}$ **22. a.** 5 **b.** 1 **24. a.** 3 **b.** 4

26. $\begin{bmatrix} 7 \\ -4 \\ 1 \\ 0 \end{bmatrix}$ in Nul A, $\begin{bmatrix} 1 \\ 0 \end{bmatrix}$ in Col A. Other answers possible.

28. **w** is in both Nul A and Col A.
$A\mathbf{w} = \mathbf{0}$, and $\mathbf{w} = -\frac{1}{2}\mathbf{a}_1 + \mathbf{a}_2$.

30. The two systems have the form $A\mathbf{x} = \mathbf{v}$ and $A\mathbf{x} = 5\mathbf{v}$. Since the first system is consistent, **v** is in Col A. Since Col A is a subspace of $\mathbb{R}^3$, $5\mathbf{v}$ is also in Col A. Thus the second system is consistent.

32. The zero vector $\mathbf{0}_W$ of W is in the range of T, because the linear transformation maps the zero vector of V onto $\mathbf{0}_W$. Typical vectors in the range of T are $T(\mathbf{x})$ and $T(\mathbf{w})$, where $\mathbf{x}, \mathbf{w}$ are in V. Since T is a linear transformation,

$$T(\mathbf{x}) + T(\mathbf{w}) = T(\mathbf{x} + \mathbf{w})$$

Thus the range of T is closed under vector addition. Also, for any scalar c, $c \cdot T(\mathbf{x}) = T(c\mathbf{x})$, since T is a linear transformation. Thus $c \cdot T(\mathbf{x})$ is in the range of T. By the Subspace Test, the range of T is a subspace of W.

34. $\mathbf{p}_1(t) = t$, $\mathbf{p}_2(t) = t^2$. The range of T is $\left\{\begin{bmatrix} a \\ a \end{bmatrix} : a \text{ real}\right\}$.

36. The kernel of T is $\{\mathbf{0}\}$.

38. Since Z is a subspace of W, the zero vector $\mathbf{0}_W$ of W is in Z. Because T is linear, T maps the zero vector $\mathbf{0}_V$ of V onto $\mathbf{0}_W$. Thus $\mathbf{0}_V$ is in $U = \{\mathbf{x} : T(\mathbf{x}) \text{ is in } Z\}$. Now take $\mathbf{u}_1, \mathbf{u}_2$ in U. Since T is linear,

$$T(\mathbf{u}_1 + \mathbf{u}_2) = T(\mathbf{u}_1) + T(\mathbf{u}_2) \qquad (*)$$

By definition of Z, $T(\mathbf{u}_1)$ and $T(\mathbf{u}_2)$ are in Z, and so the sum on the right of (*) is in Z because Z is a subspace. This proves that $\mathbf{u}_1 + \mathbf{u}_2$ is in U. For any scalar c, $c \cdot T(\mathbf{u}_1)$ is in Z because Z is a subspace. Since T is linear, $T(c\mathbf{u}_1)$ is in Z. Hence $c\mathbf{u}_1$ is in U. Thus U is a subspace of V, by the Subspace Test.

Section 5.3, page 217

2. No, the set is linearly dependent because there are more vectors in the set than entries in the vectors. However, the matrix $\begin{bmatrix} 4 & -1 & 3 \\ 0 & 1 & -5 \end{bmatrix}$ has a pivot in each row; hence its columns span $\mathbb{R}^2$.

4. No, the set is linearly dependent because the vectors are multiples. The columns of $\begin{bmatrix} -4 & 6 \\ 6 & -9 \end{bmatrix}$ do not span $\mathbb{R}^2$, by the Invertible Matrix Theorem.

6. No, the set is linearly dependent because the zero vector is in the set. The columns of $\begin{bmatrix} 1 & 0 & 0 \\ 0 & 0 & 1 \\ 1 & 0 & 0 \end{bmatrix}$ do not span $\mathbb{R}^3$, by the Invertible Matrix Theorem.

8. Yes. See Example 5 for an example of a justification.

10. No. $\begin{bmatrix} 1 & -4 \\ 2 & -5 \\ -3 & 6 \end{bmatrix} \sim \begin{bmatrix} 1 & -4 \\ 0 & 3 \\ 0 & 0 \end{bmatrix}$. The matrix does not have a pivot in each row, so its columns do not span $\mathbb{R}^3$ and hence do not form a basis. However, the columns are linearly independent because they are not multiples.

12. No, the vectors are linearly dependent because there are more than 3 vectors in $\mathbb{R}^3$.

14. $\begin{bmatrix} 5 \\ 4 \\ 1 \\ 0 \\ 0 \end{bmatrix}, \begin{bmatrix} -7 \\ -6 \\ 0 \\ 3 \\ 1 \end{bmatrix}$ **16.** $\begin{bmatrix} 1 \\ 5 \end{bmatrix}$

18. Basis for Nul A: $\begin{bmatrix} -2 \\ 1 \\ 0 \\ 0 \\ 0 \end{bmatrix}, \begin{bmatrix} -4 \\ 0 \\ 7/5 \\ 1 \\ 0 \end{bmatrix}$;

Basis for Col A: $\begin{bmatrix} 1 \\ 2 \\ 1 \\ 3 \end{bmatrix}, \begin{bmatrix} -5 \\ -5 \\ 0 \\ -5 \end{bmatrix}, \begin{bmatrix} -3 \\ 2 \\ 5 \\ -2 \end{bmatrix}$

20. $\mathbf{v}_1, \mathbf{v}_2, \mathbf{v}_3$

22. The three simplest answers are $\{\mathbf{v}_1, \mathbf{v}_2\}$ or $\{\mathbf{v}_1, \mathbf{v}_3\}$ or $\{\mathbf{v}_2, \mathbf{v}_3\}$. Other answers are possible.

24. Let $A = [\mathbf{v}_1 \ \cdots \ \mathbf{v}_n]$. Since A is square and its columns are linearly independent, its columns also span $\mathbb{R}^n$, by the Invertible Matrix Theorem. So $\{\mathbf{v}_1, \dots, \mathbf{v}_n\}$ is a basis for $\mathbb{R}^4$.

26. A basis is $\{\sin t, \sin 2t\}$ because this set is linearly independent (by inspection), and $\sin t \cos t = \frac{1}{2}\sin 2t$, as pointed out in Example 2.

28. $\{e^{-bt}, te^{-bt}\}$ The set is linearly independent because the functions are not multiples, and the set spans H.

30. There are more vectors than there are entries in each vector. By Theorem 6 in Section 2.4, the set is linearly dependent and therefore cannot be a basis for $\mathbb{R}^n$.

32. Suppose that $\{T(\mathbf{v}_1), \dots, T(\mathbf{v}_p)\}$ is linearly dependent. Then there exist $c_1, \dots, c_p$, not all zero, such that

$$c_1T(\mathbf{v}_1) + \cdots + c_pT(\mathbf{v}_p) = \mathbf{0}$$

Since T is linear and $\mathbf{0} = T(\mathbf{0})$,

$$T(c_1\mathbf{v}_1 + \cdots + c_p\mathbf{v}_p) = T(\mathbf{0})$$

By hypothesis, T is one-to-one, so this equation implies that $c_1\mathbf{v}_1 + \cdots + c_p\mathbf{v}_p = \mathbf{0}$, which shows that $\{\mathbf{v}_1, \dots, \mathbf{v}_p\}$ is linearly dependent.

Section 5.4, page 227

2. $\begin{bmatrix} 2 \\ 5 \end{bmatrix}$ **4.** $\begin{bmatrix} 0 \\ 1 \\ -5 \end{bmatrix}$ **6.** $\begin{bmatrix} -6 \\ 2 \end{bmatrix}$ **8.** $\begin{bmatrix} -2 \\ 0 \\ 5 \end{bmatrix}$

10. $\begin{bmatrix} 3 & 2 & 8 \\ -1 & 0 & -2 \\ 4 & -5 & 7 \end{bmatrix}$ **12.** $\begin{bmatrix} -7 \\ 5 \end{bmatrix}$ **14.** $\begin{bmatrix} 7 \\ -3 \\ -2 \end{bmatrix}$

16. $\begin{bmatrix} 1.3 \\ .75 \\ 1.6 \end{bmatrix}$

18. $\begin{bmatrix} 1 \\ 1 \end{bmatrix} = -5\mathbf{v}_1 + 2\mathbf{v}_2 = -4\mathbf{v}_1 + \mathbf{v}_2 + \mathbf{v}_3$ (infinitely many answers)

20. For $\mathbf{w}$ in V, there exist scalars $k_1, \dots, k_4$ such that

$$\mathbf{w} = k_1\mathbf{v}_1 + \cdots + k_4\mathbf{v}_4 \qquad (*)$$

because $\{\mathbf{v}_1, \dots, \mathbf{v}_4\}$ spans V. Also, because the set is linearly dependent, there exist scalars $c_1, \dots, c_4$, not all zero, such that

$$\mathbf{0} = c_1\mathbf{v}_1 + \cdots + c_4\mathbf{v}_4$$

Adding,

$$\mathbf{w} = \mathbf{w} + \mathbf{0} = (k_1 + c_1)\mathbf{v}_1 + \cdots + (k_4 + c_4)\mathbf{v}_4$$

At least one of the weights here differs from the corresponding weight in (*) because at least one of the c_i is nonzero. So $\mathbf{w}$ is expressed in more than one way as a linear combination of $\mathbf{v}_1, \dots, \mathbf{v}_4$.

22. Let $P_\mathcal{B} = [\mathbf{b}_1 \ \cdots \ \mathbf{b}_n]$. Then $P_\mathcal{B}[\mathbf{x}]_\mathcal{B} = \mathbf{x}$ and $[\mathbf{x}]_\mathcal{B} = P_\mathcal{B}^{-1}\mathbf{x}$. As mentioned in the text, the correspondence $\mathbf{x} \mapsto P_\mathcal{B}^{-1}\mathbf{x}$ is the coordinate mapping, so the desired matrix is $A = P_\mathcal{B}^{-1}$.

24. Given $\mathbf{y} = (y_1, \dots, y_n)$ in $\mathbb{R}^n$, let $\mathbf{u} = y_1\mathbf{b}_1 + \cdots + y_n\mathbf{b}_n$. Then, by definition, $[\mathbf{u}]_\mathcal{B} = \mathbf{y}$. So the coordinate mapping transforms $\mathbf{u}$ into $\mathbf{y}$. Since $\mathbf{y}$ was arbitrary, the coordinate mapping is onto.

26. $\mathbf{w}$ is a linear combination of $\mathbf{u}_1, \dots, \mathbf{u}_p$ if and only if there exist scalars $c_1, \dots, c_p$ such that

$$\mathbf{w} = c_1\mathbf{u}_1 + \cdots + c_p\mathbf{u}_p \qquad (*)$$

By the linearity formula (5), (*) holds if and only if

$$[\mathbf{w}]_\mathcal{B} = c_1[\mathbf{u}_1]_\mathcal{B} + \cdots + c_p[\mathbf{u}_p]_\mathcal{B}$$

for some $c_1, \dots, c_p$, which is equivalent to saying that $[\mathbf{w}]_\mathcal{B}$ is a linear combination of $[\mathbf{u}_1]_\mathcal{B}, \dots, [\mathbf{u}_p]_\mathcal{B}$.

28. Linearly dependent. It is easy to check that the coordinate vectors $\begin{bmatrix} 1 \\ 0 \\ -2 \\ -3 \end{bmatrix}, \begin{bmatrix} 0 \\ 1 \\ 0 \\ 1 \end{bmatrix}, \begin{bmatrix} 1 \\ 3 \\ -2 \\ 0 \end{bmatrix}$ are linearly dependent.

30. Linearly dependent. The coordinate vectors

$$\begin{bmatrix} 1 \\ -3 \\ 3 \\ -1 \end{bmatrix}, \begin{bmatrix} 4 \\ -12 \\ 9 \\ 0 \end{bmatrix}, \begin{bmatrix} 0 \\ 0 \\ 3 \\ -4 \end{bmatrix}$$ are linearly dependent.

Section 5.5, page 233

2. $\begin{bmatrix} 4 \\ -3 \\ 0 \end{bmatrix}, \begin{bmatrix} 0 \\ 0 \\ -1 \end{bmatrix}$; dim = 2

4. $\begin{bmatrix} 1 \\ 2 \\ 3 \\ 0 \end{bmatrix}, \begin{bmatrix} 1 \\ 0 \\ -1 \\ -1 \end{bmatrix}$; dim = 2

6. $\begin{bmatrix} 3 \\ 6 \\ -9 \\ -3 \end{bmatrix}, \begin{bmatrix} 6 \\ -2 \\ 5 \\ 1 \end{bmatrix}$; dim = 2

8. $\begin{bmatrix} 3 \\ 1 \\ 0 \\ 0 \end{bmatrix}, \begin{bmatrix} -1 \\ 0 \\ 1 \\ 0 \end{bmatrix}, \begin{bmatrix} 0 \\ 0 \\ 0 \\ 1 \end{bmatrix}$; dim = 3

10. 2 **12.** 3 **14.** 3, 3 **16.** 0, 2 **18.** 1, 2

20. Obviously, none of the Laguerre polynomials is a linear combination of the Laguerre polynomials of lower degree. By Theorem 5, the set of polynomials is linearly independent. There are exactly 4 polynomials in the four-dimensional space $\mathbb{P}_3$, so the set is a basis of $\mathbb{P}_3$, by Theorem 12.

22. $[\mathbf{p}]_{\mathcal{B}} = (5, -4, 3)$

24. If H were not all of V, then a basis for H (which is a linearly independent set) may be enlarged to a basis for V. The resulting basis would contain more than n vectors, which is impossible, by Theorem 11. So H must be all of V.

26. The space $C(\mathbb{R})$ contains the space $\mathbb{P}$ as a subspace. If $C(\mathbb{R})$ were finite-dimensional, $\mathbb{P}$ would be finite-dimensional, too, by Theorem 12. This is not true, by Exercise 25, so $C(\mathbb{R})$ is infinite-dimensional.

28. False. See Theorem 10.

30. True. If dim V were less than or equal to p, V would have a basis of not more than p elements. Such a set would span V. Since this is not the case, dim V must be greater than p. (Assume $p \geq 1$.)

32. False. *Counterexample*: Take any nonzero vector $\mathbf{v}$, and consider the set $\{\mathbf{v}, 2\mathbf{v}, 3\mathbf{v}, \ldots, (p-1)\mathbf{v}\}$. (Assume $p \geq 2$.)

34. Let $\{\mathbf{u}_1, \ldots, \mathbf{u}_p\}$ be a basis for H. Then $\{T(\mathbf{u}_1), \ldots, T(\mathbf{u}_p)\}$ spans $T(H)$, as is easily seen. Further, since T is one-to-one, Exercise 32 in Section 5.3 shows that $\{T(\mathbf{u}_1), \ldots, T(\mathbf{u}_p)\}$ is linearly independent. So this set of images is a basis for $T(H)$. So dim $H = p$ and dim $T(H) = p$.

Section 5.6, page 241

2. rank $A = 3$; dim Nul $A = 2$;

Basis for Col A: $\begin{bmatrix} 1 \\ 2 \\ -3 \\ 3 \end{bmatrix}, \begin{bmatrix} 4 \\ -6 \\ -6 \\ 4 \end{bmatrix}, \begin{bmatrix} 9 \\ -10 \\ -3 \\ 0 \end{bmatrix}$

Basis for Row A: $(1, -3, 0, 5, 7)$, $(0, 0, 2, -3, 8)$, $(0, 0, 0, 0, 5)$

Basis for Nul A: $\begin{bmatrix} 3 \\ 1 \\ 0 \\ 0 \\ 0 \end{bmatrix}, \begin{bmatrix} -5 \\ 0 \\ 3/2 \\ 1 \\ 0 \end{bmatrix}$

4. rank $A = 3$; dim Nul $A = 3$; basis for Col A : $\begin{bmatrix} 1 \\ 1 \\ 1 \\ 1 \\ 1 \end{bmatrix}, \begin{bmatrix} 1 \\ 2 \\ -1 \\ -3 \\ -2 \end{bmatrix}, \begin{bmatrix} 7 \\ 10 \\ 1 \\ -5 \\ 0 \end{bmatrix}$; Row A: $(1, 1, -3, 7, 9, -9)$, $(0, 1, -1, 3, 4, -3)$, $(0, 0, 0, 1, -1, -2)$

Basis for Nul A: $\begin{bmatrix} 2 \\ 1 \\ 1 \\ 0 \\ 0 \\ 0 \end{bmatrix}, \begin{bmatrix} -9 \\ -7 \\ 0 \\ 1 \\ 1 \\ 0 \end{bmatrix}, \begin{bmatrix} -2 \\ -3 \\ 0 \\ 2 \\ 0 \\ 1 \end{bmatrix}$

6. 0, 3, 3

8. 2. It is impossible for Col A to be $\mathbb{R}^4$ because the vectors in Col A have 5 entries. Col A is a four-dimensional subspace of $\mathbb{R}^5$.

10. 1 **12.** 2 **14.** 3, 3 **16.** 0 **18.** 0

20. No. The presence of two free variables indicates that the null space of the coefficient matrix A is two-dimensional. Since there are eight unknowns, A has eight columns and therefore must have rank 6, by the Rank Theorem. Since there are only six equations, A has six rows, and Col A is a subspace of $\mathbb{R}^6$. Since rank $A = 6$, we conclude that Col $A = \mathbb{R}^6$, which means that the equation $A\mathbf{x} = \mathbf{b}$ is consistent for all $\mathbf{b}$.

22. No. The coefficient matrix A is 10×12 and hence has rank at most 10. By the Rank Theorem, dim Nul A will have to be at least 2, so the null space cannot be spanned by one vector.

24. The coefficient matrix A in this case is 7×6. It is possible that for some $\mathbf{b}$ in $\mathbb{R}^7$, the equation $A\mathbf{x} = \mathbf{b}$ has a unique solution. In this case there are no free variables, so the rank of A must equal the number of columns, by the Rank Theorem. However, in any case the rank of A cannot exceed 6, and so Col A must be a proper subspace of $\mathbb{R}^7$. Thus there exist vectors in $\mathbb{R}^7$ that are not in Col A. For such right-hand sides, the equation $A\mathbf{x} = \mathbf{b}$ will have no solution.

26. The rank of A is n if and only if A has n pivot columns. This happens if and only if the equation $A\mathbf{x} = \mathbf{0}$ has only the trivial solution, that is, if and only if the columns of A are linearly independent.

28. **a.** dim Row A = dim Col A = rank A, by the Rank Theorem. So part (a) follows from the second part of that theorem.
b. Apply part (a) with A replaced by A^T and use the fact that Row A^T is just Col A.

30. The equation $A\mathbf{x} = \mathbf{b}$ is consistent if and only if

$$\text{rank}\,[\,A \quad \mathbf{b}\,] = \text{rank}\,A$$

because the two ranks are equal if and only if $\mathbf{b}$ is not a pivot column of $[\,A \quad \mathbf{b}\,]$. The result follows now from Theorem 1 in Section 1.2.

32. $\mathbf{v} = (1, -3, 4) = \begin{bmatrix} 1 \\ -3 \\ 4 \end{bmatrix}$

34. Since A can be reduced to an echelon form U by row operations, there exist invertible elementary matrices $E_1, \ldots, E_p$, such that $(E_p \cdots E_1)A = U$, and $A = (E_p \cdots E_1)^{-1}U$, since the product of invertible matrices is invertible. Let $E = (E_p \cdots E_1)^{-1}$. Then $A = EU$. Denote the columns of E by $\mathbf{c}_1, \ldots, \mathbf{c}_m$. Since rank $A = r$, its echelon form U has r nonzero rows, which we can denote by $\mathbf{d}_1^T, \ldots, \mathbf{d}_r^T$. By Theorem 10 in Section 3.4,

$$A = EU = [\,\mathbf{c}_1 \quad \cdots \quad \mathbf{c}_m\,] \begin{bmatrix} \mathbf{d}_1^T \\ \vdots \\ \mathbf{d}_r^T \\ 0 \\ \vdots \\ 0 \end{bmatrix} = \mathbf{c}_1\mathbf{d}_1^T + \cdots + \mathbf{c}_r\mathbf{d}_r^T$$

Section 5.7, page 247

2. **a.** $\begin{bmatrix} -1 & 5 \\ 4 & -3 \end{bmatrix}$ **b.** $\begin{bmatrix} 10 \\ 11 \end{bmatrix}$ **4.** (*i*)

6. **a.** $\begin{bmatrix} 2 & 0 & -3 \\ -1 & 3 & 0 \\ 1 & 1 & 2 \end{bmatrix}$ **b.** $\begin{bmatrix} -4 \\ -7 \\ 3 \end{bmatrix}$

8. $\underset{C\leftarrow B}{P} = \begin{bmatrix} 3 & -2 \\ -4 & 3 \end{bmatrix}$, $\underset{B\leftarrow C}{P} = \begin{bmatrix} 3 & 2 \\ 4 & 3 \end{bmatrix}$

10. $\underset{C\leftarrow B}{P} = \begin{bmatrix} 8 & 3 \\ -5 & -2 \end{bmatrix}$, $\underset{B\leftarrow C}{P} = \begin{bmatrix} 2 & 3 \\ -5 & -8 \end{bmatrix}$

12. **a.** $\underset{C\leftarrow B}{P} = \begin{bmatrix} 1 & 2 & 1 \\ 0 & 1 & 2 \\ -3 & -5 & 0 \end{bmatrix}$

b. Solve $\underset{C\leftarrow B}{P} \begin{bmatrix} x_1 \\ x_2 \\ x_3 \end{bmatrix} = \begin{bmatrix} 0 \\ 0 \\ 1 \end{bmatrix}$, and obtain $t^2 = 3(1 - 3t^2) - 2(2 + t - 5t^2) + (1 + 2t)$.

Section 5.8, page 257

2. If $y_k = 3^k$, then $y_{k+1} = 3^{k+1}$ and $y_{k+2} = 3^{k+2}$. Substituting these formulas into the left side of the equation,

$$\begin{aligned} y_{k+2} - 9y_k &= 3^{k+2} - 9\cdot 3^k \\ &= 3^k(3^2 - 9) = 3^k(0) = 0 \text{ for all } k \end{aligned}$$

Since the difference equation holds for all k, 3^k is a solution. A similar calculation works for $y_k = (-3)^k$:

$$\begin{aligned} y_{k+2} - 9y_k &= (-3)^{k+2} - 9(-3)^k \\ &= (-3)^k[(-3)^2 - 9] \\ &= (-3)^k(0) = 0 \quad \text{for all } k \end{aligned}$$

4. The signals 3^k and $(-3)^k$ are linearly independent because neither is a multiple of the other. If H is the solution space of the difference equation in Exercise 2, then $\dim H = 2$, by Theorem 18. So the two linearly independent solutions form a basis for H, by Theorem 13 in Section 5.5.

6. If $y_k = 5^k \cos(\frac{k\pi}{2})$, then

$$\begin{aligned} y_{k+2} + 25y_k &= 5^{k+2}\cos(\tfrac{(k+2)\pi}{2}) + 25\cdot 5^k\cos(\tfrac{k\pi}{2}) \\ &= 5^{k+2}[\cos(\tfrac{k\pi}{2}+\pi) + \cos(\tfrac{k\pi}{2})] \\ &= 0 \qquad \text{for all } k \end{aligned}$$

because $\cos(t+\pi) = -\cos t$ for all t. A similar calculation holds for $z_k = 5^k \sin(\frac{k\pi}{2})$, using the trigonometric identity $\sin(t+\pi) = -\sin t$. Thus y_k and z_k are both solutions of the difference equation $y_{k+2} + 25y_k = 0$. These solutions are obviously linearly independent because they are not multiples of one another. Since the solution space H is two-dimensional, y_k and z_k form a basis for H, by Theorem 13.

8. Yes **10.** Yes

12. No, two signals cannot span a four-dimensional solution space.

14. $3^k, 4^k$ **16.** $(\frac{1}{4})^k, (-\frac{3}{4})^k$

18. The auxiliary equation is $r^2 - 1.35r + .45 = 0$, with roots .75 and .6. The constant solution of the nonhomogeneous equation is found by solving $T - 1.35T + .45T = 1$, to obtain $T = 10$. The general solution of the nonhomogeneous equation is

$$Y_k = c_1(.75)^k + c_2(.6)^k + 10$$

20. Let $a = -2+\sqrt{3}$ and $b = -2-\sqrt{3}$. Then c_1 and c_2 must satisfy

$$\begin{bmatrix} a & b \\ a^N & b^N \end{bmatrix}\begin{bmatrix} c_1 \\ c_2 \end{bmatrix} = \begin{bmatrix} 5000 \\ 0 \end{bmatrix}$$

Solving, we obtain

$$y_k = c_1a^k + c_2b^k = \frac{5000}{ab^N - ba^N}(a^kb^N - a^Nb^k)$$

22. 1.4, 0, −1.4, −2, −1.4, 0, 1.4, 2, 1.4 This signal is 2 times the signal output by the filter when the input (in Example 3) was $\cos(\pi t/4)$. This is what is to be expected, since the filter is *linear*. The output should be 2 times the output from $\cos(\pi t/4)$ plus 1 times the (zero) output from $\cos(3\pi t/4)$.

24. $y_{k+1} - 1.005y_k = 200, \quad y_0 = 1{,}000$

26. $1 + k + c_1\cdot 5^k + c_2\cdot 3^k$

28. $2k - 4 + c_1\cdot(-2)^k + c_2\cdot 2^{-k}$

30. $\mathbf{x}_{k+1} = A\mathbf{x}_k$, where

$$A = \begin{bmatrix} 0 & 1 & 0 \\ 0 & 0 & 1 \\ -1/16 & 0 & 3/4 \end{bmatrix}, \mathbf{x} = \begin{bmatrix} y_k \\ y_{k+1} \\ y_{k+2} \end{bmatrix}$$

32. If $a_3 \neq 0$, the order is 3; if $a_3 = 0$ and $a_2 \neq 0$, the order is 2; if $a_3 = a_2 = 0$ and $a_1 \neq 0$, the order is 1; otherwise, the order is 0 (with only the zero signal for a solution).

34. No, the signals could be linearly dependent. *Example*: The following functions are linearly independent when considered as functions on the real line, because they have different periods and no one of the functions is a linear combination of the other two.

$$f(t) = \sin \pi t, \qquad g(t) = \sin 2\pi t, \qquad h(t) = \sin 3\pi t$$

Since f, g, and h are zero at every integer, the signals are linearly dependent in $\mathbb{S}$.

36. Given $\mathbf{z}$ in V, suppose that $\mathbf{x}_p$ in V satisfies $T(\mathbf{x}_p) = \mathbf{z}$. Also, if $\mathbf{u}$ is in the null space of T, then $T(\mathbf{u}) = \mathbf{0}$. Since T is linear, $T(\mathbf{u}+\mathbf{x}_p) = T(\mathbf{u})+T(\mathbf{x}_p) = \mathbf{z}$. So the vector $\mathbf{x} = \mathbf{u} + \mathbf{x}_p$ satisfies the nonhomogeneous equation $T(\mathbf{x}) = \mathbf{z}$.

Section 5.9, page 266

2. a. From:

$$\begin{array}{cc|l} \text{H} & \text{I} & \text{To:} \\ .95 & .45 & \text{Healthy} \\ .05 & .55 & \text{Ill} \end{array}$$

b. 15%, 12.5%

c. .925; use $\mathbf{v}_0 = \begin{bmatrix} 1 \\ 0 \end{bmatrix}$.

4. a. From:

$$\begin{array}{ccc|l} \text{G} & \text{I} & \text{B} & \text{To:} \\ .6 & .4 & .4 & \text{Good} \\ .3 & .3 & .5 & \text{Indiff.} \\ .1 & .3 & .1 & \text{Bad} \end{array}$$

b. 20% **c.** 48%

6. $\begin{bmatrix} 5/7 \\ 2/7 \end{bmatrix}$ **8.** $\begin{bmatrix} 2/5 \\ 1/5 \\ 2/5 \end{bmatrix}$ or $\begin{bmatrix} .4 \\ .2 \\ .4 \end{bmatrix}$

10. No, because P^k has a zero in the lower-left corner for all k.

12. a. $\begin{bmatrix} .9 \\ .1 \end{bmatrix}$ **b.** .10, no

14. There is a 50% chance of good weather because $\begin{bmatrix} 1/2 \\ 1/3 \\ 1/6 \end{bmatrix}$ is the steady-state vector.

16. The steady-state vector is approximately (.435, .091, .474). Of the 2000 cars, about 182 will be rented or available from the downtown location.

18. If $\alpha = \beta = 0$, then $\begin{bmatrix}1\\0\end{bmatrix}$ and $\begin{bmatrix}0\\1\end{bmatrix}$ are the steady-state vectors. Otherwise, $\frac{1}{\alpha+\beta}\begin{bmatrix}\beta\\\alpha\end{bmatrix}$ is the only steady-state vector.

20. Let $P = [\,\mathbf{p}_1 \quad \mathbf{p}_2 \quad \cdots \quad \mathbf{p}_n\,]$, so that

$$P^2 = [\,P\mathbf{p}_1 \quad P\mathbf{p}_2 \quad \cdots \quad P\mathbf{p}_n\,]$$

By Exercise 19(c), the columns of P^2 are probability vectors, so P^2 is a stochastic matrix. Alternatively, $SP = S$, by Exercise 19(b), since P is a stochastic matrix. Multiplying both sides on the right by P, we have $SP^2 = SP$. The right side is just S, so that $SP^2 = S$. Since the entries in P^2 are obviously nonnegative (they are sums of products of the nonnegative entries in P), this shows that P^2 is also a stochastic matrix.

CHAPTER 6

Section 6.1, page 278

2. Yes **4.** Yes, $\lambda = 3$ **6.** Yes, $\lambda = -2$

8. Yes, $\begin{bmatrix}3\\2\\1\end{bmatrix}$ **10.** $\begin{bmatrix}3\\2\end{bmatrix}$

12. $\lambda = 1$: $\begin{bmatrix}-2\\3\end{bmatrix}$; $\lambda = 5$: $\begin{bmatrix}-2\\1\end{bmatrix}$

14. $\begin{bmatrix}1\\1\\3\end{bmatrix}$ **16.** $\begin{bmatrix}2\\3\\1\\0\end{bmatrix}, \begin{bmatrix}0\\0\\0\\1\end{bmatrix}$ **18.** 3, 4 **20.** 4, 0, -3

22. $\lambda = 0$. Eigenvectors for $\lambda = 0$ have entries that produce linear dependence relations among the columns of A. Any nonzero vector (in $\mathbb{R}^3$) whose entries sum to 0 will work. Find any two such vectors that are not multiples, for example, $(1, 1, -2)$ and $(1, -1, 0)$.

24. Any triangular matrix with the same number in both diagonal entries, such as $\begin{bmatrix}4 & 5\\0 & 4\end{bmatrix}$

26. If $A\mathbf{x} = \lambda\mathbf{x}$ for some $\mathbf{x} \neq \mathbf{0}$, then $A^2\mathbf{x} = A(A\mathbf{x}) = A(\lambda\mathbf{x}) = \lambda A\mathbf{x} = \lambda^2\mathbf{x}$. However, $A^2\mathbf{x} = \mathbf{0}$, because $A^2 = 0$. Therefore $\mathbf{0} = \lambda^2\mathbf{x}$. Since $\mathbf{x} \neq 0$, we conclude that λ must be zero. Thus all eigenvalues of A are zero.

28. If A is lower triangular, then A^T is upper triangular and has the same diagonal entries as A. By the first part of the proof of Theorem 1, these diagonal entries are eigenvalues of A^T. By Exercise 27, they are also eigenvalues of A.

30. By Exercise 29 applied to A^T in place of A, we conclude that s is an eigenvalue of A^T. By Exercise 27, s is an eigenvalue of A.

32. You could try to write $\mathbf{x}_0$ as a linear combination of eigenvectors, $\mathbf{u}_1, \ldots, \mathbf{u}_p$, of A. If $\mathbf{x}_0 = c_1\mathbf{u}_1 + \cdots + c_p\mathbf{u}_p$, then you could define

$$\mathbf{x}_k = c_1\lambda_1^k\mathbf{u}_1 + \cdots + c_p\lambda_p^k\mathbf{u}_p$$

In this case,

$$\begin{aligned} A\mathbf{x}_k &= A(c_1\lambda_1^k\mathbf{u}_1 + \cdots + c_p\lambda_p^k\mathbf{u}_p) \\ &= c_1\lambda_1^k A\mathbf{u}_1 + \cdots + c_p\lambda_p^k A\mathbf{u}_p && \text{Linearity} \\ &= c_1\lambda_1^{k+1}\mathbf{u}_1 + \cdots + c_p\lambda_p^{k+1}\mathbf{u}_p && \text{The } \mathbf{u}_i \text{ are eigenvectors.} \\ &= \mathbf{x}_{k+1} \end{aligned}$$

Section 6.2, page 286

2. $\lambda^2 - 10\lambda + 16$; 8, 2 **4.** $\lambda^2 - 8\lambda + 3$; $4 \pm \sqrt{13}$

6. $\lambda^2 - 11\lambda + 40$; no real eigenvalues **8.** $\lambda^2 - 10\lambda + 25$; 5

10. $-\lambda^3 + 14\lambda + 12$ **12.** $-\lambda^3 + 5\lambda^2 - 2\lambda - 8$

14. $-\lambda^3 + 4\lambda^2 + 25\lambda - 28$ **16.** 5, 1, 1, -4 **18.** $h = 6$

20.
$$\begin{aligned} \det(A^T - \lambda I) &= \det(A^T - \lambda I^T) \\ &= \det(A - \lambda I)^T && \text{Property of transposes} \\ &= \det(A - \lambda I) && \text{Theorem 3(c)} \end{aligned}$$

22. First observe that if P is invertible, then Theorem 3(b) shows that $1 = \det(I) = \det(PP^{-1}) = (\det P)(\det P^{-1})$. Then, if $A = PBP^{-1}$, Theorem 3(b) again shows that

$$\det A = \det(PBP^{-1}) = (\det P)(\det B)(\det P^{-1}) = \det B$$

24. If $a \neq 0$, then $A = \begin{bmatrix}a & b\\c & d\end{bmatrix} \sim \begin{bmatrix}a & b\\0 & d - a^{-1}cb\end{bmatrix} = U$, and $\det A = (a)(d - a^{-1}cb) = ad - bc$. If $a = 0$, then $A = \begin{bmatrix}0 & b\\c & d\end{bmatrix} \sim \begin{bmatrix}c & d\\0 & b\end{bmatrix} = U$ (with one interchange), so $\det A = (-1)^1(cb) = 0 - bc$.

Section 6.3, page 295

2. $\frac{1}{16}\begin{bmatrix} 151 & 90 \\ -225 & -134 \end{bmatrix}$ **4.** $\begin{bmatrix} 4-3\cdot 2^k & 12\cdot 2^k - 12 \\ 1-2^k & 4\cdot 2^k - 3 \end{bmatrix}$

6. $\lambda = 5$: $\begin{bmatrix} -2 \\ 0 \\ 1 \end{bmatrix}, \begin{bmatrix} 0 \\ 1 \\ 0 \end{bmatrix}$; $\lambda = 4$: $\begin{bmatrix} -1 \\ 2 \\ 0 \end{bmatrix}$

When an answer involves a diagonalization, $A = PDP^{-1}$, the factors P and D are not unique, so your answer may differ from that given here.

8. Not diagonalizable

10. $P = \begin{bmatrix} 1 & -3 \\ 1 & 4 \end{bmatrix}, D = \begin{bmatrix} 5 & 0 \\ 0 & -2 \end{bmatrix}$

12. $P = \begin{bmatrix} 1 & -1 & -1 \\ 1 & 1 & 0 \\ 1 & 0 & 1 \end{bmatrix}, D = \begin{bmatrix} 8 & 0 & 0 \\ 0 & 2 & 0 \\ 0 & 0 & 2 \end{bmatrix}$

14. $P = \begin{bmatrix} -2 & 0 & -1 \\ 0 & 1 & 2 \\ 1 & 0 & 0 \end{bmatrix}, D = \begin{bmatrix} 5 & 0 & 0 \\ 0 & 5 & 0 \\ 0 & 0 & 4 \end{bmatrix}$

16. $P = \begin{bmatrix} -2 & -3 & -2 \\ 1 & 0 & -1 \\ 0 & 1 & 1 \end{bmatrix}, D = \begin{bmatrix} 2 & 0 & 0 \\ 0 & 2 & 0 \\ 0 & 0 & 1 \end{bmatrix}$

18. $P = \begin{bmatrix} 0 & -5 & 0 \\ 0 & 0 & 1 \\ 1 & 3 & 0 \end{bmatrix}, D = \begin{bmatrix} 5 & 0 & 0 \\ 0 & 0 & 0 \\ 0 & 0 & 0 \end{bmatrix}$

20. $P = \begin{bmatrix} 0 & 2 & 0 & 0 \\ 1 & 0 & 0 & 0 \\ 0 & 0 & 1 & 0 \\ 0 & 1 & 0 & 1 \end{bmatrix}, D = \begin{bmatrix} 4 & 0 & 0 & 0 \\ 0 & 4 & 0 & 0 \\ 0 & 0 & 2 & 0 \\ 0 & 0 & 0 & 2 \end{bmatrix}$

22. No. Let $\mathbf{v}_1$ and $\mathbf{v}_2$ be eigenvectors that span the two one-dimensional eigenspaces. If $\mathbf{v}$ is any other eigenvector, then it belongs to one of the eigenspaces and hence is a multiple of either $\mathbf{v}_1$ or $\mathbf{v}_2$. So there cannot exist three linearly independent eigenvectors. By the Diagonalization Theorem, A cannot be diagonalizable.

24. Yes, if the third eigenspace is only one-dimensional. In this case, any linearly independent set of eigenvectors can have no more than two vectors in the two-dimensional eigenspace, three vectors in the three-dimensional eigenspace, and one vector in the one-dimensional eigenspace. If the set contains six eigenvectors, then the set includes a basis for each eigenspace. (Apply Theorem 13 in Section 5.5 to each eigenspace.) Any seventh eigenvector would be in one of the eigenspaces and hence be a linear combination of the corresponding basis vectors. So there cannot exist a linearly independent set of seven eigenvectors. By the Diagonalization Theorem, A cannot be diagonalizable.

26. If A has n linearly independent eigenvectors, then by Theorem 5 there are an invertible P and a diagonal D such that $A = PDP^{-1}$. Using properties of transposes,

$$\begin{aligned} A^T &= (PDP^{-1})^T = (P^{-1})^T D^T P^T \\ &= (P^T)^{-1} D P^T = QDQ^{-1} \end{aligned}$$

where $Q = (P^T)^{-1}$. Thus A^T is diagonalizable. By Theorem 5, A^T has n linearly independent eigenvectors, corresponding to the eigenvalues in D.

28. A nonzero multiple of an eigenvector is another eigenvector. To produce P_2, simply multiply one or both columns of P by a nonzero scalar unequal to 1.

Section 6.4, page 301

2. $\begin{bmatrix} 2 & -4 \\ -3 & 5 \end{bmatrix}$ **4.** $\begin{bmatrix} 2 & -4 & 5 \\ 0 & -1 & 3 \end{bmatrix}$

6. a. $2 - t + 3t^2 - t^3 + t^4$

b. For any $\mathbf{p}, \mathbf{q}$ in $\mathbb{P}_2$ and any scalar c,

$$\begin{aligned} T[\mathbf{p}(t) + \mathbf{q}(t)] &= [\mathbf{p}(t) + \mathbf{q}(t)] + t^2[\mathbf{p}(t) + \mathbf{q}(t)] \\ &= [\mathbf{p}(t) + t^2\mathbf{p}(t)] + [\mathbf{q}(t) + t^2\mathbf{q}(t)] \\ &= T[\mathbf{p}(t)] + T[\mathbf{q}(t)] \end{aligned}$$

$$\begin{aligned} T[c\cdot\mathbf{p}(t)] &= [c\cdot\mathbf{p}(t)] + t^2[c\cdot\mathbf{p}(t)] = c\cdot[\mathbf{p}(t) + t^2\mathbf{p}(t)] \\ &= c\cdot T[\mathbf{p}(t)] \end{aligned}$$

c. $\begin{bmatrix} 1 & 0 & 0 \\ 0 & 1 & 0 \\ 1 & 0 & 1 \\ 0 & 1 & 0 \\ 0 & 0 & 1 \end{bmatrix}$

8. $24\mathbf{b}_1 - 20\mathbf{b}_2 + 11\mathbf{b}_3$

10. a. For any $\mathbf{p}, \mathbf{q}$ in $\mathbb{P}_2$ and any scalar c,

$$\begin{aligned} T(\mathbf{p}+\mathbf{q}) &= \begin{bmatrix} (\mathbf{p}+\mathbf{q})(-3) \\ (\mathbf{p}+\mathbf{q})(-1) \\ (\mathbf{p}+\mathbf{q})(1) \\ (\mathbf{p}+\mathbf{q})(3) \end{bmatrix} \\ &= \begin{bmatrix} \mathbf{p}(-3) \\ \mathbf{p}(-1) \\ \mathbf{p}(1) \\ \mathbf{p}(3) \end{bmatrix} + \begin{bmatrix} \mathbf{q}(-3) \\ \mathbf{q}(-1) \\ \mathbf{q}(1) \\ \mathbf{q}(3) \end{bmatrix} = T(\mathbf{p}+\mathbf{q}) \end{aligned}$$

$$T(c\cdot\mathbf{p}) = \begin{bmatrix} (c\cdot\mathbf{p})(-3) \\ (c\cdot\mathbf{p})(-1) \\ (c\cdot\mathbf{p})(1) \\ (c\cdot\mathbf{p})(3) \end{bmatrix} = c\cdot\begin{bmatrix} \mathbf{p}(-3) \\ \mathbf{p}(-1) \\ \mathbf{p}(1) \\ \mathbf{p}(3) \end{bmatrix} = c\cdot T(\mathbf{p})$$

b. $\begin{bmatrix} 1 & -3 & 9 & -27 \\ 1 & -1 & 1 & -1 \\ 1 & 1 & 1 & 1 \\ 1 & 3 & 9 & 27 \end{bmatrix}$ **12.** $\begin{bmatrix} 1 & 2 \\ -2 & 1 \end{bmatrix}$

14. $\mathbf{b}_1 = \begin{bmatrix} -1 \\ 1 \end{bmatrix}, \mathbf{b}_2 = \begin{bmatrix} 3 \\ 7 \end{bmatrix}$

16. $\mathbf{b}_1 = \begin{bmatrix} -3 \\ 1 \end{bmatrix}, \mathbf{b}_2 = \begin{bmatrix} -2 \\ 1 \end{bmatrix}$

18. If there is a basis $\mathcal{B}$ such that $[T]_{\mathcal{B}}$ is diagonal, then A is similar to a diagonal matrix, by the paragraph following Example 3. In this case, A must have three linearly independent eigenvectors. This is not necessarily the case, because A has only two distinct eigenvalues.

20. If $A = PBP^{-1}$, then $A^2 = (PBP^{-1})(PBP^{-1}) = PB(P^{-1}P)BP^{-1} = PB \cdot I \cdot BP^{-1} = PB^2P^{-1}$. So A^2 is similar to B^2.

22. If A is diagonalizable, then $A = PDP^{-1}$ for some P. Also, if B is similar to A, then $B = QAQ^{-1}$ for some Q, and

$$B = Q(PDP^{-1})Q^{-1} = (QP)D(P^{-1}Q^{-1}) = (QP)D(QP)^{-1}$$

So B is diagonalizable.

24. If $A = PBP^{-1}$, then a rank A = rank $P(BP^{-1})$ = rank BP^{-1}, by Supplementary Exercise 9 in Chapter 5. Also, rank BP^{-1} = rank B, by Supplementary Exercise 10 in Chapter 5, since P^{-1} is invertible. Thus rank A = rank B.

26. If $A = PDP^{-1}$, where D is diagonal, then $D^T = D$. By Theorem 3 in Section 3.1 and Theorem 6 in Section 3.2,

$$A^T = (PDP^{-1})^T = (P^{-1})^T D^T P^T = (P^T)^{-1} D P^T = QDQ^{-1}$$

where $Q = (P^T)^{-1}$.

28. For each j, $I(\mathbf{b}_j) = \mathbf{b}_j$, and $[I(\mathbf{b}_j)]_{\mathcal{C}} = [\mathbf{b}_j]_{\mathcal{C}}$. By formula (4), the matrix for I relative to the bases $\mathcal{B}$ and $\mathcal{C}$ is

$$M = \begin{bmatrix} [\mathbf{b}_1]_{\mathcal{C}} & [\mathbf{b}_2]_{\mathcal{C}} & \cdots & [\mathbf{b}_n]_{\mathcal{C}} \end{bmatrix}$$

In Theorem 16 of Section 5.7, this matrix was denoted by $\underset{\mathcal{C}\leftarrow\mathcal{B}}{P}$ and was called the *change-of-coordinates matrix from $\mathcal{B}$ to $\mathcal{C}$.*

Section 6.5, page 309

2. $\lambda = 3 + i, \begin{bmatrix} 2+i \\ 1 \end{bmatrix}; \quad \lambda = 3 - i, \begin{bmatrix} 2-i \\ 1 \end{bmatrix}$

4. $\lambda = 4 + i, \begin{bmatrix} 1+i \\ 1 \end{bmatrix}; \quad \lambda = 4 - i, \begin{bmatrix} 1-i \\ 1 \end{bmatrix}$

6. $\lambda = 4 - 3i, \begin{bmatrix} i \\ 1 \end{bmatrix}; \quad \lambda = 4 + 3i, \begin{bmatrix} -i \\ 1 \end{bmatrix}$

8. $\lambda = \sqrt{3} \pm 3i$, $\varphi = -\pi/3$ radians, $r = \sqrt{12} = 2\sqrt{3}$

10. $\lambda = -5 \pm 5i$, $\varphi = 3\pi/4$ radians, $r = 5\sqrt{2}$

12. $\lambda = \pm .3i$, $\varphi = -\pi/2$ radians, $r = .3$

In Exercises 14–20, other answers are possible. Any P that makes $P^{-1}AP$ equal to the given C or to C^T is a satisfactory answer. First find P; then compute $P^{-1}AP$.

14. $P = \begin{bmatrix} 2 & -1 \\ 1 & 0 \end{bmatrix}, C = \begin{bmatrix} 3 & -1 \\ 1 & 3 \end{bmatrix}$

16. $P = \begin{bmatrix} 1 & -1 \\ 1 & 0 \end{bmatrix}, C = \begin{bmatrix} 4 & -1 \\ 1 & 4 \end{bmatrix}$

18. $P = \begin{bmatrix} 1 & -3 \\ 2 & 0 \end{bmatrix}, C = \begin{bmatrix} .8 & -.6 \\ .6 & .8 \end{bmatrix}$

20. $P = \begin{bmatrix} -2 & -1 \\ 2 & 0 \end{bmatrix}, C = \begin{bmatrix} .28 & -.96 \\ .96 & .28 \end{bmatrix}$

22. $A(\mu\mathbf{x}) = \mu(A\mathbf{x}) = \mu(\lambda\mathbf{x}) = \lambda(\mu\mathbf{x})$

24. $\bar{\mathbf{x}}^T A\mathbf{x} = \bar{\mathbf{x}}^T(\lambda\mathbf{x}) = \lambda \cdot \bar{\mathbf{x}}^T\mathbf{x}$ because $\mathbf{x}$ is an eigenvector. It is easy to see that $\bar{\mathbf{x}}^T\mathbf{x}$ is real (and positive) because $\bar{z}z$ is nonnegative for every complex number z. Since $\bar{\mathbf{x}}^T A\mathbf{x}$ is real, by Exercise 23, so is λ. Next, write $\mathbf{x} = \mathbf{u} + i\mathbf{v}$, where $\mathbf{u}$ and $\mathbf{v}$ are real vectors. Then

$$A\mathbf{x} = A(\mathbf{u} + i\mathbf{v}) = A\mathbf{u} + iA\mathbf{v} \quad \text{and} \quad \lambda\mathbf{x} = \lambda\mathbf{u} + i\lambda\mathbf{v}$$

The real part of $A\mathbf{x}$ is $A\mathbf{u}$ because the entries in A, $\mathbf{u}$, and $\mathbf{v}$ are all real. The real part of $\lambda\mathbf{x}$ is $\lambda\mathbf{u}$ because λ and the entries in $\mathbf{u}$ and $\mathbf{v}$ are real. Since $A\mathbf{x}$ and $\lambda\mathbf{x}$ are equal, their real parts are equal, too. (Apply the corresponding statement about complex numbers to each entry of $A\mathbf{x}$.) Thus $A\mathbf{u} = \lambda\mathbf{u}$, which shows that the real part of $\mathbf{x}$ is an eigenvector of A.

26. a. If $\lambda = a - bi$, then

$$A\mathbf{v} = \lambda\mathbf{v} = (a - bi)(\text{Re}\,\mathbf{v} + i\,\text{Im}\,\mathbf{v}) = \underbrace{(a\,\text{Re}\,\mathbf{v} + b\,\text{Im}\,\mathbf{v})}_{\text{Re}\,A\mathbf{v}} + i\,\underbrace{(a\,\text{Im}\,\mathbf{v} - b\,\text{Re}\,\mathbf{v})}_{\text{Im}\,A\mathbf{v}}$$

By Exercise 25,

$$A(\text{Re}\,\mathbf{v}) = \text{Re}\,A\mathbf{v} = a\,\text{Re}\,\mathbf{v} + b\,\text{Im}\,\mathbf{v}$$
$$A(\text{Im}\,\mathbf{v}) = \text{Im}\,A\mathbf{v} = -b\,\text{Re}\,\mathbf{v} + a\,\text{Im}\,\mathbf{v}$$

b. Let $P = [\,\text{Re}\,\mathbf{v} \quad \text{Im}\,\mathbf{v}\,]$. By (a),

$$A(\text{Re}\,\mathbf{v}) = P\begin{bmatrix} a \\ b \end{bmatrix}, \qquad A(\text{Im}\,\mathbf{v}) = P\begin{bmatrix} -b \\ a \end{bmatrix}$$

So

$$AP = [\,A(\text{Re}\,\mathbf{v}) \quad A(\text{Im}\,\mathbf{v})\,] = \left[\, P\begin{bmatrix} a \\ b \end{bmatrix} \quad P\begin{bmatrix} -b \\ a \end{bmatrix} \right] = P\begin{bmatrix} a & -b \\ b & a \end{bmatrix} = PC$$

Section 6.6, page 320

2. $\mathbf{x}_k = 2\cdot 3^k \begin{bmatrix} 1 \\ 0 \\ -3 \end{bmatrix} + 1\cdot\left(\frac{4}{5}\right)^k \begin{bmatrix} 2 \\ 1 \\ -5 \end{bmatrix} + 2\cdot\left(\frac{3}{5}\right)^k \begin{bmatrix} -3 \\ -3 \\ 7 \end{bmatrix}$.

So $\mathbf{x}_k \approx 2\cdot 3^k \begin{bmatrix} 1 \\ 0 \\ -3 \end{bmatrix}$ for all k sufficiently large.

4. If $p = .125$, the eigenvalues are 1 and .6. An eigenvector for $\lambda = 1$ is (4, 5), so eventually the sizes of the two populations will stabilize, and there will be 4 spotted owls for every 5 (thousand) wood rats.

6. If $p = .5$, the eigenvalues are .9 and .7, and

$$\mathbf{x}_k = c_1(.9)^k \begin{bmatrix} 3 \\ 5 \end{bmatrix} + c_2(.7)^k \begin{bmatrix} 1 \\ 1 \end{bmatrix} \to 0, \qquad \text{as } k \to \infty$$

So both populations perish. If $p = .4$, the eigenvalues are 1 and .6, and

$$\mathbf{x}_k = c_1(1)^k \begin{bmatrix} 1 \\ 2 \end{bmatrix} + c_2(.6)^k \begin{bmatrix} 3 \\ 2 \end{bmatrix} \to c_1\begin{bmatrix} 1 \\ 2 \end{bmatrix}, \qquad \text{as } k \to \infty$$

Eventually, for every spotted owl there will be about 2000 flying squirrels.

8. Saddle point (because one or more eigenvalues are greater than 1, and one or more eigenvalues are less than 1, in magnitude): direction of greatest repulsion: the line through (0, 0, 0) and (1, 0, −3); direction of greatest attraction: the line through (0, 0, 0) and (−3, −3, 7)

10. Attractor; eigenvalues: .9, .5; direction of greatest attraction: the line through (0, 0) and (2, 1)

12. Saddle point; eigenvalues: 1.1, .8; greatest repulsion: line through (0, 0) and (1, 1); greatest attraction: line through (0, 0) and (2, 1)

14. Repellor; eigenvalues: 1.3, 1.1; greatest repulsion: line through (0, 0) and (−3, 2)

16. $\mathbf{v}_k = c_1 \begin{bmatrix} .435 \\ .091 \\ .474 \end{bmatrix} + c_2(.89)^k \begin{bmatrix} -1 \\ 1 \\ 0 \end{bmatrix} + c_3(.81)^k \begin{bmatrix} -1 \\ 0 \\ 1 \end{bmatrix}$

Note: The exact value of the steady-state vector is $\mathbf{q} = (91/209, 19/209, 99/209) \approx (.435, .091, .474)$.

18. a. $A = \begin{bmatrix} 0 & 0 & .42 \\ .6 & 0 & 0 \\ 0 & .75 & .95 \end{bmatrix}$

b. The long-term growth rate is $\lambda_1 = 1.105$. A corresponding eigenvector is approximately (38, 21, 100). For each 100 adults there will be approximately 38 calves and 21 yearlings.

Section 6.7, page 327

2. Eigenvector: $\mathbf{x}_4 = \begin{bmatrix} -.2520 \\ 1 \end{bmatrix}$, or $A\mathbf{x}_4 = \begin{bmatrix} -1.2536 \\ 5.0064 \end{bmatrix}$; $\lambda \approx 5.0064$

4. Eigenvector: $\mathbf{x}_4 = \begin{bmatrix} 1 \\ .7502 \end{bmatrix}$, or $A\mathbf{x}_4 = \begin{bmatrix} -.4012 \\ -.3009 \end{bmatrix}$; $\lambda \approx -.4012$

6. $\mathbf{x} = \begin{bmatrix} -.4996 \\ 1 \end{bmatrix}$, $A\mathbf{x} = \begin{bmatrix} -2.0008 \\ 4.0024 \end{bmatrix}$; estimated $\lambda = 4.0024$

8. $\mathbf{x}_k$: $\begin{bmatrix} .5 \\ 1 \end{bmatrix}, \begin{bmatrix} .2857 \\ 1 \end{bmatrix}, \begin{bmatrix} .2558 \\ 1 \end{bmatrix}, \begin{bmatrix} .2510 \\ 1 \end{bmatrix}, \begin{bmatrix} .2502 \\ 1 \end{bmatrix}$;
μ_k: 7, 6.14, 6.02, 6.0039, 6.0006

10. $\mu_5 = 9.9319$, $\mu_6 = 9.9872$; actual value: 10. *Note*: starting with $\mathbf{x}_0 = \begin{bmatrix} 0 \\ 0 \\ 1 \end{bmatrix}$ produces $\mu_4 = 9.9993$, $\mu_5 = 9.9999$

12. μ_k: −4.3333, −3.9231, −4.0196, −3.9951
$R(\mathbf{x}_k)$: −3.9231, −3.9951, −3.9997, −3.99998

14. Use the inverse power method, with $\alpha = 4$.

16. $\lambda = \alpha + 1/\mu$

18. $\nu_0 = -1.375$, $\nu_1 = -1.42623$, $\nu_2 = -1.42432$, $\nu_3 = -1.42444$. Actual: −1.424429 (accurate to 6 places)

20. a. $\mu_8 = 19.1820 = \mu_9$ to four decimal places. To six places, the largest eigenvalue is 19.182037, with eigenvector (.184416, 1, .179615, .407110).
b. $\mu_1^{-1} = .012235$, $\mu_2^{-1} = .012205$. To six places, the smallest eigenvalue is .012206, with eigenvector (1, .222610, −.917993, .660483). The other eigenvalues are −2.453128 and −1.741114, to six places.

CHAPTER 7

Section 7.1, page 340

2. 35, 5, $\frac{1}{7}$ **4.** $\begin{bmatrix} -1/5 \\ 2/5 \end{bmatrix}$ **6.** $\begin{bmatrix} 30/49 \\ -10/49 \\ 15/49 \end{bmatrix}$

8. $2\sqrt{13}$ **10.** 7 **12.** $\begin{bmatrix} -6\sqrt{61} \\ 4\sqrt{61} \\ -3\sqrt{61} \end{bmatrix}$ **14.** $\begin{bmatrix} .8 \\ .6 \end{bmatrix}$

16. $2\sqrt{17}$

18. $\mathbf{u} \cdot \mathbf{u} \geq 0$ because $\mathbf{u} \cdot \mathbf{u}$ is a sum of squares of the entries in $\mathbf{u}$. The sum of squares of numbers is zero if and only if all the numbers are themselves zero.

20. Orthogonal **22.** Not orthogonal

24.
$$\begin{aligned} \|\mathbf{u}+\mathbf{v}\|^2 &= (\mathbf{u}+\mathbf{v})\cdot(\mathbf{u}+\mathbf{v}) = \mathbf{u}\cdot\mathbf{u} + 2\mathbf{u}\cdot\mathbf{v} + \mathbf{v}\cdot\mathbf{v} \\ &= \|\mathbf{u}\|^2 + 2\mathbf{u}\cdot\mathbf{v} + \|\mathbf{v}\|^2 \\ \|\mathbf{u}-\mathbf{v}\|^2 &= (\mathbf{u}-\mathbf{v})\cdot(\mathbf{u}-\mathbf{v}) = \mathbf{u}\cdot\mathbf{u} + \mathbf{u}\cdot(-\mathbf{v}) \\ &\quad - \mathbf{v}\cdot\mathbf{u} + \mathbf{v}\cdot\mathbf{v} \\ &= \|\mathbf{u}\|^2 - 2\mathbf{u}\cdot\mathbf{v} + \|\mathbf{v}\|^2 \end{aligned}$$

When $\|\mathbf{u}+\mathbf{v}\|^2$ and $\|\mathbf{u}-\mathbf{v}\|^2$ are added, the $\mathbf{u}\cdot\mathbf{v}$ terms cancel, and the result is $2\|\mathbf{u}\|^2 + 2\|\mathbf{v}\|^2$.

26. Theorem 3 in Chapter 5, because W is the null space of the $1 \times n$ matrix $\mathbf{u}^T$. W is a plane through the origin.

28. An arbitrary $\mathbf{w}$ in Span $\{\mathbf{u}, \mathbf{v}\}$ has the form $\mathbf{w} = c_1\mathbf{u} + c_2\mathbf{v}$. If $\mathbf{y}$ is orthogonal to $\mathbf{u}$ and $\mathbf{v}$, then $\mathbf{u}\cdot\mathbf{y} = 0$ and $\mathbf{v}\cdot\mathbf{y} = 0$. By linearity of the inner product [Theorem 1(b) and 1(c)],

$$\mathbf{w}\cdot\mathbf{y} = (c_1\mathbf{u}+c_2\mathbf{v})\cdot\mathbf{y} = c_1\mathbf{u}\cdot\mathbf{y} + c_2\mathbf{v}\cdot\mathbf{y} = c_1 0 + c_2 0 = 0$$

30. a. If $\mathbf{z}$ is in $W^\perp$, $\mathbf{u}$ is in W, and c is any scalar, then $(c\mathbf{z})\cdot\mathbf{u} = c(\mathbf{z}\cdot\mathbf{u}) = c0 = 0$. Since $\mathbf{u}$ was any element of W, $c\mathbf{z}$ is in $W^\perp$.
b. Take any $\mathbf{z}_1, \mathbf{z}_2$ in $W^\perp$. Then, for any $\mathbf{u}$ in W, $(\mathbf{z}_1+\mathbf{z}_2)\cdot\mathbf{u} = \mathbf{z}_1\cdot\mathbf{u} + \mathbf{z}_2\cdot\mathbf{u} = 0 + 0 = 0$, which shows that $\mathbf{z}_1 + \mathbf{z}_2$ is in $W^\perp$.
c. Obviously $\mathbf{0}$ is in $W^\perp$, because $\mathbf{0}$ is orthogonal to every vector. This fact, together with (a) and (b), shows that $W^\perp$ is a subspace, by the Subspace Test (Section 5.1).

Section 7.2, page 350

2. Orthogonal **4.** Orthogonal **6.** Not orthogonal

8. Show $\mathbf{u}_1\cdot\mathbf{u}_2 = 0$, mention Theorem 4, and observe that two linearly independent vectors in $\mathbb{R}^2$ form a basis. Then obtain

$$\mathbf{x} = -\tfrac{15}{10}\begin{bmatrix} 3 \\ 1 \end{bmatrix} + \tfrac{30}{40}\begin{bmatrix} -2 \\ 6 \end{bmatrix} = -\tfrac{3}{2}\begin{bmatrix} 3 \\ 1 \end{bmatrix} + \tfrac{3}{4}\begin{bmatrix} -2 \\ 6 \end{bmatrix}$$

10. Show $\mathbf{u}_1\cdot\mathbf{u}_2 = 0$, $\mathbf{u}_1\cdot\mathbf{u}_3 = 0$, and $\mathbf{u}_2\cdot\mathbf{u}_3 = 0$. Mention Theorem 4, and observe that three linearly independent vectors in $\mathbb{R}^3$ form a basis. Then obtain

$$\mathbf{x} = \tfrac{24}{18}\mathbf{u}_1 + \tfrac{3}{9}\mathbf{u}_2 + \tfrac{6}{18}\mathbf{u}_3 = \tfrac{4}{3}\mathbf{u}_1 + \tfrac{1}{3}\mathbf{u}_2 + \tfrac{1}{3}\mathbf{u}_3$$

12. Not orthogonal **14.** $\begin{bmatrix} -2/3 \\ 1/3 \\ 2/3 \end{bmatrix}, \begin{bmatrix} 1/\sqrt{5} \\ 2/\sqrt{5} \\ 0 \end{bmatrix}$

16. Orthonormal **18.** $\begin{bmatrix} .4 \\ -1.2 \end{bmatrix}$

20. $\mathbf{y} = \begin{bmatrix} 14/5 \\ 2/5 \end{bmatrix} + \begin{bmatrix} -4/5 \\ 28/5 \end{bmatrix}$

22. $\mathbf{y} - \hat{\mathbf{y}} = \begin{bmatrix} -6 \\ 3 \end{bmatrix}$, dist. $= \sqrt{45} = 3\sqrt{5}$

24. If $\mathbf{v}_1\cdot\mathbf{v}_2 = 0$, then by Theorem 1(c) in Section 7.1, $(c_1\mathbf{v}_1)\cdot(c_2\mathbf{v}_2) = c_1[\mathbf{v}_1\cdot(c_2\mathbf{v}_2)] = c_1c_2(\mathbf{v}_1\cdot\mathbf{v}_2) = c_1c_2 0 = 0$.

26. $(U\mathbf{x})\cdot(U\mathbf{y}) = (U\mathbf{x})^T(U\mathbf{y}) = \mathbf{x}^TU^TU\mathbf{y} = \mathbf{x}^T\mathbf{y}$, because $U^TU = I$, by Theorem 6.

28. If U is an $n{\times}n$ orthogonal matrix, then $I = UU^{-1} = UU^T$. Since U is the transpose of U^T, Theorem 6 applied to U^T says that U^T has orthonormal columns. In particular, the columns of U^T are linearly independent and hence form a basis for $\mathbb{R}^n$, by the Invertible Matrix Theorem (see Section 5.6). That is, the rows of U form a basis (in fact, an orthonormal basis) for $\mathbb{R}^n$.

30. If U is an orthogonal matrix, its columns are orthonormal. Interchanging the columns does not change their orthonormality, so the new matrix, say V, still has orthonormal columns. By Theorem 6, $V^TV = I$. Since V is square, $V^T = V^{-1}$ by the Invertible Matrix Theorem.

Section 7.3, page 357

2. $\mathbf{v} = 2\mathbf{u}_1 + \frac{3}{7}\mathbf{u}_2 + \frac{12}{7}\mathbf{u}_3 - \frac{8}{7}\mathbf{u}_4$; $\mathbf{v} = \begin{bmatrix} 2 \\ 4 \\ 2 \\ 2 \end{bmatrix} + \begin{bmatrix} 2 \\ 1 \\ -5 \\ 1 \end{bmatrix}$

4. $\begin{bmatrix} 6 \\ 3 \\ 0 \end{bmatrix}$ **6.** $\begin{bmatrix} 6 \\ 4 \\ 1 \end{bmatrix} = \mathbf{y}$ **8.** $\mathbf{y} = \begin{bmatrix} 3/2 \\ 7/2 \\ 1 \end{bmatrix} + \begin{bmatrix} -5/2 \\ 1/2 \\ 2 \end{bmatrix}$

10. $\mathbf{y} = \begin{bmatrix} 5 \\ 2 \\ 3 \\ 6 \end{bmatrix} + \begin{bmatrix} -2 \\ 2 \\ 2 \\ 0 \end{bmatrix}$ **12.** $\begin{bmatrix} -1 \\ -5 \\ -3 \\ 9 \end{bmatrix}$

14. $\begin{bmatrix} 1 \\ 0 \\ -1/2 \\ -3/2 \end{bmatrix}$ **16.** 8

18. a. $U^TU = [1] = 1$, $UU^T = \begin{bmatrix} .1 & -.3 \\ -.3 & .9 \end{bmatrix}$

b. $\text{proj}_W \mathbf{y} = \frac{-20}{\sqrt{10}}\mathbf{u}_1 = \begin{bmatrix} -2 \\ 6 \end{bmatrix}$, and $(UU^T)\mathbf{y} = \begin{bmatrix} .7 - 2.7 \\ -2.1 + 8.1 \end{bmatrix} = \begin{bmatrix} -2 \\ 6 \end{bmatrix}$

20. Any multiple of $\begin{bmatrix} 0 \\ 4/5 \\ 2/5 \end{bmatrix}$, such as $\begin{bmatrix} 0 \\ 2 \\ 1 \end{bmatrix}$

22. a. By hypothesis, the vectors $\mathbf{w}_1, \ldots, \mathbf{w}_p$ are pairwise orthogonal, and the vectors $\mathbf{v}_1, \ldots, \mathbf{v}_q$ pairwise orthogonal. Also, $\mathbf{w}_i \cdot \mathbf{v}_j = 0$ for any i and j because the **v**'s are in the orthogonal complement of W.
b. For any **y** in $\mathbb{R}^n$, write $\mathbf{y} = \hat{\mathbf{y}} + \mathbf{z}$ as in the Orthogonal Decomposition Theorem, with $\hat{\mathbf{y}}$ in W and **z** in $W^\perp$. Then there exist scalars $c_1, \ldots, c_p$ and $d_1, \ldots, d_q$ such that

$$\mathbf{y} = \hat{\mathbf{y}} + \mathbf{z} = c_1\mathbf{w}_1 + \cdots + c_p\mathbf{w}_p + d_1\mathbf{v}_1 + \cdots + d_q\mathbf{v}_q$$

Thus $\{\mathbf{w}_1, \ldots, \mathbf{w}_p, \mathbf{v}_1, \ldots, \mathbf{v}_q\}$ spans $\mathbb{R}^n$.
c. The set $\{\mathbf{w}_1, \ldots, \mathbf{w}_p, \mathbf{v}_1, \ldots, \mathbf{v}_q\}$ is linearly independent by (a), spans $\mathbb{R}^n$ by (b), and thus is a basis for $\mathbb{R}^n$. Hence

$$\dim W + \dim W^\perp = p + q = \dim \mathbb{R}^n$$

Section 7.4, page 365

2. $\begin{bmatrix} 0 \\ 4 \\ 2 \end{bmatrix}, \begin{bmatrix} 5 \\ 4 \\ -8 \end{bmatrix}$ **4.** $\begin{bmatrix} 3 \\ -4 \\ 5 \end{bmatrix}, \begin{bmatrix} 3 \\ 6 \\ 3 \end{bmatrix}$

6. $\begin{bmatrix} 3 \\ -1 \\ 2 \\ -1 \end{bmatrix}, \begin{bmatrix} 4 \\ 6 \\ -3 \\ 0 \end{bmatrix}$ **8.** $\begin{bmatrix} 3/\sqrt{50} \\ -4/\sqrt{50} \\ 5/\sqrt{50} \end{bmatrix}, \begin{bmatrix} 1/\sqrt{6} \\ 2/\sqrt{6} \\ 1/\sqrt{6} \end{bmatrix}$

10. $\begin{bmatrix} -1 \\ 3 \\ 1 \\ 1 \end{bmatrix}, \begin{bmatrix} 3 \\ 1 \\ 1 \\ -1 \end{bmatrix}, \begin{bmatrix} 1 \\ 1 \\ -3 \\ 1 \end{bmatrix}$

12. $\begin{bmatrix} 1 \\ -1 \\ 0 \\ 1 \\ 1 \end{bmatrix}, \begin{bmatrix} -1 \\ 1 \\ 2 \\ 1 \\ 1 \end{bmatrix}, \begin{bmatrix} 1 \\ 1 \\ 0 \\ -1 \\ 1 \end{bmatrix}$ **14.** $R = \begin{bmatrix} 7 & 7 \\ 0 & 7 \end{bmatrix}$

16. $Q = \begin{bmatrix} 1/2 & -1/\sqrt{8} & 1/2 \\ -1/2 & 1/\sqrt{8} & 1/2 \\ 0 & 2/\sqrt{8} & 0 \\ 1/2 & 1/\sqrt{8} & -1/2 \\ 1/2 & 1/\sqrt{8} & 1/2 \end{bmatrix}$,

$$R = \begin{bmatrix} 2 & 8 & 7 \\ 0 & \sqrt{8} & 12/\sqrt{8} \\ 0 & 0 & 6 \end{bmatrix}$$

18. If **y** is in Col A, then $\mathbf{y} = A\mathbf{x}$ for some **x**. Then $\mathbf{y} = QR\mathbf{x} = Q(R\mathbf{x})$, which shows that **y** is a linear combination of the columns of Q using the entries in $R\mathbf{x}$ as weights. Conversely, suppose $\mathbf{y} = Q\mathbf{x}$ for some **x**. Since R is invertible, the equation $A = QR$ implies that $Q = AR^{-1}$. So $\mathbf{y} = AR^{-1}\mathbf{x} = A(R^{-1}\mathbf{x})$, which shows that **y** is in Col A.

Section 7.5, page 373

2. a. $\begin{bmatrix} 12 & 8 \\ 8 & 10 \end{bmatrix}\begin{bmatrix} x_1 \\ x_2 \end{bmatrix} = \begin{bmatrix} -24 \\ -2 \end{bmatrix}$ **b.** $\hat{\mathbf{x}} = \begin{bmatrix} -4 \\ 3 \end{bmatrix}$

4. a. $\begin{bmatrix} 3 & 3 \\ 3 & 11 \end{bmatrix}\begin{bmatrix} x_1 \\ x_2 \end{bmatrix} = \begin{bmatrix} 6 \\ 14 \end{bmatrix}$ **b.** $\hat{\mathbf{x}} = \begin{bmatrix} 1 \\ 1 \end{bmatrix}$

6. $\hat{\mathbf{x}} = \begin{bmatrix} 5 \\ -1 \\ 0 \end{bmatrix} + x_3\begin{bmatrix} -1 \\ 1 \\ 1 \end{bmatrix}$ **8.** $\sqrt{6}$

10. a. $\hat{\mathbf{b}} = \begin{bmatrix} 4 \\ -1 \\ 4 \end{bmatrix}$ **b.** $\hat{\mathbf{x}} = \begin{bmatrix} 3 \\ 1/2 \end{bmatrix}$

12. a. $\begin{bmatrix} 5 \\ 2 \\ 3 \\ 6 \end{bmatrix}$ b. $\hat{\mathbf{x}} = \begin{bmatrix} 1/3 \\ 14/3 \\ -5/3 \end{bmatrix}$

14. $A\mathbf{u} = \begin{bmatrix} 3 \\ 8 \\ 2 \end{bmatrix}$, $A\mathbf{v} = \begin{bmatrix} 7 \\ 2 \\ 8 \end{bmatrix}$, $\mathbf{b} - A\mathbf{u} = \begin{bmatrix} 2 \\ -4 \\ 2 \end{bmatrix}$,
$\mathbf{b} - A\mathbf{v} = \begin{bmatrix} -2 \\ 2 \\ -4 \end{bmatrix}$. Note that $\|\mathbf{b} - A\mathbf{u}\| = \|\mathbf{b} - A\mathbf{v}\| = \sqrt{24}$, so $A\mathbf{u}$ and $A\mathbf{v}$ are equally close to **b**. The orthogonal projection is the *unique* closest point in Col A to **b**, so neither $A\mathbf{u}$ nor $A\mathbf{v}$ can be $\hat{\mathbf{b}}$. That is, neither **u** nor **v** can be a least-squares solution of $A\mathbf{x} = \mathbf{b}$.

16. $\hat{\mathbf{x}} = \begin{bmatrix} 2.9 \\ .9 \end{bmatrix}$

18. Suppose that $A\mathbf{x} = \mathbf{0}$. Then $A^TA\mathbf{x} = A^T\mathbf{0} = \mathbf{0}$. Since A^TA is invertible, by hypothesis, **x** must be zero. Hence the columns of A are linearly independent.

20. A^TA has n columns because A does. Then

$\text{rank}\, A^TA = n - \dim \text{Nul}\, A^TA$	The Rank Theorem
$= n - \dim \text{Nul}\, A$	Exercise 17
$= \text{rank}\, A$	The Rank Theorem

22. $\hat{\mathbf{x}} = A^T\mathbf{b}$, from the normal equations, because $A^TA = I$.

24. $a_0 = a_2 = .35\underline{35}$, $a_1 = .5$ (With .707 in place of .7, $a_0 = a_2 \approx .35355339$, $a_1 = .5$.)

Section 7.6, page 382

2. $y = .7x - .6$ **4.** $y = -.7x + 4.3$

6. If the columns of X were linearly dependent, then the same dependence relation would hold for the vectors in $\mathbb{R}^3$ formed from the top three entries of the column. In this case, the *Vandermonde* matrix

$$\begin{bmatrix} 1 & x_1 & x_1^2 \\ 1 & x_2 & x_2^2 \\ 1 & x_3 & x_3^2 \end{bmatrix}$$

would be noninvertible. However, it can be shown that since x_1, x_2, and x_3 are distinct, this matrix *is* invertible, which means that the columns of X are, in fact, linearly independent. As in Exercise 5, Theorem 14 implies that there is only one least-squares solution of $\mathbf{y} = X\boldsymbol{\beta}$.

One way to show that the 3×3 matrix above is invertible is to show that its determinant is $(x_2 - x_1)(x_3 - x_1)(x_3 - x_2)$. Another way is to appeal to Supplementary Exercise 11(b) in Chapter 3.

8. $X = \begin{bmatrix} x_1 & x_1^2 & x_1^3 \\ \vdots & \vdots & \vdots \\ x_n & x_n^2 & x_n^3 \end{bmatrix}, \boldsymbol{\beta} = \begin{bmatrix} \beta_1 \\ \beta_2 \\ \beta_3 \end{bmatrix}$

10. $\mathbf{y} = X\boldsymbol{\beta} + \boldsymbol{\epsilon}$, where $\mathbf{y} = \begin{bmatrix} 21.34 \\ 20.68 \\ 20.05 \end{bmatrix}$, $X = \begin{bmatrix} e^{-.02(10)} & e^{-.07(10)} \\ e^{-.02(11)} & e^{-.07(11)} \\ e^{-.02(12)} & e^{-.07(12)} \end{bmatrix}$, $\boldsymbol{\beta} = \begin{bmatrix} M_A \\ M_B \end{bmatrix}$, $\boldsymbol{\epsilon} = \begin{bmatrix} \epsilon_1 \\ \epsilon_2 \\ \epsilon_3 \end{bmatrix}$;

MATLAB: $M_A = 20.01$, $M_B = 9.98$

12. $p = 18.55 + 19.23 \ln w$. When w is 100, p is approximately 107.

14. Write the design matrix as $X = [\mathbf{1} \quad \mathbf{x}]$. Since the residual vector, $\boldsymbol{\epsilon} = \mathbf{y} - X\boldsymbol{\beta}$ is orthogonal to Col X, we have (using the notation shown just after Exercise 14)

$$\begin{aligned} 0 = \mathbf{1} \cdot \boldsymbol{\epsilon} = \mathbf{1} \cdot (\mathbf{y} - X\hat{\boldsymbol{\beta}}) &= \mathbf{1}^T\mathbf{y} - (\mathbf{1}^T X)\hat{\boldsymbol{\beta}} \\ &= (y_1 + \cdots + y_n) - [n \quad \Sigma x]\begin{bmatrix} \hat{\beta}_0 \\ \hat{\beta}_1 \end{bmatrix} \\ &= \Sigma y - n\hat{\beta}_0 - \beta_1 \Sigma x \end{aligned}$$

Divide by $-n$, move the first term to the left side of the equation, and obtain $\overline{y} = \hat{\beta}_0 + \hat{\beta}_1 \overline{x}$.

16. The determinant of the coefficient matrix of the equations in (6) is $n\,\Sigma x^2 - (\Sigma x)^2$. Using the 2×2 formula for the inverse of the coefficient matrix, we have

$$\begin{bmatrix} \hat{\beta}_0 \\ \hat{\beta}_1 \end{bmatrix} = \frac{1}{n\Sigma x^2 - (\Sigma x)^2} \begin{bmatrix} \Sigma x^2 & -\Sigma x \\ -\Sigma x & n \end{bmatrix} \begin{bmatrix} \Sigma y \\ \Sigma xy \end{bmatrix}$$

Hence

$$\hat{\beta}_0 = \frac{\Sigma x^2\, \Sigma y - \Sigma x\, \Sigma xy}{n\,\Sigma x^2 - (\Sigma x)^2}, \quad \hat{\beta}_1 = \frac{n\Sigma\, xy - \Sigma x\, \Sigma y}{n\,\Sigma x^2 - (\Sigma x)^2}$$

Note: A simple algebraic calculation shows that $\Sigma y - (\Sigma x)\hat{\beta}_1 = n\hat{\beta}_0$, which provides a simple formula for $\hat{\beta}_0$, once $\hat{\beta}_1$ is known.

18. $X^T X = \begin{bmatrix} 1 & \cdots & 1 \\ x_1 & \cdots & x_n \end{bmatrix} \begin{bmatrix} 1 & x_1 \\ \vdots & \vdots \\ 1 & x_n \end{bmatrix} = \begin{bmatrix} n & \Sigma x \\ \Sigma x & (\Sigma x)^2 \end{bmatrix}$

This matrix is a diagonal matrix when $\Sigma x = 0$.

20. $\|X\hat{\boldsymbol{\beta}}\|^2 = (X\hat{\boldsymbol{\beta}})^T(X\hat{\boldsymbol{\beta}}) = \hat{\boldsymbol{\beta}}^T X^T X\hat{\boldsymbol{\beta}} = \hat{\boldsymbol{\beta}}^T X^T\mathbf{y}$, because $\hat{\boldsymbol{\beta}}^T$ satisfies the normal equations: $X^T X\hat{\boldsymbol{\beta}} = X^T\mathbf{y}$. Since $\|X\hat{\boldsymbol{\beta}}\|^2 = \text{SS(R)}$ and $\mathbf{y}^T\mathbf{y} = \|\mathbf{y}\|^2 = \text{SS(T)}$, Exercise 19 shows that

$$\text{SS(E)} = \text{SS(T)} - \text{SS(R)} = \mathbf{y}^T\mathbf{y} - \hat{\boldsymbol{\beta}}^T X^T\mathbf{y}$$

Section 7.7, page 392

2. $\|\mathbf{x}\|^2 = \langle \mathbf{x}, \mathbf{x} \rangle = 4(3)(3) + 5(-2)(-2) = 56$
$\|\mathbf{y}\|^2 = \langle \mathbf{y}, \mathbf{y} \rangle = 4(-2)(-2) + 5(1)(1) = 21$
$\|\mathbf{x}\|^2\|\mathbf{y}\|^2 = 56(21) = 1176$
$\langle \mathbf{x}, \mathbf{y} \rangle = 4(3)(-2) + 5(-2)(1) = -34$
$|\langle \mathbf{x}, \mathbf{y} \rangle|^2 = 1156 < 1176 = \|\mathbf{x}\|^2\|\mathbf{y}\|^2$

4. Polynomials: $3t - t^2 \quad 3 + 2t^2$

Values: $\begin{bmatrix} -4 \\ 0 \\ 2 \end{bmatrix} \quad \begin{bmatrix} 5 \\ 2 \\ 5 \end{bmatrix}$

$\langle p, q \rangle = -20 + 0 + 10 = -10$

6. $\|p\| = 2\sqrt{5}$
$\|q\| = \sqrt{59}$

8. $\dfrac{\langle q, p \rangle}{\langle p, p \rangle} p(t) = \dfrac{-10}{20} p(t) = -\dfrac{1}{2}(3t - t^2) = -\dfrac{3}{2} + \dfrac{1}{2}t^2$

10. Polynomial: $p_0 \quad p_1 \quad q \quad p(t) = t^3$

Values: $\begin{bmatrix} 1 \\ 1 \\ 1 \\ 1 \end{bmatrix} \quad \begin{bmatrix} -3 \\ -1 \\ 1 \\ 3 \end{bmatrix} \quad \begin{bmatrix} 1 \\ -1 \\ -1 \\ 1 \end{bmatrix} \quad \begin{bmatrix} -27 \\ -1 \\ 1 \\ 27 \end{bmatrix}$

$\hat{p}(t) = \frac{0}{4}p_0 + \frac{164}{20}p_1 + \frac{0}{4}q = \frac{41}{5}t$

12. Use Exercise 11 to get $t^3 - \frac{17}{5}t$. Then $5t^3 - 17t$ is also orthogonal to p_0, p_1, p_2, but its vector of values is $(-6, 12, 0, -12, 6)$. Answer: $p_3(t) = (1/6)(5t^3 - 17t)$.

14. (i) $\langle \mathbf{u}, \mathbf{v} \rangle = T(\mathbf{u}) \cdot T(\mathbf{v})$ Definition
$= T(\mathbf{v}) \cdot T(\mathbf{u})$ Property of the dot product
$= \langle \mathbf{v}, \mathbf{u} \rangle$ Definition

(ii) $\langle \mathbf{u} + \mathbf{v}, \mathbf{w} \rangle = T(\mathbf{u} + \mathbf{v}) \cdot T(\mathbf{w})$ Definition
$= [T(\mathbf{u}) + T(\mathbf{v})] \cdot T(\mathbf{w})$ Linearity of T
$= T(\mathbf{u}) \cdot T(\mathbf{w}) + T(\mathbf{v}) \cdot T(\mathbf{w})$ Property of the dot product
$= \langle \mathbf{u}, \mathbf{w} \rangle + \langle \mathbf{v}, \mathbf{w} \rangle$ Definition

(iii) $\langle c\mathbf{u}, \mathbf{v} \rangle = T(c\mathbf{u}) \cdot T(\mathbf{v})$ Definition
$= cT(\mathbf{u}) \cdot T(\mathbf{v})$ Linearity of T
$= c\langle \mathbf{u}, \mathbf{v} \rangle$ Definition

(iv) $\langle \mathbf{u}, \mathbf{u} \rangle = T(\mathbf{u}) \cdot T(\mathbf{u}) \geq 0$ Property of the dot product

If $\mathbf{u} = \mathbf{0}$, then $T(\mathbf{u}) = \mathbf{0}$, because T is linear, and $\langle \mathbf{u}, \mathbf{u} \rangle = 0$. Conversely, if $\langle \mathbf{u}, \mathbf{u} \rangle = 0$, then $T(\mathbf{u}) \cdot T(\mathbf{u}) = 0$, and hence $T(\mathbf{u}) = 0$ by a property of the dot product. Since T is one-to-one, $\mathbf{u} = \mathbf{0}$.

16. $\|\mathbf{u} - \mathbf{v}\|^2 = \langle \mathbf{u} - \mathbf{v}, \mathbf{u} - \mathbf{v} \rangle$
$= \langle \mathbf{u}, \mathbf{u} - \mathbf{v} \rangle - \langle \mathbf{v}, \mathbf{u} - \mathbf{v} \rangle$ Axioms (ii), (iii)
$= \langle \mathbf{u}, \mathbf{u} \rangle - \langle \mathbf{u}, \mathbf{v} \rangle - \langle \mathbf{v}, \mathbf{u} \rangle + \langle \mathbf{v}, \mathbf{v} \rangle$ Axioms (i–iii)
$= \langle \mathbf{u}, \mathbf{u} \rangle - 2\langle \mathbf{u}, \mathbf{v} \rangle + \langle \mathbf{v}, \mathbf{v} \rangle$ Axiom (i)
$= \|\mathbf{u}\|^2 - 2\langle \mathbf{u}, \mathbf{v} \rangle + \|\mathbf{v}\|^2$

If $\{\mathbf{u}, \mathbf{v}\}$ is orthonormal, then $\|\mathbf{u}\|^2 = \|\mathbf{v}\|^2 = 1$ and $\langle \mathbf{u}, \mathbf{v} \rangle = 0$. So $\|\mathbf{u} - \mathbf{v}\|^2 = 2$.

18. The calculation in Exercise 16 shows that

$$\|\mathbf{u} - \mathbf{v}\|^2 = \|\mathbf{u}\|^2 - 2\langle \mathbf{u}, \mathbf{v} \rangle + \|\mathbf{v}\|^2$$

Similarly,

$$\|\mathbf{u} + \mathbf{v}\|^2 = \|\mathbf{u}\|^2 + 2\langle \mathbf{u}, \mathbf{v} \rangle + \|\mathbf{v}\|^2$$

Adding, $\|\mathbf{u} + \mathbf{v}\|^2 + \|\mathbf{u} - \mathbf{v}\|^2 = 2\|\mathbf{u}\|^2 + 2\|\mathbf{v}\|^2$.

20. If $\mathbf{u} = (a, b)$ and $\mathbf{v} = (1, 1)$, then $\|\mathbf{u}\|^2 = a^2 + b^2$, $\|\mathbf{v}\|^2 = 2$, and $|\langle \mathbf{u}, \mathbf{v} \rangle| = |a + b|$. The desired inequality follows when the Cauchy–Schwarz inequality is rewritten as

$$\left(\frac{\langle \mathbf{u}, \mathbf{v} \rangle}{2}\right)^2 \leq \frac{\|\mathbf{u}\|^2 \|\mathbf{v}\|^2}{4}$$

22. $\int_0^1 (5t - 3)(t^3 - t^2)\, dt = \int_0^1 (5t^4 - 8t^3 + 3t^2)\, dt = 0$

24. $\int_0^1 (t^3 - t^2)^2\, dt = \int_0^1 (t^6 - 2t^5 + t^4)\, dt = 1/105$, $\|g\| = \sqrt{105}$

26. $1, t, 3t^2 - 4$

Section 7.8, page 399

2. Let X be the original design matrix, and let $\mathbf{y}$ be the original observation vector. Let W be the weighting matrix for the first method. Then the weighting matrix for the second method is $2W$. The weighted least-squares by the first method is equivalent to the ordinary least-squares for an equation whose normal equation is

$$(WX)^T WX\hat{\beta} = (WX)^T W\mathbf{y}$$

The second method is equivalent to the ordinary least-squares for an equation whose normal equation is

$$(2WX)^T (2W)X\hat{\beta} = (2WX)^T (2W)\mathbf{y}$$

These two equations obviously have the same solution.

4. a. The vector of values for the polynomials are

$$p_0 \leftrightarrow (1, 1, 1, 1, 1, 1), \qquad p_1 \leftrightarrow (-5, -3, -1, 1, 3, 5),$$
$$p_2 \leftrightarrow (5, -1, -4, -4, -1, 5)$$

It is easy to see that these vectors in $\mathbb{R}^6$ are mutually orthogonal.
b. $4p_0 + \frac{5}{7}p_1 + \frac{1}{14}p_2$

6. Use the identity $\sin mt \cos nt = \frac{1}{2}[\sin(m + n)t + \sin(m - n)t]$.

8. $-1 + \pi - 2\sin t - \sin 2t - \frac{2}{3}\sin 3t$

10. $\frac{4}{\pi}\sin t + \frac{4}{3\pi}\sin 3t$ (The next term is $\frac{4}{5\pi}\sin 5t$.)

12. The trigonometric identity $\cos 3t = 4\cos^3 t - 3\cos t$ shows that

$$\cos^3 t = \tfrac{3}{4}\cos t + \tfrac{1}{4}\cos 3t$$

The expression on the right is in the subspace spanned by the trigonometric polynomials of order 3 or less, so this expression *is* the third-order Fourier approximation to $\cos^3 t$.

14. g and h are both in the subspace H spanned by the trigonometric polynomials of order 2 or less. Since h is the second-order Fourier approximation to f, it is closer to f than any other function in the subspace H.

CHAPTER 8

Section 8.1, page 410

2. Not symmetric **4.** Symmetric **6.** Not symmetric

8. Orthogonal, $\begin{bmatrix} 1/\sqrt{2} & 1/\sqrt{2} \\ -1/\sqrt{2} & 1/\sqrt{2} \end{bmatrix}$ **10.** Not orthogonal

12. Orthogonal, $\begin{bmatrix} .5 & -.5 & .5 & -.5 \\ .5 & .5 & .5 & .5 \\ -.5 & -.5 & .5 & .5 \\ -.5 & .5 & .5 & -.5 \end{bmatrix}$

14. $P = \begin{bmatrix} 1/\sqrt{2} & -1/\sqrt{2} \\ 1/\sqrt{2} & 1/\sqrt{2} \end{bmatrix}, D = \begin{bmatrix} 6 & 0 \\ 0 & -4 \end{bmatrix}$

16. $P = \begin{bmatrix} 3/5 & -4/5 \\ 4/5 & 3/5 \end{bmatrix}, D = \begin{bmatrix} 25 & 0 \\ 0 & -25 \end{bmatrix}$

18. $P = \begin{bmatrix} -4/5 & 0 & 3/5 \\ 3/5 & 0 & 4/5 \\ 0 & 1 & 0 \end{bmatrix}, D = \begin{bmatrix} 25 & 0 & 0 \\ 0 & 3 & 0 \\ 0 & 0 & -50 \end{bmatrix}$

20. $P = \begin{bmatrix} 2/3 & -1/2 & 2/3 \\ -1/3 & 2/3 & 2/3 \\ 2/3 & 2/3 & -1/3 \end{bmatrix}, D = \begin{bmatrix} 13 & 0 & 0 \\ 0 & 7 & 0 \\ 0 & 0 & 1 \end{bmatrix}$

22. $P = \begin{bmatrix} -2/3 & 1/\sqrt{2} & 1/\sqrt{18} \\ 2/3 & 1/\sqrt{2} & -1/\sqrt{18} \\ 1/3 & 0 & 4/\sqrt{18} \end{bmatrix},$

$D = \begin{bmatrix} 10 & 0 & 0 \\ 0 & 1 & 0 \\ 0 & 0 & 1 \end{bmatrix}$

24. $P = \begin{bmatrix} 1 & 0 & 0 & 0 \\ 0 & 1/\sqrt{2} & 0 & -1/\sqrt{2} \\ 0 & 0 & 1 & 0 \\ 0 & 1/\sqrt{2} & 0 & 1/\sqrt{2} \end{bmatrix},$

$D = \begin{bmatrix} 2 & 0 & 0 & 0 \\ 0 & 2 & 0 & 0 \\ 0 & 0 & 2 & 0 \\ 0 & 0 & 0 & 0 \end{bmatrix}$

26. If A and B are orthogonally diagonalizable, then A and B are symmetric, by Theorem 2. If $AB = BA$, then $(AB)^T = (BA)^T = A^TB^T = AB$. So AB is symmetric and hence is orthogonally diagonalizable, by Theorem 2.

28. $A = 7\mathbf{v}_1\mathbf{v}_1^T + 7\mathbf{v}_2\mathbf{v}_2^T - 2\mathbf{v}_3\mathbf{v}_3^T$, where $\mathbf{v}_1 = \begin{bmatrix} 1/\sqrt{2} \\ 0 \\ 1/\sqrt{2} \end{bmatrix}$,

$\mathbf{v}_2 = \begin{bmatrix} -1/\sqrt{18} \\ 4/\sqrt{18} \\ 1/\sqrt{18} \end{bmatrix}$, and $\mathbf{v}_3 = \begin{bmatrix} -2/3 \\ -1/3 \\ 2/3 \end{bmatrix}$

30. $A\mathbf{x} \cdot \mathbf{y} = (A\mathbf{x})^T\mathbf{y} = \mathbf{x}^TA^T\mathbf{y} = \mathbf{x}^TA\mathbf{y} = \mathbf{x} \cdot A\mathbf{y}$, because $A^T = A$.

32. If $A = PRP^{-1}$, then $P^{-1}AP = R$. Since P is orthogonal, $R = P^TAP$. Hence $R^T = (P^TAP)^T = P^TA^TP^{TT} = P^TAP = R$, which shows that R is symmetric.

34. Given any $\mathbf{y}$ in $\mathbb{R}^n$, let $\hat{\mathbf{y}} = B\mathbf{y}$ and $\mathbf{z} = \mathbf{y} - \hat{\mathbf{y}}$. Suppose $B^T = B$ and $B^2 = B$.

a. $\mathbf{z} \cdot \hat{\mathbf{y}} = (\mathbf{y} - B\mathbf{y}) \cdot (B\mathbf{y}) = (\mathbf{y} - B\mathbf{y})^T B\mathbf{y}$
$= [\mathbf{y}^T - (B\mathbf{y})^T]B\mathbf{y} = \mathbf{y}^TB\mathbf{y} - (\mathbf{y}^TB^T)B\mathbf{y}$
$= \mathbf{y}^TB\mathbf{y} - \mathbf{y}^TBB\mathbf{y} = \mathbf{y}^TB\mathbf{y} - \mathbf{y}^TB\mathbf{y} = 0$

So $\mathbf{z}$ is orthogonal to $\mathbf{y}$.

b. Any vector in $W = \operatorname{Col} B$ has the form $B\mathbf{u}$ for some $\mathbf{u}$. To show that $\mathbf{y} - \hat{\mathbf{y}}$ is orthogonal to $B\mathbf{u}$, we can use Exercise 30, since B is symmetric:

$$(\mathbf{y} - \hat{\mathbf{y}}) \cdot B\mathbf{u} = [B(\mathbf{y} - \hat{\mathbf{y}})] \cdot \mathbf{u} = [B\mathbf{y} - BB\mathbf{y}] \cdot \mathbf{u} = 0$$

because $B^2 = B$. So $\mathbf{y} - \hat{\mathbf{y}}$ is in $W^\perp$, and the decomposition $\mathbf{y} = \hat{\mathbf{y}} + (\mathbf{y} - \hat{\mathbf{y}})$ expresses $\mathbf{y}$ as the sum of a vector in W and a vector in $W^\perp$. By the Orthogonal Decomposition Theorem in Section 7.3, this decomposition is unique, and so $\hat{\mathbf{y}}$ must be $\operatorname{proj}_W \mathbf{y}$.

Section 8.2, page 417

2. a. $4x_1^2 + 2x_2^2 + x_3^2 + 6x_1x_2 + 2x_2x_3$ **b.** 21 **c.** 5

4. a. $\begin{bmatrix} 20 & 7.5 \\ 7.5 & -10 \end{bmatrix}$ **b.** $\begin{bmatrix} 0 & .5 \\ .5 & 0 \end{bmatrix}$

6. a. $\begin{bmatrix} 5 & 5/2 & -3/2 \\ 5/2 & -1 & 0 \\ -3/2 & 0 & 7 \end{bmatrix}$ **b.** $\begin{bmatrix} 0 & -2 & 0 \\ -2 & 0 & 2 \\ 0 & 2 & 1 \end{bmatrix}$

8. $P = \frac{1}{3}\begin{bmatrix} 2 & -1 & 2 \\ -1 & 2 & 2 \\ 2 & 2 & -1 \end{bmatrix}, \mathbf{u}^TD\mathbf{u} = 15u_1^2 + 9u_2^2 + 3u_3^2$

10. Positive definite, because eigenvalues are 11 and 1
Change of variable: $\mathbf{x} = P\mathbf{u}$, with $P = \left(\frac{1}{\sqrt{5}}\right)\begin{bmatrix} 2 & 1 \\ -1 & 2 \end{bmatrix}$
New quadratic form: $11u_1^2 + u_2^2$

12. Negative definite, because eigenvalues are -1 and -6
Change of variable: $\mathbf{x} = P\mathbf{u}$, with $P = \left(\frac{1}{\sqrt{5}}\right)\begin{bmatrix} 1 & -2 \\ 2 & 1 \end{bmatrix}$
New quadratic form: $-u_1^2 - 6u_2^2$

14. Indefinite, because eigenvalues are 9 and -1
Change of variable: $\mathbf{x} = P\mathbf{u}$ where $P = \left(\frac{1}{\sqrt{10}}\right)\begin{bmatrix} 3 & -1 \\ 1 & 3 \end{bmatrix}$
New quadratic form: $9u_1^2 - u_2^2$

16. 5

18. If det $A > 0$, then by Exercise 17, $\lambda_1\lambda_2 > 0$, so that λ_1 and λ_2 have the same sign; also, $ad = \det A + b^2 > 0$.
a. If det $A > 0$ and $a > 0$, then $d > 0$, too (because $ad > 0$). By Exercise 17, $\lambda_1 + \lambda_2 = a + d > 0$. Since λ_1 and λ_2 have the same sign, they are both positive. So Q is positive definite, by Theorem 5.
b. If det $A > 0$ and $a < 0$, then $d < 0$, too. As in (a), we conclude that λ_1 and λ_2 are both negative and that Q is negative definite.
c. If det $A < 0$, then by Exercise 17, $\lambda_1\lambda_2 < 0$, which shows that λ_1 and λ_2 have opposite signs. By Theorem 5, Q is indefinite.

20. We may assume $A = PDP^T$, with $P^T = P^{-1}$. The eigenvalues of A are all positive; denote them by $\lambda_1, \ldots, \lambda_n$. Let C be the diagonal matrix with $\sqrt{\lambda_1}, \ldots, \sqrt{\lambda_n}$ on the diagonal. Then $D = C^2 = C^TC$. If $B = PCP^T$, then

$$\begin{aligned} B^TB &= (PCP^T)^T(PCP^T) = (P^{TT}C^TP^T)(PCP) \\ &= PC^TCP \qquad \text{because } P^TP = I \\ &= PDP = A \end{aligned}$$

22. The eigenvalues of A are all positive, by Theorem 5. Since the eigenvalues of A^{-1} are the reciprocals of the eigenvalues of A (see Exercise 25 in Section 6.1), the eigenvalues of A^{-1} are positive. By Theorem 5, the quadratic form $\mathbf{x}^TA^{-1}\mathbf{x}$ is positive definite.

Section 8.3, page 425

2. $\mathbf{x} = P\mathbf{y}$, where $P = \begin{bmatrix} 1/\sqrt{3} & -2/\sqrt{6} & 0 \\ 1/\sqrt{3} & 1/\sqrt{6} & 1/\sqrt{2} \\ 1/\sqrt{3} & 1/\sqrt{6} & -1/\sqrt{2} \end{bmatrix}$

4. a. 5 **b.** $\begin{bmatrix} 1/\sqrt{3} \\ 1/\sqrt{3} \\ 1/\sqrt{3} \end{bmatrix}$ **c.** 2

6. a. $\frac{15}{2}$ **b.** $\begin{bmatrix} 3/\sqrt{10} \\ 1/\sqrt{10} \end{bmatrix}$ **c.** $\frac{5}{2}$

8. Any unit vector that is a linear combination of $\begin{bmatrix} -2/\sqrt{5} \\ 1/\sqrt{5} \\ 0 \end{bmatrix}$ and $\begin{bmatrix} -1/\sqrt{2} \\ 0 \\ 1/\sqrt{2} \end{bmatrix}$

10. $1 + \sqrt{17}$

12. Let $\mathbf{x}$ be a unit eigenvector for the eigenvalue λ. Then $\mathbf{x}^TA\mathbf{x} = \mathbf{x}^T(\lambda\mathbf{x}) = \lambda$, because $\mathbf{x}^T\mathbf{x} = 1$. So λ must satisfy $m \le \lambda \le M$.

Section 8.4, page 434

2. 5, 0 **4.** 3, 1

6. $\begin{bmatrix} -2 & 0 \\ 0 & -1 \end{bmatrix} = \begin{bmatrix} -1 & 0 \\ 0 & -1 \end{bmatrix}\begin{bmatrix} 2 & 0 \\ 0 & 1 \end{bmatrix}\begin{bmatrix} 1 & 0 \\ 0 & 1 \end{bmatrix}$

8. $\begin{bmatrix} 2/\sqrt{5} & -1/\sqrt{5} \\ 1/\sqrt{5} & 2/\sqrt{5} \end{bmatrix}\begin{bmatrix} 4 & 0 \\ 0 & 1 \end{bmatrix}$
$\begin{bmatrix} 1/\sqrt{5} & 2/\sqrt{5} \\ -2/\sqrt{5} & 1/\sqrt{5} \end{bmatrix}$

10. $\begin{bmatrix} 2/\sqrt{5} & 1/\sqrt{5} & 0 \\ 1/\sqrt{5} & -2/\sqrt{5} & 0 \\ 0 & 0 & 1 \end{bmatrix}\begin{bmatrix} 5 & 0 \\ 0 & 0 \\ 0 & 0 \end{bmatrix}$
$\begin{bmatrix} 2/\sqrt{5} & -1/\sqrt{5} \\ 1/\sqrt{5} & 2/\sqrt{5} \end{bmatrix}$

12. $\begin{bmatrix} 1/\sqrt{3} & 1/\sqrt{2} & 1/\sqrt{6} \\ 1/\sqrt{3} & 0 & -2/\sqrt{6} \\ 1/\sqrt{3} & -1/\sqrt{2} & 1/\sqrt{6} \end{bmatrix}\begin{bmatrix} \sqrt{3} & 0 \\ 0 & \sqrt{2} \\ 0 & 0 \end{bmatrix}\begin{bmatrix} 0 & 1 \\ 1 & 0 \end{bmatrix}$

14. Let $A = U\Sigma V^T = U\Sigma V^{-1}$. Since A is square and invertible, rank $A = n$, and all the entries on the diagonal of Σ must be nonzero. So $A^{-1} = (U\Sigma V^{-1})^{-1} = V\Sigma^{-1}U^{-1} = V\Sigma^{-1}U^T$.

16. The determinant of an orthogonal matrix U is ± 1 because

$$\begin{aligned} 1 = \det I &= \det U^TU = (\det U^T)(\det U) \\ &= (\det U)(\det U) \end{aligned}$$

Suppose A is square and $A = U\Sigma V^T$. Then Σ is square, and

$$\begin{aligned} \det A &= (\det U)(\det \Sigma)(\det V^T) \\ &= \pm \det \Sigma = \pm \sigma_1 \cdots \sigma_n \end{aligned}$$

18. The singular values of A are the square roots of the eigenvalues of A^TA. But $A^TA = A^2$ because A is symmetric. It is easy to see that the eigenvalues of A^2 are $\lambda_1^2, \ldots, \lambda_n^2$, where $\lambda_1, \ldots, \lambda_n$ are the eigenvalues of A. Since the λ_i are positive, the square root of λ_i^2 is λ_i itself.

20. From Exercise 19, $A^T = \sigma_1\mathbf{v}_1\mathbf{u}_1^T + \cdots + \sigma_r\mathbf{v}_r\mathbf{u}_r^T$. Then

$$\begin{aligned} A^T\mathbf{u}_j &= (\sigma_j\mathbf{v}_j\mathbf{u}_j^T)\mathbf{u}_j \qquad \text{Because } \mathbf{u}_i^T\mathbf{u}_j = 0 \text{ for } i \ne j \\ &= \sigma_j\mathbf{v}_j \qquad \text{Because } \mathbf{u}_j^T\mathbf{u}_j = 1 \end{aligned}$$

22. For $2 \le k \le n$, the singular value σ_k is the maximum of $\|A\mathbf{x}\|$ as $\mathbf{x}$ varies over all unit vectors orthogonal to $\mathbf{v}_1, \ldots, \mathbf{v}_{k-1}$. *Justification*: By Theorem 7 in Section 8.3, σ_k^2 is the maximum of $\|A\mathbf{x}\|^2$ as $\mathbf{x}$ varies over all unit vectors orthogonal to $\mathbf{v}_1, \ldots, \mathbf{v}_{k-1}$, because $\|A\mathbf{x}\|^2 = \mathbf{x}^T(A^TA)\mathbf{x}$.

Section 8.5, page 442

2. $M = \begin{bmatrix} 4 \\ 9 \end{bmatrix}$; $B = \begin{bmatrix} -3 & 1 & -2 & 2 & 3 & -1 \\ 2 & 2 & -3 & -1 & 6 & 2 \end{bmatrix}$,

$S = \begin{bmatrix} 5.6 & 8 \\ 8 & 18 \end{bmatrix}$

4. $\begin{bmatrix} .44 \\ .90 \end{bmatrix}$ for $\lambda = 21.9$, $\begin{bmatrix} -.90 \\ .44 \end{bmatrix}$ for $\lambda = 1.68$

6. $u_1 = .62x_1 + .60x_2 + .51x_3$, which explains 64.9% of the total variance.

8. $u_1 = .44x_1 + .90x_2$; u_1 explains 92.9% of the variance.

10. $(BB^T)^T = (B^{TT}B^T) = BB^T$, so BB^T is symmetric. For any $\mathbf{x}$ in $\mathbb{R}^p$, $\mathbf{x}^T(BB^T)\mathbf{x} = (B^T\mathbf{x})^T(B^T\mathbf{x}) = \|B^T\mathbf{x}\|^2 \geq 0$, so BB^T is positive semidefinite.

12. By Exercise 11, the change of variable $\mathbf{U} = P\mathbf{X}$ changes the covariance matrix S of $\mathbf{X}$ into the covariance matrix P^TSP of $\mathbf{U}$. The total variance of the data, as described by $\mathbf{U}$ is $\text{tr}(P^TSP)$. However, $\text{tr}[P^T(SP)] = \text{tr}[(SP)P^T] = \text{tr}[S(PP^T)] = \text{tr}(S)$, because P is an orthogonal matrix, and $PP^T = PP^{-1} = I$. Thus the total variance of the data is unchanged by this change of variable.

Index